THE

WHO, WHEN & WHERE

OF ENGLISH
INTERNATIONAL
RUGBY

since 1947

Compiled by D.N.Stansfield

Typeset by Webmart Ltd, Bicester

Printed and bound in Great Britain by
The Bath Press, Bath

Stansfield Publishing
P.O. Box 381
Welbourn
Lincoln LN5 0GB

TABLE OF CONTENTS

TABLE OF CONTENTS (continued)

TABLE OF CONTENTS (continued)

TABLE OF CONTENTS (continued)

INTRODUCTION

Prior to the outbreak of the Second World War in 1939, England had played exactly 200 International Rugby Union matches since the first recognised match was played against Scotland at Raeburn Place, Edinburgh on Match 27th 1871.

The International Championship began in 1883, albeit informally, involving England, Scotland, Ireland and Wales but it was not until 1891 that points scoring became universally applied to all games . France joined the Championship fot the first time in 1910, but because of a serious dispute surrounding allegations of professional payments to players in France at the time, the four Home Unions excluded France from the Championship at the end of the 1930-31 season.

Of the 200 matches played by England up to 1939, only 9 were played against opposition other than Five Nations opponents. The results of those 200 matches were:

Opponents:	Matches played	England won	England lost:	Drawn
France	21	18	2	1
Ireland	58	37	18	3
Scotland	61	26	25	10
Wales	51	26	19	6
Australia	2	1	1	0
New Zealand	3	1	2	0
South Africa	3	0	2	1
NZ Maoris	1	1	0	0
Total:	200	110	69	21

Since the resumption of International competition in 1946-47, England have played a total of 276 matches up to July 31st 1997 and it is these matches with which this record is primarily concerned. The results of these post-war matches are:

Opponents:	Matches played	England won	England lost:	Drawn
France	53	22	25	6
Ireland	52	27	20	5
Scotland	53	32	14	7
Wales	52	17	29	6
Australia	18	6	12	0
New Zealand	15	3	12	0
South Africa	10	4	6	0
Argentina	9	6	2	1
Fiji	3	3	0	0
Romania	3	3	0	0
Italy	3	3	0	0
Canada	2	2	0	0
USA	2	2	0	0
Western Samoa	2	2	0	0
Japan	1	1	0	0
RFU President's XV	1	0	1	0
	279	133	121	25

These matches have been played as:

Opponents:	Matches played	Five Nations:	World Cup	Others:
France	53	51	2	
Ireland	52	51		1
Scotland	53	51	1	1
Wales	52	51	1	
Australia	18		3	15
New Zealand	15		2	13
South Africa	10			10
Argentina	9		1	8
Fiji	3			3
Romania	3			3
Italy	3		2	1
Canada	2			2
USA	2		2	
Western Samoa	2		1	1
Japan	1		1	
RFU President's XV	1			1
	279	204	16	59

Significantly, of those 279 matches, 69 have been played against opposition other than Five Nations opponents, and 43 against the senior IRB members of which only 13 have been won.

The nature, the scope and the influence, as well as the pace and the intensity of International Rugby has increased to an extent which would have been beyond the wildest dreams of those stalwarts who played in the early exchanges in the late nineteenth century. But the most significant changes have taken place within the last decade, and particularly in the last two years since, on August 27th 1995, Vernon Pugh as President of the IRB, announced to the world that Rugby Union was thenceforth an open game.

The game became different on that fateful day, and doubtless it will become even more different as the influence of professionalism, and her partner, avarice, make even heavier demands on players, referees, administrators and supporters alike, in the months and years to come.

During the last seven years, England have experienced unprecedented success at International level, in winning three Grand Slams, four Five Nations Championships, five Triple Crowns, the last three in succession, and an appearance in a World Cup Final and semi-Final in the latter two tournaments. But in spite of that success and the impetus it has given to the game in England, we are still not truly comparable with the Southern Hemisphere nations as is frequently witnessed by the results achieved against them.

This record seeks to structure within one cover the answers to all those questions which keep recurring in club rooms and bars across the land when the fortunes of the England team, particularly in retrospect, are discussed and debated long after the sun has set and the touch judges have gone home.

Perhaps it is appropriate that this record is updated and recorded at this time, because today's changes may make tomorrow's events inconsistent or incompatible with what has gone before. In that case, this record stands as testimony to the game as it was. On the other hand, if, as hopefully will be the case, mightier deeds are witnessed and greater games are played, then this record can simply be updated to encompass what is yet to come.

BIBLIOGRAPHY

Rothmans Rugby Union Yearbooks		Rothmans Headline
Playfair Rugby Football Annuals		The Dickens Press
The International Rugby Championship 1883-1983	Terry Godwin	Collins Willow
The Phoenix Book of International Rugby Records	John Griffiths	J.M.Dent & Sons
The Complete Who's Who of England Rugby Union Internationals	Raymond Maule	Breedon Books
British Lions	John Griffiths	The Crowood Press
The World of Rugby	John Reason and Carwyn James	B.B.C.
The Men in White	Wallace Reyburn	Pelham Books
Fifty Two Famous Tries	J.B.G.Thomas	Pelham Books
Rugby: Men, Matches and Moments	J.B.G.Thomas	Pelham Books
Talking of Rugby	Bill McLaren	Stanley Paul
Fran Cotton - an Autobiography	Fran Cotton	Queen Anne Press
Thanks to Rugby	Bill Beaumont	Stanley Paul
A Game and a Half	Rob Andrew	Hodder & Stoughton
Brian Moore: The Autobiography	Brian Moore with Stephen Jones	Partridge Press
Rugby - a History of Rugby Union Football	Chris Rea	Hamlyn
England's Grand Slam, 1991	Rob Andrew & Dean Richards with Ian Robertson and Mick Cleary	Stanley Paul
The Official Book of the Rugby World Cup 1991 - Heinz	Ed: Ian Robertson	Stanley Paul
The Complete Book of the Rugby World Cup 1995 - Scottish Life	Ed: Ian Robertson	Hodder & Stoughton
World Cup '95 Diary	Rob Andrew	Independent UK Sports Publications

Rugby World
Times Newspapers Ltd
The Daily Telegraph plc

International Match Programmes

SECTION 1

INTERNATIONAL MATCHES PLAYED

1947 onwards

SEQUENCE OF INTERNATIONAL MATCHES PLAYED

1947 onwards

Game:	Date:	Venue:	Opponents:	Result:	Score: Points:	Tries:	Captain:
201	January 18th 1947	Cardiff Arms Park	Wales	Won	9 - 6	1 - 2	J.Mycock
202	February 8th 1947	Lansdowne Road	Ireland	Lost	0 - 22	0 - 5	J.Mycock
203	March 15th 1947	Twickenham	Scotland	Won	24 - 5	4 - 1	J.Heaton
204	April 19th 1947	Twickenham	France	Won	6 - 3	2 - 0	J.Heaton
205	January 3rd 1948	Twickenham	Australia	Lost	0 - 11	0 - 3	E.K.Scott
206	January 17th 1948	Twickenham	Wales	Drawn	3 - 3	0 - 1	T.A.Kemp
207	February 14th 1948	Twickenham	Ireland	Lost	10 - 11	2 - 3	E.K.Scott
208	March 20th 1948	Murrayfield	Scotland	Lost	3 - 6	0 - 2	E.K.Scott
209	March 29th 1948	Stade Colombes	France	Lost	0 - 15	0 - 3	R.H.G.Weighill
210	January 15th 1949	Cardiff Arms Park	Wales	Lost	3 - 9	0 - 3	N.M.Hall
211	February 12th 1949	Lansdowne Road	Ireland	Lost	5 - 14	1 - 2	N.M.Hall
212	February 26th 1949	Twickenham	France	Won	8 - 3	1 - 0	I.Preece
213	March 19th 1949	Twickenham	Scotland	Won	19 - 3	5 - 0	I.Preece
214	January 21st 1950	Twickenham	Wales	Lost	5 - 11	1 - 2	I.Preece
215	February 11th 1950	Twickenham	Ireland	Won	3 - 0	1 - 0	I.Preece
216	February 25th 1950	Stade Colombes	France	Lost	3 - 6	1 - 2	I.Preece
217	March 18th 1950	Murrayfield	Scotland	Lost	11 - 13	2 - 3	I.Preece
218	January 20th 1951	Swansea	Wales	Lost	5 - 23	1 - 5	V.G.Roberts
219	February 10th 1951	Lansdowne Road	Ireland	Lost	0 - 3	0 - 0	J.M.Kendall-Carpenter
220	February 24th 1951	Twickenham	France	Lost	3 - 11	1 - 2	J.M.Kendall-Carpenter
221	March 17th 1951	Twickenham	Scotland	Won	5 - 3	1 - 1	J.M.Kendall-Carpenter
222	January 5th 1952	Twickenham	South Africa	Lost	3 - 8	1 - 1	N.M.Hall
223	January 19th 1952	Twickenham	Wales	Lost	6 - 8	2 - 2	N.M.Hall
224	March 15th 1952	Murrayfield	Scotland	Won	19 - 3	4 - 1	N.M.Hall
225	March 29th 1952	Twickenham	Ireland	Won	3 - 0	1 - 0	N.M.Hall
226	April 5th 1952	Stade Colombes	France	Won	6 - 3	0 - 1	N.M.Hall
227	January 17th 1953	Cardiff Arms Park	Wales	Won	8 - 3	1 - 0	N.M.Hall
228	February 14th 1953	Lansdowne Road	Ireland	Drawn	9 - 9	1 - 1	N.M.Hall
229	February 28th 1953	Twickenham	France	Won	11 - 0	3 - 0	N.M.Hall
230	March 21st 1953	Twickenham	Scotland	Won	26 - 8	6 - 2	N.M.Hall
231	January 16th 1954	Twickenham	Wales	Won	9 - 6	3 - 1	R.V.Stirling
232	January 30th 1954	Twickenham	New Zealand	Lost	0 - 5	0 - 1	R.V.Stirling
233	February 13th 1954	Twickenham	Ireland	Won	14 - 3	3 - 0	R.V.Stirling
234	March 20th 1954	Murrayfield	Scotland	Won	13 - 3	3 - 1	R.V.Stirling
235	April 10th 1954	Stade Colombes	France	Lost	3 - 11	1 - 2	R.V.Stirling
236	January 22nd 1955	Cardiff Arms Park	Wales	Lost	0 - 3	0 - 0	N.M.Hall
237	February 12th 1955	Lansdowne Road	Ireland	Drawn	6 - 6	2 - 1	N.M.Hall
238	February 26th 1955	Twickenham	France	Lost	9 - 16	1 - 2	P.D.Young
239	March 19th 1955	Twickenham	Scotland	Won	9 - 6	2 - 1	P.D.Young
240	January 21st 1956	Twickenham	Wales	Lost	3 - 8	0 - 2	E.Evans
241	February 11th 1956	Twickenham	Ireland	Won	20 - 0	3 - 0	E.Evans
242	March 17th 1956	Murrayfield	Scotland	Won	11 - 6	1 - 1	E.Evans
243	April 14th 1956	Stade Colombes	France	Lost	9 - 14	1 - 2	E.Evans
244	January 19th 1957	Cardiff Arms Park	Wales	Won	3 - 0	0 - 0	E.Evans
245	February 9th 1957	Lansdowne Road	Ireland	Won	6 - 0	1 - 0	E.Evans
246	February 23rd 1957	Twickenham	France	Won	9 - 5	3 - 1	E.Evans
247	March 16th 1957	Twickenham	Scotland	Won	16 - 3	3 - 0	E.Evans
248	January 18th 1958	Twickenham	Wales	Drawn	3 - 3	1 - 0	E.Evans
249	February 1st 1958	Twickenham	Australia	Won	9 - 6	2 - 0	E.Evans
250	February 8th 1958	Twickenham	Ireland	Won	6 - 0	1 - 0	E.Evans

Game:	Date:	Venue:	Opponents:	Result:	Score: Points:	Tries:	Captain:
251	March 1st 1958	Stade Colombes	France	Won	14 - 0	3 - 0	E.Evans
252	March 15th 1958	Murrayfield	Scotland	Drawn	3 - 3	0 - 0	E.Evans
253	January 17th 1959	Cardiff Arms Park	Wales	Lost	0 - 5	0 - 1	J.Butterfield
254	February 14th 1959	Lansdowne Road	Ireland	Won	3 - 0	0 - 0	J.Butterfield
255	February 28th 1959	Twickenham	France	Drawn	3 - 3	0 - 0	J.Butterfield
256	March 21st 1959	Twickenham	Scotland	Drawn	3 - 3	0 - 0	J.Butterfield
257	January 16th 1960	Twickenham	Wales	Won	14 - 6	2 - 0	R.E.G.Jeeps
258	February 13th 1960	Twickenham	Ireland	Won	8 - 5	1 - 1	R.E.G.Jeeps
259	February 27th 1960	Stade Colombes	France	Drawn	3 - 3	1 - 0	R.E.G.Jeeps
260	March 19th 1960	Murrayfield	Scotland	Won	21 - 12	3 - 1	R.E.G.Jeeps
261	January 7th 1961	Twickenham	South Africa	Lost	0 - 5	0 - 1	R.E.G.Jeeps
262	January 21st 1961	Cardiff Arms Park	Wales	Lost	3 - 6	1 - 2	R.E.G.Jeeps
263	February 11th 1961	Lansdowne Road	Ireland	Lost	8 - 11	2 - 1	R.E.G.Jeeps
264	February 25th 1961	Twickenham	France	Drawn	5 - 5	1 - 1	R.E.G.Jeeps
265	March 18th 1961	Twickenham	Scotland	Won	6 - 0	1 - 0	R.E.G.Jeeps
266	January 20th 1962	Twickenham	Wales	Drawn	0 - 0	0 - 0	R.E.G.Jeeps
267	February 10th 1962	Twickenham	Ireland	Won	16 - 0	3 - 0	R.E.G.Jeeps
268	February 24th 1962	Stade Colombes	France	Lost	0 - 13	0 - 3	R.E.G.Jeeps
269	March 17th 1962	Murrayfield	Scotland	Drawn	3 - 3	0 - 0	R.E.G.Jeeps
270	January 19th 1963	Cardiff Arms Park	Wales	Won	13 - 6	2 - 1	R.A.W.Sharp
271	February 9th 1963	Lansdowne Road	Ireland	Drawn	0 - 0	0 - 0	R.A.W.Sharp
272	February 23rd 1963	Twickenham	France	Won	6 - 5	0 - 1	R.A.W.Sharp
273	March 16th 1963	Twickenham	Scotland	Won	10 - 8	2 - 1	R.A.W.Sharp
274	May 25th 1963	Auckland	New Zealand	Lost	11 - 21	1 - 3	M.P.Weston
275	June 1st 1963	Christchurch	New Zealand	Lost	6 - 9	1 - 2	M.P.Weston
276	June 4th 1963	Sydney	Australia	Lost	9 - 18	3 - 4	M.P.Weston
277	January 4th 1964	Twickenham	New Zealand	Lost	0 - 14	0 - 2	J.G.Willcox
278	January 18th 1964	Twickenham	Wales	Drawn	6 - 6	2 - 2	J.G.Willcox
279	February 8th 1964	Twickenham	Ireland	Lost	5 - 18	1 - 4	J.G.Willcox
280	February 22nd 1964	Stade Colombes	France	Won	6 - 3	1 - 1	C.R.Jacobs
281	March 21st 1964	Murrayfield	Scotland	Lost	6 - 15	1 - 3	C.R.Jacobs
282	January 16th 1965	Cardiff Arms Park	Wales	Lost	3 - 14	0 - 3	D.G.Perry
283	February 13th 1965	Lansdowne Road	Ireland	Lost	0 - 5	0 - 1	D.G.Perry
284	February 27th 1965	Twickenham	France	Won	9 - 6	1 - 1	D.G.Perry
285	March 20th 1965	Twickenham	Scotland	Drawn	3 - 3	1 - 0	D.G.Perry
286	January 15th 1966	Twickenham	Wales	Lost	6 - 11	1 - 1	D.P.Rogers
287	February 12th 1966	Twickenham	Ireland	Drawn	6 - 6	1 - 1	D.P.Rogers
288	February 26th 1966	Stade Colombes	France	Lost	0 - 13	0 - 3	D.P.Rogers
289	March 19th 1966	Murrayfield	Scotland	Lost	3 - 6	0 - 1	D.P.Rogers
290	January 7th 1967	Twickenham	Australia	Lost	11 - 23	1 - 2	R.A.W.Sharp
291	February 11th 1967	Lansdowne Road	Ireland	Won	8 - 3	1 - 0	P.E.Judd
292	February 25th 1967	Twickenham	France	Lost	12 - 16	0 - 2	P.E.Judd
293	March 18th 1967	Twickenham	Scotland	Won	27 - 14	4 - 2	P.E.Judd
294	April 15th 1967	Cardiff Arms Park	Wales	Lost	21 - 34	3 - 5	P.E.Judd
295	November 4th 1967	Twickenham	New Zealand	Lost	11 - 23	2 - 5	P.E.Judd
296	January 20th 1968	Twickenham	Wales	Drawn	11 - 11	2 - 2	C.W.McFadyean
297	February 10th 1968	Twickenham	Ireland	Drawn	9 - 9	0 - 0	C.W.McFadyean
298	February 24th 1968	Stade Colombes	France	Lost	9 - 14	0 - 1	M.P.Weston
299	March 16th 1968	Murrayfield	Scotland	Won	8 - 6	1 - 0	M.P.Weston
300	February 8th 1969	Lansdowne Road	Ireland	Lost	15 - 17	1 - 2	J.R.H.Greenwood

SEQUENCE OF INTERNATIONAL MATCHES PLAYED (continued)

Game:	Date:	Venue:	Opponents:	Result:	Score: Points:	Tries:	Captain:
301	February 22nd 1969	Twickenham	France	Won	22 - 8	3 - 1	D.P.Rogers
302	March 15th 1969	Twickenham	Scotland	Won	8 - 3	2 - 0	D.P.Rogers
303	April 12th 1969	Cardiff Arms Park	Wales	Lost	9 - 30	0 - 5	D.P.Rogers
304	December 20th 1969	Twickenham	South Africa	Won	11 - 8	2 - 1	R.Hiller
305	February 14th 1970	Twickenham	Ireland	Won	9 - 3	1 - 0	R.Hiller
306	February 28th 1970	Twickenham	Wales	Lost	13 - 17	2 - 4	R.Hiller
307	March 21st 1970	Murrayfield	Scotland	Lost	5 - 14	1 - 2	R.Hiller
308	April 18th 1970	Stade Colombes	France	Lost	13 - 35	2 - 6	R.B.Taylor
309	January 16th 1971	Cardiff Arms Park	Wales	Lost	6 - 22	1 - 3	A.L.Bucknall
310	February 13th 1971	Lansdowne Road	Ireland	Won	9 - 6	0 - 2	J.S.Spencer
311	February 27th 1971	Twickenham	France	Drawn	14 - 14	1 - 2	R.Hiller
312	March 20th 1971	Twickenham	Scotland	Lost	15 - 16	2 - 3	J.S.Spencer
313	March 27th 1971	Murrayfield	Scotland	Lost	6 - 26	0 - 5	J.S.Spencer
314	April 17th 1971	Twickenham	RFU Pres XV	Lost	11 - 28	1 - 6	J.S.Spencer
315	January 15th 1972	Twickenham	Wales	Lost	3 - 12	0 - 1	R.Hiller
316	February 12th 1972	Twickenham	Ireland	Lost	12 - 16	1 - 2	R.Hiller
317	February 26th 1972	Stade Colombes	France	Lost	12 - 37	1 - 6	P.J.Dixon
318	March 18th 1972	Murrayfield	Scotland	Lost	9 - 23	0 - 2	P.J.Dixon
319	June 3rd 1972	Johannesburg	South Africa	Won	18 - 9	1 - 0	J.V.Pullin
320	January 6th 1973	Twickenham	New Zealand	Lost	0 - 9	0 - 1	J.V.Pullin
321	January 20th 1973	Cardiff Arms Park	Wales	Lost	9 - 25	0 - 5	J.V.Pullin
322	February 10th 1973	Lansdowne Road	Ireland	Lost	9 - 18	1 - 2	J.V.Pullin
323	February 24th 1973	Twickenham	France	Won	14 - 6	2 - 1	J.V.Pullin
324	March 17th 1973	Twickenham	Scotland	Won	20 - 13	4 - 2	J.V.Pullin
325	September 15th 1973	Auckland	New Zealand	Won	16 - 10	3 - 2	J.V.Pullin
326	November 17th 1973	Twickenham	Australia	Won	20 - 3	3 - 0	J.V.Pullin
327	February 2nd 1974	Murrayfield	Scotland	Lost	14 - 16	2 - 2	J.V.Pullin
328	February 16th 1974	Twickenham	Ireland	Lost	21 - 26	1 - 4	J.V.Pullin
329	March 2nd 1974	Parc des Princes	France	Drawn	12 - 12	1 - 1	J.V.Pullin
330	March 16th 1974	Twickenham	Wales	Won	16 - 12	2 - 1	J.V.Pullin
331	January 18th 1975	Lansdowne Road	Ireland	Lost	9 - 12	1 - 2	F.E.Cotton
332	February 1st 1975	Twickenham	France	Lost	20 - 27	2 - 4	F.E.Cotton
333	February 15th 1975	Cardiff Arms Park	Wales	Lost	4 - 20	1 - 3	F.E.Cotton
334	March 15th 1975	Twickenham	Scotland	Won	7 - 6	1 - 0	A.Neary
335	May 24th 1975	Sydney C.G.	Australia	Lost	9 - 16	1 - 1	A.Neary
336	May 31st 1975	Brisbane	Australia	Lost	21 - 30	2 - 5	J.V.Pullin
337	January 3rd 1976	Twickenham	Australia	Won	23 - 6	3 - 0	A.Neary
338	January 17th 1976	Twickenham	Wales	Lost	9 - 21	0 - 3	A.Neary
339	February 21st 1976	Murrayfield	Scotland	Lost	12 - 22	1 - 3	A.Neary
340	March 6th 1976	Twickenham	Ireland	Lost	12 - 13	0 - 1	A.Neary
341	March 20th 1976	Parc des Princes	France	Lost	9 - 30	1 - 6	A.Neary
342	January 15th 1977	Twickenham	Scotland	Won	26 - 6	4 - 0	R.M.Uttley
343	February 5th 1977	Lansdowne Road	Ireland	Won	4 - 0	1 - 0	R.M.Uttley
344	February 19th 1977	Twickenham	France	Lost	3 - 4	0 - 1	R.M.Uttley
345	March 5th 1977	Cardiff Arms Park	Wales	Lost	9 - 14	0 - 2	R.M.Uttley
346	January 21st 1978	Parc des Princes	France	Lost	6 - 15	0 - 2	W.B.Beaumont
347	February 4th 1978	Twickenham	Wales	Lost	6 - 9	0 - 0	W.B.Beaumont
348	March 4th 1978	Murrayfield	Scotland	Won	15 - 0	2 - 0	W.B.Beaumont
349	March 18th 1978	Twickenham	Ireland	Won	15 - 9	2 - 0	W.B.Beaumont
350	November 25th 1978	Twickenham	New Zealand	Lost	6 - 16	0 - 2	W.B.Beaumont

Game:	Date:	Venue:	Opponents:	Result:	Score: Points:	Tries:	Captain:
351	February 3rd 1979	Twickenham	Scotland	Drawn	7 - 7	1 - 1	R.M.Uttley
352	February 17th 1979	Lansdowne Road	Ireland	Lost	7 - 12	1 - 1	W.B.Beaumont
353	March 3rd 1979	Twickenham	France	Won	7 - 6	1 - 1	W.B.Beaumont
354	March 17th 1979	Cardiff Arms Park	Wales	Lost	3 - 27	0 - 5	W.B.Beaumont
355	November 24th 1979	Twickenham	New Zealand	Lost	9 - 10	0 - 1	W.B.Beaumont
356	January 19th 1980	Twickenham	Ireland	Won	24 - 9	3 - 0	W.B.Beaumont
357	February 2nd 1980	Parc des Princes	France	Won	17 - 13	2 - 2	W.B.Beaumont
358	February 16th 1980	Twickenham	Wales	Won	9 - 8	0 - 2	W.B.Beaumont
359	March 15th 1980	Murrayfield	Scotland	Won	30 - 18	5 - 2	W.B.Beaumont
360	January 17th 1981	Cardiff Arms Park	Wales	Lost	19 - 21	1 - 1	W.B.Beaumont
361	February 21st 1981	Twickenham	Scotland	Won	23 - 17	3 - 3	W.B.Beaumont
362	March 7th 1981	Lansdowne Road	Ireland	Won	10 - 6	2 - 0	W.B.Beaumont
363	March 21st 1981	Twickenham	France	Lost	12 - 16	0 - 2	W.B.Beaumont
364	May 30th 1981	Buenos Aires	Argentina	Drawn	19 - 19	3 - 2	W.B.Beaumont
365	June 6th 1981	Buenos Aires	Argentina	Won	12 - 6	1 - 1	W.B.Beaumont
366	January 2nd 1982	Twickenham	Australia	Won	15 - 11	1 - 2	W.B.Beaumont
367	January 16th 1982	Murrayfield	Scotland	Drawn	9 - 9	0 - 0	W.B.Beaumont
368	February 6th 1982	Twickenham	Ireland	Lost	15 - 16	1 - 2	S.J.Smith
369	February 20th 1982	Parc des Princes	France	Won	27 - 15	2 - 1	S.J.Smith
370	March 6th 1982	Twickenham	Wales	Won	17 - 7	2 - 1	S.J.Smith
371	January 15th 1983	Twickenham	France	Lost	15 - 19	0 - 3	S.J.Smith
372	February 5th 1983	Cardiff Arms Park	Wales	Drawn	13 - 13	1 - 1	S.J.Smith
373	March 5th 1983	Twickenham	Scotland	Lost	12 - 22	0 - 2	J.P.Scott
374	March 19th 1983	Lansdowne Road	Ireland	Lost	15 - 25	0 - 2	J.P.Scott
375	November 19th 1983	Twickenham	New Zealand	Won	15 - 9	1 - 1	P.J.Wheeler
376	February 4th 1984	Murrayfield	Scotland	Lost	6 - 18	0 - 2	P.J.Wheeler
377	February 18th 1984	Twickenham	Ireland	Won	12 - 9	0 - 0	P.J.Wheeler
378	March 3rd 1984	Parc des Princes	France	Lost	18 - 32	2 - 5	P.J.Wheeler
379	March 17th 1984	Twickenham	Wales	Lost	15 - 24	0 - 1	P.J.Wheeler
380	June 2nd 1984	Port Elizabeth	South Africa	Lost	15 - 33	0 - 3	J.P.Scott
381	June 9th 1984	Johannesburg	South Africa	Lost	9 - 35	0 - 6	J.P.Scott
382	November 3rd 1984	Twickenham	Australia	Lost	3 - 19	0 - 3	N.D.Melville
383	January 5th 1985	Twickenham	Romania	Won	22 - 15	1 - 0	P.W.Dodge
384	February 2nd 1985	Twickenham	France	Drawn	9 - 9	0 - 0	P.W.Dodge
385	March 16th 1985	Twickenham	Scotland	Won	10 - 7	1 - 1	P.W.Dodge
386	March 30th 1985	Lansdowne Road	Ireland	Lost	10 - 13	1 - 1	P.W.Dodge
387	April 20th 1985	Cardiff Arms Park	Wales	Lost	15 - 24	1 - 2	P.W.Dodge
388	June 1st 1985	Christchurch	New Zealand	Lost	13 - 18	2 - 0	P.W.Dodge
389	June 8th 1985	Wellington	New Zealand	Lost	15 - 42	2 - 6	P.W.Dodge
390	January 18th 1986	Twickenham	Wales	Won	21 - 18	0 - 1	N.D.Melville
391	February 15th 1986	Murrayfield	Scotland	Lost	6 - 33	0 - 3	N.D.Melville
392	March 1st 1986	Twickenham	Ireland	Won	25 - 20	4 - 3	N.D.Melville
393	March 15th 1986	Parc des Princes	France	Lost	10 - 29	1 - 4	N.D.Melville
394	February 7th 1987	Lansdowne Road	Ireland	Lost	0 - 17	0 - 3	R.J.Hill
395	February 21st 1987	Twickenham	France	Lost	15 - 19	0 - 2	R.J.Hill
396	March 7th 1987	Cardiff Arms Park	Wales	Lost	12 - 19	0 - 1	R.J.Hill
397	April 4th 1987	Twickenham	Scotland	Won	21 - 12	2 - 1	M.E.Harrison
398	May 23rd 1987	WC - Sydney	Australia	Lost	6 - 19	1 - 2	M.E.Harrison
399	May 30th 1987	WC - Sydney	Japan	Won	60 - 7	0 - 1	M.E.Harrison
400	June 3rd 1987	WC - Sydney	United States	Won	34 - 6	4 - 1	M.E.Harrison

Game:	Date:	Venue:	Opponents:	Result:	Score: Points:	Tries:	Captain:
401	June 8th 1987	WC - Brisbane	Wales	Lost	3 - 16	0 - 3	M.E.Harrison
402	January 16th 1988	Parc des Princes	France	Lost	9 - 10	0 - 1	M.E.Harrison
403	February 6th 1988	Twickenham	Wales	Lost	3 - 11	0 - 2	M.E.Harrison
404	March 5th 1988	Murrayfield	Scotland	Won	9 - 6	0 - 0	N.D.Melville
405	March 19th 1988	Twickenham	Ireland	Won	35 - 3	6 - 0	N.D.Melville
406	April 23rd 1988	Lansdowne Road	Ireland	Won	21 - 10	2 - 2	J.Orwin
407	May 29th 1988	Brisbane	Australia	Lost	16 - 22	2 - 1	J.Orwin
408	June 12th 1988	Sydney	Australia	Lost	8 - 28	2 - 4	J.Orwin
409	June 17th 1988	Suva	Fiji	Won	25 - 12	3 - 0	R.M.Harding
410	November 5th 1988	Twickenham	Australia	Won	28 - 19	4 - 3	W.D.C.Carling
411	February 4th 1989	Twickenham	Scotland	Drawn	12 - 12	0 - 1	W.D.C.Carling
412	February 18th 1989	Lansdowne Road	Ireland	Won	16 - 3	2 - 0	W.D.C.Carling
413	March 4th 1989	Twickenham	France	Won	11 - 0	2 - 0	W.D.C.Carling
414	March 18th 1989	Cardiff Arms Park	Wales	Lost	9 - 12	0 - 1	W.D.C.Carling
415	May 13th 1989	Bucharest	Romania	Won	58 - 3	9 - 0	C.R.Andrew
416	November 4th 1989	Twickenham	Fiji	Won	58 - 23	0 - 4	W.D.C.Carling
417	January 20th 1990	Twickenham	Ireland	Won	23 - 0	4 - 0	W.D.C.Carling
418	February 3rd 1990	Parc des Princes	France	Won	26 - 7	3 - 1	W.D.C.Carling
419	February 17th 1990	Twickenham	Wales	Won	34 - 6	4 - 1	W.D.C.Carling
420	March 17th 1990	Murrayfield	Scotland	Lost	7 - 13	1 - 1	W.D.C.Carling
421	July 28th 1990	Buenos Aires	Argentina	Won	25 - 12	2 - 0	W.D.C.Carling
422	August 4th 1990	Buenos Aires	Argentina	Lost	13 - 15	2 - 0	W.D.C.Carling
423	November 3rd 1990	Twickenham	Argentina	Won	51 - 0	7 - 0	W.D.C.Carling
424	January 19th 1991	Cardiff Arms Park	Wales	Won	25 - 6	1 - 0	W.D.C.Carling
425	February 16th 1991	Twickenham	Scotland	Won	21 - 12	1 - 0	W.D.C.Carling
426	March 2nd 1991	Lansdowne Road	Ireland	Won	16 - 7	2 - 1	W.D.C.Carling
427	March 16th 1991	Twickenham	France	Won	21 - 19	1 - 3	W.D.C.Carling
428	July 20th 1991	Suva	Fiji	Won	28 - 12	3 - 1	W.D.C.Carling
429	July 27th 1991	Sydney	Australia	Lost	15 - 40	1 - 5	W.D.C.Carling
430	October 3rd 1991	WC - Twickenham	New Zealand	Lost	12 - 18	0 - 1	W.D.C.Carling
431	October 8th 1991	WC - Twickenham	Italy	Won	36 - 6	4 - 1	W.D.C.Carling
432	October 11th 1991	WC - Twickenham	United States	Won	37 - 9	5 - 1	W.D.C.Carling
433	October 19th 1991	WC - Paris	France	Won	19 - 10	2 - 1	W.D.C.Carling
434	October 26th 1991	WC - Murrayfield	Scotland	Won	9 - 6	0 - 0	W.D.C.Carling
435	November 3rd 1991	WC - Twickenham	Australia	Lost	6 - 12	0 - 1	W.D.C.Carling
436	January 18th 1992	Murrayfield	Scotland	Won	25 - 7	2 - 1	W.D.C.Carling
437	February 1st 1992	Twickenham	Ireland	Won	38 - 9	6 - 1	W.D.C.Carling
438	February 15th 1992	Parc des Princes	France	Won	31 - 13	4 - 2	W.D.C.Carling
439	March 7th 1992	Twickenham	Wales	Won	24 - 0	3 - 0	W.D.C.Carling
440	October 17th 1992	Wembley Stadium	Canada	Won	26 - 13	4 - 1	W.D.C.Carling
441	November 14th 1992	Twickenham	South Africa	Won	33 - 16	4 - 1	W.D.C.Carling
442	January 16th 1993	Twickenham	France	Won	16 - 15	1 - 2	W.D.C.Carling
443	February 6th 1993	Cardiff Arms Park	Wales	Lost	9 - 10	0 - 1	W.D.C.Carling
444	March 6th 1993	Twickenham	Scotland	Won	26 - 12	3 - 0	W.D.C.Carling
445	March 20th 1993	Lansdowne Road	Ireland	Lost	3 - 17	0 - 1	W.D.C.Carling
446	November 27th 1993	Twickenham	New Zealand	Won	15 - 9	0 - 0	W.D.C.Carling
447	February 5th 1994	Murrayfield	Scotland	Won	15 - 14	0 - 1	W.D.C.Carling
448	February 19th 1994	Twickenham	Ireland	Lost	12 - 13	0 - 1	W.D.C.Carling
449	March 5th 1994	Parc des Princes	France	Won	18 - 14	0 - 1	W.D.C.Carling
450	March 19th 1994	Twickenham	Wales	Won	15 - 8	2 - 1	W.D.C.Carling

SEQUENCE OF INTERNATIONAL MATCHES PLAYED (continued)

Game:	Date:	Venue:	Opponents:	Result:	Score: Points:	Tries:	Captain:
451	June 4th 1994	Pretoria	South Africa	Won	32 - 15	2 - 0	W.D.C.Carling
452	June 11th 1994	Cape Town	South Africa	Lost	9 - 27	0 - 2	W.D.C.Carling
453	November 12th 1994	Twickenham	Romania	Won	54 - 3	5 - 0	W.D.C.Carling
454	December 10th 1994	Twickenham	Canada	Won	60 - 19	6 - 3	W.D.C.Carling
455	January 21st 1995	Lansdowne Road	Ireland	Won	20 - 8	3 - 1	W.D.C.Carling
456	February 4th 1995	Twickenham	France	Won	31 - 10	3 - 1	W.D.C.Carling
457	February 18th 1995	Cardiff Arms Park	Wales	Won	23 - 9	3 - 0	W.D.C.Carling
458	March 18th 1995	Twickenham	Scotland	Won	24 - 12	0 - 0	W.D.C.Carling
459	May 27th 1995	WC - Durban	Argentina	Won	24 - 18	0 - 2	W.D.C.Carling
460	May 31st 1995	WC - Durban	Italy	Won	27 - 20	2 - 2	C.R.Andrew
461	June 4th 1995	WC - Durban	Western Samoa	Won	44 - 22	4 - 3	W.D.C.Carling
462	June 10th 1995	WC - Cape Town	Australia	Won	25 - 22	1 - 1	W.D.C.Carling
463	June 17th 1995	WC - Cape Town	New Zealand	Lost	29 - 45	4 - 6	W.D.C.Carling
464	June 22nd 1995	WC - Pretoria	France	Lost	9 - 19	0 - 2	W.D.C.Carling
465	November 18th 1995	Twickenham	South Africa	Lost	14 - 24	1 - 3	W.D.C.Carling
466	December 16th 1995	Twickenham	Western Samoa	Won	27 - 9	2 - 0	W.D.C.Carling
467	January 20th 1996	Parc des Princes	France	Lost	12 - 15	0 - 0	W.D.C.Carling
468	February 3rd 1996	Twickenham	Wales	Won	21 - 15	2 - 2	W.D.C.Carling
469	March 2nd 1996	Murrayfield	Scotland	Won	18 - 9	0 - 0	W.D.C.Carling
470	March 16th 1996	Twickenham	Ireland	Won	28 - 15	1 - 0	W.D.C.Carling
471	November 23rd 1996	Twickenham	Italy	Won	54 - 21	7 - 3	P.R.de Glanville
472	December 14th 1996	Twickenham	Argentina	Won	20 - 18	1 - 0	J.Leonard
473	February 1st 1997	Twickenham	Scotland	Won	41 - 13	4 - 1	P.R.de Glanville
474	February 15th 1997	Lansdowne Road	Ireland	Won	46 - 6	6 - 0	P.R.de Glanville
475	March 1st 1997	Twickenham	France	Lost	20 - 23	1 - 2	P.R.de Glanville
476	March 15th 1997	Cardiff Arms Park	Wales	Won	34 - 13	4 - 1	P.R.de Glanville
477	May 30th 1997	Buenos Aires	Argentina	Won	46 - 20	6 - 3	P.R.de Glanville
478	June 6th 1997	Buenos Aires	Argentina	Lost	13 - 33	2 - 4	P.R.de Glanville
479	July 12th 1997	Sydney	Australia	Lost	6 - 25	0 - 4	P.R.de Glanville
480							
481							
482							
483							
484							
485							
486							
487							
488							
489							
490							
491							

Played;	279	
Won:	133	
Lost:	121	
Drawn:	25	

INTERNATIONAL MATCHES PLAYED

EACH SEASON from 1947 by category

(The season is assumed to begin on September 1st each year))

	Five Nations	World Cup	Others	Total	
1946-47	4			4	
1947-48	4		1	5	In three seasons in the Forties
1948-49	4			4	England played 13 matches.
1949-50	4			4	
1950-51	4			4	
1951-52	4		1	5	
1952-53	4			4	
1953-54	4		1	5	In ten seasons in the Fifties
1954-55	4			4	England played 43 matches.
1955-56	4			4	
1956-57	4			4	
1957-58	4		1	5	
1958-59	4			4	
1959-60	4			4	
1960-61	4		1	5	
1961-62	4			4	
1962-63	4		3	7	
1963-64	4		1	5	In ten seasons in the Sixties
1964-65	4			4	England played 47 matches.
1965-66	4			4	
1966-67	4		1	5	
1967-68	4		1	5	
1968-69	4			4	
1969-70	4		1	5	
1970-71	4		2	6	
1971-72	4		1	5	
1972-73	4		1	5	
1973-74	4		2	6	In ten seasons in the Seventies
1974-75	4		2	6	England played 51 matches.
1975-76	4		1	5	
1976-77	4			4	
1977-78	4			4	
1978-79	4		1	5	
1979-80	4		1	5	
1980-81	4		2	6	
1981-82	4		1	5	In ten seasons in the Eighties
1982-83	4			4	England played 61 matches.
1983-84	4		3	7	

INTERNATIONAL MATCHES PLAYED

EACH SEASON from 1947 by category (continued)

(The season is assumed to begin on September 1st each year))

	Five Nations	World Cup	Others	Total	
1984-85	4		4	8	
1985-86	4			4	In ten seasons in the Eighties
1986-87	4	4		8	England played 61 matches.
1987-88	4		4	8	
1988-89	4		2	6	
1989-90	4		3	7	
1990-91	4		3	7	
1991-92	4	6		10	
1992-93	4		2	6	
1993-94	4		3	7	
1994-95	4	6	2	12	In eight seasons in the Nineties
1995-96	4		2	6	England have played 64 matohes.
1996-97	4		5	9	
Total:	**204**	**16**	**59**	**279**	

INTERNATIONAL MATCHES:

ENGLAND v FRANCE

21 matches were played between England and France prior to 1947.

1948-49 Points values revised: Drop Goal reduced to 3 pts.

Match No.	Year	Cat	Date	Venue	Result	Score	England: G	T	PG	DG	France: G	T	PG	DG	Eng Won	Fra Won	Dm
						Results:									18	2	1
22	1947	5N	April 19th	Twickenham	Won	6 - 3	-	2	-	-	-	-	1	-	19	2	1
23	1948	5N	March 29th	Stade Colombes	Lost	0 - 15	-	-	-	-	1	2	-	1	19	3	1
24	1949	5N	February 26th	Twickenham	Won	8 - 3	1	1	-	-	-	1	-	-	20	3	1
25	1950	5N	February 25th	Stade Colombes	Lost	3 - 6	-	1	-	-	-	2	-	-	20	4	1
26	1951	5N	February 24th	Twickenham	Lost	3 - 11	-	1	-	-	1	1	-	-	20	5	1
27	1952	5N	April 5th	Stade Colombes	Won	6 - 3	-	2	-	-	-	1	-	-	21	5	1
28	1953	5N	February 28th	Twickenham	Won	11 - 0	1	2	-	-	-	-	-	-	22	5	1
29	1954	5N	April 10th	Stade Colombes	Lost	3 - 11	-	1	-	-	1	1	2	-	22	6	1
30	1955	5N	February 26th	Twickenham	Lost	9 - 16	-	1	2	-	2	1	2	-	22	7	1
31	1956	5N	April 14th	Stade Colombes	Lost	9 - 14	-	3	-	-	1	1	2	-	22	8	1
32	1957	5N	February 23rd	Twickenham	Won	9 - 5	1	2	1	-	1	-	-	-	23	8	1
33	1958	5N	March 1st	Stade Colombes	Won	14 - 0	-	-	-	-	-	-	-	-	24	8	1
34	1959	5N	February 28th	Twickenham	Drawn	3 - 3	-	-	1	-	-	1	1	-	24	8	2
35	1960	5N	February 27th	Stade Colombes	Drawn	3 - 3	-	1	-	-	-	1	1	-	24	8	3
36	1961	5N	February 25th	Twickenham	Drawn	5 - 5	1	-	-	-	1	-	-	-	24	8	4
37	1962	5N	February 24th	Stade Colombes	Lost	0 - 13	-	-	-	-	2	1	2	-	24	9	4
38	1963	5N	February 23rd	Twickenham	Won	6 - 5	-	1	2	-	1	-	-	-	25	9	4
39	1964	5N	February 22nd	Stade Colombes	Won	6 - 3	-	1	1	-	1	1	1	-	26	9	4
40	1965	5N	February 27th	Twickenham	Won	9 - 6	-	1	1	-	-	1	1	-	27	9	4
41	1966	5N	February 26th	Stade Colombes	Lost	0 - 13	-	-	-	-	2	1	-	-	27	10	4

ENGLAND v FRANCE (continued)

Match No.	Year	Cat:	Date:	Venue:	Result:	Score:	England: G	T	PG	DG	France: G	T	PG	DG	Eng Won	Fra Won	Drn
42	1967	5N	February 25th	Twickenham	Lost	12 - 16	-	-	3	1	2	-	1	1	27	11	4
43	1968	5N	February 24th	Stade Colombes	Lost	9 - 14	-	-	2	1	1	-	1	2	27	12	4
44	1969	5N	February 22nd	Twickenham	Won	22 - 8	2	1	3	-	1	-	-	1	28	12	4
45	1970	5N	April 18th	Stade Colombes	Lost	13 - 35	2	-	1	-	4	2	1	2	28	13	4
46	1971	5N	February 27th	Twickenham	Drawn	14 - 14	1	-	3	-	1	1	1	1	28	13	5

1971-72 Points values revised: Try increased to 4 pts.

Match No.	Year	Cat:	Date:	Venue:	Result:	Score:	England: G	T	PG	DG	France: G	T	PG	DG	Eng Won	Fra Won	Drn
47	1972	5N	February 26th	Stade Colombes	Lost	12 - 37	1	-	2	-	5	1	1	-	28	14	5
48	1973	5N	February 24th	Twickenham	Won	14 - 6	-	2	2	-	1	-	1	-	29	14	5
49	1974	5N	March 2nd	Parc des Princes	Drawn	12 - 12	1	-	1	-	1	-	1	-	29	14	6
50	1975	5N	February 1st	Twickenham	Lost	20 - 27	-	2	4	-	4	-	1	-	29	15	6
51	1976	5N	March 20th	Parc des Princes	Lost	9 - 30	1	-	1	-	3	3	-	-	29	16	6
52	1977	5N	February 19th	Twickenham	Lost	3 - 4	-	-	1	-	-	1	-	-	29	17	6
53	1978	5N	January 21st	Parc des Princes	Lost	6 - 15	-	-	-	2	2	-	1	-	29	18	6
54	1979	5N	March 3rd	Twickenham	Won	7 - 6	-	1	1	-	1	-	1	-	30	18	6
55	1980	5N	February 2nd	Parc des Princes	Won	17 - 13	-	2	1	2	1	1	1	-	31	18	6
56	1981	5N	March 21st	Twickenham	Lost	12 - 16	-	-	4	-	1	-	2	-	31	19	6
57	1982	5N	February 20th	Parc des Princes	Won	27 - 15	2	-	5	-	1	1	2	1	32	19	6
58	1983	5N	January 15th	Twickenham	Lost	15 - 19	-	-	4	1	2	-	1	-	32	20	6
59	1984	5N	March 3rd	Parc des Princes	Lost	18 - 32	2	-	2	-	3	2	2	1	32	21	6
60	1985	5N	February 2nd	Twickenham	Drawn	9 - 9	-	-	2	1	-	-	2	1	32	21	7
61	1986	5N	March 15th	Parc des Princes	Lost	10 - 29	-	1	2	-	2	2	3	-	32	22	7
62	1987	5N	February 21st	Twickenham	Lost	15 - 19	-	-	4	1	1	1	1	-	32	23	7
63	1988	5N	January 16th	Parc des Princes	Lost	9 - 10	-	-	2	1	-	-	2	-	32	24	7

ENGLAND v FRANCE (continued)

Match No.	Year	Cat:	Date:	Venue:	Result:	Score:	England: G	T	PG	DG	France: G	T	PG	DG	Eng Won	Fra Won	Drn
64	1989	5N	March 4th	Twickenham	Won	11 - 0	-	2	1	-	-	-	-	-	33	24	7
65	1990	5N	February 3rd	Parc des Princes	Won	26 - 7	-	2	4	-	-	1	-	-	34	24	7
66	1991	5N	March 16th	Twickenham	Won	21 - 19	1	-	4	1	2	1	1	-	35	24	7
67	1991	WC	October 19th	Parc des Princes	Won	19 - 10	1	1	3	-	-	1	2	-	36	24	7
68	1992	5N	February 15th	Parc des Princes	Won	31 - 13	3	1	3	-	1	1	1	-	37	24	7

1992-93 Points values revised: Try increased to 5 pts.

Match No.	Year	Cat:	Date:	Venue:	Result:	Score:	England: G	T	PG	DG	France: G	T	PG	DG	Eng Won	Fra Won	Drn
69	1993	5N	January 16th	Twickenham	Won	16 - 15	1	-	3	-	1	1	1	-	38	24	7
70	1994	5N	March 5th	Parc des Princes	Won	18 - 14	-	-	5	1	-	1	3	-	39	24	7
71	1995	5N	February 4th	Twickenham	Won	31 - 10	2	1	4	-	1	-	1	-	40	24	7
72	1995	WC	June 22nd	Pretoria	Lost	9 - 19	-	-	3	-	-	2	3	2	40	25	7
73	1996	5N	Jan 20th	Parc des Princes	Lost	12 - 15	-	-	2	2	-	-	3	2	40	26	7
74	1997	5N	March 1st	Twickenham	Lost	20 - 23	-	1	4	1	2	-	2	1	40	27	7

INTERNATIONAL MATCHES:

ENGLAND v IRELAND

Match No.	Year	Cat	Date	Venue	Result	Score	England: G	T	PG	DG	Ireland: G	T	PG	DG	Eng Won	Ire Won	Drn
			58 matches were played between England and Ireland prior to 1947.								Results:				37	18	3
59	1947	5N	February 8th	Lansdowne Road	Lost	0 - 22	-	-	-	-	2	3	1	-	37	19	3
60	1948	5N	February 14th	Twickenham	Lost	10 - 11	2	-	-	-	1	2	-	-	37	20	3
			1948-49 Points values revised: Drop Goal reduced to 3 pts.														
61	1949	5N	February 12th	Lansdowne Road	Lost	5 - 14	1	-	-	-	1	1	2	-	37	21	3
62	1950	5N	February 11th	Twickenham	Won	3 - 0	-	1	-	-	-	-	-	-	38	21	3
63	1951	5N	February 10th	Lansdowne Road	Lost	0 - 3	-	-	-	-	-	1	-	-	38	22	3
64	1952	5N	March 29th	Twickenham	Won	3 - 0	-	1	-	-	-	-	-	-	39	22	3
65	1953	5N	February 14th	Lansdowne Road	Drawn	9 - 9	-	1	2	-	-	1	2	-	39	22	4
66	1954	5N	February 13th	Twickenham	Won	14 - 3	1	2	1	-	-	-	1	-	40	22	4
67	1955	5N	February 12th	Lansdowne Road	Drawn	6 - 6	-	2	-	-	-	2	-	-	40	22	5
68	1956	5N	February 11th	Twickenham	Won	20 - 0	1	2	3	-	-	-	-	-	41	22	5
69	1957	5N	February 9th	Lansdowne Road	Won	6 - 0	-	1	1	-	-	-	-	-	42	22	5
70	1958	5N	February 8th	Twickenham	Won	6 - 0	-	1	1	-	-	-	-	-	43	22	5
71	1959	5N	February 14th	Lansdowne Road	Won	3 - 0	-	-	1	-	-	-	-	-	44	22	5
72	1960	5N	February 13th	Twickenham	Won	8 - 5	1	1	-	-	1	-	-	-	45	22	5
73	1961	5N	February 11th	Lansdowne Road	Lost	8 - 11	1	1	-	-	1	-	2	-	45	23	5
74	1962	5N	February 10th	Twickenham	Won	16 - 0	2	1	1	-	-	-	-	-	46	23	5
75	1963	5N	February 9th	Lansdowne Road	Drawn	0 - 0	-	-	-	-	-	-	-	-	46	23	6
76	1964	5N	February 8th	Twickenham	Lost	5 - 18	1	-	-	-	3	1	-	-	46	24	6
77	1965	5N	February 13th	Lansdowne Road	Lost	0 - 5	-	-	-	-	1	-	-	-	46	25	6
78	1966	5N	February 12th	Twickenham	Drawn	6 - 6	-	1	1	-	-	1	1	-	46	25	7

INTERNATIONAL MATCHES:

ENGLAND v IRELAND (continued)

Match No.	Year	Cat:	Date:	Venue:	Result:	Score:	England: G	T	PG	DG	Ireland: G	T	PG	DG	Eng Won	Ire Won	Drn
79	1967	5N	February 11th	Lansdowne Road	Won	8 - 3	1	-	1	-	-	-	1	-	47	25	7
80	1968	5N	February 10th	Twickenham	Drawn	9 - 9	-	-	2	1	-	-	3	-	47	25	8
81	1969	5N	February 8th	Lansdowne Road	Lost	15 - 17	-	1	4	-	1	1	2	1	47	26	8
82	1970	5N	February 14th	Twickenham	Won	9 - 3	-	1	-	2	-	-	1	-	48	26	8
83	1971	5N	February 13th	Lansdowne Road	Won	9 - 6	-	-	3	-	-	2	-	-	49	26	8

1971-72 Points values revised: Try increased to 4 pts.

Match No.	Year	Cat:	Date:	Venue:	Result:	Score:	England: G	T	PG	DG	Ireland: G	T	PG	DG	Eng Won	Ire Won	Drn
84	1972	5N	February 12th	Twickenham	Lost	12 - 16	1	-	2	-	1	1	2	1	49	27	8
85	1973	5N	February 10th	Lansdowne Road	Lost	9 - 18	-	-	1	-	2	-	1	1	49	28	8
86	1974	5N	February 16th	Twickenham	Lost	21 - 26	1	1	5	-	2	2	1	1	49	29	8
87	1975	5N	January 18th	Lansdowne Road	Lost	9 - 12	1	-	-	1	2	-	-	1	49	30	8
88	1976	5N	March 6th	Twickenham	Lost	12 - 13	-	-	4	-	-	1	2	-	49	31	8
89	1977	5N	February 5th	Lansdowne Road	Won	4 - 0	-	1	-	-	-	-	-	-	50	31	8
90	1978	5N	March 18th	Twickenham	Won	15 - 9	2	-	1	-	-	-	2	1	51	31	8
91	1979	5N	February 17th	Lansdowne Road	Lost	7 - 12	-	1	1	-	1	1	1	1	51	32	8
92	1980	5N	January 19th	Twickenham	Won	24 - 9	3	1	2	-	-	-	3	-	52	32	8
93	1981	5N	March 7th	Lansdowne Road	Won	10 - 6	1	1	-	2	-	-	2	-	53	32	8
94	1982	5N	February 6th	Twickenham	Lost	15 - 16	1	-	3	-	1	1	2	-	53	33	8
95	1983	5N	March 19th	Lansdowne Road	Lost	15 - 25	-	-	5	-	1	1	5	-	53	34	8
96	1984	5N	February 18th	Twickenham	Won	12 - 9	-	-	3	1	-	-	3	-	54	34	8
97	1985	5N	March 30th	Lansdowne Road	Lost	10 - 13	-	1	2	-	1	1	2	1	54	35	8
98	1986	5N	March 1st	Twickenham	Won	25 - 20	3	1	1	-	1	2	2	-	55	35	8
99	1987	5N	February 7th	Lansdowne Road	Lost	0 - 17	-	-	-	-	1	2	-	1	55	36	8
100	1988	5N	March 19th	Twickenham	Won	35 - 3	4	2	1	-	1	-	-	-	56	36	8
101	1988	Millen	April 23rd	Lansdowne Road	Won	21 - 10	2	-	3	-	1	1	-	-	57	36	8

INTERNATIONAL MATCHES:

ENGLAND v IRELAND (continued)

Match No.	Year	Cat:	Date:	Venue:	Result:	Score:	England: G	T	PG	DG	Ireland: G	T	PG	DG	Eng Won	Ire Won	Drn
102	1989	5N	February 18th	Lansdowne Road	Won	16 - 3	1	1	2	-	-	-	1	-	58	36	8
103	1990	5N	January 20th	Twickenham	Won	23 - 0	2	2	1	-	-	-	-	-	59	36	8
104	1991	5N	March 2nd	Lansdowne Road	Won	16 - 7	1	1	2	-	-	1	1	-	60	36	8
105	1992	5N	February 1st	Twickenham	Won	38 - 9	4	2	2	-	1	-	1	-	61	36	8

1992-93 Points values revised: Try increased to 5 pts.

Match No.	Year	Cat:	Date:	Venue:	Result:	Score:	England: G	T	PG	DG	Ireland: G	T	PG	DG	Eng Won	Ire Won	Drn
106	1993	5N	March 20th	Lansdowne Road	Lost	3 - 17	-	-	1	-	-	1	2	2	61	37	8
107	1994	5N	February 19th	Twickenham	Lost	12 - 13	-	-	4	-	1	-	2	-	61	38	8
108	1995	5N	January 21st	Lansdowne Road	Won	20 - 8	1	2	1	-	-	1	1	-	62	38	8
109	1996	5N	March 16th	Twickenham	Won	28 - 15	1	-	6	1	-	-	4	1	63	38	8
110	1997	5N	February 15th	Lansdowne Road	Won	46 - 6	2	4	4	-	-	-	2	-	64	38	8

INTERNATIONAL MATCHES:

ENGLAND v SCOTLAND

61 matches were played between England and Scotland prior to 1947. *(Prior totals: Eng Won 26, Sco Won 25, Drn 10)*

1948-49 Points values revised: Drop Goal reduced to 3 pts.

Match No.	Year	Cat	Date	Venue	Result	Score	England: G	T	PG	DG	Scotland: G	T	PG	DG	Eng Won	Sco Won	Drn
62	1947	5N	April 19th	Twickenham	Won	24 - 5	4	-	-	1	1	-	-	-	27	25	10
63	1948	5N	March 20th	Murrayfield	Lost	3 - 6	-	-	1	-	-	2	-	-	27	26	10
64	1949	5N	March 19th	Twickenham	Won	19 - 3	2	3	-	-	-	-	1	-	28	26	10
65	1950	5N	March 18th	Murrayfield	Lost	11 - 13	1	1	1	-	2	-	1	-	28	27	10
66	1951	5N	March 17th	Twickenham	Won	5 - 3	1	-	-	-	-	1	-	-	29	27	10
67	1952	5N	March 15th	Murrayfield	Won	19 - 3	2	3	-	-	-	-	1	-	30	27	10
68	1953	5N	March 21st	Twickenham	Won	26 - 8	4	2	-	-	1	1	-	-	31	27	10
69	1954	5N	March 20th	Murrayfield	Won	13 - 3	2	1	-	-	-	-	1	-	32	27	10
70	1955	5N	March 19th	Twickenham	Won	9 - 6	-	3	-	-	-	-	2	-	33	27	10
71	1956	5N	March 17th	Murrayfield	Won	11 - 6	1	2	-	-	-	-	2	-	34	27	10
72	1957	5N	March 16th	Twickenham	Won	16 - 3	2	2	-	-	-	-	1	-	35	27	10
73	1958	5N	March 15th	Murrayfield	Drawn	3 - 3	-	-	1	-	-	-	1	-	35	27	11
74	1959	5N	March 21st	Twickenham	Drawn	3 - 3	-	-	1	-	-	-	1	-	35	27	12
75	1960	5N	March 19th	Murrayfield	Won	21 - 12	3	2	-	-	-	1	3	-	36	27	12
76	1961	5N	March 18th	Twickenham	Won	6 - 0	-	2	-	-	-	-	-	-	37	27	12
77	1962	5N	March 17th	Murrayfield	Drawn	3 - 3	-	-	1	-	-	-	1	-	37	27	13
78	1963	5N	March 16th	Twickenham	Won	10 - 8	2	-	-	-	1	1	-	1	38	27	13
79	1964	5N	March 21st	Murrayfield	Lost	6 - 15	-	2	-	-	3	-	-	-	38	28	13
80	1965	5N	March 20th	Twickenham	Drawn	3 - 3	-	-	1	-	-	1	-	-	38	28	14
81	1966	5N	March 19th	Murrayfield	Lost	3 - 6	-	-	1	-	-	1	1	-	38	29	14

ENGLAND v SCOTLAND (continued)

Match No.	Year	Cat	Date	Venue	Result	Score	England: G	T	PG	DG	Scotland: G	T	PG	DG	Eng Won	Sco Won	Dm
82	1967	5N	March 18th	Twickenham	Won	27 - 14	3	1	2	1	1	1	2	-	39	29	14
83	1968	5N	March 16th	Murrayfield	Won	8 - 6	1	1	1	-	-	1	1	1	40	29	14
84	1969	5N	March 15th	Twickenham	Won	8 - 3	1	1	-	-	-	-	1	-	41	29	14
85	1970	5N	March 21st	Murrayfield	Lost	5 - 14	1	-	-	-	1	1	2	-	41	30	14
86	1971	5N	March 20th	Twickenham	Lost	15 - 16	-	2	3	-	2	1	-	1	41	31	14
87	1971	Cent!	March 27th	Murrayfield	Lost	6 - 26	-	-	1	-	4	1	1	-	41	32	14

1971-72 Points values revised: Try increased to 4 pts.

Match No.	Year	Cat	Date	Venue	Result	Score	England: G	T	PG	DG	Scotland: G	T	PG	DG	Eng Won	Sco Won	Dm
88	1972	5N	March 18th	Murrayfield	Lost	9 - 23	-	-	3	-	-	2	4	1	41	33	14
89	1973	5N	March 17th	Twickenham	Won	20 - 13	2	2	-	-	1	1	1	-	42	33	14
90	1974	5N	February 2nd	Murrayfield	Lost	14 - 16	-	2	1	-	1	1	2	-	42	34	14
91	1975	5N	March 15th	Twickenham	Won	7 - 6	1	1	1	-	-	-	2	-	43	34	14
92	1976	5N	February 21st	Murrayfield	Lost	12 - 22	1	1	2	-	2	1	2	-	43	35	14
93	1977	5N	January 15th	Twickenham	Won	26 - 6	2	2	2	-	-	-	2	-	44	35	14
94	1978	5N	March 4th	Murrayfield	Won	15 - 0	2	-	1	-	-	-	-	-	45	35	14
95	1979	5N	February 3rd	Twickenham	Drawn	7 - 7	-	1	1	-	-	1	1	-	45	35	15
96	1980	5N	March 15th	Murrayfield	Won	30 - 18	2	3	2	-	2	-	2	-	46	35	15
97	1981	5N	February 21st	Twickenham	Won	23 - 17	1	2	3	-	1	-	1	1	47	35	15
98	1982	5N	January 16th	Murrayfield	Drawn	9 - 9	-	-	3	-	-	1	2	1	47	35	16
99	1983	5N	March 5th	Twickenham	Lost	12 - 22	-	-	3	1	1	1	3	1	47	36	16
100	1984	5N	February 4th	Murrayfield	Lost	6 - 18	-	-	2	-	2	-	2	-	47	37	16
101	1985	5N	March 16th	Twickenham	Won	10 - 7	1	1	-	-	-	1	1	-	48	37	16
102	1986	5N	February 15th	Murrayfield	Lost	6 - 33	-	-	2	-	3	-	5	-	48	38	16
103	1987	5N	April 4th	Twickenham	Won	21 - 12	2	-	3	-	1	-	2	-	49	38	16
104	1988	5N	March 5th	Murrayfield	Won	9 - 6	-	-	2	1	-	-	2	-	50	38	16

INTERNATIONAL MATCHES:

ENGLAND v SCOTLAND (continued)

Match No.	Year:	Cat:	Date:	Venue:	Result:	Score:	England: G	T	PG	DG	Scotland: G	T	PG	DG	Eng Won	Sco Won	Drn
105	1989	5N	February 4th	Twickenham	Drawn	12 – 12	-	-	4	-	1	-	2	-	50	38	17
106	1990	5N	March 17th	Murrayfield	Lost	7 – 13	-	1	1	-	-	1	3	-	50	39	17
107	1991	5N	February 16th	Twickenham	Won	21 – 12	1	-	5	-	-	-	4	-	51	39	17
108	1991	WC	October 26th	Murrayfield	Won	9 – 6	-	-	2	1	-	-	2	-	52	39	17
109	1992	5N	January 18th	Murrayfield	Won	25 – 7	1	1	4	1	-	1	1	-	53	39	17

1992-93 Points values revised: Try Increased to 5 pts.

Match No.	Year:	Cat:	Date:	Venue:	Result:	Score:	England: G	T	PG	DG	Scotland: G	T	PG	DG	Eng Won	Sco Won	Drn
110	1993	5N	March 6th	Twickenham	Won	26 – 12	1	2	3	-	-	-	3	1	54	39	17
111	1994	5N	February 5th	Murrayfield	Won	15 – 14	-	-	5	-	-	1	2	1	55	39	17
112	1995	5N	March 18th	Twickenham	Won	24 – 12	1	-	7	1	-	-	2	2	56	39	17
113	1996	5N	March 2nd	Murrayfield	Won	18 – 9	-	-	6	-	-	-	3	-	57	39	17
114	1997	5N	February 1st	Twickenham	Won	41 – 13	3	1	5	-	1	-	2	-	58	39	17

INTERNATIONAL MATCHES:

ENGLAND v WALES

Match No.	Year	Cat	Date	Venue	Result	Score	England: G	T	PG	DG	Wales: G	T	PG	DG	Eng Won	Wal Won	Drn
				51 matches were played between England and Wales prior to 1947.							Results:				26	19	6
52	1947	5N	January 18th	Cardiff Arms Park	Won	9 - 6	1	-	-	1	-	2	-	-	27	19	6
53	1948	5N	January 17th	Twickenham	Drawn	3 - 3	-	-	1	-	-	1	-	-	27	19	7
	1948-49		Points values revised: Drop Goal reduced to 3 pts.														
54	1949	5N	January 15th	Cardiff Arms Park	Lost	3 - 9	-	1	-	-	-	3	-	-	27	20	7
55	1950	5N	January 21st	Twickenham	Lost	5 - 11	1	-	-	-	1	2	-	-	27	21	7
56	1951	5N	January 20th	St Helen's Swansea	Lost	5 - 23	1	-	-	-	4	1	-	-	27	22	7
57	1952	5N	January 19th	Twickenham	Lost	6 - 8	-	2	-	-	1	-	1	-	27	23	7
58	1953	5N	January 17th	Cardiff Arms Park	Won	8 - 3	1	1	-	-	-	-	1	-	28	23	7
59	1954	5N	January 16th	Twickenham	Won	9 - 6	-	3	-	-	-	2	-	-	29	23	7
60	1955	5N	January 22nd	Cardiff Arms Park	Lost	0 - 3	-	-	-	-	-	1	-	-	29	24	7
61	1956	5N	January 21st	Twickenham	Lost	3 - 8	-	-	1	-	1	-	1	-	29	25	7
62	1957	5N	January 19th	Cardiff Arms Park	Won	3 - 0	-	-	1	-	-	-	-	-	30	25	7
63	1958	5N	January 18th	Twickenham	Drawn	3 - 3	-	1	-	-	-	-	1	-	30	25	8
64	1959	5N	January 17th	Cardiff Arms Park	Lost	0 - 5	-	-	-	-	1	-	-	-	30	26	8
65	1960	5N	January 16th	Twickenham	Won	14 - 6	1	1	2	-	-	-	2	-	31	26	8
66	1961	5N	January 21st	Cardiff Arms Park	Lost	3 - 6	-	1	-	-	-	2	-	-	31	27	8
67	1962	5N	January 20th	Twickenham	Drawn	0 - 0	-	-	-	-	-	-	-	-	31	27	9
68	1963	5N	January 19th	Cardiff Arms Park	Won	13 - 6	2	1	-	-	-	1	1	-	32	27	9
69	1964	5N	January 18th	Twickenham	Drawn	6 - 6	-	2	-	-	-	2	-	1	32	27	10
70	1965	5N	January 16th	Cardiff Arms Park	Lost	3 - 14	-	-	1	-	1	2	-	-	32	28	10
71	1966	5N	January 15th	Twickenham	Lost	6 - 11	-	1	1	-	1	-	2	-	32	29	10

INTERNATIONAL MATCHES:

ENGLAND v WALES (continued)

Match No.	Year	Cat:	Date:	Venue:	Result:	Score:	England: G	T	PG	DG	Wales: G	T	PG	DG	Eng Won	Wal Won	Drn
72	1967	5N	April 15th	Cardiff Arms Park	Lost	21 - 34	-	3	4	-	5	-	2	1	32	30	10
73	1968	5N	January 20th	Twickenham	Drawn	11 - 11	1	1	1	-	1	1	-	1	32	30	11
74	1969	5N	April 12th	Cardiff Arms Park	Lost	9 - 30	-	-	3	-	3	2	2	1	32	31	11
75	1970	5N	February 28th	Twickenham	Lost	13 - 17	2	-	1	-	1	3	-	1	32	32	11
76	1971	5N	January 16th	Cardiff Arms Park	Lost	6 - 22	-	1	1	-	2	1	1	2	32	33	11

1971-72 Points values revised: Try increased to 4 pts.

Match No.	Year	Cat:	Date:	Venue:	Result:	Score:	England: G	T	PG	DG	Wales: G	T	PG	DG	Eng Won	Wal Won	Drn
77	1972	5N	January 15th	Twickenham	Lost	3 - 12	-	-	1	-	1	-	2	-	32	34	11
78	1973	5N	January 20th	Cardiff Arms Park	Lost	9 - 25	-	1	2	1	1	4	1	-	32	35	11
79	1974	5N	March 16th	Twickenham	Won	16 - 12	1	1	2	-	1	-	2	-	33	35	11
80	1975	5N	February 15th	Cardiff Arms Park	Lost	4 - 20	-	1	-	-	1	2	2	-	33	36	11
81	1976	5N	January 17th	Twickenham	Lost	9 - 21	-	-	3	-	3	-	1	-	33	37	11
82	1977	5N	March 5th	Cardiff Arms Park	Lost	9 - 14	-	-	3	-	-	2	2	-	33	38	11
83	1978	5N	February 4th	Twickenham	Lost	6 - 9	-	-	2	-	-	-	3	-	33	39	11
84	1979	5N	March 17th	Cardiff Arms Park	Lost	3 - 27	-	-	1	-	2	3	-	1	33	40	11
85	1980	5N	February 16th	Twickenham	Won	9 - 8	-	-	3	-	-	2	-	-	34	40	11
86	1981	5N	January 17th	Cardiff Arms Park	Lost	19 - 21	-	1	5	-	1	-	4	1	34	41	11
87	1982	5N	March 6th	Twickenham	Won	17 - 7	-	2	3	-	-	1	-	1	35	41	11
88	1983	5N	February 5th	Cardiff Arms Park	Drawn	13 - 13	-	1	2	1	-	1	2	1	35	41	12
89	1984	5N	March 17th	Twickenham	Lost	15 - 24	-	-	5	-	1	-	4	2	35	42	12
90	1985	5N	April 20th	Cardiff Arms Park	Lost	15 - 24	1	-	2	1	2	-	3	1	35	43	12
91	1986	5N	January 18th	Twickenham	Won	21 - 18	-	-	6	1	1	-	3	-	36	43	12
92	1987	5N	March 7th	Cardiff Arms Park	Lost	12 - 19	-	-	4	-	-	1	5	-	36	44	12

INTERNATIONAL MATCHES:

ENGLAND v WALES (continued)

Match No.	Year	Cat	Date	Venue	Result	Score	England: G	T	PG	DG	Wales: G	T	PG	DG	Eng Won	Wal Won	Drn
93	1987	WC	June 8th	Brisbane	Lost	3 - 16	-	-	1	-	2	1	-	-	36	45	12
94	1988	5N	February 6th	Twickenham	Lost	3 - 11	-	-	1	-	-	2	-	1	36	46	12
95	1989	5N	March 18th	Cardiff Arms Park	Lost	9 - 12	-	-	2	1	1	-	2	-	36	47	12
96	1990	5N	February 17th	Twickenham	Won	34 - 6	3	1	4	-	1	-	-	-	37	47	12
97	1991	5N	January 19th	Cardiff Arms Park	Won	25 - 6	-	1	7	-	-	-	2	-	38	47	12
98	1992	5N	March 7th	Twickenham	Won	24 - 0	3	-	2	-	-	-	-	-	39	47	12

1992-93 Points values revised: Try increased to 5 pts.

Match No.	Year	Cat	Date	Venue	Result	Score	England: G	T	PG	DG	Wales: G	T	PG	DG	Eng Won	Wal Won	Drn
99	1993	5N	February 6th	Cardiff Arms Park	Lost	9 - 10	-	-	2	1	1	-	1	-	39	48	12
100	1994	5N	March 19th	Twickenham	Won	15 - 8	1	1	1	-	-	1	1	-	40	48	12
101	1995	5N	February 18th	Cardiff Arms Park	Won	23 - 9	1	2	2	-	-	1	3	-	41	48	12
102	1996	5N	February 3rd	Twickenham	Won	21 - 15	1	1	3	-	1	1	1	-	42	48	12
103	1997	5N	March 15th	Cardiff Arms Park	Won	34 - 13	4	-	2	-	1	-	2	-	43	48	12

INTERNATIONAL MATCHES:

ENGLAND v AUSTRALIA

Match No.	Year	Cat	Date	Venue	Result	Score	England: G	T	PG	DG	Australia: G	T	PG	DG	Eng Won	Aus Won	Dm
											Results:						
	2 matches were played between England and Australia prior to 1947.														1	1	0
3	1948		January 3rd	Twickenham	Lost	0 - 11	-	-	-	-	1	2	-	-	1	2	0
	1948-49 Points values revised: Drop Goal reduced to 3 pts.																
4	1958		February 1st	Twickenham	Won	9 - 6	-	2	1	-	-	-	1	1	2	2	0
5	1963		June 4th	Sydney	Lost	9 - 18	-	3	-	-	3	1	-	-	2	3	0
6	1967		January 7th	Twickenham	Lost	11 - 23	1	-	2	-	1	1	2	3	2	4	0
	1971-72 Points values revised: Try increased to 4 pts.																
7	1973		November 17th	Twickenham	Won	20 - 3	1	2	2	-	-	-	1	-	3	4	0
8	1975		May 24th	Sydney	Lost	9 - 16	1	-	1	-	-	1	2	2	3	5	0
9	1975		May 31st	Brisbane	Lost	21 - 30	2	-	3	-	2	3	2	-	3	6	0
10	1976		January 3rd	Twickenham	Won	23 - 6	1	2	3	-	-	-	2	-	4	6	0
11	1982		January 2nd	Twickenham	Won	15 - 11	1	-	3	-	-	2	1	-	5	6	0
12	1984		November 3rd	Twickenham	Lost	3 - 19	-	-	1	-	2	1	1	-	5	7	0
13	1987	WC	May 23rd	Sydney	Lost	6 - 19	-	-	2	-	1	1	3	-	5	8	0
14	1988		May 29th	Brisbane	Lost	16 - 22	1	1	2	-	2	1	2	-	5	9	0
15	1988		June 12th	Sydney	Lost	8 - 28	-	2	-	-	3	1	2	-	5	10	0
16	1988		November 5th	Twickenham	Won	28 - 19	3	1	2	-	2	1	1	-	6	10	0
17	1991		July 27th	Sydney	Lost	15 - 40	1	-	3	-	4	1	4	-	6	11	0
18	1991	WC	November 2nd	Twickenham	Lost	6 - 12	-	-	2	-	1	-	2	-	6	12	0

INTERNATIONAL MATCHES:

ENGLAND v AUSTRALIA (continued)

1992-93 Points values revised: Try increased to 5 pts.

Match No.	Year	Cat	Date	Venue	Result	Score:	England: G	T	PG	DG	Australia: G	T	PG	DG	Eng Won	Aus Won	Drn
19	1995	WC	June 10th	Cape Town	Won	25 - 22	1	-	5	1	1	-	5	-	7	12	0
20	1997		July 12th	Sydney	Lost	6 - 25	-	-	1	1	1	3	1	-	7	13	0

INTERNATIONAL MATCHES: ENGLAND v NEW ZEALAND

Match No.	Year	Cat	Date	Venue	Result	Score	England: G	T	PG	DG	New Zealand: G	T	PG	DG	Eng Won	NZ Won	Drn
			3 matches were played between England and New Zealand prior to 1947.			Results:									1	2	0
4	1954		January 30th	Twickenham	Lost	0 - 5	-	-	-	-	1	-	-	-	1	3	0
5	1963		May 25th	Auckland	Lost	11 - 21	1	-	2	-	3	-	1	-	1	4	0
6	1963		June 1st	Christchurch	Lost	6 - 9	-	1	1	-	-	2	-	GM	1	5	0
7	1964		January 4th	Twickenham	Lost	0 - 14	-	-	-	-	1	1	2	-	1	6	0
8	1967		November 4th	Twickenham	Lost	11 - 23	1	1	1	-	4	1	-	-	1	7	0
1971-72 Points values revised: Try increased to 4 pts.																	
9	1973		January 6th	Twickenham	Lost	0 - 9	-	-	-	-	1	-	1	-	1	8	0
10	1973		September 15th	Auckland	Won	16 - 10	2	1	-	-	1	1	-	-	2	8	0
11	1978		November 25th	Twickenham	Lost	6 - 16	-	-	1	1	1	1	2	-	2	9	0
12	1979		November 24th	Twickenham	Lost	9 - 10	-	-	3	-	-	1	2	-	2	10	0
13	1983		November 19th	Twickenham	Won	15 - 9	1	1	1	-	1	-	1	-	3	10	0
14	1985		June 1st	Christchurch	Lost	13 - 18	1	1	1	-	-	3	3	1	3	11	0
15	1985		June 8th	Wellington	Lost	15 - 42	2	-	-	1	3	3	3	1	3	12	0
16	1991	WC	October 3rd	Twickenham	Lost	12 - 18	-	-	3	1	1	-	4	-	3	13	0
1992-93 Points values revised: Try increased to 5 pts.																	
17	1993		November 27th	Twickenham	Won	15 - 9	-	1	4	1	-	-	3	-	4	13	0
18	1995	WC	June 17th	Cape Town	Lost	29 - 45	3	1	1	-	3	3	1	2	4	14	0

INTERNATIONAL MATCHES:

ENGLAND v SOUTH AFRICA

Match No.	Year	Cat	Date	Venue	Result	Score	England: G	T	PG	DG	South Africa: G	T	PG	DG	Eng Won	SA Won	Drn
			3 matches were played between England and South Africa prior to 1947.				Results:										
4	1952		January 5th	Twickenham	Lost	3 - 8	-	1	-	-	1	-	1	-	0	2	1
5	1961		January 7th	Twickenham	Lost	0 - 5	-	-	-	-	1	-	-	-	0	3	1
6	1969		December 20th	Twickenham	Won	11 - 8	1	1	1	-	1	-	1	-	1	4	1
1971-72 Points values revised: Try increased to 4 pts.																	
7	1972		June 3rd	Johannesburg	Won	18 - 9	1	-	4	-	-	-	3	-	2	4	1
8	1984		June 2nd	Port Elizabeth	Lost	15 - 33	-	-	4	1	3	-	5	1	2	5	1
9	1984		June 9th	Johannesburg	Lost	9 - 35	-	-	3	-	4	2	1	-	2	6	1
1992-93 Points values revised: Try increased to 5 pts.																	
10	1992		November 14th	Twickenham	Won	33 - 16	2	2	3	-	1	-	2	1	3	6	1
11	1994		June 4th	Pretoria	Won	32 - 15	2	-	5	1	-	-	5	-	4	6	1
12	1994		June 11th	Cape Town	Lost	9 - 27	-	-	3	-	1	1	5	-	5	6	1
13	1995		November 18th	Twickenham	Lost	14 - 24	-	1	3	-	-	3	3	-	5	7	1

INTERNATIONAL MATCHES:

ENGLAND v ARGENTINA

Match No.	Year	Cat	Date	Venue	Result	Score	England: G	T	PG	DG	Argentina: G	T	PG	DG	Eng Won	Arg Won	Drn
1	1981		May 30th	Buenos Aires	Drawn	19 - 19	2	1	1	-	1	1	1	2	0	0	1
2	1981		June 6th	Buenos Aires	Won	12 - 6	1	1	2	-	1	-	-	-	1	0	1
3	1990		July 28th	Buenos Aires	Won	25 - 12	1	1	5	-	-	-	4	-	2	0	1
4	1990		August 4th	Buenos Aires	Lost	13 - 15	1	1	1	-	-	-	5	-	2	1	1
5	1990		November 3rd	Twickenham	Won	51 - 0	7	-	3	-	-	-	-	-	3	1	1

1992-93 Points values revised: Try increased to 5 pts.

Match No.	Year	Cat	Date	Venue	Result	Score	England: G	T	PG	DG	Argentina: G	T	PG	DG	Eng Won	Arg Won	Drn
6	1995	WC	May 27th	Durban	Won	24 - 18	-	-	6	2	1	1	2	-	4	1	1
7	1996		Dec 14th	Twickenham	Won	20 - 18	-	1	5	-	-	-	6	-	5	1	1
8	1997		May 30th	Buenos Aires	Won	46 - 20	5	1	2	-	1	2	-	1	6	1	1
9	1997		June 6th	Buenos Aires	Lost	13 - 33	-	2	1	-	2	2	3	-	6	2	1

ENGLAND v CANADA

Match No.	Year	Cat	Date	Venue	Result	Score	England: G	T	PG	DG	Canada: G	T	PG	DG	Eng Won	Can Won	Drn
1	1992		October 17th	Wembley	Won	26 - 13	-	4	2	-	1	-	2	-	1	0	0

1992-93 Points values revised: Try increased to 5 pts.

Match No.	Year	Cat	Date	Venue	Result	Score	England: G	T	PG	DG	Canada: G	T	PG	DG	Eng Won	Can Won	Drn
2	1994		December 10th	Twickenham	Won	60 - 19	6	-	6	-	2	1	-	-	2	0	0

INTERNATIONAL MATCHES:

ENGLAND v FIJI

Match No.	Year	Cat:	Date:	Venue:	Result:	Score:	England: G	T	PG	DG	Fiji: G	T	PG	DG	Eng Won	Fiji Won	Drn
1	1988		June 17th	Suva	Won	25 - 12	2	1	3	-	-	-	3	1	1	0	0
2	1989		November 4th	Twickenham	Won	58 - 23	6	4	2	-	2	2	1	-	2	0	0
3	1991		July 20th	Suva	Won	28 - 12	2	1	2	2	1	-	1	1	3	0	0

1992-93 Points values revised: Try increased to 5 pts.

INTERNATIONAL MATCHES:

ENGLAND v JAPAN

Match No.	Year	Cat:	Date:	Venue:	Result:	Score:	England: G	T	PG	DG	Japan: G	T	PG	DG	Eng Won	Japan Won	Drn
1	1987	WC	May 30th	Sydney	Won	60 - 7	7	3	2	-	-	1	1	-	1	0	0

1992-93 Points values revised: Try increased to 5 pts.

INTERNATIONAL MATCHES:

ENGLAND v ITALY

Match No.	Year	Cat:	Date:	Venue:	Result:	Score:	England: G	T	PG	DG	Italy: G	T	PG	DG	Eng Won	Italy Won	Drn
1	1991	WC	October 8th	Twickenham	Won	36 - 6	4	-	4	-	1	-	-	-	1	0	0
	1992-93 Points values revised: Try increased to 5 pts.																
2	1995	WC	May 31st	Durban	Won	27 - 20	1	1	5	-	2	-	2	-	2	0	0
3	1996		November 23rd	Twickenham	Won	54 - 21	5	2	3	-	3	-	-	-	3	0	0

INTERNATIONAL MATCHES:

ENGLAND v ROMANIA

Match No.	Year	Cat:	Date:	Venue:	Result:	Score:	England: G	T	PG	DG	Romania: G	T	PG	DG	Eng Won	Rom Won	Drn
1	1985		January 5th	Twickenham	Won	22 - 15	-	1	4	2	-	-	5	-	1	0	0
2	1989		May 13th	Bucharest	Won	58 - 3	8	1	1	1	-	-	1	-	2	0	0
	1992-93 Points values revised: Try increased to 5 pts.																
3	1994		November 12th	Twickenham	Won	54 - 3	6	-	4	-	-	-	1	-	3	0	0

INTERNATIONAL MATCHES:

ENGLAND v UNITED STATES OF AMERICA

Match No.	Year	Cat:	Date:	Venue:	Result:	Score:	England: G	T	PG	DG	USA: G	T	PG	DG	Eng Won	USA Won	Drm
1	1987	WC	June 3rd	Sydney	Won	34 - 6	3	1	4	-	1	-	1	-	1	0	0
2	1991	WC	October 11th	Twickenham	Won	37 - 9	4	1	3	-	1	-	1	-	2	0	0

ENGLAND v WESTERN SAMOA

Match No.	Year	Cat:	Date:	Venue:	Result:	Score:	England: G	T	PG	DG	W.Samoa G	T	PG	DG	Eng Won	WS Won	Drm
1	1995	WC	June 10th	Durban	Won	44 - 22	3	1	5	1	2	1	1	-	1	0	0
2	1995		December 16th	Twickenham	Won	27 - 9	1	1	5	-	-	-	3	-	2	0	0

ENGLAND v RFU PRESIDENT'S XV

Match No.	Year	Cat:	Date:	Venue:	Result:	Score:	England: G	T	PG	DG	RFU XV G	T	PG	DG	Eng Won	RFU Won	Drm
1	1971	Cent'l	April 17th	Twickenham	Lost	11 - 28	1	-	2	-	5	1	-	-	0	1	0

SECTION 2

INTERNATIONAL MATCH RECORDS

1947 onwards

HIGHEST SCORE BY ENGLAND IN AN INTERNATIONAL MATCH:

	Total Points:		Opponent:	Match score:	Venue:		Date:	Captain:
All Countries:								
Home:	60		Canada	60 - 19	at Twickenham		December 10th 1994	W.D.C.Carling
Away:	60		Japan	60 - 7	at Sydney	(WC)	May 30th 1987	M.E.Harrison

Individual Countries - at home:

	Total Points:		Opponent:	Match score:	Venue:		Date:	Captain:
	51		Argentina	51 - 0	at Twickenham		November 3rd 1990	W.D.C.Carling
	28		Australia	28 - 19	at Twickenham		November 5th 1988	W.D.C.Carling
	60		Canada	60 - 19	at Twickenham		December 10th 1994	W.D.C.Carling
	58	*	Fiji	58 - 23	at Twickenham		November 4th 1989	W.D.C.Carling
	31		France	31 - 10	at Twickenham		February 4th 1995	W.D.C.Carling
	38		Ireland	38 - 9	at Twickenham		February 1st 1992	W.D.C.Carling
	54		Italy	54 - 21	at Twickenham		November 23rd 1966	P.R.de Glanville
			Japan					
	15		New Zealand	15 - 9	at Twickenham		November 19th 1983	P.J.Wheeler
			New Zealand	15 - 9	at Twickenham		November 27th 1993	W.D.C.Carling
	54		Romania	54 - 3	at Twickenham		November 12th 1994	W.D.C.Carling
	41		Scotland	41 - 13	at Twickenham		February 1st 1997	P.R.de Glanville
	33		South Africa	33 - 16	at Twickenham		November 14th 1992	W.D.C.Carling
	37	*	United States	37 - 9	at Twickenham	(WC)	October 11th 1991	W.D.C.Carling
	34		Wales	34 - 6	at Twickenham		February 17th 1990	W.D.C.Carling
	27	*	Western Samoa	27 - 9	at Twickenham		December 16th 1995	W.D.C.Carling

Individual Countries - away:

	Total Points:		Opponent:	Match score:	Venue:		Date:	Captain:
	46		Argentina	46 - 20	at Buenos Aires		May 30th 1997	P.R.de Glanville
	25		Australia	25 - 22	at Cape Town	(WC)	June 10th 1995	W.D.C.Carling
			Canada					
	28		Fiji	28 - 12	at Suva		July 20th 1991	W.D.C.Carling
	31		France	31 - 13	at Parc des Princes		February 15th 1992	W.D.C.Carling
	46		Ireland	46 - 6	at Lansdowne Road		February 15th 1997	P.R.de Glanville
	27	*	Italy	27 - 20	at Durban	(WC)	May 31st 1995	W.D.C.Carling
	60	*	Japan	60 - 7	at Sydney	(WC)	May 30th 1987	M.E.Harrison
	29		New Zealand	29 - 45	at Cape Town	(WC)	June 17th 1995	W.D.C.Carling
	58	*	Romania	58 - 3	at Bucharest		May 13th 1989	C.R.Andrew
	30		Scotland	30 - 18	at Murrayfield		March 15th 1980	W.B.Beaumont
	32		South Africa	32 - 15	at Pretoria		June 4th 1994	W.D.C.Carling
	34	*	United States	34 - 6	at Sydney	(WC)	June 3rd 1987	M.E.Harrison
	34		Wales	34 - 13	at Cardiff Arms Park		March 15th 1997	P.R.de Glanville
s	44	*	Western Samoa	44 - 22	at Durban	(WC)	June 4th 1995	W.D.C.Carling

*   Only one match played to date.

HIGHEST SCORE AGAINST ENGLAND IN AN INTERNATIONAL MATCH:

Points scored:		Opponent:	Match score:	Venue:		Date:	Captain:
All Countries:							
Home: 27		by France	20 - 27	at Twickenham		February 1st 1975	F.E.Cotton
Away: 45		by New Zealand	29 - 45	at Cape Town	(WC)	June 17th 1995	W.D.C.Carling

Points scored:		Opponent:	Match score:	Venue:		Date:	Captain:
Individual Countries - at home:							
18		by Argentina	20 - 18	at Twickenham		December 14th 1996	J.Leonard
23		by Australia	11 - 23	at Twickenham		January 7th 1967	R.A.W.Sharp
19	*	by Canada	60 - 19	at Twickenham		December 12th 1995	W.D.C.Carling
23	*	by Fiji	58 - 23	at Twickenham		November 4th 1989	W.D.C.Carling
27		by France	20 - 27	at Twickenham		February 1st 1975	F.E.Cotton
26		by Ireland	21 - 26	at Twickenham		February 16th 1974	J V Pullin
21		by Italy	54 - 21	at Twickenham		November 23rd 1996	P.R.de Glanville
		Japan					
23		by New Zealand	11 - 23	at Twickenham		November 4th 1967	P.E.Judd
15		by Romania	22 - 15	at Twickenham		January 5th 1985	P.W.Dodge
22		by Scotland	12 - 22	at Twickenham		March 5th 1983	J.P.Scott
24		by South Africa	14 - 24	at Twickenham		November 18th 1995	W.D.C.Carling
9	*	by United States	37 - 9	at Twickenham	(WC)	October 11th 1991	W.D.C.Carling
24		by Wales	15 - 24	at Twickenham		March 17th 1984	P.J.Wheeler
9	*	by Western Samoa	27 - 9	at Twickenham		December 16th 1995	W.D.C.Carling

Points scored:		Opponent:	Match score:	Venue:		Date:	Captain:
Individual Countries - away:							
33		by Argentina	13 - 33	at Buenos Aires		June 6th 1997	P.R.de Glanville
40		by Australia	15 - 40	at Sydney		July 27th 1991	W.D.C.Carling
		Canada					
12		by Fiji	25 - 12	at Suva		June 17th 1988	R.M.Harding
			28 - 12	at Suva		July 20th 1991	W.D.C.Carling
37		by France	12 - 37	at Stades Colombes		February 26th 1972	P.J.Dixon
25		by Ireland	15 - 25	at Lansdowne Road		March 19th 1983	J.P.Scott
20	*	by Italy	27 - 20	at Durban	(WC)	May 31st 1995	W.D.C.Carling
7	*	by Japan	60 - 7	at Sydney	(WC)	May 30th 1987	M.E.Harrison
45		by New Zealand	29 - 45	at Cape Town	(WC)	June 17th 1995	W.D.C.Carling
3	*	by Romania	58 - 3	at Bucharest		May 13th 1989	C.R.Andrew
33		by Scotland	6 - 33	at Murrayfield		February 15th 1986	N.D.Melville
35		by South Africa	9 - 35	at Johannesburg		June 9th 1984	J.P.Scott
6	*	by United States	34 - 6	at Sydney	(WC)	June 3rd 1987	M.E.Harrison
34		by Wales	21 - 34	at Cardiff Arms Park		April 15th 1967	P.E.Judd
22	*	by Western Samoa	44 - 22	at Durban	(WC)	June 4th 1995	W.D.C.Carling

*   Only one match played to date.

HIGHEST AGGREGATE SCORE IN AN INTERNATIONAL MATCH INVOLVING ENGLAND:

	Total Points:	Opponent:	Match score:	Venue:		Date:	Captain:
All Countries:							
Home:	81 *	Fiji	58 - 23	at Twickenham		November 4th 1989	W.D.C.Carling
Away:	74	New Zealand	29 - 45	at Cape Town	(WC)	June 17th 1995	W.D.C.Carling

	Total Points:	Opponent:	Match score:	Venue:		Date:	Captain:
Individual Countries - at home:							
	51	Argentina	51 - 0	at Twickenham		November 3rd 1990	W.D.C.Carling
	47	Australia	28 - 19	at Twickenham		November 5th 1988	W.D.C.Carling
	79 *	Canada	60 - 19	at Twickenham		December 10th 1994	W.D.C.Carling
	81 *	Fiji	58 - 23	at Twickenham		November 4th 1989	W.D.C.Carling
	47	France	20 - 27	at Twickenham		February 1st 1975	F.E.Cotton
	47	Ireland	21 - 26	at Twickenham		February 16th 1974	J.V.Pullin
			38 - 9	at Twickenham		February 1st 1992	W.D.C.Carling
	75	Italy	54 - 21	at Twickenham		November 23rd 1996	P.R.de Glanville
		Japan					
	34	New Zealand	11 - 23	at Twickenham		November 4th 1967	P.E.Judd
	57	Romania	54 - 3	at Twickenham		November 12th 1994	W.D.C.Carling
	54	Scotland	41 - 13	at Twickenham		February 1st 1997	P.R.de Glanville
	49	South Africa	33 - 16	at Twickenham		November 14th 1992	W.D.C.Carling
	46 *	United States	37 - 9	at Twickenham	(WC)	October 11th 1991	W.D.C.Carling
	40	Wales	34 - 6	at Twickenham		February 17th 1990	W.D.C.Carling
	36 *	Western Samoa	27 - 9	at Twickenham		December 16th 1995	W.D.C.Carling

	Total Points:	Opponent:	Match score:	Venue:		Date:	Captain:
Individual Countries - away:							
	66	Argentina	46 - 20	at Buenos Aires		May 30th 1997	P.R.de Glanville
	55	Australia	15 - 40	at Sydney		July 27th 1991	W.D.C.Carling
		Canada					
	40	Fiji	28 - 12	at Suva		July 20th 1991	W.D.C.Carling
	50	France	18 - 32	at Parc des Princes		March 3rd 1984	P.J.Wheeler
	52	Ireland	46 - 6	at Lansdowne Road		February 15th 1997	P.R.de Glanville
	47 *	Italy	27 - 20	at Durban	(WC)	May 31st 1995	W.D.C.Carling
	67 *	Japan	60 - 7	at Sydney	(WC)	May 30th 1987	M.E.Harrison
	74	New Zealand	29 - 45	at Cape Town	(WC)	June 17th 1995	W.D.C.Carling
	61 *	Romania	58 - 3	at Bucharest		May 13th 1989	C.R.Andrew
	48	Scotland	30 - 18	at Murrayfield		March 15th 1980	W.B.Beaumont
	48	South Africa	15 - 33	at Port Elizabeth		June 2nd 1984	J.P.Scott
	40 *	United States	34 - 6	at Sydney	(WC)	June 3rd 1987	M.E.Harrison
	55	Wales	21 - 34	at Cardiff Arms Park		April 15th 1967	P.E.Judd
	66 *	Western Samoa	44 - 22	at Durban	(WC)	June 4th 1995	W.D.C.Carling

*   Only one match played to date.

HIGHEST MARGIN OF VICTORY ACHIEVED BY ENGLAND IN AN INTERNATIONAL MATCH:

		Opponent:	Match score:	Venue:	Date:	Captain:
All Countries:						
Home:	51	Argentina	51 - 0	at Twickenham	November 3rd 1990	W.D.C.Carling
	51	Romania	54 - 3	at Twickenham	November 12th 1994	W.D.C.Carling
Away:	55 *	Romania	58 - 3	at Bucharest	May 13th 1989	C.R.Andrew

		Opponent:	Match score:	Venue:	Date:	Captain:
Individual Countries - at home:						
	51	Argentina	51 - 0	at Twickenham	November 3rd 1990	W.D.C.Carling
	17	Australia	20 - 3	at Twickenham	November 17th 1973	J.V.Pullin
	41 *	Canada	60 - 19	at Twickenham	December 10th 1994	W.D.C.Carling
	35 *	Fiji	58 - 23	at Twickenham	November 4th 1989	W.D.C.Carling
	21	France	31 - 10	at Twickenham	February 4th 1995	W.D.C.Carling
	32	Ireland	35 - 3	at Twickenham	March 19th 1988	N.D.Melville
	33	Italy	54 - 21	at Twickenham	November 23rd 1996	P.R.de Glanville
		Japan				
	6	New Zealand	15 - 9	at Twickenham	November 19th 1983	P.J.Wheeler
			15 - 9	at Twickenham	November 27th 1993	W.D.C.Carling
	51	Romania	54 - 3	at Twickenham	November 12th 1994	W.D.C.Carling
	28	Scotland	41 - 13	at Twickenham	February 1st 1997	P.R.de Glanville
	17	South Africa	33 - 16	at Twickenham	November 14th 1992	W.D.C.Carling
	28 *	United States	37 - 9	at Twickenham (WC	October 11th 1991	W.D.C.Carling
	28	Wales	34 - 6	at Twickenham	February 17th 1990	W.D.C.Carling
	18 *	Western Samoa	27 - 9	at Twickenham	December 16th 1995	W.D.C.Carling

		Opponent:	Match score:	Venue:	Date:	Captain:
Individual Countries - away:						
	26	Argentina	46 - 20	at Buenos Aires	May 30th 1997	P.R.de Glanville
	3	Australia	25 - 22	at Cape Town (WC	June 10th 1995	W.D.C.Carling
		Canada				
	16	Fiji	28 - 12	at Suva	July 20th 1991	W.D.C.Carling
	19	France	26 - 7	at Parc des Princes	February 3rd 1990	W.D.C.Carling
	40	Ireland	46 - 6	at Lansdowne Road	February 15th 1997	P.R.de Glanville
	7 *	Italy	27 - 20	at Durban (WC	May 31st 1995	W.D.C.Carling
	53 *	Japan	60 - 7	at Sydney (WC	May 30th 1987	M.E.Harrison
	6	New Zealand	16 - 10	at Auckland	September 15th 1973	J.V.Pullin
	55 *	Romania	58 - 3	at Bucharest	May 13th 1989	C.R.Andrew
	18	Scotland	25 - 7	at Murrayfield	January 18th 1992	W.D.C.Carling
	17	South Africa	32 - 15	at Pretoria	June 4th 1994	W.D.C.Carling
	28 *	United States	34 - 6	at Sydney (WC	June 3rd 1987	M.E.Harrison
	21	Wales	34 - 13	at Cardiff Arms Park	March 15th 1997	P.R.de Glanville
	22 *	Western Samoa	44 - 22	at Durban (WC	June 4th 1995	W.D.C.Carling

*   Only one match played to date.

HIGHEST MARGIN OF DEFEAT SUFFERED BY ENGLAND IN AN INTERNATIONAL MATCH:

	Points Margin:	Opponent:	Match score:	Venue:	Date:	Captain:
All Countries:						
Home:	16	by Australia	3 - 19	at Twickenham	November 3rd 1984	N.D.Melville
Away:	27	by New Zealand	15 - 42	at Wellington	June 8th 1985	P.W.Dodge
	27	by Scotland	6 - 33	at Murrayfield	February 15th 1986	N.D.Melville

	Points Margin:	Opponent:	Match score:	Venue:	Date:	Captain:
Individual Countries - at home:						
		Argentina				
	16	by Australia	3 - 19	at Twickenham	November 3rd 1984	N.D.Melville
		Canada				
		Fiji				
	8	by France	3 - 11	at Twickenham	February 24th 1951	JMK Kendall -Carpenter
	13	by Ireland	5 - 18	at Twickenham	February 8th 1964	J.G.Willcox
		Italy				
*		Japan				
	14	by New Zealand	11 - 23	at Twickenham	November 4th 1967	P.E.Judd
		Romania				
	10	by Scotland	12 - 22	at Twickenham	March 5th 1983	J.P.Scott
	10	by South Africa	14 - 24	at Twickenham	November 18th 1995	W.D.C.Carling
		United States				
	12	by Wales	9 - 21	at Twickenham	January 17th 1976	A.Neary
		Western Samoa				

*   England have never played Japan in England

	Points Margin:	Opponent:	Match score:	Venue:	Date:	Captain:
Individual Countries - away:						
	20	by Argentina	13 - 33	at Buenos Aires	June 6th 1997	P.R.de Glanville
	25	by Australia	15 - 40	at Sydney	July 27th 1991	W.D.C.Carling
*		Canada				
		Fiji				
	25	by France	12 - 37	at Stade Colombes	February 26th 1972	P.J.Dixon
	22	by Ireland	0 - 22	at Lansdowne Road	February 8th 1947	J.Mycock
		Italy				
		Japan				
	27	by New Zealand	15 - 42	at Wellington	June 8th 1985	P.W.Dodge
		Romania				
	27	by Scotland	6 - 33	at Murrayfield	February 15th 1986	N.D.Melville
	26	by South Africa	9 - 35	at Johannesburg	June 9th 1984	J.P.Scott
		United States				
	24	by Wales	3 - 27	at Cardiff Arms Park	March 17th 1979	W.B.Beaumont
		Western Samoa				

*   England have never played Canada away from home.

MATCHES IN WHICH ENGLAND HAVE SCORED 25 POINTS OR MORE:

Points Scored:	Against:	Venue:		Date:	Captain:
60	Canada	Twickenham		December 10th 1994	W.D.C.Carling
60	Japan	Sydney	(WC)	May 30th 1987	M.E.Harrison
58	Fiji	Twickenham		November 4th 1989	W.D.C.Carling
58	Romania	Bucharest		May 13th 1989	C.R.Andrew
54	Italy	Twickenham		November 23rd 1996	P.R.de Glanville
54	Romania	Twickenham		November 12th 1994	W.D.C.Carling
51	Argentina	Twickenham		November 3rd 1990	W.D.C.Carling
46	Argentina	Buenos Aires		May 30th 1997	P.R.de Glanville
46	Ireland	Lansdowne Road		February 15th 1997	P.R.de Glanville
44	Western Samoa	Durban	(WC)	June 4th 1995	W.D.C.Carling
41	Scotland	Twickenham		February 1st 1997	P.R.de Glanville
38	Ireland	Twickenham		February 1st 1992	W.D.C.Carling
37	USA	Twickenham	(WC)	October 11th 1991	W.D.C.Carling
36	Italy	Twickenham	(WC)	October 8th 1991	W.D.C.Carling
35	Ireland	Twickenham		March 19th 1988	N.D.Melville
34	Wales	Cardiff Arms Park		March 15th 1997	P.R.de Glanville
34	Wales	Twickenham		February 17th 1990	W.D.C.Carling
34	USA	Sydney	(WC)	June 3rd 1987	M.E.Harrison
33	South Africa	Twickenham		November 14th 1992	W.D.C.Carling
32	South Africa	Pretoria		June 4th 1994	W.D.C.Carling
31	France	Twickenham		February 4th 1995	W.D.C.Carling
31	France	Parc des Princes		February 15th 1992	W.D.C.Carling
30	Scotland	Murrayfield		March 15th 1980	W.B.Beaumont
29	New Zealand	Cape Town	(WC)	June 17th 1995	W.D.C.Carling
28	Ireland	Twickenham		March 16th 1996	W.D.C.Carling
28	Fiji	Suva		July 20th 1991	W.D.C.Carling
28	Australia	Twickenham		November 5th 1988	W.D.C.Carling
27	Western Samoa	Twickenham		December 16th 1995	W.D.C.Carling
27	Italy	Durban	(WC)	May 31st 1995	W.D.C.Carling
27	France	Parc des Princes		February 20th 1982	S.J.Smith
27	Scotland	Twickenham		March 18th 1967	P.E.Judd
26	Scotland	Twickenham		March 6th 1993	W.D.C.Carling
26	Canada	Wembley Stadium		October 17th 1992	W.D.C.Carling
26	France	Parc des Princes		February 3rd 1990	W.D.C.Carling
26	Scotland	Twickenham		January 15th 1977	R.M.Uttley
26	Scotland	Twickenham		March 21st 1953	N.M.Hall
25	Australia	Cape Town	(WC)	June 10th 1995	W.D.C.Carling
25	Scotland	Murrayfield		January 18th 1992	W.D.C.Carling
25	Wales	Cardiff Arms Park		January 19th 1991	W.D.C.Carling
25	Argentina	Buenos Aires		July 28th 1990	W.D.C.Carling
25	Fiji	Suva		June 17th 1988	R.M.Harding
25	Ireland	Twickenham		March 1st 1986	N.D.Melville

MATCHES IN WHICH ENGLAND HAVE CONCEDED 25 POINTS OR MORE:

Points Scored:	By:	Venue:		Date:	Captain:
45	New Zealand	Cape Town	(WC)	June 17th 1995	W.D.C.Carling
42	New Zealand	Wellington		June 8th 1985	P.W.Dodge
40	Australia	Sydney		July 27th 1991	W.D.C.Carling
37	France	Stade Colombes		February 26th 1972	P.J.Dixon
35	South Africa	Johannesburg		June 9th 1984	J.P.Scott
35	France	Stade Colombes		April 18th 1970	R.B.Taylor
34	Wales	Cardiff Arms Park		April 15th 1967	P.E.Judd
33	Argentina	Buenos Aires		June 6th 1997	P.R.de Glanville
33	Scotland	Murrayfield		February 15th 1986	N.D.Melville
33	South Africa	Port Elizabeth		June 2nd 1984	J.P.Scott
32	France	Parc des Princes		March 3rd 1984	P.J.Wheeler
30	France	Parc des Princes		March 20th 1976	A.Neary
30	Australia	Brisbane		May 31st 1975	J.V.Pullin
30	Wales	Cardiff Arms Park		April 12th 1969	D.P.Rogers
29	France	Parc des Princes		March 15th 1986	N.D.Melville
28	Australia	Sydney		June 12th 1988	J.Orwin
28	President's XV	Twickenham		April 17th 1971	J.S.Spencer
27	South Africa	Cape Town		June 11th 1994	W.D.C.Carling
27	Wales	Cardiff Arms Park		March 17th 1979	W.B.Beaumont
27	France	Twickenham		February 1st 1975	F.E.Cotton
26	Ireland	Twickenham		February 16th 1974	J.V.Pullin
26	Scotland (Centenary)	Murrayfield		March 27th 1971	J.S.Spencer
25	Australia	Sydney		July 12th 1997	P.R.de Glanville
25	Ireland	Lansdowne Road		March 19th 1983	J.P.Scott
25	Wales	Cardiff Arms Park		January 20th 1973	J.V.Pullin

MATCHES IN WHICH ENGLAND HAVE SCORED 4 TRIES OR MORE:

Tries Scored:	Against:	Venue:		Date:	Captain:
10	Fiji	Twickenham		November 4th 1989	W.D.C.Carling
10	Japan	Sydney	(WC)	May 30th 1987	M.E.Harrison
9	Romania	Bucharest		May 13th 1989	C.R.Andrew
7	Italy	Twickenham		November 23rd 1996	P.R.de Glanville
7	Argentina	Twickenham		November 3rd 1990	W.D.C.Carling
6	Argentina	Buenos Aires		May 30th 1997	P.R.de Glanville
6	Ireland	Lansdowne Road		February 15th 1997	P.R.de Glanville
6	Canada	Twickenham		December 10th 1994	W.D.C.Carling
6	Ireland	Twickenham		February 1st 1992	W.D.C.Carling
6	Ireland	Twickenham		March 19th 1988	N.D.Melville
6	Scotland	Twickenham		March 21st 1953	N.M.Hall
5	Romania	Twickenham		November 12th 1994	W.D.C.Carling
5	USA	Twickenham	(WC)	October 11th 1991	W.D.C.Carling
5	Scotland	Murrayfield		March 15th 1980	W.B.Beaumont
5	Scotland	Twickenham		March 19th 1949	I.Preece
4	Wales	Cardiff Arms Park		March 15th 1997	P.R.de Glanville
4	Scotland	Twickenham		February 1st 1997	P.R.de Glanville
4	New Zealand	Cape Town	(WC)	June 17th 1995	W.D.C.Carling
4	Western Samoa	Durban	(WC)	June 4th 1995	W.D.C.Carling
4	South Africa	Twickenham		November 14th 1992	W.D.C.Carling
4	Canada	Wembley Stadium		October 17th 1992	W.D.C.Carling
4	France	Parc des Princes		February 15th 1992	W.D.C.Carling
4	Italy	Twickenham	(WC)	October 8th 1991	W.D.C.Carling
4	Wales	Twickenham		February 17th 1990	W.D.C.Carling
4	Ireland	Twickenham		January 20th 1990	W.D.C.Carling
4	Australia	Twickenham		November 5th 1988	W.D.C.Carling
4	USA	Sydney	(WC)	June 3rd 1987	M.E.Harrison
4	Ireland	Twickenham		March 1st 1986	N.D.Melville
4	Scotland	Twickenham		January 15th 1977	R.M.Uttley
4	Scotland	Twickenham		March 17th 1973	J.V.Pullin
4	Scotland	Twickenham		March 18th 1967	P.E.Judd
4	Scotland	Murrayfield		March 15th 1952	N.M.Hall
4	Scotland	Twickenham		March 15th 1947	J.Heaton

MATCHES IN WHICH ENGLAND HAVE CONCEDED 4 TRIES OR MORE:

Tries Scored:	By:	Venue:	Date:	Captain:
6	New Zealand	Cape Town (WC)	June 17th 1995	W.D.C.Carling
6	New Zealand	Wellington	June 8th 1985	P.W.Dodge
6	South Africa	Johannesburg	June 9th 1984	J.P.Scott
6	France	Parc des Princes	March 20th 1976	A.Neary
6	France	Stade Colombes	February 26th 1972	P.J.Dixon
6	President's XV	Twickenham	April 17th 1971	J.S.Spencer
6	France	Stade Colombes	April 18th 1970	R.B.Taylor
5	Australia	Sydney	July 27th 1991	W.D.C.Carling
5	France	Parc des Princes	March 3rd 1984	P.J.Wheeler
5	Wales	Cardiff Arms Park	March 17th 1979	W.B.Beaumont
5	Australia	Brisbane	May 31st 1975	J.V.Pullin
5	Wales	Cardiff Arms Park	January 20th 1973	J.V.Pullin
5	Scotland (Centenary)	Murrayfield	March 27th 1971	J.S.Spencer
5	Wales	Cardiff Arms Park	April 12th 1969	D.P.Rogers
5	New Zealand	Twickenham	November 4th 1967	P.E.Judd
5	Wales	Cardiff Arms Park	April 15th 1967	P.E.Judd
5	Wales	Swansea	January 20th 1951	V.G.Roberts
5	Ireland	Lansdowne Road	February 8th 1947	J.Mycock
4	Australia	Sydney	July 12th 1997	P.R.de Glanville
4	Argentina	Buenos Aires	June 6th 1997	P.R.de Glanville
4	Fiji	Twickenham	November 4th 1989	W.D.C.Carling
4	Australia	Sydney	June 12th 1988	J.Orwin
4	France	Parc des Princes	March 15th 1986	N.D.Melville
4	France	Twickenham	February 1st 1975	|F.E.Cotton
4	Ireland	Twickenham	February 16th 1974	J.V.Pullin
4	Wales	Twickenham	February 28th 1970	R.Hiller
4	Ireland	Twickenham	February 8th 1964	J.G.Willcox
4	Australia	Sydney	June 4th 1963	M.P.Weston

MATCHES IN WHICH ENGLAND HAVE SCORED 4 PENALTY GOALS OR MORE:

Goals Scored:	Against:	Venue:		Date:	Captain:
7	Scotland	Twickenham		March 18th 1995	W.D.C.Carling
7	Wales	Cardiff Arms Park		January 19th 1991	W.D.C.Carling
6	Ireland	Twickenham		March 16th 1996	W.D.C.Carling
6	Scotland	Murrayfield		March 2nd 1996	W.D.C.Carling
6	Argentina	Durban	(WC)	May 27th 1995	W.D.C.Carling
6	Canada	Twickenham		December 10th 1994	W.D.C.Carling
6	Wales	Twickenham		January 18th 1986	N.D.Melville
5	Scotland	Twickenham		February 1st 1997	P.R.de Glanville
5	Argentina	Twickenham		December 14th 1996	J.Leonard
5	Western Samoa	Twickenham		December 16th 1995	W.D.C.Carling
5	Australia	Cape Town	(WC)	June 10th 1995	W.D.C.Carling
5	Western Samoa	Durban	(WC)	June 4th 1995	W.D.C.Carling
5	Italy	Durban	(WC)	May 31st 1995	W.D.C.Carling
5	South Africa	Pretoria		June 4th 1994	W.D.C.Carling
5	France	Parc des Princes		March 5th 1994	W.D.C.Carling
5	Scotland	Murrayfield		February 5th 1994	W.D.C.Carling
5	Scotland	Twickenham		February 16th 1991	W.D.C.Carling
5	Argentina	Buenos Aires		July 28th 1990	W.D.C.Carling
5	Wales	Twickenham		March 17th 1984	P.J.Wheeler
5	Ireland	Lansdowne Road		March 19th 1983	J.P.Scott
5	France	Parc des Princes		February 20th 1982	S.J.Smith
5	Wales	Cardiff Arms Park		January 17th 1981	W.B.Beaumont
5	Ireland	Twickenham		February 16th 1974	J.V.Pullin
4	France	Twickenham		March 1st 1997	P.R.de Glanville
4	Ireland	Lansdowne Road		February 15th 1997	P.R.de Glanville
4	France	Twickenham		February 4th 1995	W.D.C.Carling
4	Romania	Twickenham		November 12th 1994	W.D.C.Carling
4	Ireland	Twickenham		February 19th 1994	W.D.C.Carling
4	New Zealand	Twickenham		November 27th 1993	W.D.C.Carling
4	Scotland	Murrayfield		January 18th 1992	W.D.C.Carling
4	Italy	Twickenham		October 8th 1991	W.D.C.Carling
4	France	Twickenham		March 16th 1991	W.D.C.Carling
4	Wales	Twickenham		February 17th 1990	W.D.C.Carling
4	France	Parc des Princes		February 3rd 1990	W.D.C.Carling
4	Scotland	Twickenham		February 4th 1989	W.D.C.Carling
4	USA	Sydney		June 3rd 1987	M.E.Harrison
4	Wales	Cardiff Arms Park		March 7th 1987	R.J.Hill
4	France	Twickenham		February 21st 1987	R.J.Hill
4	Romania	Twickenham		January 5th 1985	P.W.Dodge
4	South Africa	Port Elizabeth		June 2nd 1984	J.P.Scott
4	France	Twickenham		January 15th 1983	S.J.Smith
4	France	Twickenham		March 21st 1981	W.B.Beaumont
4	Ireland	Twickenham		March 6th 1976	A.Neary
4	France	Twickenham		February 1st 1975	F.E.Cotton
4	South Africa	Johannesburg		June 3rd 1972	J.V.Pullin
4	Ireland	Lansdowne Road		February 8th 1969	J.R.H.Greenwood
4	Wales	Cardiff Arms Park		April 15th 1967	P.E.Judd

MATCHES IN WHICH ENGLAND HAVE CONCEDED 4 PENALTY GOALS OR MORE:

Goals Scored:	By:	Venue:		Date:	Captain:
6	Argentina	Twickenham		December 14th 1996	J.Leonard
6	Australia	Brisbane		May 29th 1988	J.Orwin
6	New Zealand	Christchurch		June 1st 1985	P.W.Dodge
5	Australia	Cape Town	(WC)	June 10th 1995	W.D.C.Carling
5	South Africa	Cape Town		June 11th 1994	W.D.C.Carling
5	South Africa	Pretoria		June 4th 1994	W.D.C.Carling
5	Argentina	Buenos Aires		August 4th 1990	W.D.C.Carling
5	Wales	Cardiff Arms Park		March 7th 1987	R.J.Hill
5	Scotland	Murrayfield		February 15th 1986	N.D.Melville
5	Romania	Twickenham		January 5th 1985	P.W.Dodge
5	South Africa	Port Elizabeth		June 2nd 1984	J.P.Scott
5	Ireland	Lansdowne Road		March 19th 1983	J.P.Scott
4	Ireland	Twickenham		March 16th 1996	W.D.C.Carling
4	New Zealand	Twickenham	(WC)	October 3rd 1991	W.D.C.Carling
4	Australia	Sydney		July 27th 1991	W.D.C.Carling
4	Scotland	Twickenham		February 16th 1991	W.D.C.Carling
4	Argentina	Buenos Aires		July 28th 1990	W.D.C.Carling
4	Wales	Twickenham		March 17th 1984	P.J.Wheeler
4	Wales	Cardiff Arms Park		January 17th 1981	W.B.Beaumont
4	Scotland	Murrayfield		March 18th 1972	P.J.Dixon

MATCHES IN WHICH ENGLAND HAVE SCORED 2 DROP GOALS OR MORE:

Drop Goals Scored:	Against:	Venue:		Date:	Captain:
2	France	Parc des Princes		January 20th 1996	W.D.C.Carling
2	Argentina	Durban	(WC)	May 27th 1995	W.D.C.Carling
2	Fiji	Suva		July 20th 1991	W.D.C.Carling
2	Romania	Twickenham		January 5th 1985	P.W.Dodge
2	France	Parc des Princes		February 2nd 1980	W.B.Beaumont
2	France	Parc des Princes		January 21st 1978	W.B.Beaumont
2	Ireland	Twickenham		February 14th 1970	R.Hiller

MATCHES IN WHICH ENGLAND HAVE CONCEDED 2 DROP GOALS OR MORE:

Drop Goals Scored:	By:	Venue:	Date:	Captain:
3	France	Twickenham	February 2nd 1985	P.W.Dodge
3	Australia	Twickenham	January 7th 1967	R.A.W.Sharp
2	France	Parc des Princes	January 20th 1996	W.D.C.Carling
2	Scotland	Twickenham	March 18th 1995	W.D.C.Carling
2	France	Twickenham	February 21st 1987	R.J.Hill
2	Wales	Twickenham	March 17th 1984	P.J.Wheeler
2	Argentina	Buenos Aires	May 30th 1981	W.B.Beaumont
2	France	Twickenham	March 21st 1981	W.B.Beaumont
2	Ireland	Lansdowne Road	March 7th 1981	W.B.Beaumont
2	Australia	Sydney	May 24th 1975	A.Neary
2	Wales	Cardiff Arms Park	January 16th 1971	A.L.Bucknall
2	France	Stade Colombes	April 18th 1970	R.B.Taylor
2	France	Stade Colombes	February 24th 1968	M.P.Weston
2	France	Twickenham	February 26th 1955	P.D.Young

INCIDENCE OF WINNING and LOSING RUNS:

MOST CONSECUTIVE MATCHES WON:

All matches:	10	1994	Romania, Canada,
		1995	Ireland, France, Wales, Scotland, Argentina(WC),
			Italy(WC), Western Samoa(WC), Australia(WC).

England have also won: 9 successive matches once (1996-1997)
7 successive matches once (1992-1993)
6 successive matches once (1991)
5 successive matches once (1989-1990)

All matches at home:	7	1989	France, Fiji,
		1990	Ireland, Wales, Argentina,
		1991	Scotland, France.
	7	1992	Ireland, Wales, Canada, South Africa,
		1993	France, Scotland, New Zealand.

England have also won: at home, 6 successive matches once (1995-1997)

England have also played 10 successive matches at home without defeat on two occasions:
February 11th 1956 to February 13th 1960, inclusive, when 7 matches were won and three were drawn
and March 19th 1988 to March 16th 1991, inclusive, when 9 matches were won and one drawn.

All matches away:	6	1995	Ireland, Wales, Argentina(WC), Italy(WC),
			Western Samoa(WC), Australia(WC).

England have also played 6 successive matches away without defeat:
March 7th 1981 to February 5th 1983, inclusive, when three matches were won and three matches drawn.

MOST CONSECUTIVE MATCHES LOST:

All matches:	7	1971	Scotland, Scotland Centenary, President's XV.
		1972	Wales, Ireland, France, Scotland.

England have also lost: 5 successive matches three times (1948-1949), (1950-1951)
and (1984)

All matches at home:	5	1971	Scotland, President's XV,
		1972	Wales, Ireland,
		1973	New Zealand.
All matches away:	14	1983	Ireland,
		1984	Scotland, France, South Africa, South Africa,
		1985	Ireland, Wales, New Zealand, New Zealand,
		1986	Scotland, France,
		1987	Ireland, Wales, Australia(WC).

England have also lost: 9 successive matches once (1947-1951)
6 successive matches once (1975-1976)
5 successive matches twice (1964-1966) and (1969-1971)

MATCHES WITHOUT CONCEDING OR SCORING TRIES:

MOST CONSECUTIVE MATCHES WITHOUT CONCEDING A TRY:

All matches:	6	1957 - Scotland, 1958 - Wales, Australia, Ireland, France, Scotland.
	No tries scored against for	5 successive matches (1990-1991) 4 successive matches (1959-1960)
All matches at home:	7	1957 - Scotland, 1958 - Wales, Australia, Ireland, 1959 - France, Scotland 1960 - Wales.
All matches away:	4	1957 - Wales, Ireland, 1958 - France, Scotland.

MOST CONSECUTIVE MATCHES WITHOUT SCORING A TRY:

All matches:	5	1958 - Scotland, 1959 - Wales, Ireland, France, Scotland.
All matches at home:	3	1984 - Ireland, Wales, Australia.
All matches away:	4	1947 - Ireland, 1948 - Scotland, France, 1949 - Wales
	4	1965 - Wales, Ireland 1966 - France, Scotland.
	4	1993 - Wales, Ireland, 1994 - Scotland, France.

SECTION 3

THE FIVE NATIONS CHAMPIONSHIP

1947 onwards

GRAND SLAM, TRIPLE CROWN and CHAMPIONSHIP WINNERS.

GRAND SLAM WINNERS:

	ENGLAND	FRANCE	IRELAND	SCOTLAND	WALES
Prior to 1946:	6 times			once	3 times
Since 1946:	1957	1968	1948	1984	1950
	1980	1977		1990	1952
	1991	1981			1971
	1992	1987			1976
	1995	1997			1978
To date:	11 times	5 times	once	3 times	8 times

TRIPLE CROWN WINNERS:

	ENGLAND	IRELAND	SCOTLAND	WALES
Prior to 1946:	11 times	twice	8 times	7 times
Since 1946:	1954	1948	1984	1950
	1957	1949	1990	1952
	1960	1982		1965
	1980	1985		1969
	1991			1971
	1992			1976
	1995			1977
	1996			1978
	1997			1979
				1988
To date:	20 times	6 times	10 times	17 times

CHAMPIONSHIP WINNERS - OUTRIGHT:

	ENGLAND	FRANCE	IRELAND	SCOTLAND	WALES
Prior to 1946:	13 times		4 times	11 times	10 times
Since 1946:	1953	1959	1948	1984	1950
	1957	1961	1949	1990	1952
	1958	1962	1951		1956
	1963	1967	1974		1965
	1980	1968	1982		1966
	1991	1977	1985		1969
	1992	1981			1971
	1995	1987			1975
	1996	1989			1976
		1993			1978
		1997			
To date:	22 times	11 times	10 times	13 times	22 times

THE FIVE NATIONS CHAMPIONSHIP TROPHY

Until 1993 the Five Nations Tournament, although at one time the foremost International Rugby competition in the World, had no trophy, prize or reward of any kind for the winner.

The Grand Slam was a term coined by The Times newspaper from the Bridge expression meaning the taking of all tricks in a hand, in 1957 when England won that distinction for the first time in the post-war period. But there was no trophy or cup awarded to celebrate the occasion, presumably because such a materialistic gesture could be construed as being in conflict with the strict code of amateurism. Likewise, the Triple Crown, meaning victory over the other three Home Nations, carried no materialistic reward either. Only the Calcutta Cup, first played for in 1879 between England and Scotland, and much later, the Millennium Trophy for England versus Ireland matches were recognised by the RFU, and indeed the Five Nations Committee, as acceptable and appropriate accolades.

Lord Burghersh approached the Five Nations Committee in 1993 with a suggestion that there should be a Five Nations Cup, and the Committee were not averse to the idea providing that they could approve the design and providing that the trophy would not be sponsored or have any Corporate name associated with it.

It was Lord Burghersh's intention that the Cup be funded from the proceeds of the "Sport and Glory Exhibition" to be held at the Victoria and Albert Museum in 1993, and that the old firm of silversmiths, William and Comyns, be commissioned to manufacture it. In the event, the Exhibition was a failure, the funds not forthcoming and the silversmiths, having started work on the Cup, went into liquidation.

The Receivers were about to order the partially completed cup containing 200 ounces of silver, to be melted down, to raise funds to pay the Company's creditors, when Mike Davies, a London businessman stepped in and put in an unconditional offer for the partially completed trophy. This offer was accepted, and the trophy was completed on January 22nd 1993.

Davies then set up a Trust, independent of the National Unions, the Five Nations Committee and of commercial interests so that the trophy would be permanently secure, and the Trust, with Davies as Chairman received the Five Nations Championship Trophy on March 6th 1993.
A brief description of the Trophy is as follows:

- the Trophy is of classical style, distinctive in shape and is substantial, weighing nearly 14 lbs.

- it has fifteen sides - one for each player in a side, and has the emblem of each National Union around the base.

- it has three handles, one for each official - the referee and two touch judges - and the handles are large enough for the Trophy to be lifted easily.

- has a lip at the rim, and is large enough to hold the contents of five bottles of Champagne.

- the plinth has five sides - one for each Nation.

- the handle, or finial, on the lid is interchangeable and represents the current Champions. The finials of the Five Nations are kept in a hidded drawer in the plinth, where there is space for an additional (sixth) nation.

The Trophy is presented on the final day of the season to the Championship winning side, who, if two teams have won the same number of matches, is determined on points difference.

THE CALCUTTA CUP

The Calcutta Cup was donated to the Rugby Football Union, in 1878, by the Calcutta Football Club
when the Club was wound up because of diminishing support. The Cup is made from melted down
silver rupees which represented the Club's total funds at its closure.

In a letter to the President of the Rugby Football Union, dated December 20th 1877, the Club Captain,
Secretary and Treasurer, G.A.James Rothney, said:

> "I proposed at a meeting of the few remaining members of the club
> .....as the best means of doing some lasting good for the cause of
> Rugby Football..... should be devoted to the purpose of a Challenge
> Cup..... to be competed for annually in any way the Committee of the
> Rugby Union may consider best for the encouragement of Rugby Football."

The President of the RFU, A.F.Guillemard, replied:

> "The Committee accept with very great pleasure your generous offer of
> the Cup as an international challenge cup to be played for annually by
> England and Scotland - remaining the property of the Rugby Football Union."

The inscription on the Cup's wooden base reads:

**THE CALCUTTA CUP
PRESENTED TO THE RUGBY FOOTBALL UNION
BY THE CALCUTTA FOOTBALL CLUB
AS AN INTERNATIONAL CHALLENGE CUP
TO BE PLAYED FOR ANNUALLY BY ENGLAND AND
SCOTLAND
1878**

and has attached to it additional plates which record the date of each match played and also
the name of the winning country and the names of the two Captains.

The first game for the Calcutta Cup was played at Raeburn Place in Edinburgh, on March 10th
1879, and ended in a draw, England having scored a Goal and Scotland a Drop Goal.
The 100th game for the Calcutta Cup was played at Twickenham on March 6th 1993, when England
won by a Goal, two Tries and three Penalty Goals, (26 points), to three Penalty Goals and a
Drop Goal, (12 points).
The winners of the 103 games for the Calcutta Cup have been:

	England	Scotland	Drawn	
Prior to 1946:	22	24	7	
Since 1946:	32	12	7	Total - 104 matches

Although 114 matches have been played between the two countries since International matches
began in 1871, it should be noted that eight games were played before the Cup was presented,
and more recently, the Centenary Match, on March 27th 1971, and the World Cup semi-final, on
October 26th 1991, were games in which the Calcutta Cup was not at stake.

SEQUENCE OF FIVE NATIONS MATCHES PLAYED

1947 onwards

191 official matches were played against European Nations prior to 1947

Game:	Date:	Venue:	Opponents:	Result:	Score: Points:	Tries:	Captain:
192	January 18th 1947	Cardiff Arms Park	Wales	Won	9 - 6	1 - 2	J.Mycock
193	February 8th 1947	Lansdowne Road	Ireland	Lost	0 - 22	0 - 5	J.Mycock
194	March 15th 1947	Twickenham	Scotland	Won	24 - 5	4 - 1	J.Heaton
195	April 19th 1947	Twickenham	France	Won	6 - 3	2 - 0	J.Heaton
196	January 17th 1948	Twickenham	Wales	Drawn	3 - 3	0 - 1	T.A.Kemp
197	February 14th 1948	Twickenham	Ireland	Lost	10 - 11	2 - 3	E.K.Scott
198	March 20th 1948	Murrayfield	Scotland	Lost	3 - 6	0 - 2	E.K.Scott
199	March 29th 1948	Stade Colombes	France	Lost	0 - 15	0 - 3	R.H.G.Weighill
200	January 15th 1949	Cardiff Arms Park	Wales	Lost	3 - 9	0 - 3	N.M.Hall
201	February 12th 1949	Lansdowne Road	Ireland	Lost	5 - 14	1 - 2	N.M.Hall
202	February 26th 1949	Twickenham	France	Won	8 - 3	1 - 0	I.Preece
203	March 19th 1949	Twickenham	Scotland	Won	19 - 3	5 - 0	I.Preece
204	January 21st 1950	Twickenham	Wales	Lost	5 - 11	1 - 2	I.Preece
205	February 11th 1950	Twickenham	Ireland	Won	3 - 0	1 - 0	I.Preece
206	February 25th 1950	Stade Colombes	France	Lost	3 - 6	1 - 2	I.Preece
207	March 18th 1950	Murrayfield	Scotland	Lost	11 - 13	2 - 3	I.Preece
208	January 20th 1951	Swansea	Wales	Lost	5 - 23	1 - 5	V.G.Roberts
209	February 10th 1951	Lansdowne Road	Ireland	Lost	0 - 3	0 - 0	J.M.Kendall-Carpenter
210	February 24th 1951	Twickenham	France	Lost	3 - 11	1 - 2	J.M.Kendall-Carpenter
211	March 17th 1951	Twickenham	Scotland	Won	5 - 3	1 - 1	J.M.Kendall-Carpenter
212	January 19th 1952	Twickenham	Wales	Lost	6 - 8	2 - 2	N.M.Hall
213	March 15th 1952	Murrayfield	Scotland	Won	19 - 3	4 - 1	N.M.Hall
214	March 29th 1952	Twickenham	Ireland	Won	3 - 0	1 - 0	N.M.Hall
215	April 5th 1952	Stade Colombes	France	Won	6 - 3	0 - 1	N.M.Hall
216	January 17th 1953	Cardiff Arms Park	Wales	Won	8 - 3	1 - 0	N.M.Hall
217	February 14th 1953	Lansdowne Road	Ireland	Drawn	9 - 9	1 - 1	N.M.Hall
218	February 28th 1953	Twickenham	France	Won	11 - 0	3 - 0	N.M.Hall
219	March 21st 1953	Twickenham	Scotland	Won	26 - 8	6 - 2	N.M.Hall
220	January 16th 1954	Twickenham	Wales	Won	9 - 6	3 - 1	R.V.Stirling
221	February 13th 1954	Twickenham	Ireland	Won	14 - 3	3 - 0	R.V.Stirling
222	March 20th 1954	Murrayfield	Scotland	Won	13 - 3	3 - 1	R.V.Stirling
223	April 10th 1954	Stade Colombes	France	Lost	3 - 11	1 - 2	R.V.Stirling
224	January 22nd 1955	Cardiff Arms Park	Wales	Lost	0 - 3	0 - 0	N.M.Hall
225	February 12th 1955	Lansdowne Road	Ireland	Drawn	6 - 6	2 - 1	N.M.Hall
226	February 26th 1955	Twickenham	France	Lost	9 - 16	1 - 2	P.D.Young
227	March 19th 1955	Twickenham	Scotland	Won	9 - 6	2 - 1	P.D.Young
228	January 21st 1956	Twickenham	Wales	Lost	3 - 8	0 - 2	E.Evans
229	February 11th 1956	Twickenham	Ireland	Won	20 - 0	3 - 0	E.Evans
230	March 17th 1956	Murrayfield	Scotland	Won	11 - 6	1 - 1	E.Evans
231	April 14th 1956	Stade Colombes	France	Lost	9 - 14	1 - 2	E.Evans
232	January 19th 1957	Cardiff Arms Park	Wales	Won	3 - 0	0 - 0	E.Evans
233	February 9th 1957	Lansdowne Road	Ireland	Won	6 - 0	1 - 0	E.Evans
234	February 23rd 1957	Twickenham	France	Won	9 - 5	3 - 1	E.Evans
235	March 16th 1957	Twickenham	Scotland	Won	16 - 3	3 - 0	E.Evans
236	January 18th 1958	Twickenham	Wales	Drawn	3 - 3	1 - 0	E.Evans
237	February 8th 1958	Twickenham	Ireland	Won	6 - 0	1 - 0	E.Evans
238	March 1st 1958	Stade Colombes	France	Won	14 - 0	3 - 0	E.Evans
239	March 15th 1958	Murrayfield	Scotland	Drawn	3 - 3	0 - 0	E.Evans
240	January 17th 1959	Cardiff Arms Park	Wales	Lost	0 - 5	0 - 1	J.Butterfield
241	February 14th 1959	Lansdowne Road	Ireland	Won	3 - 0	0 - 0	J.Butterfield

SEQUENCE OF FIVE NATIONS MATCHES PLAYED (continued)

1947 onwards

Game:	Date:	Venue:	Opponents:	Result:	Score: Points:	Tries:	Captain:
242	February 28th 1959	Twickenham	France	Drawn	3 - 3	0 - 0	J.Butterfield
243	March 21st 1959	Twickenham	Scotland	Drawn	3 - 3	0 - 0	J.Butterfield
244	January 16th 1960	Twickenham	Wales	Won	14 - 6	2 - 0	R.E.G.Jeeps
245	February 13th 1960	Twickenham	Ireland	Won	8 - 5	1 - 1	R.E.G.Jeeps
246	February 27th 1960	Stade Colombes	France	Drawn	3 - 3	1 - 0	R.E.G.Jeeps
247	March 19th 1960	Murrayfield	Scotland	Won	21 - 12	3 - 1	R.E.G.Jeeps
248	January 21st 1961	Cardiff Arms Park	Wales	Lost	3 - 6	1 - 2	R.E.G.Jeeps
249	February 11th 1961	Lansdowne Road	Ireland	Lost	8 - 11	2 - 1	R.E.G.Jeeps
250	February 25th 1961	Twickenham	France	Drawn	5 - 5	1 - 1	R.E.G.Jeeps
251	March 18th 1961	Twickenham	Scotland	Won	6 - 0	1 - 0	R.E.G.Jeeps
252	January 20th 1962	Twickenham	Wales	Drawn	0 - 0	0 - 0	R.E.G.Jeeps
253	February 10th 1962	Twickenham	Ireland	Won	16 - 0	3 - 0	R.E.G.Jeeps
254	February 24th 1962	Stade Colombes	France	Lost	0 - 13	0 - 3	R.E.G.Jeeps
255	March 17th 1962	Murrayfield	Scotland	Drawn	3 - 3	0 - 0	R.E.G.Jeeps
256	January 19th 1963	Cardiff Arms Park	Wales	Won	13 - 6	2 - 1	R.A.W.Sharp
257	February 9th 1963	Lansdowne Road	Ireland	Drawn	0 - 0	0 - 0	R.A.W.Sharp
258	February 23rd 1963	Twickenham	France	Won	6 - 5	0 - 1	R.A.W.Sharp
259	March 16th 1963	Twickenham	Scotland	Won	10 - 8	2 - 1	R.A.W.Sharp
260	January 18th 1964	Twickenham	Wales	Drawn	6 - 6	2 - 2	J.G.Willcox
261	February 8th 1964	Twickenham	Ireland	Lost	5 - 18	1 - 4	J.G.Willcox
262	February 22nd 1964	Stade Colombes	France	Won	6 - 3	1 - 1	C.R.Jacobs
263	March 21st 1964	Murrayfield	Scotland	Lost	6 - 15	1 - 3	C.R.Jacobs
264	January 16th 1965	Cardiff Arms Park	Wales	Lost	3 - 14	0 - 3	D.G.Perry
265	February 13th 1965	Lansdowne Road	Ireland	Lost	0 - 5	0 - 1	D.G.Perry
266	February 27th 1965	Twickenham	France	Won	9 - 6	1 - 1	D.G.Perry
267	March 20th 1965	Twickenham	Scotland	Drawn	3 - 3	1 - 0	D.G.Perry
268	January 15th 1966	Twickenham	Wales	Lost	6 - 11	1 - 1	D.P.Rogers
269	February 12th 1966	Twickenham	Ireland	Drawn	6 - 6	1 - 1	D.P.Rogers
270	February 26th 1966	Stade Colombes	France	Lost	0 - 13	0 - 3	D.P.Rogers
271	March 19th 1966	Murrayfield	Scotland	Lost	3 - 6	0 - 1	D.P.Rogers
272	February 11th 1967	Lansdowne Road	Ireland	Won	8 - 3	1 - 0	P.E.Judd
273	February 25th 1967	Twickenham	France	Lost	12 - 16	0 - 2	P.E.Judd
274	March 18th 1967	Twickenham	Scotland	Won	27 - 14	4 - 2	P.E.Judd
275	April 15th 1967	Cardiff Arms Park	Wales	Lost	21 - 34	3 - 5	P.E.Judd
276	January 20th 1968	Twickenham	Wales	Drawn	11 - 11	2 - 2	C.W.McFadyean
277	February 10th 1968	Twickenham	Ireland	Drawn	9 - 9	0 - 0	C.W.McFadyean
278	February 24th 1968	Stade Colombes	France	Lost	9 - 14	0 - 1	M.P.Weston
279	March 16th 1968	Murrayfield	Scotland	Won	8 - 6	1 - 0	M.P.Weston
280	February 8th 1969	Lansdowne Road	Ireland	Lost	15 - 17	1 - 2	J.R.H.Greenwood
281	February 22nd 1969	Twickenham	France	Won	22 - 8	3 - 1	D.P.Rogers
282	March 15th 1969	Twickenham	Scotland	Won	8 - 3	2 - 0	D.P.Rogers
283	April 12th 1969	Cardiff Arms Park	Wales	Lost	9 - 30	0 - 5	D.P.Rogers
284	February 14th 1970	Twickenham	Ireland	Won	9 - 3	1 - 0	R.Hiller
285	February 28th 1970	Twickenham	Wales	Lost	13 - 17	2 - 4	R.Hiller
286	March 21st 1970	Murrayfield	Scotland	Lost	5 - 14	1 - 2	R.Hiller
287	April 18th 1970	Stade Colombes	France	Lost	13 - 35	2 - 6	R.B.Taylor
288	January 16th 1971	Cardiff Arms Park	Wales	Lost	6 - 22	1 - 3	A.L.Bucknall
289	February 13th 1971	Lansdowne Road	Ireland	Won	9 - 6	0 - 2	J.S.Spencer
290	February 27th 1971	Twickenham	France	Drawn	14 - 14	1 - 2	R.Hiller
291	March 20th 1971	Twickenham	Scotland	Lost	15 - 16	2 - 3	J.S.Spencer

SEQUENCE OF FIVE NATIONS MATCHES PLAYED (continued)

1947 onwards

Game:	Date:	Venue:	Opponents:	Result:	Score: Points:	Tries:	Captain:
292	January 15th 1972	Twickenham	Wales	Lost	3 - 12	0 - 1	R.Hiller
293	February 12th 1972	Twickenham	Ireland	Lost	12 - 16	1 - 2	R.Hiller
294	February 26th 1972	Stades Colombes	France	Lost	12 - 37	1 - 6	P.J.Dixon
295	March 18th 1972	Murrayfield	Scotland	Lost	9 - 23	0 - 2	P.J.Dixon
296	January 20th 1973	Cardiff Arms Park	Wales	Lost	9 - 25	0 - 5	J.V.Pullin
297	February 10th 1973	Lansdowne Road	Ireland	Lost	9 - 18	1 - 2	J.V.Pullin
298	February 24th 1973	Twickenham	France	Won	14 - 6	2 - 1	J.V.Pullin
299	March 17th 1973	Twickenham	Scotland	Won	20 - 13	4 - 2	J.V.Pullin
300	February 2nd 1974	Murrayfield	Scotland	Lost	14 - 16	2 - 2	J.V.Pullin
301	February 16th 1974	Twickenham	Ireland	Lost	21 - 26	1 - 4	J.V.Pullin
302	March 2nd 1974	Parc des Princes	France	Drawn	12 - 12	1 - 1	J.V.Pullin
303	March 16th 1974	Twickenham	Wales	Won	16 - 12	2 - 1	J.V.Pullin
304	January 18th 1975	Lansdowne Road	Ireland	Lost	9 - 12	1 - 2	F.E.Cotton
305	February 1st 1975	Twickenham	France	Lost	20 - 27	2 - 4	F.E.Cotton
306	February 15th 1975	Cardiff Arms Park	Wales	Lost	4 - 20	1 - 3	F.E.Cotton
307	March 15th 1975	Twickenham	Scotland	Won	7 - 6	1 - 0	A.Neary
308	January 17th 1976	Twickenham	Wales	Lost	9 - 21	0 - 3	A.Neary
309	February 21st 1976	Murrayfield	Scotland	Lost	12 - 22	1 - 3	A.Neary
310	March 6th 1976	Twickenham	Ireland	Lost	12 - 13	0 - 1	A.Neary
311	March 20th 1976	Parc des Princes	France	Lost	9 - 30	1 - 6	A.Neary
312	January 15th 1977	Twickenham	Scotland	Won	26 - 6	4 - 0	R.M.Uttley
313	February 5th 1977	Lansdowne Road	Ireland	Won	4 - 0	1 - 0	R.M.Uttley
314	February 19th 1977	Twickenham	France	Lost	3 - 4	0 - 1	R.M.Uttley
315	March 5th 1977	Cardiff Arms Park	Wales	Lost	9 - 14	0 - 2	R.M.Uttley
316	January 21st 1978	Parc des Princes	France	Lost	6 - 15	0 - 2	W.B.Beaumont
317	February 4th 1978	Twickenham	Wales	Lost	6 - 9	0 - 0	W.B.Beaumont
318	March 4th 1978	Murrayfield	Scotland	Won	15 - 0	2 - 0	W.B.Beaumont
319	March 18th 1978	Twickenham	Ireland	Won	15 - 9	2 - 0	W.B.Beaumont
320	February 3rd 1979	Twickenham	Scotland	Drawn	7 - 7	1 - 1	R.M.Uttley
321	February 17th 1979	Lansdowne Road	Ireland	Lost	7 - 12	1 - 1	W.B.Beaumont
322	March 3rd 1979	Twickenham	France	Won	7 - 6	1 - 1	W.B.Beaumont
323	March 17th 1979	Cardiff Arms Park	Wales	Lost	3 - 27	0 - 5	W.B.Beaumont
324	January 19th 1980	Twickenham	Ireland	Won	24 - 9	3 - 0	W.B.Beaumont
325	February 2nd 1980	Parc des Princes	France	Won	17 - 13	2 - 2	W.B.Beaumont
326	February 16th 1980	Twickenham	Wales	Won	9 - 8	0 - 2	W.B.Beaumont
327	March 15th 1980	Murrayfield	Scotland	Won	30 - 18	5 - 2	W.B.Beaumont
328	January 17th 1981	Cardiff Arms Park	Wales	Lost	19 - 21	1 - 1	W.B.Beaumont
329	February 21st 1981	Twickenham	Scotland	Won	23 - 17	3 - 3	W.B.Beaumont
330	March 7th 1981	Lansdowne Road	Ireland	Won	10 - 6	2 - 0	W.B.Beaumont
331	March 21st 1981	Twickenham	France	Lost	12 - 16	0 - 2	W.B.Beaumont
332	January 16th 1982	Murrayfield	Scotland	Drawn	9 - 9	0 - 0	W.B.Beaumont
333	February 6th 1982	Twickenham	Ireland	Lost	15 - 16	1 - 2	S.J.Smith
334	February 20th 1982	Parc des Princes	France	Won	27 - 15	2 - 1	S.J.Smith
335	March 6th 1982	Twickenham	Wales	Won	17 - 7	2 - 1	S.J.Smith
336	January 15th 1983	Twickenham	France	Lost	15 - 19	0 - 3	S.J.Smith
337	February 5th 1983	Cardiff Arms Park	Wales	Drawn	13 - 13	1 - 1	S.J.Smith
338	March 5th 1983	Twickenham	Scotland	Lost	12 - 22	0 - 2	J.P.Scott
339	March 19th 1983	Lansdowne Road	Ireland	Lost	15 - 25	0 - 2	J.P.Scott
340	February 4th 1984	Murrayfield	Scotland	Lost	6 - 18	0 - 2	P.J.Wheeler
341	February 18th 1984	Twickenham	Ireland	Won	12 - 9	0 - 0	P.J.Wheeler

SEQUENCE OF FIVE NATIONS MATCHES PLAYED (continued)

1947 onwards

Game:	Date:	Venue:	Opponents:	Result:	Score: Points:	Tries:	Captain:
342	March 3rd 1984	Parc des Princes	France	Lost	18 - 32	2 - 5	P.J.Wheeler
343	March 17th 1984	Twickenham	Wales	Lost	15 - 24	0 - 1	P.J.Wheeler
344	February 2nd 1985	Twickenham	France	Drawn	9 - 9	0 - 0	P.W.Dodge
345	March 16th 1985	Twickenham	Scotland	Won	10 - 7	1 - 1	P.W.Dodge
346	March 30th 1985	Lansdowne Road	Ireland	Lost	10 - 13	1 - 1	P.W.Dodge
347	April 20th 1985	Cardiff Arms Park	Wales	Lost	15 - 24	1 - 2	P.W.Dodge
348	January 18th 1986	Twickenham	Wales	Won	21 - 18	0 - 1	N.D.Melville
349	February 15th 1986	Murrayfield	Scotland	Lost	6 - 33	0 - 3	N.D.Melville
350	March 1st 1986	Twickenham	Ireland	Won	25 - 20	4 - 3	N.D.Melville
351	March 15th 1986	Parc des Princes	France	Lost	10 - 29	1 - 4	N.D.Melville
352	February 7th 1987	Lansdowne Road	Ireland	Lost	0 - 17	0 - 3	R.J.Hill
353	February 21st 1987	Twickenham	France	Lost	15 - 19	0 - 2	R.J.Hill
354	March 7th 1987	Cardiff Arms Park	Wales	Lost	12 - 19	0 - 1	R.J.Hill
355	April 4th 1987	Twickenham	Scotland	Won	21 - 12	2 - 1	M.E.Harrison
356	January 16th 1988	Parc des Princes	France	Lost	9 - 10	0 - 1	M.E.Harrison
357	February 6th 1988	Twickenham	Wales	Lost	3 - 11	0 - 2	M.E.Harrison
358	March 5th 1988	Murrayfield	Scotland	Won	9 - 6	0 - 0	N.D.Melville
359	March 19th 1988	Twickenham	Ireland	Won	35 - 3	6 - 0	N.D.Melville
360	February 4th 1989	Twickenham	Scotland	Drawn	12 - 12	0 - 1	W.D.C.Carling
361	February 18th 1989	Lansdowne Road	Ireland	Won	16 - 3	2 - 0	W.D.C.Carling
362	March 4th 1989	Twickenham	France	Won	11 - 0	2 - 0	W.D.C.Carling
363	March 18th 1989	Cardiff Arms Park	Wales	Lost	9 - 12	0 - 1	W.D.C.Carling
364	January 20th 1990	Twickenham	Ireland	Won	23 - 0	4 - 0	W.D.C.Carling
365	February 3rd 1990	Parc des Princes	France	Won	26 - 7	3 - 1	W.D.C.Carling
366	February 17th 1990	Twickenham	Wales	Won	34 - 6	4 - 1	W.D.C.Carling
367	March 17th 1990	Murrayfield	Scotland	Lost	7 - 13	1 - 1	W.D.C.Carling
368	January 19th 1991	Cardiff Arms Park	Wales	Won	25 - 6	1 - 0	W.D.C.Carling
369	February 16th 1991	Twickenham	Scotland	Won	21 - 12	1 - 0	W.D.C.Carling
370	March 2nd 1991	Lansdowne Road	Ireland	Won	16 - 7	2 - 1	W.D.C.Carling
371	March 16th 1991	Twickenham	France	Won	21 - 19	1 - 3	W.D.C.Carling
372	January 18th 1992	Murrayfield	Scotland	Won	25 - 7	2 - 1	W.D.C.Carling
373	February 1st 1992	Twickenham	Ireland	Won	38 - 9	6 - 1	W.D.C.Carling
374	February 15th 1992	Parc des Princes	France	Won	31 - 13	4 - 2	W.D.C.Carling
375	March 7th 1992	Twickenham	Wales	Won	24 - 0	3 - 0	W.D.C.Carling
376	January 16th 1993	Twickenham	France	Won	16 - 15	1 - 2	W.D.C.Carling
377	February 6th 1993	Cardiff Arms Park	Wales	Lost	9 - 10	0 - 1	W.D.C.Carling
378	March 6th 1993	Twickenham	Scotland	Won	26 - 12	3 - 0	W.D.C.Carling
379	March 20th 1993	Lansdowne Road	Ireland	Lost	3 - 17	0 - 1	W.D.C.Carling
380	February 5th 1994	Murrayfield	Scotland	Won	15 - 14	0 - 1	W.D.C.Carling
381	February 19th 1994	Twickenham	Ireland	Lost	12 - 13	0 - 1	W.D.C.Carling
382	March 5th 1994	Parc des Princes	France	Won	18 - 14	0 - 1	W.D.C.Carling
383	March 19th 1994	Twickenham	Wales	Won	15 - 8	2 - 1	W.D.C.Carling
384	January 21st 1995	Lansdowne Road	Ireland	Won	20 - 8	3 - 1	W.D.C.Carling
385	February 4th 1995	Twickenham	France	Won	31 - 10	3 - 1	W.D.C.Carling
386	February 18th 1995	Cardiff Arms Park	Wales	Won	23 - 9	3 - 0	W.D.C.Carling
387	March 18th 1995	Twickenham	Scotland	Won	24 - 12	0 - 0	W.D.C.Carling
388	January 20th 1996	Parc des Princes	France	Lost	12 - 15	0 - 0	W.D.C.Carling
389	February 3rd 1996	Twickenham	Wales	Won	21 - 15	2 - 2	W.D.C.Carling
390	March 2nd 1996	Murrayfield	Scotland	Won	18 - 9	0 - 0	W.D.C.Carling
391	March 16th 1996	Twickenham	Ireland	Won	28 - 15	1 - 0	W.D.C.Carling

1947 onwards

Game:	Date:	Venue:	Opponents:	Result:	Score: Points:	Tries:	Captain:
392	February 1st 1997	Twickenham	Scotland	Won	41 - 13	4 - 1	P.R.de Glanville
393	February 15th 1997	Lansdowne Road	Ireland	Won	46 - 6	6 - 0	P.R.de Glanville
394	March 1st 1997	Twickenham	France	Lost	20 - 23	1 - 2	P.R.de Glanville
395	March 15th 1997	Cardiff Arms Park	Wales	Won	34 - 13	4 - 1	P.R.de Glanville
396							
397							
398							
399							
400							
401							
402							
403							
404							
405							
406							
407							
408							
409							
410							
411							
412							
413							
414							
415							
416							
417							
418							
419							
420							
421							
422							
423							
424							
425							
426							
427							
428							
429							
430							
431							
432							

Played:	204
Won:	95
Lost:	85
Drawn:	24

ENGLAND'S PERFORMANCE IN THE FIVE NATIONS CHAMPIONSHIP

and THE CALCUTTA CUP

1947 onwards

Season:	Matches: W	L	D	Championship Position:	Calcutta Cup:
1946-47	3	1	0	Shared title with Wales	won Calcutta Cup
1947-48	0	3	1	Fifth - Wooden Spoon	
1948-49	2	2	0	Second equal with France and Scotland	won Calcutta Cup
1949-50	1	3	0	Fifth - Wooden Spoon	
1950-51	1	3	0	Fourth equal with Scotland	won Calcutta Cup
1951-52	3	1	0	Second	won Calcutta Cup
1952-53	3	0	1	**WON TITLE OUTRIGHT**	won Calcutta Cup
1953-54	3	1	0	Shared title with France and Wales - **TRIPLE CROWN**	won Calcutta Cup
1954-55	1	2	1	Fourth	won Calcutta Cup
1955-56	2	2	0	Second equal with France and Ireland	won Calcutta Cup
1956-57	4	0	0	**WON TITLE OUTRIGHT - GRAND SLAM and TRIPLE CROWN**	won Calcutta Cup
1957-58	2	0	2	**WON TITLE OUTRIGHT**	retained Calcutta Cup
1958-59	1	1	2	Second equal with Ireland and Wales	retained Calcutta Cup
1959-60	3	0	1	Shared title with France - **TRIPLE CROWN**	won Calcutta Cup
1960-61	1	2	1	Fourth	won Calcutta Cup
1961-62	1	1	2	Third equal with Wales	retained Calcutta Cup
1962-63	3	0	1	**WON TITLE OUTRIGHT**	won Calcutta Cup
1963-64	1	2	1	Third equal with France	
1964-65	1	2	1	Fourth	
1965-66	0	3	1	Fifth - Wooden Spoon	
1966-67	2	2	0	Second equal with Ireland and Scotland	won Calcutta Cup
1967-68	1	1	2	Third	won Calcutta Cup
1968-69	2	2	0	Third	won Calcutta Cup
1969-70	1	3	0	Fourth equal with Scotland	
1970-71	1	2	1	Third equal with Ireland	
1971-72	0	4	0	Championship not completed	
1972-73	2	2	0	Five way tie	won Calcutta Cup
1973-74	1	2	1	Fifth - Wooden Spoon	
1974-75	1	3	0	Fifth - Wooden Spoon	won Calcutta Cup
1975-76	0	4	0	Fifth - Wooden Spoon	
1976-77	2	2	0	Third	won Calcutta Cup
1977-78	2	2	0	Third	won Calcutta Cup
1978-79	1	2	1	Fourth	retained Calcutta Cup
1979-80	4	0	0	**WON TITLE OUTRIGHT - GRAND SLAM and TRIPLE CROWN**	won Calcutta Cup

ENGLAND'S PERFORMANCE IN THE FIVE NATIONS CHAMPIONSHIP

and THE CALCUTTA CUP (continued)

1947 onwards

Season:	Matches: W	L	D	Championship Position:	Calcutta Cup:
1980-81	2	2	0	Second equal with Scotland and Wales	won Calcutta Cup
1981-82	2	1	1	Second equal with Scotland	retained Calcutta Cup
1982-83	0	3	1	Fifth - Wooden Spoon	
1983-84	1	3	0	Fourth	
1984-85	1	2	1	Fourth	won Calcutta Cup
1985-86	2	2	0	Third equal with Wales	
1986-87	1	3	0	Fourth equal with Wales	won Calcutta Cup
1987-88	2	2	0	Third	won Calcutta Cup
1988-89	2	1	1	Second equal with Scotland	retained Calcutta Cup
1989-90	3	1	0	Second	
1990-91	4	0	0	**WON TITLE OUTRIGHT - GRAND SLAM and TRIPLE CROWN**	won Calcutta Cup
1991-92	4	0	0	**WON TITLE OUTRIGHT - GRAND SLAM and TRIPLE CROWN**	won Calcutta Cup
1992-93	2	2	0	Third	won Calcutta Cup
1993-94	3	1	0	Second	won Calcutta Cup
1994-95	4	0	0	**WON TITLE OUTRIGHT - GRAND SLAM and TRIPLE CROWN**	won Calcutta Cup
1995-96	3	1	0	**WON TITLE OUTRIGHT - TRIPLE CROWN**	won Calcutta Cup
1996-97	3	1	0	Second - **TRIPLE CROWN**	won Calcutta Cup

SCORING COMPARISONS BY SEASON in the FIVE NATIONS CHAMPIONSHIP

Season:	Tries	Conv	Drop Goals	Penalty Goals	Points Total: For	Against	Comments:
1946-47	7	5	2	0	39	36	No penalty goals. England share Title
1947-48	2	2	0	2	16	35	England Wooden Spoon
1948-49	7 (16)	4 (11)	2 (4)	0 (2)	35	29	No penalty goals
1949-50	5	2	0	1	22	30	J.V.Smith - 4 tries. England Wooden Spoon
1950-51	3	2	0	0	13	40	No penalty goals
1951-52	7	2	1	2	34	14	
1952-53	11	6	0	3	54	20	England win Title
1953-54	10	3	0	1	39	23	D.S.Wilson - 4 tries. England share Title
1954-55	5	0	0	3	24	31	
1955-56	6	2	0	8	43	28	
1956-57	7	2	0	3	34	8	England Grand Slam - one try conceded
1957-58	5	1	0	3	26	6	England win Title - no tries conceded
1958-59	0 (58)	0 (20)	0 (1)	3 (27)	9	11	No tries scored, only one try conceded
1959-60	7	5	2	3	46	26	England share Title
1960-61	5	2	0	1	22	22	
1961-62	3	2	0	2	19	16	
1962-63	2	2	0	3	29	19	England win Title
1963-64	5	1	0	2	23	42	
1964-65	2	0	0	3	15	28	
1965-66	2	0	1	2	15	36	England Wooden Spoon
1966-67	8	4	2	10	68	67	R.Hosen - 38 points
1967-68	3	2	2	6	37	40	
1968-69	6 (43)	3 (21)	0 (7)	10 (42)	54	58	
1969-70	6	5	2	2	40	69	England share Wooden Spoon
1970-71	4	1	0	10	44	58	Centenary season. R.Hiller - 35 pts.
1971-72	2	2	0	8	36	88	England lost all four matches - Wooden Spoon
1972-73	7	3	1	5	52	62	Five-way Championship tie
1973-74	6	3	2	9	63	66	England Wooden Spoon
1974-75	5	1	1	5	40	65	England Wooden Spoon
1975-76	2	2	0	10	42	86	England lost all four matches - Wooden Spoon
1976-77	5	2	0	6	42	24	
1977-78	4	4	2	4	42	33	
1978-79	3 (44)	0 (23)	0 (8)	4 (63)	24	52	W.N.Bennett - 20 pts out of 24

SCORING COMPARISONS BY SEASON in the FIVE NATIONS CHAMPIONSHIP

(continued)

Season:	Tries		Conv		Drop Goals		Penalty Goals		Points Total: For	Against	Comments:
1979-80	10		5		2		8		80	48	England Grand Slam
1980-81	6		2		0		12		64	60	
1981-82	5		3		0		14		68	47	
1982-83	1		0		3		14		55	79	Hare - 42 pts. One try scored - Wooden Spoon
1983-84	2		2		1		12		51	83	Hare - 44 pts.
1984-85	3		1		2		8		44	53	
1985-86	5		3		1		11		62	100	Highest ever points total against
1986-87	2		2		1		11		48	67	England share Wooden Spoon
1987-88	6		4		2		6		56	30	
1988-89	4	(44)	1	(23)	1	(13)	9	(105)	48	27	
1989-90	12		6		0		10		90	26	Highest points total to date
1990-91	5		3		1		18		83	44	England Grand Slam. S.D.Hodgkinson - 60 pts.
1991-92	15		11		1		11		118	29	England Grand Slam. J.M.Webb - 67 pts.
1992-93	4		2		1		9		54	54	
1993-94	2		1		1		15		60	49	
1994-95	9		4		1		14		98	39	England Grand Slam.
1995-96	3		2		3		17		79	54	England win Triple Crown and Title
1996-97	15	(65)	9	(38)	1	(9)	15	(109)	141	55	England win Triple Crown
Total:	270		136		42		348		2440	2212	

FINAL CHAMPIONSHIP TABLES BY SEASON from 1946-47.

Prior to the presentation of the Five Nations Championship Trophy in 1993, when two sides achieved the same number of Title points in any season, they were assumed to "share" that place in the Championship Table, Thus if Wales and England each won three matches and lost one, they would have earned six title points, and would have been declared joint Championship winners. Where this situation occurred prior to 1993, the "shared" place is shown in the tables below by an "=" sign, but the order in which the respective teams are listed is determined by points difference.

From 1993 onwards, where title points are equal, position in the Championship Table is determined by points difference, and there are no "shared" positions in the Table.

SEASON: 1946-47   **Won:**   **Share of Championship Title with Wales and Calcutta Cup.**

							Points:		Tries:		Title
			Played	Won	Lost	Drawn	For	Against	For	Against	Points
1	=	Wales	4	3	1	0	37	17	8	2	6
1	=	ENGLAND	4	3	1	0	39	36	7	8	6
3	=	Ireland	4	2	2	0	33	18	7	5	4
3	=	France	4	2	2	0	23	20	6	3	4
5		Scotland	4	0	4	0	16	57	2	12	0

Home Games: beat Scotland 24 - 5, (four tries to one); beat France 6 - 3, (two tries to nil).

Away Games: beat Wales 9 - 6, (one try to two); lost to Ireland 0 - 22, (no tries to five).

SEASON: 1947-48   **Won:**   **Nothing.**

							Points:		Tries:		Title
			Played	Won	Lost	Drawn	For	Against	For	Against	Points
1		Ireland	4	4	0	0	36	19	10	5	8
2	=	France	4	2	2	0	40	25	9	4	4
2	=	Scotland	4	2	2	0	15	31	3	6	4
4		Wales	4	1	2	1	23	20	5	5	3
5		ENGLAND	4	0	3	1	16	35	2	9	1

Home Games: drew with Wales 3 - 3, (no tries to one); lost to Ireland 10 - 11, (two tries to three).

Away Games: lost to Scotland 3 - 6, (no tries to two); lost to France 0 - 15, (no tries to three)

SEASON: 1948-49   **Won:**   **Calcutta Cup**

		Played	Won	Lost	Drawn	Points: For	Against	Tries: For	Against	Title Points
1	Ireland	4	3	1	0	41	24	5	3	6
2 =	ENGLAND	4	2	2	0	35	29	7	5	4
2 =	France	4	2	2	0	24	28	3	4	4
2 =	Scotland	4	2	2	0	20	37	4	8	4
5	Wales	4	1	3	0	17	19	5	4	2

Home Games: beat France 8 - 3, (one try to nil); beat Scotland 19 - 3, (five tries to nil).

Away Games: lost to Wales 3 - 9, (no tries to three); lost to Ireland 5 - 14, (one try to two).

SEASON: 1949-50   **Won:**   **Nothing**

		Played	Won	Lost	Drawn	Points: For	Against	Tries: For	Against	Title Points
1	Wales	4	4	0	0	50	8	10	1	8
2	Scotland	4	2	2	0	21	49	5	8	4
3 =	Ireland	4	1	2	1	27	12	3	3	3
3 =	France	4	1	2	1	14	35	3	7	3
5	ENGLAND	4	1	3	0	22	30	5	7	2

Home Games: lost to Wales 5 - 11, (one try to two); beat Ireland 3 - 0, (one try to nil).

Away Games: lost to France 3 - 6, (one try to two); lost to Scotland 11 - 13, (two tries to three).

SEASON: 1950-51   **Won:**   **Calcutta Cup**

		Played	Won	Lost	Drawn	Points: For	Against	Tries: For	Against	Title Points
1	Ireland	4	3	0	1	21	16	4	3	7
2	France	4	3	1	0	41	27	7	6	6
3	Wales	4	1	2	1	29	35	6	6	3
4 =	Scotland	4	1	3	0	39	25	7	4	2
4 =	ENGLAND	4	1	3	0	13	40	3	8	2

Home Games: lost to France 3 - 11, (one try to two); beat Scotland 5 - 3, (one try each).

Away Games: lost to Wales 5 - 23, (one try to five); lost to Ireland 0 - 3, (no tries).

SEASON: 1951-52   Won: **Calcutta Cup**

		Played	Won	Lost	Drawn	Points: For	Against	Tries: For	Against	Title Points
1	Wales	4	4	0	0	42	14	6	3	8
2	**ENGLAND**	4	3	1	0	34	14	7	4	6
3	Ireland	4	2	2	0	26	33	5	6	4
4	France	4	1	3	0	29	37	5	3	2
5	Scotland	4	0	4	0	22	55	3	10	0

Home Games: lost to Wales 6 - 8, (two tries each); beat Ireland 3 - 0, (one try to nil).

Away Games: beat Scotland 19 - 3, (four tries to one), beat France 6 - 3, (no tries to one).

SEASON: 1952-53   Won: **Championship Title and Calcutta Cup.**

		Played	Won	Lost	Drawn	Points: For	Against	Tries: For	Against	Title Points
1	**ENGLAND**	4	3	0	1	54	20	11	3	7
2	Wales	4	3	1	0	26	14	6	2	6
3	Ireland	4	2	1	1	54	25	12	3	5
4	France	4	1	3	0	17	38	1	10	2
5	Scotland	4	0	4	0	21	75	4	16	0

Home Games: beat France 11 - 0, (three tries to nil); beat Scotland 26 - 8, (six tries to two).

Away Games: beat Wales 8 - 3, (one try to nil); drew with Ireland 9 - 9, (one try each).

SEASON: 1953-54   Won: **Triple Crown, Share of Championship Title with France and Wales and Calcutta Cup.**

			Played	Won	Lost	Drawn	Points: For	Against	Tries: For	Against	Title Points
1	=	**ENGLAND**	4	3	1	0	39	23	10	4	6
1	=	France	4	3	1	0	35	22	7	3	6
1	=	Wales	4	3	1	0	52	34	7	7	6
4		Ireland	4	1	3	0	18	34	3	5	2
5		Scotland	4	0	4	0	6	37	2	10	0

Home Games: beat Wales 9 - 6, (three tries to one); beat Ireland 14 - 3, (three tries to nil).

Away Games: beat Scotland 13 - 3, (three tries to one); lost to France 3 - 11, (one try to two).

SEASON: 1954-55   **Won:**   **Calcutta Cup**

		Played	Won	Lost	Drawn	Points: For	Against	Tries: For	Against	Title Points
1 =	Wales	4	3	1	0	48	28	8	3	6
1 =	France	4	3	1	0	47	28	8	3	6
3	Scotland	4	2	2	0	32	35	4	8	4
4	**ENGLAND**	4	1	2	1	24	31	5	4	3
5	Ireland	4	0	3	1	15	44	1	8	1

Home Games: lost to France 9 - 16, (one try to two); beat Scotland 9 - 6, (two tries to one).

Away Games: lost to Wales 0 - 3, (no tries); drew with Ireland 6 - 6, (two tries to one).

SEASON: 1955-56   **Won:**   **Calcutta Cup**

		Played	Won	Lost	Drawn	Points: For	Against	Tries: For	Against	Title Points
1	Wales	4	3	1	0	25	20	6	2	6
2 =	**ENGLAND**	4	2	2	0	43	28	5	5	4
2 =	France	4	2	2	0	31	34	5	5	4
2 =	Ireland	4	2	2	0	33	47	6	7	4
5	Scotland	4	1	3	0	31	34	5	8	2

Home Games: lost to Wales 3 - 8, (no tries to two); beat Ireland 20 - 0, (three tries to nil).

Away Games: beat Scotland 11 - 6, (one try each); lost to France 9 - 14, (one try to two).

SEASON: 1956-57   **Won:**   **Grand Slam, Triple Crown, Championship Title and Calcutta Cup.**

		Played	Won	Lost	Drawn	Points: For	Against	Tries: For	Against	Title Points
1	**ENGLAND**	4	4	0	0	34	8	7	1	8
2 =	Wales	4	2	2	0	31	30	5	5	4
2 =	Ireland	4	2	2	0	21	21	4	1	4
2 =	Scotland	4	2	2	0	21	27	1	5	4
5	France	4	0	4	0	24	45	4	9	0

Home Games: beat France 9 - 5, (three tries to one); beat Scotland 16 - 3, (three tries to nil).

Away Games: beat Wales 3 - 0, (no tries), beat Ireland 6 - 0, (one try to nil).

SEASON: 1957-58   Won: **Championship Title. Retained Calcutta Cup**

		Played	Won	Lost	Drawn	Points: For	Against	Tries: For	Against	Title Points
1	**ENGLAND**	4	2	0	2	26	6	5	0	6
2	Wales	4	2	1	1	26	28	6	4	5
3	France	4	2	2	0	36	37	4	6	4
4	Scotland	4	1	2	1	23	32	4	5	3
5	Ireland	4	1	3	0	24	32	3	7	2

Home Games: drew with Wales 3 - 3, (one try to nil); beat Ireland 6 - 0, (one try to nil).

Away Games: beat France 14 - 0, (three tries to nil); drew with Scotland 3 - 3, (No tries).

SEASON: 1958-59   Won: **Retained Calcutta Cup**

		Played	Won	Lost	Drawn	Points: For	Against	Tries: For	Against	Title Points
1	France	4	2	1	1	28	15	4	1	5
2 =	Ireland	4	2	2	0	23	19	3	3	4
2 =	Wales	4	2	2	0	21	23	4	4	4
2 =	**ENGLAND**	4	1	1	2	9	11	0	1	4
5	Scotland	4	1	2	1	12	25	1	3	3

Home Games: drew with France 3 - 3, (no tries); drew with Scotland 3 - 3, (no tries).

Away Games: lost to Wales 0 - 5, (no tries to one); beat Ireland 3 - 0, (no tries).

SEASON: 1959-60   Won: **Triple Crown, Share of Championship Title with France and Calcutta Cup.**

		Played	Won	Lost	Drawn	Points: For	Against	Tries: For	Against	Title Points
1 =	France	4	3	0	1	55	28	11	6	7
1 =	**ENGLAND**	4	3	0	1	46	26	7	2	7
3	Wales	4	2	2	0	32	39	4	7	4
4	Scotland	4	1	3	0	29	47	4	8	2
5	Ireland	4	0	4	0	25	47	5	8	0

Home Games: beat Wales 14 - 6, (two tries to nil); beat Ireland 8 - 5, (one try each).

Away Games: drew with France 3 - 3, (one try to nil); beat Scotland 21 - 12, (three tries to one).

SEASON: 1960-61   **Won:**   **Calcutta Cup.**

		Played	Won	Lost	Drawn	Points: For	Against	Tries: For	Against	Title Points
1	France	4	3	0	1	39	14	5	3	7
2 =	Wales	4	2	2	0	21	14	5	4	4
2 =	Scotland	4	2	2	0	19	25	4	4	4
4	**ENGLAND**	4	1	2	1	22	22	5	4	3
5	Ireland	4	1	3	0	22	48	3	7	2

Home Games: drew with France 5 - 5, (one try each); beat Scotland 6 - 0, (one try to nil).

Away Games: lost to Wales 3 - 6, (one try to two); lost to Ireland 8 - 11, (two tries to one).

SEASON: 1961-62   **Won:**   **Retained Calcutta Cup.**

		Played	Won	Lost	Drawn	Points: For	Against	Tries: For	Against	Title Points
1	France	4	3	1	0	35	6	7	0	6
2	Scotland	4	2	1	1	34	23	5	2	5
3 =	**ENGLAND**	4	1	1	2	19	16	3	3	4
3 =	Wales	4	1	1	2	9	11	0	2	4
5	Ireland	4	0	3	1	9	50	1	9	1

Home Games: drew with Wales 0 - 0, (no tries) ; beat Ireland 16 - 0, (three tries to nil).

Away Games: lost to France 0 - 13, (no tries to three); drew with Scotland 3 - 3, (no tries)

SEASON: 1962-63   **Won:**   **Championship Title and Calcutta Cup.**

		Played	Won	Lost	Drawn	Points: For	Against	Tries: For	Against	Title Points
1	**ENGLAND**	4	3	0	1	29	19	4	3	7
2 =	France	4	2	2	0	40	25	6	2	4
2 =	Scotland	4	2	2	0	22	22	2	2	4
4	Ireland	4	1	2	1	19	33	2	5	3
5	Wales	4	1	3	0	21	32	2	4	2

Home Games: beat France 6 - 5, (no tries to one); beat Scotland 10 - 8, (two tries to one).

Away Games: beat Wales 13 - 6, (two tries to one); drew with Ireland 0 - 0, (no tries).

SEASON: 1963-64   **Won:**   **Nothing.**

			Played	Won	Lost	Drawn	Points: For	Against	Tries: For	Against	Title Points
1	=	Scotland	4	3	1	0	34	20	6	3	6
1	=	Wales	4	2	0	2	43	26	8	4	6
3	=	France	4	1	2	1	41	33	8	5	3
3	=	**ENGLAND**	4	1	2	1	23	42	5	10	3
5		Ireland	4	1	3	0	33	53	5	10	2

Home Games: drew with Wales 6 - 6, (two tries each); lost to Ireland 5 - 18, (one try to four).

Away Games: beat France 6 - 3, (one try each); lost to Scotland 6 - 15, (one try to three).

SEASON: 1964-65   **Won:**   **Nothing.**

			Played	Won	Lost	Drawn	Points: For	Against	Tries: For	Against	Title Points
1		Wales	4	3	1	0	55	45	10	5	6
2	=	France	4	2	1	1	47	33	10	7	5
2	=	Ireland	4	2	1	1	32	23	6	3	5
4		**ENGLAND**	4	1	2	1	15	28	2	5	3
5		Scotland	4	0	3	1	29	49	2	10	1

Home Games: beat France 9 - 6, (one try each); drew with Scotland 3 - 3, (one try to nil).

Away Games: lost to Wales 3 - 14, (no tries to three); lost to Ireland 0 - 5, (no tries to one).

SEASON: 1965-66   **Won:**   **Nothing.**

			Played	Won	Lost	Drawn	Points: For	Against	Tries: For	Against	Title Points
1		Wales	4	3	0	1	34	26	5	4	6
2	=	France	4	2	1	1	35	18	7	2	5
2	=	Scotland	4	2	1	1	23	17	5	2	5
4		Ireland	4	1	2	1	24	34	2	7	3
5		**ENGLAND**	4	0	3	1	15	36	2	6	1

Home Games: lost to Wales 6 - 11, (one try each); drew with Ireland 6 - 6, (one try each).

Away Games: lost to France 0 - 13, (no tries to three); lost to Scotland 3 - 6, (no tries to one).

SEASON: 1966-67 **Won:** **Calcutta Cup.**

		Played	Won	Lost	Drawn	Points: For	Against	Tries: For	Against	Title Points
1	France	4	3	1	0	55	41	8	2	6
2 =	ENGLAND	4	2	2	0	68	67	8	9	4
2 =	Scotland	4	2	2	0	37	45	4	8	4
2 =	Ireland	4	2	2	0	17	22	3	2	4
5	Wales	4	1	3	0	53	55	7	9	2

Home Games: lost to France 12 - 16, (no tries to two); beat Scotland 27 - 14, (four tries to two).

Away Games: beat Ireland 8 - 3, (one try to nil); lost to Wales 21 - 34, (three tries to five).

SEASON: 1967-68 **Won:** **Calcutta Cup.**

		Played	Won	Lost	Drawn	Points: For	Against	Tries: For	Against	Title Points
1	France	4	4	0	0	52	30	7	2	8
2	Ireland	4	2	1	1	38	37	4	2	5
3	ENGLAND	4	1	1	2	37	40	3	3	4
4	Wales	4	1	2	1	31	34	4	5	3
5	Scotland	4	0	4	0	18	35	1	7	0

Home Games: drew with Wales 11 - 11, (two tries each); drew with Ireland 9 - 9, (no tries).

Away Games: lost to France 9 - 14, (no tries to one); beat Scotland 8 - 6, (one try to nil).

SEASON: 1968-69 **Won:** **Calcutta Cup.**

		Played	Won	Lost	Drawn	Points: For	Against	Tries: For	Against	Title Points
1	Wales	4	3	0	1	79	31	14	2	7
2	Ireland	4	3	1	0	61	48	8	6	6
3	ENGLAND	4	2	2	0	54	58	6	8	4
4	Scotland	4	1	3	0	12	44	1	9	2
5	France	4	0	3	1	28	53	3	7	1

Home Games: beat France 22 - 8, (three tries to one); beat Scotland 8 - 3, (two tries to nil).

Away Games: lost to Ireland 15 - 17, (one try to two); lost to Wales 9 - 30, (no tries to five).

SEASON: 1969-70   Won: **Nothing.**

			Played	Won	Lost	Drawn	Points: For	Against	Tries: For	Against	Title Points
1	=	France	4	3	1	0	60	33	11	4	6
1	=	Wales	4	3	1	0	46	42	9	7	6
3		Ireland	4	2	2	0	33	28	6	4	4
4	=	Scotland	4	1	3	0	43	50	6	11	2
4	=	**ENGLAND**	4	1	3	0	40	69	6	12	2

Home Games: beat Ireland 9 - 3, (one try to nil); lost to Wales 13 - 17, (two tries to four).

Away Games: lost to Scotland 5 - 14, (one try to two); lost to France 13 - 35, (two tries to six).

SEASON: 1970-71   Won: **Nothing.**

			Played	Won	Lost	Drawn	Points: For	Against	Tries: For	Against	Title Points
1		Wales	4	4	0	0	73	38	13	4	8
2		France	4	1	1	2	41	40	5	5	4
3	=	Ireland	4	1	2	1	41	46	6	5	3
3	=	**ENGLAND**	4	1	2	1	44	58	4	10	3
5		Scotland	4	1	3	0	47	64	7	11	2

Home Games: drew with France 14 - 14, (one try to two); lost to Scotland 15 - 16, (two tries to three).

Away Games: lost to Wales 6 - 22, (one try to three); beat Ireland 9 - 6, (no tries to two).

SEASON: 1971-72   Won: **Nothing.**   Championship not completed due to the political situation in Ireland at the time.

	Played	Won	Lost	Drawn	Points: For	Against	Tries: For	Against	Title Points
Wales	3	3	0	0	67	21	8	1	
Ireland	2	2	0	0	30	21	4	2	
Scotland	3	2	1	0	55	53	6	6	
France	4	1	3	0	61	66	8	8	
ENGLAND	4	0	4	0	36	88	2	11	

Home Games: lost to Wales 3 - 12, (no tries to one); lost to Ireland 12 - 16, (one try to two).

Away Games: lost to France 12 - 37, (one try to six); lost to Scotland 9 - 23, (no tries to two).

SEASON: 1972-73   Won: Calcutta Cup.

			Played	Won	Lost	Drawn	Points: For	Against	Tries: For	Against	Title Points
1	=	Wales	4	2	2	0	53	43	7	3	4
1	=	France	4	2	2	0	38	36	3	3	4
1	=	Ireland	4	2	2	0	50	48	5	5	4
1	=	Scotland	4	2	2	0	55	59	6	7	4
1	=	**ENGLAND**	4	2	2	0	52	62	7	10	4

Home Games: beat France 14 - 6, (two tries to one); beat Scotland 20 - 13, (four tries to two).

Away Games: lost to Wales 9 - 25, (nil tries to five); lost to Ireland 9 - 18, (one try to two).

SEASON: 1973-74   Won: Nothing.

		Played	Won	Lost	Drawn	Points: For	Against	Tries: For	Against	Title Points
1	Ireland	4	2	1	1	50	45	5	3	5
2 =	Scotland	4	2	2	0	41	35	4	4	4
2 =	Wales	4	1	1	2	43	41	4	3	4
2 =	France	4	1	1	2	43	53	3	4	4
5	**ENGLAND**	4	1	2	1	63	66	6	8	3

Home Games: lost to Ireland 21 - 26, (one try to four); beat Wales 16 - 12, (two tries to one).

Away Games: lost to Scotland 14 - 16, (two tries each); drew with France 12 - 12, (one try each).

SEASON: 1974-75   Won: Calcutta Cup.

		Played	Won	Lost	Drawn	Points: For	Against	Tries: For	Against	Title Points
1	Wales	4	3	1	0	87	30	14	3	6
2 =	Scotland	4	2	2	0	47	40	2	5	4
2 =	Ireland	4	2	2	0	54	67	8	8	4
2 =	France	4	2	2	0	53	79	6	10	4
5	**ENGLAND**	4	1	3	0	40	65	5	9	2

Home Games: lost to France 20 - 27, (two tries to four); beat Scotland 7 - 6, (one try to nil).

Away Games: lost to Ireland 9 - 12, (one try to two); lost to Wales 4 - 20, (one try to three).

SEASON: 1975-76 **Won:** **Nothing.**

		Played	Won	Lost	Drawn	Points: For	Against	Tries: For	Against	Title Points
1	Wales	4	4	0	0	102	37	11	3	8
2	France	4	3	1	0	82	37	13	2	6
3	Scotland	4	2	2	0	49	59	4	5	4
4	Ireland	4	1	3	0	31	87	1	8	2
5	**ENGLAND**	4	0	4	0	42	86	2	13	0

Home Games: lost to Wales 9 - 21, (no tries to three); lost to Ireland 12 - 13, (no tries to one).

Away Games: lost to Scotland 12 - 22, (one try to three); lost to France 9 - 30, (one try to six).

SEASON: 1976-77 **Won:** **Calcutta Cup.**

		Played	Won	Lost	Drawn	Points: For	Against	Tries: For	Against	Title Points
1	France	4	4	0	0	58	21	8	0	8
2	Wales	4	3	1	0	66	43	7	3	6
3	**ENGLAND**	4	2	2	0	42	24	5	3	4
4	Scotland	4	1	3	0	39	85	4	11	2
5	Ireland	4	0	4	0	33	65	1	8	0

Home Games: beat Scotland 26 - 6, (four tries to nil); lost to France 3 - 4, (no tries to one).

Away Games: beat Ireland 4 - 0, (one try to nil); lost to Wales 9 - 14, (no tries to two).

SEASON: 1977-78 **Won:** **Calcutta Cup.**

		Played	Won	Lost	Drawn	Points: For	Against	Tries: For	Against	Title Points
1	Wales	4	4	0	0	67	43	8	4	8
2	France	4	3	1	0	51	47	6	4	6
3	**ENGLAND**	4	2	2	0	42	33	4	2	4
4	Ireland	4	1	3	0	46	54	2	5	2
5	Scotland	4	0	4	0	39	68	4	9	0

Home Games: lost to Wales 6 - 9, (no tries); beat Ireland 15 - 9, (two tries to nil).

Away Games: lost to France 6 - 15, (no tries to two); beat Scotland 15 - 0, (two tries to nil).

SEASON: 1978-79   Won: **Retained Calcutta Cup.**

		Played	Won	Lost	Drawn	Points: For	Against	Tries: For	Against	Title Points
1	Wales	4	3	1	0	83	51	10	5	6
2	France	4	2	1	1	50	46	7	5	5
3	Ireland	4	1	1	2	53	51	5	6	4
4	**ENGLAND**	4	1	2	1	24	52	3	8	3
5	Scotland	4	0	2	2	48	58	7	8	2

Home Games: drew with Scotland 7 - 7, (one try each); beat France 7 - 6, (one try each).

Away Games: lost to Ireland 7 - 12, (one try each); lost to Wales 3 - 27, (no tries to five).

SEASON: 1979-80   Won: **Grand Slam, Triple Crown, Championship Title and Calcutta Cup.**

		Played	Won	Lost	Drawn	Points: For	Against	Tries: For	Against	Title Points
1	**ENGLAND**	4	4	0	0	80	48	10	6	8
2 =	Wales	4	2	2	0	50	45	10	5	4
2 =	Ireland	4	2	2	0	70	65	6	8	4
4 =	Scotland	4	1	3	0	61	83	8	12	2
4 =	France	4	1	3	0	55	75	7	10	2

Home Games: beat Ireland 24 - 9, (three tries to nil); beat Wales 9 - 8, (no tries to two).

Away Games: beat France 17 - 13, (two tries each); beat Scotland 30 - 18, (five tries to two).

SEASON: 1980-81   Won: **Calcutta Cup.**

		Played	Won	Lost	Drawn	Points: For	Against	Tries: For	Against	Title Points
1	France	4	4	0	0	70	49	6	3	8
2 =	**ENGLAND**	4	2	2	0	64	60	6	6	4
2 =	Scotland	4	2	2	0	51	54	7	6	4
2 =	Wales	4	2	2	0	51	61	2	6	4
5	Ireland	4	0	4	0	36	48	4	4	0

Home Games: beat Scotland 23 - 17, (three tries each); lost to France 12 - 16, (no tries to two).

Away Games: lost to Wales 19 - 21, (one try each); beat Ireland 10 - 6, (two tries to nil).

SEASON: 1981-82   **Won:**   **Retained Calcutta Cup**

		Played	Won	Lost	Drawn	Points: For	Against	Tries: For	Against	Title Points
1		Ireland	4	3	1	0	66	61	5	5	6
2 =		ENGLAND	4	2	1	1	68	47	5	4	5
2 =		Scotland	4	2	1	1	71	55	7	2	5
4 =		France	4	1	3	0	56	74	5	4	2
4 =		Wales	4	1	3	0	59	83	4	11	2

Home Games: lost to Ireland 15 - 16, (one try to two); beat Wales 17 - 7, (two tries to one).

Away Games: drew with Scotland 9 - 9, (no tries); beat France 27 - 15, (two tries to one).

SEASON: 1982-83   **Won:**   **Nothing.**

		Played	Won	Lost	Drawn	Points: For	Against	Tries: For	Against	Title Points
1 =	France	4	3	1	0	70	61	8	4	6
1 =	Ireland	4	3	1	0	71	67	5	6	6
3	Wales	4	2	1	1	64	53	7	3	5
4	Scotland	4	1	3	0	65	65	5	5	2
5	ENGLAND	4	0	3	1	55	79	1	8	1

Home Games: lost to France 15 - 19, (no tries to three); lost to Scotland 12 - 22, (no tries to two).

Away Games: drew with Wales 13 - 13, (one try each), lost to Ireland 15 - 25, (no tries to two).

SEASON: 1983-84   **Won:**   **Nothing.**

		Played	Won	Lost	Drawn	Points: For	Against	Tries: For	Against	Title Points
1	Scotland	4	4	0	0	86	36	10	3	8
2	France	4	3	1	0	90	67	9	5	6
3	Wales	4	2	2	0	67	60	5	3	4
4	ENGLAND	4	1	3	0	51	83	2	8	2
5	Ireland	4	0	4	0	39	87	1	8	0

Home Games: beat Ireland 12 - 9, (no tries); lost to Wales 15 - 24, (no tries to one).

Away Games: lost to Scotland 6 - 18, (no tries to two); lost to France 18 - 32, (two tries to five).

SEASON: 1984-85   Won: Calcutta Cup.

		Played	Won	Lost	Drawn	Points: For	Against	Tries: For	Against	Title Points
1	Ireland	4	3	0	1	67	49	5	4	7
2	France	4	2	0	2	49	30	6	0	6
3	Wales	4	2	2	0	61	71	5	7	4
4	**ENGLAND**	4	1	2	1	44	53	3	4	3
5	Scotland	4	0	4	0	46	64	3	7	0

Home Games: drew with France 9 - 9, (no tries); beat Scotland 10 - 7, (one try each).

Away Games: lost to Ireland 10 - 13, (one try each); lost to Wales 15 - 24, (one try to two).

SEASON: 1985-86   Won: Nothing.

			Played	Won	Lost	Drawn	Points: For	Against	Tries: For	Against	Title Points
1	=	France	4	3	1	0	98	52	13	1	6
1	=	Scotland	4	3	1	0	76	54	7	4	6
3	=	Wales	4	2	2	0	74	71	4	8	4
3	=	**ENGLAND**	4	2	2	0	62	100	5	11	4
5		Ireland	4	0	4	0	50	83	5	10	0

Home Games: beat Wales 21 - 18, (no tries to one); beat Ireland 25 - 20, (four tries to three).

Away Games: lost to Scotland 6 - 33, (nil tries to three); lost to France 10 - 29, (one try to four).

SEASON: 1986-87   Won: Calcutta Cup.

			Played	Won	Lost	Drawn	Points: For	Against	Tries: For	Against	Title Points
1		France	4	4	0	0	82	59	10	4	8
2	=	Ireland	4	2	2	0	57	46	8	6	4
2	=	Scotland	4	2	2	0	71	76	7	8	4
4	=	Wales	4	1	3	0	54	65	4	6	2
4	=	**ENGLAND**	4	1	3	0	48	67	2	7	2

Home Games: lost to France 15 - 19, (no tries to two); beat Scotland 21 - 12, (two tries to one).

Away Games: lost to Ireland 0 - 17, (no tries to three), lost to Wales 12 - 19, (no tries to one).

SEASON: 1987-88   **Won:**   **Calcutta Cup.**

		Played	Won	Lost	Drawn	Points: For	Against	Tries: For	Against	Title Points
1 =	Wales	4	3	1	0	57	42	7	4	6
1 =	France	4	3	1	0	57	47	8	3	6
3	**ENGLAND**	4	2	2	0	56	30	6	3	4
4 =	Scotland	4	1	3	0	67	68	6	7	2
4 =	Ireland	4	1	3	0	43	90	4	14	2

Home Games: lost to Wales 3 - 11, (0 tries to 2); beat Ireland 35 - 3, (six tries to nil)

Away Games: lost to France 9 - 10, (no tries to one); beat Scotland 9 - 6, (no tries).

SEASON: 1988-89   **Won:**   **Retained Calcutta Cup.**

		Played	Won	Lost	Drawn	Points: For	Against	Tries: For	Against	Title Points
1	France	4	3	1	0	76	47	11	3	6
2 =	**ENGLAND**	4	2	1	1	48	27	4	2	5
2 =	Scotland	4	2	1	1	75	59	9	7	5
4 =	Ireland	4	1	3	0	64	92	6	12	2
4 =	Wales	4	1	3	0	44	82	3	9	2

Home Games: beat France 11 - 0, (two tries to nil); drew with Scotland 12 - 12, (no tries to one).

Away Games: beat Ireland 16 - 3, (two tries to nil); lost to Wales 9 - 12, (no tries to one).

SEASON: 1989-90   **Won:**   **Nothing**
                  Won: Nothing

		Played	Won	Lost	Drawn	Points: For	Against	Tries: For	Against	Title Points
1	Scotland	4	4	0	0	60	26	6	3	8
2	**ENGLAND**	4	3	1	0	90	26	12	3	6
3	France	4	2	2	0	67	78	9	6	4
4	Ireland	4	1	3	0	36	75	4	11	2
5	Wales	4	0	4	0	42	90	5	13	0

Home Games: beat Ireland 26 - 7, (four tries to nil); beat Wales 34 - 6, (four tries to one).

Away Games: beat France 26 - 7, (three tries to one), lost to Scotland 7 - 13, (one try each).

SEASON: 1990-91   Won: **Grand Slam, Triple Crown, Championship Title and Calcutta Cup.**

		Played	Won	Lost	Drawn	Points: For	Against	Tries: For	Against	Title Points
1	**ENGLAND**	4	4	0	0	83	44	5	4	8
2	France	4	3	1	0	91	46	11	2	6
3	Scotland	4	2	2	0	81	73	7	6	4
4	Ireland	4	0	3	1	66	86	8	11	1
4	Wales	4	0	3	1	42	114	5	13	1

Home Games: beat Scotland 21 - 12, (one try to nil). beat France 21 - 19, (one try to three)

Away Games: beat Wales 25 - 6, (one try to nil); beat Ireland 16 - 7, (two tries to one).

SEASON: 1991-92   Won: **Grand Slam, Triple Crown, Championship Title and Calcutta Cup.**

		Played	Won	Lost	Drawn	Points: For	Against	Tries: For	Against	Title Points
1	**ENGLAND**	4	4	0	0	118	29	15	4	8
2	France	4	2	2	0	75	62	10	5	4
2	Scotland	4	2	2	0	47	56	4	4	4
2	Wales	4	2	2	0	40	63	2	5	4
5	Ireland	4	0	4	0	46	116	3	16	0

Home Games: beat Ireland 38 - 9, (six tries to one); beat Wales 24 - 0, (three tries to nil).

Away Games: beat Scotland 25 - 7, (two tries to one); beat France 31 - 13, (four tries to two).

THE FIVE NATIONS CUP IS TO BE AWARDED FOR THE FIRST TIME IN THE 1992-93 SEASON.
IN THIS, AND FUTURE, SEASONS, IF AT THE END OF THE TOURNAMENT, TITLE POINTS ARE EQUAL,
THE OUTRIGHT WINNERS WILL BE DECIDED ON THE BASIS OF POINTS DIFFERENCE,
AND THE TROPHY WILL BE AWARDED ACCORDINGLY.   (See Section 3: Table 2)

SEASON: 1992-93 Won: **Calcutta Cup**

		Played	Won	Lost	Drawn	Points: For	Against	Tries: For	Against	Title Points	Points Diff'ce
1	France	4	3	1	0	73	35	8	2	6	+ 38
2	Scotland	4	2	2	0	50	40	3	4	4	+ 10
3	**ENGLAND**	4	2	2	0	54	54	4	4	4	=
4	Ireland	4	2	2	0	45	53	2	5	4	- 8
5	Wales	4	1	3	0	34	74	3	5	2	- 40

Home Games: beat France 16 - 15, (one try to two); beat Scotland 26 - 12, (three tries to nil)

Away Games: lost to Wales 9 - 10, (no tries to one); lost to Ireland 3 - 17, (no tries to one).

SEASON: 1993-94 Won: **Calcutta Cup**

		Played	Won	Lost	Drawn	Points: For	Against	Tries: For	Against	Title Points	Points Diff'ce
1	Wales	4	3	1	0	78	51	7	4	6	+ 27
2	**ENGLAND**	4	3	1	0	60	49	2	4	6	+ 11
3	France	4	2	2	0	84	69	9	2	4	+ 15
4	Ireland	4	1	2	1	49	70	1	5	3	- 21
5	Scotland	4	0	3	1	38	70	1	5	1	- 32

Home Games: lost to Ireland 12 - 13, (no tries to one); beat Wales 15 - 8, (two tries to one).

Away Games: beat Scotland 15 - 14, (no tries to one); beat France 18 - 14, (no tries to one).

SEASON: 1994-95 Won: **Grand Slam, Triple Crown, Championship Title and Calcutta Cup.**

		Played	Won	Lost	Drawn	Points: For	Against	Tries: For	Against	Title Points	Points Diff'ce
1	**ENGLAND**	4	4	0	0	98	39	9	2	8	+ 59
2	Scotland	4	3	1	0	87	71	6	6	6	+ 16
3	France	4	2	2	0	77	70	10	6	4	+ 7
4	Ireland	4	1	3	0	44	83	5	9	2	- 39
5	Wales	4	0	4	0	43	86	1	8	0	- 43

Home Games: beat France 31 - 10, (three tries to one); beat Scotland 24 - 12, (no tries).

Away Games: beat Ireland 20 - 8, (three tries to one); beat Wales 23 - 9, (three tries to nil).

SEASON: 1995-96   Won: **Triple Crown, Championship Title and Calcutta Cup.**

		Played	Won	Lost	Drawn	Points: For	Against	Tries: For	Against	Title Points	Points Diff'ce
1	ENGLAND	4	3	1	0	79	54	3	2	6	+ 25
2	Scotland	4	3	1	0	60	56	5	3	6	+ 4
3	France	4	2	2	0	89	57	10	3	4	+ 32
4	Wales	4	1	3	0	62	82	6	9	2	- 20
5	Ireland	4	1	3	0	65	106	5	12	2	- 41

Home Games: beat Wales 21 - 15, (two tries each); beat Ireland 28 - 15, (one try to nil)

Away Games: lost to France 12 - 15, (no tries); beat Scotland 18 - 9, (no tries)

SEASON: 1996-97   Won: **Triple Crown and Calcutta Cup**

		Played	Won	Lost	Drawn	Points: For	Against	Tries: For	Against	Title Points	Points Diff'ce
1	France	4	4	0	0	129	77	14	6	8	+ 52
2	ENGLAND	4	3	1	0	141	55	15	4	6	+ 86
3	Wales	4	1	3	0	94	106	11	12	2	- 12
4	Scotland	4	1	3	0	90	132	9	13	2	- 42
5	Ireland	4	1	3	0	57	141	4	18	2	- 84

Home Games: beat Scotland 41 - 13, (four tries to one); lost to France 20 - 23, (one try to two)

Away Games: beat Ireland 46 - 6, (six tries to nil); beat Wales 34 - 13, (four tries to one).

HIGHEST SCORE BY ENGLAND IN A FIVE NATIONS MATCH:

	Points scored:	Opponent:	Match score:	Venue:	Date:	Captain:
All Countries:						
Home:	41	Scotland	41 - 13	at Twickenham	February 1st 1997	P.R.de Glanville
Away:	46	Ireland	46 - 6	at Lansdowne Road	February 15th 1997	P.R.de Glanville

Individual Countries - at home:

	Points	Opponent	Match	Venue	Date	Captain
	31	France	31 - 10	at Twickenham	February 4th 1995	W.D.C.Carling
	22	France	22 - 8	at Twickenham	February 22nd 1969	D.P.Rogers
	21	France	21 - 19	at Twickenham	March 16th 1991	W.D.C.Carling
	38	Ireland	38 - 9	at Twickenham	February 1st 1992	W.D.C.Carling
	35	Ireland	35 - 3	at Twickenham	March 19th 1988	N.D.Melville
	28	Ireland	28 - 15	at Twickenham	March 16th 1996	W.D.C.Carling
	41	Scotland	41 - 13	at Twickenham	February 1st 1997	P.R.de Glanville
	27	Scotland	27 - 14	at Twickenham	March 18th 1967	P.E.Judd
	26	Scotland	26 - 6	at Twickenham	January 15th 1977	R.M.Uttley
	26	Scotland	26 - 12	at Twickenham	March 6th 1993	W.D.C.Carling
	34	Wales	34 - 6	at Twickenham	February 17th 1990	W.D.C.Carling
	24	Wales	24 - 0	at Twickenham	March 7th 1992	W.D.C.Carling
	21	Wales	21 - 18	at Twickenham	January 18th 1986	N.D.Melville

Individual Countries - away:

	Points	Opponent	Match	Venue	Date	Captain
	31	France	31 - 13	at Parc des Princes	February 15th 1992	W.D.C.Carling
	27	France	27 - 15	at Parc des Princes	February 20th 1982	S.J.Smith
	26	France	26 - 7	at Parc des Princes	February 3rd 1990	W.D.C.Carling
	46	Ireland	46 - 6	at Lansdowne Road	February 15th 1997	P.R.de Glanville
	21	Ireland	21 - 10	at Lansdowne Road	April 23rd 1988	J.Orwin
	20	Ireland	20 - 8	at Lansdowne Road	January 21st 1995	W.D.C.Carling
	30	Scotland	30 - 18	at Murrayfield	March 15th 1980	W.B.Beaumont
	25	Scotland	25 - 7	at Murrayfield	January 18th 1992	W.D.C.Carling
	21	Scotland	21 - 12	at Murrayfield	March 19th 1960	R.E.G.Jeeps
	34	Wales	34 - 13	at Cardiff Arms Park	March 15th 1997	P.R.de Glanville
	25	Wales	25 - 6	at Cardiff Arms Park	January 19th 1991	W.D.C.Carling
	23	Wales	23 - 9	at Cardiff Arms Park	February 18th 1995	W.D.C.Carling

HIGHEST SCORE AGAINST ENGLAND IN A FIVE NATIONS MATCH

	Points scored:		Opponent:	Match score:	Venue:	Date:	Captain:
All Countries:							
Home:	27	by	France	20 - 27	at Twickenham	February 1st 1975	F.E.Cotton
Away:	37	by	France	12 - 37	at Stades Colombes	February 26th 1972	P.J.Dixon

Individual Countries - at home:

	Points scored:		Opponent:	Match score:	Venue:	Date:	Captain:
	27	by	France	20 - 27	at Twickenham	February 1st 1975	F.E.Cotton
	23	by	France	20 - 23	at Twickenham	March 1st 1997	P.R.de Glanville
	19	by	France	21 - 19	at Twickenham	March 16th 1991	W.D.C.Carling
	19	by	France	15 - 19	at Twickenham	February 21st 1987	R.J.Hill
	19	by	France	15 - 19	at Twickenham	January 15th 1983	S.J.Smith
	26	by	Ireland	21 - 26	at Twickenham	February 16th 1974	J.V.Pullin
	20	by	Ireland	25 - 20	at Twickenham	March 1st 1986	N.D.Melville
	18	by	Ireland	5 - 18	at Twickenham	February 8th 1964	J.G.Willcox
	22	by	Scotland	12 - 22	at Twickenham	March 5th 1983	J.P.Scott
	17	by	Scotland	23 - 17	at Twickenham	February 21st 1981	W.B.Beaumont
	16	by	Scotland	15 - 16	at Twickenham	March 20th 1971	J.S.Spencer
	24	by	Wales	15 - 24	at Twickenham	March 17th 1984	P.J.Wheeler
	21	by	Wales	9 - 21	at Twickenham	January 17th 1976	A.Neary
	18	by	Wales	21 - 18	at Twickenham	January 18th 1986	N.D.Melville

Individual Countries - away:

	Points scored:		Opponent:	Match score:	Venue:	Date:	Captain:
	37	by	France	12 - 37	at Stades Colombes	February 26th 1972	P.J.Dixon
	35	by	France	13 - 35	at Stades Colombes	April 18th 1970	R.B.Taylor
	32	by	France	18 - 32	at Parc des Princes	March 3rd 1984	P.J.Wheeler
	25	by	Ireland	15 - 25	at Lansdowne Road	March 19th 1983	J.P.Scott
	22	by	Ireland	0 - 22	at Lansdowne Road	February 8th 1947	J.Mycock
	18	by	Ireland	9 - 18	at Lansdowne Road	February 10th 1973	J.V.Pullin
	33	by	Scotland	6 - 33	at Murrayfield	February 15th 1986	N.D.Melville
	23	by	Scotland	9 - 23	at Murrayfield	March 18th 1972	P.J.Dixon
	22	by	Scotland	12 - 22	at Murrayfield	February 21st 1976	A.Neary
	34	by	Wales	21 - 34	at Cardiff Arms Park	April 15th 1967	P.E.Judd
	30	by	Wales	9 - 30	at Cardiff Arms Park	April 12th 1969	D.P.Rogers
	27	by	Wales	3 - 27	at Cardiff Arms Park	March 17th 1979	W.B.Beaumont

HIGHEST AGGREGATE SCORE IN A FIVE NATIONS MATCH INVOLVING ENGLAND

	Total Points:	Opponent:	Match score:	Venue:	Date:	Captain:
All Countries:						
Home:	54	Scotland	41 - 13	at Twickenham	February 1st 1997	P.R.de Glanville
Away:	55	Wales	21 - 34	at Cardiff Arms Park	April 15th 1967	P.E.Judd

Individual Countries - at home:

	Total Points:	Opponent:	Match score:	Venue:	Date:	Captain:
	47	France	20 - 27	at Twickenham	February 1st 1975	F.E.Cotton
	43	France	20 - 23	at Twickenham	March 1st 1997	P.R.de Glanville
	41	France	31 - 10	at Twickenham	February 4th 1995	W.D.C.Carling
	47	Ireland	21 - 26	at Twickenham	February 16th 1974	J.V.Pullin
	47	Ireland	38 - 9	at Twickenham	February 1st 1992	W.D.C.Carling
	45	Ireland	25 - 20	at Twickenham	March 1st 1986	N.D.Melville
	54	Scotland	41 - 13	at Twickenham	February 1st 1997	P.R.de Glanville
	41	Scotland	27 - 14	at Twickenham	March 18th 1967	P.E.Judd
	40	Scotland	23 - 17	at Twickenham	February 21st 1981	W.B.Beaumont
	40	Wales	34 - 6	at Twickenham	February 17th 1990	W.D.C.Carling
	39	Wales	21 - 18	at Twickenham	January 18th 1986	N.D.Melville
	39	Wales	15 - 24	at Twickenham	March 17th 1984	P.J.Wheeler

Individual Countries - away:

	Total Points:	Opponent:	Match score:	Venue:	Date:	Captain:
	50	France	18 - 32	at Parc des Princes	March 3rd 1984	P.J.Wheeler
	49	France	12 - 37	at Stade Colombes	February 26th 1972	P.J.Dixon
	48	France	13 - 35	at Stades Colombes	April 18th 1970	R.B.Taylor
	52	Ireland	46 - 6	at Lansdowne Road	February 15th 1997	P.R.de Glanville
	40	Ireland	15 - 25	at Lansdowne Road	March 19th 1983	J.P.Scott
	32	Ireland	15 - 17	at Lansdowne Road	February 8th 1969	J.R.H.Greenwood
	48	Scotland	30 - 18	at Murrayfield	March 15th 1980	W.B.Beaumont
	39	Scotland	6 - 33	at Murrayfield	February 15th 1986	N.D.Melville
	34	Scotland	12 - 22	at Murrayfield	February 21st 1976	A.Neary
	55	Wales	21 - 34	at Cardiff Arms Park	April 15th 1967	P.E.Judd
	47	Wales	34 - 13	at Cardiff Arms Park	March 15th 1997	P.R.de Glanville
	40	Wales	19 - 21	at Cardiff Arms Park	January 17th 1981	W.B.Beaumont

HIGHEST MARGIN OF VICTORY ACHIEVED BY ENGLAND IN A FIVE NATIONS MATCH

	Points margin:	Opponent:	Match score:	Venue:	Date:	Captain:
All Countries:						
Home:	32	Ireland	35 - 3	at Twickenham	March 19th 1988	N.D.Melville
Away:	40	Ireland	46 - 6	at Lansdowne Road	February 15th 1997	P.R.de Glanville

Individual Countries - at home:

	Points margin:	Opponent:	Match score:	Venue:	Date:	Captain:
	21	France	31 - 10	at Twickenham	February 4th 1995	W.D.C.Carling
	14	France	22 - 8	at Twickenham	February 22nd 1969	D.P.Rogers
	11	France	11 - 0	at Twickenham	February 28th 1953	N.M.Hall
	32	Ireland	35 - 3	at Twickenham	March 19th 1988	N.D.Melville
	29	Ireland	38 - 9	at Twickenham	February 1st 1992	W.D.C.Carling
	23	Ireland	23 - 0	at Twickenham	January 20th 1990	W.D.C.Carling
	28	Scotland	41 - 13	at Twickenham	February 1st 1997	P.R.de Glanville
	20	Scotland	26 - 6	at Twickenham	January 15th 1977	R.M.Uttley
	19	Scotland	24 - 5	at Twickenham	April 19th 1947	J.Heaton
	28	Wales	34 - 6	at Twickenham	February 17th 1990	W.D.C.Carling
	24	Wales	24 - 0	at Twickenham	March 7th 1992	W.D.C.Carling
	10	Wales	17 - 7	at Twickenham	March 6th 1982	S.J.Smith

Individual Countries - away:

	Points margin:	Opponent:	Match score:	Venue:	Date:	Captain:
	19	France	26 - 7	at Parc des Princes	February 3rd 1990	W.D.C.Carling
	18	France	31 - 13	at Parc des Princes	February 15th 1992	W.D.C.Carling
	14	France	14 - 0	at Stades Colombes	March 1st 1958	E.Evans
	40	Ireland	46 - 6	at Lansdowne Road	February 15th 1997	P.R.de Glanville
	13	Ireland	16 - 3	at Lansdowne Road	February 18th 1989	W.D.C.Carling
	12	Ireland	20 - 8	at Lansdowne Road	January 21st 1995	W.D.C.Carling
	18	Scotland	25 - 7	at Murrayfield	January 18th 1992	W.D.C.Carling
	16	Scotland	19 - 3	at Murrayfield	March 15th 1952	N.M.Hall
	15	Scotland	15 - 0	at Murrayfield	March 4th 1978	W.B.Beaumont
	21	Wales	34 - 13	at Cardiff Arms Park	March 15th 1997	P.R.de Glanville
	19	Wales	25 - 6	at Cardiff Arms Park	January 19th 1991	W.D.C.Carling
	12	Wales	23 - 9	at Cardiff Arms Park	February 18th 1995	W.D.C.Carling

HIGHEST MARGIN OF DEFEAT SUFFERED BY ENGLAND IN A FIVE NATIONS MATCH

All Countries:

	Points margin:	Opponent:	Match score:	Venue:	Date:	Captain:
Home:	13	Ireland	5 - 18	at Twickenham	February 8th 1964	J.G.Willcox
Away:	27	Scotland	6 - 33	at Murrayfield	February 15th 1986	N.D.Melville

Individual Countries - at home:

8	by France	3 - 11	at Twickenham	February 24th 1951	JMK Kendall -Carpenter
7	by France	20 - 27	at Twickenham	February 1st 1975	F.E.Cotton
7	by France	9 - 16	at Twickenham	February 26th 1955	P.D.Young
13	by Ireland	5 - 18	at Twickenham	February 8th 1964	J.G.Willcox
5	by Ireland	21 - 26	at Twickenham	February 16th 1974	J.V.Pullin
4	by Ireland	12 - 16	at Twickenham	February 12th 1972	R.Hiller
10	by Scotland	12 - 22	at Twickenham	March 5th 1983	J.P.Scott
1	by Scotland	15 - 16	at Twickenham	March 20th 1971	J.S.Spencer

England have lost to Scotland only twice at Twickenham since 1947.

12	by Wales	9 - 21	at Twickenham	January 17th 1976	A.Neary
9	by Wales	15 - 24	at Twickenham	March 17th 1984	P.J.Wheeler
9	by Wales	3 - 12	at Twickenham	January 15th 1972	R.Hiller

Individual Countries - away:

25	by France	12 - 37	at Stade Colombes	February 26th 1972	P.J.Dixon
22	by France	13 - 35	at Stade Colombes	April 18th 1970	R.B.Taylor
21	by France	9 - 30	at Parc des Princes	March 20th 1976	A.Neary
22	by Ireland	0 - 22	at Lansdowne Road	February 8th 1947	J.Mycock
17	by Ireland	0 - 17	at Lansdowne Road	February 7th 1987	R.J.Hill
14	by Ireland	3 - 17	at Lansdowne Road	March 20th 1993	W.D.C.Carling
27	by Scotland	6 - 33	at Murrayfield	February 15th 1986	N.D.Melville
19	by Scotland	9 - 23	at Murrayfield	March 18th 1972	P.J.Dixon
10	by Scotland	12 - 22	at Murrayfield	February 21st 1976	A.Neary
24	by Wales	3 - 27	at Cardiff Arms Park	March 17th 1979	W.B.Beaumont
21	by Wales	9 - 30	at Cardiff Arms Park	April 12th 1969	D.P.Rogers
18	by Wales	5 - 23	at St Helen's, Swansea	January 20th 1951	V.G.Roberts

TOTAL POINTS SCORED IN A SEASON BY AND AGAINST ENGLAND

MOST POINTS SCORED:

	FOR:			AGAINST:	
Points:	Season:		Points:	Season:
141	1996-97		100	1985-86
118	1991-92		88	1971-72
98	1994-95		86	1975-76
90	1989-90		83	1983-84
83	1990-91		79	1982-83
80	1979-80		69	1969-70
79	1995-96		67	1966-67
68	1981-82		67	1986-87
68	1966-67		66	1973-74
64	1980-81		65	1974-75
63	1973-74		62	1972-73
62	1985-86		60	1980-81
60	1993-94		58	1968-69
56	1987-88		58	1970-71
55	1982-83		55	1996-97
54	1952-53		54	1992-93
54	1968-69		54	1995-96
54	1992-93		53	1984-85

LEAST POINTS SCORED:

	FOR:			AGAINST:	
Points:	Season:		Points:	Season:
9	1958-59		6	1957-58
13	1950-51		8	1956-57
15	1965-66		11	1958-59
15	1964-65		14	1951-52
16	1947-48		16	1961-62
19	1961-62		19	1962-63
22	1949-50		20	1952-53
22	1960-61		22	1960-61
23	1963-64		23	1953-54
24	1978-79		24	1976-77
24	1954-55		26	1959-60
26	1957-58		26	1989-90
29	1962-63		27	1988-89
34	1951-52		28	1955-56
34	1956-57		28	1964-65
35	1948-49		29	1948-49
36	1971-72		29	1991-92

TRIES SCORED IN A SEASON BY AND AGAINST ENGLAND

MOST TRIES SCORED:

FOR:

Tries:	Season:
15	1991-92
15	1996-97
12	1989-90
11	1952-53
10	1979-80
10	1953-54
9	1994-95
8	1966-67
7	1946-47
7	1948-49
7	1951-52
7	1956-57
7	1959-60
7	1972-73

AGAINST:

Tries:	Season:
13	1975-76
12	1969-70
11	1971-72
11	1985-86
10	1972-73
10	1970-71
10	1963-64
9	1974-75
9	1966-67
9	1947-48
8	1983-84
8	1982-83
8	1978-79
8	1973-74
8	1968-69
8	1950-51
7	1949-50
7	1986-87

LEAST TRIES SCORED:

FOR:

Tries:	Season:
0	1958-59
1	1982-83
2	1993-94
2	1986-87
2	1983-84
2	1975-76
2	1971-72
2	1965-66
2	1964-65
2	1962-63
2	1947-48
3	1995-96
3	1984-85
3	1978-79
3	1967-68
3	1961-62
3	1950-51

AGAINST:

Tries:	Season:
0	1957-58
1	1958-59
1	1956-57
2	1995-96
2	1994-95
2	1988-89
2	1977-78
2	1959-60
3	1989-90
3	1987-88
3	1976-77
3	1967-68
3	1962-63
3	1961-62
3	1952-53

PENALTY GOALS SCORED IN A SEASON BY AND AGAINST ENGLAND

MOST PENALTY GOALS SCORED:

FOR:

Goals:	Season:
18	1990-91
17	1995-96
15	1993-94
14	1994-95
14	1982-83
14	1981-82
12	1983-84
12	1980-81
11	1991-92
11	1986-87
11	1985-86
10	1989-90
10	1975-76
10	1970-71
10	1968-69
10	1966-67

AGAINST:

Goals:	Season:
13	1985-86
11	1995-96
11	1982-83
10	1983-84
9	1986-87
8	1993-94
8	1990-91
7	1994-95
7	1992-93
7	1971-72
6	1984-85
6	1981-82
6	1979-80
6	1977-78
6	1973-74
6	1966-67
6	1959-60

LEAST PENALTY GOALS SCORED:

FOR:

Goals:	Season:
0	1950-51
0	1948-49
0	1946-47
1	1960-61
1	1953-54
1	1949-50
2	1969-70
2	1965-66
2	1963-64
2	1961-62
2	1951-52
2	1947-48

AGAINST:

Goals:	Season:
0	1963-64
0	1951-52
0	1947-48
1	1964-65
1	1962-63
1	1961-62
1	1956-57
1	1950-51
1	1949-50
2	1978-79
2	1970-71
2	1960-61
2	1958-59
2	1957-58
2	1953-54
2	1946-47

MATCHES IN WHICH ENGLAND HAVE SCORED 25 POINTS OR MORE:

Points Scored:	Against:	Venue:	Date:	Captain:
46	Ireland	Landsdowne Road	February 15th 1997	P.R.de Glanville
41	Scotland	Twickenham	February 1st 1997	P.R.de Glanville
38	Ireland	Twickenham	February 1st 1992	W.D.C.Carling
35	Ireland	Twickenham	March 19th 1988	N.D.Melville
34	Wales	Cardiff Arms Park	March 15th 1997	P.R.de Glanville
34	Wales	Twickenham	February 17th 1990	W.D.C.Carling
31	France	Twickenham	February 4th 1995	W.D.C.Carling
31	France	Parc des Princes	February 15th 1992	W.D.C.Carling
30	Scotland	Murrayfield	March 15th 1980	W.B.Beaumont
28	Ireland	Twickenham	March 16th 1996	W.D.C.Carling
27	France	Parc des Princes	February 20th 1982	S.J.Smith
27	Scotland	Twickenham	March 18th 1967	P.E.Judd
26	Scotland	Twickenham	March 6th 1993	W.D.C.Carling
26	France	Parc des Princes	February 3rd 1990	W.D.C.Carling
26	Scotland	Twickenham	January 15th 1977	R.M.Uttley
26	Scotland	Twickenham	March 21st 1953	N.M.Hall
25	Scotland	Murrayfield	January 18th 1992	W.D.C.Carling
25	Wales	Cardiff Arms Park	January 19th 1991	W.D.C.Carling
25	Ireland	Twickenham	March 1st 1986	N.D.Melville

MATCHES IN WHICH ENGLAND HAVE CONCEDED 25 POINTS OR MORE:

Points Scored:	By:	Venue:	Date:	Captain:
37	France	Stade Colombes	February 26th 1972	P.J.Dixon
35	France	Stade Colombes	April 18th 1970	R.B.Taylor
34	Wales	Cardiff Arms Park	April 15th 1967	P.E.Judd
33	Scotland	Murrayfield	February 15th 1986	N.D.Melville
32	France	Parc des Princes	March 3rd 1984	P.J.Wheeler
30	France	Parc des Princes	March 20th 1976	A.Neary
30	Wales	Cardiff Arms Park	April 12th 1969	D.P.Rogers
29	France	Parc des Princes	March 15th 1986	N.D.Melville
27	Wales	Cardiff Arms Park	March 17th 1979	W.B.Beaumont
27	France	Twickenham	February 1st 1975	F.E.Cotton
26	Ireland	Twickenham	February 16th 1974	J.V.Pullin
25	Ireland	Lansdowne Road	March 19th 1983	J.P.Scott
25	Wales	Cardiff Arms Park	January 20th 1973	J.V.Pullin

MATCHES IN WHICH ENGLAND HAVE SCORED 4 TRIES OR MORE:

Tries Scored:	Against:	Venue:	Date:	Captain:
6	Ireland	Lansdowne Road	February 15th 1997	P.R.de Glanville
6	Ireland	Twickenham	February 1st 1992	W.D.C.Carling
6	Ireland	Twickenham	March 19th 1988	N.D.Melville
6	Scotland	Twickenham	March 21st 1953	N.M.Hall
5	Scotland	Murrayfield	March 15th 1980	W.B.Beaumont
5	Scotland	Twickenham	March 19th 1949	I.Preece
4	Wales	Cardiff Arms Park	March 15th 1997	P.R.de Glanville
4	France	Parc des Princes	February 15th 1992	W.D.C.Carling
4	Wales	Twickenham	February 17th 1990	W.D.C.Carling
4	Ireland	Twickenham	January 20th 1990	W.D.C.Carling
4	Ireland	Twickenham	March 1st 1986	N.D.Melville
4	Scotland	Twickenham	February 1st 1997	P.R.de Glanville
4	Scotland	Twickenham	January 15th 1977	R.M.Uttley
4	Scotland	Twickenham	March 17th 1973	J.V.Pullin
4	Scotland	Twickenham	March 18th 1967	P.E.Judd
4	Scotland	Murrayfield	March 15th 1952	N.M.Hall
4	Scotland	Twickenham	March 15th 1947	J.Heaton

MATCHES IN WHICH ENGLAND HAVE CONCEDED 4 TRIES OR MORE:

Tries Scored:	By:	Venue:	Date:	Captain:
6	France	Parc des Princes	March 20th 1976	A.Neary
6	France	Stade Colombes	February 26th 1972	P.J.Dixon
6	France	Stade Colombes	April 18th 1970	R.B.Taylor
5	France	Parc des Princes	March 3rd 1984	P.J.Wheeler
5	Wales	Cardiff Arms Park	March 17th 1979	W.B.Beaumont
5	Wales	Cardiff Arms Park	January 20th 1973	J.V.Pullin
5	Wales	Cardiff Arms Park	April 12th 1969	D.P.Rogers
5	Wales	Cardiff Arms Park	April 15th 1967	P.E.Judd
5	Wales	Swansea	January 20th 1951	V.G.Roberts
5	Ireland	Lansdowne Road	February 8th 1947	J.Mycock
4	France	Parc des Princes	March 15th 1986	N.D.Melville
4	France	Twickenham	February 1st 1975	|F.E.Cotton
4	Ireland	Twickenham	February 16th 1974	J.V.Pullin
4	Wales	Twickenham	February 28th 1970	R.Hiller
4	Ireland	Twickenham	February 8th 1964	J.G.Willcox

MATCHES IN WHICH ENGLAND HAVE SCORED 4 PENALTY GOALS OR MORE:

Goals Scored:	Against:	Venue:	Date:	Captain:
7	Scotland	Twickenham	March 18th 1995	W.D.C.Carling
7	Wales	Cardiff Arms Park	January 19th 1991	W.D.C.Carling
6	Ireland	Twickenham	March 16th 1996	W.D.C.Carling
6	Scotland	Murrayfield	March 2nd 1966	W.D.C.Carling
6	Wales	Twickenham	January 18th 1986	N.D.Melville
5	France	Parc des Princes	March 5th 1994	W.D.C.Carling
5	France	Parc des Princes	February 20th 1982	S.J.Smith
5	Ireland	Lansdowne Road	March 19th 1983	J.P.Scott
5	Ireland	Twickenham	February 16th 1974	J.V.Pullin
5	Scotland	Twickenham	February 1st 1997	P.R.de Glanville
5	Scotland	Murrayfield	February 5th 1994	W.D.C.Carling
5	Scotland	Twickenham	February 16th 1991	W.D.C.Carling
5	Wales	Twickenham	March 17th 1984	P.J.Wheeler
5	Wales	Cardiff Arms Park	January 17th 1981	W.B.Beaumont
4	France	Twickenham	March 1st 1997	P.R.de Glanville
4	France	Twickenham	February 4th 1995	W.D.C.Carling
4	France	Twickenham	March 16th 1991	W.D.C.Carling
4	France	Parc des Princes	February 3rd 1990	W.D.C.Carling
4	France	Twickenham	February 21st 1987	R.J.Hill
4	France	Twickenham	January 15th 1983	S.J.Smith
4	France	Twickenham	March 21st 1981	W.B.Beaumont
4	France	Twickenham	February 1st 1975	F.E.Cotton
4	Ireland	Lansdowne Road	February 15th 1997	P.R.de Glanville
4	Ireland	Twickenham	February 19th 1994	W.D.C.Carling
4	Ireland	Twickenham	March 6th 1976	A.Neary
4	Ireland	Lansdowne Road	February 8th 1969	J.R.H.Greenwood
4	Scotland	Murrayfield	January 18th 1992	W.D.C.Carling
4	Scotland	Twickenham	February 4th 1989	W.D.C.Carling
4	Wales	Twickenham	February 17th 1990	W.D.C.Carling
4	Wales	Cardiff Arms Park	March 7th 1987	R.J.Hill
4	Wales	Cardiff Arms Park	April 15th 1967	P.E.Judd

MATCHES IN WHICH ENGLAND HAVE CONCEDED 4 PENALTY GOALS OR MORE:

Goals Scored:	By:	Venue:	Date:	Captain:
5	Wales	Cardiff Arms Park	March 7th 1987	R.J.Hill
5	Scotland	Murrayfield	February 15th 1986	N.D.Melville
5	South Africa	Port Elizabeth	June 2nd 1984	J.P.Scott
5	Ireland	Lansdowne Road	March 19th 1983	J.P.Scott
4	Ireland	Twickenham	March 16th 1996	W.D.C.Carling
4	Scotland	Twickenham	February 16th 1991	W.D.C.Carling
4	Wales	Twickenham	March 17th 1984	P.J.Wheeler
4	Wales	Cardiff Arms Park	January 17th 1981	W.B.Beaumont
4	Scotland	Murrayfield	March 18th 1972	P.J.Dixon

MATCHES IN WHICH ENGLAND HAVE SCORED 2 DROP GOALS OR MORE:

Drop Goals Scored:	Against:	Venue:	Date:	Captain:
2	France	Parc des Princes	January 20th 1996	W.D.C.Carling
2	France	Parc des Princes	February 2nd 1980	W.B.Beaumont
2	France	Parc des Princes	January 21st 1978	W.B.Beaumont
2	Ireland	Twickenham	February 14th 1970	R.Hiller

MATCHES IN WHICH ENGLAND HAVE CONCEDED 2 DROP GOALS OR MORE:

Drop Goals Scored:	By:	Venue:	Date:	Captain:
3	France	Twickenham	February 2nd 1985	P.W.Dodge
2	France	Parc des Princes	January 20th 1996	W.D.C.Carling
2	Scotland	Twickenham	March 18th 1995	W.D.C.Carling
2	France	Twickenham	February 21st 1987	R.J.Hill
2	Wales	Twickenham	March 17th 1984	P.J.Wheeler
2	France	Twickenham	March 21st 1981	W.B.Beaumont
2	Ireland	Lansdowne Road	March 7th 1981	W.B.Beaumont
2	Wales	Cardiff Arms Park	January 16th 1971	A.L.Bucknall
2	France	Stade Colombes	April 18th 1970	R.B.Taylor
2	France	Stade Colombes	February 24th 1968	M.P.Weston
2	France	Twickenham	February 26th 1955	P.D.Young

INCIDENCE OF WINNING AND LOSING RUNS

MOST CONSECUTIVE MATCHES WON:

All Five Nations matches:	9	1991 - Wales, Scotland, Ireland, France
		1992 - Scotland, Ireland, France, Wales
		1993 - France
Five Nations matches at home:	9	1989 - France
		1990 - Ireland, Wales
		1991 - Scotland, France
		1992 - Ireland, Wales
		1993 - France, Scotland
Five Nations matches away:	4	1991 - Wales, Ireland
		1992 - Scotland, France

MOST CONSECUTIVE DEFEATS:

All Five Nations matches:	7	1971 - Scotland
		1972 - Wales, Ireland, France, Scotland.
		1973 - Wales Ireland
Five Nations matches at home:	3	1971 - Scotland
		1972 - Wales, Ireland,
Five Nations matches away:	10	1983 - Ireland,
		1984 - Scotland, France
		1985 - Ireland, Wales,
		1986 - Scotland, France,
		1987 - Ireland, Wales
		1988 - France

MATCHES WITHOUT CONCEDING OR SCORING TRIES

MOST CONSECUTIVE MATCHES WITHOUT CONCEDING A TRY:

All Five Nations matches:	5	1957 - Scotland
		1958 - Wales, Ireland, France, Scotland.
Five Nations matches at home:	6	1957 - Scotland,
		1958 - Wales, Ireland,
		1959 - France, Scotland
		1960 - Wales.
Five Nations matches away:	4	1957 - Wales, Ireland,
		1958 - France, Scotland.

MOST CONSECUTIVE MATCHES WITHOUT SCORING A TRY:

All Five Nations matches:	5	1958 - Scotland,
		1959 - Wales, Ireland, France, Scotland.
Five Nations matches at home:	5	1983 - France, Scotland
		1984 - Ireland, Wales
		1985 - France
Five Nations matches away:	4	1947 - Ireland,
		1948 - Scotland, France,
		1949 - Wales
	4	1965 - Wales, Ireland
		1966 - France, Scotland.
	4	1987 - Ireland, Wales,
		1988 - France, Scotland
	4	1993 - Wales, Ireland,
		1994 - Scotland, France.

LEADING INDIVIDUAL SCORERS BY SEASON:

Season:		Player:	Club:	Points scored:		
1947	(	J.Heaton	(Waterloo)	8	(4c)	
	(	N.M.Hall	(St Mary's Hospital)	8	(2dg)	
1948		R.Uren	(Waterloo)	7	(2c,1pg)	
1949		C.B.van Ryneveld	(Oxford University)	9	(3t)	
1950		J.V.Smith	(Cambridge University)	12	(4t)	RECORD
1951						
1952		N.M.Hall	(Richmond)	10	(2c,2pg)	
1953		N.M.Hall	(Richmond)	18	(6c,2pg)	RECORD
1954		D.S.Wilson	(Metropolitan Police)	12	(4t)	
1955		D.St G.Hazell	(Leicester)	9	(3pg)	
1956		J.D.Currie	(Harlequins)	16	(2c,4pg)	
1957		R.Challis	(Bristol)	10	(2c,2pg)	
1958		P.H.Thompson	(Headingley)	9	(3t)	
1959		A.B.W.Risman	(Manchester University)	6	(2pg)	
1960		D.Rutherford	(Percy Park)	19	(5c,3pg)	RECORD
1961		J.Roberts	(Sale)	6	(2t)	
1962		R.A.W.Sharp	(Oxford University)	10	(t,2c,1pg)	
1963	(	R.A.W.Sharp	(Wasps)	10	(t,2c,1dg)	
	(	J.G.Willcox	(Oxford University)	10	(2c,2pg)	
1964	(	D.P.Rogers	(Bedford)	6	(2t)	
	(	R.W.Hosen	(Northampton)	6	(2pg)	
1965		D.Rutherford	(Gloucester)	9	(3pg)	
1966		D.Rutherford	(Gloucester)	6	(2pg)	
1967		R.W.Hosen	(Bristol)	38	(4c,10pg)	RECORD
1968		R.Hiller	(Harlequins)	22	(2c,6pg)	
1969		R.Hiller	(Harlequins)	36	(3c,10pg)	
1970		R.Hiller	(Harlequins)	15	(3c,2dg,1pg)	
1971		R.Hiller	(Harlequins)	35	(2t,1c,9pg)	
1972		A.G.B.Old	(Middlesborough)	17	(1c,5pg)	
1973		A.M.Jordan	(Blackheath)	15	(3c,3pg)	
1974		A.G.B.Old	(Leicester)	33	(3c,9pg)	
1975		P.A.Rossborough	(Coventry)	16	(1t,4pg)	
1976		A.G.B.Old	(Middlesborough)	20	(1c,6pg)	
1977		A.J.Hignell	(Bristol)	22	(2c,6pg)	
1978		M.Young	(Gosforth)	11	(4c,1pg)	
1979		W.N.Bennett	(London Welsh)	20	(2t,4pg)	
1980		W.H.Hare	(Leicester)	34	(5c,8pg)	

LEADING INDIVIDUAL SCORERS BY SEASON: (continued)

Season:	Player:	Club:	Points scored:		
1981	W.H.Hare	(Leicester)	30	(1t,1c,8pg)	
1982	W.H.Hare	(Leicester)	28	(2c,8pg)	
1983	W.H.Hare	(Leicester)	42	(14pg)	RECORD
1984	W.H.Hare	(Leicester)	44	(1t,2c,12pg)	RECORD
1985	C.R.Andrew	(Cambridge University)	32	(2dg,1c,8pg)	
1986	C.R.Andrew	(Nottingham)	36	(1dg,3c,9pg)	
1987	W.M.H.Rose	(Harlequins)	41	(1t,2c,11pg)	
1988	J.M.Webb	(Bristol)	20	(1c,6pg)	
1989	C.R.Andrew	(Wasps)	26	(1dg,1c,7pg)	
1990	S.D.Hodgkinson	(Nottingham)	42	(6c,10pg)	
1991	S.D.Hodgkinson	(Nottingham)	60	(3c,18pg)	RECORD
1992	J.M.Webb	(Bath)	67	(3t,11c,11pg)	RECORD
1993	J.M.Webb	(Bath)	31	(2c,9pg)	
1994	J.E.B.Callard	(Bath)	27	(9pg)	
1995	C.R.Andrew	(Wasps)	53	(1dg,4c,14pg)	
1996	P.J.Grayson	(Northampton)	64	(3dg,2c,17pg)	
1997	P.J.Grayson	(Northampton)	52	(1dg, 2c, 13pg)	

SECTION 4

INDIVIDUAL RECORDS

1947 onwards

LEADING CAP WINNERS FROM 1947:

Name:	Club:	Total Caps:	Five Nations	World Cup	Others	As a Replcmt	Period:
R.Underwood	RAF/Leicester	85	50	15	20		1984 - 1996
W.D.C.Carling	Durham Univ/Harlequins	72	40	11	21		1988 - 1997
C.R.Andrew	Cambridge U/Nottingham/ Wasps/Newcastle	71	40	13	18	2	1985 - 1997
B.C.Moore	Nottingham/Harlequins	64	33	14	17	1	1987 - 1995
P.J.Winterbottom	Headingley/Harlequins	58	37	9	12		1982 - 1993
W.A.Dooley	Preston G'hoppers	55	33	8	14	1	1985 - 1993
J.Leonard	Saracens/Harlequins	55	28	11	16		1990 - 1997
J.C.Guscott	Bath	48	26	10	12	2	1989 - 1997
D.Richards	Leicester	48	26	10	12	2	1986 - 1996
A.Neary	Broughton Park	43	34		9	1	1971 - 1980
J.V.Pullin	Bristol	42	33		9	1	1966 - 1976
P.J.Wheeler	Leicester	41	36		5		1975 - 1984
J.A.Probyn	Wasps	37	22	5	10	1	1988 - 1993
D.J.Duckham	Coventry	36	29		7		1969 - 1976
G.S.Pearce	Northampton	36	22	4	10		1979 - 1991
W.B.Beaumont	Fylde	34	26		8	1	1975 - 1982
D.P.Rogers	Bedford	34	28		6		1961 - 1969
J.P.Scott	Rosslyn Park/Cardiff	34	27		7	1	1978 - 1984
B.B.Clarke	Bath/Richmond	33	16	5	12	2	1992 - 1997
J.M.Webb	Bristol/Bath	33	16	9	8	1	1987 - 1993
P.W.Dodge	Leicester	32	24		8		1978 - 1985
T.A.K.Rodber	Army/Northampton	32	16	6	10	3	1992 - 1997
M.C.Bayfield	Northampton	31	16	5	10		1991 - 1996
F.E.Cotton	Loughboro' Coll/Coventry	31	25		6		1971 - 1981
M.A.C.Slemen	Liverpool	31	27		4		1976 - 1984
E.Evans	Sale	30	26		4		1948 - 1958
M.O.Johnson	Leicester	30	17	6	7		1993 - 1997
R.J.Hill	Bath	29	13	7	9	3	1984 - 1991
C.R.Jacobs	Northampton	29	24		5		1956 - 1964
P.J.Squires	Harrogate	29	23		6		1973 - 1979
M.P.Weston	Richmond/Durham City	29	24		5		1963 - 1968

RORY UNDERWOOD
England's most capped player with 85 caps
earned between February 1984 and March 1996
50 Five Nations; 15 World Cup; and 20 others.

WILL CARLING
72 caps earned between November 1988 and
March 1997, and 59 of them as Captain.
40 Five Nations; 11 World Cup; and 21 others.

ROB ANDREW
71 caps earned between January 1985 and
March 1997, Captain on two occasions.
40 Five Nations; 13 World Cup; and 18 others.

BRIAN MOORE
64 caps earned between April 1987 and June
1995, and England's most capped forward.
33 Five Nations; 14 World Cup; and 17 others.

LEADING CAP WINNERS FROM 1947 (continued):

Name:	Club:	Total Caps:	Five Nations	World Cup	Others	As a Replcmt	
J.Butterfield	Northampton	28	26		2		1953 - 1959
P.A.G.Rendall	Wasps	28	18	4	6	1	1984 - 1991
S.J.Smith	Sale	28	23		5	2	1973 - 1983
M.C.Teague	Gloucester	27	16	5	6	1	1985 - 1993
J.Carleton	Orrell	26	20		6		1979 - 1984
C.D.Morris	Liverpool/St Helen's/Orrell	26	15	5	6	1	1988 - 1995
M.J.Colclough	Angouleme/Wasps	25	22		3		1978 - 1986
J.D.Currie	Oxford U/'Quins/Bristol	25	23		2		1956 - 1962
W.H.Hare	Nottingham/Leicester	25	18		7		1974 - 1984
M.S.Phillips	Oxford Univ/Fylde	25	20		5		1958 - 1964
C.B.Stevens	Penzance-Newlyn	25	19		6		1969 - 1975
T.Underwood	Leicester/Newcastle	25	13	4	8		1992 - 1997
P.R de Glanville	Bath	24	11	3	10	7	1992 - 1997
R.E.G.Jeeps	Northampton	24	22		2		1956 - 1962
P.J.Larter	Northampton	24	17		7		1967 - 1973
A.G.Ripley	Rosslyn Park	24	17		7		1972 - 1976
M.J.Catt	Bath	23	10	6	7	2	1994 - 1997
S.J.Halliday	Bath/Harlequins	23	15	3	5	1	1986 - 1992
J.M.Kendall-Carpenter	Oxford U/Penzance-	23	21		2		1949 - 1954
R.W.D.Marques	Cambridge U/Harlequins	23	21		2		1956 - 1961
G.W.Rees	Nottingham	23	8	5	10	6	1984 - 1991
R.M.Uttley	Gosforth	23	18		5		1973 - 1980
P.J.Ackford	Harlequins	22	12	5	5		1988 - 1991
P.J.Dixon	Gosforth	22	20		2		1971 - 1978
P.E.Judd	Coventry	22	16		6		1962 - 1967
C.W.Ralston	Richmond	22	16		6		1971 - 1975
G.H.Davies	Cambridge U/Coventr	21	13		8	1	1981 - 1986
J.P.Hall	Bath	21	14		7	1	1984 - 1994
M.G.Skinner	Harlequins	21	12	4	5	1	1988 - 1992
V.E.Ubogu	Bath	21	8	5	8		1992 - 1995
C.R.Woodward	Leicester	21	17		4	1	1980 - 1984
N.E.Horton	Moseley/Toulouse	20	20				1969 - 1980
P.B.Jackson	Coventry	20	19		1		1956 - 1963
N.C.Redman	Bath	20	5	5	10	1	1984 - 1997
P.J.Blakeway	Gloucester	19	17		2		1980 - 1985
L.B.Cannell	Northampton/Oxford U	19	18		1		1948 - 1957
R.Hiller	Harlequins	19	16		3		1968 - 1972
P.G.D.Robbins	Oxford Univ/Coventry	19	17		2		1956 - 1962
S.Bainbridge	Gosforth	18	13	2	3		1982 - 1987
J.Roberts	Old Millhillians/Sale	18	16		2		1960 - 1964
R.V.Stirling	RAF/Leicester	18	16		2		1951 - 1954

LEADING CAP WINNERS FROM 1947 (continued):

Name:	Club:	Total Caps:	Five Nations	World Cup	Others	As a Replcmt	
M.A.Burton	Gloucester	17	13		4		1972 - 1978
N.M.Hall	St Mary's Hosp/Richmond	17	16		1		1947 - 1955
M.Rafter	Bristol	17	13		4	1	1977 - 1981
C.E.Smart	Newport	17	13		4		1979 - 1983
P.H.Thompson	Headingley	17	16		1		1956 - 1959
A.Ashcroft	Waterloo	16	15		1		1956 - 1959
A.M.Davis	Torquay Ath/Harlequins	16	11		5		1963 - 1970
W.A.Holmes	Nuneaton	16	15		1		1950 - 1953
A.G.B.Old	Middlesborough/Leicester	16	12		4		1972 - 1978
V.G.Roberts	Penryn/Harlequins	16	16				1947 - 1956
R.B.Taylor	Northampton	16	13		3		1966 - 1971
J.G.Willcox	Oxford University	16	15		1		1961 - 1964
M.E.Harrison	Wakefield	15	9	4	2		1985 - 1988
D.G.Perry	Bedford	15	11		4		1963 - 1966
G.C.Rowntree	Leicester	15	9	2	4	1	1995 - 1997
K.G.Simms	Cambridge U/Liverpool	15	11	3	1		1985 - 1988
J.E.Woodward	Wasps	15	13		2		1952 - 1956
K.P.P.Bracken	Bristol/Saracens	14	6	2	6	2	1993 - 1997
G.J.Chilcott	Bath	14	7	3	4	4	1984 - 1989
A.J.Hignell	Cambridge Univ/Bristol	14	12		2		1975 - 1979
S.D.Hodgkinson	Nottingham	14	8	1	5		1989 - 1991
N.C.Jeavons	Moseley	14	11		3		1981 - 1983
J.Orwin	Gloucester	14	8		6		1985 - 1988
J.E.Owen	Coventry	14	11		3		1963 - 1967
D.Rutherford	Percy Park/Gloucester	14	12		2		1960 - 1967
R.A.W.Sharp	Oxford University/Wasps	14	13		1		1960 - 1967
J.S.Spencer	Cambridge U/Headingley	14	11		3		1969 - 1971
D.F.White	Northampton	14	13		1		1947 - 1953
S.E.Brain	Coventry	13	8		5	1	1984 - 1986
S.J.S.Clarke	Cambridge U/Blackheath	13	9		4		1963 - 1965
J.F.Finlan	Moseley	13	11		2		1967 - 1973
G.W.D.Hastings	Gloucester	13	12		1		1955 - 1958
R.Higgins	Liverpool	13	12		1		1954 - 1959
J.P.Horton	Bath	13	10		3		1978 - 1984
N.D.Melville	Wasps	13	10		3		1984 - 1988
C.Oti	Cambridge Univ/Wasps	13	6	2	5		1988 - 1991
M.P.Regan	Bristol	13	8		5		1995 - 1997
K.F.Savage	Northampton	13	11		2		1966 - 1968
D.T.Wilkins	Roundhay/US Portsmouth	13	12		1		1951 - 1953
T.P.Wright	Blackheath	13	12		1		1960 - 1962
D.H.Cooke	Harlequins	12	9		3		1981 - 1985
L.Cusworth	Leicester	12	10		2		1979 - 1988
L.B.N.Dallaglio	Wasps	12	7		5	1	1995 - 1997
K.E.Fairbrother	Coventry	12	11		1		1969 - 1971
R.M.Harding	Bristol	12	4	3	5	1	1985 - 1988
J.P.A.G.Janion	Bedford/Richmond	12	6		6		1971 - 1975

LEADING CAP WINNERS FROM 1947 (continued):

Name:	Club:	Total Caps:	Five Nations	World Cup	Others	As a Replcmt	
I.Preece	Coventry	12	12				1948 - 1951
P.S.Preece	Coventry	12	8		4	1	1972 - 1976
M.Regan	Liverpool	12	11		1		1953 - 1956
G.Rimmer	Waterloo	12	10		2		1949 - 1954
J.L.B.Salmon	Harlequins	12	6	4	2		1985 - 1987
J.M.Sleightholme	Bath	12	8		4		1996 - 1997
R.E.Webb	Coventry	12	11		1		1967 - 1972
M.J.Cooper	Moseley	11	9		2	1	1973 - 1977
W.P.C.Davies	Harlequins	11	10		1		1953 - 1958
H.O.Godwin	Coventry	11	6		5		1959 - 1967
S.A.M.Hodgson	Durham City	11	10		1		1960 - 1964
C.W.McFadyean	Moseley	11	9		2		1966 - 1968
S.O.Ojomoh	Bath	11	4	4	3	3	1994 - 1996
D.L.Powell	Northampton	11	10		1		1966 - 1971
D.M.Rollitt	Bristol	11	9		2		1967 - 1975
R.E.Syrett	Wasps	11	10		1		1958 - 1962
J.G.Webster	Moseley	11	8		3		1972 - 1975
S.Barnes	Bristol/Bath	10	5		5	4	1984 - 1993
R.C.Bazley	Waterloo	10	10				1952 - 1955
A.L.Bucknall	Richmond	10	8		2		1969 - 1971
B.J.Corless	Coventry/Moseley	10	9		1	1	1976 - 1978
K.J.Fielding	Loughboro' Coll/Moseley	10	9		1		1969 - 1972
R.H.Guest	Waterloo	10	9		1		1947 - 1949
R.Hesford	Bristol	10	8		2	3	1981 - 1985
N.J.Heslop	Orrell	10	5	2	3	1	1990 - 1992
R.W.Hosen	Northampton/Bristol	10	6		4		1963 - 1967
A.O.Lewis	Bath	10	9		1		1952 - 1954
J.R.C.Matthews	Harlequins	10	9		1		1949 - 1952
C.M.Payne	Harlequins	10	10				1964 - 1966
W.M.H.Rose	Cambridge U/Harlequins	10	8	1	1		1981 - 1987
M.Young	Gosforth	10	9		1		1977 - 1979
B.Boobbyer	Oxford Univ/Rosslyn Park	9	9				1950 - 1952
M.J.Coulman	Moseley	9	8		1		1967 - 1968
G.W.Evans	Coventry	9	8		1	1	1972 - 1974
A.P.Henderson	Cambridge U/Edinburgh W	9	9				1947 - 1949
J.P.Horrocks-Taylor	Cambridge U/Leics/M'boro	9	4		5		1958 - 1964
W.D.G.Morgan	Medicals	9	8		1		1960 - 1961
S.B.Richards	Richmond	9	8		1		1965 - 1967
D.L.Sanders	Harlequins	9	8		1		1954 - 1956
S.T.Smith	Wasps	9	6		3		1985 - 1986
M.R.Steele-Bodger	Cambridge & Edinburgh U	9	8		1		1947 - 1948
H.W.Walker	Coventry	9	8		1		1947 - 1948
J.E.Williams	Old Millhilians	9	9				1954 - 1965
J.R.C.Young	Oxford Univ/Harlequins	9	8		1		1958 - 1961
P.D.Young	Dublin Wanderers	9	8		1		1954 - 1955
T.J.Brophy	Liverpool	8	8				1964 - 1966
R.J.Cowling	Leicester	8	7		1		1977 - 1979

LEADING CAP WINNERS FROM 1947 (continued):

Name:	Club:	Total Caps:	Five Nations	World Cup	Others	As a Replcmt	
N.J.Drake-Lee	Cambridge U/Leicester	8	7		1		1963 - 1965
P.J.Grayson	Northampton	8	7		1		1995 - 1997
A.B.W.Risman	Manchr U/Loughboro' C	8	7		1		1959 - 1961
R.A.Robinson	Bath	8	4		4		1988 - 1995
D.B.Vaughan	Headingley/D'port Servs	8	7		1		1948 - 1950
B.R.West	Loughboro' C/Northampton	8	7		1		1968 - 1970
D.S.Wilson	Met Police	8	7		1		1953 - 1955
C.E.Winn	Rosslyn Park	8	7		1		1952 - 1954
S.J.Adkins	Coventry	7	7				1950 - 1953
A.E.Agar	Harlequins	7	6		1		1952 - 1953
D.F.Allison	Coventry	7	7				1956 - 1958
M.D.Bailey	Cambridge U/Wasps	7	3	1	3	1	1984 - 1990
B.Barley	Wakefield	7	3		4		1984 - 1988
R.M.Bartlett	Harlequins	7	7				1957 - 1958
N.O.Bennett	St Mary's Hosp/US Ptsm'th	7	6		1		1947 - 1948
W.N.Bennett	Bedford	7	6		1	1	1975 - 1979
D.W.Egerton	Bath	7	1		6	2	1988 - 1990
A.L.Horton	Blackheath	7	6		1		1965 - 1967
I.G.Hunter	Northampton	7	4	2	1		1992 - 1995
A.M.Jorden	Camb U/B'khth/Bedford	7	7				1970 - 1975
A.W.Maxwell	New Brighton/Headingley	7	5		2		1975 - 1978
W.K.T.Moore	Devonport Servs/Leicester	7	7				1947 - 1950
A.J.Morley	Bristol	7	3		4		1972 - 1975
S.V.Perry	Cambridge Univ	7	6		1		1947 - 1948
J.M.Ranson	Rosslyn Park	7	4		3		1963 - 1964
P.A.Rossborough	Coventry	7	5		2		1971 - 1975
S.D.Shaw	Bristol	7	4		3		1996 - 1997
N.C.Starmer-Smith	Harlequins	7	4		3		1969 - 1971
P.W.Sykes	Wasps	7	7				1948 - 1953
J.A.Watkins	Gloucester	7	3		4		1972 - 1975
A.M.Bond	Sale	6	4		2		1978 - 1982
M.J.S.Dawson	Northampton	6	4		2		1995 - 1997
A.C.T.Gomarsall	Wasps	6	3		3	1	1996 - 1997
V.S.J.Harding	Cambridge U/Saracens	6	6				1961 - 1962
R.D.Hearn	Bedford	6	6				1966 - 1967
A.J.Herbert	Wasps	6	6				1958 - 1959
J.G.G.Hetherington	Northampton	6	5		1		1958 - 1959
B.G.Nelmes	Cardiff	6	3		3		1975 - 1978
R.D.A.Pickering	Bradford	6	6				1967 - 1968
T.W.Price	Gloucester/Cheltenham	6	6				1948 - 1949
E.L.Rudd	Oxford Univ/Liverpool	6	6				1965 - 1966
T.R.G.Stimpson	Newcastle	6	4		2		1996 - 1997
D.W.Swarbrick	Oxford University	6	5		1		1947 - 1949
A.M.Swift	Swansea	6	3		3		1981 - 1984
P.J.Taylor	Northampton	6	6				1955 - 1962
B.H.Travers	Oxford Univ/Harlequins	6	5		1		1947 - 1949
C.S.Wardlow	Northampton	6	4		2	1	1969 - 1971
P.J.Warfield	Rosslyn Park/Cambridge U	6	5		1		1973 - 1975
R.M.Wilkinson	Bedford	6	4		2		1975 - 1976
N.C.Youngs	Leicester	6	5		1		1983 - 1984

LEADING CAP WINNERS FROM 1947 (continued):

Name:	Club:	Total Caps:	Five Nations	World Cup	Others	As a Replcmt	
N.A.Back	Leicester	5	2	3		1	1994 - 1995
J.E.B.Callard	Bath	5	2	1	2		1993 - 1995
A.R.Cowman	Coventry/Loughboro' Coll	5	3		2		1971 - 1973
R.G.R.Dawe	Bath	5	3	2			1987 - 1995
J.R.H.Greenwood	Waterloo	5	4		1		1966 - 1969
R.A.Hill	Saracens	5	4		1		1997
G.R.d'A.Hosking	Devonport Services	5	5				1949 - 1950
C.P.Kent	Rosslyn Park	5	5			1	1977 - 1978
P.J.Kingston	Gloucester	5	3		2		1977 - 1979
N.Labuschagne	Harlequins/Guy's Hospital	5	5				1953 - 1955
R.H.Lloyd	Harlequins	5	4		1		1967 - 1968
H.F.Luya	Headingley	5	5				1948 - 1949
S.G.F.Mills	Gloucester	5	1		4		1981 - 1984
J.Mycock	Sale	5	4		1		1947 - 1948
J.J.Page	Bedford	5	5				1971 - 1975
J.P.Quinn	New Brighton	5	4		1		1954
L.I.Rimmer	Bath	5	4		1		1961
D.W.A.Rosser	Cambridge U/Wasps	5	5				1965 - 1966
E.K.Scott	St Mary's Hosp/Redruth	5	4		1		1947 - 1948
C.M.A.Sheasby	Wasps	5	1		4	3	1996 - 1997
S.R.Smith	Cambridge U/Richmond	5	5				1959 - 1964
J.S.Steeds	Middlesex Hosp/Saracens	5	5				1949 - 1950
N.C.Stringer	Wasps	5			5	3	1982 - 1985
A.M.Underwood	Northampton/Exeter	5	5				1962 - 1964
B.J.Wightman	Moseley	5	3		2		1959 - 1963
T.C.Wintle	Northampton	5	5				1966 - 1969
P.G.Yarranton	RAF/Wasps	5	4		1		1954 - 1955

The International careers of fourteen England players have extended over a period of ten years or more.

Nigel Redman	20 caps	14 years from 1984 to 1987
Rory Underwood	85 caps	13 years from 1984 to 1996
Rob Andrew	71 caps	13 years from 1985 to 1997
Gary Pearce	36 caps	13 years from 1979 to 1991
Peter Winterbottom	58 caps	12 years from 1982 to 1993
Dean Richards	48 caps	11 years from 1986 to 1996
John Pullin	42 caps	11 years from 1966 to 1976
Fran Cotton	31 caps	11 years from 1971 to 1981
Eric Evans	30 caps	11 years from 1948 to 1958
Steve Smith	28 caps	11 years from 1973 to 1983
Dusty Hare	25 caps	11 years from 1974 to 1984
Will Carling	72 caps	10 years from 1988 to 1987
Tony Neary	43 caps	10 years from 1971 to 1980
Peter Wheeler	41 caps	10 years from 1975 to 1984

LEADING CAP WINNERS - FIVE NATIONS

R.Underwood	RAF/Leicester	50
C.R.Andrew	Cambridge Univ/Nottingham/Wasps/Newcastle	40
W.D.C.Carling	Durham University/Harlequins	40
P.J.Winterbottom	Headingley/Harlequins	37
P.J.Wheeler	Leicester	36
A.Neary	Broughton Park	34
W.A.Dooley	Preston Grasshoppers	33
B.C.Moore	Nottingham/Harlequins	33
J.V.Pullin	Bristol	33
D.J.Duckham	Coventry	29
J.Leonard	Saracens/Harlequins	28
D.P.Rogers	Bedford	28
J.P.Scott	Rosslyn Park/Cardiff	27
M.A.C.Slemen	Liverpool	27
W.B.Beaumont	Fylde	26
J.Butterfield	Northampton	26
E.Evans	Sale	26
J.C.Guscott	Bath	26
D.Richards	Leicester	26
F.E.Cotton	Loughborough Coll/Coventry/Sale	25
P.W.Dodge	Leicester	24
C.R.Jacobs	Northampton	24
M.P.Weston	Richmond/Durham City	24
J.D.Currie	Oxford University/Harlequins/Bristol	23
S.J.Smith	Sale	23
P.J.Squires	Harrogate	23
M.J.Colclough	Angouleme/Wasps	22
R.E.G.Jeeps	Northampton	22
G.S.Pearce	Northampton	22
J.A.Probyn	Wasps	22
J.M.Kendall-Carpenter	Oxford University/Penzance-Newlyn	21
R.W.D.Marques	Cambridge University/Harlequins	21
J.Carleton	Orrell	20
P.J.Dixon	Gosforth	20
N.E.Horton	Moseley/Toulouse	20
M.S.Phillips	Oxford University/Fylde	20

LEADING CAP WINNERS - FIVE NATIONS (continued)

P.B.Jackson	Coventry	19
C.B.Stevens	Penzance-Newlyn	19
L.B.Cannell	Northampton/Oxford University	18
W.H.Hare	Nottingham/Leicester	18
P.A.G.Rendall	Wasps	18
R.M.Uttley	Gosforth	18
P.J.Blakeway	Gloucester	17
M.O.Johnson	Leicester	17
P.J.Larter	Northampton	17
A.G.Ripley	Rosslyn Park	17
P.G.D.Robbins	Oxford University/Coventry	17
C.R.Woodward	Leicester	17
M.C.Bayfield	Northampton	16
B.B.Clarke	Bath/Richmond	16
N.M.Hall	St Mary's Hospital/Richmond	16
R.Hiller	Harlequins	16
P.E.Judd	Coventry	16
C.W.Ralston	Richmond	16
J.Roberts	Old Millhillians/Sale	16
V.G.Roberts	Penryn/Harlequins	16
T.A.K.Rodber	Army/Northampton	16
R.V.Stirling	RAF/Leicester	16
M.C.Teague	Gloucester	16
P.H.Thompson	Headingley	16
J.M.Webb	Bristol/Bath	16
A.Ashcroft	Waterloo	15
S.J.Halliday	Bath/Harlequins	15
W.A.Holmes	Nuneaton	15
C.D.Morris	Liverpool St Helen's/Orrell	15
J.G.Willcox	Oxford University	15
J.P.Hall	Bath	14
S.Bainbridge	Gosforth	13
M.A.Burton	Gloucester	13
G.H.Davies	Cambridge University/Coventry/Wasps	13
R.J.Hill	Bath	13
M.Rafter	Bristol	13
R.A.W.Sharp	Oxford University/Wasps	13
C.E.Smart	Newport	13
R.B.Taylor	Northampton	13
T.Underwood	Leicester/Newcastle	13
D.F.White	Northampton	13
J.E.Woodward	Wasps	13

LEADING CAP WINNERS - FIVE NATIONS (continued)

P.J.Ackford	Harlequins	12
G.W.D.Hastings	Gloucester	12
R.Higgins	Liverpool	12
A.J.Hignell	Cambridge University/Bristol	12
A.G.B.Old	Middlesborough/Leicester	12
I.Preece	Coventry	12
D.Rutherford	Percy Park/Gloucester	12
M.G.Skinner	Harlequins	12
D.T.Wilkins	Roundhay/US Portsmouth	12
T.P.Wright	Blackheath	12
A.M.Davis	Torquay Athletic/Harlequins	11
K.E.Fairbrother	Coventry	11
J.F.Finlan	Moseley	11
P.R de Glanville	Bath	11
N.C.Jeavons	Moseley	11
J.E.Owen	Coventry	11
D.G.Perry	Bedford	11
M.Regan	Liverpool	11
K.F.Savage	Northampton	11
K.G.Simms	Cambridge University/Liverpool	11
J.S.Spencer	Cambridge University/Headingley	11
R.E.Webb	Coventry	11
R.C.Bazley	Waterloo	10
M.J.Catt	Bath	10
L.Cusworth	Leicester	10
W.P.C.Davies	Harlequins	10
S.A.M.Hodgson	Durham City	10
J.P.Horton	Bath	10
N.D.Melville	Wasps	10
C.M.Payne	Harlequins	10
D.L.Powell	Northampton	10
G.Rimmer	Waterloo	10
R.E.Syrett	Wasps	10
B.Boobbyer	Oxford University/Rosslyn Park	9
S.J.S.Clarke	Cambridge University/Blackheath	9
D.H.Cooke	Harlequins	9
M.J.Cooper	Moseley	9
B.J.Corless	Coventry/Moseley	9
K.J.Fielding	Loughborough Coll/Moseley	9
R.H.Guest	Waterloo	9
M.E.Harrison	Wakefield	9
A.P.Henderson	Cambridge University/Edinburgh Wanderers	9
A.O.Lewis	Bath	9
C.W.McFadyean	Moseley	9
J.R.C.Matthews	Harlequins	9
D.M.Rollitt	Bristol	9
G.C.Rowntree	Leicester	9
J.E.Williams	Old Millhillians	9
M.Young	Gosforth	9

LEADING CAP WINNERS - FIVE NATIONS (continued)

S.E.Brain	Coventry	8
T.J.Brophy	Liverpool	8
A.L.Bucknall	Richmond	8
M.J.Coulman	Moseley	8
G.W.Evans	Coventry	8
R.Hesford	Bristol	8
S.D.Hodgkinson	Nottingham	8
W.D.G.Morgan	Medicals	8
J.Orwin	Gloucester	8
P.S.Preece	Coventry	8
G.W.Rees	Nottingham	8
M.P.Regan	Bristol	8
S.B.Richards	Richmond	8
W.M.H.Rose	Cambridge University/Harlequins	8
D.L.Sanders	Harlequins	8
J.M.Sleightholme	Bath	8
M.R.Steele-Bodger	Cambridge University/Edinburgh University	8
V.E.Ubogu	Bath	8
H.W.Walker	Coventry	8
J.G.Webster	Moseley	8
J.R.C.Young	Oxford University/Harlequins	8
P.D.Young	Dublin Wanderers	8
S.J.Adkins	Coventry	7
D.F.Allison	Coventry	7
R.M.Bartlett	Harlequins	7
G.J.Chilcott	Bath	7
R.J.Cowling	Leicester	7
L.B.N.Dallaglio	Wasps	7
N.J.Drake-Lee	Cambridge University/Leicester	7
P.J.Grayson	Northampton	7
A.M.Jorden	Cambridge University/Blackheath/Bedford	7
W.K.T.Moore	Devonport Services/Leicester	7
A.B.W.Risman	Manchester University/Loughborough Coll	7
P.W.Sykes	Wasps	7
D.B.Vaughan	Headingley/Devonport Services	7
B.R.West	Loughborough Coll/Northampton	7
D.S.Wilson	Metropolitan Police	7
C.E.Winn	Rosslyn Park	7
A.E.Agar	Harlequins	6
N.O.Bennett	St Mary's Hospital/US Portsmouth	6
W.N.Bennett	Bedford	6
K.P.P.Bracken	Bristol/Saracens	6
H.O.Godwin	Coventry	6
V.S.J.Harding	Cambridge University/Saracens	6
R.D.Hearn	Bedford	6
A.J.Herbert	Wasps	6
A.L.Horton	Blackheath	6
R.W.Hosen	Northampton/Bristol	6
J.P.A.G.Janion	Bedford/Richmond	6
C.Oti	Cambridge University/Wasps	6

LEADING CAP WINNERS - FIVE NATIONS (continued)

S.V.Perry	Cambridge University	6
R.D.A.Pickering	Bradford	6
T.W.Price	Gloucester/Cheltenham	6
E.L.Rudd	Oxford University/Liverpool	6
J.L.B.Salmon	Harlequins	6
S.T.Smith	Wasps	6
P.J.Taylor	Northampton	6
S.Barnes	Bristol/Bath	5
N.J.Heslop	Orrell	5
J.G.G.Hetherington	Northampton	5
G.R.d'A.Hosking	Devonport Services	5
C.P.Kent	Rosslyn Park	5
N.Labuschagne	Harlequins/Guy's Hospital	5
H.F.Luya	Headingley	5
A.W.Maxwell	New Brighton/Headingley	5
J.J.Page	Bedford	5
N.C.Redman	Bath	5
P.A.Rossborough	Coventry	5
D.W.A.Rosser	Cambridge University/Wasps	5
S.R.Smith	Cambridge University/Richmond	5
J.S.Steeds	Middlesex Hospital/Saracens	5
D.W.Swarbrick	Oxford University	5
B.H.Travers	Oxford University/Harlequins	5
A.M.Underwood	Northampton/Exeter	5
P.J.Warfield	Rosslyn Park/Cambridge University	5
T.C.Wintle	Northampton	5
N.C.Youngs	Leicester	5

In the 204 Five Nations matches played since 1947, 3,118 caps have been awarded to 400 different players.

Of those 3,118 caps, 58 have been awarded to players who have replaced originally selected players during the course of a match.

LEADING CAP WINNERS - WORLD CUP MATCHES

R.Underwood	RAF/Leicester	15
B.C.Moore	Nottingham/Harlequins	14
C.R.Andrew	Cambridge Univ/Nottingham/Wasps/Newcastle	13
W.D.C.Carling	Durham University/Harlequins	11
J.Leonard	Saracens/Harlequins	11
J.C.Guscott	Bath	10
D.Richards	Leicester	10
J.M.Webb	Bristol/Bath	9
P.J.Winterbottom	Headingley/Harlequins	9
W.A.Dooley	Preston Grasshoppers	8
R.J.Hill	Bath	7
M.J.Catt	Bath	6
M.O.Johnson	Leicester	6
T.A.K.Rodber	Army/Northampton	6
P.J.Ackford	Harlequins	5
M.C.Bayfield	Northampton	5
B.B.Clarke	Bath/Richmond	5
C.D.Morris	Liverpool/St Helen's/Orrell	5
J.A.Probyn	Wasps	5
N.C.Redman	Bath	5
G.W.Rees	Nottingham	5
M.C.Teague	Gloucester	5
V.E.Ubogu	Bath	5
M.E.Harrison	Wakefield	4
S.O.Ojomoh	Bath	4
G.S.Pearce	Northampton	4
P.A.G.Rendall	Wasps	4
J.L.B.Salmon	Harlequins	4
M.G.Skinner	Harlequins	4
T.Underwood	Leicester/Newcastle	4
N.A.Back	Leicester	3
G.J.Chilcott	Bath	3
P.R de Glanville	Bath	3
S.J.Halliday	Bath/Harlequins	3
R.M.Harding	Bristol	3
K.G.Simms	Cambridge University/Liverpool	3
P.N.Williams	Orrell	3

LEADING CAP WINNERS - WORLD CUP MATCHES
(continued)

S.Bainbridge	Gosforth	2
K.P.P.Bracken	Bristol/Saracens	2
F.J.Clough	Cambridge University	2
R.G.R.Dawe	Bath	2
N.J.Heslop	Orrell	2
I.G.Hunter	Northampton	2
C.Oti	Cambridge University/Wasps	2
G.C.Rowntree	Leicester	2
M.D.Bailey	Cambridge University/Wasps	1
J.E.B.Callard	Bath	1
S.D.Hodgkinson	Nottingham	1
D.P.Hopley	Wasps	1
J.Mallett	Bath	1
C.J.Olver	Northampton	1
W.M.H.Rose	Cambridge University/Harlequins	1

In the three World Cup Tournaments played so far, England have played 16 matches and 253 caps have been awarded to 52 different players.

Of those 253 caps, 33 have been awarded to players who have replaced originally selected players during the course of a match.

Four England players have played in all three tournaments. They are:

	Matches played in:		
	1987	**1991**	**1995**
R.Underwood	3	6	6
B.C.Moore	3	5	6
C.R.Andrew	2	6	5
D.Richards	4	3	3

R.G.R.Dawe has the unique distinction of having played in both the 1987 and the 1995 World Cups, but not that of 1991. Thus, his two World Cup caps were earned in a span of eight years.

Name:	Club:	Total Caps	1	2	3	4	5	6	7	8	9	10	Five Nations	World Cup	Others	As a Rplcmt
P.J.Ackford	Harlequins	22	A 88/3 S 90 {S 91} IT96	S 89 AR90/3 {A 91}	I 89 W 91	F 89 S 91	W 89 I 91	RO89 F 91	FI89 A 91	I 90 {NZ91}	F 90 {IT91}	W 90 {F 91}	12	5	5	
A.A.Adebayo	Bath	3	IT96	AR97/1	AR97/2										3	
G.D.Adey	Leicester	2	I76	F76									2			
S.J.Adkins	Coventry	7	I50	F50	S50	W53	I53	F53	S53				7			
A.E.Agar	Harlequins	7	SA52	W52	S52	I52	F52	W53	I53				6		1	
D.F.Allison	Coventry	7	W56	I56	S56	F56	W57	W58	S58				7			
W.F.Anderson	Orrell	1	NZ73/1												1	
C.R.Andrew	Cambridge U/Nottingham /Wasps/Newcastle	71	RO85 F 87 A 88/3 S 90 {US91} F 93 CA94 W 97r	F 85 W 87 S 89 AR90/3 {F 91} W 93 I 95	S 85 {J 87r} I 89 W 91 {S 91} NZ293 F 95	I 85 {US87} S 91 {A 91} S 94 W 95	W 85 S 88 W 89 I 91 I 94 S 95	W 86 I 88 RO89-C F 91 I 92 F 94 {AR95}	S 86 IM88 FI89 FI91 F 92 W 94 {IT95-C}	I 86 A 88/1 I 90 A 91 S 92 SA94/1 {A 95}	F 86 A 88/2 F 90 {NZ91} CA92 SA94/2 {NZ95}	I 87 FI88 W 90 {IT91} SA92 RO94 {F 95}	40	13	18	2
G.S.Archer	Bristol	2	S 96	I 96									2			
T.G.Arthur	Wasps	2	W 66	I 66									2			
R.C.Ashby	Wasps	3	I 66	F 66	A 67								2		1	
A.Ashcroft	Waterloo	16	W56 I 58	I 56 F 58	S 56 S 58	F 56 I 59	W 57 F 59	I 57 S 59	F 57	S 57	W 58	A 58	15		1	
N.A.Back	Leicester	5	S 94	I 94	{AR95}	{IT95}	{WS95}						2	3		
M.D.Bailey	Cambridge U/Wasps	7	SA84/1	SA84/2	{US87}	FI89	I 90	F 90	S 90r				3	1	3	1
S.Bainbridge	Gosforth	18	F 82	W 82	F 83	W 83	S 83	I 83	NZ283 {J 87}	S 84 {US87}	I 84	F 84	13	2	3	1
D.G.S.Baker	Old Merchant Taylors'	4	W 55	I 55	F 55	S 55							4			
J.F.Bance	Bedford	1	S 54										1			
B.Barley	Wakefield	7	I 84	F 84	W 84	A 84	A 88/1	A 88/2	FI88				3		4	
S.Barnes	Bristol/Bath	10	A 84	RO85/1	NZ85/1	NZ85/2	S 86r	F 86r	I 87r	FI88	S 93	I 93	5		5	4
J.T.Bartlett	Waterloo	1	W 51										1			
R.M.Bartlett	Harlequins	7	W 57	I 57	F 57	S 57	I 58	F 58	S 58				7			

CAPS GAINED BY MATCH (continued)

Total Caps:

Name:	Club:	Total Caps	1	2	3	4	5	6	7	8	9	10	Five Nations	World Cup	Others	As a Replcmt
J.Barton	Coventry	4	I67	F67	W67	F72							4			
S.M.Bates	Wasps	1	RO89												1	
J.L.Baume	Northern	1	S50										1			
M.C.Bayfield	Northampton	31	FI91 S93 W95 W96	A91 I93 S95	S92 S94 {AR95}	I92 I94 {IT95}	F92 SA94/1 {A95}	W92 SA94/2 {NZ95}	CA92 RO94 {F96}	SA92 CA94 SA95	F93 I95 WS95	W93 F95 F96	16	5	10	
R.C.Bazley	Waterloo	10	I52	F52	W53	I53	F53	S53	W55	I55	F55	S55	10			
N.D.Beal	Northampton	2	AR96	A97											2	
W.B.Beaumont	Fylde	34	I75 F77 W79-C AR81/1C	A75/1r W77 NZ79-C AR81/2C	A75/2 F78-C I80-C A82-C	A76 W78-C F80-C S82-C	W76 S78-C W80-C	S76 I78-C S80-C	I76 NZ78-C W81-C	F76 S79 S81-C	S77 I79-C I81-C	I77 F79-C F81-C	26		8	1
I.D.S.Beer	Harlequins	2	F55	S55									2			
M.C.Beese	Liverpool	3	W72	I72	F72								3			
P.J.Bell	Blackheath	4	W68	I68	F68	S68							4			
G.J.Bendon	Wasps	4	W59	I59	F59	S59							4			
N.O.Bennett	St Mary's Hosp/US Ptsmt	7	W47	S47	F47	A48	W48	I48	S48				6		1	
W.N.Bennett	Bedford	7	S75	A75/1r	S76r	S79	I79	F79	W79				6		1	1
J.Bentley	Sale	3	IM88	A88/1	A97										3	
M.J.Berridge	Northampton	2	W49	I49									2			
P.J.Blakeway	Gloucester	19	I80 W82	F80 I84	W80 F84	S80 W84	W81 SA84/1	S81 RO85	I81 F85	F81 S85	I82 I85	F82	17		2	
A.M.Bond	Sale	6	NZ78	S79	I79	NZ79	I80	I82					4		2	
B.Boobbyer	Oxford Univ/Rosslyn Park	9	W50	I50	F50	S50	W51	F51	S52	I52			9			
I.J.Botting	Oxford University	2	W50	I50									2			
S.B.Boyle	Gloucester	3	W83	S83	I83								3			
K.P.P.Bracken	Bristol/Saracens	14	NZ93 SA95	S94 IT96r	I94 AR97/1	CA94 AR97/2	I95	F95	W95	S95	{IT95}	{WS95r}	6	2	6	2
S.E.Brain	Coventry	13	SA84/2 S86	A84r I86	RO85 F86	F85	S85	I85	W85	NZ85/1	NZ85/2	W86	8		5	1
B.Braithwaite-Exley	Headingley	1	W49										1			
A.Brinn	Gloucester	3	W72	I72	S72								3			

CAPS GAINED BY MATCH (continued)

Name:	Club:	Total Caps	1	2	3	4	5	6	7	8	9	10	Total Caps:			
													Five Nations	World Cup	Others	As a Replcmt
T.J.Brooke	Richmond	2	F 88	S 68									2			
T.J.Brophy	Liverpool	8	I 64	F 64	S 64	W 65	I 65	W 66	I 66	F 66			8			
A.L.Bucknall	Richmond	10	SA69	I 70	W 70	S 70	F 70	W 71-C	I 71	F 71	S 71	SC71	8		2	
J.R.D.Buckton	Saracens	3	A88/3r	AR90/1	AR90/2										3	1
M.P.Bulpitt	Blackheath	1	S 70										1			
M.A.Burton	Gloucester	17	W 72	I 72	F 72	S 72	SA72	F 74	W 74	S 75	A 75/1	A 75/2	13		4	
			A 76	W 76	S 76	I 76	F 76	F 78	W 78							
C.J.S.Butcher	Harlequins	3	SA84/1	SA84/2	A 84										3	
P.E.Butler	Gloucester	2	A 75/1	F 76									1		1	
J.Butterfield	Northampton	28	F 53	S 53	W 54	NZ254	I 54	S 54	F 54	W 55	I 55	F 55	26		2	
			S 55	W 56	I 56	S 56	F 56	W 57	I 57	F 57	S 57	W 58				
			A 58	I 58	F 58	S 58	W 59-C	I59-C	F 59-C	S 59-C						
J.J.Cain	Waterloo	1	W 50										1			
J.E.B.Callard	Bath	5	NZ63	S 94	I 94	{WS95}	SA95						2	1	2	
L.B.Cannell	Northampton/Oxford U /St Mary's Hosp	19	F 48	W 49	I 49	F 49	S 49	W 50	I 50	F 50	S 50	SA52	18		1	
			W 52	W 53	I 53	F 53	I 56	S 56	F 56	W 57	I 57					
D.W.N.Caplan	Headingley	2	S 78	I 78									2			
R.M.Cardus	Roundhay	2	F 79	W 79									2			
J.Carleton	Orrell	26	NZ79	I 80	F 80	W 80	S 80	W 81	S 81	I 81	F 81	AR81/1	20		6	
			AR81/2	A 82	S 82	I 82	F 82	W 82	F 83	W 83	S 83	I 83				
			NZ83													
W.D.C.Carling	Durham Univ/Harlequins	72	F 88	S 88	S 88	I 88	IM88	A 88/2	FI88	A88/3C	S 89-C	I 89-C	40	11	21	
			F 89-C	W 89-C	FI89-C	I 90-C	F 90-C	W 90-C	S 90-C	AR90/1C	AR90/2C	AR90/3C				
			W 91-C	S 91-C	I 91-C	F 91-C	FI91-C	A 91-C	{NZ91-C}	{IT91-C}	{US91-C}	{F 91-C}				
			{S 91-C}	{A 91-C}	S 92-C	I 92-C	F 92-C	W 92-C	CA92-C	SA92-C	F 93-C	W 93-C				
			S 93-C	I 93-C	NZ93-C	S 94-C	I 94-C	F 94-C	W 94-C	SA94/1C	SA94/2C	RO94-C				
			CA94-C	I 95-C	F 95-C	W 95-C	S 95-C	{AR95-C}	{WS95-C}	{A 95-C}	{NZ95-C}	{F 95-C}				
			CA95-C	WS95-C	F 96-C	W 96-C	S 96-C	I 96-C	IT96	AR96	S 97	I 97				
			F 97	W 97												
M.J.Catt	Bath	23	W 94r	CA94r	I 95	F 95	W 95	S 95	{AR95}	{IT95}	{WS95}	{A 95}	10	6	7	2
			{N295}	{F 95}	SA95	WS95	F 96	W 96	S 96	I 96	IT96	AR96				
			W 97	AR97/1	A 97											
R.Challis	Bristol	3	I 57	F 57	S 57								3			

CAPS GAINED BY MATCH (continued)

Total Caps:

Name:	Club:	Total Caps	1	2	3	4	5	6	7	8	9	10	Five Nations	World Cup	Others	As a Replcmt
G.J.Chilcott	Bath	14	A 84 I 89r	I 86 F 89	F 86 W 89	F 87r RO89	W 87	{J 87}	{US87}	{W 87r}	IM88r	FI88	7	3	4	4
B.B.Clarke	Bath/Richmond	33	SA92 SA94/2 {NZ95} AR97/1	F 93 RO94 {F 95} AR97/2	W 93 CA94 SA95 A 97	S 93 I 95 WS95	I 93 F 95 F 96	NZ93 W 95 W 96	S 94 S 95 I 96	F 94 {AR95} I 96	W 94 {IT95} AR96r	SA94/1 {A 95} W 97	16	5	12	2
S.J.S.Clarke	Cambridge U/Blackheath	13	W 63 I 65	I 63 F 65	F 63 S 65	S 63	NZ63/1	NZ63/2	A 63	NZ64	W 64	I 64	9		4	
J.W.Clements	Old Cranleighans	3	I 59	F 59	S 59								3			
F.J.Clough	Cambridge Univ	4	I 86	F 86	{J 87r}	{US87}							2	2		1
R.Cockerill	Leicester	2	AR97/1r	AR97/2											2	1
M.J.Colclough	Angouleme/Wasps/Swansea	25	S 78 A 82 W 84	I 78 S 82 W 86	NZ79 I 82 S 86	F 80 F 82 I 86	W 80 W 82 F 86	S 80 F 83	W 81 NZ283	S 81 S 84	I 81 I 84	F 81 F 84	22		3	1
P.J.Collins	Camborne	3	S 52	I 52	F 52								3			
P.W.Cook	Richmond	2	I 65	F 65									2			
D.A.Cooke	Harlequins	4	W 76	S 76	I 76	F 76							4			
D.H.Cooke	Harlequins	12	W 81 NZ85/1	S 81 NZ285/2	I 81	F 81	I 84	RO85	F 85	S 85	I 85	W 85	9		3	
M.J.Cooper	Moseley	11	F 73 W 77	S 73	NZ73/2r	F 75	W 75	A 76	W 76	S 77	I 77	F 77	9		2	1
B.J.Corless	Coventry/Moseley	10	A 76	I 76r	S 77	I 77	F 77	W 77	F 78	W 78	S 78	I 78	9		1	1
M.Corry	Bristol	2	AR97/1	AR97/2											2	
F.E.Cotton	Loughboro' Coll/Coventry/Sale	31	S 71 I 74 I 77 W 81	SC71 I 75-C F 77	PR71 F 75-C W 77	W 73 W 75-C S 78	I 73 A 76 I 78	F 73 W 76 NZ79	S 73 S 76 I 80	NZ73/2 I 76 F 80	A 73 F 76 W 80	S 74 S 77 S 80	25		6	
M.J.Coulman	Moseley	9	A 67	I 67	F 67	S 67	W 67	W 68	I 68	F 68	S 68		8		1	
R.J.Cowling	Leicester	8	S 77	I 77	F 77	W 77	F 78	NZ78	S 79	I 79			7		1	
A.R.Cowman	Coventry/Loughboro' Coll	5	S 71	SC71	PR71	W 73	I 73						3		2	
R.N.Creed	Coventry	1	PR71												1	
J.D.Currie	Oxford U/Quins/Bristol	25	W 56 I 58 S 60	I 56 F 58 SA61	S 56 S 58 W 62	F 56 W 59 I 62	W 57 I 59 F 62	I 57 F 59	F 57 S 59	S 57 W 60	W 58 I 60	A 58 F 60	23		2	

CAPS GAINED BY MATCH (continued)

Total Caps:

Name:	Club:	Total Caps	1	2	3	4	5	6	7	8	9	10	Five Nations	World Cup	Others	As a Replcmt
D.A.Cusani	Orrell	1	I 87										1			
L.Cusworth	Leicester	12	NZ79 F 88	F 82 W 88	W 82	F 83	W 83	NZ83	S 84	I 84	F 84	W 84	10		2	
L.B.N.Dallaglio	Wasps	12	SA95r F 97	WS95 A 97	F 96	W 96	S 96	I 96	IT96	AR96	S 97	I 97	7		5	1
T.J.Dalton	Coventry	1	S 69r										1			
T.Danby	Harlequins	1	W 49										1			1
G.H.Davies	Cambridge U/Coventr /Wasps	21	S 81 S 83 F 86	I 81 S 84	F 81 SA84/1	AR81/1 SA84/2	AR81/2 RO85r	A 82 NZ85/1	S 82 NZ85/2	I 82 W 86	F 83 S 86	W 83 I 86	13		8	1
W.P.C.Davies	Harlequins	11	S 53 W 58	NZ54	I 54	W 55	I 55	F 55	S 55	W 56	F 57	S 57	10		1	
A.M.Davis	Torquay Ath/Harlequins	16	W 63 W 66	I 63 A 67	S 63 SA69	NZ63/1 I 70	NZ63/2 W 70	NZ64 S 70	W 64	I 64	F 64	S 64	11		5	
R.G.R.Dawe	Bath	5	I 87	F 87	W 87	{US87}	{WS95}						3	2		
M.J.S.Dawson	Northampton	6	WS95	F 96	W 96	S 96	I 96	A 97					4		2	
J.M.Dee	Hartlepool Rovers	2	S 62	NZ63/1									1		1	
A.J.Diprose	Saracens	2	AR97/1	AR97/2											2	
P.J.Dixon	Gosforth	22	PR71 F 74 I 78	W 72 W 74 NZ78	I 72 I 75	F 72-C F 76	S 72-C S 77	I 73 I 77	F 73 F 77	S 73 W 77	S 74 F 78	I 74 S 78	20		2	
S.A.Doble	Moseley	3	SA72	NZ73/1	W 73								1		2	
P.W.Dodge	Leicester	32	W 78 W 81 F 83 NZ85/1C	S 78 S 81 W 83 NZ85/2C	I 78 I 81 S 83	NZ78 F 81 I 83	S 79 AR81/1 NZ83	I 79 AR81/2 RO85-C	F 79 A 82 F 85-C	W 79 S 82 S 85-C	W 80 F 82 I 85-C	S 80 W 82 W 85-C	24		8	
M.P.Donnelly	Oxford University	1	I 47										1			
W.A.Dooley	Preston G'hoppers	55	RO85 F 87 A 88/1 I 90 F 91 CA92	F 85 W 87 A 88/2 F 90 {NZ91} SA92	S 85 {A 87} FI88 W 90 {US91} W 93	I 85 {US87} A 88/3 S 90 {F 91} S 93	W 85 {W 87} S 89 AR90/1 {S 91} I 93	NZ85/2r F 88 I 89 AR90/2 {A 91}	W 86 W 88 F 89 AR90/3 S 92	S 86 S 88 W 89 W 91 I 92	I 86 I 88 RO89 S 91 F 92	F 86 IM88 FI89 I 91 W 92	33	8	14	1

CAPS GAINED BY MATCH (continued)

Total Caps:

Name:	Club:	Total Caps	1	2	3	4	5	6	7	8	9	10	Five Nations	World Cup	Others	As a Replcmt
B.A.Dovey	Rosslyn Park	2	W 63	I 63									2			
N.J.Drake-Lee	Cambridge U/Leicester	8	W 63	I 63	F 63	S 63	NZ264	W 64	I 64	W 65			7		1	
D.J.Duckham	Coventry	36	I 69 I 71 W 73 I 75	F 69 F 71 I 73 F 75	S 69 S 71 F 73 W 75	W 69 SC71 S 73 A 76	SA69 PR 71 NZ73/2 W 76	I 70 W 72 A 73 S 76	W 70 I 72 S 74	S 70 F 72 I 74	F 70 S 72 F 74	W 71 NZ73/1 W 74	29		7	
A.F.Dun	Wasps	1	W 84										1			
D.W.Egerton	Bath	7	IM88	A 88/1	FI88r	A 88/3	FI89	I 90	AR90/2r				1		6	2
N.S.D.Estcourt	Blackheath	1	S 55										1			
B.J.Evans	Leicester	2	A 88/2	FI88											2	
E.Evans	Sale	30	A 48 I 53 F 56-C	W 50 F 53 W 57-C	I 51 S 53 I57-C	F 51 S 54 F 57-C	S 51 NZ254 S 57-C	SA52 I 54 W 58-C	W 52 F 54 A 58-C	S 52 W 56-C I 58-C	I 52 I 56-C F 58-C	F 52 S 56-C S 58-C	26		4	
G.W.Evans	Coventry	9	S 72	W 73r	I 73	S 73	NZ73/2	S 74	I 74	F 74	W 74		8		1	1
K.E.Fairbrother	Coventry	12	I 69 I 71	F 69 F 71	S 69	W 69	SA69	I 70	W 70	S 70	F 70	W 71	11		1	
K.J.Fielding	Loughboro' Coll/Moseley	10	I 69	F 69	S 69	SA69	I 70	F 70	W 72	I 72	F 72	S 72	9		1	
J.H.Fidler	Gloucester	4	AR81/1	AR81/2	SA84/1	SA84/2									4	
J.F.Finlan	Moseley	13	I 67 W 69	F 67 F 70	S 67 NZ73/1	W 67	NZ267	W 68	I 68	I 69	F 69	S 69	11		2	
P.J.Ford	Gloucester	4	W 64	I 64	F 64	S 64							4			
G.P.Frankcom	Cambridge Univ	4	W 65	I 65	F 65	S 65							4			
R.J.French	St Helen's	4	W 61	I 61	F 61	S 61							4			
D.J.Garforth	Leicester	4	W 97r	AR97/1	AR97/2	A 97									3	1
M.N.Gavins	Leicester	1	W 61										1			
D.J.Gay	Bath	4	W 68	I 68	F 68	S 68							4			
J.T.George	Falmouth	3	S 47	F 47	I 49								3			
G.A.Gibbs	Bristol	2	F 47	I 48									2			
N.Gibbs	Harlequins	2	S 54	F 54									2			
W.J.Gittings	Coventry	1	NZ267												1	
P.R de Glanville	Bath	24	SA92r {AR95r} W 97-C	W 93r {IT95} AR97/1-C	NZ393 {WS95} AR97/2-C	S 94 SA95r A97-C	I 94 W 96r	F 94 I 96r	W 94 IT96-C	SA94/1 S 97-C	SA94/2 I 97-C	CA94r F 97-C	11	3	10	7

CAPS GAINED BY MATCH (continued)

Total Caps:

Name:	Club:	Total Caps	1	2	3	4	5	6	7	8	9	10	Five Nations	World Cup	Others	As a Replcmt
P.B.Glover	RAF/Bath	3	A 67	F 71	PR71								1		2	
H.O.Godwin	Coventry	11	F 59 NZ267	S 59	S 63	NZ263	NZ263/2	A 63	NZ264	I 64	F 64	S 64	6		5	
A.C.T.Gomarsall	Wasps	6	IT96	AR96	S 97	I 97	F 97	AR97/2r					3		3	1
A.Gray	Otley	3	W 47	I 47	S 47								3			
P.J.Grayson	Northampton	8	WS95	F 96	W 96	S 96	I 96	S 97	I 97	F 97			7		1	
P.B.T.Greening	Gloucester	3	IT96r	W 97r	AR97/1								1		2	2
N.J.J.Greenstock	Wasps	3	AR97/1	AR97/2	A 97										3	
J.R.H.Greenwood	Waterloo	5	I 66	F 66	S 66	A 67	I 69-C						4		1	
J.A.Gregory	Blackheath	1	W 49										1			
D.J.Grewcock	Coventry	1	AR97/2												1	
R.H.Guest	Waterloo	10	W 47	I 47	S 47	F 47	A 48	W 48	I 48	S 48	F 49	S 49	9		1	
J.C.Guscott	Bath	48	RO89 F 91 F 92 I 95 WS95	FI89 FI91 W 92 F 95 F 96	I 90 A 91 CA92 W 95 W 96	F 90 {NZ291} SA92 S 95 S 96	W 90 {IT91} F 93 {AR95} I 96	S 90 {F 91} W 93 {IT95} AR96	AR90/3 {S 91} S 93 {A 95} I 97r	S 48 W 91 {A 91} I 93 {NZ295} W 97r	F 49 S 91 S 92 RO94 {F 95}	S 49 I 91 I 92 CA94 SA95	26	10	12	2
M.Haag	(Bath)	2	AR97/1	AR97/2											2	
P.M.Hale	Moseley	3	SA69	I 70	W 70								2		1	
J.P.Hall	Bath	21	S 84r W 85 S 94	I 84 NZ285/1	F 84 NZ285/2	SA84/1 W 86	SA84/2 S 86	A 84 I 87	RO85 F 87	F 85 W 87	S 85 S 87	I 85 AR90/3	14		7	1
N.M.Hall	St Mary's Hosp/Richmond	17	W 47 F 52-C	I 47 W 53-C	S 47 I 53-C	F 47 F 53-C	W 49-C S 53-C	I 49-C W 55-C	SA52-C I 55-C	W 52-C	S 52-C	I 52-C	16		1	
S.J.Halliday	Bath/Harlequins	23	W 86 F 89 I 92	S 86 W 89 F 92	S 87 RO89 W 92	S 88 FI89r	I 88 W 90	IM88 S 90	A 88/1 {US91}	A 88/3 {S 81}	S 89 {A 91}	I 89 S 92	15	3	5	1
A.W.Hancock	Northampton	3	F 65	S 65	F 66								3			
J.H.Hancock	Newport	2	W 55	I 55									2			
R.C.Hannaford	Bristol	3	W 71	I 71	F 71								3			
R.M.Harding	Bristol	12	RO85 A 88/2	F 85 FI88-C	S 85	S 87	{A 87}	{J 87}	{W 87}	I 88r	IM88	A 88/1	4	3	5	1
V.S.J.Harding	Cambridge U/Saracens	6	F 61	S 61	W 62	I 62	F 62	S 62					6			

CAPS GAINED BY MATCH (continued)

Total Caps:

Name:	Club:	Total Caps	1	2	3	4	5	6	7	8	9	10	Five Nations	World Cup	Others	As a Replcmt
R.J.K.Hardwick	Coventry	1	IT96r												1	1
E.M.P.Hardy	Blackheath	3	I 51	F 51	S 51								3			
W.H.Hare	Nottingham/Leicester	25	W 74 / AR81/1 / I 84	F 78 / AR82/2 / F 84	NZ78 / F 82 / W 84	NZ79 / W 82 / SA84/1	I 80 / F 83 / SA84/2	F 80 / W 83	W 80 / S 83	S 80 / I 83	W 81 / NZ83	S 81 / S 84	18		7	
A.T.Harriman	Harlequins	1	A 88/3												1	
M.E.Harrison	Wakefield	15	NZ85/1 / {J 87-C}	NZ85/2 / {US87-C}	S 86 / {W 87-C}	I 86 / F 88-C	F 86 / W 88-C	I 87	F 87	W 87	S 87-C	{A87-C}	9	4	2	
G.W.D.Hastings	Gloucester	13	W 55 / I 58	I 55 / F 58	F 55 / S 58	S 55	W 57	I 57	F 57	S 57	W 58	A 58	12		1	
D.St G.Hazell	Leicester	4	W 55	I 55	F 55	S 55							4			
A.Healey	Leicester	3	I 97r	W 97	A 97r								2		1	2
R.D.Hearn	Bedford	6	F 66	S 66	I 67	F 67	S 67	W 67					6			
J.Heaton	Waterloo	3	I 47	S 47-C	F 47-C								3			
A.P.Henderson	Cambridge U/Edinburgh	9	W 47	I 47	S 47	F 47	I 48	S 48	F 48	W 49	I 49		9			
A.J.Herbert	Wasps	6	F 58	S 58	W 59	I 59	F 59	S 59					6			
R.Hesford	Bristol	10	S 81r	A 82	S 82	F 82r	F 83r	RO85	F 85	S 85	I 85	W 85	8		2	3
N.J.Heslop	Orrell	10	AR90/1	AR90/2	AR90/3	W 91	S 91	I 91	F 91	{US91}	{F 91}	W 92r	5	2	3	1
J.G.G.Hetherington	Northampton	6	A 58	I 58	W 59	I 59	F 59	S 59					5		1	
E.N.Hewitt	Coventry	3	W 51	I 51	F 51								3			
R.Higgins	Liverpool	13	W 54 / F 57	NZ54 / S 57	I 54 / W 59	S 54	W 55	I 55	F 55	S 55	W 57	I 57	12		1	
A.J.Hignell	Cambridge Univ/Bristol	14	A 75/2 / S 79	A 76 / I 79	W 76 / F 79	S 76 / W 79	I 76	S 77	I 77	F 77	W 77	W 78	12		2	
R.A.Hill	Saracens	5	S 97	I 97	F 97	W 97	A 97						4		1	
R.J.Hill	Bath	29	SA84/1 / I 90 / F 91	SA84/2 / F 90 / FI91	I 85r / W 90 / A 91	NZ85/2r / S 90 / {N291}	AR90/1 / {TI91}	AR90/2 / {US91}	AR90/3 / {F 91}	W 91 / {S 91}	{US87} / S 91 / {A 91}	FI89 / I 91	13	7	9	3
R.Hiller	Harlequins	19	W 68 / W 70-C	I 68 / S 70-C	F 68 / I 71	S 68 / F 71-C	I 69 / S 71	F 69 / SC71	S 69 / PR71	W 69 / W 72	SA69-C / I 72	I 70-C	16		3	
S.D.Hodgkinson	Nottingham	14	RO89 / S 91	FI89 / I 91	I 90 / F 91	F 90 / {US91}	AR90/1 / W 90	S 90	AR90/1	AR90/2	AR90/3	W 91	8	1	5	
S.A.M.Hodgson	Durham City	11	W 60 / W 64	I 60	F 60	S 60	SA61	W 61	W 62	I 62	F 62	S 62	10		1	

CAPS GAINED BY MATCH (continued)

Total Caps:

Name:	Club:	Total Caps	1	2	3	4	5	6	7	8	9	10	Five Nations	World Cup	Others	As a Replcmt
M.B.Hofmeyr	Oxford University	3	W 50	F 50	S 50								3			
C.B.Holmes	Manchester	3	S 47	I 48	F 48								3			
W.A.Holmes	Nuneaton	16	W 50 I 52	I 50 F 52	F 50 W 53	S 50 I 53	W 51 F 53	I 51 S 53	F 51	S 51	SA52	S 52	15		1	
W.B.Holmes	Cambridge Univ	4	W 49	I 49	F 49	S 49							4			
W.G.Hook	Gloucester	3	S 51	SA52	W 52								2		1	
D.P.Hopley	Wasps	3	{WS95r}	SA95	WS95									1	2	1
J.P.Horrocks-Taylor	Cambridge U/Leics/M'boro	9	W 58	A 58	S 61	S 62	NZ63/1	NZ63/2	A 63	NZ64	W 64		4		5	
E.L.Horsfall	Harlequins	1	W 49										1			
A.L.Horton	Blackheath	7	W 65	I 65	F 65	S 65	F 66	S 66					6		1	
J.P.Horton	Bath	13	W 78 I 83	S 78 SA84/1	I 78 SA84/2	NZ78	I 80	F 80	W 80	S 80	W 81	S 83	10		3	
N.E.Horton	Moseley/Toulouse	20	I 69 I 77	F 69 F 77	S 69 W 77	W 69 F 78	I 71 W 78	F 71 S 79	S 71 I 79	S 74 F 79	W 75 W 79	S 77 I 80	20			
R.W.Hosen	Northampton/Bristol	10	NZ63/1	NZ63/2	A 63	F 64	S 64	A 67	I 67	F 67	S 67	W 67	6		4	
G.R.d'A.Hosking	Devonport Services	5	W 49	I 49	F 49	S 49	W 50						6			
P.Hull	RAF/Bristol	4	SA94/1	SA94/2	RO94	CA94									4	
I.G.Hunter	Northampton	7	CA92	F 93	W 93	I 94	W 94	{WS95}	{F 95}				4	2	1	
R.P.Huntsman	Headingley	2	NZ85/1	NZ85/2											2	
A.C.B.Hurst	Wasps	1	S 62										1			
J.P.Hyde	Northampton	2	F 50	S 50									2			
B.S.Jackson	Broughton Park	2	S 70r	F 70									2			
P.B.Jackson	Coventry	20	W 56 S 58	I 56 W 59	F 56 I 59	W 57 F 59	I 57 S 59	F 57 I 61	S 57 W 63	W 58 I 63	A 58 F 63	F 58 S 63	19		1	1
C.R.Jacobs	Northampton	29	W 56 F 58 S 61	I 56 S 58 W 62	F 56 W 60 I 62	W 57 I 60 F 62	I 57 F 60 S 62	F 57 S 60 NZ63/1	S 57 SA61 NZ63/2	W 58 W 61 A 63	A 58 I 61 F 64	I 58 F 61	24		5	
J.P.A.G.Janion	Bedford/Richmond	12	W 71 A 75/1	I 71 A 75/2	F 71	S 71	SC71	PR71	W 72	S 72	SA72	A 73	6		6	
N.C.Jeavons	Moseley	14	S 81 F 83	I 81 W 83	F 81 S 83	AR81/1 I 83	AR81/2	A 82	S 82	I 82	F 82	W 82	11		3	
R.E.G.Jeeps	Northampton	24	I 59 W 62-C	W 57 I 62-C	I 57 F 62-C	F 57 S 62-C	S 57	W 58 SA61-C	A 58 W 61-C	I 58 I 61-C	F 58 F 61-C	S 58 S 61-C	22		2	

Total Caps:

Name:	Club:	Total Caps	1	2	3	4	5	6	7	8	9	10	Five Nations	World Cup	Others	As a Replcmt
C.R.Jennins	Waterloo	3	A 67	I 67	F 67								2		1	
M.O.Johnson	Leicester	30	F 93 W 95 F 96	NZ293 S 95 W 96	S 94 (AR95) S 96	I 94 (IT95) I 96	F 94 (WS95) IT96	W 94 (A 95) AR96	RO94 (NZ295) S 97	CA94 (F 96) I 97	I 95 SA95 F 97	F 95 WS95 W 97	17	6	7	1
H.A.Jones	Barnstaple	3	W 50	I 50	F 50								3			
A.M.Jorden	Camb U/B'khth/Bedford	7	F 70	I 73	F 73	S 73	F 74	W 75	S 75				7			
P.E.Judd	Coventry	22	W 62 F 65 W 67-C	I 62 S 65 NZ67-C	F 62 W 66	I 66	F 66	S 66	A 67	I 67-C	NZ64 F 67-C	I 65 S 67-C	16		6	
J.H.Keeling	Guy's Hospital	2	A 48	W 48									1		1	
B.W.Keen	Newcastle Univ	4	W 68	I 68	F 68	S 68							4			
G.A.Kelly	Bedford	4	W 47	I 47	S 47	W 48							4			
T.A.Kemp	Richmond	2	A 48	W 48-C									1		1	
J.M.Kendall-Carpenter	Oxford U/Penzance-Newlyn/Bath	23	I 49 SA52 NZ254	F 49 W 52 I 54	S 49 S 52 F 54	W 50 I 52	I 50 F 52	F 50 W 53	S 50 I 53	I 51-C F 53	F 51-C S 53	S 51-C W 54	21		2	
R.D.Kennedy	Camborne	3	I 49	F 49	S 49								3			
C.P.Kent	Rosslyn Park	5	S 77	I 77	F 77	W 77	F 78r						5			1
M.Keyworth	Swansea	4	A 76	W 76	S 76	I 76							3		1	
A.D.King	Wasps	1	AR97/2r												1	1
I.King	Harrogate	3	W 54	NZ254	I 54								2		1	
P.J.Kingston	Gloucester	5	A 75/1	A 75/2	I 79	F 79	W 79						3		2	
P.M.Knight	Bristol	3	F 72	S 72	SA72								2		1	
N.Labuschagne	Harlequins/Guy's Hospital	5	W 53	W 55	I 55	F 55	S 55						5			
M.S.Lampkowski	Headingley	4	A 76	NZ267	S 76	I 76							3		1	
P.J.Larter	Northampton	24	A 67 SA69 PR71	I 70 SA72	W 68 W 70 NZ73/1	I 68 S 70 W 73	F 68 F 70	S 68 W 71	I 69 I 71	F 69 F 71	S 69 S 71	W 69 SC71	17		7	
M.M.Leadbetter	Broughton Park	1	F 70										1			
V.H.Leadbetter	Edinburgh Wanderers	2	S 54	F 54									2			

CAPS GAINED BY MATCH (continued)

Total Caps:

Name:	Club:	Total Caps	1	2	3	4	5	6	7	8	9	10	Five Nations	World Cup	Others	As a Replcmt
J.Leonard	Saracens/Harlequins	55	AR90/1 {IT91} SA92 SA94/1 {A 95} AR96-C	AR90/2 {US91} F 93 SA94/2 {NZ95} S 97	AR90/3 {F 91} W 93 RO94 {F 95} I 97	W 91 {S 91} S 93 CA94 SA95 F 97	S 91 {A 91} I 93 I 95 WS95 W 97	I 91 S 92 NZ93 F 95 F 96	F 91 I 92 S 94 W 95 W 96	FI91 F 92 I 94 S 95 S 96	A 91 S 92 F 94 {AR95} I 96	{NZ91} CA92 W 94 {IT95} IT96	28	11	16	
A.O.Lewis	Bath	10	SA52	W 52	S 52	I 52	F 52	W 53	I 53	F 53	S 53	F 54	9		1	
M.S.Linnett	Moseley	1	FI89												1	
R.H.Lloyd	Harlequins	5	NZ67	W 68	I 68	F 68	S 68						4		1	
R.A.P.Lozowski	Wasps	1	A 84												1	
H.F.Luya	Headingley	5	W 48	I 48	S 48	F 48	W 49						5			
C.W.McFadyean	Moseley	11	I 66 I 68-C	F 66	S 66	A 67	I 67	F 67	S 67	W 67	NZ67	W 68-C	9		2	
R.J.P.Madge	Exeter	4	A 48	W 48	I 48	S 48							3		1	
J.Mallett	Bath	1	{WS95r}											1		1
J.Mallinder	Sale	2	AR97/1	AR97/2											2	
D.C.Manley	Exeter	4	W 63	I 63	F 63	S 63							4		1	
N.D.Mantell	Rosslyn Park	1	A 75/1												1	
M.S.Mapletoft	Gloucester	1	AR97/2													
R.W.D.Marques	Cambridge U/Harlequins	23	W 56 I 58 S 60	I 56 F 58 SA61	S 56 S 58 W 61	F 56 W 59	W 57 I 59	I 57 F 59	F 57 S 59	S 57 W 60	W 58 I 60	A 58 F 60	21		2	
V.R.Marriott	Harlequins	4	NZ63/1	NZ63/2	A 63	NZ64									4	
C.R.Martin	Bath	4	F 85	S 85	I 85	W 85							4			
N.O.Martin	Harlequins	1	F 72r										1			1
J.R.C.Matthews	Harlequins	10	F 49	S 49	I 50	F 50	S 50	SA52	W 52	S 52	I 52	F 52	9		1	
A.W.Maxwell	New Brighton/Headingley	7	A 75/1	A 76	W 76	S 76	I 76	F 76	F 78				5		2	
N.D.Melville	Wasps	13	A 84-C W 88	I 85 S 88-C	W 85 I 88-C	NZ85/1	NZ85/2	W 86-C	S 86-C	I 86-C	F 86-C	F 88	10		3	
S.G.F.Mills	Gloucester	5	AR81/1	AR81/2	W 83	SA84/1	A 84						1		4	

Total Caps:

Name:	Club:	Total Caps	1	2	3	4	5	6	7	8	9	10	Five Nations	World Cup	Others	As a Replcmt
B.C.Moore	Nottingham/Harlequins	64	S 87 A 88/2 F 90 A 91 SA92 SA94/1 {WS95r}	{A 87} FI88 W 90 {NZ91} F 93 SA94/2 {A 95}	{J 87} A 88/3 S 90 {IT91} W 93 RO94 {NZ95}	{W 87} S 89 AR90/1 {F 91} S 93 CA94 {F 95}	F 88 I 89 AR90/2 {S 91} I 93 I 95	W 88 F 89 W 91 {A 91} NZ93 F 95	S 88 W 89 S 91 S 92 S 94 W 95	I 88 RO89 I 91 I 92 I 94 S 95	IM88 FI89 F 91 F 92 F 94 {AR95}	A 88/1 I 90 FI91 W 92 W 94 {IT95}	33	14	17	1
P.B.C.Moore	Blackheath	1	W 51										1			
W.K.T.Moore	Devonport Servs/Leicester	7	W 47	I 47	F 49	S 49	I 50	F 50	S 50				7			
R.J.Mordell	Rosslyn Park	1	W 78										1			
W.D.G.Morgan	Medicals	9	W 60	I 60	F 60	S 60	SA61	W 61	I 61	F 61	S 61		8		1	
A.J.Morley	Bristol	7	SA72	NZ73/1	W 73	I 73	S 75	A 75/1	A 75/2				3		4	
C.D.Morris Liverpool	St Helen's/Orrell	26	A 88/3 SA92 S 95r {WS95r}	S 89 F 93 {AR95}	I 89 W 93 {WS95}	F 89 S 93 {A 95}	W 89 I 93 {NZ95}	S 92 F 94 {F 95}	I 92 W 94	F 92 SA94/1	S 92 SA94/2	CA92 RO94	15	5	6	1
A.R.Mullins	Harlequins	1	FI89												1	
J.Mycock	Sale	5	W 47-C	I 47-C	S 47	F 47	A 48						4		1	
B.A.Neale	Rosslyn Park/Army	3	I 51	F 51	S 51								3			
A.Neary	Broughton Park	43	W 71 SA72 F 74 I 76-C F 80	I 71 NZ73/1 W 74 F 76-C W 80	F 71 W 73 I 75 I 77 S 80	S 71 I 73 F 75 F 78r	SC71 F 73 W 75 S 79	PR71 S 73 S 75-C I 79	W 72 NZ73/2 A75/1-C F 79	I 72 A 73 A76-C W 79	F 72 S 74 W 76-C NZ79	S 72 I 74 S 76-C I 80	34		9	1
B.G.Nelmes	Cardiff	6	A 75/1	A 75/2	W 78	S 78	I 78	NZ78					3		3	
S.C.Newman	Oxford University	3	F 47	A 48	W 48								2		1	
J.O.Newton-Thompson	Oxford University	2	S 47	F 47									2			
B.F.Ninnes	Coventry	1	W 71										1			
M.J.Novak	Harlequins	3	W 70	S 70	F 70								3			
L.F.L.Oakley	Bedford	1	W 51										1			
S.O.Ojomoh	Bath	11	I 94 F 96	F 94	SA94/1r	SA94/2	RO94	S 95r	{AR95}	{WS95}	{A 95r}	{F 95}	4	4	3	3
A.G.B.Old	Middlesborough/Leicester	16	W 72 W 74	I 72 I 75	F 72 A 75/2	S 72 S 76	SA72 I 76	NZ73/2 F 78	A 73	S 74	I 74	F 74	12		4	

CAPS GAINED BY MATCH (continued)

Total Caps:

Name:	Club:	Total Caps	1	2	3	4	5	6	7	8	9	10	Five Nations	World Cup	Others	As a Replcmt
C.J.Olver	Northampton	3	AR90/3	{US91}	CA92										2	
J.Orwin	Gloucester	14	RO85	F 85	S 85	I 85	W 85	NZ85/1	NZ85/2	F 88	W 88	S 88	8	1	6	
C.Oti	Cambridge Univ/Wasps	13	I 88	IM88-C	A88/1-C	A88/2-C	F 89	W 89	RO89	AR90/1	AR90/2	FI91	6	2	5	
			A 91	(NZ291)	(IT91)											
J.E.Owen	Coventry	14	W 63	I 63	F 63	S 63	A 63	NZ64	W 65	I 65	F 65	S 65	11		3	
			I 66	F 66	S 66	NZ67										
J.J.Page	Bedford	5	W 71	I 71	F 71	S 71	S 75						5			
J.N.Pallant	Nottingham	3	I 67	F 67	S 67								3			
J.A.Palmer	Bath	3	SA84/1	SA84/2	I 86r								1		2	1
T.A.Pargetter	Coventry	3	S 62	F 63	NZ63/1								2		1	
M.J.Parsons	Northampton	4	W 68	I 68	F 68	S 68							4			
W.M.Patterson	Sale	2	SA61	S 61									1		1	
C.M.Payne	Harlequins	10	I 64	F 64	S 64	I 65	F 65	S 65	W 66	I 66	F 66	S 66	10			
G.S.Pearce	Northampton	36	S 79	I 79	NZ83	W 79	AR81/1	AR81/2	A 82	S 82	F 83	W 83	22	4	10	
			S 83	I 83	NZ85/2	S 84	SA84/2	A 84	RO85	F 85	S 85	I 85				
			W 85	NZ85/1	(US87)	W 86	S 86	I 86	RO85	F 85	S 85	I 85				
			S 87	(A 87)	F 92r	{W 87}	FI88	(US91)	F 86	I 87	F 87	W 87				
D.Pears	Harlequins	4	AR90/1	AR90/2									2		2	
T.G.A.H.Peart	Hartlepool Rovers	2	F 64	S 64									2			
D.G.Perry	Bedford	15	F 63	S 63	NZ263/1	NZ263/2	A 63	NZ264	W 64	I 64	W 65-C	I 65-C	11		4	
			F 65-C	S 65-C	W 66	I 66	F 66									
S.V.Perry	Cambridge Univ	7	W 47	I 47	A 48	W 48	I 48	S 48	F 48	F 59			6		1	
M.S.Phillips	Oxford Univ/Fylde	25	A 58	I 58	F 58	S 58	W 59	I 59	F 59	S 59	W 60	I 60	20		5	
			F 60	S 60	W 61	W 63	I 63	F 63	S 63	NZ263/1	NZ263/2	A 63				
			NZ64	W 64	I 64											
R.D.A.Pickering	Bradford	6	I 67	F 67	S 67	W 67	F 68	S 68					6			
K.C.Plummer	Bristol	4	W 69	S 76	I 76	F 76							4			
D.L.Powell	Northampton	11	W 66	I 66	I 69	F 69	S 69	W 69	W 71	I 71	F 71	S 71	10		1	
			SC71													
I.Preece	Coventry	12	I 48	S 48	F 48	F 49-C	S 49-C	W 50-C	I 50-C	F 50-C	S 50-C	W 51	12			
			I 51	F 51												
P.S.Preece	Coventry	12	SA72	NZ73/1	W 73	I 73	F 73	S 73	NZ73/2	I 75	F 75	W 75	8		4	1
			A 75/2	W 76r												

CAPS GAINED BY MATCH (continued)

Total Caps:

Name:	Club:	Total Caps	1	2	3	4	5	6	7	8	9	10	Five Nations	World Cup	Others	As a Replcmt
M.Preedy	Gloucester	1	SA84/1												1	
N.J.Preston	Richmond	3	NZ79	I80	F80								2		1	
J.Price	Coventry	1	I61										1			
T.W.Price	Gloucester/Cheltenham	6	S48	F48	W49	I49	F49	S49					6			
J.A.Probyn	Wasps	37	F88 RO89r I91 I92	W88 I90 F91 F92	S88 F90 FI91 W92	I88 W90 A91 F93	IM88 S90 {NZ91} W93	A88/1 AR90/1 {IT91} S93	A88/2 AR90/2 {F91} I93	A88/3 AR90/3 {S81}	S89 W91 {A91}	I89 S91 S92	22	5	10	1
D.H.Prout	Northampton	2	W68	I68									2			
J.V.Pullin	Bristol	42	W66 I70 W72 NZ73-C A75/2-C	W68 W70 I72 A73-C F76	I68 S70 F72 S74-C	F68 F70 S72 I74-C	S68 W71 SA72-C F74-C	I69 I71 NZ73-C W74-C	F69 F71 W73-C I75	S69 S71 I73-C W75r	W69 SC71 F73-C S75	SA69 PR71 S73-C A75/1	33		9	1
S.J.Purdy	Rugby	1	S62										1			
J.P.Quinn	New Brighton	5	W54	NZ54	I54	S54	F54						4		1	
M.Rafter	Bristol	17	S77 F79	F77 W79	W77 NZ79	F78 W80r	W78 W81	S78 AR81/1	I78 AR81/2	NZ78	S79	I79	13		4	1
C.W.Ralston	Richmond	22	SC71 F73 W75	PR71 S73 S75	W72 NZ73/2	I72 A73	F52 S74	S72 I74	SA72 F74	NZ73/1 W74	W73 I75	I73 F75	16		6	
J.M.Ranson	Rosslyn Park	7	NZ63/1	NZ63/2	A63	W64	I64	F64	S64				4		3	
S.Redfern	Leicester	1	I84r										1			1
N.C.Redman	Bath	20	A84 FI91	S86r {IT91}	I87 {US91}	S87 NZ93	{A87} F94	{J87} W94	{W87} SA94/1	FI88 SA94/2	AR90/1 AR97/1	AR90/2 A97	5	5	10	1
G.F.Redmond	Cambridge University	1	F70										1			
B.W.Redwood	Bristol	2	W68	I68									2			
G.W.Rees	Nottingham	23	SA84/2r (W87) AR90/3r	A84 S88r FI91	I86 I88 {US91}	F86 IM88	F87 A88/1	W87 A88/2	S87 FI88	{A87} W89r	{J87} RO89r	{US87} FI89r	8	5	10	6
M.Regan	Liverpool	12	W53 S56	I53 F56	F53	S53	W54	NZ54	I54	S54	F54	I56	11		1	
M.P.Regan	Bristol	13	SA95 F97	WS95 W97	F96 A97	W96	S96	I96	IT96	AR96	S97	I97	8		5	

CAPS GAINED BY MATCH (continued)

Total Caps:

Name:	Club:	Total Caps	1	2	3	4	5	6	7	8	9	10	Five Nations	World Cup	Others	As a Replcmt
P.A.G.Rendall	Wasps	28	W 84	SA84/2	W 86	S 86	I 87	F 87	S 87	{A 87}	{J 87}	{W 87}	18	4	6	1
			F 88	W 88	S 88	I 88	IM88	A 88/1	A 88/2	A 88/3	S 89	I 89				
			F 89	W 89	RO89	I 90	F 90	W 90	S 90	{IT91r}						
D.Richards	Leicester	48	I 86	F 86	S 87	{A 87}	{J 87}	{US87}	{W 87}	F 88	W 88	S 88	26	10	12	2
			I 88	A 88/1	A 88/2	FI88	A 88/3	S 89	I 89	F 89	W 89	RO89				
			AR90/3	W 91	S 91	I 91	F 91	FI91	A 91	{NZ91}	{IT91}	{US91}				
			S 92r	F 92	W 92	CA92	NZ93	W 94	SA94/1	CA94	I 95	F 95				
			W 95	S 95	{WS95}	{A 95}	{NZ95}	F 96r	S 96	I 96						
S.B.Richards	Richmond	9	W 65	I 65	F 65	S 65	A 67	I 67	F 67	S 67	W 67		8		1	
G.Rimmer	Waterloo	12	W 49	I 49	W 50	W 51	I 51	F 51	SA52	W 52	W 54	NZ54	10		2	
			I 54	S 54												
L.I.Rimmer	Bath	5	SA61	W 61	I 61	F 61	S 61						4		1	
A.G.Ripley	Rosslyn Park	24	W 72	I 72	F 72	S 72	SA72	NZ73/1	W 73	I 73	F 73	S 73	17		7	
			NZ73/2	A 73	S 74	I 74	F 74	W 74	I 75	F 75	S 75	A 75/1				
			A 75/2	A 76	W 76	S 76										
A.B.W.Risman	Manchr U/Loughboro' C	8	W 59	I 59	F 59	S 59	SA61	W 61	I 61	F 61			7		1	
G.C.Rittson-Thomas	Oxford University	3	W 51	I 51	F 51								3			
G.L.Robbins	Coventry	2	W 86	S 86									2			
P.G.D.Robbins	Oxford Univ/Coventry	19	W 56	I 56	S 56	F 56	W 57	I 57	F 57	S 57	W 58	A 58	17		2	
			I 58	S 58	W 60	I 60	F 60	S 60	SA61	W 61	S 62					
J.Roberts	Old Millilians/Sale	18	W 60	I 60	F 60	S 60	SA61	W 61	I 61	F 61	S 61	W 62	16		2	
			I 62	F 62	S 62	W 63	I 63	F 63	S 63	NZ64						
V.G.Roberts	Penryn/Harlequins	16	F 47	W 49	I 49	F 49	S 49	I 50	F 50	S 50	W 51-C	I 51	16			
			F 51	S 51	W 56	I 56	S 56	F 56								
E.F.Robinson	Coventry	4	S 54	I 61	F 61	S 61							4			
R.A.Robinson	Bath	8	A 88/1	A 88/2	A 88/3	FI88	S 89	I 89	F 89	W 89			4		4	
T.A.K.Rodber	Army/Northampton	32	S 92	I 92	NZ93	I 94	F 94	W 94	SA94/1	SA94/2	RO94	CA94	16	6	10	3
			I 95	WS95	W 95	W 95	{AR95}	{IT95}	{WS95r}	SA95	{NZ95}	{F 95}				
			SA95	A 97	W 96	S 96r	I 96r	IT96	AR96	{A 95}	I 97	F 97				
			W 97							S 97						
D.P.Rogers	Bedford	34	I 61	F 61	S 61	W 62	I 62	F 62	W 63	I 63	F 63	S 63	28		6	
			NZ63/1	NZ63/2	A 63	NZ64	W 64	I 64	F 64	S 64	W 65	I 65				
			F 65	S 65	W 66-C	I 66-C	F 66-C	S 66-C	A 67	S 67	W 67	NZ67				
			I 69	F 69-C	S 69-C	W 69-C										

CAPS GAINED BY MATCH (continued)

Total Caps:

Name:	Club:	Total Caps	1	2	3	4	5	6	7	8	9	10	Five Nations	World Cup	Others	As a Replcmt
D.M.Rollitt	Bristol	11	I67, A75/2	F67	S67	W67	I69	F69	S69	W69	S75	A75/1	9		2	
W.M.H.Rose	Cambridge U/Harlequins	10	I81	F81	A82	S82	I82	I87	F87	W87	S87	{A87}	8	1	1	
P.A.Rossborough	Coventry	7	W71	NZ73/2	A73	S74	I74	I75	F75				5		2	
D.W.A.Rosser	Cambridge U/Wasps	5	W65	I65	F65	S65	W66						5			
D.F.K.Roughley	Liverpool	3	A73	S74	I74								2		1	
R.E.Rowell	Leicester	2	W64	W65									2			
G.C.Rowntree	Leicester	15	S95r, S97	{IT95}, I97	{WS95}, F97	WS95, W97	F96, A97	W96	S96	I96	IT96	AR96	9	2	4	1
E.L.Rudd	Oxford Univ/Liverpool	6	W65	I65	S65	W66	I66	S66					6			
D.Rutherford	Percy Park/Gloucester	14	W60	I60	F60	S60	SA61	W65	I65	F65	S65	W66	12		2	
D.Ryan	Wasps	3	AR90/1	AR90/2	CA92										3	
P.H.Ryan	Richmond	2	W55	I55									2			
C.B.van Ryneveld	Oxford University	4	W49	I49	F49	S49							4			
J.L.B.Salmon	Harlequins	12	NZ285/1, {US87}	NZ285/2, {W87}	W86	S86	I87	F87	W87	S87	{A87}	{J87}	6	4	2	
D.L.Sanders	Harlequins	9	W54	NZ54	I54	S54	F54	W56	I56	S56	F56		8		1	
R.D.Sangwin	Hull & East Riding	2	NZ64	W64									1		1	
G.A.F.Sargent	Gloucester	1	I81r										1			1
K.F.Savage	Northampton	13	W66, W68	I66, F68	F66, S68	S66	A67	I67	F67	S67	W67	NZ267	11		2	
E.K.Scott	St Mary's Hosp/Redruth	5	W47, F55	A48-C	W48	I48-C	S48-C						4		1	
H.Scott	Manchester	1	F55										1			
J.P.Scott	Rosslyn Park/Cardiff	34	F78, I80, I82, F84	W78, F80, F82, W84	S78, W80, W82, SA84/1C	I78, S80, F83, SA84/2C	NZ278, W81, W83	S79r, S81, S83-C	I79, I81, I83-C	F79, F81, NZ83	W79, AR81/1, S84	NZ279, AR81/2, I84	27		7	1
J.S.M.Scott	Oxford University	1	F58										1			
I.R.Shackleton	Harrogate	4	SA69	I70	W70	S70							3		1	
R.A.W.Sharp	Oxford University/Wasps	14	W60, I63-C	I60, F63-C	F60, S63-C	S60, A67-C	I61	F61	W62	I62	F62	W63-C	13		1	
S.D.Shaw	Bristol	7	IT96	AR96	S97	I97	F97	W97	A97				4		3	

CAPS GAINED BY MATCH (continued)

Total Caps:

Name:	Club:	Total Caps	1	2	3	4	5	6	7	8	9	10	Five Nations	World Cup	Others	As a Replcmt
C.M.A.Sheasby	Wasps	5	IT96	AR96	W97r	AR97/1r	AR97/2r						1		4	3
A.Sheppard	Bristol	2	W81r	W85									2			1
G.A.Sherriff	Saracens	3	S66	A67	NZ67								1		2	
D.W.Shuttleworth	Headingley	2	S51	S53									2			
N.Silk	Harlequins	4	W65	I65	F65	S65							4			
K.G.Simms	Cambridge U/Liverpool /Wasps	15	RO85 / {A87}	F85 / {J87}	S85 / {W87}	I85 / F88	W85 / W88	I86	F86	I87	F87	W87	11	3	1	
C.P.Simpson	Harlequins	1	W65										1			
P.D.Simpson	Bath	3	NZ83	S84	I87								2		1	
M.G.Skinner	Harlequins	21	F88 / AR90/1 / W92	W88 / AR90/2	S88 / FI91r	I88 / {US91}	IM88 / {F91}	FI89 / {S91}	I90 / {A91}	F90 / S92	W90 / I92	S90 / F92	12	4	5	1
J.M.Sleightholme	Bath	12	F96 / AR97/1	W96 / AR97/2	S96	I96	IT96	AR96	S97	I97	F97	W97	8		4	
M.A.C.Slemen	Liverpool	31	I76 / NZ78 / W81 / S84	F76 / S79 / S81	S77 / I79 / I81	I77 / F79 / F81	F77 / W79 / A82	W77 / NZ79 / S82	F78 / I80 / I82	W78 / F80 / F82	S78 / W80 / W82	I78 / S80 / NZ83	27		4	
H.D.Small	Oxford University	4	W50	I50	F50	S50							4			
C.E.Smart	Newport	17	F79 / I82	W79 / F82	NZ79 / W82	S81 / F83	I81 / W83	F81 / S83	AR81/1 / I83	AR81/2	A82	S82	13		4	
J.V.Smith	Cambridge University	4	W50	I50	F50	S50							4			
K.Smith	Roundhay	4	F74	W74	W75	S75							4			
M.J.K.Smith	Oxford University	1	W56										1			
S.J.Smith	Sale	28	I73 / I80 / A82	F73 / F80 / S82	S73 / W80 / I82-C	A73 / S80 / F82-C	I74 / W81 / W82-C	F74 / S81 / F83-C	W75r / I81 / W83-C	F76 / F81 / S83	F77r / AR81/1	NZ79 / AR81/2	23		5	2
S.R.Smith	Cambridge U/Richmond	5	W59	F59	S59	F64	S64						5			
S.T.Smith	Wasps	9	RO85	F85	S85	I85	W85	NZ85/1	NZ85/2	W86	S86		6		3	
T.A.Smith	Northampton	1	W51										1			
J.Spencer	Harlequins	1	W66										1			
J.S.Spencer	Cambridge U/Headingley	14	I69 / I71-C	F69 / S71-C	S69 / SC71-C	W69 / PR71-C	SA69	I70	W70	S70	F70	W71	11		3	

CAPS GAINED BY MATCH (continued)

Total Caps:

Name:	Club:	Total Caps	1	2	3	4	5	6	7	8	9	10	Five Nations	World Cup	Others	As a Replcmt
P.J.Squires	Harrogate	29	F73	S73	NZ73/2	A73	S74	I74	F74	W74	I75	F75	23		6	
			W75	S75	A75/1	A75/2	A76	W76	S77	I77	F77	W77				
			F78	W78	S78	I78	NZ78	S79	I79	F79	W79					
N.C.Starmer-Smith	Harlequins	7	SA69	I70	W70	S70	F70	SC71	PR71				4		3	
J.S.Steeds	Middlesex Hosp/Saracens	5	F49	S49	I50	F50	S50						5			
M.R.Steele-Bodger	Cambridge & Edinburgh U	9	W47	I47	S47	F47	A48	W48	I48	S48	F48		8		1	
C.B.Stevens	Penzance-Newlyn /Harlequins	25	SA69	I70	W70	S70	PR71	W72	I72	F72	S72	SA72	19		6	
			NZ73/1	W73	I73	F73	S73	NZ73/2	A73	S74	I74	F74				
			W74	I75	F75	W75	S75									
T.R.G.Stimpson	Newcastle	6	IT96	S97	I97	F97	W97	A97					4		2	
R.V.Stirling	RAF/Leicester	18	W51	I51	F51	S51	SA52	W52	S52	I52	F52	W53	16		2	
			I53	F53	S53	W54-C	NZ254-C	I54-C	S54-C	F54-C						
N.C.Stringer	Wasps	5	A82r	NZ283r	SA84/1r	A84	RO85								5	3
D.W.Swarbrick	Oxford University	6	W47	I47	F47	A48	W48	I49					5		1	
A.M.Swift	Swansea	6	AR81/1	AR81/2	F83	W83	S83	SA84/2					3		3	
J.P.Syddall	Waterloo	2	I82	A84									1		1	
F.D.Sykes	Northampton	4	F55	S55	NZ63/2	A63							2		2	
P.W.Sykes	Wasps	7	F48	S52	I52	F52	W53	I53	F53				7			
R.E.Syrett	Wasps	11	W58	A58	I58	F58	W60	I60	F60	S60	W62	I62	10		1	
			F62													
P.J.Taylor	Northampton	6	W55	I55	W62	I62	F62	S62					6			
R.B.Taylor	Northampton	16	W66	I67	F67	S67	W67	NZ67	F69	S69	W69	SA69	13		3	
			I70	W70	S70	F70	S71	SC71								
M.C.Teague	Gloucester	27	F85r	NZ85/1	NZ285/2	S89	I89	F89	W89	RO89	F90	W90	16	5	6	1
			S90	S91	SA92	I91	F91	FI91	A91	{NZ291}	{IT91}	{F91}				
			{S91}	{A91}		F93	W93	S93	I93							
P.H.Thompson	Headingley	17	W56	I56	S56	F56	W57	I57	F57	S57	W58	A58	16		1	
			I58	F58	S58	W59	I59	F59	S59							
J.D.Thorne	Bristol	3	W63	I63	F63								3			
V.R.Tindall	Liverpool University	4	W51	I51	F51	S51							4			
A.C.Towell	Bedford	2	F48	S51									2			
B.H.Travers	Oxford Univ/Harlequins	6	W47	I47	A48	W48	F49	S49					5		1	
W.T.Treadwell	Wasps	3	I66	F66	S66								3			

CAPS GAINED BY MATCH (continued)

Total Caps:

Name:	Club:	Total Caps	1	2	3	4	5	6	7	8	9	10	Five Nations	World Cup	Others	As a Replcmt
D.M.Trick	Bath	2	I 83	SA84/1									1		1	
M.F.Turner	Blackheath	2	S 48	F 48									2			
V.E.Ubogu	Bath	21	CA92 SA94 SA95	SA92 I 95	NZ293 F 95	S 94 W 95	I 94 S 95	F 94 {AR95}	W 94 {WS95}	SA94/1 {A 95}	SA94/2 {NZ95}	RO94 {F 95}	8	5	8	
A.M.Underwood	Northampton/Exeter	5	W 62	I 62	F 62	S 62	I 64						5			
R.Underwood	RAF/Leicester	85	I 84 I 86 W 88 F 89 S 91 {A 91} NZ93 F 95 WS95	I 62 F 84 F 86 S 88 W 89 I 91 S 92 S 94 W 95 F 96	F 62 W 84 I 87 I 88 RO89 F 91 I 92 I 94 S 95 W 96	S 62 A 84 F 87 IM88 FI89 FI91 F 92 F 94 {AR95} S 96	RO85 W 87 A 88/1 I 90 A 91 W 92 W 94 {IT95} I 96	F 85 S 87 A 88/2 F 90 {NZ91} SA92 SA94/1 {WS95}	S 85 {A 87} FI88 W 90 {IT91} F 93 SA94/2 {A 95}	I 85 {J 87} A 88/3 S 90 {US91} W 93 RO94 {NZ95}	W 85 {W 87} S 89 AR90/3 {F 91} S 93 CA94 {F 95}	W 86 F 88 I 89 W 91 {S 91} I 93 I 95 SA95	50	15	20	
T.Underwood	Leicester/Newcastle	25	CA92 RO94 AR96	SA92 CA94 S 97	S 93 I 95 I 97	I 93 F 95 F 97	NZ93 W 95 W 97	S 94 S 95	I 94 {AR95}	W 94 {IT95}	SA94/1 {A 95}	SA94/2 {NZ95}	13	4	8	
R.Uren	Waterloo	4	I 48	S 48	F 48	I 50							4			
D.B.Vaughan	Headingley/D'port Servs	8	A 48	W 48	I 48	S 48	I 49	F 49	S 49	W 50			7		1	
R.M.Uttley	Gosforth	23	I 73 S 75 F 80	F 73 A 75/1 W 80	S 73 A 75/2 S 80	NZ73/2 S 77-C	A 73 I 77-C	I 74 F 77-C	W 74 W 77-C	W 74 NZ78	F 75 S 79-C	W 75 I 80	18		5	
J.A.S.Wackett	Rosslyn Park	2	W 59	I 59									2			
M.R.Wade	Cambridge Univ	3	W 62	I 62	F 62								3			
H.W.Walker	Coventry	9	W 47	I 47	S 47	F 47	A 48	W 48	I 48	S 48	F 48		8		1	
C.S.Wardlow	Northampton	6	SA69r	W 71	I 71	F 71	S 71	SC71					4		2	1
P.J.Warfield	Rosslyn Park/Cambridge	6	NZ73/1	W 73	I 73	I 75	F 75	S 75					5		1	
J.A.Watkins	Gloucester	7	SA72	NZ73/1	W 73	NZ73/2	A 73	F 75	W 75				3		4	
D.E.J.Watt	Bristol	4	I 67	F 67	S 67	W 67							4			
J.M.Webb	Bristol/Bath	33	{A87r} A 88/2 {F 91} W 93	{J 87} A 88/3 {S 91} S 93	{US87} S 89 {A 91} I 93	{W 87} I 89 S 92	F 88 F 89 I 92	W 88 W 89 F 92	S 88 FI91 W 92	I 88 A 91 CA92	IM88 {NZ291} SA92	A 88/1 {IT91} F 93	16	9	8	1

CAPS GAINED BY MATCH (continued)

Total Caps:

Name:	Club:	Total Caps	1	2	3	4	5	6	7	8	9	10	Five Nations	World Cup	Others	As a Replcmt
L.H.Webb	Bedford	4	W 59	I 59	F 59	S 59							4			
R.E.Webb	Coventry	12	S 67	W 67	NZ267	I 68	F 68	S 68	I 69	F 69	S 69	W 69	11		1	
J.G.Webster	Moseley	11	I 72 W 72 W 75	F 72 I 72	SA72	NZ73/1	W 73	NZ73/2	S 74	W 74		F 75	8		3	
R.H.G.Weighill	Harlequins	4	S 47	F 47	S 48	F 48-C							4			
B.R.West	Loughboro' C/Northampto	8	W 68	I 68	F 68	S 68	SA69	I 70	W 70	S 70			7		1	
R.I.West	Gloucester	1	(WS95)											1		
L.E.Weston	West of Scotland	2	F 72	S 72									2			
M.P.Weston	Richmond/Durham City	29	W 60 I 62 W 64	I 60 F 62 I 64	F 60 W 63 F 64	S 60 I 63 S 64	SA61 F 63 F 65	W 61 S 63 S 65	I 61 Z63/1C S 66	F 61 NZ263/2C F 68-C	S 61 A63-C S 68-C	W 62 NZ64	24		5	
P.J.Wheeler	Leicester	41	F 75 F 78 I 80 I 82 W 84	W 75 W 78 F 80 F 82	A 76 S 78 W 80 W 82	W 76 I 78 S 80 F 83	S 76 NZ78 W 81 S 83	I 76 S 79 S 81 I 83	S 77 I 79 I 81 NZ283-C	I 77 F 79 F 81 S 84-C	F 77 W 79 A 82 I 84-C	W 77 NZ79 S 82 F 84-C	36		5	
C.White	Gosforth	4	NZ283	S 84	I 84	F 84							3		1	
D.F.White	Northampton	14	W 47 F 52	I 47 W 53	S 47 I 53	I 48 S 53	F 48	S 51	SA52	W 52	S 52	I 52	13		1	
B.J.Wightman	Moseley	5	W 59	W 53	I 53	NZ263/2	A 63						3		2	
J.G.Wilcox	Oxford University	16	I 61 S 63	F 61 NZ264-C	S 61 I 63	W 62 I 64-C	I 62 F 64	S 64	S 62	W 63	I 63	F 63	15		1	
C.G.Williams	Gloucester	1	F 76										1			
J.E.Williams	Old Millhilians	9	F 54	W 55	I 55	F 55	S 55	I 56	S 56	F 56	W 65		9			
J.M.Williams	Penzance-Newlyn	2	I 51	S 51									2			
P.N.Williams	Orrell	4	S 87	{A 87}	{J 87}	{W 87}							1	3		
D.T.Wilkins	Roundhay/US Portsmouth	13	W 51 I 53	I 51 F 53	F 51 S 53	S 51 NZ254	W 52	I 52	S 52	I 52	F 52	W 53	12		1	
R.M.Wilkinson	Bedford	6	A 75/2	A 76	W 76	S 76	I 76	F 76					4		2	
D.S.Wilson	Met Police	8	F 53	W 54	NZ254	I 54	S 54	F 54	F 55	S 55			7		1	
K.J.Wilson	Gloucester	1	F 63										1			
C.E.Winn	Rosslyn Park	8	SA52	W 52	S 52	I 52	F 52	W 54	S 54	F 54			7		1	

CAPS GAINED BY MATCH (continued)

Total Caps:

Name:	Club:	Total Caps	1	2	3	4	5	6	7	8	9	10	Five Nations	World Cup	Others	As a Replcmt
P.J.Winterbottom	Headingley/Harlequins	58	A 82	S 82	I 82	F 82	W 82	F 83	W 83	S 83	I 83	NZ83	37	9	12	
			S 84	F 84	W 84	SA84/1	SA84/2	W 86	S 86	I 86	F 86	I 87				
			F 87	W 87	{A 87}	{J87}	{US87}	{W 87}	F 88	W 88	S 88	RO89				
			FI89	I 90	F 90	W 90	S 90	AR90/1	AR90/2	AR90/3	W 91	S 91				
			I 91	F 91	A 91	{NZ91}	{I91}	{F 91}	{S 91}	{A 91}	S 92	I 92				
			F 92	W 92	CA92	SA92	F 93	W 93	S 93	I 93						
T.C.Wintle	Northampton	5	S 66	I 69	F 69	S 69	W 69						5			
E.E.Woodgate	Paignton	1	W 52										1			
C.G.Woodruff	Harlequins	4	W 51	I 51	F 51	S 51							4			
C.R.Woodward	Leicester	21	I 80r	F 80	W 80	S 80	W 81	S 81	I 81	F 81	AR81/1	AR81/2	17		4	
			A 82	S 82	I 82	F 82	W 82	I 83	NZ83	S 84	I 84	F 84				
			W 84													
J.E.Woodward	Wasps	15	SA52	W 52	S 52	W 53	I 53	F 53	S 53	W 54	NZ54	I 54	13		2	
			S 54	F 54	W 55	I 55	S 56									
A.J.Wordsworth	Cambridge University	1	A75/1r												1	1
D.F.B.Wrench	Harlequins	2	F 64	S 64									2			
I.D.Wright	Northampton	4	W 71	I 71	F 71	S 71r							4		1	1
T.P.Wright	Blackheath	13	W 60	I 60	F 60	S 60	SA61	W 61	I 61	F 61	S 61	W 62	12		1	
			I 62	F 62	S 62											
D.M.Wyatt	Bedford	1	S 76r										1			1
P.G.Yarranton	RAF/Wasps	5	W 54	NZ54	I 54	F 55	S 55						4		1	
K.Yates	Bath	2	AR97/1	AR97/2											2	
J.R.C.Young	Oxford Univ/Harlequins	9	I 58	W 60	I 60	F 60	S 60	SA61	W 61	I 61	F 61		8		1	
M.Young	Gosforth	10	S 77	I 77	F 77	W 77	F 78	W 78	S 78	I 78	NZ78	S 79	9		1	
P.D.Young	Dublin Wanderers	9	W 54	NZ54	I 54	S 54	F 54	W 55	I 55	F 55-C	S 55-C		8		1	
N.C.Youngs	Leicester	6	I 83	NZ83	S 84	I 84	F 84	W 84					5		1	
Total Caps:		4296											3118	253	925	111

CAPS GAINED BY MATCH (continued)

Since 1947, in the 279 matches played, 4,296 caps have been awarded to 437 different players.

Of those 4,296 caps, 111 have been awarded to players who have replaced originally selected players during the course of a match.

NOTES:

Suffix " r " after the match opponent and year indicates a replacement player - 1969 onwards.

Suffix "C" after the match opponent and year indicates the Captain.

Five Nations: F - France;   I - Ireland;   S - Scotland;   W - Wales.

World Cup: A - Australia;   AR - Argentina;   F - France;   IT - Italy;   J - Japan;   NZ - New Zealand;   S - Scotland;   US - United States;   W - Wales;

WS - Western Samoa;

All World Cup matches are shown in Brackets, e.g. (W 87).

Other Matches: A - Australia;   AR - Argentina;   CA - Canada;   FI - Fiji;   IM - Ireland (Millenium);   IT - Italy;   NZ - New Zealand;   PR - RFU President's Overseas XV;

RO - Romania;   SA - South Africa;   SC - Centenary Match v. Scotland, 1971;   WS - Western Samoa.

Three International players gained caps both before and after the Second World War. They are:

R.H.Guest (Waterloo):   Three caps in 1939, Wales, Ireland and Scotland; and ten post-war,

J.Heaton (Waterloo):   Three caps in 1935, Wales, Ireland and Scotland; three caps in 1939, Wales, Ireland and Scotland; and three post-war.

T.A.Kemp (Richmond):   Two caps in 1937, Wales and Ireland; one cap in 1939, Scotland; and two post-war.

CAPS EARNED AS A REPLACEMENT

P.R de Glanville	Bath	7
G.W.Rees	Nottingham	6
S.Barnes	Bristol/Bath	4
G.J.Chilcott	Bath	4
R.Hesford	Bristol	3
R.J.Hill	Bath	3
S.O.Ojomoh	Bath	3
T.A.K.Rodber	Army/Northampton	3
C.M.A.Sheasby	Wasps	3
N.C.Stringer	Wasps	3
C.R.Andrew	Cambridge Univ/Nottingham/Wasps/Newcastle	2
K.P.P.Bracken	Bristol/Saracens	2
M.J.Catt	Bath	2
B.B.Clarke	Bath/Richmond	2
D.W.Egerton	Bath	2
P.B.T.Greening	Gloucester	2
J.C.Guscott	Bath	2
A.Healey	Leicester	2
D.Richards	Leicester	2
S.J.Smith	Sale	2
N.A.Back	Leicester	1
M.D.Bailey	Cambridge University/Wasps	1
W.B.Beaumont	Fylde	1
W.N.Bennett	Bedford	1
S.E.Brain	Coventry	1
J.R.D.Buckton	Saracens	1
F.J.Clough	Cambridge University	1
R.Cockerill	Leicester	1
M.J.Cooper	Moseley	1
B.J.Corless	Coventry/Moseley	1
L.B.N.Dallaglio	Wasps	1
* T.J.Dalton	Coventry	1
G.H.Davies	Cambridge University/Coventry/Wasps	1
W.A.Dooley	Preston Grasshoppers	1
G.W.Evans	Coventry	1
D.J.Garforth	Leicester	1
A.C.T.Gomarsall	Wasps	1
J.P.Hall	Bath	1
S.J.Halliday	Bath/Harlequins	1
R.M.Harding	Bristol	1
* R.J.K.Hardwick	Coventry	1
N.J.Heslop	Orrell	1
D.P.Hopley	Wasps	1
B.S.Jackson	Broughton Park	1
C.P.Kent	Rosslyn Park	1
* A.D.King	Wasps	1
* J.Mallett	Bath	1

PHIL de GLANVILLE

Gained most caps for England as a Replacement

de Glanville has also Captained England eight times since the retirement of Will Carling as England Captain in March 1996.

CAPS EARNED AS A REPLACEMENT (continued)

*	N.O.Martin	Harlequins	1
	B.C.Moore	Nottingham/Harlequins	1
	C.D.Morris Liverpool	St Helen's/Orrell	1
	A.Neary	Broughton Park	1
	J.A.Palmer	Bath	1
	D.Pears	Harlequins	1
	P.S.Preece	Coventry	1
	J.A.Probyn	Wasps	1
	J.V.Pullin	Bristol	1
	M.Rafter	Bristol	1
*	S.Redfern	Leicester	1
	N.C.Redman	Bath	1
	P.A.G.Rendall	Wasps	1
	G.C.Rowntree	Leicester	1
*	G.A.F.Sargent	Gloucester	1
	J.P.Scott	Rosslyn Park/Cardiff	1
	A.Sheppard	Bristol	1
	M.G.Skinner	Harlequins	1
	M.C.Teague	Gloucester	1
	C.S.Wardlow	Northampton	1
	J.M.Webb	Bristol/Bath	1
	C.R.Woodward	Leicester	1
*	A.J.Wordsworth	Cambridge University	1
	I.D.Wright	Northampton	1
*	D.M.Wyatt	Bedford	1

*   Players whose only cap this was.

LEADING CAP WINNERS - BY POSITION

(caps shown do not include caps gained as a replacement because the player was not an original selection and because the replacement position will not necessarily be the same.

Position:	Name:	Club:	Caps:	
Full-back:				
	J.M.Webb	Bristol/Bath	32	+ 1 cap as a replacement - WC A 87
	W.H.Hare	Nottingham/Leicester	25	
	R.Hiller	Harlequins	19	
	J.G.Willcox	Oxford Univ/Harlequins	16	
	M.J.Catt		14	see Note 1
	A.J.Hignell	Cambridge Univ/Bristol	14	
	S.D.Hodgkinson	Nottingham	14	
	D.Rutherford	Percy Park/Gloucester	14	
	R.W.Hosen	Northampton/Bristol	10	
	W.M.H.Rose	Cambridge Univ/Harlequins	10	
Wing-threequarter:				
	R.Underwood	RAF/Leicester	85	
	M.A.C.Slemen	Liverpool	31	
	P.J.Squires	Harrogate	29	
	J.Carleton	Orrell	26	
	T.Underwood	Leicester	25	
	D.J.Duckham	Coventry	22	see Note 1
	P.B.Jackson	Coventry	20	
	J.Roberts	Old Millhillians/Sale	18	
	P.H.Thompson	Headingley	17	- all successive
	M.E.Harrison	Wakefield	15	
	J.E.Woodward	Wasps	15	
	C.Oti	Cambridge Univ/Wasps	13	
	K.F.Savage	Northampton	13	
	R.E.Webb	Coventry	12	
	R.C.Bazley	Waterloo	10	
	K.F.Fielding	Loughborough Coll/Moseley	10	
	R.H.Guest	Waterloo	13	+ 3 caps pre-war
	J.M.Sleightholme	Bath	12	
Centre-threequarter:				
	W.D.C.Carling	Durham Univ/Harlequins	72	
	J.C.Guscott	Bath	46	+ 2 caps as a replacement, I 97, W 97
	P.W.Dodge	Leicester	32	
	J.Butterfield	Northampton	28	- all successive
	M.P.Weston	Richmond/Durham City	24	see Note 1
	M.S.Phillips	Oxford Univ/Fylde	23	see Note 1
	C.R.Woodward	Leicester	20	+ 1 cap as a replacement - I 80
	L.B.Cannell	Nthmptn/Oxford U/St Mary's H	19	
	P.R.de Glanville	Bath	17	+ 7 caps as a replacement, SA 92, W 93
				CA 94, WC AR 95, SA 95, W 96, I 96
	K.G.Simms	Cambridge Univ/Liverpool/Wasp	15	
	D.J.Duckham	Coventry	14	see Note 1
	S.J.Halliday	Bath/Harlequins	14	see Note 1
	J.S.Spencer	Cambridge Univ/Headingley	14	

JONATHAN WEBB

England's most-capped Full-back with 32 caps plus one cap (his first in the 1987 World Cup) as a replacement at Full-back for Marcus Rose.

RORY UNDERWOOD

England's most-capped Wing-threequarter with 85 caps. Throughout his entire career, Rory Underwood never sat on the bench for for England, he was always an original selection.

ROB ANDREW

England's most-capped Fly-half with 68 caps.
In addition, Rob Andrew gained one cap at Full-back (against Fiji in 1988)
and two caps as a replacement.

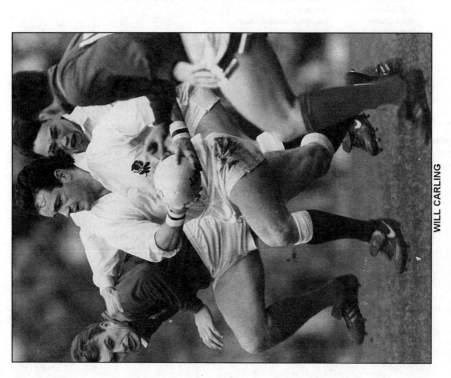

WILL CARLING

England's most-capped Centre-threequarter with 72 caps, all original
selections as he never sat on the Bench.
Carling played in **44** successive International matches - an England record.

LEADING CAP WINNERS - BY POSITION (continued)

Position:	Name:	Club:	Caps:	
Centre-threequarter:				
	J.L.B.Salmon	Harlequins	12	
	P.S.Preece	Coventry	11	+ 1 cap as a replacement - W 76
	W.P.C.Davies	|Harlequins	11	
Fly-half:				
	C.R.Andrew	Cambridge U/Nottingham/Wasps	68	see Note 1
	A.G.B.Old	Middlesborough/Leicester	16	
	R.A.W.Sharp	Oxford Univ/Wasps	14	
	J.F.Finlan	Moseley	13	
	J.P.Horton	Bath	13	
	L.Cusworth	Leicester	12	
	M.Regan	Liverpool	12	
	N.M.Hall	St Mary's Hosp/Richmond	11	see Note 1
	M.J.Cooper	Moseley	10	+ 1 cap as a replacement - NZ73/2
	I.Preece	Coventry	10	see Note 1
Scrum half:				
	R.J.Hill	Bath	26	+ 3 caps as replacement - I 85, NZ85/2, and F 86
	S.J.Smith	Sale	26	+ 2 caps as a replacement - W 75, F 77
	C.D.Morris	Liverpool-St Helen's/Orrell	25	+ 1 cap as a replacement - S 95
	R.E.G.Jeeps	Northampton	24	
	S.J.S.Clarke	Cambridge Univ/Blackheath	13	
	N.D.Melville	Wasps	13	
	G.Rimmer	Waterloo	12	
	K.P.P.Bracken	Bristol	12	+ 2 caps as a replacement WC WS95, and I 96
	R.M.Harding	Bristol	11	+ 1 cap as a replacement - I 88
	J.G.Webster	Moseley	11	
	M.Young	Gosforth	10	- all successive
Note 1:	C.R.Andrew	Cambridge U/Nottingham/Wasps	69	68 at fly-half; 1 at full-back and 2 caps as a replacement - WC J 87, W 9
Players capped				
in more than	D.J.Duckham	Coventry	36	22 on the wing; 14 as a centre
one position	M.P.Weston	Richmond/Durham City	29	24 as a centre; 5 at fly-half
- backs:	M.S.Phillips	Oxford Univ/Fylde	25	23 as a centre; 2 on the wing
	S.J.Halliday	Bath/Harlequins	22	14 as a centre; 8 on the wing and 1 cap as a replacement - FI89
	M.J.Catt	Bath	21	14 as full-back; 7 as fly-half + 2 caps as replacement - W 94, CA94
	G.H.Davies	Cambridge Univ/Coventry/Wasp	20	8 at fly-half; 6 as a centre; 6 at full-back and 1 cap as a replacement - RO85
	N.M.Hall	St Mary's Hosp/Richmond	17	11 at fly-half; 6 at full-back
	J.P.A.G.Janion	Bedford/Richmond	12	7 as a centre; 5 on the wing
	I.Preece	Coventry	12	10 at fly-half; 2 as a centre
	C.W.McFadyean	Moseley	11	9 as a centre; 2 on the wing

LEADING CAP WINNERS - BY POSITION (continued)

Position:	Name:	Club:	Caps:	
Prop:				
	J Leonard	Saracens/Harlequins	55	
	J.A.Probyn	Wasps	36	+ 1 cap as a replacement - RO89
	G.S.Pearce	Northampton	36	
	F.E.Cotton	Loughborough Col/Coventry/Sale	31	
	C.R.Jacobs	Northampton	29	
	P.A.G.Rendall	Wasps	27	+ 1 cap as a replacement - WC IT91
	C.B.Stevens	Penzance-Newlyn/Harlequins	25	
	P.E.Judd	Coventry	22	
	V.E.Ubogu	Bath	21	
	P.J.Blakeway	Gloucester	19	
	R.V.Stirling	RAF/Leicester	18	- all successive
	M.A.Burton	Gloucester	17	
	C.E.Smart	Newport	17	
	W.A.Holmes	Nuneaton	16	
	G.C.Rowntree	Leicester	14	+ 1 cap as a replacement, S 95
	G.W.D.Hastings	Gloucester	13	
	T.P.Wright	Blackheath	13	- all successive
	K.E.Fairbrother	Coventry	12	- all successive
	D.L.Powell	Northampton	11	
	G.J.Chilcott	Bath	10	+ 4 caps as a replacement - F 87, WC W 87, IM88 and I 89
Hooker:				
	B.C.Moore	Nottingham/Harlequins	63	+ 1 cap as a replacement - WC WS 95
	J.V.Pullin	Bristol	41	+ 1 cap as a replacement - W 75
	P.J.Wheeler	Leicester	41	
	E.Evans	Sale	29	see Note 2
	M.P.Regan	Bristol	13	
	S.E.Brain	Coventry	12	+ 1 cap as a replacement - A 84
	H.O.Godwin	Coventry	11	
	S.A.M.Hodgson	Durham City	11	
Lock:				
	W.A.Dooley	Preston Grasshoppers	54	+ 1 cap as a replacement - NZ85/2
	W.B.Beaumont	Fylde	33	+ 1 cap as a replacement - A 75/1
	M.C.Bayfield	Northampton	31	
	M.O.Johnson	Leicester	30	
	M.J.Colclough	Angouleme/Wasps/Swansea	25	
	J.D.Currie	Oxford Univ/Harlequins/Bristol	25	
	P.J.Larter	Northampton	25	
	R.W.D.Marques	Cambridge Univ/Harlequins	23	- all successive
	P.J.Ackford	Harlequins	22	
	C.W.Ralston	Richmond	22	- all successive
	N.E.Horton	Moseley/Toulouse	20	
	N.C.Redman	Bath	19	+ 1 cap as a replacement - S 86
	S.Bainbridge	Gosforth	18	
	A.M.Davis	Torquay Athletic/Harlequins	16	
	J.Orwin	Gloucester	14	
	J.E.Owen	Coventry	14	
	D.T.Wilkins	Roundhay/US Portsmouth	13	- all successive

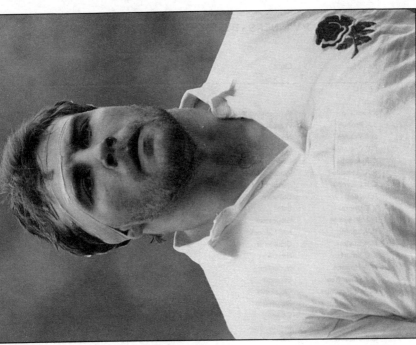

JASON LEONARD

England's most-capped Prop forward with 55 caps, 40 of which were gained in successive matches. Jason Leonard was equally competent at tight-head as he was at loose-head which was his favoured, and original, position.

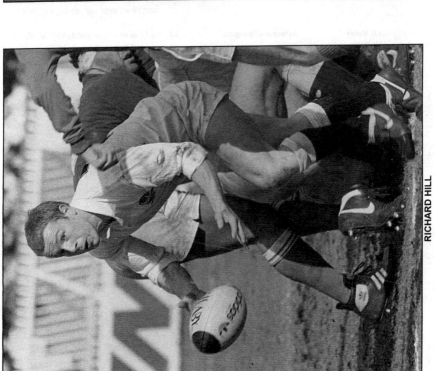

RICHARD HILL

England's most-capped Scrum-half with 26 caps. In addition, Richard Hill also gained three caps as a replacement.

WADE DOOLEY

England's most-capped Lock forward with 54 caps and one additional cap as a replacement. 28 of Dooley's caps were successive.

BRIAN MOORE

England's most-capped Hooker with 63 caps and one additional cap as a replacement.

DEAN RICHARDS

England's most-capped No.8 with 46 caps and an additional two caps as a replacement.

PETER WINTERBOTTOM

England's most-capped Flank forward with 58 caps and never a seat on the Bench. Peter Winterbottom's International career spanned 12 years from 1982 to 1993, inclusive, longer than any other England forward.

Position:	Name:	Club:	Caps:	
Lock:				
	J.R.C.Matthews	Harlequins	10	
	C.M.Payne	Harlequins	10	
Flanker:				
	P.J.Winterbottom	Headingley/Harlequins	58	
	A.Neary	Broughton Park	42	+ 1 cap as a replacement - F 78
	D.P.Rogers	Bedford	34	
	T.A.K.Rodber	Northampton	24	see Note 2
	P.J.Dixon	Gosforth/Harlequins	21	see Note 2
	M.G.Skinner	Harlequins	20	+ 1 cap as a replacement - FI91
	P.G.D.Robbins	Oxford Univ/Coventry	19	
	J.P.Hall	Bath	18	see Note 2
	M.C.Teague	Gloucester/Moseley	18	see Note 2
	G.W.Rees	Nottingham	17	+ 6 caps as a replacement - SA84/2, S 88, W 89, RO89, FI89 and AR90/3
	M.Rafter	Bristol	16	+ 1 cap as a replacement - W 80
	V.G.Roberts	Penryn/Harlequins	16	
	B.B.Clarke	Bath	15	see Note 2
	N.C.Jeavons	Moseley	14	- all successive
	D.F.White	Northampton	14	
	R.Higgins	Liverpool	13	
	D.H.Cooke	Harlequins	12	
	R.E.Syrett	Wasps	11	
	L.B.N.Dallaglio	Wasps	11	+ 1 cap as a replacement, SA 95
	A.L.Bucknall	Richmond	10	- all successive
	A.O.Lewis	Bath	10	
	R.B.Taylor	Northampton	10	see Note 2
No 8:				
	D.Richards	Leicester	46	+ 2 caps as replacement - S 92, F 96
	J.P.Scott	Rosslyn Park/Cardiff	30	see Note 2
	A.G.Ripley	Rosslyn Park	24	
	J.M.Kendall-Carpenter	Oxford U/Penzance-Newlyn/Bath	18	see Note 2
	A.Ashcroft	Waterloo	16	
	B.B.Clarke	Bath	15	see Note 2
	D.G.Perry	Bedford	13	see Note 2

Position:	Name:	Club:	Caps:	
Note 2: Players capped in more than one position - forwards:	J.P.Scott	Rosslyn Park/Cardiff	33	30 at No 8; 3 as a lock + 1 cap as a replacement - S 79
	B.B.Clarke	Bath	31	16 as flanker; 15 at No 8; + 2 caps as a replacement AR 96, A 97
	E.Evans	Sale	30	29 at hooker; 1 as a prop
	T.A.K.Rodber	Army/Northampton	29	24 as a flanker; 5 at No 8; + 3 caps as a replacement, WC WS 95, S 96, I 96
	M.C.Teague	Gloucester/Moseley	26	18 as a flanker; 8 at No 8 + 1 cap as a replacement - F 85
	J.M.Kendall-Carpenter	Oxford U/Penzance-Newlyn/Bath	23	18 at No 8; 5 as a prop
	R.M.Uttley	Gosforth	23	9 as a lock; 9 at No 8 and 5 as a flanker
	P.J.Dixon	Gosforth/Harlequins	22	21 as a flanker; 1 at No 8
	J.P.Hall	Bath	20	18 as a flanker; 2 at No 8 + 1 cap as a replacement - S 84
	R.B.Taylor	Northampton	16	10 as a flanker; 6 at No 8
	D.G.Perry	Bedford	15	13 at No 8; 2 as a lock
	D.M.Rollitt	Bristol	11	6 at No 8; 5 as a flanker

PLAYERS WHO HAVE APPEARED IN TEN OR MORE

SUCCESSIVE INTERNATIONAL MATCHES

(not including matches in which the player appeared as a replacement for which he was not an original selection)

Successive matches:	Name:	Club:	Succession of matches:
44	W.D.C.Carling	Harlequins	Fiji, Nov 1989 to Argentina (WC), May 1995
40	J.Leonard	Saracens/Harlequins	Argentina/1, Jul 1990 to Italy (WC), May 1995
36	J.V.Pullin	Bristol	Wales, Jan 1968 to Ireland, Jan 1975
32	W.B.Beaumont	Fylde	Australia, May 1975 to Scotland, Jan 1982
30	R.Underwood	RAF/Leicester	South Africa, Nov 1992 to Ireland, March 1966
28	J.Butterfield	Northampton	France, Feb 1953 to Scotland, March 1959
28	W.A.Dooley	Preston Grasshoppers	USA (WC), Jun 1987 to France, Mar 1991
27	A.Neary	Broughton Park	Wales, Jan 1971 to Australia/1, May 1975
25	J.Carleton	Orrell	New Zealand, Nov 1979 to France, Mar 1984
24	M.O.Johnson	Leicester	Romania, Nov 1994 to Wales, March 1997
24	M.A.C.Slemen	Liverpool	Ireland, Mar 1976 to France, March 1981
23	R.W.D.Marques	Cambridge U/Harlequins	Wales, Jan 1956 to Wales, Jan 1961
22	J.D.Currie	Oxford U/Harlequins	Wales, Jan 1956 to South Africa, Jan 1961
22	B.C.Moore	Nottingham/Harlequins	Wales (WC), Jun 1987 to Argentina, Aug 1990
22	C.W.Ralston	Richmond	Scotland (Centenary), Mar 1971 to Scotland, Mar 1975
22	P.J.Wheeler	Leicester	Scotland, Jan 1977 to France, Mar 1981
21	C.R.Andrew	Wasps	Argentina, Nov 1990 to Wales, Feb 1993
21	D.P.Rogers	Bedford	Wales, Jan 1963 to Australia, Jan 1967
21	C.B.Stevens	Penzance-N/Harlequins	RFU Presidents, Apr 1971 to Scotland, Mar 1975
20	R.J.Hill	Bath	Fiji, Nov 1989 to Australia (WC), Nov 1991
20	P.J.Larter	Northampton	New Zealand, Nov 1967 to RFU President's, Apr 1971
20	B.C.Moore	Nottingham/Harlequins	South Africa, Nov 1992 to Italy (WC), May 1995
20	R.Underwood	RAF/Leicester	Wales (WC), Jun 1987 to Scotland, Mar 1990
19	D.J.Duckham	Coventry	Ireland, Feb 1969 to Scotland, Mar 1972
19	S.J.Smith	Sale	New Zealand, Nov 1979 to Scotland, Mar 1983
18	M.J.Catt	Bath	Ireland, Jan 1995 to Argentina, Dec 1996
18	G.S.Pearce	Northampton	South Africa/2, Jun 1984 to Australia (WC),May 1987
18	A.G.Ripley	Rosslyn Park	Wales, Jan 1972 to France, Feb 1975
18	R.V.Stirling	RAF/Leicester	Wales, Jan 1951 to France, Apr 1954

WILL CARLING

44 successive matches
from November 1989 to May 1995

JASON LEONARD

40 successive matches
July 1990 to May 1995

JOHN PULLIN

36 successive matches
January 1968 to January 1975

BILL BEAUMONT

32 successive matches
May 1975 to January 1982

PLAYERS WHO HAVE MADE THE MOST SUCCESSIVE INTERNATIONAL MATCH APPEARANCES

(not including matches in which the player appeared as a replacement for which he was not an original selection)

Successive matches:	Name:	Club:	Succession of matches:
17	C.R.Andrew	Wasps	Scotland, Mar 1988 to Scotland, Mar 1990
17	J.Roberts	Old Millhillians/Sale	Wales, Jan 1960 to Scotland, Mar 1963
17	P.H.Thompson	Headingley	Wales, Jan 1956 to Scotland, Mar 1959
17	R.Underwood	RAF/Leicester	Argentina, Nov 1990 to Wales, Mar 1992
16	W.D.C.Carling	Harlequins	Western Samoa (WC), May 1995 to Wales, March 1997
16	P.J.Squires	Harrogate	France, Feb 1973 to Wales, Jan 1976
15	C.R.Andrew	Wasps	New Zealand, Nov 1993 to Italy (WC), May 1995
15	J.M.K.Kendall-Carpenter	Oxford U/Penzance-N/Bath	Ireland, Feb 1951 to Ireland,Feb 1954
15	J.Leonard	Harlequins	Australia (WC) 1995, to Wales, March 1997
15	J.A.Probyn	Wasps	Ireland, Jan 1990 to Italy (WC) Oct 1991
14	D.J.Duckham	Coventry	New Zealand, Jan 1973 to Wales, Feb 1975
14	N.C.Jeavons	Moseley	Scotland, Feb 1981 to Ireland, March 1983
14	J.P.Scott	Cardiff	Ireland, Feb 1979 to Argentina/2, Jun 1981
14	J.P.Scott	Cardiff	Ireland, Feb 1982 to South Africa/2, Jun 1984
14	C.E.Smart	Newport	Scotland, February 1981, to Ireland, Mar 1983
14	V.E.Ubogu	Bath	New Zealand, Nov 1993 to Argentina (WC), May 1995
14	C.R.Woodward	Leicester	France, Feb 1980 to Wales, Mar 1982
13	A.Ashcroft	Waterloo	Wales, Jan 1956 to Scotland, Mar 1958
13	E.Evans	Sale	Wales, Jan 1956 to Scotland, Mar 1958
13	K.E.Fairbrother	Coventry	Ireland, Feb 1969 to France, Feb 1971
13	J.C.Guscott	Bath	France (WC), Oct 1991 to Ireland, Mar 1993
13	W.H.Hare	Leicester	France, Feb 1982 to South Africa/2, Jun 1984
13	M.E.Harrison	Wakefield	Scotland, Feb 1986 to Wales, Feb 1988
13	S.D.Hodgkinson	Nottingham	Romania, 1989 to France, March 1991
13	C.R.Jacobs	Northampton	Wales, Jan 1956 to Scotland, Mar 1958
13	R.E.G.Jeeps	Northampton	Wales, Jan 1960 to Scotland, Mar 1962
13	P.E.Judd	Coventry	Ireland, Feb 1965 to New Zealand, Nov 1967
13	T.A.K.Rodber	Northampton	Ireland, Feb 1994 to Italy (WC), May 1995
13	K.F.Savage	Northampton	Wales, Jan 1966 to Wales, Jan 1968
13	P.J.Squires	Harrogate	Scotland, Jan 1977 to Wales, March 1979
13	J.M.Webb	Bath	France (WC), Oct 1991 to Ireland, Mar 1993
13	D.T Wilkins	Roundhay/US Portsmouth	Wales, Jan 1951 to Scotland, Mar 1953
13	P.J.Winterbottom	Headingley/Harlequins	Romania, Jun 1989 to France, Mar 1991
13	P.J.Winterbottom	Harlequins	France (WC, Oct 1991 to Ireland, Mar 1993
13	T.P.Wright	Blackheath	Wales, Jan 1960 to Scotland, March 1962
12	B.B.Clarke	Bath	Wales, Mar 1994 to Italy (WC), May 1995
12	R.Hiller	Harlequins	Wales, Jan 1968 to Scotland, Mar 1970
12	M.S.Phillips	Oxford University	Australia, Feb 1958 to Scotland, March 1960
12	M.S.Phillips	Fylde	Wales, Jan 1963 to Scotland, March 1964
12	M.Rafter	Bristol	France, Feb 1977 to New Zealnd, Nov 1989
12	M.P.Regan	Bristol	South Africa, Nov 1995 to Wales, March 1997
12	M.P.Weston	Richmond	Wales, Jan 1960 to France, Feb 1962
12	M.P.Weston	Durham City	Wales, Jan 1963 to Scotland, Mar 1964

PLAYERS WHO HAVE APPEARED IN TEN OR MORE

SUCCESSIVE INTERNATIONAL MATCHES (continued)

(not including matches in which the player appeared as a replacement for which he was not an original selection)

Successive matches:	Name:	Club:	Succession of matches:
11	P.J.Ackford	Harlequins	Australia, Nov 1988 to Scotland, Mar 1990
11	S.Bainbridge	Gosforth	France, Feb 1982 to Wales, Mar 1984
11	S.E.Brain	Coventry	Romania, Jan 1985 to France, Mar 1986
11	J.P.Hall	Bath	South Africa/1, Jun 1984 to Scotland, Feb 1986
11	C.W.McFadyean	Moseley	Ireland, Feb 1966 to Ireland, Feb 1968
11	J.S.Spencer	Canbridge U/Headingley	Ireland, Feb 1969 to Ireland, Feb 1961
11	P.G.D.Robbins	Oxford University	Wales, Jan 1956 to Ireland Feb 1958
11	G.C.Rowntree	Leicester	Western Samoa, Dec 1995 to Wales, March 1997
11	J.G.Willcox	Oxford U/Harlequins	Ireland, Feb 1961 to Scotland, Mar 1963
11	P.J.Winterbottom	Headingley	Australia, Jan 1982 to Scotland, Feb 1984
11	J.E.Woodward	Wasps	Wales, Jan 1953 to Ireland, Feb 1955
10	M.C.Bayfield	Northampton	South Africa/1, June 1994 to Italy (WC), May 1995
10	M.C.Bayfield	Northampton	Scotland, Jan 1992 to Ireland, Mar 1993
10	A.L.Bucknall	Richmond	South Africa, Dec 1969 to Scotland, Mar 1971
10	S.J.S.Clarke	Cambridge University	Wales, Jan 1963 to Ireland, Feb 1964
10	L.B.N.Dallaglio	Wasps	Western Samoa, Dec 1995 to France, Mar 1997
10	P.W.Dodge	Leicester	Wales, Feb 1980 to Scotland, Jan 1982
10	W.A.Dooley	Preston Grasshoppers	USA (WC), Oct 1991 to South Africa, Nov 1992
10	C.D.Morris	Liverpool-St Helen's/Orrell	Scotland, Jan 1992 to Ireland, Mar 1993
10	D.Richards	Leicester	Argentina/3, Nov 1990 to USA (WC) Oct 1991
10	J.M.Sleightholme	Bath	France, Jan 1996 to Wales, Mar 1997
10	J.M.Webb	Bristol	Japan (WC), May 1987 to Australia/2, Jun 1988
10	M.Young	Gosforth	Scotland, Jan 1977 to Scotland, Feb 1979

ENGLAND CAPTAINS:

			Matches: Won	Lost	Drawn	Age on appointment as Captain
W.D.C.Carling	(Harlequins)	Fifty nine matches	44	14	1	22 years 10 months
W.B.Beaumont	(Fylde)	Twenty one matches	11	8	2	25 years 9 months
E.Evans	(Sale)	Thirteen matches	9	2	2	30 years 11 months
N.M.Hall	(Richmond)	Thirteen matches	6	5	2	24 years 5 months
R.E.G.Jeeps	(Northampton)	Thirteen matches	5	4	4	28 years 2 months
J.V.Pullin	(Bristol)	Thirteen matches	6	6	1	30 years 11 months
P.R.de Glanville	(Bath)	Eight matches	5	3	-	28 years 1 month
P.W.Dodge	(Leicester)	Seven matches	2	4	1	26 years 11 months
M.E.Harrison	(Wakefield)	Seven matches	3	4	-	31 years
R.Hiller	(Harlequins)	Seven matches	2	4	1	27 years 2 months
N.D.Melville	(Wasps)	Seven matches	4	3	-	23 years 10 months
A.Neary	(Broughton Park)	Seven matches	2	5	-	25 years 4 months
D.P.Rogers	(Bedford)	Seven matches	2	4	1	30 years 7 months
I Preece	(Coventry)	Six matches	3	3	-	28 years 2 months
P.E.Judd	(Coventry)	Five matches	2	3	-	32 years 10 months
R.A.W.Sharp	(Wasps and Bristol)	Five matches	3	1	1	24 years 5 months
S.J.Smith	(Sale)	Five matches	2	2	1	30 years 7 months
R.V.Stirling	(RAF/Leicester)	Five matches	3	2	-	34 years 4 months
R.M.Uttley	(Gosforth)	Five matches	2	2	1	27 years 4 months
M.P.Weston	(Durham City)	Five matches	1	4	-	24 years 10 months
P.J.Wheeler	(Leicester)	Five matches	2	3	-	35 years
J.Butterfield	(Northampton)	Four matches	1	1	2	29 years 5 months
D.G.Perry	(Bedford)	Four matches	1	2	1	27 years 1 month
J.P.Scott	(Cardiff)	Four matches	-	4	-	28 years 6 months
J.S.Spencer	(Headingley)	Four matches	1	3	-	23 years 6 months
F.E.Cotton	(Coventry)	Three matches	-	3	-	27 years
R.J.Hill	(Bath)	Three matches	-	3	-	25 years 9 months
J.M.Kendall Carpenter	(Bath)	Three matches	-	2	-	25 years 5 months
J.Orwin	(Bedford)	Three matches	1	2	-	34 years 1 month
E.K.Scott	(St Mary's Hospital)	Three matches	-	3	-	29 years 6 months
J.G.Willcox	(Harlequins)	Three matches	-	2	1	26 years 10 months

ENGLAND CAPTAINS: (continued)

			Won	Lost	Drawn	Age on appointment as Captain
C.R.Andrew	(Wasps)	Two matches	2	-	-	26 years 3 months
P.J.Dixon	(Gosforth)	Two matches	-	2	-	27 years 10 months
J.Heaton	(Waterloo)	Two matches	2	-	-	34 years 7 months
C.R.Jacobs	(Northampton)	Two matches	1	1	-	35 years 4 months
C.W.McFadyean	(Moseley)	Two matches	-	-	2	24 years 10 months
J.Mycock	(Sale)	Two matches	1	1	-	31 years
P.D.Young	(Dublin Wanderers)	Two matches	1	1	-	27 years 5 months
A.L.Bucknall	(Richmond)	One match	-	1	-	25 years 7 months
J.R.H.Greenwood	(Waterloo)	One match	-	1	-	27 years 5 months
R.M.Harding	(Bristol)	One match	1	-	-	24 years 9 months
T.A.Kemp	(Richmond)	One match	-	-	1	32 years 5 months
J.Leonard	(Harlequins)	One Match	1	-	-	29 years 4 months
V.G.Roberts	(Penryn)	One match	-	1	-	26 years 5 months
R.B.Taylor	(Northampton)	One match	-	1	-	27 years 11 months
R.H.G.Weighill	(RAF/Harlequins)	One match	-	1	-	27 years 6 months

WILL CARLING

59 matches as Captain - 44 matches won.

BILL BEAUMONT

21 matches as Captain - 11 matches won.

LEADING BY EXAMPLE - ENGLAND'S LONGEST SERVING CAPTAINS

ENGLAND CAPTAINCY RECORDS:

WILLIAM DAVID CHARLES CARLING   (Harlequins)   72 caps - 59 matches as Captain

Born: December 12th 1965   First match as Captain: November 5th 1988 v Australia at Twickenham.
                                           Last match as Captain: March 16th 1996 v Ireland at Twickenham

Record as Captain: Won the **GRAND SLAM** three times, 1991, 1992, and 1995
                                           Won the **TRIPLE CROWN** four times, 1991, 1992, 1995, and 1996
                                           Won the **CHAMPIONSHIP TITLE** outright four times, 1991, 1992, 1995 and 1996
                                           Won the **CALCUTTA CUP** six times, 1991, 1992, 1993, 1994, 1995 and 1996
                                           Retained the **CALCUTTA CUP** once, 1989

                                           Captain for forty four successive matches, 1989 to 1995

                                           The first England Captain to lead his side to victory over all seven
                                           senior IRB member nations.

Five Nations: **Won twenty five matches:**   **Lost six matches:**   **Drew one match:**

                         Ireland 1989   (a) (16 - 3)   Wales 1989   (a) (9 - 12)   Scotland 1989   (h) (12 - 12)
                         France 1989   (h) (11 - 0)   Scotland 1990 (a) (7 - 13)
                         |Ireland 1990   (h) (23 - 0)   Wales 1993   (a) (9 - 10)
                         France 1990   (a) (26 - 7)   Ireland 1993   (a) (3 - 17)
                         Wales 1990   (h) (34 - 6)   Ireland 1994   (h) (12 - 13)
                         Wales 1991   (a) (25 - 6)   France 1996   (a) (12 - 15)
                         Scotland 1991   (h) (21 - 12)
                         Ireland 1991   (a) (16 - 7)
                         France 1991   (h) (21 - 19)
                         Scotland 1992   (a) (25 - 7)
                         Ireland 1992   (h) (38 - 9)
                         France 1992   (a) (31 - 13)
                         Wales 1992   (h) (24 - 0)
                         France 1993   (h) (16 - 15)
                         Scotland 1993   (h) (26 - 12)
                         Scotland 1994   (a) (15 - 14)
                         France 1994   (a) (18 - 14)
                         Wales 1994   (h) (15 - 8)
                         Ireland 1995   (a) (20 - 8)
                         France 1995   (h) (31 - 10)
                         Wales 1995   (a) (23 - 9)
                         Scotland 1995   (h) (24 - 12)
                         Wales 1996   (h) (21 - 15)
                         Scotland 1996   (a) (18 - 9)
                         Ireland 1996   (h) (28 - 15)

ENGLAND CAPTAINCY RECORDS: (continued)

WILLIAM DAVID CHARLES CARLING (continued):

World Cup:

Won seven matches:			Lost four matches:		
Italy 1991	(h)	(35 - 6)	N Zealand 1991	(h)	(12 - 18)
USA 1991	(h)	(37 - 9)	Australia 1991	(h)	(6 - 12)
France 1991	(a)	(19 - 10)	N Zealand 1995	SA	(45 - 29)
Scotland 1991	(a)	(9 - 6)	France 1995	SA	(9 - 19)
Argentina 1995	SA	(24 - 18)			
W Samoa 1995	SA	(44 - 22)			
Australia 1995	SA	(25 - 22)			

Other matches:

Won twelve matches:			Lost four matches:		
Australia 1988	(h)	(28 - 19)	Argentina 1990	(a)	(13 - 15)
Fiji 1989	(h)	(58 - 23)	Australia 1991	(a)	(15 - 40)
Argentina 1990	(a)	(25 - 12)	S Africa 1994	(a)	(9 - 27)
Argentina 1990	(h)	(51 - 0)	S Africa 1995	(h)	(14 - 24)
Fiji 1991	(a)	(28 - 12)			
Canada 1992	(h)	(26 - 13)			
S Africa 1992	(h)	(33 - 16)			
N Zealand 1993	(h)	(15 - 9)			
S Africa 1994	(a)	(32 - 15)			
Romania 1994	(h)	(54 - 3)			
Canada 1994	(h)	(60 - 19)			
W Samoa 1995	(h)	(27 - 9)			

IN TOTAL: **WON FORTY FOUR MATCHES**   **LOST FOURTEEN MATCHES**   **DREW ONE MATCH**

Without any doubt whatsoever, Will Carling was the most outstanding of all the 46 individuals who have led England in the 51 seasons since 1947. When Geoff Cooke appointed him in November 1988, Carling was the youngest post-war England Captain, at the age of 22 years and 10 months, and England rugby was in a sorry state indeed, having lost five of their previous nine matches and in that time having had four different captains. Carling then led England for 59 of the next 61 matches, and in doing so, he was to lead England to two World Cups, including one final, to three Grand Slams and to four Triple Crowns and was to become the first England Captain ever to lead his side to victory over all seven of the senior IRB member nations. Even if England failed during his stewardship to match the three sides from the Southern hemisphere, his Captaincy record is likely to remain unequalled in the future.

The high points of his career were undoubtedly the three Grand Slams and, in adversity, the way in which he led the England side back to respectability from the brink of ignominy in the 1995 World Cup semi-final in South Africa when, shortly after half-time, England were 35 points to 3 down. Carling then inspired England to score 26 points against New Zealand's 10, in the latter stages, with two tries himself. Against that, he failed to inspire his side either to win the Grand Slam at Murrayfield in 1990, or to win the World Cup at Twickenham in 1991, both of which prizes were within the grasp of the then England side had their approach and their leadership on the day, been right. Finally, Carling bore his greatest burden, the insufferable, and corrosive attention of the media, with dignity and composure which alone did great service to the game as a whole as, during his period of office, it ground slowly and agonisingly to the threshold of professionalism.

When he finally retired from International rugby in 1997, he was England's most capped centre, with 72 caps, and England's fourth highest try scorer, with 12 tries, and he had played in 44 successive International matches , more than any other England player. A remarkable record, and one which made him, really, England's first rugby Super-Star.

WILLIAM BLACKLEDGE BEAUMONT   (Fylde)   34 caps - 21 matches as Captain

Born: March 9th 1952   First match as Captain: January 21st 1978 v France at Parc des Princes
                                   Last match as Captain: January 16th 1982 v Scotland at Murrayfield

Record as Captain: Won the **GRAND SLAM** once, 1980
                                   Won the **TRIPLE CROWN** once, 1980
                                   Won the **CHAMPIONSHIP TITLE** outright once, 1980
                                   Won the **CALCUTTA CUP** three times, 1978, 1980 and 1981
                                   Retained the **CALCUTTA CUP** once, 1982

                                   Captain for sixteen successive matches, 1979 to 1982

Five Nations:

Won nine matches:			Lost six matches:			Drew one match:		
Scotland 1978	(a)	(15 - 0)	France 1978	(a)	(6 - 15)	Scotland 1982	(h)	(9 - 9)
Ireland 1978	(h)	(15 - 9)	Wales 1978	(h)	(6 - 9)			
France 1979	(h)	(7 - 6)	Ireland 1979	(a)	(7 - 12)			
Ireland 1980	(h)	(24 - 9)	Wales 1979	(a)	(3 - 27)			
France 1980	(a)	(17 - 13)	Wales 1981	(a)	(19 - 21)			
Wales 1980	(h)	(9 - 8)	France 1981	(h)	(12 - 16)			
Scotland 1980	(a)	(30 - 18)						
Scotland 1981	(h)	(23 - 17)						
Ireland 1981	(a)	(10 - 6)						

Other matches:

Won two matches:			Lost two matches:			Drew one match:		
Argentina 1981	(a)	(12 - 6)	N Zealand 1978	(h)	(6 - 16)	Argentina 1981	(a)	(19 - 19)
Australia 1982	(h)	(15 - 11)	N Zealand 1979	(h)	(9 - 10)			

IN TOTAL: **WON ELEVEN MATCHES**   **LOST EIGHT MATCHES**   **DREW TWO MATCHES**

Bill Beaumont became almost a legend in his time because of his tremendous contribution to the game of rugby, his personal integrity and immense popularity amongst all the members of the many teams which he led and his record as a Captain of England, but above all for the outstanding example which he set to his teammates in literally leading from the front and never, ever, expecting more from his charges than he himself was prepared to contribute. His record as England Captain is not as good as many in that he won only 11 of the 21 matches in which he captained the side. But he led England to a Grand Slam for the first timwe for 23 years and he became the first English Captain of the British Lions for 50 years since F.D.Prentice of Leicester led the newly named "Lions" to Australia and New Zealand in 1930.

His contribution to Lancashire and North of England rugby was equally significant, leading Lancashire to two County Championship finals and the North fo England to that memorable win over the All Blacks at Otley on November 17th 1979, the only match they lost on that tour.

His career was tragically cut short on medical advice after suffering a head injury in the County Final of 1982. After leading England at Murrayfield on January 16th, leading Lancashire at Moseley on January 30th, only nine days later, Bill Beaumont had to announce to an astonished nation, his complete retirement from the game. He bore this disaster with the same courage, fortitude and level-headedness which he had shown in the face of the triumphs and high points of his career. He went on to endear himself to a much wider audience with his participation with Ian Botham and David Coleman in BBC TV's "A Question of Sport", and as Bill McLaren's expert opinion provider in many a TV match commentary.   May his outboard motor, as his ample backside became affectionately known, power him to greater heights in the administration of the game in the years to come.

ERIC EVANS   (Sale)   30 caps - 13 matches as Captain

Born: **February 1st 1925**   First match as Captain: January 21st 1956 v Wales at Twickenham
Died: **January 12th 1991**   Last match as Captain: March 15th 1958 v Scotland at Murrayfield

Record as Captain:

Won the **GRAND SLAM** once, 1957
Won the **TRIPLE CROWN** once, 1957
Won the **CHAMPIONSHIP TITLE** outright twice, 1957 and 1958
Won the **CALCUTTA CUP** twice, 1956 and 1957
Retained the **E160** once, 1958

Captain for thirteen successive matches

Five Nations:	Won eight matches:		Lost two matches:		Drew two matches:	
	Ireland 1956	(h) (20 - 0)	Wales 1956	(h) (3 - 8)	Wales 1958	(h) (3 - 3)
	Scotland 1956	(a) (11 - 6)	France 1956	(a) (9 - 14)	Scotland 1958	(a) (3 - 3)
	Wales 1957	(a) (3 - 0)				
	Ireland 1957	(a) (6 - 0)				
	France 1957	(h) (9 - 5)				
	Scotland 1957	(h) (16 - 3)				
	Ireland 1958	(h) (6 - 0)				
	France 1958	(a) (14 - 0)				

Other matches:	Won one match:	
	Australia 1958	(9 - 6)

IN TOTAL :   **WON NINE MATCHES**   **LOST TWO MATCHES**   **DREW TWO MATCHES**

Eric Evans' International career extended over a period of eleven years from January 3rd 1948, when he gained his first cap as a loose head prop against Australia, to March 15th 1958 when he led England to a try-less draw against Scotland at Murrayfield. After his first cap he had to wait two years for his second and a further year for his third after which he became England's first choice hooker. His record as captain of England is second only to that of Will Carling in terms of matches won as a proportion of matches played, he won nine out of thirteen. Under his stewardship, England won the Grand Slam in 1957, and prior to the triumphs of Will Carling and Bill Beaumont, Eric Evans thus became the first captain to lead England to a Grand Slam post-war. The following season, England won the Five Nations Championship outright a feat unique in England International rugby since 1947 until Will Carling's side won two successive Championships (and Grand Slams) in 1991 and 1992.
He scored five tries in his International career - only two other hookers have scored a try for England in the post-war period - Brian Moore and John Pullin- and they only scored one try each. Like Bill Beaumont, he was a pillar of strength in Lancashire County rugby and played 85 times for the County side.
Eric Evans never went on a Lions' Tour although he must have been close to selection for the 1955 tour to South Africa, but with Brynn Meredith and Robin Roe in contention, the competition was certainly tough.

NORMAN MACLEOD HALL	(Richmond)	17 caps - 13 matches as Captain

Born: **August 2nd 1925**	First match as Captain:	January 15th 1949 v Wales at Cardiff
Died: **June 26th 1972**	Last match as Captain:	February 12th 1955 v Ireland at Lansdowne Road

Record as Captain:

Won the **CHAMPIONSHIP TITLE** outright once, 1953
Won the **CALCUTTA CUP** twice, 1952 and 1953

Captain for nine successive matches

Five Nations:	**Won six matches:**		**Lost four matches:**		**Drew two matches:**	
	Scotland 1952	(a) (19 - 3)	Wales 1949	(a) (3 - 9)	Ireland 1953	(a) (9 - 9)
	Ireland 1952	(h) (3 - 0)	Ireland 1949	(a) (5 - 14)	Ireland 1955	(a) (6 - 6)
	France 1952	(a) (6 - 3)	Wales 1952	(h) (6 - 8)		
	Wales 1953	(a) (8 - 3)	Wales 1953	(a) (0 - 3)		
	France 1953	(h) (11 - 0)				
	Scotland 1953	(h) (26 - 8)				

Other matches:	**Lost one match:**	
	S Africa 1952	(h) (3 - 8)

IN TOTAL:	**WON SIX MATCHES**	**LOST FIVE MATCHES**	**DREW TWO MATCHES**

"Nim" Hall was probably the most put upon of all England's post-war Captains in that the Selectors appeared to treat him as a necessary evil to be employed only as a last resort and to be dispensed with as soon as any reasonable alternative became available.

He played only seventeen times for England and on thirteen of those occasions was Captain. He made his debut in the first post-war International against Wales and scored a drop goal to help England win by 9 points to 6 in Cardiff. He played in all the four Five Nations matches that season then was dropped for the whole of the following season in favour of, first, Tommy Kemp, who was Captain for one match, and then Ivor Preece. The 1949 season saw him back at fly-half and now as Captain for two matches when he was again dropped in favour of Ivor Preece in both capacities. Two more seasons in the wilderness followed when the England Captaincy passed from Ivor Preece to Vic Roberts and to John Kendall-Carpenter, but in 1952 the Selectors came back cap in hand to request his services again. This time the tenure of office was somewhat longer and Hall captained the side in 1952 from fly-half, and in 1953 when Martin Regan ousted him from fly-half, from full-back. Another year as a pariah to allow Bob Stirling to lead England to their first post-war Triple Crown, and then "Nim" was called upon again in 1955 at the age of 30 to lead the side from full back, to make the crucial tackles and to kick the goals, and it all proved too much for the ageing stalwart. He, with help from the fickle Selectors, stepped down from the Captaincy and retired from International rugby after the Ireland match in 1955.

Like Eric Evans, "Nim" Hall never made a Lions' Tour, but was a universally respected player. He died, aged only 47 years, in 1972, in St Mary's Hospital.

RICHARD ERIC GAUTREY JEEPS   (Northampton)   24 caps - 13 matches as Captain

Born: November 25th 1931   First match as Captain: January 16th 1960 v Wales at Twickenham

Last match as Captain: March 17th 1962 v Scotland at Murrayfield

Record as Captain: Won the **TRIPLE CROWN** once, 1960

Shared the **CHAMPIONSHIP TITLE** with France once, 1960

Won the **CALCUTTA CUP** twice, 1960 and 1961

Retained the **CALCUTTA CUP** once, 1962

Captain for thirteen successive matches

Five Nations:	**Won five matches:**		**Lost three matches:**		**Drew four matches:**	
	Wales 1960	(h) (14 - 6)	Wales 1961	(a) (3 - 6)	France 1960	(a) (3 - 3)
	Ireland 1960	(h) (8 - 5)	Ireland 1961	(a) (8 - 11)	France 1961	(h) (5 - 5)
	Scotland 1960	(a) (21 - 12)	France 1962	(a) (0 - 13)	Wales 1962	(h) (0 - 0)
	Scotland 1961	(h) (6 - 0)			Scotland 1962	(a) (0 - 0)
	Ireland 1962	(h) (16 - 0)				

Other matches: Lost one match:

S Africa 1961   (h) (0 - 5)

IN TOTAL: **WON FIVE MATCHES**   **LOST FOUR MATCHES**   **DREW FOUR MATCHES**

Dickie Jeeps donned the mantle of the England Captaincy immediately following the disastrous season when Jeff Butterfield had led England to two draws and one win in the 1959 Five Nations Championship and when England had failed to score a try during the entire season. In his first season as Captain, England scored seven tries and shared the Championship title with France, missing the Grand Slam only because of the drawn game at Stade Colombes, but taking the Triple Crown. Subsequent seasons were not quite so successful however, and his record of winning only five matches out of thirteen does not reflect creditably on his capabilities as a leader and most certainly not on his ability as a player.

Dickie Jeeps was perhaps the most resilient player of his day and indeed it was said of him by more than one of his opponents that when Dickie Jeeps was tackled or barged or otherwise knocked to the ground, he did not just hit the deck, he bounced, and was on his feet again immediately. It was undoubtedly this resilience that earned him selection for three Lions' tours and rewarded him with thirteen Lions' caps, more than any other England player and second only to Willie John McBride in Lions history. He gained his first four Lions' caps in South Africa in 1955 before he was capped for England against Wales in 1956. He played at scrum half for the Lions with six different fly-halves and had the distinction of leading the Lions in the fourth and last Test against South Africa in 1962 when Arthur Smith was indisposed.

When he retired from the game, Jeeps became an England selector for six years and Predident of the RFU in 1976-77. For many years he was Chairman of the Sports Council and served as a County Councillor and Justice of the Peace.

JOHN VIVIAN PULLIN   (Bristol)   42 caps - 13 matches as Captain

Born: **November 1st 1941**   First match as Captain: June 3rd 1972 v South Africa in Johannesburg
                                         Last match as Captain: May 31st 1975 v Australia in Brisbane

Record as Captain: Shared the **CHAMPIONSHIP TITLE** with the other four Nations, 1973
                           Won the **CALCUTTA CUP** once, 1973

                           Captain for twelve successive matches

**Apart from Will Carling, John Pullin is the only England Captain to have led his
team to victory over the three major Southern hemisphere Nations, New Zealand,
South Africa and Australia. Two of these three victories were away from home.**

Five Nations:

Won three matches:		Lost four matches:		Drew one match:	
France 1973	(h) (14 - 6)	Wales 1973	(a) (9 - 25)	France 1974	(a) (12 - 12)
Scotland 1973	(h) (20 - 13)	Ireland 1973	(a) (9 - 18)		
Wales 1974	(h) (16 - 12)	Scotland 1974	(a) (14 - 16)		
		Ireland 1974	(h) (21 - 26)		

Other matches:

Won three matches:		Lost two matches:	
S Africa 1972	(a) (18 - 9)	N Zealand 1973	(h) (0 - 9)
N Zealand 1973	(a) (16 - 10)	Australia 1975	(a) (21 - 30)
Australia 1973	(h) (20 - 3)		

IN TOTAL: **WON SIX MATCHES**   **LOST SIX MATCHES**   **DREW ONE MATCH**

Twelve of John Pullin's matches as England Captain were successive, and 36 of his 42 International caps were also gained in consecutive matches. He was, by any standards, a remarkably consistent player and this earned him a position amongst the most exalted players of his age when he embarked on his second Lions' Tour to Australia and New Zealand in 1971, playing in all four Tests, having played in three of the four in South Africa in 1968.

After that triumphant 1971 Lions' Tour, and even with five Lions in the side, England had a disastrous season and for the first time in history lost all four Five Nations matches. Thus, not without a sense of foreboding, did an England party of 25 players. nine of them uncapped, and under the Captaincy of John Pullin, embark on a punishing seventeen day tour to South Africa, the first ever, concluding with an International match at Ellis Park, Johannesburg. They returned unbeaten having seen off South Africa by 18 points to 9, and by one try to nil, against all the odds. That it was a team effort is undeniable, but John Pullin's leadership and example were a major contribution to a remarkable achievement.

The following season saw a defeat by the Seventh All Blacks and a 'middle-of-the-table' performance in the Five Nations. Then, at the beginning of the 1973-74 season, in September, another short tour was arranged, to New Zealamd. One game in Fiji and three in New Zealand preceded the only Test Match in Auckland at the end of the tour. The three provincial matches in New Zealand were lost, but, yet again, John Pullin inspired his side to a sublime effort in beating New Zealand by eighteen points to ten and three tries to two. Just over 12 months later, Australia came to Twickenham to experience the formidable power and influence of Pullin's leadership, only to fall, as had their illustrious southern hemisphere colleagues, to another mighty England effort.

John Pullin can have no finer testimony to his career as England Captain than that he led his side to victories over all three senior IRB sides from the southern hemisphere at a time when England International rugby had recently plumbed the depths by losing all four Five Nations matches in one season.

John Pullin was called upon again, for the second match of the 1975 Australian tour, to Captain the side following the injury in the first Test to Tony Neary, but the disadvantage of losing Mike Burton early in the match created an obstacle which even his powers of leadership and inspiration were unable to overcome.

PHILIP RANULPH de GLANVILLE   (Bath)   23 caps - 8 matches as Captain

Born: **October 1st 1968**   First match as Captain: November 23rd 1996 v Italy at Twickenham

                                 Last match as Captain: July 12th 1997 v Australia in Sydney

Record as Captain: Won the **TRIPLE CROWN** once, 1997

                                 Won the **CALCUTTA CUP** once, 1997

Five Nations: **Won three matches**   **Lost one match**

                 Scotland 1997   (h) (41 - 13)   France, 1997   (h) (20 - 23)

                 Ireland, 1997   (a) (46 - 6)

                 Wales, 1997   (a) (34 - 13)

Other Matches: **Won two matches**   **Lost two matches:**

                 Italy, 1996   (h) (54 - 21)   Argentina, 1997   (a) (13 - 33)

                 Argentina, 1997   (a) (46 - 20)   Australia, 1997   (a) (6 - 25)

IN TOTAL: **WON FIVE MATCHES**   **LOST THREE MATCHES**

PAUL WILLIAM DODGE   (Leicester)   32 caps - 7 matches as Captain

Born: **February 28th 1958**   First match as Captain: January 5th 1985 v Romania at Twickenham

                                 Last match as Captain: June 8th 1985 v New Zealand at Wellington

Record as Captain: Won **CALCUTTA CUP** once, 1985

                                 Captain for seven successive matches.

Five Nations: **Won one match:**   **Lost two matches:**   **Drew one match:**

                 Scotland 1985   (h) (10 - 7)   Ireland 1985   (a) (10 - 13)   France 1985   (h) (9 - 9)

Other matches: **Won one match:**   **Lost two matches:**

                 Romania 1985   (h) (22 - 15)   N Zealand 1985   (a) (13 - 18)

                                            N Zealand 1985   (a) (15 - 42)

IN TOTAL: **WON TWO MATCHES**   **LOST FOUR MATCHES**   **DREW ONE MATCH**

MICHAEL EDWARD HARRISON (Wakefield) 15 caps - 7 matches as Captain

Born: April 9th 1956 First match as Captain: April 4th 1987 v Scotland at Twickenham
Last match as Captain: February 6th 1988 v Wales at Twickenham

Record as Captain: Won the **CALCUTTA CUP** once, 1987
Led England in the first World Cup in 1987

Captain for seven successive matches

Five Nations:	Won one match:		Lost two matches:		
	Scotland 1987	(h) (21 - 12)	France 1988	(a) (9 - 10)	
			Wales 1988	(h) (3 - 11)	

World Cup:	Won two matches:		Lost two matches:	
	Japan 1987	U (60 - 7)	Australia 1987	U (6 - 19)
	USA 1987	U (34 - 6)	Wales 1987	U (3 - 16)

IN TOTAL: **WON THREE MATCHES** **LOST FOUR MATCHES**

ROBERT HILLER (Harlequins) 19 caps - 7 matches as Captain

Born: October 14th 1942 First match as Captain: December 20th 1969 v South Africa at Twickenham
Last match as Captain: February 12th 1972 v Ireland at Twickenham

Record as Captain: Captain for four successive matches

Five Nations:	Won one match:		Lost four matches:		Drew one match:	
	Ireland 1970	(h) (9 - 3)	Wales 1970	(h) (13 - 17)	France 1971	(h) (14 - 14)
			Scotland 1970	(a) (5 - 14)		
			Wales 1972	(h) (3 - 12)		
			Ireland 1972	(h) (12 - 16)		

Other matches:	Won one match:	
	S Africa 1969	(h) (11 - 8)

IN TOTAL: **WON TWO MATCHES** **LOST FOUR MATCHES** **DREW ONE MATCH**

ENGLAND CAPTAINCY RECORDS: (continued)

NIGEL DAVID MELVILLE   (Wasps)   13 caps - 7 matches as Captain

Born: January 6th 1961   First match as Captain: November 3rd 1984 v Australia at Twickenham
                                       Last match as Captain: March 19th 1988 v Ireland at Twickenham

Record as Captain: Won the CALCUTTA CUP once, 1988
                                       Captain for four successive nmatches

Nigel Melville was the second player since 1947 to have captained England in first International match. Joe Mycock was the first to achieve this distinction in the first game after the Second World War in 1947.

Five Nations:	Won four matches:			Lost two matches:		
	Wales 1986	(h)	(21 - 18)	Scotland 1986	(a)	(6 - 33)
	Ireland 1986	(h)	(25 - 20)	France 1986	(a)	(10 - 29)
	Scotland 1988	(a)	(9 - 6)			
	Ireland 1988	(h)	(35 - 3)			

Other matches:			Lost one match:		
			Australia 1984	(h)	(3 - 19)

IN TOTAL: WON FOUR MATCHES   LOST THREE MATCHES

ANTHONY NEARY   (Broughton Park)   43 caps - 7 matches as Captain

Born: November 25th 1949   First match as captain: March 15th 1975 v Scotland at Twickenham
                                         Last match as Captain: March 20th 1975 v France at Parc des Princes

Record as Captain: Won the **CALCUTTA CUP** once, 1975
                                         Captain for four successive matches

Tony Neary has the unfortunate distinction to be the only Captain to have led England to four defeats in a single Five Nations season, 1976. England also also lost all four matches in 1972, but after the first two defeats the Captaincy was taken from Bob Hiller and given to Peter Dixon.

Five Nations:	Won one match:			Lost four matches:		
	Scotland 1975	(h)	(7 - 6)	Wales 1976	(h)	(9 - 21)
				Scotland 1976	(a)	(12 - 22)
				Ireland 1976	(h)	(12 - 13)
				France 1976	(a)	(9 - 30)

Other matches:	Won one match:			Lost one match:		
	Australia 1976	(h)	(23 - 6)	Australia 1975	(a)	(9 - 16)

IN TOTAL: WON TWO MATCHES   LOST FIVE MATCHES

DEREK PRIOR ROGERS (Bedford) 34 caps - 7 matches as Captain

Born: June 20th 1935

First match as Captain: January 15th 1966 v Wales at Twickenham
Last match as Captain: April 12th 1969 v Wales at Cardiff

Record as Captain: Won **CALCUTTA CUP** once, 1969
Captain for four successive matches

Five Nations: Won two matches: Lost four matches: Drew one match:

France 1969	(h) (22 - 8)	Wales 1966	(h) (6 - 11)	Ireland 1966	(a) (6 - 6)
Scotland 1969	(h) (8 - 3)	France 1966	(a) (0 - 13)		
		Scotland 1966	(a) (3 - 6)		
		Wales 1969	(a) (9 - 30)		

IN TOTAL: **WON TWO MATCHES** **LOST FOUR MATCHES** **DREW ONE MATCH**

IVOR PREECE (Coventry) 12 caps - 6 matches as Captain

Born: December 15th 1920
Died: March 14th 1987

First match as Captain: February 26th 1949 v France at Twickenham
Last match as Captain: March 18th 1950 v Scotland at Murrayfield

Record as Captain: Won the **CALCUTTA CUP** once, 1949
Captain for six successive matches

Five Nations: Won three matches Lost three matches:

France 1949	(h) (8 - 3)	Wales 1950	(h) (5 - 11)
Scotland 1949	(h) (19 - 3)	France 1950	(a) (3 - 6)
Ireland 1950	(h) (3 - 0)	Scotland 1950	(a) (11 - 13)

IN TOTAL: **WON THREE MATCHES** **LOST THREE MATCHES**

PHILIP EDWARD JUDD   (Coventry)   22 caps - 5 matches as Captain

Born: April 8th 1934   First match as Captain: February 11th 1967 v Ireland at Twickenham

           Last match as Captain: November 4th 1967 v New Zealand at Twickenham

Record as Captain: Won the **CALCUTTA CUP** once, 1967

           Captain for five successive matches

Five Nations: **Won two matches:**   **Lost two matches:**

      Ireland 1967 (a) (8 - 3) France 1967 (h) (12 - 16)

      Scotland 1967 (h) (27 - 14) Wales 1967 (a) (21 - 34)

Other matches: **Lost one match:**

               N Zealand 1967 (h) (11 - 23)

IN TOTAL: **WON TWO MATCHES** **LOST THREE MATCHES**

RICHARD ADRIAN WILLIAM SHARP (Wasps and Bristol) 14 caps - 5 matches as Captain

Born: September 9th 1938 First match as Captain: January 19th 1963 v Wales at Cardiff

           Last match as Captain: January 7th 1967 v Australia at Twickenham

Record as Captain: Won the **CHAMPIONSHIP TITLE** outright once, 1963

           Won the **CALCUTTA CUP** once, 1963

           Captain for four successive matches

Five Nations: **Won three matches:**   **Drew one match:**

      Wales 1963 (a) (13 - 6)

      France 1963 (h) (6 - 5)   Ireland 1963 (a) (0 - 0)

      Scotland 1963 (h) (10 - 8)

Other matches: **Lost one match:**

            Australia 1967 (h) (11 - 23)

IN TOTAL: **WON THREE MATCHES** **LOST ONE MATCH** **DREW ONE MATCH**

STEPHEN JAMES SMITH (Sale) 28 caps - 5 matches as Captain

Born: **July 22nd 1951** First match as Captain: February 6th 1982 v Ireland at Twickenham
Last match as Captain: February 5th 1983 v Wales at Cardiff

Record as Captain: Captain for five successive matches

Five Nations:	Won two matches:		Lost two matches:		Drew one match:	
	France 1982	(a) (27 - 15)	Ireland 1982	(h) (15 - 16)	Wales 1983	(a) (13 - 13)
	Wales 1982	(h) (17 - 7)	France 1983	(h) (15 - 19)		

ROBERT VICTOR STIRLING (RAF/Leicester) 18 caps - 5 matches as Captain

Born: **September 4th 1919** First match as Captain: January 16th 1954 v Wales at Twickenham
Last match as Captain: April 10th 1954 v France at Parc des Princes

Record as Captain: Shared the **CHAMPIONSHIP TITLE** with France and Wales 1954
Won the **TRIPLE CROWN** once, 1954
Won the **CALCUTTA CUP** once, 1954

Captain for five successive matches

Five Nations:	Won three matches:		Lost one match:	
	Wales 1954	(h) (9 - 6)	France 1954	(a) (3 - 11)
	Ireland 1954	(h) (14 - 3)		
	Scotland 1954	(a) (13 - 3)		

Other matches:		Lost one match:	
		N Zealand 1954	(h) (0 - 5)

IN TOTAL: **WON THREE MATCHES** **LOST TWO MATCHES**

ROGER MILES UTTLEY (Gosforth) 23 caps - 5 matches as Captain

Born: **September 11th 1949** First match as Captain: January 15th 1977 v Scotland at Twickenham
Last match as Captain: February 3rd 1979 v Scotland at Twickenham

Record as Captain: Won the **CALCUTTA CUP** once, 1977

Captain for four successive matches

Five Nations:	Won two matches:		Lost two matches:		Drew one match:	
	Scotland 1977	(h) (26 - 6)	France 1977	(h) (3 - 4)	Scotland 1979	(h) (7 - 7)
	Ireland 1977	(a) (4 - 0)	Wales 1977	(a) (9 - 14)		

MICHAEL PHILIP WESTON   (Durham City)   29 caps - 5 matches as Captain

Born: **August 21st 1938**   First match as Captain: May 25th 1963 v New Zealand at Auckland

Last match as Captain: March 16th 1968 v Scotland at Murrayfield

Record as Captain: Won the **CALCUTTA CUP** once, 1968

Captain for three successive matches

Mike Weston led England's first ever tour overseas to New Zealand and Australia in the summer of 1963.

Five Nations:	**Won one match:**		**Lost one match:**	
	Scotland 1968	(a) (8 - 6)	France 1968	(a) (9 - 14)

Other matches:		**Lost three matches:**	
		N Zealand 1963	(a) (11 - 21)
		N Zealand 1963	(a) (6 - 9)
		Australia 1963	(a) (9 - 18)

IN TOTAL: **WON ONE MATCH**   **LOST FOUR MATCHES**

PETER JOHN WHEELER   (Leicester)   41 caps - 5 matches as Captain

Born: **November 26th 1948**   First match as Captain: November 19th 1983 v New Zealand at Twickenham

Last match as Captain: March 17th 1984 v Wales at Twickenham

Record as Captain: Captain for five successive matches

Five nations:	**Won one match:**		**Lost three matches:**	
	Ireland 1984	(h) (12 - 9)	Scotland 1984	(a) (6 - 18)
			France 1984	(a) (18 - 32)
			Wales 1984	(h) (15 - 24)

Other matches:	**Won one match:**
	N Zealand 1983 (h) (15 - 9)

IN TOTAL: **WON TWO MATCHES**   **LOST THREE MATCHES**

JEFFREY BUTTERFIELD   (Northampton)   28 caps - 4 matches as Captain

Born: August 9th 1929   First match as Captain: January 17th 1959 v Wales at Cardiff
                                 Last match as Captain: March 21st 1959 v Scotland at Twickenham

Record as Captain: Retained the **CALCUTTA CUP** once, 1959
                                 Captain for four successive matches

                                 **It was Jeff Butterfield's misfortune to lead England through a Five Nations
                                 season in which no tries were scored, and in which only nine points were
                                 scored in the four matches played.**

Five Nations: **Won one match:**   **Lost one match:**   **Drew two matches:**

                      Ireland 1959   (a) (3 - 0)   Wales 1959   (a) (0 - 5)   France 1959   (h) (3 - 3)
                                                                                 Scotland 1959 (h) (3 - 3)

DAVID GORDON PERRY   (Bedford)   15 caps - 4 matches as Captain

Born: December 26th 1937   First match as Captain: January 16th 1965 v Wales at Cardiff
                                 Last match as Captain: March 20th 1965 v Scotland at Twickenham

Record as Captain: Captain for four successive matches

Five Nations: **Won one match:**   **Lost two matches:**   **Drew one match:**

                      France 1965   (h) (9 - 6)   Wales 1965   (a) (3 - 14)   Scotland 1965 (h) (3 - 3)
                                                    Ireland 1965 (a) (0 - 5)

JOHN PHILIP SCOTT   (Cardiff)   34 caps - 4 matches as Captain

Born: September 28th 1954   First match as Captain: March 5th 1983 v Scotland at Twickenham
                                 Last match as Captain: June 9th 1984 v South Africa in Johannesburg

Record as Captain: Captain for two successive matches (twice)

Five Nations: **Lost two matches:**

                                           Scotland 1983   (h) (12 - 22)
                                           Ireland 1983   (h) (15 - 25)

Other matches: **Lost two matches:**

                                           S Africa 1984   (a) (15 - 33)
                                           S Africa 1984   (a) (9 - 35)

IN TOTAL: **LOST FOUR MATCHES**

JOHN SOTHERN SPENCER   (Headingley)   14 caps - 4 matches as Captain

Born: **August 10th 1947**

First match as Captain: February 13th 1971 v Ireland at Lansdowne Road
Last Match as Captain: April 17th 1971 v RFU President's XV at Twickenha

Record as Captain: Captain for three successive matches

Five Nations: **Won one match:**   **Lost one match:**

Ireland 1971   (a) (9 - 6)   Scotland 1971   (h) (15 - 16)

Other matches: **Lost two matches:**

Scotland 1971   (a) (6 - 26)   (Centenary)
RFU Presdt's X V ((11 - 28)

IN TOTAL: **WON ONE MATCH**   **LOST THREE MATCHES**

FRANCIS EDWARD COTTON   (Coventry)   31 caps - 3 matches as Captain

Born: **January 3rd 1948**

First match as Captain: January 18th 1975 v Ireland at Lansdowne Road
Last match as Captain: February 15th 1975 v Wales at Cardiff

Record as Captain: Captain for three successive matches

Five Nations: **Lost three matches:**

Ireland 1975   (a) (9 - 12)
France 1975   (h) (20 - 27)
Wales 1975   (a) (4 - 20)

RICHARD JOHN HILL   (Bath)   27 caps - 3 matches as Captain

Born: **May 4th 1961**

First match as Captain: February 7th 1987 v Ireland at Lansdowne Road
Last match as Captain: March 7th 1987 v Wales at Cardiff

Record as Captain: Captain for three successive matches

Five Nations: **Lost three matches:**

Ireland 1987   (a) (0 - 17)
France 1987   (h) (15 - 19)
Wales 1987   (a) (12 - 19)

JOHN MacGREGOR KENDALL-CARPENTER (Bath) 23 caps - 3 matches as Captain

Born: September 25th 1925
First match as Captain: February 10th 1951 v Ireland at Lansdowne Road
Last match as Captain: March 17th 1951 v Scotland at Twickenham

Record as Captain: Won the CALCUTTA CUP once. 1951
Captain for three successive matches

Five Nations:	Won one match:		Lost two matches:		
	Scotland 1951	(h) (5 - 3)	Ireland 1951	(a) (0 - 3)	
			France 1951	(h) (3 - 11)	

JOHN ORWIN (Bedford) 14 caps - 3 matches as Captain

Born: March 20th 1954
First match as Captain: April 23rd 1988 v Ireland at Lansdowne Road
Last match as Captain: June 12th 1988 v Australia in Sydney

Record as Captain: Captain for three successive matches

Other matches:	Won one match:		Lost two matches:		
	Ireland 1988	(a) (21 - 12)	Australia 1988	(a) (16 - 22)	
	(Dublin Millennium)		Australia 1988	(a) (8 - 28)	

EDWARD KEITH SCOTT (St Mary's Hospital) 5 caps - 3 matches as Captain

Born: June 14th 1918
First match as Captain: January 3rd 1948 v Australia at Twickenham
Last match as Captain: March 20th 1948 v Scotland at Murrayfield

Record as Captain: Captain for two successive matches

Five Nations:		Lost two matches:	
		Ireland 1948	(h) (10 - 11)
		Scotland 1948	(a) (3 - 6)

Other matches:		Lost one match:	
		Australia 1948	(h) (0 - 11)

IN TOTAL: **LOST THREE MATCHES**

JOHN GRAHAM WILLCOX   (Harlequins)   15 caps - 3 matches as Captain

Born: February 16th 1937

First match as Captain: January 4th 1964 v New Zealand at Twickenham
Last match as Captain: February 8th 1964 v Ireland at Twickenham

Record as Captain: Captain for three successive matches

Five Nations:

	Lost one match:		Drew one match:	
	Ireland 1964	(h) (5 - 18)	Wales 1964	(h) (6 - 6)

Other matches: Lost one match:

N Zealand 1964 (h) (0 - 14)

IN TOTAL: **LOST TWO MATCHES**   **DREW ONE MATCH**

CHRISTOPHER ROBERT ANDREW   (Wasps)   71 caps - 2 matches as Captain

Born: February 18th 1963

First match as Captain: May 13th 1989 v Romania in Bucharest
Last match as Captain: May 31st 1995 v Italy (WC) in Durban

World Cup: Won one match:

Italy 1965   SA (27 - 20)

Other matches: Won one match:

Romania 1989 (a) (58 - 3)

IN TOTAL: **WON TWO MATCHES**

PETER JOHN DIXON   (Gosforth)   22 caps - 2 matches as Captain

Born: April 30th 1944

First match as Captain: February 26th 1972 v France at Stade Colombes
Last match as Captain: March 18th 1972 v Scotland at Murrayfield

Record as Captain: Captain for two successive matches

Five Nations: Lost two matches:

France 1972   (a) (12 - 37)
Scotland 1972 (a) (9 - 23)

JACK HEATON   (Waterloo)   9 caps - 2 matches as Captain

Born: August 30th 1912   First match as Captain: March 15th 1947 v Scotland at Twickenham
                                   Last match as Captain: April 19th 1947 v France at Twickenham

Record as Captain: Won the **CALCUTTA CUP** once, 1947
                                   Two successive matches as Captain

Five Nations: **Won two matches:**

                        Scotland 1947   (h) (24 - 5)
                        France 1947   (h) (6 - 3)

CHARLES RONALD JACOBS   (Northampton)   29 caps - 2 matches as Captain

Born: October 28th 1928   First match as Captain: February 22nd 1964 v France at Stades Colombes
                                   Last match as Captain: March 21st 1964 v Scotland at Murrayfield

Record as Captain: Captain for two successive matches

Five Nations: **Won one match:**   **Lost one match:**

                        France 1964   (a) (6 - 3)   Scotland 1964   (a) (6 - 15)

COLIN WILLIAM McFADYEAN   (Moseley)   11 caps - 2 matches as Captain

Born: March 11th 1943   First match as Captain: January 20th 1968 v Wales at Twickenham
                                   Last match as Captain: February 10th 1968 v Ireland at Twickenham

Record as Captain: Captain for two successive matches

Five Nations: **Drew two matches:**

                                                        Wales 1968   (h) (11 - 11)
                                                        Ireland 1968   (h) (9 - 9)

JOSEPH MYCOCK (Sale) 5 caps - 2 matches as Captain

Born: **January 17th 1916** First match as Captain: January 18th 1947 v Wales at Cardiff
Last match as Captain: February 8th 1947 v Ireland at Lansdowne Road

Record as Captain: Joe Mycock was only the third England player to Captain the side in his
first International match and the first to do so since 1891.
Captain for two successive matches

Five Nations: **Won one match:** **Lost one match:**

Wales 1974 (a) (9 - 6) Ireland 1947 (a) (0 - 22)

PETER DALTON YOUNG (Dublin Wanderers) 9 caps - 2 matches as Captain

Born: **September 11th 1927** First match as Captain: February 26th 1955 v France at Twickenham
Last match as Captain: March 19th 1955 v Scotland at Twickenham

Record as Captain: Won the CALCUTTA CUP once, 1955
Captain for two successive matches

Five Nations: **Won one match:** **Lost one match:**

Scotland 1955 (h) (9 - 6) France 1955 (h) (9 - 16)

ANTHONY LAUNCE BUCKNALL (Richmond) 10 caps - one match as Captain

Born: **June 7th 1945**

Five Nations: January 17th 1971 v Wales at Cardiff. Match lost (6 - 22)

JOHN RICHARD HEATON GREENWOOD (Waterloo) 5 caps - one match as Captain

Born: **September 11th 1941**

Five Nations: February 8th 1969 v Ireland at Lansdowne Road. Match lost (15 - 17)

RICHARD MARK HARDING (Bristol) 12 caps - one match as Captain

Born: **August 28th 1963**

Tour to Australia and Fiji: June 17th 1988 v Fiji at Suva. Match won (25 - 12)

THOMAS ARTHUR KEMP   (Richmond)   5 caps - one match as Captain

Born: August 12th 1915

Five Nations: January 17th 1948 v Wales at Twickenham.   Match drawn (3 - 3)

JASON LEONARD   (Harlequins)   55 caps - one match as Captain

Born: August 14th 1968

Other Matches   December 14th 1996 v Argentina at Twickenham   Match won (20 - 18)

VICTOR GEORGE ROBERTS   (Penryn)   16 caps - one match as Captain

Born: August 6th 1924

Five Nations: January 20th 1951 v Wales at Swansea.   Match lost (5 - 23)

ROBERT BAINBRIDGE TAYLOR   (Northampton)   16 caps - one match as Captain

Born: April 30th 1942

Five Nations: April 18th 1970 v France at Stade Colombes.   Match lost (13 - 35)

ROBERT HAROLD GEORGE WEIGHILL   (RAF/Harlequins   4 caps - one match as Captain

Born: September 9th 1920

Five Nations: March 29th 1948 v France at Stade Colombes.   Match lost (0 - 15)

LEADING POINTS SCORERS - ALL MATCHES

Name:	Club:	Total Points:	Five Nations:	World Cup:	Others:	Tries:	Pn'lty Goals:	Drop Goals:	Convs
C.R.Andrew	Cam U/Ntt'm/Wasps	396	185	85	126	2	86	21	33
J.M.Webb	Bristol/Bath	296	124	99	73	4	66		41
W.H.Hare	Leicester	240	178		62	2	67	1	14
R.Underwood	RAF/Leicester	210	77	49	84	49			
S.D.Hodgkinson	Nottingham	203	102	17	84	1	43		35
R.Hiller	Harlequins	138	119		19	3	33	2	12
P.J.Grayson	Northampton	133	116		17		35	4	8
A.G.B.Old	M'boro'/Leicester	98	81		17	1	23	3	8
M.J.Catt	Bath	85	14	3	68	3	12	2	14
J.C.Guscott	Bath	83	37	8	38	18		2	
W.M.H.Rose	Cam U/Harlequins	82	73		9	2	22		4
J.E.B.Callard	Bath	69	27	21	21		21		
T.Underwood	Leicester	65	35	10	20	13			
R.W.Hosen	Northampton	63	44		19		17		6
W.D.C.Carling	Harlequins	54	26	18	10	12			
A.J.Hignell	Cambridge U/Bristol	48	37		11		14		3
N.M.Hall	St Mary's H/Hddrsfd	39	39				4	3	8
D.J.Duckham	Coventry	36	32		4	10			
D.Rutherford	Percy Park	36	34		2		8		6
S.Barnes	Bristol/Bath	34	6		28		7	1	5
P.A.Rossborough	Coventry	34	22		12	1	7	1	3
C.Otl	Cambridge U/Wasps	32	12		20	8			
M.A.C.Slemen	Liverpool	32	32			8			
J.Carleton	Orrell	28	28			7			
M.E.Harrison	Wakefield	28		20	8	7			
R.A.W.Sharp	Oxford U/Wasps	26	26			2	1	3	4
D.Richards	Leicester	24	12	4	8	6			
P.J.Squires	Harrogate	24	12		12	6			

ROB ANDREW
396 points
2 Tries; 88 Penalty Goals;
21 Drop Goals and 33 Conversions

JONATHAN WEBB
296 points
4 Tries; 66 Penalty Goals
and 41 conversions.

"DUSTY" HARE
240 points
2 Tries; 67 Penalty Goals;
1 Drop Goal and 14 Conversions.

RORY UNDERWOOD
210 points
49 tries.

ENGLAND'S LEADING POINTS SCORERS IN ALL MATCHES.

LEADING POINTS SCORERS - ALL MATCHES (continued)

Name:	Club:	Total Points:	Five Nations:	World Cup:	Others:	Tries:	Pn'lty Goals:	Drop Goals:	Convs
W.N.Bennett	Bedford/Lndn Wlsh	23	23			2	5		
A.M.Jorden	Cam U/Blackheath	22	22				4		5
C.D.Morris	L'pool-St Hlns/Orrell	21	12		9	5			
J.E.Woodward	Wasps	21	21			6			
S.A.Doble	Moseley	20	6		14		6		1
A.C.T.Gomarsall	Wasps	20	10		10	4			
J.M.Sleightholme	Bath	20	15		5	4			
A.Neary	Broughton Park	19	11		8	5			
P.B.Jackson	Coventry	18	15		3	6			
J.Roberts	Old Millhillians	18	18			6			
J.G.Willcox	Oxford U/Harlequins	17	17				3		4
J.D.Currie	Oxford University	16	16				4		2
G.H.Davies	Cambridge U/Wasps	16	8		8	4			
P.J.Dixon	Gosforth	16	16			4			
C.R.Woodward	Leicester	16	8		8	4			
D.F.Allison	Coventry	15	15				5		
J.Butterfield	Northampton	15	15			5			
B.B.Clarke	Bath/Richmond	15	5		10	3			
L.B.N.Dallaglio	Wasps	15	5		10	3			
P.W.Dodge	Leicester	15	13		2	1	3		1
E.Evans	Sale	15	15			5			
P.R.de Glanville	Bath	15	10		5	3			
R.H.Guest	Waterloo	15	15			5			
I.G.Hunter	Northampton	15	5		10	3			
C.W.McFadyean	Moseley	15	15			4		1	
M.S.Phillips	Oxford U/Fylde	15	6		9	5			
T.A.K.Rodber	Northampton	15	5		10	3			
P.H.Thompson	Headingley	15	15			5			
M.Young	Gosforth	15	15			1	1		4
P.J.Winterbottom	Headingley/Quins	13		8	5	3			
L.Cusworth	Leicester	12	12						
W.A.Dooley	Preston G'hoppers	12	8	4		3			
N.J.Heslop	Orrell	12	4	4	4	3			
J.P.Horton	Bath	12	9		3			4	
J.A.Probyn	Wasps	12	4		8	3			
M.G.Skinner	Harlequins	12	4	4	4	3			
J.V.Smith	Cambridge Univ	12	12			4			
S.T.Smith	Wasps	12	8		4	3			
M.C.Teague	Gloucester	12	8		4	3			
D.S.Wilson	Met Police	12	12			4			

LEADING POINTS SCORERS - FIVE NATIONS MATCHES

Name:	Club:	Total Points:	Tries:	Pn'lty Goals:	Drop Goals:	Convs:
C.R.Andrew	Cam U/Ntt'm/Wasps	185		44	9	13
W.H.Hare	Leicester	178	2	50		10
J.M.Webb	Bristol/Bath	124	3	28		14
R.Hiller	Harlequins	119	2	29	2	10
P.J.Grayson	Northampton	116		30	4	7
S.D.Hodgkinson	Nottingham	102		28		9
A.G.B.Old	M'boro'/Leicester	81		20	3	6
R.Underwood	RAF/Leicester	77	18			
W.M.H.Rose	Cam U/Harlequins	73	2	19		4
R.W.Hosen	Northampton	44		12		4
N.M.Hall	St Mary's H/Hddrsfd	39		4	3	8
J.C.Guscott	Bath	37	7		2	
A.J.Hignell	Cambridge U/Bristol	37		11		2
T.Underwood	Leicester	35	7			
D.Rutherford	Percy Park	34		8		5
D.J.Duckham	Coventry	32	9			
M.A.C.Slemen	Liverpool	32	8			
J.Carleton	Orrell	28	7			
J.E.B.Callard	Bath	27		9		
W.D.C.Carling	Harlequins	26	6			
R.A.W.Sharp	Oxford U/Wasps	26	2	1	3	4
W.N.Bennett	Bedford/Lndn Wlsh	23	2	5		
A.M.Jorden	Cam U/Blackheath	22		4		5
P.A.Rossborough	Coventry	22	1	5	1	
J.E.Woodward	Wasps	21	6	1		
J.Roberts	Old Millhillians	18	6			

LEADING POINTS SCORERS - FIVE NATIONS MATCHES (continued)

Name:	Club:	Total Points:	Tries:	Pn'lty Goals:	Drop Goals:	Convs
J.G.Willcox	Oxford U/Harlequins	17		3		4
J.D.Currie	Oxford University	16		4		2
P.J.Dixon	Gosforth	16	4			
D.F.Allison	Coventry	15		5		
J.Butterfield	Northampton	15	5			
E.Evans	Sale	15	5			
R.H.Guest	Waterloo	15	5			
P.B.Jackson	Coventry	15	5			
C.W.McFadyean	Moseley	15	4		1	
J.M.Sleightholme	Bath	15	3			
P.H.Thompson	Headingley	15	5			
M.Young	Gosforth	15	1	1		4
M.J.Catt	Bath	14		2		4
P.W.Dodge	Leicester	13	1	3		
L.Cusworth	Leicester	12			4	
C.Oti	Cambridge U/Wasps	12	3			
D.Richards	Leicester	12	3			
J.V.Smith	Cambridge Univ	12	4			
P.J.Squires	Harrogate	12	3			
D.S.Wilson	Met Police	12	4			

LEADING POINTS SCORERS - WORLD CUP MATCHES

Name:	Club:	Total Points:	Tries	Pn'lty Goals	Drop Goals	Convs:
J.M.Webb	Bristol/Bath	99	1	21		16
C.R.Andrew	Cam U/Ntt'm/Wasps	85		20	5	5
R.Underwood	RAF/Leicester	49	11			
J.E.B.Callard	Bath	21		5		3
M.E.Harrison	Wakefield	20	5			
W.D.C.Carling	Harlequins	18	4			
S.D.Hodgkinson	Nottingham	17		3		4
T.Underwood	Leicester	10	2			
J.C.Guscott	Bath	8	2			
P.J.Winterbottom	Headingley/'Quins	8	2			

POINTS SCORED FOR ENGLAND IN ALL INTERNATIONAL MATCHES:

Name:	Club:	Total Points:	Five Nations:	World Cup:	Other Matches:
P.J.Ackford	Harlequins	4			FI89 4
A.A.Adebayo	Bath	10			AR97/1 10
S.J.Adkins	Coventry	3	S53 3		
A.E.Agar	Harlequins	6	W52 3, S52 3		
D.F.Allison	Coventry	15	W56 3, I56 3, F56 6, W57 3		
C.R.Andrew	Cam U/Ntt'm/Wasps	396	F85 9, S85 6, I85 6, W85 11, W86 21, S86 6, I86 9, F87 3, S88 3, I88 6, S89 6, I89 8, F89 3, W89 9, F91 3, F94 18, W94 5, I95 5, F95 16, W95 8, S95 24	NZ91 3, S91 3, AR95 24, IT95 17, A95 20, NZ95 9, F95 9	R085 18, R089 3, FI89 2, FI91 10, NZ93 3, SA94 27, SA94 9, R094 24, CA94 30
R.C.Ashby	Wasps	3			A67 3
A.Ashcroft	Waterloo	3	I58 3		
N.A.Back	Leicester	5		WS95 5	
M.D.Bailey	Wasps	4			FI89 4
B.Barley	Wakefield	4			FI88 4
S.Barnes	Bristol/Bath	34	F86 6		A84 3, N285 5, N285 7, FI88 13
J.Barton	Coventry	6	W67 6		
R.C.Bazley	Waterloo	6	S53 6		
I.D.S.Beer	Harlequins	3	S55 3		
M.C.Beese	Liverpool	4	F72 4		
N.O.Bennett	St Mary's Hospital	3	S47 3		
W.N.Bennett	Bedford/Lndn Wlsh	23	S75 3, S79 3, I79 7, F79 7, W79 3		
J.Bentley	Sale	4			A88 4
B.Boobbyer	Oxf U/Rosslyn Park	6	F51 3, I52 3		
K.P.P.Bracken	Bristol	5			CA94 5
P.E.Butler	Gloucester	10	F76 5		A75 5
J.Butterfield	Northampton	15	F53 3, S53 3, I54 3, I55 3, I56 3		
J.E.B.Callard	Bath	69	S94 15, I94 12	WS95 21	NZ93 12, SA95 9
L.B.Cannell	Oxf U/St Mary's H	6	F49 3, W53 3		
J.Carleton	Orrell	28	F80 4, S80 12, F82 4, W82 4, W83 4		
W.D.C.Carling	Harlequins	54	F89 4, F90 4, W90 4, W92 4, I95 5, S97 5	US91 4, F91 4, N295 10	SA92 5, R094 5
M.J.Catt	Bath	85	W97 14	WS95 3	CA94 10, IT96 19, AR96 15, AR97/1 21, A97 3

POINTS SCORED FOR ENGLAND IN ALL INTERNATIONAL MATCHES (continued):

Name:	Club:	Total Points:	Five Nations:	World Cup:	Other Matches:
R.Challis	Bristol	10	I57 3 S57 7		
B.B.Clarke	Bath	15	I95 5		SA94 5 R97/1 5
S.J.S.Clarke	Cambridge Univ	3			A63 3
M.J.Colclough	Wasps	4			NZ63 4
M.J.Cooper	Moseley	4	I77 4		
B.J.Corless	Coventry	4	S74 4		
F.E.Cotton	Coventry	4			A76 4
M.J.Coulman	Moseley	3	S68 3		
A.R.Cowman	L'boro' Coll/Coventry	6	W73 3		S71 3
J.D.Currie	Oxford University	16	I56 8 S56 8		
L.Cusworth	Leicester	12	F83 3 W83 3 I84 3 F88 3		
L.B.N.Dallaglio	Wasps	15	F97 5		WS95 5 IT96 5
G.H.Davies	Cambridge U/Wasps	16	S81 4 I86 4		AR81 4 AR81 4
W.P.C.Davies	Harlequins	3	S57 3		
A.J.Diprose	Saracens	5			AR97/1 5
P.J.Dixon	Gosforth	16	S73 8 F76 4 I78 4		
S.A.Doble	Moseley	20	W73 6		SA72 14
P.W.Dodge	Leicester	15	S78 3 I81 4 S82 6		A82 2
W.A.Dooley	Preston G'hoppers	12	F86 4 W92 4	US87 4	
N.J.Drake-Lee	Cambridge Univ	3	S63 3		
D.J.Duckham	Coventry	36	I69 3 S69 6 W70 3 F73 8 F74 4 W74 4 F75 4		A76 4
D.W.Egerton	Bath	4	I90 4		
E.Evans	Sale	15	S52 3 I53 3 F53 3 I56 3 F57 3		
G.W.Evans	Coventry	7	S73 4 F74 3		
K.J.Fielding	Loughborough Coll	3	F69 3		
J.F.Finlan	Moseley	9	F67 3 S67 3 I68 3		
N.Gibbs	Harlequins	4	S54 4		
P.R.de Glanville	Bath	15	S97 5 W97 5		SA95 5
H.O.Godwin	Coventry	3			A63 3
A.C.T.Gomarsall	Wasps	20	S97 5 I97 5		IT96 10
A.Gray	Otley	2	W47 2		
P.J.Grayson	Northampton	133	F96 12 W96 11 S96 18 I96 23 S97 21 I97 16 F97 15		WS95 17
N.J.J.Greenstock	Wasps	5			AR97/1 5
J.R.H.Greenwood	Waterloo	3	I66 3		
D.J.Grewcock	Coventry	5			AR97/2 5

POINTS SCORED FOR ENGLAND IN ALL INTERNATIONAL MATCHES (continued):

Name:	Club:	Total Points:	Five Nations:	World Cup:	Other Matches:
R.H.Guest	Waterloo	15	S47 3, F47 3, I48 6, S49 3		
J.C.Guscott	Bath	83	I90 4, F90 4, S90 4, S92 3, I92 4, W93 3, S93 5, F95 5, W96 5	IT91 8	RO89 12, FI89 4, AR90 8, A91 4, CA92 5, SA92 5
J.P.Hall	Bath	8			NZ85 4, AR90 4
N.M.Hall	St Mary's H/H'drsfd /Richmond	39	W47 4, S47 4, W49 3, S52 4, F52 6, W53 2, I53 6, F53 2, S53 8		
S.J.Halliday	Bath/Harlequins	8	I92 4		A88 4
A.W.Hancock	Northampton	3	S65 3		
R.C.Hannaford	Bristol	3	W71 3		
R.M.Harding	Bristol	4			IM88 4
V.S.J.Harding	Cambridge Univ	3	F61 3		
W.H.Hare	Leicester	240	I80 12, F80 9, W80 9, S80 10, W81 19, S81 11, F82 19, W82 9, F83 12, W83 6, S83 9, I83 15, S84 6, I84 9, F84 14, W84 15		NZ78 6, NZ79 9, AR81 7, AR81 8, NZ83 11, SA84 12, SA84 9
M.E.Harrison	Wakefield	28		A87 4, J87 12, US87 4	NZ85 4, NZ85 4
G.W.D.Hastings	Gloucester	11	I55 3, F58 5, S58 3		
D.St G.Hazell	Leicester	9	F55 6, S55 3		
J.Heaton	Waterloo	8	S47 8		
A.P.Henderson	Cambridge Univ	3	S47 3		
N.J.Heslop	Orrell	12	S91 4	US91 4	AR90 4
J.G.G.Hetherington	Northampton	9	I58 3, F59 3		A58 3
E.N.Hewitt	Coventry	2	W51 2		
R.Higgins	Liverpool	6	F55 3, S57 3		
A.J.Hignell	Cambridge U/Bristol	48	W76 9, S77 10, F77 3, W77 9, W78 6		A76 11
R.A.Hill	(Saracens)	10	I97 5, W97 5		
R.J.Hill	Bath	8	W90 4		AR90 4
R.Hiller	Harlequins	138	W68 5, I68 6, F68 6, S68 5, I69 12, F69 13, S69 2, W69 9, I70 6, W70 7, S70 2, I71 9, F71 14, S71 12, W72 3, I72 8		SA69 5, SC71 3, PR71 11
S.D.Hodgkinson	Nottingham	203	I90 7, F90 14, W90 18, S90 3, W91 21, S91 17, I91 8, F91 14	US91 17	RO89 19, FI89 16, AR90 17, AR90 9, AR90 23
M.B.Hofmeyr	Oxford University	7	W50 2, S50 5		
C.B.Holmes		3	S47 3		
W.B.Holmes	Cambridge Univ	4	I49 2, F49 2		
W.G.Hook	Gloucester	2	S51 2		

POINTS SCORED FOR ENGLAND IN ALL INTERNATIONAL MATCHES (continued):

Name:	Club:	Total Points:	Five Nations:	World Cup:	Other Matches:
J.P.Horrocks-Taylor	Leicester	3	S61 3		
J.P.Horton	Bath	12	F80 6 S83 3		SA84 3
N.E.Horton,	Moseley	4	W75 4		
R.W.Hosen	Northampton	63	F64 3 S64 3 I67 5 F67 9 S67 12 W67 12		NZ63 8 NZ63 3 A67 8
G.R.d'A.Hosking	Devonport Services	3	S49 3		
I.G.Hunter	Northampton	15	F93 5		CA92 10
P.B.Jackson	Coventry	18	I56 3 I57 3 F57 6 F58 3		A58 3
N.C.Jeavons	Moseley	4			A82 4
M.O.Johnson	Leicester	5			IT96 5
A.M.Jorden	Cam U/Blackheath	22	F70 7 I73 5 F73 6 S73 4		
J.M.Kendall-Carpenter	Penzance-Newlyn	3	S52 3		
R.D.Kennedy	Camborne	3	S49 3		
C.P.Kent	Rosslyn Park	4	S77 4		
A.D.King	Wasps	5			AR97/2 5
I.King	Harrogate	5	I54 5		
M.S.Lampkowski	Headingley	4			A76 4
P.J.Larter	Northampton	6			NZ67 3 SA69 3
J.Leonard	Harlequins	5			AR96 5
M.S.Linnett	Moseley	4			FI89 4
R.H.Lloyd	Harlequins	6			NZ67 6
C.W.McFadyean	Moseley	15	S66 3 I67 3 S67 6 W68 3		
M.S.Mapletoft	Gloucester	3			AR97/2 3
R.W.D.Marques	Harlequins	3	I60 3		
A.W.Maxwell	Headingley	4	S76 4		
B.C.Moore	Nottingham	4	I89 4		
A.J.Morley	Bristol	8	S75 4		SA72 4
C.D.Morris	L'pool-St Hlns/Orrell	21	S92 4 I92 4 F92 4		A88 4 SA92 5
A.Neary	Broughton Park	19	S71 3 I73 4 S74 4		NZ73 4 A73 4
B.G.Nelmes	Cardiff	4	S78 4		
S.C.Newman	Oxford University	3	W48 3		
M.J.Novak	Harlequins	3	W70 3		
A.G.B.Old	M'boro/Leicester /Sheffield	98	F72 8 S72 9 I74 17 F74 5 W74 8 I75 5 S76 8 I76 12 F78 6		A73 4 A75 13
C.Oti	Cambridge U/Wasps	32	I88 12		R089 16 AR90 4

POINTS SCORED FOR ENGLAND IN ALL INTERNATIONAL MATCHES (continued):

Name:	Club:	Total Points:	Five Nations:	World Cup:	Other Matches:
J.E.Owen	Coventry	3	W63 3		
C.M.Payne	Harlequins	3	F65 3		
D.G.Perry	Bedford	6	W64 3 W66 3		
M.S.Phillips	Oxford U/Fylde	15	W63 3 F64 3		A58 3 NZ63 3 A63 3
I.Preece	Coventry	3	F49 3		
N.J.Preston	Richmond	4	F80 4		
J.A.Probyn	Wasps	12	I90 4		R089 4 FI91 4
J.V.Pullin	Bristol	3			SA69 3
C.W.Ralston	Richmond	4	I72 4		
J.M.Ranson	Rosslyn Park	6	W64 3		NZ63 3
N.C.Redman	Bath	4		J87 4	
B.W.Redwood	Bristol	3	W68 3		
G.W.Rees	Nottingham	4	I88 4		
M.Regan	Liverpool	3	I54 3		
D.Richards	Leicester	24	I86 8 I89 4	J87 4	A88 4 R089 4
A.G.Ripley	Rosslyn Park	8	W74 4		A73 4
A.B.W.Risman	Manchr U/L'boro' C	8	I59 3 S59 3 I61 2		
G.C.Rittson-Thomas	Oxford University	3	W51 3		
J.Roberts	Old Millhillians	18	W60 6 S60 3 I61 3 S61 3 I62 3		
V.G.Roberts	Penryn	6	F47 3 I50 3		
R.A.Robinson	Bath	4	F89 4		
T.A.K.Rodber	Northampton	15	F94 5		R094 5 IT96 5
D.P.Rogers	Bedford	9	I61 3 I64 3 S64 3		
D.M.Rollitt	Bristol	3	F69 3		
W.M.H.Rose	Cam U/Harlequins	82	I81 6 F81 12 S82 3 I82 11 F87 12 W87 12 S87 17		A82 9
P.A.Rossborough	Coventry	34	W71 3 S74 3 F75 16		NZ273 4 A73 8
D.Rutherford	Percy Park	36	W60 8 I60 2 S60 9 W65 3 F65 6 W66 3 I66 3		NZ267 2
D.Ryan	Wasps	4			AR90 4
C.B.van Ryneveld	Oxford University	9	I49 3 S49 6		
J.L.B.Salmon	Harlequins	4		J87 4	
K.F.Savage	Northampton	3	W67 3		
J.P.Scott	Cardiff	4	I80 4		
I.R.Shackleton	Harrogate	3	I70 3		
R.A.W.Sharp	Oxford U/Wasps	26	I60 3 S60 3 I62 10 W63 7 S63 3		
C.M.A.Sheasby	Wasps	5			IT96 5

POINTS SCORED FOR ENGLAND IN ALL INTERNATIONAL MATCHES (continued):

Name:	Club:	Total Points:	Five Nations:	World Cup:	Other Matches:
K.G.Slmms	Wasps	4		J87 4	
M.G.Skinner	Harlequins	12	W92 4	US91 4	FI89 4
J.M.Sleightholme	Bath	20	I96 5 I97 10		IT96 5
M.A.C.Slemen	Liverpool	32	S77 4 I78 4 S79 4 I80 4 S80 4 S81 4 I82 4 W82 4		
J.V.Smith	Cambridge Univ	12	W50 3 F50 3 S50 6		
S.J.Smith	Sale	8	I80 3 S80 4		
S.T.Smith	Wasps	12	S85 4 W85 4		R085 4
J.S.Spencer	Headingley	6	S70 3 F70 3		
P.J.Squires	Harrogate	24	S73 4 I74 4 S78 4		NZ73 4 A75 4 A75 4
C.B.Stevens	Penzance-Newlyn	8	I75 4		NZ73 4 A75 4
T.R.G.Stimpson	Newcastle	8	W97 5		A 97 3
R.V.Stirling	RAF/Leicester	3	S53 3		
F.D.Sykes	Northampton	3	S55 3		
R.E.Syrett	Wasps	3	S60 3		
R.B.Taylor	Northampton	6	S67 3 F70 3		
M.C.Teague	Gloucester	12	W91 4 I91 4		NZ85 4
P.H.Thompson	Headingley	15	F56 3 S57 3 W58 3 F58 6		
P.H.Thompson	Headingley	15	F56 3 S57 3 W58 3 F58 6		
B.H.Travers	Harlequins	4	S49 4		
V.E.Ubogu	Bath	5	W95 5		
R.Underwood	RAF/Leicester	210	F84 4 I85 4 I88 8 I90 4 F90 4 W90 8 I91 4 F91 4 S92 4 I92 4 F92 4 S93 5 W94 5 W95 10 W96 5	J87 8 IT91 4 US91 8 F91 4 IT95 5 WS95 10 NZ95 10	IM88 4 A88 4 A88 4 FI88 8 A88 8 FI89 20 AR90 12 FI91 4 R094 5 CA94 10 WS95 5 CA94 5
T.Underwood	Leicester	65	S93 5 I95 5 F95 10 I97 10 W97 5	IT95 5 A95 5	SA92 5 R094 10 CA94 5
R.Uren	Waterloo	7	I48 4 S48 3		
R.M.Uttley	Gosforth	8	S77 4		A75 4
M.R.Wade	Cambridge Univ	3	I62 3		
J.M.Webb	Bristol/Bath	296	F88 6 W88 3 I88 5 S89 6 S92 14 I92 22 F92 19 W92 12 F93 11 W93 6 S93 11 I93 3	A87 2 J87 20 US87 18 W87 3 NZ91 9 IT91 24 F91 11 S91 6 A91 6	IM88 13 A88 8 A88 12 FI91 10 A91 11 CA92 6 SA92 13
R.E.Webb	Coventry	6	S67 3 F69 3		
M.P.Weston	Richmond/Durham C	6	F60 3 F68 3		
D.F.White	Northampton	6	W47 3 S51 3		

POINTS SCORED FOR ENGLAND IN ALL INTERNATIONAL MATCHES (continued):

Name:	Club:	Total Points:	Five Nations:	World Cup:	Other Matches:
J.G.Willcox	Oxford U/Harlequins	17	F61 2 S62 3 F63 6 S63 4 I64 2		
J.E.Williams	Old Millhilians	3	S56 3		
D.S.Wilson	Met Police	12	I54 3 S54 6 F54 3		
C.E.Winn	Rosslyn Park	9	S52 3 W54 3		SA52 3
P.J.Winterbottom	Headingley/Quins	13		US87 8	CA92 5
C.R.Woodward	Leicester	16	S81 4 F82 4		AR81 8
J.E.Woodward	Wasps	21	W52 3 S52 3 W53 3 F53 3 S53 3 W54 6		
J.R.C.Young	Harlequins	6	S60 3 W61 3		
M.Young	Gosforth	15	S77 4 S78 4 I78 7		
P.D.Young	Dublin Wanderers	3	S54 3		

LEGEND:

A - Australia   AR - Argentina   CA - Canada   F - France   FI - Fiji   I - Ireland   IT - Italy   J - Japan   NZ - New Zealand   RO - Romania   S - Scotland

SA- South Africa   US - United States   W - Wales   WS - Western Samoa   PR - President's Overseas XV   IM - Ireland (Millennium)   SC - Centenary Match v Scotland, 1971

LEADING TRY SCORERS - ALL MATCHES

Name:	Club:	Total Tries:	Five Nations:	World Cup:	Others:
R.Underwood	RAF/Leicester	49	18	11	20
J.C.Guscott	Bath	18	7	2	9
T.Underwood	Leicester	13	7	2	4
W.D.C.Carling	Harlequins	12	6	4	2
D.J.Duckham	Coventry	10	9		1
C.Oti	Cambridge U/Wasps	8	3		5
M.A.C.Slemen	Liverpool	8	8		
J.Carleton	Orrell	7	7		
M.E.Harrison	Wakefield	7		5	2
P.B.Jackson	Coventry	6	5		1
D.Richards	Leicester	6	3	1	2
J.Roberts	Old Millhillians	6	6		
P.J.Squires	Harrogate	6	3		3
J.E.Woodward	Wasps	6	6		
J.Butterfield	Northampton	5	5		
E.Evans	Sale	5	5		
R.H.Guest	Waterloo	5	5		
C.D.Morris	L'pool St Helens/Orrell	5	3		2
A.Neary	Broughton Park	5	3		2
M.S.Phillips	Oxford U/Fylde	5	2		3
P.H.Thompson	Headingley	5	5		
G.H.Davies	Cambridge U/Wasps	4	2		2
P.J.Dixon	Gosforth	4	4		
A.C.T.Gomarsall	Wasps	4	2		2
C.W.McFadyean	Moseley	4	4		
J.M.Sleightholme	Bath	4	3		1
J.V.Smith	Cambridge University	4	4		
J.M.Webb	Bath	4	3	1	
D.S.Wilson	Met Police	4	4		
C.R.Woodward	Leicester	4	2		2
M.J.Catt	Bath	3			3
B.B.Clarke	Bath/Richmond	3			3
L.B.N.Dallaglio	Wasps	3	1		2
W.A.Dooley	Preston G'hoppers	3	2	1	
P.R.de Glanville	Bath	3	2		1
N.J.Heslop	Orrell	3	1	1	1
R.Hiller	Harlequins	3	2		1

RORY UNDERWOOD

49 Tries in 89 matches.
18 Five Nations; 11 World Cup; 20 others.

JEREMY GUSCOTT

18 Tries in 48 matches.
7 Five Nations; 2 World Cup; 9 others.

TONY UNDERWOOD

13 Tries in 25 matches
7 Five Nations; 2 World Cup; 4 others.

WILL CARLING

12 Tries in 72 matches
6 Five Nations; 4 World Cup; 2 opthers.

ENGLAND'S LEADING TRY SCORERS IN ALL INTERNATIONAL MATCHES..

LEADING TRY SCORERS - ALL MATCHES (continued)

Name:	Club:	Total Tries:	Five Nations:	World Cup:	Others:
I.G.Hunter	Northampton	3	1		2
J.A.Probyn	Wasps	3	1		2
T.A.K.Rodber	Northampton	3	1		2
D.P.Rogers	Bedford	3	3		
C.B.van Ryneveld	Oxford University	3	3		
M.G.Skinner	Harlequins	3	1	1	1
S.T.Smith	Wasps	3	2		1
M.C.Teague	Gloucester	3	2		1
C.E.Winn	Rosslyn Park	3	2		1
P.J.Winterbottom	Headingley/'Quins	3		2	1
A.A.Adebayo	Bath	2			2
C.R.Andrew	Wasps	2			2
J.Barton	Coventry	2	2		
R.C.Bazley	Waterloo	2	2		
W.N.Bennett	London Welsh	2	2		
B.Boobbyer	Oxford U/Rosslyn Pk	2	2		
L.B.Cannell	Oxford U/St Mary's H	2	2		
M.J.Catt	Bath	2			2
B.B.Clarke	Bath	2	1		1
J.P.Hall	Bath	2			2
S.J.Halliday	Bath/Harlequins	2	1		1
W.H.Hare	Leicester	2	2		
R.Higgins	Liverpool	2	2		
R.A.Hill	Saracens	2	2		
R.J.Hill	Bath	2	1		1
R.H.Lloyd	Harlequins	2			2
A.J.Morley	Bristol	2	1		1
D.G.Perry	Bedford	2	2		
J.M.Ranson	Rosslyn Park	2	1		1
G.W.Rees	Nottingham	2	1	1	
A.G.Ripley	Rosslyn Park	2	1		1
V.G.Roberts	Penryn	2	2		
W.M.H.Rose	Cambridge U/'Quins	2	2		
R.A.W.Sharp	Oxford U/Wasps	2	2		
S.J.Smith	Sale	2	2		
J.S.Spencer	Headingley	2	2		
C.B.Stevens	Penzance-Newlyn	2	1		1
R.B.Taylor	Northampton	2	2		
R.M.Uttley	Gosforth	2	1		1
R.E.Webb	Coventry	2	2		
D.F.White	Northampton	2	2		
J.R.C.Young	Harlequins	2	2		
Penalty Tries		6	4	1	1

LEADING TRY SCORERS - FIVE NATIONS MATCHES

Name:	Club:	Total Tries:
R.Underwood	RAF/Leicester	18
D.J.Duckham	Coventry	9
M.A.C.Slemen	Liverpool	8
J.Carleton	Orrell	7
J.C.Guscott	Bath	7
T.Underwood	Leicester	7
W.D.C.Carling	Harlequins	6
J.Roberts	Old Millhillians	6
J.E.Woodward	Wasps	6
J.Butterfield	Northampton	5
E.Evans	Sale	5
R.H.Guest	Waterloo	5
P.B.Jackson	Coventry	5
P.H.Thompson	Headingley	5
P.J.Dixon	Gosforth	4
C.W.McFadyean	Moseley	4
J.V.Smith	Cambridge University	4
D.S.Wilson	Met Police	4
C.D.Morris	L'pool St Helens/Orrell	3
A.Neary	Broughton Park	3
C.Oti	Cambridge U/Wasps	3
D.Richards	Leicester	3
D.P.Rogers	Bedford	3
C.B.van Ryneveld	Oxford University	3
J.M.Sleightholme	Bath	3
P.J.Squires	Harrogate	3
J.M.Webb	Bath	3
J.Barton	Coventry	2
R.C.Bazley	Waterloo	2
W.N.Bennett	London Welsh	2
B.Boobbyer	Oxford U/Rosslyn Pk	2
L.B.Cannell	Oxford U/St Mary's H	2
G.H.Davies	Cambridge U/Wasps	2
W.A.Dooley	Preston G'hoppers	2
P.R.de Glanville	Bath	2
A.C.T.Gomarsall	Wasps	2
W.H.Hare	Leicester	2
R.Higgins	Liverpool	2
R.A.Hill	Saracens	2
R.Hiller	Harlequins	2

Name:	Club:	Total Tries:
D.G.Perry	Bedford	2
M.S.Phillips	Oxford U/Fylde	2
V.G.Roberts	Penryn	2
W.M.H.Rose	Cambridge U/'Quins	2
R.A.W.Sharp	Oxford U/Wasps	2
S.J.Smith	Sale	2
S.T.Smith	Wasps	2
J.S.Spencer	Headingley	2
R.B.Taylor	Northampton	2
M.C.Teague	Gloucester	2
R.E.Webb	Coventry	2
D.F.White	Northampton	2
C.E.Winn	Rosslyn Park	2
C.R.Woodward	Leicester	2
J.R.C.Young	Harlequins	2
Penalty Tries		4

LEADING TRY SCORERS - WORLD CUP MATCHES

Name:	Club:	Total Tries:
R.Underwood	RAF/Leicester	11
M.E.Harrison	Wakefield	5
W.D.C.Carling	Harlequins	4
J.C.Guscott	Bath	2
T.Underwood	Leicester	2
P.J.Winterbottom	Headingley/'Quins	2
N.A.Back	Leicester	1
W.A.Dooley	Preston G'hoppers	1
N.J.Heslop	Orrell	1
N.C.Redman	Bath	1
G.W.Rees	Nottingham	1
D.Richards	Leicester	1
J.L.B.Salmon	Harlequins	1
K.G.Simms	Wasps	1
M.G.Skinner	Harlequins	1
J.M.Webb	Bath	1
Penalty Tries		1

TRIES SCORED FOR ENGLAND IN ALL INTERNATIONAL MATCHES:

Name:	Club:	Total Tries:	Five Nations:	World Cup:	Other Matches:
P.J.Ackford	Harlequins	1			FI89 1
A.A.Adebayo	Bath	2			AR97/1 2
S.J.Adkins	Coventry	1	S53 1		
A.E.Agar	Harlequins	1	W52 1		
C.R.Andrew	Wasps	2			FI91 1 SA94 1
R.C.Ashby	Wasps	1			A67 1
A.Ashcroft	Waterloo	1	I58 1		
N.A.Back	Leicester	1		WS95 1	
M.D.Bailey	Wasps	1			FI89 1
B.Barley	Wakefield	1			FI88 1
J.Barton	Coventry	2	W67 2		
R.C.Bazley	Waterloo	2	S53 2		
I.D.S.Beer	Harlequins	1	S55 1		
M.C.Beese	Liverpool	1	F72 1		
N.O.Bennett	St Mary's Hospital	1	S47 1		
W.N.Bennett	London Welsh	2	I79 1 F79 1		
J.Bentley	Sale	1			A88 1
B.Boobbyer	Oxford U/Rosslyn Pk	2	F51 1 I52 1		
K.P.P.Bracken	Bristol	1			CA94 1
J.Butterfield	Northampton	5	F53 1 S53 1 I54 1 I55 1 I56 1		
L.B.Cannell	Oxford U/St Mary's H	2	F5 1 W53 1		
J.Carleton	Orrell	7	F49 1 S80 3 F82 1 W82 1 W83 1		
W.D.C.Carling	Harlequins	12	F89 1 F90 1 W90 1 W92 1 I95 1	US91 1 F 91- 1 NZ95- 2 S97 1	SA92 1 CA94 2 R094 1
M.J.Catt	Bath	3			CA94 2 AR97/1 1
B.B.Clarke	Bath	3	I95 1		SA94 1 AR97/1 1
S.J.S.Clarke	Cambridge University	1			A63 1
M.J.Colclough	Wasps	1			NZ83 1
M.J.Cooper	Moseley	1	I77 1		
B.J.Corless	Coventry	1			A76 1
F.E.Cotton	Coventry	1	S74 1		
M.J.Coulman	Moseley	1	S68 1		
L.B.N.Dallaglio	Wasps	3	F97 1		WS95 1 IT96 1

TRIES SCORED FOR ENGLAND IN ALL INTERNATIONAL MATCHES (continued):

Name:	Club:	Total Tries:	Five Nations:	World Cup:	Other Matches:
G.H.Davies	Cambridge U/Wasps	4	S81 1, I86 1		AR81 1, AR81 1
W.P.C.Davies	Harlequins	1	S57 1		
A.J.Diprose	Saracens	1			AR97/1 1
P.J.Dixon	Gosforth	4	S73 2, F76 1, I78 1		
P.W.Dodge	Leicester	1	I81 1		
W.A.Dooley	Preston G'hoppers	3	F86 1, W92 1	US87 1	
N.J.Drake-Lee	Cambridge University	1	S63 1		
D.J.Duckham	Coventry	10	I69 1, S69 2, W70 1, F73 2, F74 1, W74 1, F75 1		A76 1
D.W.Egerton	Bath	1	I90 1		
E.Evans	Sale	5	S52 1, F53 1, I53 1, I56 1, F57 1		
G.W.Evans	Coventry	1	S73 1		
K.J.Fielding	Loughboro' Coll	1	F69 1		
P.R.de Glanville	Bath	3	S97 1, W97 1		SA95 1
H.O.Godwin	Coventry	1			A63 1
A.C.T.Gomarsall	Wasps	4	S97 1, I97 1		IT96 2, AR97/1 1
N.J.J.Greenstock	Wasps	1			AR97/1 1
J.R.H.Greenwood	Waterloo	1	I66 1		
D.J.Grewcock	Gloucester	1			AR97/2 1
R.H.Guest	Waterloo	5	S47 1, F47 1, I48 2, S49 1		
J.C.Guscott	Bath	18	I90 1, F90 1, S90 1, I92 1, S93 1, F95 1, W96 1	IT91 2	R089 3, A91 1, FI89 1, CA92 1, AR90 1, R90 2
J.P.Hall	Bath	2	I92 1		NZ285 1
S.J.Halliday	Bath/Harlequins	2			A88 1, A92 1
A.W.Hancock	Northampton	1	S65 1		
R.C.Hannaford	Bristol	1	W71 1		
R.M.Harding	Bristol	1			IM88 1
V.S.J.Harding	Cambridge University	1	F61 1		
W.H.Hare	Leicester	2	W81 1, F84 1		
M.E.Harrison	Wakefield	7		A87 1, J87 3, US87 1	NZ285 1
G.W.D.Hastings	Gloucester	1	I55 1		
A.P.Henderson	Cambridge University	1	S47 1		
N.J.Heslop	Orrell	3	S91 1	US91 1	AR90 1
R.Higgins	Liverpool	2	F55 1, S57 1		
R.A.Hill	Saracens	2	I97 1, W97 1		
R.J.Hill	Bath	2	W90 1		AR90 1
R.Hiller	Harlequins	3	F71 1, S71 1		PR71 1

TRIES SCORED FOR ENGLAND IN ALL INTERNATIONAL MATCHES (continued):

Name:	Club:	Total Tries:	Five Nations:	World Cup:	Other Matches:
S.D.Hodgkinson	Nottingham	1			AR90 1
C.B.Holmes	Manchester	1	S47 1		
N.E.Horton	Moseley	1	W75 1		
G.R.d'A.Hosking	Devonport Services	1	S49 1		
I.G.Hunter	Northampton	3	F93 1		CA92 2
P.B.Jackson	Coventry	6	I56 1 I57 1 F57 2 F58 1		A58 1
N.C.Jeavons	Moseley	1			A82 1
M.O.Johnson	Leicester	1			IT96 1
J.M.Kendall-Carpent	Penzance-Newlyn	1	S52 1		
R.D.Kennedy	Camborne	1	S49 1		
C.P.Kent	Rosslyn Park	1	S77 1		
A.D.King	Wasps	1			AR97/2 1
M.S.Lampkowski	Headingley	1			A76 1
P.J.Larter	Northampton	1			SA69 1
J.Leonard	Harlequins	1			AR96 1
M.S.Linnett	Moseley	1			FI89 1
R.H.Lloyd	Harlequins	2			NZ67 2
C.W.McFadyean	Moseley	4	I67 1 S67 2 W68 1		
R.W.D.Marques	Harlequins	1	I60 1		
A.W.Maxwell	Headingley	1	S76 1		
B.C.Moore	Nottingham	1	I89 1		
A.J.Morley	Bristol	2	S75 1		SA72 1
C.D.Morris	L'pool St Helens/Orrell	5	S92 1 I92 1 F92 1		A88 1 SA92 1
A.Neary	Broughton Park	5	S71 1 I73 1 S74 1		NZ73 1 A73 1
B.G.Nelmes	Cardiff	1	S78 1		
M.J.Novak	Harlequins	1	W70 1		
A.G.B.Old	Leicester	1			A73 1
C.Oti	Cambridge U/Wasps	8	I88 3		RO89 4 AR90 1
J.E.Owen	Coventry	1	W63 1		
C.M.Payne	Harlequins	1	F65 1		
D.G.Perry	Bedford	2	W64 1 W66 1		
M.S.Phillips	Oxford U/Fylde	5	W63 1 F64 1		A58 1 NZ63 1 A63 1
N.J.Preston	Richmond	1	F80 1		
J.A.Probyn	Wasps	3	I90 1		RO89 1 FI91 1
J.V.Pullin	Bristol	1			SA69 1
C.W.Raiston	Richmond	1	I72 1		

TRIES SCORED FOR ENGLAND IN ALL INTERNATIONAL MATCHES (continued):

Name:	Club:	Total Tries:	Five Nations:	World Cup:	Other Matches:
J.M.Ranson	Rosslyn Park	2	W64 1		NZ63 1
N.C.Redman	Bath	1	W68 1	J87 1	
B.W.Redwood	Bristol	1	I88 1		
G.W.Rees	Nottingham	2	I54 1	J87 1	
M.Regan	Liverpool	1	I54 1		
D.Richards	Leicester	6	I86 2 I89 1	J87 1	A88 1 R089 1
A.G.Ripley	Rosslyn Park	2	W74 1		A73 1
G.C.Rittson-Thomas	Oxford University	1	W51 1		
J.Roberts	Old Millhilians	6	W60 2 S60 1 I61 1 S61 1 I62 1		
V.G.Roberts	Penryn	2	F47 1 I50 1		
R.A.Robinson	Bath	1	F89 1		
T.A.K.Rodber	Northampton	3	W94 1		R094 1 IT96 1
D.P.Rogers	Bedford	3	I61 1 I64 1 S64 1		
D.M.Rollitt	Bristol	1	F69 1		
W.M.H.Rose	Cambridge U/Quins	2	I81 1 S87 1		
P.A.Rossborough	Coventry	1	F75 1		
D.Ryan	Wasps	1			AR90 1
C.B.van Ryneveld	Oxford University	3	I49 1 S49 2		
J.L.B.Salmon	Harlequins	1		J87 1	
K.F.Savage	Northampton	1	W67 1		
J.P.Scott	Cardiff	1	I80 1		
I.R.Shackleton	Harrogate	1	I70 1		
R.A.W.Sharp	Oxford U/Wasps	2	I62 1 S63 1		
C.M.A.Sheasby	Wasps	1			IT96 1
K.G.Simms	Wasps	3		J87 1	
M.G.Skinner	Harlequins	3	W92 1	US91 1	FI89 1
M.A.C.Slemen	Liverpool	7	S77 1 I78 1 I80 1 S80 1 S81 1 I82 1		
J.M.Sleightholme	Bath	4	I96 1 I97 2		IT96 1
S.J.Smith	Sale	2	I80 1 S80 1		
S.T.Smith	Wasps	3	S85 1 W85 1		R085 1
J.V.Smith	Cambridge University	4	W50 1 F50 1 S50 2		
J.S.Spencer	Headingley	2	S70 1 F70 1		
P.J.Squires	Harrogate	6	S73 1 I74 1 S78 1		NZ73 1 A75 1 A75 1
C.B.Stevens	Penzance-Newlyn	2	I75 1		NZ73 1
T.R.G.Stimpson	Newcastle	1	W97 1		
R.V.Stirling	RAF/Leicester	1	S53 1		

TRIES SCORED FOR ENGLAND IN ALL INTERNATIONAL MATCHES (continued):

Name:	Club:	Total Tries:	Five Nations:	World Cup:	Other Matches:
F.D.Sykes	Northampton	1	S55 1		
R.E.Syrett	Wasps	1	S60 1		
R.B.Taylor	Northampton	2	S67 1, F70 1		
M.C.Teague	Gloucester	3	W91 1, I91 1		NZ85 1
P.H.Thompson	Headingley	5	F56 1, S57 1, W58 1, F58 2		
V.E.Ubogu	Bath	1	W95 1		
R.Underwood	RAF/Leicester	49	F84 1, I85 1, I88 2, I90 1, F90 1, W90 2, I91 1, F91 1, S92 1, I92 1, F92 1, S93 1, W94 1, W95 2, W96 1	J87 2, IT91 1, US91- 2, F91 1, IT95 1, S95- 2, NZ95 2	IM88 1, A88 1, A88 1, FI88 2, A88 2, FI89 5, AR90 3, FI91 1, O94 1, CA94 2, WS95 1, SA92 1, RO94 2, A94 1
T.Underwood	Leicester	13	S93 1, I95 1, F95 2, I97 2, W97 1	IT95 1, A95 1	SA92 1, A75 1
R.M.Uttley	Gosforth	2	S77 1, S77 1		
M.R.Wade	Cambridge University	1	I62 1		
J.M.Webb	Bath	4	I92 2, F92 1	IT91 1	
R.E.Webb	Coventry	2	S67 1, F69 1		
M.P.Weston	Richmond	1	F60 1		
D.F.White	Northampton	2	W47 1, S51 1		
J.E.Williams	Old Millhilians	1	S56 1		
D.S.Wilson	Met Police	4	I54 1, S54 2, F54 1		
C.E.Winn	Rosslyn Park	3	S52 1, W54 1		SA52 1
P.J.Winterbottom	Headingley/Quins	3		US87 2	CA92 1
C.R.Woodward	Leicester	4	S81 1, F82 1		AR91 2
J.E.Woodward	Wasps	6	W52 1, S52 1, F53 1, S53 1, W54 2		
J.R.C.Young	Harlequins	2	S60 1, W61 1		
M.Young	Gosforth	1	S77 1		
P.D.Young	Dublin Wanderers	1	S54 1		
Penalty Tries		6	I86 1, S87 1, F92 1, S97 1	WS95 1	RO94 1
Total tries scored since 1947:		434	271	37	126

TRIES SCORED FOR ENGLAND IN ALL INTERNATIONAL MATCHES (continued):

LEGEND:

A - Australia   AR - Argentina   CA - Canada   F - France   FI - Fiji   I - Ireland   IT - Italy   J - Japan   NZ - New Zealand   RO - Romania   S - Scotland

SA - South Africa   US - United States   W - Wales   WS - Western Samoa   PR - President's Overseas XV   IM - Ireland (Millennium)   SC - Centenary Match v Scotland, 1971

LEADING PENALTY GOAL SCORERS - ALL MATCHES

Name:	Club:	Total Penalties	Five Nations:	World Cup	Others
C.R.Andrew	Camb U/Nott'm/Wasps	86	44	20	22
W.H.Hare	Leicester	67	50		17
J.M.Webb	Bristol/Bath	66	28	21	17
S.D.Hodgkinson	Nottingham	43	28	3	12
P.J.Grayson	Northampton	35	30		5
R.Hiller	Harlequins	33	29		4
A.G.B.Old	M'boro/Leicester	23	20		3
W.M.H.Rose	Cambridge U/'Quins	22	19		3
J.E.B.Callard	Bath	21	9	5	7
R.W.Hosen	Northampton	17	12		5
A.J.Hignell	Cambridge U/Bristol	14	11		3
M.J.Catt	Bath	12	2		10
D.Rutherford	Percy Park	8	8		
S.Barnes	Bristol/Bath	7	2		5
P.A.Rossborough	Coventry	7	5		2
S.A.Doble	Moseley	6	2		4
D.F.Allison	Coventry	5	5		
W.N.Bennett	Bedford/Lndn Welsh	5	5		
J.D.Currie	Oxford University	4	4		
N.M.Hall	Richmond	4	4		
A.M.Jorden	Camb U/Blackheath	4	4		
P.W.Dodge	Leicester	3	3		
D.St G.Hazell	Leicester	3	3		
J.G.G.Hetherington	Northampton	3	2		1
J.G.Willcox	Oxford University	3	3		
P.E.Butler	Gloucester	2	1		1
R.Challis	Bristol	2	2		
G.W.D.Hastings	Gloucester	2	2		
A.B.W.Risman	Manchester Univ	2	2		

ROB ANDREW

86 Penalty Goals
44 Five Nations; 20 World Cup; 22 others.

"DUSTY" HARE

67 Penalty Goals
50 Five Nations; 17 others.

JONATHAN WEBB

66 Penalty Goals
28 Five Nations; 21 World Cup; 17 others.

SIMON HODGKINSON

43 Penalty Goals
28 Five Nations; 3 World Cup; 12 others.

ENGLAND'S MOST SUCCESSFUL PENALTY GOAL EXPONENTS.

LEADING PENALTY GOAL SCORERS

- FIVE NATIONS MATCHES

Name:	Club:	Total Penalties
W.H.Hare	Leicester	50
C.R.Andrew	Camb U/Nott'm/Wasps	44
P.J.Grayson	Northampton	30
R.Hiller	Harlequins	29
J.M.Webb	Bristol/Bath	28
S.D.Hodgkinson	Nottingham	28
A.G.B.Old	M'boro/Leicester	20
W.M.H.Rose	Cambridge U/'Quins	19
R.W.Hosen	Northampton	12
A.J.Hignell	Cambridge U/Bristol	11
J.E.B.Callard	Bath	9
D.Rutherford	Percy Park	8
P.A.Rossborough	Coventry	5
D.F.Allison	Coventry	5
W.N.Bennett	Bedford/Lndn Welsh	5
J.D.Currie	Oxford University	4
N.M.Hall	Richmond	4
A.M.Jorden	Camb U/Blackheath	4
P.W.Dodge	Leicester	3
D.St G.Hazell	Leicester	3
J.G.Willcox	Oxford University	3
M.J.Catt	Bath	2
S.Barnes	Bristol/Bath	2
S.A.Doble	Moseley	2
J.G.G.Hetherington	Northampton	2
R.Challis	Bristol	2
G.W.D.Hastings	Gloucester	2
A.B.W.Risman	Manchester Univ	2
P.E.Butler	Gloucester	1

LEADING PENALTY GOAL SCORERS

- WORLD CUP MATCHES

Name:	Club:	Total Penalties
J.M.Webb	Bristol/Bath	21
C.R.Andrew	Camb U/Nott'm/Wasps	20
J.E.B.Callard	Bath	5
S.D.Hodgkinson	Nottingham	3

PENALTY GOALS SCORED FOR ENGLAND IN ALL INTERNATIONAL MATCHES:

Name:	Club:	Total Penalties	Five Nations:	World Cup:	Other Matches:
D.F.Allison	Coventry	5	W56 1, I56 1, F56 2, W57 1		
C.R.Andrew	Camb U/Nott'm/Wasp	86	F85 1, S85 2, I85 2, W85 2, W86 6, S86 2, I86 1, S89 2, I89 2, F89 1, W89 2, F94 5, W94 1, I95 1, F95 4, W95 2, S95 7	AR95 6, NZ95 1, IT95 5, F95 3, A95 5	R085 4, R094 4, SA94 5, CA94 6, SA94 3
S.Barnes	Bristol/Bath	7	F86 2		A84 1, NZ85 1, Fl88 3
W.N.Bennett	Bedford/Lndn Welsh	5	S75 1, S79 1, I79 1, F79 1, W79 1		
P.E.Butler	Gloucester	2	F76 1		A75 1
J.E.B.Callard	Bath	21	S94 5, I94 4	WS95 5	NZ93 4, SA95 3
M.J.Catt	Bath	12	W97 2		AR96 5, IT96 3, AR97/1 2
R.Challis	Bristol	2	I57 1, S57 1		
J.D.Currie	Oxford University	4	I56 2, S56 2		
S.A.Doble	Moseley	6	W73 2		SA72 4
P.W.Dodge	Leicester	3	S78 1, S82 2		
P.J.Grayson	Northampton	35	F96 2, W96 3, S96 6, I96 6, S97 5, I97 4, F97 4		WS95 5
N.M.Hall	Richmond	4	F52 2, I53 2		
W.H.Hare	Leicester	67	I80 2, F80 1, W80 3, S80 2, W81 5, S81 3, F82 5, F83 4, W83 2, S83 3, I83 5, W82 3, I84 3, S84 2, F84 2, W84 5		NZ78 1, AR81 2, SA84 3, AR81 1, NZ79 3, NZ83 3, SA84 4
G.W.D.Hastings	Gloucester	2	F58 1, S58 1		
D.St G.Hazell	Leicester	3	F55 2, S55 1		
J.G.G.Hetherington	Northampton	3	F59 1, I58 1		A58 1
A.J.Hignell	Cambridge U/Bristol	14	W76 3, S77 2, F77 1, W77 3, W78 2		A76 3
R.Hiller	Harlequins	33	W68 1, I68 2, W70 1, I71 3, W71 3, S71 3, F71 3, W72 1, I72 2, I69 4, F69 3, W69 3		SA69 1, SC71 1, PR71 2
S.D.Hodgkinson	Nottingham	43	W90 4, S90 1, I90 1, F90 4, W91 7, S91 5, I91 2, F91 4	US91 3	R089 1, AR90 1, Fl89 2, AR90 3, AR90 5
M.B.Hofmyer	Oxford University	1	S50 1		
J.P.Horrocks-Taylor	Leicester	1	S61 1		
R.W.Hosen	Northampton	17	F64 1, S64 1, I67 1, F67 3, S67 2, W67 4		NZ63 2, NZ63 1, A67 2

PENALTY GOALS SCORED FOR ENGLAND IN ALL INTERNATIONAL MATCHES: (continued)

Name:	Club:	Total Penalties	Five Nations:	World Cup:	Other Matches:
A.M.Jorden	Camb U/Blackheath	4	F70 1, I73 1, F73 2		
I.King	Harrogate	1	I54 1		NZ67 1
P.J.Larter	Northampton	1			AR97/2 1
M.S.Mapletoft	Gloucester	1			
S.C.Newman	Oxford University	1	W48 1		
A.G.B.Old	Mboro/Leicester	23	F72 2, I76 4, S72 3, S74 1, I74 5, F74 1, W74 2, S76 2		A75 3
A.B.W.Risman	Manchester Univ	2	I59 1, S59 1		
W.M.H.Rose	Cambridge U/'Quins	22	F81 4, S82 1, I82 3, F87 4, W87 4, S87 3		A82 3
P.A.Rossborough	Coventry	7	W71 1, F75 4		A73 2
D.Rutherford	Percy Park	8	W60 2, S60 1, W65 1, F65 2, W66 1, I66 1		
R.A.W.Sharp	Oxford University	1	I62 1		
T.R.G.Stimpson	Newcastle	1			A 97 1
R.Uren	Waterloo	1	S48 1		
J.M.Webb	Bristol/Bath	66	F88 2, W88 1, S88 2, I88 1, S89 2, S92 4, I92 2, F92 3, W92 2, F93 3, W93 2, S93 3, I93 1	J87 2, US87 4, W87 1, NZ291 3, IT91 4, F91 3, S91 2, A91 2	IM88 3, A88 2, A88 2, FI91 2, A91 3, CA92 2, SA92 3
J.G.Willcox	Oxford University	3	S62 1, F63 2		
J.E.Woodward	Wasps	1	W53 1		
M.Young	Gosforth	1	I78 1		
Total Penalty Goals scored since 1947:		**520**	**347**	**49**	**124**

A - Australia   AR - Argentina   CA - Canada   F - France   FI - Fiji   I - Ireland   IT - Italy   J - Japan   NZ - New Zealand   RO - Romania

S - Scotland   SA - South Africa   US - United States   W - Wales   WS - W Samoa   PR - President's Overseas XV   IM - Ireland (Millennium)   SC - Centenary Match v Scotland, 1971

DROP GOALS SCORED FOR ENGLAND IN ALL INTERNATIONAL MATCHES:

Name:	Club:	Drop Goals:	Five Nations:	World Cup:	Other Matches:
A.E.Agar	Harlequins	1	S52 1		
C.R.Andrew	Cam U/Nott'm/Wasps	21	F85 1, W85 1, W86 1, F87 1, S88 1, W89 1, F91 1, F94 1, S95 1	NZ91 1, A95 1, S91 1, AR95 2	R085 2, NZ93 1, R089 1, SA94 1, FI91 2
S.Barnes	Bristol	1			NZ85 1
M.J.Catt	Bath	2		WS95 1	AR97/1 1
A.R.Cowman	Loughbro' C/Coventry	2	W73 1		SC71 1
L.Cusworth	Leicester	4	F83 1, W83 1, I84 1, F88 1		
G.W.Evans	Coventry	1	F74 1		
J.F.Finlan	Moseley	3	F67 1, S67 1, I68 1		
P.J.Grayson	Northampton	4	F96 2, I96 1, F97 1		
J.C.Guscott	Bath	2	S92 1, W93 1		
N.M.Hall	St Mary's H/Huddrsfld	3	W47 1, S47 1, W49 1		
W.H.Hare	Leicester	1			NZ78 1
R.Hiller	Harlequins	2	I70 2		
J.P.Horton	Bath	4	F80 2, S83 1		SA84 1
C.W.McFadyean	Moseley	1	S66 1		
A.G.Old	Midddlesbro'/Sheffield	3	I75 1, F78 2		
I.Preece	Coventry	1	F49 1		
P.A.Rossborough	Coventry	1	S74 1		
R.A.W.Sharp	Oxford U/Wasps	3	I60 1, S60 1, W63 1		
M.P.Weston	Durham City	1	F68 1		
Total Drop Goals scored		60	43	6	11

LEGEND:

A - Australia   AR - Argentina   CA - Canada   F - France   FI - Fiji   I - Ireland   IT - Italy   J - Japan   NZ - New Zealand   RO - Romania   S - Scotland

SA - South Africa   US - United States   W - Wales   WS - Western Samoa   PR - President's Overseas XV   IM - Ireland (Millennium)   SC - Centenary Match v Scotland, 1971

TRY CONVERSIONS SCORED FOR ENGLAND IN ALL INTERNATIONAL MATCHES:

Name:	Club:	Total Conver'ns	Five Nations:	World Cup:	Other Matches:
C.R.Andrew	Camb U/Nott'm /Wasps	33	W85 1, W95 1, I 86 3, I 88- 3, I 89- 1, W 9 1, I 95- 1, F 95- 2	IT95- 1, A 95- 1, NZ95- 3	FI89 1, CA94 6, SA94 2, RO94 6
S.Barnes	Bristol/Bath	5			NZ285 1, NZ285 2, FI88 2
P.E.Butler	Gloucester	2	F76 1		A75 1
J.E.B.Callard	Bath	3		WS95 3	
M.J.Catt	Bath	14	W97 4		IT95 5, AR97/1 5
R.Challis	Bristol	2	S57 2		
J.D.Currie	Oxford University	2	I 56 1, S56 1		
S.A.Doble	Moseley	1			SA72 1
P.W.Dodge	Leicester	1			A82 1
N.Gibbs	Harlequins	2	S54 2		
A.Gray	Otley	1	W47 1		
P.J.Grayson	Northampton	8	W96 1, I 96 1, S97 3, I 97 2		WS95 1
N.M.Hall	Richmond	8	S52 2, W53 1, F53 1, S53 4		
W.H.Hare	Leicester	14	I 80 3, S80 2, S81 1, F82 2, F84 2		AR81 2, AR81 1, NZ83 1
G.W.D.Hastings	Gloucester	1	F58 1		
J.Heaton	Waterloo	4	S47 4		
E.N.Hewitt	Coventry	1	W51 1		
A.J.Hignell	Cambridge U/Bristol	3	S77 2		A76 1
R.Hiller	Harlequins	12	W68 1, I 72 1, S68 1, F69 2, S69 1, W70 2, S70 1, F71 1		SA69 1, PR71 1
S.D.Hodgkinson	Nottingham	35	I 90 2, F90 1, W90 3, S91 1, I 91 1, F91 1	US91 4	R089 8, AR90 1, FI89 5, AR90 7, AR90 1
M.B.Hofmyer	Oxford University	2	W50 1, S50 1		
W.B.Holmes	Cambridge Univ	2	I 49 1, F49 1		
W.G.Hook	Gloucester	1	S51 1		
R.W.Hosen	Northampton	6	I 67 1, S67 3		NZ63 1, A67 1
A.M.Jorden	Camb U/Blackheath	5	F70 2, I 73 1, S73 2		

TRY CONVERSIONS SCORED FOR ENGLAND IN ALL INTERNATIONAL MATCHES: (continued)

Name:	Club:	Total Conver'ns	Five Nations:	World Cup:	Other Matches:
I.King	Harrogate	1	I 54 1		
A.G.B.Old	Middlesbro'/Leicester	8	F72 1 I74 1 F74 1 W74 1 I75 1 S76 1		A75 2
A.B.W.Risman	Loughboro' Coll	1	I 61 1		
W.M.H.Rose	Cambridge U/'Quins	4	I 81 1 I 82 1 S87 2		
P.A.Rossborough	Coventry	3			NZ73 2 A73 1
D.Rutherford	Percy Park	6	W60 1 I 60 1 S60 3		NZ67 1
R.A.W.Sharp	Oxford U/Wasps	4	I 62 2 W63 2		
B.H.Travers	Harlequins	2	S49 2		
R.Uren	Waterloo	2	I 48 2		
J.M.Webb	Bristol/Bath	41	I 88 1 S92 1 I 92 4 F92 3 W92 3 F93 1 S93 1	A87 1 J87 7 US87 3 IT91 4 F91 1	IM88 2 A88 1 A88 3 FI91 2 A91 1 SA92 2
J.G.Willcox	Oxford U/Harlequins	4	F61 1 S63 2 I 64 1		
M.Young	Gosforth	4	S78 2 I 78 2		
Total Conversions made since 1947:		**248**	**138**	**28**	**77**

LEGEND:

A - Australia   AR - Argentina   CA - Canada   F - France   FI - Fiji   I - Ireland   IT - Italy   J - Japan   NZ - New Zealand   RO - Romania   S - Scotland

SA - South Africa   US - United States   W - Wales   WS - Western Samoa   PR - President's Overseas XV   IM - Ireland (Millennium)   SC - Centenary Match v Scotland, 1971

JEREMY GUSCOTT

Jeremy Guscott scored three tries on his International debut against Romania
in Bucharest on May 13th 1989.
This feat has not been accomplished by any other England player in the last fifty years.

ENGLAND PLAYERS WHO SCORED A TRY IN THEIR FIRST INTERNATIONAL MATCH:

Name:	Club:	Match details:		

THREE TRIES ON DEBUT:

| **J.C.Guscott** | Bath | v Romania | at Bucharest | May 13th 1989 |

TWO TRIES ON DEBUT:

J.Roberts	Old Millhillians	v Wales	at Twickenham	January 16th 1960
R.H.Lloyd	Harlequins	v New Zealand	at Twickenham	November 4th 1967
D.Richards	Leicester	v Ireland	at Twickenham	March 1st 1986
I.G.Hunter	Northampton	v Canada	at Wembley Stadium	October 17th 1992
A.C.T.Gomarsall	Wasps	v Italy	at Twickenham	November 23rd 1996

TRY ON FIRST and ONLY INTERNATIONAL MATCH:

| **M.S.Linnett** | Moseley | v Fiji | at Twickenham | November 4th 1989 |

TRY ON DEBUT:

D.F.White	Northampton	v Wales	at Cardiff Arms Park	January 18th 1947
C.B.Holmes	Manchester	v Scotland	at Twickenham	March 15th 1947
V.G.Roberts	Penryn	v France	at Twickenham	April 19th 1947
J.V.Smith	Cambridge University	v Wales	at Twickenham	January 21st 1950
G.C.Rittson-Thomas	Oxford University	v Wales	at Swansea	January 20th 1951
C.E.Winn	Rosslyn Park	v South Africa	at Twickenham	January 5th 1952
J.Butterfield	Northampton	v France	at Twickenham	February 28th 1953
M.S.Phillips	Oxford University	v Australia	at Twickenham	February 1st 1958
D.P.Rogers	Bedford	v Ireland	at Lansdowne Road	February 11th 1961
V.S.J.Harding	Cambridge University	v France	at Twickenham	February 25th 1961

ENGLAND PLAYERS WHO SCORED A TRY IN THEIR FIRST INTERNATIONAL MATCH:
(continued)

Name:	Club:	Match details:		
J.E.Owen	Coventry	v Wales	at Cardiff Arms Park	January 19th 1963
J.M.Ranson	Rosslyn Park	v New Zealand	at Auckland	May 25th 1963
J.R.H.Greenwood	Waterloo	v Ireland	at Twickenham	February 12th 1966
R.E.Webb	Coventry	v Scotland	at Twickenham	March 18th 1967
B.W.Redwood	Bristol	v Wales	at Twickenham	January 20th 1968
D.J.Duckham	Coventry	v Ireland	at Lansdowne Road	February 8th 1969
M.J.Novak	Harlequins	v Wales	at Twickenham	February 28th 1970
R.C.Hannaford	Bristol	v Wales	at Cardiff Arms Park	January 16th 1971
A.J.Morley	Bristol	v South Africa	at Johannesburg	June 3rd 1972
B.J.Corless	Coventry	v Australia	at Twickenham	January 3rd 1976
M.S.Lampowski	Headingley	v Australia	at Twickenham	January 3rd 1976
M.Young	Gosforth	v Scotland	at Twickenham	January 15th 1977
C.P.Kent	Rosslyn Park	v Scotland	at Twickenham	January 15th 1977
G.H.Davies	Cambridge University	v Scotland	at Twickenham	February 21st 1981
W.M.H.Rose	Cambridge University	v Ireland	at Lansdowne Road	March 7th 1981
S.T.Smith	Wasps	v Romania	at Twickenham	January 5th 1955
M.E.Harrison	Wakefield	v New Zealand	at Christchurch	June 1st 1985
C.D.Morris	Liverpool St Helen's	v Australia	at Twickenham	November 5th 1988
M.S.Linnett	Moseley	v Fiji	at Twickenham	November 4th 1989
D.Ryan	Wasps	v Argentina	at Buenos Aires	July 28th 1990
C.M.A.Sheasby	Wasps	v Italy	at Twickenham	November 23rd 1996
N.J.J.Greenstock	Wasps	v Argentina	at Buenos Aires	May 30th 1997
A.J.Diprose	Saracens	v Argentina	at Buenos Aires	May 30th 1997
A.D.King	Wasps	v Argentina	at Buenos Aires	June 6th 1997
D.J.Grewcock	Coventry	v Argentina	at Buenos Aires	June 6th 1997

ENGLAND PLAYERS WHO HAVE SCORED ALL THE TEAM'S POINTS
IN AN INTERNATIONAL MATCH
(when more than one score has occured)

Name:	Club:	Points:		Match details:			
C.R.Andrew	Wasps	24	(dg,7pg)	v Scotland		at Twickenham	March 18th 1995
C.R.Andrew	Wasps	24	(2dg, 6pg)	v Argentina	WC)	at Durban	May 27th 1995
C.R.Andrew	Nottingham	21	(dg, 6pg)	v Wales		at Twickenham	January 18th 1986
W.H.Hare	Leicester	19	(t, 5pg)	v Wales		at Cardiff Arms Park	January 17th 1981
C.R.Andrew	Wasps	18	(dg, 5pg)	v France		at Parc des Princes	March 5th 1994
P.J.Grayson	Northampton	18	(6pg)	v Scotland		at Murrayfield	March 2nd 1996
W.H.Hare	Leicester	15	(5pg)	v Ireland		at Lansdowne Road	March 19th 1983
W.H.Hare	Leicester	15	(5pg)	v Wales		at Twickenham	March 17th 1984
J.E.B.Callard	Bath	15	(5pg)	v Scotland		at Murrayfield	February 5th 1994
R.Hiller	Harlequins	14	(t,c,3pg)	v France		at Twickenham	February 27th 1971
A.G.B.Old	Sheffield	12	(4pg)	v Ireland		at Twickenham	March 6th 1976
W.H.M.Rose	Camdridge Univ	12	(4pg)	v France		at Twickenham	March 21st 1981
W.H.M.Rose	Harlequins	12	(4pg)	v Wales		at Cardiff Arms Park	March 7th 1987
J.E.B.Callard	Bath	12	(4pg)	v Ireland		at Twickenham	February 19th 1994
P.J.Grayson	Northampton	12	(2dg, 2pg)	v France		at Parc des Princes	January 20th 1996
R.Hiller	Harlequins	11	(t,c,2pg)	v President's XV		at Twickenham	April 17th 1971
R.Hiller	Harlequins	9	(3pg)	v Wales		at Cardiff Arms Park	April 12th 1969
R.Hiller	Harlequins	9	(3pg)	v Ireland		at Lansdowne Road	February 13th 1971
A.G.B.Old	Middlesboro'	9	(3pg)	v Scotland		at Murrayfield	March 18th 1972
A.J.Hignell	Cambridge Univ	9	(3pg)	v Wales		at Twickenham	January 17th 1976
A.J.Hignell	Cambridge Univ	9	(3pg)	v Wales		at Cardill Arms Park	March 5th 1977
W.H.Hare	Leicester	9	(3pg)	v New Zealand		at Twickenham	November 24th 1979
W.H.Hare	Leicester	9	(3pg)	v Wales		at Twickenham	February 16th 1980
W.H.Hare	Leicester	9	(3pg)	v South Africa		at Johannesburg	June 9th 1984
C.R.Andrew	Cambridge Univ	9	(dg, 2pg)	v France		at Twickenham	Februarey 2nd 1985
C.R.Andrew	Wasps	9	(dg, 2pg)	v Wales		at Cardiff Arms Park	March 18th 1989
C.R.Andrew	Wasps	9	(3pg)	v South Africa		at Cape Town	June 11th 1994
C.R.Andrew	Wasps	9	(3pg)	v France	WC)	at Pretoria	June 22nd 1995
W.N.Bennett	London Welsh	7	(t, pg)	v Ireland		at Lansdowne Road	February 17th 1979
W.N.Bennett	London Welsh	7	(t, pg)	v France		at Twickenham	March 3rd 1979
N.M.Hall	Richmond	6	(2pg)	v France		at Stade Colombes	April 5th 1952
J.G.Willcox	Oxford Univ	6	(2pg)	v France		at Twickenham	February 23rd 1963
A.G.B.Old	Sheffiled	6	(2dg)	v France		at Parc des Princes	January 21st 1978
A.J.Hignell	Bristol	6	(2pg)	v Wales		at Twickenham	February 4th 1978
W.H.Hare	Leicester	6	(dg, pg)	v New Zealand		at Twickenham	November 25th 1978
W.H.Hare	Leicester	6	(2pg)	v Scotland		at Murrayfield	February 4th 1984
C.R.Andrew	Nottingham	6	(2pg)	v Scotland		at Murrayfield	February 15th 1986
J.M.Webb	Bath	6	(2pg)	v Australia	WC)	at Twickenham	November 2nd 1991

MOST POINTS SCORED BY AN ENGLAND PLAYER IN AN INTERNATIONAL MATCH:

Name:	Club:	Points:		Match details:			
C.R.Andrew	Wasps	30	(6c,6pg)	v Canada		at Twickenham	December 10th 1994
C.R.Andrew	Wasps	27	(t,c,dg,5pg)	v South Africa		at Pretoria	June 4th 1994
J.M.Webb	Bath	24	(t, 4c, 4pg)	v Italy	(WC	at Twickenham	October 8th 1991
C.R.Andrew	Wasps	24	(6c,4pg)	v Romania		at Twickenham	November 12th 1994
C.R.Andrew	Wasps	24	(dg,7pg)	v Scotland		at Twickenham	March 18th 1995
C.R.Andrew	Wasps	24	(2dg,6pg)	v Argentina	(WC	at Durban	May 27th 1995
S.D.Hodgkinson	Nottingham	23	(7c, 3pg)	v Argentina		at Twickenham	November 3rd 1990
P.J.Grayson	Northampton	23	(dg, c, 6pg)	v Ireland		at Twickenham	March 16th 1996
J.M.Webb	Bath	22	(2t, 4c, 2pg)	v Ireland		at Twickenham	February 1st 1992
C.R.Andrew	Nottingham	21	(dg, 6pg)	v Wales		at Twickenham	January 18th 1986
S.D.Hodgkinson	Nottingham	21	(7pg)	v Wales		at Cardiff Arms Park	January 19th 1991
J.E.B.Callard	Bath	21	(3c,5pg)	v W Samoa	(WC	at Durban	June 4th 1995
P.J.Grayson	Northampton	21	(3c,5pg)	v Scotland		at Twickenham	February 1st 1997
M.J.Catt	Bath	21	(5c, 2pg)	v Argentina		at Buenos Aires	May 30th 1997
J.M.Webb	Bristol	20	(7c, 2pg)	v Japan	(WC	at Sydney	May 30th 1987
R.Underwood	RAF/Leicester	20	(5t)	v Fiji		at Twickenham	November 4th 1989
C.R.Andrew	Wasps	20	(dg,c,5pg)	v Australia	(WC	at Cape Town	June 10th 1995
W.H.Hare	Leicester	19	(t, 5pg)	v Wales		at Cardiff Arms Park	January 17th 1981
W.H.Hare	Leicester	19	(2c, 5pg)	v France		at Parc des Princes	February 20th 1982
S.D.Hodgkinson	Nottingham	19	(8c, pg)	v Romania		at Bucharest	May 13th 1989
J.M.Webb	Bath	19	(t, 3c, 3pg)	v France		at Parc des Princes	February 15th 1992
M.J.Catt	Bath	19	(5c,3pg)	v Italy		at Twickenham	November 23rd 1996
C.R.Andrew	Cambridge Univ	18	(2dg, 4pg)	v Romania		at Twickenham	January 5th 1985
J.M.Webb	Bristol	18	(3c, 4pg)	v U.S.A	(WC	at Sydney	June 3rd 1987
S.D.Hodgkinson	Nottingham	18	(6c, 2pg)	v Fiji		at Twickenham	November 4th 1989
S.D.Hodgkinson	Nottingham	18	(3c, 4pg)	v Wales		at Twickenham	February 17th 1990
C.R.Andrew	Wasps	18	(dg, 5pg)	v France		at Parc des Princes	March 5th 1994
P.J.Grayson	Northampton	18	(6pg)	v Scotland		at Murrayfield	March 2nd 1996
A.G.B.Old	Leicester	17	(c, 5pg)	v Ireland		at Twickenham	February 16th 1974
W.M.H.Rose	Harlequins	17	(t, 2c, 3pg)	v Scotland		at Twickenham	April 4th 1978
S.D.Hodgkinson	Nottingham	17	(c, 5pg)	v Argentina		at Buenos Aires	July 28th 1990
S.D.Hodgkinson	Nottingham	17	(c, 5pg)	v Scotland		at Twickenham	February 16th 1991
S.D.Hodgkinson	Nottingham	17	(4c, 3pg)	v U.S.A	(WC	at Twickenham	October 11th 1991
C.R.Andrew	Wasps	17	(c,5pg)	v Italy	(WC	at Durban	May 31st 1995
P.J.Grayson	Northampton	17	(c, 5pg)	v Western Samoa		at Twickenham	December 16th 1995
P.A.Rossborough	Coventry	16	(t, 4pg)	v France		at Twickenham	February 1st 1975
C.Oti	Wasps	16	(4t)	v Romania		at Bucharest	May 13th 1989
C.R.Andrew	Wasps	16	(2c,4pg)	v France		at Twickenham	February 4th 1995
P.J.Grayson	Northampton	16	(2c,4pg)	v Ireland		at Lansdowne Road	February 15th 1997

MOST POINTS SCORED BY AN ENGLAND PLAYER IN AN INTERNATIONAL MATCH:

(continued)

Name:	Club:	Points:		Match details:		
W.H.Hare	Leicester	15	(5pg)	v Ireland	at Lansdowne Road	March 19th 1983
W.H.Hare	Leicester	15	(5pg)	v Wales	at Twickenham	March 17th 1984
J.E.B.Callard	Bath	15	(5pg)	v Scotland	at Murrayfield	February 5th 1994
M.J.Catt	Bath	15	(5pg)	v Argentina	at Twickenham	December 14th 1996
P.J.Grayson	Northampton	15	(dg,4pg)	v France	at Twickenham	March 1st 1997
R.Hiller	Harlequins	14	(t, c, 3pg)	v France	at Twickenham	February 27th 1971
S.A.Doble	Moseley	14	(c, 4pg)	v South Africa	at Johannesburg	June 3rd 1972
W.H.Hare	Leicester	14	(t, 2c, 2pg)	v France	at Parc des Princes	March 3rd 1984
S.D.Hodgkinson	Nottingham	14	(c, 4pg)	v France	at Parc des Princes	February 3rd 1990
S.D.Hodgkinson	Nottingham	14	(c, 4pg)	v France	at Twickenham	March 16th 1991
J.M.Webb	Bath	14	(c, 4pg)	v Scotland	at Murrayfield	January 18th 1992
M.J.Catt	Bath	14	(4c,2pg)	v Wales	at Cardiff Arms Park	March 15th 1997
R.Hiller	Harlequins	13	(2c, 3pg)	v France	at Twickenham	February 22nd 1969
A.G.B.Old	Middlesbro'	13	(t, 3pg)	v Australia	at Brisbane	May 31st 1975
J.M.Webb	Bristol	13	(2c, 3pg)	v Ireland	at Lansdowne Road	April 23rd 1988
S.Barnes	Bath	13	(2c, 3pg)	v Fiji	at Suva	June 17th 1988
J.M.Webb	Bath	13	(2c, 3pg)	v South Africa	at Twickenham	November 14th 1992
R.W.Hosen	Bristol	12	(3c, 2pg)	v Scotland	at Twickenham	March 18th 1967
R.W.Hosen	Bristol	12	(4pg)	v Wales	at Cardiff Arms Park	April 15th 1967
R.Hiller	Harlequins	12	(4pg)	v Ireland	at Lansdowne Road	February 8th 1969
R.Hiller	Harlequins	12	(t, 3pg)	v Scotland	at Twickenham	March 20th 1971
A.G.B.Old	Sheffield	12	(4pg)	v Ireland	at Twickenham	March 6th 1976
W.H.Hare	Leicester	12	(3c, 2pg)	v Ireland	at Twickenham	January 19th 1980
J.Carleton	Orrell	12	(3t)	v Scotland	at Murrayfield	March 15th 1980
W.M.H.Rose	Cambridge Univ	12	(4pg)	v France	at Twickenham	March 21st 1981
W.H.Hare	Leicester	12	(4pg)	v France	at Twickenham	January 15th 1983
W.H.Hare	Leicester	12	(4pg)	v South Africa	at Port Elizabeth	June 4th 1984
W.M.H.Rose	Harlequins	12	(4pg)	v France	at Twickenham	February 21st 1987
W.M.H.Rose	Harlequins	12	(4pg)	v Wales	at Cardiff Arms Park	March 7th 1987
M.E.Harrison	Wakefield	12	(3t)	v Japan (WC	at Sydney	May 30th 1987
C.Oti	Cambridge Univ	12	(3t)	v Ireland	at Twickenham	March 19th 1988
J.M.Webb	Bristol	12	(3c, 2pg)	v Australia	at Twickenham	Novemnber 5th 1988
J.C.Guscott	Bath	12	(3t)	v Romania	at Bucharest	May 13th 1989
R.Underwood	RAF/Leicester	12	(3t)	v Argentina	at Twickenham	November 3rd 1990
J.M.Webb	Bath	12	(3c, 2pg)	v Wales	at Twickenham	March 7th 1992
J.E.B.Callard	Bath	12	(4pg)	v New Zealand	at Twickenham	November 27th 1993
J.E.B.Callard	Bath	12	(4pg)	v Ireland	at Twickenham	February 19th 1994
P.J.Grayson	Northampton	12	(2dg, 2pg)	v France	at Parc des Princes	January 20th 1996

MOST POINTS SCORED BY AN OPPOSING PLAYER IN AN INTERNATIONAL MATCH AGAINST ENGLAND

Name:	Country:		Points scored:	Match details:	
S.O.Campbell	Ireland		21	(t, c, 5pg)	at Lansdowne Road	March 19th 1983
J.W.Heunis	South Africa		21	(3c, 5pg)	at Port Elizabeth	June 2nd 1984
A.G.Hastings	Scotland		21	(3c, 5pg)	at Murrayfield	February 15th 1986
M.P.Lynagh	Australia		20	(4c, 4pg)	at Sydney	July 27th 1991
J.Lomu	New Zealand	(WC)	20	(4t)	at Cape Town	June 17th 1995
K.S.Jarrett	Wales		19	(t, 5c, 2pg)	at Cardiff Arms Park	April 15th 1967
K.J.Crowley	New Zealand		18	(6 pg)	at Christchurch	June 1st 1985
M.P.Lynagh	Australia		18	(6 pg)	at Brisbane	May 29th 1988
G.Queseda	Argentina		18	(6pg)	at Twickenham	December 14th 1996
C.Lamaison	France		18	(t, 2c, dg, 2pg)	at Twickenham	March 1st 1997
M.P.Lynagh	Australia	(WC)	17	(c,5pg)	at Cape Town	June 10th 1995
G.Laporte	France		17	(t, 2c, 3pg)	at Parc des Princes	March 15th 1986
M.P.Lynagh	Australia		16	(t, 3c, 2pg)	at Sydney	June 12th 1988
D.B.Clarke	New Zealand		15	(t, 3c, dg, pg)	at Auckland	May 25th 1963
K.J.Crowley	New Zealand		15	(3c, 3pg)	at Wellington	June 8th 1985
M.A.Wyatt	Wales		15	(5pg)	at Cardiff Arms Park	March 7th 1987
H.Vidou	Argentina		15	(5pg)	at Buenos Aires	August 4th 1990
A.J.Joubert	South Africa		15	(5pg)	at Pretoria	June 4th 1994
P.Villepreux	France		14	(4c, dg, pg)	at Stades Colombes	April 18th 1970
S.P.Fenwick	Wales		14	(c, 4pg)	at Cardiff Arms Park	January 17th 1981
H.Davies	Wales		14	(c, 4pg)	at Twickenham	March 17th 1984
G.J.Fox	New Zealand	(WC)	14	(c, 4pg)	at Twickenham (WC)	October 3rd 1991
H.P.le Roux	South Africa		14	(t,3pg)	at Cape Town	June 11th 1994
B.Mullan	Ireland		13	(2t, 2c, pg)	at Lansdowne Road	February 8th 1947
P.Villepreux	France		13	(5c, pg)	at Stades Colombes	February 26th 1972
P.C.Brown	Scotland		13	(t, 3pg)	at Murrayfield	March 18th 1972
P.H.Thorburn	Wales		13	(2c, 3pg)	at Cardiff Arms Park	April 20th 1985
A.J.Joubert	South Africa		13	(t,c,2pg)	at Cape Town	June 11th 1994
L.Arbizu	Argentina	(WC)	13	(t,c,2pg)	at Durban	May 27th 1995
G.Queseda	Argentina		13	(2c, 3pg)	at Buenos Aires	June 6th 1997
P.F.Hawthorne	Australia		12	(3 dg, pg)	at Twickenham	January 7th 1967
K.S.Jarrett	Wales		12	(3c, 2pg)	at Cardiff Arms Park	April 12th 1969
M.C.R.Richards	Wales		12	(4t)	at Cardiff Arms Park	April 12th 1969
A.R.Irvine	Scotland		12	(t, c, 2pg)	at Murrayfield	February 2nd 1974
C.M.H.Gibson	Ireland		12	(2t, 2c)	at Twickenham	February 16th 1974
J-P.Romeu	France		12	(t, c, dg, p)	at Parc des Princes	March 2nd 1974
J-P.Lescarboura	France		12	(3c, dg, pg)	at Parc des Princes	March 3rd 1984
D.M.Gerber	South Africa		12	(3t)	at Johannesburg	June 9th 1984
H.Vidou	Argentina		12	(4pg)	at Buenos Aires	July 28th 1990

MOST POINTS SCORED BY AN OPPOSING PLAYER IN AN INTERNATIONAL MATCH
AGAINST ENGLAND (continued)

Name:	Country:		Points scored:		Match details:	
C.M.Chalmers	Scotland		12	(4pg)	at Twickenham	February 16th 1991
E.Ellwood	Ireland		12	(2dg, 2pg)	at Lansdowne Road	March 20th 1993
A.Mehrtens	New Zealand	(WC)	12	(dg,3c,pg)	at Cape Town	June 17th 1995
T.Lacroix	France		12	(dg, 3pg)	at Parc des Princes	January 20th 1996
S.J.P.Mason	Ireland		12	(4pg)	at Twickenham	March 16th 1996

MOST TRIES SCORED BY AN ENGLAND PLAYER IN AN INTERNATIONAL MATCH:

Name:	Club:	Tries:	Match details:		
R.Underwood	RAF/Leicester	5	v Fiji	at Twickenham	November 4th 1989
C.Oti	Wasps	4	v Romania	at Bucharest	May 13th 1989
J.Carleton	Orrell	3	v Scotland	at Murrayfield	March 15th 1980
M.E.Harrison	Wakefield	3	v Japan (WC)	at Sydney	May 30th 1987
C.Oti	Cambridge Universit	3	v Ireland	at Twickenham	March 19th 1988
J.C.Guscott	Bath	3	v Romania	at Bucharest	May 13th 1989
R.Underwood	RAF/Leicester	3	v Argentina	at Twickenham	November 3rd 1990
R.H.Guest	Waterloo	2	v Ireland	at Twickenham	February 14th 1948
C.B.van Ryneveld	Oxford University	2	v Scotland	at Twickenham	March 19th 1949
J.V.Smith	Cambridge Universit	2	v Scotland	at Murrayfield	March 18th 1950
R.C.Bazley	Waterloo	2	v Scotland	at Twickenham	March 21st 1953
J.E.Woodward	Wasps	2	v Wales	at Twickenham	January 16th 1954
D.S.Wilson	Met Police	2	v Scotland	at Murrayfield	March 20th 1954
P.B.Jackson	Coventry	2	v France	at Twickenham	February 23rd 1957
P.H.Thompson	Headingley	2	v France	at Stade Colombes	March 1st 1958
J.Roberts	Old Millhillians	2	v Wales	at Twickenham	January 16th 1960
C.W.McFadyean	Moseley	2	v Scotland	at Twickenham	March 18th 1967
J.Barton	Coventry	2	v Wales	at Cardiff Arms Park	April 15th 1967
R.H.Lloyd	Harlequins	2	v New Zealand	at Twickenham	November 4th 1967
D.J.Duckham	Coventry	2	v Scotland	at Twickenham	March 15th 1969
D.J.Duckham	Coventry	2	v France	at Twickenham	February 24th 1973
P.J.Dixon	Gosforth	2	v Scotland	at Twickenham	March 17th 1973
C.R.Woodward	Leicester	2	v Argentina	at Buenos Aires	May 30th 1981
D.Richards	Leicester	2	v Ireland	at Twickenham	March 1st 1986
R.Underwood	RAF/Leicester	2	v Japan (WC)	at Sydney	May 30th 1987
P.J.Winterbottom	Headingley	2	v United States (WC)	at Sydney	June 3rd 1987
R.Underwood	RAF/Leicester	2	v Ireland	at Twickenham	March 19th 1988
R.Underwood	RAF/Leicester	2	v Fiji	at Suva	June 17th 1988
R.Underwood	RAF/Leicester	2	v Australia	at Twickenham	November 5th 1988
R.Underwood	RAF/Leicester	2	v Wales	at Twickenham	February 17th 1990
I.G.Hunter	Northampton	2	v Canada	at Wembley Stadium	October 17th 1990
J.C.Guscott	Bath	2	v Argentina	at Twickenham	November 3rd 1990
J.C.Guscott	Bath	2	v Italy (WC)	at Twickenham	October 8th 1991
R.Underwood	RAF/Leicester	2	v United States (WC)	at Twickenham	October 11th 1991
J.M.Webb	Bath	2	v Ireland	at Twickenham	February 1st 1992
T.Underwood	Leicester	2	v Romania	at Twickenham	November 12th 1994
M.J.Catt	Bath	2	v Canada	at Twickenham	December 10th 1994
R.Underwood	RAF/Leicester	2	v Canada	at Twickenham	December 10th 1994
T.Underwood	Leicester	2	v France	at Twickenham	February 4th 1995
R.Underwood	RAF/Leicester	2	v Wales	at Cardiff Arms Park	February 18th 1995
R.Underwood	RAF/Leicester	2	v Western Samoa (WC)	at Durban	June 4th 1995
W.D.C.Carling	Harlequins	2	v New Zealand (WC)	at Cape Town	June 17th 1995
R.Underwood	RAF/Leicester	2	v New Zealand (WC)	at Cape Town	June 17th 1995
A.C.T.Gomarsall	Wasps	2	v Italy	at Twickenham	November 23rd 1996
J.M.Sleightholme	Bath	2	v Ireland	at Lansdowne Road	February 15th 1997
T.Underwood	Newcastle	2	v Ireland	at Lansdowne Road	February 15th 1997
A.A.Adebayo	Bath	2	v Argentina	at Buenos Aires	May 30th 1997

MOST PENALTY GOALS SCORED BY AN ENGLAND PLAYER IN AN INTERNATIONAL MATCH:

Name:	Club:	Penalty Goals:	Match details:			
S.D.Hodgkinson	Nottingham	7	v Wales		at Cardiff Arms Park	January 19th 1991
C.R.Andrew	Wasps	7	v Scotland		at Twickenham	March 18th 1995
C.R.Andrew	Nottingham	6	v Wales		at Twickenham	January 18th 1986
C.R.Andrew	Wasps	6	v Canada		at Twickenham	December 10th 1994
C.R.Andrew	Wasps	6	v Argentina	(WC)	at Durban	May 27th 1995
P.J.Grayson	Northampton	6	v Scotland		at Murrayfield	March 2nd 1996
P.J.Grayson	Northampton	6	v Ireland		at Twickenham	March 16th 1996
A.G.B.Old	Leicester	5	v Ireland		at Twickenham	February 16th 1974
W.H.Hare	Leicester	5	v Wales		at Cardiff Arms Park	January 17th 1981
W.H.Hare	Leicester	5	v France		at Parc des Princes	February 20th 1982
W.H.Hare	Leicester	5	v Ireland		at Lansdowne Road	March 19th 1983
W.H.Hare	Leicester	5	v Wales		at Twickenham	March 17th 1984
S.D.Hodgkinson	Nottingham	5	v Argentina		at Buenos Aires	July 28th 1990
S.D.Hodgkinson	Nottingham	5	v Scotland		at Twickenham	February 16th 1991
J.E.B.Callard	Bath	5	v Scotland		at Murrayfield	February 5th 1994
C.R.Andrew	Wasps	5	v France		at Parc des Princes	March 5th 1994
C.R.Andrew	Wasps	5	v South Africa		at Pretoria	June 4th 1994
C.R.Andrew	Wasps	5	v Italy	(WC)	at Durban	May 31st 1995
J.E.B.Callard	Bath	5	v Western Samoa	(WC)	at Durban	June 4th 1995
C.R.Andrew	Wasps	5	v Australia	(WC)	at Cape Town	June 10th 1995
P.J.Grayson	Northampton	5	v Western Samoa		at Twickenham	December 16th 1995
M.J.Catt	Bath	5	v Argentina		at Twickenham	December 14th 1996
P.J.Grayson	Northampton	5	v Scotland		at Twickenham	February 1st 1997
R.W.Hosen	Northampton	4	v Wales		at Cardiff Arms Park	April 15th 1967
R.Hiller	Harlequins	4	v Ireland		at Lansdowne Road	February 8th 1969
S.A.Doble	Moseley	4	v South Africa		at Johannesburg	June 3rd 1972
P.A.Rossborough	Coventry	4	v France		at Twickenham	February 1st 1975
A.G.B.Old	Sheffield	4	v Ireland		at Twickenham	March 6th 1976
W.M.H.Rose	Cambridge Univ	4	v France		at Twickenham	March 21st 1981
W.H.Hare	Leicester	4	v France		at Twickenham	January 15th 1983
W.H.Hare	Leicester	4	v South Africa		at Port Elizabeth	June 2nd 1984
C.R.Andrew	Cambridge Univ	4	v Romania		at Twickenham	January 5th 1985
W.M.H.Rose	Harlequins	4	v France		at Twickenham	February 21st 1987
J.M.Webb	Bath	4	v United States	(WC)	at Sydney	June 3rd 1987
S.D.Hodgkinson	Nottingham	4	v France		at Parc des Princes	February 3rd 1990
S.D.Hodgkinson	Nottingham	4	v Wales		at Twickenham	February 17th 1990
S.D.Hodgkinson	Nottingham	4	v France		at Twickenham	March 16th 1991
J.M.Webb	Bath	4	v Italy	(WC)	at Twickenham	October 8th 1991
J.M.Webb	Bath	4	v Scotland		at Murrayfield	January 18th 1992
J.E.B.Callard	|Bath	4	v New Zealand		at Twickenham	November 27th 1993
J.E.B.Callard	Bath	4	v Ireland		at Twickenham	February 19th 1994
C.R.Andrew	Wasps	4	v Romania		at Twickenham	November 12th 1994
C.R.Andrew	Wasps	4	v France		at Twickenham	February 4th 1995
P.J.Grayson	Northampton	4	v Ireland		at Lansdowne Road	February 15th 1997
P.J.Grayson	Northampton	4	v France		at Twickenham	March 1st 1997

MOST PENALTY GOALS SCORED BY AN ENGLAND PLAYER IN AN INTERNATIONAL MATCH:
(continued)

Name:	Club:	Penalty Goals:	Match details:			
R.W.Hosen	Bristol	3	v France		at Twickenham	February 25th 1967
R.Hiller	Harlequins	3	v France		at Twickenham	February 22nd 1969
R.Hiller	Harlequins	3	v Wales		at Cardiff Arms Park	April 12th 1969
R.Hiller	Harlequins	3	v Ireland		at Lansdowne Road	February 13th 1971
R.Hiller	Harlequins	3	v France		at Twickenham	February 27th 1971
R.Hiller	Harlequins	3	v Scotland		at Twickenham	March 20th 1971
A.G.B.Old	Middlesborough	3	v Scotland		at Murrayfield	March 18th 1972
A.G.B.Old	Middlesborough	3	v Australia		at Brisbane	May 31st 1975
A.J.Hignell	Cambridge Univ	3	v Australia		at Twickenham	January 3rd 1976
A.J.Hignell	Cambridge Univ	3	v Wales		at Twickenham	January 17th 1976
A.J.Hignell	Bristol	3	v Wales		at Cardiff Arms Park	March 5th 1977
W.H.Hare	Leicester	3	v New Zealand		at Twickenham	November 24th 1979
W.H.Hare	Leicester	3	v Wales		at Twickenham	February 16th 1980
W.H.Hare	Leicester	3	v Scotland		at Twickenham	February 21st 1981
W.M.H.Rose	Cambridge Univ	3	v Australia		at Twickenham	January 2nd 1982
W.M.H.Rose	Cambridge Univ	3	v Ireland		at Twickenham	February 6th 1982
W.H.Hare	Leicester	3	v Wales		at Twickenham	March 6th 1982
W.H.Hare	Leicester	3	v Scotland		at Twickenham	March 5th 1983
W.H.Hare	Leicester	3	v New Zealand		at Twickenham	November 19th 1983
W.H.Hare	Leicester	3	v Ireland		at Twickenham	February 18th 1984
W.H.Hare	Leicester	3	v South Africa		at Johannesburg	June 9th 1984
W.M.H.Rose	Harlequins	3	v Scotland		at Twickenham	April 4th 1987
J.M.Webb	Bristol	3	v Ireland (Mill)		at Lansdowne Road	April 23rd 1988
S.Barnes	Bath	3	v Fiji		at Suva	June 17th 1988
S.D.Hodgkinson	Nottingham	3	v Argentina		at Twickenham	November 3rd 1990
J.M.Webb	Bath	3	v Australia		at Sydney	July 27th 1991
J.M.Webb	Bath	3	v New Zealand	(WC)	at Twickenham	October 3rd 1991
S.D.Hodgkinson	Nottingham	3	v United States	(WC)	at Twickenham	October 11th 1991
J.M.Webb	Bath	3	v France	(WC)	at Parc des Princes	October 19th 1991
J.M.Webb	Bath	3	v France		at Parc des Princes	February 15th 1992
J.M.Webb	Bath	3	v South Africa		at Twickenham	November 14th 1992
J.M.Webb	Bath	3	v France		at Twickenham	January 16th 1993
J.M.Webb	Bath	3	v Scotland		at Twickenham	March 6th 1993
C.R.Andrew	Wasps	3	v South Africa		at Cape Town	June 11th 1994
C.R.Andrew	Wasps	3	v France	(WC)	at Pretoria	June 22nd 1995
J.E.B.Callard	Bath	3	v South Africa		at Twickenham	November 18th 1995
P.J.Grayson	Northampton	3	v Wales		at Twickenham	February 3rd 1996
M.J.Catt	Bath	3	v Italy		at Twickenham	November 23rd 1996

MOST TRY CONVERSIONS SCORED BY AN ENGLAND PLAYER IN AN INTERNATIONAL MATCH:

Name:	Club:	Conversions	Match details:		
S.D.Hodgkinson	Nottingham	8	v Romania	at Bucharest	May 13th 1989
J.M.Webb	Bath	7	v Japan (WC)	at Sydney	May 30th 1987
S.D.Hodgkinson	Nottingham	7	v Argentina	at Twickenham	November 3rd 1990
S.D.Hodgkinson	Nottingham	6	v Fiji	at Twickenham	November 4th 1989
C.R.Andrew	Wasps	6	v Romania	at Twickenham	November 12th 1994
C.R.Andrew	Wasps	6	v Canada	at Twickenham	December 10th 1994
M.J.Catt	Bath	5	v Italy	at Twickenham	November 23rd 1996
M.J.Catt	Bath	5	v Argentina	at Buenos Aires	May 30th 1997
J.Heaton	Waterloo	4	v Scotland	at Twickenham	March 15th 1947
N.M.Hall	Richmond	4	v Scotland	at Twickenham	March 21st 1953
J.M.Webb	Bath	4	v Italy (WC)	at Twickenham	October 8th 1991
S.D.Hodgkinson	Nottingham	4	v United States (WC)	at Twickenham	October 11th 1991
J.M.Webb	Bath	4	v Ireland	at Twickenham	February 1st 1992
M.J.Catt	Bath	4	v Wales	at Cardiff Arms Park	March 15th 1997
D.Rutherford	Percy Park	3	v Scotland	at Murrayfield	March 19th 1960
R.W.Hosen	Northampton	3	v Scotland	at Twickenham	March 18th 1967
W.H.Hare	Leicester	3	v Ireland	at Twickenham	January 19th 1980
C.R.Andrew	Nottingham	3	v Ireland	at Twickenham	March 1st 1986
J.M.Webb	Bath	3	v United States (WC)	at Sydney	June 3rd 1987
C.R.Andrew	Wasps	3	v Ireland	at Twickenham	March 19th 1988
J.M.Webb	Bath	3	v Australia	at Twickenham	November 5th 1988
S.D.Hodgkinson	Nottingham	3	v Wales	at Twickenham	February 17th 1990
J.M.Webb	Bath	3	v France	at Parc des Princes	February 15th 1992
J.M.Webb	Bath	3	v Wales	at Twickenham	March 7th 1992
J.E.B.Callard	Bath	3	v Western Samoa (WC)	at Durban	June 4th 1995
C.R.Andrew	Wasps	3	v New Zealand (WC)	at Cape Town	June 17th 1995
P.J.Grayson	Northampton	3	v Scotland	at Twickenham	February 1st 1997
R.Uren	Waterloo	2	v Ireland	at Twickenham	February 14th 1948
B.H.Travers	Harlequins	2	v Scotland	at Twickenham	March 19th 1949
N.M.Hall	Richmond	2	v Scotland	at Murrayfield	March 15th 1952
N.Gibbs	Harlequins	2	v Scotland	at Murrayfield	March 20th 1954
R.Challis	Bristol	2	v Scotland	at Twickenham	March 16th 1957
R.A.W.Sharp	Oxford University	2	v Ireland	at Twickenham	February 10th 1962
R.A.W.Sharp	Wasps	2	v Wales	at Cardiff Arms Park	January 19th 1963
J.G.Willcox	Harlequins	2	v Scotland	at Twickenham	March 16th 1963
R.Hiller	Harlequins	2	v France	at Twickenham	February 22nd 1969
R.Hiller	Harlequins	2	v Wales	at Twickenham	February 28th 1970
A.M.Jordan	Cambridge Unive	2	v France	at Stades Colombes	April 18th 1970
A.M.Jordan	Blackheath	2	v Scotland	at Twickenham	March 17th 1973
P.A.Rossborough	Coventry	2	v New Zealand	at Auckland	September 15th 1973
A.G.B.Old	Middlesborough	2	v Australia	at Brisbane	May 31st 1975
A.J.Hignell	Bristol	2	v Scotland	at Twickenham	January 15th 1977
M.Young	Gosforth	2	v Scotland	at Murrayfield	March 4th 1978

MOST TRY CONVERSIONS SCORED BY AN ENGLAND PLAYER IN AN INTERNATIONAL MATCH: (continued)

Name:	Club:	Conversions	Match details:		
M.Young	Gosforth	2	v Ireland	at Twickenham	March 18th 1978
W.H.Hare	Leicester	2	v Scotland	at Murrayfield	March 15th 1980
W.H.Hare	Leicester	2	v Argentina	at Buenos Aires	May 30th 1981
W.H.Hare	Leicester	2	v France	at Parc des Princes	February 20th 1982
W.H.Hare	Leicester	2	v France	at Parc des Princes	March 3rd 1984
S.Barnes	Bristol	2	v New Zealand	at Wellington	June 8th 1985
W.M.H.Rose	Harlequins	2	v Scotland	at Twickenham	April 4th 1987
J.M.Webb	Bath	2	v Ireland (Mill)	at Lansdowne Road	April 23rd 1988
S.Barnes	Bath	2	v Fiji	at Suva	June 17th 1988
S.D.Hodgkinson	Nottingham	2	v Ireland	at Twickenham	January 20th 1990
J.M.Webb	Bath	2	v Fiji	at Suva	July 20th 1991
J.M.Webb	Bath	2	v South Africa	at Twickenham	November 14th 1992
C.R.Andrew	Wasps	2	v South Africa	at Pretoria	June 4th 1994
C.R.Andrew	Wasps	2	v France	at Twickenham	February 4th 1995

PLAYERS WHO HAVE TOURED WITH THE BRITISH LIONS

(including the 1997 tour to South Africa)

Name:	Club:	Tours:		Caps:	
R.E.G.Jeeps	Northampton	3	South Africa 1955	13	All four Tests
			Australia/New Zealand 1959		Australia 1st & 2nd Tests
					New Zealand, 1st, 2nd & 3rd Tests
			South Africa 1962		All four Tests
	Dickie Jeeps captained the side in the fourth Test in 1962 in the absence of Arthur Smith.				
J.C.Guscott	Bath	3	Australia 1989	8	2nd & 3rd Tests
			New Zealand 1993		All three Tests
			South Africa 1997		All three Tests
	Scored a try in the second Test v Australia on his debut.				
	Scored a drop goal to win the match in the second Test v South Africa				
M.J.Colclough	Angouleme	2	South Africa 1980	8	All four Tests
			New Zealand 1983		All four Tests
F.E.Cotton	Coventry/Sale	3	South Africa 1974	7	All four Tests
			New Zealand 1977		2nd, 3rd & 4th Tests
			South Africa 1980		No Tests
W.B.Beaumont	Fylde	* 2	New Zealand 1977	7	2nd, 3rd & 4th Tests
			South Africa 1980		All four Tests
	Bill Beaumont was Captain of the 1980 British Lions in South Africa.				
J.V.Pullin	Bristol	2	South Africa 1968	7	2nd, 3rd & 4th Tests
			New Zealand 1971		All four Tests
P.J.Wheeler	Leicester	2	New Zealand 1977	7	2nd, 3rd & 4th Tests
			South Africa 1980		All four Tests
P.J.Winterbottom	Headingley/Harlequins	2	New Zealand 1983	7	All four Tests
			New Zealand 1993		All three Tests
J.Carleton	Orrell	2	South Africa 1980	6	1st, 2nd & 4th Tests
			New Zealand 1983		2nd, 3rd & 4th Tests
D.Richards	Leicester	2	Australia 1989	6	All three Tests
			New Zealand 1993		All three Tests
R.Underwood	RAF/Leicester	2	Australia 1989	6	All three Tests
			New Zealand 1993		All three Tests
	Scored one try in the 2nd Test v New Zealand 1993.				
M.P.Weston	Durham City	2	South Africa 1962	6	All four Tests
			Australia/New Zealand 1966		Aust 1st & 2nd Tests

PLAYERS WHO HAVE TOURED WITH THE BRITISH LIONS (continued)

Name:	Club:		Tours:		Caps:	
C.R.Andrew	Wasps	*	2	Australia 1989 New Zealand 1993	5	2nd & 3rd Tests All three Tests
B.C.Moore	Nottingham/Harlequins		2	Australia 1989 New Zealand 1993	5	All three Tests 2nd & 3rd Tests
M.O.Johnson	Leicester	*	2	New Zealand 1993 South Africa 1997	5	2nd & 3rd Tests All three Tests

Martin Johnson was Captain of the 1997 British Lions in South Africa

P.B.Jackson	Coventry		1	Australia/New Zealand 1959	5	Australia, 1st & 2nd Tests New Zealand, 1st, 3rd & 4th Tests

Scored a try in each of the 1st and 4th Tests v New Zealand.

J.Butterfield	Northampton		2	South Africa 1955 Australia/New Zealand 1959	4	All four Tests No Tests

Scored a try in each of his first three Tests - and a drop goal too, in the third.

K.F.Savage	Northampton		2	Australia/New Zealand 1966 South Africa 1968	4	No Tests All four Tests
C.W.McFadyean	Moseley		1	Australia/New Zealand 1966	4	All New Zealand Tests

Scored a try in the 4th Test v New Zealand.

A.B.W.Risman	Manchester University		1	Australia/New Zealand 1959	4	Australia, 1st & 2nd Tests New Zealand, 1st & 4th Tests

Scored a try in the 2nd Test v Australia, and also in the 4th Test v New Zealand.

R.B.Taylor	Northampton		1	South Africa 1968	4	All four Tests
R.M.Uttley	Gosforth		1	South Africa 1974	4	All four Tests

Scored a try in the 4th test.

J.Leonard	Harlequins		2	New Zealand 1993 South Africa 1997	3	2nd & 3rd Tests 1st Test (replacement)
M.C.Teague	Gloucester		2	Australia 1989 New Zealand 1993	3	2nd & 3rd Tests 2nd Test (temp replacement)
P.J.Ackford	Harlequins		1	Australia 1989	3	All three Tests
M.C.Bayfield	Northampton		1	New Zealand 1993	3	All three Tests
B.B.Clarke	Bath		1	New Zealand 1993	3	All three Tests
L.B.N.Dallaglio	Wasps		1	South Africa 1997	3	All three Tests
M.J.S.Dawson	Northampton		1	South Africa 1997	3	All three Tests

Scored a try in the 1st Test on his debut, and another in the 3rd Test

W.P.C.Davies	Harlequins		1	South Africa 1955	3	1st, 2nd & 3rd Tests
P.J.Dixon	Harlequins		1	New Zealand 1971	3	1st, 2nd & 4th Tests

Scored a try in the 4th Test.

PLAYERS WHO HAVE TOURED WITH THE BRITISH LIONS (continued)

Name:	Club:		Tours:		Caps:	
D.J.Duckham	Coventry		1	New Zealand 1971	3	2nd, 3rd & 4th Tests
A.L.Horton	Blackheath		1	South Africa 1968	3	2nd, 3rd & 4th Tests
C.D.Morris	Orrell		1	New Zealand 1993	3	All three Tests
J.G.Willcox	Oxford University		1	South Africa 1962	3	1st, 2nd & 4th Tests
M.C.Teague	Gloucester		2	Australia 1989	3	2nd & 3rd Tests
				New Zealand 1993		2nd Test (temp replacement)
W.A.Dooley	Preston Grasshoppers		2	Australia 1989	2	2nd & 3rd Tests
				New Zealand 1993		No Tests
C.R.Woodward	Leicester		2	South Africa 1980	2	2nd & 3rd Tests
				New Zealand 1983		No Tests
A.Ashcroft	Waterloo		1	Australia/New Zealand 1959	2	Australia, 1st Test
						New Zealand, 2nd Test
N.A.Back	Leicester		1	South Africa 1997	2	2nd Test (replacement), 3rd Test
S.Bainbridge	Gosforth		1	New Zealand 1983	2	3rd & 4th Tests
D.G.S.Baker	Old Merchant Taylor's		1	South Africa 1955	2	3rd & 4th Tests
J.Bentley	Newcastle		1	South Africa 1997	2	2nd & 3rd Tests
P.W.Dodge	Leicester	*	1	South Africa 1980	2	3rd & 4th Tests
A.Healey	Leicester		1	South Africa 1997	2	2nd Test (replacement)
						3rd Test (replacement)
R.A.Hill	Saracens		1	South Africa 1997	2	1st & 2nd Tests
R.W.D.Marques	Harlequins		1	Australia/New Zealand 1959	2	Australia, 2nd Test
						New Zealand, 2nd Test
T.A.K.Rodber	Northampton		1	South Africa 1997	2	1st & 2nd Test
D.P.Rogers	Bedford		1	South Africa 1962	2	1st & 4th Tests
R.A.W.Sharp	Oxford University		1	South Africa 1962	2	3rd & 4th Tests
A.Neary	Broughton Park		2	South Africa 1974	1	No Tests
				New Zealand 1977		4th Test
T.Underwood	Leicester		2	New Zealand 1993	1	No Tests
				South Africa 1997		3rd Test
W.D.C.Carling	Harlequins		1	New Zealand 1993	1	1st Test
M.J.Catt	Bath	*	1	South Africa 1997	1	3rd Test

Name:	Club:	Tours:		Caps:	
M.J.Coulman	Moseley	1	South Africa 1968	1	3rd Test
R.Higgins	Liverpool	1	South Africa 1955	1	1st Test
J.P.Horrocks-Taylor	Leicester	1	Australia/New Zealand 1959	1	New Zealand, 3rd Test
P.J.Larter	Northampton	1	South Africa 1968	1	2nd Test
W.M.Patterson	Sale	1	Australia/New Zealand 1959	1	New Zealand, 2nd Test
I.Preece	Coventry	1	Australia/New Zealand 1950	1	New Zealand, 1st Test
C.W.Ralston	Richmond	1	South Africa 1974	1	4th Test
M.P.Regan	Bristol	1	South Africa 1997	1	3rd Test
G.Rimmer	Waterloo	1	Australia/New Zealand 1950	1	3rd Test
D.Rutherford	Gloucester	1	Australia/New Zealand 1966	1	Australia, 1st Test
M.A.C.Slemen	Liverpool	1	South Africa 1980	1	1st Test
P.J.Squires	Harrogate	1	New Zealand 1977	1	1st Test
T.R.G.Stimpson	Newcastle	1	South Africa 1997	1	3rd Test (replacement)
J.R.C.Young	Oxford University	1	Australia/New Zealand 1959	1	New Zealand, 2nd Test
	Scored a try in his first and only Test.				
R.Hiller	Harlequins	2	South Africa 1968	0	No Tests
			New Zealand 1971		No Tests
S.J.Smith	Sale	* 2	South Africa 1980	0	No Tests
		*	New Zealand 1983		No Tests
S.Barnes	Bristol	1	New Zealand 1993	0	No Tests
N.D.Beal	Northampton	1	South Africa 1997	0	No Tests
P.J.Blakeway	Gloucester	1	South Africa 1980	0	No Tests
S.B.Boyle	Gloucester	1	New Zealand 1983	0	No Tests
K.P.P.Bracken	Saracens	* 1	South Africa 1997	0	No Tests
M.A.Burton	Gloucester	1	South Africa 1974	0	No Tests
G.J.Chilcott	Bath	1	Australia 1989	0	No Tests
J.M.Dee	Hartlepool Rovers	1	South Africa 1982	0	No Tests
A.J.Diprose	Saracens	* 1	South Africa 1997	0	No Tests
G.W.Evans	Coventry	1	South Africa 1974	0	No Tests

PLAYERS WHO HAVE TOURED WITH THE BRITISH LIONS (continued)

Name:	Club:		Tours:		Caps:	
H.O.Godwin	Coventry	*	1	South Africa 1962	0	No Tests
P.J.Grayson	Northampton		1	South Africa 1997	0	No Tests
W.J.H.Greenwood	Leicester		1	South Africa 1997	0	No Tests
W.H.Hare	Leicester		1	New Zealand 1983	0	No Tests
S.A.M.Hodgson	Durham City		1	South Africa 1962	0	No Tests
N.E.Horton	Moseley		1	New Zealand 1977	0	No Tests
I.G.Hunter	Northampton		1	New Zealand 1993	0	No Tests
N.C.Jeavons	Moseley	*	1	New Zealand 1983	0	No Tests
N.D.Melville	Wasps	*	1	New Zealand 1983	0	No Tests
A.J.Morley	Bristol	*	1	South Africa 1974	0	No Tests
A.G.B.Old	Leicester		1	South Africa 1974	0	No Tests
C.Oti	Wasps		1	Australia 1989	0	No Tests
D.L.Powell	Northampton		1	Australia/New Zealand 1966	0	No Tests
J.P.Quinn	New Brighton		1	South Africa 1955	0	No Tests
N.C.Redman	Bath	*	1	South Africa 1997	0	No Tests
A.G.Ripley	Rosslyn Park		1	South Africa 1974	0	No Tests
V.G.Roberts	Penryn		1	Australia/New Zealand 1950	0	No Tests
R.A.Robinson	Bath		1	Australia 1989	0	No Tests
G.C.Rowntree	Leicester		1	South Africa 1997	0	No Tests
S.D.Shaw	Bristol		1	South Africa 1997	0	No Tests
J.S.Spencer	Headingley		1	New Zealand 1971	0	No Tests
C.B.Stevens	Penz & N'lyn/Quins	*	1	New Zealand 1971	0	No Tests
F.D.Sykes	Northampton		1	South Africa 1955	0	No Tests
B.R.West	Northampton	*	1	South Africa 1968	0	No Tests
J.E.Williams	Old Millhillians		1	South Africa 1955	0	No Tests
D.S.Wilson	Metropolitan Police		1	South Africa 1955	0	No Tests
T.P.Wright	Blackheath		1	South Africa 1962	0	No Tests

*   Indicates a tour to which a player was called to rpelace an injured player.

DICKIE JEEPS

3 TOURS and 13 MATCHES.
South Africa 1955, Australia/New Zealand 1959,
South Africa 1992.

JEREMY GUSCOTT

3 TOURS and 8 MATCHES
Australia 1989, New Zealand 1993
South Africa 1997

MAURICE COLCLOUGH

2 TOURS and 8 MATCHES
South Africa 1980, New Zealand 1983

FRAN COTTON

3 TOURS and 7 MATCHES
South Africa 1974, New Zealand 1977
South Africa 1980

ENGLAND'S LEADING LION'S TEST PLAYERS.

BILL BEAUMONT

2 TOURS and 7 MATCHES
New Zealand 1977, South Africa 1980
Captain in 1980

JOHN PULLIN

2 TOURS and 7 MATCHES
South Africa 1968, New Zealand 1971

PETER WHEELER

2 TOURS and 7 MATCHES
New Zealand 1977, South Africa 1980

PETER WINTERBOTTOM

2 TOURS and 7 MATCHES
New Zealand 1983, New Zealand 1993

ENGLAND'S LEADING LION'S TEST PLAYERS.

ENGLAND PLAYERS REPRESENTED ON LIONS' TOURS:

1950 TOUR TO NEW ZEALAND AND AUSTRALIA

Only three England players were invited to join Karl Mullen's Lions tour to the Antipodes in the summer of 1950.

They were:

I.Preece	(Coventry)	9 caps	Fly half/Centre
G.Rimmer	(Waterloo)	3 caps	Scrum-half
V.G.Roberts	(Penryn)	8 caps	Flanker

Ivor Preece played in the 1st Test against New Zealand
Gordon Rimmer played in the 3rd Test against New Zealand.
Vic Roberts did not play in a Test match

1955 TOUR TO SOUTH AFRICA

Nine England players were invited to join Ronnie Thompson's 1955 Tour to South Africa

They were:

J.Butterfield	(Northampton)	11 caps	Centre
W.P.C.Davies	(Harlequins)	7 caps	Centre
J.P.Quinn	(New Brighton)	5 caps	Centre
F.D.Sykes	(Northampton)	2 caps	Wing
D.G.S.Baker	(O.M.T's.)	4 caps	Utility back
R.E.G.Jeeps	(Northampton)	uncapped	Scrum-half
J.E.Williams	(Old Millhillians)	5 caps	Scrum-half
R.Higgins	(Liverpool)	8 caps	Flanker
D.S.Wilson	(Metropolitan Police)	8 caps	Flanker

Jeff Butterfield played in all four Tests, scored a try in each of the first three, and a drop goal in the third.
Dickie Jeeps played in all four Tests at a time when he was uncapped for England.
Phil Davies played in the first three Tests.
Douglas Baker played at full-back in the 3rd and 4th Tests, kicking one penalty goal in the third.
Reg Higgins played in the 1st Test

ENGLAND PLAYERS REPRESENTED ON LIONS' TOURS (continued)

THE 1959 TOUR TO AUSTRALIA AND NEW ZEALAND

Seven England players were originally selected for the 1959 tour led by Ronnie Dawson.

They were:

J.Butterfield	(Northampton)	28 caps	Centre
P.B.Jackson	(Coventry)	15 caps	Wing
J.R.C.Young	(Oxford University)	1 cap	Wing
A.B.W.Risman	(Manchester Univ)	4 caps	Fly-half
R.E.G.Jeeps	(Northampton)	11 caps	Scrum-half
R.W.D.Marques	(Harlequins)	17 caps	Lock
A.Ashcroft	(Waterloo)	16 caps	No 8

in addition two England players were later called upon to join the party as replacements:

W.M.Patterson	(Sale)	uncapped	Centre
J.P.Horrocks-Taylor	(Leicester)	2 caps	Fly-half

Peter Jackson played in 5 Tests, missing only the 2nd v New Zealand due to injury.

He scored a try in each of the 1st and 4th Tests against New Zealand.

Dickie Jeeps played in five Tests, missing only the last of the tour due to injury.

Bev Risman played in both Tests against Australia, scoring a conversion in the first and a try in the second, and in the 1st and the 4th against New Zealand scoring a conversion in the first and a try in the fourth.

Alan Ashcroft played in the 1st Test against Australia and the 2nd Test against New Zealand.

David Marques played in the 2nd Test against Australia and the 2nd Tast against New Zealand, both in the unaccustomed position of No 8.

John Young played in his only Lions' Test in the 2nd against New Zealand and scored a try.

Bill Patterson, after arriving as an uncapped replacement, played in the 2nd and 3rd Tests against New Zealand.

Phil Horrocks-Taylor played in the 3rd Test against New Zealand - his only Lions' Test appearance.

ENGLAND PLAYERS REPRESENTED ON LIONS' TOURS (continued)

THE 1962 TOUR TO SOUTH AFRICA

Eight England players were selected for Arthur Smith's Lions party to tour South Africa in 1962.

They were:

J.G.Willcox	(Oxford University)	7 caps	Full-back
J.M.Dee	(Hartlepool Rovers)	1 cap	Centre
M.P.Weston	(Durham City)	12 caps	Utility back
R.A.W.Sharp	(Oxford University)	9 caps	Fly-half
R.E.G.Jeeps	(Northampton)	24 caps	Scrum-half
S.A.M.Hodgson	(Durham City)	10 caps	Hooker
T.P.Wright	(Blackheath)	13 caps	Prop
D.P.Rogers	(Bedford)	6 caps	Flanker

in addition two England players were later called upon to join the party as replacements:

H.J.C.Brown	(RAF/Blackheath)	uncapped	Centre
H.O.Godwin	(Coventry)	2 caps	Hooker

Dickie Jeeps played in all four Tests bringing his total Test appearances for the Lions to 13, a record for an English player which still stands. In the final Test he led the side in the absence of Arthur Smith, thus becoming the first English player to Captain the Lions since 1947.
Mike Weston played in all four Tests in the centre.
John Willcox played in the 1st, 2nd and final Tests, scoring 5 points with a conversion and a penalty goal in the last.
Richard Sharp played in the 3rd and 4th Tests, scoring a drop goal on his debut.
"Budge" Rogers played in the 1st and 4th Tests.

THE 1966 TOUR TO AUSTRALIA AND NEW ZEALAND

Only five England players were invited to join the 1966 tour to Australia and New Zealand under Mike Campbell-Lamerton

They were:

D.Rutherford	(Gloucester)	13 caps	Full-back
C.W.McFadyean	(Moseley)	3 caps	Centre
K.F.Savage	(Northampton)	4 caps	Wing
M.P.Weston	(Durham City)	27 caps	Utility back
D.L.Powell	(Northampton)	2 caps	Prop

Colin McFadyean played in all four Tests against New Zealand and scored a try in the last.
Mike Weston played in both Tests against Australia in the centre.
Don Rutherford played in the 1st Test against Australia and scored 5 points with a conversion and a penalty goal.

THE 1968 TOUR TO SOUTH AFRICA

Seven England players were selected for the 1968 tour to South Africa led by Tom Kiernan.

They were:

R.Hiller	**(Harlequins)**	4 caps	Full-back
K.F.Savage	**(Northampton)**	13 caps	Wing
J.V.Pullin	**(Bristol)**	5 caps	Hooker
M.J.Coulman	**(Moseley)**	9 caps	Prop
A.L.Horton	**(Blackheath)**	6 caps	Prop
P.J.Larter	**(Northampton)**	6 caps	Lock
R.B.Taylor	**(Northampton**	6 caps	Lock

in addition one further England player was later called upon to join the party as a replacement:

B.R.West	**(Northampton)**	4 caps	Flanker

Keith Savage and Bob Taylor both played in all four Tests.
John Pullin and Tony Horton played together in the front row in the last three Tests.
Peter Larter played in the 2nd Test and Mike Coulman in the 3rd.

THE 1971 TOUR TO NEW ZEALAND

Only five England players were originally selected to go on John Dawes' 1971 tour to New Zealand.

They were:

R.Hiller	**(Harlequins)**	17 caps	Full-back
D.J.Duckham	**(Coventry)**	15 caps	Centre/Wing
J.S.Spencer	**(Headingley)**	14 caps	Centre
J.V.Pullin	**(Bristol**	20 caps	Hooker
P.J.Dixon	**(Harlequins)**	1 cap	Flanker

in addition one further England player was later called upon to join the party as a replacement:

C.B.Stevens	**(Penzance-Newlyn**	5 caps	Prop
	/Harlequins)		

John Pullin played in all four Tests.
David Duckham played in the last three Tests on the wing.
Peter Dixon played in the 1st, 2nd and 4th Tests.

ENGLAND PLAYERS REPRESENTED ON LIONS' TOURS (continued)

THE 1974 TOUR TO SOUTH AFRICA

Seven England players were invited to join Willie-John McBride's Lions side in South Africa in 1974

They were:

A.G.B.Old	(Leicester)	11 caps	Fly-half
M.A.Burton	(Gloucester)	7 caps	Prop
F.E.Cotton	(Coventry)	11 caps	Prop
C.W.Ralston	(Richmond)	18 caps	Lock
A.Neary	(Broughton Park)	22 caps	Flanker
R.M.Uttley	(Gosforth)	8 caps	Flanker/No 8
A.G.Ripley	(Rosslyn Park)	16 caps	No 8

in addition one further England player was later called upon to join the party as a replacement:

A.J.Morley	(Bristol)	4 caps	Wing

Fran Cotton and Roger Uttley played in all four Tests and Roger Uttley scored a try in the 4th.
Chris Ralston played in the 4th Test.

THE 1977 TOUR TO NEW ZEALAND

Only five England players were originally selected for the 1977 Lions' Tour to New Zealand led by Phil Bennett.

They were:

P.J.Squires	(Harrogate)	20 caps	Wing
P.J.Wheeler	(Leicester)	10 caps	Hooker
F.E.Cotton	(Sale)	23 caps	Prop
N.E.Horton	(Moseley)	13 caps	Lock
A.Neary	(Broughton Park)	33 caps	Flanker

in addition one further England player was later called upon to join the party as a replacement:

W.B.Beaumont	(Fylde)	12 caps	Lock

Fran Cotton and Peter Wheeler played together in the front row in the 2nd, 3rd and 4th Tests.
Bill Beaumont played in the three last Tests behind them.
Peter Squires played in the 1st Test, and Tony Neary played in the last Test.

ENGLAND PLAYERS REPRESENTED ON LIONS' TOURS (continued)

THE 1980 TOUR TO SOUTH AFRICA

Eight England players including the Captain, Bill Beaumont, were selected for the 1980 Lions Tour to South Africa.

They were:

C.R.Woodward	(Leicester)	4 caps	Centre
J.Carleton	(Orrell)	5 caps	Wing
M.A.C.Slemen	(Liverpool)	20 caps	Wing
P.J.Wheeler	(Leicester)	24 caps	Hooker
P.J.Blakeway	(Gloucester)	4 caps	Prop
F.E.Cotton	(Sale)	30 caps	Prop
W.B.Beaumont (Capt)	(Fylde)	26 caps	Lock
M.J.Colclough	(Angouleme)	6 caps	Lock

in addition two further England players were later called upon to join the party as replacements:

P.W.Dodge	(Leicester)	10 caps	Centre
S.J.Smith	(Sale)	14 caps	Scrum-half

Bill Beaumont and Maurice Colclough played together in all four Tests matches at lock.
In front of them, Peter Wheeler played in all four Tests at hooker.
John Carleton played in the 1st, 2nd and 4th Tests.
Clive Woodward played in the 2nd Test at centre and the 3rd Test on the wing.
Paul Dodge played in the centre in the 3rd and 4th Tests
Mike Slemen played in the 1st Test.

THE 1983 TOUR TO NEW ZEALAND

Seven England players were originally selected for the 1983 tour to New Zealand led by Ciaran Fitzgerald

They were:

W.H.Hare	(Leicester)	18 caps	Full-back
C.R.Woodward	(Leicester)	16 caps	Centre
J.Carleton	(Orrell)	20 caps	Wing
S.Bainbridge	(Gosforth)	6 caps	Lock
S.B.Boyle	(Gloucester)	3 caps	Lock
M.J.Colclough	(Angouleme)	16 caps	Lock
P.J.Winterbottom	(Headingley)	9 caps	Flanker

in addition three further England players were later called upon to join the party as replacements:

N.D.Melville	(Wasps)	uncapped	Scrum-half
S.J.Smith	(Sale)	28 caps	Scrum-half
N.C.Jeavons	(Moseley)	14 caps	Flanker

Maurice Colclough and Peter Winterbottom played in all four Tests.
John Carleton played in the 2nd, 3rd and 4th Tests.
Steve Bainbridge played in the 3rd and 4th Tests.

ENGLAND PLAYERS REPRESENTED ON LIONS' TOURS (continued)

The intended 1986 tour by the Lions to South Africa was cancelled by the Four Home Unions in response to political pressure and popular opinion.

A Lions squad was selected in 1986 to play a match at Cardiff against an Overseas Unions XV to celebrate the Centenary of the IRB. The squad of 27 was managed by Clive Rowlands and Colin Deans was nominated Captain.

Four England players were named in the squad: they were:

R.Underwood	(RAF/Leicester)	12 caps	Wing
R.J.Hill	(Bath)	5 caps	Scrum-half
S.E.Brain	(Gloucester)	13 caps	Hooker.
W.A.Dooley	(Preston Grasshoppers)	10 caps	Lock

Only Wade Dooley and Rory Underwood played in the match.

Lions' Caps were not awarded for this match.

THE 1989 TOUR TO AUSTRALIA

Ten England players were originally selected for the Lions Tour to Australia in 1989 led by Finlay Calder.

They were:

J.C.Guscott	(Bath)	1 cap	Centre
C.Oti	(Wasps)	7 caps	Wing
R.Underwood	(RAF/Leicester)	33 caps	Wing
B.C.Moore	(Nottingham)	18 caps	Hooker
G.J.Chilcott	(Bath)	14 caps	Prop
W.A.Dooley	(Preston Grasshoppers)	29 caps	Lock
P.J.Ackford	(Harlequins)	6 caps	Lock
R.A.Robinson	(Bath)	7 caps	Flanker
M.C.Teague	(Gloucester)	8 caps	Flanker
D.Richards	(Leicester)	20 caps	No 8

in addition one further England player was later called upon to join the party as a replacement:

C.R.Andrew	(Wasps)	26 caps	Fly-half

Eight England players were selected for the 2nd and 3rd Tests.
Rory Underwood, Brian Moore, Paul Ackford and Dean Richards played in all three Tests.
Jeremy Guscott, Rob Andrew, Wade Dooley and Mike Teague joined them for the 2nd and 3rd Tests.
Jeremy Guscott scored a try in the 2nd Test, his debut.
Rob Andrew, also on his debut, scored 8 points in the 2nd Test, with a conversion, a penalty goal and a drop goal.

THE 1993 TOUR TO NEW ZEALAND

A record sixteen England players were invited to join the 1993 tour to New Zealand led by Gavin Hastings

They were:

R.Underwood	(RAF/Leicester)	60 caps	Wing
T.Underwood	(Leicester)	4 caps	Wing
I.G.Hunter	(Northampton)	3 caps	Wing
W.D.C.Carling	(Harlequins)	42 caps	Centre
J.C.Guscott	(Bath)	28 caps	Centre
S.Barnes	(Bath)	10 caps	Fly-half
C.R.Andrew	(Wasps)	52 caps	Fly-half
C.D.Morris	(Orrell)	15 caps	Scrum-half
B.C.Moore	(Harlequins)	45 caps	Hooker
J.Leonard	(Harlequins)	25 caps	Prop
W.A.Dooley	(Preston Grasshoppers)	55 caps	Lock
M.C.Bayfield	(Northampton)	12 caps	Lock
P.J.Winterbottom	(Harlequins)	58 caps	Flanker
M.C.Teague	(Moseley)	27 caps	Flanker/No 8
B.B.Clarke	(Bath)	5 caps	Flanker/No 8
D.Richards	(Leicester)	34 caps	No 8

in addition one further England player was later called upon to join the party as a replacement:

M.O.Johnson	(Leicester)	1 cap	Lock

Nine England players played in the 1st Test and eleven in each of the 2nd and 3rd Tests.
Rory Underwood, Jeremy Guscott, Rob Andrew, Dewi Morris, Martin Bayfield, Ben Clarke, Peter Winterbottom and Dean Richards played in all three Tests.
Brian Moore, Jason Leonard and Martin Johnson each played in the 2nd and 3rd Tests
Will Carling played in only the 1st Test.
Mike Teague played as a temporary replacement in the 2nd Test.
Rory Underwood scored a try in the 2nd Test, and in the same match, Rob Andrew scored with a drop goal.

ENGLAND PLAYERS REPRESENTED ON LIONS' TOURS (continued)

THE 1997 TOUR TO SOUTH AFRICA

Eighteen England players including the Captain, Martin Johnson, were selected for the 1997 Lions Tour to South Africa.

They were:

T.R.G.Stimpson	(Newcastle)	5 caps	Full-back
J.C.Guscott	(Bath)	48 caps	Centre
W.J.H.Greenwood	(Leicester)	uncapped	Centre
J.Bentley	(Newcastle)	2 caps	Wing
T.Underwood	(Newcastle)	25 caps	Wing
N.D.Beal	(Northampton)	1 cap	Utility back
P.J.Grayson	(Northampton)	8 caps	Fly-half
M.J.S.Dawson	(Northampton)	5 caps	Scrum-half
A.Healey	(Leicester)	2 caps	Scrum-half
M.P.Regan	(Bristol)	12 caps	Hooker
J.Leonard	(Harlequins)	55 caps	Prop
G.C.Rowntree	(Leicester)	14 caps	Prop
M.O.Johnson (Capt)	(Leicester)	30 caps	Lock
S.D.Shaw	(Bristol)	6 caps	Lock
N.A.Back	(Leicester)	5 caps	Flanker
L.B.N.Dallaglio	(Wasps)	11 caps	Flanker
R.A.Hill	(Saracens)	4 caps	Flanker
T.A.K.Rodber	(Northampton)	31 caps	Flanker/No 8

Never before has a Lions party contained eighteen England players, and never before have six players from the same Club, in this case Leicester, been named in a Lions' squad.

in addition four further England players were later called upon to join the party as replacements:

M.J.Catt	(Bath)	22 caps	Fly-half
K.P.P.Bracken	(Saracens)	14 caps	Scrum-half
N.C.Redman	(Bath)	19 caps	Lock
A.J.Diprose	(Saracens)	2 caps	Flanker/No 8

Six England players played in the 1st Test, seven in the 2nd and nine in the 3rd.
Jeremy Guscott, Matt Dawson, Martin Johnson and Lawrence Dallaglio played in all three Tests.
Matt Dawson scored a tri in the 1st Test and another in the 3rd.
Jeremy Guscott dropped a goal late in the 2nd Test to win the match.
Tim Rodber and Richard Hill each played in both the 1st and 2nd Tests.
John Bentley played in the 2nd and 3rd Tests.
Tony Underwood, Neil Back, Mike Catt and Mark Regan played in only the 3rd Test.
Four England players appeared in the Tests as replacements: Jason Leonard once in the 1st; Neil Back once in the 2nd; Austin Healy twice in the 2nd and the 3rd; and Tim Stimpson once in the 3rd.

SECTION 5

DETAIL OF EACH INTERNATIONAL MATCH

PLAYED BY ENGLAND

SEASON 1946-47 to SEASON 1996-97 inclusive

including summaries for each season, each tour and each World Cup

52nd match   **ENGLAND   9 pts**   v   **WALES   6 pts**

	Caps					Caps		
15	1st	A.Gray	(Otley)	.		3rd	C.H.Davies	(Llanelli)
14	4th	R.H.Guest	(Waterloo)	.		1st	K.J.Jones	(Newport)
13	1st	N.O.Bennett	(St Mary's Hospital)	.		1st	J.Matthews	(Cardiff)
12	1st	E.K.Scott	(St Mary's Hospital)	.		1st	W.B.Cleaver	(Cardiff)
11	1st	D.W.Swarbrick	(Oxford University)	.		1st	W.L.T.Williams	(Llanelli)
10	1st	N.M.Hall	(St Mary's Hospital)	.		1st	B.L.Williams	(Cardiff)
9	1st	W.K.T.Moore	(Devonport Serv's)	.		14th	H.Tanner (Capt)	(Cardiff)
1	1st	G.A.Kelly	(Bedford)	.		1st	D.Jones	(Swansea)
2	1st	A.P.Henderson	(Cambridge Univ)	.		1st & only	R.E.Blakemore	(Newport)
3	1st	H.W.Walker	(Coventry)	.		1st & only	G.W.Bevan	(Llanelli)
4	1st	J.Mycock (Capt)	(Sale)	.		1st	S.Williams	(Llanelli)
5	1st	S.V.Perry	(Cambridge Univ)	.		1st & only	G.W.Parsons	(Newport)
6	1st	M.R.Steele-Bodger	(Cambridge Univ)	.		1st	O.Williams	(Llanelli)
7	1st	D.F.White	(Northampton)	.		1st	G.Evans	(Cardiff)
8	1st	B.H.Travers	(Oxford University)	.		1st	J.R.G.Stephens	(Neath)

Referee: R.A.Beattie   (Scotland)

SCORERS:

D.F.White	Try	(1st)	3 - 0			
A.Gray	Conversion		5 - 0			
			5 - 3	J.R.G.Stephens	Try	
			Half-time			
			5 - 6	.	G.Evans	Try
N.M.Hall	Drop Goal	(1st)	9 - 6			

POINTS:

N.M.Hall	4 points	(4)		J.R.G.Stephens	3 points
D.F.White	3 points	(3)		G.Evans	3 points
A.Gray	2 points	(2)			

MATCH COMMENTARY:

Fourteen new caps in the England side, and thirteen for Wales was the inevitable result of the interruption to the Five Nations Championship caused by the Second World War. For England, only Dick Guest, in this side, and later Jack Heaton and Tommy Kemp were capped both before and after the war. Joe Mycock became only the third player ever to lead England on the occasion of his first cap, the previous incidence of which was in 1891. The Welsh side included "legends-to-be" in Ken Jones, Billy Cleaver, Bleddyn Williams and Rees Stephens led by the already legendary Hadyn Tanner, first capped in 1935, whose International career was to span fourteen seasons.

In spite of their potential and the reputations to come, the Welsh back play was of very poor International standard, and they could not take advantage of the fact that England were reduced to fourteen men for much of the match. Scott damaged his knee and had to leave the field after 15 minutes, Steele-Bodger withdrew to the centre and the battle really commenced. The Welsh tries came either side of half-time and both came from back row moves against a depleted England pack, but, with only fourteen men, England hung on and Wales could not overcome an heroic English defence. Nim Hall's late drop goal secured the first of England's very infrequent post-war victories at Cardiff.

59th match   **ENGLAND   0 pts**   v   **IRELAND   22 pts**

	Caps				Caps		
15	2nd	**A.Gray**	(Otley)	.	5th & last	**C.J.Murphy (Capt)**	(Lansdowne)
14	5th	**R.H.Guest**	(Waterloo)	.	1st	**B.R.O'Hanlon**	(Dolphin)
13	7th	**J.Heaton**	(Waterloo)	.	1st	**J.D.E.Monteith**	(Queen's U Belfast)
12	1st & only	**M.P.Donnelly**	(Oxford University)	.	2nd	**J.Harper**	(Instonians)
11	2nd	**D.W.Swarbrick**	(Oxford University)	.	2nd	**B.Mullan**	(Clontarf)
10	2nd	**N.M.Hall**	(St Mary's Hospital)	.	2nd	**J.W.Kyle**	(Queen's U Belfast)
9	2nd	**W.K.T.Moore**	(Devonport Services)	.	1st	**E.Strathdee**	(Queen's U Belfast)
1	2nd	**H.W.Walker**	(Coventry)	.	2nd	**M.R.Neely**	(Collegians)
2	2nd	**A.P.Henderson**	(Cambridge Univ)	.	2nd	**K.D.Mullen**	(Old Belvedere)
3	2nd	**G.A.Kelly**	(Bedford)	.	2nd	**J.C.Daly**	(London Irish)
4	2nd	**J.Mycock (Capt)**	(Sale)	.	2nd	**C.P.Callan**	(Lansdowne)
5	2nd	**S.V.Perry**	(Cambridge Univ)	.	2nd	**E.Keeffe**	(Sunday's Well)
6	2nd	**M.R.Steele-Bodger**	(Cambridge Univ)	.	2nd	**D.J.Hingerty**	(UC Dublin)
7	2nd	**D.F.White**	(Northampton)	.	2nd	**J.W.McKay**	(Queen's U Belfast)
8	2nd	**B.H.Travers**	(Oxford University)	.	2nd	**R.D.Agar**	(Malone)

Referee: M.A.Allan   (Scotland)

SCORERS:

	0 - 3	**B.Mullan**	Penalty Goal
	0 - 6	**B.R.O'Hanlon**	Try
	Half-time		
	0 - 9	**B.Mullan**	Try
	0 - 12	**B.R.O'Hanlon**	Try
	0 - 15	**J.W.McKay**	Try
	0 - 17	**B.Mullan**	Conversion
	0 - 20	**B.Mullan**	Try
	0 - 22	**B.Mullan**	Conversion

POINTS:

	B.Mullan	13 points
	B.R.O'Hanlon	6 points
	J.W.McKay	3 points

MATCH COMMENTARY:

The Irish back division showing three changes from the team which had been beaten by four tries to one by the French two weeks previously, were faster, more alert and far more enterprising than their English counterparts, in front of whom the English pack were well beaten. Twenty two points still stands as the biggest Irish winning margin over England, and Ireland have not scored five tries in a match against England since. This was an overwhelming triumph by the Irish pack and they gained complete ascendancy in the second half despite the icy wind which seemed to immobilise England. Not so the Irish backs, who prospered to the tune of four tries, two from each wing but were gracious enough to allow a representative from the pack, who had served them so well, onto the score sheet in the closing minutes. This was the last of captain Con Murphy's five caps and he was the only Irish player to have won caps both before and after the Second World War. Martin Donnelly gained his first and only English cap in this match; he had already played in three cricket Test Matches for New Zealand in 1937 at the age of 20, and was to tour England with the Kiwis in 1949 and score 206 runs in the Lords Test Match. Bernard Mullan's 13 points in this game will stand as the highest individual points total against England for twenty years until the eighteen-year-old Welsh full-back, Keith Jarrett, improves upon it.

62nd match   **ENGLAND   24 pts**   v   **SCOTLAND   5 pts**

54th Calcutta Cup

		Caps					Caps		
15	3rd & last	A.Gray	(Otley)	.		4th & last	K.I.Geddes	(London Scottish)
14	1st	C.B.Holmes	(Manchester)	.		3rd	T.G.H.Jackson	(London Scottish)
13	2nd	N.O.Bennett	(St Mary's Hospital)	.		4th	C.W.Drummond	(Melrose)
12	8th	J.Heaton (Capt)	(Waterloo)	.		2nd & last	W.H.Munro	(Glasgow HSFP)
11	6th	R.H.Guest	(Waterloo)	.		3rd	D.D.Mackenzie	(Edinburgh Univ)
10	3rd	N.M.Hall	(St Mary's Hospital)	.		4th	C.R.Bruce (Capt)	(Glasgow Acad'ls)
9	1st	J.O.Newton-Thompson	(Oxford University)	.		2nd & last	E.Anderson	(Stewarts Coll FP)
1	3rd	H.W.Walker	(Coventry)	.		3rd	T.P.L.McGlashan	(Royal HSFP)
2	3rd	A.P.Henderson	(Cambridge Univ)	.		2nd & last	A.T.Fisher	(Waterloo)
3	3rd	G.A.Kelly	(Bedford)	.		2nd	H.H.Campbell	(Cambridge Univ)
4	3rd	J.Mycock	(Sale)	.		5th	I.C.Henderson	(Edinburgh Acad'ls)
5	1st	J.T.George	(Falmouth)	.		3rd & last	F.H.Coutts	(Melrose)
6	3rd	M.R.Steele-Bodger	(Edinburgh Univ)	.		2nd & last	D.D.Valentine	(Hawick)
7	3rd	D.F.White	(Northampton)	.		3rd	W.I.D.Elliot	(Edinburgh Acad'ls)
8	1st	R.H.G.Weighill	(Harlequins)	.		2nd & last	D.I.McLean	(Royal HSFP)

Referee: I. David   (Wales)

SCORERS:

N.M.Hall	Drop Goal	(2nd)	4 - 0			
C.B.Holmes	Try	(1st & only)	7 - 0			
J.Heaton	Conversion		9 - 0			
R.H.Guest	Try	(1st)	12 - 0			
J.Heaton	Conversion		14 - 0			
			Half-time			
A.P.Henderson	Try	(1st & only)	17 - 0			
J.Heaton	Conversion		19 - 0			
N.O.Bennett	Try	(1st & only)	22 - 0			
J.Heaton	Conversion		24 - 0			
			24 - 3	T.G.H.Jackson	Try	
			24 - 5	K.I.Geddes	Conversion	

POINTS:

J.Heaton	8 points	(17)		T.G.H.Jackson	3 points
N.M.Hall	4 points	(8)		K.I.Geddes	2 points
C.B.Holmes, N.O.Bennett,	3 points	(3),(3)			
R.H.Guest, A.P.Henderson	each	(3),(3)			

MATCH COMMENTARY:

After the heavy defeat at Lansdowne Road five weeks earlier, England made six changes for this match, one of them positional, with Dickie Guest switching wings. The pitch was very icy and conditions were difficult, but the English pack took almost total control and inflicted upon the Scots their fourth, and heaviest defeat of the season. Jack Heaton's four conversions created a new record for England against Scotland and the winning margin of 19 points was to remain the highest for the next thirty years. The frozen pitch took its toll of injuries - at one stage during the match there were four players, two from each side, off the field receiving treatment - and of reputations - seven of the Scottish side were never selected again. One of those was David Valentine who turned to Rugby League for Huddersfield and captained the victorious Great Britain side in the 1954 World Cup.

The game finished in a blizzard as Scotland just managed to restore some dignity by scoring a converted try in the last minute.

22nd match   **ENGLAND   6 pts**   v   **FRANCE   3 pts**

	Caps				Caps		
15	1st	S.C.Newman	(Oxford University)	.	9th	A.Alvarez	(Tyrosse)
14	3rd	D.W.Swarbrick	(Oxford University)	.	8th & last	E-J.Pebeyre	(Brive)
13	3rd	N.O.Bennett	(St Mary's Hospital)	.	10th	L.Junquas (Capt)	(Bayonne)
12	9th & last	J.Heaton (Capt)	(Waterloo)	.	5th	L-M.Sorondo	(Montauban)
11	7th	R.H.Guest	(Waterloo)	.	4th	H.Dutrain	(Toulouse)
10	4th	N.M.Hall	(St Mary's Hospital)	.	9th	M-M.Terreau	(Bressanne)
9	2nd & last	J.O.Newton-Thompson	(Oxford University)	.	10th	Y.R.Bergougnan	(Toulouse)
1	1st	G.A.Gibbs	(Bristol)	.	1st	L.Caron	(Lyon)
2	4th	A.P.Henderson	(Cambridge Univ)	.	4th	M.Jol	(Biarritz)
3	4th	H.W.Walker	(Coventry)	.	6th	C-E.Buzy	(Lourdes)
4	4th	J.Mycock	(Sale)	.	11th	A-M-A.Moga	(Begles)
5	2nd	J.T.George	(Falmouth)	.	10th	R.Soro	(Lourdes)
6	4th	M.R.Steele-Bodger	(Edinburgh Univ)	.	11th	J.Prat	(Lourdes)
7	1st	V.G.Roberts	(Penryn)	.	9th	J.Matheu-Cambas	(Castres)
8	2nd	R.H.G.Weighill	(Harlequins)	.	9th	G.Basquet	(Agen)

Referee: T.Jones   (Wales)

SCORERS:	R.H.Guest	Try	(2nd)	3 - 0		
				Half-time		
				3 - 3	J.Prat	Penalty Goal
	V.G.Roberts	Try	(1st)	6 - 3		

POINTS:	R.H.Guest	3 points	(6)		J.Prat	3 points
	V.G.Roberts	3 points	(6)			

MATCH COMMENTARY:

The match was originally scheduled to be played on February 23rd but the severe winter necessitated postponement until late April.
The match was very close and was only settled when the newly capped Vic Roberts scored England's second try very late in the second half. France, who had started the season so promisingly by scoring six tries in victories over Scotland and Ireland, did not live up to their potential and seemed to lack purpose, penetration and confidence. Thus the visitors allowed England to control events because they never attempted to do so themselves. It was a disappointing French performance and they played as if they did not expect to win at Twickenham - a self-fulfilling prophesy, because their first win at Twickenham was not to come for another four years.
England's third win of the season gave them a share of the Championship title with Wales which flattered somewhat because, although England had scored seven tries, they had conceded eight, whereas Wales had scored eight and conceded only two.
This was the last of Jack Heaton's nine caps for England, unremarkable in itself, but he was first capped against Wales in 1935, gained three caps that year, gained his next three caps four years later in 1939, and his final three caps eight years later in 1947, a career span of thirteen years.

SUMMARY OF THE SEASON - 1946 - 47:

The 1946-47 season heralded the resumption of full International Rugby after the end of the Second World war, and the welcome return of France to the restored Five Nations Championship. France had been excluded since 1931, when the Four Home Unions had issued an ultimatum to the French Federation to either eradicate alleged illegal payments to players and professionals at Club level, or face the severance of all ties and association with the Home Unions. The hapless French Federation had been either unable or unwilling to influence the clubs and, as a result, France had languished in the International wilderness from the end of the 1931 season. Several "Victory" Internationals took place in both 1945 and 1946 involving British, and other, teams, principally against France, but the four Home Unions did not recognise these as full Internationals and caps were not awarded - but they were by France !

England introduced fourteen new caps for the first match against Wales in Cardiff, and eight more in the remaining three matches, using 24 different players in total during the season. Jack Heaton, now 34 years old, and Dickie Guest, now 28, both of Waterloo, and who were cousins, had appeared in Internationals before the war.

England started the season very well with a commendable victory in Cardiff, the first of only six post-war wins in the Principality. Then, with exactly the same pack and two changes in the centre, they crumbled at Lansdowne Road and lost to Ireland by 22 points, the biggest margin ever, before or since. The French match should have taken place next but the severe winter weather necessitated a postponement, and it was not much better in March when Scotland came to Twickenham. The pitch was very hard and the match was fraught with injuries, but England handed the Scots their fourth and heaviest defeat of the season. England's performance seemed to have picked up where it left off in Cardiff, with the reverse in Dublin merely an aberration. The Selectors had made five changes and had switched Dickie Guest from one wing to the other, to accommodate the Manchester and Lancashire winger, C.B.Holmes, who duly obliged with a try on his debut. In dominating the match, inspite of the conditions, England ran in four tries in all. The final match against France, postponed to April, was very tight, and although the French seemed strangely hesitant and lacking in confidence, the result was always in doubt even after Vic Roberts' try established an England lead late in the second half.

The end of the season saw England in possession of the Calcutta Cup, and sharing the Five Nations Championship with Wales, each having won three matches. A try count, however, is more indicative of the merits of the two sides as Wales scored eight tries and conceded only two whereas England scored one less try than Wales - as had been the case in Cardiff although they won the match - but they had conceded five of them in that disastrous game in Dublin.

Four players gained their last caps in this first post-war season; Jack Heaton after a career spanning thirteen seasons (including the war years) and nine caps; Arthur Gray, the Otley full-back, with three caps, who later joined Wakefield Trinity Rugby League Club; John Newton-Thompson, a South African who won the DFC during the War, with two caps; and Martin Donnelly, the New Zealand cricketer who won only one cap.

Of the season's 22 new caps, three scored tries on their debut; Don White, the Northampton flanker; Cyril Holmes, the Olympic sprinter from Manchester; and the ebullient and skillful Cornish flanker, Vic Roberts. Jack Heaton and Nim Hall each scored eight points and Dickie Guest was the leading try scorer with two. There were never less than five students in the side, and against Wales there were eight, five from Oxbridge and three from St Mary's Hospital.

FIVE NATIONS CHAMPIONSHIP TABLE:

Won: **Share of Championship Title with Wales, Calcutta Cup.**

						Points:		Tries:		Title
		Played	Won	Lost	Drawn	For	Against	For	Against	Points
1 =	Wales	4	3	1	0	37	17	8	2	6
1 =	ENGLAND	4	3	1	0	39	36	7	8	6
3 =	Ireland	4	2	2	0	33	18	7	5	4
3 =	France	4	2	2	0	23	20	6	3	4
5	Scotland	4	0	4	0	16	57	2	12	0

Home Games: beat Scotland 24 - 5, (four tries to one); beat France 6 - 3, (two tries to nil).

Away Games: beat Wales 9 - 6, (one try to two); lost to Ireland 0 - 22, (no tries to five).

3rd match   **ENGLAND 0 pts**   v   **AUSTRALIA 11 pts**

	Caps					Caps		
15	2nd	S.C.Newman	(Oxford University)	.		7th	B.J.C.Piper	(New South Wales)
14	8th	R.H.Guest	(Waterloo)	.		4th	A.E.J.Tonkin	(New South Wales)
13	4th	N.O.Bennett	(St Mary's Hospital)	.		8th	T.Allan (Capt)	(New South Wales)
12	2nd	E.K.Scott (Capt)	(St Mary's Hospital)	.		2nd	A.K.Walker	(New South Wales)
11	4th	D.W.Swarbrick	(Oxford University)	.		9th	J.W.T.McBride	(New South Wales)
10	4th	T.A.Kemp	(Richmond)	.		5th	N.A.Emery	(New South Wales)
9	1st	R.J.P.Madge	(Exeter)	.		7th	C.T.Burke	(New South Wales)
1	1st	E.Evans	(Sale)	.		2nd	N.M.Shehadie	(New South Wales)
2	1st	J.H.Keeling	(Guy's Hospital)	.		6th	K.H.Kearney	(New South Wales)
3	5th	H.W.Walker	(Coventry)	.		6th	E.Tweedale	(New South Wales)
4	5th & last	J.Mycock	(Sale)	.		5th	D.F.Kraefft	(New South Wales)
5	3rd	S.V.Perry	(Cambridge Univ)	.		12th	G.M.Cooke	(Queensland)
6	5th	M.R.Steele-Bodger	(Cambridge Univ)	.		5th	D.H.Keller	(New South Wales)
7	1st	D.B.Vaughan	(Headingley)	.		8th	A.J.Buchan	(New South Wales)
8	3rd	B.H.Travers	(Oxford University)	.		7th	C.J.Windon	(New South Wales)

Referee: N.H.Lambert   (Ireland)

SCORERS:

0 - 3	C.J.Windon	Try
Half-time		
0 - 6	A.K.Walker	Try
0 - 9	C.J.Windon	Try
0 - 11	A.E.J.Tonkin	Conversion

POINTS:

C.J.Windon	6 points
A.K.Walker	3 points
A.E.J.Tonkin	2 points

MATCH COMMENTARY:

Following the relatively successful previous season, and having seen the Australians lose at Cardiff where, last year, England, had won, the team could perhaps be excused for approaching this match with a high level of confidence. The Selectors made eight team and two positional changes for the match. Dickie Guest was asked to change wings, again, this time with Swarbrick, Tommy Kemp appeared at fly-half, Keith Scott took over the Captaincy from Jack Heaton, and a promising young front row forward from Sale, Eric Evans, acquired the first of many caps. Events proved the pre-match confidence somewhat mis-placed - as was to be the case in several later, and more high profile confrontations with Australia, in future years. It was an undistinguished match for England and they were well beaten at the start of what was to be a poor season. Australia proved themselves faster, fitter and, surprisingly, better able to handle the cold wet ball than were England. After Australia's first try by the athletic and highly mobile Windon, England exerted considerable pressure in the latter part of the first half but could not transform pressure into points as had been the case against France in the previous match. After half-time, it was a totally different story as Australia remorselessly turned the screw and scored 8 points in the last ten minutes when England collapsed. A dramatic solo try by Walker sealed the match for Australia when he ran 75 yards down the left touchline, kicked ahead, gathered the rolling ball and rounded Newman to score in the corner. Three minutes later, Windon completed a remarkable match by scoring his second try. Although they had lost to Wales, Australia had not conceded a try in their four matches against the Home Nations.

53rd match   **ENGLAND   3 pts**   v   **WALES   3 pts**

	Caps					Caps		
15	3rd & last	S.C.Newman	(Oxford University)	.	1st	R.F.Trott	(Cardiff)
14	9th	R.H.Guest	(Waterloo)	.	6th	K.J.Jones	(Newport)
13	5th	N.O.Bennett	(US Portsmouth)	.	6th	B.L.Williams	(Cardiff)
12	3rd	E.K.Scott	(Redruth)	.	6th	W.B.Cleaver	(Cardiff)
11	5th	D.W.Swarbrick	(Oxford University)	.	3rd	J.Matthews	(Cardiff)
10	5th & last	T.A.Kemp (Capt)	(Richmond)	.	3rd	G.Davies	(Pontypridd)
9	2nd	R.J.P.Madge	(Exeter)	.	18th	H.Tanner (Capt)	(Cardiff)
1	6th	H.W.Walker	(Coventry)	.	1st	L.Anthony	(Neath)
2	2nd & last	J.H.Keeling	(Guy's Hospital)	.	2nd	M.James	(Cardiff)
3	4th & last	G.A.Kelly	(Bedford)	.	5th	C.Davies	(Cardiff)
4	1st	H.F.Luya	(Headingley)	.	1st & only	W.D.Jones	(Llanelli)
5	4th	S.V.Perry	(Cambridge Univ)	.	5th	W.E.Tamplin	(Cardiff)
6	6th	M.R.Steele-Bodger	(Edinburgh Univ)	.	4th	O.Williams	(Llanelli)
7	4th	B.H.Travers	(Oxford University)	.	6th	G.W.Evans	(Cardiff)
8	2nd	D.B.Vaughan	(Devonport Services)	.	4th	L.Manfield	(Cardiff)

Referee: R.A.Beattie   (Scotland)

SCORERS: S.C.Newman   Penalty Goal   3 - 0
                                                          Half-time
                                                           3 - 3   K.J.Jones   Try

POINTS: S.C.Newman   3 points   (3)   K.J.Jones   3 points

MATCH COMMENTARY:

After the disappointing performance against Australia, the Selectors saw fit to change the Captain for the third successive match giving the poisoned chalice to Tommy Kemp who was not to play for England again following his refusal to play against Ireland in the next match. A poor England side was unable to make any real impact against a potentially good Welsh side which included ten players from the Cardiff club. A vast crowd of 73,000 at Twickenham saw England lucky to gather what was to be their only Championship point of the season. After Newman gave England the lead, Wales gradually wore the English resistance down until eventually Ken Jones ran in the try which levelled the score. Tamplin missed the conversion, but Wales were distinctly unfortunate not add more points to that solitary try during the course of the last fifteen minutes of the match. They often got very close indeed, but, once more the England defence was resolute, but they never really looked like scoring a try. It is not enough, however, to have a stout defence, attacking enterprise must be cultivated as well. Despite the preponderance of Cardiff players, the try was scored by a Newport player, Ken Jones, who, in the circumstances, should consider himself fortunate to have got a pass, let alone score a try. This match was the last for the England Captain, Tommy Kemp, of Richmond who was first capped against Wales in 1936, and was one of only three English players who were capped both before and after the war, the others A29being the cousins Dick Guest and Jack Heaton, both of Waterloo.

60th match

ENGLAND 10 pts   v   IRELAND 11 pts

	Caps				Caps		
15	1st	R.Uren	(Waterloo)	.	1st & only	J.A.Mattsson	(Wanderers)
14	10th	R.H.Guest	(Waterloo)	.	5th	B.R.O'Hanlon	(Dolphin)
13	6th	N.O.Bennett	(US Portsmouth)	.	3rd	W.D.McKee	(NIFC)
12	4th	E.K.Scott (Capt)	(Redruth)	.	3rd	P.J.Reid	(Garryowen)
11	2nd	C.B.Holmes	(Manchester)	.	6th	B.Mullan	(Clontarf)
10	1st	I.Preece	(Coventry)	.	7th	J.W.Kyle	(Queen's U Belfast)
9	3rd	R.J.P.Madge	(Exeter)	.	1st	H.de Lacy	(Harlequins)
1	7th	H.W.Walker	(Coventry)	.	3rd	A.A.McConnell	(Collegians)
2	5th	A.P.Henderson	(Cambridge Univ)	.	7th	K.D.Mullen (Capt)	(Old Belvedere)
3	2nd & last	G.A.Gibbs	(Bristol)	.	5th	J.C.Daly	(London Irish)
4	2nd	H.F.Luya	(Headingley)	.	6th	C.P.Callan	(Lansdowne)
5	5th	S.V.Perry	(Cambridge Univ)	.	2nd	J.E.Nelson	(Malone)
6	7th	M.R.Steele-Bodger	(Edinburgh Univ)	.	7th	J.W.McKay	(Queen's U Belfast)
7	4th	D.F.White	(Northampton)	.	2nd	J.S.McCarthy	(Dolphin)
8	3rd	D.B.Vaughan	(Devonport Services)	.	1st	D.J.O'Brien	(London Irish)

Referee: T.Jones   (Wales)

SCORERS:

R.H.Guest	Try	(3rd)	3 - 0				
R.Uren	Conversion		5 - 0				
			5 - 3	W.D.McKee	Try		
			5 - 5	B.Mullan	Conversion		
			Half-time				
			5 - 8	J.W.Kyle	Try		
			5 - 11	J.W.McKay	Try		
R.H.Guest	Try	(4th)	8 - 11				
R.Uren	Conversion		10 - 11				

POINTS:

R.H.Guest	6 points	(12)	W.D.McKee, J.W.Kyle		
R.Uren	4 points	(4)	and J.W.McKay	3 points each	
			B.Mullan	2 points	

MATCH COMMENTARY:

Five changes, including, yet again, a change of captain, and the selectors decided that more play-making may be appropriate, so when Tommy Kemp declined to play against ireland, they wrote him off and pinned their faith in the Coventry fly-half, Ivor Preece. Despite the changes, it was still a mediocre performance by England, again in front of a capacity crowd at Twickenham whose only memorable moment came when Dicky Guest intercepted in the England 25 and ran 60 yards to beat the cover and score his second try under the posts for Richard Uren to convert. This was, nevertheless, against the run of play and resulted in acloser score line than England really deserved. This was the beginning of a period of Irish dominance in the Five Nations Championship with the Captaincy with Karl Mullen for the first time, the genius of Jackie Kyle and the remarkable ability of the Irish back row of McKay, O'Brien and McCarthy playing together also for the first time in this match. The Irish forwards aggressive and mobile play in the loose put England on the back foot for most of the match, and although England gained the lead in the first quarter through Dickey Guest's first try, it was never a convincing lead. Ireland went on to win the Grand Slam. Optimists in the England camp could seek consolation in that losing by the odd point in 21 to the eventual Grand Slam winners, is no mean feat, but, in truth, England flattered to deceive.

63rd match
55th Calcutta Cup

ENGLAND 3 pts   v   SCOTLAND 6 pts

	Caps					Caps		
15	2nd	**R.Uren**	(Waterloo)	.	9th & last	**W.C.W.Murdoch**	(Hillhead HSFP)
14	11th	**R.H.Guest**	(Waterloo)	.	8th	**T.G.H.Jackson**	(London Scottish)
13	7th & last	**N.O.Bennett**	(US Portsmouth)	.	8th & last	**J.R.S.Innes (Capt)**	(Aberdeen GSFP)
12	5th & last	**E.K.Scott (Capt)**	(Redruth)	.	1st	**L.Bruce-Lockhart**	(London Scottish)
11	1st	**M.F.Turner**	(Blackheath)	.	7th	**C.W.Drummond**	(Melrose)
10	2nd	**I.Preece**	(Coventry)	.	5th	**D.P.Hepburn**	(Woodford)
9	4th & last	**R.J.P.Madge**	(Exeter)	.	3rd	**A.W.Black**	(Edinburgh Univ)
1	8th	**H.W.Walker**	(Coventry)	.	8th & last	**I.C.Henderson**	(Edinburgh Acad'ls)
2	6th	**A.P.Henderson**	(Edinburgh Wand'rs)	.	5th & last	**G.G.Lyall**	(Gala)
3	1st	**T.W.Price**	(Gloucester)	.	4th & last	**H.H.Campbell**	(London Scottish)
4	3rd	**H.F.Luya**	(Headingley)	.	1st	**R.Finlay**	(Watsonians)
5	6th	**S.V.Perry**	(Cambridge Univ)	.	4th	**W.P.Black**	(Glasgow HSFP)
6	8th	**M.R.Steele-Bodger**	(Edinburgh Univ)	.	8th	**W.I.D.Elliot**	(Edinburgh Acad'ls)
7	4th	**D.B.Vaughan**	(Devonport Services)	.	10th & last	**W.B.Young**	(London Scottish)
8	3rd	**R.H.G.Weighill**	(Harlequins)	.	5th	**J.B.Lees**	(Gala)

Referee: N.H.Lambert   (Ireland)

SCORERS:	R.Uren	Penalty Goal	3 - 0			
			Half-time			
			3 - 3		C.W.Drummond	Try
			3 - 6		W.B.Young	Try

POINTS:	R.Uren	3 points	(7)	C.W.Drummond	3 points
				W.B.Young	3 points

MATCH COMMENTARY:

The selectors made a further three changes for this match, but allowed Keith Scott to retain the Captaincy, but England's hopes were doomed from the outset. Injuries which cause a player to leave the field for the remainder of the match, at a time when substitutes are not permitted does seriously inhibit team performance. Such was England's fate in this match, for scrum-half Madge had to retire with torn ligaments after only ten minutes, and Keith Scott, although he did not leave the field, played much of the match with a broken jaw. In the circumstances, and with Mickey Steele-Bodger suffering concussion early in the second half, England's options were severely limited, but, even so, there were many handling and kicking errors and the lack of teamwork and cohesion was very evident. But the defence, with only thirteen men, and with Steele-Bodger concussed, maybe only twelve men able to make a serious tackle, did remarkably well to hold Scotland to only two tries in the second half. The London Scottish flanker, W.B.Young, who had been capped nine times before the war, was recalled to the side for only this match, and it was he who scored the winning try with only fifteen minutes of the match remaining. The injuries, and the consequent reduction to twelve fit men on the field, denied England any hope of winning a match which, despite three disappointing performances recently, they had felt confident of winning. But, as some other Scot was once inspired to remark " the best laid plans......"

23rd match   **ENGLAND   0 pts**   v   **FRANCE   15 pts**

	Caps				Caps		
15	3rd	**R.Uren**	(Waterloo)		14th	**A.Alvarez**	(Bayonne)
14	2nd & last	**M.F.Turner**	(Blackheath)		5th	**M.Pomathios**	(Agen)
13	1st	**L.B.Cannell**	(Oxford University)		13th	**M-M.Terreau**	(Bressane)
12	1st	**A.C.Towell**	(Bedford)		3rd	**P.Dizabo**	(Tyrosse)
11	3rd & last	**C.B.Holmes**	(Manchester)		1st	**M.Siman**	(Montferrand)
10	3rd	**I.Preece**	Coventry)		4th	**L.Bordenave**	(Toulon)
9	1st	**P.W.Sykes**	(Wasps)		13th	**Y.R.Bergougnan**	(Toulouse)
1	9th & last	**H.W.Walker**	(Coventry)		5th	**L.Caron**	(Castres)
2	7th	**A.P.Henderson**	(Edinburgh Wand'rs)		5th	**L.Martin**	(Pau)
3	2nd	**T.W.Price**	(Gloucester)		11th	**C-E.Buzy**	(Lourdes)
4	4th	**H.F.Luya**	(Headingley)		16th	**A-M-A.Moga**	(Begles)
5	7th & last	**S.V.Perry**	(Cambridge Univ)		15th	**R.Soro**	(Romans)
6	9th & last	**M.R.Steele-Bodger**	(Edinburgh Univ)		16th	**J.Prat**	(Lourdes)
7	5th	**D.F.White**	(Northampton)		14th	**J.Matheu-Cambas**	(Castres)
8	4th & last	**R.H.G.Weighill (Capt)**	(Harlequins)		14th	**G.Basquet (Capt)**	(Agen)

Referee: T.Jones   (Wales)

SCORERS:

0 - 3		**M.Pomathios**	Try
Half-time			
0 - 6		**R.Soro**	Try
0 - 9		**J.Prat**	Try
0 - 11		**A.Alvarez**	Conversion
0 - 15		**Y.R.Bergougnan**	Drop Goal

POINTS:

Y.R.Bergougnan	4 points
M.Pomathios, R.Soro	
and J.Prat	3 points each
A.Alvarez	2 points

MATCH COMMENTARY:

This match, somewhat unusually, was played on Easter Monday and only nine days after England's previous match. England made five changes, two because of injury, to the somewhat unfortunate team which had lost at Murrayfield the previous week. Included in these changes was, of course, another change of Captain, as a result of Keith Scott's broken jaw. All to no avail, however, as England allowed France to compile their highest ever score and winning margin in the series of matches between the two countries, and it was only the second time that England has failed to score against France. England had no answer to the powerful and highly mobile French pack, the tight French marking, the dominant presence of Jean Prat and the elusive running of Pomathios who scored one of the French tries - his third of the season. The injury jinx struck at England again when Mickey Steel-Bodger almost scored, but failed to ground the ball properly and, in attempting to do so, broke his wrist and inevitably had to leave the field.

From sharing the Championship last season with Wales, England found themselves in the unenviable position at the foot of the Table, clutching the Wooden Spoon and with only one point to show from four games, and having scored only two tries and conceded nine. They also failed to score a point against Australia in the first match of the season. Surely, a season to forget !

SUMMARY OF THE SEASON - 1947 - 48:

Just as this was a season of total triumph for the Irish, in winning their first and, to date, only Grand Slam, so it was a season of disaster and humiliation dressed with a generous dose of misfortune for England. The misfortune took the form of injuries to key players which affected the team's performance for the remainder of the match and limited selection options for the next match. This was particularly true for the final two matches of the season when England suffered a spate of injuries against Scotland and were scheduled to play France - in Paris a mere nine days later.

Four new caps were introduced for the match against Australia, and eight more for the Five Nations matches. In all, England used twenty-nine different players during the course of the season, five more than the previous year, and, again of those, nine were students at either University or Teaching Hospital where rugby was never stronger than it was at this time. In the five matches played throughout the season, only three players took part in all five matches. They were, Harry Walker, Mickey Steele-Bodger and Vic Perry. The team was led by three different Captains during the season, Scott three times, Kemp and Weighhill, not the surest foundation for a successful season.

When Australia came to Twickenham in January, England should have known what to expect for they had scored four tries against both Scotland and Ireland, and although Wales had beaten them by two penalty goals to nil, they had not conceded a try. England failed to score a point, never mind a try, and Australia joyfully scored three. Only two changes were made when Wales visited Twickenham two weeks later but England fared badly and got away with a fortunate draw. Although the score was close against Ireland, the difference between the two teams was immense., but at least the massive crowd of over 70,000 at Twickenham that day, were able to cheer the only two tries England were able to score all season, both by the resourceful Dickie Guest. The 70,000 crowds at the other two home matches were less fortunate ! At Murrayfield, England should and probably would have won the match had they not been plagued by injuries and five more changes were made for the match in Paris on Easter Monday. But on that occasion, the power of the French pack and the pace of the French backs were altogether too much for England.

Thus ended a dismal season and England had nothing to show for it but an ignominious Wooden Spoon and a resolve to do better next time. Only two tries were scored in five matches, twelve conceded and only sixteen points in total were scored, a sad but accurate commentary on England's performance throughout the season.

Not surprisingly, fifteen of the twenty-nine players who pulled on the white jersey during the season did so for the last time and retired from the International scene. Among them were Mickey Steele-Bodger and Harry Walker, both of whom had played in all nine of England's post war matches. Steele-Bodger later became a selector, President of the RFU and Chairman of the IRB, and Harry Walker went back to his pub. Norman Bennett, a Royal Navy Surgeon-Lieutenant, and Vic Perry, an academic at Birmingham University, retired with seven caps each; Tommy Kemp, who had played in three Internationals before the war, for some reason declined to play against Ireland, and retired with five caps, but later became a selector and RFU President; Joe Mycock who had been England Captain for the first post-war International on his debut also had five caps to his credit; Bob Weighhill, with four caps, was a wartime DFC, and later became a selector and RFU and IRB member; Scott and Madge with four caps each, both retired after the injuries received in the match against Scotland, and Scott went on to play first class cricket for Gloucestershire; Sydney Newman took his three caps back to his native South Africa; Cyril Holmes added three caps to his trophy cupboard - he had held Empire records for both the 100 yards and 220 yards sprints, and ran in the 100 metres in the Berlin Olympics in 1936; and Martin Turner, with two caps, later became a selector.

With only sdixteen points scored in the whole season, no scoring records were broken, indeed only three players scored any points at all. Richard Uren scored seven, Dickie Guest six (the two tries), and Sydney Newman three points.

FIVE NATIONS CHAMPIONSHIP TABLE:

Won: Nothing

		Played	Won	Lost	Drawn	Points: For	Against	Tries: For	Against	Title Points
1	Ireland	4	4	0	0	36	19	10	5	8
2 =	France	4	2	2	0	40	25	9	4	4
2 =	Scotland	4	2	2	0	15	31	3	6	4
4	Wales	4	1	2	1	23	20	5	5	3
5	**ENGLAND**	4	0	3	1	16	35	2	9	1

Home Games: drew with Wales 3 - 3 (no tries to one); lost to Ireland 10 - 11, (two tries to three)

Away Games: lost to Scotland 3 - 6, (no tries to two); lost to France 0 - 15, (no tries to three)

54th match　　　　**ENGLAND　3 pts**　　　v　　　**WALES　9 pts**

	Caps					Caps		
15	1st	**W.B.Holmes**	(Cambridge Univ)	.	5th	**R.F.Trott**	(Cardiff)
14	1st & only	**J.A.Gregory**	(Blackheath)	.	10th	**K.J.Jones**	(Newport)
13	2nd	**L.B.Cannell**	(Oxford University)	.	10th	**B.L.Williams**	(Cardiff)
12	1st	**C.B.van Ryneveld**	(Oxford University)	.	6th	**J.Matthews**	(Cardiff)
11	1st & only	**T.Danby**	(Harlequins)	.	7th & last	**W.L.T.Williams**	(Llanelli)
10	5th	**N.M.Hall (Capt)**	(Huddersfield)	.	7th	**G.Davies**	(Cambridge Univ)
9	1st	**G.Rimmer**	(Waterloo)	.	22nd	**H.Tanner (Capt)**	(Cardiff)
1	3rd	**T.W.Price**	(Cheltenham)	.	1st	**E.Coleman**	(Newport)
2	8th	**A.P.Henderson**	(Edinburgh Wand'rs)	.	9th	**W.H.Travers**	(Newport)
3	1st	**M.J.Berridge**	(Northampton)	.	4th	**D.Jones**	(Swansea)
4	5th & last	**H.F.Luya**	(Headingley)	.	1st	**D.J.Hayward**	(Newbridge)
5	1st	**G.R.d'A.Hosking**	(Devonport Services)	.	1st	**A.Meredith**	(Devonport Services)
6	1st & only	**E.L.Horsfall**	(Harlequins)	.	1st	**W.R.Cale**	(Newbridge)
7	2nd	**V.G.Roberts**	(Penryn)	.	10th	**G.W.Evans**	(Cardiff)
8	1st & only	**B.Braithwaite-Exley**	Headingley)	.	3rd	**J.A.Gwilliam**	(Cambridge Univ)

Referee:　　N.H.Lambert　　　(Ireland)

SCORERS:

			0 - 3	**W.L.T.Williams**	Try
N.M.Hall	D'p Goal (3rd & last)	3 - 3			
		Half-time			
		3 - 6	**A.Meredith**	Try
		3 - 9	**W.L.T.Williams**	Try

POINTS:

N.M.Hall	3 points	(11)	**W.L.T.Williams**	6 points
			A.Meredith	3 points

MATCH COMMENTARY:

England brought in nine new caps for this game (four of whom would not be capped again), and the whole of the back division with the exception of Lewis Cannell, was changed. All to no avail, however, as England conceded three unconverted tries and lost the match. The England side played a solid and largely faultless game, but Wales were exceptional and the difference was flair - that quality, as Cliff Morgan would later pronounce, which distinguishes the mediocre from the truly great. Scintillating running by the Welsh backs and inspired half-back play by Glyn Davies, led by Hadyn Tanner, provided Les Williams with the opportunity to run in two excellent tries. Within days of the match, Les Williams was to sign terms with Hunslet Rugby League Club. "Bunny" Travers (aged only 35) was recalled to the Welsh pack ten years after his previous appearance in 1939. Each of the England wings gained their first and only caps in this match, and both had Rugby League connections. Tom Danby was to sign for Salford in the following August, and later played in three tests for Great Britain. John Gregory had already played Rugby League for Huddersfield and in 1946 was banned by the RFU for his pains. He was re-instated in April 1948, the same year as he won a silver medal in the 1948 Olympics in the 4 x 100 metres relay. The English back row was torn apart by the Welsh half-backs and Braithwaite-Exley and Horsfall paid the inevitable penalty and vanished from the International scene !

61st match   **ENGLAND   5 pts   v   IRELAND   14 pts**

	Caps				Caps		
15	2nd	**W.B.Holmes**	(Cambridge Univ)	.	2nd	**G.W.Norton**	(Bective Rangers)
14	6th & last	**D.W.Swarbrick**	(Oxford University)	.	3rd	**M.F.Lane**	(UC Cork)
13	3rd	**L.B.Cannell**	(Oxford University)	.	7th	**W.D.McKee**	(NIFC)
12	2nd	**C.B.van Ryneveld**	(Oxford University)	.	2nd & last	**T.J.Gavin**	(London Irish)
11	1st	**R.D.Kennedy**	(Camborne)	.	9th	**B.R.O'Hanlon**	(Dolphin)
10	6th	**N.M.Hall (Capt)**	(Huddersfield)	.	11th	**J.W.Kyle**	(Queen's U Belfast)
9	2nd	**G.Rimmer**	(Waterloo)	.	7th	**E.Strathdee**	(Queen's U Belfast)
1	4th	**T.W.Price**	(Cheltenham)	.	7th & last	**A.A.McConnell**	(Collegians)
2	9th & last	**A.P.Henderson**	(Edinburgh Wand'rs)	.	11th	**K.D.Mullen (Capt)**	(Old Belvedere)
3	2nd & last	**M.J.Berridge**	(Northampton	.	2nd	**J.T.Clifford**	(Young Munster)
4	3rd & last	**J.T.George**	(Falmouth)	.	10th & last	**C.P.Callan**	(Lansdowne)
5	2nd	**G.R.d'A.Hosking**	(Devonport Services)	.	6th	**J.E.Nelson**	(Malone)
6	5th	**D.B.Vaughan**	(Headingley)	.	11th	**J.W.McKay**	(Queen's U Belfast)
7	3rd	**V.G.Roberts**	(Penryn)	.	6th	**J.S.McCarthy**	(Dolphin)
8	1st	**J.M.Kendall-Carpenter**	(Oxford University)	.	5th	**D.J.O'Brien**	(London Irish)

Referee: R.A.Beattie   (Scotland)

SCORERS:

				0 - 3	G.W.Norton	Penalty Goal
C.B.van Ryneveld	Try	(1st)		3 - 3		
W.B.Holmes	Conversion			5 - 3		
				5 - 6	G.W.Norton	Penalty Goal
				Half-time		
				5 - 9	B.R.O'Hanlon	Try
				5 - 12	W.D.McKee	Try
				5 - 14	G.W.Norton	Conversion

POINTS:

C.B.van Ryneveld	3 points	(3)	G.W.Norton	8 points	
W.B.Holmes	2 points	(2)	W.D.McKee	3 points	
			B.R.O'Hanlon	3 points	

MATCH COMMENTARY:

Five more changes to the England side following the defeat by Wales in January, was the tactic adopted to try to contain last season's Grand Slam Champions on their home ground in Dublin. Another folorn hope for, as previously, the leadership of Karl Mullen, the vision of Jack Kyle and the increasingly formidable Irish back row saw England off without too much trouble. There were a few encouraging signs in the running of the England backs and one delightful move resulted in Clive van Ryneveld's try, but, generally the team effort was disjointed, the forwards were slow and ponderous, the backs lacked flair and, above all, there was a conspicuous lack of authority from Nim Hall. This was England's fourth successive defeat at the hands of the Irish, the fifth successive Five Nations defeat, and the seventh successive match against all opposition without a win. Sad days indeed, but better times were ahead, but before that there has to be some consistency selection and some positive leadership on the field from the Captain who, himself, must be confident of retaining his place.

24th match   **ENGLAND   8 pts**   v   **FRANCE   3 pts**

	Caps					Caps	
15	3rd	W.B.Holmes	(Cambridge Univ)	.	16th	A.Alvarez	(Tyrosse)
14	12th	R.H.Guest	(Waterloo)	.	8th	M.Pomathios	(Lyon)
13	4th	L.B.Cannell	(Oxford University)	.	6th	P.Dizabo	(Tyrosse)
12	3rd	C.B.van Ryneveld	(Oxford University)	.	6th	H.Dutrain	(Toulouse)
11	2nd	R.D.Kennedy	(Camborne)	.	7th	J.Lassegue	(Toulouse)
10	4th	I.Preece (Capt)	(Coventry)	.	1st	J.Pilon	(Perigeux)
9	3rd	W.K.T.Moore	(Leicester)	.	15th	Y.R.Bergougnan	(Toulouse)
1	5th	T.W.Price	(Cheltenham)	.	8th	L.Caron	(Lyon)
2	1st	J.H.Steeds	(Middlesex Hospital)	.	7th	M.Jol	(Biarritz)
3	2nd	J.M.Kendall-Carpenter	(Oxford University)	.	14th	C-E.Buzy	(Lourdes)
4	1st	J.R.C.Matthews	(Harlequins)	.	19th	A-M-A.Moga	(Begles)
5	3rd	G.R.d'A.Hosking	(Devonport Services)	.	18th	R.Soro	(Romans)
6	5th	B.H.Travers	(Harlequins)	.	19th	J.Prat	(Lourdes)
7	4th	V.G.Roberts	(Penryn)	.	17th	J.Matteu-Cambas	(Castres)
8	6th	D.B.Vaughan	(Headingley)	.	17th	G.Basquet (Capt)	(Agen)

Referee: T.Jones   (Wales)

SCORERS:	L.B.Cannell	Try	(1st)	3 - 0		
	W.B.Holmes	Conversion		5 - 0		
				Half-time		
	I.Preece	D'p Goal (1st & only)		8 - 0		
				8 - 3	A.Alvarez	Drop Goal

POINTS:	L.B.Cannell	3 points	(3)		A.Alvarez	3 points
	I.Preece	3 points	(3)			
	W.B.Holmes	2 points	(4)			

MATCH COMMENTARY:

England made another six changes for this match, most notably at half back where Nim Hall and Gordon Rimmer were replaced by Ivor Preece and the Leicester scrum-half Moore. Preece was given the Captaincy and three of the front five were replaced and these moves included playing John Kendall-Carpenter in the front row at tight head where he was to play the next five Internationals.

Under Preece's Captaincy, the team performance was altogether more robust and vigorous than had been the case in the Ireland match, but the back play as a whole was still disappointing. The English pack held their own against the mobile and powerful French eight, and indeed they improved as the game went on, but it was significant that the French scrum-half, Bergougnan, had to leave the field just before half-time and, because Jean Prat took up the scrum-half position, France were reduced to seven forwards. Nevertheless some stout tackling combined with French hesitancy in mid-field denied the dangerous Pomathios and Lassegue. Lewis Cannell's try was the highlight of the match for England when he cut inside the defence twice with two men heavily marked outside him to score near the posts, and for France it was Alvarez' drop goal from full-back and fully fifty yards which soared through the uprights. A competent, encouraging and very welcome win for England, before a home crowd, at last, and France have yet to win at Twickenham !

64th match   **ENGLAND   19 pts   v   SCOTLAND   3 pts**
56th Calcutta Cup

	Caps					Caps		
15	4th & last	**W.B.Holmes**	(Cambridge Univ)	.	7th & last	**I.J.M.Lumsden**	(Bath)
14	13th & last	**R.H.Guest**	(Waterloo)	.	12th & last	**T.G.H.Jackson**	(London Scottish)
13	5th	**L.B.Cannell**	(Oxford University)	.	4th & last	**L.G.Gloag**	(Cambridge Univ)
12	4th & last	**C.B.van Ryneveld**	(Oxford University)	.	9th & last	**D.P.Hepburn**	(Woodford)
11	3rd & last	**R.D.Kennedy**	(Camborne)	.	4th	**D.W.C.Smith**	(London Scottish)
10	5th	**I.Preece (Capt)**	(Coventry)	.	8th & last	**C.R.Bruce**	(Glasgow Acads)
9	4th	**W.K.T.Moore**	(Leicester)	.	8th & last	**W.D.Allardice**	Aberdeen GSFP
1	6th & last	**T.W.Price**	(Cheltenham)	.	1st & only	**S.T.H.Wright**	(Stewart's Coll FP)
2	2nd	**J.H.Steeds**	(Saracens)	.	1st	**J.A.R.MacPhail**	(Edinburgh Acads)
3	3rd	**J.M.Kendall-Carpenter**	(Oxford University)	.	5th & last	**S.Coltman**	(Hawick)
4	2nd	**J.R.C.Matthews**	(Harlequins)	.	8th & last	**L.R.Currie**	(Dunfermline)
5	4th	**G.R.d'A.Hosking**	(Devonport Services)	.	3rd & last	**G.A.Wilson**	(Oxford University)
6	6th & last	**B.H.Travers**	(Harlequins)	.	12th	**W.I.D.Elliot**	(Edinburgh Acads)
7	5th	**V.G.Roberts**	(Penryn)	.	4th	**D.H.Keller**	(London Scottish)
8	7th	**D.B.Vaughan**	(Headingley)	.	4th	**P.W.Kinninmonth**	(Oxford University)

Referee: N.H.Lambert   (Ireland)

SCORERS:	**R.D.Kennedy**	Try	(1st & only)	3 - 0		
				Half-time		
	C.B.van Ryneveld	Try	(2nd)	6 - 0		
	B.H.Travers	Conversion		8 - 0		
				8 - 3	**G.A.Wilson**	Penalty Goal
	C.B.van Ryneveld	Try	(3rd & last)	11 - 3		
	G.R.d'A.Hosking	Try	(1st & only)	14 - 3		
	B.H.Travers	Conversion		16 - 3		
	R.H.Guest	Try	(5th & last)	19 - 3		

POINTS:	**C.B.van Ryneveld**	6 points	(9)		**G.A.Wilson**	3 points
	B.H.Travers	4 points	(4)			
	R.H.Guest, R.D.Kennedy		(15),(3)			
	and G.R.d'A.Hosking	3 points ach	(3)			

MATCH COMMENTARY:

England fielded an unchanged side for this match for the first time since the war, and the confidence of the selectors was fully justified. England scored five tries without reply, and the two scored by Clive van Ryneveld were particularly spectacular following counter-attacks by Ivor Preece. Dickie Guest's try was a perfect illustration of why he was still playing International rugby ten years after he was first capped. Although he has lost some speed with the advancing years, his side-step and balance were as lethal as ever and were justly rewarded as he scored his fifth and last try for England. Robert Kennedy's try was the result of a brief burst of astonishing pace and Hosking's direct result of commendable backing up. In every respect it was a first class performance by the England side, backs and forwards alike. Scotland were led by D.H.Keller, an Australian (with very strong Scottish connections) who had played in all five Internationals for the 47-48 Wallabies, and who was studying medicine at Guy's Hospital. England regained possession of the Calcutta Cup once more, and shared second place in the Championship table with Scotland and France, both of whom they had beaten.

SUMMARY OF THE SEASON - 1948 - 49:

England's performance went from the ridiculous to the sublime in this season of total contrast. Similarly their supporters must have experienced extremes of emotion from the depths of despair following the defeat by Ireland at Lansdowne Road to the euphoria which acclaimed the defeat of Scotland at Twickenham by five tries to nil - more tries than England have scored in total in their last eight matches.

There were eleven changes and five new caps for the first match of the season against Wales at Cardiff, and four other new caps were awarded during the remainder of the season. Throughout the season in the four matches, England used twenty-six players, but the number of students in their ranks had fallen to six. Six players were ever-present for the four matches of the Championship, they were: Barry Holmes Lewis Cannell, Clive van Ryneveld, Tom Price, Geoffrey Hosking and Vic Roberts.

The defeat in the first match at the hands of the Welsh at Cardiff was entirely due to Welsh superiority and there was nothing that the England side could do about it. They were outplayed in every respect and, although they played correctly and almost without fault, they never looked even remotely capable of winning. In complete contrast, the match against Ireland in Dublin was lost because they were slow and ponderous and lacked imagination, initiative and leadership. The five changes for the match in Dublin were followed by a further six for the first home game of the season against France. Ivor Preece was recalled at fly-half and was given the Captaincy and his authority and leadership produced a much more robust, aggressive and disciplined performance, especially from the pack. It was fortunate for England that Bergougnan, the French scrum-half, had to leave the field, and with Jean Prat moving to fill his place, the French had to play the whole of the second half with one forward short. But it is an ill wind........because the confidence generated by that win over France was to see the hapless Scots completely torn apart when England fielded an unchanged side for the last match of the season.

Two wins and two matches lost gave England a share of second place with Scotland and France, having scored more tries in the season than any other nation. The Calcutta Cup had been recovered from Scotland and a degree of contentment had replaced the abject despair in the England camp following the results of the previous season.

As last season, fifteen players were to leave the International stage. Most prominent of these was Dickie Guest who retired with thirteen caps, three of which he had won before the war, and his ten post-war caps were a record at the time. A.P Henderson, the Cambridge University hooker, who later lived and worked in Scotland and played his rugby with Edinburgh Wanderers, gained nine caps; David Swarbrick, who had to retire from the game with a severe head injury, "Jika" Travers, who returned to his native Australia, there to captain New South Wales against the 1950 British Lions, and Tom Price of the Cheltenham club, had each earned six caps; Humphrey Luya bowed out with five; Clive van Ryneveld, after four caps during his year at Oxford, returned to South Africa to become a Test Cricketer, Barrister and Member of Parliament; and the promising Cambridge University full-back, Barry Holmes, four caps, who tragically died of typhoid later in the year on returning to Argentina, his country of birth, aged only 21 years. It has been suggested in other quarters that Holmes' death was not of natural causes, but was indirectly attributable to the dictator, Peron. Seven other players retired with three, or less, caps, four of whom were selected for the Welsh match, and were promptly dropped immediately afterwards.

Clive van Ryneveld was the sides' leading scorer in both points and tries for the season with three tries and nine points. The remainder of England's thirty-five points for the season were shared among seven other players, none scoring more than four points or more that one try. England did not score a penalty goal throughout the entire season.

FIVE NATIONS CHAMPIONSHIP TABLE:

Won: **Calcutta Cup**

		Played	Won	Lost	Drawn	Points: For	Against	Tries: For	Against	Title Points
1	Ireland	4	3	1	0	41	24	5	3	6
2 =	**ENGLAND**	4	2	2	0	35	29	7	5	4
2 =	France	4	2	2	0	24	28	3	4	4
2 =	Scotland	4	2	2	0	20	37	4	8	4
5	Wales	4	1	3	0	17	19	5	4	2

Home Games: beat France 8 - 3, (one try to nil); beat Scotland 19 - 3, (five tries to nil)

Away Games: lost to Wales 3 - 9, (no tries to three); lost to Ireland 5 - 14, (one try to two)

55th match   **ENGLAND   5 pts**   v   **WALES   11 pts**

	Caps				Caps		
15	1st	M.B.Hofmeyr	(Oxford University)		1st	B.L.Jones	(Devonport Services)
14	1st	J.V.Smith	(Cambridge Univ)		14th	K.J.Jones	(Newport)
13	1st	B.Boobbyer	(Oxford University)		2nd	M.C.Thomas	(Newport)
12	6th	L.B.Cannell	(Oxford University)		10th	J.Matthews	(Cardiff)
11	1st	I.J.Botting	(Oxford University)		1st	T.J.Brewer	(Newport
10	6th	I.Preece (Capt)	(Coventry)		11th	W.B.Cleaver	(Cardiff)
9	3rd	G.Rimmer	(Waterloo)		1st	W.R.Willis	(Cardiff)
1	4th	J.M.Kendall-Carpenter	(Oxford University)		1st	J.D.Robins	(Birkenhead Park)
2	2nd	E.Evans	(Sale)		1st	D.M.Davies	(Somerset Police)
3	1st	W.A.Holmes	(Nuneaton)		10th	C.Davies	(Cardiff)
4	5th & last	G.R.d'A.Hosking	(Devonport Services)		1st	E.R.John	(Neath)
5	1st	H.A.Jones	(Barnstaple)		3rd	D.J.Hayward	(Newbridge)
6	1st	H.D.Small	(Oxford University)		4th	W.R.Cale	(Newbridge)
7	1st & Only	J.J.Cain	(Waterloo)		3rd	R.T.Evans	(Newport)
8	8th & last	D.B.Vaughan	(Headingley)		7th	J.A.Gwilliam (Capt)	(Edinburgh Wand'rs)

Referee: N.H.Lambert   (Ireland)

SCORERS:	J.V.Smith	Try	(1st)	3 - 0		
	M.B.Hofmeyr	Conversion		5 - 0		
				5 - 3	C.Davies	Try
				Half-time		
				5 - 6	B.L.Jones	Penalty Goal
				5 - 9	W.R.Cale	Try
				5 - 11	B.L.Jones	Conversion

POINTS:	J.V.Smith	3 points	(3)		B.L.Jones	5 points
	M.B.Hofmeyr	2 points	(2)		C.Davies	3 points
					W.R.Cale	3 points

MATCH COMMENTARY:

England fielded eight new caps for the opening match of the 1949-50 Championship with high hopes that the successes of the latter part of the previous season would be continued. Alas, inspite of the contentious presence of "Dominion" players in the side, two South Africans (Hofmeyr and Small), and one All Black (Botting). - there were also six Oxford University students in the team - England fell at the first hurdle. The Welsh side led by John Gwilliam, and including new cap eighteen year old Lewis Jones at full-back, won at Twickenham for only the second time since 1910, and went on to take the Triple Crown and the Grand Slam. It was a poor performance by the English pack who could not compete with John Gwilliam or his inspired leadership, and the backs, therefore, had little opportunity to run with the ball - even Smith's try, on his debut, came from an interception. Murray Hofmeyr had an outstanding game at full-back and never put a foot wrong although sometimes under intense pressure. The match attracted a record crowd of 75,532 - one third of whom, it was estimated, were Welsh - and this prompted the RFU to decree that all future Internationals at Twickenham would be all-ticket. The police also imposed a maximum to the crowd of 72,500 for all future matches.

62nd match   **ENGLAND   3 pts**   v   **IRELAND   0 pts**

	Caps					Caps		
15	4th & last	**R.Uren**	(Waterloo)	.		6th	**G.W.Norton**	(Bective Rangers)
14	2nd	**J.V.Smith**	(Cambridge Univ)	.		7th	**M.F.Lane**	(UC Cork)
13	2nd	**B.Boobbyer**	(Oxford University)	.		11th	**W.D.McKee**	(NIFC)
12	7th	**L.B.Cannell**	(Oxford University)	.		1st	**G.C.Phipps**	(Army)
11	2nd & last	**I.J.Botting**	(Oxford University)	.		1st	**L.Crowe**	(Old Belvedere)
10	7th	**I.Preece (Capt)**	(Coventry)	.		15th	**J.W.Kyle**	(Queens U Belfast)
9	5th	**W.K.T.Moore**	(Leicester)	.		2nd	**J.H.Burges**	(Rosslyn Park)
1	5th	**J.M.Kendall-Carpenter**	(Oxford University)	.		6th	**J.T.Clifford**	(Young Munster)
2	3rd	**J.H.Steeds**	(Saracens)	.		15th	**K.D.Mullen (Capt)**	(Old Belvedere)
3	2nd	**W.A.Holmes**	(Nuneaton)	.		2nd	**D.McKibbin**	(Instonians)
4	3rd	**J.R.C.Matthews**	(Harlequins)	.		10th	**J.E.Nelson**	(Malone)
5	2nd	**H.A.Jones**	(Barnstaple)	.		9th	**R.D.Agar**	(Malone)
6	2nd	**H.D.Small**	(Oxford University)	.		15th	**J.W.McKay**	(Queens U Belfast)
7	6th	**V.G.Roberts**	(Penryn)	.		2nd	**A.B.Curtis**	(Oxford University)
8	1st	**S.J.Adkins**	(Coventry)	.		9th	**D.J.O'Brien**	(London Irish)

Referee: R.A.Beattie   (Scotland)

SCORERS: **V.G.Roberts**   Try   (2nd & last)   3 - 0
                                                                Half-time
                                                                3 - 0

POINTS: V.G.Roberts   3 points   (6)

MATCH COMMENTARY:
After the disappointing performance against Wales, the selectors made six changes, but two of these, Hofmeyr and Rimmer, were
necessitated by injury, in an attempt to reverse the trend of Irish post-war victories over England, and in this respect they were successful.
Ireland, holders of the triple Crown for two years, and victors over England for the last three, had begun the season as hot favourites to
continue their successes, but a drawn match in Paris in near arctic conditions had already tempered those expectations with reality.
This match was hard and very even, with Karl Mullen again an inspiring leader, and Jack Kyle at the peak of his considerable form, but it
was Ivor Preece creating a break from counter-attack who opened up the field for Vic Roberts to score the only try of the match. England
owed their success as much to the unfortunate injury to Irish centre-threequarter Des McKee who was compelled to leave the field just
before half-time, thus reducing the Irish pack to seven, as they did to any strategy and plan of attack of their own. England, before
McKee's departure were pressed and Norton was desperately close with both a drop goal and a penalty attempt. The second half was
a thrilling encounter, but Ireland could not manage the vital break-through, and England were really a shade fortunate to win this match,
their only success of the season.

25th match   **ENGLAND   3 pts**   **v**   **FRANCE   6 pts**

	Caps					Caps		
15	2nd	**M.B.Hofmeyr**	(Oxford University)	.		1st	**G.Brun**	(Vienne)
14	3rd	**J.V.Smith**	(Cambridge Univ)	.		5th	**M.Siman**	(Castres)
13	3rd	**B.Boobbyer**	(Oxford University)	.		3rd	**P.Lauga**	(Vichy)
12	8th	**L.B.Cannell**	(Oxford University)	.		3rd	**J.Merquey**	(Toulon)
11	1st	**J.P.Hyde**	(Northampton)	.		1st	**F.Cazenave**	(Racing Club)
10	8th	**I.Preece (Capt)**	(Coventry)	.		2nd	**J.Pilon**	(Perigueux)
9	6th	**W.K.T.Moore**	(Leicester)	.		6th	**G.Dufau**	(Racing Club)
1	6th	**J.M.Kendall-Carpenter**	(Oxford University)	.		3rd	**R.Bienes**	(Cognac)
2	4th	**J.H.Steeds**	(Saracens)	.		2nd	**P.Pascalin**	(Mont-de-Marsan)
3	3rd	**W.A.Holmes**	(Nuneaton)	.		3rd	**R.Ferrien**	(Tarbes)
4	4th	**J.R.C.Matthews**	(Harlequins)	.		5th	**P.Aristouy**	(Pau)
5	3rd & last	**H.A.Jones**	(Barnstaple)	.		3rd	**F.Bonnus**	(Toulon)
6	3rd	**H.D.Small**	(Oxford University)	.		25th	**J.Prat**	(Lourdes)
7	7th	**V.G.Roberts**	(Penryn)	.		21st	**J.Matheu-Cambas**	(Castres)
8	2nd	**S.J.Adkins**	(Coventry)	.		22nd	**G.Basquet (Capt)**	(Agen)

Referee: N.H.Lambert   (Ireland)

SCORERS:

				0 - 3	**J.Pilon**		Try
	J.V.Smith	Try	(2nd)	3 - 3			
				Half-time			
				3 - 6	**F.Cazenave**		Try

POINTS:

J.V.Smith	3 points	(6)		**J.Pilon**	3 points
				F.Cazenave	3 points

MATCH COMMENTARY:

England made two changes after the solid performance against the Irish, restoring the previously injured Murray Hofmeyr to full-back and introducing John Hyde in place of the New Zealander Ian Botting. There had been torrential rain in the previous two days, the Seine was full, and, true to form, Stade Colombes was little more than a quagmire. France gave England a torrid time, and England did well to hold them to two unconverted tries. Dealing with a very slippery ball led to many handling mistakes but even so Lauga and Pilon attempted several drop goals and the frequent appearance of the new French full-back, Georges Brun, into the line at pace, stretched the English defence to the limit. Hofmeyr was sorely pressed with high kicks of pinpoint accuracy and ferocious forward rushes but he never flinched and must have denied France at least a dozen points. As the "Times" correspondent reported   " .....he had to excel himself if he was not to appear slow". Smith's try came from a kick ahead and a follow up at pace which, even by French standards, was electric. Cazenave's winning try for France late in the second half was a touch dubious as he appeared to have been driven into the corner flag before he touched down. A creditable performance by England against a formidable French XV in appalling conditions.

65th match
57th Calcutta Cup

ENGLAND　11 pts　　v　　SCOTLAND　13 pts

	Caps				Caps		
15	3rd & last	M.B.Hofmeyr	(Oxford University)	.	1st	T.Gray	(Northampton)
14	4th & last	J.V.Smith	(Cambridge Univ)	.	2nd	D.M.Scott	(Langholm)
13	4th	B.Boobbyer	(Oxford University)	.	4th & last	R.Macdonald	(Edinburgh Univ)
12	9th	L.B.Cannell	(Oxford University)	.	3rd	D.A.Sloan	(Edinburgh Acad)
11	2nd & last	J.P.Hyde	(Northampton)	.	11th & last	C.W.Drummond	(Melrose)
10	9th	I.Preece (Capt)	(Coventry)	.	3rd	A.Cameron	(Glasgow HSFP)
9	7th & last	W.K.T.Moore	(Leicester)	.	6th & last	A.W.Black	(Edinburgh Univ)
1	1st & only	J.L.Baume	(Northern)	.	10th	J.C.Dawson	(Glasgow Acad)
2	5th & last	J.H.Steeds	(Saracens)	.	7th	J.G.Abercrombie	(Edinburgh Univ)
3	4th	W.A.Holmes	(Nuneaton)	.	4th & last	G.M.Budge	(Edinburgh Wand'rs)
4	5th	J.R.C.Matthews	(Harlequins)	.	4th	R.Gemmill	(Glasgow HSFP)
5	3rd	S.J.Adkins	(Coventry)	.	4th	D.E.Muir	(Heriots)
6	4th & last	H.D.Small	(Oxford University)	.	16th	W.I.D.Elliot	(Edinburgh Acad)
7	8th	V.G.Roberts	(Penryn)	.	1st & only	J.S.Scott	(St Andrew's Univ)
8	7th	J.M.Kendall-Carpenter	(Oxford University)	.	8th	P.W.Kinninmonth	(Richmond)
							(Capt)

Referee:　　M.J.Dowling　　　(Ireland)

SCORERS:

				0 - 3	D.A.Sloan	Try
J.V.Smith	Try	(3rd)		3 - 3		
				3 - 6	J.G.Abercrombie	Try
				3 - 8	T.Gray	Conversion
				Half-time		
M.B.Hofmeyr	Penalty Goal			6 - 8		
J.V.Smith	Try	(4th & last)		9 - 8		
M.B.Hofmeyr	Conversion			11 - 8		
				11 - 11	D.A.Sloan	Try
				11 - 13	T.Gray	Conversion

POINTS:

J.V.Smith	6 points	(12)	D.A.Sloan	6 points	
M.B.Hofmeyr	5 points	(7)	T.Gray	4 points	
			J.G.Abercrombie	3 points	

MATCH COMMENTARY:

England lost an exciting match and the Calcutta Cup, and ended a poor season in wet and muddy conditions in Edinburgh. Scotland dramatically came from behind ten minutes from time to win the match when Tom Gray, who played his club rugby for Northampton at fly-half, converted the third Scottish try. Gray had had a foot severely injured during the war and played with a specially built up boot, and it was he who peppered the English posts with penalty and drop goal attempts before Sloan scored his second and decisive try. All five tries were opportunist as handling the wet ball was a very risky business and it is doubtful whether any of the four wings received a pass from a running movement during the entire match. Some observers, it is said, thought England deserved to win, and indeed they came close to doing so, but, at the end of the day, a try count of three to two tells the true story. In this match, for the first time, John Kendall-Carpenter, having gained six earlier caps at loose-head prop, played at No 8 (then called lock) where he was to play sixteen more times for England with great distinction. J.V.Smith had scored four tries in the Five Nations season - no mean feat at any time. England collected the Wooden Spoon for the second time in three years, but it would be fourteen years before they lost to Scotland again.

SUMMARY OF THE SEASON - 1949 - 50:

Following the two very good performances at the end of the previous season, hopes were high for a successful Five Nations campaign when England prepared to entertain Wales at Twickenham for the opening match of the season. Six players were no longer available of the fifteen who so handsomely beat Scotland the previous March, but ten changes were made and eight new caps introduced. The bandwagon was rolling, but, by the final whistle, unfortunately the wheels had fallen off and the season became another disappointment for England with only one win from the four matches.

Eleven new caps were awarded throughout the season but England used a total of only twenty-two players for the four Five Nations matches, seven of then students at Oxbridge. During the season controversy raged , mainly from beyond the English borders, regarding the preference shown by the English selectors for Dominion players. For the Welsh match there were three - All Black Ian Botting and two South Africans, Hofmeyr and Small. However, the tumult died down when it became apparent that England's only achievement was going to be the Wooden Spoon.

Wales, the season's Grand Slam winners, were far too good for England especially up front, and the consequent lack of possession gave the England backs very little chance. But the Welsh pressure was remorseless and England's early five point lead from J.V.Smith's interception try did not trouble John Gwilliam and his men at all. Six changes for the match with Ireland certainly had the desired effect, although Ireland had to play with only fourteen men for more than half the match, but it was a solid and tight performance. Only two changes were made for the encounter with France, and for Scotland only one, but there were two positional changes of significance. John Kendall-Carpenter switched from loose-head prop to No 8, and Stan Adkins from No 8 to lock. The moves undoubtedly strengthened the England pack but not enough, it transpired, for Scotland inflicted upon England their third defeat of a disappointing season. It was not that England had played badly, and their performance had improved with each match, it was simply that the opposition was just too good - except for those fourteen Irishmen !

For the second time in three seasons England finished in sole possession of the Wooden Spoon and had not even the Calcutta Cup as consolation. But there will undoubtedly be future seasons when they will play less well and finish in a more respectable position in the Championship Table.

Thirteen players played their last for England this season. D.B.Vaughan, a Royal Navy officer, and later England selector, retired with eight caps; W.K.T.Moore, the Leicester scrum-half, who was first capped for the first match after the Second World War, had been awarded seven; Harold Steeds, Registrar at the Middlesex Hospital, and the first Saracens player to be capped, and Geoffrey Hosking, formerly a Royal Marine, and latterly a farmer in Australia, each had five caps; J.V.Smith, the scorer of four tries in the season, a feat only to be accomplished by three other players in future years, H.D.Small, a native South African mining engineer, and Dick Uren, the Cheshire full-back, each earned four caps. Six other players retired with three caps or less, most distinguished of whom was Murray Hofmeyr, the immaculate full-back from South Africa, who was spending a year at Oxford. He would undoubtedly have won many more caps had he stayed in the UK.

J.V.Smith's four tries set a post-war record for England on two counts, tries and total points, and he also enjoyed the distinction of scoring on his debut against Wales.

FIVE NATIONS CHAMPIONSHIP TABLE:

Won: **Nothing**

		Played	Won	Lost	Drawn	Points: For	Against	Tries: For	Against	Title Points
1	Wales	4	4	0	0	50	8	10	1	8
2	Scotland	4	2	2	0	21	49	5	8	4
3 =	Ireland	4	1	2	1	27	12	3	3	3
3 =	France	4	1	2	1	14	35	3	7	3
5	**ENGLAND**	4	1	3	0	22	30	5	7	2

Home Games: lost to Wales 5 - 11, (one try to two); beat Ireland 3 - 0, (one try to nil)

Away Games: lost to France 3 - 6, (one try to two); lost to Scotland 11 - 13, (two tries to three)

56th match   **ENGLAND   5 pts**   v   **WALES   23 pts**

	Caps					Caps		
15	1st	E.N.Hewitt	(Coventry)	.	3rd	G.Williams	(London Welsh)
14	1st	C.G.Woodruff	(Harlequins)	.	18th	K.J.Jones	(Newport)
13	1st & only	L.F.L.Oakley	(Bedford)	.	5th	B.L.Jones	(Devonport Services)
12	5th	B.Boobbyer	(Oxford University)	.	14th	J.Matthews	(Cardiff)
11	1st	V.R.Tindall	(Liverpool Univ)	.	6th	M.C.Thomas	(Devonport Services)
10	10th	I.Preece	(Coventry)	.	10th	G.Davies	(Cambridge Univ)
9	4th	G.Rimmer	(Waterloo)	.	5th	W.R.Willis	(Cardiff)
1	1st	R.V.Stirling	(RAF/Leicester)	.	5th	J.D.Robins	(Birkenhead Park)
2	1st & only	T.A.Smith	(Northampton)	.	5th	D.M.Davies	(Somerset Police)
3	5th	W.A.Holmes	(Nuneaton)	.	14th	C.Davies	(Cardiff)
4	1st	D.T.Wilkins	(Roundhay)	.	5th	E.R.John	(Neath)
5	1st & only	J.T.Bartlett	(Waterloo)	.	7th	D.J.Hayward	(Newbridge)
6	9th	V.G.Roberts (Capt)	(Penryn)	.	1st	P.D.Evans	(Llannelli)
7	1st	G.C.Rittson-Thomas	(Oxford University)	.	7th	R.T.Evans	(Newport)
8	1st & only	P.B.C.Moore	(Blackheath)	.	11th	J.A.Gwilliam (Capt)	(Edinburgh Wand'rs)

Referee: M.Dowling   (Ireland)

SCORERS:

			0 - 3	J.Matthews	Try
			0 - 5	B.L.Jones	Conversion
			0 - 8	M.C.Thomas	Try
			Half-time		
			0 - 11	J.Matthews	Try
			0 - 13	B.L.Jones	Conversion
G.C.Rittson-Thomas	Try	(1st)	3 - 13		
E.N.Hewitt	Conversion		5 - 13		
			5 - 16	K.J.Jones	Try
			5 - 18	B.L.Jones	Conversion
			5 - 21	M.C.Thomas	Try
			5 - 23	B.L.Jones	Conversion

POINTS:

G.C.Rittson-Thomas	3 points	(3)	B.L.Jones	8 points
E.N.Hewitt	2 points	(2)	J.Matthews	6 points
			M.C.Thomas	6 points
			K.J.Jones	3 points

MATCH COMMENTARY:

England fielded ten new caps, and for four of them it was to be their only International appearance. Not surprisingly, England went down by five tries to one in their last match at St Helen's. The Welsh were able to do almost what they pleased, so inept was the English performance, but this was not the magnificent triumph that the Welsh press cracked it up to be - as would shortly be clearly demonstrated by the Scots. Nevertheless, Lewis Jones put in a performance which clearly illustrated his class and genius when he created three of the five tries and converted four. Not since 1922 had England lost by such a margin to Wales, and this was the highest points total against since Scotland scored 28 in 1931, and the second time since the war that England have conceded five tries in a match. England have now won only three matches in the last fourteen, and the selectors must be in even more of a muddle than were the English team in this match.

63rd match   **ENGLAND   0 pts**   v   **IRELAND   3 pts**

	Caps					Caps		
15	2nd	E.N.Hewitt	(Coventry)	.	10th	G.W.Norton	(Bective Rangers)
14	2nd	C.G.Woodruff	(Harlequins)	.	2nd & last	C.S.Griffin	(London Irish)
13	11th	I.Preece	(Coventry)	.	5th	N.J.Henderson	(Queen's U Belfast)
12	1st	J.M.Williams	(Penzance/Newlyn)	.	2nd	R.R.Chambers	(Instonians)
11	2nd	V.R.Tindall	(Liverpool Univ	.	1st	W.H.J.Millar	(Queen's U Belfast)
10	1st	E.M.P.Hardy	(Blackheath)	.	19th	J.W.Kyle	(Queen's U Belfast)
9	5th	G.Rimmer	(Waterloo)	.	2nd	J.A.O'Meara	(UC Cork)
1	2nd	R.V.Stirling	(RAF/Leicester)	.	10th	J.T.Clifford	(Young Munster)
2	3rd	E.Evans	(Sale)	.	19th	K.D.Mullen (Capt)	(Old Belvedere)
3	6th	W.A.Holmes	(Nuneaton)	.	2nd	J.H.Smith	(Queen's U Belfast)
4	2nd	D.T.Wilkins	(Roundhay)	.	14th	J.E.Nelson	(Malone)
5	1st	B.A.Neale	(Rosslyn Park)	.	6th	D.McKibbin	(Instonians)
6	10th	V.G.Roberts	(Penryn)	.	19th	J.W.McKay	(Queen's U Belfast)
7	2nd	G.C.Rittson-Thomas	(Oxford University)	.	11th	J.S.McCarthy	(Dolphin)
8	8th	J.M.Kendall-Carpenter	(Oxford University)	.	13th	D.J.O'Brien	(London Irish)
		(Capt)					

Referee: T.Jones   (Wales)

SCORERS:

	0 - 0		
	Half-time		
	0 - 3	D.McKibbin	Penalty Goal

POINTS: D.McKibbin   3 points

MATCH COMMENTARY:

A better performance by England after a further six changes, and a change of Captain, including a positional change to put Ivor Preece in the centre and bring in Hardy, the Yorkshire fly-half. The improvement, however, was mainly in the pack who looked purposeful and resolute compared with recent performances. The Irish pack, though were rumbustious and aggressive and, in general, played at a formidable pace. Jack Kyle was masterminding Irish attacks all afternoon and they were camped on the English line for the greater part of the match, but could not get that elusive try. The unfortunate Gordon Rimmer provided the Irish with a opportunity which the whole English defence had denied them, by committing an offence at his put-in to a scrum and conceding the penalty goal which proved decisive.

Rittson-Thomas and Roberts, the England flankers, created several breakaways from the siege on England's line, and on one such occasion, Hardy hit the post high up with a drop goal attempt, but every time Ireland worked their remoresless weay back to the England line only to be foiled again. England were the only side, during the season, to deny Ireland at least one try, and only a draw at Cardiff denied Ireland the Triple Crown and Grand Slam. But, this was England's ninth successive defeat away from home since they beat Wales in the first full International match since the second world war.

26th match   **ENGLAND   3 pts**   v   **FRANCE   11 pts**

	Caps					Caps		
15	3rd & last	E.N.Hewitt	(Coventry)	.		4th	R.Arcalis	(Brive)
14	3rd	C.G.Woodruff	(Harlequins)	.		2nd	A.Porthault	(Racing Club)
13	12th & last	I.Preece	(Coventry)	.		4th	G.Brun	(Vienne)
12	6th	B.Boobbyer	(Oxford University)	.		2nd	G.Belletante	(Nantes)
11	3rd	V.R.Tindall	(Liverpool Univ)	.		17th	M.Pomathios	(Lyon)
10	2nd	E.M.P.Hardy	(Blackheath)	.		19th	A.Alvarez	(Tyrosse)
9	6th	G.Rimmer	(Waterloo)	.		10th	G.Dufau	(Racing Club)
1	3rd	R.V.Stirling	(RAF/Leicester)	.		3rd	R.Bernard	(Bergerac)
2	4th	E.Evans	(Sale)	.		6th	P.Pascalin	(Mont-de-Marsan)
3	7th	W.A.Holmes	(Nuneaton)	.		2nd	P.Bertrand	(Bressanne)
4	3rd	D.T.Wilkins	(Roundhay)	.		3rd	L.Mias	(Mazamet)
5	2nd	B.A.Neale	(Rosslyn Park)	.		3rd	H.Foures	(Toulouse)
6	11th	V.G.Roberts	(Penryn)	.		28th	J.Prat	(Lourdes)
7	3rd & last	G.C.Rittson-Thomas	(Oxford University)	.		7th	R.Bienes	(Cognac)
8	9th	J.M.Kendall-Carpenter	(Penzance-Newlyn)	.		26th	G.Basquet (Capt)	(Agen)
		(Capt)						

Referee: V.S.Llewellyn   (Wales)

SCORERS:	B.Boobbyer	Try	(1st)	3 - 0			
				3 - 3	G.Basquet	Try	
				3 - 5	J.Prat	Conversion	
				Half-time			
				3 - 8	J.Prat	Try	
				3 - 11	J.Prat	Drop Goal	

POINTS:	B.Boobbyer	3 points	(3)		J.Prat	8 points
					G.Basquet	3 points

MATCH COMMENTARY:

This was France's first ever victory at Twickenham, and the match, played in driving rain, was dominated and won by the French flanker, Jean Prat. On the occasion of his 28th cap, Prat contributed a try, a conversion and a drop goal to a very well earned victory. England had retained the same pack after the narrow defeat in Dublin and there were more encouraging signs that the eight were beginning to function very well as a unit, but, on this occasion, the French were much quicker to the slippery ball and were able to handle it to better effect. England showed great promise early in the match, after Brian Boobbyer's try, when several breaks drove the French back to their own line. Prominent in these breakaways was Chris Rittson-Thomas who had played very well in his first two games in an England jersey, but who, unfortunately, had to leave the field injured before half-time. His departure and the resultant reduction to seven in the England pack - indeed at one stage in the second half England were down to six forwards - does not detract from the performance of the French in general, or that of Jean Prat in particular. No-one would deny France their first success at Twickenham after this performance, but their triumph put England in the unenviable position of having lost five successive Five Nations matches for the second time in five years

66th match   **ENGLAND**   **5 pts**   **v**   **SCOTLAND**   **3 pts**
58th Calcutta Cup

	Caps					Caps		
15	1st	W.G.Hook	(Gloucester)	.	3rd & last	T.Gray	(Heriots FP)
14	4th & last	C.G.Woodruff	(Harlequins)	.	2nd	K.J.Dalgleish	(Edinburgh Wand'rs)
13	2nd & last	A.C.Towell	(Bedford)	.	6th	D.A.Sloan	(Edinburgh Acad)
12	2nd & last	J.M.Williams	(Penzance-Newlyn)	.	5th	D.M.Scott	(Langholm)
11	4th & last	V.R.Tindall	(Liverpool Univ)	.	4th	D.M.Rose	(Jedforest)
10	3rd & last	E.M.P.Hardy	(Blackheath)	.	7th	A.Cameron	(Glasgow HSFP)
9	1st	D.W.Shuttleworth	(Headingley)	.	4th & last	I.A.Ross	(Hillhead HSFP)
1	4th	R.V.Stirling	(RAF/Leicester)	.	14th	J.C.Dawson	(Glasgow Acad)
2	5th	E.Evans	(Sale)	.	4th & last	N.G.R.Mair	(Edinburgh Univ)
3	8th	W.A.Holmes	(Nuneaton)	.	4th	R.L.Wilson	(Gala)
4	4th	D.T.Wilkins	(Roundhay)	.	4th	H.M.Inglis	(Edinburgh Acad)
5	3rd & last	B.A.Neale	(Rosslyn Park)	.	5th & last	W.P.Black	(Glasgow HSFP)
6	12th	V.G.Roberts	(Penryn)	.	20th	W.I.D.Elliot	(Edniburgh Acad)
7	6th	D.F.White	(Northampton)	.	3rd	R.C.Taylor	(Kelvinside-West)
8	10th	J.M.Kendall-Carpenter	(Penzance-Newlyn)	.	12th	P.W.Kinninmonth	(Richmond)
		(Capt)				**(Capt)**	

Referee: M.J.Dowling   (Ireland)

SCORERS: D.F.White   Try   (2nd & last)   3 - 0
                 W.G.Hook   Conversion   5 - 0
                                                    Half-time
                                                             5 - 3   A.Cameron   Try

POINTS: D.F.White   3 points   (6)   A.Cameron   3 points
                 W.G.Hook   2 points   (2)

MATCH COMMENTARY:

England won the Calcutta Cup with a convincing display of resolute forward play in both loose and tight, and some imaginative and attacking play from the Yorkshire half-back pair who, strangely, were never to play together for England again. It was a hard and fast game with drenching rain in the second half.   England's try came late in the first half and Scotland's even later in the second half when the fourteen stone fly-half, Angus Cameron, forced his way over in the corner. Hamish Inglis could not convert from the touch-line and England won a very close encounter. England had their chances with both Hook and Hardy going desperately close with drop and penalty goal attempts throughout the second half. After five successive defeats, any win would have been very satisfactiory, and indeed this was. But, it is only the fourth win England have recorded in the last four Five Nations Championships, average one per season. Not a record of which to be proud ! The England half-back pairing of Evan Hardy and Dennis Shuttleworth was unique in that, not only did they play together for Yorkshire, they were both in the Army and were both in the same regiment, the Duke of Wellington's. As well as Hardy, five other players played their last for England in this match, including the entire three-quarter line !

SUMMARY OF THE SEASON - 1950 - 51:

In many respects this season was worse for England than either of the other two Wooden Spoon seasons, 1947-48 and 1949-50, because they were humiliated by Wales, generally run off their feet by Ireland (not for the last time) and allowed France to win for the first time at Twickenham before pulling themselves together and beating Scotland in a determined fashion in the last match of the season. England scored fewer and conceded more tries and points in the season than any other side in the Championship, and by some monstrous injustice had to share the Wooden Spoon with Scotland, who had also won only one game, but who had scored more than twice as many tries as England and had conceded only half as many.

The opening match against Wales was the last time England were to play a match at St Helen's, Swansea, and it was not one they would wish to remember. England made eleven changes and introduced ten new caps for this match and for the season awarded a total of fifteen new caps and played 25 different players. Wales inflicted a humiliating defeat on England because not only did England allow Wales to do almost anything they liked during the course of the match, not only did they give Lewis Jones the freedom of the park, but because Wales' capability was put into perspective in their next match when Scotland beat them by an even bigger margin, and because they failed to win another match in the Championship. After that four of the new caps at Swansea were promptly dropped, and six changes and three more new caps formed the side for the visit to Lansdowne Road, where England had not won since 1938, and, at least in defence, the team performance was very much improved. Much of the game was played on the England line, but the defence held and they successfully denied Ireland a try - the only side to do so this season. Then to Twickenham, and France, and Jean Prat who master-minded his side to their first ever victory at Twickenham. The England pack, unchanged from the visit to Dublin, acquitted themselves very well when they were all on the field - at one time they were reduced to six in number - but the French were quicker to man and ball and dealt with the wet ball very much better. England's last chance of closing the season with any credibility whatsoever depended not so much on the performance, but the result against Scotland. A further five changes and the Yorkshire and Army pairing of Hardy and Shuttleworth at half-back, was the basis of a determined and resolute performance by the front ten in extremely wet conditions, and a very close match was just, but deservedly, won.

Even so, England had now won only four matches in the last four Five Nations Championships, and during the five seasons since the Championship resumed after the war, had won only once away from home. So, again, the honours were the Calcutta Cup and a share of the Wooden Spoon. Three tries and only thirteen points in total for the season's effforts was very poor reward, but, in truth, it was no less than the side deserved.

Ivor Preece, the versatile and innovative Coventry player, not available through injury for the last match of the season, did not play for England again. With twelve caps he was England's most capped post-war player, had played at fly-half ten times and in the centre twice and he had captained the side for six of the twenty matches since the war. Ivor Preece was one of only three Englishmen to tour Australia and New Zealand with the 1950 Lions, the others being Gordon Rimmer and Vic Roberts. Preece and Roberts each played in only one Test. Another twelve players gained their last caps during the season. Among them were, Vic Tindall, still an undergraduate at Liverpool University, retired with four caps and continued to play club rugby for many years after he became a consultant obstetrician; Charlie Woodruff, also with four caps, having been in the RAF, continued to work for the Air Ministry; Walter Hewitt, an excellent oarsman, gained three caps as did Bruce Neale a serving officer in the Royal Artillery; Chris Rittson-Thomas, three caps, having scored a try on his debut against Wales, on graduating from Oxford went to work for Lloyds Bank; and the thrice capped Evan Hardy continued his career in the Army and achieved the rank of Colonel. Alan Towell, a Bedford schoolteacher, retired with two caps, one in 1948, and one in 1951; and John Williams took his two caps back to his solicitor's office in Cornwall. The remaining four, Brian Braithwaite-Exley, Jasper Bartlett, Harvey Smith and Philip Moore, who was later to become Private Secretary to Her Majesty The Queen and was elevated to the peerage in 1986, all belonged to that unfortunate band of men who, due to circumstances or lack of ability, earned only one cap each. In their case, the rock upon which their ambitions perished was that disastrous match against Wales at St Helen's.

FIVE NATIONS CHAMPIONSHIP TABLE:

Won: **Calcutta Cup**

		Played	Won	Lost	Drawn	Points: For	Against	Tries: For	Against	Title Points
1	Ireland	4	3	0	1	21	16	4	3	7
2	France	4	3	1	0	41	27	7	6	6
3	Wales	4	1	2	1	29	35	6	6	3
4 =	Scotland	4	1	3	0	39	25	7	4	2
4 =	ENGLAND	4	1	3	0	13	40	3	8	2

Home Games: lost to France 3 - 11, (one try to two); beat Scotland 5 - 5, (one try each).

Away Games: lost to Wales 5 - 23, (one try to five); lost to Ireland 0 - 3, (no tries)

4th match   **ENGLAND   3 pts**   v   **SOUTH AFRICA   8 pts**

	Caps					Caps		
15	2nd	W.G.Hook	(Gloucester)			4th	J.U.Buchler	(Transvaal)
14	1st	J.E.Woodward	(Wasps)			4th	P.G.A.Johnstone	(Western Province)
13	1st	A.E.Agar	(Harlequins)			7th	R.A.M.van Schoor	(Rhodesia)
12	10th	L.B.Cannell	(St Mary's Hospital)			8th	M.T.Lategan	(Western Province)
11	1st	C.E.Winn	(Rosslyn Park)			3rd	J.K.Ochse	(Western Province)
10	7th	N.M.Hall (Capt)	(Richmond)			8th	J.D.Brewis	(Northern Transvaal)
9	7th	G.Rimmer	(Waterloo)			7th	P.A.du Toit	(Northern Transvaal)
1	9th	W.A.Holmes	(Nuneaton)			1st	H.P.J.Bekker	(Northern Transvaal)
2	6th	E.Evans	(Sale)			4th	W.H.Delport	(Eastern Province)
3	5th	R.V.Stirling	(RAF/Leicester)			7th	A.C.Koch	(Boland)
4	6th	J.R.C.Matthews	(Harlequins)			6th	J.A.du Rand	(Rhodesia)
5	5th	D.T.Wilkins	(US Portsmouth)			3rd	E.E.Dinklemann	(Northern Transvaal)
6	7th	D.F.White	(Northampton)			4th	S.P.Fry	(Western Province)
7	1st	A.O.Lewis	(Bath)			4th	C.J.van Wyk	(Transvaal)
8	11th	J.M.Kendall-Carpenter	(Penzance-Newlyn)			8th	H.S.V.Muller (Capt)	(Transvaal)

Referee: W.C.W.Murdoch   (Scotland)

SCORERS:

			0 - 3	P.A.du Toit	Try
			0 - 5	H.S.V.Muller	Conversion
C.E.Winn	Try	(1st)	3 - 5		
			Half-time		
			3 - 8	H.S.V.Muller	Penalty Goal

POINTS:

C.E.Winn	3 points	(3)		H.S.V.Muller	5 points
				P.A.du Toit	3 points

MATCH COMMENTARY:

There were eight changes from the side which had beaten Scotland in the previous match in March, two in the pack, all the three-quarter line and both half-backs, but there were only four new caps. Nim Hall was recalled at fly-half , and given the Captaincy, to inject some depth of experience in that pivotal position against some formidable opponents.

England put up a fine performance to hold the mighty South Africans, who had won their first three Tests (and were later to beat France as well), to one try apiece. The English pack lived up to all the high expectations of last season, and although Nim Hall at fly-half had been, and would be, criticised, and not for the first time, for being unable to make the decisive break to release his backs and the powerful Ted Woodward and Chris Winn on the wings, Winn, nonetheless, scored the English try on his debut. In spite of the soft and slippery ground, there was a good deal of open play, and further tries were almost scored by both sides. Both Albert Agar and Ochse, the South African wing, managed to cross the line but both failed to ground the ball at the last moment. Muller's penalty goal in the second half hit the post and rebounded over. It was a close thing, and in the end the match was won by the magnificent South African pack - but England gave a very good account of themselves.

57th match   **ENGLAND   6 pts**   v   **WALES   8 pts**

		<u>Caps</u>				<u>Caps</u>		
15	3rd & last	**W.G.Hook**	(Gloucester)	.	8th	**G.Williams**	(Llanelli)
14	2nd	**J.E.Woodward**	(Wasps)	.	25th	**K.J.Jones**	(Newport)
13	2nd	**A.E.Agar**	(Harlequins)	.	1st	**A.G.Thomas**	(Swansea)
12	11th	**L.B.Cannell**	(St Mary's Hospital)	.	11th	**M.C.Thomas**	(Newport)
11	2nd	**C.E.Winn**	(Rosslyn Park)	.	8th	**B.L.Jones**	(Llanelli)
10	8th	**N.M.Hall (Capt)**	(Richmond)	.	4th	**C.I.Morgan**	(Cardiff)
9	8th	**G.Rimmer**	(Waterloo)	.	10th	**W.R.Willis**	(Cardiff)
1	1st & only	**E.E.Woodgate**	(Paignton)	.	3rd	**W.O.G.Williams**	(Swansea)
2	7th	**E.Evans**	(Sale)	.	10th	**D.M.Davies**	(Somerset Police)
3	6th	**R.V.Stirling**	(RAF/Leicester)	.	12th	**D.J.Hayward**	(Newbridge)
4	7th	**J.R.C.Matthews**	(Harlequins)	.	10th	**E.R.John**	(Neath)
5	6th	**D.T.Wilkins**	(US Portsmouth)	.	11th	**J.R.G.Stephens**	(Neath)
6	8th	**D.F.White**	(Northampton)	.	2nd	**L.Blyth**	(Swansea)
7	2nd	**A.O.Lewis**	(Bath)	.	3rd	**A.Forward**	(Pontypool)
8	12th	**J.M.Kendall-Carpenter**	(Penzance-Newlyn)	.	15th	**J.A.Gwilliam (Capt)**	(Edinburgh Wand'rs)

Referee: N.H.Lambert   (Ireland)

SCORERS:	**A.E.Agar**	Try	(1st & only)	3 - 0		
	J.E.Woodward	Try	(1st)	6 - 0		
				6 - 3	**K.J.Jones**	Try
				6 - 5	**M.C.Thomas**	Conversion
				Half-time		
				6 - 8	**K.J.Jones**	Try

POINTS:	**A.E.Agar**	3 points	(3)		**K.J.Jones**	6 points
	J.E.Woodward	3 points	(3)		**M.C.Thomas**	2 points

MATCH COMMENTARY:

England had not beaten Wales since 1947, and hopes were high that, at home, this unfortunate trend could be reversed. Alas, it was not to be. The eventual Triple Crown and Grand Slam winners were dominant and England could not contain the genius of Cliff Morgan or the wizardry of Ken Jones, who scored both the Welsh tries, the second being quite spectacular. Again, the England pack aquitted themselves well, although perhaps missing the strength of Holmes in the tight following his withdrawal from the side at the last minute. Despite the reservations about Nim Hall, the England backs scored two tries, both on Lewis Jones' wing, the first when he was limping badly before treatment and the second when he was off the field getting it.

In an enthralling second half, Wales fought back to gain the lead and win the match primarily on the basis of possession won by Roy John in the lines-out. Ironically, the movement which resulted in the match winning try scored by Ken Jones was initiated by the limping Lewis Jones which more than atoned for his temporary absence when the second English try was scored. In the last minute it appeared that Alec Lewis had scored a sensational winning try from a Gordon Rimmer cross-kick, but the referee adjudged him off-side and the try was disallowed.

67th match   **ENGLAND   19 pts   v   SCOTLAND   3 pts**
59th Calcutta Cup

	Caps				Caps		
15	1st	P.J.Collins	(Camborne)		1st	N.W.Cameron	(Glasgow University)
14	3rd	J.E.Woodward	(Wasps)		5th	R.A.Gordon	(Edinburgh Wand'rs)
13	3rd	A.E.Agar	(Harlequins)		4th & last	I.F.Cordial	(Edinburgh Wand'rs)
12	7th	B.Boobbyer	(Rosslyn Park)		2nd & last	I.D.F.Coutts	(Old Aleynians)
11	3rd	C.E.Winn	(Rosslyn Park)		1st	T.G.Weatherstone	(Stewart's Coll FP)
10	9th	N.M.Hall (Capt)	(Richmond)		4th	J.N.G.Davidson	(Edinburgh Univ)
9	2nd	P.W.Sykes	(Wasps)		5th	A.F.Dorward	(Gala)
1	10th	W.A.Holmes	(Nuneaton)		19th	J.C.Dawson	(Glasgow Acad'ls)
2	8th	E.Evans	(Sale)		4th & last	J.Fox	(Gala)
3	7th	R.V.Stirling	(RAF/Leicester)		1st & only	J.M.Inglis	(Selkirk)
4	8th	J.R.C.Matthews	(Harlequins)		5th & last	J.Johnston	(Melrose)
5	7th	D.T.Wilkins	(US Portsmouth)		7th & last	D.E.Muir	(Heriot's)
6	9th	D.F.White	(Northampton)		25th	W.I.D.Elliot	(Edinburgh Acad'ls)
7	3rd	A.O.Lewis	(Bath)		1st & only	D.S.Gilbert-Smith	(London Scottish)
8	13th	J.M.Kendall-Carpenter	(Penzance-Newlyn)		1st & only	J.P.Friebe	(Glasgow HSFP)

Referee: M.J.Dowling   (Ireland)

SCORERS:

C.E.Winn	Try	(2nd)	3 - 0			
N.M.Hall	Conversion		5 - 0			
			Half-time			
E.Evans	Try	(1st)	8 - 0			
J.E.Woodward	Try	(2nd)	11 - 0			
J.M.Kendall-Carpenter	Try	(1st & only)	14 - 0			
N.M.Hall	Conversion		16 - 0			
			16 - 3		J.Johnston	Try
A.E.Agar	D'p Goal (1st & only)		19 - 3			

POINTS:

N.M.Hall	4 points	(15)		J.Johnston	3 points
J.E.Woodward, C.E.Winn		(6),(6)			
A.E.Agar, E.Evans and	3 points	(6),(3)			
J.M.Kendall-Carpenter	each				

MATCH COMMENTARY:

It had been a disastrous season for Scotland in which thet had lost all five games, including the 44 - 0 defeat by South Africa the previous November, but this did not detract from England's substantial performance. Four tries were scored including one from each wing. All the promise of the last few matches since this pack was put together at the beginning of the previous season, was now being realised, and the team , the selectors and the long-suffering English supporters could be well-pleased with the outcome. It was suggested by some that perhaps England were flattered by this result because the heels were slow and the lines-out were untidy. Even so, the fact of the matter is that England were good enough to run nineteen points past another International side, and having won only two of their previous ten matches, the critics, for the time being, could be contemptuously ignored. In gaining his thirteenth cap, John Kendall-Carpenter became England's most-capped post-war player, exceeding Ivor Preece's total of twelve. Nim Hall emulated Dickie Guest's record of fifteen post-war points for England.

64th match   **ENGLAND 3 pts**   v   **IRELAND 0 pts**

	Caps				Caps		
15	2nd	P.J.Collins	(Camborne)	.	4th	J.G.M.W.Murphy	(Dublin University)
14	4th	C.E.Winn	(Rosslyn Park)	.	1st & only	M.F.Hillary	(UC Dublin)
13	4th	A.E.Agar	(Harlequins)	.	12th	N.J.Henderson	(Queen's U Belfast)
12	8th	B.Boobbyer	(Rosslyn Park)	.	5th & last	G.C.Phipps	(Rosslyn Park)
11	1st	R.C.Bazley	(Waterloo)	.	1st & only	N.Bailey	(Northampton)
10	10th	N.M.Hall (Capt)	(Richmond)	.	26th	J.W.Kyle	(NIFC)
9	3rd	P.W.Sykes	(Wasps)	.	9th	J.A.O'Meara	(UC Cork)
1	11th	W.A.Holmes	(Nuneaton)	.	1st	W.A.O'Neill	(UC Dublin)
2	9th	E.Evans	(Sale)	.	1st	R.Roe	(Dublin University)
3	8th	R.V.Stirling	(RAF/Leicester)	.	9th	J.H.Smith	(Collegians)
4	9th	J.R.C.Matthews	(Harlequins)	.	6th	P.J.Lawler	(Clontarf)
5	8th	D.T.Wilkins	(US Portsmouth)	.	3rd & last	A.F.O'Leary	(Cork Constitution)
6	10th	D.F.White	(Northampton)	.	1st	P.J.Kavanagh	(UC Dublin)
7	4th	A.O.Lewis	(Bath)	.	18th	J.S.McCarthy	(Dolphin)
8	14th	J.M.Kendall-Carpenter	(Penzance-Newlyn)	.	20th & last	D.J.O'Brien (Capt)	(Cardiff)

Referee: I.David   (Wales)

SCORERS: B.Boobbyer   Try   (2nd & last)   3 - 0
                                          Half-time
                                          3 - 0

POINTS: B.Boobbyer   3 points   (6)

MATCH COMMENTARY:

Ireland had been Five Nations Champions for three out of the last four seasons, and had achieved this success not least because of their powerful and very mobile pack, which had undoubtedly been the best in the tournament in recent years. England's performance against these formidable opponents was of a very high order, as it had also been two years previously when both result and score were exactly the same. Again, England's try was scored by the back division, and was the sixth scored by the backs in the four games so far this season. The match was scheduled to have been played on February 9th, but had been postponed due to the death of King George VI, and in the event, was played in near blizzard conditions. At the time it was decided to start the match, only half the pitch had been cleared of snow, but the officials (and the teams) were so fearful of another postponement that it was decided to get the match going as soon as possible. As it was conditions at one end of the pitch were completely different from conditions at the other. At the south end, the ball would skid on the slippery surface, and at the north end it would stop dead in the snow. It was a pity that conditions should have been so inhibiting to open running rugby in the last International appearance of Des O'Brien whose contributions to Ireland's recent successes had been immense, and who had set new standards in back row mobility and tenacity in the loose.

27th match   **ENGLAND   6 pts**   v   **FRANCE   3 pts**

	Caps				Caps		
15	3rd & last	P.J.Collins	(Camborne)	.	10th	G.Brun	(Vienne)
14	5th	C.E.Winn	(Rosslyn Park)	.	20th	M.Pomathios	(Lyon)
13	5th	A.E.Agar	(Harlequins)	.	3rd	J.Mauran	(Castres)
12	9th & last	B.Boobbyer	(Rosslyn Park)	.	6th	M.Prat	(Lourdes)
11	2nd	R.C.Bazley	(Waterloo)	.	3rd & last	J.Colombier	(St Junien)
10	11th	N.M.Hall (Capt)	(Richmond)	.	5th	J.Carbignac	(Agen)
9	4th	P.W.Sykes	(Wasps)	.	4th	P.Lasoasa	(Dax)
1	12th	W.A.Holmes	(Nuneaton)	.	13th	R.Bienes	(Cognac)
2	10th	E.Evans	(Sale)	.	5th	P.Labadie	(Bayonne)
3	9th	R.V.Stirling	(RAF/Leicester)	.	5th	R.Brejassou	(Tarbes)
4	10th & last	J.R.C.Matthews	(Harlequins)	.	8th	L.Mias	(Mazamet)
5	9th	D.T.Wilkins	(US Portsmouth)	.	5th	B.Chevallier	(Montferrand)
6	11th	D.F.White	(Northampton)	.	34th	J.Prat	(Lourdes)
7	5th	A.O.Lewis	(Bath)	.	5th	J.R.Bordeu	(Lourdes)
8	15th	J.M.Kendall-Carpenter	(Penzance-Newlyn)	.	32nd	G.Basquet (Capt)	(Agen)

Referee: W.C.W.Murdoch   (Scotland)

SCORERS:

			0 - 3	M.Pomathios	Try
			Half-time		
N.M.Hall		Penalty Goal	3 - 3		
N.M.Hall		Penalty Goal	6 - 3		

POINTS: N.M.Hall   6 points   (21)   M.Pomathios   3 points

MATCH COMMENTARY:

After the blizzard at Twickenham only a week previously, conditions were near perfect for the match at Stades Colombes and England won their first game in Paris since 1929, with a competent but unspectacular performance, although conceding the only try of the match. Nim Hall accomplished an unusual feat in modern times by scoring with a penalty goal from a drop kick from some fifty yards. After scoring his early try Pomathios had to retire and leave the French a forward short, but even so England could not get across the French line. In the closing stages, France were pressing strongly, but nothing seemed to go right for them. England were a trifle lucky to get away with this result, but after the paucity of success in recent years, no-one would decry it. This had been a much improved season for England. Having had hold of the Wooden Spoon for the last two seasons, it was a major achievement to finish this season as runners up to Grand Slam winning Wales. This was Guy Basquet's last Five Nations match. He had done much to raise the standard of the game in France and to improve the performance of the National side. He had played in every International match for France, bar one, since 1945, and had led the side on twenty three occasions.

Nim Hall became England's leading post-war points scorer with twenty-one points in eleven International matches.

SUMMARY OF THE SEASON - 1951 - 52

England's much improved performance this season and their relative success in the Five Nations Championship had its origins in the development of a sound pack, despite the results, during the course of last season, and consistent selection this season in spite of early set-backs.

Four new caps were introduced for the first match against South Africa, and only three more for the four Five Nations matches. In all only twenty players were used throughout the five matches, the lowest total in the post-war period. More significantly, the same pack played together four times in the new and effective 3-4-1 formation, and it would have been five had not Edmund Woodgate played in the front row against Wales in place of the injured Holmes.

Eight changes from the side which narrowly beat Scotland the previous season were made for the match against South Africa. All four three-quarters and both half-backs were replaced, but only two of the pack. South Africa, who had already won three, and were to win all five Internationals on this their fourth tour, were held by a very sound performance by the England pack and some staunch defence to only one try, and Muller's penalty goal to win the match went in off the post ! Much encouraged by this performance, it was a confident and, bar one (Woodgate for Holmes), unchanged side which faced Wales at Twickenham for the opening Five Nations encounter two weeks later. The packs were evenly balanced except in the lines-out where Roy John dominated but England could not contain either Cliff Morgan or Ken Jones and Wales won despite a debilitating injury to Lewis Jones. Then the wheel of fortune turned, and the selectors' faith in making only three changes, including the return of Holmes, was fully justified and Scotland were turned over by 19 points to 3, and four tries to one, at Murrayfield. As a result only one change was made for the match against Ireland at Twickenham, Reg Bazley in for Ted Woodward on the left wing. The match had been postponed from February due to the death of the King. In a near blizzard and on atrocious ground conditions, England, as they had two years previously, subdued the tenacious Irish pack and won the match. Finally, only one week later, an unchanged team beat France competently at Stade Colombes to complete their best performance in the Five Nations Championship for five years.

England finished second in the Championship table to the Grand Slam winners, Wales, and retained the Calcutta Cup. In their five matches England had scored eight tries, one more even than Wales, and had conceded only five. After the disappointments of previous years, this had been a very satisfactory season.

As a measure of selection consistency, and as an optimistic portent for next season, only five players ended their International careers this season. J.R.C.Matthews, the naval dentist with ten caps, continued to play with Harlequins and Middlesex for some time to come; Brian Boobbyer, with nine caps, was shortly to give up all sporting activities - he was also a very fine cricketer with four Oxford Blues - and he stayed in Japan after the Oxford tour there later in the year and worked for ten years for Moral Rearmament before returning to these shores. Philip Collins and Gordon Hook, with three caps each, joined the succession of short-lived English full-backs. Since 1947, England have chosen eight different full-backs none of whom have won more than four caps, nor less than three. The fifth swansong was that of Edmund Woodgate who gained his only cap against Wales as a last minute replacement for Walter Holmes.

During the season, John Kendall-Carpenter became England's most-capped post-war player, he now has fifteen caps. Nim Hall has now led England seven times, a post-war record, and has accumulated a record twenty-one individual points in eleven matches. He was also this season's leading points scorer with ten points. The two England wings, Ted Woodward and Chris Winn, who scored his first try on his debut, shared the top of the try scoring list with two tries each.

FIVE NATIONS CHAMPIONSHIP TABLE:

Won: **Calcutta Cup**

						Points:		Tries:		Title
		Played	Won	Lost	Drawn	For	Against	For	Against	Points
1	Wales	4	4	0	0	42	14	6	3	8
2	**ENGLAND**	4	3	1	0	34	14	7	4	6
3	Ireland	4	2	2	0	26	33	5	6	4
4	France	4	1	3	0	29	37	5	3	2
5	Scotland	4	0	4	0	22	55	3	10	0

Home Games: lost to Wales 6 - 8, (two tries each); beat Ireland 3 - 0, (one try to nil).

Away Games: beat Scotland 19 - 3, (four tries to one); beat France 6 - 3, (no tries to one).

58th match   **ENGLAND   8 pts**   v   **WALES   3 pts**

	Caps				Caps		
15	12th	**N.M.Hall (Capt)**	(Richmond)	.	1st	**T.J.Davies**	(Swansea)
14	4th	**J.E.Woodward**	(Wasps)	.	29th	**K.J.Jones**	(Newport)
13	6th	**A.E.Agar**	(Harlequins)	.	16th	**B.L.Williams**	(Cardiff)
12	12th	**L.B.Cannell**	(St Mary's Hospital)	.	15th	**M.C.Thomas**	(Newport)
11	3rd	**R.C.Bazley**	(Waterloo)	.	1st	**G.M.Griffiths**	(Cardiff)
10	1st	**M.Regan**	(Liverpool)	.	1st & only	**R.Burnett**	(Newport)
9	5th	**P.W.Sykes**	(Wasps)	.	3rd & last	**W.A.Williams**	(Newport)
1	13th	**W.A.Holmes**	(Nuneaton)	.	9th	**J.D.Robins**	(Bradford)
2	1st	**N.Labuschagne**	(Harlequins)	.	1st	**G.Beckingham**	(Cardiff)
3	10th	**R.V.Stirling**	(RAF/Leicester)	.	7th	**W.O.G.Williams**	(Swansea)
4	4th	**S.J.Adkins**	(Coventry)	.	14th	**E.R.John**	(Neath)
5	10th	**D.T.Wilkins**	(US Portsmouth)	.	15th	**J.R.G.Stephens**	(Neath)
6	12th	**D.F.White**	(Northampton)	.	1st & only	**W.D.Johnson**	(Swansea)
7	6th	**A.O.Lewis**	(Bath)	.	1st	**S.Judd**	(Cardiff)
8	16th	**J.M.Kendall-Carpenter**	(Bath)	.	19th	**J.A.Gwilliam (Capt)**	(Gloucester)

Referee: M.J.Dowling   (Ireland)

SCORERS:

			0 - 3	**T.J.Davies**	Penalty Goal
L.B.Cannell	Try	(2nd & last)	3 - 3		
N.M.Hall	Conversion		5 - 3		
			Half-time		
J.E.Woodward	Penalty Goal		8 - 3		

POINTS:

L.B.Cannell	3 points	(6)	**T.J.Davies**	3 points
J.E.Woodward	3 points	(9)		
N.M.Hall	2 points	(23)		

MATCH COMMENTARY:

It was a daunting prospect, despite England's recent successes, to travel to Cardiff to face the reigning Grand Slam Champions, and the selectors, seeking to attack, brought in Martin Regan, the mercurial Liverpool fly-half, and moved Captain Nim Hall to full-back. But Wales had introduced six new caps to the team, some in critical positions. Lewis Jones had signed for Leeds Rugby League Club the previous October, and the Welsh selectors really shot themselves in the foot by dropping Cliff Morgan on the grounds that he could not play effectively without Rex Willis who was injured and genuinely unavailable ! In the event, the game went England's way not because of the Welsh selectors' incompetence but because England played well and deserved to win. The team was settled, played well together and had that vitally necessary mutual understanding. Lewis Cannell's try was spectacular; Martin Regan put out a long pass to Reg Bazley and Cannell looped round the outside to scorch down the touch-line with the Welsh defence floundering. At the other end with ten minutes to go, Ken Jones surprisingly dropped a scoring pass from Malcolm Thomas, and England had secured their second post-war victory at Cardiff. This was England's fourth successive Five Nations win; quite remarkable when one considers that less than two years ago they had suffered a losing streak of five.

65th match   **ENGLAND   9 pts**   v   **IRELAND   9pts**

	Caps					Caps		
15	13th	N.M.Hall (Capt)	(Richmond)	.		2nd	R.J.Gregg	(Queen's U Belfast)
14	5th	J.E.Woodward	(Wasps)	.		17th & last	M.F.Lane	(UC Cork)
13	7th & last	A.E.Agar	(Harlequins)	.		14th	N.J.Henderson	(NIFC)
12	13th	L.B.Cannell	(St Mary's Hospital)	.		4th	K.N.Quinn	(Old Belvedere)
11	4th	R.C.Bazley	(Waterloo)	.		2nd	M.Mortell	(Bective Rangers)
10	2nd	M.Regan	(Liverpool)	.		28th	J.W.Kyle (Capt)	(NIFC)
9	6th	P.W.Sykes	(Wasps)	.		11th	J.A.O'Meara	(UC Cork)
1	14th	W.A.Holmes	(Nuneaton)	.		3rd	W.A.O'Neill	(UC Dublin)
2	11th	E.Evans	(Sale)	.		3rd	R.Roe	(Dublin University)
3	11th	R.V.Stirling	(RAF/Leicester)	.		2nd	F.E.Anderson	(Queen's U Belfast)
4	5th	S.J.Adkins	(Coventry)	.		1st	T.E.Reid	(Garryowen)
5	11th	D.T.Wilkins	(US Portsmouth)	.		4th	J.R.Brady	(CIYMS)
6	13th	D.F.White	(Northampton)	.		2nd	W.E.Bell	(Collegians)
7	7th	A.O.Lewis	(Bath)	.		20th	J.S.McCarthy	(Dolphin)
8	17th	J.M.Kendall-Carpenter	(Bath)	.		2nd	J.R.Kavanagh	(UC Dublin)

Referee: A.W.C.Austin   (Scotland)

SCORERS:

E.Evans	Try	(2nd)	3 - 0			
			Half-time			
			3 - 3	N.J.Henderson	Penalty Goal	
N.M.Hall	Penalty Goal		6 - 3			
			6 - 6	M.Mortell	Try	
			6 - 9	N.J.Henderson	Penalty Goal	
N.M.Hall	Penalty Goal		9 - 9			

POINTS:

N.M.Hall	6 points	(29)	N.J.Henderson	6 points	
E.Evans	3 points	(6)	M.Mortell	3 points	

MATCH COMMENTARY:

There was only one change from tthe team which had performed so creditably at Cardiff, Eric Evans returned to replace Nick Labuschagne at hooker. England went to Lansdowne Road seeking their second win of the season away from home, but Ireland, now under the captaincy of Jack Kyle, were determined that this should not be England's day. In the event, justice was done, for after a very even match where neither side gained any real advantage at any time, the scores finished exactly even at one try and two penalty goals each. England got off to a tremendous start and almost scored two further tries after Eric Evans had scored the first. After twenty minutes Ireland began to assert themselves and the struggle began. By half-time Ireland were putting England under considerable pressure. The second half was a see-saw with the honours, the pressure and the territorial advantage fluctuating. In the end, honours were even and the result was a fair one.

Lewis Cannell and Nim Hall both overtook Ivor Preece's total of 12 post-war caps as a back, in this match, and John Kendall-Carpenter extended further his record of all post-war caps.

28th match   **ENGLAND   11 pts   v   FRANCE   0 pts**

	Caps					Caps		
15	14th	N.M.Hall (Capt)	(Richmond)			12th	G.Brun	(Vienne)
14	6th	J.E.Woodward	(Wasps)			9th & last	J.R.Bourdeu	(Lourdes)
13	1st	J.Butterfield	(Northampton)			6th & last	J.Mauran	(Castres)
12	14th	L.B.Cannell	(St Mary's Hospital)			9th	M.Prat	(Lourdes)
11	5th	R.C.Bazley	(Waterloo)			2nd	L.Roge	(Beziers)
10	3rd	M.Regan	(Liverpool)			1st	A.Haget	(PUC)
9	7th & last	P.W.Sykes	(Wasps)			16th	G.Dufau	(Racing Club)
1	15th	W.A.Holmes	(Nuneaton)			6th	P.Bertrand	(Bourg)
2	12th	E.Evans	(Sale)			1st	J.Arrieta	(Stade Francais)
3	12th	R.V.Stirling	(RAF/Leicester)			1st	R.Carrere	(Mont-de-Marsan)
4	6th	S.J.Adkins	(Coventry)			7th	R.Brejassou	(Tarbes)
5	12th	D.T.Wilkins	(US Portsmouth)			7th	B.Chevallier	(Montferrand)
6	1st	D.S.Wilson	(Harlequins)			38th	J.Prat (Capt)	(Lourdes)
7	8th	A.O.Lewis	(Bath)			17th	R.Bienes	(Cognac)
8	18th	J.M.Kendall-Carpenter	(Bath)			1st	M.Celaya	(Biarritz)

Referee: V.J.Parfitt   (Wales)

SCORERS:

J.E.Woodward	Try	(3rd)	3 - 0	
E.Evans	Try	(3rd)	6 - 0	
J.Butterfield	Try	(1st)	9 - 0	
N.M.Hall	Conversion		11 - 0	
			Half-time	
			11 - 0	

POINTS:

J.E.Woodward	3 points	(12)
J.Butterfield	3 points	(3)
E.Evans	3 points	(9)
N.M.Hall	2 points	(31)

MATCH COMMENTARY:

Two changes from the side which drew with Ireland, Jeff Butterfield for Albert Agar in the centre, and "Tug" Wilson, the policeman, for Donald White, the Northampton flanker. For an International match the rugby on display this afternoon was of poor quality. England scored a try in the second minute when Haget threw a high pass to Mauran who dropped it and Jeff Butterfield simply had to pick up the ball and pass for Ted Woodward to score. A few minutes later Eric Evans forced his way over and French heads went down and they looked hopelessly beaten. A further excellent try on his debut, by Jeff Butterfield, could really have dispirited the French, but Jean Prat, standing in for the injured Haget at fly-half, somehow inspired his troops and France fought back strongly in the second half, but to no avail. Conceding two tries in the first few minutes must have reminded all Frenchmen present of the Twickenham "hoodoo" and from the moment when Eric Evans scored his try, France were psychologically beaten. All the more credit to Jean Prat for effectively shutting the door on England at half-time. After last year's reversal of fortunes, England, at last, appear to have a very real chance of at least sharing the Championship by beating Scotland at home in the final match of the season.

68th match
60th Calcutta Cup

ENGLAND 26 pts   v   SCOTLAND 8 pts

	Caps					Caps		
15	15th	N.M.Hall (Capt)	(Richmond)	.	7th & last	I.H.M.Thomson	(Heriot's FP)
14	7th	J.E.Woodward	(Wasps)	.	3rd	T.G.Weatherstone	(Stewart's Coll FP)
13	2nd	J.Butterfield	(Northampton)	.	10th	A.Cameron (Capt)	(Glasgow HSFP)
12	1st	W.P.C.Davies	(Harlequins)	.	2nd	D.Cameron	(Glasgow HSFP)
11	6th	R.C.Bazley	(Waterloo)	.	1st	J.S.Swan	(St Andrew's Univ)
10	4th	M.Regan	(Liverpool)	.	5th & last	L.Bruce-Lockhart	(London Scottish)
9	2nd & last	D.W.Shuttleworth	(Headingley)	.	8th	A.F.Dorward	(Gala)
1	13th	R.V.Stirling	(RAF/Leicester)	.	20th & last	J.C.Dawson	(Glasgow Acad'ls)
2	13th	E.Evans	(Sale)	.	3rd	J.H.F.King	(Selkirk)
3	16th & last	W.A.Holmes	(Nuneaton)	.	8th & last	R.L.Wilson	(Gala)
4	7th & last	S.J.Adkins	(Coventry)	.	4th	J.H.Henderson	(Oxford University)
5	13th & last	D.T.Wilkins	(US Portsmouth)	.	5th	J.J.Hegarty	(Hawick)
6	14th & last	D.F.White	(Northampton)	.	1st & only	W.Kerr	(London Scottish)
7	9th	A.O.Lewis	(Bath)	.	4th & last	K.H.D.MacMillan	(Sale)
8	19th	J.M.Kendall-Carpenter	(Bath)	.	1st & only	W.L.K.Cowie	(Edinburgh Wand'rs)

Referee: M.J.Dowling   (Ireland)

SCORERS:	R.C.Bazley	Try	(1st)	3 - 0			
	N.M.Hall	Conversion		5 - 0			
				5 - 3	T.G.Weatherstone	Try	
	R.C.Bazley	Try	(2nd & last)	8 - 3			
	S.J.Adkins	Try	(1st & only)	11 - 3			
			Half-time				
	R.V.Stirling	Try	(1st & only)	14 - 3			
	N.M.Hall	Conversion		16 - 3			
	J.Butterfield	Try	(2nd)	19 - 3			
	N.M.Hall	Conversion		21 - 3			
				21 - 6	J.H.Henderson	Try	
				21 - 8	I.H.M.Thomson	Conversion	
	J.E.Woodward	Try	(4th)	24 - 8			
	N.M.Hall	Conversion		26 - 8			

POINTS:	N.M.Hall	8 points	(39)	T.G.Weatherstone	3 points
	R.C.Bazley	6 points	(6)	J.H.Henderson	3 points
	J.E.Woodward, J.Butterfield,	3 points	(15),(6)	I.H.M.Thomson	2 points
	S.J.Adkins and R.V.Stirling	each	(3),(3)		

MATCH COMMENTARY:

England won the Championship outright for the first time since 1937, in fine style, completely overwhelming Scotland by six tries to two. The game was a splendid spectacle of all that is best in running rugby. Stan Adkin's try was the 100th try scored in England v Scotland Championship matches. Never before have England scored six tries in a match against Scotland, but it is the fourth time that England have scored four tries or more against them since 1947. Scotland were willing to run the ball at every opportunity from the limited possession allowed them by the England pack, but their mid-field marking and tackling was very poor and England were allowed to score almost at will. This was England's highest score in all matches since 1947, and their highest try total since 1938.

SUMMARY OF THE SEASON - 1952 - 53:

Confidence and consistency were again the features of an even more successful season for England than the last, and they came within a whisker of winning the Grand Slam, but for Irish determination and that mysterious dedication that all Celts have, not to let the English get away with anything if it can be helped !

Again only twenty players were used throughout the season, and four new caps were awarded. The decline in the influence of student rugby, nationally, was now confirmed by the fact that only one student, and a mature one at that, Lewis Cannell, played in the England side either last season or this. Students, like children, of course, grow up, and many of yesterday's students are the senior club members of today, but never since has student rugby been as dominant an influence on the national scene as it was in the immediate post-war years.

The team selected for the first match and the daunting prospect of facing the Grand Slam Champions in Wales, showed six changes from the side which had won competently in Paris last March. Aided by Welsh selectorial blunders and a dropped pass by Ken Jones, England won their second post-war match at Cardiff. Eric Evans replaced Nick Labuschagne for the match at Lansdowne Road, and this really was a titanic struggle with no quarter asked, or given, by either side. The balance shifted from time to time but never decisively, and a draw based on identical scores was a just result to an enthralling match. There were two changes for the French match at Twickenham, both of which were to have a lasting impact on English International rugby, the appearance on the International scene of Jeff Butterfield and "Tug" Wilson. England were six poiints up in no time at all, and although Jean Prat inspired the French to hold on, the match was over by half-time The match against Scotland was a showpiece in which eight tries were scored and was a credit to every player on the field and the referee.

England had won the Five Nations Championship outright for the first time since 1937, and had come as close as it is possible to get to a Grand Slam without actually achieving it. In scoring fifty-four points and eleven tries, England had done better than any side in the previous post-war Championship seasons, although in this season, not to be outdone, Ireland had scored the same number of points and one more try !

All good things have to come to an end, however, and seven players decided to hang up their International boots at the close of the season, including a substantial representation of the successful England pack, the front row of which had played together ten times and the back row, eight times. Walter Holmes, with sixteen caps, at only twenty-seven years old, was England's most capped prop. Don White fourteen caps, was first capped in the first post-war International in 1947, against Wales. He continued to play for Northampton for another eight years, and later became an England selector and a first class coach. Dennis Wilkins, known to friend and foe alike as the "Squire", stepped down with thirteen caps. Stan Adkins, Albert Agar and Patrick Sykes had each earned seven caps; Agar later gave dedicated service to the game as an administrator both nationally and internationally; Stan Adkins, wartime colleague and friend of Bill McLaren, and a great bowls player, became a pub landlord in Coventry, and Patrick Sykes was long associated with Middlesex County rugby. With two caps, Dennis Shuttleworth was the least capped of the famous half-back pairings from Yorkshire and Lancashire at that time. Evan Hardy and Dennis Shuttleworth for Yorkshire, and Martin Regan and Gordon Rimmer for Lancashire, had many a classic County confrontation when the County Championship was the premier tournament in England.

Nim Hall continued to set the standards for others to follow when he set the record for individual points scored in a season with eighteen, became England's most capped post-war back with fifteen caps, England's highest post-war points scorer with thirty-nine, and the longest serving captain having led the side on eleven occasions. John Kendall-Carpenter continued as England's most capped post-war player with nineteen caps. Four players scored two tries in the season, Eric Evans, Ted Woodward, Reg Bazley and Jeff Butterfield, the first of which was on his debut.

FIVE NATIONS CHAMPIONSHIP TABLE:

Won: **Championship Title, Calcutta Cup**

		Played	Won	Lost	Drawn	Points: For	Against	Tries: For	Against	Title Points
1	ENGLAND	4	3	0	1	54	20	11	3	7
2	Wales	4	3	1	0	26	14	6	2	6
3	Ireland	4	2	1	1	54	25	12	3	5
4	France	4	1	3	0	17	38	1	10	2
5	Scotland	4	0	4	0	21	75	4	16	0

Home Games: beat France 11 - 0, (three tries to nil); beat Scotland 26 - 8, (six tries to two)

Away Games: beat Wales 8 - 3, (one try to nil); drew with Ireland 9 - 9, (one try each).

59th match   **ENGLAND   9 pts**   v   **WALES   6 pts**

	Caps					Caps		
15	1st	**I.King**	(Harrogate)	.	13th & last	**G.Williams**	(London Welsh)
14	8th	**J.E.Woodward**	(Wasps)	.	32nd	**K.J.Jones**	(Newport)
13	1st	**J.P.Quinn**	(New Brighton)	.	8th	**A.G.Thomas**	(Cardiff)
12	3rd	**J.Butterfield**	(Northampton)	.	1st	**G.John**	(St Luke's Exeter)
11	6th	**C.E.Winn**	(Rosslyn Park)	.	2nd	**G.Rowlands**	(Cardiff)
10	5th	**M.Regan**	(Liverpool)	.	11th	**C.I.Morgan**	(Cardiff)
9	9th	**G.Rimmer**	(Waterloo)	.	14th	**W.R.Willis**	(Cardiff)
1	14th	**R.V.Stirling (Capt)**	(RAF/Leicester)	.	12th	**W.O.G.Williams**	(Swansea)
2	14th	**E.Evans**	(Sale)	.	17th & last	**D.M.Davies**	(Somerset Police)
3	1st	**D.L.Sanders**	(Harlequins)	.	3rd	**C.C.Meredith**	(Neath)
4	1st	**P.D.Young**	(Dublin Wanderers)	.	19th & last	**E.R.John**	(Neath)
5	1st	**P.G.Yarranton**	(RAF/Wasps)	.	20th	**J.R.G.Stephens (Capt)**	(Neath)
6	2nd	**D.S.Wilson**	(Metropolitan Police)	.	8th	**R.C.C.Thomas**	(Swansea)
7	1st	**R.Higgins**	(Liverpool)	.	6th	**S.Judd**	(Cardiff)
8	20th	**J.M.Kendall-Carpenter**	(Bath)	.	23rd	**J.A.Gwilliam**	(Gloucester)

Referee: M.J.Dowling   (Ireland)

SCORERS:						
				0 - 3	**G.Rowlands**	Try
J.E.Woodward	Try	{5th}		3 - 3		
				Half-time		
J.E.Woodward	Try	(6th & last)		6 - 3		
				6 - 6	**G.Rowlands**	Penalty Goal
C.E.Winn	Try	(3rd & last)		9 - 6		

POINTS:					
J.E.Woodward	6 points	(21)		**G.Rowlands**	6 points
C.E.Winn	3 points	(9)			

MATCH COMMENTARY:

Wales made two changes from the team which had beaten New Zealand in December, and England fielded six new caps, four of them in the pack. Nim Hall was out of favour again and had been replaced by Ian King, the Yorkshire full-back, so Bob Stirling was given the Captaincy. Again the English backs, with more than a fair share of possession, ran impressively at all times, and always threatened. There was an early disaster when Gwyn Rowlands latched on to a loose ball and dribbled cleverly for the touch-down. England recovered from this set-back and three tries were scored, all by the wings, but the winning try by Chris Winn came only in injury time in the corner. Wales had an unusually high incidence of restricting injuries, at times they were down to thirteen men with Rex Willis off the field for good and both Billy Williams and Gerwyn Williams off the field periodically, and this inevitably adversely affected their performance and thus must have helped England towards recording their first win over Wales at Twickenham since 1939. England have now played eight successive Five Nations matches without defeat. This match was the first all-ticket game to be held at Twickenham. The RFU had decided after the 1950 match against Wales when 75,532 people crammed into Twickenham, that all future matches would be all-ticket. It had taken four years to put this decision into effect !

4th match   **ENGLAND   0 pts**   v   **NEW ZEALAND   5 pts**

	Caps					Caps		
15	2nd	I.King	(Harrogate)		15th	R.W.H.Scott	(Auckland)
14	9th	J.E.Woodward	(Wasps)		2nd	M.J.Dixon	(Canterbury)
13	2nd	J.P.Quinn	(New Brighton)		2nd	C.J.Loader	(Wellington)
12	4th	J.Butterfield	(Northampton)		1st	D.D.Wilson	(Canterbury)
11	2nd	W.P.C.Davies	((Harlequins)		7th	R.A.Jarden	(Wellington)
10	6th	M.Regan	(Liverpool)		8th	L.S.Haig	(Otago)
9	10th	G.Rimmer	(Waterloo)		4th	K.Davis	(Auckland)
1	15th	R.V.Stirling (Capt)	(RAF/Leicester)		2nd	H.L.White	(Auckland)
2	15th	E.Evans	(Sale)		3rd	R.C.Hemi	(Waikato)
3	2nd	D.L.Sanders	(Harlequins)		16th	K.L.Skinner	(Otago)
4	2nd	P.D.Young	(Dublin Wanderers)		3rd	G.N.Dalzell	(Canterbury)
5	2nd	P.G.Yarranton	(RAF/Wasps)		14th	R.A.White	(Poverty Bay)
6	3rd	D.S.Wilson	(Metropolitan Police)		1st	P.F.H.Jones	(North Auckland)
7	2nd	R.Higgins	(Liverpool)		3rd	W.H.Clark	(Wellington)
8	21st	J.M.Kendall-Carpenter	(Bath)		5th	R.C.Stuart (Capt)	(Canterbury)

Referee: I.David   (Wales)

SCORERS:

0 - 3	G.N.Dalzell	Try
0 - 5	R.W.H.Scott	Conversion
Half-time		
0 - 5		

POINTS:

G.N.Dalzell	3 points
R.W.H.Scott	2 points

MATCH COMMENTARY:

The Fourth All Blacks were probably the most popular New Zealand team to tour the Five Nations, but they were not the best in rugby playing terms, and they had to work extremely hard to beat England by the only try of the match. England made only one change, understandably, from the side which had beaten Wales, on the grounds that Wales had beaten the All Blacks anyway, and put Phil Davies on the wing in place of the injured Chris Winn. New Zealand certainly had a superior pack but they won the match because the back row effectively put the pressure on the England half-backs, especially Regan, so that the three-quarters were receiving the ball with the New Zealand defence on top of them and opportunities for taking the pass at pace and attacking the opposition were almost totally eliminated. England were always prepared to counter-attack even though they were always under pressure but the New Zealand tackling and cover defence was very effective. The pack, good though they were, were too light in the set pieces and too slow in the loose. New Zealand came very close to scoring additional tries in the second half, including a near push-over try, but the home side heroically held them off. England, on the other hand, despite their spirited endeavours, never really looked like scoring a try, and the result was no surprise and certainly no injustice.

66th match   **ENGLAND   14 pts   v   IRELAND   3 pts**

	Caps					Caps		
15	3rd & last	I.King	(Harrogate)	.	6th	R.J.Gregg	(Queen's U Belfast)
14	10th	J.E.Woodward	(Wasps)	.	7th	M.Mortell	(Bective Rangers)
13	3rd	J.P.Quinn	(New Brighton)	.	19th	N.J.Henderson	(NIFC)
12	5th	J.Butterfield	(Northampton)	.	4th	A.C.Pedlow	(Queen's U Belfast)
11	3rd	W.P.C.Davies	((Harlequins)	.	3rd	J.T.Gaston	(Dublin University)
10	7th	M.Regan	(Liverpool)	.	1st	W.J.Hewitt	(Instonians)
9	11th	G.Rimmer	(Waterloo)	.	16th	J.A.O'Meara	(Dolphin)
1	16th	R.V.Stirling (Capt)	(Wasps)	.	7th	F.E.Anderson	(Queen's U Belfast)
2	16th	E.Evans	(Sale)	.	7th	R.Roe	(Lansdowne)
3	3rd	D.L.Sanders	(Harlequins)	.	1st	B.G.M.Wood	(Garryowen)
4	3rd	P.D.Young	(Dublin Wanderers)	.	9th	P.J.Lawler	(Clontarf)
5	3rd	P.G.Yarranton	(RAF/Wasps)	.	5th	R.H.Thompson	(Instonians)
6	4th	D.S.Wilson	(Metropolitan Police)	.	3rd	G.F.Reidy	(Lansdowne)
7	3rd	R.Higgins	(Liverpool)	.	24th	J.S.McCarthy (Capt)	(Dolphin)
8	22nd	J.M.Kendall-Carpenter	(Bath)	.	1st & only	J.Murphy-O'Connor	(Bective Rangers)

Referee: A.I.Dickie   (Scotland)

SCORERS:	M.Regan	Try	(1st & only)	3 - 0		
	J.Butterfield	Try	(3rd)	6 - 0		
				6 - 3	J.Murphy-O'Connor	Penalty Goal
				Half-time		
	I.King	Penalty Goal		9 - 3		
	D.S.Wilson	Try	(1st)	12 - 3		
	I.King	Conversion		15 - 3		

POINTS:	I.King	5 points	(5)	J.Murphy-O'Connor	3 points
	M.Regan, D.S.Wilson	3 points	(3),(3)		
	and J.Butterfield	each	(9)		

MATCH COMMENTARY:

England fielded an unchanged side from that which had lost narrowly to the All Blacks two weeks previously, but the match was very much closer than the score might suggest. Ireland were without Jack Kyle, due to injury, who had played thirty-two successive Internationals, and his absence undoubtedly was a major factor in Ireland's defeat.   The Irish forwards got the better of a lack-lustre English pack on the day, but they could not get their backs moving effectively.   This was largely due to the efforts of Reg Higgins and "Tug" Wilson in their intimidation of the Irish half-backs, especially the inexperienced Hewitt. The English backs took their limited chances and scored two tries with the third coming from the very impressive Wilson, to win the match. Ireland had failed to score any points at all on their two previous visits to Twickenham, nor were they to score on their next two visits either ! So James Murphy-O'Connor's penalty goal in this match was to represent the only points scored by Ireland in five successive matches at Twickenham from 1950 to 1958.

This was England's fifth successive Five Nations win at Twickenham and sent them off to Murrayfield and Paris respectively in pursuit of the ultimate Five Nations prize with confidence riding very high.

69th match
61st Calcutta Cup

ENGLAND 13 pts v SCOTLAND 3 pts

	Caps				Caps		
15	1st	N.Gibbs	(Harlequins)	.	4th	J.C.Marshall	(London Scottish)
14	11th	J.E.Woodward	(Wasps)	.	5th	J.S.Swan	(London Scottish)
13	4th	J.P.Quinn	(New Brighton)	.	3rd	M.K.Elgie	(London Scottish)
12	6th	J.Butterfield	(Northampton)	.	6th & last	D.Cameron	(Glasgow HSFP)
11	7th	C.E.Winn	(Rosslyn Park)	.	7th	T.G.Weatherstone	(Stewart's Coll FP)
10	8th	M.Regan	(Liverpool)	.	3rd	G.T.Ross	(Watsonians)
9	12th & last	G.Rimmer	(Waterloo)	.	3rd	L.P.MacLachlan	(Oxford University)
1	17th	R.V.Stirling (Capt)	(Wasps)	.	7th	T.P.L.McGlashan	(Royal HSFP)
2	1st	E.F.Robinson	(Coventry)	.	4th & last	J.H.F.King	(Selkirk)
3	4th	D.L.Sanders	(Harlequins)	.	4th	H.F.McLeod	(Hawick)
4	4th	P.D.Young	(Dublin Wanderers)	.	4th	E.A.J.Ferguson	(Oxford University)
5	1st & only	J.F.Bance	(Bedford)	.	4th	E.J.S.Michie	(Aberdeen Univ)
6	5th	D.S.Wilson	(Metropolitan Police)	.	28th	W.I.D.Elliot (Capt)	(Edinburgh Acad)
7	4th	R.Higgins	(Liverpool)	.	8th	J.H.Henderson	(Richmond)
8	1st	V.H.Leadbetter	(Edinburgh Wand'rs)	.	20th	P.W.Kininmonth	(Richmond)

Referee: O.B.Glasgow   (Ireland)

SCORERS:

P.D.Young	Try	(1st & only)	3 - 0			
N.Gibbs	Conversion		5 - 0			
			Half-time			
D.S.Wilson	Try	(2nd)	8 - 0			
N.Gibbs	Conversion		10 - 0			
			10 - 3	M.K.Elgie	Try	
D.S.Wilson	Try	(3rd)	13 - 3			

POINTS:

D.S.Wilson	6 points	(9)	M.K.Elgie	3 points
N.Gibbs	4 points	(4)		
P.D.Young	3 points	(3)		

MATCH COMMENTARY:

Five changes were made to the side for the all-important visit to Murrayfield, some by necessity because of injury, others not so. Ian King suffered the fate of most English full-backs in the post-war period and lost his place after three caps to Nigel Gibbs of Harlequins. Chris Winn regained his place on the wing over Phil Davies, and Ernie Robinson, John Bance and Vic Leadbetter replaced the injured parties Eric Evans, Peter Yarranton and John Kendall-Carpenter respectively. The forwards recovered from their off-day against Ireland and led England to a decisive win at Murrayfield to secure at least the Triple Crown this year, for the first time since 1937, to follow the Championship title won last year. Following England's first try, there was some very entertaining rugby with both sides launching penetrative attacks with good positional play and solid tackling the appropriate response. In the second half, England gradually raised their game, and Wilson's two tries, the second from an interception, secured the match. "Tug" Wikson had again been quite outstanding in the loose and Martin Regan, the play-maker, was still very effective although he now commands much more respectful attention from opposing back rows than before. This was, sadly, Scotland's fifteenth successive defeat, and their fourth successive defeat by England. On the other hand, it was England's fifth successive Five Nations win and their tenth in succession without defeat.

29th match   **ENGLAND   3 pts**   v   **FRANCE   11 pts**

	Caps				Caps		
15	2nd & last	N.Gibbs	(Harlequins)	.	1st	P.Albaladejo	(Dax)
14	12th	J.E.Woodward	(Wasps)	.	6th & last	F.Cazenave	(Racing Club)
13	5th & last	J.P.Quinn	(New Brighton)		13th	M.Prat	(Lourdes)
12	7th	J.Butterfield	(Northampton)		9th	R.Martine	(Lourdes)
11	8th & last	C.E.Winn	(Rosslyn Park)	.	4th	A.Boniface	(Mont-de-Marsan)
10	9th	M.Regan	(Liverpool)	.	4th	A.Haget	(PUC)
9	1st	J.E.Williams	(Old Millhillians)	.	22nd	G.Dufau	(Racing Club)
1	18th & last	R.V.Stirling (Capt)	(Leicester)	.	22nd	R.Bienes	(Cognac)
2	17th	E.Evans	(Sale)	.	14th	P.Labadie	(Bayonne)
3	5th	D.L.Sanders	(Harlequins)	.	2nd	A.Domenech	(Vichy)
4	5th	P.D.Young	(Dublin Wanderers)	.	4th	A.Sanac	(Perpignan)
5	2nd & last	V.H.Leadbetter	(Edinburgh Wand'rs)	.	4th	R.Baulon	(Vienne)
6	6th	D.S.Wilson	(Metropolitan Police)	.	45th	J.Prat (Capt)	(Lourdes)
7	10th & last	A.O.Lewis	(Bath)	.	7th	H.Domec	(Lourdes)
8	23rd & last	J.M.Kendall-Carpenter	(Bath)	.	5th	M.Celaya	(Biarritz)

Referee: I.David   (Wales)

SCORERS:

				0 - 3	A.Boniface	Try
	D.S.Wilson	Try	(4th & last)	3 - 3		
				Half-time		
				3 - 6	J.Prat	Drop Goal
				3 - 9	M.Prat	Try
				3 - 11	J.Prat	Conversion

POINTS:

	D.S.Wilson	3 points	(12)		J.Prat	5 points
					M.Prat	3 points
					A.Boniface	3 points

MATCH COMMENTARY:

Three down and one to go for the elusive ultimate prize in Five Nations rugby, and with this in mind the selectors restored John Kendall-Carpenter, dropped Reg Higgins, and, the biggest mistake of all, replaced Gordon Rimmer with John Williams at scrum-half ! Nonetheless, all the high hopes for a Grand Slam were strewn to the winds in the noisy confines of the Stade Colombes and England met their match in all facets of the game and their undoing was the same as it had been against the All Blacks. The mobile French back row pressured Regan to such an extent that the English backs never got moving with space to run. With Cazenave a passenger for most of the match, and Baulon filling the gap on the wing, seven French forwards effectively outplayed their eight English opposite numbers, but the game was not won until Jeff Butterfield, completely out of character, put out a very loose pass, Martine gathered it and sent Maurice Prat across the line untouched. Dufau, the French scrum-half, with good ball, was able to get his backs moving to force England on to the defensive and to concede two tries. Thus England shared the title with France and Wales each having won three matches, but England took the Triple Crown for the first time since 1937. "Tug" Wilson's four tries in the Five Nations matches equalled J.V.Smith's feat in the '49-50 season.

SUMMARY OF THE SEASON - 1953 - 54:

Despite the loss of seven seasoned International players, who retired from International rugby at the end of the previous season, England, again, enjoyed considerable success, although not quite to the same extent, in winning three of their Five Nations matches, and holding Bob Stuart's popular All Black side to a very tight game.

Six new caps took the field for the first match against Wales, and four others were so honoured during the course of the season. Twenty-two players were used for the five matches in total. Nim Hall was discarded again , although not yet for the last time, and Bob Stirling was deservedly given the Captaincy. There was a galaxy of talent in the England three-quarters, with as much try-scoring potential amongst them as the 1992 Grand Slam side were to enjoy.

Against Wales, Martin Regan, who already had four caps, but was now playing with his Lancashire scrum-half, Gordon Rimmer, commanded the field and the match. The abundant possession which the excellent pack, half of them new caps, provided, gave Regan all sorts of opportunities to display his attacking flair, and the English wings scored three tries. There was only one change for the match with New Zealand, Phil Davies replacing Chris Winn, but the pack had to share possession this time, and the All Black back row gave Regan precious little room. The same pack struggled against Ireland, but with the limited possession he got, Regan still found enough space and England, again, scored three tries. In facing Scotland, the pack, with three necessary changes, once more did the business and three tries were scored. But it was a different story against France. With Yarranton and Higgins missing but with Evans restored, the strong English pack met their match, and the French back row, like New Zealand's were determined to contain the ebullient England fly-half, now with a new scrum-half, John Williams, and in that they were very successful.

England took the Triple Crown, for the first time since 1937, and shared the Five Nations Championship with France and Wales, with Wales having lost to England, England having lost to France, who, in turn had lost to Wales. England had won nine of their last twelve Five Nations matches, whereas in the four seasons prior to that, they had won only four matches out of sixteen.

The season saw the end of ten England International's careers, most prominent amongst whom was John Kendall-Carpenter, capped twenty-three times at prop and No.8, and fifteen time in succession, who was England's most capped post-war player, and had led the side three times in the 1951-52 season. He became President of the RFU and Chairman of the IRB, as well as the Chairman of the Rugby World Cup organising Committee in 1987. Bob Stirling finished the season with eighteen caps, all in successive matches - another post-war record. Gordon Rimmer, who with Ivor Preece, was one of only two English players to play in a Test on the 1950 Lions Tour to New Zealand and Australia, retired with twelve caps but continued to play county rugby for Lancashire for whom he appeared seventy-eight times. Alec Lewis, with ten caps, became a selector and managed the triumphant England tour to South Africa in 1972. Chris Winn the Sussex and MCC cricketer, ended his International career with eight caps, and Pat Quinn, the crash-tackling Lancashire centre, won five caps, and, although he did not play for England again, went on the 1955 Lions Tour to South Africa, and then joined Leeds Rugby League club in 1956. Ian King became the tenth English full-back since the war to win no less than three and no more than four caps. Nigel Gibbs, the brother of George Gibbs who won two caps at prop, one in 1947 and one in 1948, was an Oxford Cricket Blue and a master at Charterhouse, and was another unfortunate full-back, although he won only two caps. Victor Leadbetter and John Bance, the Bedfordshire farmer, also completed their International careers with two caps and one cap respectively.

"Tug" Wilson was the season's leading tries and points scorer with four tries, emulating J.V.Smith's feat in 1949-50. Other try scorers were Ted Woodward with two, and Chris Winn, Martin Regan, Jeff Butterfield and Peter Young with one each.

FIVE NATIONS CHAMPIONSHIP TABLE:

Won: **Triple Crown, share of Championship Title with France and Wales, Calcutta Cup.**

		Played	Won	Lost	Drawn	Points: For	Against	Tries: For	Against	Title Points
1 =	**ENGLAND**	4	3	1	0	39	23	10	4	6
1 =	France	4	3	1	0	35	22	7	3	6
1 =	Wales	4	3	1	0	52	34	7	7	6
4	Ireland	4	1	3	0	18	34	3	5	2
5	Scotland	4	0	4	0	6	37	2	10	0

Home Games: beat Wales 9 - 6, (three tries to one); beat Ireland 14 - 3, (three tries to nil).

Away Games: beat Scotland 13 - 3, (three tries to one); lost to France 3 - 11, (one try to two).

60th match   **ENGLAND   0 pts   v   WALES   3 pts**

	Caps					Caps		
15	16th	N.M.Hall (Capt)	(Richmond)	.	1st	A.B.Edwards	(London Welsh)
14	13th	J.E.Woodward	(Wasps)	.	36th	K.J.Jones	(Newport)
13	8th	J.Butterfield	(Northampton)	.	1st	G.T.Wells	(Cardiff)
12	4th	W.P.C.Davies	(Harlequins)	.	22nd & last	B.L.Williams (Capt)	(Cardiff)
11	7th	R.C.Bazley	(Waterloo)	.	2nd	T.J.Brewer	(Newport)
10	1st	D.G.S.Baker	(OMT's)	.	14th	C.I.Morgan	(Bective Rangers)
9	2nd	J.E.Williams	(Old Millhillians)	.	18th	W.R.Willis	(Cardiff)
1	1st	G.W.D.Hastings	(Gloucester)	.	16th	W.O.G.Williams	(Swansea)
2	2nd	N.A.Labuschagne	(Guy's Hospital)	.	4th	B.V.Meredith	(St Luke's Exeter)
3	1st	D.St G.Hazell	(Leicester)	.	7th	C.C.Meredith	(Neath)
4	6th	P.D.Young	(Dublin Wanderers)	.	22nd	J.R.G.Stephens	(Neath)
5	1st	J.H.Hancock	(Newport)	.	4th	R.J.Robins	(Pontypridd)
6	1st	P.H.Ryan	(Richmond)	.	1st & only	N.G.Davies	(London Welsh)
7	5th	R.Higgins	(Liverpool)	.	2nd	B.Sparks	(Neath)
8	1st	P.J.Taylor	(Northampton)	.	9th	S.Judd	(Cardiff)

Referee: O.B.Glasgow   (Ireland)

SCORERS: 0 - 3   A.B.Edwards   Penalty Goal
                                         Half-time
                                            0 - 3

POINTS: A.B.Edwards   3 points

MATCH COMMENTARY:

The match had been postponed from a week earlier due to heavy snow, and the subsequent thaw and steady drizzle made conditions very wet and muddy. Retirements and injury compelled England to introduce six new caps, five of them in the forwards - all eight of the pack had only eighteen caps between them. Only two of last season's pack were on the field for the first match of the new season, Peter Young and Reg Higgins. In the conditions there were very few passages of open play and the match was won by a penalty goal by Arthur Edwards, the new Welsh full-back, from in front of the posts after only ten minutes, when England were deemed to be offside during a forward rush. Both sides generated a lot of pressure, first England, and latterly, Wales, but the conditions really prevented further scoring. England had recalled Nim Hall, now in his 30th year, in an attempt to ensure successful goal-kicking, to improve and strengthen the defence at full-back and to lead the side following Bob Stirling's retirement. As the season progressed it became apparent both that Hall was getting too old and that there was no suitable replacement in the land !

This was the occasion of Bleddyn Williams' last cap for Wales,. He had been one of the finest players ever to grace the International stage.

67th match   **ENGLAND   6 pts   v   IRELAND   6 pts**

	Caps				Caps		
15	17th & last	**N.M.Hall (Capt)**	(Richmond)	.	2nd	**W.R.Tector**	(Wanderers)
14	14th	**J.E.Woodward**	(Wasps)	.	1st	**R.E.Roche**	(UC Galway)
13	9th	**J.Butterfield**	(Northampton)	.	23rd	**N.J.Henderson**	(NIFC)
12	5th	**W.P.C.Davies**	(Harlequins)	.	2nd	**A.J.F.O'Reilly**	(Old Belvedere)
11	8th	**R.C.Bazley**	(Waterloo)	.	6th	**A.C.Pedlow**	(CIYMS)
10	2nd	**D.G.S.Baker**	(OMT's)	.	34th	**J.W.Kyle**	(NIFC)
9	3rd	**J.E.Williams**	(Old Millhillians)	.	19th	**J.A.O'Meara**	(Dolphin)
1	2nd	**G.W.D.Hastings**	(Gloucester)	.	11th	**F.E.Anderson**	(NIFC)
2	3rd	**N.A.Labuschagne**	(Guy's Hospital)	.	11th	**R.Roe**	(Lansdowne)
3	2nd	**D.St G.Hazell**	(Leicester)	.	2nd	**P.J.O'Donoghue**	(Bective Rangers)
4	7th	**P.D.Young**	(Dublin Wanderers)	.	6th	**T.E.Reid**	(London Irish)
5	2nd & last	**J.H.Hancock**	(Newport)	.	1st	**M.N.Madden**	(Sunday's Well)
6	2nd & last	**P.H.Ryan**	(Richmond)	.	2nd	**M.J.Cunningham**	(UC Cork)
7	6th	**R.Higgins**	(Liverpool)	.	28th & last	**J.S.McCarthy (Capt)**	(Dolphin)
8	2nd	**P.J.Taylor**	(Northampton)	.	9th	**J.R.Kavanagh**	(Wanderers)

Referee: A.I.Dickie   (Scotland)

SCORERS:

J.Butterfield	Try	(4th)	3 - 0			
G.W.D.Hastings	Try	(1st & only)	6 - 0			
			6 - 3	**A.C.Pedlow**	Try	
			Half-time			
			6 - 6	**N.J.Henderson**	Penalty Goal	

POINTS:

J.Butterfield	3 points	(12)		**A.C.Pedlow**	3 points
G.W.D.Hastings	3 points	(3)		**N.J.Henderson**	3 points

MATCH COMMENTARY:

England retained the same team who had lost narrowly at the Arms Park three weeks ago, but this game was of poor international quality. Ireland should have won but for uncharacteristic uncertainty at half-back (Kyle and O'Meara were both dropped for the next match). Nim Hall, normally a very reliable goal kicker, failed to convert either of the English tries, both of which were scored in the first twenty minutes of the match, when England were completely on top.

Ireland gradually came to life and when an Irish penalty attempt fell short, Jeff Butterfield, again out of character, knocked on under the posts. From the ensuing scrum, Cecil Pedlow scored, and from then on England seemed to lose confidence, and, despite Jackie Kyle's uncertainty, Ireland came back to draw the match. If only Nim Hall had converted just one of his side's two tries - if only.......

The first try was Jeff Butterfield's fourth International try. But little else was memorable.

Strangely, both captains, both of long standing and vast international experience, lost their places after this match and vacated the International stage.

30th match   **ENGLAND   9 pts**   **v**   **FRANCE   16 pts**

	Caps					Caps		
15	1st & only	H.Scott	(Manchester)	.	8th	M.Vannier	(Racing Club)
14	1st	F.D.Sykes	(Northampton)	.	1st	H.Rancoule	(Lourdes)
13	10th	J.Butterfield	(Northampton)	.	17th	M.Prat	(Lourdes)
12	6th	W.P.C.Davies	(Harlequins)	.	2nd	J.Bouquet	(Bourg)
11	9th	R.C.Bazley	(Waterloo)	.	4th	J.Lepatey	(Mazamet)
10	3rd	D.G.S.Baker	(OMT's)	.	6th	A.Haget	(PUC)
9	4th	J.E.Williams	(Old Millhillians)	.	22nd	G.Dufau	(Racing Club)
1	3rd	G.W.D.Hastings	(Gloucester)	.	13th	R.Brejassou	(Tarbes)
2	4th	N.A.Labuschagne	(Guy's Hospital)	.	18th	P.Labadie	(Bayonne)
3	3rd	D.St G.Hazell	(Leicester)	.	6th	A.Domenech	(Vichy)
4	8th	P.D.Young (Capt)	(Dublin Wanderers)	.	11th	M.Celaya	(Biarritz)
5	4th	P.G.Yarranton	(RAF/Wasps)	.	17th	B.Chevallier	(Montferrand)
6	7th	D.S.Wilson	(Metropolitan Police)	.	49th	J.Prat (Capt)	(Lourdes)
7	7th	R.Higgins	(Liverpool)	.	11th	H.Domec	(Lourdes)
8	1st	I.D.S.Beer	(Harlequins)	.	7th	R.Baulon	(Vienne)

Referee: R.Mitchell   (Ireland)

SCORERS:

R.Higgins	Try	(1st)	3 - 0			
D.St G.Hazell	Penalty Goal		6 - 0			
			6 - 3	J.Prat	Drop Goal
			Half-time		
			6 - 6	M.Celaya	Try
			6 - 8	M.Vannier	Conversion
D.St G.Hazell	Penalty Goal		9 - 8		
			9 - 11	R.Baulon	Try
			9 - 13	M.Vannier	Conversion
			9 - 16	J.Prat	Drop Goal

POINTS:

D.St G.Hazell	6 points	(6)	J.Prat	6 points
R.Higgins	3 points	(3)	M.Vannier	4 points
			M.Celaya and R.Baulon	3 points each

MATCH COMMENTARY:

Despite five changes, England could not stop France recording their second victory and their highest score at Twickenham. The five changes included the dropping of Nim Hall, the reliable goal kicker, but Hazell assumed his mantle (and his boots) effectively and landed two penalty goals. England were thoroughly out-played, in good conditions, but were deservedly in the lead at half-time. Then France got their act together and England began to make mistakes sometimes enforced by French pressure. But England still held a one point lead with ten minutes to go. This was where French weight, strength and particularly fitness took their toll. Baulon crossed for a try, Vannier was successful with the kick, and it was left to the inimitable Jean Prat to seal England's fate with an immaculate drop goal, his second of the match. "Monsieur Rugby" gained his 49th cap in this match and it was his last appearance against England. He had opposed England nine times since 1947, three times as Captain, and had scored twenty-seven points including two tries and four drop goals.

70th match

ENGLAND 9 pts   v   SCOTLAND 6 pts

62nd Calcutta Cup

	Caps				Caps		
15	1st & only	N.S.D.Estcourt	(Blackheath)	2nd	R.W.T.Chisholm	(Melrose)
14	2nd	F.D.Sykes	(Northampton)	3rd	A.R.Smith	(Cambridge Univ)
13	11th	J.Butterfield	(Northampton)	8th & last	M.K.Elgie	(London Scottish)
12	7th	W.P.C.Davies	(Harlequins)	3rd & last	R.G.Charters	(Hawick)
11	10th & last	R.C.Bazley	(Waterloo)	10th	J.S.Swan	(Army)
10	4th & last	D.G.S.Baker	(OMT's)	14th	A.Cameron (Capt)	(Glasgow HSFP)
9	5th	J.E.Williams	(Old Millhillians)	3rd & last	J.A.Nichol	(Royal HSFP)
1	4th	G.W.D.Hastings	(Gloucester)	9th	H.F.McLeod	(Hawick)
2	5th & last	N.A.Labuschagne	(Guy's Hospital)	4th & last	W.K.L.Relph	(Stewart's Coll FP)
3	4th & last	D.St G.Hazell	(Leicester)	3rd	T.Elliot	(Gala)
4	9th & last	P.D.Young (Capt)	(Dublin Wanderers)	7th	E.J.S.Michie	(Aberdeen GSFP)
5	5th & last	P.G.Yarranton	(RAF/Wasps)	5th	J.W.Y.Kemp	(Glasgow HSFP)
6	8th & last	D.S.Wilson	(Metropolitan Police)	2nd	I.A.A.MacGregor	(Hillhead HSFP)
7	8th	R.Higgins	(Liverpool)	5th	A.Robson	(Hawick)
8	2nd & last	I.D.S.Beer	(Harlequins)	5th	J.T.Greenwood	(Dunf'lne & Perth A)

Referee: D.C.Johnson   (Wales)

SCORERS:	D.St G.Hazell	Penalty Goal		3 - 0		
	F.D.Sykes	Try	(1st & only)	6 - 0		
				6 - 3	A.Cameron	Penalty Goal
	I.D.S.Beer	Try	(1st & only)	9 - 3		
				Half-time		
				9 - 6	A.Cameron	Try

POINTS:	F.D.Sykes	3 points	(3)	A.Cameron	6 points
	I.D.S.Beer	3 points	(3)		
	D.St G.Hazell	3 points	(9)		

MATCH COMMENTARY:

Scotland came to Twickenham for the Triple Crown and England were still looking for their first win of the season. The match proved to be a dour struggle, and Scotland, despite an outstanding performance by Angus Cameron, could not recapture the form that had inspired them to victories over Wales and Ireland. England's performance was solid but unimaginative, and the flair which Martin Regan had inspired in the backs in the past two seasons was missing. England were dominant in the first half, with Scotland feeling the pace, and only an Angus Cameron drop goal penalty (a la Nim Hall) kept them in touch. In the second half Scotland fought back and when only 9 - 6 behind, Tom Elliot was convinced that he had scored under the posts, but the referee ruled otherwise. Immediately after that, Reg Higgins all but forced his way over at the other end, and the match then became tense and exciting to the final whistle. The England pack were not yet a settled unit - neither were they to become one for only two were to play for England again !

After the successes of the last two years, England had to be content with a disappointing fourth place in the Five Nations Table, but it was their fifth successive win over Scotland.

SUMMARY OF THE SEASON - 1954 - 55:

The mass exodus of experienced Internationals, especially from the England pack, at the end of the previous season, left the selectors with little alternative but to blood a lot of new pplayers, some in critical positions and at the same time, and still they had not solved the goal kicking problem in finding a suitable replacement for Nim Hall. Not surprisingly, England did not have a successful season, winning only one match and drawing another.

The selectors made eleven changes for the first match at Cardiff, and introduced six new caps, five of them in the pack. Nim Hall was invited to take up the full-back berth, and the Captaincy, again. The inexperienced pack acquitted themselves well in a dour struggle in very wet conditions at the Arms Park, in a match in which there was hardly any running with the ball in hand at all. The England pack had only eighteen caps among them compared with sixty-five among the Welsh forwards, and the "juniors" did themselves proud, but the match was decided by the only score, a penalty goal. The same side was sent to Lansdowne Road and would have won the match had Nim Hall done that which he was brought into the side to do - kick the goals. He failed, lost his place and left the International stage forthwith. Five changes and three new caps formed the side to face France but they were well beaten by a side with over two hundred caps to their credit. The only change for the Scotland match was at full-back where the search was still on for an adequate replacement for Nim Hall, and, Scotland, looking for the Triple Crown, were the fall guys yet again to England, and went down by two tries to one. Even though England took the Calcutta Cup for the fifth successive year, they could only manage fourth place in the Five Nations Championship Table.

In all twenty-one players were used and ten new caps were awarded. The two unfortunate full-backs chosen to succeed Nim Hall, Harry Scott of Manchester, and Nick Estcourt of Blackheath, a Rhodesian, lasted only one match each. After four matches, the pack had, at last, begun to gather some cohesion and permanence, but, again, it was to be decimated when six of its members retired at the end of the season.

Apart from Scott and Estcourt, eleven other players ended their International careers. Nim Hall, the much maligned and yet frequently called upon and mild-mannered scapegoat escaped with seventeen caps, thirteen as Captain and with thirty-nine points for England to his credit. He was England's most capped post-war back, highest points scorer and had led England as many times as had Wavell Wakefield. Reg Bazley, the Waterloo winger, and Civil Engineer, had ten caps; Peter Young, who took over from Hall as Captain, and who, after getting his Cambridge Blue, played much of his rugby in Ireland, had nine; "Tug" Wilson, the undercover policeman, had eight caps, had scored four tries in three successive Internationals, and then returned to his native South Africa, as did Nick Labuschagne with his five caps; Wilson, Labuschagne and Estcourt were the last of the "Dominion" players who had been chosen for England and about whom so much fuss had been made in previous seasons; Peter Yarranton, five caps, became a Knight, President of the RFU and a broadcaster on BBC Radio London; Douglas Baker, four caps, was born in Las Palmas (hardly a Dominion) and was a schoolmaster at Oundle; David Hazell, the Leicester prop, who was also a schoolmaster, at Taunton, also had four caps; Ian Beer, later Headmaster of Harrow and RFU President, had two, as did Peter Ryan and Jack Hancock, who joined Salford Rugby League Club for whom he played over one hundred matches.

England were much better represented on the forthcoming Lions tour to South Africa than they had been on the 1950 tour to New Zealand and Australia. Nine players were invited to join the touring party, Jeff Butterfield, Phil Davies, Pat Quinn, Frank Sykes, Douglas Baker, John Williams, Reg Higgins, "Tug" Wilson and Dickie Jeeps, who, at the time was uncapped. Five of them played in the Test Matches; Jeff Butterfield and Dickie Jeeps in all four; Phil Davies in three; Douglas Baker in two, at full-back and Reg Higgins in one. Strangely, the two Test matches with the highest England representation, were the two Test Matches which the Lions won !

FIVE NATIONS CHAMPIONSHIP TABLE:

Won: **Calcutta Cup**

		Played	Won	Lost	Drawn	Points: For	Against	Tries: For	Against	Title Points
1 =	Wales	4	3	1	0	48	28	8	3	6
1 =	France	4	3	1	0	47	28	8	3	6
3	Scotland	4	2	2	0	32	35	4	8	4
4	**ENGLAND**	4	1	2	1	24	31	5	4	3
5	Ireland	4	0	3	1	15	44	1	8	1

Home Games: lost to France 9 - 16, (one try to two); beat Scotland 9 - 6, (two tries to one).

Away Games: lost to Wales 0 - 3, (no tries); drew with Ireland 6 - 6, (two tries to one).

61st match   **ENGLAND   3 pts**   **v**   **WALES   8 pts**

	Caps				Caps		
15	1st	D.F.Allison	(Coventry)	3rd	G.D.Owen	(Newport)
14	1st	P.B.Jackson	(Coventry)	40th	K.J.Jones	(Newport)
13	12th	J.Butterfield	(Northampton)	1st	H.P.Morgan	(Newport)
12	8th	W.P.C.Davies	(Harlequins)	16th	M.C.Thomas	(Newport)
11	1st	P.H.Thompson	(Headingley)	1st	C.L.Davies	(Cardiff)
10	1st & only	M.J.K.Smith	(Oxford University)	18th	C.I.Morgan (Capt)	(Cardiff)
9	1st	R.E.G.Jeeps	(Northampton)	1st	D.O.Brace	(Oxford University)
1	6th	D.L.Sanders	(Harlequins)	20th	W.O.G.Williams	(Swansea)
2	18th	E.Evans (Capt)	(Sale)	8th	B.V.Meredith	(Newport)
3	1st	C.R.Jacobs	(Northampton)	11th	C.C.Meredith	(Neath)
4	1st	J.D.Currie	(Oxford University)	7th	R.H.Williams	(Llanelli)
5	1st	R.W.D.Marques	(Cambridge Univ)	8th	R.J.Robins	(Pontypridd)
6	1st	P.G.D.Robbins	(Oxford University)	14th	R.C.C.Thomas	(Swansea)
7	13th	V.G.Roberts	(Harlequins)	4th	B.Sparks	(Neath)
8	1st	A.Ashcroft	(Waterloo)	2nd	L.H.Jenkins	(Newport)

Referee: R.Mitchell   (Ireland)

SCORERS:

			0 - 3	R.J.Robins	Try
			0 - 5	G.D.Owen	Conversion
			Half-time		
D.F.Allison		Penalty Goal	3 - 5		
			3 - 8	C.L.Davies	Try

POINTS:

D.F.Allison	3 points	(3)		C.L.Davies	3 points
				R.J.Robins	3 points
				G.D.Owen	2 points

MATCH COMMENTARY:

England introduced ten new caps to the first game of the season under Eric Evans, in an attempt to build for the future rather than to aim for immediate success - Vic Roberts was also recalled to provide some experience and stability amongst the new caps in the back five. The tactic was certainly going to pay off, although not on this day, for six members of this pack as well as Jeff Butterfield and Peter Thompson in the backs were to play together in the next eleven Internationals. It was not a very convincing performance by Wales, but it was a very encouraging one for England, the new pack knitted together well considering that they had only got together in the Trials (squad week-ends had not, at this stage, become standard preparation for International matches) and were well led by Eric Evans ably and willingly assisted by the veteran Vic Roberts whose enthusiasm was almost tangible. Application did not diminish when England found themselves five points down after only ten minutes after a series of Welsh drives and territorial gain in loose play had allowed Russell Robins to crash over. Thereafter the match was evenly contested. There were five current Oxbridge Blues on the field that day, the most fascinating being the brilliant Oxford half-backs, Mike Smith and Onllwyn Brace - but they were on opposite sides. Brace went on to win nine Welsh caps over this and the next five seasons, but for Mike Smith this was his first and only International rugby cap.

68th match   **ENGLAND   20 pts   v   IRELAND   0 pts**

	Caps				Caps		
15	2nd	**D.F.Allison**	(Coventry)	.	2nd & last	**J.M.McKelvey**	(Queen's U Belfast)
14	2nd	**P.B.Jackson**	(Coventry)	.	2nd	**S.V.J.Quinlan**	(Highfield)
13	13th	**J.Butterfield**	(Northampton)	.	6th	**A.J.F.O'Reilly**	(Old Belvedere)
12	15th	**L.B.Cannell**	(St Mary's Hospital)	.	10th	**A.C.Pedlow**	(Queen's U Belfast)
11	2nd	**P.H.Thompson**	(Headingley)	.	8th & last	**J.T.Gaston**	(Monkstown)
10	10th	**M.Regan**	(Liverpool)	.	37th	**J.W.Kyle**	(NIFC)
9	6th	**J.E.Williams**	(Old Millhillians)	.	2nd	**A.A.Mulligan**	(Cambridge Univ)
1	7th	**D.L.Sanders**	(Harlequins)	.	2nd	**W.B.C.Fagan**	(Morley)
2	19th	**E.Evans (Capt)**	(Sale)	.	15th	**R.Roe**	(Lansdowne)
3	2nd	**C.R.Jacobs**	(Northampton)	.	4th	**B.G.M.Wood**	(Garryowen)
4	2nd	**J.D.Currie**	(Oxford University)	.	12th & last	**P.J.Lawler**	(Clontarf)
5	2nd	**R.W.D.Marques**	(Cambridge Univ)	.	9th	**T.E.Reid**	(London Irish)
6	2nd	**P.G.D.Robbins**	(Oxford University)	.	1st & only	**N.Feddis**	(Lansdowne)
7	14th	**V.G.Roberts**	(Harlequins)	.	2nd & last	**J.S.Ritchie (Capt)**	(London Irish)
8	2nd	**A.Ashcroft**	(Waterloo)	.	10th	**J.R.Kavanagh**	(Wanderers)

Referee: A.I.Dickie   (Scotland)

SCORERS:	D.F.Allison	Penalty Goal		3 - 0
				Half-time
	P.B.Jackson	Try	(1st)	6 - 0
	E.Evans	Try	(4th)	9 - 0
	J.D.Currie	Conversion		11 - 0
	J.D.Currie	Penalty Goal		14 - 0
	J.Butterfield	Try	(5th & last)	17 - 0
	J.D.Currie	Penalty Goal		20 - 0

POINTS:	J.D.Currie	8 points	(8)
	P.B.Jackson, D.F.Allison	3 points	(3),(6)
	J.Butterfield and E.Evans	each	(15),(12)

MATCH COMMENTARY:

From Ireland's point of view, this game was a complete disaster, but from England's it was an outstanding result. Twenty points was England's biggest winning margin since they beat Ireland in 1938 in Dublin by 36 points to 14. It was also England's highest winning margin in all Internationals since the Second World War. Despite the dominance, Regan and the centres did not look as sharp as previously, and Jeff Butterfield, after an outstandingly successful Lions Tour to South Africa, was perhaps a little jaded. The pack were looking more and more solid and cohesive and the selectors would be content with their bold changes at the beginning of the season. Another bold move this time, was to bring back another veteran to join Vic Roberts in the successful blend of youth and experience. Lewis Cannell, one of the finest creators of opportunities in the post-war game, with his superbly timed passes, came back after a three year gap having been capped first in 1948. Ireland held England to a solitary penalty goal in the first half, but apparently exhausted themselves in doing so and the floodgates opened in the second half. After the disappointment against Wales, the Twickenham crowd went home very satisfied indeed.

71st match　　　　　**ENGLAND　11 pts**　　　v　　　**SCOTLAND　6 pts**

63rd Calcutta Cup

	Caps					Caps		
15	3rd	D.F.Allison	(Coventry)		6th	R.W.T.Chisholm	(Melrose)
14	15th & last	J.E.Woodward	(Wasps)		7th	A.R.Smith	(Cambridge Univ)
13	14th	J.Butterfield	(Northampton)		3rd	J.T.Docherty	(Glasgow HSFP)
12	16th	L.B.Cannell	(St Mary's Hospital)		1st	G.D.Stevenson	(Hawick)
11	3rd	P.H.Thompson	(Headingley)		14th	J.S.Swan	(Coventry)
10	11th	M.Regan	(Liverpool)		2nd	T.McClung	(Edinburgh Acad)
9	7th	J.E.Williams	(Old Millhillians)		11th	A.F.Dorward	(Gala)
1	8th	D.L.Sanders	(Harlequins)		13th	H.F.McLeod	(Hawick)
2	20th	E.Evans (Capt)	(Sale)		8th	R.K.G.MacEwen	(London Scottish)
3	3rd	C.R.Jacobs	(Northampton)		7th	T.Elliot	(Gala)
4	3rd	J.D.Currie	(Oxford University)		11th	E.J.S.Michie	(Aberdeen GSFP)
5	3rd	R.W.D.Marques	(Cambridge Univ)		9th	J.W.Y.Kemp	(Glasgow HSFP)
6	3rd	P.G.D.Robbins	(Oxford University)		6th	I.A.A.MacGregor	(Llanelli)
7	15th	V.G.Roberts	(Harlequins)		9th	A.Robson	(Hawick)
8	3rd	A.Ashcroft	(Waterloo)		9th	J.T.Greenwood (Capt)	(Dunfermline)

Referee:　　M.J.Dowling　　　(Ireland)

SCORERS:

J.D.Currie	Penalty Goal	3 - 0			
J.E.Williams	Try　　(1st & only)	6 - 0			
J.D.Currie	Conversion	8 - 0			
		8 - 3	A.R.Smith	Penalty Goal
J.D.Currie	Penalty Goal	11 - 3			
		11 - 6	G.D.Stevenson	Try
		Half-time			
		11 - 6			

POINTS:

J.D.Currie	8 points	(16)	G.D.Stevenson	3 points
J.E.Williams	3 points	(3)	A.R.Smith	3 points

MATCH COMMENTARY:

England continued their improving performances by beating the Scots at Murrayfield, for the third successive time, but they only managed to share the try count, one each. England's forwards were certainly developing into a formidable unit, but still Martin Regan with much good possession, could not get his back division moving as he would have liked and as they had shown themselves to be capable. John Currie was proving to be a reliable goal kicker and with Dennis Allison available too, that shortcoming seemed to have been eliminated. Both tries were opportunistic and very well taken but owed nothing to set piece moves. Scotland were not without several opportunities to win the match because, in all, five penalty goal attempts were missed, and any two of those could have won the match. As it was, there was no scoring in the second half, but England could never shake off the tenacious Scots who constantly threatened to narrow the slender five point margin. In the end, the Scots were contained, and England deserved their second victory of the season, and their sixth successive win over Scotland, but the team and all Sassenachs at Murrayfield that day must have been mightily relieved to hear the final whistle. This was Ted Woodward's last cap for England and he retired as England's most capped post-war wing three-quarter.

31st match   **ENGLAND   9 pts**   v   **FRANCE   14 pts**

	Caps				Caps		
15	4th	D.F.Allison	(Coventry)	.	15th	M.Vannier	(Racing Club)
14	3rd	P.B.Jackson	(Coventry)	.	5th	J.Dupuy	(Tarbes)
13	15th	J.Butterfield	(Northampton)	.	7th	J.Bouquet	(Vienne)
12	17th	L.B.Cannell	(St Mary's Hospital)	.	3rd	G.Stener	(PUC)
11	4th	P.H.Thompson	(Headingley)	.	12th	L.Roge	(Beziers)
10	12th & last	M.Regan	(Liverpool)	.	4th	A.Labazuy	(Lourdes)
9	8th	J.E.Williams	(Old Millhillians)	.	1st & only	G.Pauthe	(Graulhet)
1	9th & last	D.L.Sanders	(Harlequins)	.	12th	A.Domenech	(Brive)
2	21st	E.Evans (Capt)	(Sale)	.	4th	R.Vigier	(Montferrand)
3	4th	C.R.Jacobs	(Northampton)	.	29th & last	R.Bienes	(Cognac)
4	4th	J.D.Currie	(Oxford University)	.	18th	M.Celaya (Capt)	(Biarritz)
5	4th	R.W.D.Marques	(Cambridge Univ)	.	24th	B.Chevallier	(Montferrand)
6	4th	P.G.D.Robbins	(Oxford University)	.	7th	J.Barthe	(Lourdes)
7	16th & last	V.G.Roberts	(Harlequins)	.	14th	R.Baulon	(Bayonne)
8	4th	A.Ashcroft	(Waterloo)	.	3rd	H.Lazies	(Toulouse)

Referee: I.David   (Wales)

SCORERS:

			3 - 6	A.Labazuy	Penalty Goal
D.F.Allison	Penalty Goal		6 - 6		
			Half-time		
			6 - 9	G.Pauthe	Try
			6 - 11	A.Labazuy	Conversion
			6 - 14	J.Dupuy	Try
D.F.Allison	Penalty Goal		9 - 14		

POINTS:

D.F.Allison	6 points	(12)		A.Labazuy	8 points
P.H.Thompson	3 points	(3)		J.Dupuy	3 points
				G.Pauthe	3 points

MATCH COMMENTARY:

The English pack, unchanged for the four Championship games this season, gave the French a very hard game indeed, but the essential difference between the two sides was the fluency of running of the back divisions and the space they had in which to do it, and, as usual, the clear evidence that the French were faster and fitter than their opponents.   For an undisclosed reason Messieurs Dufau, Boniface, Haget and Prat chose to withdraw from the originally selected side, but in spite of this, the French XV were masters of the situation, and pressured the English forwards and denied space to the backs.   Pauthe, who had replaced Dufau, the French scrum-half and Captain, playing in his first and only international, was a admirable substitute, got his backs moving and scored the decisive try in the second half. By this time England were run ragged and had nothing left and were probably a trifle fortunate to lose by only five points.   England had now lost three successive games to France for the first time, and, as a result, had to settle for a share of second place in the Championship Table with France and Ireland.

SUMMARY OF THE SEASON - 1955 - 56:

The season was essentially one of consolidation for England, and had one been clairvoyant at the time, one would have been quite content with two matches won and two matches lost, in view of the successes which the team, now being put together, were to enjoy in the future. As it was, the mere mortals among us were a trifle disappointed at the results and at the quality of rugby played in the Five Nations Championship after the magnificent Lions tour to South Africa the previous summer.

Ten new caps appeared in the opening match against Wales, at full-back, on both wings, both half-backs, both locks as well as a prop, a flanker and the No. 8. Eric Evans, the most experienced player was appointed Captain. Also included was Vic Roberts to lend experience to an otherwise somewhat raw pack - in International terms. The match was lost - England have beaten Wales only once at Twickenham since the war - but the pack showed immense promise. For the Ireland match, Lewis Cannell replaced Phil Davies and the half-back pairing of Martin Regan and John Williams came back to take over from Mike Smith and the injured Dickie Jeeps, but the pack remained unchanged. In the second half the play flowed, England had abundant possession, scored three tries and beat Ireland by a twenty point margin, the highest by England against all opposition since the war. Against Scotland, the same pack was beginning to exert some real influence, but the backs never played to their potential and the match was won due to some wayward Scottish goal-kicking. In Paris, the forwards competed most effectively but the backs were outplayed by French speed of thought and deed, and flair and fitness.

Over the season, the only new caps awarded were the ten in the first match, the pack remained unchanged during the entire season, and only eighteen different players were used. This must indicate sound selection policy, and it was certainly to pay off in the longer term.

England finished the season, with France and Ireland, in equal second place to Wales, all three having won two matches. England scored five tries and the highest points total in the Championship with forty-three. In this total were eight penalty goals - a sign of things to come ! John Currie was the leading England points scorer with sixteen points from four penalty goals and two conversions, and Dennis Allison followed with twelve points from four penalty goals. The five England tries were scored by five different players.

Only five players retired at the end of the season. Vic Roberts, after an inspired performance following his recall five years after his previous cap and nine years after his first, had sixteen caps. Ted Woodward, the heavy-weight Wasps wing three-quarter and butcher, gained fifteen. Martin Regan, a fly-half of considerable flair, with twelve caps, joined Warrington Rugby League Club later in the year. "Sandy" Sanders had earned nine caps and later became Chairman of the England selectors, President of the RFU and Manager of the England touring side which was to beat New Zealand in Auckland in 1973. Mike Smith (MJK) earned his only Rugby Union cap against Wales this season, but his principle sport was, of course, cricket, and he played fifty Test matches for England and was Captain for twenty five of them.

This had been an excellent season of team building and consolidation for England, but only in retrospect; it was not very satisfactory at all in terms of this season's results. Five tries had been scored and five conceded, and over half the points scored had been by penalty goals. This particular phenomena would hardly merit comment in the future, but at this stage it was regarded by many as ominous. Nevertheless, England had now established a sound pack who had no peers either in the set piece or in the lines-out, and there was, still, considerable potential in the back division. Six of the pack were expected to be available the following season, only "Sandy" Sanders and Vic Roberts had stated their intention to retire, and with Dickie Jeeps restored to full fitness, the next season was eagerly anticipated.

FIVE NATIONS CHAMPIONSHIP TABLE:

Won: **Calcutta Cup**

		Played	Won	Lost	Drawn	Points: For	Against	Tries: For	Against	Title Points
1	Wales	4	3	1	0	25	20	6	2	6
2 =	**ENGLAND**	4	2	2	0	43	28	5	5	4
2 =	France	4	2	2	0	31	34	5	5	4
2 =	Ireland	4	2	2	0	33	47	6	7	4
5	Scotland	4	1	3	0	31	34	5	8	2

Home Games: lost to Wales 3 - 8, (no tries to two); beat Ireland 20 - 0, (three tries to nil)

Away Games: beat Scotland 11 - 6, (one try each); lost to France 9 - 14, (one try to two).

62nd match   **ENGLAND 3 pts**   v   **WALES 0 pts**

	Caps					Caps		
15	5th	D.F.Allison	(Coventry)	.		5th	T.J.Davies	(Llanell)
14	4th	P.B.Jackson	(Coventry)	.		1st	W.G.Howells	(Llanelli)
13	16th	J.Butterfield	(Northampton)	.		20th	M.C.Thomas (Capt)	(Newport)
12	18th	L.B.Cannell	(St Mary's Hospital)	.		11th	G.M.Griffiths	(Cardiff)
11	5th	P.H.Thompson	(Headingley)	.		1st & only	K.Maddocks	(Neath)
10	1st	R.M.Bartlett	(Harlequins)	.		22nd	C.I.Morgan	(Cardiff)
9	2nd	R.E.G.Jeeps	(Northampton)	.		5th	D.O.Brace	(Newport)
1	5th	C.R.Jacobs	(Northampton)	.		3rd	T.R.Prosser	(Pontypool)
2	22nd	E.Evans (Capt)	(Sale)	.		12th	B.V.Meredith	(Newport)
3	5th	G.W.D.Hastings	(Gloucester)	.		13th	C.C.Meredith	(Neath)
4	5th	J.D.Currie	(Oxford University)	.		10th	R.H.Williams	(Llanelli)
5	5th	R.W.D.Marques	(Cambridge Univ)	.		29th	J.R.G.Stephens	(Neath)
6	5th	P.G.D.Robbins	(Oxford University)	.		17th	R.C.C.Thomas	(Swansea)
7	9th	R.Higgins	(Liverpool)	.		1st & only	R.O'Connor	(Aberavon)
8	5th	A.Ashcroft	(Waterloo)	.		10th	R.J.Robins	(Pontypridd)

Referee: A.I.Dickie   (Scotland)

SCORERS: D.F.Allison   Penalty Goal   3 - 0
                                                        Half-time
                                                        3 - 0

POINTS: D.F.Allison   3 points   (15)

MATCH COMMENTARY:

The last time Wales failed to score in an International match at Cardiff Arms Park was in 1934, when they lost by nine points to nothing also to England. There was little constructive rugby in the game as a whole, with the Welsh, even with several illustrious names on the field, strangely hesitant and lacking confidence. The English pack, on the other hand never looked in trouble, but the backs, Ricky Bartlett, in particular, will have to be more enterprising and innovative to capitalise on this ascendancy.

England's winning penalty goal was given away by Keith Maddocks who unwittingly stepped off-side at a line-out. To be the singular cause of Wales' demise had to merit almost the ultimate sanction, and the hapless Maddocks found that he had played his first, and last, International for Wales.

Although England failed to score a try in this match, for the third successive time they prevented Wales from scoring a try against them in an International at Cardiff Arms Park, no mean feat by anybody's standards..

69th match   **ENGLAND   6 pts**   v   **IRELAND   0 pts**

	Caps					Caps		
15	1st	R.Challis	(Bristol)			6th	P.J.Berkery	(Lansdowne)
14	5th	P.B.Jackson	(Coventry)			10th	A.J.F.O'Reilly	(Old Belvedere)
13	17th	J.Butterfield	(Northampton)			29th	N.J.Henderson (Capt)	(NIFC)
12	19th & last	L.B.Cannell	(St Mary's Hospital)			14th	A.C.Pedlow	(CIYMS)
11	6th	P.H.Thompson	(Headingley)			2nd	N.H.Brophy	(UC Dublin)
10	2nd	R.M.Bartlett	(Harlequins)			41st	J.W.Kyle	(NIFC)
9	3rd	R.E.G.Jeeps	(Northampton)			4th	A.A.Mulligan	(Cambridge Univ)
1	6th	C.R.Jacobs	(Northampton)			7th	P.J.O'Donoghue	(Bective Rangers)
2	23rd	E.Evans (Capt)	(Sale)			19th	R.Roe	(London Irish)
3	6th	G.W.D.Hastings	(Gloucester)			8th	B.G.M.Wood	(Garryowen)
4	6th	J.D.Currie	(Oxford University)			11th	T.E.Reid	(London Irish)
5	6th	R.W.D.Marques	(Cambridge Univ)			10th	J.R.Brady	(CIYMS)
6	6th	P.G.D.Robbins	(Oxford University)			2nd	H.S.O'Connor	(Dublin University)
7	10th	R.Higgins	(Liverpool)			14th	J.R.Kavanagh	(Wanderers)
8	6th	A.Ashcroft	(Waterloo)			2nd	P.J.A.O'Sullivan	(Galwegians)

Referee: A.I.Dickie   (Scotland)

SCORERS: P.B.Jackson   Try   (2nd)   3 - 0
                                                                  Half-time
                       R.Challis   Penalty Goal   6 - 0

POINTS: P.B.Jackson   3 points   (6)
                     R.Challis   3 points   (3)

MATCH COMMENTARY:

Only one change was made in the team for Lansdowne Road, Robert Challis replacing Dennis Allison at full-back. Challis was the first of several full-backs to adopt the practice of taking a place kick for a penalty kick to touch, and indeed did this in this match.

The Irish back division was as powerful and experienced as any in the Five Nations this season, and they were particularly strong in defence. Nevertheless, Peter Jackson scored the only try which Ireland conceded all season, and this evidenced the increasing confidence of the English backs. The English forwards never allowed the Irish pack to gain any control although honours were fairly even in the lines-out. This was a considerable performance because for almost half the match Peter Thompson was off the field with several broken ribs and Alan Ashcroft took his place on the wing, thus the English pack were down to seven men. England had not beaten Ireland at Lansdowne Road since 1938, and they had started this season by winning both away matches without conceding a point. A very warm welcome would await them at Twickenham.

Lewis Cannell made his nineteenth and last appearance for England. His career had spanned ten seasons and he had shown himself to be a very shrewd tactician with a genius for timing his pass and creating try scoring opportunities for others.

32nd match   **ENGLAND   9 pts**   **v**   **FRANCE   5 pts**

	Caps					Caps		
15	2nd	**R.Challis**	(Bristol)	.	18th	**M.Vannier**	(Racing Club)
14	6th	**P.B.Jackson**	(Coventry)	.	2nd	**C.Darrouy**	(Mont-de-Marsan)
13	18th	**J.Butterfield**	(Northampton)	.	10th	**J.Bouquet**	(Vienne)
12	9th	**W.P.C.Davies**	(Harlequins)	.	2nd & last	**R.Monie**	(Perpignan)
11	7th	**P.H.Thompson**	(Headingley)	.	9th	**J.Dupuy**	(Tarbes)
10	3rd	**R.M.Bartlett**	(Harlequins)	.	10th	**A.Haget**	(PUC)
9	4th	**R.E.G.Jeeps**	(Northampton)	.	35th	**G.Dufau**	(Racing Club)
1	7th	**C.R.Jacobs**	(Northampton)	.	16th	**A.Domenech**	(Brive)
2	24th	**E.Evans (Capt)**	(Sale)	.	7th	**R.Vigier**	(Montferrand)
3	7th	**G.W.D.Hastings**	(Gloucester)	.	8th	**A.Sanac**	(Perpignan)
4	7th	**J.D.Currie**	(Oxford University)	.	22nd	**M.Celaya (Capt)**	(Biarritz)
5	7th	**R.W.D.Marques**	(Cambridge Univ)	.	2nd	**M.Hoche**	(PUC)
6	7th	**P.G.D.Robbins**	(Oxford University)	.	3rd	**F.Moncla**	(Racing Club)
7	11th	**R.Higgins**	(Liverpool)	.	2nd	**J.Carrere**	(Vichy)
8	7th	**A.Ashcroft**	(Waterloo)	.	11th	**J.Barthe**	(Lourdes)

Referee: R.C.Williams   (Ireland)

SCORERS:

P.B.Jackson	Try	(3rd)	3 - 0			
P.B.Jackson	Try	(4th)	6 - 0			
			Half-time			
			6 - 3	**C.Darrouy**		Try
			6 - 5	**M.Vannier**		Conversion
E.Evans	Try	(5th & last)	9 - 6			

POINTS:

P.B.Jackson	6 points	(12)		**C.Darrouy**	3 points
E.Evans	3 points	(15)		**M.Vannier**	2 points

MATCH COMMENTARY:

Again only one change from the side who had played so splendidly in Dublin, Phil Davies replacing Lewis Cannell, and the pack, for the third match in succession, remained the same.

It seemed that almost two seasons of preparation and planning had at last come to fruition, when England beat France, at Twickenham, much more comprehensively than the score suggests. The, forwards, as they had in previous games, dominated the tight and the lines-out and were very effective in the loose. Abundant possession for Jeeps and Bartlett gave them the confidence to play an expansive game. Peter Jackson's two tries, and one from the captain, were just reward for some enterprising play and brilliant running by Ricky Bartlett. There was a ferocious French onslaught on the English line in the last quarter of the match which failed to yield any points, and England recorded their third win of the season. The ground was heavy and the ball greasy, and it was to the credit of both sides that three tries were scored by the backs. It was also refreshing that penalty goals had no bearing on the result !

Eric Evans became England's most-capped post-war player, beating John Kendall-Carpenter's record of 23 caps.

72nd match

64th Calcutta Cup

ENGLAND 16 pts   v   SCOTLAND 3 pts

	Caps					Caps		
15	3rd & last	R.Challis	(Bristol)	.	4th	K.J.F.Scotland	(Heriot's)	
14	7th	P.B.Jackson	(Coventry)	.	11th	A.R.Smith	(Cambridge Univ)	
13	19th	J.Butterfield	(Northampton)	.	5th	T.McClung	(Edinburgh Acad'ls)	
12	10th	W.P.C.Davies	(Harlequins)	.	6th & last	K.R.MacDonald	(Stewart's Coll FP)	
11	8th	P.H.Thompson	(Headingley)	.	2nd & last	J.L.F.Allen	(Cambridge Univ)	
10	4th	R.M.Bartlett	(Harlequins)	.	1st	G.H.Waddell	(London Scottish)	
9	5th	R.E.G.Jeeps	(Northampton)	.	15th & last	A.F.Dorward	(Gala)	
1	8th	C.R.Jacobs	(Northampton)	.	17th	H.F.McLeod	(Hawick)	
2	25th	E.Evans (Capt)	(Sale)	.	12th	R.K.G.MacEwen	(London Scottish)	
3	8th	G.W.D.Hastings	(Gloucester)	.	11th	T.Elliot	(Gala)	
4	8th	J.D.Currie	(Oxford University)	.	15th & last	E.J.S.Michie	(London Scottish)	
5	8th	R.W.D.Marques	(Cambridge Univ)	.	13th	J.W.Y.Kemp	(Glasgow HSFP)	
6	8th	P.G.D.Robbins	(Oxford University)	.	2nd	G.K.Smith	(Kelso)	
7	12th	R.Higgins	(Liverpool)	.	13th	A.Robson	(Hawick)	
8	8th	A.Ashcroft	(Waterloo)	.	12th	J.T.Greenwood (Capt)	(Perthshire Acad)	

Referee: R.Mitchell   (Ireland)

SCORERS: W.P.C.Davies   Try   (1st & only)   3 - 0

Half-time

	R.Challis	Penalty Goal	6 - 0			
			6 - 3	K.J.F.Scotland	Penalty Goal	
	P.H.Thompson	Try	(2nd)	9 - 3		
	R.Challis	Conversion	11 - 3			
	R.Higgins	Try	(2nd & last)	14 - 3		
	R.Challis	Conversion	16 - 3			

POINTS: R.Challis   7 points   (14)   K.J.F.Scotland   3 points

R.Higgins, P.H Thompson   3 points   (6),(6)

and W.P.C.Davies   each   (3)

MATCH COMMENTARY:

England fielded an unchanged side for the final match of the season - they had used only 17 players for the four matches. The forwards, unchanged throughout the season, took complete control, in both the tight and the loose although they were up against an even more experienced Scottish pack. The England backs moved the ball with courage and confidence and, although with limited possession, so did Scotland and it was a spectacular and invigorating match. England won comfortably by three tries to one and the result provided them with all manner of rewards - the seventh Calcutta Cup in succession, the Championship, the Triple Crown for the thirteenth time and the second time in four years and the Grand Slam for the seventh time and for the first time for twenty-nine years - since 1928.

In achieving this, England had conceded only eight points - one converted try and a penalty goal - and had themselves scored thirty-four points and seven tries. In their report of this match, The Times coined the Bridge term "Grand Slam" (meaning the taking of all tricks) in the Rugby context. It was the first time that this expression had been used and it certainly stuck !

Jeff Butterfield beat Bob Stirlings post-war record of eighteen successive caps in this match.

SUMMARY OF THE SEASON - 1956 - 57:

The groundwork and team-building undertaken last season and a series of very satisfactory trial matches set England up for the pinnacle of achievement in the Five Nations Championship, the Grand Slam.. This was the seventh time that England have achieved the feat, and the first time since 1928, twenty-nine years ago, and it had only been done three times since then, by Wales in 1950 and again in 1952, and by Ireland in 1948. The expression "Grand Slam" is, of course, a term from the game of Bridge - or Whist - meaning the taking of all tricks. The term was coined by The Times in their report of the match and is now widely understood to mean the winning of all matches in the Five Nations Championship, two at home and two away, in any one season.

Perhaps the most fortunate aspect of the success of the England side this season was that, although two very experienced forwards had retired at the end of the previous season, "Sandy" Sanders and Vic Roberts, their replacements, Reg Higgins and George Hastings were already seasoned Internationals with nine caps and five caps resepctively, (indeed Reg Higgins was a British Lion who had played in the first Test in South Africa in 1955). Both, of course, fitted into the England pack as if to the manner born.
England introduced only one new cap for the opening match against Wales at Cardiff, Ricky Bartlett, the Harlequins fly-half, and such was the stability of the side at this time, that eleven of the side had played in the corresponding fixture at Twickenham in the previous season. It was fortunate, perhaps, for the half-backs that the forwards gained such ascendancy, because, as a pair, they did not play well. Neither, on the other hand did Wales, and one penalty goal was sufficient to decide the issue. Only one change, at full-back, was made to the side to travel to Dublin, and Ricky Bartlett, in particular, grew in confidence, Peter Jackson scored the only try, and having won both away matches, the English bandwagon was rolling. This time the wheels did not fall off. Phil Davies replaced Lewis Cannell for the match against France, and the forwards dominated. Ricky Bartlett's confidence was never higher and England won decisively by scoring three tries to one. The last match, for the Grand Slam, with Scotland, was the best of the season by far, and Scotland played their part to the full but could not match England's confidence, courage and craftsmanship and England won a most entertaining match comfortably by scoring three tries with no reply from Scotland.

Apart from the supreme accolade of the Grand Slam of course, England won the Triple Crown, as they had in 1954, and denied Scotland the Calcutta Cup for the seventh successive season. They had conceded only one try, to France, and had scored seven in the four matches, six of them, fittingly, at Twickenham, and had conceded only eight points in all.

During the season Eric Evans had become England's most-capped post-war player, passing John Kendall-Carpenter's record of twenty-three he now has twenty-five caps, Lewis Cannell became England's most-capped post-war back beating Nim Hall's seventeen caps with nineteen and by the end of the season Jeff Butterfield had emulated that achievement and had beaten Bob Stirling's record of eighteen successive caps.

Robert Challis was England's leading points scorer with ten points, and Peter Jackson followed close behind with nine points from three tries, the remaining four tries were scored by Eric Evans (against France) and Reg Higgins, Peter Thompson and Phil Davies (all against Scotland)

Only two players quit International rugby at the end of this season, Lewis Cannell, with nineteen caps earned over ten seasons, eventually settled in South Africa and practised medicine there. Robert Challis, the full-back from Bristol, yet another of England's short-tenure full-backs, earned all his caps in this Grand Slam season, and was one of the first players to adopt the ultra-cautious practice of taking a place kick to find touch after the award of a penalty kick.

It had been a magnificent season, and while tributes are due to all members of the side, none can have earned them more than Eric Evans, an inspirational player and Captain - who was not finished yet !

FIVE NATIONS CHAMPIONSHIP TABLE:

Won: **Grand Slam, Triple Crown, Championship Title and Calcutta Cup.**

		Played	Won	Lost	Drawn	Points: For	Points: Against	Tries: For	Tries: Against	Title Points
1	ENGLAND	4	4	0	0	34	8	7	1	8
2 =	Wales	4	2	2	0	31	30	5	5	4
2 =	Ireland	4	2	2	0	21	21	4	1	4
2 =	Scotland	4	2	2	0	21	27	1	5	4
5	France	4	0	4	0	24	45	4	9	0

Home Games: beat France 9 - 5, (three tries to one); beat Scotland 16 - 3, (three tries to none).

Away Games: beat Wales 3 - 0, (no tries); beat Ireland 6 - 0, (one try to none).

63rd match   **ENGLAND   3 pts**   v   **WALES   3 pts**

	Caps					Caps		
15	6th	D.F.Allison	(Coventry)	.		10th	T.J.Davies	(Llanelli)
14	8th	P.B.Jackson	(Coventry)	.		2nd	J.R.Collins	(Aberavon)
13	20th	J.Butterfield	(Northampton)	.		22nd	M.C.Thomas	(Newport)
12	11th & last	W.P.C.Davies	(Harlequins)	.		3rd	C.A.H.Davies	(Cardiff)
11	9th	P.H.Thompson	(Headingley)	.		6th	G.T.Wells	(Cardiff)
10	1st	J.P.Horrocks-Taylor	(Cambridge Univ)	.		26th	C.I.Morgan	(Cardiff)
9	6th	R.E.G.Jeeps	(Northampton)	.		4th	L.H.Williams	(Cardiff)
1	9th	C.R.Jacobs	(Northampton)	.		8th	T.R.Prosser	(Pontypool)
2	26th	E.Evans (Capt)	(Sale)	.		17th	B.V.Meredith	(Newport)
3	9th	G.W.D.Hastings	(Gloucester)	.		2nd	D.Devereux	(Neath)
4	9th	J.D.Currie	(Oxford University)	.		15th	R.H.Williams	(Llanelli)
5	9th	R.W.D.Marques	(Cambridge Univ)	.		2nd	W.R.Evans	(Cardiff)
6	9th	P.G.D.Robbins	(Oxford University)	.		19th	R.C.C.Thomas (Capt)	(Swansea)
7	1st	R.E.Syrett	(Wasps)	.		1st	H.J.Morgan	(Abertillery)
8	9th	A.Ashcroft	(Waterloo)	.		4th	J.Faull	(Swansea)

Referee: R.C.Williams   (Ireland)

SCORERS: 0 - 3   T.J.Davies   Penalty Goal
                                                     Half-time
                    P.H.Thompson   Try   (3rd)   3 - 3

POINTS: P.H.Thompson   3 points   (9)   T.J.Davies   3 points

MATCH COMMENTARY:

There were only three changes from the previous season's Grand Slam side for the opening match of the season against Wales, Dennis Allison returning at full-back, and new caps Phil Horrocks-Taylor at fly-half and Ron Syrett on the open side flank, but even so, the Champions of last season did not quite live up to their reputation against a strong Welsh XV. England did score the only try of the match midway through the second half, but the new young fly-half, Phil Horrocks-Taylor could not get his backs moving as had Ricky Bartlett in the previous Grand Slam season. The forwards performance was no more than adequate, and it was almost pedestrian compared with the two previous games. The Welsh tactics were essentially to play 10-man rugby, and Cliff Morgan's vast touch kicks and the very able playing of the touch line by himself and Lloyd Williams made for effective but not memorable rugby. This was not a game to remember. It was however, the last occasion on which Jeff Butterfield and Phil Davies played together in the centre for England. On nine occasions had their flair, powerful running and determined tackling been seen to advantage in the white jerseys and had it not been for the availability of equally talented centres at the same time, Pat Quinn and Lewis Cannell, they may well have worn the England shirt together on twice as many occasions.

4th match   **ENGLAND   9 pts**   v   **AUSTRALIA   6 pts**

	Caps					Caps		
15	1st	**J.G.G.Hetherington**	(Northampton)	.		5th	**T.G.P.Curley**	(New South Wales)
14	9th	**P.B.Jackson**	(Coventry)	.		4th	**K.J.Donald**	(Queensland)
13	21st	**J.Butterfield**	(Northampton)	.		2nd	**J.K.Lenehan**	(New South Wales)
12	1st	**M.S.Phillips**	(Oxford University)	.		4th	**S.W.White**	(New South Wales)
11	10th	**P.H.Thompson**	(Headingley)	.		9th	**R.Phelps**	(New South Wales)
10	2nd	**J.P.Horrocks-Taylor**	(Cambridge Univ)	.		3rd	**A.J.Summons**	(New South Wales)
9	7th	**R.E.G.Jeeps**	(Northampton)	.		3rd	**D.M.Connor**	(Queensland)
1	10th	**G.W.D.Hastings**	(Gloucester)	.		1st	**G.N.Vaughan**	(Victoria)
2	27th	**E.Evans (Capt)**	(Sale)	.		7th	**J.V.Brown**	(New South Wales)
3	10th	**C.R.Jacobs**	(Northampton)	.		10th	**R.A.L.Davidson (Capt)**	(New South Wales)
4	10th	**J.D.Currie**	(Oxford University)	.		19th	**A.R.Millar**	(New South Wales)
5	10th	**R.W.D.Marques**	(Cambridge Univ)	.		4th	**D.M.Emanuel**	(New South Wales)
6	10th	**P.G.D.Robbins**	(Oxford University)	.		12th	**N.M.Hughes**	(New South Wales)
7	2nd	**R.E.Syrett**	(Wasps)	.		4th	**P.T.Fenwicke**	(New South Wales)
8	10th	**A.Ashcroft**	(Waterloo)	.		1st	**K.J.Ryan**	(Queensland)

Referee: R.C.Williams   (Ireland)

SCORERS:

				0 - 3	**J.K.Lenehan**		Penalty Goal
				Half-time			
M.S.Phillips		Try	(1st)	3 - 3			
				3 - 6	**T.G.P.Curley**		Drop Goal
J.G.G.Hetherington		Penalty Goal		6 - 6			
P.B.Jackson		Try	(5th)	9 - 6			

POINTS:

P.B.Jackson	3 points	(15)	**T.G.P.Curley**	3 points	
M.S.Phillips	3 points	(3)	**J.K.Lenehan**	3 points	
J.G.G.Hetherington	3 points	(3)			

MATCH COMMENTARY:

The Fourth Wallabies eventually lost all five international matches on their tour, but this game was very close, was played at a frenetic pace and was one of the hardest and most exciting ever seen at Twickenham. Early in the match, Phil Horrocks-Taylor had to leave the field and Jeff Butterfield took over at fly-half. The backs seemed to move more freely after this but Jeff Butterfield was taking a severe battering from the Australian back row. Twice Australia took the lead and twice England clawed their way back to level terms, firstly through Malcolm Phillips' excellent debut try and secondly through John Hetherington's penalty goal kicked when he appeared to be seriously concussed, and with only ten minutes of the match remaining. The final bruising minutes reached a dramatic climax when Peter Jackson, breaking out near the right touchline, swerved and feinted his way over in the corner for the decisive score in the last minute of the match. Immediately on the final whistle, John Hetherington fell forward flat on his face, totally exhausted and lay inert on the pitch, a testimony to the Herculean effort that not only he, but the happy few, the band of brothers, had put in to achieve this remarkable result. The magnificent performance of the pack can be attributed, no doubt, to the fact that six of them had played in all the previous ten Internationals together - the thread of continuity, previously lacking, had yielded the Grand Slam last season and was not faded yet.

70th match   **ENGLAND 6 pts**   v   **IRELAND 0 pts**

	Caps					Caps		
15	2nd	J.G.G.Hetherington	(Northampton)	.	10th	P.J.Berkery	(London Irish)
14	1st	J.R.C.Young	(Oxford University)	.	14th	A.J.F.O'Reilly	(Old Belvedere)
13	22nd	J.Butterfield	(Northampton)	.	33rd	N.J.Henderson (Capt)	(NIFC)
12	2nd	M.S.Phillips	(Oxford University)	.	2nd	D.Hewitt	(Queen's U Belfast)
11	11th	P.H.Thompson	(Headingley)	.	18th	A.C.Pedlow	(CIYMS)
10	5th	R.M.Bartlett	(Harlequins)	.	45th	J.W.Kyle	(NIFC)
9	8th	R.E.G.Jeeps	(Northampton)	.	9th	A.A.Mulligan	(London Irish)
1	11th	C.R.Jacobs	(Northampton)	.	9th	P.J.O'Donoghue	(Bective Rangers)
2	28th	E.Evans (Capt)	(Sale)	.	2nd	A.R.Dawson	(Wanderers)
3	11th	G.W.D.Hastings	(Gloucester)	.	12th	B.G.M.Wood	(Garryowen)
4	11th	J.D.Currie	(Oxford University)	.	2nd	J.B.Stevenson	(Instonians)
5	11th	R.W.D.Marques	(Cambridge Univ)	.	2nd	W.A.Mulcahy	(UC Dublin)
6	11th	P.G.D.Robbins	(Oxford University)	.	2nd	J.A.Donaldson	(Belfast Collegians)
7	3rd	R.E.Syrett	(Wasps)	.	2nd	N.A.A.Murphy	(Cork Constitution)
8	11th	A.Ashcroft	(Waterloo)	.	18th	J.R.Kavanagh	(Wanderers)

Referee: G.Burrell   (Scotland)

SCORERS:	J.G.G.Hetherington	Penalty Goal		3 - 0
	A.Ashcroft	Try	(1st & only)	6 - 0
			Half-time	6 - 0

POINTS:	A.Ashcroft	3 points	(3)
	J.G.G.Hetherington	3 points	(6)

MATCH COMMENTARY:

After the Lord Mayor's Show only a week previously, England failed to make a significant mark on this rather featureless match. The pack was unchanged but the physical Australians had seen to it that Phil Horrocks-Taylor and Peter Jackson needed more than just a week to recover. John Hetherington played, but should not have done so after suffering concussion in that same match.

The forwards played an excellent game as a pack, as indeed they had over the past two seasons, but, despite the recall of Ricky Bartlett, running rugby and spectacular tries which had been the hallmark of the previous five matches, was not the order of the day on this occasion. England were totally dominant for the first ten minutes and Ireland for the last ten, but in between was a somewhat tedious stalemate. Ireland's onslaught at the end was very ferocious and a splendid passing movement involving O'Reilly, Henderson and Pedlow resulted in Kavanagh touching down only to be called back for a forward pass somewhere along the line.

This was Jack Kyle's penultimate international and his last at Twickenham where he had appeared five times for Ireland in the twelve seasons since the end of the war, having missed the match in 1954.

33rd match   **ENGLAND   14 pts**   v   **FRANCE   0 pts**

	Caps					Caps		
15	1st & only	**J.S.M.Scott**	(Oxford University)	.	24th	**M.Vannier**	(Racing Club)
14	10th	**P.B.Jackson**	(Coventry)		5th	**G.Mauduy**	(Perigueux)
13	23rd	**J.Butterfield**	(Northampton)		20th	**A.Boniface**	(Mont-de-Marsan)
12	3rd	**M.S.Phillips**	(Oxford University)		4th & last	**C.Vignes**	(Racing Club)
11	12th	**P.H.Thompson**	(Headingley)		14th	**J.Dupuy**	(Tarbes)
10	6th	**R.M.Bartlett**	(Harlequins)		14th	**J.Bouquet**	(Vienne)
9	9th	**R.E.G.Jeeps**	(Northampton)		5th	**P.Danos**	(Beziers)
1	12th	**C.R.Jacobs**	(Northampton)		22nd	**A.Domenech**	(Brive)
2	29th	**E.Evans (Capt)**	(Sale)		13th	**R.Vigier**	(Montferrand)
3	12th	**G.W.D.Hastings**	(Gloucester)		3rd	**A.Quaglio**	(Mazamet)
4	12th	**J.D.Currie**	(Oxford University)		20th	**L.Mias**	(Mazamet)
5	12th	**R.W.D.Marques**	(Cambridge Univ)		26th	**M.Celaya (Capt)**	(Biarritz)
6	1st	**A.J.Herbert**	(Wasps)		4th	**M.Crauste**	(Racing Club)
7	4th	**R.E.Syrett**	(Wasps)		16th	**H.Domec**	(Lourdes)
8	12th	**A.Ashcroft**	(Waterloo)		16th	**J.Barthe**	(Lourdes)

Referee: W.J.Evans   (Wales)

SCORERS:
P.H.Thompson	Try	(4th)	3 - 0
G.W.D.Hastings	Conversion		5 - 0
P.H.Thompson	Try	(5th & last)	8 - 0
P.B.Jackson	Try	(6th & last)	11 - 0
			Half-time
G.W.D.Hastings	Penalty Goal		14 - 0

POINTS:
P.H.Thompson	6 points	(15)
G.W.D.Hastings	5 points	(8)
P.B.Jackson	3 points	(18)

MATCH COMMENTARY:

Three further changes were considered necessary for the trip to Paris, the most significant being the return of Peter Jackson on the wing. The first half was England's most impressive performance for some time, including last year's Grand Slam victories. The forwards started well and improved up to half-time and Ricky Bartlett was able to get the three-quarter line moving to such an extent that three tries had been scored before the interval in a memorable display of high quality rugby. Although the French tightened up on their defence and their forward play in the second half, England, for some inexplicable reason, slackened off and the aggressive running and confident handling of the first half was no longer in evidence. Another score early in the second half would have knocked all the stuffing out of the French, but England failed to take the advantage. As it was, France gradually came back and the longer the match went on the less likely it seemed that England could score again. So the match ended as something of an anticlimax after that splendid first half.

This was England's biggest victory in Paris since 1914 - and their highest post-war winning margin against France but it could have been so very much more. It was also the sixth successive defeat for France, a statistic to which the French crowd at Stade Colombes did not take very kindly, and there were all sorts of protests against the selectors, the President of the FFRU, the team and others, after the match !

73rd match   **ENGLAND   3 pts**   v   **SCOTLAND   3 pts**

65th Calcutta Cup

	Caps					Caps		
15	7th & last	D.F.Allison	(Coventry)	.	5th	K.J.F.Scotland	(Heriot's FP)
14	11th	P.B.Jackson	(Coventry)	.	1st	C.Elliot	(Langholm)
13	24th	J.Butterfield	(Northampton)	.	7th	G.D.Stevenson	(Hawick)
12	4th	M.S.Phillips	(Oxford University)	.	8th & last	J.T.Docherty	(Glasgow HSFP)
11	13th	P.H.Thompson	(Headingley)	.	13th	T.G.Weatherstone	(Stewart's Coll FP)
10	7th & last	R.M.Bartlett	(Harlequins)	.	6th	G.H.Waddell	(Devonport Services)
9	10th	R.E.G.Jeeps	(Northampton)	.	5th	J.A.T.Rodd	(US Portsmouth)
1	13th	C.R.Jacobs	(Northampton)	.	22nd	H.F.McLeod	(Hawick)
2	30th & last	E.Evans (Capt)	(Sale)	.	4th	N.S.Bruce	(Army/Blackheath)
3	13th & last	G.W.D.Hastings	(Gloucester)	.	3rd	I.R.Hastie	(Kelso)
4	13th	J.D.Currie	(Oxford University)	.	5th	M.W.Swan	(London Scottish)
5	13th	R.W.D.Marques	(Cambridge Univ)	.	18th	J.W.Y.Kemp	(Glasgow HSFP)
6	12th	P.G.D.Robbins	(Oxford University)	.	4th & last	D.C.Macdonald	(Edinburgh Univ)
7	2nd	A.J.Herbert	(Wasps)	.	17th	A.Robson	(Hawick)
8	13th	A.Ashcroft	(Waterloo)	.	17th	J.T.Greenwood (Capt)	(Perthshire Acad)

Referee: R.C.Williams   (Ireland)

SCORERS:

			0 - 0		
			Half-time		
G.W.D.Hastings	Penalty Goal		3 - 0		
			3 - 3	C.Elliot	Penalty Goal

POINTS:

G.W.D.Hastings	3 points	(11)		C.Elliot	3 points

MATCH COMMENTARY:

This was an uneventful match in complete contrast to the thrilling display in the first half in Paris. The draw was sufficient, however, to give England the Championship title with six points as, unlike other nations, they were unbeaten having drawn two uneventful and uninspiring matches - hardly the apogee of success !! England won the title for the second successive year, largely due to their solid defence and determined first time tackling. The effectiveness of this is amply demonstrated in that they conceded no tries and only two penalty goals in the four Championship matches. In those terms this is the best season England have ever had. In spite of that achievement, this match was an eminently unsatisfactory affair featuring only two penalty goals - and the first half did not even have that !

England's possession was slow, and the passing when it occurred was erratic. Peter Thompson and Peter Jackson on the wings must have had a very frustrating afternoon. To their credit, the Scots back row was very aggressive and typically tenacious and did much to knock England out of her stride.

This match also completed a record post-war sequence for England of nine matches without defeat covering two complete seasons, and including six Five Nations wins, draws against Wales and Scotland, and a win over Australia.

SUMMARY OF THE SEASON - 1957 - 58:

There had been some meddling with the laws of the game before the International season began this year, the principal change being that it was no longer necessary to play the ball with the foot after a tackle. The intention was to speed up the game and make it more free-flowing but the unforeseen effect, at least in the Five Nations Championship, was to place the emphasis on defensive rugby rather than the reverse. Thus, often, are the rewards of the reformer.

It was a dull Championship on the whole, and no more so than on Wales' visit to Twickenham for the first match of the season. England introduced one new cap, Phil Horrocks-Taylor, the Cambridge University fly-half, but there were only two other changes from the side which had met Wales the previous season. It was a dour match, the Welsh played ten man rugby, and the English forwards had, for the moment lost the cohesiveness and authority of last season, so a draw was a just, if unsatisfactory, result. The Australians came to Twickenham having already lost in Dublin and Cardiff, but England with the same pack and changes at full-back and centre, had to draw on all their resources to keep pace and eventually triumph by a narrow margin but by two tries to nil. The final match winning try scored by Peter Jackson in the last minute after a dramatic and evasive run, was a thrilling climax to a very hard, entertaining and exciting encounter. Only a week later, with Peter Jackson injured and Ricky Bartlett recalled, England could not attain the same heights as the Australians had inspired them to, and the match against Ireland was another dull affair with brief intensive flurries of activity at the beginning and at the end, but with little in between. In Paris, especially in the first half, England displayed again all the poise, confidence courage and enterprise which had brought them success last season, and although they slackened off in the second half, they ran out worthy winners by three tries to nil. Then, against Scotland, another complete contrast - a dull and tedious match of shared penalty goals and precious little else. Scotland partially achieved their objective by denying England victory, but not in a memorable fashion.

For the five matches, England had awarded seven new caps, and had used twenty-one players, amongst them three different full-backs, but only nine forwards, and the nucleus of the side, particularly the pack, had been together for three seasons.

England won the Championship for the second successive season, but not in as spectacular manner as previously, because, although they drew two matches, they did not lose one. They also denied Scotland the Calcutta Cup for the eighth successive time. Their defensive record was certainly exemplary in having conceded no tries at all and only six points in the Five Nations and a further six against Australia. No side since the war, in twelve Five Nations Championships has had no tries scored against them, nor conceded so few points. In the years to come, only France would emulate this record - no-one would beat it.

Six players came to the end of their International careers. Eric Evans had enjoyed a remarkable career having earned thirty caps, one short of Wavell Wakefield's all time record, having led England on thirteen occasions, the same as Wakefield and Nim Hall, but with a far better record than either Wakefield or Hall, having won nine of those matches (Wakefield won seven and Hall only six). Strangely, Eric Evans was never a British Lion although his career spanned two Lions tours, 1950 and 1955. George Hastings retired with thirteen caps having missed one season completely when the selectors preferred "Sandy" Sanders; Phil Davies, a British Lion in 1955 with three Test caps, whose centre partnership with Jeff Butterfield on nine occasions had been one of the best centre-threequarter pairings, retired after the match against Wales with eleven caps; Dennis Allison, seven caps, pursued his career with ICI and became a Director of the Company; Ricky Bartlett, also with seven caps, a pig farmer and schoolmaster at Millfield, enjoyed the unique distinction of having played seven times for England and never on the losing side; John Scott, later a solicitor and an Americas Cup crew member in 1964, enjoyed a different moment of glory, and his only cap, in the best match of the season against France.

FIVE NATIONS CHAMPIONSHIP TABLE:

Won: **Championship Title,. Retained Calcutta Cup.**

		Played	Won	Lost	Drawn	Points: For	Against	Tries: For	Against	Title Points
1	**ENGLAND**	4	2	0	2	26	6	5	0	6
2	Wales	4	2	1	1	26	28	6	4	5
3	France	4	2	2	0	36	37	4	6	4
4	Scotland	4	1	2	1	23	32	4	5	3
5	Ireland	4	1	3	0	24	32	3	7	2

Home Games: drew with Wales 3 - 3, (one try to nil); beat Ireland 6 - 0, (one try to nil).

Away Games: beat France 14 - 0, (three tries to nil); drew with Scotland 3 - 3, (no tries)

64th match   **ENGLAND   0 pts**   v   **WALES   5 pts**

	Caps					Caps		
15	3rd	J.G.G.Hetherington	(Northampton)	.	13th	T.J.Davies	(Llanelli)	
14	12th	P.B.Jackson	(Coventry)	.	5th	J.Collins	(Aberavon)	
13	5th	M.S.Phillips	(Oxford University)	.	1st	H.J.Davies	(Cambridge Univ.)	
12	25th	J.Butterfield (Capt)	(Northampton)	.	1st	M.J.Price	(Pontypool)	
11	14th	P.H.Thompson	(Waterloo)	.	1st	D.I.E.Bebb	(Carmarthen TC)	
10	1st	A.B.W.Risman	(Manchester Univ)	.	1st	C.Ashton	(Aberavon)	
9	1st	S.R.Smith	(Cambridge Univ)	.	8th	L.H.Williams	|(Cardiff)	
1	1st	L.H.Webb	(Bedford)	.	12th	T.R.Prosser	(Pontypool)	
2	1st	J.A.S.Wackett	(Rosslyn Park)	.	20th	B.V.Meredith	(Newport)	
3	1st	G.J.Bendon	(Wasps)	.	1st	D.R.Main	(London Welsh)	
4	14th	J.D.Currie	(Harlequins)	.	19th	R.H.Williams	(Llanelli)	
5	14th	R.W.D.Marques	(Harlequins)	.	1st	I.Ford	(Newport)	
6	3rd	A.J.Herbert	(Wasps)	.	23rd	R.C.C.Thomas (Capt)	(Swansea)	
7	13th & last	R.Higgins	(Liverpool)	.	1st	J.Leleu	(London Welsh)	
8	1st	B.J.Wightman	(Moseley)	.	8th	J.Faull	(Swansea)	

Referee: R.C.Williams   (Ireland)

SCORERS:

0 - 3	D.I.E.Bebb	Try
0 - 5	T.J.Davies	Conversion
Half-time		
0 - 5		

POINTS:

D.I.E.Bebb	3 points
T.J.Davies	2 points

MATCH COMMENTARY:

England fielded six new caps for this game and Wales seven. In spite of a considerable degree of inexperience, the Welsh side played an extremely aggressive game in very wet and muddy conditions, and their victory was well earned. It was not an auspicious start for Jeff Butterfield's year of captaincy, but the team, as a whole, showed promise and much was expected from the line-out combination of John Currie and David Marques now together at Harlequins. Clem Thomas masterminded this Welsh victory by marshalling his forwards to keep it extremely tight and by having a totally dependable full-back in Terry Price whose performance was outstanding. So effective was the Welsh control, and so evident was the outcome, that the crowd were inspired almost to a man, to a rendering of "Land of my Fathers" with fifteen minutes of the match still to go. It was very emotive, and once that started, England had no chance at all.

Strangley enough, Dewi Bebb's try, on his debut, was the first scored by Wales against England at Cardiff for ten years. It was exactly four years since England had last failed to score a point in an International match - also against Wales on this awesome ground.

This was only England's second defeat in twelve Five Nations matches since 1956.

71st match   **ENGLAND   3 pts**   **v**   **IRELAND   0 pts**

	Caps					Caps		
15	4th	J.G.G.Hetherington	(Northampton)	.		37th	N.J.Henderson	(NIFC)
14	13th	P.B.Jackson	(Coventry)	.		22nd	A.C.Pedlow	(CIYMS)
13	6th	M.S.Phillips	(Oxford University)	.		1st	J.F.Dooley	(Galwegians)
12	26th	J.Butterfield (Capt)	(Northampton)	.		18th	A.J.F.O'Reilly	(Old Belvedere)
11	15th	P.H.Thompson	(Waterloo)	.		3rd	N.H.Brophy	(UC Dublin)
10	2nd	A.B.W.Risman	(Manchester Univ)	.		3rd	M.A.F.English	(Lansdowne)
9	11th	R.E.G.Jeeps	(Northampton)	.		12th	A.A.Mulligan	(London Irish)
1	2nd	L.H.Webb	(Bedford)	.		16th	B.G.M.Wood	(Garryowen)
2	2nd & last	J.A.S.Wackett	(Rosslyn Park)	.		6th	A.R.Dawson	(Wanderers)
3	2nd	G.J.Bendon	(Wasps)	.		2nd	S.Millar	(Ballymena)
4	15th	J.D.Currie	(Harlequins)	.		6th	W.A.Mulcahy	(UC Dublin)
5	15th	R.W.D.Marques	(Harlequins)	.		1st	M.G.Culliton	(Wanderers)
6	4th	A.J.Herbert	(Wasps)	.		6th	N.A.A.Murphy	(Cork Constitution)
7	1st	J.W.Clements	(Old Cranleighans)	.		21st	J.R.Kavanagh	(Wanderers)
8	14th	A.Ashcroft	(Waterloo)	.		5th	P.J.A.O'Sullivan	(Galwegians)

Referee: D.G.Walters   (Wales)

SCORERS: **A.B.W.Risman**   Penalty Goal   3 - 0
                                                            Half-time
                                                            3 - 0

POINTS: **A.B.W.Risman**   3 points   (3)

MATCH COMMENTARY:

The English pack continued to show marked signs of improvement and cohesion with Ashcroft back after injury and with Marques and Currie solid in the tight and impressive in the line-out. But the Irish eight played very well and matched England in nearly all respects. However, Ireland appeared to have no tactic other than to move the ball out to O'Reilly and hope that he could smash his way through the middle. The English defence was ready for him and he could not break through because Jeff Butterfield and Malcolm Phillips hardly missed a tackle. On the other hand, England were no more successful in breaching the Irish defence although not for the want of trying. Malcolm Phillips was probably to get as near as anyone to scoring a try when a perfect break and blistering pace was only thwarted by an excellent covering tackle just short of the line. In the end, the only penalty goal was decisive.

Improvement in the pack or not, the match was an immense disappointment because, quite simply, England again failed to score a try. The entire back division has, in previous seasons, shown itself capable of scoring tries, so why, with a steadily improving pack, does it not continue to do so ?

34th match

ENGLAND　3 pts　　v　　FRANCE　3 pts

	Caps				Caps		
15	5th	J.G.G.Hetherington	(Northampton)		4th	P.Lacaze	(Lourdes)
14	14th	P.B.Jackson	(Coventry)		6th	C.Darrouy	(Mont-de-Marsan)
13	7th	M.S.Phillips	(Oxford University)		21st	A.Boniface	(Mont-de-Marsan)
12	27th	J.Butterfield (Capt)	(Northampton)		5th	A.Marquesuzaa	(Racing Club)
11	16th	P.H.Thompson	(Waterloo)		18th	J.Dupuy	(Tarbes)
10	3rd	A.B.W.Risman	(Manchester Univ)		9th	A.Labazuy	(Lourdes)
9	2nd	S.R.Smith	(Cambridge Univ)		12th	P.Danos	(Beziers)
1	3rd	L.H.Webb	(Bedford)		10th	A.Quaglio	(Mazamet)
2	1st	H.O.Godwin	(Coventry)		21st	R.Vigier	(Montferrand)
3	3rd	G.J.Bendon	(Wasps)		8th	A.Roques	(Cahors)
4	16th	J.D.Currie	(Harlequins)		31st	M.Celaya	(Biarritz)
5	16th	R.W.D.Marques	(Harlequins)		6th	B.Mommejat	(Cahors)
6	5th	A.J.Herbert	(Wasps)		9th	M.Crauste	(Racing Club)
7	2nd	J.W.Clements	(Old Cranleighans)		10th	F.Moncla	(Racing Club)
8	15th	A.Ashcroft	(Waterloo)		24th	J.Barthe (Capt)	(Lourdes)

Referee:　R.C.Williams　　(Ireland)

SCORERS:

			0 - 3	A.Labazuy	Penalty Goal
J.G.G.Hetherington	Penalty Goal		3 - 3		
		Half-time			
			3 - 3		

POINTS:　J.G.G.Hetherington　3 points　　(9)　　　A.Labazuy　3 points

MATCH COMMENTARY:

The selectors were certainly not going to be rushed into rash decisions in making multiple changes to the team in an attempt to put some tries on the score sheet. Only one change was made, Herbert Godwin replacing John Wackett at hooker.

It was a warm and sunny spring day at Twickenham, and the capacity crowd had high expectations that England's try famine was about to end, and that they would be entertained by some enterprising rugby. Alas, it was not to be. The French had developed a big and very mobile set of forwards and they gave England a very severe test in this game. The English eight performed very creditably against the eventual Championship winners, but had to be satisfied with the draw and could not, yet again, score a try for the fourth match in succession. Again, penalty goals prevailed and the second half, this time, was scoreless.

It was also the first time in fifteen matches against France at Twickenham that England had failed to score a try.

74th match   **ENGLAND   3 pts   v   SCOTLAND   3 pts**

66th Calcutta Cup

	Caps					Caps		
15	6th & last	J.G.G.Hetherington	(Northampton)	.	9th	K.J.F.Scotland	(Cambridge Univ.)
14	15th	P.B.Jackson	(Coventry)	.	19th	A.R.Smith	(Ebbw Vale)
13	8th	M.S.Phillips	(Oxford University)	.	1st	J.A.P.Shackleton	(London Scottish)
12	28th & last	J.Butterfield (Capt)	(Northampton)	.	10th	G.D.Stevenson	(Hawick)
11	17th & last	P.H.Thompson	(Waterloo)	.	16th & last	T.G.Weatherstone	(Stewart's Coll FP)
10	4th	A.B.W.Risman	(Manchester Univ)	.	10th	G.H.Waddell (Capt)	(Cambridge Univ.)
9	3rd	S.R.Smith	(Cambridge Univ)	.	4th	S.Coughtrie	(Edinburgh Acad)
1	4th & last	L.H.Webb	(Bedford)	.	1st	D.M.D.Rollo	(Howe of Fife)
2	2nd	H.O.Godwin	(Coventry)	.	8th	N.S.Bruce	(Army/Blackheath)
3	4th & last	G.J.Bendon	(Wasps)	.	26th	H.F.McLeod	(Hawick)
4	17th	J.D.Currie	(Harlequins)	.	1st	F.H.ten Bos	(Oxford University)
5	17th	R.W.D.Marques	(Harlequins)	.	22nd	J.W.Y.Kemp	(Glasgow HSFP)
6	6th & last	A.J.Herbert	(Wasps)	.	9th	G.K.Smith	(Kelso)
7	3rd & last	J.W.Clements	(Old Cranleighans)	.	21st	A.Robson	(Hawick)
8	16th & last	A.Ashcroft	(Waterloo)	.	1st	J.A.Davidson	(London Scottish)

Referee: D.G.Walters   (Wales)

SCORERS: A.B.W.Risman   Penalty Goal   3 - 0

Half-time

3 - 3   K.J.F.Scotland   Penalty Goal

POINTS: A.B.W.Risman   3 points   (6)   K.J.F.Scotland   3 points

MATCH COMMENTARY:

An unchanged side met the Scots at Twickenham to try to win the Calcutta Cup, the only trophy now available to either side this season. Even that matter had to pass unresolved as the two teams drew yet another tryless game for the second year in succession. There were passages of exciting and attacking play - Ken Scotland was called upon to make two outstanding tackles, saving certain tries by Bev Risman and Malcolm Phillips - and Scotland, with limited possession did all they could to move the ball, but, all in all, it was a very dull game indeed. Jim Swanton reported in the Daily Telegraph that there were 78 lineout, 71 set scrums and 25 penalties awarded during the match. Not, by any stretch of the imagination, inspiring rugby.

In the four Championship games England had scored only nine points from three penalty goals and no try had been scored for five consecutive matches. It was ironic that Jeff Butterfield, one of England's best centre three-quarters, should Captain the side and end his twenty-eight successive cap career in a season when no tries were scored, for the first and only time. This dearth of tries was not, however, a peculiarly English phenomenon - England had conceded only one try in the whole season - for only twelve tries were scored in the ten Championship matches.

SUMMARY OF THE SEASON - 1958 - 59:

This had been a desperately disappointing season for England, and particularly for the Captain, Jeff Butterfield, in his last International season He, who had done so much for English rugby, not least as England's most capped three-quarter, who had played twenty-eight successive International matches and had scored five tries for England - and three tries for the British Lions - was destined to lead England in what was in many respects their poorest post-war season when not one try was scored, and only one victory was accomplished. Such a performance was particularly difficult for the England following to stomach after the successes of the last two years when England had won the Tittle twice and the Grand Slam in 1957. As T.S.Eliot said "This is the way the world ends, not with a bang but a whimper."
But the season, and the Championship as a whole had been of a very poor standard. The Title was taken outright by France with only five points and a record of having won two, drawn one and lost one match. Only twelve tries, and ninety three points, were scored in all of the ten Championship matches.

It was not surprising that only seven England players were invited to join Ronnie Dawson's British Lions tour to Australia and New Zealand during the summer of 1959. They were Jeff Butterfield, Peter Jackson, Bev Risman, Dickie Jeeps, Alan Ashcroft, David Marques and John Young although Phil Horrocks-Taylor and Bill Patterson, at that time uncapped, were to join the party later.

The selectors had used only nineteen players throughout the Five Nations season, and the back division remained unchanged except for the match against Ireland when Dickie Jeeps played his only International match of the season. Six new caps were introduced for the formidable trip to Cardiff, where Clem Thomas and the fervent Welsh crowd conspired to deny England. In Dublin, they had their defence to thank, especially Malcolm Phillips and Jeff Butterfield, but the last two matches, both at Twickenham, were dismal affairs with no tries and only four penalty goals scored.

Ten players came to the end of their International careers for England at the end of the season although Jeff Butterfield and Alan Ashcroft did not retire until after the Lions Tour.
When he retired, Jeff Butterfield continued his career as PE Master at Worksop College, and, likewise, Alan Ashcroft, with sixteen caps, returned to Liverpool College to teach Art and coach rugby. Peter Thompson, having scored five tries in his seventeen Internationals, continued to play many more County matches for his native Yorkshire. Reg Higgins, thirteen caps, the Liverpool flanker, whose father and uncle were both Rugby League Internationals, had his career interrupted when he suffered a severe knee injury in the first Test of the 1955 Lions tour to South Africa and was unable to play for almost two years and missed the whole of the 1956 International season.
John Herbert, with six caps, and with three rugby Blues from Cambridge, eventually went to Australia where he taught at Geelong Grammar School. James Hetherington, the former Cambridge University full-back, earned six caps. Lawrence Webb, the Bedford prop, who gained four caps, and who was later in business with John Wackett, died with many others when a Turkish airliner returning from the England match in Paris in 1974, crashed just after take-off. Gordon Bendon, the Wasps tight head prop, who won four caps, was said by many of his contemporaries to be one of the best and strongest scrummagers that England had ever produced, yet his talents were inadequately recognised at International level - at least by the selectors, presumably opposing loose heads thought differently !
Jeffrey Clements, three caps, having spent some considerable time in the Royal Navy, returned to his alma mater, Cranleigh, to pursue a teaching career.

So ended a miserable season for England, and one which did not contain much in terms of accomplishment for the other nations in the Championship either. France, perhaps, could see the beginnings of the development of the unique style of play which was to become thier hallmark in years to come, but for the rest, it was a season not to be remembered.

FIVE NATIONS CHAMPIONSHIP TABLE:

Won: **Retained Calcutta Cup.**

		Played	Won	Lost	Drawn	Points: For	Points: Against	Tries: For	Tries: Against	Title Points
1	France	4	2	1	1	28	15	4	1	5
2 =	Ireland	4	2	2	0	23	19	3	3	4
2 =	Wales	4	2	2	0	21	23	4	4	4
2 =	**ENGLAND**	4	1	1	2	9	11	0	1	4
5	Scotland	4	1	2	1	12	25	1	3	3

Home Games: drew with France 3 - 3, (no tries); drew with Scotland 3 - 3, (no tries).

Away Games: lost to Wales 0 - 5, (no tries to one); beat Ireland 3 - 0, (no tries).

65th match   **ENGLAND   14 pts**   v   **WALES   6 pts**

	Caps				Caps		
15	1st	D.Rutherford	(Percy Park)	.	17th	T.J.Davies	(Llanelli)
14	2nd	J.R.C.Young	(Harlequins)	.	9th	J.Collins	(Aberavon)
13	9th	M.S.Phillips	(Oxford University)	.	1st	G.W.Lewis	(Richmond)
12	1st	M.P.Weston	(Richmond)	.	5th	M.J.Price	(Pontypool)
11	1st	J.Roberts	(Old Millhillians)	.	5th	D.I.E.Bebb	(Swansea)
10	1st	R.A.W.Sharp	(Oxford University)	.	4th	C.Ashton	(Aberavon)
9	12th	R.E.G.Jeeps (Capt)	(Northampton)	.	1st & only	C.Evans	(Pontypool)
1	14th	C.R.Jacobs	(Northampton)	.	16th	T.R.Prosser	(Pontypool)
2	1st	S.A.M.Hodgson	(Durham City)	.	24th	B.V.Meredith	(Newport)
3	1st	T.P.Wright	(Blackheath)	.	1st	L.J.Cunningham	(Aberavon)
4	18th	R.W.D.Marques	(Harlequins)	.	23rd & last	R.H.Williams (Capt)	(Llanelli)
5	18th	J.D.Currie	(Harlequins)	.	1st	G.W.Payne	(Pontypridd)
6	13th	P.G.D.Robbins	(Moseley)	.	1st	B.Cresswell	(Newport)
7	5th	R.E.Syrett	(Wasps)	.	7th	H.J.Morgan	(Abertillery)
8	1st	W.D.G.Morgan	(Medicals)	.	11th	J.Faull	(Swansea)

Referee: J.A.S.Taylor   (Scotland)

SCORERS:

D.Rutherford	Penalty Goal		3 - 0	
J.Roberts	Try	(1st)	6 - 0	
D.Rutherford	Conversion		8 - 0	
D.Rutherford	Penalty Goal		11 - 0	
J.Roberts	Try	(2nd)	14 - 0	
			Half-time	
			14 - 3	T.J.Davies Penalty Goal
			14 - 6	T.J.Davies Penalty Goal

POINTS:

D.Rutherford	8 points	(8)	T.J.Davies	6 points
J.Roberts	6 points	(6)		

MATCH COMMENTARY:

The seven new caps in the English side helped to make a sensational start to the season, when at half-time, England were fourteen points ahead of Wales having scored two tries. The England forwards were dominant in the set-piece and in the loose, but the back row was where England had the greatest advantage with the Welsh back three looking disappointingly ineffective. Richard Sharp, at fly-half, who only came into the side as a last minute replacement for Bev Risman, had a marvellous debut and was undoubtedly the man of the match, running smoothly and setting up his backs on the basis of solid possession, and with all the space he could wish for, courtesy of the Welsh back row. Wales fought back with some determination in the second half, but were ragged and unco-ordinated and could only achieve two Terry Davies penalty goals, and towards the end England reasserted themselves, but failed to add to their half-time score.

Jim Roberts scored both the England tries on his International debut. This was England's highest score against Wales since 1924, and it was a pity that Rhys Williams, the Welsh Captain, should have to end his International career on what - for Wales - was such a disastrous day !

This was England's seventh successive home match without having conceded a try.

72nd match   **ENGLAND   8 pts**   v   **IRELAND   5 pts**

	Caps					Caps		
15	2nd	D.Rutherford	(Percy Park)	.		1st	T.J.Kiernan	(UC Cork)
14	3rd	J.R.C.Young	(Harlequins)	.		1st	W.W.Bornemann	(Wanderers)
13	10th	M.S.Phillips	(Oxford University)	.		23rd	A.C.Pedlow	(CIYMS)
12	2nd	M.P.Weston	(Richmond)	.		8th	D.Hewitt	(Queens U Belfast)
11	2nd	J.Roberts	(Old Millhillians)	.		22nd	A.J.F.O'Reilly	(Leicester)
10	2nd	R.A.W.Sharp	(Oxford University)	.		6th	M.A.F.English	(Bohemians)
9	13th	R.E.G.Jeeps (Capt)	(Northampton)	.		16th	A.A.Mulligan (Capt)	(London Irish)
1	15th	C.R.Jacobs	(Northampton)	.		20th	B.G.M.Wood	(Lansdowne)
2	2nd	S.A.M.Hodgson	(Durham City)	.		1st	B.McCallan	(Ballymena)
3	2nd	T.P.Wright	(Blackheath)	.		6th	S.Millar	(Ballymena)
4	19th	R.W.D.Marques	(Harlequins)	.		10th	W.A.Mulcahy	(UC Dublin)
5	19th	J.D.Currie	(Harlequins)	.		5th	M.G.Culliton	(Wanderers)
6	14th	P.G.D.Robbins	(Moseley)	.		10th	N.A.A.Murphy	(Cork Constitution)
7	6th	R.E.Syrett	(Wasps)	.		25th	J.R.Kavanagh	(Wanderers)
8	2nd	W.D.G.Morgan	(Medicals)	.		3rd	T.McGrath	(Garryowen)

Referee: D.G.Walters   (Wales)

SCORERS:

			0 - 3	M.G.Culliton	Try
			0 - 5	T.J.Kiernan	Conversion
			Half-time		
R.A.W.Sharp	D'p Goal	(1st)	3 - 5		
R.W.D.Marques	Try	(1st & only)	6 - 5		
D.Rutherford	Conversion		8 - 5		

POINTS:

R.W.D.Marques	3 points	(3)	M.G.Culliton	3 points	
R.A.W.Sharp	3 points	(3)	T.J.Kiernan	2 points	
D.Rutherford	2 points	(10)			

MA MATCH COMMENTARY:

There was much debate after this game as to whether England won the game on merit, or whether Ireland lost it by default. Ireland dominated eighty per cent of the match but England's resilience was rewarded when Ireland flagged in the closing stages. After the Irish try, the first for Ireland at Twickenham for 12 years, and only the second conceded by England in twelve matches, Ireland appeared too intent on preserving their advantage rather than adding to it, and Mick English tended to kick too often. Richard Sharp's drop goal, the first for England for eight years, gave the side some encouragement, but David Marques, who had been immense throughout the match, put the seal on an England victory with a try only two minutes from the final whistle. The try came from a second drop goal attempt by Richard Sharp, which was blocked and then recovered by Sharp, who passed to Peter Robbins who, in turn, found Malcolm Phillips outside him. Phillips wrong-footed the whole Irish defence and gave David Marques, in support, the scoring pass. So England won her fifth successive victory over Ireland, but only just, and only because they lasted a little bit longer than the Irish. The match was memorable in that not only were no penalty goals scored, none were even attempted.

35th match   **ENGLAND   3 pts**   v   **FRANCE   3 pts**

	Caps				Caps		
15	3rd	D.Rutherford	(Percy Park)	.	30th	M.Vannier	(Racing Club)
14	4th	J.R.C.Young	(Harlequins)	.	15th & last	L.Roge	(Beziers)
13	11th	M.S.Phillips	(Oxford University)	.	20th	J.Bouquet	(Vienne)
12	3rd	M.P.Weston	(Richmond)	.	9th	A.Marquesuzaa	(Lourdes)
11	3rd	J.Roberts	(Old Millhillians)	.	3rd	S.Mericq	(Agen)
10	3rd	R.A.W.Sharp	(Oxford University)	.	22nd	R.Martine	(Lourdes)
9	14th	R.E.G.Jeeps (Capt)	(Northampton)	.	17th & last	P.Danos	(Beziers)
1	16th	C.R.Jacobs	(Northampton)	.	26th	A.Domenech	(Brive)
2	3rd	S.A.M.Hodgson	(Durham City)	.	2nd	J.de Gregorio	(Grenoble)
3	3rd	T.P.Wright	(Blackheath)	.	12th	A.Roques	(Cahors)
4	20th	R.W.D.Marques	(Harlequins)	.	33rd	M.Celaya	(SBUC)
5	20th	J.D.Currie	(Harlequins)	.	11th	B.Mommejat	(Cahors)
6	15th	P.G.D.Robbins	(Moseley)	.	15th	F.Moncla (Capt)	(Pau)
7	7th	R.E.Syrett	(Wasps)	.	5th & last	G-S.Meyer	(Perigueux)
8	3rd	W.D.G.Morgan	(Medicals)	.	14th	M.Crauste	(Lourdes)

Referee: J.A.S.Taylor   (Scotland)

SCORERS:

				0 - 3	M.Vannier	Penalty Goal
M.P.Weston	Try	(1st & only)		3 - 3		
				Half-time		
				3 - 3		

POINTS: M.P.Weston   3 points   (3)   M.Vannier   3 points

MATCH COMMENTARY:

The match was fast and exciting, but never skillful, there was no quarter asked, or given, on either side, and there was an abundance of unforced errors and missed chances. England's try was well taken and came from well set-up and constructive open play and a fine, apparently casual break by Richard Sharp, but it was the only time that the English backs were allowed to threaten the French line. Don Rutherford missed the easiest of conversion kicks which could have won the match. Michel Vannier missed two further penalty goal attempts and Jim Roberts came desperately close to a try in the closing minutes when the bounce which had already beaten Vannier, beat him. It might have been different had not John Young been hobbling on the right wing for most of the second half with a severely bruised thigh. As it was, it was a fitting result to a keenly fought match between two teams who were to share the Championship, neither having lost a game, and both of whom, apart from this match, played some sparkling rugby.

75th match

ENGLAND   21 pts   v   SCOTLAND   12 pts

67th Calcutta Cup

	Caps				Caps		
15	4th	D.Rutherford	(Percy Park)	13th	K.J.F.Scotland	(Cambridge Univ)
14	5th	J.R.C.Young	(Harlequins)	23rd	A.R.Smith	(Ebbw Vale)
13	12th	M.S.Phillips	(Oxford University)	13th	G.D.Stevenson	(Hawick)
12	4th	M.P.Weston	(Richmond)	5th	I.H.P.Laughland	(London Scottish)
11	4th	J.Roberts	(Old Millhillians)	2nd	R.H.Thomson	(London Scottish)
10	4th	R.A.W.Sharp	(Oxford University)	12th	G.H.Waddell (Capt)	(Cambridge Univ)
9	15th	R.E.G.Jeeps (Capt)	(Northampton)	2nd	R.B.Shillinglaw	(Army/Gala)
1	17th	C.R.Jacobs	(Northampton)	5th	D.M.D.Rollo	(Howe of Fife)
2	4th	S.A.M.Hodgson	(Durham City)	12th	N.S.Bruce	(London Scottish)
3	4th	T.P.Wright	(Blackheath)	30th	H.F.McLeod	(Hawick)
4	21st	R.W.D.Marques	(Harlequins)	2nd	T.O.Grant	(Hawick)
5	21st	J.D.Currie	(Harlequins)	26th	J.W.Y.Kemp	(Glasgow HSFP)
6	16th	P.G.D.Robbins	(Moseley)	13th	G.K.Smith	(Kelso)
7	8th	R.E.Syrett	(Wasps)	2nd	D.B.Edwards	(Heriot's FP)
8	4th	W.D.G.Morgan	(Medicals)	3rd & last	J.A.Davidson	(London Scottish)

Referee: R.C.Williams   (Ireland)

SCORERS:						
R.A.W.Sharp	D'p Goal	(2nd)	3 - 0			
R.E.Syrett	Try	(1st & only)	6 - 0			
D.Rutherford	Conversion		8 - 0			
J.Roberts	Try	(3rd)	11 - 0			
D.Rutherford	Conversion		13 - 0			
D.Rutherford	Penalty Goal		16 - 0			
			16 - 3	K.J.F.Scotland	Penalty Goal	
			16 - 6	K.J.F.Scotland	Penalty Goal	
			Half-time			
			16 - 9	K.J.F.Scotland	Penalty Goal	
J.R.C.Young	Try	(1st)	19 - 9			
D.Rutherford	Conversion		21 - 9			
			21 - 12	A.R.Smith	Try	

POINTS:					
D.Rutherford	9 points	(19)	K.J.F.Scotland	9 points	
R.A.W.Sharp	3 points	(6)	A.R.Smith	3 points	
J.Roberts, J.R.C.Young	3 points	(9),(3)			
and R.E.Syrett	each	(3)			

MATCH COMMENTARY:

England fielded an unchanged side for the fourth time this season, and in an explosive start they scored sixteen points in the first twenty minutes. It was another excellent display of running rugby based on solid possession from a pack who were masters of their craft. England collected the Calcutta Cup and the Triple Crown, but shared the Championship title with France after the draw in Paris. What a contrast to last season, forty-six points compared to nine, and seven tries compared to none. It is now ten years since England lost to Scotland.

SUMMARY OF THE SEASON - 1959 - 60:

This season the England side remained unchanged throughout all four matches in the Five Nations Championship, a degree of consistency, and absence of injury, which had not occured before. Furthermore this was also the first season at the end of, or during which, no English player had retired from the International scene, either voluntarily or involuntarily. Such consistency surely deserved the highest honour, but the ultimate prize of the Grand Slam evaded both England and France as they drew an uneventful match in Paris. Nevertheless, England collected their third Triple Crown in fourteen seasons since the end of the Second World War - no other side had achieved as much at the time.

The season was unique in another respect as well, in that all seven of the new caps who played in the opening match against Wales, remained in the side throughout the season. Apart from 1946-47, such selectorial faith has not been in evidence in the post-war years. Several times have more new caps been exposed to the rigours of International rugby, for the first match of the season, but never have so many original choices fully justified their selection and kept their place in the side all season; in 1948-49 there were nine new caps; in 1949-50, eight; and in 1950-51 and 1955-56 there were ten in each year. These stalwarts would have been perceived to have been good enough at the beginning of the season but, as is so often the case, the anticipation was better than the event, and most of them failed to last the course. In 1948-49 only three gained four caps in the season, and four of the original selections were dropped after the first match. The following season, four survived, and in 1950-51 a further four lasted the pace. 1955-56 saw ten new caps selected and seven of those played throughout the season, but this season, all the original new caps at the beginning of the season held their place throughout the season. It is true, that an injury to any one of those players at any time during the course of the season could have spoiled the record, but that did not happen and all seven prevailed.

The player of the season was, undoubtedly, one Richard Adrian William Sharp who only came into the side in the first match against Wales as a last minute replacement for the injured Bev Risman, who himself had played with no little distinction in four of the Tests in the previous summer's Lions tour of Australia and New Zealand. Richard Sharp grasped his opportunity magnificently. The twenty-one year old Oxford under-graduate showed himself to be one of the most elegant of England fly-halves, and, while not wishing to detract from his performance in any way, he did enjoy the considerable advantage of playing outside that most competent of scrum-halves, Dickie Jeeps.

The whole side, although arguably a scratch side at the outset, played commendably well together. Seven tries were scored and two drop goals, and, although such scoring is by no means exceptional, it does indicate the style of play adopted by England in giving Richard Sharp the freedom to exploit his talents behind a pack, and a scrum-half, all of whom gave him plenty of opportunity. The three penalty goals, remarkable by modern standards, passed almost unnoticed.

Of the nine English Lions (including two replacements) who went on the 1959 Lions tour, only three, Dickie Jeeps, John Young and David Marques, continued playing International rugby in this, the following, season. Bev Risman, of course, had every intention of doing so, but, after the first match for which he was selected but could not play, he could not get into the side ! Phil Horrocks-Taylor and Bill Patterson did not play in this season, but were to gain caps in subsequent seasons.

So to the end of a remarkable, and very successful season.. It was remarkable too that in a period of four years 1957 to 1960, during which time England won the Grand Slam once, won the Triple Crown twice, won, or shared, the Five Nations Championship three times, that they should have such a lean year in 1959. Significantly, in the last four seasons, England have lost only one match, but they have drawn five, and have conceded only four tries in four years, one to each of the other four nations. This must reflect highly on their defensive qualities.

Don Rutherford's nineteen points in the season sets a new record for England, beating Nim Hall's eighteen points in 1953.

FIVE NATIONS CHAMPIONSHIP TABLE:

Won: **Triple Crown, Share of Championship Title with France, Calcutta Cup.**

		Played	Won	Lost	Drawn	Points: For	Points: Against	Tries: For	Tries: Against	Title Points
1 =	France	4	3	0	1	55	28	11	6	7
1 =	**ENGLAND**	4	3	0	1	46	26	7	2	7
3	Wales	4	2	2	0	32	39	4	7	4
4	Scotland	4	1	3	0	29	47	4	8	2
5	Ireland	4	0	4	0	25	47	5	8	0

Home Games: beat Wales 14 - 6, (two tries to nil); beat Ireland 8 - 5, (one try each).

Away Games: drew with France 3 - 3, (one try to nil); beat Scotland 21 - 12, (three tries to nil).

5th match   **ENGLAND   0 pts   v   SOUTH AFRICA   5 pts**

	Caps				Caps		
15	5th	D.Rutherford	(Percy Park)	.	5th	L.G.Wilson	(Western Province)
14	6th	J.R.C.Young	(Harlequins)	.	4th	J.P.Englebrecht	(Western Province)
13	1st	W.M.Patterson	(Sale)	.	11th	A.I.Kirkpatrick	(Orange Free State)
12	5th	M.P.Weston	(Richmond)	.	8th	J.L.Gainsford	(Western Province)
11	5th	J.Roberts	(Old Millhillians)	.	6th	H.J.van Zyl	(Transvaal)
10	5th	A.B.W.Risman	(Loughborough Coll)	.	2nd	D.A.Stewart	(Western Province)
9	16th	R.E.G.Jeeps (Capt)	(Northampton)	.	2nd	P.de W.Uys	(Northern Transvaal)
1	18th	C.R.Jacobs	(Northampton)	.	9th	P.S.du Toit	(Boland)
2	5th	S.A.M.Hodgson	(Durham City)	.	5th	G.F.Malan	(Western Province)
3	5th	T.P.Wright	(Blackheath)	.	5th	S.P.Kuhn	(Transvaal)
4	22nd	R.W.D.Marques	(Harlequins)	.	7th	A.S.Malan (Capt)	(Transvaal)
5	22nd	J.D.Currie	(Harlequins)	.	19th	J.T.Claassen	(Western Transvaal)
6	17th	P.G.D.Robbins	(Moseley)	.	9th	G.H.van Zyl	(Western Province)
7	1st	L.I.Rimmer	(Bath)	.	1st	F.C.H.du Preez	(Northern Transvaal)
8	5th	W.G.D.Morgan	(Medicals)	.	5th	D.J.Hopwood	(Western Province)

Referee: G.J.Treharne   (Wales)

SCORERS:

0 - 3	D.J.Hopwood	Try
0 - 5	F.C.H.du Preez	Conversion
Half-time		
0 - 5		

POINTS:

D.J.Hopwood	3 points
F.C.du Preez	2 points

MATCH COMMENTARY:

South Africa played to win this match and refused to exploit the many opportunities they had to open up play. The English backs were disappointing in attack, in that their continued attempts to break out always came to grief either in the face of strong determined tackling or because of unforced errors - perhaps they were almost too anxious to succeed - but they were very competent in defence. The stronger South African pack gradually wore the English eight down, and as the game wore on, South Africa gained more and more control.

Hopwood's decisive try came just before half-time, when the English pack, attempting a wheel, lost the ball. Claassen gathered it and sent Hopwood racing in from fifteen yards, beating two would-be tacklers on the way. Frik du Preez added the two points, but he missed several attempts to convert penalty goal opportunities in each half which would have given the score a more realistic appearance. Significantly, England were awarded no penalties throughout the entire match within scoring range. England were well beaten and the margin certainly illustrates the South African approach to the game which appeared to be: Win at all costs; risk nothing; and preserve the unbeaten record. Such seriousness does not make for attractive, enterprising and open rugby - quite the reverse.

This match was the last in which the formidable second-row partnership of John Currie and David Marques appeared. They had played with distinction for England for 22 successive matches since first being capped together against Wales, at Twickenham, in January 1956.

66th match   **ENGLAND   3 pts   v   WALES   6 pts**

	Caps					Caps		
15	1st & only	M.N.Gavins	(Leicester)			19th	T.J.Davies (Capt)	(Llanelli)
14	7th	J.R.C.Young	(Harlequins)			1st	P.M.Rees	(Newport)
13	13th	M.S.Phillips	(Fylde)			7th & last	C.A.H.Davies	(Cardiff)
12	6th	M.P.Weston	(Richmond)			2nd	H.M.Roberts	(Cardiff)
11	6th	J.Roberts	(Old Millhillians)			10th	D.I.E.Bebb	(Swansea)
10	6th	A.B.W.Risman	(Loughborough Coll)			2nd	K.H.L.Richards	(Bridgend)
9	17th	R.E.G.Jeeps (Capt)	(Northampton)			2nd	A.O'Connor	(Aberavon)
1	19th	C.R.Jacobs	(Northampton)			1st	P.E.J.Morgan	(Aberavon)
2	6th	S.A.M.Hodgson	(Durham City)			28th	B.V.Meredith	(Newport)
3	6th	T.P.Wright	(Blackheath)			2nd	K.D.Jones	(Cardiff)
4	23rd & last	R.W.D.Marques	(Harlequins)			7th	D.J.E.Harris	(Cardiff)
5	1st	R.J.French	(St Helen's)			7th	W.R.Evans	(Bridgend)
6	18th	P.G.D.Robbins	(Moseley)			6th	G.D.Davidge	(Newport)
7	2nd	L.I.Rimmer	(Bath)			8th	H.J.Morgan	(Abertillery)
8	6th	W.G.D.Morgan	(Medicals)			2nd	D.Nash	(Ebbw Vale)

Referee: K.D.Kelleher   (Ireland)

SCORERS:							
				0 - 3	D.I.E.Bebb	Try
				0 - 6	D.I.E.Bebb	Try
				Half-time		
	J.R.C.Young	Try	(2nd)	3 - 6		

POINTS:	J.R.C.Young	3 points	(6)		D.I.E.Bebb	6 points

MATCH COMMENTARY:

Following the defeat by South Africa, two weeks ago, the Selectors made two changes in restoring Malcolm Phillips to centre in place of Bill Patterson and, inexplicably, dropping Don Rutherford. John Currie was compelled to withdraw due to illness shortly before the game. It was a most entertaining match in which both teams showed willingness to play open rugby in spite of the very heavy ground. In the first half, Wales dominated in almost every phase of the game, especially up front where the Welsh pack gave England a severe lesson in the art, and the science, of forward play. As a result, Dewi Bebb scored two tries after clever running by Keith Richards, switches of direction and slick handling of the very slippery ball. England's game plan of "Give the ball to Young", as well as being somewhat simplistic and naive, was severely overplayed, although he did score a try in the second half from a charged down kick, and came close again towards the end. But by then Wales were a man short because Cyril Davies sustained a leg injury and had to leave the field early in the second half. This reduced the Welsh pack to seven men and seriously limited their attacking options. England have had a good run in recent years with consistent selection and an established team, and this was only their second defeat in the last seventeen Five Nations matches, but now, it seems, some changes are becoming necessary.

| 73rd match | | **ENGLAND** | **8 pts** | **v** | **IRELAND** | **11 pts** | |

<u>Caps</u>   <u>Caps</u>

15	1st	**J.G.Willcox**	(Oxford University)	.	6th	**T.J.Kiernan**	(UC Cork)
14	8th	**J.R.C.Young**	(Harlequins)	.	1st	**R.J.McCarten**	(London Irish)
13	7th	**A.B.W.Risman**	(Loughborough Coll)	.	12th	**D.Hewitt**	(Queens U Belfast)
12	7th	**M.P.Weston**	(Richmond)	.	3rd	**J.C.Walsh**	(UC Cork)
11	7th	**J.Roberts**	(Sale)	.	23rd	**A.J.F.O'Reilly**	(Dolphin)
10	5th	**R.A.W.Sharp**	(Oxford University)	.	2nd & last	**W.K.Armstrong**	(NIFC)
9	18th	**R.E.G.Jeeps (Capt)**	(Northampton)	.	1st	**J.W.Moffett**	(Ballymena)
1	20th	**C.R.Jacobs**	(Northampton)	.	25th	**B.G.M.Wood**	(Lansdowne)
2	2nd	**E.F.Robinson**	(Coventry)	.	12th	**A.R.Dawson (Capt)**	(Wanderers)
3	7th	**T.P.Wright**	(Blackheath)	.	11th	**S.Millar**	(Ballymena)
4	1st & only	**J.Price**	(Coventry)	.	14th	**W.A.Mulcahy**	(UC Dublin)
5	2nd	**R.J.French**	(St Helen's)	.	10th	**M.G.Culliton**	(Wanderers)
6	1st	**D.P.Rogers**	(Bedford)	.	15th	**N.A.A.Murphy**	(Cork Constitution)
7	3rd	**L.I.Rimmer**	(Bath)	.	30th	**J.R.Kavanagh**	(Wanderers)
8	7th	**W.D.G.Morgan**	(Medicals)	.	10th	**P.J.A.O'Sullivan**	(Galwegians)

Referee: G.J.Treharne   (Wales)

SCORERS:

				0 - 3	J.W.Moffett	Penalty Goal
				0 - 6	J.W.Moffett	Penalty Goal
				Half-time		
				0 - 9	J.R.Kavanagh	Try
				0 - 11	J.W.Moffett	Conversion
J.Roberts	Try	(4th)	3 - 11		
D.P.Rogers	Try	(1st)	6 - 11		
A.B.W.Risman	Conversion		8 - 11		

POINTS:

D.P.Rogers	3 points	(3)	J.W.Moffett	8 points
J.Roberts	3 points	(12)	J.R.Kavanagh	3 points
A.B.W.Risman	2 points	(8)		

MATCH COMMENTARY:

This was a fast and furious match full of excitement and mistakes which Ireland deserved to win if only because they established an eleven point lead before England began to settle down. England made six changes following the disappointing result against Wales, and, at first, the team did not knit well together. The recall of Richard Sharp, putting Bev Risman at centre, was not an immediate success, but into the second half the team seemed to find their feet. First a break by Jeeps, supported by Morgan, led to a try when Jim Roberts squeezed into the corner and several minutes later Budge Rogers charged down a clearance kick and scored a try on his international debut. England threw everything at Ireland in the closing stages and in the last minute John Young crossed the line but failed to ground the ball and Ireland held out. Ernie Robinson, the Coventry hooker, was recalled to the side for only his second cap, having won his first against Scotland seven years earlier. England's only consolation from this match was that they won the try count by two tries to one, but nevertheless lost the game !

36th match   **ENGLAND   5 pts**   **v**   **FRANCE   5 pts**

	Caps					Caps		
15	2nd	J.G.Willcox	(Oxford University)	.		38th	M.Vannier	(Chalon)
14	9th & last	J.R.C.Young	(Harlequins)	.		18th	H.Rancoule	(Toulon)
13	8th & last	A.B.W.Risman	(Loughborough Coll)	.		10th	G.Boniface	(Mont-de-Marsan)
12	8th	M.P.Weston	(Richmond)	.		26th	J.Bouquet	(Vienne)
11	8th	J.Roberts	(Sale)	.		29th	J.Dupuy	(Tarbes)
10	6th	R.A.W.Sharp	(Oxford University)	.		9th	P.Albaladejo	(Dax)
9	19th	R.E.G.Jeeps (Capt)	(Northampton)	.		11th	P.Lacroix	(Agen)
1	21st	C.R.Jacobs	(Northampton)	.		36th	A.Domenech	(Brive)
2	3rd	E.F.Robinson	(Coventry)	.		11th	J.de Gregorio	(Grenoble)
3	8th	T.P.Wright	(Blackheath)	.		21st	A.Roques	(Cahors)
4	1st	V.S.J.Harding	(Cambridge Univ.)	.		2nd	G.Bouguyon	(Grenoble)
5	3rd	R.J.French	(St Helen's)	.		6th	J-P.Saux	(Pau)
6	2nd	D.P.Rogers	(Bedford)	.		23rd	M.Crauste	(Lourdes)
7	4th	L.I.Rimmer	(Bath)	.		25th	F.Moncla (Capt)	(Pau)
8	8th	W.D.G.Morgan	(Medicals)	.		42nd	M.Celaya	(SBUC)

Referee: D.G.Walters   (Wales)

SCORERS:

			0 - 0		
			Half-time		
V.S.J.Harding	Try	(1st & only)	3 - 0		
J.G.Willcox	Conversion		5 - 0		
			5 - 3	M.Crauste	Try
			5 - 5	M.Vannier	Conversion

POINTS:

V.S.J.Harding	3 points	(3)		M.Crauste	3 points
J.G.Willcox	2 points	(2)		M.Vannier	2 points

MATCH COMMENTARY:

Torrential rain immediately before the kick-off flooded the pitch and the first half was a dour struggle and no points were scored. The French came into this game only one week after their titanic struggle with South Africa, and, after a furious first half, the strain began to show. It was much to England's credit that they withstood the early onslaught, and in the second half, were able to score the first points of the match. After some muddled passing among the England backs, Mike Weston picked the ball off his toes at full stretch, broke through the first line of defence and passed to Vic Harding, following up on the inside, for his debut try. Only five minutes later the French replied when Michel Vannier, who had been a terrier snapping at England's heels all day, broke, cross-kicked and Michel Crauste just won the race for the touchdown with Vannier. Thus a draw it was, and the third in succession against France, but, on balance, the French were a trifle fortunate. Nevertheless, it was England's tenth successive match at Twickenham without defeat.

76th match

68th Calcutta Cup

ENGLAND 6 pts   v   SCOTLAND 0 pts

	Caps					Caps		
15	3rd	J.G.Willcox	(Oxford University)	.	18th	K.J.F.Scotland	(Heriot's FP)
14	16th	P.B.Jackson	(Coventry)	.	29th	A.R.Smith	(Edinburgh Wand'rs)
13	2nd & last	W.M.Patterson	(Sale)	.	6th & last	E.McKeating	(Heriot's FP)
12	9th	M.P.Weston	(Richmond)	.	19th	G.D.Stevenson	(Hawick)
11	9th	J.Roberts	(Sale)	.	8th	R.H.Thomson	(London Scottish)
10	3rd	J.P.Horrocks-Taylor	(Leicester)	.	9th	I.H.P.Laughland	(London Scottish)
9	20th	R.E.G.Jeeps (Capt)	(Northampton)	.	3rd	A.J.Hastie	(Melrose)
1	22nd	C.R.Jacobs	(Northampton)	.	36th	H.F.McLeod	(Hawick)
2	4th & last	E.F.Robinson	(Coventry)	.	18th	N.S.Bruce	(London Scottish)
3	9th	T.P.Wright	(Blackheath)	.	11th	D.M.D.Rollo	(Howe of Fife)
4	2nd	V.S.J.Harding	(Cambridge Univ.)	.	9th	F.H.ten Bos	(London Scottish)
5	4th & last	R.J.French	(St Helen's)	.	5th	J.Douglas	(Stewart's Coll FP)
6	3rd	D.P.Rogers	(Bedford)	.	1st & only	J.C.Brash	(Cambridge Univ.)
7	5th & last	L.I.Rimmer	(Bath)	.	4th	K.I.Ross	(Boroughmuir)
8	9th & last	W.D.G.Morgan	(Medicals)	.	18th & last	G.K.Smith	(Kelso)

Referee: K.D.Kelleher   (Ireland)

SCORERS: J.Roberts   Try   (5th)   3 - 0
                                                              Half-time
                    J.P.Horrocks-Taylor   Penalty Goal   6 - 0

POINTS: J.Roberts   3 points)   (15)
                    J.P.Horrocks-Taylor   3 points   (3)

MATCH COMMENTARY:

Scotland came to Twickenham looking for the Triple Crown again, as they had in 1955, but, because Ken Scotland missed four kicks at goal, and because Phil Horrocks-Taylor had other ideas, their ambition was to be frustrated. England had wrestled with selection problems during the season, and this time re-instated Horrocks-Taylor because Richard Sharp was unfit, and Bev Risman had followed his father's footsteps into Rugby League. Peter Jackson was also recalled but spent much of the game limping on the wing. Horrocks-Taylor took full advantage of his good fortune and played an excellent game, to all intents and purposes controlling the match. This was due firstly to his ability, secondly to Dickie Jeeps' revitalised, accurate and bullet-like service, and, not least, to John Brash's lack of confidence (or ability) in trying to nail him. Horrocks-Taylor evaded Brash all afternoon, and this set up the England victory.

The Scottish defence, particularly the back line, deserve more credit than they got in the press subsequently, for holding England at bay, for even with Horrocks-Taylor consistently outwitting Brash, England scored only one try, and with that sort of advantage, it should have been many more. This was England's first win in a disappointing season and they finished fourth in the Championship Table, but kept hold of the Calcutta Cup for the eleventh successive season.

SUMMARY OF THE SEASON - 1960 - 61:

After the successes of three of the previous four seasons, one Grand Slam, two Triple Crowns and at least a share of the Championship Title on three occasions, this was indeed a disappointing season for England. The only saving grace was that, in this era of a general paucity of tries (not yet, thankfully overwhelmed by penalty goals) England scored five tries in the four matches. One try was scored in each match except the Ireland game in which England scored two and lost ! No team scored more than five tries and only France, the Title winners, scored more than twenty-two points. In other words, no-one in the Five Nations Championship had played inspiring rugby during the course of the season.

England, too, were beset with selection problems, not least at fly-half where Bev Risman, Richard Sharp and Phil Horrocks-Taylor all held office. In all, in the five matches played, England used twenty-six players but seven played in all five matches, and eight in all four Five Nations games. Eight new caps were awarded in the season, two of whom were discarded after one game. The team to play South Africa, in the first match of the season, contained two new caps, Bill Patterson and Laurie Rimmer, and showed only one other change where Bev Risman replaced Richard Sharp at fly-half. The match was lost to a powerful, determined and single-minded South African side who deserved to win the match, but failed to win many friends; only grudging admiration for their power play. Three changes and two new caps for the trip to Cardiff, John Currie became ill just before the game, failed to solve the basic problems and the overall impression was that the team looked jaded and badly in need of inspiration. So, five changes and three new caps were made to face Ireland, and the team began to knit together in the second half, but not before they had gone eleven points down. Then, as they started to fight back, England began to look good, but to claw back an eleven point deficit was asking a bit too much - but they got close. In gaining his first cap, Vic Harding was the only change against France, and, in spite of a very wet pitch, it was a good match and an honorable draw a fair result. At last, against Scotland, with three more changes and Horrocks-Taylor recalled at fly-half, England achieved their first win of the season, but that was as much to do with the inadequacy of the Scottish back row as it was to England's supremacy. In the circumstances, England should have scored a hatful of tries. But they did not, and largely because they did not when they should, it really was a most disappointing season.

After this season, ten players were not to appear in the International arena again. David Marques, who with John Currie had played in twenty-two successive matches in the second row with great distinction, finished with twenty-three caps. He had had a very distinguished rugby career at Cambridge where he gained three blues, with England, with the Barbarians and with the British Lions for whom he played in two Tests on the 1959 tour, in both of which he played at No 8. He was later a crew member aboard the America's Cup Challenger "Sovereign" in 1964 together with John Scott who had gained one cap against France in 1958. Derek Morgan, the Welsh dentist, retired with nine caps, and managed the England tour to New Zealand in 1985; also with nine caps was John Young, one of the fastest wingers of his day and a former AAA sprint champion, who retired after having qualified as a Barrister. Bev Risman would have earned many more than his eight caps had he not followed his father's example and signed for Leigh, and later Leeds, Rugby League Clubs. He was to Captain, from full-back, the Great Britain side in the 1968 Rugby League World Cup. Laurie Rimmer, the Bath schoolteacher, retired after this, his only International season, with five caps. Ernie Robinson and Ray French had four caps each; Robinson had earned his first cap seven years earlier in 1954, and Ray French turned to Rugby League and became Great-Britain Vice-Captain to Bev Risman for the 1968 Rugby League World Cup, and later emulated Eddie Waring as a knowledgeable and distinctive Radio and TV commentator. Bill Patterson, who like Dickie Jeeps, had earned a Lions Cap before he was capped for England, had two caps, and although he went on the England tour of Canada in 1967, which was not a full tour, he gained no further full caps. Neil Gavins and John Price, who emigrated to Australia, each gained their one International cap this season.

A poor season in most respects, and not what the England Captain and inspiring scrum-half, Dickie Jeeps, either would have wished, or deserved. He, no doubt, along with the rest of us, hoped for better things next time.

FIVE NATIONS CHAMPIONSHIP TABLE:

Won: **Calcutta Cup.**

		Played	Won	Lost	Drawn	Points: For	Points: Against	Tries: For	Tries: Against	Title Points
1	France	4	3	0	1	39	14	5	3	7
2 =	Wales	4	2	2	0	21	14	5	4	4
2 =	Scotland	4	2	2	0	19	25	4	4	4
4	**ENGLAND**	4	1	2	1	22	22	5	4	3
5	Ireland	4	1	3	0	22	48	3	7	2

Home Games: drew with France 5 - 5, (one try each); beat Scotland 6 - 0, (one try to nil).

Away Games: lost to Wales 3 - 6, (one try to two); lost to Ireland 8 - 11, (two tries to one).

FIVE NATIONS CHAMPIONSHIP, 1961-62 January 20th 1962, at Twickenham

67th match **ENGLAND** **0 pts** v **WALES** **0 pts**

	Caps					Caps		
15	4th	J.G.Willcox	(Oxford University)	.		1st	K.Coslett	(Aberavon)
14	1st	A.M.Underwood	(Northampton)	.		1st	D.R.R.Morgan	(Llanelli)
13	1st	M.R.Wade	(Cambridge Univ)	.		1st	D.K.Jones	(Llanelli)
12	10th	M.P.Weston	(Richmond)			9th & last	M.J.Price	(RAF/Pontypool)
11	10th	J.Roberts	(Sale)	.		14th	D.I.E.Bebb	(Swansea)
10	7th	R.A.W.Sharp	(Oxford University)	.		1st	A.Rees	(Maesteg)
9	21st	R.E.G.Jeeps (Capt)	(Northampton)	.		12th	L.H.Williams (Capt)	(Cardiff)
1	1st	P.E.Judd	(Coventry)			5th	K.D.Jones	(Cardiff)
2	7th	S.A.M.Hodgson	(Durham City)	.		31st	B.V.Meredith	(Newport)
3	10th	T.P.Wright	(Blackheath)	.		5th	L.J.Cunningham	(Aberavon)
4	3rd	V.S.J.Harding	(Saracens)	.		3rd	B.Price	(Newport)
5	23rd	J.D.Currie	(Bristol)	.		11th	W.R.Evans	(Bridgend)
6	4th	D.P.Rogers	(Bedford)	.		5th	R.H.Davies	(London Welsh)
7	9th	R.E.Syrett	(Wasps)	.		12th	H.J.Morgan	(Abertillery)
8	3rd	P.J.Taylor	(Northampton)	.		2nd	A.E.I.Pask	(Abertillery)

Referee: J.A.S.Taylor (Scotland)

SCORERS:

POINTS:

MATCH COMMENTARY:

The game ended in a scoreless draw - the first for England since 1936, also against Wales, but at Swansea. The England pack, despite the loss of Derek Morgan, Ray French and Laurie Rimmer and the non-availability of the mighty Ron Jacobs, was still a reasonable force although the selectors had brought back old hands in Phil Taylor after a seven year gap and Ron Syrett who thought his International days were over two years ago. There were, in total, seven new caps on the field, six behind the scrum, yet no-one managed to distinguish themselves in this tedious match. The essence of the game was the titanic srtuggle between two almost perfectly matched sets of forwards neither of whom could gain the slightest advantage over the other. The Welsh backs had a fair share of possession but could not find room to make an incisive break. Their English counterparts, on the other hand, too often confused and bamboozled themselves with over-elaborate passing movements which rarely made any progress. Both sides had their chances; Richard Sharp tried and failed with four drop goal attempts, two of which could have resulted in tries for Jim Roberts; and the new Welsh full-back, Kevin Coslett, failed in the swirling Twickenham wind with five penalty kicks.

Of the seven new caps on the field, four Welsh and three English, only Phil Judd was to make a serious impact on the International scene.

74th match   **ENGLAND   16 pts**   v   **IRELAND   0 pts**

	Caps					Caps		
15	5th	**J.G.Willcox**	(Oxford University)	.		11th	**T.J.Kiernan**	(UC Cork)
14	2nd	**A.M.Underwood**	(Northampton)	.	1st & only	**L.P.F.L'Estrange**	(Dublin U)
13	2nd	**M.R.Wade**	(Cambridge Univ)	.	3rd	**M.K.Flynn**	(Wanderers)
12	11th	**M.P.Weston**	(Richmond)	.	1st	**W.R.Hunter**	(CIYMS)
11	11th	**J.Roberts**	(Sale)	.	11th	**N.H.Brophy**	(Blackrock College)
10	8th	**R.A.W.Sharp**	(Oxford University)	.	1st	**F.G.Gilpin**	(Queens U Belfast)
9	22nd	**R.E.G.Jeeps (Capt)**	(Northampton)	.	1st	**J.M.T.Quirke**	(Blackrock College)
1	2nd	**P.E.Judd**	(Coventry)	.	16th	**S.Millar**	(Ballymena)
2	8th	**S.A.M.Hodgson**	(Durham City)	.	1st & only	**J.S.Dick**	(Queens U Belfast)
3	11th	**T.P.Wright**	(Blackheath)	.	1st	**R.J.McLoughlin**	(UC Dublin)
4	4th	**V.S.J.Harding**	(Saracens)	.	18th	**W.A.Mulcahy (Capt)**	(Bohemians)
5	24th	**J.D.Currie**	(Bristol)	.	1st	**W.J.McBride**	(Ballymena)
6	5th	**D.P.Rogers**	(Bedford)	.	1st & only	**P.N.Turley**	(Blackrock College)
7	10th	**R.E.Syrett**	(Wasps)	.	18th	**N.A.A.Murphy**	(Cork Constitution)
8	4th	**P.J.Taylor**	(Northampton)	.	1st	**M.L.Hipwell**	(Terenure College)

Referee: D.G.Walters   (Wales)

SCORERS:	**M.R.Wade**	Try	(1st & only)	3 - 0
	R.A.W.Sharp	Conversion		5 - 0
				Half-time
	J.Roberts	Try	(6th & last)	8 - 0
	R.A.W.Sharp	Penalty Goal		11 - 0
	R.A.W.Sharp	Try	(1st)	14 - 0
	R.A.W.Sharp	Conversion		16 - 0

POINTS:	**R.A.W.Sharp**	10 point	(16)
	M.R.Wade	3 points	(3)
	J.Roberts	3 points	(3)

MATCH COMMENTARY:

After the drab and pointless draw with Wales, England put out the same side and they played a totally different game. The forwards dominated, Jeeps was highly efficient and Richard Sharp played one of his best games in an England jersey. The Times said of Sharp, ".....there is a languid grace about this modest young man which is fascinatingly deceptive. Opponents realise this only after he has passed them. He does not punch holes in the opposition; lissom and beautifully balanced, he glides like a silent wraith through gaps which nobody else has spotted. Even when punting, he does not kick the ball, he elegantly persuades it to do his bidding." Expansive rugby produced three tries and a fine display, and the hapless Irish could only watch but, territorially, the match was by no means as one sided as the score would suggest.

Ireland awarded nine new caps for this game, three of whom played only once, but amongst the others were Willie-John McBride and Ray McLoughlin both of whom were to dominate Irish forward play for the next 14 seasons. Also included was Johnny Quirk at scrum-half, Ireland's youngest post-war player who was 17 years 7 months and 14 days old on the day of the match. This was England's seventh successive victory over Ireland at Twickenham and, in all of those matches, Ireland had managed to score only one try and a total of eight points. Richard Sharp's ten points in the match was a post-war record for an England player.

37th match　　　　**ENGLAND　0 pts　　v　　FRANCE　13 pts**

	Caps					Caps		
15	6th	J.G.Willcox	(Oxford University)	.		5th	C.Lacaze	(Lourdes)
14	3rd	A.M.Underwood	(Northampton)	.		24th	H.Rancoule	(Tarbes)
13	3rd & last	M.R.Wade	(Cambridge Univ)	.		26th	A.Boniface	(Mont-de-Marsan)
12	12th	M.P.Weston	(Richmond)	.		32nd	J.Bouquet	(Vienne)
11	12th	J.Roberts	(Sale)	.		33rd	J.Dupuy	(Tarbes)
10	9th	R.A.W.Sharp	(Oxford University)	.		16th	P.Albaladejo	(Dax)
9	23rd	R.E.G.Jeeps (Capt)	(Northampton)	.		20th	P.Lacroix (Capt)	(Agen)
1	3rd	P.E.Judd	(Coventry)	.		46th	A.Domenech	(Brive)
2	9th	S.A.M.Hodgson	(Durham City)	.		16th	J.de Gregorio	(Grenoble)
3	12th	T.P.Wright	(Blackheath)	.		26th	A.Roques	(Cahors)
4	5th	V.S.J.Harding	(Saracens)	.		15th	B.Mommejat	(Albi)
5	25th & last	J.D.Currie	(Harlequins)	.		15th	J-P.Saux	(Pau)
6	6th	D.P.Rogers	(Bedford)	.		2nd	R.Gensane	(Beziers)
7	11th & last	R.E.Syrett	(Wasps)	.		33rd	M.Crauste	(Lourdes)
8	5th	P.J.Taylor	(Northampton)	.		2nd	H.Romero	(Montauban)

Referee:　　D.G.Walters　　(Wales)

SCORERS:

0 - 3	M.Crauste	Try
0 - 5	P.Albaladejo	Conversion
Half-time		
0 - 8	M.Crauste	Try
0 - 11	M.Crauste	Try
0 - 13	P.Albaladejo	Conversion

POINTS:

	M.Crauste	9 points
	P.Albaladejo	4 points

MATCH COMMENTARY:

After the sparkling display against Ireland two weeks earlier, the same England side again looked completely different as they were totally out-played in this match. Only John Willcox in any way, distinguished himself with some heroic tackling, and without his contribution the score would surely have been very much greater. By scoring three tries in the match, Michel Crauste equalled the Championship record for a forward, set in 1903 by Jehoida Hodges of Wales against England (although he had been moved to the wing to replace an injured player at the time) - such was the superiority of the French pack in open play. At the set pieces, England held their own convincingly. So much so, and so well was Hodgson hooking, that the French flankers stood off the scrum on England's ball.

Three England players were dropped after this performance including John Currie who, mostly with David Marques, had made a monumental contribution to English forward and line-out play for seven seasons.

77th match   **ENGLAND   3 pts   v   SCOTLAND   3 pts**

69th Calcutta Cup

	Caps					Caps		
15	7th	J.G.Willcox	(Oxford University)	.	22nd	K.J.F.Scotland	(Leicester)
14	1st & only	A.C.B.Hurst	(Wasps)	.	33rd & last	A.R.Smith (Capt)	(Edinburgh W'd'rs)
13	4th	A.M.Underwood	(Exeter)	.	6th & last	J.J.McPartlin	(Oxford University)
12	1st	J.M.Dee	(Hartlepool Rovers)	.	13th	I.H.P.Laughland	(London Scottish)
11	13th	J.Roberts	(Sale)	.	5th & last	R.C.Cowan	(Selkirk)
10	4th	J.P.Horrocks-Taylor	(Leicester)	.	18th & last	G.H.Waddell	(Cambridge Univ)
9	24th & last	R.E.G.Jeeps (Capt)	(Northampton)	.	7th	S.Coughtrie	(Edinburgh Acad)
1	4th	P.E.Judd	(Coventry)	.	40th & last	H.F.McLeod	(Hawick)
2	10th	S.A.M.Hodgson	(Durham City)	.	22nd	N.S.Bruce	(London Scottish)
3	13th & last	T.P.Wright	(Blackheath)	.	14th	D.M.D.Rollo	(Howe of Fife)
4	6th & last	V.S.J.Harding	(Saracens)	.	13th	F.H.ten Bos	(London Scottish)
5	1st	T.A.Pargetter	(Coventry)	.	8th	M.J.Campbell-Lamerton	(Halifax)
6	19th & last	P.G.D.Robbins	(Coventry)	.	4th	R.J.C.Glasgow	(Dunfermline)
7	1st & only	S.J.Purdy	(Rugby)	.	8th	K.I.Ross	(Boroughmuir)
8	6th & last	P.J.Taylor	(Northampton)	.	9th	J.Douglas	(Stewart's Coll FP)

Referee: K.D.Kelleher   (Ireland)

SCORERS:	J.G.Willcox	Penalty Goal	3 - 0		
			3 - 3	K.J.F.Scotland	Penalty Goal
			Half-time		
			3 - 3		

POINTS:	J.G.Willcox	3 points	(5)	K.J.F.Scotland	3 points

MATCH COMMENTARY:

Having made six changes from the team so comprehensively beaten by France, England could only manage a draw, the third in five years, against an unconvincing Scottish side, to deny them the Triple Crown and to retain the Calcutta Cup which England had held since 1951. Scotland failed largely because of England's resolute defence. Richard Sharp had to withdraw through injury at the last minute, and, as last year, Phil Horrocks-Taylor stepped in to replace him but not with the same result. The match was an exciting one with thrust and counter-thrust from both sides, but perhaps the essential ingredients of skill and flair were conspicuous by their absence. There was always the expectation, or perhaps the hope, that something dramatic would occur to establish a commanding advantage for one side or the other, but the match, and the season, finished as an anticlimax after much promise but little to remember - except for the outstanding performance against Ireland. Thus England finished the season in third place in the Championship Table after a rather inconclusive and, again, very disappointing season.

SUMMARY OF THE SEASON - 1961 - 62:

This season was arguably one of England's least memorable and certainly the most frustrating season in recent memory. Of the four Five Nations Championship matches, one was won, one was lost and two were drawn. That statistic in itself did not make history for exactly the same results had been achieved in 1959, and drawn matches seemed to have become *a la mode* at this time. In this and the previous four seasons, England have played twenty Five Nations matches of which eight have been drawn. The 1959 season was probably the nadir, when only nine points and no tries were scored in the four matches. This time, nineteen points and three tries were scored, but it was not what was done but the manner of its doing which gave rise to the frustration. Consider the sequence of events: the first match was a pointless draw, in both senses of the word, played at Twickenham, which had little to commend it at all; the second was a spectacle of running rugby and a delight to behold in which England scored three tries, delighted their home supporters and thoroughly defeated their opponents; the third was exactly the reverse with England on the receiving end of a three-try thrashing, and the last another deadly dull draw of one penalty goal each.

Three new caps were introduced for the opening game against Wales at Twickenham, as well as the recall of the ageing veterans Ron Syrett and Phil Taylor, now aged thirty, whose previous caps were earned in 1955. The selectors were rewarded by England trying to be too clever by half, and where it was assumed that all things were possible, nothing, in fact, was achieved. Strangely, for the second match of the season, also at home, against Ireland, the selectors made no changes, and their faith was entirely justified, when England provided sparkling expansive rugby and Richard Sharp, in particular, played, to use the vernacular, a blinder. Then, in Paris, exactly the same side were on the receiving end of a masterful display by the French pack in general, and Michel Crauste in particular, and went down by three tries to none, all scored by the ubiquitous Monsieur Crauste. From England's point of view the result was wrong, but the rugby on display was excellent. Finally, at Murrayfield, with only the Calcutta Cup to play for, neither side displayed any vestige of talent or flair and the game spluttered very briefly and fizzled out into a draw - one penalty goal each. For this match, the selectors abandoned their previous faith and made six changes and for two of them it was to be their only International.

Equal third place in the Championship table was probably just about what England deserved, and they were flattered to be able to retain the Calcutta Cup. Twenty-one players were used in the four matches in all, the same team playing in the first three matches, and six changes being made, one enforced through injury, for the final match of the season. Seven new caps were awarded.

Eight players quit the International arena at the end of the season, two of them stalwarts of English rugby by any standards. John Currie, with twenty-three caps had been with David Marques, the backbone of the side for five seasons and twenty-two successive matches. He became an England selector and was Chairman of Harlequins for many years. He had also played first class cricket both for Oxford and, briefly, for Somerset. Dickie Jeeps, whose twenty-four caps stood as a record for a scrum half until surpassed by Steve Smith some twenty years later, had Captained England on thirteen occasions in successive matches, emulating both Nim Hall and Eric Evans. He became a selector and President of the RFU, and Chairman of the Sports Council. By the end of the forthcoming Lions tour to South Africa, Dickie Jeeps had earned thirteen Lions Caps, and Captained the side in the fourth and final Test in Bloemfontein. Peter Robbins retired with nineteen caps, lived for some years in France, and later was Rugby Correspondent for the Financial Times and the Observer; Peter Wright had earned thirteen caps in the dark shadows of the front row; Ron Syrett, eleven caps, Ted Woodward's brother-in-law, and one time butcher, became a retail sports outfitter; Phil Taylor, a schoolteacher at Northampton Grammar School, retired with six caps, as did Vic Harding, to add to his three Cambridge Blues; Mike Wade, a contemporary of Harding's at Cambridge, added three caps to his four Blues; and Andy Hurst, of Wasps, and John Purdy, who continued to play club rugby for Rugby until 1972, each earned only one cap.

Eight England players, Dickie Jeeps, John Willcox, John Dee, Mike Weston, Richard Sharp, Sam Hodgson (who broke his leg on the first match of the tour), Budge Rogers and Peter Wright were invited to tour with the Lions to South Africa in the summer of 1962. In addition, Bert Godwin and H.J.C.Brown of the RAF and Blackheath, who was uncapped, were called up as replacements.

FIVE NATIONS CHAMPIONSHIP TABLE:

Won: **Retained Calcutta Cup.**

		Played	Won	Lost	Drawn	Points: For	Against	Tries: For	Against	Title Points
1	France	4	3	1	0	35	6	7	0	6
2	Scotland	4	2	1	1	34	23	5	2	5
3 =	**ENGLAND**	4	1	1	2	19	16	3	3	4
3 =	Wales	4	1	1	2	9	11	0	2	4
5	Ireland	4	0	3	1	9	50	1	9	1

Home Games: drew with Wales 0 - 0, (no tries); beat Ireland 16 - 0, (three tries to nil).

Away Games: lost to France 0 - 13, (no tries to three); drew with Scotland 3 - 3, (no tries).

68th match   **ENGLAND   13 pts**   v   **WALES   6 pts**

	Caps				Caps		
15	8th	J.G.Willcox	(Oxford University)	.	2nd	G.T.R.Hodgson	(Neath)
14	17th	P.B.Jackson	(Coventry)	.	5th	D.R.R.Morgan	(Llanelli)
13	14th	M.S.Phillips	(Fylde)	.	5th	D.K.Jones	(Llanelli)
12	13th	M.P.Weston	(Durham City)	.	2nd	D.B.Davies	(Llanelli)
11	14th	J.Roberts	(Sale)	.	18th	D.I.E.Bebb	(Swansea)
10	10th	R.A.W.Sharp (Capt)	(Wasps)	.	1st	D.Watkins	(Newport)
9	1st	S.J.S.Clarke	(Cambridge Univ)	.	1st	D.C.T.Rowlands (Capt)	(Pontypool)
1	1st	N.J.Drake-Lee	(Cambridge Univ)	.	7th	K.D.Jones	(Cardiff)
2	1st	J.D.Thorne	(Bristol)	.	2nd	N.R.Gale	(Llanelli)
3	1st	B.A.Dovey	(Rosslyn Park)	.	1st	D.Williams	(Ebbw Vale)
4	1st	A.M.Davis	(Torquay Athletic)	.	5th	B.Price	(Newport)
5	1st	J.E.Owen	(Coventry)	.	1st	B.E.Thomas	(Neath)
6	7th	D.P.Rogers	(Bedford)	.	6th	A.E.I.Pask	(Abertillery)
7	1st	D.C.Manley	(Exeter)	.	1st	D.J.Hayward	(Cardiff)
8	2nd	B.J.Wightman	(Coventry)	.	1st & only	R.C.B.Michaelson	(Cambridge Univ)

Referee: K.D.Kelleher   (Ireland)

SCORERS:

M.S.Phillips	Try	(1st)	3 - 0			
R.A.W.Sharp	Conversion		5 - 0			
			Half-time			
J.E.Owen	Try	(1st & only)	8 - 0			
R.A.W.Sharp	Conversion		10 - 0			
			10 - 3	G.T.R.Hodgson	Penalty Goal	
R.A.W.Sharp	D'p Goal (3rd & last)		13 - 3			
			13 - 6	D.J.Hayward	Try	

POINTS:

R.A.W.Sharp	7 points	(23)	D.J.Hayward	3 points	
M.S.Phillips	3 points	(6)	G.T.R.Hodgson	3 points	
J.E.Owen	3 points	(3)			

MATCH COMMENTARY:

England awarded seven new caps for this game, six of them in the pack - a courageous gamble for a trip to Cardiff. The conditions after recent severe blizzards, were hardly conducive to good rugby, but England adapted better. Wales, with five new caps, through dropped passes and the slippery turf, missed several early chances, and England gradually asserted their authority on the proceedings. Clive Rowlands, captain on his debut, got little help, or sympathy, from his pack, whereas the new England eight (the front five were all new caps) performed well, and the back row had the freedom of the park. It was entirely appropriate that one of the front five - John Owen - should score a try on his debut. Malcolm Phillip's try was brilliantly conceived and executed when Mike Weston chipped ahead, Phillips gathered and passed to Peter Jackson on the scissors who drew Graham Hodgson perfectly and passed back to Phillips who scored in the corner. Hodgson gave Wales a glimmer of hope with a penalty goal midway through the second half, but Richard Sharp's drop goal sealed the match and Dai Hayward's try, direct from a line-out, came far too late to further Wales' cause. Basically, Wales played badly, although to win at Cardiff is never a mean achievement and England were not to win again at Cardiff Arms Park for twenty-eight years !!

75th match   **ENGLAND   0 pts**   **v**   **IRELAND   0 pts**

	Caps					Caps		
15	9th	J.G.Willcox	(Oxford University)	.	1st & only	B.D.E.Marshall	(Queens U Belfast)
14	18th	P.B.Jackson	(Coventry)	.	6th	W.R.Hunter	(CIYMS)
13	15th	M.S.Phillips	(Fylde)	.	7th	J.C.Walsh	(UC Cork)
12	14th	M.P.Weston	(Durham City)	.	2nd	P.J.Casey	(UC Dublin)
11	15th	J.Roberts	(Sale)	.	14th	N.H.Brophy	(Blackrock College)
10	11th	R.A.W.Sharp (Capt)	(Wasps)	.	13th	M.A.F.English	(Lansdowne)
9	2nd	S.J.S.Clarke	(Cambridge Univ)	.	4th	J.C.Kelly	(UC Dublin)
1	2nd	N.J.Drake-Lee	(Cambridge Univ)	.	4th	R.J.McLoughlin	(Blackrock College)
2	2nd	J.D.Thorne	(Bristol)	.	21st	A.R.Dawson	(Wanderers)
3	2nd & last	B.A.Dovey	(Rosslyn Park)	.	20th	S.Millar	(Ballymena)
4	2nd	A.M.Davis	(Torquay Athletic)	.	23rd	W.A.Mulcahy (Capt)	(Bective Rangers)
5	2nd	J.E.Owen	(Coventry)	.	6th	W.J.McBride	(Ballymena)
6	8th	D.P.Rogers	(Bedford)	.	1st	E.P.McGuire	(UC Galway)
7	2nd	D.C.Manley	(Exeter)	.	3rd	M.D.Kiely	(Lansdowne)
8	3rd	B.J.Wightman	(Coventry)	.	6th	C.J.Dick	(Ballymena)

Referee: H.B.Laidlaw   (Scotland)

SCORERS:

POINTS:

MATCH COMMENTARY:

An unchanged England side could not emulate the standards they had set in the opening match of the season at Cardiff Arms Park. In contrast to the icy conditions then, the pitch in Dublin was heavy mud and the forwards were out-paced by a furious Irish pack. Mick English's line and tactical kicking was of a very high order indeed, and, again, England had cause to be grateful for John Willcox's solid defence. Marshall, deputising for Kiernan at full-back, missed three penalty attempts, any one of which would have seen Ireland home. Nevertheless, the match had little chance of becoming an enjoyable spectacle even before the start, due to the really atrocious weather and the state of the pitch. Were it not for the difficulty of dispersing a large crowd without undue disappointment, the case for postponement would have been very strong.

This was the second scoreless draw in the post-war period, and, fortunately, so far, is the last.

38th match   ENGLAND   6 pts   v   FRANCE   5 pts

	Caps					Caps		
15	10th	J.G.Willcox	(Oxford University)	.	1st	P.Dedieu	(Beziers)
14	19th	P.B.Jackson	(Coventry)	.	3rd	P.Besson	(Brive)
13	16th	M.S.Phillips	(Fylde)	.	21st	G.Boniface	(Mont-de-Marsan)
12	15th	M.P.Weston	(Durham City)	.	33rd	A.Boniface	(Mont-de-Marsan)
11	16th	J.Roberts	(Sale)	.	10th	C.Darrouy	(Mont-de-Marsan)
10	12th	R.A.W.Sharp (Capt)	(Wasps)	.	21st	P.Albaladejo	(Dax)
9	3rd	S.J.S.Clarke	(Cambridge Univ)	.	26th	P.Lacroix (Capt)	(Agen)
1	1st & only	K.J.Wilson	(Gloucester)	. .	4th	F.Mas	(Beziers)
2	3rd & last	J.D.Thorne	(Bristol)	.	1st & only	R.Rebujent	(Racing Club)
3	3rd	N.J.Drake-Lee	(Cambridge Univ)	.	2nd & last	F.Zago	(Montauban)
4	2nd	T.A.Pargetter	(Coventry)	.	3rd	M.Lira	(La Voulte)
5	3rd	J.E.Owen	(Coventry)	.	21st	J-P.Saux	(Pau)
6	9th	D.P.Rogers	(Bedford)	.	3rd	J.Fabre	(Toulouse)
7	3rd	D.C.Manley	(Exeter)	.	40th	M.Crauste	(Lourdes)
8	1st	D.G.Perry	(Bedford)	.	7th & last	H.Romero	(Montauban)

Referee: D.C.J.MacMahon   (Scotland)

SCORERS:

			0 - 3	G.Boniface	Try
			0 - 5	P.Albaladejo	Conversion
J.G.Willcox	Penalty Goal		3 - 5		
			Half-time		
J.G.Willcox	Penalty Goal		6 - 5		

POINTS:

J.G.Willcox	6 points	(11)	G.Boniface	3 points
			P.Albaladejo	2 points

MATCH COMMENTARY:

After the less than satisfactory forward display in Dublin, and with Phil Judd still unavailable, the selectors juggled about with the front row, dropping Dovey and moving Nick Drake-Lee to tight head, and also brought in David Perry at No 8.

England controlled this game very effectively. They denied France any worthwhile possession and, for the most part, kept them well out of range of the posts to thwart any attempted French drop goals and to deny any penalty goal conversions should English discipline waver a little. Even so, Pierre Albaladejo came close with several attempts from difficult positions. After Guy Boniface's early try, John Willcox failed with three penalty goal attempts before he was successful both before and just after half-time. But there the scoring, but not the interest in the match, ended. Towards the end of the game, French pressure from the Boniface brothers and from Albaladejo increased, but the English defence was resolute and, yet again, especially that of John Willcox.

England had made a conscious decision to play the game very tight indeed to deny the French, at Twickenham, once more, and, in that respect, they were outstandingly successful. The victory by the narrowest of margins was satisfactory but far from spectacular and, not for the last time, England lost the try count to France, but won the match. Both sides knew that the result would have a significant effect on their title hopes and risk-taking was minimal.

78th match   **ENGLAND   10 pts**   v   **SCOTLAND   8 pts**

70th Calcutta Cup

	Caps				Caps		
15	11th	J.G.Willcox	(Harlequins)	.	2nd	C.F.Blaikie	(Heriot's FP)
14	20th & last	P.B.Jackson	(Coventry)	.	4th	C.Elliott	(Langholm)
13	17th	M.S.Phillips	(Fylde)	.	1st	B.C.Henderson	(Edinburgh W'd'rs)
12	16th	M.P.Weston	(Durham City)	.	4th & last	D.M.White	(Kelvinside Acad)
11	17th	J.Roberts	(Sale)	.	12th	R.H.Thomson	(London Scottish)
10	13th	R.A.W.Sharp (Capt)	(Wasps)	.	26th	K.J.F.Scotland (Capt)	(Heriot's FP)
9	4th	S.J.S.Clarke	(Cambridge Univ)	.	11th & last	S.Coughtrie	(Edinburgh Acad)
1	5th	P.E.Judd	(Coventry)	.	1st	J.B.Neill	(Edinburgh Acad)
2	3rd	H.O.Godwin	(Coventry)	.	26th	N.S.Bruce	(London Scottish)
3	4th	N.J.Drake-Lee	(Cambridge Univ)	.	18th	D.M.D.Rollo	(Howe of Fife)
4	3rd	A.M.Davis	(Torquay Athletic)	.	17th & last	F.H.ten Bos	(London Scottish)
5	4th	J.E.Owen	(Coventry)	.	12th	M.J.Campbell-Lamerton	(Halifax)
6	10th	D.P.Rogers	(Bedford)	.	11th	K.I.Ross	(Boroughmuir)
7	4th & last	D.C.Manley	(Exeter)	.	10th & last	R.J.C.Glasgow	Stewart's Coll FP
8	2nd	D.G.Perry	(Bedford)	.	1st	J.P.Fisher	(Royal HSFP)

Referee: D.G.Walters   (Wales)

SCORERS:

			0 - 3	R.J.C.Glasgow	Try
			0 - 5	S.Coughtrie	Conversion
			0 - 8	K.J.F.Scotland	Drop Goal
N.J.Drake-Lee	Try	(1st & only)	3 - 8		
J.G.Willcox	Conversion		5 - 8		
		Half-time			
R.A.W.Sharp	Try	(2nd & last)	8 - 8		
J.G.Willcox	Conversion		10 - 8		

POINTS:

J.G.Willcox	4 points	(15)	R.J.C.Glasgow	3 points	
N.J.Drake-Lee	3 points	(3)	K.J.F.Scotland	3 points	
R.A.W.Sharp	3 points	(26)	S.Coughtrie	2 points	

MATCH COMMENTARY:

This match was the Championship decider although there was no Triple Crown at stake because Scotland had lost to Wales and England had drawn with Ireland. The Scots started out as if they were convinced that the title was theirs for the taking. Within twenty minutes of the start they were eight points up and getting plenty of possession. But some typical wizardry by Peter Jackson in supporting Richard Sharp led to Nick Drake-Lee scoring near the posts before half-time. Shortly after came the decisive strike for England; Richard Sharp from a set piece cut through the Scottish defence like a knife through butter beating first Ross, the Scottish flanker, who was coming straight at him, then, having run a dummy scissors with Malcolm Phillps, he accelerated to run between the two Scottish centres, Henderson and White, and was left with only Blaikie, the Scottish full-back, to beat. Jim Roberts was outside Sharp to the left and could have scored with ease had he been given the pass. Blaikie, rightly, went for the man with the ball and Sharp sold him an outrageous dummy and ran between the posts without accelerating further. A truly magnificent try. It inspired England, deflated Scotland, and England only had to defend to to take the title outright.

Thus for the thirteenth successive match, Scotland had failed to beat England, and had left Twickenham empty-handed, but at least they had scored their first try on the Auld Enemy's ground since 1955.

SUMMARY OF THE SEASON - 1962 - 63:

Despite the recurrance of that nightmare, the pointless draw, England deserrved to win the Championship outright with three good and merited wins over Wales, France and Scotland. After the disappointments of the previous few seasons, the taste of success was sweet indeed. Nevertheless only four tries were scored and a mere twenty-nine points registered over the four Championship matches against three tries and nineteen points, so it was by no means a vintage season of stimulating rugby. But the results show that England came within a whisker of winning another Grand Slam to add to that achieved in 1957. Only the second pointless draw in two seasons stood between this side and the ultimate goal.

Seven new caps were introduced for the opening match at Cardiff, and six of those were in the pack including all the front five, and recalled to the colours were Peter Jackson, who had been out of the side for two years, for his seventeenth cap, and Malcolm Phillips whose previous cap had been on the previous visit to Cardiff, two years ago. The only non-forward new cap was Simon Clarke, the Cambridge scrum-half. England's cause was assisted by a mediocre Welsh performance, but no victory against the Welsh at Cardiff Arms Park should ever be underrated, or under-valued. Then, after the Lord Mayor's Show, and with an unchanged side, came the next draw in the recent tedious incidence of inconclusive matches - the ninth in six seasons and the second in two years with no score at all. Bad as the conditions were, one side or the other should have risen above them to some degree. For the visit of France to Twickenham, three changes were made, all in the pack, and two new caps made thier debut. The result was satisfactory and England controlled the match well. It was a close encounter and the score reflected that accurately, but certainly, England deserved their victory on account of their better discipline and the extent to which they limited the French options. The tension before the final match had begun to mount with both sides facing the opportunity to win the Championship outright by winning the match. Although Scotland were eight points up in twenty minutes, they had no answer either to Peter Jackson's wizardry which led to the first English try, nor to Richard Sharp's magnificent solo effort from a set piece in scoring one of the finest tries ever seen at Twickenham. Comparisons are odious, and as far as the scoring of tries is concerned, irrelevant, and they may come differently and as good as this one, but they won't come any better !!

For the Championship England called upon twenty players and awarded nine new caps in all, seven for the first match against Wales and a further two for the third game against France. The whole of the back division played unchanged throughout the season, but only four of the pack survived the season.

With the prospect of selection for England's first overseas tour to Australia and New Zealand to take place in the following summer, an added incentive, only five players left International rugby at the end of the season. Most conspicuous of these was Peter Jackson, the brilliant and very elusive Coventry winger, who had justly earned twenty caps. He was thirty-three years old when he played in his twentieth International match and had first attracted the selectors' interest when he played in an England trial in 1950, thirteen years previously. He went to Australia and New Zealand on the 1959 Lions Tour, played in five of the six tests and scored tries in the first and fourth Tests against New Zealand. His finest hour came, however, in the match against Australia at Twickenham in 1958 when he scored the winning try with a dazzling run in the final minutes of a vey hard match. As was Richard Sharp's this season, this was one of the most memorable tries ever seen at Twickenham. Also leaving the stage were Dick Manley, the Exeter cabinet maker, who gained four caps, played in seven England trials, represented Devon fifty-six times and made over 450 appearances for his club, Exeter; John Thorne, the Bristol hooker and shoemaker, won three caps, and played in many England trials; B.A.Dovey, a schoolmaster at Merchant Taylors' School, Northwood, had two caps, and the once-capped Ken Wilson, a former RAF heavyweight boxing Champion, later joined Oldham Rugby League Club.

It had been a very good season for England, and the tour to Australia and New Zealand, although offering a very demanding itinerary, was eagerly anticipated.

FIVE NATIONS CHAMPIONSHIP TABLE:

Won: **Championship Title, Calcutta Cup.**

		Played	Won	Lost	Drawn	Points: For	Against	Tries: For	Against	Title Points
1	ENGLAND	4	3	0	1	29	19	4	3	7
2 =	France	4	2	2	0	40	25	6	2	4
2 =	Scotland	4	2	2	0	22	22	2	2	4
4	Ireland	4	1	2	1	19	33	2	5	3
5	Wales	4	1	3	0	21	32	2	4	2

Home Games: beat France 6 - 5, (no tries to one); beat Scotland 10 - 8, (two tries to one).

Away Games: beat Wales 13 - 6, (two tries to one); drew with Ireland 0 - 0, (no tries).

ENGLAND TOUR TO NEW ZEALAND and AUSTRALIA, 1963.

THE TOUR PARTY:

Manager:	**J.W.T.Berry**	Assistant::		**M.R.Steele-Bodger**	Captain:		**M.P.Weston**	
Full-back:	**R.W.Hosen**	(Northampton)	no caps	Forwards:	**C.R.Jacobs**	(Northampton)	22 caps	
					P.E.Judd	(Coventry)	5 caps	
Three-quarters:	**F.D.Sykes**	(Northampton)	2 caps		**J.E.Highton**	(US Portsmouth)	no caps	
	M.S.Phillips	(Fylde)	20 caps		**H.O.Godwin**	(Coventry)	3 caps	
	M.P.Weston	(Durham City)	16 caps		**J.D.Thorne**	(Bristol)	3 caps	
	G.C.Gibson	(US Portsmouth)	no caps		**J.E.Owen**	(Coventry)	4 caps	
	J.M.Dee	(Hartlepool Rov)	2 caps		**T.A.Pargetter**	(Coventry)	2 caps	
	J.M.Ranson	(Rosslyn Park)	no caps		**A.M.Davis**	(Torquay Athletic)	3 caps	
					D.P.Rogers	(Bedford)	10 caps	
Half-backs:	**J.P.Horrocks**	(Leicester)	4 caps		**D.G.Perry**	(Bedford)	2 caps	
	-Taylor				**B.J.Wightman**	(Coventry)	3 caps	
	R.F.Read	(Harlequins)	no caps		**V.R.Marriott**	(Harlequins)	no caps	
	T.C.Wintle	(St Mary's Hosp)	4 caps					
	S.J.S.Clarke	(Cambridge Univ)	4 caps					

Reports on the three Test matches appear in the appropriate International match sequence.

Scotland, Ireland and France had preceded England in embarking on short tours to the Southern Hemisphere, and the RFU can be criticised for not having understood that an itinerary of six hard matches including three Test matches in a mere eighteen days is somewhat severe, especially when two Test matches, against different countries, fall within four days at the end of the trip.

The tour began very encouragingly with a victory against Wellington where the uncapped Roger Hosen excelled himself by kicking two penalty goals, one from fifty yards, a very wide angled drop goal and, finally the conversion of Simon Clarke's try. The jet lag after a very long flight was evident in other members of the side, but it was a good start.

Otago, four days later were a different proposition, and they played a very hard game indeed, determined not to be upstaged by a mere England side. Again Roger Hosen plundered a drop goal and a penalty and put England into the lead by 6 points to 3 at the interval. In the second half, Otago turned the screws and some formidable forward rushes put them in front with a converted try and two further penalty goals. The relatively inexperienced half-back pairing of Read and Wintle restored England's pride with a fine try towards the end from a clever scissors movement.

After the Frist Test it was a battered but not dispirited England side who faced a very young Hawke's Bay team, but the backs made a multitude of unforced errors, especially the unfortunate Mike Weston, by dropping passes frequently, and Roger Hosen by missing five penalty kicks at goal. England's solitary try came from Brian Wightman after one of the few passes from Weston which did not go down, and the England side were well beaten - but it was only three days after the first Test and seven England players played in both matches. This, the first overseas tour England had ever made, was hardly an outstanding success interms of the results achieved but it was an invaluable lesson for the selectors and the RFU and it was invaluable experience for the players, none more so than the forwards, all of whom, except Brian Wightman and Tom Pargetter who retired after the tour, were to become better players in future seasons.

Those retiring at the end of the tour were: Brain Wightman, with five caps, a schoolteacher who emigrated to Canada in 1964; Frank Sykes had four caps and he, too, emigrated but to the States and continued his PE teaching career and his club rugby there; Tom Pargetter, the Coventry baker had earned three caps; and John Dee, another schoolteacher, and a British Lion, retired to Hartlepool with his two caps.

TOUR RESULTS:

May 18th	Wellington	at Wellington	WON	14 - 9	(one try each)
May 22nd	Otago	at Dunedin	LOST	9 - 14	(one try each)
May 25th	**NEW ZEALAND**	**at Auckland**	**LOST**	**11 - 21**	**(one try to three)**
May 28th	Hawke's Bay	at Napier	LOST	5 - 20	(one try to four)
June 1st	**NEW ZEALAND**	**at Christchurch**	**LOST**	**6 - 9**	**(one try to two)**
June 4th	**AUSTRALIA**	**at Sydney**	**LOST**	**9 - 18**	**(three tries to four)**

5th match   **ENGLAND   11 pts   v   NEW ZEALAND   21 pts**

	Caps					Caps		
15	1st	R.W.Hosen	(Northampton)		23rd	D.B.Clarke	(Waikato)
14	1st	J.M.Ranson	(Rosslyn Park)		4th	D.W.McKay	(Auckland)
13	18th	M.S.Phillips	(Fylde)		1st	I.N.Uttley	(Wellington)
12	17th	M.P.Weston (Capt)	(Durham City)		6th & last	T.N.Wolfe	(Taranaki)
11	2nd & last	J.M.Dee	(Hartlepool Rovers)		7th	R.W.Caulton	(Wellington)
10	5th	J.P.Horrocks-Taylor	(Leicester)		3rd	B.A.Watt	(Canterbury)
9	5th	S.J.S.Clarke	(Cambridge Univ)		9th	D.M.Connor	(Auckland)
1	23rd	C.R.Jacobs	(Northampton)		22nd	W.J.Whineray (Capt)	(Auckland)
2	4th	H.O.Godwin	(Coventry)		16th	D.Young	(Canterbury)
3	6th	P.E.Judd	(Coventry)		23rd	I.J.Clarke	(Waikato)
4	3rd & last	T.A.Pargetter	(Coventry)		20th	C.E.Meads	(King Country)
5	4th	A.M.Davis	(Torquay Athletic)		1st	A.J.Stewart	(Canterbury)
6	11th	D.P.Rogers	(Bedford)		6th	W.J.Nathan	(Auckland)
7	1st	V.R.Marriott	(Harlequins)		13th	K.R.Tremain	(Hawke's Bay)
8	3rd	D.G.Perry	(Bedford)		13th	D.J.Graham	(Canterbury)

Referee: C.F.Robson   (New Zealand)

SCORERS:	R.W.Hosen	Penalty Goal		3 - 0		
	R.W.Hosen	Penalty Goal		6 - 0		
				Half-time		
				6 - 3	D.B.Clarke	Penalty Goal
	J.M.Ranson	Try	(1st)	9 - 3		
	R.W.Hosen	Conversion		11 - 3		
				11 - 6	D.B.Clarke	Try
				11 - 8	D.B.Clarke	Conversion
				11 - 11	R.W.Caulton	Try
				11 - 13	D.B.Clarke	Conversion
				11 - 16	R.W.Caulton	Try
				11 - 18	D.B.Clarke	Conversion
				11 - 21	D.B.Clarke	Drop Goal

POINTS:	R.W.Hosen	8 points	(8)		D.B.Clarke	15 points
	J.M.Ranson	3 points	(3)		R.W.Caulton	6 points

MATCH COMMENTARY:

England, as Five Nations Champions, were making their first overseas tour but it was a brutal itinerary involving six matches in seventeen days including three Tests. Ahead by six points at half-time, it just began to look as if England might be able to spring a major surprise. After a fair bit of vocal abuse from the 55,000 crowd at half-time, New Zealand in general, and Don Clarke in particular, began to stir themselves. Following Clarke's 40 yard penalty goal, England were able to extend their lead even further when Roger Hosen converted Ranson's try after Budge Rogers had broken away from a loose maul some thirty-five yards out, but in the last quarter the All Black forward power and strength began to tell. England defended desperately and well, but could not stem the tide of continuous attacks. Don Clarke scored by four different means, a try, a drop goal, a penalty goal and a conversion in amassing 15 points.

6th match   **ENGLAND   6 pts**   v   **NEW ZEALAND   9 pts**

	Caps					Caps		
15	2nd	R.W.Hosen	(Northampton)	.	24th	D.B.Clarke	(Waikato)
14	2nd	J.M.Ranson	(Rosslyn Park)	.	5th & last	D.W.McKay	(Auckland)
13	19th	M.S.Phillips	(Fylde)	.	2nd & last	I.N.Uttley	(Wellington)
12	18th	M.P.Weston (Capt)	(Durham City)	.	13th & last	P.T.Walsh	(Counties)
11	3rd	F.D.Sykes	(Northampton)	.	8th	R.W.Caulton	(Wellington)
10	6th	J.P.Horrocks-Taylor	(Leicester)	.	4th	B.A.Watt	(Canterbury)
9	6th	S.J.S.Clarke	(Cambridge Univ)	.	10th	D.M.Connor	(Auckland)
1	24th	C.R.Jacobs	(Northampton)	.	23rd	W.J.Whineray (Capt)	(Auckland)
2	5th	H.O.Godwin	(Coventry)	.	17th	D.Young	(Canterbury)
3	7th	P.E.Judd	(Coventry)	.	24th & last	I.J.Clarke	(Waikato)
4	4th	D.G.Perry	(Bedford)	.	21st	C.E.Meads	(King Country)
5	5th	A.M.Davis	(Torquay Athletic)	.	2nd	A.J.Stewart	(Canterbury)
6	12th	D.P.Rogers	(Bedford)	.	7th	W.J.Nathan	(Auckland)
7	2nd	V.R.Marriott	(Harlequins)	.	14th	K.R.Tremain	(Hawke's Bay)
8	4th	B.J.Wightman	(Coventry)	.	14th	D.J.Graham	(Canterbury)

Referee: J.P.Murphy   (New Zealand)

SCORERS:

			0 - 3	D.W.McKay	Try
R.W.Hosen	Penalty Goal		3 - 3		
			3 - 6	P.T.Walsh	Try
			Half-time		
M.S.Phillips	Try	(3rd)	6 - 6		
			6 - 9	D.B.Clarke	Penalty Goal

POINTS:

R.W.Hosen	3 points	(11)	D.W.McKay	3 points
M.S.Phillips	3 points	(9)	P.T.Walsh	3 points
			D.B.Clarke	3 points

MATCH COMMENTARY:

For the second Test, only seven days later, three changes, one of them positional, were made. John Dee gave way to Frank Sykes on the left wing, David Perry moved to lock with Mike Davis and Brian Wightman returned at No 8. England played their best rugby of the tour and were very unlucky to lose in the manner in which they did. Excellent tries were scored in each half, and Malcolm Phillips' try to tie the scores was particularly spectacular, and, at that stage, the match appeared to be heading towards a draw. England were well on top and stifling all New Zealand's attacks, when Don Clarke called a "Mark" ten yards inside his own half of the field and with only a few minutes of the match remaining. As he prepared to kick for goal, the two stalwart English props, Phil Judd and Ron Jacobs questioned the referee on their right to charge the kicker, but by some strange quirk of fate, completely misunderstood his statement and charged - illegally. Another penalty resulted, and a prodigious kick of all of sixty yards soared between the posts from Don Clarke's boot, and New Zealand had won the match. This was a courageous and committed display of the very highest order by the England team, but it had been a disappointing tour as England had managed to win only one match, the first, against Wellington. Frank Sykes, the Northampton winger, won his third cap in this match eight years after he had won his second against Scotland in 1955.

5th match   **ENGLAND 9 pts**   **v**   **AUSTRALIA 18 pts**

	Caps					Caps		
15	3rd	R.W.Hosen	(Northampton)	.	1st	P.F.Ryan	(New South Wales)
14	4th & last	F.D.Sykes	(Northampton)	.	2nd & last	K.P.Walsham	(New South Wales)
13	20th	M.S.Phillips	(Fylde)	.	3rd	R.J.P.Marks	(Queensland)
12	19th	M.P.Weston (Capt)	(Durham City)	.	1st	P.A.Jones	(New South Wales)
11	3rd	J.M.Ranson	(Rosslyn Park)	.	4th	J.S.Boyce	(New South Wales)
10	7th	J.P.Horrocks-Taylor	(Leicester)	.	4th	P.F.Hawthorne	(New South Wales)
9	7th	S.J.S.Clarke	(Cambridge Univ)	.	3rd	K.V.McMullen	(New South Wales)
1	25th	C.R.Jacobs	(Northampton)	.	15th	J.P.L.White	(New South Wales)
2	6th	H.O.Godwin	(Coventry)	.	14th	P.G.Johnson	(New South Wales)
3	8th	P.E.Judd	(Coventry)	.	1st & only	L.R.Austin	(New South Wales)
4	5th	D.G.Perry	(Bedford)	.	25th	J.E.Thornett (Capt)	(New South Wales)
5	5th	J.E.Owen	(Coventry)	.	2nd	J.M.Miller	(New South Wales)
6	13th	D.P.Rogers	(Bedford)	.	9th	E.L.Heinrich	(New South Wales)
7	3rd	V.R.Marriott	(Harlequins)	.	1st	G.V.Davis	(New South Wales)
8	5th & last	B.J.Wightman	(Coventry)	.	6th	J.F.O'Gorman	(New South Wales)

Referee: C.F.Ferguson   (Australia)

SCORERS:

				0 - 3	P.A.Jones	Try
				0 - 5	P.F.Ryan	Conversion
				0 - 8	K.P.Walsham	Try
				0 - 10	P.F.Ryan	Conversion
				0 - 13	E.L.Heinrich	Try
				0 - 16	G.V.Davis	Try
				0 - 18	P.F.Ryan	Conversion
S.J.S.Clarke	Try	(1st & only)	3 - 18			
H.O.Godwin	Try	(1st & only)	6 - 18			
			Half-time			
M.S.Phillips	Try	(4th)	9 - 18			

POINTS:

S.J.S.Clarke	3 points	(3)		P.F.Ryan	6 points
H.O.Godwin	3 points	(3)		P.A.Jones, K.P.Walsham,	
M.S.Phillips	3 points	(12)		E.L.Heinrich and G.V.Davis	3 points each

MATCH COMMENTARY:

Only three days after the second Test against the All Blacks, England found themselves facing Australia for the first time on Australian soil in a sea of mud at the Sydney Sports Ground. Such was England's lethargy that within thirty minutes Australia had run up a total of eighteen points including four tries, due to a fine display of finger-tip passing and handling in conditions as dreadful as can have been witnessed anywhere. England did very well to respond and pulled back two tries before half-time, and a third midway into the second half. But it must be said that the young Australian side played excellent rugby in very trying conditions and were too fast in thought and deed for England. Valuable lessons had been learned from the tour and such an ambitious and demanding itinerary will surely not be permitted again. Three Internationals and three major provincial games in seventeen days cannot be in anybody's interests - except perhaps the opposition !!

7th match   **ENGLAND   0 pts   v   NEW ZEALAND   14 pts**

Caps

15	12th	**J.G.Willcox (Capt)**	(Harlequins)	.	27th	**D.B.Clarke**	(Waikato)
14	21st	**M.S.Phillips**	(Fylde)	.	3rd	**M.J.Dick**	Auckland)
13	20th	**M.P.Weston**	(Durham City)	.	8th	**P.F.Little**	Auckland)
12	1st	**R.D.Sangwin**	(Hull & East Riding)	.	3rd	**D.A.Arnold**	(Canterbury)
11	18th & last	**J.Roberts**	(Sale)	.	11th	**R.W.Caulton**	(Wellington)
10	8th	**J.P.Horrocks-Taylor**	(Middlesborough)	.	6th	**B.A.Watt**	(Canterbury)
9	8th	**S.J.S.Clarke**	(Cambridge Univ)	.	8th	**K.C.Briscoe**	(Taranaki)
1	9th	**P.E.Judd**	(Coventry)	.	26th	**W.J.Whineray (Capt)**	(Auckland)
2	7th	**H.O.Godwin**	(Coventry)	.	20th	**D.Young**	(Canterbury)
3	5th	**N.J.Drake-Lee**	(Cambridge Univ)	.	3rd	**K.F.Gray**	(Wellington)
4	6th	**A.M.Davis**	(Torquay Athletic)	.	24th	**C.E.Meads**	(King Country)
5	6th	**J.E.Owen**	(Coventry)	.	5th	**A.J.Stewart**	(Canterbury)
6	14th	**D.P.Rogers**	(Bedford)	.	17th	**D.J.Graham**	(Canterbury)
7	4th & last	**V.R.Marriott**	(Harlequins)	.	17th	**K.R.Tremain**	(Hawke's Bay)
8	6th	**D.G.Perry**	(Bedford)	.	1st	**B.J.Lochore**	(Wairarapa)

Referee: D.C.J.McMahon   (Scotland)

SCORERS:

0 - 3		**D.B.Clarke**	Penalty Goal
0 - 6		**D.B.Clarke**	Penalty Goal
0 - 9		**R.W.Caulton**	Try
Half-time			
0 - 12		**C.E.Meads**	Try
0 - 14		**D.B.Clarke**	Conversion

POINTS:

D.B.Clarke	8 points
R.W.Caulton	3 points
C.E.Meads	3 points

MATCH COMMENTARY:

After last summer's tour to New Zealand and Australia, England had high hopes for a successful season, but the Fifth All Blacks destroyed that dream by inflicting on England their biggest defeat ever at Twickenham.   England showed six team and one positional change from the side which had narrowly lost the Second Test on the recent tour to New Zealand, but they were severely demoralised when, once again, the mighty Don Clarke "put the boot in" and secured the lead for New Zealand with a penalty goal from almost fifty yards in the first five minutes, and then another from closer range shortly afterwards. England never recovered from these two early setbacks and their failure lay largely in the pack whose slow and ponderous heels gave the New Zealand defence, already lying up to the gain line, ample time to smother whatever attacking intentions Horrocks-Taylor or Clarke may have had. As the game went on the visitors became more powerful in the loose, and England never looked like scoring any points at all. The fatal blow must have been the sight of Colin Meads irresistably powering his way to the line for the second New Zealand try. The few fitful attacks which England managed to put together came to nothing, and John Willcox missed three penalty attempts. It was not that the England side lacked experience - eleven had been on the summer tour and the remainder had thirty-two caps amongst them, but, as the Times correspondent said "....New Zealand were too fit, too fast and too fiery". England could not come to terms with the constant harrying of the man in possession, giving him little, if any, time to do anything constructive with the ball - even if he had been able to think quickly enough.

69th match   **ENGLAND   6 pts**   v   **WALES   6 pts**

	Caps					Caps		
15	13th	**J.G.Willcox (Capt)**	(Harlequins)	.		7th	**G.T.R.Hodgson**	(Neath)
14	22nd	**M.S.Phillips**	(Fylde)	.		1st & only	**D.Weaver**	(Swansea)
13	21st	**M.P.Weston**	(Durham City)	.		8th	**D.K.Jones**	(Llanelli)
12	2nd & last	**R.D.Sangwin**	(Hull & East Riding)	.		1st	**K.Bradshaw**	(Bridgend)
11	4th	**J.M.Ranson**	(Rosslyn Park)	.		21st	**D.I.E.Bebb**	(Swansea)
10	9th & last	**J.P.Horrocks-Taylor**	(Middlesborough)	.		6th	**D.Watkins**	(Newport)
9	9th	**S.J.S.Clarke**	(Cambridge Univ)	.		6th	**D.C.T.Rowlands (Capt)**	(Pontypool)
1	26th	**C.R.Jacobs**	(Northampton)	.		5th	**D.Williams**	(Ebbw Vale)
2	11th & last	**S.A.M.Hodgson**	(Durham City)	.		6th	**N.R.Gale**	(Llanelli)
3	6th	**N.J.Drake-Lee**	(Cambridge Univ)	.		10th	**L.J.Cunningham**	(Aberavon)
4	7th	**A.M.Davis**	(Torquay Athletic)	.		9th	**B.Price**	(Newport)
5	1st	**R.E.Rowell**	(Leicester)	.		6th	**B.E.Thomas**	(Neath)
6	15th	**D.P.Rogers**	(Bedford)	.		2nd & last	**A.Thomas**	(Newport)
7	1st	**P.J.Ford**	(Gloucester)	.		1st	**J.T.Mantle**	(Loughborough Coll)
8	7th	**D.G.Perry**	(Bedford)	.		11th	**A.E.I.Pask**	(Abertillery)

Referee: K.D.Kelleher   (Ireland)

SCORERS:

J.M.Ranson	Try	(2nd & last)	3 - 0			
D.G.Perry	Try	(1st)	6 - 0			
			6 - 3	**D.I.E.Bebb**	Try	
			Half-time			
			6 - 6	**D.I.E.Bebb**	Try	

POINTS:

J.M.Ranson	3 points	(6)		**D.I.E.Bebb**	6 points
D.G.Perry	3 points	(3)			

MATCH COMMENTARY:

Five changes, four in the pack, was the result of the dismal showing against the All Blacks and all appeared to be justified when England found themselves six points up in as many minutes through two tries both scored directly from breaks by Phil Horrocks-Taylor on the blind side, neither of which John Willcox could convert. Gradually, Wales recovered and Dewi Bebb scored a try in his corner before half-time. But a lead of three points at half-time did not seem to be enough. Wales tried to turn up the pace in the second half and although they never looked really convincing, Bebb crossed for his second try when a sliced drop goal attempt form Dai Watkins bounced awkwardly for Malcolm Phillips and the resultant confusion allowed Ken Jones to scoop up a loose ball and send Bebb away. It was an entertaining game between two teams who seemed willing to attack and run with the ball in hand at every available opportunity. As the tension increased, John Willcox missed a relatively easy penalty opportunity, and in the dying seconds Graham Hodgson missed from twenty yards right in front of the posts. So, the draw was an appropriate result. Dewi Bebb became the second Welshman to score two tries at Twickenham, Ken Jones being the first in 1952, and Bebb had also scored two against England at Cardiff three years previously. England have now played sixteen successive matches at Twickenham in the Five Nations Championship without defeat.

76th match   **ENGLAND 5 pts**   **v**   **IRELAND 18 pts**

	Caps					Caps		
15	14th	J.G.Willcox (Capt)	(Harlequins)	.	17th	T.J.Kiernan		(Cork Constitution)
14	5th & last	A.M.Underwood	(Exeter)	.	6th	P.J.Casey		(UC Dublin)
13	23rd	M.S.Phillips	(Fylde)	.	11th	J.C.Walsh		(UC Cork)
12	22nd	M.P.Weston	(Durham City)	.	7th	M.K.Flynn		(Wanderers)
11	5th	J.M.Ranson	(Rosslyn Park)	.	2nd	J.J.Fortune		(Clontarf)
10	1st	T.J.Brophy	(Liverpool)	.	1st	C.M.H.Gibson		(Cambridge Univ)
9	10th	S.J.S.Clarke	(Cambridge Univ)	.	8th	J.C.Kelly		(UC Dublin)
1	27th	C.R.Jacobs	(Northampton)	.	2nd	M.P.O'Callaghan		(London Irish)
2	8th	H.O.Godwin	(Coventry)	.	25th	A.R.Dawson		(Wanderers)
3	7th	N.J.Drake-Lee	(Cambridge Univ)	.	8th	R.J.McLoughlin		(Gosforth)
4	8th	A.M.Davis	(Torquay Athletic)	.	10th	W.J.McBride		(Ballymena)
5	1st	C.M.Payne	(Harlequins)	.	27th	W.A.Mulcahy (Capt)		(Bective Rangers)
6	16th	D.P.Rogers	(Bedford)	.	5th	E.P.McGuire		(UC Galway)
7	2nd	P.J.Ford	(Gloucester)	.	20th	N.A.A.Murphy		(Cork Constitution)
8	8th	D.G.Perry	(Bedford)	.	16th	M.G.Culliton		(Wanderers)

Referee: D.G.Walters   (Wales)

SCORERS:

			0 - 3	N.A.A.Murphy	Try
			Half-time		
D.P.Rogers	Try	(2nd)	3 - 3		
J.G.Willcox	Conversion		5 - 3		
			5 - 6	M.K.Flynn	Try
			5 - 8	T.J.Kiernan	Conversion
			5 - 11	P.J.Casey	Try
			5 - 13	T.J.Kiernan	Conversion
			5 - 16	M.K.Flynn	Try
			5 - 18	T.J.Kiernan	Conversion

POINTS:

D.P.Rogers	3 points	(6)	M.K.Flynn	6 points
J.G.Willcox	2 points	(17)	T.J.Kiernan	6 points
			P.J.Casey and N.A.A.Murphy	3 points each

MATCH COMMENTARY:

Another five changes, one positional, to the England XV failed to improve England's performance against an Irish side inspired by a young Cambridge undergraduate at fly-half, of whom much more was to be heard in the future.   England were one try down at half-time, and they fought back well to level and go ahead through a splendid try by Budge Rogers converted by John Willcox. England almost scored again when Colin Payne was brought down inches from the Irish line. Ireland then launched a series of devastating attacks, scored three tries, all of them converted and England were swept aside. Ireland achieved, and merited, their first victory at Twickenham since 1938. This was said, by those present, to have been the most fluid match seen at Twickenham in recent years. Indeed, both Five Nations matches this season have been perfect advertisements for the game, with four tries in the Welsh match and five in this, and no penalty goals in either ! But joy was hardly unconfined, for England had not lost a Five Nations match at Twickenham for eight years, since Wales won in 1956, and this was the highest Five Nations margin of defeat ever at Twickenham and the highest points total against since 1938.

39th match   **ENGLAND   6 pts   v   FRANCE   3 pts**

	Caps					Caps		
15	15th	J.G.Willcox	(Harlequins)	.	13th	C.Lacaze	(Angouleme)
14	4th	R.W.Hosen	(Northampton)	.	6th	J.Gachassin	(Lourdes)
13	24th	M.S.Phillips	(Fylde)	.	7th	J.Pique	(Pau)
12	23rd	M.P.Weston	(Durham City)	.	39th	A.Boniface	(Mont-de-Marsan)
11	6th	J.M.Ranson	(Rosslyn Park)	.	14th	C.Darrouy	(Mont-de-Marsan)
10	2nd	T.J.Brophy	(Liverpool)	.	1st & only	J-C.Hiquet	(Agen)
9	4th	S.R.Smith	(Richmond)	.	4th	J-C.Lasserre	(Dax)
1	28th	C.R.Jacobs (Capt)	(Northampton)	.	2nd & last	J-B.Amestoy	(Mont-de-Marsan)
2	9th	H.O.Godwin	(Coventry)	.	22nd & last	J.de Gregorio	(Grenoble)
3	1st	D.F.B.Wrench	(Harlequins)	.	3rd & last	J.Bayardon	(Chalon)
4	9th	A.M.Davis	(Torquay Athletic)	.	3rd	B.Dauga	(Mont-de-Marsan)
5	2nd	C.M.Payne	(Harlequins)	.	5th	J.le Droff	(Auch)
6	17th	D.P.Rogers	(Bedford)	.	3rd	A.Herrero	(Toulon)
7	3rd	P.J.Ford	(Gloucester)	.	46th	M.Crauste	(Lourdes)
8	1st	T.G.A.H.Peart	(Hartlepool Rovers)	.	8th & last	J.Fabre (Capt)	(Beziers)

Referee: D.G.Walters   (Wales)

SCORERS: R.W.Hosen   Penalty Goal   3 - 0
                                                       3 - 3   C.Darrouy   Try
                                                       Half-time
              M.S.Phillips   Try   (5th & last) 6 - 3

POINTS: M.S.Phillips   3 points   (15)   C.Darrouy   3 points
              R.W.Hosen   3 points   (14)

MATCH COMMENTARY:
Another four changes to the team seemed to have found the right combination, at least for this match. The change of Captain had little visible effect, but the apparent folly of placing a player out of position in an International match, on this occasion, was an outstanding success. Roger Hosen had an excellent match kicking an early penalty goal and giving Malcolm Phillips the scoring pass for a fine try. He could have provoked another kind of revolution in France had he landed two penalty goal attempts from fifty yards, both of which went desperately close. The French had been in disarray all season, having drawn with Romania and lost to Scotland and New Zealand, and could not not cope with sound English forward play, in which Godwin took six strikes against the head. However, it was England's only win of the season, but it must be said that this was a poor French side. After the match, a large crowd of French supporters gathered in front of the Committee box and shouted for the dismissal of the French selectors. This would never have happened at Twickenham !!

79th match

71st Calcutta Cup

ENGLAND   6 pts   v   SCOTLAND   15 pts

	Caps				Caps		
15	16th & last	J.G.Willcox	(Harlequins)	.	5th	S.Wilson	(Oxford University)
14	5th	R.W.Hosen	(Northampton)	.	9th	C.Elliott	(Langholm)
13	25th & last	M.S.Phillips	(Fylde)	.	4th	B.C.Henderson	(Edinburgh W'ndrs)
12	24th	M.P.Weston	(Durham City)	.	21st	I.H.P.Laughland	(London Scottish)
11	7th & last	J.M.Ranson	(Rosslyn Park)	.	23rd	G.D.Stevenson	(Hawick)
10	3rd	T.J.Brophy	(Liverpool)	.	2nd	D.H.Chisholm	(Melrose)
9	5th & last	S.R.Smith	(Richmond)	.	5th	A.J.Hastie	(Melrose)
1	29th & last	C.R.Jacobs (Capt)	(Northampton)	.	6th	J.B.Neill (Capt)	(Edinburgh Acad)
2	10th	H.O.Godwin	(Coventry)	.	31st	N.S.Bruce	(London Scottish)
3	2nd & last	D.F.B.Wrench	(Harlequins)	.	23rd	D.M.D.Rollo	(Howe of Fife)
4	10th	A.M.Davis	(Torquay Athletic)	.	5th	P.C.Brown	(West of Scotland)
5	3rd	C.M.Payne	(Harlequins)	.	14th	M.J.Campbell-Lamerton	(London Scottish)
6	18th	D.P.Rogers	(Bedford)	.	6th	J.P.Fisher	(Royal HSFP)
7	4th & last	P.J.Ford	(Gloucester)	.	8th	R.J.C.Glasgow	(Dunfermline)
8	2nd & last	T.G.A.H.Peart	(Hartlepool Rovers)	.	5th	J.W.Telfer	(Melrose)

Referee: R.C.Williams   (Ireland)

SCORERS:

			0 - 3	R.J.C.Glasgow	Try	
			0 - 5	S.Wilson	Conversion	
			0 - 8	N.S.Bruce	Try	
			0 - 10	S.Wilson	Conversion	
			Half-time			
R.W.Hosen	Penalty Goal		3 - 10			
			3 - 13	J.W.Telfer	Try	
			3 - 15	S.Wilson	Conversion	
D.P.Rogers	Try	(3rd & last)	6 - 15			

POINTS:

D.P.Rogers	3 points	(9)	S.Wilson	6 points	
R.W.Hosen	3 points	(17)	R.J.C.Glasgow	3 points	
			N.S.Bruce	3 points	
			J.W.Telfer	3 points	

MATCH COMMENTARY:

England fielded the same XV which had beaten France, but found that they were up against very different opposition in this match. The Scottish forwards, to a man, gave their English counterparts a torrid time and created many scoring opportunities for their own backs whilst putting the English backs under enormous pressure, but all four tries were scored by forwards. After half an hour, the England effort appeared to be beginning to wilt, and sure enough Scotland scored two tries before half-time. Roger Hosen's successful penalty attempt early in the second half failed to rally England, and Scottish forward power again paid off when Jim Telfer went over for their third try. The push-over try at the end, scored by Budge Rogers, was certainly to England's credit, but they were soundly beaten amidst much jubilation at Murrayfield. Scotland took the Calcutta Cup for the first time since 1950, when they last beat England at home, and in sharing the title with Wales, finished at the top of the Table for the first time since 1938. England had to settle for a share of third place with France.

SUMMARY OF THE SEASON - 1963 - 64:

Not a good season for England at all, and another disappointing one because, following last seasons successes and with the invaluable but onerous experience of the first short Antipodean tour the previous summer, there were hopes that this could be an exceptional season for England. But, yet again, it was not to be.

The Fifth All Blacks, under Wilson Whineray, probably had as much to do with this disappointment as anybody. In December, the All Blacks had beaten Ireland by the odd point in eleven, each side scoring a try, and had followed that by beating Wales by six points to nil, and, in so doing, failed to score a try. On that basis, and mindful of the fact that England had lost by only three points in the second Test on the recent tour to New Zealand, there was an optimism that a potentially outstanding season could be prefaced by a famous win over the redoubtable All Blacks for only the second time. There were six changes from the side which had played in that second Test, amongst them the return of John Willcox and Jim Roberts, both of whom had been unable to tour, and John Owen restored to fitness. In the event, All Black forward power proved too much in all respects for England and they suffered their worst defeat ever at Twickenham and provided their opponents with the highest Test winning margin of their tour. Five changes were made for the first Five Nations match against Wales at Twickenham, and although it was an entertaining game with four tries scored, the distribution of those tries, two to each side, was not to the selectors', or the supporters', liking. Accordingly, five more changes, one of them positional, were made for the visit of the Irish, and this time five tries were scored in an excellent match, but Ireland scored four of them. Another four changes for the trip to Paris seemed to have struck the right formula, for the only win of the season was recorded, and at Stade Colombes, but the same team could do nothing to halt the rampaging Scots at Murrayfield. England had used twenty seven players in the season's five matches, twenty-three in the four Five Nations games and seven new caps were awarded, four of whom were to gain only two caps each.

England were flattered to finish equal third with France in the Championship Table and their try and points scoring record was significantly worse than that of France. England scored five tries and conceded ten; France scored eight and conceded five. For total points, England's record was 23 for and 42 against; and France 41 for and 33 against. This year, although at the time unrecognised, was the first in a long succession of years during which England never won more than two of their Championship games in any one season, and it was to be sixteen years before the Championship Title was to be won again - by Bill Beaumont and his 1980 Grand Slam side.

Fourteen players played their last International match during the course of this season. Ron Jacobs, England's most capped prop with twenty-nine caps, retired to his farm, and later became an England selector, as did Malcolm Phillips, with twenty-five caps, who also served on the Barbarians Committee and had scored a try on his debut against Australia in 1958; Jim Roberts, who had scored two tries on his debut against Wales in 1960, in all earned eighteen caps. John Willcox, sixteen caps, was the most proficient, reliable and fearless of all England's post-war full-backs. He was a British Lion, and, at Oxford, had won, in addition to his four rugby blues, a Blue for boxing at heavyweight; Stan Hodgson earned eleven caps and played on with Durham City for many years after his International career was over; Phil Horrocks-Taylor would probably have won many more than his nine caps had his career not coincided with that of Bev Risman and Richard Sharp; John Ranson, a teacher, who scored a try on his debut in the first Test of the 1963 tour to New Zealand, gained seven caps; Martin Underwood, a PE teacher, no relation to the latterday Underwoods, gained four of his five caps on the wing for England, but played in the centre for his club, Northampton; Stephen Smith won five caps and taught at Harrow before he decided to become a missionary in India with his wife; Vic Marriott, with the Army Educational Corps, won four caps, as did Peter Ford who did not win his first cap until he was thirty-one, and who became an England selector; Roger Sangwin, an architect, David Wrench, a schoolteacher and Tony Peart each earned their two caps during the course of this season. With fourteen players having reached the end of their International careers, it is to be expected that there will be an influx of new caps, and therefore inexperience, into the England ranks next season which may not augur well for England's Championship prospects, in the immediate future, at any rate.

FIVE NATIONS CHAMPIONSHIP TABLE:

Won: **Nothing.**

		Played	Won	Lost	Drawn	Points: For	Against	Tries: For	Against	Title Points
1 =	Scotland	4	3	1	0	34	20	6	3	6
1 =	Wales	4	2	0	2	43	26	8	4	6
3 =	France	4	1	2	1	41	33	8	5	3
3 =	**ENGLAND**	4	1	2	1	23	42	5	10	3
5	Ireland	4	1	3	0	33	53	5	10	2

Home Games: drew wirh Wales 6 - 6, (two tries each); lost to Ireland 5 - 18, (one try to four)

Away Games: beat France 6 - 3, (one try each); lost to scvotland 6 - 15, (one try to three)

70th match   **ENGLAND   3 pts**   v   **WALES   14 pts**

	Caps					Caps		
15	6th	D.Rutherford	(Gloucester)	.		1st	T.G.Price	(Llanelli)
14	1st	E.L.Rudd	(Oxford University)	.		4th	S.J.Watkins	(Newport)
13	1st	D.W.A.Rosser	(Cambridge Univ)	.		4th	S.J.Dawes	(London Welsh)
12	1st	G.P.Frankcom	(Cambridge Univ)	.		2nd	J.R.Uzzell	(Newport)
11	1st & only	C.P.Simpson	(Harlequins)	.		25th	D.I.E.Bebb	(Swansea)
10	4th	T.J.Brophy	(Liverpool)	.		11th	D.Watkins	(Newport)
9	9th & last	J.E.Williams	(Sale)	.		11th	D.C.T.Rowlands (Capt)	(Pontypool)
1	1st	A.L.Horton	(Blackheath)	.		10th	D.Williams	(Ebbw Vale)
2	1st	S.B.Richards	(Richmond)	.		11th	N.R.Gale	(Llanelli)
3	8th & last	N.J.Drake-lee	(Leicester)	.		1st	R.Waldron	(Neath)
4	7th	J.E.Owen	(Coventry)	.		14th	B.Price	(Newport)
5	2nd & last	R.E.Rowell	(Leicester)	.		11th	B.E.Thomas	(Neath)
6	19th	D.P.Rogers	(Bedford)	.		4th	G.J.Prothero	(Bridgend)
7	1st	N.Silk	(Harlequins)	.		19th	H.J.Morgan	(Abertillery)
8	9th	D.G.Perry (Capt)	(Bedford)	.		16th	A.E.I.Pask	(Abertillery)

Referee: K.D.Kelleher   (Ireland)

SCORERS:

			0 - 3	D.Watkins	Drop Goal
			Half-time		
			0 - 6	S.J.Watkins	Try
			0 - 8	T.G.Price	Conversion
D.Rutherford	Penalty Goal		3 - 8		
			3 - 11	H.J.Morgan	Try
			3 - 14	S.J.Watkins	Try

POINTS:

D.Rutherford	3 points	(22)	S.J.Watkins	6 points
			H.J.Morgan	3 points
			D.Watkins	3 points
			T.G.Price	2 points

MATCH COMMENTARY:

The selectors tried to blend experience with youth in recalling Don Rutherford and John Williams to join the seven new caps in making the trip to Cardiff to meet Wales. The rain was very heavy and so was the pitch and England could not adapt to the conditions or to the new laws which had been framed to encourage more open play.

David Watkins, on the other hand, was untroubled by the mud underfoot and exploited the new rules cleverly to provide Wales with three good tries to England's none. Terry Price, another astonishingly talented Welsh prodigy made his debut in, and a substantial impression on, this match. Would that England had the facility that Max Boyce was later to dub "the fly-half factory" in which to rear such talent !!

England's recall of John Williams at scrum-half after a nine year break and eleven years after his first cap against France in 1954, was not an unqualified success, nor could anybody seriously expect it to be. Such selections can hardly be expected to improve England's mediocre performance of last season in the Five Nations Championship. On the other hand, Don Rutherford's recall, four years after his previous cap, was successful, and for him, this was the first of a further ten International caps, nine of them successive.

77th match   **ENGLAND 0 pts**   **v**   **IRELAND 5 pts**

	Caps					Caps		
15	7th	D.Rutherford	(Gloucester)	.		20th	T.J.Kiernan	(Cork Constitution)
14	2nd	E.L.Rudd	(Oxford University)	.		11th	P.J.Casey	(Lansdowne)
13	2nd	D.W.A.Rosser	(Cambridge Univ)	.		12th	M.K.Flynn	(Wanderers)
12	2nd	G.P.Frankcom	(Cambridge Univ)	.		5th	K.J.Houston	(Oxford University)
11	1st	P.W.Cook	(Richmond)	.		1st	P.J.McGrath	(UC Cork)
10	5th	T.J.Brophy	(Liverpool)	.		6th	C.M.H.Gibson	(Cambridge Univ)
9	11th	S.J.S.Clarke	(Blackheath)	.		2nd	R.M.Young	(Queen's U Belfast)
1	2nd	A.L.Horton	(Blackheath)	.		2nd	S.McHale	(Lansdowne)
2	2nd	S.B.Richards	(Richmond)	.		2nd	K.W.Kennedy	(Queen's U Belfast)
3	10th	P.E.Judd	(Coventry)	.		11th	R.J.McLoughlin (Capt)	(Gosforth)
4	8th	J.E.Owen	(Coventry)	.		14th	W.J.McBride	(Ballymena)
5	4th	C.M.Payne	(Harlequins)	.		32nd	W.A.Mulcahy	(Bective Rangers)
6	20th	D.P.Rogers	(Bedford)	.		2nd	M.G.Doyle	(UC Dublin)
7	2nd	N.Silk	(Harlequins)	.		25th	N.A.A.Murphy	(Cork Constitution)
8	10th	D.G.Perry (Capt)	(Bedford)	.		2nd	R.A.Lamont	(Instonians)

Referee: H.B.Laidlaw   (Scotland)

SCORERS:

	0 - 0		
	Half-time		
	0 - 3	R.A.Lamont	Try
	0 - 5	T.J.Kiernan	Conversion

POINTS:

	R.A.Lamont	3 points
	T.J.Kiernan	2 points

MATCH COMMENTARY:

Having made four changes after the disappointing performance in Cardiff four weeks previously, England faced different but equally hostile conditions with a very strong ice-cold wind, and again could not adapt as well as the opposition. Ireland's dominance was not overwhelming as had been Wales', but England were outplayed and well beaten. Young and Gibson at half-back for Ireland, controlled the game, and the darting opportunism of Tom Brophy was never apparent at any time, and he was uncharacteristically indecisive. Even in the set pieces, England appeared hesitant and as a result, Clarke and Brophy were continually exposed to the marauding Irish back row. But the Irish defence was the team's stoutest quality, with Tom Kiernan, as ever, leading by example. It was because the defence by the whole team, and in all areas of the field was so solid and uncompromising, that England were prevented from playing any form of constructive rugby. Thus, for the second successive year, England were unable to score at Lansdowne Road. In the ten games between the two countries in Dublin, in the last twenty years, England have failed to score four times, have won only twice, and have scored only thirty-seven points in all.

40th match   ## ENGLAND   9 pts   v   FRANCE   6 pts

	Caps					Caps		
15	8th	D.Rutherford	(Gloucester)	.	11th	P.Dedieu	(Beziers)
14	1st	A.W.Hancock	(Northampton)	.	15th	J.Gachassin	(Lourdes)
13	3rd	D.W.A.Rosser	(Cambridge Univ)	.	28th	G.Boniface	(Mont-de-Marsan)
12	3rd	G.P.Frankcom	(Cambridge Univ)	.	16th	J.Pique	(Pau)
11	2nd & last	P.W.Cook	(Richmond)	.	23rd	C.Darrouy	(Mont-de-Marsan)
10	25th	M.P.Weston	(Durham City)	.	6th & last	J.P.Capdouze	(Pau)
9	12th	S.J.S.Clarke	(Blackheath)	.	5th & last	C.Laborde	(Racing Club)
1	3rd	A.L.Horton	(Blackheath)	.	9th	A.Gruarin	(Toulon)
2	3rd	S.B.Richards	(Richmond)	.	5th	Y.Menthiller	(Romans)
3	11th	P.E.Judd	(Coventry)	.	11th	J-C.Berejnoi	(Tulle)
4	9th	J.E.Owen	(Coventry)	.	12th	B.Dauga	(Mont-de-Marsan)
5	5th	C.M.Payne	(Harlequins)	.	6th	W.Spanghero	(Narbonne)
6	21st	D.P.Rogers	(Bedford)	.	4th	J-J.Rupert	(Tyrosse)
7	3rd	N.Silk	(Harlequins)	.	55th	M.Crauste (Capt)	(Lourdes)
8	11th	D.G.Perry (Capt)	(Bedford)	.	12th	A.Herrero	(Toulon)

Referee: R.W.Gilliland   (Ireland)

SCORERS:	D.Rutherford	Penalty Goal		3 - 0		
			3 - 3	P.Dedieu	Penalty Goal
			Half-time		
			3 - 6	C.Darrouy	Try
C.M.Payne	Try	(1st & only)	6 - 6		
D.Rutherford	Penalty Goal		9 - 6		

POINTS: | D.Rutherford | 6 points | (28) | C.Darrouy | 3 points |
|---|---|---|---|---|
| C.M.Payne | 3 points | (3) | P.Dedieu | 3 points |

MATCH COMMENTARY:

The selectors decided to go into this game against France with the same pack, and made only two changes in the back division, bringing Mike Weston back at fly-half in preference to Tom Brophy and putting Andy Hancock on the wing in place of Edward Rudd. Against all expectations and the form book, England managed to contain and subdue a mighty and experienced French pack. This was done to such good effect that Steve Richards, the Richmond hooker, said to be the fastest striker in the game, and earning only his third cap, was able to take ten strikes against the head. Payne's try matched that of Darrouy and Don Rutherford's accurate place kicking enabled England to win the match. This was a much more competent, though not spectacular, English performance than had been seen for some considerable time. Simon Clarke was subjected to much pressure following his recall for the match in Dublin and his performance there, but the selectors had retained him and their faith was amply justified as he revelled in the possession provided by the pack and his control of the match really decided the result.

France's record at Twickenham was rapidly deteriorating, they had not won there for ten years, and had won only twice in eleven visits. This was only England's second win in the last eleven matches.

80th match   **ENGLAND** **3 pts**   **v**   **SCOTLAND** **3 pts**

72nd Calcutta Cup

	Caps					Caps		
15	9th	D.Rutherford	(Gloucester)	.		8th	S.Wilson (Capt)	(London Scottish)
14	3rd	E.L.Rudd	(Oxford University)	.		3rd	D.J.Whyte	(Edinburgh W'ndrs)
13	4th	D.W.A.Rosser	(Cambridge Univ)	.		8th	B.C.Henderson	(Edinburgh W'ndrs)
12	4th & last	G.P.Frankcom	(Cambridge Univ)	.		25th	I.H.P.Laughland	(London Scottish)
11	2nd	A.W.Hancock	(Northampton)	.		2nd	W.D.Jackson	(Hawick)
10	26th	M.P.Weston	(Durham City)	.		3rd	D.H.Chisholm	(Melrose)
9	13th & last	S.J.S.Clarke	(Blackheath)	.		6th	A.J.Hastie	(Melrose)
1	4th	A.L.Horton	(Blackheath)	.		3rd	N.Suddon	(Hawick)
2	4th	S.B.Richards	(Richmond)	.		4th	F.A.L.Laidlaw	(Melrose)
3	12th	P.E.Judd	(Coventry)	.		27th	D.M.D.Rollo	(Howe of Fife)
4	10th	J.E.Owen	(Coventry)	.		3rd	P.K.Stagg	(Sale)
5	6th	C.M.Payne	(Harlequins)	.		18th	M.J.Campbell-Lamerton	(London Scottish)
6	22nd	D.P.Rogers	(Bedford)	.		10th	J.P.Fisher	(London Scottish)
7	4th & last	N.Silk	(Harlequins)	.		2nd	D.Grant	(Hawick)
8	12th	D.G.Perry (Capt)	(Bedford)	.		7th	P.C.Brown	(West of Scotland)

Referee: D.G.Walters   (Wales)

SCORERS:

				0 - 0			
				Half-time			
				0 - 3	D.H.Chisholm	Drop Goal
	A.W.Hancock	Try	(1st & only)	3 - 3		

POINTS: A.W.Hancock   3 points   (3)   D.H.Chisholm   3 points

MATCH COMMENTARY:

The only change to the team which had beaten France was the return of Rudd, and the switch of wings for Hancock to accomodate him. Mike Weston showed again his fine tactical sense at fly-half, but the match was controlled, not for the first time this season, by the opposition half-backs, this time the Melrose pair, Hastie and Chisholm. The first half was hard, clean and featureless and the kicking of both fly-halves inhibited running rugby and was leading to stalemate. As the second half progressed, England had to pull out all the stops to keep the Scots out. Chisholm's drop goal was the only score of the match when very late in the game, Andy Hancock, "....unheralded and unsung galloped into history". Scotland were attacking, as they had for most of the second half, when Mike Weston mis-kicked a clearance and Whyte, the Scottish wing, attempted to run the ball back but he was tackled and the ball went loose. Mike Weston picked it up and Andy Hancock accepted his optimistic pass well inside his own 25, and set off down the touch-line, stumbling along the way, and avoiding the cover defence by a hair's-breadth. He seemed to realise that a try was possible only after he crossed the half-way line, in front of the Queen in the Royal Box, and resolutely fought his way against fatigue and weariness for the remainder of his magnificent ninety yard run to score one of the most amazing tries ever seen at Twickenham. The roar of the crowd encouraging him along the way could have been heard in Edinburgh, mingled with the agonised groans of those Scots present, but Andy Hancock claimed not to have heard a thing.

This try lifted England into fourth place in the Championship table, and consigned the Wooden Spoon to a brave and unfortunate Scotland.

SUMMARY OF THE SEASON - 1964 - 65:

There was not much, as they say, to laugh at during the course of this season apart from a workman-like win over France and, of course, the unanticipated drama of Andy Hancock's match-saving try in the closing minutes of the Calcutta Cup match at Twickenham - at least the spectators had something positive to talk about in the close season.

For the opening match of the season at Cardiff, only two of the side who played in that memorable match at the end of the previous season were called upon to pull on the white jersey again, Tom Brophy and Budge Rogers. Of the others, seven were new caps - all the three-quarter line, two of the front row and a flanker, and David Perry was given the Captaincy. The recall of Don Rutherford at full-back was a masterstroke and he played throughout the season giving substance to the defence and immense support to the younger backs in front of him. John Williams, recalled at scrum-half nine years after his previous cap against France in 1956 was on a hiding to nothing as soon as his name was written on the team sheet. He had a sorry afternoon and like the rest of the England side, could not adapt to the difficult conditions in which the match was played. The team with four changes and another new cap on the wing, arrived in Dublin to find the weather different but no more kind than it had been in Cardiff with a very strong and very cold north wind. Again, England failed to rise to the occasion largely because, with possession shared evenly, the Irish back row completely negated the activities and indeed the presence of Brophy and Clarke at half-back for England and prevented them doing anything constructive at all. For the first match at Twickenham against France, the selectors recalled Mike Weston who had gained all his earlier caps in the centre, at fly-half. The efforts of the unchanged pack in providing a regular flow of quality possession, and Weston's tactical kicking saw France off with Steve Richards taking ten strikes against the head ! For the Scotland match, essentially for the Wooden Spoon rather than for the Calcutta Cup, the same pack again served the side well, but the Scottish tackling and defence generally, was demoniac, until that is, Andy Hancock got the ball - and the rest is history. Strange though, that the selectors had switched wings and put Hancock on the left wing to accomodate Edward Rudd on the right. Strange too that the two finest tries seen at Twickenham since Prince Obolensky made his mark against New Zealand in 1936, should be scored within two years of each other nearly thirty years later, and should both be against Scotland. The Scots must have been wondering just what they had to do to win at Twickenham where their efforts had been thwarted since 1938.

The outcome of that drama was that Scotland took the Wooden Spoon and England were place fourth in the Championship table having scored only two tries and fifteen points in the four matches. Only twenty-one players were used during the season, and nine new caps were awarded. The Captaincy of David Perry, the ex-paratrooper, could not be faulted, and the fact that he failed to inspire his charges in the two games in Cardiff and Dublin says much more about their lack of ability to respond rather than the inadequacy of Perry's exhortations, or, indeed, his example.

Eight players were to play no more for England after the season's close. Simon Clarke had earned thirteen caps, ten of them when he was still an undergraduate at Cambridge University, including three on the 1963 England tour to New Zealand and Australia; as well as two rugby Blues he also played cricket for the University. John Williams, who could really have done without his ninth cap this season, was a British Lion in South Africa in 1955, although Dickie Jeeps kept him out of the Test side, and was first capped in 1954; Nick Drake-Lee was only twenty years old when he gained his first cap at prop against Wales in 1963, and was only twenty-two when his eight-cap International career came to an end; Geoff Frankcom, with three Cambridge Blues and Nick Silk, with three Oxford Blues, each earned four caps. Early in the following season Nick Silk suffered a severe injury to his knee which finished his rugby playing career at a stroke. The other three players not to appear for England again were Peter Cook, an Engineering student form Richmond with two caps, the Leicester schoolmaster, Bob Rowell, also with two caps, and Colin Simpson whose only cap was earned when he was a cadet at Sandhurst.

FIVE NATIONS CHAMPIONSHIP TABLE:

Won: **Nothing.**

		Played	Won	Lost	Drawn	Points: For	Against	Tries: For	Against	Title Points
1	Wales	4	3	1	0	55	45	10	5	6
2 =	France	4	2	1	1	47	33	10	7	5
2 =	Ireland	4	2	1	1	32	23	6	3	5
4	**ENGLAND**	4	1	2	1	15	28	2	5	3
5	Scotland	4	0	3	1	29	49	2	10	1

Home Games: beat France 9 - 6, (one try each); drew with Scotland 3 - 3, (one try to nil).

Away Games: lost to Wales 3 - 14 (no tries to three); lost to Ireland 0 - 5, (no tries to one).

71st match   **ENGLAND   6 pts**   v   **WALES   11 pts**

	Caps				Caps		
15	10th	D.Rutherford	(Gloucester)	.	5th	T.G.Price	(Llanelli)
14	4th	E.L.Rudd	(Liverpool)	.	8th	S.J.Watkins	(Newport)
13	1st	T.G.Arthur	(Wasps)	.	11th	D.K.Jones	(Cardiff)
12	5th & last	D.W.A.Rosser	(Wasps)	.	6th	K.Bradshaw	(Bridgend)
11	1st	K.F.Savage	(Northampton)	.	1st	L.Davies	(Bridgend)
10	6th	T.J.Brophy	(Liverpool)	.	15th	D.Watkins	(Newport)
9	1st & only	J.Spencer	(Harlequins)	.	1st	A.R.Lewis	(Abertillery)
1	13th	P.E.Judd	(Coventry)	.	14th	D.Williams	(Ebbw Vale)
2	1st	J.V.Pullin	(Bristol)	.	15th	N.R.Gale	(Llanelli)
3	1st	D.L.Powell	(Northampton)	.	1st	D.J.LLoyd	(Bridgend)
4	7th	C.M.Payne	(Harlequins)	.	18th	B.Price	(Newport)
5	11th	A.M.Davis	(Devonport Services)	.	12th	B.E.Thomas	(Neath)
6	23rd	D.P.Rogers (Capt)	(Bedford)	.	8th	G.J.Prothero	(Bridgend)
7	1st	R.B.Taylor	(Northampton)	.	23rd	H.J.Morgan	(Abertillery)
8	13th	D.G.Perry	(Bedford)	.	20th	A.E.I.Pask (Capt)	(Abertillery)

Referee: R.W.Gilliland   (Ireland)

SCORERS:

			0 - 3	T.G.Price	Penalty Goal
D.Rutherford	Penalty Goal		3 - 3		
			Half-time		
			3 - 6	T.G.Price	Penalty Goal
			3 - 9	A.E.I.Pask	Try
			3 - 11	T.G.Price	Conversion
D.G.Perry	Try	(2nd & last)	6 - 11		

POINTS:

D.G.Perry	3 points	(6)	T.G.Price	8 points
D.Rutherford	3 points	(31)	A.E.I.Pask	3 points

MATCH COMMENTARY:

There were six new caps, and eight changes from the side which had just managed to draw with Scotland - thanks to Andy Hancock - in the previous match at Twickenham, and all the omens pointed to a dour forward struggle on a grey winter afternoon. England started tentatively, and the forwards in particular never seemed sure of themselves and this lack of confidence inhibited Jeremy Spencer and thus Tom Brophy. On the other hand, the Welsh, rarely looking confident initially, grew in stature as they watched England continually choose the wrong options and hesitiate. By half-time the score was level but Don Rutherford was having an agonising day in missing two penalty goal attempts and putting a drop goal wide, but, more ominously, the Welsh pack were in the ascendent and English heads were down. Early in the second half, as if to underline his pack's superiority, Alun Pask scored a splendid try in the corner, well converted by Terry Price who followed this with another penalty goal. England struggled to compete and failed, although the injured Perry, even though deprived of the Captaincy, scored his try, Rutherford missed the conversion and another penalty attempt, and England faded away. The England pack were soundly beaten, especially in the second half, and for the hapless Jeremy Spencer, his first cap turned into a nightmare, from which he must think that he will never emerge because the Selectors decided that he had been largely responsible for England's demise and refused to pick him again. This was only England's second defeat in the last twenty Five Nations matches at Twickenham.

78th match   **ENGLAND   6 pts   v   IRELAND   6 pts**

	Caps					Caps		
15	11th	D.Rutherford	(Gloucester)	.	25th	T.J.Kiernan	(Cork Constitution)
14	5th	E.L.Rudd	(Liverpool)	.	9th	W.R.Hunter	(CIYMS)
13	2nd & last	T.G.Arthur	(Wasps)	.	17th	M.K.Flynn	(Wanderers)
12	1st	C.W.McFadyean	(Moseley)	.	1st	F.P.K.Bresnihan	(UC Dublin)
11	2nd	K.F.Savage	(Northampton)	.	6th	P.J.McGrath	(UC Cork)
10	7th	T.J.Brophy	(Liverpool)	.	11th	C.M.H.Gibson	(Cambridge Univ)
9	1st	R.C.Ashby	(Wasps)	.	7th	R.M.Young	(Queen's U Belfast)
1	14th	P.E.Judd	(Coventry)	.	7th	S.MacHale	(Lansdowne)
2	1st	W.T.Treadwell	(Wasps)	.	7th	K.W.Kennedy	(CIYMS)
3	2nd	D.L.Powell	(Northampton)	.	16th	R.J.McLoughlin (Capt)	(Gosforth)
4	8th	C.M.Payne	(Harlequins)	.	2nd	M.G.Molloy	(UC Galway)
5	11th	J.E.Owen	(Coventry)	.	19th	W.J.McBride	(Ballymena)
6	24th	D.P.Rogers (Capt)	(Bedford)	.	7th	M.G.Doyle	(Cambridge Univ)
7	1st	J.R.H.Greenwood	(Waterloo)	.	30th	N.A.A.Murphy	(Cork Constitution)
8	14th	D.G.Perry	(Bedford)	.	5th	R.A.Lamont	(Instonians)

Referee: B.Marie   (France)

SCORERS:

J.R.H.Greenwood	Try	(1st & only)	3 - 0			
			3 - 3	T.J.Kiernan	Penalty Goal
D.Rutherford	Penalty Goal		6 - 3			
			Half-time			
			6 - 6	P.J.McGrath	Try

POINTS:

J.R.H.Greenwood	3 points	(3)	T.J.Kiernan	3 points
D.Rutherford	3 points	(34)	P.J.McGrath	3 points

MATCH COMMENTARY:

Five changes in all, three of them in the pack, and four new caps, was the result of the Selectors' deliberations following the disappointing performance against Wales four weeks ago. The match started well for England and Dick Greenwood had the dubious pleasure of meeting those two imposters, triumph and disaster, within a few minutes in the first-half. First, following up a Brophy free-kick which Tom Kiernan failed to gather cleanly, he pounced on the loose ball and dived over to score an early try in his first International. Then, only a few minutes later he was caught off-side and Tom Kiernan levelled the score. Don Rutherford's penalty goal set the Irish back on their heels just before half-time, but there was certainly no room for complacency in the England camp. In the second half, the Irish defence held, although England never really put it to the test, and Irish persistence and cunning got McGrath in to the corner for a try to level the score, and there it remained. The eagerly anticipated confrontation between the mercurial Tom Brophy and the precocious genius of Mike Gibson unfortunately came to nothing and the match finished as another inconclusive draw - the eleventh in the last thirty six Five Nations matches.

Again, there was lack of harmony and confidence at half-back for England, where a little more authority from Tom Brophy could have exploited England's three-quarter strength to better effect. But Ashby had poor and slow service from his pack at both scrum and line-out (as had Jeremy Spencer in the previous match) and he was able to provide Brophy with very little good ball. So, England had failed to win either of their home games, and, already, the season's prospects had faded away.

This was the first Five Nations Championship match for which a French referee had been appointed.

41st match   **ENGLAND   0 pts**   v   **FRANCE   13 pts**

	Caps					Caps		
15	12th	D.Rutherford	(Gloucester)	.	18th	C.Lacaze	(Angouleme)
14	3rd & last	A.W.Hancock	(Northampton)	.	1st	B.Duprat	(Bayonne)
13	1st	R.D.Hearn	(Bedford)	.	34th	G.Boniface	(Mont-de-Marsan)
12	2nd	C.W.McFadyean	(Moseley)	.	47th	A.Boniface	(Mont-de-Marsan)
11	3rd	K.F.Savage	(Northampton)	.	28th	C.Darrouy	(Mont-de-Marsan)
10	8th & last	T.J.Brophy	(Liverpool)	.	21st	J.Gachassin	(Lourdes)
9	2nd	R.C.Ashby	(Wasps)	.	4th	L.Camberabero	(La Voulte)
1	15th	P.E.Judd	(Coventry)	.	14th	A.Gruarin	(Toulon)
2	2nd	W.T.Treadwell	(Wasps)	.	11th	J-M.Cabanier	(Montauban)
3	5th	A.L.Horton	(Blackheath)	.	17th	J-C.Berejnoi	(Tulle)
4	9th	C.M.Payne	(Harlequins)	.	3rd	E.Cester	(Toulouse)
5	12th	J.E.Owen	(Coventry)	.	12th	W.Spanghero	(Narbonne)
6	25th	D.P.Rogers (Capt)	(Bedford)	.	9th	J-J.Rupert	(Tyrosse)
7	2nd	J.R.H.Greenwood	(Waterloo)	.	61st	M.Crauste (Capt)	(Lourdes)
8	15th & last	D.G.Perry	(Bedford)	.	18th	B.Dauga	(Mont-de-Marsan)

Referee: D.G.Walters   (Wales)

SCORERS:

0 - 3	J.Gachassin	Try
0 - 5	C.Lacaze	Conversion
Half-time		
0 - 8	A.Gruarin	Try
0 - 11	A.Boniface	Try
0 - 13	C.Lacaze	Conversion

POINTS:

C.Lacaze	4 points
J.Gachassin	3 points
A.Gruarin	3 points
A.Boniface	3 points

MATCH COMMENTARY:

Three more changes were made in an attempt to stop the rot of England's already disastrous season, but to no avail. England really never looked like winning this game, primarily because they failed to score when playing with the wind in the first half. During that time, they conceded a very soft try when Gachassin, who had a magnificent match, scored a try underneath the posts without the English defence appearing to know what he was doing. In the second half, with the wind and five points, against them already, England were extremely unfortunate in that Perry, Hancock, Horton and Rogers were all injured with the former two almost immobile. France took advantage and ran the ball at every opportunity, sometimes with bewildering flair and pace linking players across the field irrespective of playing position or status, as only the French can, and it is much to the credit of the other eleven Englishmen who defended stoutly, that the scoring was limited to only two tries in that second half. It was unfortunate for England that everything went wrong, not entirely because of their own shortcomongs, just when they needed a fair slice of luck to have a hope of reversing the first half score and the season's depressing trend. This was Gwynne Walters' nineteenth and last Championship match as a referee, and as a committed advocate of open play, he could not have wished for a better display than that provided by those fifteen Frenchmen in the second half of this match.

81st match   **ENGLAND   3 pts   v   SCOTLAND   6 pts**

73rd Calcutta Cup

	Caps				Caps		
15	13th	D.Rutherford	(Gloucester)		3rd	C.F.Blaikie	(Heriot's FP)
14	6th & last	E.L.Rudd	(Liverpool)		4th	A.J.W.Hinshelwood	(London Scottish)
13	2nd	R.D.Hearn	(Bedford)		12th & last	B.C.Henderson	(Edinburgh W'ndrs)
12	3rd	C.W.McFadyean	(Moseley)		30th	I.H.P.Laughland (Capt)	(London Scottish)
11	4th	K.F.Savage	(Northampton)		8th	D.J.Whyte	(Edinburgh W'ndrs)
10	27th	M.P.Weston	(Durham City)		7th	D.H.Chisholm	(Melrose)
9	1st	T.C.Wintle	(Northampton)		11th	A.J.Hastie	(Melrose)
1	6th	A.L.Horton	(Blackheath)		4th	J.D.Macdonald	(London Scottish)
2	3rd & last	W.T.Treadwell	(Wasps)		9th	F.A.L.Laidlaw	(Melrose)
3	16th	P.E.Judd	(Coventry)		32nd	D.M.D.Rollo	(Howe of Fife)
4	10th & last	C.M.Payne	(Harlequins)		8th	P.K.Stagg	(Sale)
5	13th	J.E.Owen	(Coventry)		23rd & last	M.J.Campbell-Lamerton	(London Scottish)
6	26th	D.P.Rogers (Capt)	(Bedford)		15th	J.P.Fisher	(London Scottish)
7	3rd	J.R.H.Greenwood	(Waterloo)		7th	D.Grant	(Hawick)
8	1st	G.A.Sherriff	(Saracens)		12th	J.W.Telfer	(Melrose)

Referee: K.D.Kelleher   (Ireland)

SCORERS: 0 - 3   C.F.Blaikie   Penalty Goal
                                                  Half-time
                 C.W.McFadyean   D'p Goal (1st & only)   3 - 3
                                                  3 - 6   D.J.Whyte   Try

---

POINTS: C.W.McFadyean   3 points   (3)   D.J.Whyte   3 points
                                                                C.F.Blaikie   3 points

---

MATCH COMMENTARY:

With four changes from the team beaten by France, England had now used 26 players during the course of this season, and three different scrum-halves. The return of Mike Weston at fly-half improved England's use of the possession they obtained, but the initial tactic of putting up high balls to unnerve Colin Blaikie under the Scottish posts failed miserably as Blaikie was as solid as a rock and he had little trouble dealing with Weston's tactical kicking in other parts of the field. It was the same player who put Scotland into a three point lead at half time with a penalty kick in off the post. In the second half Colin McFadyean dropped a fine goal, but this paled into insignificance compared with Scotland's excellent winning try. The more England attacked as the game went on, the better they looked, but it was always too little, too late in the match, and too late in the season, and the sooner the season is forgotten, the better !

This had been England's poorest Five Nations performance since the war and they were rightly and firmly alone at the foot of the Five Nations Championship table, and collected the Wooden Spoon for the first time in sixteen years.   It had hardly been a sudden fall from grace, for, of the last sixteen International matches in which England have played, they have won only two, both against France, have drawn three, and have failed to score a try in five.   Dark days indeed !

SUMMARY OF THE SEASON - 1965 - 66:

Since International rugby re-commenced after the Second World War in 1946-47, only once have England had as unsuccessful a season as this, and that was in 1948, when the results were exactly the same. Played four, won none, drawn one and lost three. This time the draw was with Ireland, last time it was with Wales. Each time only two tries were scored in the season. This time one point less in total was scored, fifteen in four matches, sixteen last time. England finished rightly and firmly alone at the foot of the Championship table for the first time since 1951. The reason for this dismal performance really lay at half-back where Tom Brophy failed to realise his potential, where the various scrum-halves, three in the four matches, failed to capitalise on the reasonable amount of possession which was provided by the pack, and the opposition back rows fed voraciously upon the lack of confidence displayed by the English half-back pairing of whatever combination.

Eight changes from the side representing England at the end of the previous season, including six new caps, did nothing to further England's interests and the side stumbled to defeat for only the second time in twenty Five Nations matches at Twickenham. Jeremy Spencer, the new scrum-half for Tom Brophy did not manage to make a mark on the match at all, not entirely his own fault, and it seemed that everything round about him failed to function properly, and he paid the price. Five changes for Ireland - and a new scrum-half - improved matters slightly in that England did not lose the match but hardly any chances were created and the match finished as yet another uninspiring and inconclusive draw - the eleventh in thirty-six Five Nations matches. Three more changes in the side to travel to Stade Colombes, and still the means of arresting the downward slide was to elude the selectors. But it is true to say that no side could have resisted the free-flowing onslaught of the French XV, backs and forward alike, with which England were faced in the second half of the match. Finally to Murrayfield and the battle for the Calcutta Cup, or, more accurately on this occasion, the battle to avoid the Wooden Spoon, and England lost this one too !. There were four more changes including the selection of Mike Weston at fly-half in place of Tom Brophy, presumably to utilise Weston's tactical kicking skills, The strategy was not successful because Colin Blaikie was more than capable of dealing with whatever question Weston posed and England, not for the first time, had no secondary plan to fall back on when Plan "A" failed.

Twenty-six players played in the four matches, thirteen new caps were awarded and only five players held their place for all four matches. Amongst the new caps, John Pullin and Bob Taylor were to make a significant mark on English rugby in future seasons, but each played only one game this season - the first against Wales which was not an auspicious start.

Come the end of the season, nine players had seen all they were going to see of International rugby for a variety of reasons. David Perry, England's Captain the previous season, and an ex-Paratrooper retired with fifteen caps; Colin Payne, a TV engineer, left the scene with ten caps; Tom Brophy, a gifted player who fell well short of his true potential when clad in an England shirt, signed for Barrow Rugby League club having earned eight caps; Ted Rudd, six caps, continued his career in banking; David Rosser, a schoolteacher and Army Instructor bowed out with five caps. All these players, with the exception of Tom Brophy had gained one or more Blue at Oxbridge. Andy Hancock, hero one season, has-been the next, had earned three caps and a certain degree of immortality; Bill Treadwell, a dental surgeon, won three caps as a hooker; Terry Arthur, another ex-Blue, with two caps was an actuary; and the unfortunate Jeremy Spencer was the scapegoat of the season, and in his spare time was an artist who was said to live in a converted double-decker bus !

The 1966 British Lions touring party to Australia and New Zealand, under Mike Campbell-Lamerton called upon only five English players, Don Rutherford, Colin McFadyean, Keith Savage, Mike Weston, and David Powell, the only forward. Mike Weston played in both the Tests in Australia, and Don Rutherford in only the first of those, but Colin McFadyean played in the in all four Tests against New Zealand, in the first on the wing, and in the last three in the centre alongside Mike Gibson, scoring a fine try in the last one.

FIVE NATIONS CHAMPIONSHIP TABLE:

Won: **Nothing.**

						Points:		Tries:		Title
		Played	Won	Lost	Drawn	For	Against	For	Against	Points
1	Wales	4	3	1	0	34	26	5	4	6
2 =	France	4	2	1	1	35	18	7	2	5
2 =	Scotland	4	2	1	1	23	17	5	2	5
4	Ireland	4	1	2	1	24	34	2	7	3
5	**ENGLAND**	4	0	3	1	15	36	2	6	1

Home Games: lost to Wales 6 - 11, (one try each); drew with Ireland 6 - 6, (one try each)

Away Games: lost to France 0 - 13, (no tries to three); lost to Scotland 3 - 6, (no tries to one).

6th match   **ENGLAND   11 pts**   v   **AUSTRALIA   23 pts**

	Caps				Caps		
15	6th	R.W.Hosen	(Bristol)		21st	J.K.Lenehan	(New South Wales)
14	1st	P.B.Glover	(RAF/Bath)		10th	E.S.Boyce	(New South Wales)
13	4th	C.W.McFadyean	(Moseley)		14th	R.J.P.Marks	(Queensland)
12	1st	C.R.Jennins	(Waterloo)		4th	J.E.Brass	(New South Wales)
11	5th	K.F.Savage	(Northampton)		5th	A.M.Cardy	(New South Wales)
10	14th & last	R.A.W.Sharp (Capt)	(Bristol)		17th	P.F.Hawthorne	(New South Wales)
9	3rd & last	R.C.Ashby	(Wasps)		22nd	K.W.Catchpole (Capt)	(New South Wales)
8	17th	P.E.Judd	(Coventry)		6th	J.M.Miller	(New South Wales)
7	5th	S.B.Richards	(Richmond)		28th	P.G.Johnson	(New South Wales)
6	1st	M.J.Coulman	(Moseley)		1st	R.B.Prosser	(New South Wales)
5	12th	A.M.Davis	(US Portsmouth)		3rd	R.G.Teitzel	(Queensland)
4	1st	P.J.Larter	(Northampton)		14th	P.C.Crittle	(New South Wales)
3	27th	D.P.Rogers	(Bedford)		10th	J.Guerassimoff	(Queensland)
2	4th	J.R.H.Greenwood	(Waterloo)		14th	G.V.Davis	(New South Wales)
1	2nd	G.A.Sherriff	(Saracens)		15th	J.F.O'Gorman	(New South Wales)

Referee: K.D.Kelleher   (Ireland)

SCORERS:	R.W.Hosen	Penalty Goal	3 - 0		
	R.W.Hosen	Penalty Goal	6 - 0		
			6 - 3	P.F.Hawthorne	Drop Goal
			6 - 6	P.F.Hawthorne	Penalty Goal
			6 - 9	J.K.Lenehan	Penalty Goal
			Half-time		
			6 - 12	P.F.Hawthorne	Drop Goal
			6 - 15	P.F.Hawthorne	Drop Goal
			6 - 18	J.E.Brass	Try
	R.C.Ashby	Try (1st & only)	9 - 18		
	R.W.Hosen	Conversion	11 - 18		
			11 - 21	K.W.Catchpole	Try
			11 - 23	J.K.Lenehan	Conversion

POINTS:	R.W.Hosen	8 points	(25)	P.F.Hawthorne	12 points
	R.C.Ashby	3 points	(3)	J.K.Lenehan	5 points
				J.E.Brass and K.W.Catchpole	3 points each

MATCH COMMENTARY:

The Fifth Wallabies demonstrated, in this game, as they had against Wales, that International matches can be won by playing attractive open rugby. The game was most notable though, for the very high standard of goal kicking on both sides. Three drop goals from Hawthorne, two conversions by Lenehan and Hosen from very wide out, and four perfectly struck penalty goals provided a fine demonstration of the art.

In all other respects, England were simply outplayed, and could not match the cohesion, enterprise and teamwork of the Australians, backs and forwards alike. England started the match at an unsustainable pace, and Australia waited. Gradually, England became dispirited, the back row fell out amongst themselves and started playing as individuals and Richard Sharp, notwithstanding the selectors' faith in him, was a shadow of his former self. It was yet another poor England performance.

Twenty three points equals the highest post-war score, by Wales, against England and is the highest ever at Twickenham.

79th match   **ENGLAND   8 pts**   v   **IRELAND   3 pts**

	Caps				Caps		
15	7th	R.W.Hosen	(Bristol)		29th	T.J.Kiernan	(Cork Constitution)
14	6th	K.F.Savage	(Northampton)		1st	R.D.Scott	(Queens U Belfast)
13	3rd	R.D.Hearn	(Bedford)		4th	F.P.K.Bresnihan	(UC Dublin)
12	2nd	C.R.Jennins	(Waterloo)		22nd	J.C.Walsh	(Sunday's Well)
11	5th	C.W.McFadyean	(Moseley)		16th	N.H.Brophy	(Blackrock College)
10	1st	J.F.Finlan	(Moseley)		15th	C.M.H.Gibson	(NIFC)
9	1st	R.D.A.Pickering	(Bradford)		2nd	B.F.Sherry	(Terenure College)
1	18th	P.E.Judd (Capt)	(Coventry)		3rd & last	T.A.Moroney	(UC Dublin)
2	6th	S.B.Richards	(Richmond)		10th	K.W.Kennedy	(CIYMS)
3	2nd	M.J.Coulman	(Moseley)		2nd	P.O'Callaghan	(Dolphin)
4	1st	J.Barton	(Coventry)		23rd	W.J.McBride	(Ballymena)
5	1st	D.E.J.Watt	(Bristol)		4th	M.G.Molloy	(UC Galway)
6	1st	D.M.Rollitt	(Bristol)		11th	M.G.Doyle	(Edinburgh Wand'rs)
7	2nd	R.B.Taylor	(Northampton)		34th	N.A.A.Murphy (Capt)	(Cork Constitution)
8	1st	J.N.Pallant	(Nottingham)		2nd	K.G.Goodall	(Newcastle Univ)

Referee: D.M.Hughes   (Wales)

SCORERS:	R.W.Hosen	Penalty Goal		3 - 0			
				Half-time			
				3 - 3		T.J.Kiernan	Penalty Goal
	C.W.McFadyean	Try	(1st)	6 - 3			
	R.W.Hosen	Conversion		8 - 3			

POINTS:	R.W.Hosen	5 points	(30)		T.J.Kiernan	3 points
	C.W.McFadyean	3 points	(6)			

MATCH COMMENTARY:

Seven of the side so soundly beaten by Australia in January, were dropped for this game, and six new caps were awarded. The England team had 57 caps between them, but the more experienced Irish boasted more than three times that with 178.   Ireland played very well; McBride ruled the lines-out; Gibson made the plays and the Irish attacks came in wave upon wave but the English tackling was exemplary and heroic. All Ireland could hardly believe their eyes - or ears - when Roger Hosen converted a penalty goal to give England a three point half-time lead. Tom Kiernan replied in kind early in the second half, and England had to tackle for their lives again. Gaelic credulity was stretched a little further when an Irish try was disallowed, but it reached breaking point when, with the score still tied at 3 - 3 in the closing seconds yet another Irish passing movement began and broke down, Colin McFadyean booted ahead, and with all Ireland on the wrong foot, the ball bounced perfectly into his hands as he raced to the line. Hosen converted with the last kick of the match and Ireland were denied. Rough justice, perhaps, but England tackled heroically, withstood some intense and prolonged Irish pressure, took their chance and ended a miserable succession of six matches without a win. The pack was solid enough in the tight, but, as the Australians had shown, was significantly slower, man for man, about the field. It was a much better performance than the dispirited performance against Australia, and the win, especially in Dublin, was most welcome - and most enjoyable !

42nd match   **ENGLAND 12 pts**   v   **FRANCE 16 pts**

	Caps					Caps		
15	8th	R.W.Hosen	(Bristol)	.		23rd	C.Lacaze	(Angouleme)
14	7th	K.F.Savage	(Northampton)	.		7th	B.Duprat	(Bayonne)
13	4th	R.D.Hearn	(Bedford)	.		1st	J-P.Lux	(Tyrosse)
12	3rd & last	C.R.Jennins	(Waterloo)	.		4th	C.Dourthe	(Dax)
11	6th	C.W.McFadyean	(Moseley)	.		34th	C.Darrouy (Capt)	(Mont-de-Marsan)
10	2nd	J.F.Finlan	(Moseley)	.		5th	G.Camberabero	(La Voulte)
9	2nd	R.D.A.Pickering	(Bradford)	.		7th	L.Camberabero	(La Voulte)
1	19th	P.E.Judd (Capt)	(Coventry)	.		20th	A.Gruarin	(Toulon)
2	7th	S.B.Richards	(Richmond)	.		17th	J-M.Cabanier	(Montauban)
3	3rd	M.J.Coulman	(Moseley)	.		23rd	J-C.Berejnoi	(Tulle)
4	2nd	J.Barton	(Coventry)	.		24th	B.Dauga	(Mont-de-Marsan)
5	2nd	D.E.J.Watt	(Bristol)	.		18th	W.Spanghero	(Narbonne)
6	2nd	D.M.Rollitt	(Bristol)	.		8th	M.Sitjar	(Agen)
7	3rd	R.B.Taylor	(Northampton)	.		4th	C.Carrere	(Toulon)
8	2nd	J.N.Pallant	(Nottingham)	.		19th	A.Herrero	(Toulon)

Referee: D.P.d'Arcy   (Ireland)

SCORERS:

			0 - 3	C.Dourthe	Try
			0 - 5	G.Camberabero	Conversion
R.W.Hosen	Penalty Goal		3 - 5		
J.F.Finlan	D'p Goal	(1st)	6 - 5		
			6 - 8	B.Duprat	Try
			6 - 10	G.Camberabero	Conversion
R.W.Hosen	Penalty Goal		9 - 10		
			9 - 13	G.Camberabero	Drop Goal
			Half-time		
R.W.Hosen	Penalty Goal		12 - 13		
			12 - 16	G.Camberabero	Penalty Goal

POINTS:

R.W.Hosen	9 points	(39)		G.Camberabero	10 points
J.F.Finlan	3 points	(3)		C.Dourthe and B.Duprat	3 points each

MATCH COMMENTARY:

An unchanged England XV, hard though they tried, could not generate as much luck as had enabled them to win in Dublin, but, although France scored the two tries of the game, England were well in contention and this was a magnificent match. The first half was a fierce contest with England having most of the territorial advantage, and France's first try coming from loose play at great pace did not dishearten England. In the second half, France exerted tremendous pressure in the first ten minutes and restored their half-time lead of four points with Guy Camberabero's penalty goal in the 48th minute. After that it was all England, but in very heavy rain and against the wind, they could not quite raise their game to the necessary level to score a try and possibly win the match. England had held the lead once, and got to within one point on two occasions, but in the end had to accept France's first win at Twickenham since 1955. The Camberabero brothers at half-back had a major influence on the match, with the accuracy of Guy's kicking and his brother's long pass. It was an extremely exciting match and a credit to both teams and to the game as a whole.

With his final penalty goal, Roger Hosen equalled Nim Hall's record of 39 points in his International career.

82nd match
74th Calcutta Cup

ENGLAND   27 pts   v   SCOTLAND   14 pts

	Caps					Caps		
15	9th	R.W.Hosen	(Bristol)	.		17th	S.Wilson	(London Scottish)
14	8th	K.F.Savage	(Northampton)	.		9th	A.J.W.Hinshelwood	(London Scottish)
13	5th	R.D.Hearn	(Bedford)	.		6th	J.W.C.Turner	(Gala)
12	7th	C.W.McFadyean	(Moseley)	.		2nd & last	R.B.Welsh	(Hawick)
11	1st	R.E.Webb	(Coventry)	.		13th & last	D.J.Whyte	(Edinburgh Wand'rs)
10	3rd	J.F.Finlan	(Moseley)	.		31st & last	I.H.P.Laughland	(London Scottish)
9	3rd	R.D.A.Pickering	(Bradford)	.		1st	I.G.McRae	(Gordonians)
1	20th	P.E.Judd (Capt)	(Coventry)	.		8th & last	J.D.MacDonald	(London Scottish)
2	8th	S.B.Richards	(Richmond)	.		14th	F.A.L.Laidlaw	(Melrose)
3	4th	M.J.Coulman	(Moseley)	.		36th	D.M.D.Rollo	(Howe of Fife)
4	3rd & last	J.N.Pallant	(Nottingham)	.		13th	P.K.Stagg	(Sale)
5	3rd	D.E.J.Watt	(Bristol)	.		7th & last	W.J.Hunter	(Hawick)
6	28th	D.P.Rogers	(Bedford)	.		20th	J.P.Fisher (Capt)	(London Scottish)
7	4th	R.B.Taylor	(Northampton)	.		12th	D.Grant	(Hawick)
8	3rd	D.M.Rollitt	(Bristol)	.		15th	J.W.Telfer	(Melrose)

Referee: D.P.d'Arcy   (Ireland)

SCORERS:

R.W.Hosen	Penalty Goal		3 - 0			
			3 - 3	J.W.C.Turner	Try	
			3 - 6	A.J.W.Hinshelwood	Try	
			3 - 8	S.Wilson	Conversion	
C.W.McFadyean	Try	(2nd)	6 - 8			
R.W.Hosen	Conversion		8 - 8			
			8 - 11	S.Wilson	Penalty Goal	
			Half-time			
R.B.Taylor	Try	(1st)	11 - 11			
R.W.Hosen	Conversion		13 - 11			
			13 - 14	S.Wilson	Penalty Goal	
R.W.Hosen	Penalty Goal		16 - 14			
R.E.Webb	Try	(1st)	19 - 14			
C.W.McFadyean	Try	(3rd)	22 - 14			
R.W.Hosen	Conversion		24 - 14			
J.F.Finlan	D'p Goal	(2nd)	27 - 14			

POINTS:

R.W.Hosen	12 points	(51)		S.Wilson	8 points
C.W.McFadyean	6 points	(12)		A.J.W.Hinshelwood	3 points
R.E.Webb, J.F.Finlan, R.B.Taylor	3 points	(3),(6),(3)		J.W.C.Turner	3 points
	each				

MATCH COMMENTARY:

A thrilling game with 41 points and six tries to delight the capacity crowd. Coiln McFadyean, restored to the centre, had a magnificent match, his second try, as a result of John Finlan's interception near halfway, was breathtaking. Scotland led 14 - 13 with about 25 minutes to go but then succumbed to a flurry of English attacks and conceded eleven points in the last five minutes. For the fifth time since 1947, England scored four tries against Scotland and this was the highest points total in that period. Scotland have not won at Twickenham in that time. Roger Hosen's twelve points is the highest individual points total in a match since 1947, beating Richard Sharp's record of ten.

72nd match   ## ENGLAND   21 pts   v   WALES   34 pts

	Caps					Caps		
15	10th & last	R.W.Hosen	(Bristol)	.	1st	K.S.Jarrett	(Newport)
				.			
14	9th	K.F.Savage	(Northampton)	.	16th	S.J.Watkins	(Newport)
13	6th & last	R.D.Hearn	(Bedford)	.	4th	W.H.Raybould	(London Welsh)
12	8th	C.W.McFadyean	(Moseley)	.	5th	T.G.R.Davies	(Cardiff)
11	2nd	R.E.Webb	(Coventry)	.	34th & last	D.I.E.Bebb	(Swansea)
10	4th	J.F.Finlan	(Moseley)	.	21st & last	D.Watkins (Capt)	(Newport)
9	4th	R.D.A.Pickering	(Bradford)	.	2nd	G.O.Edwards	(Cardiff Training Coll)
1	21st	P.E.Judd (Capt)	(Coventry)	.	19th	D.Williams	(Ebbw Vale)
2	9th & last	S.B.Richards	(Richmond)	.	20th	N.R.Gale	(Llanelli)
3	5th	M.J.Coulman	(Moseley)	.	9th	D.J.Lloyd	(Bridgend)
4	3rd	J.Barton	(Coventry)	.	26th	B.Price	(Newport)
5	4th & last	D.E.J.Watt	(Bristol)	.	4th	W.T.Mainwaring	(Aberavon)
6	29th	D.P.Rogers	(Bedford)	.	2nd	R.E.Jones	(Coventry)
7	5th	R.B.Taylor	(Northampton)	.	4th	J.Taylor	(London Welsh)
8	4th	D.M.Rollitt	(Bristol)	.	2nd	W.D.Morris	(Neath)

Referee: D.C.J.MacMahon   (Scotland)

SCORERS:

			0 - 3	K.S.Jarrett	Penalty Goal	
			0 - 6	W.D.Morris	Try	
			0 - 8	K.S.Jarrett	Conversion	
			0 - 11	K.S.Jarrett	Penalty Goal	
J.Barton	Try	(1st)	3 - 11			
R.W.Hosen	Penalty Goal		6 - 14			
			6 - 14	W.H.Raybould	Drop Goal	
			Half-time			
R.W.Hosen	Penalty Goal		9 - 14			
			9 - 17	T.G.R.Davies	Try	
			9 - 19	K.S.Jarrett	Conversion	
K.F.Savage	Try	(1st & only)	12 - 19			
R.W.Hosen	Penalty Goal		15 - 19			
			15 - 22	K.S.Jarrett	Try	
			15 - 24	K.S.Jarrett	Conversion	
			15 - 27	D.I.E.Bebb	Try	
			15 - 29	K.S.Jarrett	Conversion	
			15 - 32	T.G.R.Davies	Try	
			15 - 34	K.S.Jarrett	Conversion	
R.W.Hosen	Penalty Goal		18 - 34			
J.Barton	Try	(2nd & last)	21 - 34			

POINTS:

R.W.Hosen	12 points	(63)		K.S.Jarrett	19 points	
J.Barton	6 points	(6)		T.G.R.Davies	6 points	
K.F.Savage	3 points	(3)		D.I.E.Bebb, W.D.Morris, and W.H.Raybould	3 points each	

MATCH COMMENTARY:

A magnificent fast open match, postponed from January, with records falling galore. Wales' highest score ever against England and their highest ever score at Cardiff. Keith Jarrett, an eighteen year old from Newport, scored nineteen points in the match including a spectacular individual try. It was always going to be Keith Jarrett's day when his first penalty goal attempt hit the post and went over, and thereafter, he could no wrong and everything he touched, so to speak, turned, Midas-like, to gold. From a 14 points to 6 lead at half-time, Wales extended that lead to ten points when Gerald Davies scored an excellent try, following a second penalty from Roger Hosen, but England came back and got to within four points with a Keith Savage try and a third penalty goal. Four points adrift and fourteen minutes to go, and many present were beginning to wonder whether England were about to turn the match around. Keith Jarrett did not subscribe to that view and scored as magnificent an individual try as has ever been seen at Cardiff when he gathered a poor kick for touch in the right hand corner from Colin McFadyean which bounced infield. Jarrett took the ball at full speed inside the Welsh 22 and raced down the touchline shaking off several desperate tackles and leaving the English defence way out of position and flat-footed. Two more tries from Dewi Bebb and another from Gerald Davies, all converted by Jarrett, and England had conceded nineteen points in eight minutes or so. But even then, they did not give up and a further penalty goal and a second try for John Barton, the best forward on the field that day, reduced the deficit to an mere thirteen points. The Welsh were inspired, but, in the face of their onslaught, England stood their ground and fought back.

The game was a credit to both sides and a joy to the Cardiff crowd. There will be other, equally spectacular, team efforts, to come in Cardiff but such an inspired individual performance will not be witnessed again for many a long day.

Roger Hosen had kicked ten penalty goals and scored thirty-eight points in the Five Nations season and sixty three in his career - all post-war records - and he never played for England again ! Nor did three other members of this brave side.

SUMMARY OF THE SEASON - 1966 - 67:

In every respect a substantial improvement in both fortunes and performance for the England side following the previous season's humiliation. The results were moderate from England's point of view but the quality of rugby played and the excitement and spectacle of the contests increased dramatically as the season progressed. The International season started with the match against the touring Australians on the first Saturday in January 1967 when the Wallabies gave England a lesson in the art of open rugby and a fine sight it was to see the Australian forwards linking with their backs especially from the back of the line-outs. The England side became noticeably dispirited, especially in the back row and seven changes were made for the match against Ireland in Dublin in February, the first match against Wales in January having been postponed due to the weather. Ireland made all the running and dominated the play but England won the match thanks largely to their heroic and determined defence and the opportunism of Colin McFadyean. Against France, the same team did not enjoy the same rub of the green, and, although the whole side played with great fervour and determination and competed throughout, they could not deny France their first win at Twickenham for twelve years. The Calcutta Cup match was a six try feast with Scotland scoring the first two, and going into the second half with a three point lead, and then England gradually edging ahead and finally scoring eleven points in the last five minutes. But the climax of the whole Five Nations season came belatedly when the postponed match against Wales was played at Cardiff on April 15th. Both sides scored more points than either had done in this fixture this century and an unknown eighteen year old lad from Newport, Keith Jarrett, equalled John Bancroft's record set in 1910, by scoring nineteen points in an International match. Jarrett almost certainly would not have been in the Welsh side had the match been played as originallty scheduled, in January, for this was his first cap. It was a magnificent match and as fitting a climax as possible to a much-improved Five Nations season - in all respects.

Richard Sharp was recalled to lead the side for the first match against Australia following Budge Roger's apparent inability to inspire his side during the previous season, but it was four years since Sharp had earned his previous cap when he was captain for the 1962-63 season, and for Sharp himself it was a match too far and a rather ignominious end to a fine International career. For the Five Nations Tournament, the Selectors settled on a better balanced side and maintained faith with them with Phil Judd leading, as always, by example from the front. In the five matches, England used twenty four different players (the front row of Judd, Richards and Coulman played in all five matches), but for the Five Nations only seventeen players were called upon.

Roger Hosen scored forty six points in the season and a record thirty eight in the Five Nations Championship - a record which was to stand for sixteen years until beaten by Dusty Hare in 1983. His career points tally for England of sixty three is also an individual record and, in the Calcutta Cup match, he became the first player to reach a total of fifty points in an International jersey for England.

Eight players came to the end of their International careers of whom the most notable was Danny Hearn, the Bedford centre, who, when playing for Midland and Home Counties against the touring All Blacks at Leicester in the following October, tragically broke his neck and has been paralysed ever since. With enormous courage, he subsequently learned to walk and resumed his teaching career at Haileybury. He still maintains a keen interest in schoolboy rugby. He earned six caps. Richard Sharp, after an unfortunate return to the International scene, had won fourteen caps and was, and still is, the Redruth club's most capped player. He was a schoolmaster at Sherborne. Roger Hosen, by now 34 years of age, retired with ten caps and the England points total record. He, too, was a schoolmaster. Steve Richards, a solicitor and Richmond hooker, had gained nine caps playing in all matches in the seasons 1964-65 and 1966-67. Dave Watt, four caps, continued play club rugby for Bristol for a further eight years and in all made over 500 appearances for the club. Clive Ashby, born in Mozambique, and later adopting South African nationality, won three caps. Also with three caps each, Chris Jennins, was an accountant in Merseyside, and John Pallant, a fine all-round athlete, basketball player and All England schools champion hammer-thrower, was a schoolmaster at Merchant Taylor's although he played for Nottingham.

Similar progress next season should augur well for England - providing one Keith Jarrett has an off day !!

FIVE NATIONS CHAMPIONSHIP TABLE:

Won: **Calcutta Cup**

		Played	Won	Lost	Drawn	Points: For	Against	Tries: For	Against	Title Points
1	France	4	3	1	0	55	41	8	2	6
2 =	**ENGLAND**	4	2	2	0	68	67	8	9	4
2 =	Scotland	4	2	2	0	37	45	4	8	4
2 =	Ireland	4	2	2	0	17	22	3	2	4
5	Wales	4	1	3	0	53	55	7	9	2

Home Games: lost to France 12 - 16, (no tries to two); beat Scotland 27 - 14, (four tries to two).

Away Games: beat Ireland 8 - 3, (one try to nil); lost to Wales 21 - 34, (three tries to five).

8th match　　　　# ENGLAND　11 pts　　v　　NEW ZEALAND　23 pts

	Caps					Caps		
15	14th & last	D.Rutherford	(Gloucester)	.		2nd	W.F.McCormick	(Canterbury)
14	10th	K.F.Savage	(Northampton)	.		9th	M.J.Dick	(Auckland)
13	9th	C.W.McFadyean	(Moseley)	.		2nd	W.L.Davis	(Hawke's Bay)
12	1st	R.H.Lloyd	(Harlequins)	.		6th	I.R.MacRae	(Hawke's Bay)
11	3rd	R.E.Webb	(Coventry)	.		5th	W.M.Birtwistle	(Canterbury)
10	5th	J.F.Finlan	(Moseley)	.		1st	E.W.Kirton	(Otago)
9	1st & only	W.J.Gittings	(Coventry)	.		11th	C.R.Laidlaw	(Otago)
1	7th & last	A.L.Horton	(Blackheath)	.		2nd	B.L.Muller	(Taranaki)
2	11th & last	H.O.Godwin	(Coventry)	.		12th	B.E.McLeod	(Counties)
3	22nd & last	P.E.Judd (Capt)	(Coventry)	.		6th & last	E.J.Hazlett	(Southland)
4	2nd	P.J.Larter	(Northampton)	.		2nd	S.C.Strahan	(Manawatu)
5	14th & last	J.E.Owen	(Coventry)	.		39th	C.E.Meads	(King Country)
6	30th	D.P.Rogers	(Bedford)	.		1st	G.C.Williams	(Wellington)
7	6th	R.B.Taylor	(Northampton)	.		32nd	K.R.Tremain	(Hawke's Bay)
8	3rd & last	G.A.Sherriff	(Saracens)	.		12th	B.J.Lochore (Capt)	(Wairarapa)

Referee:　　D.C.J.MacMahon　　(Scotland)

SCORERS:

				0 - 3	E.W.Kirton	Try
				0 - 5	W.F.McCormick	Conversion
				0 - 8	W.M.Birtwistle	Try
				0 - 10	W.F.McCormick	Conversion
				0 - 13	C.R.Laidlaw	Try
				0 - 16	E.W.Kirton	Try
				0 - 18	W.F.McCormick	Conversion
R.H.Lloyd	Try	(1st)		3 - 18		
D.Rutherford	Conversion			5 - 18		
			Half-time			
				5 - 21	M.J.Dick	Try
				5 - 23	W.F.McCormick	Conversion
P.J.Larter	Penalty Goal			8 - 23		
R.H.Lloyd	Try	(2nd & last)		11 - 23		

POINTS:

R.H.Lloyd	6 points	(6)	W.F.McCormick	8 points	
P.J.Larter	3 points	(3)	E.W.Kirton	6 points	
D.Rutherford	2 points	(36)	M.J.Dick, W.M.Birtwistle,		
			and C.R.Laidlaw	3 points each	

MATCH COMMENTARY:

The Sixth All Blacks were an extremely competent side coached by Fred Allen, perhaps the first of the modern coaches, who had an abundance of talent to work with. England did not acquit themselves well as the try count indicates. The feed from the set pieces was slow and cumbersome and Gittings, the Coventry scrum-half had a torrid time. With limited possession, Bob Lloyd, replacing Danny Hearn who had broken his neck playing for the Midlands against the All Blacks the previous week, scored two tries on his debut. Five tries had been conceded for the second successive match. Predictably, seven of this side were not capped again and the least fortunate of these must be Bill Gittings who had not asked to play behind a soundly beaten pack ! Budge Rogers equalled Eric Evans' record of 30 post-war caps.

73rd match   **ENGLAND   11 pts**   v   **WALES   11 pts**

	Caps					Caps		
15	1st	R.Hiller	(Harlequins)	.		2nd	P.J.Wheeler	(Aberavon)
14	1st	D.H.Prout	(Northampton)	.		18th	S.J.Watkins	(Cardiff)
13	10th	C.W.McFadyean (Capt)	(Moseley)	.		2nd	K.S.Jarrett	(Newport)
12	2nd	R.H.Lloyd	(Harlequins)	.		6th	T.G.R.Davies	(Cardiff)
11	11th	K.F.Savage	(Northampton)	.		2nd	W.K.Jones	(Cardiff)
10	6th	J.F.Finlan	(Moseley)	.		4th	B.John	(Cardiff)
9	1st	B.W.Redwood	(Bristol)	.		4th	G.O.Edwards	(Cardiff)
1	1st	B.W.Keen	(Newcastle Univ)	.		21st	D.Williams	(Ebbw Vale)
2	2nd	J.V.Pullin	(Bristol)	.		22nd	N.R.Gale (Capt)	(Llanelli)
3	6th	M.J.Coulman	(Moseley)	.		1st	B.J.James	(Brigend)
4	1st	M.J.Parsons	(Northampton)	.		2nd	M.Wiltshire	(Aberavon)
5	3rd	P.J.Larter	(Northampton)	.		6th	W.T.Mainwaring	(Aberavon)
6	1st	B.R.West	(Loughborough Coll)	.		3rd	W.D.Morris	(Neath)
7	1st	P.J.Bell	(Blackheath)	.		1st	A.J.Gray	(London Welsh)
8	1st	D.J.Gay	(Bath)	.		1st	R.Wanbon	(Aberavon)

Referee: D.P.d'Arcy   (Ireland)

SCORERS:

C.W.McFadyean	Try	(4th & last)	3 - 0				
			3 - 3		G.O.Edwards	Try	
B.W.Redwood	Try	(1st & only)	6 - 3				
R.Hiller	Conversion		8 - 3				
			Half-time				
R.Hiller	Penalty Goal		11 - 3				
			11 - 6		R.Wanbon	Try	
			11 - 8		K.S.Jarrett	Conversion	
			11 - 11		B.John	Drop Goal	

POINTS:

R.Hiller	5 points	(5)		G.O.Edwards	3 points
C.W.McFadyean	3 points	(15)		R.Wanbon	3 points
B.W.Redwood	3 points	(3)		B.John	3 points
				K.S.Jarrett	2 points

MATCH COMMENTARY:

Eight new caps came into the side after the disappointing performance against the All Blacks the previous autumn, and they exceeded all reasonable expectations. Wales, as their first coach, David Nash, would be sure to agree, were fortunate to escape with a draw. Keith Jarrett missed only two penalty kicks at goal, and each time an English player knocked-on and from both succeeding scrums, Wales scored a try, the first by Gareth Edwards and the second by Bob Wanbon. Jarrett converted the second try and thus sparked a Welsh revival and they drew level with a Barry John drop goal. Prior to this, the England pack had provided much more than a fair share of possession, but the backs were unable to do anything with it. When the scores were level, tension increased, risk-taking disappeared and kicking prevailed, and, as The Times correspondent reported, "with a soft sigh or two, the game died".

Amongst the new caps was Bob Hiller at full-back, who was to set a new points scoring record for England. John Pullin gained his second cap, having played against Wales two years ago, and he was to play in the next 36 Internationals, and eventually win 42 caps as hooker.

80th match   ENGLAND   9 pts   v   IRELAND   9 pts

	Caps					Caps		
15	2nd	R.Hiller	(Harlequins)		35th	T.J.Kiernan (Capt)	(Cork Constitution)
14	2nd & last	D.H.Prout	(Northampton)	.	9th	A.T.A.Duggan	(Lansdowne)
13	11th & last	C.W.McFadyean (Capt)	(Moseley)	.	2nd	B.A.P.O'Brien	(Shannon)
12	3rd	R.H.Lloyd	(Harlequins)	.	9th	F.P.K.Bresnihan	(UC Dublin)
11	4th	R.E.Webb	(Coventry)	.	4th	R.D.Scott	(Queen's U Belfast)
10	7th	J.F.Finlan	(Moseley)	.	20th	C.M.H.Gibson	(NIFC)
9	2nd & last	B.W.Redwood	(Bristol)	.	6th & last	B.F.Sherry	(Terenure College)
1	2nd	B.W.Keen	(Newcastle Univ)	.	25th	S.Millar	(Ballymena)
2	3rd	J.V.Pullin	(Bristol)	.	2nd	A.M.Brady	(Malone)
3	7th	M.J.Coulman	(Moseley)	.	5th	P.O'Callaghan	(Dolphin)
4	2nd	M.J.Parsons	(Northampton)	.	29th	W.J.McBride	(Ballymena)
5	4th	P.J.Larter	(Northampton)	.	10th	M.G.Molloy	(UC Galway)
6	2nd	B.R.West	(Loughborough Coll)	.	17th	M.G.Doyle	(Blackrock College)
7	2nd	P.J.Bell	(Blackheath)	.	1st	T.J.Doyle	(Wanderers)
8	2nd	D.J.Gay	(Bath)	.	8th	K.G.Goodall	(Newcastle Univ)

Referee: M.Joseph   (Wales)

SCORERS:

			0 - 3	T.J.Kiernan	Penalty Goal
J.F.Finlan	D'p Goal	rd & last)	3 - 3		
			3 - 6	T.J.Kiernan	Penalty Goal
R.Hiller	Penalty Goal		6 - 6		
			Half-time		
			6 - 9	T.J.Kiernan	Penalty Goal
R.Hiller	Penalty Goal		9 - 9		

POINTS:

R.Hiller	6 points	(11)	T.J.Kiernan	9 points
J.F.Finlan	3 points	(9)		

MATCH COMMENTARY:

The match probably never would have been a memorable one, but when after thirty minutes, Bill Redwood, the England scrum half, had to leave the field, England were only concerned with damage limitation. Peter Bell went to scrum half and struggled in all respects. So, not surprisingly, did the English pack and they were flagging well before the end of the match. But the Irish backs, even with Mike Gibson restored at fly-half after recovering from a viral infection, could not take advantage of the situation. The ultimate indignity for Ireland came right at the end of the match when Brendan Sherry, the Irish scrum-half, was adjudged to have deliberately thrown the ball into touch when defending on his own 25 yard line. Merion Joseph, the referee, awarded the penalty and Bob Hiller converted the kick with superb aplomb from the touchline to earn the draw. This time England were fortunate, and the hapless Sherry was cast into the wilderness as a sacrificial offering to atone for the opportunity missed by, not only him, but also the other fourteen Irish players.

Brian Redwood, who, quite remarkably for an International sportsman, was unsighted in one eye, did not play for England again.

43rd match   **ENGLAND   9 pts**   v   **FRANCE   14 pts**

	Caps				Caps		
15	3rd	R.Hiller	(Harlequins)	.	29th	C.Lacaze	(Angouleme)
14	12th	K.F.Savage	(Northampton)	.	1st	J-M.Bonal	(Toulouse)
13	1st	T.J.Brooke	(Richmond)	.	10th	J-P.Lux	(Tyrosse)
12	4th	R.H.Lloyd	(Harlequins)	.	30th	J.Gachassin	(Lourdes)
11	5th	R.E.Webb	(Coventry)	.	5th	A.Campaes	(Lourdes)
10	28th	M.P.Weston (Capt)	(Durham City)	.	13th	G.Camberabero	(La Voulte)
9	5th	R.D.A.Pickering	(Bradford)	.	12th	L.Camberabero	(La Voulte)
1	3rd	B.W.Keen	(Newcastle Univ)	.	1st	J-C.Noble	(La Voulte)
2	4th	J.V.Pullin	(Bristol)	.	1st	M.Yachvili	(Tulle)
3	8th	M.J.Coulman	(Moseley)	.	3rd	M.Lassere	(Agen)
4	3rd	M.J.Parsons	(Northampton)	.	6th	A.Plantefol	(Agen)
5	5th	P.J.Larter	(Northampton)	.	7th	E.Cester	(Toulouse)
6	3rd	B.R.West	(Loughborough Coll)	.	4th	J-P.Salut	(Toulouse)
7	3rd	P.J.Bell	(Blackheath)	.	14th	C.Carrere (Capt)	(Toulon)
8	3rd	D.J.Gay	(Bath)	.	26th	W.Spanghero	(Narbonne)

Referee: H.B.Laidlaw   (Scotland)

SCORERS:	M.P.Weston	D'p Goal (1st & only)	3 - 0			
	R.Hiller	Penalty Goal	6 - 0			
			6 - 3		G.Camberabero	Penalty Goal
			Half-time			
	R.Hiller	Penalty Goal	9 - 3			
			9 - 6		J.Gachassin	Try
			9 - 8		G.Camberabero	Conversion
			9 - 11		C.Lacaze	Drop Goal
			9 - 14		L.Camberabero	Drop Goal

POINTS:	R.Hiller	6 points	(17)		G.Camberabero	5 points
	M.P.Weston	3 points	(6)		L.Camberabero	3 points
					J.Gachassin	3 points
					C.Lacaze	3 points

MATCH COMMENTARY:

England kept the same pack but made two changes in the three-quarters and changed both half backs. The decision to bring back Mike Weston, first capped over eight years ago, as a tactician at fly-half, was partially but not wholly successful. The French, generally, on their way to their first Grand Slam, were better in all areas of the game, and England were not quite quick enough to deal with the Camberabero brothers at half-back, who, as they had the previous year at Twickenham, structured the game for France. Almost all the play in the first half of the match was in French territory and, appropriately, England led 9 - 3 until late in the game, and, indeed, created even further opportunities to score. But then the brothers Camberabero decided that something had to be done, Together, they raised their game, and that of the whole team, and some brilliant switches and support play turned the match in favour of France such that they scored eleven points in the last quarter of the match.   A deserved French win, and a much more encouraging England performance.

Mike Weston achieved the distinction of equalling Jeff Butterfield's record of 28 post-war caps, as a back.

83rd match

ENGLAND　8 pts　　v　　**SCOTLAND　6 pts**

75th Calcutta Cup

	Caps				Caps		
15	4th	R.Hiller	(Harlequins)	.	22nd & last	S.Wilson	(London Scottish)
14	13th & last	K.F.Savage	(Northampton)	.	14th	A.J.W.Hinshelwood	(London Scottish)
13	2nd & last	T.J.Brooke	(Richmond)	.	11th	J.W.C.Turner	(Gala)
12	5th & last	R.H.Lloyd	(Harlequins)	.	5th	J.N.M.Frame	(Gala)
11	6th	R.E.Webb	(Coventry)	.	2nd & last	C.G.Hodgson	(London Scottish)
10	29th & last	M.P.Weston (Capt)	(Durham City)	.	1st	I.Robertson	(London Scottish)
9	6th & last	R.D.A.Pickering	(Bradford)	.	1st	G.C.Connell	(Trinity Acad'ls)
1	4th & last	B.W.Keen	(Newcastle Univ)	.	6th	N.Suddon	(Hawick)
2	5th	J.V.Pullin	(Bristol)	.	1st & only	D.T.Deans	(Hawick)
3	9th & last	M.J.Coulman	(Moseley)	.	6th	A.B.Carmichael	(West of Scotland)
4	4th & last	M.J.Parsons	(Northampton)	.	18th	P.K.Stagg	(Sale)
5	6th	P.J.Larter	(Northampton)	.	2nd	A.F.McHarg	(West of Scotland)
6	4th	B.R.West	(Loughborough Coll)	.	25th & last	J.P.Fisher	(London Scottish)
7	4th & last	P.J.Bell	(Blackheath)	.	2nd	R.J.Arneil	(Edinburgh Acad'ls)
8	4th & last	D.J.Gay	(Bath)	.	16th	J.W.Telfer (Capt)	(Melrose)

Referee:　　D.P.d'Arcy　　(Ireland)

SCORERS:

			0 - 3	S.Wilson	Penalty Goal
			0 - 6	G.C.Connell	Drop Goal
			Half-time		
M.J.Coulman	Try	(1st & only)	3 - 6		
R.Hiller	Conversion		5 - 6		
R.Hiller	Penalty Goal		8 - 6		

POINTS:

R.Hiller	5 points	(22)		S.Wilson	3 points
M.J.Coulman	3 points	(3)		G.C.Connell	3 points

MATCH COMMENTARY:

England's best performance, in the only match which they won in an undistinguished season. Mike Weston was able to control events without too much trouble, but as Scotland had also had a very poor season, losing all five matches, England's narrow win was no cause for wild and unrestrained celebration. The match, though, had several highlights. Amongst them were scrum-half Gordon Connell's remarkable drop goal from barely six feet from the posts and Mike Coulman's opportunistic try when he broke through a line-out, fully thirty yards out, and reached the line at great speed with not a finger laid upon him. Jock Turner had the opportunity to deny England in the last minute, but he failed to score from a penalty goal from only 25 yards. England had kept the same pack for the four Five Nations matches, but they never dominated the opposition in any area of the game - or of the field. This was not a good England performance, and they had played a better quality of rugby and with greater determination and apparent enthusiasm in both their drawn matches than they displayed in this their only success of the season.

Thus, England finished in third place in the Championship table having drawn two and won one of their four matches.

SUMMARY OF THE SEASON - 1967 - 68:

Following the heightened expectations generated by the quality of rugby played towards the end of the previous season, this was another anti-climactic season for England. Strangely, the season started in much the same way as had the previous one with a dispiriting defeat at the hands of another southern hemisphere side - this time New Zealand. For this match, played in early November, Phil Judd retained the captaincy, but there were eight changes in the side which had somewhat fortuitously beaten Scotland the previous March. The side were well beaten, with England seemingly moving at half the pace exhibited by the fitter, faster All Blacks. Bob Lloyd grasped his opportunity commendably with two tries on his debut, but the side conceded five for the second successive match. As formerly, after the defeat at the hands of Australia, wholesale changes were made for the first match of the Five Nations tournament with eight new caps coming into the side against Wales at Twickenham in January - in fact the whole side selected had only 33 caps amongst them ! Phil Judd was deposed and Colin McFadyean was nominated to replace him as captain, and one wondered whether the selectors really knew what they were doing.

In the event, the match against Wales, although drawn, gave much encouragement to the England faithful, but yet gain the early efforts in the first half could not be sustained either throughout the match nor for the rest of the season. If, as was the popular opinion, Wales were fortunate to escape from Twickenham with a draw, Ireland were equally unfortunate to achieve the same result. England certainly raised their level of commitment in accommodating the loss of Bill Redwood after half an hour's play but it was passive rather than active commitment, and possession was consistently lost in all areas of play. Ireland, and especially Mike Gibson, should have taken advantage of the situation but failed to do so and then presented a generous gift to England with Brendan Sherry's indiscretion.

Two draws in the two home matches was not considered satisfactory so the unfortunate Colin McFadyean was summarily despatched and Mike Weston was recalled to give tactical direction on the field for the trip to Stade Colombes. Although it was not known at the time, France were en route to their first ever Grand Slam and the Camberabero brothers demonstrated precisely why in this match. England, as on previous occasions, started very well, and led 9 - 3 until France stepped up a gear and England quietly subsided. The final fixture against Scotland produced the right result for England, at last, but it was a hollow victory against a very poor Scotland side, who were "whitewashed" in the season, and even then Scotland would have won had Jock Turner succeeded with a relatively easy penalty goal attempt in the closing stages. So, another undistinguished season for England drew to a close - not with a bang, but almost a whimper.

England used twenty eight players in the five matches but only eighteen for the Five Nations encounters where the pack played unchanged. Three different captains led their charges and only Bob Lloyd and Peter Larter played in all five matches. Twenty of those twenty eight players were not called upon to turn out for England again. No previous season had seen such a mass exodus from the England ranks. Mike Weston's 29 caps were a record for a back; he captained England five times, went on two Lions tours and played in six Tests, and became a Lions' and England selector. Phil Judd, who also led England five times, was a pattern-maker by trade and a county water polo and squash player. Don Rutherford and John Owen both gained fourteen caps; Rutherford was England's most capped full-back, and became RFU Coaching Director, and Owen, a former double blue, who had scored a try on his debut against Wales in 1963, was employed at Jaguar in Coventry. Keith Savage, thirteen caps, went on two Lions tours and played in all four Tests in South Africa on the 1968 tour. Colin McFadyean, England captain twice, British Lion for four Tests in 1966, retired with eleven caps to his career as a PE Instructor. Herbert Godwin, also earned eleven caps and was employed at the Standard motor works in Coventry. Mike Coulman, having won nine caps, joined Salford RL Club and had an outstandingly successful career in the game for a further fifteen years. He played 441 matches for Salford, scored 135 tries and represented Great Britain. Twelve other players were not to appear for England again - all had less than eight caps each Eight England players were invited to tour with the 1968 Lions to South Africa. They were: Bob Hiller, Keith Savage, Mike Coulman, Tony Horton, Peter Larter, John Pullin, Bob Taylor and Bob Lloyd who, unfortunately, was unable to go. Brian West later joined the tour as a replacement. Six played in the Tests; Bob Taylor and Keith Savage (all four); Tony Horton and John Pullin (three); and Mike Coulman and Peter Larter each played in one Test.

FIVE NATIONS CHAMPIONSHIP TABLE:

Won: **Calcutta Cup**

		Played	Won	Lost	Drawn	Points: For	Points: Against	Tries: For	Tries: Against	Title Points
1	France	4	4	0	0	52	30	7	2	8
2	Ireland	4	2	1	1	38	37	4	2	5
3	**ENGLAND**	4	1	1	2	37	40	3	3	4
4	Wales	4	1	2	1	31	34	4	5	3
5	Scotland	4	0	4	0	18	35	1	7	0

Home Games: drew with Wales 11 - 11, (two tries each); drew with Ireland 9 - 9, (no tries)

Away Games: lost to France 9 - 14, (no tries to one); beat Scotland 8 - 6, (one try to nil)

81st match   **ENGLAND   15 pts**   v   **IRELAND   17 pts**

	Caps					Caps		
15	5th	R.Hiller	(Harlequins)	.		40th	T.J.Kiernan (Capt)	(Cork Constitution)
14	1st	K.J.Fielding	(Loughboro' Coll)	.		13th	A.T.A.Duggan	(Lansdowne)
13	1st	J.S.Spencer	(Cambridge Univ)	.		14th	F.P.K.Bresnihan	(UC Dublin)
12	1st	D.J.Duckham	(Coventry)	.		24th	C.M.H.Gibson	(NIFC)
11	7th	R.E.Webb	(Coventry)	.		4th	J.C.M.Moroney	(London Irish)
10	8th	J.F.Finlan	(Moseley)	.		2nd	B.J.McGann	(Lansdowne)
9	2nd	T.C.Wintle	(Northampton)	.		15th	R.M.Young	(Queen's U Belfast)
1	3rd	D.L.Powell	(Northampton)	.		30th	S.Millar	(Ballymena)
2	6th	J.V.Pullin	(Bristol)	.		18th	K.W.Kennedy	(London Irish)
3	1st	K.E.Fairbrother	(Coventry)	.		9th	P.O'Callaghan	(Dolphin)
4	7th	P.J.Larter	(Northampton)	.		34th	W.J.McBride	(Ballymena)
5	1st	N.E.Horton	(Moseley)	.		22nd	M.G.Molloy	(London Irish)
6	31st	D.P.Rogers	(Bedford)	.		2nd	J.C.Davidson	(Dungannon)
7	5th & last	J.R.H.Greenwood (Capt)	(Waterloo)	.		39th	N.A.A.Murphy	(Cork Constitution)
8	5th	D.M.Rollitt	(Bristol)	.		13th	K.G.Goodall	(City of Derry)

.   1st & only   C.Grimshaw (Queen's U Belf) for Young - 24

Referee: R.P.Burrell   (Scotland)

SCORERS:

R.Hiller	Penalty Goal		3 - 0			
			3 - 3	T.J.Kiernan	Penalty Goal	
R.Hiller	Penalty Goal		6 - 3			
			6 - 6	T.J.Kiernan	Penalty Goal	
R.Hiller	Penalty Goal		9 - 6			
			9 - 9	F.P.K.Bresnihan	Try	
			Half-time			
D.J.Duckham	Try	(1st)	12 - 9			
			12 - 12	B.J.McGann	Drop Goal	
			12 - 15	N.A.A.Murphy	Try	
			12 - 17	T.J.Kiernan	Conversion	
R.Hiller	Penalty Goal		15 - 17			

POINTS:

R.Hiller	12 point	(34)	T.J.Kiernan	8 points	
D.J.Duckham	3 point	(3)	F.P.K.Bresnihan	3 points	
			N.A.A.Murphy and B.J.McGann	3 points each	

MATCH COMMENTARY:

Five new caps were introduced, three of whom were to make a substantial contribution to the game in years to come, Keith Fielding, David Duckham and John Spencer. The task, against a formidable Irish side, particularly the pack with 167 caps amongst them, unbeaten since drawing with England last year, was a daunting one. England acquitted themselves well and Duckham's debut try heralded a new-found confidence and determination which was also evident in the staunch defence against Ireland's powerful attacks. But, overall, England were competent but Ireland were inspired. England held the lead on four occasions, but, as so often in the past, could not conjure up the decisive strike to win the match. It appears from the scoreline that the difference between the two teams lay in the fact that Ireland converted a try whereas England did not. But it was much, much more than that. Bob Hiller scored 12 points in the match, emulating Roger Hosen's feat in 1967 and Budge Rogers equalled Wavell Wakefield's record in being capped 31 times for England.

44th match   **ENGLAND   22 pts**   v   **FRANCE   8 pts**

	Caps					Caps		
15	6th	R.Hiller	(Harlequins)	.	13th	P.Villepreux	(Toulouse)
14	2nd	K.J.Fielding	(Loughborough Coll)	.	1st	B.Moraitis	(Toulon)
13	2nd	J.S.Spencer	(Cambridge Univ)	.	18th	J-P.Lux	(Tyrosse)
12	2nd	D.J.Duckham	(Coventry)	.	12th	J.Trillo	(Begles)
11	8th	R.E.Webb	(Coventry)	.	11th	J-M.Bonal	(Toulouse)
10	9th	J.F.Finlan	(Moseley)	.	33rd & last	C.Lacaze	(Angouleme)
9	3rd	T.C.Wintle	(Northampton)	.	15th	M.Puget (Capt)	(Toulouse)
1	4th	D.L.Powell	(Northampton)	.	12th	M.Lassere	(Agen)
2	7th	J.V.Pullin	(Bristol)	.	1st	C.Swierczinski	(Begles)
3	2nd	K.E.Fairbrother	(Coventry)	.	10th & last	J-M.Esponda	(Perpignan)
4	8th	P.J.Larter	(Northampton)	.	10th	A.Plantefol	(Agen)
5	2nd	N.E.Horton	(Moseley)	.	18th	E.Cester	(Toulouse)
6	32nd	D.P.Rogers (Capt)	(Bedford)	.	1st	P.Biemouret	(Agen)
7	7th	R.B.Taylor	(Northampton)	.	1st & only	M.Hauser	(Lourdes)
8	6th	D.M.Rollitt	(Bristol)	.	45th	B.Dauga	(Mont-de-Marsan)

Referee: D.P.d'Arcy   (Ireland)

SCORERS:	R.Hiller	Penalty Goal		3 - 0			
	R.Hiller	Penalty Goal		6 - 0			
				6 - 3	J-M.Bonal	Try	
				6 - 5	C.Lacaze	Conversion	
	D.M.Rollitt	Try	(1st & only)	9 - 5			
	R.Hiller	Conversion		11 - 5			
				Half-time			
	K.J.Fielding	Try	(1st & only)	14 - 5			
	R.Hiller	Conversion		16 - 5			
	R.E.Webb	Try	2nd & only)	19 - 5			
				19 - 8	C.Lacaze	Drop Goal	
	R.Hiller	Penalty Goal		22 - 8			

POINTS:	R.Hiller	13 points	(47)		C.Lacaze	5 points	
	R.E.Webb	3 points	(6)		J-M.Bonal	3 points	
	K.J.Fielding and D.M.Rollitt	3 points	(3),(3)				

MATCH COMMENTARY:

Since July 1968, when they started their tour of New Zealand, France have lost nine successive matches, and their low morale was evident for all to see in this match. England were able to play a free flowing game and were rewarded with a try for each wing and one for Dave Rollitt Thus, England achieved their highest points total against France for 55 years and equalled their highest post-war winning margin. The dependable Bob Hiller demonstrated his kicking ability and consistency, in scoring a record thirteen points in the match, and the confidence of the whole team must have received a substantial boost from this and his previous worthy performance in Dublin. England had scored only three tries in the previous five games against France, and had lost the last three matches, so this result was just cause for celebration. The strong running of David Duckham and John Spencer could have led to more tries had it not been for the courageous tackling of Villepreux.

84th match

ENGLAND 8 pts   v   SCOTLAND 3 pts

76th Calcutta Cup

	Caps					Caps		
15	7th	R.Hiller	(Harlequins)	.	8th & last	C.F.Blaikie	(Heriot's)
14	3rd	K.J.Fielding	(Loughborough Coll)	.	1st	W.C.C.Steele	(Langholm)
13	3rd	J.S.Spencer	(Headingley)	.	8th	J.N.M.Frame	(Gala)
12	3rd	D.J.Duckham	(Coventry)	.	2nd	I.Robertson	(Watsonians)
11	9th	R.E.Webb	(Coventry)	.	8th & last	W.D.Jackson	(Hawick)
10	10th	J.F.Finlan	(Moseley)	.	5th	C.M.Telfer	(Hawick)
9	4th	T.C.Wintle	(Northampton)	.	4th	G.C.Connell	(London Scottish)
1	5th	D.L.Powell	(Northampton)	.	1st	J.McLauchlan	(Jordanhill)
2	8th	J.V.Pullin	(Bristol)	.	23rd	F.A.L.Laidlaw	(Melrose)
3	3rd	K.E.Fairbrother	(Coventry)	.	11th	A.B.Carmichael	(West of Scotland)
4	9th	P.J.Larter	(Northampton)	.	11th	P.C.Brown	(Gala)
5	3rd	N.E.Horton	(Moseley)	.	7th	A.F.McHarg	(London Scottish)
6	33rd	D.P.Rogers (Capt)	(Bedford)	.	2nd	W.Lauder	(Neath)
7	8th	R.B.Taylor	(Northampton)	.	7th	R.J.Arneil	(Edinburgh Acad'ls)
8	7th	D.M.Rollitt	(Bristol)	.	21st	J.W.Telfer (Capt)	(Melrose)

1st & only   T.J.Dalton (Coventry) for Fielding - 30

Referee: C.Durand   (France)

SCORERS:	D.J.Duckham	Try	(2nd)	3 - 0		
	R.Hiller	Conversion		5 - 0		
				Half-time		
	D.J.Duckham	Try	(3rd)	8 - 0		
				8 - 3	P.C.Brown	Penalty Goal

POINTS:	D.J.Duckham	6 points	(9)		P.C.Brown	3 points
	R.Hiller	2 points	(49)			

MATCH COMMENTARY:

Not surprisingly, England fielded an unchanged side following the convincing win over France three weeks earlier. David Duckham's two tries (he has now scored three in three matches) were well taken but the team were not co-ordinated, and it could not be said that they played well. Scotland, on the other hand did play well together, but totally failed to take their chances. They dominated the lines-out through Peter Brown and Alastair McHarg, and in the rucks and in loose play the Scots went in horizontally whereas England went in vertically and lost both footing and possession. With two very competent props, of whom much more was to be heard, the Scottish locks, giving away four stones nevertheless controlled the tight. But, for all that they never seriously threatened the English line and it became another disappointment in the long succession of Scottish lost causes at Twickenham where they have not won since the war.

Tim Dalton of Coventry, whose only cap this was to be, became the first replacement used by England in an International match when he took Keith Fielding's place following his retirement with an ankle injury during the first half.

74th match   **ENGLAND   9 pts**   v   **WALES   30 pts**

	Caps					Caps		
15	8th	R.Hiller	(Harlequins)	.		4th	J.P.R.Williams	(London Welsh)
14	1st	K.C.Plummer	(Bristol)	.		23rd	S.J.Watkins	(Newport)
13	4th	J.S.Spencer	(Headingley)	.		7th	K.S.Jarrett	(Newport)
12	4th	D.J.Duckham	(Coventry)	.		11th	S.J.Dawes	(London Welsh)
11	10th	R.E.Webb	(Coventry)	.		6th	M.C.R.Richards	(Cardiff)
10	11th	J.F.Finlan	(Moseley)	.		11th	B.John	(Cardiff)
9	5th & last	T.C.Wintle	(Northampton)	.		11th	G.O.Edwards (Capt)	(Cardiff)
1	6th	D.L.Powell	(Northampton)	.		25th	D.Williams	(Ebbw Vale)
2	9th	J.V.Pullin	(Bristol)	.		7th	J.Young	(Harrogate)
3	4th	K.E.Fairbrother	(Coventry)	.		16th	D.J.Lloyd	(Bridgend)
4	10th	P.J.Larter	(Northampton)	.		5th	W.D.Thomas	(Llanelli)
5	4th	N.E.Horton	(Moseley)	.		19th	B.E.Thomas	(Neath)
6	34th & last	D.P.Rogers (Capt)	(Bedford)	.		10th	W.D.Morris	(Neath)
7	9th	R.B.Taylor	(Northampton)	.		11th	J.Taylor	(London Welsh)
8	8th	D.M.Rollitt	(Bristol)	.		4th	T.M.Davies	(London Welsh)

Referee: D.P.d'Arcy   (Ireland)

SCORERS:

R.Hiller	Penalty Goal	3 - 0			
		3 - 3	M.C.R.Richards	Try	
		Half-time			
		3 - 6	K.S.Jarrett	Penalty Goal	
		3 - 9	K.S.Jarrett	Penalty Goal	
		3 - 12	B.John	Try	
		3 - 14	K.S.Jarrett	Conversion	
		3 - 17	M.C.R.Richards	Try	
R.Hiller	Penalty Goal	6 - 17			
		6 - 20	B.John	Drop Goal	
		6 - 23	M.C.R.Richards	Try	
		6 - 25	K.S.Jarrett	Conversion	
		6 - 28	M.C.R.Richards	Try	
		6 - 30	K.S.Jarrett	Conversion	
R.Hiller	Penalty Goal	9 - 30			

POINTS: R.Hiller   9 points   (58)   K.S.Jarrett and M.C.R.Richards   12 points each
       B.John   6 points

MATCH COMMENTARY:

Again, England placed their faith in the same XV who had performed so creditably against France and Scotland, except for Plummer who replaced the injured Fielding. The match was most notable for Maurice Richards' remarkable feat in scoring four tries, but it was also unusual in that the score at half-time was three points each and the deluge of points in the second half saw England go down to their heaviest defeat against Wales since 1922, and their second successive drubbing at Cardiff. This was the fifth time that England had conceded five tries since the war, and the third time to the Welsh.

SUMMARY OF THE SEASON - 1968 - 69:

For the third successive season England finished the Five Nations Championship with four points from the four matches played, but the results were somewhat unusual in that England had beaten France soundly at Twickenham, and lost to Wales by an even greater margin in Cardiff, yet France had drawn with Wales in Paris, thus denying them the Grand Slam. In similar vein, the England pack who had acquitted themselves reasonably well in three matches were utterly outplayed in every respect by the Scots at Twickenham, and yet managed to win the match. Such is the unpredictability - and the joy - of the Five Nations.

Two significant changes to the laws of the game had been introduced during the close season in the Northern Hemisphere. In the event of a player being injured during a match and having to leave the field and withdraw from the game, the new rule now allowed a replacement to take the field. The second change was the universal adoption of what had become known as the Australian dispensation rule which had been adopted in Australia some years ago in local matches. This allowed kicking directly into touch only from within the defending side's 22 metre line, kicks to touch from all other parts of the field were now required to bounce in the field of play before crossing the touch line. Whether the latter rule change was directly responsible for a much more free-flowing style of rugby in this year's Five Nations Championship is a matter for conjecture, but the fact remains that 32 tries were scored in the 1968-69 Five Nations compared with an average of slightly less than 23 in the previous ten years.

Only seventeen players were used for the four Five Nations matches, and eighteen if the first ever replacement, Tim Dalton of Coventry, who replaced the injured Keith Fielding in the Scottish match, is included. It was injury only which led to any changes being made in the team at all, and if ever a player suffered misfortune through injury, it was Dick Greenwood, the England captain in the first match of the season against Ireland. For the second match, against France, the selectors had announced an unchanged team. On the day before the match, Greenwood was playing squash and was hit in the eye by his opponent's racquet, and suffered an injury which compelled him to withdraw from the side. Budge Rogers was appointed captain in his stead and the unfortunate Greenwood, although quickly recovering from his injury, did not play for England again, either as captain, or in any other capacity.

Two other milestones of some significance were passed during the season; Budge Rogers, for the match against France, gained his 32nd cap, thus beating Wavell Wakefield's all time record of 31 caps, and becoming England's most capped player. "Wakers" record was achieved in eight seasons, whereas Budge Rogers set his record in his ninth season. In the final match of the season, against Wales, Bob Hiller became only the second player to score fifty points for England, Roger Hosen having been the first, two years previously.

Only four players were not to play in the white jersey for England again after this season. Most eminent, of course, was Budge Rogers whose record of thirty four caps would stand for five years until John Pullin surpassed it in 1974. He had had a very distinguished International career, scored a try on his debut against Ireland in 1961, and captained England seven times. He went on the 1962 Lions' tour to South Africa and played in two Tests. He became an England selector and was one of the youngest men ever to be appointed to the selection panel and was awarded an OBE for services to rugby. He is a senior executive in the engineering industry.
Dick Greenwood had gained five caps and captained England only once before his unfortunate pre-match injury, and he, too, scored a try on his debut against Ireland, but in 1966. He played 26 times for Lancashire and was a schoolmaster, and later Bursar, at Stonyhurst. Trevor Wintle, the Northampton scrum-half with five caps, was one of the early exponents of the diving pass from the base of the scrum. Least conspicuous of all, but nevertheless with a place in the record books, was Tim Dalton, the Coventry wing, whose only cap was earned as the first replacement used by England following the introduction of that rule by the IRB at the beginning of the season.

Evidence of a much more stable selection policy, both in terms of players used during the season, and the numbers leaving the International stage, should, it was hoped, augur well for England in the immediate future.

FIVE NATIONS CHAMPIONSHIP TABLE:

Won: **Calcutta Cup**

		Played	Won	Lost	Drawn	Points: For	Against	Tries: For	Against	Title Points
1	Wales	4	3	0	1	79	31	4	2	7
2	Ireland	4	3	1	0	61	48	8	6	6
3	**ENGLAND**	4	2	2	0	54	58	6	8	4
4	Scotland	4	1	3	0	12	44	1	9	2
5	France	4	0	3	1	28	53	3	7	1

Home Games: beat France 22 - 8, (three tries to one); beat Scoptland 8 - 3, (two tries to nil)

Away Games: lost to Ireland 15 - 17, (one try to two); lost to Wales 9 - 30, (no tries to five)

6th match   **ENGLAND   11 pts**   v   **SOUTH AFRICA   8 pts**

	Caps					Caps		
15	9th	R.Hiller (Capt)	(Harlequins)			12th	H.O.de Villiers	(Western Province)
14	4th	K.J.Fielding	(Moseley)			13th	S.H.Nomis	(Transvaal)
13	5th	J.S.Spencer	(Headingley)			2nd	O.A.Roux	(Northern Transvaal)
12	5th	D.J.Duckham	(Coventry)			16th & last	E.Olivier	(Western Province)
11	1st	P.M.Hale	(Moseley)			2nd	A.E.van der Watt	(Western Province)
10	1st	I.R.Shackleton	(Harrogate)			16th	P.J.Visagie	(Griqualand West)
9	1st	N.C.Starmer-Smith	(Harlequins)			19th	D.J.de Villiers (Capt)	(Western Province)
1	1st	C.B.Stevens	(Penzance-Newlyn)			14th	J.L.Myburgh	(Northern Transvaal)
2	10th	J.V.Pullin	(Bristol)			8th & last	D.C.Walton	(Natal)
3	5th	K.E.Fairbrother	(Coventry)			18th	J.F.K.Marais	(Western Province)
4	13th	A.M.Davis	(Harlequins)			3rd & last	A.E.de Wet	(Western Province)
5	11th	P.J.Larter	(Northampton)			1st	I.J.de Klerk	(Transvaal)
6	5th	B.R.West	(Northampton)			13th	P.J.F.Greyling	(Orange Free State)
7	1st	A.L.Bucknall	(Richmond)			1st	A.J.Bates	(Western Transvaal)
8	10th	R.B.Taylor	(Northampton)			21st	T.P.Bedford	(Natal)
	1st	C.S.Wardlow (Northampton) for Hiller - 77				2nd	M.J.Lawless (West'n Prov) for Olivier -	

Referee:	K.D.Kelleher	(Ireland)

SCORERS:

			0 - 3	P.J.Visagie	Penalty Goal
			0 - 6	P.J.F.Greyling	Try
			0 - 8	P.J.Visagie	Conversion
P.J.Larter	Try	(1st & only)	3 - 8	
			Half-time	
R.Hiller	Penalty Goal		6 - 8	
J.V.Pullin	Try	(1st & only)	9 - 8	
R.Hiller	Conversion		11 - 8	

POINTS:

R.Hiller	5 points	(63)	P.J.Visagie	5 points
J.V.Pullin	3 points	(3)	P.J.F.Greyling	3 points
P.J.Larter	3 points	(6)		

MATCH COMMENTARY:

For the first time England adopted a squad system for this game, preparing with a squad of 30 players. As a result, the team were well prepared and fully deserved to win the match. The South Africans were not seen at their best because the whole tour had suffered disruption at the hands of anti-apartheid demonstrators wherever they went and they were seriously affected by an unusually high incidence of niggling injuries The match was really played, not only in two halves, but also in two distinct parts. South Africa dominated the first half and powered to an impressive eight point lead in 35 minutes. English doggedness was amply rewarded, and the team was immensely heartened by Peter Larter's try immediately before half-time. In the second half it was all England. They more than matched the legendary South African forward power and John Pullin's try emphasised the forwards' superiority. Bob Hiller's usually reliable boot secured the conversion and a three point lead, and despite ferocious South African onslaughts in the closing stages, England withstood all that their opponents could muster and emerged victorious.

In converting John Pullin's try, Bob Hiller equalled Roger Hosen's record of 63 points in International matches.

82nd match   **ENGLAND   9 pts**   v   **IRELAND   3 pts**

	Caps					Caps		
15	10th	R.Hiller (Capt)	(Harlequins)	.		45th	T.J.Kiernan (Capt)	(Cork Constitutio
14	5th	K.J.Fielding	(Moseley)	.		18th	A.T.A.Duggan	(Lansdowne)
13	6th	J.S.Spencer	(Headingley)	.		19th	F.P.K.Bresnihan	(London Irish)
12	6th	D.J.Duckham	(Coventry)	.		29th	C.M.H.Gibson	(NIFC)
11	2nd	P.M.Hale	(Moseley)	.		29th & last	A.J.F.O'Reilly	(London Irish)
10	2nd	I.R.Shackleton	(Harrogate)	.		7th	B.J.McGann	(Lansdowne)
9	2nd	N.C.Starmer-Smith	(Harlequins)	.		20th	R.M.Young	(Collegians)
1	2nd	C.B.Stevens	(Penzance-Newlyn)	.		35th	S.Millar	(Ballymena)
2	11th	J.V.Pullin	(Bristol)	.		23rd	K.W.Kennedy	(London Irish)
3	6th	K.E.Fairbrother	(Coventry)	.		14th	P.O'Callaghan	(Dolphin)
4	14th	A.M.Davis	(Harlequins)	.		19th	M.G.Molloy	(London Irish)
5	12th	P.J.Larter	(Northampton)	.		39th	W.J.McBride	(Ballymena)
6	6th	B.R.West	(Northampton)	.		10th	R.A.Lamont	(Instonians)
7	2nd	A.L.Bucknall	(Richmond)	.		3rd	J.F.Slattery	(UC Dublin)
8	11th	R.B.Taylor	(Northampton)	.		17th	K.G.Goodall	(City of Derry)

Referee: A.R.Lewis   (Wales)

SCORERS:

				0 - 3	T.J.Kiernan Penalty Goal
				Half-time	
R.Hiller	D'p Goal	(1st)	3 - 3		
R.Hiller	D'p Goal	(2nd & last)	6 - 3		
I.R.Shackleton	Try	(1st & only)	9 - 3		

POINTS:

R.Hiller	6 points	(69)	T.J.Kiernan	3 points
I.R.Shackleton	3 points	(3)		

MATCH COMMENTARY:

The same side which had beaten South Africa in December took the field on a bright dry day against Ireland. The Irish selectors sprung a surprise by inviting Tony O'Reilly to take the place of Bill Brown, who had to withdraw at the last minute, to gain his 29th cap after a gap of seven years. As it happened, he had little to do during the game, he barely got a pass and there was no fairy-tale ending. It is said that Johnny Quirke, Ireland's youngest post-war cap when he played at scrum-half against England in 1962 aged 17, sent a telegram to Tony O'Reilly before the match offering the observation that "Heinz beans are Has-beens". O'Reilly's response is not recorded.

The match was played on a slippery surface and in a strong wind, and Ireland fully deserved their lead at half-time. The English pack did not look half as capable as they had against South Africa in December. England generated a little more fire and aggression in the second half, and when the ball came loose following a strong run into the Irish half by David Duckham, the ball came back to Bob Hiller who dropped a towering goal from 45 yards and near touch to level the score. Ninety seconds later, he did exactly the same thing again, and England were, surprisingly, in the lead. England's victory was sealed when, after the ball went loose following John Spencer's tackle on Tom Kiernan, Roger Shackleton scooped it up to score. A fortuitous victory for England after a very promising start against South Africa.

75th match   **ENGLAND   13 pts**   v   **WALES   17 pts**

	Caps					Caps		
15	11th	R.Hiller (Capt)	(Harlequins)	.		10th	J.P.R.Williams	(London Welsh)
14	1st	M.J.Novak	(Harlequins)	.		25th	S.J.Watkins	(Cardiff)
13	7th	J.S.Spencer	(Headingley)	.		16th	S.J.Dawes	(London Welsh)
12	7th	D.J.Duckham	(Coventry)	.		9th	W.H.Raybould	(Newport)
11	3rd & last	P.M.Hale	(Moseley)	.		4th	I.Hall	(Aberavon)
10	3rd	I.R.Shackleton	(Harrogate)	.		17th	B.John	(Cardiff)
9	3rd	N.C.Starmer-Smith	(Harlequins)	.		17th	G.O.Edwards (Capt)	(Cardiff)
1	3rd	C.B.Stevens	(Penzance-Newlyn)	.		31st	D.Williams	(Ebbw Vale)
2	12th	J.V.Pullin	(Bristol)	.		9th	J.Young	(Harrogate)
3	7th	K.E.Fairbrother	(Coventry)	.		3rd	D.B.Llewellyn	(Newport)
4	15th	A.M.Davis	(Harlequins)	.		3rd	T.G.Evans	(London Welsh)
5	13th	P.J.Larter	(Northampton)	.		10th	W.D.Thomas	(Llanelli)
6	7th	B.R.West	(Northampton)	.		16th	W.D.Morris	(Neath)
7	3rd	A.L.Bucknall	(Richmond)	.		5th	W.D.Hughes	(Newbridge)
8	12th	R.B.Taylor	(Northampton)	.		10th	T.M.Davies	(London Welsh)

1st & only   R.Hopkins (Maesteg) for Edwards - 60

Referee: R.Calmet   (France)
                 replaced by R.F.Johnson   (England)

SCORERS: D.J.Duckham   Try   (4th)   3 - 0
               R.Hiller   Conversion   5 - 0
                                                  5 - 3   T.M.Davies   Try
               M.J.Novak   Try   (1st & only) 8 - 3
               R.Hiller   Conversion   10 - 3
               R.Hiller   Penalty Goal   13 - 3
                                                  Half-time
                                                  13 - 6   B.John   Try
                                                  13 - 9   J.P.R.Williams Try
                                                  13 - 12   R.Hopkins   Try
                                                  13 - 14   J.P.R.Williams Conversion
                                                  13 - 17   B.John   Drop Goal

POINTS: R.Hiller   7 points   (76)   B.John   6 points
              D.J.Duckham   3 point   (12)   J.P.R.Williams   5 points
              M.J.Novak   3 points   (3)   T.M.Davies and R.Hopkins   3 points each

MATCH COMMENTARY:

England made only one change from the team which had won the last two matches, that of Novak for the injured Keith Fielding and they started the game very purposefully. At half-time England held a commanding 13 points to 3 lead and a third successive win seemed almost certain. But then Barry John wove his magic and scored a try. Welsh hearts and hopes were raised. Half way into the second half, Gareth Edwards had to leave the field and Welsh hearts sank. On came Ray "Chico" Hopkins of Maesteg, for his first (and only) cap, and he must have thought that this was the day for which he had been born. He inspired Wales, made a try for J.P.R.Williams and then scored one himself. Finally Hopkins gave Barry John a pass which gave him time, and room, to drop a goal to secure a tremendous Welsh triumph. During the match, the French referee, M. Calmet, suffered a broken leg after a collision with a player, and was replaced by a Englishman !!

85th match   **ENGLAND 5 pts**   v   **SCOTLAND 14 pts**

77th Calcutta Cup

	Caps					Caps		
15	12th	R.Hiller (Capt)	(Harlequins)	.	5th	I.S.G.Smith	(London Scottish)
14	2nd	M.J.Novak	(Harlequins)	.	3rd	M.A.Smith	(London Scottish)
13	8th	J.S.Spencer	(Headingley)	.	13th	J.N.M.Frame	(Gala)
12	8th	D.J.Duckham	(Coventry)	.	14th	J.W.C.Turner	(Gala)
11	1st & only	M.P.Bulpitt	(Blackheath)	.	4th	A.G.Biggar	(London Scottish)
10	4th & last	I.R.Shackleton	(Harrogate)	.	7th	I.Robertson	(Watsonians)
9	4th	N.C.Starmer-Smith	(Harlequins)	.	3rd	D.S.Paterson	(Gala)
1	4th	C.B.Stevens	(Penzance-Newlyn)	.	12th	N.Suddon	(Hawick)
2	13th	J.V.Pullin	(Bristol)	.	28th	F.A.L.Laidlaw (Capt)	(Melrose)
3	8th	K.E.Fairbrother	(Coventry)	.	16th	A.B.Carmichael	(West of Scotland)
4	16th & last	A.M.Davis	(Harlequins)	.	27th	P.K.Stagg	(Sale)
5	14th	P.J.Larter	(Northampton)	.	5th	G.L.Brown	(West of Scotland)
6	8th & last	B.R.West	(Northampton)	.	5th & last	T.G.Elliott	(Langholm)
7	4th	A.L.Bucknall	(Richmond)	.	12th	R.J.Arneil	(Leicester)
8	13th	R.B.Taylor	(Northampton)	.	13th	P.C.Brown	(Gala)

1st   B.S.Jackson (Broughton Park) for West -

Referee: M.Joseph   (Wales)

SCORERS:

			0 - 3	P.C.Brown	Penalty Goal
			0 - 6	A.G.Biggar	Try
			Half-time		
			0 - 9	P.C.Brown	Penalty Goal
J.S.Spencer	Try	(1st)	3 - 9		
R.Hiller	Conversion		5 - 9		
			5 - 12	J.W.C.Turner	Try
			5 - 14	P.C.Brown	Conversion

POINTS:

J.S.Spencer	3 points	(3)	P.C.Brown	8 points
R.Hiller	2 points	(78)	J.W.C.Turner	3 points
			A.G.Biggar	3 points

MATCH COMMENTARY:

Although Scotland had beaten South Africa, they had lost all three Five Nations matches this season, and England went to Murrayfield confident that the late second half humiliation against Wales had been a temporary lapse and that normal service would be resumed today. Complacency never pays off, nor did it on this occasion. The England pack were completely outplayed by a very lively and mobile Scottish eight and England had little possession and little chance to score. The chance that they had, they took, when John Spencer, receiving a short pass from a tapped penalty by Roger Shackleton, ran 70 yards to touch down in the corner. Bob Hiller converted with casual aplomb but he had missed four penalty goal opportunities and seemed strangely out of touch. He failed to lead his team effectively and on occasions they showed signs of falling out amongst themselves. At best it was a very indifferent performance by England.

Strangely, exactly twenty years later, England were to make exactly the same mistake in complacently and completely under-estimating the Scots, only on this later occasion, there was a Grand Slam at stake !!

45th match   **ENGLAND 13 pts**   v   **FRANCE 35 pts**

	Caps					Caps		
15	1st	A.M.Jorden	(Blackheath)		19th	P.Villepreux	(Toulouse)
14	6th	K.J.Fielding	(Moseley)		4th	R.Bourgarel	(Toulouse)
13	9th	J.S.Spencer	(Headingley)		15th	J.Trillo	(Begles)
12	9th	D.J.Duckham	(Coventry)		22nd	J-P.Lux	(Tyrosse)
11	3rd & last	M.J.Novak	(Harlequins)		14th & last	J-M.Bonal	(Toulouse)
10	12th	J.F.Finlan	(Moseley)		5th	J-L.Berot	(Toulouse)
9	5th	N.C.Starmer-Smith	(Harlequins)		1st	M.Pebeyre	(Vichy)
1	2nd & last	B.S.Jackson	(Broughton Park)		13th	M.Lasserre	(Agen)
2	14th	J.V.Pullin	(Bristol)		6th	R.Benesis	(Narbonne)
3	9th	K.E.Fairbrother	(Coventry)		11th	J.Iracabal	(Bayonne)
4	1st & only	M.M.Leadbetter	(Broughton Park)		6th	J.Le Droff	(Auch)
5	15th	P.J.Larter	(Northampton)		23rd	E.Cester	(Toulouse)
6	14th	R.B.Taylor (Capt)	(Northampton)		5th	P.Biemouret	(Agen)
7	5th	A.L.Bucknall	(Richmond)		25th	C.Carrere (Capt)	(Toulon)
8	1st & only	G.F.Redmond	(Cambridge Univ)		50th	B.Dauga	(Mont-de-Marsan)

Referee: W.K.M.Jones   (Wales)

SCORERS:

		0 - 3	P.Villepreux	Penalty Goal
		0 - 6	R.Bougarel	Try
		0 - 9	J-P.Lux	Try
		0 - 11	P.Villepreux	Conversion
		0 - 14	J-L.Berot	Drop Goal
		Half-time		
		0 - 17	J.Trillo	Try
		0 - 19	P.Villepreux	Conversion
R.B.Taylor	Try (2nd & last)	3 - 19		
A.M.Jorden	Conversion	5 - 19		
J.S.Spencer	Try (2nd & last)	8 - 19		
A.M.Jorden	Conversion	10 - 19		
A.M.Jorden	Penalty Goal	13 - 19		
		13 - 22	P.Villepreux	Drop Goal
		13 - 25	B.Dauga	Try
		13 - 28	J-M.Bonal	Try
		13 - 30	P.Villepreux	Conversion
		13 - 33	J-L.Berot	Try
		13 - 35	P.Villepreux	Conversion

POINTS:

A.M.Jorden	7 points	(7)	P.Villepreux	14 points
J.S.Spencer	3 points	(6)	J-L.Berot	6 points
R.B.Taylor	3 points	(6)	R.Bourgarel, J.Trillo, J-P.Lux,	
			J-M.Bonal and B.Dauga	3 points each

MATCH COMMENTARY:

The Selectors decided that they could do better in finding not only a different full-back but also a different Captain and dispensed with the services of Bob Hiller along with five others and they made two positional changes. In spite of all that, there was no perceptible difference other than that England lost by an even greater margin. England made no impression at all on a French side in superb form and were soundly thrashed by six tries to two. England had a remarkable purple patch in the third quarter when they scored 13 points in eight minutes, but the then France scored another 16 !! Never had England conceded 35 points before, and they had not been beaten by a margin of 22 points since Ireland won by 22 points to nil at Lansdowne Road in 1947. It was a humiliating display, but the French, with the sun on their backs, in Paris, in the spring, were unstoppable and they had a field day. To celebrate Benoit Dauga's 50th cap, France won their third Championship title sharing it with Wales - the other year - last year, they picked up the Wooden Spoon. This was the first time England had conceded six tries in a match since 1931.

SUMMARY OF THE SEASON - 1969 - 70:

Whatever encouragement may have grown out of England's rather more consistent selection policy during the course of last season was seriously undermined when the selectors brought in five new caps and made eight changes in total for the first match of the season against South Africa. As the season progressed all hopes of an improvement in England's fortunes were dashed and the humiliation of the final match against France in Paris was the beginning of a very sorry chapter in the history of English International rugby.

Against South Africa, in spite of the many changes, England fared well. The pack, in particular, excelled themselves, and although it can certainly be argued that the South African side were dispirited on tour with all the aggravation they had to suffer on the apartheid issue, it was, nevertheless, a commendable victory. The same side took the field against Ireland, but they looked a totally different team, and had it not been for the laconic Bob Hiller grasping the nettle with two superbly struck drop goals within two minutes in the second half, England's cause would have been well and truly lost. As it was, Hiller's vision inspired England to raise their game just enough and two Championship points were in the bag. Regrettably nothing more was to be added to that collection for the remainder of the season. The first half against Wales was eminently satisfactory and England turned round with a ten point lead. Wales began to recover after the break, and Barry John scored a try with casual ease, but when Ray Hopkins came on to the pitch for his first and only cap, to replace the injured Gareth Edwards, he somehow managed to control events such that Wales scored a further eleven points and won the match at a canter. For Hopkins, it was the match of a lifetime; for England, it was the end of the season. Only one change for the trip to Edinburgh, and to all outward appearances it seemed that England expected to win. The Scottish pack thought differently and proceeded to trample England into the ground. Only John Spencer's try after a run of all of seventy yards, gave any heart to England, and indeed, with the Scottish pack so dominant, this was about the only opportunity that the strong-running backs got throughout the match. Six changes, three in the pack, made not a whit of difference to the result in Paris, England let in six tries and were soundly thrashed. Bob Hiller being dropped, the unfortunate Bob Taylor was nominated as captain for this match. The result did not destroy his International career, he played two more International matches - but not as Captain !

The Championship as a whole, although producing more tries than in any season since the war, seemed to contain more coach-inspired stereotype play, more rigid game plans, than before - with the notable exception of Ray Hopkins' contribution at Twickenham . Despite the number of tries scored, it was not an inspirational Championship.

In the five matches, and in the Five Nations Championship alone, England used a total of twenty-two players, and one replacement, Chris Wardlow who came on to replace Bob Hiller in the match against South Africa to gain his first cap. In all, in addition to Wardlow, ten new caps were awarded; for three of these it was to be their only cap, Mike Bulpitt, Gerry Redmond and Mike Leadbetter; and Mike Novak joined that distinguised band of players who scored a try in their debut match, in his case in that memorable match against Wales.

Nine players were not to represent England again in their remaining rugby careers. Alec Davis, with sixteen caps, did a great deal of work in coaching at schoolboy level for many years, and later became an England coach. He was a schoolteacher. Bryan West, a British Lion in 1968, won eight caps, joined Wakefield Trinity Rugby League Club in 1971, but played with them for only one season. A product of Loughborough College, he was a PE teacher. Ian Shackleton, four caps, had had the distinction of scoring the winning try on his debut for Cambridge in 1968, the first of his three Blues. Mike Novak and Peter Hale both earned three caps and Barry Jackson, whose first cap was as a substitute, had two.

It had been an extremely disappointing season for England, after reasonably high expectations and a promising start, but the fall from grace in the last two matches at Murrayfield and Stade Colombes was a bitter pill for the devoted England following to swallow - but they were to get used to that in the seasons to come !

FIVE NATIONS CHAMPIONSHIP TABLE:

Won: **Calcutta Cup**

		Played	Won	Lost	Drawn	Points: For	Against	Tries: For	Against	Title Points
1 =	France	4	3	1	0	60	33	11	4	6
1 =	Wales	4	3	1	0	46	42	9	7	6
3	Ireland	4	2	2	0	33	28	6	4	4
4 =	Scotland	4	1	3	0	43	50	6	11	2
4 =	ENGLAND	4	1	3	0	40	69	6	12	2

Home Games: beat Ireland 9 - 3, (one try to nil); lost to Wales 13 - 17, (two tries to four)

Away Games: lost to Scotland 5 - 14, (one try to two); lost to France 13 - 35, (two tries to six)

CENTENARY SEASON

76th match   **ENGLAND   6 pts**   v   **WALES   22 pts**

	Caps				Caps		
15	1st	P.A.Rossborough	(Coventry)	.	13th	J.P.R.Williams	(London Welsh)
14	1st	J.P.A.G.Janion	(Bedford)	.	14th	T.G.R.Davies	(London Welsh)
13	2nd	C.S.Wardlow	(Northampton)	.	19th	S.J.Dawes (Capt)	(London Welsh)
12	10th	J.S.Spencer	(Headingley)	.	2nd	A.J.Lewis	(Ebbw Vale)
11	10th	D.J.Duckham	(Coventry)	.	1st	J.C.Bevan	(Cardiff)
10	1st	I.D.Wright	(Northampton)	.	19th	B.John	(Cardiff)
9	1st	J.J.Page	(Bedford)	.	20th	G.O.Edwards	(Cardiff)
1	7th	D.L.Powell	(Northampton)	.	6th	D.B.Llewellyn	(Newport)
2	15th	J.V.Pullin	(Bristol)	.	12th	J.Young	(London Welsh)
3	10th	K.E.Fairbrother	(Coventry)	.	33rd	D.Williams	(Ebbw Vale)
4	16th	P.J.Larter	(Northampton)	.	1st	M.G.Roberts	(London Welsh)
5	1st & only	B.F.Ninnes	(Coventry)	.	13th	W.D.Thomas	(Llanelli)
6	6th	A.L.Bucknall (Capt)	(Richmond)	.	19th	W.D.Morris	(Neath)
7	1st	A.Neary	(Broughton Park)	.	15th	J.Taylor	(London Welsh)
8	1st	R.C.Hannaford	(Bristol)	.	13th	T.M.Davies	(London Welsh)

Referee: D.P.d'Arcy   (Ireland)

SCORERS:

				0 - 3	B.John	Drop Goal
	R.C.Hannaford	Try	(1st & only)	3 - 3		
				3 - 6	T.G.R.Davies	Try
				3 - 8	J.Taylor	Conversion
				3 - 11	J.C.Bevan	Try
				3 - 14	T.G.R.Davies	Try
				3 - 16	J.Taylor	Conversion
				Half-time		
				3 - 19	J.P.R.Williams	Penalty Goal
	P.A.Rossborough	Penalty Goal		6 - 19		
				6 - 22	B.John	Drop Goal

POINTS:

	R.C.Hannaford	3 points	(3)	T.G.R.Davies	6 points
	P.A.Rossborough	3 points	(3)	B.John	6 points
				J.Taylor	4 points
				J.C.Bevan and J.P.R.Williams	3 points each

MATCH COMMENTARY:

Seven new caps, for the opening match of this Centenary season, in the cauldron at Cardiff never had a chance against this formidable Welsh team, claimed by many to be the best ever assembled, who were to go on to win the Grand Slam this season and form the nucleus of the successful British Lions side in New Zealand later in the year. England just could not match the skill, flair and pure quality of this fine side. The Welsh pack were all powerful, frequently pushing England back despite the half-stone per man disadvantage, and this was the basis of the Welsh victory. Only in the lines-out did England compete effectively. Jeremy Janion had the misfortune to drop a scoring pass with the line at his mercy just before half-time, but nothing England did or could have done would have knocked the Welsh out of their stride that day, even had they been able to overcome the trauma of conceding three tries before half-time; that no more were conceded does them credit

CENTENARY SEASON

83rd match   **ENGLAND   9 pts**   v   **IRELAND   6 pts**

	Caps					Caps		
15	13th	**R.Hiller**	(Harlequins)			2nd	**B.J.O'Driscoll**	(Manchester)
14	2nd	**J.P.A.G.Janion**	(Bedford)			22nd	**A.T.A.Duggan**	(Lansdowne)
13	11th	**J.S.Spencer (Capt)**	(Headingley)			23rd	**F.P.K.Bresnihan**	(London Irish)
12	3rd	**C.S.Wardlow**	(Northampton)			33rd	**C.M.H.Gibson (Capt)**	(NIFC)
11	11th	**D.J.Duckham**	(Coventry)			2nd	**E.L.Grant**	(CIYMS)
10	2nd	**I.D.Wright**	(Northampton)			11th	**B.J.McGann**	(Lansdowne)
9	2nd	**J.J.Page**	(Bedford)			24th	**R.M.Young**	(Collegians)
1	8th	**D.L.Powell**	(Northampton)			20th	**R.J.McLoughlin**	(Blackrock Coll)
2	16th	**J.V.Pullin**	(Bristol)			27th	**K.W.Kennedy**	(London Irish)
3	11th	**K.E.Fairbrother**	(Coventry)			2nd	**J.F.Lynch**	(St Mary's College)
4	17th	**P.J.Larter**	(Northampton)			43rd	**W.J.McBride**	(Ballymena)
5	5th	**N.E.Horton**	(Moseley)			23rd	**M.G.Molloy**	(London Irish)
6	7th	**A.L.Bucknall**	(Richmond)			9th	**M.L.Hipwell**	(Tenerure College)
7	2nd	**A.Neary**	(Broughton Park)			7th	**J.F.Slattery**	(UC Dublin)
8	2nd	**R.C.Hannaford**	(Bristol)			2nd	**D.J.Hickie**	(St Mary's College)

Referee: M.Joseph   (Wales)

SCORERS:	R.Hiller	Penalty Goal	3 - 0		
			3 - 3	**E.L.Grant**	Try
	R.Hiller	Penalty Goal	6 - 3		
	R.Hiller	Penalty Goal	9 - 3		
			Half-time		
			9 - 6	**A.T.A.Duggan**	Try

POINTS:	R.Hiller	9 points (87)		**A.T.A.Duggan**	3 points
				E.L.Grant	3 points

MATCH COMMENTARY:

It was only thanks to the reliable boot of Bob Hiller that England were able to record this their only victory in their Centenary season. England conceded two tries, although there is a strong suspicion that Grant knocked on in intercepting the pass which led to his try. England, on the other hand, did not come close to scoring a try, certainly not from among the backs because they were denied possession because the forwards again lost the battle up front. The record books will show the win, but it was not an convincing one. England played with the gale force wind in the first half and Bob Hiller took as much advantage as he could in kicking three penalty goals, two of them from all of fifty yards Even so, a six point lead at half-time did not look enough, but the Irish backs squandered their chances and the defence of Wardlow and Duckham, in particular, was outstanding.

This was the second occasion on which Bob Hiller has scored all England's points in a match, and in the last four matches against Ireland, he has scored 33 of the 42 points scored.

CENTENARY SEASON

46th match   **ENGLAND   14 pts**   v   **FRANCE   14 pts**

	Caps				Caps		
15	14th	R.Hiller (Capt)	(Harlequins)	.	23rd	P.Villepreux	(Toulouse)
14	3rd	J.P.A.G.Janion	(Bedford)	.	6th	J.Sillieres	(Tarbes)
13	4th	C.S.Wardlow	(Northampton)	.	1st	R.Bertranne	(Bagneres)
12	12th	D.J.Duckham	(Coventry)	.	26th	J-P.Lux	(Tyrosse)
11	2nd	P.B.Glover	(Bath)	.	5th	J.Cantoni	(Beziers)
10	3rd	I.D.Wright	(Northampton)	.	9th	J-L.Berot	(Toulouse)
9	3rd	J.J.Page	(Bedford)	.	2nd	M.Barrau	(Beaumont)
1	9th	D.L.Powell	(Northampton)	.	9th	J-L.Azarete	(St Jean-de-Luz)
2	17th	J.V.Pullin	(Bristol)	.	10th	R.Benesis	(Narbonne)
3	12th & last	K.E.Fairbrother	(Coventry)	.	14th	M.Lassere	(Agen)
4	18th	P.J.Larter	(Northampton)	.	39th	W.Spanghero	(Narbonne)
5	6th	N.E.Horton	(Moseley)	.	1st	C.Spanghero	(Narbonne)
6	8th	A.L.Bucknall	(Richmond)	.	10th	M.Yachvili	(Brive)
7	3rd	A.Neary	(Broughton Park)	.	26th	C.Carrere (Capt)	(Toulon)
8	3rd & last	R.C.Hannaford	(Bristol)	.	54th	B.Dauga	(Mont-de-Marsan)

Referee: A.R.Lewis   (Wales)

SCORERS:

R.Hiller	Penalty Goal		3 - 0			
R.Hiller	Penalty Goal		6 - 0	J.Cantoni	Try	
R.Hiller	Penalty Goal		9 - 0	P.Villepreux	Conversion	
R.Hiller	Try	(1st)	12 - 0			
R.Hiller	Conversion		14 - 0			
			14 - 3	P.Villepreux	Penalty Goal	
			14 - 6	R.Bertranne	Try	
			Half-time			
			14 - 9	J-L.Berot	Drop Goal	
			14 - 12	J.Cantoni	Try	
			14 - 14	P.Villepreux	Conversion	

POINTS: R.Hiller   14 points   (101)   P.Villepreux   5 points
                                        R.Bertranne, J.Cantoni and J-L.Berot 3 points each

MATCH COMMENTARY:

For the second successive match, Bob Hiller scored all England's points and thus salvaged a creditable draw with France, especially creditable after the severe defeat at Stade Colombes last year. France played enterprising rugby and their exciting running produced two good tries, and although England matched them and took all their scoring opportunities, they were fortunate to emerge with a draw as Pierre Villepreux missed four possible penalty goal attempts which normally he could be expected to convert with ease.   In addition, the French backs were so superior in running and handling skills that they should have scored at least three more tries late in the second half and two further drop goals where the attempts went narrowly wide.   Cantoni's try was arguably one of the finest ever seen at Twickenham starting from a missed touch kick by David Duckham which Berot and Villepreux ran back at England before sending Cantoni away en route to the posts. The England defence in the latter stages was heroic and unyielding and effectively denied France. With his final score Bob Hiller became the first England player to score 100 points in International matches. In scoring 14 points in the match he established a new England individual points scoring record, exceeding the 13 points he scored in the corresponding match 3 years ago.

CENTENARY SEASON

86th match   **ENGLAND**   **15 pts**   v   **SCOTLAND**   **16 pts**

78th Calcutta Cup

	Caps					Caps		
15	15th	R.Hiller	(Harlequins)	.		1st	A.R.Brown	(Gala)
14	4th	J.P.A.G.Janion	(Bedford)			5th	W.C.C.Steele	(RAF/Bedford)
13	5th	C.S.Wardlow	(Northampton)	.		18th	J.N.M.Frame	(Gala)
12	12th	J.S.Spencer (Capt)	(Headingley)	.		12th	C.W.W.Rea	(Headingley)
11	13th	D.J.Duckham	(Coventry)	.		9th	A.G.Biggar	(London Scottish)
10	1st	A.R.Cowman	(Loughborough Coll)	.		19th	J.W.C.Turner	(Gala)
9	4th	J.J.Page	(Bedford)	.		9th	D.S.Paterson	(Gala)
1	10th	D.L.Powell	(Northampton)	.		8th	J.McLauchlan	(Jordanhill)
2	18th	J.V.Pullin	(Bristol)	.		1st	Q.Dunlop	(West of Scotland)
3	1st	F.E.Cotton	(Loughborough Coll)	.		21st	A.B.Carmichael	(West of Scotland)
4	19th	P.J.Larter	(Northampton)	.		11th	A.F.McHarg	(London Scottish)
5	7th	N.E.Horton	(Moseley)	.		10th	G.L.Brown	(West of Scotland)
6	9th	A.L.Bucknall	(Richmond)	.		4th	N.A.MacEwan	(Gala)
7	4th	A.Neary	(Broughton Park)	.		17th	R.J.Arneil	(Leicester)
8	15th	R.B.Taylor	(Northampton)	.		17th	P.C.Brown (Capt)	(Gala)

4th & last   I.D.Wright (Northampton) for Wardlow -   .   1st & only   A.S.Turk (Langholm) for Frame -

Referee: C.Durand   (France)

SCORERS:

R.Hiller	Try	(2nd)	3 - 0			
			3 - 3	P.C.Brown	Try	
			3 - 5	P.C.Brown	Conversion	
R.Hiller	Penalty Goal		6 - 5			
R.Hiller	Penalty Goal		9 - 5			
			Half-time			
			9 - 8	D.S.Paterson	Drop Goal	
A.Neary	Try	(1st)	12 - 8			
R.Hiller	Penalty Goal		15 - 8			
			15 - 11	D.S.Paterson	Try	
			15 - 14	C.W.W.Rea	Try	
			15 - 16	P.C.Brown	Conversion	

POINTS:

R.Hiller	12 point	(113)	P.C.Brown	7 points	
A.Neary	3 points	(3)	D.S.Paterson	6 points	
			C.W.W.Rea	3 points	

MATCH COMMENTARY:

A most entertaining game played in near perfect conditions at Twickenham, but again it was Bob Hiller's boot which kept England in touch.
Going into the last few minutes of the game, England were in fact ahead by fifteen points to eleven when Chris Rea broke away to score halfway out and Peter Brown with supreme nonchalance converted to get Scotland home by the narrowest of margins, to win the Calcutta Cup again, and, much more importantly, to win at Twickenham for the first time since 1938. Again, the England pack were poor, and even with a weight advantage, allowed Scotland to get the better of them. Bobn Hiller's remarkable consistency continues; of England's last 38 points, he has scored 35.
England shared third place in the Championship table with Ireland and had had another disappointing season in this their Centenary year.

CENTENARY SEASON

87th match   **ENGLAND**   **6 pts**   v   **SCOTLAND**   **26 pts**

	Caps					Caps		
15	16th	R.Hiller	(Harlequins)	.	2nd	A.R.Brown	(Gala)
14	5th	J.P.A.G.Janion	(Bedford)	.	6th	W.C.C.Steele	(RAF/Bedford)
13	6th & last	C.S.Wardlow	(Northampton)	.	19th	J.N.M.Frame	(Gala)
12	13th	J.S.Spencer (Capt)	(Headingley)	.	13th & last	C.W.W.Rea	(West of Scotland)
11	14th	D.J.Duckham	(Coventry)	.	10th	A.G.Biggar	(London Scottish)
10	2nd	A.R.Cowman	(Loughborough Coll)	.	20th & last	J.W.C.Turner	(Gala)
9	6th	N.C.Starmer-Smith	(Harlequins)	.	10th	D.S.Paterson	(Gala)
1	11th & last	D.L.Powell	(Northampton)	.	9th	J.McLauchlan	(Jordanhill)
2	19th	J.V.Pullin	(Bristol)	.	2nd & last	Q.Dunlop	(West of Scotland)
3	2nd	F.E.Cotton	(Loughborough Coll)	.	22nd	A.B.Carmichael	(West of Scotland)
4	20th	P.J.Larter	(Northampton)	.	12th	A.F.McHarg	(London Scottish)
5	1st	C.W.Ralston	(Richmond)	.	11th	G.L.Brown	(West of Scotland)
6	10th & last	A.L.Bucknall	(Richmond)	.	6th	N.A.MacEwan	(Gala)
7	5th	A.Neary	(Broughton Park)	.	18th	R.J.Arneil	(Leicester)
8	16th & last	R.B.Taylor	(Northampton)	.	18th	P.C.Brown (Capt)	(Gala)
				.	1st	G.M.Strachan (Jordanhill) for G.L.Brown -	

Referee: M.Joseph   (Wales)

SCORERS:

			0 - 3	J.N.M.Frame	Try
			0 - 5	A.R.Brown	Conversion
			0 - 8	P.C.Brown	Penalty Goal
A.R.Cowman	D'p Goal	(1st)	3 - 8		
			Half-time		
			3 - 11	J.N.M.Frame	Try
			3 - 13	A.R.Brown	Conversion
			3 - 16	P.C.Brown	Try
			3 - 19	W.C.C.Steele	Try
			3 - 21	A.R.Brown	Conversion
			3 - 24	C.W.W.Rea	Try
			3 - 26	A.R.Brown	Conversion
R.Hiller	Penalty Goal		6 - 26		

POINTS:

R.Hiller	3 points	(116)	A.R.Brown	8 points
A.R.Cowman	3 points	(3)	J.N.M.Frame and P.C.Brown	6 points each
			W.C.C.Steele and C.W.W.Rea	3 points each

MATCH COMMENTARY:

For the first of England's two Centenary matches, Scotland fielded the same side which had, at long last, won at Twickenham, so it was hardly surprising that, with home advantage, Scotland completely outplayed England to the tune of five tries to nil. There was only one team on the pitch who was celebrating anything and that was Scotland who rejoiced in displaying their handling and running skills while England either practiced poor tackling or stood and watched. The Scots crowd were, of course, delighted that the "Auld Enemy" were shown up to such an extent and it was a delightful day - as long as you were not English !! This was Scotland's highest score against England since 1931 and their highest ever winning margin. For the seventh time since 1947, England have conceded five or more tries in an International match.

CENTENARY SEASON

ENGLAND   11 pts   v   RFU PRESIDENT'S
OVERSEAS XV   28 pts

	Caps					
15	17th	R.Hiller	(Harlequins)	.	P.Villepreux	(France)
14	6th	J.P.A.G.Janion	(Bedford)	.	S.O.Knight	(Australia)
13	14th & last	J.S.Spencer (Capt)	(Headingley)	.	J.Maso	(France)
12	15th	D.J.Duckham	(Coventry)	.	J.S.Janses	(South Africa)
11	3rd & last	P.B.Glover	(Bath)	.	B.G.Williams	(New Zealand)
10	3rd	A.R.Cowman	(Loughborough Coll)	.	W.D.Cottrell	(New Zealand)
9	7th & last	N.C.Starmer-Smith	(Harlequins)	.	D.J.De Villiers	(South Africa)
1	5th	C.B.Stevens	(Penzance-Newlyn)	.	R.B.Prosser	(Australia)
2	20th	J.V.Pullin	(Bristol)	.	P.G.Johnson	(Australia)
3	3rd	F.E.Cotton	(Loughborough Coll)	.	J.F.K.Marais	(South Africa)
4	21st	P.J.Larter	(Northampton)	.	C.E.Meads	(New Zealand)
5	2nd	C.W.Ralston	(Richmond)	.	F.C.H.Du Preez	(South Africa)
6	1st & only	R.N.Creed	(Coventry)	.	G.V.Davis	(Australia)
7	6th	A.Neary	(Broughton Park)	.	I.A.Kirkpatrick	(New Zealand)
8	1st	P.J.Dixon	(Harlequins)	.	B.J.Lochore (Capt)	(New Zealand)

Referee: M.H.Titcomb   (England)

SCORERS:

			0 - 3	J.F.K.Marais	Try
R.Hiller	Penalty Goal		3 - 3	
		Half-time		
			3 - 6	I.A.Kirkpatrick	Try
			3 - 8	P.Villepreux	Conversion
R.Hiller	Penalty Goal		6 - 8	
			6 - 11	B.G.Williams	Try
			6 - 13	P.Villepreux	Conversion
R.Hiller	Try rd & last)		9 - 13	
R.Hiller	Conversion		11 - 13	
			11 - 16	I.A.Kirkpatrick	Try
			11 - 18	P.Villepreux	Conversion
			11 - 21	B.G.Williams	Try
			11 - 23	P.Villepreux	Conversion
			11 - 26	B.G.Williams	Try
			11 - 28	P.Villepreux	Conversion

POINTS:

R.Hiller	11 points (127)	
		P.Villepreux	10 points
		B.G.Williams	9 points
		I.A.Kirkpatrick	6 points
		J.F.K.Marais	3 points

MATCH COMMENTARY:
Although England were thoroughly out-classed in this the second Centenary match, by six tries to one, this was their best performance of the season. Bob Hiller again made an immense contribution scoring England's only try and all their points. It was the fourth time that he has achieved this feat. England creditably held the score to 11 - 13 until the last quarter, when experience and class finally told and Bryan Williams scored two tries in injury time. Four great Overseas players appeared for the last time at Twickenham, Dawie De Villiers, Colin Meads, Frik du Preez and Brian Lochore and at the end of the match, the crowd gave them all a stirring and richly deserved farewell.

SUMMARY OF THE SEASON - 1970 - 71

England's Centenary season, planned to be such a joyous occasion, became an embarrassment, particularly in the two Centenary matches when England conceded eleven tries, which provided a very sharp reminder that England's current performance at International level was somewhat less than adequate. Throughout the season, the team was never a cohesive unit, and with three different captains in the Five Nations and twenty one different players, increased by a further five for the Centenary matches, the lack of understanding and consistent direction on the field was perhaps understandable. Without Bob Hiller, England would have been in dire straits. In the Five Nations, although he did not play in the first match against Wales, he scored 35 of England's 44 points, and in the two Centenary matches he scored 14 of the team's 17 points. Without him, England scored 12 points in six matches !! Not surprisingly, in every match he played, Hiller set a new record for Individual points scoring for England. In the match against France, he became the first England player to score 100 points in an International jersey.

The season had started with an impossible task in the away fixture against Wales whose team had been building and improving for some years and were now at the peak of their considerable powers. England were simply outplayed in the early stages, and the impression was that Wales eased up in the second half. A notable match for Charlie Hannaford who scored a try on his debut, and at Cardiff !! The captaincy switched to John Spencer and Bob Hiller was recalled for the second match in Dublin. Hiller showed his appreciation by scoring all England's points in a match in which they lost the try count 0 - 2. It was a win, but it was the only win of the season and a somewhat unmeritted one. France at Twickenham was next and was little better. Again Bob Hiller scored all England's points by converting his own try and kicking three penalty goals to achieve a draw. But the ultimate indignity was kept to the end when Scotland came to Twickenham, scored three tries and left with the Calcutta Cup won on English soil for the first time for 33 years. Not a season to remember.

The Centenary matches were played in an adventurous spirit, but England's opponents had substantially more of that than England could muster. Scotland ran riot at Murrayfield, scoring five tries without reply. The match at Twickenham was an emotive affair, marking, as it did, the retirement form these shores of several internationall stalwarts of the game, and it was a fine advertisement for the game of Rugby Union despite the less than satisfactory England performance. The President's XV won without stretching themselves and allowed Bryan Williams to score three of his side's six tries.

Twelve players called it an International day, voluntarily or otherwise, at the end of the season. Bob Taylor, having earned sixteen caps, and captained England just once when they were thrashed by France at Stades Colombes by six tries to two in 1970, nevertheless had four Lion's caps to his credit from the 1968 tour to South Africa and he was a very versatile back row forward. John Spencer gained fourteen caps and captained England on four occasions during this last unfortunate Centenary season. He went on the 1971 Lions tour to New Zealand but was not capped. He is a solicitor. Keith Fairbrother, twelve caps, whose motto was alleged to be "I hate Welshmen",went on the 1968 Lions' tour to South Africa, joined Leigh Rugby League Club in 1975, but the association was very short-lived. Dave Powell, the Northampton prop, who won eleven caps and had been on the 1966 Lions' tour of Australia and New Zealand, retired to his farm. Tony Bucknall won ten caps and had the thankless task of leading England against Wales at Cardiff this season. He was a boxing, as well as a rugby blue at Oxford and is a stockbroker and brother-in-law to Allan Lamb, the England cricketer. Nigel Starmer-Smith earned seven caps as a Harlequin, and became Editor of the magazine Rugby World and Post and a BBC TV Commentator. Chris Wardlow really deserved more than his six caps as a hard tackling hard-running centre or full-back, and missed the 1971 Lions' tour with cartilege problems. Ian Wright, four caps, was a schoolteacher in Northampton. Peter Glover, with three caps , was a RAF Flying Instructor and a fine athlete. Charlie Hannaford, who scored a try on his debut in Cardiff, gained three caps, was a teacher at Clifton College until he emigrated to New Zealand in 1975 and did a great deal of coaching work there. Barry Ninnes and Roger Creed each took their single caps into retirement. Both could have chosen better seasons to make their mark on English International rugby.

Only five England players were invited to tour New Zealand with the British Lions later in the year, Hiller, Duckham, Spencer, Pullin and Dixon with "Stack" Stevens joining the party as a replacement. John Pullin played in all four Tests, and David Duckham and Peter Dixon in three.

FIVE NATIONS CHAMPIONSHIP TABLE:

Won: **Nothing**

		Played	Won	Lost	Drawn	Points: For	Against	Tries: For	Against	Title Points
1	Wales	4	4	0	0	73	38	13	4	8
2	France	4	1	1	2	41	40	5	5	4
3 =	Ireland	4	1	2	1	41	46	6	5	3
3 =	**ENGLAND**	4	1	2	1	44	58	4	10	3
5	Scotland	4	1	3	0	47	64	7	11	2

Home Games: drew with France 14 - 14, (one try to two); lost to Scotland 15 - 16, (two tries to three)

Away Games: lost to Wales 6 - 22, (one try to three); beat Ireland 9 - 6, (no tries to two)

77th match   **ENGLAND**   **3 pts**   v   **WALES**   **12 pts**

	Caps					Caps		
15	18th	**R.Hiller (Capt)**	(Harlequins)	.	17th	**J.P.R.Williams**	(London Welsh)
14	7th	**J.P.A.G.Janion**	(Bedford)	.	18th	**T.G.R.Davies**	(London Welsh)
13	1st	**M.C.Beese**	(Liverpool)	.	1st	**R.T.E.Bergiers**	(Cardiff Coll of Ed)
12	16th	**D.J.Duckham**	(Coventry)	.	5th	**A.J.Lewis**	(Ebbw Vale)
11	7th	**K.J.Fielding**	(Moseley)	.	5th	**J.C.Bevan**	(Cardiff)
10	1st	**A.G.B.Old**	(Middlesborough)	.	23rd	**B.John**	(Cardiff)
9	1st	**J.G.Webster**	(Moseley)	.	24th	**G.O.Edwards**	(Cardiff)
1	6th	**C.B.Stevens**	(Harlequins)	.	20th	**D.J.Lloyd (Capt)**	(Bridgend)
2	21st	**J.V.Pullin**	(Bristol)	.	16th	**J.Young**	(Harrogate)
3	1st	**M.A.Burton**	(Gloucester)	.	10th	**D.B.Llewellyn**	(Llanelli)
4	1st	**A.Brinn**	(Gloucester)	.	17th	**W.D.Thomas**	(Llanelli)
5	3rd	**C.W.Ralston**	(Richmond)	.	5th	**T.G.Evans**	(London Welsh)
6	2nd	**P.J.Dixon**	(Harlequins)	.	23rd	**W.D.Morris**	(Neath)
7	7th	**A.Neary**	(Broughton Park)	.	19th	**J.Taylor**	(London Welsh)
8	1st	**A.G.Ripley**	(Rosslyn Park)	.	17th	**T.M.Davies**	(London Welsh)

Referee: J.Young   (Scotland)

SCORERS: **R.Hiller**   Penalty Goal   3 - 0

			3 - 3	**B.John**	Penalty Goal
			3 - 6	**B.John**	Penalty Goal
			Half-time		
			3 - 10	**J.P.R.Williams**	Try
			3 - 12	**B.John**	Conversion

POINTS: **R.Hiller**   3 points   (130)   **B.John**   8 points

J.P.R.Williams   4 points

MATCH COMMENTARY:

Six new caps in a side to face a Welsh XV which contained ten of the victorious 1971 Lions squad and six of the side which played in the final test - such was the magnitude of the task facing England. On the other hand, England had five of the Lions' squad in their side, three of whom, Duckham, Pullin and Dixon, played in the final Test Match, and Bob Hiller had been the second highest points scorer on the tour. After the disappointment of last season, there were high hopes that England could at last begin to make a mark on the Championship in which they had had no success for nine years. England lost but were by no means disgraced and held the Welsh to only one try by determination and relentless tackling. England put Wales under considerable pressure early in the match and were first on the scoreboard with Bob Hiller's 31st penalty goal, but Barry John reciprocated twice and Wales were ahead at half-time. Then Wales turned the screw and England conceded the only try of the match. At a scrum in the England 22, Barry John drifted to the open side and a drop goal attempt was on, but J.P.R.Williams had crept up on the blind side, Edwards passed and he was over in a trice. Barry John converted and England were beaten. The England pack, with only 42 caps between, and John Pullin had half of those, appeared for the first time for several seasons to have some stability and, more importantly, some mobility. In fact, this match saw the beginning of a back row partnership which was to last for several years. Peter Dixon, Tony Neary and Andy Ripley were to play together for 12 matches, and the Neary/Ripley combination would be together 23 times, 18 of them successive. The points value of the try had been increased to four during the close season.

84th match   **ENGLAND   12 pts**   v   **IRELAND   16 pts**

	Caps					Caps		
15	19th & last	R.Hiller (Capt)	(Harlequins)	.	50th	T.J.Kiernan	(Cork Constitution)
14	8th	K.J.Fielding	(Moseley)	.	2nd	T.O.Grace	(UC Dublin)
13	2nd	M.C.Beese	(Liverpool)	.	37th	C.M.H.Gibson	(NIFC)
12	17th	D.J.Duckham	(Coventry)	.	20th	M.K.Flynn	(Wanderers)
11	11th	R.E.Webb	(Coventry)	.	2nd	A.W.McMaster	(Ballymena)
10	2nd	A.G.B.Old	(Middlesborough)	.	15th	B.J.McGann	(Cork Constitution)
9	2nd	J.G.Webster	(Moseley)	.	2nd	J.J.Moloney	(St Mary's College)
1	7th	C.B.Stevens	(Harlequins)	.	6th	J.F.Lynch	(St Mary's College)
2	22nd	J.V.Pullin	(Bristol)	.	31st	K.W.Kennedy	(London Irish)
3	2nd	M.A.Burton	(Gloucester)	.	24th	R.J.McLoughlin	(Blackrock College)
4	2nd	A.Brinn	(Gloucester)	.	47th	W.J.McBride	(Ballymena)
5	4th	C.W.Ralston	(Richmond)	.	2nd	C.F.P.Feighery	(Lansdowne)
6	3rd	P.J.Dixon	(Harlequins)	.	2nd	S.A.McKinney	(Dungannon)
7	8th	A.Neary	(Broughton Park)	.	11th	J.F.Slattery	(Blackrock College)
8	2nd	A.G.Ripley	(Rosslyn Park)	.	6th & last	D.J.Hickie	(St Mary's College)

Referee: R.Austry   (France)

SCORERS:

			0 - 3	T.J.Kiernan	Penalty Goal
R.Hiller	Penalty Goal		3 - 3		
C.W.Ralston	Try	(1st & only)	7 - 3		
R.Hiller	Conversion		9 - 3		
			Half-time		
			9 - 7	T.O.Grace	Try
R.Hiller	Penalty Goal		12 - 7		
			12 - 10	B.J.McGann	Drop Goal
			12 - 14	M.K.Flynn	Try
			12 - 16	T.J.Kiernan	Conversion

POINTS:

R.Hiller	8 points	(138)	T.J.Kiernan	5 points
C.W.Ralston	4 points	(4)	T.O.Grace and M.K.Flynn	4 points each
			B.J.McGann	3 points

MATCH COMMENTARY:

After the encouraging, but losing, performance against Wales, England made only one change for this match, keeping the pack intact and bringing in Webb for Janion with Keith Fielding switching wings. A lively and enjoyable game played in the very best of spirits saw England lose only late in injury time when Kevin Flynn (who was first capped in 1959, 13 years previously) ripped through a gap between the English centres to score the winning try. Until then it had been a very even contest which could have gone either way, and the result was a fitting tribute to Tom Keirnan who was winning his 50th cap - the first Irish player to achieve that worthy distinction. England played well and courageously until the Irish pack gained ascendancy in the last quarter, and then came England's fatal mistake. In an attempt to field a missed penalty attempt by Mike Gibson, England knocked on behind the goal line, and from the subsequent five yard scrum Barry McGann dropped a goal. Ireland maintained the pressure on the England line and injury time seemed to go on for ever. Too long, as it happened, and that was when Kevin Flynn beat the England defence. This was only the third Irish victory at Twickenham in thirteen visits since the war. England, again, had failed to win either of their home matches, and it was almost inevitable that the Captain would become the scapegoat.

FIVE NATIONS CHAMPIONSHIP, 1971-72 February 26th 1972, at Stade Colombes

47th match   **ENGLAND   12 pts**   v   **FRANCE   37 pts**

	Caps					Caps		
15	1st	**P.M.Knight**	(Bristol)	.		30th	**P.Villepreux**	(Toulouse)
14	9th	**K.J.Fielding**	(Moseley)	.		12th	**B.Duprat**	(Bayonne)
13	3rd & last	**M.C.Beese**	(Liverpool)	.		19th	**J.Maso**	(Narbonne)
12	18th	**D.J.Duckham**	(Coventry)	.		32nd	**J-P.Lux**	(Dax)
11	12th & last	**R.E.Webb**	(Coventry)	.		7th	**J.Sillieres**	(Tarbes)
10	3rd	**A.G.B.Old**	(Middlesborough)	.		18th	**J-L.Berot**	(Toulouse)
9	1st	**L.E.Weston**	(West of Scotland)	.		4th	**M.Barrau**	(Beaumont)
1	8th	**C.B.Stevens**	(Harlequins)	.		13th	**J-L.Azarete**	(St Jean-de-Luz)
2	23rd	**J.V.Pullin**	(Bristol)	.		16th	**R.Benesis**	(Agen)
3	3rd	**M.A.Burton**	(Gloucester)	.		17th	**J.Iracabal**	(Bayonne)
4	4th & last	**J.Barton**	(Coventry)	.		3rd	**A.Esteve**	(Beziers)
5	5th	**C.W.Ralston**	(Richmond)	.		9th	**C.Spanghero**	(Narbonne)
6	4th	**P.J.Dixon (Capt)**	(Harlequins)	.		10th	**P.Biemouret**	(Agen)
7	9th	**A.Neary**	(Broughton Park)	.		5th	**J-C.Skrela**	(Toulouse)
8	3rd	**A.G.Ripley**	(Rosslyn Park)	.		42nd	**W.Spanghero (Capt)**	(Narbonne)

1st & only   N.O.Martin (Harlequins) for Neary -

Referee: T.F.E.Grierson   (Scotland)

SCORERS:

			0 - 3	P.Villepreux	Penalty Goal
			0 - 7	B.Duprat	Try
			0 - 9	P.Villepreux	Conversion
			0 - 13	P.Biemouret	Try
			0 - 15	P.Villepreux	Conversion
M.C.Beese	Try	(1st & only)	4 - 15		
A.G.B.Old	Conversion		6 - 15		
			Half-time		
A.G.B.Old	Penalty Goal		9 - 15		
			9 - 19	J.Sillieres	Try
			9 - 23	J-P.Lux	Try
			9 - 25	P.Villepreux	Conversion
			9 - 29	W.Spanghero	Try
			9 - 31	P.Villepreux	Conversion
A.G.B.Old	Penalty Goal		12 - 31		
			12 - 35	B.Duprat	Try
			12 - 37	P.Villepreux	Conversion

POINTS:

A.G.B.Old	8 points	(8)	P.Villepreux	13 points
M.C.Beese	4 points	(4)	B.Duprat	8 points
			P.Biemouret, W.Spanghero,	
			J.Sillieres and J-P.Lux	4 points each

MATCH COMMENTARY:

England were thrashed by six tries to one by a French side showing ten changes from that beaten by Ireland four weeks ago. France had also lost to Scotland by 20 points to 9 (and three tries to one) so should have approached this match with something of an inferiority complex. But England too, had just lost to Ireland and in response their selectors had dropped Bob Hiller - not for the first time - and had replaced Jan Webster with Lionel Weston at scrum-half, and had brought in John Barton for Alec Brinn at lock.

Irrespective of the selectors' deliberations, the fact is that England were thrashed by six tries to one by a French side showing no trace whatsoever of inferiority. The English defence was paper-thin and Peter Knight replacing the dropped Bob Hiller was out of his depth. Only once did England get even close at 9 points to 15 early in the second half. and the French gleefully ran up the highest score ever by any side against England, and also achieved a record 25 point margin equalling that set by Wales 67 years ago in 1905.

For the second successive match in France, England conceded six tries - Bob Hiller was dropped for that match too !

88th match

79th Calcutta Cup

ENGLAND   9 pts   v   SCOTLAND   23 pts

	Caps				Caps		
15	2nd	P.M.Knight	(Bristol)	.	5th & last	A.R.Brown	(Gala)
14	10th & last	K.J.Fielding	(Moseley)	.	9th	W.C.C.Steele	(RAF/Bedford)
13	8th	J.P.A.G.Janion	(Bedford)	.	22nd	J.N.M.Frame	(Gala)
12	1st	G.W.Evans	(Coventry)	.	3rd	J.M.Renwick	(Hawick)
11	19th	D.J.Duckham	(Coventry)	.	2nd	L.G.Dick	(Loughborough Coll)
10	4th	A.G.B.Old	(Middlesborough)	.	8th	C.M.Telfer	(Hawick)
9	2nd & last	L.E.Weston	(West of Scotland)	.	2nd	A.J.M.Lawson	(Edinburgh Wand'rs)
1	9th	C.B.Stevens	(Harlequins)	.	12th	J.McLauchlan	(Jordanhill)
2	24th	J.V.Pullin	(Bristol)	.	3rd	R.L.Clark	(Edinburgh Wand'rs)
3	4th	M.A.Burton	(Gloucester)	.	25th	A.B.Carmichael	(West of Scotland)
4	3rd & last	A.Brinn	(Gloucester)	.	14th	A.F.McHarg	(London Scottish)
5	6th	C.W.Ralston	(Richmond)	.	14th	G.L.Brown	(West of Scotland)
6	5th	P.J.Dixon (Capt)	(Harlequins)	.	8th	N.A.McEwan	(Gala)
7	10th	A.Neary	(Broughton Park)	.	21st	R.J.Arneil	(Northampton)
8	4th	A.G.Ripley	(Rosslyn Park)	.	21st	P.C.Brown (Capt)	(Gala)

Referee: M.Joseph   (Wales)

SCORERS:

			0 - 4	N.A.McEwan	Try
A.G.B.Old	Penalty Goal		3 - 4		
			3 - 7	P.C.Brown	Penalty Goal
			3 - 11	P.C.Brown	Try
			3 - 14	C.M.Telfer	Drop Goal
			Half-time		
A.G.B.Old	Penalty Goal		6 - 14		
A.G.B.Old	Penalty Goal		9 - 14		
			9 - 17	A.R.Brown	Penalty Goal
			9 - 20	P.C.Brown	Penalty Goal
			9 - 23	P.C.Brown	Penalty Goal

POINTS:

A.G.B.Old	9 points	(17)		P.C.Brown	13 points
				N.A.McEwan	4 points
				A.R.Brown and C.M.Telfer	3 points each

MATCH COMMENTARY:

England gave the impression at Murrayfield that they did not believe that they could win this match - and so it proved. Scotland won their fourth successive Calcutta Cup and achieved their highest Five Nations points total against England since 1931. The Scottish pack, including four Lions, were significantly superior to their English counterparts, and were very ably led by Peter Brown who kicked three penalty goals and scored a try. Nairn McEwan's try was the direct result of sloppy defence by England, and there must have been five players in a position to stop Peter Brown driving over the line from a line-out, but none made a serious attempt. The match ended unsatisfactorily with five penalty goals scored in the second half and no tries. It was a fine Scottish team effort, but it has to be said that there was little evidence that the England side had any heart for the contest, and it came as no surprise that England were completely "whitewashed" in the Five Nations for the very first time.

SUMMARY OF THE SEASON - 1971 - 72:

The 1971-72 season will be seen by posterity as a sad one from any point of view because the political situation in Ireland, and the fear of repercussions, convinced both Wales and Scotland that their scheduled visits to Lansdowne Road should not take place. This meant that Wales and Scotland each played only three matches, and Ireland only two. Wales could argue that they were denied a Grand Slam having won the three games played, and so indeed could Ireland who won both their away matches at Twickenham and in Paris. The situation, nor the outcome spared England the embarrassment of losing all four matches in the Five Nations Championship for the first time ever. In so doing, England conceded a record 88 points and in all four matches scored less points (36) than France totalled against them (37) in the humiliating match which was the last International to be played at Stades Colombes. England have now lost seven successive matches against all opposition, and have won only one match in the last thirteen. Not since 1906 have England suffered such a losing streak.

For the first match against Wales six new caps were selected, a centre, both half-backs, a prop, lock and No 8, in a side which showed ten changes from that which had allowed Scotland to leave Twickenham with the Calcutta Cup last March. Despite three of the victorious Lions in the side, Peter Dixon, John Pullin and David Duckham, England were unable to make a lasting impression on the Welsh side which contained ten of the Lions' squad. The first twenty minutes though were all England and Bob Hiller put them into the lead for a short time, but gradually Wales took over and won comfortably. Keith Fielding's return was the only change for the visit of Ireland and again England flattered to deceive by leading for most of the match until Irish fitness, determination and opportunism, none of which England could match, secured victory for the men in green. With the two home matches lost, the England selectors decided that desperate situations demand desperate remedies and for the forthcoming visit to Paris made three changes, including the dropping of Bob Hiller and appointing Peter Dixon as captain. Their thinking, presumably, was that a repetition of the thrashing two years ago in Paris, for which match Bob Hiller had also been dropped, could not possibly happen. In a word, they were wrong - very wrong. France scored more points than any other side had ever done against England and that total included six tries for the second time in the two most recent matches in Paris. For the final engagement of this disastrous season, the selectors in their infinite wisdom, changed the two centres putting David Duckham on the wing, and recalled Alec Brinn at lock to partner Chris Ralston again in preference to John Barton. Such decisive and incisive action deserved success. Not so. Peter Brown marshalled his forces in such a way that England were allowed no chance whatever to redeem themselves, and they sank without trace. The casual, independent observer could well have gained the impression that having got to the brink of a "whitewash" England were resigned to the fact that it was inevitable. And so it proved.

In four disastrous matches, England had used only twenty players, and had awarded nine new caps. Such was the selectorial inconsistency, again, that there had been two captains, two full-backs, two scrum-halves, and three different three-quarter combinations. Only the pack remained reasonably stable, and at times, showed promising signs of becoming a formidable unit, especially in the first two matches. The forthcoming trip to South Africa for a one Test tour in May will be as demanding a test as they have had so far this season.

Eight players said farewell to International rugby at the end, or during the course of the season. Bob Hiller had said, following his omission from the side to play France, that he would retire from International rugby, and so he did with nineteen caps. In the nineteen matches in which he played, England had scored exactly 200 points, and Bob Hiller's contribution to that total was 138. On four separate occasions he had scored all England's points and in his last seven matches he had scored 60 out of England's 70 points and had scored three of their five tries. His 138 points total is more than double that of his closest rival, Roger Hosen. Rodney Webb, 12 caps, had scored a try on his debut against Scotland in 1967, and his brother had toured England with Australia in 1966. Keith Fielding, a schoolteacher and product of Loughborough College, won ten caps and was one of the finest runners on the rugby field of his day. He joined Salford Rugby League Club in 1973 and played with them for ten years scoring 253 tries. John Barton retired with four caps earned over five years, and his fellow lock Alec Brinn, a sports outfitter, had earned three. Mike Beese had three caps, Lionel Weston, the six foot scrum half, had two, and Nick Martin just one, as a replacement for Tony Neary in that eminently forgettable match against France.

FIVE NATIONS CHAMPIONSHIP TABLE: Championship not completed due to the political situation
                                                                                    in Ireland at the time.

Won: **Nothing**

	Played	Won	Lost	Drawn	Points: For	Against	Tries: For	Against	Title Points
Wales	3	3	0	0	67	21	8	1	
Ireland	2	2	0	0	30	21	4	2	
Scotland	3	2	1	0	55	53	6	6	
France	4	1	3	0	61	66	8	8	
ENGLAND	4	0	4	0	36	88	2	11	

Home Games: lost to Wales 3 - 12, (no tries to one); lost to Ireland 12 - 16, (one try to two)

Away Games: lost to France 12 - 37, (one try to six); lost to Scotland 9 - 23, (no tries to two)

ENGLAND TOUR TO SOUTH AFRICA, 1972

THE TOUR PARTY:

Manager:	**A.O.Lewis**	Assistant:	**J.Elders**	Captain:	**J.V.Pullin**		

Full-backs:	**S.A.Doble**	(Moseley)	no caps	Forwards:	**J.Barton**	(Coventry)	4 caps
	D.Whibley	(Leicester)	no caps		**A.V.Boddy**	(Met Police)	no caps
					M.A.Burton	(Gloucester)	4 caps
Three-quarters:	**J.P.A.G.Janion**	(Bedford)	8 caps		**F.E.Cotton**	(Loughboro Coll)	3 caps
	P.M.Knight	(Bristol)	2 caps		**T.Cowell**	(Rugby)	no caps
	A.J.Morley	(Bristol)	no caps		**P.J.Larter**	(Northampton)	21 caps
	P.S.Preece	(Coventry)	no caps		**A.Neary**	(Broughton Park)	10 caps
	A.A.Richards	(Fylde)	no caps		**J.V.Pullin**	(Bristol)	24 caps
	J.S.Spencer	(Headingley)	15 caps		**C.W.Ralston**	(Richmond)	6 caps
					A.G.Ripley	(Rosslyn Park)	4 caps
Half-backs:	**A.G.B.Old**	(Middlesboro)	4 caps		**C.B.Stevens**	(Harlequins)	9 caps
	T.Palmer	(Gloucester)	no caps		**J.A.Watkins**	(Gloucester)	no caps
	L.E.Weston	(W of Scotland)	2 caps		**D.E.J.Watt**	(Bristol)	4 caps
	J.G.Webster	(Moseley)	2 caps				

Replacement:	**S.J.Smith**	(Wilmslow)	no caps

This first tour undertaken by England to South Africa was really a very demanding schedule, although with only one Test match. Within two weeks and three days, seven matches were to be played, the first four at sea level, and the last three, including the Test match, at altitude in the High Veldt with only two days to acclimatise before a demanding fixture against Northern Transvaal. From the outset, under captain John Pullin and the management of Alec Lewis and John Elders, there was a buoyant and optimistic spirit in the squad, as if they were determined to erase the memories of the last few seasons of undistinguished English performances.

The squad consisted of twenty four players originally with Chris Ralston named later and Steve Smith replacing the injured Lionel Weston, and this meant that several of them were called upon to play in three successive matches. Indeed, three players, Alan Morley, "Stack" Stevens and John Watkins played in each of the last three matches including the Test - having had no altitude preparation. The first match was relatively easy with the forwards in outstanding form and Andy Ripley a veritable giant, but the second, against Western Province in Cape Town was a very different proposition. The opposition pack were much tougher than that of Natal, and with a 40,000 crowd yelling abuse and derision, the side really had to "screw themselves to the sticking place". This they succeeded in doing and also managed to silence the crowd with a fine try from Peter Knight and Sam Doble's place-kicking. In the third match, the Federation side, now known as the Proteas, for whom the notable Errol Tobias was at fly-half, provided a frustrating afternoon aided by a referee who seemed dedicated to awarding penalty kicks to the home side often as as possible. The match against the Bantu XV was the first ever played in South Africa between a European side and one consisting entirely of native Africans. The enthusiasm was infectious, the atmosphere electric and the result emphatic. Then the trip to the High Veldt and England were 3 - 13 down to Northern Transvaal fifteen minutes into the second half when the match became a test of character for the whole England side. John Pullin called for the supreme effort, the pack responded to a man, Sam Doble kicked two more penalty goals and Andy Ripley scored the equalising try. Creditable though it was, an even more Herculean effort was to be witnessed in the Test match a week later after a festival of a match against Griqualand West midweek when Alan Old achieved a record personal points tally of 24. A report on the Test match appears in the appropriate International match sequence. Unlike England, South Africa had previously enjoyed a run of seven matches undefeated, with three wins over Australia, two over New Zealand and one over France, and with whom they had drawn in Durban. In that respect, England's win was even more commendable. Only Peter Knight, with three caps, played no further International rugby after the tour, although he did go to New Zealand in 1973.

TOUR RESULTS:

May 17th	Natal	in Durban	WON	19 - 0	(three tries to nil)
May 20th	Western Province	in Cape Town	WON	9 - 6	(one try to nil)
May 22nd	South African Federation XV	in Cape Town	WON	11 - 6	(two tries to nil)
May 24th	South African (Bantu) XV	in Port Elizabeth	WON	36 - 3	(six tries to nil)
May 27th	Northern Transvaal	in Pretoria	DREW	13 - 13	(one try each)
May 30th	Griqualand West	in Kimberley	WON	60 - 21	(nine tries to two)
June 3rd	**SOUTH AFRICA**	**in Johannesburg**	**WON**	**18 - 9**	**(one try to nil)**

7th match   **ENGLAND   18 pts**   v   **SOUTH AFRICA   9 pts**

	Caps					Caps		
15	1st	S.A.Doble	(Moseley)	.	1st & last	R.A.Carlson	(Western Province)
14	3rd & last	P.M.Knight	(Bristol)	.	25th & last	S.H.Nomis	(Transvaal)
13	1st	P.S.Preece	(Coventry)	.	10th & last	J.S.Jansen	(Orange Free State)
12	9th	J.P.A.G.Janion	(Bedford)	.	5th	O.A.Roux	(Northern Transvaal)
11	1st	A.J.Morley	(Bristol)	.	11th	G.H.Muller	(Western Province)
10	5th	A.G.B.Old	(Middlesborough)	.	1st	D.S.L.Snyman	(Western Province)
9	3rd	J.G.Webster	(Moseley)	.	6th & last	J.F.Viljoen	(Griqualand West)
1	10th	C.B.Stevens	(Harlequins)	.	1st	N.S.E.Bezuidenhoudt	(Northern Transvaal)
2	25th	J.V.Pullin (Capt)	(Bristol)	.	10th	J.F.B.van Wyk	(Northern Transvaal)
3	5th	M.A.Burton	(Gloucester)	.	4th	J.T.Sauermann	(Transvaal)
4	22nd	P.J.Larter	(Northampton)	.	6th	J.G.Williams	(Northern Transvaal)
5	7th	C.W.Ralston	(Richmond)	.	1st & only	P.G.du Plessis	(Northern Transvaal)
6	1st	J.A.Watkins	(Gloucester)	.	25th & last	P.J.F.Greyling (Capt)	(Orange Free State)
7	11th	A.Neary	(Broughton Park)	.	31st	J.H.Ellis	(South West Africa)
8	5th	A.G.Ripley	(Rosslyn Park)	.	4th & last	A.J.Bates	(Western Transvaal)

Referee: J.Moolman   (South Africa)

SCORERS:

				0 - 3	D.S.L.Snyman	Penalty Goal
S.A.Doble	Penalty Goal			3 - 3		
				3 - 6	D.S.L.Snyman	Penalty Goal
S.A.Doble	Penalty Goal			6 - 6		
S.A.Doble	Penalty Goal			9 - 6		
			Half-time			
A.J.Morley	Try	(1st)		13 - 6		
S.A.Doble	Conversion			15 - 6		
S.A.Doble	Penalty Goal			18 - 6		
				18 - 9	D.S.L.Snyman	Penalty Goal

POINTS:

S.A.Doble	14 points	(14)	D.S.L.Snyman	9 points
A.J.Morley	4 points	(4)		

MATCH COMMENTARY:

Although they were unbeaten over the first five matches, England were not expected to provide very serious opposition to the Springboks in the sixth and last match of the tour. England astounded the rugby world and every South African by winning handsomely, having controlled the match throughout. Sam Doble, in particular, was a pillar of strength at full-back, his goal kicking was nerveless and deadly accurate and his 14 points in the match equalled Bob Hiller's record individual points total set against France in 1971. Jan Webster, at scrum-half, also had an outstanding match tormenting the Springbok defence, and the pack gave him excellent service and protection. The cover defence was tireless and impenetrable and South Africa were quite unable to cross the England line. With a slender lead of 9 - 6 going into the second half, England's confidence soared when Alan Morley scored a fine try in the corner which was well converted by Sam Doble. Then another penalty gave them a 12 point lead and this seemed to motivate their defence to even greater heights of endeavour and all South Africa could claim was a solitary penalty goal. The whole England side showed remarkable resilience and application, qualities which have been conspicuously lacking in some of the recent matches, and this performance compensated fully for all the sins of the past.

9th match   ENGLAND   0 pts   v   NEW ZEALAND   9 pts

	Caps				Caps		
15	2nd	S.A.Doble	(Moseley)	.	3rd	J.F.Karam	(Wellington)
14	2nd	A.J.Morley	(Bristol)	.	13th	B.G.Williams	(Auckland)
13	1st	P.J.Warfield	(Rosslyn Park)	.	4th	B.J.Robertson	(Counties)
12	2nd	P.S.Preece	(Coventry)	.	6th	R.M.Parkinson	(Poverty Bay)
11	20th	D.J.Duckham	(Coventry)	.	3rd	G.B.Batty	(Wellington)
10	13th & last	J.F.Finlan	(Moseley)	.	2nd	I.N.Stevens	(Wellington)
9	4th	J.G.Webster	(Moseley)	.	17th	S.M.Going	(North Auckland)
1	11th	C.B.Stevens	(Penzance-Newlyn)	.	4th	G.J.Whiting	(King Country)
2	26th	J.V.Pullin (Capt)	(Bristol)	.	10th	R.W.Norton	(Canterbury)
3	1st & only	W.F.Anderson	(Orrell)	.	2nd	K.K.Lambert	(Manawatu)
4	23rd	P.J.Larter	(Northampton)	.	3rd	H.H.MacDonald	(Canterbury)
5	8th	C.W.Ralston	(Richmond)	.	9th	P.J.Whiting	(Auckland)
6	2nd	J.A.Watkins	(Gloucester)	.	22nd	I.A.Kirkpatrick (Capt)	(Canterbury)
7	12th	A.Neary	(Broughton Park)	.	8th	A.J.Wylie	(Canterbury)
8	6th	A.G.Ripley	(Rosslyn Park)	.	8th	A.R.Sutherland	(Marlborough)

Referee: J.Young   (Scotland)

SCORERS:

0 - 3	I.A.Kirkpatrick	Try
0 - 6	J.F.Karam	Conversion
Half-time		
0 - 9	B.G.Williams	Drop Goal

POINTS:

I.A.Kirkpatrick	4 points
B.G.Williams	3 points
J.F.Karam	2 points

MATCH COMMENTARY:

After the euphoria of the successful tour to South Africa, expectations were perhaps a little unreasonably high when the Seventh All Blacks came to Twickenham. England played well and courageously, and never gave up, but they could not match the awesome forward power of the New Zealand pack, against whom they lost threee strikes against the head. Other difficulties were found to be the sniping runs of Sid Going, interacting with his substantial back row and the pace of Bryan Williams and Grant Batty on the wings.

Nevertheless, England put up a creditable performance and almost scored a try when Peter Preece broke through on a marginally forward pass from Warfield and that was the only time that England had an opportunity to breach the All Black defence. England were badly let down by the usually totally reliable Sam Doble who missed four penalty goal attempts - had he landed them, it might have been a very different story. The truth of the matter is that, as any good side must, New Zealand took their opportunities, whereas England did not.

Unfortunately England were the only International side to fail to score against this powerful New Zealand side.

But the sad story continues. This was England's fifth successive defeat at home and the seventh match without a win at Twickenham. There was a real danger that the faithful would become disillusioned !

78th match   **ENGLAND 9 pts**   v   **WALES 25 pts**

	Caps					Caps		
15	3rd & last	**S.A.Doble**	(Moseley)	.		21st	**J.P.R.Williams**	(London Welsh)
14	3rd	**A.J.Morley**	(Bristol)	.		22nd	**T.G.R.Davies**	(London Welsh)
13	2nd	**P.J.Warfield**	(Rosslyn Park)	.		5th	**R.T.E.Bergiers**	(Llanelli)
12	3rd	**P.S.Preece**	(Coventry)	.		8th	**A.J.Lewis (Capt)**	(Ebbw Vale)
11	21st	**D.J.Duckham**	(Coventry)	.		9th	**J.C.Bevan**	(Cardiff)
10	4th	**A.R.Cowman**	(Coventry)	.		7th	**P.Bennett**	(Llanelli)
9	5th	**J.G.Webster**	(Moseley)	.		28th	**G.O.Edwards**	(Cardiff)
1	12th	**C.B.Stevens**	(Penzance-Newlyn)	.		2nd	**G.Shaw**	(Neath)
2	27th	**J.V.Pullin (Capt)**	(Bristol)	.		20th	**J.Young**	(London Welsh)
3	4th	**F.E.Cotton**	(Loughborough Coll)	.		23rd	**D.J.Lloyd**	(Bridgend)
4	24th & last	**P.J.Larter**	(Northampton)	.		21st	**W.D.Thomas**	(Llanelli)
5	9th	**C.W.Ralston**	(Richmond)	.		3rd	**D.L.Quinnell**	(Llanelli)
6	3rd	**J.A.Watkins**	(Gloucester)	.		27th	**W.D.Morris**	(Neath)
7	13th	**A.Neary**	(Broughton Park)	.		23rd	**J.Taylor**	(London Welsh)
8	7th	**A.G.Ripley**	(Rosslyn Park)	.		21st	**T.M.Davies**	(London Welsh)
	2nd	G.W.Evans (Coventry) for Warfield -						

Referee: G.Domercq   (France)

SCORERS:	A.R.Cowman	D'p Goal (2nd & last)	3 - 0		
			3 - 4	J.C.Bevan	Try
			3 - 8	T.G.R.Davies	Try
	S.A.Doble	Penalty Goal	6 - 8		
			6 - 12	G.O.Edwards	Try
			Half-time		
			6 - 15	J.Taylor	Penalty Goal
	S.A.Doble	Penalty Goal	9 - 15		
			9 - 19	A.J.Lewis	Try
			9 - 21	P.Bennett	Conversion
			9 - 25	J.C.Bevan	Try

POINTS:	S.A.Doble	6 points	(20)	J.C.Bevan	8 points
	A.R.Cowman	3 points	(6)	T.G.R.Davies, A.J.Lewis	
				and G.O.Edwards	4 points each
				J.Taylor	3 points
				P.Bennett	2 points

MATCH COMMENTARY:

England were thoroughly beaten by five tries to nil on a fine afternoon in Cardiff. Wales seemed to pile on increasing pressure throughout the game and finished the match with a flourish and two tries in injury time. England started off at a cracking pace and immediately before Cowman's drop goal, Fran Cotton had just been denied a try by Roy Begiers' splendid tackle only inches short, when he had two men outside him. But as far as Wales was concerned that was as far as England were to get and they gradually took complete control. The two tries in injury time were spectacular, none more so than the last when eleven Welshmen including all seven backs, handled the ball from a set piece before giving John Bevan the honour of rounding off the move. Another wonderful performance by another fine Welsh side.

85th match   **ENGLAND   9 pts**   v   **IRELAND   18 pts**

	Caps					Caps		
15	2nd	A.M.Jorden	(Blackheath)	.		53rd	T.J.Kiernan (Capt)	(Cork Constitution)
14	4th	A.J.Morley	(Bristol)			4th	T.O.Grace	(St Mary's College)
13	3rd	P.J.Warfield	(Rosslyn Park)	.		1st	R.A.Milliken	(Bangor)
12	4th	P.S.Preece	(Coventry)	.		40th	C.M.H.Gibson	(NIFC)
11	22nd	D.J.Duckham	(Coventry)	.		5th	A.W.McMaster	(Ballymena)
10	5th & last	A.R.Cowman	(Coventry)	.		18th	B.J.McGann	(Cork Constitution)
9	1st	S.J.Smith	(Sale)	.		5th	J.J.Moloney	(St Mary's College)
1	13th	C.B.Stevens	(Penzance-Newlyn)	.		27th	R.J.McLoughlin	(Blackrock College)
2	28th	J.V.Pullin (Capt)	(Bristol)	.		34th	K.W.Kennedy	(London Irish)
3	5th	F.E.Cotton	(Loughborough Coll)	.		9th	J.F.Lynch	(St Mary's College)
4	1st	R.M.Uttley	(Gosforth)	.		50th	W.J.McBride	(Ballymena)
5	10th	C.W.Ralston	(Richmond)	.		2nd	K.M.A.Mays	(UC Dublin)
6	6th	P.J.Dixon	(Gosforth)	.		1st	J.H.Buckley	(Sunday's Well)
7	14th	A.Neary	(Broughton Park)	.		14th	J.F.Slattery	(Blackrock College)
8	8th	A.G.Ripley	(Rosslyn Park)	.		3rd	T.A.P.Moore	(Highfield)

Referee: A.M.Hosie   (Scotland)

SCORERS:

A.M.Jorden	Penalty Goal	3 - 0			
		3 - 4	T.O.Grace	Try	
		3 - 6	B.J.McGann	Conversion	
		3 - 10	R.A.Milliken	Try	
		3 - 12	B.J.McGann	Conversion	
		Half-time			
		3 - 15	B.J.McGann	Drop Goal	
A.Neary	Try	7 - 15			
A.M.Jorden	Conversion	9 - 15			
		9 - 18	B.J.McGann	Penalty Goal	

POINTS:

A.M.Jorden	5 points	(12)	B.J.McGann	10 points	
A.Neary	4 points	(8)	T.O.Grace	4 points	
			R.A.Milliken	4 points	

MATCH COMMENTARY:

After the difficulties of last season's Five Nations, the English team were given a very warm welcome when they ran onto the pitch at Lansdowne Road. But when the game started England were given rough treatment and the forwards were overrun by the fast and ferocious Irish eight. There was excellent control and pace in the Irish backs and Barry McGann was in fine form with his boot. Once again, England opened the scoring, but it was another false dawn, because as the match progressed Ireland became more and more dominant. The score does not reflect the gulf between the sides, and such was Ireland's dominance in the second half, that they came desperately close to scoring four further tries and, even more significantly, in the second forty minutes, Tom Kiernan did not touch the ball at all !!

All in all an object lesson for England and a worthy celebration of Willie-John McBride's fiftieth and Mike Gibson's fortieth caps for Ireland. England have not won a game in the Five Nations Championship since they beat Ireland on this ground in 1971, so this was their seventh successive Five Nations defeat. In all matches, in the last seventeen, England have won only two.

　FIVE NATIONS CHAMPIONSHIP, 1972-73　February 24th 1973, at Twickenham

48th match　　　**ENGLAND　14 pts**　　v　　**FRANCE　6 pts**

	Caps				Caps		
15	3rd	A.M.Jorden	(Blackheath)	.	3rd	M.Droitecourt	(Montferrand)
14	1st	P.J.Squires	(Harrogate)	.	9th	R.Bertranne	(Toulon)
13	3rd	G.W.Evans	(Coventry)	.	25th	C.Dourthe	(Dax)
12	5th	P.S.Preece	(Coventry)	.	28th & last	J.Trillo	(Begles)
11	23rd	D.J.Duckham	(Coventry)	.	40th	J-P.Lux	(Dax)
10	1st	M.J.Cooper	(Moseley)	.	4th	J-P.Romeu	(Montferrand)
9	2nd	S.J.Smith	(Sale)	.	11th	M.Barrau	(Toulouse)
1	14th	C.B.Stevens	(Penzance-Newlyn)	.	1st & only	A.Darrieussecq	(Biarritz)
2	29th	J.V.Pullin (Capt)	(Bristol)	.	22nd	R.Benesis	(Agen)
3	6th	F.E.Cotton	(Loughborough Coll)	.	24th	J.Iracabal	(Bayonne)
4	2nd	R.M.Uttley	(Gosforth)	.	10th	J-P.Bastiat	(Dax)
5	11th	C.W.Ralston	(Richmond)	.	10th	A.Esteve	(Beziers)
6	7th	P.J.Dixon	(Gosforth)	.	8th	O.Saisset	(Beziers)
7	15th	A.Neary	(Broughton Park)	.	17th	J-P.Biemouret	(Agen)
8	9th	A.G.Ripley	(Rosslyn Park)	.	49th	W.Spanghero (Capt)	(Narbonne)
				.	3rd	R.Astre (Beziers) for Barrau -	

Referee:　K.H.Clark　　　(Ireland)

SCORERS:	A.M.Jorden	Penalty Goal		3 - 0			
	D.J.Duckham	Try	(5th)	7 - 0			
				Half-time			
	D.J.Duckham	Try	(6th)	11 - 0			
	A.M.Jorden	Penalty Goal		14 - 0			
				14 - 4		R.Bertranne	Try
				14 - 6		J-P.Romeu	Conversion

POINTS:	D.J.Duckham	8 points	(20)		R.Bertranne	4 points	
	A.M.Jorden	6 points	(18)		J-P.Romeu	2 points	

MATCH COMMENTARY:

France had impressed with their highly mobile pack, especially in beating New Zealand, but they were out-played by a determined England eight. This was England's first win in eight Championship games and came as a welcome relief. There were heartening signs that the pack was knitting well together, much as five of them had in South Africa the previous summer, and Steve Smith at scrum-half appeared to be developing a fine understanding with his back row, who had already played together six times. In addition, Martin Coper, the new fly-half looked composed and, with the help of Smith's long pass, was able to get his backs moving. Peter Preece looked sharper than he had done before in an England jersey and Geoff Evans, as one would expect of a club centre partnership, complemented him well. It is perhaps a pertinent commentary on England's recent performances to note that it had been fifteen matches since David Duckham had scored a try for England, and today he got two. As for the French, Peter West summed up admirably in The Times by saying that "......their forwards were slow, the backs perfunctory and their handling fallible". Once again, England opened the scoring, but this time they did not flatter to deceive, and went on tto record their first victory at Twickenham since 1970 !!

John Pullin was playing in his 29th successive match for England overtaking Jeff Butterfield's record of 28 successive caps.

89th match

80th Calcutta Cup

ENGLAND 20 pts v SCOTLAND 13 pts

	Caps					Caps		
15	4th	A.M.Jorden	(Blackheath)	.		5th	A.R.Irvine	(Heriot's FP)
14	2nd	P.J.Squires	(Harrogate)	.		14th	W.C.C.Steele	(RAF/Bedford)
13	4th	G.W.Evans	(Coventry)	.		5th	I.R.McGeechan	(Headingley)
12	6th	P.S.Preece	(Coventry)	.		5th	I.W.Forsyth	(Stewart's-Melville)
11	24th	D.J.Duckham	(Coventry)	.		5th	D.Shedden	(West of Scotland)
10	2nd	M.J.Cooper	(Moseley)	.		11th	C.M.Telfer	(Hawick)
9	3rd	S.J.Smith	(Sale)	.		3rd	D.W.Morgan	(Stewart's-Melville)
1	15th	C.B.Stevens	(Penzance-Newlyn)	.		17th	J.McLauchlan (Capt)	(Jordanhill)
2	30th	J.V.Pullin (Capt)	(Bristol)	.		8th	R.L.Clark	(Edinburgh Wand'rs)
3	7th	F.E.Cotton	(Loughborough Coll)	.		30th	A.B.Carmichael	(West of Scotland)
4	3rd	R.M.Uttley	(Gosforth)	.		19th	A.F.McHarg	(London Scottish)
5	12th	C.W.Ralston	(Richmond)	.		26th	P.C.Brown	(Gala)
6	8th	P.J.Dixon	(Gosforth)	.		13th	N.A.MacEwan	(Gala)
7	16th	A.Neary	(Broughton Park)	.		3rd & last	J.G.Millican	(Edinburgh Univ)
8	10th	A.G.Ripley	(Rosslyn Park)	.		4th	G.M.Strachan	(Jordanhill)
				.		15th	G.L.Brown (W of Scotland) for Millican - 73	

Referee: J.C.Kelleher   (Wales)

SCORERS:	P.J.Squires	Try	(1st)	4 - 0		
	P.J.Dixon	Try	(1st)	8 - 0		
				Half-time		
	P.J.Dixon	Try	(2nd)	12 - 0		
	A.M.Jorden	Conversion		14 - 0		
				14 - 3	D.W.Morgan	Penalty Goal
				14 - 7	W.C.C.Steele	Try
				14 - 11	W.C.C.Steele	Try
				14 - 13	A.R.Irvine	Conversion
	G.W.Evans	Try	(1st & only)	18 - 13		
	A.M.Jorden	Conversion		20 - 13		

POINTS:	P.J.Dixon	8 points	(8)		W.C.C.Steele	8 points
	P.J.Squires, G.W.Evans	4 points	(4),(4)		D.W.Morgan	3 points
	and A.M.Jorden	each	(22)		A.R.Irvine	2 points

MATCH COMMENTARY:

For the third time in recent years, Scotland came to Twickenham in search of the Triple Crown, and, for the third time left empty-handed. Martin Cooper had another excellent game at fly-half and, as they had against France, the England pack played an influential game, dominating and controlling the opposition, and the consequence was an outstanding free-flowing match producing six tries.

Tony Neary, Andy Ripley and Peter Dixon were able to put considerable pressure on the Scottish half-backs as well as being commanding in the loose, and this was the platform for the English success. Peter Dixon's second try was perfectly executed, linking with Fran Cotton from a line-out peel. But it became a desperately close thing when Peter Brown put Billy Steele in for his second try of the match, making the score 14 - 13 to England. It could have gone either way, but England had the luck of the bounce from a diagonal kick and Geoff Evans touched down. This was the sixth time since 1947 that England have scored four, or more, tries against Scotland.

SUMMARY OF THE SEASON - 1972 - 73:

The prospect of facing New Zealand even if it was the next match after the triumph against South Africa in the previous June was a mouth-watering one, and, as New Zealand had already seen off both Scotland and Wales, perhaps the expectations were from the hearts rather than the heads of the now bouyant England supporters. Ten of the side who had returned victorious from South Africa were selected again, and only Mike Burton was missing from the pack. Frank Anderson, ther first player to be capped from the Orrell Club, was unfortunate in having to face the might of the All Black pack on the occasion of his first International, and, with respect, his inexperience may have contributed to England's downfall. For the opening match in the Five Nations, against Wales, two changes were made, Fran Cotton replacing the unfortunate Anderson and Dick Cowman came in at fly-half in place of John Finlan. The result was no better than had been experienced at the hands of the All Blacks, but this time it was the Welsh backs who did the damage rather than the All Black pack. Four changes for the trip to Dublin, including first caps for two future stalwarts, Steve Smith at scrum-half and Roger Uttley at lock, did not help England's cause at all, they were very soundly beaten by a rampant Ireland, and the score does not reflect the true difference between the two sides on the pitch. So all the pre-Christmas euphoria had dissipated, and England could only reflect on seven successive Five Nations matches lost and only two wins against all opposition in the last seventeen matches, those being against Ireland at Lansdowne Road two years ago and the match against South Africa. At the end of the season prospects were not quite so gloomy and it was perhaps unfortunate that England's first two matches of the Five Nations season were away from home, for, in common with each of the other nations, the home matches were won, and won well. For France, the selectors, wisely, kept the same pack but brought in Peter Squires, for his first cap, and Geoff Evans in the threequarters, and Martin Cooper for his International baptism at fly-half. Their faith in the pack was justified and their experiments in the backs, successful, for the forwards outplayed a surprisingly ponderous French eight, who failed to provide their always dangerous runners with any worthwhile possession. For the first time for several years, an English fly-half was able to get his backs moving and the direct result was two tries for David Duckham who must have had more passes in this match than he had in the previous ten. The same side, not surprisingly, faced Scotland at Twickenham three weeks later and continued their new-found winning ways with a very entertaining match in which six tries were scored. Geoff Evans' final, winning, try was ultimately down to a bounce which favoured England rather than the defending Scots, and this was the nail in the Scottish coffin once again at Twickenham, which also prevented the Triple Crown going across the Border for the first time since 1938.

This season was the first and only season, thus far, that the Five Nations Championship has finished with all five Nations winning their home matches and losing both fixtures away from home. So in points terms, the Championship was a "quintuple tie" in the words of one of the popular national dailies. Had the title been decided on points difference, as today, then Wales would have been Champions, but at the time, others half-heartedly claimed the glory; Scotland, on the grounds that they had scored most points, and England (!), on the grounds that they (with Wales) had scored the most tries. As it was, the title was considered to have been shared amongst all participants.

In all five matches, England used twenty-four players, twenty-two for the four Five Nations matches, and awarded caps for the first time to five players. Only five players stepped down from International level at the end of the season, the proposed tour to Argentina next September no doubt providing an incentive not to retire in cases where that was an option. Peter Larter had earned 24 caps, had been a British Lion in 1968 and, although he played regularly for Northampton, was serving in the RAF, for whom he also played Basketball. John Finlan, thirteen caps, later became an England selector, had played for England with six different scrum-halves and his career spanned seven seasons. Dick Cowman, once of Loughborough Colleges, and a schoolteacher by profession, had five caps. Sam Doble, although a prodigious points scorer for Club and County, was awarded only three England caps. The previous season, (1971-72) he had set a world club record of 450 points in a season. A schoolteacher, he tragically died of cancer in 1977. Frank Anderson was the remaining ex-International at the end of the season, and his one and only jersey occupies a place of honour in the Orrell Clubhouse.

The proposed tour to Argentina was cancelled later in the year, and a hastily arranged alternative to New Zealand took place.

FIVE NATIONS CHAMPIONSHIP TABLE:

Won: **Nothing**

	Played	Won	Lost	Drawn	Points: For	Against	Tries: For	Against	Title Points
Wales	4	2	0	2	53	43	7	3	4
France	4	2	0	2	38	36	3	3	4
Ireland	4	2	0	2	50	48	5	5	4
Scotland	4	2	0	2	55	59	4	7	4
ENGLAND	4	2	0	2	52	62	7	10	4

Home Games: beat France 14 - 6, (two tries to one); beat Scotland 20 - 13, (four tries to two)

Away Games: lost to Wales 25 - 9, (no tries to five); lost to Ireland 9 - 18, (one try to two)

ENGLAND TOUR TO FIJI and NEW ZEALAND, 1973

THE TOUR PARTY:

Manager: **D.L.Sanders**   Assistant: **J.Elders**   Captain: **J.V.Pullin**

Full-backs:	P.A.Rossborough	(Coventry)	1 cap	Forwards:	M.A.Burton	(Gloucester)	5 caps
	A.M.Jorden	(Blackheath)	4 caps		F.E.Cotton	(Coventry)	7 caps
					P.J.Hendy	(St Ives)	no caps
Three-quarters:	D.J.Duckham	(Coventry)	24 caps		N.O.Martin	(Bedford)	1 cap
	G.W.Evans	(Coventry)	4 caps		A.Neary	(Broughton Park)	16 caps
	J.P.A.G.Janion	(Richmond)	9 caps		J.V.Pullin	(Bristol)	30 caps
	P.M.Knight	(Bristol)	3 caps		C.W.Ralston	(Richmond)	12 caps
	P.S.Preece	(Coventry)	6 caps		A.G.Ripley	(Rosslyn Park)	10 caps
	P.J.Squires	(Harrogate)	2 caps		C.B.Stevens	(Harlequins)	15 caps
					R.M.Uttley	(Gosforth)	3 caps
Half-backs:	M.J.Cooper	(Moseley)	2 caps		J.A.Watkins	(Gloucester)	3 caps
	A.G.B.Old	(Leicester)	5 caps		J.White	(Bristol)	no caps
	S.J.Smith	(Sale)	3 caps		R.M.Wilkinson	(Cambridge Univ)	no caps
	J.G.Webster	(Moseley)	5 caps				

This tour was rather hastily arranged at very little notice when the originally planned tour to Argentina was cancelled due to terrorist threats against the players. A squad of 25 was selected, all but three being capped, and nine of whom (six in the pack) had played in the match against the All Blacks at Twickenham nine months ago, in January. David Duckham and "Stack" Stevens had been, with John Pullin, on the 1971 Lions' tour.

The contrast of a mild late summer in England with the high humidity of Suva, combined with the jet-lag, meant that a near Test side struggled to beat Fiji by the odd point in 25, towards which each side scored two tries. Four days later they were in the rain and mud at New Plymouth and the second contrast took its toll. Taranaki's tactics were almost exclusively to drive thorugh the English lines-out, and they achieved an unspectacular victory by two penalty goals to one. Wellington was a different proposition altogether, and the try they scored in the third minute gave the side the confidence they needed to play an open and expansive game. At half-time Wellington led by 21 points to 3, and the signs were ominous for England, especially as Jeremy Janion had squandered a try-scoring opportunity just before the break. For the second half, Fran Cotton, captain in John Pullin's absence, had to pull his team up by the bootstraps, and did so as England score thirteen points in the last fifteen minutes with tries from Peter Knight and Chris Ralston and a conversion and a penalty goal from Tony Jorden. Arguably, England could have won that one but didn't, but they certainly could have beaten Canterbury in the fourth match of the tour had the goal-kicking been up to the usual standard. England scored three tries, one from Peter Rossborough, and two from Peter Squires, against two by Canterbury, but Alan Old and Peter Rossborough missed nine kicks at goal between them, three conversions and six penalty goal attempts. Matches are not won by such extravagance.

But the ultimate task was at hand, and with a week to prepare, England were well ready to face the All Blacks in Auckland. A full report on the Test match appears in the appropriate International match sequence. England's performance was a magnificent example of teamwork and proper and thorough match perparation, and it was a tribue to the vision and determination of the tour management, John Pullin, John Elders and "Sandy" Sanders. England had only ever beaten New Zealand once, thirty-seven years ago when Prince Obolensky had a say in the matter, and to win in this manner on New Zealand soil was a tremendous achievement - even better, John Pullin said, than Johannesburg in June 1972 - and who would gainsay him ?

TOUR RESULTS:

August 28th	Fiji	in Suva	WON	13 - 12	(two tries each)
September 1st	Taranaki	in New Plymouth	LOST	3 - 6	(no tries)
September 5th	Wellington	in Wellington	LOST	16 - 25	(two tries to three)
September 8th	Canterbury	in Christchurch	LOST	12 - 19	(three tries to two)
September 15th	**NEW ZEALAND**	**in Auckland**	**WON**	**16 - 10**	**(three tries to two)**

10th match   **ENGLAND   16 pts**   v   **NEW ZEALAND   10 pts**

	Caps					Caps		
15	2nd	P.A.Rossborough	(Coventry)	.	1st & only	R.N.Lendrum	(Counties)
14	3rd	P.J.Squires	(Harrogate)		16th	B.G.Williams	(Auckland)
13	5th	G.W.Evans	(Coventry)	.	3rd	I.A.Hurst	(Canterbury)
12	7th	P.S.Preece	(Coventry)		7th & last	R.M.Parkinson	(Poverty Bay)
11	25th	D.J.Duckham	(Coventry)	.	6th	G.B.Batty	(Wellington)
10	6th	A.G.B.Old	(Leicester)	.		J.P.Dougan	(Wellington)
9	6th	J.G.Webster	(Moseley)	.	20th	S.M.Going	(North Auckland)
1	16th	C.B.Stevens	(Penzance-Newlyn)	.	5th	K.K.Lambert	(Manawatu)
2	31st	J.V.Pullin (Capt)	(Bristol)	.	13th	R.W.Norton	(Canterbury)
3	8th	F.E.Cotton	(Coventry)	.	1st & only	M.G.Jones	(North Auckland)
4	4th	R.M.Uttley	(Gosforth)	.	6th	H.H.Macdonald	(Canterbury)
5	13th	C.W.Ralston	(Richmond)	.	17th & last	S.C.Strahan	(Manawatu)
6	4th	J.A.Watkins	(Gloucester)	.	1st	K.W.Stewart	(Southland)
7	17th	A.Neary	(Broughton Park)	.	25th	I.A.Kirkpatrick (Capt)	(Poverty Bay)
8	11th	A.G.Ripley	(Rosslyn Park)	.	11th & last	A.J.Wylie	(Canterbury)

	3rd	M.J.Cooper (Moseley) for Evans - 20	.	1st & only	T.G.Morrison (Otago) for Parkinson - 54

Referee: R.F.McMullen   (New Zealand)

SCORERS:

				0 - 4	G.B.Batty	Try
P.J.Squires	Try	(2nd)		4 - 4		
P.A.Rossborough	Conversion			6 - 4		
				6 - 8	I.A.Hurst	Try
				6 - 10	R.N.Lendrum	Conversion
				Half-time		
C.B.Stevens	Try	(1st)		10 - 10		
A.Neary	Try	(3rd)		14 - 10		
P.A.Rossborough	Conversion			16 - 10		

POINTS:

P.J.Squires, C.B.Stevens,	4 points	(8),(4)	I.A.Hurst and G.B.Batty	4 points each
A.Neary and P.A.Rossborough	each	(11),(7)	R.N.Lendrum	2 points

MATCH COMMENTARY:

England had lost all three provincial matches, had beaten Fiji on the way by only one point, so, no doubt, they went into this match as underdogs. There is no doubt either that all New Zealand were astonished and dismayed at the result, describing their team's performance as "the worst in an International for years." That is as may be, but such sentiments cannot be allowed to detract from the England's titanic achievement in which every aspect of their game was of the highest order. John Pullin led by example an England team which played and beat the All Blacks at 10-man rugby with Jan Webster, who completely eclipsed Sid Going, and the England back row controlling the game. Webster, virtrually single-handed, created all three tries, the first when he gathered possession from a loose ball and gave the scoring pass to Peter Squires, the second from behind a powerful England forward drive with a pass to "Stack" Stevens, and the third from a blind side move started by him and finishing with the try by Tony Neary. This decisive try, and the way it was scored, was a bitter pill for New Zealand to swallow for it was straight out of the All Blacks manual. New Zealand's half-time lead, after they had played with the wind, always looked insufficient on the evidence of the England pack performance in the first half. And so it proved. If anything, all eight raised their game another notch in the second half, much due, no doubt, to John Pullin's experiences in New Zealand with the Lions two years ago.

7th match   **ENGLAND   20 pts**   v   **AUSTRALIA   3 pts**

	Caps					Caps		
15	3rd	P.A.Rossborough	(Coventry)	.	8th & last	R.L.Fairfax	(New South Wales)
14	4th	P.J.Squires	(Harrogate)	.	1st	L.E.Monaghan	(New South Wales)
13	10th	J.P.A.G.Janion	(Richmond)	.	9th	R.D.L'Estrange	(Queensland)
12	1st	D.F.K.Roughley	(Liverpool)	.	10th	G.A.Shaw	(New South Wales)
11	26th	D.J.Duckham	(Coventry)	.	12th	J.J.McLean	(Queensland)
10	7th	A.G.B.Old	(Leicester)	.	2nd & last	P.G.Rowles	(New South Wales)
9	4th	S.J.Smith	(Sale)	.	20th	J.N.B.Hipwell (Capt)	(New South Wales)
1	17th	C.B.Stevens	(Penzance-Newlyn)	.	4th	R.Graham	(New South Wales)
2	32nd	J.V.Pullin (Capt)	(Bristol)	.	2nd	C.M.Carberry	(New South Wales)
3	9th	F.E.Cotton	(Coventry)	.	2nd	S.G.MacDougall	(New South Wales)
4	5th	R.M.Uttley	(Gosforth)	.	16th & last	S.C.Gregory	(New South Wales)
5	14th	C.W.Ralston	(Richmond)	.	8th	G.Fay	(New South Wales)
6	5th	J.A.Watkins	(Gloucester)	.	9th	M.R.Cocks	(Queensland)
7	18th	A.Neary	(Broughton Park)	.	1st & only	B.R.Battishall	(New South Wales)
8	12th	A.G.Ripley	(Rosslyn Park)	.	2nd	A.A.Shaw	(Queensland)

6th & last   M.E.Freney (Queensland) for Carberry - 61

Referee: A.R.Lewis   (Wales)

SCORERS:					
A.Neary	Try	(4th)	4 - 0		
P.A.Rossborough	Penalty Goal		7 - 0		
			Half-time		
A.G.Ripley	Try	(1st)	11 - 0		
P.A.Rossborough	Conversion		13 - 0		
			13 - 3	R.L.Fairfax	Penalty Goal
A.G.B.Old	Try	(1st & only)	17 - 3		
P.A.Rossborough	Penalty Goal		20 - 3		

POINTS:					
P.A.Rossborough	8 points	(15)	R.L.Fairfax	3 points
A.G.B.Old	4 points	(21)		
A.Neary	4 points	(15)		
A.G.Ripley	4 points	(4)		

MATCH COMMENTARY:

This was not a very good Australian side, as before this short tour, they had lost to Tonga, and on this tour had been well beaten by Wales the previous week. Nevertheless, England's progress continued and the forwards again provided the solid basis on which the victory by three tries to nothing was built, but if the backs had made the most of their opportunities, the margin could have been very much greater. England had little cohesion and rhythm in mid-field where Dave Roughley and Jeremy Janion were substituting for the injured Coventry pair, Peter Preece and Geoff Evans, and David Duckham, on the wing, saw very little of the ball. But with the forward dominance, the match was not really a contest, although it could have been different too, if McLean had not missed five penalty goal attempts before Fairfax took over the kicking duties late in the second half. This win gave John Pullin the unique distinction of having led an England side to victory over the three major southern hemisphere nations, South Africa, New Zealand and Australia and all in less than eighteen months ! Six players were privileged to assist him in achieving this feat, Alan Old, "Stack" Stevens, Chris Ralston and the back row of John Watkins, Andy Ripley and Tony Neary. Even more remarkable was the fact that in those three matches, England had conceded a mere 22 points and only two tries.

90th match   **ENGLAND   14 pts**   v   **SCOTLAND   16 pts**

81st Calcutta Cup

	Caps					Caps		
15	4th	P.A.Rossborough	(Coventry)	.		8th	A.R.Irvine	(Heriot's FP)
14	5th	P.J.Squires	(Harrogate)	.		3rd	A.D.Gill	(Gala)
13	2nd	D.F.K.Roughley	(Liverpool)	.		7th	J.M.Renwick	(Hawick)
12	6th	G.W.Evans	(Coventry)	.		8th	I.R.McGeechan	(Headingley)
11	27th	D.J.Duckham	(Coventry)	.		4th	L.G.Dick	(Jordanhill)
10	8th	A.G.B.Old	(Leicester)	.		14th	C.M.Telfer	(Hawick)
9	7th	J.G.Webster	(Moseley)	.		5th	A.J.M.Lawson	(Edinburgh Wand'rs)
1	18th	C.B.Stevens	(Penzance-Newlyn)	.		20th	J.McLauchlan (Capt)	(Jordanhill)
2	33rd	J.V.Pullin (Capt)	(Bristol)	.		2nd	D.F.Madsen	(Gosforth)
3	10th	F.E.Cotton	(Coventry)	.		33rd	A.B.Carmichael	(West of Scotland)
4	8th	N.E.Horton	(Moseley)	.		18th	G.L.Brown	(West of Scotland)
5	15th	C.W.Ralston	(Richmond)	.		22nd	A.F.McHarg	(London Scottish)
6	9th	P.J.Dixon	(Gosforth)	.		16th	N.A.MacEwan	(Highland)
7	19th	A.Neary	(Broughton Park)	.		10th	W.Lauder	(Neath)
8	13th	A.G.Ripley	(Rosslyn Park)	.		2nd	W.S.Watson	(Boroughmuir)

Referee: M.J.St.Guilhem   (France)

SCORERS:

			0 - 3	A.R.Irvine	Penalty Goal
			0 - 7	W.Lauder	Try
			0 - 9	A.R.Irvine	Conversion
F.E.Cotton	Try	(1st & only)	4 - 9		
A.G.B.Old	Penalty Goal		7 - 9		
			Half-time		
A.Neary	Try	(5th & last)	11 - 9		
			11 - 13	A.R.Irvine	Try
P.A.Rossborough	D'p Goal (1st & only)		14 - 13		
			14 - 16	A.R.Irvine	Penalty Goal

POINTS: F.E.Cotton and A.Neary   4 points each   (4),(15)   A.R.Irvine   12 points

          P.A.Rossborough and A.G.B.Old   3 points each (18),(24)   W.Lauder   4 points

MATCH COMMENTARY:

After the remarkable results earlier in the season when both New Zealand and Australia had been beaten, there were, again, high hopes for the Five Nations season. Alas, although the rugby was good, the results, from England's point of view were somewhat disappointing. This was a fascinating match with the result in doubt until the last seconds. Good though the England pack were, they met their match against the Scots front five who knew exactly what to do and went about it with gusto and purpose. Scotland got off to an explosive start and were nine points up in only thirteen minutes before England got their act together and hauled themselves back to 7 - 9 at half-time. England's ferocious third quarter attacks were resisted by stout and courageous Scottish defence in which Ian McGeechan was very prominent. But a rampaging Andy Ripley run produced a try for Tony Neary, giving England the lead. This was quickly followed by a dazzling riposte by Andy Irvine for a try to restore the Scottish lead. Then with five minutes remaining, Peter Rossborough dropped a speculative goal from 40 yards (shades of Bob Hiller) to put England ahead again. In the last minute, a relatively minor infringement on the touch-line near half-way resulted in a penalty kick for Scotland. In total silence, Andy Irvine kicked the goal to reclaim the Calcutta Cup, and the respectful silence became a jubilant roar.

86th match   **ENGLAND   21 pts**   v   **IRELAND   26 pts**

	Caps					Caps		
15	5th	**P.A.Rossborough**	(Coventry)	.	5th	**A.H.Ensor**	(Lansdowne)
14	6th	**P.J.Squires**	(Harrogate)	.	7th	**T.O.Grace**	(UC Dublin)
13	3rd & last	**D.F.K.Roughley**	(Liverpool)	.	46th	**C.M.H.Gibson**	(NIFC)
12	7th	**G.W.Evans**	(Coventry)	.	7th	**R.A.Milliken**	(Bangor)
11	28th	**D.J.Duckham**	(Coventry)	.	10th	**A.W.McMaster**	(Ballymena)
10	9th	**A.G.B.Old**	(Leicester)	.	4th	**M.A.M.Quinn**	(Lansdowne)
9	5th	**S.J.Smith**	(Sale)	.	11th	**J.J.Moloney**	(St Mary's College)
1	19th	**C.B.Stevens**	(Penzance-Newlyn)	.	33rd	**R.J.McLoughlin**	(Blackrock College)
2	34th	**J.V.Pullin (Capt)**	(Bristol)	.	40th	**K.W.Kennedy**	(London Irish)
3	11th	**F.E.Cotton**	(Coventry)	.	14th	**J.F.Lynch**	(St Mary's College)
4	6th	**R.M.Uttley**	(Gosforth)	.	56th	**W.J.McBride (Capt)**	(Ballymena)
5	16th	**C.W.Ralston**	(Richmond)	.	3rd	**M.I.Keane**	(Lansdowne)
6	10th	**P.J.Dixon**	(Gosforth)	.	7th	**S.A.McKinney**	(Dungannon)
7	20th	**A.Neary**	(Broughton Park)	.	20th	**J.F.Slattery**	(Blackrock College)
8	14th	**A.G.Ripley**	(Rosslyn Park)	.	9th	**T.A.P.Moore**	(Highfield)

Referee: M.Joseph   (Wales)

SCORERS:

A.G.B.Old	Penalty Goal		3 - 0			
			3 - 3	**A.H.Ensor**	Penalty Goal	
A.G.B.Old	Penalty Goal		6 - 3			
			6 - 6	**T.A.P.Moore**	Try	
			6 - 10	**M.A.M.Quinn**	Drop Goal	
			Half-time			
			6 - 14	**J.J.Moloney**	Try	
			6 - 18	**C.M.H.Gibson**	Try	
			6 - 20	**C.M.H.Gibson**	Conversion	
			6 - 24	**C.M.H.Gibson**	Try	
			6 - 26	**C.M.H.Gibson**	Conversion	
A.G.B.Old	Penalty Goal		9 - 26			
A.G.B.Old	Penalty Goal		12 - 26			
A.G.B.Old	Penalty Goal		15 - 26			
P.J.Squires	Try	(3rd)	19 - 26			
A.G.B.Old	Conversion		21 - 26			

POINTS:

A.G.B.Old	17 points	(41)	**C.M.H.Gibson**	12 points	
P.J.Squires	4 points	(12)	**J.J.Moloney and T.A.P.Moore**	4 points each	
			A.H.Ensor and M.A.M.Quinn	3 points each	

MATCH COMMENTARY:

The score may be close, but the try count of four to one for Ireland is much more indicative of the course and the outcome of the match. Ireland's front five dominated the forward battle and secured abundant possession for the Irish backs, outstanding amongst whom was Mike Gibson who scored two fine tries. The England backs looked pedestrian in comparison, and, significantly, all Irelands points originated from English errors - many of them unforced. Several records were set during the course of the match; Alan Old's 17 points in the game was a post-war individual record; five penalty goals in a match was also an (unwanted) English record: and this was the highest aggregate points total so far in an International match at Twickenham.

49th match   **ENGLAND   12 pts**   v   **FRANCE   12 pts**

	Caps					Caps		
15	5th	A.M.Jorden	(Blackheath)	.		4th	M.Droitecourt	(Montferrand)
14	7th	P.J.Squires	(Harrogate)	.		14th	R.Bertranne	(Bagneres)
13	1st	K.Smith	(Roundhay)	.		2nd	J.Pecune	(Tarbes)
12	8th	G.W.Evans	(Coventry)	.		43rd	J-P.Lux	(Dax)
11	29th	D.J.Duckham	(Coventry)	.		6th	A.Dubertrand	(Montferrand)
10	10th	A.G.B.Old	(Leicester)	.		9th	J-P.Romeu	(Montferrand)
9	6th	S.J.Smith	(Sale)	.		4th	J.Fouroux	(La Voulte)
1	20th	C.B.Stevens	(Penzance-Newlyn)	.		7th	A.Vaquerin	(Beziers)
2	35th	J.V.Pullin (Capt)	(Bristol)	.		29th	R.Benesis	(Narbonne)
3	6th	M.A.Burton	(Gloucester)	.		30th	J.Iracabal	(Bayonne)
4	7th	R.M.Uttley	(Gosforth)	.		14th	A.Esteve	(Beziers)
5	17th	C.W.Ralston	(Richmond)	.		34th	E.Cester (Capt)	(Valence)
6	11th	P.J.Dixon	(Gosforth)	.		13th	J-C.Skrela	(Toulouse)
7	21st	A.Neary	(Broughton Park)	.		9th	V.Boffelli	(Aurillac)
8	15th	A.G.Ripley	(Rosslyn Park)	.		16th	C.Spanghero	(Narbonne)

Referee: J.C.Kelleher   (Wales)

SCORERS:

			0 - 3	J-P.Romeu	Drop Goal
			0 - 6	J-P.Romeu	Penalty Goal
			Half-time		
G.W.Evans	D'p Goal (1st & only)	3 - 6			
			3 - 10	J-P.Romeu	Try
			3 - 12	J-P.Romeu	Conversion
A.G.B.Old	Penalty Goal	6 - 12			
D.J.Duckham	Try	(7th)	10 - 12		
A.G.B.Old	Conversion	12 - 12			

POINTS:

A.G.B.Old	5 points	(46)	J-P.Romeu	12 points
D.J.Duckham	4 points	(24)		
G.W.Evans	3 points	(7)		

MATCH COMMENTARY:

England had not beaten France in Paris since 1964, but in this their first visit to the new Parc des Princes, they came desperately close. Again it was a case of the pack providing sufficient possession but the backs being unable to capitalise on their opportunities. Just after half-time, England were 12 points to 3 down and looking beaten when Alan Old slotted a penalty goal from 40 yards and a wide angle, and almost immediately following that, England moved the ball quickly alomng the line and David Duckham found himself just clear with 35 yards to go; Alan Old converted and the scores were level with 20 minutes to play. There followed some fine rugby from both sides but neither could score and the game ended in an honourable draw. The French fly-half, Romeu, had a remarkable match, not only scoring all his side's points, but doing so by scoring by every possible means, a feat only accomplished four times previously. John Pullin became England's most capped player with 35 caps beating "Budge" Roger's record 34, and David Duckham equalled Mike Weston's record of 29 caps for a back. The next day, a Turkish aircraft taking fans back to London, crashed just after take-off near Paris. Amongst many killed were Larry Webb, the Bedford prop capped four times in 1959, and Welsh rugby correspondent Lloyd Lewis.

79th match   **ENGLAND   16 pts**   v   **WALES   12 pts**

	Caps				Caps		
15	1st	**W.H.Hare**	(Nottingham)		1st	**W.R.Blyth**	(Swansea)
14	8th	**P.J.Squires**	(Harrogate)		29th	**T.G.R.Davies**	(London Welsh)
13	9th & last	**G.W.Evans**	(Coventry)		10th	**R.T.E.Bergiers**	(Llanelli)
12	2nd	**K.Smith**	(Roundhay)		3rd & last	**A.A.J.Finlayson**	(Cardiff)
11	30th	**D.J.Duckham**	(Coventry)		6th	**J.J.Williams**	(Llanelli)
10	11th	**A.G.B.Old**	(Leicester)		15th	**P.Bennett**	(Llanelli)
9	8th	**J.G.Webster**	(Moseley)		36th	**G.O.Edwards (Capt)**	(Cardiff)
1	21st	**C.B.Stevens**	(Penzance-Newlyn)		10th	**G.Shaw**	(Neath)
2	36th	**J.V.Pullin (Capt)**	(Bristol)		5th	**R.W.Windsor**	(Pontypool)
3	7th	**M.A.Burton**	(Gloucester)		5th & last	**P.D.Llewellyn**	(Swansea)
4	8th	**R.M.Uttley**	(Gosforth)		2nd & last	**I.R.Robinson**	(Cardiff)
5	18th	**C.W.Ralston**	(Richmond)		25th & last	**W.D.Thomas**	(Llanelli)
6	12th	**P.J.Dixon**	(Gosforth)		34th & last	**W.D.Morris**	(Neath)
7	22nd	**A.Neary**	(Broughton Park)		4th	**T.J.Cobner**	(Pontypool)
8	16th	**A.G.Ripley**	(Rosslyn Park)		29th	**T.M.Davies**	(Swansea)

Referee: J.R.West   (Ireland)

SCORERS:

D.J.Duckham	Try	(8th)	4 - 0			
A.G.B.Old	Penalty Goal		7 - 0			
			7 - 4	T.M.Davies	Try	
			7 - 6	P.Bennett	Conversion	
			7 - 9	P.Bennett	Penalty Goal	
			Half-time			
A.G.Ripley	Try	(2nd & last)	11 - 9			
A.G.B.Old	Conversion		13 - 9			
A.G.B.Old	Penalty Goal		16 - 9			
			16 - 12	P.Bennett	Penalty Goal	

POINTS:

A.G.B.Old	8 points	(54)		P.Bennett	8 points
D.J.Duckham and A.G.Ripley	4 points each	(28),(8)		T.M.Davies	4 points

MATCH COMMENTARY:

England certainly deserved their first victory over Wales at Twickenham since 1960, by playing solid sensible, albeit unspectacular rugby and by giving very little away. The pack was solid and the defence was sound, and this was the basis of the English victory. There were, regrettably, several questionable refereeing decisions in that both sides claimed tries which were disallowed - but, the referee is the sole arbiter. The high point came, for England, having trailed by two points at half-time, when Andy Ripley capped an outstanding display by scoring the all important try to give England the lead they were not to relinquish. This first win of the Championship season could not prevent England finishing with the Wooden Spoon - a far cry from the hopes and expectations after the triumphs over New Zealand on tour and over Australia at the beginning of the season. In fact, over the last five Five Nations Championships, England have won only five matches, beating Ireland twice, France, Scotland and Wales today. In gaining his 30th cap, David Duckham became England's most capped back. With his conversion of Andy Ripley's try, Alan Old became only the third England player to score 50 points in International matches, only Roger Hosen and Bob Hiller having accomplished the feat before.

SUMMARY OF THE SEASON - 1973 - 74:

The Five Nations Committee had decreed that this season would see the start of a revised format for the Championship in that all matches would be played in rotation, on specific Saturdays with two weeks between each. The cycle of match combinations would take five years to complete, and then would be repeated. Most significantly, of course, this meant that each Nation would play alternately home and away in perpetuity.

Before the Five Nations, however, England had some unfinished business and a fixture against the touring Australians in November would offer the possibility of lowly England beating all three southern hemisphere nations within a period of eighteen months - and this one would be the only match at home !! The match was won emphatically by a team consisting of the same pack as had faced New Zealand in Auckland in September and three changes in the backs, two of which were necessary because of injury. John Pullin's feat in leading England to these three victories, two of them away from home, was to be emulated by Will Carling some twenty one years later.
But, as frequently after the Lord Mayor's show, disappointment was to follow, for the in Five Nations Championship in 1974, although some excellent and exciting rugby was on display, indeed some of the matches were memorable, the results from England's point of view were miserable and they finished at the bottom of the pile with a firm grip on the Wooden Spoon. So mediocre was the fare on the whole that only nineteen tries were scored in the entire Championship, yet England, at the bottom of the Table, scored more than any other side - they also conceded twice as many as anybody else. Nevertheless, the first match at Murrayfield, was a cracker with four tries and excitement to almost the last kick of the match. England had made three changes and made a further two for the second match at home to Ireland which provided fascinating rugby, and set several records including another defeat for England at Twickenham with Ireland scoring more points against England than ever before. Barring injuries, and Peter Dixon's succession to John Watkins after the Australia game, the pack had been unchanged, and in Paris, where England had not won since 1964, and had taken some terrible beatings in the meantime, they gave the backs every opportunity to win the match, but again, the backs could not take advantage. As it was, a draw was a fair result, but it could have been so different. Finally a visit by Wales to Twickenham and England had not beaten Wales on English soil for fourteen years. At least that bogey was put to bed, courtesy, again, of the unchanged pack, and as they were two points down at the break, it was heartening to witness the effort and application that went in to reversing that position by the final whistle - especially against Wales !!

Several milestones were passed during the course of the season, John Pullin became England's most capped player, overtaking Budge Rogers, and has earned 36 caps, and 35 of those, that is all bar his first, have been successive. Similarly David Duckham, now with 30 caps, is the country's most capped back, having passed Mike Weston's twenty nine. Alan Old emulated the feat of both Roger Hosen and Bob Hiller in registering 50 points scored in International matches for England.

Twenty five players were called upon to do or die for England this season, twenty one for the Five Nations, and included in these were three new caps, one of whom, "Dusty" Hare, although he was not to be capped again for four years, was to make a substantial mark on English International rugby. Only two players, Dave Roughley and Geoff Evans, were to say farewell to International rugby this season. Geoff Evans was awarded the first of his nine caps in 1972 at Murrayfield when he was only 21 years of age. He was a fine athlete and a former schools long jump champion. Dave Roughley, three caps, was a stalwart of the Liverpool Club and played 34 times for Lancashire.

Eight players were invited to tour with Willie-John McBride's 1974 Lions side to South Africa. They were: Geoff Evans, Alan Old, Mike Burton, Fran Cotton, Tony Neary, Chris Ralston, Andy Ripley, and Roger Uttley. In addition, Alan Morley was called up as a replacement to join the tour at a later stage. Of those Fran Cotton and Roger Uttley, as a flanker, played in all four Tests, and Chris Ralston played in the Final Test with Willie-John McBride at lock.

FIVE NATIONS CHAMPIONSHIP TABLE:

Won: **Nothing**

		Played	Won	Lost	Drawn	Points: For	Against	Tries: For	Against	Title Points
1	Ireland	4	2	1	1	50	45	5	3	5
2 =	Scotland	4	2	2	0	41	35	4	4	4
2 =	Wales	4	1	1	2	43	41	4	3	4
2 =	France	4	1	1	2	43	53	3	4	4
5	ENGLAND	4	1	2	1	63	66	6	8	3

Home Games: lost to Ireland 21 - 26, (one try to four); beat Wales 16 - 12, (two tries to one)

Away Games: lost to Scotland 14 - 16, (two tries each); drew with France 12 - 12, (one try each)

87th match   ENGLAND   9 pts   v   IRELAND   12 pts

	Caps					Caps		
15	6th	P.A.Rossborough	(Coventry)	.		9th	A.H.Ensor	(Wanderers)
14	9th	P.J.Squires	(Harrogate)	.		11th	T.O.Grace	(St Mary's College)
13	4th	P.J.Warfield	(Cambridge Univ)	.		11th	R.A.Milliken	(Bangor)
12	8th	P.S.Preece	(Coventry)	.		49th	C.M.H.Gibson	(NIFC)
11	31st	D.J.Duckham	(Coventry)	.		2nd	S.P.Dennison	(Garryowen)
10	12th	A.G.B.Old	(Middlesborough)	.		2nd	W.M.McCombe	(Bangor)
9	9th	J.G.Webster	(Moseley)	.		15th	J.J.Moloney	(St Mary's College)
1	22nd	C.B.Stevens	(Penzance-Newlyn)	.		37th	R.J.McLoughlin	(Blackrock College)
2	37th	J.V.Pullin	(Bristol)	.		1st	P.C.Whelan	(Garryowen)
3	12th	F.E.Cotton (Capt)	(Coventry)	.		2nd	R.J.Clegg	(Bangor)
4	1st	W.B.Beaumont	(Fylde)	.		60th	W.J.McBride (Capt)	(Ballymena)
5	19th	C.W.Ralston	(Richmond)	.		7th	M.I.Keane	(Lansdowne)
6	13th	P.J.Dixon	(Gosforth)	.		11th	S.A.McKinney	(Dungannon)
7	23rd	A.Neary	(Broughton Park)	.		24th	J.F.Slattery	(Blackrock College)
8	17th	A.G.Ripley	(Rosslyn Park)	.		1st	W.P.Duggan	(Blackrock College)

Referee: F.Palmade   (France)

SCORERS:

C.B.Stevens	Try	(2nd & last)	4 - 0			
A.G.B.Old	Conversion		6 - 0			
			6 - 4	C.M.H.Gibson	Try
			6 - 6	W.M.McCombe	Conversion
A.G.B.Old	D'p Goal	(1st)	9 - 6		
			Half-time		
			9 - 10	W.M.McCombe	Try
			9 - 12	W.M.McCombe	Conversion

POINTS:

A.G.B.Old	5 points	(59)	W.M.McCombe	8 points
C.B.Stevens	4 points	(8)	C.M.H.Gibson	4 points

MATCH COMMENTARY:

England lost their fourth successive game to Ireland largely because of one major error in defence. The packs were well matched both with considerable experience - seven Lions amongst them - and England had done well to turn round at half-time, having faced the wind, leading by nine points to six. Ireland had done most of the attacking when England unexpectedly took the lead. Jan Webster had sent Peter Squires away on the right, and he beat two men before passing to "Stack" Stevens in support. who did remarkably well to be there at all, and he scored for Alan Old to convert. Joy was short-lived, however, as Mike Gibson, running with characterisrtic flair and vision, looped round his wing to take the overlap pass and scored from forty yards. Then, just before half-time, Alan Old dropped a 35 yard goal to give England a half-time lead, nine points to six. The Irish forwards stepped up a gear in the second half, McCombe's tactical kicking was becoming more effective and Mike Gibson's running and covering was frustrating England. But still the score held until, with only ten minurtes to go, the backs, under pressure, let McCombe nip in for the decisive try after Rossborough slipped and let Webster's pass go loose under the posts. Willie-John McBride, leader of the successful Lions in South Africa, gained his 60th cap in this match, whereas Bill Beaumont, his opposite number who would lead the next Lions tour to South Africa, was earning his first - a daunting baptism for anybody !!

50th match   **ENGLAND   20 pts**   v   **FRANCE   27 pts**

	Caps					Caps		
15	7th & last	P.A.Rossborough	(Coventry)	.		2nd	M.Taffary	(Racing Club)
14	10th	P.J.Squires	(Harrogate)	.		8th	J-F.Gourdon	(Racing Club)
13	5th	P.J.Warfield	(Cambridge Univ)	.		32nd	C.Dourthe (Capt)	(Dax)
12	9th	P.S.Preece	(Coventry)	.		3rd	J-M.Etchenique	(Biarritz)
11	32nd	D.J.Duckham	(Coventry)	.		22nd	R.Bertranne	(Bagneres)
10	4th	M.J.Cooper	(Moseley)	.		6th	L.Paries	(Narbonne)
9	10th	J.G.Webster	(Moseley)	.		4th	R.Astre	(Beziers)
1	23rd	C.B.Stevens	(Penzance-Newlyn)	.		15th	A.Vaquerin	(Beziers)
2	1st	P.J.Wheeler	(Leicester)	.		7th	A.Paco	(Beziers)
3	13th	F.E.Cotton (Capt)	(Coventry)	.		1st	G.Cholley	(Castres)
4	9th	R.M.Uttley	(Gosforth)	.		20th & last	A.Esteve	(Beziers)
5	20th	C.W.Ralston	(Richmond)	.		1st	A.Guilbert	(Toulon)
6	6th	J.A.Watkins	(Gloucester)	.		1st	J-P.Rives	(Toulouse)
7	24th	A.Neary	(Broughton Park)	.		18th	J-C.Skrela	(Toulouse)
8	18th	A.G.Ripley	(Rosslyn Park)	.		20th	C.Spanghero	(Narbonne)

Referee: T.F.E.Grierson   (Scotland)

SCORERS:

			0 - 4	A.Guilbert	Try
			0 - 6	L.Paries	Conversion
			0 - 10	J-F.Gourdon	Try
			0 - 12	L.Paries	Conversion
P.A.Rossborough	Try	(1st & last)	4 - 12		
P.A.Rossborough	Penalty Goal		7 - 12		
P.A.Rossborough	Penalty Goal		10 - 12		
			Half-time		
			10 - 16	C.Spanghero	Try
			10 - 18	L.Paries	Conversion
			10 - 22	J-M.Etchenique	Try
			10 - 24	L.Paries	Conversion
			10 - 27	L.Paries	Penalty Goal
P.A.Rossborough	Penalty Goal		13 - 27		
P.A.Rossborough	Penalty Goal		16 - 27		
D.J.Duckham	Try	(9th)	20 - 27		

POINTS:

P.A.Rossborough	16 points	(34)	L.Paries	11 points
D.J.Duckham	4 points	(32)	J-F.Gourdon, J-M.Etchenique,	
			C.Spanghero and A.Guilbert	4 points each

MATCH COMMENTARY:

England missed the opportunity to score a possible 12 points in the opening stages of the match when Rossborough missed penalties from 35 and 40 yards and Peter Preece chose the wrong option with the line at his mercy. Thereafter, England let France play with all the flair and confidence of which they are frequently capable. The score lines suggest that England kept in touch, but they flatter to deceive as England were indecisive and seemingly incapable of putting a respectable attack together. The dithering which surrounded a series of tap penalties near the French line typified England's dearth of ideas. David Duckham's try at the end was very well taken when Peter Preece kicked through and Duckham picked up brilliantly, but it was no consolation. Peter Rossborough, in spite of his early lapses, scored 16 points in the match and was never capped again; in that respect he must hold a unique place in the history of the game.

80th match   **ENGLAND   4 pts**   v   **WALES   20 pts**

	Caps					Caps		
15	6th	A.M.Jorden	(Bedford)	.		30th	J.P.R.Williams	(London Welsh)
14	11th	P.J.Squires	(Harrogate)	.		31st	T.G.R.Davies	(London Welsh)
13	3rd	K.Smith	(Roundhay)	.		2nd	S.P.Fenwick	(Bridgend)
12	10th	P.S.Preece	(Coventry)	.		2nd	R.W.R.Gravell	(Llanelli)
11	33rd	D.J.Duckham	(Coventry)	.		8th	J.J.Williams	(Llanelli)
10	5th	M.J.Cooper	(Moseley)	.		2nd	J.D.Bevan	(Aberavon)
9	11th & last	J.G.Webster	(Moseley)	.		38th	G.O.Edwards	(Cardiff)
1	24th	C.B.Stevens	(Penzance-Newlyn)	.		2nd	G.Price	(Pontypool)
2	2nd	P.J.Wheeler	(Leicester)	.		7th	R.W.Windsor	(Pontypool)
3	14th	F.E.Cotton (Capt)	(Coventry)	.		2nd	A.G.Faulkner	(Pontypool)
4	9th	N.E.Horton	(Moseley)	.		5th	A.J.Martin	(Aberavon)
5	21st	C.W.Ralston	(Richmond)	.		4th	G.A.D.Wheel	(Swansea)
6	7th & last	J.A.Watkins	(Gloucester)	.		6th	T.J.Cobner	(Pontypool)
7	25th	A.Neary	(Broughton Park)	.		2nd	T.P.Evans	(Swansea)
8	10th	R.M.Uttley	(Gosforth)	.		31st	T.M.Davies (Capt)	(Swansea)
	7th	S.J.Smith (Sale) for Webster - 20		.		8th	D.L.Quinnell (Llanelli) for Wheel - 25	
	38th	J.V.Pullin (Bristol) for Wheeler - 44		.				

Referee: A.M.Hosie   (Scotland)

SCORERS:							
				0 - 3	A.J.Martin		Penalty Goal
				0 - 6	A.J.Martin		Penalty Goal
				0 - 10	J.J.Williams		Try
				0 - 14	T.G.R.Davies		Try
				0 - 16	A.J.Martin		Conversion
				Half-time			
	N.E.Horton	Try	(1st & only)	4 - 16			
				4 - 20	S.P.Fenwick		Try

POINTS:	N.E.Horton	4 points	(4)	A.J.Martin	8 points
				T.G.R.Davies, S.P.Fenwick	
				and J.J.Williams	4 points each

MATCH COMMENTARY:

The Welsh forwards had been in powerful mood in Paris, and they were no less so at Cardiff Arms Park against England. The first half saw England almost swept away by the mighty pack and the enterprising Welsh backs running as if their lives depended on it. Fortunately for England, the pace slackened somewhat in the second half, or the result could have been considerably worse. There was no further scoring at all until, with five minutes to go, Nigel Horton scored England's only points with a try from a line-out. This seemed to galvanise the Welsh and in the last minute Steve Fenwick scored after at least six players had handled the ball. England used two substitutes which perhaps disrupted their game to a certain extent, but this did not influence the result of the match. The backs had let England down badly against France, and, with only one change, they did so again at Cardiff. There was no authority at half-back, and Jan Webster who had destroyed the All Blacks almost on his own eighteen months ago, was a shadow of his former self and did not play for England again.

England must be able to do better than this, indeed, if they do not, then another Five Nations "whitewash" must certainly be on the cards

91st match
82nd Calcutta Cup

ENGLAND 7 pts   v   SCOTLAND 6 pts

	Caps				Caps		
15	7th & last	A.M.Jorden	(Bedford)	14th	A.R.Irvine	(Heriot's FP)
14	12th	P.J.Squires	(Harrogate)	18th	W.C.C.Steele	(London Scottish)
13	6th & last	P.J.Warfield	(Cambridge Univ)	13th	J.M.Renwick	(Hawick)
12	4th & last	K.Smith	(Roundhay)	4th & last	D.L.Bell	(Watsonians)
11	5th	A.J.Morley	(Bristol)	10th	L.G.Dick	(Jordanhill)
10	1st	W.N.Bennett	(Bedford)	13th	I.R.McGeechan	(Headingley)
9	5th & last	J.J.Page	(Northampton)	10th	D.W.Morgan	(Stewart's-Melville)
1	25th & last	C.B.Stevens	(Penzance-Newlyn)	26th	J.McLauchlan (Capt)	(Jordanhill)
2	39th	J.V.Pullin	(Bristol)	8th	D.F.Madsen	(Gosforth)
3	8th	M.A.Burton	(Gloucester)	39th	A.B.Carmichael	(West of Scotland)
4	11th	R.M.Uttley	(Gosforth)	28th	A.F.McHarg	(London Scottish)
5	22nd & last	C.W.Ralston	(Richmond)	24th	G.L.Brown	(West of Scotland)
6	8th	D.M.Rollitt	(Bristol)	4th	M.A.Biggar	(London Scottish)
7	26th	A.Neary (Capt)	(Broughton Park)	20th & last	N.A.MacEwan	(Highland)
8	19th	A.G.Ripley	(Rosslyn Park)	4th	D.G.Leslie	(Dundee HSFP)
				3rd	I.A.Barnes (Hawick) for MacEwan - 4	

Referee: D.P.d'Arcy   (Ireland)

SCORERS:

			0 - 3	D.W.Morgan Penalty Goal
W.N.Bennett	Penalty Goal		3 - 3	
			Half-time	
			3 - 6	D.W.Morgan Penalty Goal
A.J.Morley	Try	(2nd & last)	7 - 6	

POINTS:

A.J.Morley	4 points	(8)	D.W.Morgan	6 points
W.N.Bennett	3 points	(3)		

MATCH COMMENTARY:

In desperation, to try to inject some life and sense of purpose and urgency into the side, the selectors made nine changes, one positional, and some occasioned by injury, but a damage limitation exercise seemed certainly to be the underlying intention. Among the changes in personnel were, Jacko Page, recalled at scrum-half to partner tne new fly-half, Neil Bennett, four years since his previous cap, and Dave Rollitt, the Bristol flanker, whose previous cap was six years ago.. The Captaincy, that poisoned chalice, was handed to Tony Neary. Scotland had come to Twickenham in search of the Triple Crown, for the fourth time since 1947, with high hopes, but the whole occasion proved to be a disappointing anti-climax. The day was dull and grey, and the play was little better. The Scots had marginally the upper hand with their pack providing plenty of possession which the backs either kicked away or lost with over-complicated moves. England, with less possession achieved even less. Early in the second half, the slippery ball bounced cruelly over Andy Irvine's head and Alan Morley just won the race to score the only try of the match. In the closing minutes, Douglas Morgan had two penalty goal chances to steal the match for Scotland but on each occasion, he hooked the ball wide. Scotland had to leave with no trophies at all, but England collected the Calcutta Cup and the Wooden Spoon for the second successive year, but at least the dreaded "whitewash" had been avoided.

SUMMARY OF THE SEASON - 1974 - 75:

Yet another disappointing season for England after the summer had been spent in pumping up expectations following the disappointments of the previous season. The Championship was not without drama, the title was not decided until the results of the final series of matches were known, and there was some very enterprising and attractive rugby on display, even from England. But, on the whole, England's contribution to that which will be remembered from the season was minimal. The problem, it would seem, was anglo-saxon reserve which tended to inhibit England's style of play, and the brave, whom fortune favoured, finished very much higher up the Championship Table !

No tourists this season, following the dramatic and successful Lions' tour to South Africa, so four Five Nations matches was the only available fare for the England faithful. For the first match in Dublin, England fielded only one new cap, one W.B.Beaumont, and pitted him against the invincible Lions' captain, Willie-John McBride, There were five changes from the side which had beaten Wales at the end of the previous season, and there were five Lions in the side. The match was evenly balanced until Rossborough's fatal mistake let McCombe, the Irish fly-half, in for the winning try. This was the fourth successive match that England have lost to Ireland. Roger Uttley and John Watkins returned to the pack for the first home match against France, and Alan Old gave way to Martin Cooper. All to no avail, for it was a very disappointing display all round. Ten points were squandered very early in the match, before France got onto the scoresheet, and no side can expect to win with that degree of generosity towards their opponents. One notable French debutant was Jean-Pierre Rives. Including this one, England have beaten France only twice in the last ten matches. But this season, two defeats out of two and the next requirement was a trip to Cardiff where England had not won since 1963. Three changes, including the switch of Roger Uttley to No 8, were considered necessary, but, nevertheless Wales ran riot, completely demolished England in the first half and then, fortunately, eased off and the second half saw one try apiece, but it was, again, a poor England performance. In a last despairing effort, bordering on panic, the selectors made nine changes for the final match at Twickenham against Scotland, and saw fit to recall John Pullin, over whom Peter Wheeler had been preferred for the last two matches; Jacko Page whose last cap had been against Scotland four years ago; Mike Rafter whose last cap had been against Wales six years ago; Alan Morley who had been out of favour thus far in the season, and Mike Burton replaced captain Cotton with Tony Neary being given that dubious honour. In the event, England won. The dreaded "whitewash" was avoided but honour was hardly satisfied, and Scotland, who had had high hopes of a Triple Crown, left Twickenham somewhat aggrieved at the cruel twist of fate in the bounce of a ball which left Andy Irvine standing and allowed Alan Morley to score the only try of the match. But, it must be said, Douglas Morgan could have won both the match and the Triple Crown had he been successful with either of two penalty goal attempts towards the end of the match. So, prior to the forthcoming tour to Australia, England had cause to reflect on two Wooden Spoons in two years, yet they had won the Calcutta Cup twice, and the very urgent and necessary prospect of rebuilding the team from the abundance of talent available based on the nucleus of what was still a very good pack.

With an amazing inconsistency in selection policy, England had used twenty-seven players in four Five Nations matches, and yet had awarded only three new caps. Two of them were not retained in the side, Bill Beaumont played only one match and Peter Wheeler only two. Nine players, inspite of the forthcoming tour, ended their International careers. Claud Brian Stevens, know to friend and foe alike as "Stack", not a particularly athletic figure, but a fine exponent of the dark art of front-row play, and a Cornwall farmer, earned 25 caps. Chris Ralston who had the distinction of being the 1,000th player to be capped by England, and was the first England player to score a four-point try, against Ireland in 1972 He had 22 caps , and played in one Lions Test in South Africa in 1974. Jan Webster, a Midlands sports outfitter, gained 11 caps and was England captain twice. He was only 5ft 5 inches tall, yet had been the scourge of the All Blacks in that memorable match in Auckland in 1973. With seven caps, Peter Rossborough, a Coventry solicitor, and Tony Jorden, an Essex cricketer of some note, both retired. John Watkins, also with seven caps, and a cricketer, was one of the first of the new breed of fast flankers with good ball recycling skills. Peter Warfield, another fine athlete, won six caps, and Jacko Page, a tenacious scrum-half, won five. Keith Smith joined Wakefield Rugby League Club and played for England in the thirteen-a-side code.

FIVE NATIONS CHAMPIONSHIP TABLE:

Won: **Calcutta Cup**

		Played	Won	Lost	Drawn	Points: For	Against	Tries: For	Against	Title Points
1	Wales	4	3	1	0	87	30	14	3	6
2 =	Scotland	4	2	2	0	47	40	2	5	4
2 =	Ireland	4	2	2	0	54	67	8	8	4
2 =	France	4	2	2	0	53	79	6	10	4
5	**ENGLAND**	4	1	3	0	40	65	5	9	2

Home Games: lost to France 20 - 27, (two tries to four); beat Scotland 7 - 6, (one try to none)

Away Games: lost to Ireland 9 - 12, (one try to two); lost to Wales 4 - 20, (one try to three)

ENGLAND TOUR TO AUSTRALIA, 1975

THE TOUR PARTY:

Manager:	A.O.Lewis	Assistant:	J.Burgess		Captain:	A.Neary	
Full-backs:	P.E.Butler	(Gloucester)	no caps	Forwards:	W.B.Beaumont	(Fylde)	1 cap
	A.J.Hignell	(Cambridge U)	no caps		P.J.Blakeway	(Gloucester)	no caps
					M.A.Burton	(Gloucester)	8 caps
Three-quarters:	A.W.Maxwell	(New Brighton)	no caps		S.R.Callum	(Upper Clapton)	no caps
	A.J.Morley	(Bristol)	5 caps		F.E.Cotton	(Coventry)	14 caps
	P.S.Preece	(Coventry)	10 caps		N.D.Mantell	(Rosslyn Park)	no caps
	K.Smith	(Roundhay)	4 caps		A.Neary	(Broughton Park)	26 caps
	P.J.Squires	(Harrogate)	12 caps		J.V.Pullin	(Bristol)	39 caps
	D.M.Wyatt	(Bedford)	no caps		J.A.G.D.Raphael	(Northampton)	no caps
					A.G.Ripley	(Rosslyn Park)	19 caps
Half-backs:	W.B.Ashton	(Orrell)	no caps		D.M.Rollitt	(Bristol)	9 caps
	W.N.Bennett	(Bedford)	1 cap		R.M.Uttley	(Gosforth)	11 caps
	P.Kingston	(Gloucester)	no caps		R.M.Wilkinson	(Bedford)	no caps
	A.J.Wordsworth	(Cambridge U)	no caps				
Replacements:	J.P.A.G.Janion	(Richmond)	10 caps		P.J.Dixon	(Gosforth)	13 caps
	A.G.B.Old	(Middlesboro')	12 caps		B.G.Nelmes	(Cardiff)	no caps
	I.N.Orum	(Roundhay)	no caps				

The England selectors boldly, and in the circumstances quite rightly, chose an experimental squad for this, England's first tour of Australia. That the experiment was not altogether successful, nor the tour the team buiding exercise it had been intended to be, was largely due to the extraordinary number of injuries suffered by the England squad, frequently to key players. This disrupted cohesion in the team, prevented a policy of selection and development in the build up to the two Test matches, and also engendered a degree of animosity between the teams, particularly in the International matches which culminated in Mike Burton being sent off the field in the second minute of the second International at Brisbane.

The first match, en route in Perth, was not indicative of what was to come.. A very strong England side ran amok, scored nine tries (of which Alan Morley scored four) and provided Neil Bennett with the opportunity to score 36 points during the match, 12 more than Alan Old had scored in South Africa to set the previous record.. The second match against Sydney was a different proposition altogether, and Fran Cotton suffered a back injury which kept him out of the rest of the tour, and England lost by four points. New South Wales provided stiff opposition too but England ran out winners in an entertaining match with Peter Preece scoring four out of England's five tries. Against the Country XV in Goulburn, Neil Bennett had to leave the field in an ill-tempered match which was lost by one point. There was no respite from the demoralising sequence of physical ailments and in the first Test Tony Neary and Neil Bennett suffered injuries which prevented either playing any further part in the tour. Thus it was that England had to call for five replacements during the course of a tour lasting only three and a half weeks. However, the tour, disrupted as it was, was an invaluable experience for those fortunate enough to have taken part, but it did not do a great deal for England team-building for the future.

At the conclusion of the tour, four players bad farewell to the International stage. Jeremy Janion, with 12 caps, played both in the centre and on the wing, in a career which spanned five years. Dave Rollitt, a Bristol schoolteacher, earned 11 caps, and his career had spanned nine years with a gap of six years prior to 1975. Alan Morley, played over 500 times for Bristol, scored a try on his England debut in Souith Africa, and retired with 7 caps. Neil Mantell won his one and only cap in the first Test.

TOUR RESULTS:

May 10th	Western Australia	in Perth	WON	64 - 12	(nine tries to one)
May 13th	Sydney	in Sydney	LOST	10 - 14	(two tries to three)
May 17th	New South Wales	in Sydney	WON	29 - 24	(five tries to four)
May 20th	N.S.W.Country XV	in Goulburn	LOST	13 - 14	(two tries to three)
May 27th	Queensland	in Brisbane	WON	29 - 3	(five tries to none)
June 3rd	Queensland Country	in Townsville	WON	42 - 6	(eight tries to one)
May 24th	**AUSTRALIA**	in Sydney	LOST	9 - 16	(one try each)
May 31st	**AUSTRALIA**	in Brisbane	LOST	21 - 30	(two tries to five)

8th match   **ENGLAND 9 pts**   v   **AUSTRALIA 16 pts**

	Caps					Caps		
15	1st	P.E.Butler	(Gloucester)	.	1st	R.C.Brown	(New South Wales)
14	13th	P.J.Squires	(Harrogate)	.	5th	L.E.Monaghan	(New South Wales)
13	11th	J.P.A.G.Janion	(Richmond)	.	1st	L.J.Weatherstone	(ACT)
12	1st	A.W.Maxwell	(New Brighton)	.	14th	G.A.Shaw	(Queensland)
11	6th	A.J.Morley	(Bristol)	.	1st	D.H.Osborne	(Victoria)
10	2nd	W.N.Bennett	(Bedford)	.	1st	K.J.Wright	(New South Wales)
9	1st	P.J.Kingston	(Gloucester)	.	24th	J.N.B.Hipwell (Capt)	(New South Wales)
1	1st	B.G.Nelmes	(Cardiff)	.	6th	S.G.MacDougall	(ACT)
2	40th	J.V.Pullin	(Bristol)	.	4th	P.A.Horton	(New South Wales)
3	9th	M.A.Burton	(Gloucester)	.	1st	S.C.Finnane	(New South Wales)
4	1st & only	N.D.Mantell	(Rosslyn Park)	.	9th	R.A.Smith	(New South Wales)
5	12th	R.M.Uttley	(Gosforth)	.	12th	G.Fay	(New South Wales)
6	10th	D.M.Rollitt	(Bristol)	.	3rd	A.A.Shaw	(Queensland)
7	27th	A.Neary (Capt)	(Broughton Park)	.	4th	R.A.Price	(New South Wales)
8	20th	A.G.Ripley	(Rosslyn Park)	.	4th	M.E.Loane	(Queensland)

1st & only	A.J.Wordsworth (Camb U) for Bennett - 15		
2nd	W.B.Beaumont (Fylde) for Neary - 23	.	

Referee: W.M.Cooney   (Australia)

SCORERS:

				0 - 4	M.E.Loane	Try
	P.J.Squires	Try	(4th)	4 - 4		
	P.E.Butler	Conversion		6 - 4		
				6 - 7	R.C.Brown	Penalty Goal
				Half-time		
				6 - 10	K.J.Wright	Drop Goal
				6 - 13	R.C.Brown	Drop Goal
				6 - 16	R.C.Brown	Penalty Goal
	P.E.Butler	Penalty Goal		9 - 16		

POINTS:

	P.E.Butler	5 points	(5)	R.C.Brown	9 points
	P.J.Squires	4 points	(12)	M.E.Loane	4 points
				K.J.Wright	3 points

MATCH COMMENTARY:

England sent a young squad to Australia for this short tour, and they had a series of misfortunes and injuries which seriously demoralised the side. Nevertheless, in front of a crowd of 40,000 at the Sydney Cricket Ground, England put up brave resistance but the Australian backs held sway throughout the match. The try count was only one each and, bearing in mind that England lost both their captain, Tony Neary, and their fly-half during the game due to injury, this was not a bad performance by a side which was a team of contrasts, seven players had 133 caps amongst them, and the remaining eight only 22, with five new caps. The England backs did not see a great deal of the ball, and when they did the possession was frittered away, and they failed to capitalise on the pace on their wings. The Australian running and handling on the other hand, was of a very high order. Ironically, England's try came, not from enterprise by the England backs, but from a dropped pass by the Australians which Peter Squires was very quick to pounce upon.

The match got a little abrasive towards the end and there was one particularly fierce brawl involving almost all sixteen forwards. Unfortunately, this ill-feeling was carried over to the second International of the tour.

9th match   # ENGLAND   21 pts   v   AUSTRALIA   30 pts

	Caps					Caps		
15	1st	A.J.Hignell	(Cambridge Univ)	.	2nd & last	R.C.Brown	(New South Wales)
14	14th	P.J.Squires	(Harrogate)	.	6th	L.E.Monaghan	(New South Wales)
13	12th & last	J.P.A.G.Janion	(Richmond)	.	2nd	L.J.Weatherstone	(ACT)
12	11th	P.S.Preece	(Coventry)	.	15th	G.A.Shaw	(Queensland)
11	7th & last	A.J.Morley	(Bristol)	.	2nd	D.H.Osborne	(Victoria)
10	13th	A.G.B.Old	(Middlesborough)	.	2nd	K.J.Wright	(New South Wales)
9	2nd	P.J.Kingston	(Gloucester)	.	25th	J.N.B.Hipwell (Capt)	(New South Wales)
1	2nd	B.G.Nelmes	(Cardiff)	.	7th	S.G.MacDougall	(ACT)
2	41st	J.V.Pullin (Capt)	(Bristol)	.	5th	P.A.Horton	(New South Wales)
3	10th	M.A.Burton	(Gloucester)	.	7th	R.Graham	(New South Wales)
4	1st	R.M.Wilkinson	(Bedford)	.	10th	R.A.Smith	(New South Wales)
5	3rd	W.B.Beaumont	(Fylde)	.	13th	G.Fay	(New South Wales)
6	11th & last	D.M.Rollitt	(Bristol)	.	4th	A.A.Shaw	(Queensland)
7	13th	R.M.Uttley	(Gosforth)	.	5th	R.A.Price	(New South Wales)
8	21st	A.G.Ripley	(Rosslyn Park)	.	5th	M.E.Loane	(Queensland)

Referee: R.T.Burnett   (Australia)

SCORERS:

				Score		
				0 - 3	R.C.Brown	Penalty Goal
A.G.B.Old	Penalty Goal			3 - 3		
A.G.B.Old	Penalty Goal			6 - 3		
P.J.Squires	Try	(5th)		10 - 3		
A.G.B.Old	Conversion			12 - 3		
				12 - 7	R.A.Price	Try
				12 - 9	R.C.Brown	Conversion
A.G.B.Old	Penalty Goal			15 - 9		
				Half-time		
				15 - 13	R.A.Smith	Try
				15 - 17	L.J.Weatherstone	Try
				15 - 21	G.Fay	Try
				15 - 23	K.J.Wright	Conversion
				15 - 26	K.J.Wright	Penalty Goal
				15 - 30	L.E.Monaghan	Try
R.M.Uttley	Try	(1st)		19 - 30		
A.G.B.Old	Conversion			21 - 30		

POINTS:

A.G.B.Old	13 points	(72)	R.C.Brown and K.J.Wright	5 points each
P.J.Squires	4 points	(20)	L.E.Monaghan, R.A.Smith, G.Fay	
R.M.Uttley	4 points	(4)	L.J.Weatherstone and R.A.Price	4 points each

---

MATCH COMMENTARY:

England made five changes from the side beaten the previous week, primarily due to injury. The match started at a ferocious pace, and within a minute the referee had to warn several players for brawling. Seconds later Mike Burton was adjudged to have tackled late and was sent off, the first England player ever to suffer this fate. With 14 men, England did remarkably well to lead 15 - 9 at half-time but were then overrun.

10th match   **ENGLAND   23 pts**   v   **AUSTRALIA   6 pts**

	Caps				Caps		
15	2nd	A.J.Hignell	(Cambridge Univ)		8th	P.E.McLean	(Queensland)
14	15th	P.J.Squires	(Harrogate)		3rd	P.G.Batch	(Queensland)
13	2nd	A.W.Maxwell	(New Brighton)		1st	W.A.McKid	(New South Wales)
12	1st	B.J.Corless	(Coventry)		19th	G.A.Shaw (Capt)	(New South Wales)
11	34th	D.J.Duckham	(Coventry)		9th	L.E.Monaghan	(New South Wales)
10	6th	M.J.Cooper	(Moseley)		5th	L.J.Weatherstone	(ACT)
9	1st	M.S.Lampkowski	(Headingley)		4th	R.G.Hauser	(Queensland)
1	11th	M.A.Burton	(Gloucester)		2nd	S.C.Finnane	(New South Wales)
2	3rd	P.J.Wheeler	(Leicester)		10th	P.A.Horton	(New South Wales)
3	15th	F.E.Cotton	(Coventry)		8th & last	S.G.MacDougall	(New South Wales)
4	4th	W.B.Beaumont	(Fylde)		15th	R.A.Smith	(New South Wales)
5	2nd	R.M.Wilkinson	(Bedford)		2nd	D.W.Hillhouse	(Queensland)
6	1st	M.Keyworth	(Swansea)		6th	G.Cornelsen	(New South Wales)
7	28th	A.Neary (Capt)	(Broughton Park)		8th	A.A.Shaw	(Queensland)
8	22nd	A.G.Ripley	(Rosslyn Park)		7th	M.E.Loane	(Queensland)

Referee: M.Joseph   (Wales)

SCORERS:

A.J.Hignell	Penalty Goal		3 - 0			
			3 - 3	P.E.McLean	Penalty Goal	
A.J.Hignell	Penalty Goal		6 - 3			
			Half-time			
B.J.Corless	Try	(1st & only)	10 - 3			
M.S.Lampkowski	Try	(1st & only)	14 - 3			
D.J.Duckham	Try	(10th & last)	18 - 3			
A.J.Hignell	Conversion		20 - 3			
			20 - 6	P.E.McLean	Penalty Goal	
A.J.Hignell	Penalty Goal		23 - 6			

POINTS:

A.J.Hignell	11 points	(11)		P.E.McLean	6 points
B.J.Corless, D.J.Duckham	4 points	(4),(36)			
and M.S.Lampkowski	each	(4)			

MATCH COMMENTARY:

The Sixth Wallabies were almost as plagued by injuries as England had been on tour the previous year, but they were a far less effective side than that which had beaten England soundly twice on that tour.   The England side had been well coached by Peter Colston, and looked full of confidence at the beginning of the game, and the pack gradually achieved the ascendancy and played some very solid and determined football. As a result the forwards provided an abundance of quality possession, Wheeler winning four against the head, yet apart from a purple patch in the second half when they scored three tries in seven minutes, the backs looked hesitant and unimaginative. David Duckham's try was the only one that came from a good thrusting three-quarter movement. But England were deserving winners and the result, three tries to nil, and some of the play, was adequate compensation for the disappointments in Australia and was a welcome and refreshing change from some of the spectacles that England supporters have been compelled to witness in the recent past. England should now go into the Five Nations with greater and justifiable confidence.

81st match **ENGLAND 9 pts**   v   **WALES 21 pts**

	Caps				Caps		
15	3rd	A.J.Hignell	(Cambridge Univ)	.	34th	J.P.R.Williams	(London Welsh)
14	16th	P.J.Squires	(Harrogate)	.	34th	T.G.R.Davies	(Cardiff)
13	3rd	A.W.Maxwell	(Headingley)	.	6th	R.W.R.Gravell	(Llanelli)
12	1st	D.A.Cooke	(Harlequins)	.	5th	S.P.Fenwick	(Bridgend)
11	35th	D.J.Duckham	(Coventry)	.	12th	J.J.Williams	(Llanelli)
10	7th	M.J.Cooper	(Moseley)	.	18th	P.Bennett	(Llanelli)
9	2nd	M.S.Lampkowski	(Headingley)	.	42nd	G.O.Edwards	(Cardiff)
1	16th	F.E.Cotton	(Sale)	.	6th	G.Price	(Pontypool)
2	4th	P.J.Wheeler	(Leicester)	.	11th	R.W.Windsor	(Pontypool)
3	12th	M.A.Burton	(Gloucester)	.	6th	A.G.Faulkner	(Pontypool)
4	5th	W.B.Beaumont	(Fylde)	.	9th	A.J.Martin	(Aberavon)
5	3rd	R.M.Wilkinson	(Bedford)	.	7th	G.A.D.Wheel	(Swansea)
6	2nd	M.Keyworth	(Swansea)	.	10th	T.J.Cobner	(Pontypool)
7	29th	A.Neary (Capt)	(Broughton Park)	.	6th	T.P.Evans	(Swansea)
8	23rd	A.G.Ripley	(Rosslyn Park)	.	35th	T.M.Davies (Capt)	(Swansea)

12th & last P.S.Preece (Coventry) for Squires - 30

Referee: G.Domercq (France)

SCORERS:

		0 - 4	G.O.Edwards	Try
		0 - 6	S.P.Fenwick	Conversion
		0 - 9	A.J.Martin	Penalty Goal
A.J.Hignell	Penalty Goal	3 - 9		
		3 - 13	J.P.R.Williams	Try
		3 - 15	S.P.Fenwick	Conversion
A.J.Hignell	Penalty Goal	6 - 15		
		Half-time		
A.J.Hignell	Penalty Goal	9 - 15		
		9 - 19	J.P.R.Williams	Try
		9 - 21	S.P.Fenwick	Conversion

POINTS:

A.J.Hignell	9 points	(20)	J.P.R.Williams	8 points
			S.P.Fenwick	6 points
			G.O.Edwards	4 points
			A.J.Martin	3 points

MATCH COMMENTARY:

After the euphoria following the win over Australia only two weeks previously, England came down to earth with a thump. This was, of course the beginning of Wales' total ascendancy when they won four Triple Crowns in succession, but this was not known at the time ! Well though England played, they were out-played especially at scrum-half where Gareth Edwards' superb line-kicking and long, fast passes to Phil Bennett kept England at bay, and at full-back from where J.P.R.Williams scored two tries, the first full-back ever to do so in an International match, as well as being rock-solid in defence. England's defence too, was, for the most part, determined and courageous, but some glaring and fundamental errors were made - Gareth Edwards scored from a five yard scrum on an England ball ! This was Wales' highest winning score and margin ever at Twickenham.

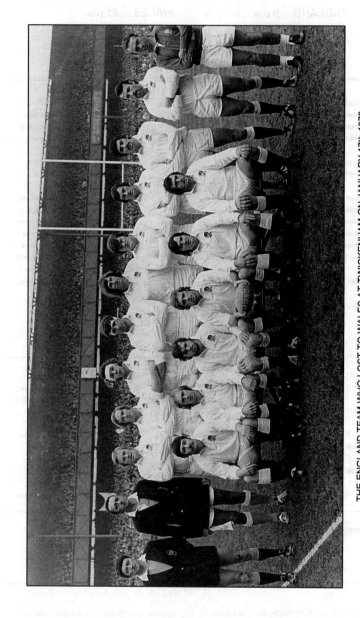

THE ENGLAND TEAM WHO LOST TO WALES AT TWICKENHAM ON JANUARY 17th 1976

Standing: Touch Judges, P.J.Wheeler, D.J.Duckham, W.B.Beaumont, R.M.Wilkinson, A.G.Ripley, F.E.Cotton, M.Keyworth, M.J.Cooper, A.W.Maxwell, G.Domercq (Referee),
Seated: D.A.Cooke, P.J.Squires, A.J.Hignell, A.Neary (Capt), M.S.Lampkowski, M.A.Burton.

92nd match   **ENGLAND   12 pts**   v   **SCOTLAND   22 pts**

83rd Calcutta Cup

	Caps					Caps		
15	4th	A.J.Hignell	(Cambridge Univ)	.	19th	A.R.Irvine	(Heriot's FP)
14	2nd	K.C.Plummer	(Bristol)	.	20th	W.C.C.Steele	(London Scottish)
13	4th	A.W.Maxwell	(Headingley)	.	2nd	A.G.Cranston	(Hawick)
12	2nd	D.A.Cooke	(Harlequins)	.	18th	I.R.McGeechan	(Headingley)
11	36th & last	D.J.Duckham	(Coventry)	.	8th	D.Shedden	(West of Scotland)
10	14th	A.G.B.Old	(Middlesborough)	.	1st	R.Wilson	(London Scottish)
9	3rd	M.S.Lampkowski	(Headingley)	.	8th	A.J.M.Lawson	(London Scottish)
1	17th	F.E.Cotton	(Sale)	.	31st	J.McLauchlan (Capt)	(Jordanhill)
2	5th	P.J.Wheeler	(Leicester)	.	4th	C.D.Fisher	(Waterloo)
3	13th	M.A.Burton	(Gloucester)	.	44th	A.B.Carmichael	(West of Scotland)
4	6th	W.B.Beaumont	(Fylde)	.	1st	A.J.Tomes	(Hawick)
5	4th	R.M.Wilkinson	(Bedford)	.	28th	G.L.Brown	(West of Scotland)
6	3rd	M.Keyworth	(Swansea)	.	6th	M.A.Biggar	(London Scottish)
7	30th	A.Neary (Capt)	(Broughton Park)	.	9th	D.G.Leslie	(West of Scotland)
8	24th & last	A.G.Ripley	(Rosslyn Park)	.	33rd	A.F.McHarg	(London Scottish)

	1st & only	D.M.Wyatt (Bedford) for Duckham - 10			18th	J.M.Renwick (Hawick) for Shedden - 32
	3rd	W.N.Bennett (Bedford) for Maxwell - 45				

Referee: D.M.Lloyd   (Wales)

A.W.Maxwell	Try	(1st & only)	4 - 0	
A.G.B.Old	Conversion		6 - 0	
			6 - 3	A.R.Irvine	Penalty Goal
A.G.B.Old	Penalty Goal		9 - 3	
			9 - 7	A.J.M.Lawson	Try
			9 - 9	A.R.Irvine	Conversion
A.G.B.Old	Penalty Goal		12 - 9	
			Half-time	
			12 - 12	A.R.Irvine	Penalty Goal
			12 - 16	D.G.Leslie	Try
			12 - 20	A.J.M.Lawson	Try
			12 - 22	A.R.Irvine	Conversion

POINTS:						
	A.G.B.Old	8 points	(80)		A.R.Irvine	10 points
	A.W.Maxwell	4 points	(4)		A.J.M.Lawson	8 points
					D.G.Leslie	4 points

MATCH COMMENTARY:

The Queen, Prince Philip and a crowd of some 70,000 saw England fail at Murrayfield for the fifth successive time. But it was a splendid match. The forwards were evenly matched but, not for the first time, the English backs never threatened and the departure of David Duckham further sapped their confidence. Scotland always had the upper hand and kept the initiative. Alan Lawson, Bill MacLaren's son-in-law, after a two year absence, scored two fine tries and the decisive score came when David Leslie charged down Alan Old's clearance kick and ran in twenty yards to score. But England held a deserved half-time lead. In the second half, Mike Lampowski perhaps tried to do too much on his own and consequently the quality of ball available to Alan Old deteriorated. To a demoralised back line this was the last straw, and England failed to add to their score in a poor, but if you were Scottish excellent, second half !

88th match   ENGLAND   12 pts   v   IRELAND   13 pts

	Caps					Caps		
15	5th	A.J.Hignell	(Cambridge Univ)	.	16th	A.H.Ensor	(Lansdowne)
14	3rd	K.C.Plummer	(Bristol)	.	18th	T.O.Grace (Capt)	(St Mary's College)
13	5th	A.W.Maxwell	(Headingley)	.	1st	J.A.Brady	(Wanderers)
12	3rd	D.A.Cooke	(Harlequins)	.	56th	C.M.H.Gibson	(NIFC)
11	1st	M.A.C.Slemen	(Liverpool)	.	1st	S.E.F.Blake-Knox	(NIFC)
10	15th	A.G.B.Old	(Sheffield)	.	23rd	B.J.McGann	(Cork Constitution)
9	4th & last	M.S.Lampkowski	(Headingley)	.	2nd & last	D.M.Canniffe	(Lansdowne)
1	18th	F.E.Cotton	(Sale)	.	3rd	P.A.Orr	(Old Wesley)
2	6th	P.J.Wheeler	(Leicester)	.	4th	J.L.Cantrell	(UC Dublin)
3	14th	M.A.Burton	(Gloucester)	.	19th	P.O'Callaghan	(Dolphin)
4	7th	W.B.Beaumont	(Fylde)	.	14th	M.I.Keane	(Lansdowne)
5	5th	R.M.Wilkinson	(Bedford)	.	2nd	B.O.Foley	(Shannon)
6	4th & last	M.Keyworth	(Swansea)	.	16th	S.A.McKinney	(Dungannon)
7	31st	A.Neary (Capt)	(Broughton Park)	.	4th	S.M.Deering	(Garryowen)
8	1st	G.J.Adey	(Leicester)	.	1st	H.W.Steele	(Ballymena)

	2nd	B.J.Corless (Coventry) for Hignell - 38

Referee:	A.M.Hosie	(Scotland)

SCORERS:	A.G.B.Old	Penalty Goal	3 - 0		
	A.G.B.Old	Penalty Goal	6 - 0		
	A.G.B.Old	Penalty Goal	9 - 0		
			Half-time		
			9 - 3	B.J.McGann	Penalty Goal
			9 - 7	T.O.Grace	Try
			9 - 10	B.J.McGann	Penalty Goal
			9 - 13	B.J.McGann	Drop Goal
	A.G.B.Old	Penalty Goal	12 - 13		

POINTS:	A.G.B.Old	12 points	(92)	B.J.McGann	9 points
				T.O.Grace	4 points

MATCH COMMENTARY:

An uninspiring game saw England lose their second home game of the season, and their third overall, to a poor Irish side whose only win in the Championship this was to be. England should have had a settled pack - the front five were playing together for the fourth time, whereas Ireland were still struggling to come to terms with the retirement at the end of last season of Willie-John McBride, Ken Kennedy and Ray McLoughlin and the absence through injury of Fergus Slattery. England were convincing enough in the first half, and turned round with a nine point lead, but in the second half, with only one minute gone, Mike Gibson was tackled from behind without the ball by Peter Wheeler and Barry McGann converted the penalty - which should arguably have been a penalty try. Then, all within the space of fifteen minutes, the same Barry McGann structured a fine try for Tom Grace, kicked another penalty and dropped a goal to give Ireland a four point lead, and the way England were playing at the time, the match. England sparked something of a revival and, in the last minute, were awarded a penalty some 35 yards out, but, instead of running the ball, and going for the try to win the match, Tony Neary elected to kick for goal. Alan Old converted the kick and England closed to within one point, but, in so doing, lost a match they could have won. This was Ireland's fifth successive win over England and their third in a row at Twickenham. Eight tries conceded so far this season, and only one scored !

51st match   **ENGLAND   9 pts**   v   **FRANCE   30 pts**

	Caps				Caps		
15	2nd & last	P.E.Butler	(Gloucester)	.	13th	J-M.Aguirre	(Bagneres)
14	4th & last	K.C.Plummer	(Bristol)	.	15th	J-F.Gourdon	(Racing Club)
13	4th & last	D.A.Cooke	(Harlequins)	.	33rd	R.Bertranne	(Bagneres)
12	6th	A.W.Maxwell	(Headingley)	.	9th	J.Pecune	(Tarbes)
11	2nd	M.A.C.Slemen	(Liverpool)	.	7th	J-L.Averous	(La Voulte)
10	1st & only	C.G.Williams	(RAF/Gloucester)	.	24th	J-P.Romeu	(Montferrand)
9	8th	S.J.Smith	(Sale)	.	16th	J.Fouroux (Capt)	(La Voulte)
1	19th	F.E.Cotton	(Sale)	.	12th	G.Cholley	(Castres)
2	42nd & last	J.V.Pullin	(Bristol)	.	14th	A.Paco	(Beziers)
3	15th	M.A.Burton	(Gloucester)	.	9th	R.Paparemborde	(Pau)
4	8th	W.B.Beaumont	(Fylde)	.	3rd	J-F.Imbernon	(Perpignan)
5	6th & last	R.M.Wilkinson	(Bedford)	.	9th	M.Palmie	(Beziers)
6	14th	P.J.Dixon	(Gosforth)	.	10th	J-P.Rives	(Toulouse)
7	32nd	A.Neary (Capt)	(Broughton Park)	.	29th	J-C.Skrela	(Toulouse)
8	2nd & last	G.J.Adey	(Leicester)	.	21st	J-P.Bastiat	(Dax)

1st & only   R.Berges-Cau (Lourdes) for Aguirre - 38

Referee: K.H.Clark   (Ireland)

SCORERS:	P.E.Butler	Penalty Goal		3 - 0			
				3 - 4	J-P.Romeu	Try	
				3 - 6	J-P.Romeu	Conversion	
				3 - 10	R.Paparemborde	Try	
				Half-time			
				3 - 14	J.Fouroux	Try	
				3 - 16	J-P.Romeu	Conversion	
				3 - 20	J-P.Bastiat	Try	
				3 - 22	J-P.Romeu	Conversion	
				3 - 26	R.Paparemborde	Try	
				3 - 30	J-F.Gourdon	Try	
	P.J.Dixon	Try	(3rd)	7 - 30			
	P.E.Butler	Conversion		9 - 30			

POINTS:	P.E.Butler	5 points	(10)		J-P.Romeu	10 points
	P.J.Dixon	4 points	(12)		R.Paparemborde	8 points
					J-P.Bastiat, J-F.Gourdon,	
					and J.Fouroux	4 points each

MATCH COMMENTARY:

The power of the French scrummaging in the tight and in the loose was far too much for England. Three of the six tries were scored by the forwards, one from a pushover, by Paparemborde, and one direct from a scrum by Bastiat. England have now conceded 30 points, or more, and six tries to France in three of the last four games in Paris. In all, this was a very poor performance by England. Only Slemen, Plummer, and Dixon emerged with any credit. England's season of high promise and expectation had come to nothing, and they had lost all four Championship matches for only the second time, but within five seasons, and claimed the Wooden Spoon for the third successive year.

SUMMARY OF THE SEASON 1975 - 76:

Disappointing seasons are becoming the norm for England supporters these days, but even by current standards, this was a big one. For only the second time ever, but for the second time in the last five years, England were whitewashed, in that they lost all four Five Nations matches in the season. In fact, in the last ten years, England have played 40 Five Nations matches, have won 11, drawn 4 and lost 25. In that time, they have beaten Wales only once, France only twice, Ireland three times and Scotland five times. By any standards, an appalling performance.

Yet the season had started encouragingly, with a well merited win over the touring Australians. Fot that match, the selectors chose only six of the side who has played in that abrasive match in Brisbane the previous May, and included Mike Burton. The side was well coached, the forwards gained the lion's share of possession and England won by 23 points to 6 and three tries to nil. The backs did not look razor sharp, but nowhere were there signs of imminent disaster. David Cooke in the centre for Barry Corless was the only change made for the Five Nations opener against Wales at Twickenham. It was a magnificent, and Grand Slam winning Welsh side and England were well beaten and there were some fundamental errors made which should not be witnessed on an International field of play. For the trip to Murrayfield, Alan Old replaced Martin Cooper at fly-half, and Keith Plummer came in for the injured Peter Squires, but little else changed. There were still too many fundamental errors, even with adequate posession, and having turned round at half-time with a three point lead, England offered little opposition in the second half and Scotland scored thirteen points without reply. However, the selectors persisted and the only changes for the visit of Ireland to Twickenham were necessitated by injury to David Duckham and Andy Ripley, with Gary Adey and Mike Slemen making their International debuts. Again, the first half saw a reasonable performance by the England side and they went into the second half with a nine point lead, albeit by three penalty goals from Alan Old. Then, in the second half, the side went to pieces yet again and allowed Ireland to score thirteen points in the second half to win the match. Confusion was rife and direction was lost - and so were the last three matches. Selectorial panic became evident, five changes were made for the last match of the season against France in Paris, and not without reason, because in the course of the last three visits to Paris, England had conceded 84 points and 13 tries ! Changes were made at full-back, both half-backs, hooker, with John Pullin recalled to stiffen English resistance, and at wing-forward or flanker, where Peter Dixon was re-installed. All to no avail. Another humiliating Parisian thrashing had to be endured. This time there was no lead at half-time and twenty points were conceded in the second half - and another six tries in all.

The season was disastrous, and in the last three matches there were worrying signs that the side lost interest in competing in the second-half It was a tragedy for Tony Neary, too, who had the misfortune to be appointed captain for the season, but, on the other hand, he was unable to arrest the decline. At the end of the season, the Chairman of Selectors, Alec Lewis, resigned.

England had called upon twenty five players during the course of the five matches in the season, and twenty four for the Five Nations. Seven new caps were awarded, three in the first match against Australia when Mike Lampowski and Barry Corless both scored a try on their debut. Not surprisingly in view of the season's results, twelve players did not appear for England again. John Pullin won a record 42 caps as hooker, 36 of them successive - another record - having led England 13 times and his record of victories over each of the major southern hemisphere nations has been emulated since only by Will Carling. He went on two Lions' tours and played in seven Tests. David Duckham, England's most capped back, gained 36 caps, 22 on the wing, 14 as a centre, scored a record 10 tries, and went on the 1971 Lions' tour, playing in three Tests. Andy Ripley, with 24 caps, was England's most capped No 8, and a very fine athlete excelling in many sports. Bob Wilkinson, 6 caps, came to prominence when he was the only uncapped player in the 1973 Barbarians side for that memorable match against the All Blacks in Cardiff. Also retiring, with four caps, were David Cooke, the Harlequin centre and schoolteacher; Mark Keyworth, the Swansea flanker; Mike Lampowski, who went to Wakefield RL Club; and Keith Plummer, the Bristol wing. Peter Butler, the prolific points-scoring Gloucester full-back and Gary Adey, the Leicester flanker, both had two caps, and Chris Williams and Derek Wyatt each gained one cap, the latter as a replacement.

FIVE NATIONS CHAMPIONSHIP TABLE:

Won: **Nothing**

		Played	Won	Lost	Drawn	Points: For	Against	Tries: For	Against	Title Points
1	Wales	4	4	0	0	102	37	11	3	8
2	France	4	3	1	0	82	37	13	2	6
3	Scotland	4	2	2	0	49	59	4	5	4
4	Ireland	4	1	3	0	31	87	1	8	2
5	**ENGLAND**	4	0	4	0	42	86	2	13	0

Home Games: lost to Wales 9 - 21, (no tries to three); lost to Ireland 12 - 13, (no tries to one)

Away Games: lost to Scotland 12 - 22, (one try to three); lost to France 9 - 30, (one try to six)

93rd match
84th Calcutta Cup

ENGLAND 26 pts   v   SCOTLAND 6 pts

	Caps				Caps		
15	6th	A.J.Hignell	(Bristol)	21st	A.R.Irvine	(Heriot's FP)
14	17th	P.J.Squires	(Harrogate)	23rd & last	W.C.C.Steele	(RAF/Ldn Scottish)
13	3rd	B.J.Corless	(Moseley)	21st	I.R.McGeechan (Capt)	(Headingley)
12	1st	C.P.Kent	(Rosslyn Park)	4th	A.G.Cranston	(Hawick)
11	3rd	M.A.C.Slemen	(Liverpool)	14th & last	L.G.Dick	(Swansea)
10	8th	M.J.Cooper	(Moseley)	3rd	R.Wilson	(London Scottish)
9	1st	M.Young	(Gosforth)	8th	A.J.M.Lawson	(London Scottish)
1	1st	R.J.Cowling	(Leicester)	1st	J.Aitken	(Gala)
2	7th	P.J.Wheeler	(Leicester)	10th	D.F.Madsen	(Gosforth)
3	20th	F.E.Cotton	(Sale)	46th	A.B.Carmichael	(West of Scotland)
4	9th	W.B.Beaumont	(Fylde)	3rd	A.J.Tomes	(Hawick)
5	10th	N.E.Horton	(Moseley)	35th	A.F.McHarg	(London Scottish)
6	15th	P.J.Dixon	(Gosforth)	18th & last	W.Lauder	(Neath)
7	1st	M.Rafter	(Bristol)	1st	A.K.Brewster	(Stewart's-Melville)
8	14th	R.M.Uttley (Capt)	(Gosforth)	1st	D.S.M.MacDonald	(Oxford University)

Referee: M.Joseph   (Wales)

SCORERS:

			0 - 3	A.R.Irvine	Penalty Goal
M.A.C.Slemen	Try	(1st)	4 - 3		
A.J.Hignell	Penalty Goal		7 - 3		
			7 - 6	A.R.Irvine	Penalty Goal
M.Young	Try	(1st & only)	11 - 6		
A.J.Hignell	Conversion		13 - 6		
		Half-time			
A.J.Hignell	Penalty Goal		16 - 6		
C.P.Kent	Try	(1st & only)	20 - 6		
R.M.Uttley	Try	(2nd & last)	24 - 6		
A.J.Hignell	Conversion		26 - 6		

POINTS:

A.J.Hignell	10 points	(30)	A.R.Irvine	6 points
C.P.Kent, M.A.C.Slemen	4 points	(4),(4)		
M.Young and R.M.Uttley	each	(4),(8)		

MATCH COMMENTARY:

Under Roger Uttley's inspiring captaincy, England looked, at times, as if they might be in serious contention for the Championship. The tactic for this game had been to establish solid possession from the set pieces and secure secondary possession behind Charles Kent's crash-ball run and exploit the subsequent openings. The game plan worked extremely well and England secured their biggest ever winning margin against Scotland. All the tries were well executed and well taken, although it must be said that sterner Scottish defence, and, especially, tackling, could have saved them quite a lot of embarrassment. Four tries to one was, nevertheless, a highly satisfactory opening to the new season, especially after the humiliations of recent years. But, there were sterner tests to come, and, after this result, much of the optimism in the press, proved to be somewhat misplaced. This was the seventh time that England had scored four tries or more in a Championship match in the post-war period and each time Scotland have been on the receiving end.

　　　FIVE NATIONS CHAMPIONSHIP, 1976-77

89th match　　　　　　**ENGLAND　4 pts**　　　v　　　**IRELAND　0 pts**

	Caps					Caps		
15	7th	A.J.Hignell	(Bristol)	.		2nd	F.Wilson	(CIYMS)
14	18th	P.J.Squires	(Harrogate)	.		22nd	T.O.Grace (Capt)	(St Mary's College)
13	4th	B.J.Corless	(Moseley)	.		2nd	A.R.McKibbin	(Instonians)
12	2nd	C.P.Kent	(Rosslyn Park)	.		5th & last	J.A.McIlrath	(Ballymena)
11	4th	M.A.C.Slemen	(Liverpool)	.		2nd	D.St J.Bowen	(Cork Constitution)
10	9th	M.J.Cooper	(Moseley)			60th	C.M.H.Gibson	(NIFC)
9	2nd	M.Young	(Gosforth)			2nd	R.J.M.McGrath	(Wanderers)
1	2nd	R.J.Cowling	(Leicester)			7th	P.A.Orr	(Old Wesley)
2	8th	P.J.Wheeler	(Leicester)			5th	P.C.Whelan	(Garryowen)
3	21st	F.E.Cotton	(Sale)	.		2nd & last	T.A.O.Feighery	(St Mary's College)
4	10th	W.B.Beaumont	(Fylde)			18th	M.I.Keane	(Lansdowne)
5	11th	N.E.Horton	(Moseley)			5th	R.F.Hakin	(CIYMS)
6	16th	P.J.Dixon	(Gosforth)	.		20th	S.A.McKinney	(Dungannon)
7	33rd	A.Neary	(Broughton Park)	.		7th	S.M.Deering	(Garryowen)
8	15th	R.M.Uttley (Capt)	(Gosforth)	.		11th	W.P.Duggan	(Blackrock College)

Referee:　　F.Palmade　　　　　(France)

SCORERS:　　　　　　　　　　　　　　0 - 0
　　　　　　　　　　　　　　　　　　　Half-time
　　　　M.J.Cooper　　　Try　　(1st & only)　4 - 0

POINTS:　　　M.J.Cooper　　　4 points　　　(4)

MATCH COMMENTARY:

In damp and drizzling conditions, at Lansdowne Road, this was never going to be a free-running and free-scoring game. The spirited, spoiling terrier-like forward play of the Irish was as much in evidence in this match as at any time in the past, and England, unchanged except for Mike Rafter's late withdrawal, coped with the fire and brimstone very well, and gradually imposed a calming influence on proceedings. Ireland had the better of the scoreless first-half, but in the second, the strength and stamina of the English pack damped down the Irish fire. The decisive, and only, score came midway through the second half after a prolonged period of intense English pressure. Martin Cooper gained possession from a ruck on the far left and started the movement. Mike Slemen looped round to take Cooper's pass, Alistair Hignell joined the line and chipped ahead for Peter Squires. He fed the ball back and Nigel Horton booted on for Cooper, following up very well, to gather the ball and dive over on the far right. Hignell failed with the kick, and with two penalty goal attempts, and there the scoring ended. All in all, an impressive English performance, which gave them their first win against Ireland for six years, and it was the first time for seventeen years that they had won both their first two matches in the Five Nations. Mike Gibson today gained his 60th cap for Ireland, and was playing in his 50th Five Nations Championship match.

52nd match   **ENGLAND 3 pts**   v   **FRANCE 4 pts**

	Caps					Caps		
15	8th	A.J.Hignell	(Bristol)	.	18th	J-M.Aguirre	(Bagneres)
14	19th	P.J.Squires	(Harrogate)	.	7th	D.Harize	(Toulouse)
13	5th	B.J.Corless	Moseley	.	39th	R.Bertranne	(Bagneres)
12	3rd	C.P.Kent	(Rosslyn Park)	.	9th	F.Sangalli	(Narbonne)
11	5th	M.A.C.Slemen	(Liverpool)	.	13th	J-L.Averous	(La Voulte)
10	10th	M.J.Cooper	(Moseley)	.	27th	J-P.Romeu	(Montferrand)
9	3rd	M.Young	(Gosforth)	.	20th	J.Fouroux (Capt)	(Auch)
1	3rd	R.J.Cowling	(Leicester)	.	17th	G.Cholley	(Castres)
2	9th	P.J.Wheeler	(Leicester)	.	20th	A.Paco	(Beziers)
3	22nd	F.E.Cotton	(Sale)	.	15th	R.Paparemborde	(Pau)
4	11th	W.B.Beaumont	(Fylde)	.	7th	J-F.Imbernon	(Perpignan)
5	12th	N.E.Horton	(Moseley)	.	12th	M.Palmie	(Beziers)
6	17th	P.J.Dixon	(Gosforth)	.	16th	J-P.Rives	(Toulouse)
7	2nd	M.Rafter	(Bristol)	.	35th	J-C.Skrela	(Toulouse)
8	16th	R.M.Uttley (Capt)	(Gosforth)	.	26th	J-P.Bastiat	(Dax)

     9th   S.J.Smith (Sale) for Young - 40

Referee: J.C.Kelleher   (Wales)

SCORERS:

			0 - 0	
			Half-time	
			0 - 4	F.Sangalli Try
A.J.Hignell		Penalty Goal	3 - 4	

POINTS: A.J.Hignell   3 points   (33)   F.Sangalli   4 points

MATCH COMMENTARY:

France came to Twickenham, having beaten Wales, as they saw it en route to the Grand Slam. Indeed, they eventually won that honour, but not before a titanic struggle against England, who in all fairness should have won the match. The first half was very tight and scoreless but twice England had an overlap and took the wrong option when a try was almost certain, first, Barry Corless cut inside into a wall of defenders, with Peter Squires unmarked outside him; and later, Mike Slemen decided to go on his own, and failed, with Peter Dixon free on his left. In the second half, France were the first to score with a well-worked try for Sangalli down the blind side. For the last thirty minutes England exerted tremendous pressure on the French line and, in so doing forced the French to concede six penalty kicks all within range for Alastair Hignell. Unfortunately the hapless full-back could convert only one of them, when just one more success would have won the match. Twickenham fell silent with understandable disappointment at the end and the crowd departed dreaming of the might-have-beens. However, it has been said before, and it will surely be said again, that no team can afford to squander chances and expect to win International matches.

82nd match   **ENGLAND   9 pts**   v   **WALES   14 pts**

	Caps					Caps		
15	9th	A.J.Hignell	(Bristol)		40th		J.P.R.Williams	(Bridgend)
14	20th	P.J.Squires	(Harrogate)		40th		T.G.R.Davies	(Cardiff)
13	6th	B.J.Corless	(Moseley)		11th		S.P.Fenwick	(Bridgend)
12	4th	C.P.Kent	(Rosslyn Park)		3rd		D.H.Burcher	(Newport)
11	6th	M.A.C.Slemen	(Liverpool)		18th		J.J.Williams	(Llanelli)
10	11th & last	M.J.Cooper	(Moseley)		24th		P.Bennett (Capt)	(Llanelli)
9	4th	M.Young	(Gosforth)		48th		G.O.Edwards	(Cardiff)
1	4th	R.J.Cowling	(Leicester)		1st		C.Williams	(Aberavon)
2	10th	P.J.Wheeler	(Leicester)		17th		R.W.Windsor	(Pontypool)
3	23rd	F.E.Cotton	(Sale)		12th		G.Price	(Pontypool)
4	12th	W.B.Beaumont	(Fylde)		15th		A.J.Martin	(Aberavon)
5	13th	N.E.Horton	(Moseley)		12th		G.A.D.Wheel	(Swansea)
6	18th	P.J.Dixon	(Gosforth)		13th		T.J.Cobner	(Pontypool)
7	3rd	M.Rafter	(Bristol)		3rd		R.C.Burgess	(Ebbw Vale)
8	17th	R.M.Uttley (Capt)	(Gosforth)		11th		D.L.Quinnell	(Llanelli)

Referee: D.I.H.Burnett   (Ireland)

SCORERS:

A.J.Hignell	Penalty Goal	3 - 0		
A.J.Hignell	Penalty Goal	6 - 0		
		6 - 4	G.O.Edwards	Try
		6 - 7	S.P.Fenwick	Penalty Goal
		Half-time		
A.J.Hignell	Penalty Goal	9 - 7		
		9 - 10	S.P.Fenwick	Penalty Goal
		9 - 14	J.P.R.Williams	Try

POINTS:

A.J.Hignell	9 points	(42)	S.P.Fenwick	6 points
			J.P.R.Williams	4 points
			G.O.Edwards	4 points

MATCH COMMENTARY:

England had not won in Cardiff since 1963, but came with confidence on this occasion to take the Triple Crown as the prize for victory. England acquitted themselves well - but not well enough - and conceded two tries without crossing the Welsh line. Alastair Hignell had found his kicking touch again, and put England into an early lead with two fine penalty goals. Gareth Edwards amply demonstrated his power from the base of the scrum when he scored a try down the blind side from a set piece, taking England defender, Mike Slemen, with him, body and soul. Wales slipped into a half-time lead with Steve Fenwick's first penalty goal and the lead changed hands twice in the second half before J.P.R.Williams scored the decisive try, the sixth in his career and his fifth against England.

The English backs, with plenty of possession, wasted what scoring opportunities may have arisen by kicking far too much - the result, one suspects, of lack of imagination and perception to spot the potential opening. With one exception, England had played an unchanged team throughout the season and the benefit of this was evident in stronger team work as the season progressed, and particularly in this match, at Cardiff, where England could find little confidence based on recent experience. The Triple Crown bid had failed, but the season , as a whole, was very much more encouraging than the previous five had been.

SUMMARY OF THE SEASON 1976 - 77:

After the depressing results and performances of recent seasons, this was a very much more encouraging season for England, even though as England's abysmal performance last year contrasted sharply with Wales' Grand Slam, so, this season, England's improved fortunes paled into insignificance against the tremendous achievement of France in winning the Grand Slam with the same fifteen players and without conceding a try.   Bearing in mind that England held France to a single point at Twickenham, and that England could have won the match had Alastair Hignell been successful with but one more of his six penalty goal attempts, England had certainly competed with the best on equal terms.   More than could be said for their efforts in recent years.

The opening Five Nations match at Twickenham against Scotland provided a wonderful pick-me-up for the jaded England supporters who had begun to wonder exactly when England's fortunes would begin to change.   They did not expect what they got as soon as this, and it was very welcome.   Of the side who had experienced the crushing defeat at Parc des Princes at the end of last season, only four, Mike Slemen, Fran Cotton, Bill Beaumont, and Peter Dixon retained their places, and the captaincy was given to Roger Uttley.   He provided some inspired, and inspiring, leadership, and the introduction of Charles Kent and the "crash-ball" tactic was very successful. So much so that England scored four tries, twice as many as they had scored in the previous Five Nations season.   The same side was chosen for the match against Ireland in Dublin, three weeks later but Mike Rafter had to withdraw at the eleventh hour and was replaced by Tony Neary.   The match was close fought in depressing conditions and England managed to contain both the foraging, bustling and aggressive Irish forwards and the potential creative genius of Mike Gibson, playing at fly-half.   In the end, Martin Cooper's try was the only score in the match.   This result gave England their first away win in the Championship for six years, their first win over Ireland for six years and it was the first time for seventeen years that England had won both of their first two matches in the Five Nations Championship.

Mike Rafter came back for the match against France, and England really made more of a meal of the match than was necessary as they could so easily have won it.   The forwards to a man, played an excellent game, with Nigel Horton a tower of strength and influence in the lines-out.   There was no score in the first-half, but England squandered two almost certain tries by taking the wrong option at the critical time, and the one try which the French scored in the second half was enough to win the match for them against Alastair Hignell's solitary penalty goal.   The unfortunate Hignell missed five penalty goal attempts, whereas Romeu, the French kicker, missed only three and a conversion.   England played well enough to win, but Internationals are not won by losing opportunities.   The side remained unchanged for the final match in Cardiff and acquitted themselves very much better than their predecessors had done for the past thirteen years, but still they did not win.   Wales were just too good, and picked up their second successive Triple Crown.   Nevertheless, Wales had to work extremely hard for their victory, for with only twenty minutes to go in the match, England led by 9 points to 7, but then Steve Fenwick landed a penalty goal and J.P.R.Williams scored yet another try against England (his fifth).

Roger Uttley had been an excellent choice as captain, always leading from the front and by example, and he inspired his team to play to the very best of their individual, if not always their collective, capabilities.   It was unfortunate that a back injury sustained during the first half at Cardiff severely inhibited his personal performance for the remainder of that match.

England finished the season in the middle of the Table, and regained the Calcutta Cup.   The try count of five against three, and the points difference of 42 points for to a mere 24 against, certainly reflects a much improved performance over recent seasons.

Only sixteen players were used for the four matches of the Championship plus one replacement, Steve Smith, who replaced Malcolm Young who broke his nose during the match against France.   A remarkable tribute to selectorial consistency - and picking the right team in the first place !!   Four new caps were awarded for the first match of the season and three, Malcolm Young, Charles Kent and Robin Cowling played throughout the season.   Mike Rafter missed one match, Ireland, because of sickness.   Only Martin Cooper quit the International arena at the end of the season.   He had eleven caps .

Five players were invited to tour with the 1977 Lions to New Zealand; Peter Squires, Fran Cotton, Nigel Horton, Tony Neary and Peter Wheeler; Bill Beaumont joined as a replacement.   Cotton, Wheeler and Beaumont, 3 each, and Neary and Squires, one, played in the Tests.

FIVE NATIONS CHAMPIONSHIP TABLE:

Won: **Calcutta Cup**

		Played	Won	Lost	Drawn	Points: For	Against	Tries: For	Against	Title Points
1	France	4	4	0	0	58	21	8	0	8
2	Wales	4	3	1	0	66	43	7	3	6
3	ENGLAND	4	2	2	0	42	24	5	3	4
4	scotland	4	1	3	0	39	85	4	11	2
5	Ireland	4	0	4	0	33	65	1	8	0

Home Games: beat Scotland 26 - 6, (four tries to nil); lost to France 3 - 4, (no tries to one)

Away Games: beat Ireland 4 - 0, (one try to nil); lost to Wales 9 - 14, (no tries to two)

53rd match   **ENGLAND   6 pts**   v   **FRANCE   15 pts**

	Caps					Caps		
15	2nd	W.H.Hare	(Leicester)			26th	J-M.Aguirre	(Bagneres)
14	21st	P.J.Squires	(Harrogate)			16th	J-F.Gourdon	(Bagneres)
13	7th	B.J.Corless	(Moseley)			47th	R.Bertranne	(Bagneres)
12	7th & last	A.W.Maxwell	(Headingley)			2nd	C.Belascain	(Bayonne)
11	7th	M.A.C.Slemen	(Liverpool)			18th	J-L.Averous	(La Voulte)
10	16th & last	A.G.B.Old	(Sheffield)			1st	B.Vivies	(Agen)
9	5th	M.Young	(Gosforth)			1st	J.Gallion	(Toulon)
1	5th	R.J.Cowling	(Leicester)			25th	G.Cholley	(Castres)
2	11th	P.J.Wheeler	(Leicester)			26th	A.Paco	(Beziers)
3	16th	M.A.Burton	(Gloucester)			21st	R.Paperamborde	(Pau)
4	13th	W.B.Beaumont (Capt)	(Fylde)			14th	J-F.Imbernon	(Perpignan)
5	14th	N.E.Horton	(Toulouse)			20th	M.Palmie	(Beziers)
6	19th	P.J.Dixon	(Gosforth)			22nd	J-P.Rives	(Toulouse)
7	4th	M.Rafter	(Bristol)			43rd	J-C.Skrela	(Toulouse)
8	1st	J.P.Scott	(Rosslyn Park)			29th	J-P.Bastiat (Capt)	(Dax)

5th & last	C.P.Kent (Rosslyn Park) for Maxwell - 34	
34th	A.Neary (Broughton Park) for Dixon - 34	

Referee: N.R.Sanson   (Scotland)

SCORERS:

A.G.B.Old	D'p Goal	(2nd)	3 - 0			
			3 - 3	J-M.Aguirre	Penalty Goal	
A.G.B.Old	D'p Goal	(3rd & last)	6 - 3			
			Half-time			
			6 - 7	J-L.Averous	Try	
			6 - 9	J-M.Aguirre	Conversion	
			6 - 13	J.Gallion	Try	
			6 - 15	J-M.Aguirre	Conversion	

POINTS:

A.G.B.Old	6 points	(98)	J-M.Aguirre	7 points	
			J-L.Averous	4 points	
			J.Gallion	4 points	

MATCH COMMENTARY:

A trip to Paris for the first match of the season, where they had not won since 1964, was not an ideal start to the Five Nations Championship. The nucleus of the pack was the same as last season, with Mike Burton replacing Cotton, and Scott coming in for Roger Uttley and powerful as they were, with a good mutual understanding which had developed significantly during the previous season, they found themselves facing eight forwards who were playing together for the eighth time - and showed the expected cohesion. England, though, did not let France have it all their own way and were deservedly leading at half-time through Alan Old's two drop goals and in spite of having lost Andy Maxwell with a knee injury which was to end his career and Peter Dixon with a sprung collar bone, both after just half an hour's play. It would have been a very tight and interesting game had Robin Cowling not suffered a dislocated shoulder early in the second half. He refused to leave the field because England had already used their two replacements and he continued to prop against the French pack with a dislocated shoulder. France grabbed this advantage and scored two tries to win the match without much difficulty. For new captain Bill Beaumont, England put up a creditable performance, even so, this was their fourth successive defeat by France.

When Tony Neary replaced Peter Dixon, he equalled Budge Rogers' record of 34 caps as a flank forward.

83rd match   **ENGLAND   6 pts**   v   **WALES   9 pts**

	Caps					Caps		
15	10th	**A.J.Hignell**	(Bristol)	.	42nd	**J.P.R.Williams**	(Bridgend)
14	22nd	**P.J.Squires**	(Harrogate)	.	42nd	**T.G.R.Davies**	(Cardiff)
13	8th	**B.J.Corless**	(Moseley)	.	10th	**R.W.R.Gravell**	(Llanelli)
12	1st	**P.W.Dodge**	(Leicester)	.	13th	**S.P.Fenwick**	(Bridgend)
11	8th	**M.A.C.Slemen**	(Liverpool)	.	20th	**J.J.Williams**	(Llanelli)
10	1st	**J.P.Horton**	(Bath)	.	26th	**P.Bennett (Capt)**	(Llanelli)
9	6th	**M.Young**	(Gosforth)	.	50th	**G.O.Edwards**	(Cardiff)
1	3rd	**B.G.Nelmes**	(Cardiff)	.	14th	**G.Price**	(Pontypool)
2	12th	**P.J.Wheeler**	(Leicester)	.	19th	**R.W.Windsor**	(Pontypool)
3	17th & last	**M.A.Burton**	(Gloucester)	.	10th	**A.G.Faulkner**	(Pontypool)
4	14th	**W.B.Beaumont (Capt)**	(Fylde)	.	17th	**A.J.Martin**	(Aberavon)
5	15th	**N.E.Horton**	(Toulouse)	.	14th	**G.A.D.Wheel**	(Swansea)
6	1st & only	**R.J.Mordell**	(Rosslyn Park)	.	15th	**T.J.Cobner**	(Pontypool)
7	5th	**M.Rafter**	(Bristol)	.	3rd	**J.Squire**	(Newport)
8	2nd	**J.P.Scott**	(Rosslyn Park)	.	13th	**D.L.Quinnell**	(Llanelli)

Referee: N.R.Sanson   (Scotland)

SCORERS:

A.J.Hignell	Penalty Goal	3 - 0			
		3 - 3	**P.Bennett**	Penalty Goal
A.J.Hignell	Penalty Goal	6 - 3			
		Half-time			
		6 - 6	**P.Bennett**	Penalty Goal
		6 - 9	**P.Bennett**	Penalty Goal

POINTS: **A.J.Hignell**   6 points   (48)   **P.Bennett**   9 points

MATCH COMMENTARY:

This could hardly be an inspiring match played as it was in appalling conditions with the pitch almost under water.   A handling game was totally out of the question and the match was decided on penalty goals and on the strike rate of the respective kickers.

Phil Bennett kicked three out of four attempts and Alastair Hignell was successful with only two out of six.   Gareth Edwards, in his fiftieth successive International, was the most influential man on the field, for, particularly in the second half, his positional kicking from the base of the scrum drove England back into their 22 on countless occasions, and though Bill Beaumont led a spirited rearguard action, England could not escape from the territorial advantage which Gareth Edwards gave the Welsh side. In spite of this, Wales were on their way to their second Grand Slam and their third Triple Crown in only three years - a remarkable achievement by some remarkable players. Bob Mordell gained his first and only cap in this match. Apparently he had disputed the referee's decision when a penalty was awarded against him for handling in a ruck. From there, Phil Bennet kicked the winning penalty goal. Whether his departure from the International scene and this incident were connected, can only be a subject of speculation.

94th match   **ENGLAND   15 pts**   v   **SCOTLAND   0 pts**

85th Calcutta Cup

	Caps					Caps		
15	1st	D.W.N.Caplan	(Headingley)	.		25th	A.R.Irvine	(Heriot's FP)
14	23rd	P.J.Squires	(Harrogate)	.	5th & last	W.B.B.Gammell	(Edinburgh Wand'rs)
13	9th	B.J.Corless	(Moseley)	.	25th	J.M.Renwick	(Hawick)
12	2nd	P.W.Dodge	(Leicester)	.	8th	A.G.Cranston	(Hawick)
11	9th	M.A.C.Slemen	(Liverpool)	.	7th	B.H.Hay	(Boroughmuir)
10	2nd	J.P.Horton	(Bath)	.	1st & only	R.W.Breakey	(Gosforth)
9	7th	M.Young	(Gosforth)	.	21st & last	D.W.Morgan (Capt)	(Stewart's-Melville)
1	4th	B.G.Nelmes	(Cardiff)	.	37th	J.McLauchlan	(Jordanhill)
2	13th	P.J.Wheeler	(Leicester)	.	3rd	C.T.Deans	(Hawick)
3	24th	F.E.Cotton	(Sale)	.	4th & last	N.E.K.Pender	(Hawick)
4	15th	W.B.Beaumont (Capt)	(Fylde)	.	7th	A.J.Tomes	(Hawick)
5	1st	M.J.Colclough	(Angouleme)	.	1st	D.Gray	(West of Scotland)
6	20th	P.J.Dixon	(Gosforth)	.	14th	M.A.Biggar	(London Scottish)
7	6th	M.Rafter	(Bristol)	.	4th & last	C.B.Hegarty	(Hawick)
8	3rd	J.P.Scott	(Rosslyn Park)	.	7th & last	D.S.M.MacDonald	(West of Scotland)

Referee: J.R.West   (Ireland)

SCORERS: P.J.Squires   Try   (6th & last)   4 - 0

M.Young   Conversion   6 - 0

P.W.Dodge   Penalty Goal   9 - 0

Half-time

B.G.Nelmes   Try   (1st & only)   13 - 0

M.Young   Conversion   15 - 0

POINTS: P.J.Squires   4 points   (24)

B.G.Nelmes   4 points   (4)

M.Young   4 points   (8)

P.W.Dodge   3 points   (3)

MATCH COMMENTARY:

Four changes and two more new caps were contained in the side which went to Murrayfield in search of its first win on that ground for ten years - and they were successful. The return of Fran Cotton and Peter Dixon and the introduction of Maurice Colclough steadied the pack and gave it more weight. David Caplan at full-back had an impressive debut following Alastair Hignell's late withdrawal, and altogether the team combined well to deny the Scots too many opportunities, although those they had, particularly with the wind in the second half, Richard Breakey was inclined to waste by continually kicking and ignoring the attacking potential of Andy Irvine.

In the first half David Caplan came very close to scoring in the first two minutes, but it was thirty minutes before the first England try for five matches came when Peter Squires cut inside to score near the posts after some fine handling from the forwards and the scoring pass from the captain.   Malcolm Young converted and a little later, Paul Dodge landed a huge penalty goal from well over fifty metres to give England a half-time lead of nine points. This time it was not surrendered, as in previous seasons, for Scotland failed to take advantage of the wind in the second half and Barry Nelmes' converted try was the extent of further scoring.

England broke their self-imposed try famine, and fully deserved their achievement in retaining the Calcutta Cup.

90th match   **ENGLAND   15 pts**   v   **IRELAND   9 pts**

	Caps					Caps		
15	2nd & last	D.W.N.Caplan	(Headingley)	.		22nd & last	A.H.Ensor	(Wanderers)
14	24th	P.J.Squires	(Harrogate)	.		65th	C.M.H.Gibson	(NIFC)
13	3rd	P.W.Dodge	(Leicester)	.		7th	A.R.McKibbin	(London Irish)
12	10th & last	B.J.Corless	(Moseley)	.		4th	P.P.McNaughton	(Greystones)
11	10th	M.A.C.Slemen	(Liverpool)	.		5th	A.C.McLennan	(Wanderers)
10	3rd	J.P.Horton	(Bath)	.		4th	A.J.P.Ward	(Garryowen)
9	8th	M.Young	(Gosforth)	.		23rd	J.J.Moloney (Capt)	(St Mary's College)
1	5th	B.G.Nelmes	(Cardiff)	.		13th	P.A.Orr	(Old Wesley)
2	14th	P.J.Wheeler	(Leicester)	.		11th	P.C.Whelan	(Garryowen)
3	25th	F.E.Cotton	(Sale)	.		5th	E.M.J.Byrne	(Blackrock College)
4	16th	W.B.Beaumont (Capt)	(Fylde)	.		24th	M.I.Keane	(Lansdowne)
5	2nd	M.J.Colclough	(Angouleme)	.		5th	H.W.Steele	(Ballymena)
6	21st	P.J.Dixon	(Gosforth)	.		25th & last	S.A.McKinney	(Dungannon)
7	7th	M.Rafter	(Bristol)	.		34th	J.F.Slattery	(Blackrock College)
8	4th	J.P.Scott	(Rosslyn Park)	.		17th	W.P.Duggan	(Blackrock College)

Referee: F.Palmade   (France)

SCORERS:	P.J.Dixon	Try	(4th & last)	4 - 0		
	M.Young	Conversion		6 - 0		
				Half-time		
				6 - 3	A.J.P.Ward	Penalty Goal
				6 - 6	A.J.P.Ward	Drop Goal
	M.Young	Penalty Goal		9 - 6		
				9 - 9	A.J.P.Ward	Penalty Goal
	M.A.C.Slemen	Try	(2nd)	13 - 9		
	M.Young	Conversion		15 - 9		

POINTS:	M.Young	7 points	(15)		A.J.P.Ward	9 points
	M.A.C.Slemen	4 points	(8)			
	P.J.Dixon	4 points	(16)			

MATCH COMMENTARY:

An unchanged side proved to be too strong for Ireland, and England's second win of the season was based entirely on their forward supremacy in both the tight and the loose. Only Wales had a better pack this season, and they won the Grand Slam.

This was a bright and entertaining game, played in the best of spirits, and, although Ireland failed to score a try, the quality and potential of their new fly-half, Tony Ward, was very apparent. England had not beaten Ireland at Twickenham since 1970, and there was a purpose and urgency about England's play. Ireland played with the wind in the first half, but failed to score a point. England went ahead through Peter Dixon's converted try after he and Maurice Colclough had ably supported John Horton's blind side break.. Tony Ward brought Ireland level with a penalty goal and a drop goal, and then he and Malcolm Young exchanged penalties again. The scores were thus level when Mike Slemen supported a three-quarter move by coming right round from the left wing to the right, took the final pass outside Peter Squires and crossed the line in the corner. Malcolm Young converted to complete a competent win for England who again finished the season third in the Five Nations Championship table.

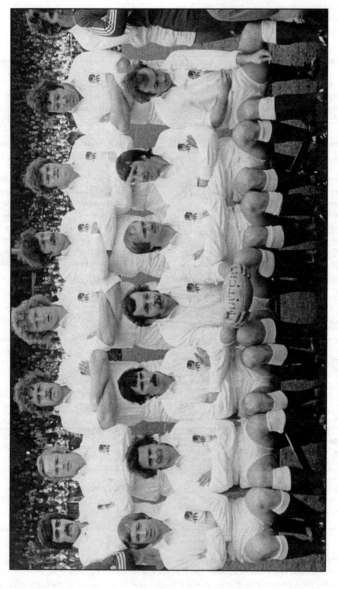

THE ENGLAND TEAM WHO BEAT IRELAND AT TWICKENHAM ON MARCH 18th 1978
Standing: D.W.N.Caplan, P.J.Wheeler, J.P.Scott, M.J.Colclough, P.J.Dixon, F.E.Cotton, B.G.Nelmes, P.W.Dodge,
Seated: M.Young, J.P.Horton, M.A.C.Slemen, W.B.Beaumont (Capt), P.J.Squires, B.J.Corless, M.Rafter.

SUMMARY OF THE SEASON 1977 - 78:

England's results this season were not far from identical to those of last season in that they won two of the four Five Nations Championship matches; the two matches won were those against Scotland and Ireland, and the two lost those against Wales and France; they scored 42 points against 24 last season, and 42 points against 33 this season; and they scored two more tries than they conceded, 5 to 3 last season, and 4 to 2 this. The notable difference between the two seasons was that whereas in 1977, England won their first two matches and lost the last two, the reverse applied in 1978 when they lost the first two and won the third and fourth. Nevertheless, it was still a "middle-of-road" season, finishing in third place in the Table with four points, but still a welcome change from previous achievements.

The first match in Paris was a formidable prospect and any hopes of a first win in Paris for fourteen years were dashed with the series of injuries to Peter Dixon, Andy Maxwell and Robin Cowling who stayed on the field with a dislocated shoulder and continued to scrummage !! With that latter misfortune went any chance of winning the match and to concede only 12 points in the second half was an achievement in itself. For the visit of Wales to Twickenham, three changes were necessary due to the injuries suffered in Paris and, in addition, John Horton replaced Alan Old at fly-half, and Alastair Hignell returned in place of "Dusty" Hare. The condi+A42tions for the match were truly appalling, possibly the worst ever experienced at Twickenham, and there was no possibility of a handling spectacle for the entertainment of the brave souls who turned out in torrential rain. In the event, no tries were scored and the match was decided by a goal kicking contest between Phil Bennett and Alastair Hignell which Phil Bennett won 3 - 2, and Gareth Edwards' immaculate line kicking. But it cannot be without significance that England denied the Grand Slam champions a try. So the first two matches had been lost, in direct contrast to last season, but this did not give rise to gloom and despondency for the performances had been creditable although, especially in the first match, tinged with misfortune. The approach to the Scotland match at Murrayfield was buoyant and optimistic, and rightly so. Four further changes were made; David Caplan, the Headingley full-back, replaced Alastair Hignell who had to withdraw at the last minute. Fran Cotton returned to the front row, Maurice Colclough gained his first cap alongside Bill Beaumont at lock, and Peter Dixon had recovered from his shoulder injury. England played well and confidently and took their opportunities, whereas Scotland did not; it was as simple as that. England had not won at Murrayfield for ten years. Finally, for Ireland, the selectors kept faith and named an unchanged team, and in conditions totally different from those which had prevailed for the Wales match, England won a bright and entertaining game by two tries to nil to record, surprisingly enough, their first win over Ireland at home since 1970. The four newcomers to the side, Paul Dodge, John Horton, Maurice Colclough and John Scott had all not only earned their places in the side but each, in his own way, had contributed to a better team performance, and in the future were to continue that contribution significantly in the next couple of years. In Bill Beaumont, England had found a leader of considerable potential who led by example and shirked no task at all.

Twenty four players had represented England during the course of the season, five new caps had been awarded, and eight players had kept their places for all four matches - had it not been for the injuries sustained in the first match in Paris, the ever-presents may well have had Peter Dixon, Robin Cowling and Andy Maxwell added to their number. Seven players came to the end of their International careers during or at the end of the season. The most unfortunate was certainly Andy Maxwell who had won seven caps when he sustained a serious knee injury in Paris which ended his playing career altogether. Mike Burton, who came to the end of his striking International career with seventeen caps , has the unfortunate distinction of being the only England player to have been sent off in an International match, (Australia, 1975, in Brisbane), and now runs a Corporate Hospitality Agency for, amongst other things, International Rugby matches. Alan Old earned sixteen caps and later became coach and Technical Administrator for the North of England and the RFU. He was, along with his brother, Chris, a fine cricketer. Barry Corless, a Coventry schoolmaster, scored a try on his debut against Australia and earned ten caps. Charles Kent, five caps, had a short but spectacular career when his crash-ball tactics became England's main strike weapon during the 1977 season. His final cap this season was as a replacement for Andy Maxwell. David Caplan, a Yorkshire dentist, earned only two caps, but, had he had a mind to do so, could possibly have won many more, and Bob Mordell, one cap, went to Oldham and later Kent Invicta Rugby League Clubs, and later, having defected, was one of the few players to be re-instated by the IB, and played for Rosslyn Park.

FIVE NATIONS CHAMPIONSHIP TABLE:

Won: **Calcutta Cup**

		Played	Won	Lost	Drawn	Points: For	Against	Tries: For	Against	Title Points
1	Wales	4	4	0	0	67	43	8	4	8
2	France	4	3	1	0	51	47	6	4	6
3	**ENGLAND**	4	2	2	0	42	33	4	2	4
4	Ireland	4	1	3	0	46	54	2	5	2
5	Scotland	4	0	4	0	39	68	4	9	0

Home Games: lost to Wales 6 - 9, (no tries); beat Ireland 15 - 9, (two tries to nil)

Away Games: lost to France 6 - 15. (no tries to two); beat Scotland 15 - 0, (two tries to nil)

11th match   **ENGLAND   6 pts**   v   **NEW ZEALAND   16 pts**

	Caps				Caps		
15	3rd	W.H.Hare	(Leicester)		6th	B.J.McKechnie	(Southland)
14	25th	P.J.Squires	(Harrogate)		8th	S.S.Wilson	(Wellington)
13	1st	A.M.Bond	(Sale)		25th	B.J.Robertson	(Counties)
12	4th	P.W.Dodge	(Leicester)		12th	W.M.Osborne	(Wanganui)
11	11th	M.A.C.Slemen	(Liverpool)		37th	B.G.Williams	(Auckland)
10	4th	J.P.Horton	(Bath)		13th	O.D.Bruce	(Canterbury)
9	9th	M.Young	(Gosforth)		7th	M.W.Donaldson	(Manawatu)
1	6th	R.J.Cowling	(Leicester)		9th	B.R.Johnstone	(Auckland)
2	15th	P.J.Wheeler	(Leicester)		7th	A.G.Dalton	(Counties)
3	6th & last	B.G.Nelmes	(Cardiff)		6th	G.A.Knight	(Manawatu)
4	17th	W.B.Beaumont (Capt)	(Fylde)		12th	A.M.Haden	(Auckland)
5	5th	J.P.Scott	(Cardiff)		13th	F.J.Oliver	(Otago)
6	22nd & last	P.J.Dixon	(Gosforth)		7th	G.N.K.Mourie (Capt)	(Taranaki)
7	8th	M.Rafter	(Bristol)		6th	L.M.Rutledge	(Southland)
8	18th	R.M.Uttley	(Gosforth)		8th	G.A.Seear	(Otago)

Referee: N.R.Sanson   (Scotland)

SCORERS:	W.H.Hare	D'p Goal (1st & only)	3 - 0			
			3 - 4	F.J.Oliver	Try	
	W.H.Hare	Penalty Goal	6 - 4			
			6 - 8	B.R.Johnstone	Try	
			6 - 10	B.J.McKechnie	Conversion	
			Half-time			
			6 - 13	B.J.McKechnie	Penalty Goal	
			6 - 16	B.J.McKechnie	Penalty Goal	

POINTS:	W.H.Hare	6 points	(6)	B.J.McKechnie	8 points
				B.R.Johnstone	4 points
				F.J.Oliver	4 points

MATCH COMMENTARY:

This game, and indeed Graeme Mourie's All blacks Tour, demonstrated quite clearly the significant difference in the quality and power of forward play between the Northern and Southern hemispheres. The All Blacks won all four "Tests" on the back of complete control up front. But, it must be said, in this match New Zealand had some considerable assistance from the England selectors who decided to play Barry Nelmes, a loose-head prop, at tight-head, and John Scott, a No 8, at lock, and furthermore, went into the game with no true line-out specialist. It came as no surprise that the England pack were well and truly beaten, and gave away two tries from lines-out near their own line, the second on the England throw.   The little possession that England did obtain was largely wasted by John Horton's inaccurate kicking and when the ball did reach the three-quarters it had taken so long to get there that All Black defenders were just waiting to pounce. Mike Slemen and Peter Squires, on the wings, did not receive a decent pass for the whole of the match - not a new experience for England wing three-quarters. Second half scoring was limited to two New Zealand penalty goals, and England could have had one too had "Dusty" Hare's long range effort not hit the cross-bar and rebounded out.

The All Blacks wasted some of their chances too, and had they been taken, the winning margin could have doubled - or trebled.

95th match   **ENGLAND   7 pts**   v   **SCOTLAND   7 pts**

86th Calcutta Cup

	Caps					Caps		
15	11th	**A.J.Hignell**	(Bristol)	.		30th	**A.R.Irvine**	(Heriot's FP)
14	26th	**P.J.Squires**	(Harrogate)	.		3rd	**K.W.Robertson**	(Melrose)
13	2nd	**A.M.Bond**	(Sale)	.		28th	**J.M.Renwick**	(Hawick)
12	5th	**P.W.Dodge**	(Leicester)	.		30th	**I.R.McGeechan (Capt)**	(Headingley)
11	12th	**M.A.C.Slemen**	(Liverpool)	.		10th	**B.H.Hay**	(Boroughmuir)
10	4th	**W.N.Bennett**	(London Welsh)	.		2nd	**J.Y.Rutherford**	(Selkirk)
9	10th & last	**M.Young**	(Gosforth)	.		11th	**A.J.M.Lawson**	(London Scottish)
1	7th	**R.J.Cowling**	(Leicester)	.		40th	**J.McLauchlan**	(Jordanhill)
2	16th	**P.J.Wheeler**	(Leicester)	.		6th	**C.T.Deans**	(Hawick)
3	1st	**G.S.Pearce**	(Northampton)	.		3rd & last	**R.F.Cunningham**	(Gala)
4	18th	**W.B.Beaumont**	(Fylde)	.		10th	**A.J.Tomes**	(Hawick)
5	16th	**N.E.Horton**	(Toulouse)	.		44th & last	**A.F.McHarg**	(London Scottish)
6	35th	**A.Neary**	(Broughton Park)	.		17th	**M.A.Biggar**	(London Scottish)
7	9th	**M.Rafter**	(Bristol)	.		3rd	**G.Dickson**	(Gala)
8	19th	**R.M.Uttley (Capt)**	(Gosforth)	.		3rd	**I.K.Lambie**	(Watsonians)

	6th	J.P.Scott (Cardiff) for Uttley - 70	.

Referee: C.Norling   (Wales)

SCORERS:

M.A.C.Slemen	Try	(3rd)	4 - 0			
W.N.Bennett	Penalty Goal		7 - 0			
			7 - 4	**J.Y.Rutherford**	Try
		Half-time			
			7 - 7	**A.R.Irvine**	Penalty Goal

POINTS:

M.A.C.Slemen	4 points	(12)	**J.Y.Rutherford**	4 points
W.N.Bennett	3 points	(6)	**A.R.Irvine**	3 points

MATCH COMMENTARY:

This was a very undistinguished performance, although the England pack dominated the rucks and the lines-out, the backs could not turn this possession to advantage. Both tries in the match, one for each side, were spectacular, but they were both flashes of inspiration rather than the result of worthy endeavour. England's, in the third minute, was a classic with the ball moving quickly along the line after a finger-tip deflection at the line-out by Nigel Horton. Hignell came into the line at pace, created the overlap, and passed to Slemen who went in at the corner flag. But there was little else to cheer in the England backs' performance even though they had more possession than they could have dreamed of. Bennett was inclined to kick far too much and when he did move the ball, Tony Bond and Paul Dodge, in the centre, tried to cut inside too much, thus failing to exploit the two powerful wings. Roger Uttley, who had been given the captaincy in preference to Bill Beaumont, was far below his best at No 8 where he often confused his scrum-half with his pick-up attempts at the base of the scrum - and they both played for the same club, Gosforth !!

Neither side deserved to win this match; not England because they wasted their opportunities and their possession, and not Scotland because they could not get any !

There had not been a draw in a Calcutta Cup match since 1965, but England, having won last year, retained the Cup.

ENGLAND 7 pts   v   IRELAND 12 pts

91st match

	Caps					Caps		
15	12th	A.J.Hignell	(Bristol)		3rd & last	R.M.Spring	(Lansdowne)
14	27th	P.J.Squires	(Harrogate)		1st	M.C.Finn	(UC Cork)
13	3rd	A.M.Bond	(Sale)		11th	A.R.McKibbin	(London Irish)
12	6th	P.W.Dodge	(Leicester)		7th	P.P.McNaughton	(Greystones)
11	13th	M.A.C.Slemen	(Liverpool)		9th	A.C.McLennan	(Wanderers)
10	5th	W.N.Bennett	(London Welsh)		8th	A.J.P.Ward	(Garryowen)
9	3rd	P.J.Kingston	(Gloucester)		4th	C.S.Patterson	(Instonians)
1	8th & last	R.J.Cowling	(Leicester)		17th	P.A.Orr	(Old Wesley)
2	17th	P.J.Wheeler	(Leicester)		15th	P.C.Whelan	(Garryowen)
3	2nd	G.S.Pearce	(Northampton)		3rd	G.A.J.McLoughlin	(Shannon)
4	19th	W.B.Beaumont (Capt)	(Fylde)		28th	M.I.Keane	(Lansdowne)
5	17th	N.E.Horton	(Toulouse)		8th	H.W.Steele	(Ballymena)
6	36th	A.Neary	(Broughton Park)		19th	W.P.Duggan	(Blackrock College)
7	10th	M.Rafter	(Bristol)		38th	J.F.Slattery (Capt)	(Blackrock College)
8	7th	J.P.Scott	(Cardiff)		3rd	M.E.Gibson	(Lansdowne)

Referee: A.M.Hosie   (Scotland)

SCORERS:

			0 - 4	A.C.McLennan	Try
			0 - 6	A.J.P.Ward	Conversion
W.N.Bennett	Penalty Goal		3 - 6		
			Half-time		
			3 - 9	A.J.P.Ward	Drop Goal
			3 - 12	A.J.P.Ward	Penalty Goal
W.N.Bennett	Try	(1st)	7 - 12		

POINTS:

W.N.Bennett	7 points	(13)		A.J.P.Ward	8 points
				A.C.McLennan	4 points

MATCH COMMENTARY:

In spite of another change at half-back and the replacement of the virus stricken Uttley by John Scott, England's performance was even less impressive than against Scotland. The forwards, led once more by Bill Beaumont, played better, and against sterner opposition than Scotland had provided, but the back play and goal-kicking were well below International standard. The day began in the worst possible manner for England when Tony Ward kicked ahead, Alistair Hignell gathered and tried to find Peter Squires with a long floated pass. The intentions were spotted well in advance by the Irish left wing, McLennan, who simply intercepted the pass and ran 35 metres to score unopposed and under the posts to make Tony Ward's conversion a formality. Neil Bennett pulled back three points before half-time with a penalty goal, but in the second half a drop goal and another penalty goal from the immaculate Tony Ward took the game well out of England's reach. Neil Bennett's consolation try towards the end was just that, and even though the score looks close, England never seriously threatened. Neil Bennett missed five of his six attempted goals, and although it is true that a 50% success rate would have won the match for England, the confidence necessary to do so was never in evidence. Compare that with Tony Ward's success in scoring with every attempted kick - except one, a drop goal attempt from 45 metres which struck the post !

54th match   **ENGLAND   7 pts**   v   **FRANCE   6 pts**

	Caps					Caps		
15	13th	A.J.Hignell	(Bristol)	.		33rd	J-M.Aguirre	(Bagneres)
14	28th	P.J.Squires	(Harrogate)	.		19th	J-F.Gourdon	(Bagneres)
13	1st	R.M.Cardus	(Roundhay)	.		54th	R.Bertranne	(Bagneres)
12	7th	P.W.Dodge	(Leicester)	.		9th	C.Belascain	(Bayonne)
11	14th	M.A.C.Slemen	(Liverpool)	.		1st	F.Costes	(Montferrand)
10	6th	W.N.Bennett	(London Welsh)	.		4th	A.Caussade	(Lourdes)
9	4th	P.J.Kingston	(Gloucester)	.		7th	J.Gallion	(Toulon)
1	1st	C.E.Smart	(Newport)	.		24th	A.Vaquerin	(Beziers)
2	18th	P.J.Wheeler	(Leicester)	.		33rd	A.Paco	(Beziers)
3	3rd	G.S.Pearce	(Northampton)	.		28th	R.Paparemborde	(Pau)
4	20th	W.B.Beaumont (Capt)	(Fylde)	.		14th	F.Haget	(Biarritz)
5	18th	N.E.Horton	(Toulouse)	.		2nd	A.Maleig	(Oloron)
6	37th	A.Neary	(Broughton Park)	.		29th	J-P.Rives (Capt)	(Toulouse)
7	11th	M.Rafter	(Bristol)	.		5th	J-L.Joinel	(Brive)
8	8th	J.P.Scott	(Cardiff)	.		14th	A.Guilbert	(Toulon)

Referee: J.R.West   (Ireland)

SCORERS:

W.N.Bennett	Penalty Goal		3 - 0				
			Half-time				
W.N.Bennett	Try	(2nd & last)	7 - 0				
			7 - 4	F.Costes	Try		
			7 - 6	J-M.Aguirre	Conversion		

POINTS:

W.N.Bennett	7 points	(20)	F.Costes	4 points
			J-M.Aguirre	2 points

MATCH COMMENTARY:

A vastly improved, and unexpected, performance by England gave them a richly deserved win over a powerful French side.   The forwards were immense, especially in the lines-out, the half-backs played much better than previously, and the backs, although sometimes confused in attack, defended heroically, none more so than Alastair Hignell.   France, playing with the wind, failed to capitalise on this advantage in the first half, and the only score was a well-struck penalty goal by Neil Bennett from some 40 metres.   In the second half, France turned up the pressure and played some attractive rugby in an attempt to get the breakthrough.   The English defence held and Neil Bennett extended the England lead with an opportunist try when he gathered a loose ball after Richard Cardus had made a half-break before he was tackled. France redoubled their efforts and scored a converted try with six minutes remaining. The tension was tangible for the last few minutes, but England held out to the immense relief of the crowd whose roar of triumph at the final whistle was like an escape of steam from a pressure vessel. Like Bennett against Ireland, Jean-Michel Aguirre could have won the match had he kicked his goals. Neil Bennett scored all England's points in exactly the same way as he had done against Ireland two weeks previously, with an unconverted try and a penalty goal, but the circumstances and the result were very different.

84th match   **ENGLAND   3 pts**   v   **WALES   27 pts**

	Caps					Caps		
15	14th & last	A.J.Hignell	(Bristol)		52nd	J.P.R.Williams (Capt)	(Bridgend)
14	29th & last	P.J.Squires	(Harrogate)		4th	H.E.Rees	(Neath)
13	2nd & last	R.M.Cardus	(Roundhay)		2nd	D.S.Richards	(Swansea)
12	8th	P.W.Dodge	(Leicester)		23rd	S.P.Fenwick	(Bridgend)
11	15th	M.A.C.Slemen	(Liverpool)		30th	J.J.Williams	(Llanelli)
10	7th & last	W.N.Bennett	(London Welsh)		7th	W.G.Davies	(Cardiff)
9	5th & last	P.J.Kingston	(Gloucester)		6th	T.D.Holmes	(Cardiff)
1	2nd	C.E.Smart	(Newport)		2nd & last	S.J.Richardson	(Aberavon)
2	19th	P.J.Wheeler	(Leicester)		1st	A.J.Phillips	(Cardiff)
3	4th	G.S.Pearce	(Northampton)		24th	G.Price	(Pontypool)
4	21st	W.B.Beaumont (Capt)	(Fylde)		27th	A.J.Martin	(Aberavon)
5	19th	N.E.Horton	(Toulouse)		8th & last	M.G.Roberts	(London Welsh)
6	38th	A.Neary	(Broughton Park)		12th	J.Squire	(Pontypool)
7	12th	M.Rafter	(Bristol)		5th	P.Ringer	(Llanelli)
8	9th	J.P.Scott	(Cardiff)		22nd	D.L.Quinnell	(Llanelli)

1st & only   C.Griffiths (Llanelli) for J.P.R.Williams - 60

Referee: J-P.Bonnet   (France)

SCORERS:

		0 - 3	W.G.Davies	Drop Goal
		0 - 7	D.S.Richards	Try
W.N.Bennett	Penalty Goal	3 - 7		
		Half-time		
		3 - 11	M.G.Roberts	Try
		3 - 15	P.Ringer	Try
		3 - 19	J.J.Williams	Try
		3 - 21	A.J.Martin	Conversion
		3 - 25	H.E.Rees	Try
		3 - 27	S.P.Fenwick	Conversion

POINTS:

W.N.Bennett	3 points	(23)	D.S.Richards, J.J.Williams, H.E.Rees, M.G.Roberts, P.Ringer	4 points each
			W.G.Davies	3 points
			S.P.Fenwick and A.J.Martin	2 points each

MATCH COMMENTARY:

Despite all the optimism following the win over France, England were soundly thrashed again at Cardiff by five tries to nil and a 24 point margin which was the highest Wales had achieved against England since 1905. In every respect, up front, England were outplayed, yet for sixty minutes of the game they were in contention, four points down with twenty minutes to go and J.P.R.off the field. The Welsh thereupon changed gear and piled on 20 points, including four tries, in those fateful last twenty minutes and England had no answer at all. The man who made the greatest contribution to England's demise on this occasion was Mike Roberts, called upon to replace Geoff Wheel, four years after his previous cap and eight years after his first, he subdued Bill Beaumont, let every England forward know he was there and crowned his day with a try ! Wales thus collected their fourth successive Triple Crown and England finished fourth in the Championship Table. In their last eight matches at Cardiff, England have scored 5 tries and conceded 31 !!

SUMMARY OF THE SEASON 1978 - 79:

For the past decade, it seems, England have frequently promised much, but without exception, season by season, have achieved little. The underlying reason for this string of continuing disappointments has been the failure of the backs in general, and the midfield in particular, to capitalise on what was more often than not, a generous share of possession provided by a competent pack who frequently won their contest with the opposing eight. England's Five Nations record supports this hypothesis, for in the last ten years England have won only 11 of their 40 Five Nations matches and have lost 26. During this time they have scored on average, just over one try per match and have conceded just over two.

This season was no exception, the only difference being that this season had not started off on an optimistic note following a victory over a touring side or a successful overseas tour, it had started with a sound defeat by Graham Mourie's All Blacks in November. The side for this match showed only four changes from that which had beaten Ireland in the final match of last season, and included one new cap, Tony Bond, but the playing of Barry Nelmes and John Scott out of position against such formidable opponents had a predictable result. As it was, New Zealand wasted many chances, particularly in the second half, and had they not done so, the margin of defeat could have been seriously embarrassing. The Five Nations opened with an extremely disappointing draw against Scotland at Twickenham, even though the selection gaffes made for the previous match were not repeated, although the selectors, in their wisdom, had deprived Bill Beaumont of the captaincy and passed it to Roger Uttley. He was unavailable for the next match against Ireland, so Beaumont reclaimed the crown which he was not then to relinquish until he retired in 1982. The performance against Ireland, in a match dominated by Tony Ward, was very poor, almost entirely because of poor play in midfield. Then the contrast against France. The side with two changes, in the centre and at loose-head, giving first caps to Richard Cardus and Colin Smart, produced a significantly improved performance to beat a very strong French side by the odd point in thirteen. Then an unchanged side went to Cardiff and were unceremoniously torn apart by the Welsh. It was suggested before the match, as Wales were without Charlie Faulkner, Bobby Windsor and Geoff Wheel, all injured, and many of the stars of yesteryear had retired at the end of the previous season, that this was a very weak Welsh XV. Not so, as events proved. England competed well until last quarter of the match when the score was as it had been at half-time, and JPR had to leave the field. In the next nightmarish twenty minutes, Wales scored 20 points including four tries. Such situations usually come about because the winning side is substantially fitter than their opponents, and there was no evidence to the contrary in England's defence. Wales took their fourth successive Triple Crown and England returned over the Severn Bridge to lick their wounds - yet again.

Twenty four players were used in the season's five matches, nineteen in the Five Nations. Four new caps were awarded, to two centres, Tony Bond of Sale, and Richard Cardus of Roundhay, and to two new props, Gary Pearce at tight-head and Colin Smart on the loose side. Neil Bennett, in a very undistinguished season overall, nevertheless achieved a remarkable distinction in that he scored all England's points in three successive matches, seven against Ireland, seven against France and three against Wales. Even Bob Hiller had not managed to do that in three successive matches.

Nine players had represented England for the last time during the course of the season. Peter Squires, was England's most capped wing-threequarter, with 29 caos, and was a British Lion on the 1977 tour to New Zealand and played in one Test. He was a schoolteacher and also had time to play for Yorkshire on 56 occasions at Rugby and on 49 occasions at cricket. Peter Dixon's career spanned nine seasons, yet he won only 22 caps. He captained England twice, in 1972, and went on the 1971 Lions' Tour to New Zealand before he was capped by England. He then played in the back row with Andy Ripley and Tony Neary on 12 occasions. Alastair Hignell, 14 caps, was a Cambridge Blue at cricket as well as rugby, and he played 137 matches for Gloucester CCC. He is a sports commentator. Malcolm Young, the Gosforth scrum-half, won 10 caps and scored a try on his debut against Scotland in 1977. Robin Cowling, a courageous loose-head prop, who played on with a dislocated shoulder against France in 1978, won 8 caps. Neil Bennet, 7 caps, had had a successful tour in Australia in 1975 and held the record for points scored on an England tour, of 48. Barry Nelmes returned to Cardiff with 6 caps, and Peter Kingston a PE teacher, retired with 5. Richard Cardus, 2 caps, continued to play for many more years, and captained his new club, Wasps.

FIVE NATIONS CHAMPIONSHIP TABLE:

Won: **Retained Calcutta Cup**

		Played	Won	Lost	Drawn	Points: For	Against	Tries: For	Against	Title Points
1	Wales	4	3	1	0	83	51	10	5	6
2	France	4	2	1	1	50	46	7	5	5
3	Ireland	4	1	1	2	53	51	5	6	4
4	**ENGLAND**	4	1	2	1	24	52	3	8	3
5	Scotland	4	0	2	2	48	58	7	8	2

Home Games: drew with Scotland 7 - 7, (one try each); beat France 7 - 6, (one try each)

Away Games: lost to Ireland 7 - 12, (one try each), lost to Wales 3 - 27, (no tries to five)

12th match   **ENGLAND**   **9 pts**   v   **NEW ZEALAND**   **10 pts**

	Caps				Caps		
15	4th	W.H.Hare	(Leicester)	2nd & last	R.G.Wilson	(Canterbury)
14	1st	J.Carleton	(Orrell)	4th & last	B.R.Ford	(Marlborough)
13	4th	A.M.Bond	(Sale)	14th	S.S.Wilson	(Wellington)
12	1st	N.J.Preston	(Richmond)	2nd	G.R.Cunningham	(Auckland)
11	16th	M.A.C.Slemen	(Liverpool)	2nd	B.G.Fraser	(Wellington)
10	1st	L.Cusworth	(Leicester)	5th	M.B.Taylor	(Waikato)
9	10th	S.J.Smith	(Sale)	3rd	D.S.Loveridge	(Taranaki)
1	3rd	C.E.Smart	(Newport)	13th & last	B.R.Johnstone	(Auckland)
2	20th	P.J.Wheeler	(Leicester)	1st & only	P.H.Sloane	(North Auckland)
3	26th	F.E.Cotton	(Sale)	2nd	J.E.Spiers	(Counties)
4	22nd	W.B.Beaumont (Capt)	(Fylde)	2nd	J.K.Fleming	(Wellington)
5	3rd	M.J.Colclough	(Angouleme)	18th	A.M.Haden	(Auckland)
6	39th	A.Neary	(Broughton Park)	11th	K.W.Stewart	(Southland)
7	13th	M.Rafter	(Bristol)	13th	G.N.K.Mourie (Capt)	(Taranaki)
8	10th	J.P.Scott	(Cardiff)	2nd	M.G.Mexted	(Wellington)

Referee: N.R.Sanson   (Scotland)

SCORERS:

			0 - 3	R.G.Wilson	Penalty Goal
			0 - 7	J.K.Fleming	Try
W.H.Hare	Penalty Goal		3 - 7		
			3 - 10	R.G.Wilson	Penalty Goal
			Half-time		
W.H.Hare	Penalty Goal		6 - 10		
W.H.Hare	Penalty Goal		9 - 10		

POINTS:

W.H.Hare	9 points	(15)	R.G.Wilson	6 points
			J.K.Flemimg	4 points

MATCH COMMENTARY:

This was as unspectacular and uninspiring a match as one could ever wish to see. Neither side seemed capable of introducing any flair or innovation whatsoever, and the game became a dour forward struggle. Graham Mourie and Bill Beaumont, the respective captains, did their best to raise their teams' efforts but tight refereeing and an abundance of penalty kicks - 35 penalties were awarded during the game, 20 to England and 15 to New Zealand - frustrated their efforts. Dave Loveridge had an excellent game for the All Blacks at scrum-half, but even he could do nothing to get his backs moving constructively. Richard Wilson scored with two kicks from a possible six, and Dusty Hare with three from six. It was that sort of game, but as New Zealand scored the only try of the match, they must have deserved to win. Even that was a little fortuitous. Dave Loveridge hoisted a high kick from behind his pack into the "box", and the ball bounced, (it should never have been allowed to bounce) behind the England goal line and back in to the field of play. It fell straight into the hands of the All Black lock, Fleming, who just had to fall forward to score. Late in the second half, "Dusty" Hare missed a final penalty goal attempt, having succeeded with the previous three, and the match, thankfully, was over.

There were six England players on the field today who took part in the corresponding match twelve months ago

92nd match   ## ENGLAND 24 pts v IRELAND 9 pts

	Caps					Caps		
15	5th	**W.H.Hare**	(Leicester)	.	1st	**K.A.O'Brien**	(Broughton Park)
14	2nd	**J.Carleton**	(Orrell)	.	7th	**T.J.Kennedy**	(St Mary's College)
13	5th	**A.M.Bond**	(Sale)	.	13th	**A.R.McKibbin**	(London Irish)
12	2nd	**N.J.Preston**	(Richmond)	. .	11th	**P.P.McNaughton**	(Greystones)
11	17th	**M.A.C.Slemen**	(Liverpool)	.	11th	**A.C.McLennan**	(Wanderers)
10	5th	**J.P.Horton**	(Bath)	.	4th	**S.O.Campbell**	(Old Belvedere)
9	11th	**S.J.Smith**	(Sale)	.	8th	**C.S.Patterson**	(Instonians)
1	27th	**F.E.Cotton**	(Sale)	.	21st	**P.A.Orr**	(Old Wesley)
2	21st	**P.J.Wheeler**	(Leicester)	.	3rd	**C.F.Fitzgerald**	(St Mary's College)
3	1st	**P.J.Blakeway**	(Gloucester)	.	7th	**G.A.J.McLoughlin**	(Shannon)
4	23rd	**W.B.Beaumont (Capt)**	(Fylde)	.	32nd	**M.I.Keane**	(Lansdowne)
5	20th & last	**N.E.Horton**	(Moseley)	.	1st	**J.J.Glennon**	(Skerries)
6	20th	**R.M.Uttley**	(Wasps)	.	4th	**J.B.O'Driscoll**	(London Irish)
7	40th	**A.Neary**	(Broughton Park)	.	42nd	**J.F.Slattery (Capt)**	(Blackrock College)
8	11th	**J.P.Scott**	(Cardiff)	.	23rd	**W.P.Duggan**	(Blackrock College)

  1st C.R.Woodward (Leicester) for Bond - 61 . 1st & only I.J.Burns (Wanderers) for McNaughton - 33

Referee: C.Thomas (Wales)

SCORERS:

W.H.Hare	Penalty Goal		3 - 0			
			3 - 3	**S.O.Campbell**	Penalty Goal	
			3 - 6	**S.O.Campbell**	Penalty Goal	
			3 - 9	**S.O.Campbell**	Penalty Goal	
S.J.Smith	Try	(1st)	7 - 9			
W.H.Hare	Conversion		9 - 9			
M.A.C.Slemen	Try	(4th)	13 - 9			
W.H.Hare	Conversion		15 - 9			
			Half-time			
W.H.Hare	Penalty Goal		18 - 9			
J.P.Scott	Try	(1st & only)	22 - 9			
W.H.Hare	Conversion		25 - 9			

POINTS:

W.H.Hare	12 points	(27)		**S.O.Campbell**	9 points
J.P.Scott, S.J.Smith	4 points	(4),(4)			
and M.A.C.Slemen	each	(16)			

MATCH COMMENTARY:

This match was undoubtedly won by the English forwards, who decisively beat their opponents in every facet of play and provided Steve Smith and John Horton with abundant possession which they used well. As a result, England scored as many points, and tries, in this game as they had in the entire Five Nations Championship last season. Phil Blakeway had an excellent debut, and his presence gave the front five even more stability, and therefore the back row more freedom because their opposite numbers were tied down. Steve Smith's try and his kick to provide the opportunity for Mike Slemen were a result of this freedom. Dusty Hare was in good goal kicking form, succeeding with five out of six attempts, and the performance of the whole side was excellent. Tony Bond, winning his fifth cap, saw his season come to an abrupt and untimely end when he fractured his leg in the second half. Not since 1938 have England scored as many points against Ireland.

55th match   **ENGLAND   17 pts**   v   **FRANCE   13 pts**

	Caps					Caps		
15	6th	W.H.Hare	(Leicester)	.	1st	S.Gabernet	(Toulouse)
14	3rd	J.Carleton	(Orrell)	.	8th	D.Bustaffa	(Carcassonne)
13	2nd	C.R.Woodward	(Leicester)	.	58th	R.Bertranne	(Bagneres)
12	3rd & last	N.J.Preston	(Richmond)	.	5th	D.Codorniou	(Narbonne)
11	18th	M.A.C.Slemen	(Liverpool)	.	23rd	J-L.Averous	(La Voulte)
10	6th	J.P.Horton	(Bath)	.	9th	A.Caussade	(Lourdes)
9	12th	S.J.Smith	(Sale)	.	12th	J.Gallion	(Toulon)
1	28th	F.E.Cotton	(Sale)	.	5th	P.Salas	(Narbonne)
2	22nd	P.J.Wheeler	(Leicester)	.	4th	P.Dintrans	(Tarbes)
3	2nd	P.J.Blakeway	(Gloucester)	.	34th	R.Paparemborde	(Pau)
4	24th	W.B.Beaumont (Capt)	(Fylde)	.	1st & only	Y.Duhard	(Bagneres)
5	4th	M.J.Colclough	(Angouleme)	.	4th	A.Maleig	(Oloron)
6	21st	R.M.Uttley	(Wasps)	.	11th	J-L.Joinel	(Brive)
7	41st	A.Neary	(Broughton Park)	.	35th	J-P.Rives (Capt)	(Toulouse)
8	12th	J.P.Scott	(Cardiff)	.	1st	M.Carpentier	(Lourdes)

Referee: C.Norling   (Wales)

SCORERS:

			0 - 4	J-P.Rives	Try
W.H.Hare	Penalty Goal		3 - 4		
			3 - 7	A.Caussade	Penalty Goal
N.J.Preston	Try	(1st & only)	7 - 7		
J.Carleton	Try	(1st)	11 - 7		
J.P.Horton	D'p Goal	(1st)	14 - 7		
			Half-time		
J.P.Horton	D'p Goal	(2nd)	17 - 7		
			17 - 11	J-L.Averous	Try
			17 - 13	A.Caussade	Conversion

POINTS:

J.P.Horton	6 points	(6)	A.Caussade	5 points
N.J.Preston	4 points	(4)	J-P.Rives	4 points
J.Carleton	4 points	(4)	J-L.Averous	4 points
W.H.Hare	3 points	(30)		

MATCH COMMENTARY:

Apart from Clive Woodward for the injured Tony Bond, England made only one change for Paris, restoring Maurice Colclough at lock in preference to Nigel Horton. The forwards, Beaumont and Scott in particular, played very well and subdued the French eight, again giving Smith and Horton at half-back, time and space in which to move. England did well to recover from Jean-Pierre Rives' try in the second minute of the match. After an exchange of penalty goals between Hare and Caussade, Nick Preston's try when he broke through two weak tackles levelled the score. Only minutes later a break from a scrum by John Scott with Colclough and Beaumont in support resulted in Steve Smith giving the scoring pass to John Carleton who ran in from 10 metres out. John Horton's drop goals either side of half-time put England well in the driving seat. Both drop goals were scored when Roger Uttley was off the field having stitches inserted in a cut on his head. England then had to withstand the furious French onslaught at the end, and did well to concede only Averous' converted try.

85th match   **ENGLAND 9 pts**   v   **WALES 8 pts**

	Caps					Caps		
15	7th	W.H.Hare	(Leicester)	.		4th	W.R.Blyth	(Swansea)
14	4th	J.Carleton	(Orrell)	.		6th	H.E.Rees	(Neath)
13	3rd	C.R.Woodward	(Leicester)	.		4th	D.S.Richards	(Swansea)
12	9th	P.W.Dodge	(Leicester)	.		25th	S.P.Fenwick	(Bridgend)
11	19th	M.A.C.Slemen	(Liverpool)	.		2nd	L.Keen	(Aberavon)
10	7th	J.P.Horton	(Bath)	.		9th	W.G.Davies	(Cardiff)
9	13th	S.J.Smith	(Sale)	.		8th	T.D.Holmes	(Cardiff)
1	29th	F.E.Cotton	(Sale)	.		4th	C.Williams	(Swansea)
2	23rd	P.J.Wheeler	(Leicester)	.		3rd	A.J.Phillips	(Cardiff)
3	3rd	P.J.Blakeway	(Gloucester)	.		26th	G.Price	(Pontypool)
4	25th	W.B.Beaumont (Capt)	(Fylde)	.		29th	A.J.Martin	(Aberavon)
5	5th	M.J.Colclough	(Angouleme)	.		24th	G.A.D.Wheel	(Swansea)
6	22nd	R.M.Uttley	(Wasps)	.		14th	J.Squire (Capt)	(Pontypool)
7	42nd	A.Neary	(Broughton Park)	.		7th	P.Ringer	(Llanelli)
8	13th	J.P.Scott	(Cardiff)	.		2nd	E.T.Butler	(Pontypool)

      14th   M.Rafter (Bristol) for Uttley - 40

Referee: D.I.H.Burnett   (Ireland)

SCORERS:

W.H.Hare	Penalty Goal	3 - 0			
		3 - 4	J.Squire	Try	
		Half-time			
W.H.Hare	Penalty Goal	6 - 4			
		6 - 8	H.E.Rees	Try	
W.H.Hare	Penalty Goal	9 - 8			

POINTS:

W.H.Hare	9 points	(39)	J.Squire	4 points	
			H.E.Rees	4 points	

MATCH COMMENTARY:

England can count themselves only lucky to have won this match without scoring a try, and having conceded two. Wales were doomed when Paul Ringer was sent off for a high tackle on John Horton after a bad-tempered opening to a rough and abrasive game. Ringer was only the second International player to be sent off at Twickenham, the first being Cyril Brownlee of New Zealand 55 years previously, and he was unfortunate because his crime was not a malevolent one, he was the necessary example "pour discourager les autres". His departure was significant because thereafter Terry Holmes, shorn of defence, was constantly in trouble and could not get his backs moving. Dusty Hare opened the scoring for England with a penalty goal immediately following Ringer's departure. Shortly after that, on a heel from a scrum almost on his own line, Steve Smith was dispossessed by Jeff Squire who touched down to score. So Wales led at half-time, with only 14 men. Hare's second penalty goal restored England's lead only for Elgan Rees to snatch it back after a superb break by Alan Phillips. Gareth Davies failed with the conversion, as he had with six other scoring opportunities during the match. It fell to Dusty Hare to win the match for England with a fine kick from the touch-line in injury time. In the circumstances, Wales played very well, but England won the match, their third of the season, but they had ridden their luck to get to Murrayfield for the Grand Slam.

96th match

87th Calcutta Cup

ENGLAND   30 pts   v   SCOTLAND   18 pts

	Caps					Caps		
15	8th	W.H.Hare	(Leicester)	.		37th	A.R.Irvine	(Heriot's FP)
14	5th	J.Carleton	(Orrell)	.		8th	K.W.Robertson	(Melrose)
13	4th	C.R.Woodward	(Leicester)	.		35th	J.M.Renwick	(Hawick)
12	10th	P.W.Dodge	(Leicester)	.		5th	D.I.Johnston	(Watsonians)
11	20th	M.A.C.Slemen	(Liverpool)	.		17th	B.H.Hay	(Boroughmuir)
10	8th	J.P.Horton	(Bath)	.		8th	J.Y.Rutherford	(Selkirk)
9	14th	S.J.Smith	(Sale)	.		4th	R.J.Laidlaw	(Jedforest)
1	30th	F.E.Cotton	(Sale)	.	4th & last	J.N.Burnett	(Heriot's FP)
2	24th	P.J.Wheeler	(Leicester)	.	3rd & last	K.G.Lawrie	(Gala)
3	4th	P.J.Blakeway	(Gloucester)	.	2nd	N.A.Rowan	(Boroughmuir)
4	26th	W.B.Beaumont (Capt)	(Fylde)	.	16th	A.J.Tomes	(Hawick)
5	6th	M.J.Colclough	(Angouleme)	.	8th	D.Gray	(West of Scotland)
6	23rd & last	R.M.Uttley	(Wasps)	.	12th	D.G.Leslie	(Gala)
7	43rd & last	A.Neary	(Broughton Park)	.	24th & last	M.A.Biggar	(London Scottish)
8	14th	J.P.Scott	(Cardiff)	.	4th	J.R.Beattie	Glasgow Acad'ls)

.   1st & only   J.S.Gossman (W of Scotland) for Hay - 50

Referee: J-P.Bonnet   (France)

SCORERS:

				England	Scotland		
J.Carleton	Try	(2nd)	4 - 0			
W.H.Hare	Conversion		6 - 0			
M.A.C.Slemen	Try	(5th)	10 - 0			
W.H.Hare	Conversion		12 - 0			
J.Carleton	Try	(3rd)	16 - 0			
			16 - 3	A.R.Irvine	Penalty Goal
W.H.Hare	Penalty Goal		19 - 3			
			Half-time			
			19 - 6	A.R.Irvine	Penalty Goal
S.J.Smith	Try	(2nd & last)	23 - 6			
			23 - 10	A.J.Tomes	Try
			23 - 12	A.R.Irvine	Conversion
W.H.Hare	Penalty Goal		26 - 12			
J.Carleton	Try	(4th)	30 - 12			
			30 - 16	J.Y.Rutherford	Try
			30 - 18	A.R.Irvine	Conversion

POINTS:

J.Carleton	12 point	(16)	A.R.Irvine	10 points
W.H.Hare	10 point	(49)	A.J.Tomes and J.Y.Rutherford	4 points each
M.A.C.Slemen and S.J.Smith	4 points each	(20),(8)		

MATCH COMMENTARY:

This was a classic match in every sense of the word. Attack, counter-attack, and splendid running by backs and forwards alike. A hat-trick of tries for John Carleton, the first for England since 1924, and four tries in the season equalling existing records. Bill Beaumont led England for the thirteenth time into this Grand Slam match, certainly the most dramatic confrontation of his outstanding career to date. England picked an unchanged side, and from the early stages it became very apparent that the English pack were going to have a significant say in the course of events that afternoon. The pack pushed Scotland around almost at will and, as a direct result of that, England had accumulated a lead of 16 points to nil within the first half-hour. Two tries for John Carleton and one for Mike Slemen were testimony to the quality of English possession and to the pace an ability of the England backs. The onslaught continued in the second half until England had extended their half-time lead of 19 - 3 to 23 - 6 with a try from Steve Smith. Then Scotland decided that two could play at this game and in the last half-hour scored two converted tries with John Carleton's third coming in between them. The first Scottish try came after a jinking elusive run by Jim Renwick every bit as enthralling as those by Clive Woodward in the first half leading to England's first two tries. The second was a classic fly-half break and touchdown under the posts by John Rutherford for the last of the seven tries scored in this magnificent match. John Carleton's hat-trick was the first for England since H.P.Jacobs scored three against France at Twickenham in 1924.

It had been 23 years since England last won the Grand Slam, and 20 years since the last Triple Crown, so it was a good night in Edinburgh in which the Scots were not altogether reluctant to join !!

SUMMARY OF THE SEASON 1979 - 80:

It all came good for England this season, as with some spectacular play and a generous slice of good fortune, all the false dawns of previous years disappeared into history and oblivion, for not only was the Championship Title secured outright for the first time in 17 years, with it came the Triple Crown for the first time in 20 years and the ultimate accolade, the Grand Slam, for the first time in 23 years and for only the second time since the Second World War.   In doing so, the side scored more points (80), and more tries (10) than in any other season since the War.   It was an excellent achievement.   Two matches, Ireland and Scotland, particularly the latter, stand out as first rate examples of how the game should be played in terms of attacking rugby and sparkling entertainment.   The match against France was a prime example of application of all fifteen players for the full 80 minutes and determination not to be disheartened or dispirited by conceding a try in only the second minute of the match.   The game against Wales at Twickenham was the one where the luck ran England's way for once.   Wales came with the intention of spoiling England's party by any means at their disposal and feelings were bitter and ran high.   The only tries were scored by Wales, but England won the match.   Paul Ringer was not a lone villain, but in a match played in such bad grace, somebody had to go - and he was caught.   Wales failed with many of their kicks at goal, and "Dusty" Hare got the one that mattered.   This does not detract from the worthiness of England's achievement, in any respect, but it does serve as a cogent reminder that Lady Fortune has a part to play even on the International rugby field.   Bill Beaumont's leadership was exemplary.   By the end of the season, he had captained England thirteen times, emulating the records set by Wavell Wakefield, Nim Hall, Dickie Jeeps and John Pullin.   Not least of the contributory factors to England's success was the appointment of "Budge" Rogers as Chairman of Selectors and Mike Davis as Coach.   Two actions of theirs certainly had a significant effect on England's fortunes this season.   Firstly, the "A" tour to Japan and the Far East the previous summer had blended a cohesive squad with Bill Beaumont firmly established as leader, and secondly, the continuation of that team spirit into the much more frequent squad sessions which were held throughout the season.

The first International of the season, against New Zaeland in November, gave no hint of the success which was round the corner, for the side showed little cohesion even though nine of those who had benefitted from the Far East tour were in the side, and seven of the north-western stalwarts who had beaten New Zealand at Otley only the previous week.   A few squad sessions later, it was a very different and purposeful side, showing four changes, who demonstrated a strong will to win over Ireland in the first Five Nations match.   That solidarity was very evident for the remainder of the season, albeit in three very different kinds of match, culminating in the final spectacle at Murrayfield.   A very shrewd selection was made after the All Black match in bringing into the side Phil Blakeway, the Gloucester tight-head prop, and moving Fran Cotton to loose-head.   This move gave the England pack an even more secure platform than they had previously enjoyed, and paid handsome dividends, for Blakeway was to be a permanent fixture in the side for the best part of the next five seasons.   Some sympathy must be felt for Tony Bond whose potential Grand Slam season was sadly and abruptly ended when he broke his leg in the Irish match.   England played 22 different players during the course of the five matches, and 19, including one replacement, for the Five Nations. Five new caps were awarded, John Carleton, Nick Preston, Clive Woodward, Les Cusworth and Phil Blakeway.   With one exception, Horton for Colclough for one match, the pack was unchanged for the Five Nations.   Nine players played in all five matches and twelve played in all Five Nations matches.   Only four players came to the end of their International careers; Tony Neary, with 43 caps, had become England's most-capped player in the last match of the season, overtaking John Pullin's record 42.   His career had spanned 10 seasons and he had captained England seven times.   He went on two Lions' tours, 1974 and 1977, playing in one Test, and was one of the finest open-side flankers of his time.   A solicitor, he is a partner in Cotton Traders.   Roger Uttley won 23 caps and captained the side five times.   He went on the 1974 Lions' tour and played in all four Tests.   He was a schoolmaster at Harrow, Lions' coach in Australia in 1989, and England coach in 1991, thus becoming the only player to have played in and coached a Grand Slam side.   Nigel Horton, a policeman, was awarded the first of his 20 caps at the age of twenty.   Nick Preston, the Richmond centre, retired with three caps.

Eight players, including the worthy captain, Bill Beaumont, were invited to tour with the Lions to South Africa. Paul Dodge and Steve Smith were later called upon as replacements. Of those eight, Bill Beaumont, Peter Wheeler and Maurice Colclough played in all four Tests.

FIVE NATIONS CHAMPIONSHIP TABLE:

Won: **Grand Slam, Triple Crown, Championship Title and Calcutta Cup**

		Played	Won	Lost	Drawn	Points: For	Against	Tries: For	Against	Title Points
1	ENGLAND	4	4	0	0	80	48	10	6	8
2 =	Wales	4	2	2	0	50	45	10	5	4
2 =	Ireland	4	2	2	0	70	65	6	8	4
4 =	Scotland	4	1	3	0	61	83	8	12	2
4 =	France	4	1	3	0	55	75	7	10	2

Home Games: beat Ireland 24 - 9, (three tries to nil); beat Wales 9 - 8, (no tries to two)

Away Games: beat France 17 - 13, (two tries each); beat Scotland 30 - 18, (five tries to two)

86th match   **ENGLAND   19 pts**   v   **WALES   21 pts**

	Caps				Caps		
15	9th	W.H.Hare	(Leicester)	.	54th	J.P.R.Williams	(Bridgend)
14	6th	J.Carleton	(Orrell)	.	2nd	R.A.Ackerman	(Newport)
13	5th	C.R.Woodward	(Leicester)	.	8th	D.S.Richards	(Swansea)
12	11th	P.W.Dodge	(Leicester)	.	29th	S.P.Fenwick (Capt)	(Bridgend)
11	21st	M.A.C.Slemen	(Liverpool)	.	1st	D.L.Nicholas	(Llanelli)
10	9th	J.P.Horton	(Bath)	.	12th	W.G.Davies	(Cardiff)
9	15th	S.J.Smith	(Sale)	.	2nd	D.B.Williams	(Swansea)
1	31st & last	F.E.Cotton	(Sale)	.	30th	G.Price	(Pontypool)
2	25th	P.J.Wheeler	(Leicester)	.	7th	A.J.Phillips	(Cardiff)
3	5th	P.J.Blakeway	(Gloucester)	.	1st	I.Stephens	(Bridgend)
4	27th	W.B.Beaumont (Capt)	(Fylde)	.	2nd	C.E.Davis	(Newbridge)
5	7th	M.J.Colclough	(Angouleme)	.	27th	G.A.D.Wheel	(Swansea)
6	15th	M.Rafter	(Bristol)	.	18th	J.Squire	(Pontypool)
7	1st	D.H.Cooke	(Harlequins)	.	1st	J.R.Lewis	(S Glamorgan Inst)
8	15th	J.P.Scott	(Cardiff)	.	2nd	G.P.Williams	(Bridgend)

    1st   A.Sheppard   (Bristol)   for Cotton - 17

Referee: J.B.Anderson   (Scotland)

SCORERS:

			0 - 3		S.P.Fenwick	Penalty Goal
			0 - 7		C.E.Davis	Try
			0 - 9		S.P.Fenwick	Conversion
W.H.Hare	Penalty Goal		3 - 9			
			3 - 12		S.P.Fenwick	Penalty Goal
W.H.Hare	Penalty Goal		6 - 12			
W.H.Hare	Try	(1st)	10 - 12			
			Half-time			
W.H.Hare	Penalty Goal		13 - 12			
			13 - 15		W.G.Davies	Drop Goal
			13 - 18		S.P.Fenwick	Penalty Goal
W.H.Hare	Penalty Goal		16 - 18			
W.H.Hare	Penalty Goal		19 - 18			
			19 - 21		S.P.Fenwick	Penalty Goal

POINTS:

W.H.Hare	19 points	(68)	S.P.Fenwick	14 points
			C.E.Davis	4 points
			W.G.Davies	3 points

MATCH COMMENTARY:

An immensely exciting match in which the result was in doubt until the very last seconds, but a game in which there was little enterprising play. The Welsh forwards gave the strong England pack a very hard time, and Gareth Davies was always a threat with his tactical kicking. The game largely hinged on penalty goals right to the end when Clive Woodward was lured off-side in the middle of the pitch at a set scrum, and the Steve Fenwick's penalty put Wales back in the lead. Then "Dusty" Hare had a similar chance in the last seconds but pulled the kick and Wales had won. Fran Cotton had to leave the field, and the International scene, with a torn hamstring early in the match.

97th match   **ENGLAND   23 pts**   v   **SCOTLAND   17 pts**

88th Calcutta Cup

	Caps					Caps		
15	10th	W.H.Hare	(Leicester)			40th	A.R.Irvine (Capt)	(Heriot's FP)
14	7th	J.Carleton	(Orrell)			5th	S.Munro	(Ayr)
13	6th	C.R.Woodward	(Leicester)			38th	J.M.Renwick	(Hawick)
12	12th	P.W.Dodge	(Leicester)			11th	K.W.Robertson	(Melrose)
11	22nd	M.A.C.Slemen	(Liverpool)			20th	B.H.Hay	(Boroughmuir)
10	1st	G.H.Davies	(Cambridge Univ)			11th	J.Y.Rutherford	(Selkirk)
9	16th	S.J.Smith	(Sale)			7th	R.J.Laidlaw	(Jedforest)
1	4th	C.E.Smart	(Newport)			6th	J.Aitken	(Gala)
2	26th	P.J.Wheeler	(Leicester)			14th	C.T.Deans	(Hawick)
3	6th	P.J.Blakeway	(Gloucester)			5th	N.A.Rowan	(Boroughmuir)
4	28th	W.B.Beaumont (Capt)	(Fylde)			3rd	W.Cuthbertson	(Kilmarnock)
5	8th	M.J.Colclough	(Angouleme)			19th	A.J.Tomes	(Hawick)
6	1st	N.C.Jeavons	(Moseley)			3rd	J.H.Calder	(Stewart's-Melville)
7	2nd	D.H.Cooke	(Harlequins)			14th	D.G.Leslie	(Gala)
8	16th	J.P.Scott	(Cardiff)			7th	J.R.Beattie	(Heriot's FP)

1st   R.Hesford (Bristol) for Jeavons - 14

Referee: D.I.H.Burnett   (Ireland)

SCORERS:

			0 - 3	A.R.Irvine	Penalty Goal
W.H.Hare	Penalty Goal		3 - 3		
			3 - 7	S.Munro	Try
C.R.Woodward	Try	(1st)	6 - 7		
W.H.Hare	Conversion		9 - 7		
			Half-time		
			9 - 11	S.Munro	Try
			9 - 13	A.R.Irvine	Conversion
W.H.Hare	Penalty Goal		12 - 13		
M.A.C.Slemen	Try	(6th)	16 - 13		
			16 - 17	J.H.Calder	Try
G.H.Davies	Try	(1st)	20 - 17		
W.H.Hare	Penalty Goal		23 - 17		

POINTS:

W.H.Hare	11 points	(79)	S.Munro	8 points
M.A.C.Slemen, G.H.Davies	4 points	(24),(4)	A.R.Irvine	5 points
and C.R.Woodward	each	(4)	J.H.Calder	4 points

MATCH COMMENTARY:

In complete contrast to the match against Wales, this game provided scintillating rugby and six excellent tries. The English pack, although missing Uttley, Neary and, recently Cotton, played well and were superbly led by Bill Beaumont, leading England for the 15th time. The match started, as these things usually do, with an exchange of penalty goals, and a defensive error by "Dusty" Hare let in Munro, to give Scotland the lead. Just before half-time, Clive Woodward received the ball in a conventional three-quarter movement, and with nothing looking on, he jinked, side-stepped and otherwise evaded six would-be tacklers to cut clean through to score a magnificent individual try. Four tries in the second half rounded off a wonderful match with England worthy winners.

93rd match   **ENGLAND   10 pts**   v   **IRELAND   6 pts**

	Caps					Caps		
15	1st	W.M.H.Rose	(Cambridge Univ)	.	3rd	H.P.McNeill	(Dublin University)
14	8th	J.Carleton	(Orrell)	.	3rd & last	F.P.Quinn	(Old Belvedere)
13	7th	C.R.Woodward	(Leicester)	.	5th	D.G.Irwin	(Queen's U Belfast)
12	13th	P.W.Dodge	(Leicester)	.	10th	S.O.Campbell	(Old Belvedere)
11	23rd	M.A.C.Slemen	(Liverpool)	.	15th	A.C.McLennan	(Wanderers)
10	2nd	G.H.Davies	(Cambridge Univ)	.	11th	A.J.P.Ward	(Garryowen)
9	17th	S.J.Smith	(Sale)	.	8th	J.C.Robbie	(Greystones)
1	5th	C.E.Smart	(Newport)	.	27th	P.A.Orr	(Old Wesley)
2	27th	P.J.Wheeler	(Leicester)	.	19th & last	P.C.Whelan	(Garryowen)
3	7th	P.J.Blakeway	(Gloucester)	.	7th	M.P.Fitzpatrick	(Wanderers)
4	29th	W.B.Beaumont (Capt)	(Fylde)	.	38th	M.I.Keane	(Lansdowne)
5	9th	M.J.Colclough	(Angouleme)	.	7th	B.O.Foley	(Shannon)
6	2nd	N.C.Jeavons	(Moseley)	.	10th	J.B.O'Driscoll	(London Irish)
7	3rd	D.H.Cooke	(Harlequins)	.	48th	J.F.Slattery (Capt)	(Blackrock College)
8	17th	J.P.Scott	(Cardiff)	.	26th	W.P.Duggan	(Blackrock College)

1st & only   G.A.F.Sargent (Glo'ster) for Blakeway - 26

Referee: J-P.Bonnet   (France)

SCORERS:

				0 - 3	H.P.McNeill	Drop Goal
				0 - 6	S.O.Campbell	Drop Goal
W.M.H.Rose	Try	(1st)	4 - 6		
			Half-time		
P.W.Dodge	Try	(1st & only)	8 - 6		
W.M.H.Rose	Conversion		10 - 6		

POINTS:

W.M.H.Rose	6 points	(6)	H.P.McNeill	3 points
P.W.Dodge	4 points	(7)	S.O.Campbell	3 points

MATCH COMMENTARY:

Although Ireland led until the last quarter of the game, it never seemed likely that they would win the contest. The English pack coped adequately with their opponents despite losing Phil Blakeway with a neck injury in the first half. He was replaced by Gordon Sargent, the Gloucester loose-head, who got into all sorts of trouble, and Colin Smart (who seven years previously had been offered a place in the Welsh squad), had to switch heads occasionally to relieve the pressure. The Irish pack failed to take advantage of this situation, and the England forwards maintained control, but it was the flair, the running and handling skills of the backs which won the match. Not least among these was Marcus Rose in his first International, who appeared to be suffering acutely from nerves early in the game, yet it was he who scored the first and made the second try. The first came from a three-quarter movement when Rose appeared outsdie Mike Slemen, took the pass and rounded Hugo McNeill at pace to score in the corner. Ollie Campbell's long drop-out midway through the second half, with Ireland still in the lead, was gathered by Rose and, when all Ireland expected him to kick, he set the backs moving, and a fine try by Paul Dodge was the outcome. England had to dig deep into their reserves to keep the Irish out in the last quarter, and they succeeded well. England's backs have emerged this season as a creative, innovative force and the team as a whole is less dependent on its powerful pack to grind down the opposition. This has resulted in much better rugby, enjoyed by players and spectators alike.

56th match   **ENGLAND   12 pts**   v   **FRANCE   16 pts**

	Caps					Caps		
15	2nd	W.M.H.Rose	(Cambridge Univ)	.		6th	S.Gabernet	(Toulouse)
14	9th	J.Carleton	(Orrell)	.		5th	S.Blanco	(Biarritz)
13	8th	C.R.Woodward	(Leicester)	.		66th	R.Bertranne	(Bagneres)
12	14th	P.W.Dodge	(Leicester)	.		10th	D.Codorniou	(Narbonne)
11	24th	M.A.C.Slemen	(Liverpool)	.		6th	L.Pardo	(Bayonne)
10	3rd	G.H.Davies	(Cambridge Univ)	.		3rd	G.Laporte	(Graulhet)
9	18th	S.J.Smith	(Sale)	.		4th	P.Berbizier	(Lourdes)
1	6th	C.E.Smart	(Newport)	.		6th	P.Dospital	(Bayonne)
2	28th	P.J.Wheeler	(Leicester)	.		12th	P.Dintrans	(Tarbes)
3	8th	P.J.Blakeway	(Gloucester)	.		41st	R.Paparemborde	(Pau)
4	30th	W.B.Beaumont (Capt)	(Fylde)	.		4th	D.Revallier	(Graulhet)
5	10th	M.J.Colclough	(Angouleme)	.		20th	J-F.Imbernon	(Perpignan)
6	3rd	N.C.Jeavons	(Moseley)	.		42nd	J-P.Rives (Capt)	(Toulouse)
7	4th	D.H.Cooke	(Harlequins)	.		3rd	P.Lacans	(Beziers)
8	18th	J.P.Scott	(Cardiff)	.		18th	J-L.Joinel	(Brive)

Referee: A.M.Hosie   (Scotland)

SCORERS:

			0 - 3	G.Laporte	Drop Goal
			0 - 7	P.Lacans	Try
			0 - 9	G.Laporte	Conversion
			0 - 13	L.Pardo	Try
			0 - 16	G.Laporte	Drop Goal
			Half-time		
W.M.H.Rose	Penalty Goal		3 - 16		
W.M.H.Rose	Penalty Goal		6 - 16		
W.M.H.Rose	Penalty Goal		9 - 16		
W.M.H.Rose	Penalty Goal		12 - 16		

POINTS:

W.M.H.Rose	12 points	(18)	G.Laporte	8 points
			P.Lacans and L Pardo	4 points each

MATCH COMMENTARY:

The strong south-westerly wind was a decisive factor in this match for which England fielded an unchanged side. England chose to play against the very strong wind in the first half in the hope of containing the French, and failed. This was the essence of the difference between the two sides in that with the wind in the first half, France scored two fine tries and 16 points, whereas, in the second half, England could only manage four penalty goals. It is true that the first French try, which came from a quick throw-in, but using a different ball, was somewhat suspect, but of the second, by Pardo, there was no doubt at all. England gained an abundance of possession from the lines-out but the backs, unlike the last two matches, ignored the basics and tried to over-elaborate by complicated moves and long and looped passes which, inevitably, went astray in the strong wind. In the second half, the French, sensibly, played a contained game and limited England to those four penalty goals from Marcus Rose, with two chances missed.

There can be no doubt that France deserved to win, because they did the basics properly and adapted themselves to the conditions far better than did England. France proceeded to their third Grand Slam and England had to settle for equal second place in the Championship Table.

SUMMARY OF THE SEASON 1980 - 81:

In most respects this was a disappointing Championship, and probably the most uninteresting for some considerable time. This does not detract from France's achievement in winning their third Grand Slam, and their second in five years, but apart from occasional flashes of inspired play, and Clive Woodward's try against Scotland was one such, the season had little to commend it. This was the beginning of the long period in the eighties and into the nineties when the penalty goal dominated, and the result became more important than the means of its achievement. This season England scored 12 penalty goals, more than any previous season, and 41 were scored in total in the ten Championship matches. England's performance in the Championship, joint second in the Table having won two matches, had been influenced by a series of misfortunes in the front row of the scrum. In the first match at Cardiff, Fran Cotton had to leave the field after 13 minutes and his replacement, Austin Sheppard, was the Bristol tight-head. Thus it was that Phil Blakeway had to move to loose-head to accommodate him and this disruption must have had a detrimental effect on England's normal powerful scrummaging, particularly in the set piece. Similarly against Ireland, Phil Blakeway had to leave the field after 26 minutes, and the replacement this time was Gordon Sargent, the Gloucester loose-head, so Colin Smart had to switch to tight-head, and this again disrupted the pack who were looking very forceful in the first quarter. Again, in the French match, Blakeway was injured after fifteen minutes, and although he did not leave the field, his performance was well below par and must have affected the England performance and, arguably, the result.

It was the same Grand Slam team, with the exception of the retired Tony Neary and Roger Uttley, who took the field for the first match, at Cardiff. Mike Rafter, an old hand with 15 caps and a new flanker David Cooke form Harlequins, were selected to succeed them. England were a trifle unfortunate to lose at the very last gasp, but lose they did for the ninth successive time at Cardiff. "Dusty" Hare's 19 points set a new individual record for points scored during a match, beating Alan Old's total of 17 points against Ireland in 1974. Hare also became the fourth England player to score fifty individual points for England - it had taken him nine matches. Fran Cotton had to leave the field with hamstring problems, but because of his cardiac condition, which had become evident on the Lions tour in South Africa, and a recurring infection in his left leg, he never graced the International stage again. Three changes were made for the Scotland match, Colin Smart replacing Fran Cotton, Huw Davies coming in at fly-half because of an injury to John Horton and Nick Jeavons replacing Mike Rafter on the blind-side flank. The unfortunate Jeavons had to leave the field with double vision after only 14 minutes, but it was by far the best match of the whole Championship with six fine tries, three for each side. Clive Woodward's try was simply individual genius and flair, all impromptu and off-the-cuff, whereas that by Huw Davies on his debut, showed vision and beautifully balanced running to beat the defence. Bob Hesford, the Bristol flanker, gained his first cap as a replacement for Nick Jeavons. The only change for the Ireland match was the introduction of Marcus Rose, another Cambridge undergraduate to join Huw Davies, in place of "Dusty" Hare who, although his kicking had been highly dependable, had been considered to be at fault for Wales' try and one of those scored by Scotland in the two previous matches. The pack had been badly disrupted by the Blakeway injury and Steve Smith and the back five forwards in particular had done extremely well to contain the Irish pack, and with Ireland leading 6 - 0, it was Marcus Rose's flair and confidence, after a shaky start, which won the match for England. So, no change for the final match at Twickenham against France. No contest either, really, for the injury to Phil Blakeway removed any chance England may have had of overhauling France's 16 point lead when playing with the wind in the second half. A disappointing end to a disappointing season - but then a season following a Grand Slam, unless it is repeated, is bound to be a disappointment.

Nineteen players were used during the four Five Nations matches as well as three players who came on as replacements only. The entire three-quarter line, the scrum half, and six of the pack played in all four matches. Only Fran Cotton retired from International rugby this season and that as a direct result of his health problems. He had gained 31 caps and was England's most capped prop and was to remain so until he lost that record to Gary Pearce in 1987. He founded the liesurewear group Cotton Traders which he now runs with Tony Neary and Steve Smith. Gordon Sargent gained his only cap when he replaced Phil Blakeway against Ireland in Dublin.

FIVE NATIONS CHAMPIONSHIP TABLE:

Won: **Calcutta Cup**

		Played	Won	Lost	Drawn	Points: For	Against	Tries: For	Against	Title Points
1	France	4	4	0	0	70	49	6	3	8
2 =	**ENGLAND**	4	2	2	0	64	60	6	6	4
2 =	Scotland	4	2	2	0	51	54	7	6	4
2 = ●	Wales	4	2	2	0	51	61	2	6	4
5	Ireland	4	0	4	0	36	48	4	4	0

Home Games: beat Scotland 23 - 17, (three tries each); lost to france 12 - 16, (no tries to two)

Away Games: lost to Wales 19 - 21, (one try each); beat Ireland 10 - 6, (two tries to nil)

ENGLAND TOUR TO ARGENTINA - 1981

THE TOUR PARTY:

Manager:	W.G.D.Morgan	Assistant:	A.M.Davis		Captain:		W.B.Beaumont	
Full-backs:	W.H.Hare	(Leicester)	10 caps	Forwards:	S.J.Bainbridge	(Gosforth)		no caps
	B.Patrick	(Gosforth)	no caps		W.B.Beaumont	(Fylde)		30 caps
					D.H.Cooke	(Harlequins)		4 caps
Three-quarters:	J.Carleton	(Orrell)	9 caps		J.H.Fidler	(Gloucester)		no caps
	P.W.Dodge	(Leicester)	14 caps		R.J.Hesford	(Bristol)		1 cap
	N.J.Prestom	(Richmond)	3 caps		N.C.Jeavons	(Moseley)		3 caps
	A.M.Swift	(Swansea)	no caps		C.M.McGregor	(Angouleme)		no caps
	D.M.Trick	(Bath)	no caps		S.G.F.Mills	(Gloucester)		no caps
	C.R.Woodward	(Leicester)	8 caps		G.S.Pearce	(Northampton)		4 caps
					M.Rafter	(Bristol)		15 caps
Half-backs:	G.H.Davies	(Cambridge U)	3 caps		P.A.G.Rendall	(Wasps)		no caps
	J.P.Horton	(Bath)	9 caps		J.P.Scott	(Cardiff)		18 caps
	N.D.Melville	(Wasps)	no caps		A.Simpson	(Sale)		no caps
	S.J.Smith	(Sale)	18 caps		C.E.Smart	(Newport)		6 caps

England were the first of the Home Nations to tour Argentina, and to take advantage of the recent International Board ruling that full caps could be awarded for matches against non-IB countries. It had been the intention to tour Argentina in 1973, but terrorist threats had necessitated cancellation and the side had gone to New Zealand instead. This first tour was a success, with England remaining unbeaten and drawing one game. For the most part the provincial games caused no problems, but in the two Tests, England had to pull out all the stops to draw the first and win the second.

Three of last season's regular England pack were unavailable to tour, Blakeway, Wheeler and Colclough. Mike Slemen and Marcus Rose were also absent. There were some pre-tour fears that, especially in the Tests, England might struggle without three strong pack members But the fears were unfounded as all the newly capped players acquitted themselves extremely well. The first two matches, against the San Isidro Club and the Northern Region were entertaining and, particularly the first, competitive, with England scoring four tries in the first and eight in the second. The third match, against the Buenos Aires Selection, was a dull affair, high scoring but containing far too many penalty awards and nine successful penalty kicks. England did not play well and were a trifle fortunate to win. The fourth match was another run-away win with eight tries scored without reply, and in the final provincial game, England, again, were a trifle lucky to win with a 60 metre run by David Trick to score a try in the last minute to avoid an embarrassing draw.

However, in spite of somewhat mediocre performances otherwise, England raised their game in both the Tests and the results were appropriate and deserved. The side took few risks, their defence was rock solid and they denied Hugo Porta any space, or time, to weave his particular brand of magic. The new caps, John Fidler, Tony Swift and Steve Mills rose to the occasions splendidly and of the established players, Steve Smith, John Scott and "Dusty" Hare each played exceptionally well. All the matches were well-contested and clean and played in a good spirit. Brian Patrick, from three appearances, not including a Test, was top scorer with 41 points, and Hare followed him with 37 points. David Trick grabbed five tries. John Carleton and Paul Dodge played in all seven games, and Bill Beaumont, Nick Jeavons and Gary Pearce appeared in six. Only Mike Rafter quit the International scene after the tour with 17 caps.

The Test matches had attracted enormous interest in Argentine with over 30,000 people attending the first, rather less for the second, no doubt due to the weather, and touring in this country, as England discovered, was no free holiday - as New Zealand and France were to learn to their cost in the next few years when both lost a Test match on Argentinian soil.

TOUR RESULTS:

May 16th	San Isidro Club	in Buenos Aires	WON	20 - 14	(four tries to two)
May 19th	Northern Region XV	in Cordoba	WON	36 - 12	(eight tries to one)
May 23rd	Buenos Aires Selection	in Buenos Aires	WON	34 - 25	(four tries to two)
May 25th	Southern Region XV	in Mar del Plata	WON	47 - 3	(eight tries to nil)
May 30th	**ARGENTINA**	**in Buenos Aires**	**DREW**	**19 - 19**	**(three tries to two)**
June 2nd	Littoral Region XV	in Rosario	WON	25 - 21	(two tries each)
June 6th	**ARGENTINA**	**in Buenos Aires**	**WON**	**12 - 6**	(one try each)

1st match **ENGLAND 19 pts** v **ARGENTINA 19 pts**

	Caps					Caps	
15	11th	**W.H.Hare**	(Leicester)	.		**D.Baetti**	(Atletico Rosario)
14	10th	**J.Carleton**	(Orrell)	.		**M.Campo**	(Pueyrredon)
13	15th	**P.W.Dodge**	(Leicester)	.		**R.Madero**	(San Isidro)
12	9th	**C.R.Woodward**	(Leicester)	.		**M.Loffreda**	(San Isidro)
11	1st	**A.M.Swift**	(Swansea)	.		**A.Cappelletti**	(Banco Nacion)
10	4th	**G.H.Davies**	(Cambridge Univ)	.		**H.Porta (Capt)**	(Banco Nacion)
9	19th	**S.J.Smith**	(Sale)	.		**T.R.Landajo**	(Pueyrredon)
1	7th	**C.E.Smart**	(Newport)	.		**F.Morel**	(CA San Isidro)
2	1st	**S.G.F.Mills**	(Gloucester)	.		**J.Perez Cobo**	(San Isidro)
3	5th	**G.S.Pearce**	(Northampton)	.		**E.E.Rodriguez**	(El Tala, Cordoba)
4	31st	**W.B.Beaumont (Capt)**	(Fylde)	.		**A Iachetti**	(Hindu)
5	1st	**J.H.Fidler**	(Gloucester)	.		**E.N.Branca**	(CA San Isidro)
6	4th	**N.C.Jeavons**	(Moseley)	.		**T.Petersen**	(San Isidro)
7	16th	**M.Rafter**	(Bristol)	.		**E.Ure**	(Buenos Aires Univ)
8	19th	**J.P.Scott**	(Cardiff)	.		**G.Travaglini**	(CA San Isidro)

Referee: J-P.Bonnet   (France)

SCORERS:						
G.H.Davies	Try	(2nd)	4 - 0			
			4 - 3	**H.Porta**	Drop Goal	
			4 - 7	**M.Campo**	Try	
			Half-time			
			4 - 10	**H.Porta**	Penalty Goal	
C.R.Woodward	Try	(2nd)	8 - 10			
W.H.Hare	Conversion		10 - 10			
			10 - 14	**M.Campo**	Try	
			10 - 16	**H.Porta**	Conversion	
W.H.Hare	Penalty Goal		13 - 16			
			13 - 19	**T.R.Landajo**	Drop Goal	
C.R.Woodward	Try	(3rd)	17 - 19			
W.H.Hare	Conversion		19 - 19			

POINTS:						
C.R.Woodward	8 points	(12)		**H.Porta**	8 points	
W.H.Hare	7 points	(86)		**M.Campo**	8 points	
G.H.Davies	4 points	(8)		**T.R.Landajo**	3 points	

MATCH COMMENTARY:

For the first International of their first tour to Argentina, England made six changes, four in the pack, from the side beaten by France in March There were fears that the depleted pack might suffer, but they rose to the occasion. Huw Davies' early try looked easy, but it did not stay as easy as that. On three occasions Argentina gained a lead of six points, and England had to fight back to draw level and showed a lot of character in doing so. Steve Smith was a pillar of strength at scrum-half, and the backs defended well. Down by 7 points to 4 at half-time, they gave away another penalty but within two minutes were on level terms again when a high kick from Huw Davies was misfielded by Baetti and Clive Woodward gathered the loose ball and scored. With five minutes left, and England still six points adrift, Paul Dodge set up Clive Woodward's second try. Hare converted and the match was saved. The sides were evenly matched and, in truth, a draw was a just result.

2nd match   **ENGLAND   12 pts**   v   **ARGENTINA   6 pts**

Caps   Caps

15	12th	W.H.Hare	(Leicester)		D.Baetti	(Atletico Rosario)
14	11th	J.Carleton	(Orrell)		M.Campo	(Pueyrredon)
13	16th	P.W.Dodge	(Leicester)		R.Madero	(San Isidro)
12	10th	C.R.Woodward	(Leicester)		M.Loffreda	(San Isidro)
11	2nd	A.M.Swift	(Swansea)		A.Cappelletti	(Banco Nacion)
10	5th	G.H.Davies	(Cambridge Univ)		H.Porta (Capt)	(Banco Nacion)
9	20th	S.J.Smith	(Sale)		T.R.Landajo	(Pueyrredon)
1	8th	C.E.Smart	(Newport)		F.Morel	(CA San Isidro)
2	2nd	S.G.F.Mills	(Gloucester)		J.Perez Cobo	(San Isidro)
3	6th	G.S.Pearce	(Northampton)		E.E.Rodriguez	(El Tala, Cordoba)
4	32nd	W.B.Beaumont (Capt)	(Fylde)		A.Iachetti	(Hindu)
5	2nd	J.H.Fidler	(Gloucester)		E.N.Branca	(CA San Isidro)
6	5th	N.C.Jeavons	(Moseley)		T.Petersen	(San Isidro)
7	17th & last	M.Rafter	(Bristol)		E.Ure	(Buenos Aires Univ)
8	20th	J.P.Scott	(Cardiff)		G.Travaglini	(CA San Isidro)

J.P.Picardo (Hindu) for Madero - 55

Referee: J-P.Bonnet   (France)

SCORERS:

W.H.Hare	Penalty Goal		3 - 0		
W.H.Hare	Penalty Goal		6 - 0		
			Half-time		
G.H.Davies	Try	(3rd)	10 - 0		
W.H.Hare	Conversion		12 - 0		
			12 - 4	G.Travaglini	Try
			12 - 6	H.Porta	Conversion

POINTS:

W.H.Hare	8 points	(94)	G.Travaglini	4 points
G.H.Davies	4 points	(12)	H.Porta	2 points

MATCH COMMENTARY:

This was a very different match from the first International, and was played in very different conditions. Sunshine and a dry ball were replaced by drizzle, wet grass and heavy ground. England had the better of the first half, with all the territorial advantage. Tony Swift got as close to scoring in the corner as it is possible to get before a heroic last-ditch tackle by the Argentinian No 8, put him into the corner flag. A six point half-time lead from two Dusty Hare penalty goals was increased almost immediately when Steve Smith made a powerful break from a ruck and fed Huw Davies who scored his third International try. Dusty Hare converted and England looked to be comfortable winners with a 12 point lead. In response, the Argentinian pack raised their game and penned England back in their own half for long periods. In this time, Hugo Porta, uncharacteristically, missed two possible penalty goals and only an unlucky bounce denied Cappelletti, on the right wing, a try. Eventually, after more sustained pressure, England suffered the indignity of conceding a push-over try. But this seemed to have exhausted all Argentina's resources of determination and stamina, for thereafter the game fluctuated around midfield and there was no further scoring. The England defence had held out extremely well, with Hare, in particular, deserving of the highest praise. He did not put a foot wrong, and his line-kicking and fielding were immaculate.

11th match   **ENGLAND** **15 pts**   v   **AUSTRALIA** **11 pts**

	Caps					Caps		
15	3rd	W.M.H.Rose	(Cambridge Univ)	.		29th	P.E.McLean	(Queensland)
14	12th	J.Carleton	(Orrell)	.		10th	M.D.O'Connor	(Queensland)
13	11th	C.R.Woodward	(Leicester)	.		12th	A.G.Slack	(Queensland)
12	17th	P.W.Dodge	(Leicester)	.		9th	M.J.Hawker	(New South Wales)
11	25th	M.A.C.Slemen	(Liverpool)	.		17th	B.J.Moon	(Queensland)
10	6th	G.H.Davies	(Cambridge Univ)	.		6th	M.G.Ella	(New South Wales)
9	21st	S.J.Smith	(Sale)	.		36th & last	J.N.B.Hipwell	(New South Wales)
1	9th	C.E.Smart	(Newport)	.		17th	J.E.C.Meadows	(Victoria)
2	29th	P.J.Wheeler	(Leicester)	.		13th & last	C.M.Carberry	(Queensland)
3	7th	G.S.Pearce	(Northampton)	.		8th	A.M.D'Arcy	(Queensland)
4	33rd	W.B.Beaumont (Capt)	(Fylde)	.		6th	S.A.Williams	(New South Wales)
5	11th	M.J.Colclough	(Angouleme)	.		14th	P.W.McLean	(Queensland)
6	6th	N.C.Jeavons	(Moseley)	.		10th	S.P.Poidevin	(New South Wales)
7	1st	P.J.Winterbottom	(Headingley)	.		25th & last	G.Cornelsen	(New South Wales)
8	2nd	R.Hesford	(Bristol)	.		26th	M.E.Loane (Capt)	(Queensland)

1st   N.C.Stringer (Wasps) for Slemen - 63

Referee: A.Richards   (Wales)

SCORERS:

W.M.H.Rose	Penalty Goal		3 - 0			
			3 - 3	P.E.McLean	Penalty Goal	
W.M.H.Rose	Penalty Goal		6 - 3			
			Half-time			
			6 - 7	B.J.Moon	Try	
N.C.Jeavons	Try	(1st & last)	10 - 7			
P.W.Dodge	Conversion		12 - 7			
W.M.H.Rose	Penalty Goal		15 - 7			
			15 - 11	B.J.Moon	Try	

POINTS:

W.M.H.Rose	9 points	(27)	B.J.Moon	8 points	
N.C.Jeavons	4 points	(4)	P.E.McLean	3 points	
P.W.Dodge	2 points	(2)			

MATCH COMMENTARY:

An exciting game and a powerful display from the English pack, and Australia found, not for the first time on this tour that their forwards were under-strength. The Wallabies won the try count by two to one, but only one of the three, the Australian second, came from a direct attack. After a rather slow start, the first half served only to show that England were on top up front, especially in the lines-out, and that Steve Smith, at scrum-half, was in cracking form. It was a wet and windy day, and it was no surpise when Huw Davies dropped a pass and the Australian mid-field booted on and followed up at great speed for Brendan Moon to score his first try. England responded aggressively, and Mike Slemen almost crossed in the corner and was concussed for his trouble. While he was off the field, before being replaced by Nick Stringer, Mark Ella was caught in possession, Maurice Colclough and Peter Winterbottom drove on and Nick Jeavons scored a try, converted by Paul Dodge, to put England back in the lead. Rose's third penalty goal added more points before, in the closing minutes, Brendan Moon got his second try from a well-executed blind-side move by John Hipwell. Despite the try count, Australia were well beaten, but they had cause to reflect ruefully that Paul McLean had missed four out of a possible five penalty goal opportunities.

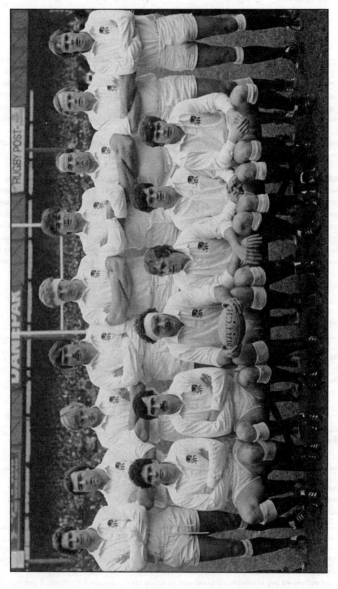

THE ENGLAND TEAM WHO BEAT AUSTRALIA AT TWICKENHAM ON JANUARY 2nd 1982

Standing: P.W.Dodge, G.S.Pearce, P.J.Winterbottom, R.Hesford, M.J.Colclough, N.C.Jeavons, C.E.Smart, P.J.Wheeler, C.R.Woodward,

Seated: W.M.H.Rose, M.A.C.Slemen, W.B.Beaumont (Captain), S.J.Smith, G.H.Davies, J.Carleton.

98th match

89th Calcutta Cup

ENGLAND 9 pts v SCOTLAND 9 pts

	Caps					Caps		
15	4th	W.M.H.Rose	(Cambridge Univ)	.	46th	A.R.Irvine (Capt)	(Heriot's FP)
14	13th	J.Carleton	(Orrell)	.	15th	K.W.Robertson	(Melrose)
13	12th	C.R.Woodward	(Leicester)	.	44th	J.M.Renwick	(Hawick)
12	18th	P.W.Dodge	(Leicester)	.	8th	D.I.Johnston	(Watsonians)
11	26th	M.A.C.Slemen	(Liverpool)	.	2nd	G.R.T.Baird	(Kelso)
10	7th	G.H.Davies	(Cambridge Univ)	.	16th	J.Y.Rutherford	(Selkirk)
9	22nd	S.J.Smith	(Sale)	.	13th	R.J.Laidlaw	(Jedforest)
1	10th	C.E.Smart	(Newport)	.	12th	J.Aitken	(Gala)
2	30th	P.J.Wheeler	(Leicester)	.	20th	C.T.Deans	(Hawick)
3	8th	G.S.Pearce	(Northampton)	.	10th	I.G.Milne	(Heriot's FP)
4	34th & last	W.B.Beaumont (Capt)	(Fylde)	.	9th	W.Cuthbertson	(Kilmarnock)
5	12th	M.J.Colclough	(Angouleme)	.	25th	A.J.Tomes	(Hawick)
6	7th	N.C.Jeavons	(Moseley)	.	9th	J.H.Calder	(Stewart's-Melville)
7	2nd	P.J.Winterbottom	(Headingley)	.	20th	D.G.Leslie	(Gala)
8	3rd	R.Hesford	(Bristol)	.	5th	I.A.M.Paxton	(Selkirk)

Referee: K.Rowlands   (Wales)

SCORERS:

		0 - 3	J.Y.Rutherford	Drop Goal
P.W.Dodge	Penalty Goal	3 - 3		
		3 - 6	A.R.Irvine	Penalty Goal
P.W.Dodge	Penalty Goal	6 - 6		
W.M.H.Rose	Penalty Goal	9 - 6		
		Half-time		
		9 - 9	A.R.Irvine	Penalty Goal

POINTS:

P.W.Dodge	6 points	(15)	A.R.Irvine	6 points
W.M.H.Rose	3 points	(3)	J.Y.Rutherford	3 points

MATCH COMMENTARY:

England were unchanged from the team which beat Australia and looked to have the beating of Scotland when they took the lead late in the first half, and held it for most of the second. The game, possible only due to the electric "blanket" at Murrayfield, was played at a fast and furious pace and there were many understandable mistakes in mid-field in the very cold conditions. The second half, with England holding a slender three point lead, was as tense as many other high-scoring matches, and there were thrills and errors in abundance, and still all at lightning pace. Nevertheless, both defences were almost faultless, however, and, in the last minute, Scotland launched yet another assault on the English line, but the ball was cleared to half-way, and all the signs and expectations were that England were going to win. In the middle of the field, in injury time, Colin Smart saw fit to knock Iain Paxton to the ground without the ball. Penalty awarded and Andy Irvine placed tha ball with meticulous care two metres inside the Scotland half, took the kick and the ball soared between the posts to ensure the draw. It was a phenomenal effort, worthy of rank with the best of Andy Irvine's audacious scores for Scotland, and Murrayfield, understandably, erupted - the "Auld Enemy" had been denied. This was to be the last match that Bill Beaumont was to play for England, although it was not known at the time. He had to retire on medical advice following a head injury sustained during the County Championship final on January 30th, two weeks later.

94th match   **ENGLAND   15 pts**   v   **IRELAND   16 pts**

	Caps					Caps		
15	5th	W.M.H.Rose	(Cambridge Univ)	.		7th	H.P.McNeill	(Dublin University)
14	14th	J.Carleton	(Orrell)	.		3rd	T.M.Ringland	(Queen's U Belfast)
13	13th	C.R.Woodward	(Leicester)	.		2nd	M.J.Kiernan	(Dolphin)
12	6th & last	A.M.Bond	(Sale)	.		5th	P.M.Dean	(St Mary's College)
11	27th	M.A.C.Slemen	(Liverpool)	.		3rd	M.C.Finn	(Cork Constitution)
10	8th	G.H.Davies	(Cambridge Univ)	.		10th	S.O.Campbell	(Old Belvedere)
9	23rd	S.J.Smith (Capt)	(Sale)	.		8th	R.J.M.McGrath	(Wanderers)
1	11th	C.E.Smart	(Newport)	.		11th	G.A.J.McLoughlin	(Shannon)
2	31st	P.J.Wheeler	(Leicester)	.		8th	C.F.Fitzgerald (Capt)	(St Mary's College)
3	9th	P.J.Blakeway	(Gloucester)	.		33rd	P.A.Orr	(Old Wesley)
4	1st	J.P.Syddall	(Waterloo)	.		41st	M.I.Keane	(Lansdowne)
5	13th	M.J.Colclough	(Angouleme)	.		3rd	D.G.Lenihan	(UC Cork)
6	8th	N.C.Jeavons	(Moseley)	.		54th	J.F.Slattery	(Blackrock College)
7	3rd	P.J.Winterbottom	(Headingley)	.		16th	J.B.O'Driscoll	(London Irish)
8	21st	J.P.Scott	(Cardiff)	.		32nd	W.P.Duggan	(Blackrock College)

Referee: A.M.Hosie   (Scotland)

SCORERS:

				0 - 3	S.O.Campbell	Penalty Goal
				0 - 7	H.P.McNeill	Try
	W.M.H.Rose	Penalty Goal		3 - 7		
				3 - 10	S.O.Campbell	Penalty Goal
				Half-time		
	W.M.H.Rose	Penalty Goal		6 - 10		
				6 - 14	G.A.J.McLoughlin	Try
				6 - 16	S.O.Campbell	Conversion
	W.M.H.Rose	Penalty Goal		9 - 16		
	M.A.C.Slemen	Try	(7th)	13 - 16		
	W.M.H.Rose	Conversion		15 - 16		

POINTS:

W.M.H.Rose	11 points	(41)	S.O.Campbell	8 points
M.A.C.Slemen	4 points	(28)	H.P.McNeill	4 points
			G.A.J.McLoughlin	4 points

MATCH COMMENTARY:

A much more one-sided game than the score would suggest, with Ireland controlling the game for most of the match with their "aged" but quicker and more mobile pack, with 198 caps between them, more than twice the total of the England pack, and the tactical expertise of Ollie Campbell.   Ireland were fully in command when they went 16 - 6 up in the middle of the second half, and Rose's penalty and Slemen's converted try in the very last minute, were mere consolation for England. Steve Smith did a good job in taking over from the departed Bill Beaumont, but Beaumont was obviously missed. Tony Bond, whose leg was broken in the corresponding fixture in the Grand Slam season two years ago, gained his sixth cap when Paul Dodge had to withdraw with hamstring trouble just before the match.   Jim Syddall, a stalwart of Waterloo and Lancashire, had the unenviable task of following Beaumont, but he certainly did as well as could be expected of him. England were well beaten by Ireland at Twickenham, again, for the fourth time in the last six visits.

57th match

ENGLAND 27 pts   v   FRANCE 15 pts

	Caps					Caps		
15	13th	W.H.Hare	(Leicester)	.		3rd	M.Sallefranque	(Dax)
14	15th	J.Carleton	(Orrell)	.		12th	S.Blanco	(Biarritz)
13	14th	C.R.Woodward	(Leicester)	.		2nd	P.Perrier	(Bayonne)
12	19th	P.W.Dodge	(Leicester)	.		12th	C.Belascain	(Bayonne)
11	28th	M.A.C.Slemen	(Liverpool)	.		9th	L.Pardo	(Bayonne)
10	2nd	L.Cusworth	(Leicester)	.		2nd	J-P.Lescarboura	(Dax)
9	24th	S.J.Smith (Capt)	(Sale)	.		2nd	G.Martinez	(Toulouse)
1	12th	C.E.Smart	(Newport)	.		3rd	D.Dubroca	(Agen)
2	32nd	P.J.Wheeler	(Leicester)	.		19th	P.Dintrans	(Tarbes)
3	10th	P.J.Blakeway	(Gloucester)	.		4th & last	J-P.Wolff	(Beziers)
4	1st	S.Bainbridge	(Gosforth)	.		7th	M.Carpentier	(Lourdes)
5	14th	M.J.Colclough	(Angouleme)	.		7th	L.Rodriguez	(Mont-de-Marsan)
6	9th	N.C.Jeavons	(Moseley)	.		45th	J-P.Rives (Capt)	(Toulouse)
7	4th	P.J.Winterbottom	(Headingley)	.		2nd	E.Buchet	(Nice)
8	22nd	J.P.Scott	(Cardiff)	.		22nd	J-L.Joinel	(Brive)

	4th	R.Hesford (Bristol) for Jeavons - 59		.

Referee:	M.D.M.Rea	(Ireland)

SCORERS:	W.H.Hare	Penalty Goal		3 - 0			
	W.H.Hare	Penalty Goal		6 - 0			
	C.R.Woodward	Try	(4th & last)	10 - 0			
	W.H.Hare	Conversion		12 - 0			
				12 - 4	L.Pardo	Try	
				12 - 6	M.Sallefranque	Conversion	
				Half-time			
	W.H.Hare	Penalty Goal		15 - 6			
				15 - 9	J-P.Lescarboura	Drop Goal	
	W.H.Hare	Penalty Goal		18 - 9			
				18 - 12	M.Sallefranque	Penalty Goal	
				18 - 15	M.Sallefranque	Penalty Goal	
	W.H.Hare	Penalty Goal		21 - 15			
	J.Carleton	Try	(4th)	25 - 15			
	W.H.Hare	Conversion		27 - 15			

POINTS:	W.H.Hare	19 points	(113)		M.Sallefranque	8 points
	C.R.Woodward	4 points	(16)		L.Pardo	4 points
	J.Carleton	4 points	(20)		J-P.Lescarboura	3 points

MATCH COMMENTARY:

Dusty Hare, recalled after the first choice, Nick Stringer cried off, was the thorn in France's side in this game. Hare scored 19 points for the second time in his international career, and took his points total in matches for England past 100, second only to Bob Hiller. He had a first class game as well, and this and the English forwards' denial of any worthwhile possession to France with which to get their backs moving proved to be the decisive factors. Both tries were well worked and well taken, and both were superbly converted.

87th match   **ENGLAND   17 pts**   v   **WALES   7 pts**

	Caps				Caps		
15	14th	W.H.Hare	(Leicester)	.	7th	G.Evans	(Maesteg)
14	16th	J.Carleton	(Orrell)	.	7th	R.A.Ackerman	(Newport)
13	15th	C.R.Woodward	(Leicester)	.	22nd	R.W.R.Gravell	(Llanelli)
12	20th	P.W.Dodge	(Leicester)	.	4th	A.J.Donovan	(Swansea)
11	29th	M.A.C.Slemen	(Liverpool)	.	8th	C.F.W.Rees	(London Welsh)
10	3rd	L.Cusworth	(Leicester)	.	17th	W.G.Davies (Capt)	(Cardiff)
9	25th	S.J.Smith (Capt)	(Sale)	.	15th	T.D.Holmes	(Cardiff)
1	13th	C.E.Smart	(Newport)	.	37th	G.Price	(Pontypool)
2	33rd	P.J.Wheeler	(Leicester)	.	14th	A.J.Phillips	(Cardiff)
3	11th	P.J.Blakeway	(Gloucester)	.	8th	I.Stephens	(Bridgend)
4	15th	M.J.Colclough	(Angouleme)	.	2nd	S.Sutton	(Pontypool)
5	2nd	S.Bainbridge	(Gosforth)	.	4th	R.D.Moriarty	(Swansea)
6	10th	N.C.Jeavons	(Moseley)	.	8th	R.C.Burgess	(Ebbw Vale)
7	5th	P.J.Winterbottom	(Headingley)	.	6th	J.R.Lewis	(Cardiff)
8	23rd	J.P.Scott	(Cardiff)	.	25th	J.Squire	(Pontypool)
				.	3rd	G.Williams (Bridgend) for Holmes - 49

Referee: F.Palmade   (France)

SCORERS:

M.A.C.Slemen	Try	(8th & last)	4 - 0	
W.H.Hare	Penalty Goal		7 - 0	
J.Carleton	Try	(6th)	11 - 0	
			11 - 4	J.R.Lewis Try
W.H.Hare	Penalty Goal		14 - 4	
			14 - 7	W.G.Davies Drop Goal
			Half-time	
W.H.Hare	Penalty Goal		17 - 7	

POINTS:

W.H.Hare	9 points	(122)	J.R.Lewis	4 points	
J.Carleton	4 points	(24)	W.G.Davies	3 points	
M.A.C.Slemen	4 points	(32)			

MATCH COMMENTARY:

Wales decided to give an unchanged England side their chance with the stiff breeze in the first half and found themselves seven points down at half-time. Each of the England wings had scored a try, although John Carleton's came from the scrum-half position, with Steve Smith under the ruck, and he ran in to score from 40 yards without a finger laid upon him. Mike Slemen, whose 29 caps today equalled Peter Squires record for a wing three-quarter, scored the first try in the thirteenth minute in the corner from an excellent scoring pass from Steve Smith. In the second half, try as they might having lost Terry Holmes with a shoulder injury, Wales could not breach the solid English defence. The England pack had settled very well since Bill Beaumont's untimely departure and, as against France, they dominated their opponents in this match - no easy task against the Welsh ! Steve Smith revelled in his captaincy and had played very well especially behind his dominant pack. But in the second half it was the solid defence of the English backs and Peter Winterbottom which prevented the Welsh from capitalising on their turn with the wind in their favour, but they could not even score a single point. No doubt, Terry Holmes' absence diluted the Welsh potency, but it was not the cause of their demise.

A margin of only ten points, but it was England's biggest margin of victory over Wales since 1921.

SUMMARY OF THE SEASON 1981 - 82:

The 1981-82 season was a seaon of uncertainty and change most of which arose out of the extraordinary sequence of injuries sustained by England players and potential players at various stages of the season. Not least of these, of course, was the tragedy of Bill Beaumont's withdrawal from the side to play Ireland and eventual total retirement from the game, in the middle of the season.

The season started on a reasonably optimistic note. The tour to Agrentina had been successful, and, although the opposition had been somewhat stiffer than had been anticipated by some, the side returned unbeaten having secured a draw in the first Test and won the second. The team for the match against Australia showed six changes from that which had represented England in both the Tests in Argentina. Wheeler, Colclough and Slemen who had been unable to tour, returned, Marcus Rose was preferred to "Dusty" Hare, John Scott had recently had surgery on an ankle and was replaced by Bob Hesford and Peter Winterbottom gained the first of many caps in the place of Mike Rafter who had retired after the tour. Australia had beaten Ireland (the eventual Triple Crown winners) and had lost to Wales (the season's shared Wooden Spoonists) and Scotland, so it was not a surprise when the England pack proved far to strong for the Australians, and the touring side were well beaten. With the Argentinian and the Australian scalps in the bag, so to speak, England embarked upon the Five Nations tournament with high hopes and buoyant optimism. It did not all go to plan for the unchanged England side at an extremely cold Murrayfield where only the "electric blanket" had made play possible at all. The match was exciting and tense, and with the second half scoreless until injury time, the atmosphere was electric when Andy Irvine slotted his dramatic long-range last-minute penalty goal. It was not all Colin Smart's fault for England were stumbling before that. Maurice Colclough injured a knee early in the second half, and knowing that Bill Beaumont had been unwell at the start of the match, declined to go off, and with their "boilerhouse" somewhat off-colour, the England pack's dominance began to decline. This may have had more to do with the result than Colin Smart's momentary indiscretion resulting in Andy Irvine's momentous penalty kick. At that point, the season was facing anti-climax anyway, for all hopes of a Triple Crown had gone. But, there was more to come. The team for the Ireland match was announced ten days beforehand and the Selectors assumed that Maurice Colclough would recover in time, brought Phil Blakeway back at tight-head instead of Gary Pearce and picked John Scott even though he had played only one first-class match since his surgery. Then Bill Beaumont had to withdraw from the side following his injury in the County Championship final the previous Saturday; on the prior Thursday, Paul Dodge pulled a hamstring and stepped down and Peter Wheeler strained his back in training. He eventually played, but Tony Bond and Jim Sydall came into the side at the last minute and Steve Smith was given the captaincy. With all that pre-match disruption, it was hardly surprising that England failed to match the Irish as a whole, and particularly the tactical expertise of Ollie Campbell. A few days later Beaumont's retirement form the game for medical reasons was announced and for Parc des Princes the selectors wielded the axe. Out went the Cambridge pair, Huw Davies and Marcus Rose, and back came Les Cusworth and Nick Stringer, each with one cap previously. Paul Dodge returned and Jim Syddall was thanked for his short notice services and Beaumont's place went to Steve Bainbridge. Then Nick Stringer had to withdraw, and fortunately, "Dusty" Hare was restored to full-back from where he scored 19 points, to equal his own International match record, and England won handsomely and for the second successive time at Parc des Princes, scoring their highest points total against France since 1914. The highlight of the season came in the last match when Wales were soundly beaten by the biggest margin since 1921. The resurgence in confidence and performance must be in large measure due to the influence of Mike Davis, the coach, and Steve Smith, the captain, pitched into the maelstrom, as he was, with little notice. In the last match he became England's most capped scrum-half beating Dickie Jeeps' record of 24 appearances. England had used only 21 players for the season (22 including Nick Stringer, a replacement in the match against Australia), and awarded new caps to Peter Winterbottom, Steve Bainbridge, Jim Syddall and Nick Stringer. Only two players left the International stage in the season. Bill Beaumont had gained 34 caps, a record for a lock forward, 32 of them in successive matches,. He had led England on a record 21 occasions to eleven victories which included the Grand Slam and Triple Crown in 1980 and four Calcutta Cups. He went on two Lions' tours to New Zealand in 1977 and as captain to South Africa in 1980, and played in seven Test matches. He became a BBC commentator, and with Ian Botham, provided many hours of entertainment on David Coleman's TV programme "A Question of Sport". He was later awarded the OBE. Tony Bond had gained six caps, but only one after he tragically broke his leg in the Ireland match during the Grand Slam season of 1980.

FIVE NATIONS CHAMPIONSHIP TABLE:

Won: **Retained Calcutta Cup**

		Played	Won	Lost	Drawn	Points: For	Against	Tries: For	Against	Title Points
1	Ireland	4	3	1	0	66	61	5	5	6
2 =	**ENGLAND**	4	2	1	1	68	47	5	4	5
2 =	Scotland	4	2	1	1	71	55	7	2	5
4 =	France	4	1	3	0	56	74	5	4	2
4 =	Wales	4	1	3	0	59	83	4	11	2

Home Games: lost to Ireland 15 - 16, (one try to two); beat Wales 17 - 7, (two tries to one)

Away Games: drew with Scotland 9 - 9, (no tries); beat France 27 - 15, (two tries to one)

58th match   **ENGLAND   15 pts**   v   **FRANCE   19 pts**

	Caps					Caps		
15	15th	**W.H.Hare**	(Leicester)	.		18th	**S.Blanco**	(Biarritz)
14	17th	**J.Carleton**	(Orrell)	.		4th	**P.Sella**	(Agen)
13	9th	**G.H.Davies**	(Coventry)	.		15th	**C.Belascain**	(Bayonne)
12	21st	**P.W.Dodge**	(Leicester)	.		12th	**D.Codorniou**	(Narbonne)
11	3rd	**A.H.Swift**	(Swansea)	.		4th	**P.Esteve**	(Narbonne)
10	4th	**L.Cusworth**	(Leicester)	.		4th	**D.Camberabero**	(La Voulte)
9	26th	**S.J.Smith (Capt)**	(Sale)	.		6th	**G.Martinez**	(Toulouse)
1	14th	**C.E.Smart**	(Newport)	.		11th	**P.Dospital**	(Bayonne)
2	34th	**P.J.Wheeler**	(Leicester)	.		25th	**P.Dintrans**	(Tarbes)
3	9th	**G.S.Pearce**	(Northampton)	.		52nd	**R.Paparemborde**	(Pau)
4	16th	**M.J.Colclough**	(Angouleme)	.		3rd	**J-C.Orso**	(Nice)
5	3rd	**S.Bainbridge**	(Gosforth)	.		2nd	**J.Condom**	(Boucau)
6	11th	**N.C.Jeavons**	(Moseley)	.		49th	**J-P.Rives (Capt)**	(Racing Club)
7	6th	**P.J.Winterbottom**	(Headingley)	.		11th	**L.Rodriguez**	(Mont-de-Marsan)
8	24th	**J.P.Scott**	(Cardiff)	.		26th	**J-L.Joinel**	(Brive)

5th   R.Hesford (Bristol) for Colclough - 50

Referee: D.I.H.Burnett   (Ireland)

SCORERS:

W.H.Hare	Penalty Goal		3 - 0				
W.H.Hare	Penalty Goal		6 - 0				
L.Cusworth	D'p Goal	(1st)	9 - 0				
			9 - 3		D.Camberabero	Penalty Goal	
			Half-time				
			9 - 7		P.Esteve	Try	
			9 - 9		S.Blanco	Conversion	
			9 - 13		R.Paparemborde	Try	
			9 - 15		S.Blanco	Conversion	
			9 - 19		P.Sella	Try	
W.H.Hare	Penalty Goal		12 - 19				
W.H.Hare	Penalty Goal		15 - 19				

POINTS:

W.H.Hare	12 points	(134)	R.Paparemborde, P.Sella,	4 points	
L.Cusworth	3 points	(3)	P.Esteve and S.Blanco	each	
			D.Camberabero	3 points	

MATCH COMMENTARY:

England were well beaten by a very capable French side, and by three tries to nil. The French backs had great pace and were innovative, and their forwards provided them with adequate possession. The English pack were mere shadows of their former selves, especially as Maurice Colclough had to leave the field through injury. "Dusty" Hare, normally metronomically accurate, was successful with only four out of ten penalty attempts, but had he been more successful it would have been a travesty of justice if England had, as a result, won the match. Didier Camberabero, too, had a very poor game, but he achieved the now unusual feat of scoring a penalty goal with a drop kick. Serge Blanco and Didier Codorniou between them really structured the French victory and England never threatened to score a try. France won for the fourth time in their last five visits to Twickenham. Three of Bob Hesford's five caps have been won as a replacement.

88th match   **ENGLAND   13 pts**   v   **WALES   13 pts**

	Caps					Caps		
15	16th	**W.H.Hare**	(Leicester)	.	1st	**M.A.Wyatt**	(Swansea)
14	18th	**J.Carleton**	(Orrell)	.	10th	**H.E.Rees**	(Neath)
13	10th	**G.H.Davies**	(Coventry)	.	14th	**D.S.Richards**	(Swansea)
12	22nd	**P.W.Dodge**	(Leicester)	.	1st	**M.G.Ring**	(Cardiff)
11	4th	**A.H.Swift**	(Swansea)	.	10th	**C.F.W.Rees**	(London Welsh)
10	5th	**L.Cusworth**	(Leicester)	.	1st	**M.Dacey**	(Swansea)
9	27th	**S.J.Smith (Capt)**	(Sale)	.	16th	**T.D.Holmes**	(Cardiff)
1	15th	**C.E.Smart**	(Newport)	.	8th & last	**C.Williams**	(Swansea)
2	3rd	**S.G.F.Mills**	(Gloucester)	.	1st	**W.J.James**	(Aberavon)
3	10th	**G.S.Pearce**	(Northampton)	.	39th	**G.Price**	(Pontypool)
4	1st	**S.B.Boyle**	(Gloucester)	.	2nd	**R.L.Norster**	(Cardiff)
5	4th	**S.Bainbridge**	(Gosforth)	.	6th	**R.D.Moriarty**	(Swansea)
6	12th	**N.C.Jeavons**	(Moseley)	.	26th	**J.Squire**	(Pontypool)
7	7th	**P.J.Winterbottom**	(Headingley)	.	1st	**D.F.Pickering**	(Llanelli)
8	25th	**J.P.Scott**	(Cardiff)	.	7th	**E.T.Butler (Capt)**	(Pontypool)

Referee: J.R.West   (Ireland)

SCORERS:

J.Carleton	Try	(7th & last)	4 - 0			
			4 - 3	**M.A.Wyatt**	Penalty Goal
			4 - 6	**M.Dacey**	Drop Goal
W.H.Hare	Penalty Goal		7 - 6		
L.Cusworth	D'p Goal	(2nd)	10 - 6		
			Half-time		
			10 - 9	**M.A.Wyatt**	Penalty Goal
			10 - 13	**J.Squire**	Try
W.H.Hare	Penalty Goal		13 - 13		

POINTS:

W.H.Hare	6 points	(140)	**M.A.Wyatt**	6 points
J.Carleton	4 points	(28)	**J.Squire**	4 points
L.Cusworth	3 points	J'(6)	**M.Dacey**	3 points

MATCH COMMENTARY:

England probably just deserved to win this match, although the scores were even in all respects. The revised England pack forced the Welsh onto the back foot, and prevented Malcolm Dacey and the Welsh backs from running the ball as had been Coach John Bevan's declared intention. Having established a solid lead, starting with John Carleton's classic try - the only memorable move of the match - England lost the advantage and allowed Wales to come back, and the Welsh need no such second invitation at Cardiff.   The match and the result were highly unsatisfactory for both teams and for the crowd, but at least England had broken a 20 year losing streak in Wales.   Clive Rowlands, Chairman of the Welsh Selectors, probably summed it all up when he said that the replay would be next Saturday but that he, for one, would not be attending ! England, surprisingly, have now played six away games without defeat.   "Dusty" Hare's second penalty goal took his International points total to 140, thus overtaking Bob Hiller's record of 138 points.

This was the first sponsored Home International, on this occasion by British Telecom.

99th match   **ENGLAND 12 pts**   v   **SCOTLAND 22 pts**

90th Calcutta Cup

	Caps					Caps		
15	17th	W.H.Hare	(Leicester)	.		4th	P.W.Dods	(Gala)
14	19th	J.Carleton	(Orrell)	.		2nd	J.A.Pollock	(Gosforth)
13	11th	G.H.Davies	(Coventry)	.		51st	J.M.Renwick	(Hawick)
12	23rd	P.W.Dodge	(Leicester)	.		23rd	K.W.Robertson	(Melrose)
11	5th	A.H.Swift	(Swansea)	.		11th	G.R.T.Baird	(Kelso)
10	10th	J.P.Horton	(Bath)	.		22nd	J.Y.Rutherford	(Selkirk)
9	28th & last	S.J.Smith	(Sale)	.		22nd	R.J.Laidlaw	(Jedforest)
1	16th	C.E.Smart	(Newport)	.		18th	J.Aitken (Capt)	(Gala)
2	35th	P.J.Wheeler	(Leicester)	.		29th	C.T.Deans	(Hawick)
3	11th	G.S.Pearce	(Northampton)	.		19th	I.G.Milne	(Heriot's FP)
4	2nd	S.B.Boyle	(Gloucester)	.		1st	T.J.Smith	(Gala)
5	5th	S.Bainbridge	(Gosforth)	.		12th	I.A.M.Paxton	(Selkirk)
6	13th	N.C.Jeavons	(Moseley)	.		18th	J.H.Calder	(Stewart's-Melville)
7	8th	P.J.Winterbottom	(Headingley)	.		24th	D.G.Leslie	(Gala)
8	26th	J.P.Scott (Capt)	(Cardiff)	.		11th	J.R.Beattie	(Glasgow Acad'ls)

Referee: T.F.Doocey   (New Zealand)

SCORERS:

J.P.Horton	D'p Goal	(3rd)	3 - 0				
			3 - 3	P.W.Dods	Penalty Goal		
			3 - 6	P.W.Dods	Penalty Goal		
			3 - 9	P.W.Dods	Penalty Goal		
W.H.Hare	Penalty Goal		6 - 9				
W.H.Hare	Penalty Goal		9 - 9				
			Half-time				
			9 - 13	R.J.Laidlaw	Try		
			9 - 15	P.W.Dods	Conversion		
W.H.Hare	Penalty Goal		12 - 15				
			12 - 18	K.W.Robertson	Drop Goal		
			12 - 22	T.J.Smith	Try		

POINTS:

W.H.Hare	9 points	(149)	P.W.Dods	11 points	
J.P.Horton	3 points	(9)	R.J.Laidlaw, T.J.Smith	4 points	
			K.W.Robertson	3 points	

MATCH COMMENTARY:

England dropped both half-backs following the draw in Cardiff, although Steve Smith was recalled to replace the injured Nigel Melville a few days before the game. The dropping of Les Cusworth was hard to understand because he had played well at Cardiff and his understanding with Paul Dodge and "Dusty" Hare had led to England's only try of the season - so far. But the English performance was lack-lustre and the lively Scottish pack ran them ragged. Roy Laidlaw scored the decisive try early in the second half to give Scotland the lead and by that time England were well beaten. Scotland achieved their highest ever score against England at Twickenham and this was only their second win in England since 1947. Four times have Scotland been to Twickenham since the War, looking for the Triple Crown, and four times have they failed - this time having lost their first three matches, they win !! - and England, in truth did little to prevent them doing so.

　　　　FIVE NATIONS CHAMPIONSHIP, 1982-83　　　　March 19th 1983, at Lansdowne Road

95th match　　　　　**ENGLAND**　**15 pts**　　v　　**IRELAND**　**25 pts**

	Caps					Caps		
15	18th	**W.H.Hare**	(Leicester)	.		13th	**H.P.McNeill**	(Blackrock College)
14	20th	**J.Carleton**	(Orrell)	.		8th	**T.M.Ringland**	(Ballymena)
13	16th	**C.R.Woodward**	(Leicester)	.		14th	**D.G.Irwin**	(Instonians)
12	24th	**P.W.Dodge**	(Leicester)	.		8th	**M.J.Kiernan**	(Dolphin)
11	1st	**D.M.Trick**	(Bath)	.		9th	**M.C.Finn**	(Cork Constitution)
10	11th	**J.P.Horton**	(Bath)	.		20th	**S.O.Campbell**	(Old Belvedere)
9	1st	**N.G.Youngs**	(Leicester)	.		14th	**R.J.M.McGrath**	(Wanderers)
1	17th & last	**C.E.Smart**	(Newport)	.		39th	**P.A.Orr**	(Old Wesley)
2	36th	**P.J.Wheeler**	(Leicester)	.		14th	**C.F.Fitzgerald (Capt)**	(St Mary's College)
3	12th	**G.S.Pearce**	(Northampton)	.		17th	**G.A.J.McLoughlin**	(Shannon)
4	3rd & last	**S.B.Boyle**	(Gloucester)	.		9th	**D.G.Lenihan**	(Cork Constitution)
5	6th	**S.Bainbridge**	(Gosforth)	.		48th	**M.I.Keane**	(Lansdowne)
6	14th & last	**N.C.Jeavons**	(Moseley)	.		60th	**J.F.Slattery**	(Blackrock College)
7	9th	**P.J.Winterbottom**	(Headingley)	.		22nd	**J.B.O'Driscoll**	(Manchester)
8	27th	**J.P.Scott (Capt)**	(Cardiff)	.		37th	**W.P.Duggan**	(Blackrock College)
						14th	A.J.P.Ward (St Mary's College) for Campbell -

Referee:　　J.B.Anderson　　(Scotland)

SCORERS:	**W.H.Hare**	Penalty Goal	3 - 0		
	W.H.Hare	Penalty Goal	6 - 0		
			6 - 4	**J.F.Slattery**	Try
	W.H.Hare	Penalty Goal	9 - 4		
	W.H.Hare	Penalty Goal	12 - 4		
			12 - 7	**S.O.Campbell**	Penalty Goal
			12 - 10	**S.O.Campbell**	Penalty Goal
			Half-time		
			12 - 14	**S.O.Campbell**	Try
			12 - 16	**S.O.Campbell**	Conversion
			12 - 19	**S.O.Campbell**	Penalty Goal
			12 - 22	**S.O.Campbell**	Penalty Goal
	W.H.Hare	Penalty Goal	15 - 22		
			15 - 25	**S.O.Campbell**	Penalty Goal

POINTS:	**W.H.Hare**	15 points	(164)	**S.O.Campbell**	21 points
				J.F.Slattery	4 points

MATCH COMMENTARY:

Yet again, despite three changes in the backs, England were well beaten and could not score a try. Ollie Campbell had an amazing match, scoring 21 points, to which England had no answer at all. This total is the highest ever individual points tally against England, beating Keith Jarrett's 19 for Wales in 1967. It was also Ireland's highest ever points total against England in Dublin. England showed no enterprise, no initiative and precious little inclination to face up to the challenge of the Irish. "Dusty" Hare's five penalty goals equalled his own and Alan Old's previous record. Had it not been for Hare's prodigious goal kicking, the defeat would have been an enormous embarrassment to the team and their now somewhat disillusioned supporters, not many of whom, mercifully, had travelled to Dublin.

SUMMARY OF THE SEASON 1982 - 83:

Not only did the season end with the Wooden Spoon for England because the side failed to win a match, and the only entry on the credit side was a draw with Wales in Cardiff, but, worse, in four matches, the side only managed to score one try, that by John Carleton in the drawn match.   This abject performance compares with the Championship in 1959 when England failed to score even one try, but at least in that season they won a game.   It was a sad, sad season, and it seemed to get progressively worse as the weeks dragged agonisingly by !

For the first match of the season, when France came toTwickenham, there were only three changes from the side which had beaten Wales convincingly at the end of the previous Championship.   Mike Slemen was dropped - and inexplicably remained so for the rest of the season - Huw Davies was called into the centre to replace Clive Woodward and Gary Pearce came back at tight-head because Phil Blakeway was still having problems with his neck vertebrae.   Nevertheless, the forwards were annihilated by their French opposite numbers, and in the front row in particular.   Just after half-time Maurice Colclough had to leave the field and that was the death knell for England.   There followed an electrifying spell when France scored 16 points in 13 minutes including three tries, and England were sunk without trace.   The selectors had wanted to make no changes for the trip to Cardiff, because Wales were in the process of restructuring the side, having come down firmly in favour of Malcolm Dacey in preference to Gareth Davies at outside-half.   In the event, injury forced two changes in the England pack, Steve Mills for Peter Wheeler and Steve Boyle for Maurice Colclough.   The result was a moderately better performance from the forwards, but it was a desperately dull and uninspiring match.   Only two aspects are worthy of mention; firstly, the try, early in the match was a cracker and came from a depth of understanding between the Leicester trio of Cusworth, Dodge and Hare which left John Carleton with a huge overlap on the right and in he went near the corner flag.   It was just as well that the try was memorable, because it was the only one for England throughout the season and there remained precious little else to cheer or even to laugh about.   Secondly, "Dusty" Hare became only the second England player after Bob Hiller to score 100 points for England.   It took Hiller 14 matches, it took Hare 13 !!

The selectors came to the surprising conclusion that both half-backs had to be cast in the role of scapegoat for the poor showing in Cardiff and proposed that John Horton return at fly-half to be partnered by the very promising 22-year-old, Nigel Melville.   They persisted with Tony Swift in preference to Mike Slemen, the recovered Peter Wheeler returned to hook, and the captaincy was handed to John Scott - a selectorial form of hospital pass.   As it was, someone had to go to Steve Smith, cap in hand, and ask him to turn out after all.   A less devoted enthusiast than Steve Smith might have had something to say !   But, although improvement was sought, it was not achieved and Scotland returned victorious from Twickenham for only the second time in 37 years !   The Scottish back row, as had the French front row, saw to it that England never got into their stride, and they chased and foraged and worried, terrier-like, all afternoon, and England quietly subsided, as has been said before, not with a bang, but a whimper.   Finally, for the trip to Dublin, and mindful of the pitfalls that awaited on that emerald turf, the selectors meddled again.   Huw Davies was dropped in favour of Clive Woodward, Tony Swift gave way, not to Mike Slemen, but to David Trick on the unfamiliar, to him, left wing !   Steve Smith was discarded for the second time in two selectorial meetings, and Nick Youngs was called up to partner not his club fly-half, Les Cusworth, but John Horton, who had failed against the Scots.   The pack remained the same.   The Irish, as you might say, saw them coming and none more clearly than the Irish half-backs Campbell and McGrath who set about demolishing England with a precision and clinical perception that was almost uncanny.   Again, England's back was broken when Ireland scored 12 points in 15 minutes shortly after half-time, and England slipped quietly into obscurity.   "Dusty" Hare was not to be distracted, and his five penalty goals were a worthy achievement.   Twenty one players were used during the season, plus one replacement, and three new caps were awarded.   Four players came to the end of their International careers.   Steve Smith, England's most capped scrum-half with 28 caps, had led the side five times, and had been on two Lions' tours as a replacement both times.   Colin Smart, 17 caps, had the choice of going for Welsh or English representation.   Nick Jeavons, earned 14 caps and Jilly Cooper's admiration as "the body beautiful", and Steve Boyle, with neither a beautiful body, nor dual nationality was awarded three caps, and was chosen for the 1983 Lions' tour.

There had been some debate as to whether Peter Wheeler or Ciaran Fitzgerald had the better credentials to lead the Lions in 1983, but after this season, Fitzgerald was the only candidate.   Seven English players were chosen to tour, with, in fairness, several not available, and three English replacements were called upon, Nick Jeavons, Nigel Melville (at that time uncapped), and the ubiquitous Steve Smith.

Maurice Colclough and Peter Winterbottom played in all four Tests, John Carleton in three, and Steve Bainbridge in two.

FIVE NATIONS CHAMPIONSHIP TABLE:

Won: **Nothing**

		Played	Won	Lost	Drawn	Points: For	Against	Tries: For	Against	Title Points
1 =	France	4	3	1	0	70	61	8	4	6
1 =	Ireland	4	3	1	0	71	67	5	6	6
3	Wales	4	2	1	1	64	53	7	3	5
4	Scotland	4	1	3	0	65	65	5	5	2
5	**ENGLAND**	4	0	3	1	55	79	1	8	1

Home Games: lost to France 15 - 19, (no tries to three); lost to Scotland 12 - 22, (no tries to two)

Away Games: drew with Wales 13 - 13, (one try each); lost to Ireland 15 - 25, (no tries to two)

13th match   **ENGLAND   15 pts**   v   **NEW ZEALAND   9 pts**

	Caps					Caps		
15	19th	W.H.Hare	(Leicester)	.		2nd	R.M.Deans	(Canterbury)
14	21st	J.Carleton	(Orrell)	.		34th & last	S.S.Wilson (Capt)	(Wellington)
13	17th	C.R.Woodward	(Leicester)	.		11th	S.T.Pokere	(Southland)
12	25th	P.W.Dodge	(Leicester)	.		2nd	C.I.Green	(Canterbury)
11	30th	M.A.C.Slemen	(Liverpool)	.		22nd	B.G.Fraser	(Wellington)
10	6th	L.Cusworth	(Leicester)	.		8th	W.R.Smith	(Canterbury)
9	2nd	N.G.Youngs	(Leicester)	.		2nd	A.J.Donald	(Wanganui)
1	1st	C.White	(Gosforth)	.		2nd	B.McGrattan	(Wellington)
2	37th	P.J.Wheeler (Capt)	(Leicester)	.		5th	H.R.Ried	(Bay of Plenty)
3	13th	G.S.Pearce	(Northampton)	.		2nd & last	S.A.Crichton	(Wellington)
4	17th	M.J.Colclough	(Wasps)	.		2nd & last	G.J.Braid	(Bay of Plenty)
5	7th	S.Bainbridge	(Gosforth)	.		2nd	A.Anderson	(Canterbury)
6	1st	P.D.Simpson	(Bath)	.		21st	M.W.Shaw	(Manawatu)
7	10th	P.J.Winterbottom	(Headingley)	.		7th	M.J.B.Hobbs	(Canterbury)
8	28th	J.P.Scott	(Cardiff)	.		24th	M.G.Mexted	(Wellington)
	2nd	N.C.Stringer (Wasps) for Carleton - 38		.	1st & only	M.Davie (Canterbury) for Crichton - 15		

Referee: A.M.Hosie   (Scotland)

SCORERS:

				0 - 3	R.M.Deans		Penalty Goal
W.H.Hare	Penalty Goal			3 - 3			
W.H.Hare	Penalty Goal			6 - 3			
				Half-time			
M.J.Colclough	Try	(1st & only)		10 - 3			
W.H.Hare	Conversion			12 - 3			
				12 - 7	M.Davie		Try
				12 - 9	R.M.Deans		Conversion
W.H.Hare	Penalty Goal			15 - 9			

POINTS:

W.H.Hare	11 points	(175)	R.M.Deans	5 points	
M.J.Colclough	4 points	(4)	M.Davie	4 points	

MATCH COMMENTARY:

England did extremely well to win a very hard match against an ill-disciplined New Zealand side. Nick Youngs, at scrum-half, had an excellent match, as he had had for the victorious Midlands Division side against the All Blacks ten days earlier, and Paul Simpson had an impressive and tough debut. This was the first time England had beaten New Zealand at Twickenham since Obolensky's match in 1936, and this time it was Maurice Colclough who added a try against the All Blacks to his many claims to fame. It was a very physical match indeed, several England players required stitches which had been inflicted by various devious means, and it was a pity that New Zealand allowed their normally high standards of self-discipline to slip to such an extent. The England performance, and the result, were a great encouragement to supporters and to the new England management team which had taken over at the beginning of the season, Derek Morgan as Chairman of Selectors, Dick Greenwood as Coach and Peter Wheeler as Captain. After last season's catastrophe in the Five Nations, this result came as a very welcome surprise and, hopefully, a portent of better things to come.

THE ENGLAND TEAM WHO BEAT NEW ZEALAND AT TWICKENHAM ON NOVEMBER 19th 1983
Standing: W.H.Hare, N.G.Youngs, G.S.Pearce, P.D.Simpson, S.Bainbridge, M.J.Colclough, J.P.Scott, P.J.Winterbottom, C.White,
Seated: L.Cusworth, P.W.Dodge, M.A.C.Slemen, P.J.Wheeler (Captain), C.R.Woodward, J.Carleton

100th match

91st Calcutta Cup

ENGLAND 6 pts   v   SCOTLAND 18 pts

	Caps					Caps		
15	20th	W.H.Hare	(Leicester)	.		7th	P.W.Dods	(Gala)
14	22nd	J.Carleton	(Orrell)	.		24th	K.W.Robertson	(Melrose)
13	12th	G.H.Davies	(Wasps)	.		3rd	A.E.Kennedy	(Watsonians)
12	18th	C.R.Woodward	(Leicester)	.		19th	D.I.Johnston	(Watsonians)
11	31st & last	M.A.C.Slemen	(Liverpool)	.		14th	G.R.T.Baird	(Kelso)
10	7th	L.Cusworth	(Leicester)	.		25th	J.Y.Rutherford	(Selkirk)
9	3rd	N.G.Youngs	(Leicester)	.		25th	R.J.Laidlaw	(Jedforest)
1	2nd	C.White	(Gosforth)	.		21st	J.Aitken (Capt)	(Gala)
2	38th	P.J.Wheeler (Capt)	(Leicester)	.		32nd	C.T.Deans	(Hawick)
3	14th	G.S.Pearce	(Northampton)	.		22nd	I.G.Milne	(Heriot's)
4	18th	M.J.Colclough	(Wasps)	.		20th	W.Cuthbertson	(Harlequins)
5	8th	S.Bainbridge	(Gosforth)	.		35th	A.J.Tomes	(Hawick)
6	2nd	P.D.Simpson	(Bath)	.		21st	J.H.Calder	(Stewart's-Melville)
7	11th	P.J.Winterbottom	(Headingley)	.		26th	D.G.Leslie	(Gala)
8	29th	J.P.Scott	(Cardiff)	.		15th	I.A.M.Paxton	(Selkirk)
	1st	J.P.Hall (Bath) for Winterbottom - 50		.		13th	J.R.Beattie (G'gow A) for Cuthbertson - 40	
				.		4th	J.A.Pollock (Gosforth) for Kennedy - 60	
	Referee:	D.I.H.Burnett	(Ireland)	.				

SCORERS:

			0 - 4	D.I.Johnston	Try
			0 - 6	P.W.Dods	Conversion
W.H.Hare		Penalty Goal	3 - 6		
			Half-time		
			3 - 10	A.E.Kennedy	Try
			3 - 12	P.W.Dods	Conversion
W.H.Hare		Penalty Goal	6 - 12		
			6 - 15	P.W.Dods	Penalty Goal
			6 - 18	P.W.Dods	Penalty Goal

POINTS:

W.H.Hare	6 points	(181)	P.W.Dods	10 points
			D.I.Johnston	4 points
			A.E.Kennedy	4 points

MATCH COMMENTARY:

England went to Murrayfield brimful of confidence following their impressive win over New Zealand, but the Scots had very different ideas, and proceeded to do exactly what England had planned to do - dominate up front. The forward battle was intriguing with Scotland gradually and visibly gaining the ascendancy, and when they had surrendered the initiative, England had no other recourse to bring into play. John Rutherford had a magnificent game and the Scottish back row were too quick by half for their English opposite numbers and for the English half-backs. "Dusty" Hare had an off day with the boot, kicking only two out of eight penalty goal attempts and fate certainly and correctly decreed that England were not going to win the match that way. The Scottish pack, as they had been against New Zealand, were very fast in the loose and rucked very effectively, drawing the English back row in and creating space for themselves. It was a very impressive demonstration. "Dusty" Hare's second penalty goal took his total for England to 50 penalty goals, a unique achievement. This was the 100th match between England and Scotland since the first took place on March 27th 1871 at Raeburn Place, Edinburgh This, of course, was not the 100th match for the Calcutta Cup which was first played for in 1879.

96th match   **ENGLAND   12 pts**   v   **IRELAND   9 pts**

		Caps					Caps		
15	21st	**W.H.Hare**	(Leicester)	.		16th	**H.P.McNeill**	(Blackrock College)
14	23rd	**J.Carleton**	(Orrell)	.		11th	**T.M.Ringland**	(Ballymena)
13	1st	**B.Barley**	(Wakefield)	.		9th	**M.J.Kiernan**	(Lansdowne)
12	19th	**C.R.Woodward**	(Leicester)	.		10th	**M.C.Finn**	(Cork Constitution)
11	1st	**R.Underwood**	(RAF/Leicester)	.		4th	**K.D.Crossan**	(Instonians)
10	8th	**L.Cusworth**	(Leicester)	.		15th	**A.J.P.Ward**	(St Mary's College)
9	4th	**N.G.Youngs**	(Leicester)	.		1st	**J.A.P.Doyle**	(Greystones)
1	3rd	**C.White**	(Gosforth)	.		42nd	**P.A.Orr**	(Old Wesley)
2	39th	**P.J.Wheeler (Capt)**	(Leicester)	.		2nd	**H.T.Harbison**	(Bective Rangers)
3	12th	**P.J.Blakeway**	(Gloucester)	.		1st	**D.C.Fitzgerald**	(Lansdowne)
4	19th	**M.J.Colclough**	(Wasps)	.		50th	**M.I.Keane**	(Lansdowne)
5	9th	**S.Bainbridge**	(Gosforth)	.		12th	**D.G.Lenihan**	(Cork Constitution)
6	2nd	**J.P.Hall**	(Bath)	.	2nd & last	**W.R.Duncan**	(Malone)
7	5th	**D.H.Cooke**	(Harlequins)	.		25th	**J.B.O'Driscoll**	(London Irish)
8	30th	**J.P.Scott**	(Cardiff)	.		40th	**W.P.Duggan (Capt)**	(Blackrock College)

1st & only   S.Redfern (Leicester) for White - 59

Referee: R.Hourquet   (France)

SCORERS:	**W.H.Hare**	Penalty Goal		3 - 0			
				3 - 3	**A.J.P.Ward**	Penalty Goal
	L.Cusworth	D'p Goal	(3rd)	6 - 3		
	W.H.Hare	Penalty Goal		9 - 3		
				9 - 6	**A.J.P.Ward**	Penalty Goal
				Half-time		
	W.H.Hare	Penalty Goal		12 - 6		
				12 - 9	**A.J.P.Ward**	Penalty Goal

POINTS:	**W.H.Hare**	9 points	(190)		**A.J.P.Ward**	9 points
	L.Cusworth	3 points	(9)			

MATCH COMMENTARY:

Five changes were made from the side which had so abjectly lost their way against Scotland at Murrayfield, two weeks previously. In the backs, Bryan Barley replaced Huw Davies in the centre, and Rory Underwood succeeded Mike Slemen for his first cap in what was to be a record-breaking career. Phil Blakeway replaced Gary Pearce, and with Peter Winterbottom injured, David Cooke returned on the open side. and Paul Simpson gave way to club-mate John Hall.   This was a much more exciting and entertaining game than the score might suggest. Both fly-halves tried, and to some extent succeeded, in getting their back lines moving and there was some good running both on and off the ball. Rory Underwood had little to do (and not for the last time in his illustrious career) for most of the passing movements went to John Carleton's wing, and Brian Barley and John Hall made good impressions. But for the fourth successive Championship game, England failed to score a try. But at half-time with the score 9 points 6 in England's favour, there was every possibility that Les Cusworth's expansive game might become England's pattern of play in the second-half, or if that hope was a forlorn one, perhaps Tony Ward would be able to ignite the Irish backs. Alas, neither hope was to be fulfilled, and all the second-half could offer was a penalty goal for each side instead of the anticipated spectacular bucketful of tries !!

FIVE NATIONS CHAMPIONSHIP, 1983-84

59th match   # ENGLAND 18 pts   v   # FRANCE 32 pts

	Caps					Caps		
15	22nd	**W.H.Hare**	(Leicester)	.		24th	**S.Blanco**	(Biarritz)
14	24th	**J.Carleton**	(Orrell)	.		2nd	**J.Begu**	(Dax)
13	20th	**C.R.Woodward**	(Wakefield)	.		13th	**P.Sella**	(Agen)
12	2nd	**B.Barley**	(Wakefield)	.		21st	**D.Codorniou**	(Narbonne)
11	2nd	**R.Underwood**	(RAF/Leicester)	.		13th	**P.Esteve**	(Narbonne)
10	9th	**L.Cusworth**	(Leicester)	.		10th	**J-P.Lescarboura**	(Dax)
9	5th	**N.G.Youngs**	(Leicester)	.		20th	**J.Gallion**	(Toulon)
1	4th & last	**C.White**	(Gosforth)	.		15th	**P.Dospital**	(Bayonne)
2	40th	**P.J.Wheeler (Capt)**	(Leicester)	.		32nd	**P.Dintrans**	(Tarbes)
3	13th	**P.J.Blakeway**	(Gloucester)	.		6th	**D.Dubroca**	(Agen)
4	20th	**M.J.Colclough**	(Wasps)	.		10th	**A.Lorieux**	(Grenoble)
5	10th	**S.Bainbridge**	(Gosforth)	.		11th	**J.Condom**	(Boucau)
6	3rd	**J.P.Hall**	(Bath)	.		58th	**J-P.Rives (Capt)**	(Racing Club)
7	12th	**P.J.Winterbottom**	(Headingley)	.		14th	**D.Erbani**	(Agen)
8	31st	**J.P.Scott**	(Cardiff)	.		35th	**J-L.Joinel**	(Brive)
				.		6th	J-C.Orso (Nice) for Lorieux - 32	

Referee: A.M.Hosie   (Scotland)

SCORERS:

W.H.Hare	Penalty Goal		3 - 0			
			3 - 4	**D.Codorniou**	Try	
			3 - 6	**J-P.Lescarboura**	Conversion	
W.H.Hare	Penalty Goal		6 - 6			
			6 - 9	**J-P.Lescarboura**	Penalty Goal	
			Half-time			
R.Underwood	Try	(1st)	10 - 9			
W.H.Hare	Conversion		12 - 9			
			12 - 13	**P.Sella**	Try	
			12 - 15	**J-P.Lescarboura**	Conversion	
			12 - 18	**J-P.Lescarboura**	Drop Goal	
			12 - 22	**P.Esteve**	Try	
			12 - 26	**J.Begu**	Try	
			12 - 30	**J.Gallion**	Try	
			12 - 32	**J-P.Lescarboura**	Conversion	
W.H.Hare	Try	(2nd & last)	16 - 32			
W.H.Hare	Conversion		18 - 32			

POINTS:

W.H.Hare	14 point	(204)		**J-P.Lescarboura**	12 points
R.Underwood	4 points	(4)	**P.Sella, J.Begu, P.Esteve**		
			J.Gallion and D.Codorniou		4 points each

MATCH COMMENTARY:

The two earlier Five Nations matches had hinted at major weaknesses in the England side, and these were all cruelly exposed in Paris on a warm spring afternoon. The French just cut loose and scored five tries to England's opportunistic two and won the match decisively. Each of the four French three-quarters scored tries in as fine an exhibition of running back play as one could wish to see. At half-time, the score was 9 points to 6 to France but things were already looking ominous for England. The French front five were coming to the fore, and the French backs were beginning to get faster and better ball. But in the second-half, England actually took the lead with Rory Underwood's first try for England which was well taken with clever dribbling and a smart pick-up before he glided past Begu and cut inside Blanco. The conversion gave Englands a three point lead and the faintest glimmer of hope. But it was short-lived, for France turned on the charm and ran in four tries before England again got on to the scoresheet, and Hare's try after all that was a meagre consolation. For the fourth time in eight visits to Paris, England have concede at least 30 points and five tries or more in the match.

"Dusty" Hare , when he kicked his second penalty goal in the first half, became the first England player to score 200 points in International Rugby. A remarkable achievement accomplished during the course of 22 matches.

89th match   **ENGLAND 15 pts**   v   **WALES 24 pts**

	Caps				Caps		
15	23rd	W.H.Hare	(Leicester)	.	4th & last	H.Davies	(Bridgend)
14	25th	J.Carleton	(Orrell)	.	5th	M.H.Titley	(Bridgend)
13	3rd	B.Barley	(Wakefield)	.	16th	R.A.Ackerman	(London Welsh)
12	21st & last	C.R.Woodward	(Leicester)	.	5th	B.Bowen	(South Wales P
11	3rd	R.Underwood	(RAF/Leicester)	.	5th	A.M.Hadley	(Cardiff)
10	10th	L.Cusworth	(Leicester)	.	9th	M.Dacey	(Swansea)
9	6th & last	N.G.Youngs	(Leicester)	.	20th	T.D.Holmes	(Cardiff)
1	1st	P.A.G.Rendall	(Wasps)	.	12th	I.Stephens	(Bridgend)
2	41st & last	P.J.Wheeler (Capt)	(Leicester)	.	3rd	M.J.Watkins (Capt)	(Newport)
3	14th	P.J.Blakeway	(Gloucester)	.	5th	I.H.Eidman	(Cardiff)
4	21st	M.J.Colclough	(Wasps)	.	8th	S.J.Perkins	(Pontypool)
5	11th	S.Bainbridge	(Gosforth)	.	9th	R.L.Norster	(Cardiff)
6	1st & only	A.F.Dun	(Wasps)	.	10th	R.D.Moriarty	(Swansea)
7	13th	P.J.Winterbottom	(Headingley)	.	9th	D.F.Pickering	(Llanelli)
8	32nd	J.P.Scott	(Cardiff)	.	15th	E.T.Butler	(Pontypool)

Referee: F.Palmade   (France)

SCORERS:

W.H.Hare	Penalty Goal	3 - 0				
		3 - 3		H.Davies	Penalty Goal	
W.H.Hare	Penalty Goal	6 - 3				
		6 - 6		H.Davies	Penalty Goal	
W.H.Hare	Penalty Goal	9 - 6				
		Half-time				
		9 - 9		H.Davies	Penalty Goal	
		9 - 13		A.M.Hadley	Try	
		9 - 15		H.Davies	Conversion	
		9 - 18		H.Davies	Penalty Goal	
W.H.Hare	Penalty Goal	12 - 18				
W.H.Hare	Penalty Goal	15 - 18				
		15 - 21		M.Dacey	Drop Goal	
		15 - 24		M.Dacey	Drop Goal	

POINTS:

W.H.Hare	15 points	(219)	H.Davies	14 points	
			M.Dacey	6 points	
			A.M.Hadley	4 points	

MATCH COMMENTARY:
The margin was narrow but the defeat was total in this match as Wales achieved their highest ever points total at Twickenham. England were beaten comprehensively up front and especially in the lines-out where they did not win a throw-in until after half-time. Only "Dusty" Hare emerged with any credit, succeeding with all five of his goal attempts. Hare had scored 44 points during the Five Nations season surpassing his own record of 42 points. The season, which had started so promisingly with the win over New Zealand in November, had disappointed from that point on, and England finished fourth in the Championship Table, scoring only two tries and conceding eight.

SUMMARY OF THE SEASON - 1983 - 84:

Once again, England strove hard to disappoint their supporters by providing a very promising start to the season in beating New Zealand for only the second time ever at Twickenham, then losing away to Scotland, beating Ireland at home in a cheerful match, and finally losing heavily, and with some embarrassment, to both France and Wales. The New Zealand game was, indeed, a false dawn and those who took heart from it had failed to recognise the effect on the All Black's performance of being without their first choice front five, all of whom were unable to tour. The All Blacks resort to almost overt intimidation did them no credit, and the satisfaction born of England's ability to overcome that aspect of their game failed to recognise that in other areas, England were somewhat exposed. In due course the Five Nations Championship revealed just those fundamental weaknesses, and England's performance was far from creditable. Maybe they were a trifle unfortunate in having to face a very confident Scottish side at Murrayfield for the first match of the Championship. The Scots taught England a lesson in mobility, ball recycling, and how to retain and gain possession, but, undeniably, thereafter, their season, to coin a phrase, fell apart This, perhaps inherited, problem was particularly unfortunate for the new management team of Derek Morgan and Dick Greenwood The side to face New Zealand contained two new caps, Paul Simpson of Bath and Colin White, the Gosforth loose-head prop. Simpsom was exactly the right choice for this match for he revelled in the physical contact, within or without the rules, written or unspoken, and thoroughly enjoyed himself - he was rarely seen throughout the match without a broad grin on his face which, alone, would have frustrated the All Blacks and probably contributed to their demise. Colin White was an enormously courageous but very light-weight loose-head prop, with three fingers missing on one hand ! For the trip to Murrayfield, only one change was made, Huw Davies coming in to the centre for Paul Dodge. The truth of the matter is that, no matter what side England had chosen, Scotland, en route to their Grand Slam, would have destroyed England's season in any event. The game against Ireland gave England their only win of the Championship - but no tries - and continually promised much but failed to deliver. The Irish, of course, were on their way to a whitewash, so the inability to score a try against them and to win by only, in effect, a drop goal, does not say much for England's ability, even though the match was entertaining. Peter Winterbottom returned from injury to face France at Parc des Princes and probably wished that he hadn't. It was a very poor display by England in allowing the French to cut loose in the last quarter of the match to inflict nothing short of humiliation on the visitors. Finally Wales, at Twickenham, were not going to miss the opportunity to put one over on England, and indeed they did not. The margin 24 points to 15 was not great, but Wales achieved their highest ever points total at Twickenham and completely dictated the course of events. "Dusty" Hare scored with all his penalty attempts and had he not done so, the margin would have reflected more accurately the totality of the defeat. Howell Davies persistently kept pace with Hare's penalties, and then Wales took over in the second half and there was nothing that England could do about it - except "Dusty" Hare who kicked the goals available to him, but Malcolm Dacey's two drop goals towards the end were testimony to his effective control the match. Hare had had a memorable season, scoring 44 points and so beating his own record, and becoming the first player to score 50 penalty goals and exceed 200 points in total, in Internationals for England.

Twenty four players were called upon by England for the five matches of the season and, in addition, two players acted as replacements without being original selections. For the Five Nations Championship, twenty three players and one additional replacement, were involved. Seven new caps were awarded during the season, the most notorious of whom were Rory Underwood, Paul Rendall and John Hall. Similarly seven players pulled on the white jersey for the last time. Peter Wheeler, with 41 caps, just failed to emulate John Pullin's record of 42 caps as England's most capped hooker and, at the time of his retirement was England's third highest cap winner, one less than John Pullin, and two less thanTony Neary's 43.   He had captained England on five occasions, went on two Lions' tours (1977 and 1980) and played in seven Test matches. He is an Insurance Broker. Mike Slemen was England's most capped wing at that time, having won 31 caps. He went on one Lions' tour in 1980 and played in one Test, He is a schoolteacher at Merchant Taylor's, Crosby and had many offers from Rugby League Clubs. Clive Woodward, one of the most elusive of post-war centres, earned 21 caps, and went on the 1980 and 1983 Lions' tours playing in two Tests. He was employed by Rank Xerox and maintains his association with the game in various coaching roles. Nick Youngs, the resilient Leicester scrum-half, earned six caps, Colin White, a Newcastle PE teacher, won four caps at loose-head prop. Andy Dun won only one cap, as did Steve Redfern as a replacement. For those remaining, and available, the forthcoming tour to South Africa would be, in all likelihood, as severe a test as any they had faced in their careers to date.

FIVE NATIONS CHAMPIONSHIP TABLE:

Won: **Nothing**

		Played	Won	Lost	Drawn	Points: For	Against	Tries: For	Against	Title Points
1	Scotland	4	4	0	0	86	36	10	3	8
2	France	4	3	1	0	90	67	9	5	6
3	Wales	4	2	2	0	67	60	5	3	4
4	**ENGLAND**	4	1	3	0	51	83	2	8	2
5	Ireland	4	0	4	0	39	87	1	8	0

Home Games: beat Ireland 12 - 9, (no tries); lost to Wales 15 - 24, (no tries to one)

Away Games: lost to Scotland 6 - 18, (no tries to two): lost to France 18 - 32, (two tries to five)

ENGLAND TOUR TO SOUTH AFRICA - 1984

THE TOUR PARTY:

Tour Manager:	C.R.Jacobs	Team Manager:	W.G.D.Morgan	Captain:		J.P.Scott	
		Coach:	J.R.H.Greenwood				

Full-backs:	W.H.Hare	(Leicester)	23 caps	Forwards:	P.J.Blakeway	(Gloucester)	14 caps
	N.C.Stringer	(Wasps)	2 caps		S.E.Brain	(Coventry)	no caps
					C.J.S.Butcher	(Harlequins)	no caps
Three-quarters:	M.D.Bailey	(Cambridge U)	no caps		D.A.Cusani	(Orrell)	no caps
	S.B.Burnhill	(Loughboro' C)	no caps		J.H.Fidler	(Gloucester)	2 caps
	P.W.Dodge	(Leicester)	25 caps		J.P.Hall	(Bath)	3 caps
	J.A.Palmer	(Bath)	no caps		S.G.F.Mills	(Gloucester)	3 caps
	A.H.Swift	(Swansea)	5 caps		G.S.Pearce	(Northampton)	14 caps
	D.M.Trick	(Bath)	1 cap		M.Preedy	(Gloucester)	no caps
					P.A.G.Rendall	(Wasps)	1 cap
Half-backs:	G.H.Davies	(Wasps)	12 caps		G.W.Rees	(Nottingham)	no caps
	R.J.Hill	(Bath)	no caps		J.P.Scott	(Cardiff)	32 caps
	J.P.Horton	(Bath)	11 caps		M.C.Teague	(Gloucester)	no caps
	N.C.Youngs	(Leicester)	6 caps		P.J.Winterbottom	(Headingley)	13 caps
Replacement:	B.Barley	(Wakefield)	3 caps				

In the face of much criticism, and in spite of covert political pressure, the RFU decided that the tour to South Africa should go ahead, but probably with hindsight, in the light of the results, later wished that they had not. Many players were unable to tour (not for political reasons, only Ralph Knibbs of Bristol stood up to be counted in that respect) and the squad was relatively inexperienced. Ten of the twenty six players were uncapped before the tour and seven gained their first caps in South Africa.

By far England's best performance was in the match against Western Province, the third of the tour. Western Province were the defending Currie Cup Champions, and although the match was drawn fifteen points each, England scored two tries to their opponents none. The side showed imagination and enterprise to a degree not seen in an England side since the 1980 Grand Slam season, and, even more importantly showed determination and courage in the tackle, really for the only time on the tour. In the Test matches, in particular, the first time tackling especially in midfield was way below international standard, and Danie Gerber, above others, relished the opportunities which that shortcoming offered him, and scored four tries in those two Test Matches.

It was in this series of matches that the South African Rugby Union began to bow to the inevitable and to recognise that the practise of *apartheid* could no longer be perpetrated on the rugby field, and two coloured players appeared in the Springbok jersey in both Tests. Avril Williams of Western Province was one, and the other was the immaculate Errol Tobias of Boland. Tobias was no stranger to British rugby having played in both matches against Ireland in 1981, toured South Wales with the Barbarians at Easter in 1983 and visited Britain with the Proteas on two occasions and played for them against the Lions in 1984. He played four times against England on this tour, but never more impressively than in the second Test when his breaks and half-breaks and immaculate passing presented Danie Gerber with three tries before he crowned his afternoon with a magnificent try of his own.

The tour was a sobering experience for England, learning yet again, at first hand, of the increasing superiority of southern-hemisphere rugby Eight players quit the International stage at the end of the tour most conspicuous of whom were John Scott, 34 caps and four times captain, who had played at No 8 on a record 31 occasions, and was to captain his club, Cardiff for four successive seasons. "Dusty" Hare, with 25 caps was England's most-capped full-back and had set the Individual points scoring record of 240 points, including 67 penalty goals. Others retiring were John Horton, 13 caps, Tony Swift, six caps, John Fidler, four caps, David Trick, two caps, and Malcolm Preedy whose only cap made him the youngest ever England prop at 23 years and 8 months.

TOUR RESULTS:

May 19th	Currie Cup "B" Section	at Durban	WON	31 - 21	(four tries to three)
May 23rd	South African Federation	at Stellenbosch	WON	23 - 21	(two tries each)
May 26th	Western Province	at Cape Town	DREW	15 - 15	(two tries to nil)
May 29th	South African Rugby Association	at East London	WON	30 - 8	(five tries to two)
June 2nd	**SOUTH AFRICA**	**at Port Elizabeth**	**LOST**	**15 - 33**	**(no tries to three)**
June 5th	Country Districts	at Sasolburg	WON	33 - 12	(six tries to two)
June 9th	**SOUTH AFRICA**	**at Johannesburg**	**LOST**	**9 - 35**	**(no tries to six)**

8th match   **ENGLAND**   **15 pts**   v   **SOUTH AFRICA**   **33 pts**

Caps   Caps

15	24th	**W.H.Hare**	(Leicester)	.	5th	**J.W.Heunis**	(Northern Transvaal)
14	1st	**M.D.Bailey**	(Cambridge Univ)	.	1st	**A.P.Williams**	(Western Province)
13	1st	**J.A.Palmer**	(Bath)	.	12th	**D.M.Gerber**	(Eastern Province)
12	13th	**G.H.Davies**	(Wasps)	.	1st	**J.V.Villet**	(Western Province)
11	2nd & last	**D.M.Trick**	(Bath)	.	3rd	**C.J.du Plessis**	(Western Province)
10	12th	**J.P.Horton**	(Bath)	.	3rd	**E.G.Tobias**	(Boland)
9	1st	**R.J.Hill**	(Bath)	.	16th	**D.J.Serfontein**	(Western Province)
1	1st & only	**M.Preedy**	(Gloucester)	.	8th	**O.W.Oosthuizen**	(Transvaal)
2	4th	**S.G.F.Mills**	(Gloucester)	.	1st	**C.D.Rogers**	(Transvaal)
3	15th	**P.J.Blakeway**	(Gloucester)	.	4th	**P.G.du Toit**	(Western Province)
4	33rd	**J.P.Scott (Capt)**	(Cardiff)	.	1st	**S.W.P.Burger**	(Western Province)
5	3rd	**J.H.Fidler**	(Gloucester)	.	1st	**R.G.Visagie**	(Orange Free State)
6	4th	**J.P.Hall**	(Bath)	.	16th	**R.J.Louw**	(Western Province)
7	14th	**P.J.Winterbottom**	(Headingley)	.	20th	**M.T.S.Stofberg (Capt)**	(Western Province)
8	1st	**C.J.S.Butcher**	(Harlequins)	.	2nd	**G.H.H.Sonnekus**	(Orange Free State)

3rd   N.C.Stringer (Wasps) for Bailey -

Referee: R.Hourquet   (France)

SCORERS:

		0 - 3	J.W.Heunis	Penalty Goal
		0 - 7	C.J.du Plessis	Try
		0 - 9	J.W.Heunis	Conversion
W.H.Hare	Penalty Goal	3 - 9		
J.P.Horton	D'p Goal (3rd & last)	6 - 9		
W.H.Hare	Penalty Goal	9 - 9		
		9 - 12	J.W.Heunis	Penalty Goal
W.H.Hare	Penalty Goal	12 - 12		
		Half-time		
		12 - 15	J.W.Heunis	Penalty Goal
		12 - 18	J.W.Heunis	Penalty Goal
		12 - 22	D.M.Gerber	Try
		12 - 24	J.W.Heunis	Conversion
W.H.Hare	Penalty Goal	15 - 24		
		15 - 27	J.W.Heunis	Penalty Goal
		15 - 31	R.J.Louw	Try
		15 - 33	J.W.Heunis	Conversion

POINTS:

W.H.Hare	12 points	(231)	**J.W.Heunis**	21 points
J.P.Horton	3 points	(12)	**D.M.Gerber, R.J.Louw**	
			and C.J.du Plessis	4 points each

MATCH COMMENTARY:

There were five new caps on both sides, but England were by far the less experienced at this level - and it showed. South African power play was always too much for the England side, and they were able to control events. For the first time, the England front row all came from the same club, Gloucester, but despite their club understanding, they could make no impression. The game was, somewhat disappointingly, dominated by penalty goals, nine in all, for South Africa had the possession and the opportunities to make more of a running game out of it. Four of the penalties awarded to South Africa were unnecessary infringements on England's part, amongst them clumsy line-out barging, interference with play from a totally off-side position, and one very late tackle. England could have gone into a reasonable lead just after half-time when "Dusty" Hare and John Horton respectively missed straight-forward penalty goal and drop goal opportunities.

Errol Tobias, the first black player to be capped by South Africa, launched his backs frequently and the powerful centres Gerber and Villet took full advantage of England's fragile mid-field defence but then lost probably four try-scoring opportunities by being over-elaborate.

A disappointing result, but there was worse to come.

9th match **ENGLAND 9 pts** v **SOUTH AFRICA 35 pts**

	Caps					Caps		
15	25th & last	**W.H.Hare**	(Leicester)	.	6th	**J.W.Heunis**	(Northern Transvaal)
14	2nd	**M.D.Bailey**	(Cambridge Univ)	.	2nd & last	**A.P.Williams**	(Western Province)
13	2nd	**J.A.Palmer**	(Bath)	.	13th	**D.M.Gerber**	(Eastern Province)
12	14th	**G.H.Davies**	(Wasps)	.	2nd & last	**J.V.Villet**	(Western Province)
11	6th & last	**A.H.Swift**	(Swansea)	.	4th	**C.J.du Plessis**	(Western Province)
10	13th & last	**J.P.Horton**	(Bath)	.	4th	**E.G.Tobias**	(Boland)
9	2nd	**R.J.Hill**	(Bath)	.	17th	**D.J.Serfontein**	(Western Province)
1	2nd	**P.A.G.Rendall**	(Wasps)	.	9th & last	**O.W.Oosthuizen**	(Transvaal)
2	1st	**S.E.Brain**	(Coventry)	.	2nd	**C.D.Rogers**	(Transvaal)
3	15th	**G.S.Pearce**	(Northampton)	.	5th & last	**P.G.du Toit**	(Western Province)
4	34th & last	**J.P.Scott (Capt)**	(Cardiff)	.	2nd	**S.W.P.Burger**	(Western Province)
5	4th & last	**J.H.Fidler**	(Gloucester)	.	2nd	**R.G.Visagie**	(Orange Free State)
6	5th	**J.P.Hall**	(Bath)	.	17th	**R.J.Louw**	(Western Province)
7	15th	**P.J.Winterbottom**	(Headingley)	.	21st & last	**M.T.S.Stofberg (Capt)**	(Western Province)
8	2nd	**C.J.S.Butcher**	(Harlequins)	.	3rd & last	**G.H.H.Sonnekus**	(Orange Free State)

  1st G.W.Rees (Nottingham) for Hall - 35

Referee: R.Hourquet (France)

SCORERS:

			0 - 4	M.T.S.Stofberg	Try
			0 - 6	J.W.Heunis	Conversion
W.H.Hare		Penalty Goal	3 - 6		
			3 - 10	D.M.Gerber	Try
			3 - 12	J.W.Heunis	Conversion
			3 - 16	D.M.Gerber	Try
			3 - 20	D.M.Gerber	Try
			3 - 22	J.W.Heunis	Conversion
			Half-time		
			3 - 26	E.G.Tobias	Try
W.H.Hare		Penalty Goal	6 - 26		
			6 - 29	J.W.Heunis	Penalty Goal
W.H.Hare		Penalty Goal	9 - 29		
			9 - 33	G.H.H.Sonnekus	Try
			9 - 35	E.G.Tobias	Conversion

POINTS:

W.H.Hare	9 points	(240)		D.M.Gerber	12 points
				J.W.Heunis	9 points
				E.G.Tobias	6 points
				G.H.H.Sonnekus and M.T.S.Stofberg	4 points each

MATCH COMMENTARY:

The pattern set in the first match was repeated at Johannesburg despite England having replaced the entire front row.   This was England's highest ever losing margin, and South Africa's 35 points was the highest total conceded by England except for France's 37 points in 1972. England seemed to have no defence at all, especially in the first half when swift passing and powerful straight running, allowed Danie Gerber to score three tries in 18 minutes in a demoralising passage of play for England.   The ball moved very quickly through the hands from scrum-half to scorer, each pass was taken at pace and the English defence was left floundering.   Classical rugby, and strenuously avoiding the sins of over-elaboration which had denied South Africa tries in the First Test.   South Africa had learned their lessons from that match but England, A29unfortunately, had not.

Although they had scored 19 tries in the five Provincial matches, England had failed to score a try in either of the two Test matches and had conceded nine - four of them scored by Danie Gerber.

12th match   **ENGLAND**   **3 pts**   v   **AUSTRALIA**   **19 pts**

	Caps				Caps		
15	4th	N.C.Stringer	(Wasps)	.	18th	R.G.Gould	(Queensland)
14	26th & last	J.Carleton	(Orrell)	.	15th	D.I.Campese	(ACT)
13	1st & only	R.A.P.Lozowski	(Wasps)	.	24th	A.G.Slack (Capt)	(Queensland)
12	4th	B.Barley	(Wakefield)	.	2nd	M.P.Lynagh	(Queensland)
11	4th	R.Underwood	(RAF/Leicester)	.	31st & last	B.J.Moon	(Queensland)
10	1st	S.Barnes	(Bristol)	.	22nd	M.G.Ella	(New South Wales)
9	1st	N.D.Melville (Capt)	(Wasps)	.	1st	N.C.Farr-Jones	(New South Wales)
1	1st	G.J.Chilcott	(Bath)	.	5th	E.E.Rodriguez	(New South Wales)
2	5th & last	S.G.F.Mills	(Gloucester)	.	7th	T.A.Lawton	(Queensland)
3	16th	G.S.Pearce	(Northampton)	.	10th	A.J.McIntyre	(Queensland)
4	2nd & last	J.P.Syddall	(Waterloo)	.	20th	S.A.Williams	(New South Wales)
5	1st	N.C.Redman	(Bath)	.	5th	S.A.G.Cutler	(New South Wales)
6	6th	J.P.Hall	(Bath)	.	25th	S.P.Poidevin	(New South Wales)
7	2nd	G.W.Rees	(Nottingham)	.	2nd	D.Codey	(Queensland)
8	3rd & last	C.J.S.Butcher	(Harlequins)	.	3rd	S.N.Tuynman	(New South Wales)
	2nd	S.E.Brain (Coventry) for Mills -		.	1st	M.P.Burke (New South Wales) for Moon -	

Referee: R.C.Francis   (New Zealand)

SCORERS:

S.Barnes	Penalty Goal	3 - 0			
		3 - 3	M.P.Lynagh	Penalty Goal	
		Half-time			
		3 - 7	S.P.Poideven	Try	
		3 - 11	M.G.Ella	Try	
		3 - 13	M.P.Lynagh	Conversion	
		3 - 17	M.P.Lynagh	Try	
		3 - 19	M.P.Lynagh	Conversion	

POINTS:

S.Barnes	3 points	(3)	M.P.Lynagh	11 points	
			M.G.Ella	4 points	
			S.P.Poidevin	4 points	

MATCH COMMENTARY:

For the first of eight matches during this season, England selected five new caps against Australia, including Nigel Melville who was captaining the side on his debut, the first England player to do so since Joe Mycock in 1947.   The Australians, though, were at their peak, with powerful forwards, fast running backs and a supreme play-maker at fly-half, Mark Ella.   England never got close to scoring a try and succumbed quietly to their fifth successive international defeat and the fourth without an English try. The score also posted England's highest post-war margin of defeat at Twickenham and, at that time, the highest margin of defeat against Australia .

1st match   **ENGLAND   22 pts**   v   **ROMANIA   15 pts**

<u>Caps</u>

15	5th & last	**N.C.Stringer**	(Wasps)	.	**S.Podarescu**	(Dynamo Bucharest)
14	1st	**S.T.Smith**	(Wasps)	.	**M.Toader**	(Steaua Bucharest)
13	1st	**K.G.Simms**	(Cambridge Univ)	.	**A.Lungu**	(Farul Constanta)
12	26th	**P.W.Dodge (Capt)**	(Leicester)	.	**M.Marghescu**	(Dynamo Bucharest)
11	5th	**R.Underwood**	(RAF/Leicester)	.	**M.Aidea**	(Dynamo Bucharest)
10	1st	**C.R.Andrew**	(Cambridge Univ)	.	**D.Alexandru**	(Steaua Bucharest)
9	1st	**R.M.Harding**	(Bristol)	.	**M.Parachiv (Captain)**	(Dynamo Bucharest)
1	16th	**P.J.Blakeway**	(Gloucester)		**I.Bucan**	(Dynamo Bucharest)
2	3rd	**S.E.Brain**	(Coventry)	.	**E.Grigore**	(Farul Constanta)
3	17th	**G.S.Pearce**	(Northampton)	.	**G.Leonte**	(Steaua Bucharest)
4	1st	**J.Orwin**	(Gloucester)	.	**F.Murariu**	(Steaua Bucharest)
5	1st	**W.A.Dooley**	(Preston G'hoppers)	.	**G.Dumitru**	(Farul Constanta)
6	7th	**J.P.Hall**	(Bath)	.	**G.Caraagea**	(Dynamo Bucharest)
7	6th	**D.H.Cooke**	(Harlequins)	.	**A.Radulescu**	(Steaua Bucharest)
8	6th	**R.Hesford**	(Bristol)	.	**L.Constantin**	(Steaua Bucharest)

2nd	S.Barnes (Bristol) for Stringer -		.	H.Dumitras (Suceava) for Dumitru -
15th	G.H.Davies (Wasps) for Simms -		.	

Referee: W.D.Bevan   (Wales)

SCORERS:

C.R.Andrew	D'p Goal	(1st)	3 - 0		
C.R.Andrew	D'p Goal	(2nd)	6 - 0		
			6 - 3	**D.Alexandru**	Penalty Goal
C.R.Andrew	Penalty Goal		9 - 3		
			9 - 6	**D.Alexandru**	Penalty Goal
C.R.Andrew	Penalty Goal		12 - 6		
C.R.Andrew	Penalty Goal		15 - 6		
			15 - 9	**D.Alexandru**	Penalty Goal
			Half-time		
C.R.Andrew	Penalty Goal		18 - 9		
			18 - 12	**D.Alexandru**	Penalty Goal
			18 - 15	**D.Alexandru**	Penalty Goal
S.T.Smith	Try	(1st)	22 - 15		

POINTS:

C.R.Andrew	18 points	(18)		
S.T.Smith	4 points	(4)		15 points

MATCH COMMENTARY:

England made eleven changes following the inept performance against Australia, including six new caps and the recall of Paul Dodge to assume the mantle of captaincy. England won their first match against Romania comfortably but not convincingly, and managed to score only one try - by Simon Smith on his debut. Rob Andrew had a memorable game, scoring eighteen points on his debut - a record for an England player. The lack of cohesion in the side was due to there only being three days preparation beforehand and Gary Rees' last minute withdrawal with suspected appendicitis. There were only two players in this team who had played in the last Five Nations match against Wales, and in the four games since, 17 new caps had been awarded !

60th match   **ENGLAND   9 pts**   v   **FRANCE   9 pts**

	Caps					Caps		
15	1st	C.R.Martin	(Bath)			29th	S.Blanco	(Biarritz)
14	2nd	S.T.Smith	(Wasps)			18th	P.Esteve	(Narbonne)
13	2nd	K.G.Simms	(Cambridge Univ)			18th	P.Sella	(Agen)
12	27th	P.W.Dodge (Capt)	(Leicester)			25th	D.Codorniou	(Narbonne)
11	6th	R.Underwood	(RAF/Leicester)			2nd & last	B.Lavigne	(Agen)
10	2nd	C.R.Andrew	(Cambridge Univ)			15th	J-P.Lescarboura	(Dax)
9	2nd	R.M.Harding	(Bristol)			22nd	J.Gallion	(Toulon)
1	17th	P.J.Blakeway	(Gloucester)			19th	P.Dospital	(Bayonne)
2	4th	S.E.Brain	(Coventry)			35th	P.Dintrans (Capt)	(Tarbes)
3	18th	G.S.Pearce	(Northampton)			8th	J-P.Garuet-Lempirou	(Lourdes)
4	2nd	J.Orwin	(Gloucester)			26th	F.Haget	(Biarritz)
5	2nd	W.A.Dooley	(Preston G'hoppers)			16th	J.Condom	(Boucau)
6	8th	J.P.Hall	(Bath)			3rd	J.Gratton	(Agen)
7	7th	D.H.Cooke	(Harlequins)			17th	L.Rodriguez	(Montois)
8	7th	R.Hesford	(Bristol)			16th	D.Erbani	(Agen)

	1st	M.C.Teague (Gloucester) for Hall - 55	

Referee: D.I.H.Burnett   (Ireland)

SCORERS:	C.R.Andrew	D'p Goal	(3rd)	3 - 0		
				3 - 3	J-P.Lescarboura	D'p Goal
				Half-time		
				3 - 6	J-P.Lescarboura	D'p Goal
	C.R.Andrew	Penalty Goal		6 - 6		
				6 - 9	J-P.Lescarboura	D'p Goal
	C.R.Andrew	Penalty Goal		9 - 9		

POINTS:	C.R.Andrew	9 points	(27)		J-P.Lescarboura	9 points

MATCH COMMENTARY:

An unremarkable match with an unremarkable result, yet a match in which remarkable feats were achieved. In this game, all of each sides' points were scored by the two fly-halves. There were four drop goals in the match, three of which were scored by Jean Lescarboura, a Championship record. But the most remarkable occurance came in the second half when Patrick Esteve had crossed the English line after a flowing French three-quarter movement, and was about to touch down when Richard Harding leapt on him in a smothering tackle and knocked the ball from his grasp thus saving a certain try, and, as it happened, the match. Steve Smith came desperately close to scoring a try on his wing but he was very well tackled into touch and subsequently was off the field for fully seven minutes for attention to a head wound. While he was off, England did not pull a forward out of the pack, yet France could not exploit the yawning gap on their left. In the second half, as the French became more and more frustrated at their inability to score the decisive points, their discipline began to fade and England were awarded fifteen penalties to only one against. Rob Andrew managed to score from two, but it was not enough On the whole it was a good performance from England, even though the match had few sparks of excitement, and they showed much character, courage and no little confidence in achieving this result.

101st match   **ENGLAND 10 pts**   v   **SCOTLAND 7 pts**

92nd Calcutta Cup

	Caps					Caps		
15	2nd	C.R.Martin	(Bath)	.		15th	P.W.Dods	(Gala)
14	3rd	S.T.Smith	(Wasps)	.		4th & last	P.D.Steven	(Heriot's FP)
13	3rd	K.G.Simms	(Cambridge Univ)	.		3rd	D.S.Wylie	(Stewart's-Melville)
12	28th	P.W.Dodge (Capt)	(Leicester)	.		32nd	K.W.Robertson	(Melrose)
11	7th	R.Underwood	(RAF/Leicester)	.		20th	G.R.T.Baird	(Kelso)
10	3rd	C.R.Andrew	(Cambridge Univ)	.		32nd	J.Y.Rutherford	(Selkirk)
9	3rd	R.M.Harding	(Bristol)	.		4th & last	I.G.Hunter	(Selkirk)
1	18th	P.J.Blakeway	(Gloucester)	.		7th & last	G.M.McGuinness	(West of Scotland)
2	5th	S.E.Brain	(Coventry)	.		39th	C.T.Deans	(Hawick)
3	19th	G.S.Pearce	(Northampton)	.		28th	I.G.Milne	(Harlequins)
4	3rd	J.Orwin	(Gloucester)	.		7th	A.J.Campbell	(Hawick)
5	3rd	W.A.Dooley	(Preston G'hoppers)	.		41st	A.J.Tomes	(Hawick)
6	9th	J.P.Hall	(Bath)	.		3rd	J.Jeffrey	(Kelso)
7	8th	D.H.Cooke	(Harlequins)	.		32nd & last	D.G.Leslie (Capt)	(Gala)
8	8th	R.Hesford	(Bristol)	.		21st	I.A.M.Paxton	(Selkirk)

Referee: C.Norling   (Wales)

SCORERS:

C.R.Andrew	Penalty Goal	3 - 0			
C.R.Andrew	Penalty Goal	6 - 0			
		6 - 4		K.W,.Robertson	Try
		Half-time			
		6 - 7		P.W.Dods	Penalty Goal
S.T.Smith	Try	(2nd)	10 - 7		

POINTS:

C.R.Andrew	6 points	(33)		K.W.Robertson	4 points
S.T.Smith	4 points	(8)		P.W.Dods	3 points

MATCH COMMENTARY:

England kept the same team that had drawn with France early in February, but this was not an inspiring performance until the last ten minutes when Steve Smith scored his second International try for England to give them a three point lead with the match drawing to a close. Scotland then threw everything into attack in an effort to gain their second successive win at Twickenham and their third successive Calcutta Cup. And they came desperately close. After a series of Scottish attacks, the match entered injury time, and Iain Paxton, the burly Scottish No 8 broke away from a maul and approached the English line with only Rory Underwood to beat. Somehow, Underwood stole the ball from him in the tackle and a dramatic winning try was denied. The England pack had controlled events for over three quarters of the match and the talented Scottish backs had to live with only scraps of possession and very close marking from the England back row. The lines-out too, went very much England's way with Wade Dooley becoming a formidable presence in the middle. But behind the scrum England showed indecision and little creative ability at half-back, such that both sets of three-quarters were starved of both ball and opportunity and as a result the match became, for the most part, tedious and uninspiring. But, nevertheless, Scotland were denied. Because the Welsh match was postponed due to the weather, England have both away matches yet to come - neither will be easy.

97th match   **ENGLAND   10 pts**   v   **IRELAND   13 pts**

	Caps					Caps		
15	3rd	C.R.Martin	(Bath)		21st	H.P.McNeill	(Blackrock College)
14	4th	S.T.Smith	(Wasps)		17th	T.M.Ringland	(Queens U Belfast)
13	4th	K.G.Simms	(Cambridge Univ)		4th	B.J.Mullin	(UC Dublin)
12	29th	P.W.Dodge (Capt)	(Leicester)		15th	M.J.Kiernan	(Dolphin)
11	8th	R.Underwood	(RAF/Leicester)		9th	K.D.Crossan	(Instonians)
10	4th	C.R.Andrew	(Cambridge Univ)		12th	P.M.Dean	(St Mary's College)
9	2nd	N.D.Melville	(Wasps)		5th	M.T.Bradley	(Cork Constitution)
1	19th & last	P.J.Blakeway	(Gloucester)		48th	P.A.Orr	(Old Wesley)
2	6th	S.E.Brain	(Coventry)		21st	C.F.Fitzgerald (Capt)	(St Mary's College)
3	20th	G.S.Pearce	(Northampton)		6th	J.J.McCoy	(Dungannon)
4	4th	J.Orwin	(Gloucester)		18th	D.G.Lenihan	(Cork Constitution)
5	4th	W.A.Dooley	(Preston G'hoppers)		5th	W.A.Anderson	(Dungannon)
6	10th	J.P.Hall	(Bath)		5th	P.M.Matthews	(Wanderers)
7	9th	D.H.Cooke	(Harlequins)		4th	N.J.Carr	(Ards)
8	9th	R.Hesford	(Bristol)		4th	B.J.Spillane	(Bohemians)

3rd   R.J.Hill (Bath) for Melville - 18

Referee: J.M.Fleming   (Scotland)

SCORERS:

C.R.Andrew	Penalty Goal		3 - 0				
			3 - 4		B.J.Mullin	Try	
			3 - 7		M.J.Kiernan	Penalty Goal	
			Half-time				
R.Underwood	Try	(2nd)	7 - 7				
C.R.Andrew	Penalty Goal		10 - 7				
			10 - 10		M.J.Kiernan	Penalty Goal	
			10 - 13		M.J.Kiernan	Drop Goal	

POINTS:

C.R.Andrew	6 points	(39)	M.J.Kiernan	9 points	
R.Underwood	4 points	(8)	B.J.Mullin	4 points	

MATCH COMMENTARY:

The return of Nigel Melville was the only change in the side which went to Lansdowne Road to face a buoyant Ireland seeking the Triple Crown. This had been and was, a very good Irish side said by some to be the most complete side Ireland had ever had. In the event, England made them work hard for their sixth Triple Crown and the match was only settled by Michael Kiernan's drop goal very late in the game. The unfortunate Nigel Melville was injured yet again and was replaced by the young Richard Hill whose first two caps were won in South Africa. The secret of England's success in restricting Ireland's normally expansive game was the dominance of the pack in tight and loose which effectively tied in the Irish back row and denied them the opportunity of foraging around the field creating havoc as they are wont to do. The England line-out, however, was not as effective as previously, which was probably due to the effectiveness of the Irish spoiling as much as any shortcoming on England's part. As the game went on, it became more and more apparent that England were not going to win, and Michael Kiernan's drop goal was a mighty relief, but no great surprise to the Dublin faithful.

90th match   **ENGLAND   15 pts**   v   **WALES   24 pts**

	Caps					Caps		
15	4th & last	C.R.Martin	(Bath)			2nd	P.H.Thorburn	(Neath)
14	5th	S.T.Smith	(Wasps)			5th	P.I.Lewis	(Llanelli)
13	5th	K.G.Simms	(Cambridge Univ)			21st	R.A.Ackerman	(London Welsh)
12	30th	P.W.Dodge (Capt)	(Leicester)			1st	K.Hopkins	(Cardiff)
11	9th	R.Underwood	(RAF/Leicester)			7th	A.M.Hadley	(Cardiff)
10	5th	C.R.Andrew	(Cambridge Univ)			1st	J.Davies	(Neath)
9	3rd	N.D.Melville	(Wasps)			24th	T.D.Holmes (Capt)	(Cardiff)
1	2nd & last	A.Sheppard	(Bristol)			5th	J.Whitefoot	(Cardiff)
2	7th	S.E.Brain	(Coventry)			10th	W.J.James	(Aberavon)
3	21st	G.S.Pearce	(Northampton)			2nd	S.Evans	(Swansea)
4	5th	J.Orwin	(Gloucester)			13th	S.J.Perkins	(Pontypool)
5	5th	W.A.Dooley	(Preston G'hoppers)			14th	R.L.Norster	(Cardiff)
6	11th	J.P.Hall	(Bath)			2nd	G.J.Roberts	(Cardiff)
7	10th	D.H.Cooke	(Harlequins)			14th	D.F.Pickering	(Llanelli)
8	10th & last	R.Hesford	(Bristol)			1st	P.T.Davies	(Llanelli)

Referee: F.Palmade   (France)

SCORERS:

C.R.Andrew	Penalty Goal		3 - 0			
S.T.Smith	Try	(3rd & last)	7 - 0			
C.R.Andrew	Conversion		9 - 0			
			9 - 3	P.H.Thorburn	Penalty Goal	
			9 - 6	P.H.Thorburn	Penalty Goal	
C.R.Andrew	Penalty Goal		12 - 6			
			12 - 9	P.H.Thorburn	Penalty Goal	
			12 - 12	J.Davies	Drop Goal	
			Half-time			
C.R.Andrew	D'p Goal	(4th)	15 - 12			
			15 - 16	J.Davies	Try	
			15 - 18	P.H.Thorburn	Conversion	
			15 - 22	G.J.Roberts	Try	
			15 - 24	P.H.Thorburn	Conversion	

POINTS:

C.R.Andrew	11 points	(50)	P.H.Thorburn	13 points	
S.T.Smith	4 points	(12)	J.Davies	7 points	
			G.J.Roberts	4 points	

MATCH COMMENTARY:

England had high hopes winning a match at Cardiff for the first time since 1963, against a Welsh side which, by normal standards had had a dreadful season, winning only one game out of four. Simon Smith scored an excellent try, probably the best of the whole season, but elementary defensive lapses, the inspiration of the new Welsh fly-half, Jonathan Davies, and a rejuvenated Welsh pack, ensured that England's hopes for that elusive win at Cardiff were to be dashed yet again, and they finished fourth in the Table for the second successive season. Rob Andrew, in only his fifth International, scored his 50th point for England - a remarkable feat.

SUMMARY OF THE SEASON - 1984 - 85:

For the first time in over 100 years of International rugby, this year England played six International matches during the course of the domestic season, and, with the tour to New Zealand following next May and into June, in the calendar year from July 1984 eight International matches will have been played, and this trend will continue with the World Cup and more frequent matches with southern hemisphere nations Following the return of a rather disillusioned squad from a decisive hammering in South Africa the previous summer, the selectors had quite a task on their hands both to chose a side and to attempt to restore confidence for the opening match with Australia early in November. The team chosen, with Nigel Melvelle selected to lead it on his debut, contained only three players who had been in the side at Ellis Park the previous July, Gary Pearce, John Hall and Chris Butcher, together with five new caps. The match achieved little for England other than a fifth successive defeat and the fourth successive match without an English try, but it did help Australia towards their own Grand Slam in beating all four Home Nations on this tour. For the first ever match against Romania, early in January, eleven changes were made, six new caps were awarded, yet still only three players who had been on the South African tour held their places, and Paul Dodge was given the captaincy following Nigel Melville's injury. At least the sequence of losing matches was broken, but it was a far from convincing victory over a raw but hard and aggressive Romanian side, and only one try was scored. For the opening Five Nations encounter with France selection stability was restored with just one change made, Chris Martin replacing Nick Stringer at full-back. It was a better all-round performance with distinct signs of confidence returning and an almost inspirational moment when Richard Harding denied Patrick Esteve the winning try for France by refusing to give up and be beaten. The encounter with Wales at Cardiff had to be postponed due to weather, so there was a six week break for England between their first and second Five Nations match. An unchanged side was selected and they squeezed past Scotland at Twickenham, with again a remarkable tackle, this time by Rory Underwood on Iain Paxton, denying the Scots a last minute try to win the match. Commendably too, Simon Smith, scored his second try for England and the side's first in a Five Nations match at Twickenham since March 1982. So, in a much more buoyant frame of mind, England set off for Dublin in an attempt to deny Ireland their second Triple Crown in four years with again an unchanged side except that Nigel Melville returned at scrum-half but Paul Dodge retained the captaincy. The unfortunate Melville lasted only fifteen minutes and was replaced by Richard Hill, and although England were up against a a very strong Irish side with all-round strengths, they restricted Irish activity as no other side had done during the season, except possibly France, and the result was only determined at the very last minute with Michael Kiernan's drop goal. Between the Irish and the Welsh matches Phil Blakeway had decided, or Phil Blakeway's neck had decided that it had taken enough punishmnet, and Alan Sheppard came in for his second cap as the only team change.. Sheppard has a unique distinctioin in that he won only two England caps, but both against the Welsh at Cardiff, the first being when he replaced Fran Cotton there in 1983. Wales had won only one match, against Scotland, so England crossed the Severn with a degree of confidence inconsistent with their record at that awesome ground. Sure enough, the fickle finger of the Welsh dragon pointed again at England and they came away empty handed, as they had every year since 1963.

England finished a disappointing fourth in the Championship Table having won only one match and having scored only three tries in the four matches. Indeed in the six matches, England had scored only four tries, and Simon Smith got three of them.

In the six matches played, England called upon the services of 29 players and three additional replacements, but for the four Five Nations matches only 17 players were used, and two additional replacements. Thirteen new caps were awarded during the season, and nine players came to the end of their International careers. John Carleton retired after the match against Australia with 29 caps, and having scored seven International tries. He went on two Lions' tours, 1980 and 1983, and played in 6 Tests Phil Blakeway eventually retired with 19 caps - he had announced his retirement on two previous occasions, and later changed his mind. He was one of the strongest scrummagers of his day despite having broken his neck in 1978, and having continued trouble with it since. He went on the 1980 Lions' tour, but a broken rib in the early matches caused him to return home. Bob Hesford, from a family of professional soccer goalkeepers, had won 10 caps. Nick Stringer retired on medical grounds, having suffered repeated concussion. Of his five caps, three were won as a replacement, Steve Mills, the Gloucester hooker was unfortunate to be playing in the International shadow of Peter Wheeler and won only five caps. Chris Butcher, three caps, having tasted the delights of South Africa on the 1984 tour, returned there as soon as he could after the tour and makes his living as a fisherman. Jim Sydall and Alan Sheppard each gained two caps, and Rob Lozowski only one.

FIVE NATIONS CHAMPIONSHIP TABLE:

Won: **Calcutta Cup**

		Played	Won	Lost	Drawn	Points: For	Against	Tries: For	Against	Title Points
1	Ireland	4	3	0	1	67	49	5	4	7
2	France	4	2	0	2	49	30	6	0	6
3	Wales	4	2	2	0	61	71	5	7	4
4	**ENGLAND**	4	1	2	1	44	53	3	4	3
5	Scotland	4	0	4	0	46	64	3	7	0

Home Games: drew with France 9 - 9, (no tries);   beat Scotland 10 - 7, (one try each)

Away Games: lost to Ireland 10 - 13, (one try each);   lost to Wales 15 - 24, (one try to two)

ENGLAND TOUR TO NEW ZEALAND - 1985

THE TOUR PARTY:

Manager:	W.D.G.Morgan	Coach:	M.J.Green		Captain:		P.W.Dodge
		Assistant:	W.B.Ashton				

Full-backs:	C.R.Martin	(Bath)	4 caps	Forwards:	S.Bainbridge	(Fylde)	11 caps
	I.J.Metcalfe	(Moseley)	no caps		S.E.Brain	(Coventry)	7 caps
					D.H.Cooke	(Harlequins)	10 caps
Three-quarters:	B.Barley	(Wakefield)	4 caps		W.A.Dooley	(Preston G'hoppers	5 caps
	P.W.Dodge	(Leicester)	30 caps		J.P.Hall	(Bath)	11 caps
	J.M.Goodwin	(Moseley)	no caps		R.Hesford	(Bristol)	10 caps
	M.E.Harrison	(Wakefield)	no caps		P.Huntsman	(Headingley)	no caps
	J.L.B.Salmon	(Harlequins)	no caps		J.Orwin	(Gloucester)	5 caps
	S.T.Smith	(Wasps)	5 caps		G.S.Pearce	(Northamptom)	21 caps
					M.Preedy	(Gloucester)	1 cap
Half-backs:	S.Barnes	(Bath)	2 caps		G.W.Rees	(Nottingham)	2 caps
	G.H.Davies	(Wasps)	15 caps		A.Sheppard	(Bristol)	2 caps
	R.J.Hill	(Bath)	2 caps		A.Simpson	(Sale)	no caps
	N.D.Melville	(Wasps)	3 caps		M.C.Teague	(Gloucester)	1 cap

The preliminaries to this tour were shrouded in uncertainty and selection announcements containing players whose availability had not been confirmed. Dick Greenwood, England's current coach, announced he was not available having just taken a new job, and eventually two coaches were appointed under Derek Morgan, Martin Green and Brian Ashton. The party as a whole was very short of experience, and only three players had previous experience of New Zealand rugby at Test level, Jamie Salmon, who had three All Black caps, and Paul Dodge and Steve Bainbridge who had both played in the 1983 match at Twickenham.

The first two matches against North Auckland and Poverty Bay were won reasonably easily, but against Auckland , in the third match, England never got even close and were thoroughly beaten by three tries to one. It must be said that Auckland had won their last fifteen matches against overseas opponents, including the 1983 British Lions so, to them, the win was no surprise, but it did English confidence no good at all. Following that upset, the tour management had a radical re-think of their tactics, and as a result, and as unusually, eight of the players chosen for the First Test played in the mid-week game earlier that week. The reward was a very much improved England performance in the First Test and in many respects England were unlucky to lose. Two opportunist tries were scored in the match, and England did not fall behind until the last quarter. But it was a very different story in the Second Test when the same team suffered England's heaviest ever Test defeat in total points and margin despite having scored first with John Hall's first International try. New Zealand played power rugby, highly physical, intimidating and aggressive and England crumbled. The All Blacks were assisted somewhat by referee Fitzgerald's metaphorically blind eye, but there were players on both sides who were fortunate to remain on the field, especially after the mass fight which broke out right at the end of the match inviolving some twenty players. Nevertheless, "Burglar" Bill Harrison managed another interception try almost identical to the one he scored in the First Test.

Strangely, the tours to South Africa and New Zealand in 1984 and 1985 had resulted in record defeats on both tours, whereas the previous tours to the same countries in 1972 and 1973 had seen well-earned victories on both occasions. An illustration, perhaps, of how far southern hemisphere rugby has progressed in those twelve years.

At the end of the tour, Paul Dodge, the Leicester book-binder, retired with 32 caps as England's most capped centre. He hed led England seven times and played in two Tests on the 1980 Lions tour after having been summoned as a replacement. David Cooke, an Estate Agent had earned twelve caps and Paul Huntsman after winning his two caps on this tour, yielded to the temptations of Rugby League.

TOUR RESULTS:

May 18th	North Auckland	at Whangarei	WON	27 - 14	(four tries to three)
May 22nd	Poverty Bay	at Gisborne	WON	45 - 0	(seven tries to nil)
May 25th	Auckland	at Auckland	LOST	6 - 24	(one try to three)
May 28th	Otago	at Dunedin	WON	25 - 16	(four tries to two)
June 1st	NEW ZEALAND	at Christchurch	LOST	13 - 18	(two tries to nil)
June 4th	Southland	at Invercargill	WON	15 - 9	(no tries)
June 8th	NEW ZEALAND	at Wellington	LOST	15 - 42	(two tries to six)

THE ENGLAND SQUAD FOR THE SEVEN MATCH TOUR TO NEW ZEALAND IN 1985

Back Row: R.J.Hill, B.Barley, J.L.B.Salmon, S.T.Smith, M.E.Harrison, J.M.Goodwin, A.Simpson, G.W.Rees, M.Preedy, N.D.Melville,

Middle Row: P.Huntsman, D.H.Cooke, M.C.Teague, J.P.Hall, J.Orwin, W.A.Dooley, S.Bainbridge, R.Hesford, I.J.Metcalfe, C.R.Martin, A.Sheppard,

Seated: W.B.Ashton (Asst Coach), G.H.Davies, S.E.Brain, M.J.Green (Coach), P.W.Dodge (Captain), W.D.G.Morgan (Manager), G.S.Pearce, S.Barnes

14th match   **ENGLAND   13 pts**   v   **NEW ZEALAND   18 pts**

	Caps					Caps		
15	16th	**G.H.Davies**	(Wasps)	.	1st	**K.J.Crowley**	(Taranaki)
14	6th	**S.T.Smith**	(Wasps)	.	3rd	**J.J.Kirwan**	(Auckland)
13	31st	**P.W.Dodge (Capt)**	(Leicester)	.	16th	**S.T.Pokere**	(Auckland)
12	1st	**J.L.B.Salmon**	(Harlequins)	.	11th	**W.T.Taylor**	(Canterbury)
11	1st	**M.E.Harrison**	(Wakefield)	.	6th	**C.I.Green**	(Canterbury)
10	3rd	**S.Barnes**	(Bath)	.	14th	**W.R.Smith**	(Canterbury)
9	4th	**N.D.Melville**	(Wasps)	.	1st	**D.E.Kirk**	(Auckland)
1	1st	**R.P.Huntsman**	(Headingley)	.	22nd	**J.C.Ashworth**	(Hawkes' Bay)
2	8th	**S.E.Brain**	(Coventry)	.	33rd	**A.G.Dalton (Capt)**	(Counties)
3	22nd	**G.S.Pearce**	(Northampton)	.	32nd	**G.A.Knight**	(Manawatu)
4	6th	**J.Orwin**	(Gloucester)	.	1st	**M.J.Pierce**	(Wellington)
5	12th	**S.Bainbridge**	(Gosforth)	.	15th	**G.W.Whetton**	(Auckland)
6	12th	**J.P.Hall**	(Bath)	.	25th	**M.W.Shaw**	(Hawkes' Bay)
7	11th	**D.H.Cooke**	(Harlequins)	.	13th	**M.J.B.Hobbs**	(Canterbury)
8	2nd	**M.C.Teague**	(Gloucester)	.	30th	**M.G.Mexted**	(Wellington)

Referee: K.V.J.Fitzgerald   (Australia)

SCORERS:

S.Barnes	Penalty Goal		3 - 0			
			3 - 3	**K.J.Crowley**	Penalty Goal
M.E.Harrison	Try	(1st)	7 - 3		
S.Barnes	Conversion		9 - 3		
			9 - 6	**K.J.Crowley**	Penalty Goal
			9 - 9	**K.J.Crowley**	Penalty Goal
M.C.Teague	Try	(1st)	13 - 9		
			13 - 12		
			13 - 12	**K.J.Crowley**	Penalty Goal
			Half-time		
			13 - 15	**K.J.Crowley**	Penalty Goal
			13 - 18	**K.J.Crowley**	Penalty Goal

POINTS:

S.Barnes	5 points	(8)	**K.J.Crowley**	18 points
M.C.Teague	4 points	(4)		
M.E.Harrison	4 points	(4)		

MATCH COMMENTARY:

Huw Davies became the first England player to gain caps in three different positions, full-back, centre and fly-half - a measure of his superb versatility. Jamie Salmon gained his first England cap having won three with New Zealand in Europe in 1981. England, although undoubtedly the weaker side, acquitted themselves very well indeed scoring two tries to none, the first of which was a spectacular interception by Mike Harrison from a determined New Zealand attack. He ran 50 yards to score. Mike Teague's try was less spectacular but just as valuable and that put England in the lead at half-time. Unfortunately Kieran Crowley's fifth and sixth penalty goals were yet to come and England were denied a famous and wholly unexpected victory. There were some unusual refereeing decisions, generally not in England's favour, but Stuart Barnes did miss penalty goal attempts which might have swung the game England's way. A much improved performance over the Auckland match, but the second Test will be the basis on which the success of the tour will be judged.

15th match   **ENGLAND   15 pts**   v   **NEW ZEALAND   42 pts**

	Caps					Caps		
15	17th	**G.H.Davies**	(Wasps)	.		2nd	**K.J.Crowley**	(Taranaki)
14	7th	**S.T.Smith**	(Wasps)	.		4th	**J.J.Kirwan**	(Auckland)
13	32nd & last	**P.W.Dodge (Capt)**	(Leicester)	.		17th	**S.T.Pokere**	(Auckland)
12	2nd	**J.L.B.Salmon**	(Harlequins)	.		12th	**W.T.Taylor**	(Canterbury)
11	2nd	**M.E.Harrison**	(Wakefield)	.		7th	**C.I.Green**	(Canterbury)
10	4th	**S.Barnes**	(Bristol)	.		15th	**W.R.Smith**	(Canterbury)
9	5th	**N.D.Melville**	(Wasps)	.		2nd	**D.E.Kirk**	(Auckland)
1	2nd & last	**R.P.Huntsman**	(Headingley)	.		23rd	**J.C.Ashworth**	(Hawkes' Bay)
2	9th	**S.E.Brain**	(Coventry)	.		34th	**A.G.Dalton (Capt)**	(Counties)
3	23rd	**G.S.Pearce**	(Northampton)	.		33rd	**G.A.Knight**	(Manawatu)
4	7th	**J.Orwin**	(Gloucester)	.		2nd	**M.J.Pierce**	(Wellington)
5	13th	**S.Bainbridge**	(Gosforth)	.		16th	**G.W.Whetton**	(Auckland)
6	13th	**J.P.Hall**	(Bath)	.		26th	**M.W.Shaw**	(Hawkes' Bay)
7	12th & last	**D.H.Cooke**	(Harlequins)	.		14th	**M.J.B.Hobbs**	(Canterbury)
8	3rd	**M.C.Teague**	(Gloucester)	.		31st	**M.G.Mexted**	(Wellington)

	4th	R.J.Hill (Bath) for Melville - 40		.
	6th	W.A.Dooley (Preston G) for Orwin - 65		.

Referee: K.V.J.Fitzgerald   (Australia)

SCORERS:

J.P.Hall	Try	(1st)	4 - 0		
S.Barnes	Conversion		6 - 0		
			6 - 4	**J.J.Kirwan**	Try
			6 - 7	**K.J.Crowley**	Penalty Goal
			6 - 10	**W.R.Smith**	Drop Goal
S.Barnes	D'p Goal	(1st & only)	9 - 10		
			9 - 13	**K.J.Crowley**	Penalty Goal
			Half-time		
			9 - 17	**M.J.B.Hobbs**	Try
			9 - 19	**K.J.Crowley**	Conversion
			9 - 23	**M.G.Mexted**	Try
			9 - 25	**K.J.Crowley**	Conversion
			9 - 29	**C.I.Green**	Try
			9 - 31	**K.J.Crowley**	Conversion
M.E.Harrison	Try	(2nd)	13 - 31		
S.Barnes	Conversion		15 - 31		
			15 - 34	**K.J.Crowley**	Penalty Goal
			15 - 38	**C.I.Green**	Try
			15 - 42	**M.W.Shaw**	Try

POINTS:

S.Barnes	7 points	(15)		**K.J.Crowley**	15 points
M.E.Harrison	4 points	(8)		**C.I.Green**	8 points
J.P.Hall	4 points	(4)		J.J.Kirwan, M.J.B.Hobbs,	
				M.W.Shaw and M.G.Mexted	4 points each
				W.R.Smith	3 points

MATCH COMMENTARY:

Both sides were unchanged for this the second match in the two Test series, and so, for that matter, was the referee, Kerry Fitzgerald. But this time England were totally out-played and soundly thrashed. Although they scored two tries, including another interception by Mike Harrison ("Burglar Bill" to his teammates and to the New Zealand press), they conceded six including one each for the All Black back row. England got an ideal start through a converted try by John Hall after just two minutes, but seven minutes later New Zealand were in the lead and never intended to relinquish it. The classic New Zealand driving pack triumphed. The match was not without its somewhat petulant punch-ups especially at the very end, when referee Fitzgerald almost lost all control, but there can be no doubt that England were well beaten in all aspects of play. England's tactics were somewhat questionable in that all through the second half they persisted in kicking the ball into touch, yet knowing that New Zealand were totally dominant in the line-out. On those rare occasions when England did run the ball New Zealand looked distinctly less comfortable.

This was the highest score ever against England and the biggest ever margin of defeat, one point more than that suffered against South Africa twelve months ago. The difference in pace and performance between the two matches by the All Blacks was awesome, and England could not match the quality or the pace of the play.

91st match   **ENGLAND   21 pts**   v   **WALES   18 pts**

	Caps				Caps		
15	18th	**G.H.Davies**	(Wasps)	.	4th	**P.H.Thorburn**	(Neath)
14	8th	**S.T.Smith**	(Wasps)	.	6th	**P.I.Lewis**	(Llanelli)
13	1st	**S.J.Halliday**	(Bath)	.	1st	**J.A.Devereux**	(Sth Glamorgan Inst)
12	3rd	**J.L.B.Salmon**	(Harlequins)	.	7th	**B.Bowen**	(South Wales Police)
11	10th	**R.Underwood**	(RAF/Leicester)	.	9th	**A.M.Hadley**	(Cardiff)
10	6th	**C.R.Andrew**	(Nottingham)	.	3rd	**J.Davies**	(Neath)
9	6th	**N.D.Melville (Capt)**	(Wasps)	.	1st	**R.N.Jones**	(Swansea)
1	3rd	**P.A.G.Rendall**	(Wasps)		7th	**J.Whitefoot**	(Cardiff)
2	10th	**S.E.Brain**	(Coventry)	.	12th	**W.J.James**	(Aberavon)
3	24th	**G.S.Pearce**	(Northampton)	.	10th	**I.H.Eidman**	(Cardiff)
4	7th	**W.A.Dooley**	(Preston G'Hoppers)	.	15th	**S.J.Perkins**	(Pontypool)
5	22nd	**M.J.Colclough**	(Swansea)	.	1st	**D.R.Waters**	(Newport)
6	14th	**J.P.Hall**	(Bath)	.	2nd	**M.Brown**	(Pontypool)
7	16th	**P.J.Winterbottom**	(Headingley)	.	16th	**D.F.Pickering (Capt)**	(Llanelli)
8	1st	**G.L.Robbins**	(Coventry)	.	3rd	**P.T.Davies**	(Llanelli)

Referee: R.J.Fordham   (Australia)

SCORERS:

SCORERS:	C.R.Andrew	Penalty Goal	3 - 0			
			3 - 3	**P.H.Thorburn**	Penalty Goal	
			3 - 6	**P.H.Thorburn**	Penalty Goal	
	C.R.Andrew	Penalty Goal	6 - 6			
	C.R.Andrew	Penalty Goal	9 - 6			
			9 - 9	**J.Davies**	Drop Goal	
	C.R.Andrew	Penalty Goal	12 - 9			
			Half-time			
	C.R.Andrew	Penalty Goal	15 - 9			
			15 - 12	**P.H.Thorburn**	Penalty Goal	
			15 - 16	**B.Bowen**	Try	
			15 - 18	**P.H.Thorburn**	Conversion	
	C.R.Andrew	Penalty Goal	18 - 18			
	C.R.Andrew	D'p Goal	(5th)	21 - 18		

POINTS:

POINTS:	C.R.Andrew	21 points	(71)	**P.H.Thorburn**	11 points
				B.Bowen	4 points
				J.Davies	3 points

MATCH COMMENTARY:

Eight changes from the side humiliated in New Zealand the previous June duly inspired England to a creditable performance against a bright and alert Welsh team. England, through Dooley and Colclough, dominated the lines-out, and as the game progressed, this dominance extended to all areas of forward play. Rob Andrew played exceptionally well with a fine demonstration of the art of kicking both at goal and out of hand. The newest of the inexperienced Welsh backs, Robert Jones, Jonathan Davies and John Devereux showed immense promise, and despite only one try, the game was exciting and entertaining.   England just deserved their victory on the strength of Rob Andrew's late drop goal. His six penalties in a match equalled the match record, and his 21 points is the highest individual points total in any match for England.

102nd match   **ENGLAND 6 pts**   v   **SCOTLAND 33 pts**

93rd Calcutta Cup

	Caps					Caps		
15	19th	**G.H.Davies**	(Wasps)	.		3rd	**A.G.Hastings**	(Watsonians)
14	9th & last	**S.T.Smith**	(Wasps)	.		3rd	**M.D.F.Duncan**	(West of Scotland)
13	2nd	**S.J.Halliday**	(Bath)	.		25th	**D.I.Johnston**	(Watsonians)
12	4th	**J.L.B.Salmon**	(Harlequins)	.		3rd	**S.Hastings**	(Watsonians)
11	3rd	**M.E.Harrison**	(Wakefield)	.		23rd	**G.R.T.Baird**	(Kelso)
10	7th	**C.R.Andrew**	(Nottingham)	.		35th	**J.Y.Rutherford**	(Selkirk)
9	7th	**N.D.Melville (Capt)**	(Wasps)	.		34th	**R.J.Laidlaw**	(Jedforest)
1	4th	**P.A.G.Rendall**	(Wasps)	.		4th	**A.K.Brewster**	(Stewart's-Melville)
2	11th	**S.E.Brain**	(Coventry)	.		42nd	**C.T.Deans (Capt)**	(Hawick)
3	25th	**G.S.Pearce**	(Northampton)	.		31st	**I.G.Milne**	(Harlequins)
4	8th	**W.A.Dooley**	(Preston G'Hoppers)	.		10th	**A.J.Campbell**	(Hawick)
5	23rd	**M.J.Colclough**	(Swansea)	.		23rd	**I.A.M.Paxton**	(Selkirk)
6	15th	**J.P.Hall**	(Bath)	.		6th	**J.Jeffrey**	(Kelso)
7	17th	**P.J.Winterbottom**	(Headingley)	.		3rd	**F.Calder**	(Stewart's-Melville)
8	2nd & last	**G.L.Robbins**	(Coventry)	.		19th	**J.R.Beattie**	(Glasgow Acad'ls)

	5th	S.Barnes (Bath) for Davies - 40	
	2nd	N.C.Redman (Bath) for Hall - 76	

Referee: R.C.Francis   (New Zealand)

SCORERS:	C.R.Andrew	Penalty Goal	3 - 0			
			3 - 3	A.G.Hastings	Penalty Goal
			3 - 6	A.G.Hastings	Penalty Goal
			3 - 9	A.G.Hastings	Penalty Goal
	C.R.Andrew	Penalty Goal	6 - 9		
			6 - 12	A.G.Hastings	Penalty Goal
			Half-time		
			6 - 16	M.D.F.Duncan	Try
			6 - 18	A.G.Hastings	Conversion
			6 - 21	A.G.Hastings	Penalty Goal
			6 - 25	J.Y.Rutherford	Try
			6 - 27	A.G.Hastings	Conversion
			6 - 31	S.Hastings	Try
			6 - 33	A.G.Hastings	Conversion

POINTS:	C.R.Andrew	6 points	(77)	A.G.Hastings	21 points
				M.D.F.Duncan, S.Hastings	
				and J.Y.Rutherford	4 points each

MATCH COMMENTARY:

The second half of this match was no contest at all. England, with the notable exceptions of Nigel Melville, Steve Brain and Peter Winterbottom seemed just to give up. In this half, Scotland scored three tries but must have come desperately close to six more. John Rutherford and the Scottish backs were immense, none more so than Gavin Hastings who did not miss a kick at goal for his 21 points. Two defeats for England by a record 27 point margin, in less than a year, will, one imagines, give the Selectors something to think about. at their next meeting, for the heavy pack which had beaten Wales had become a liability against Scotland !!

98th match   **ENGLAND   25 pts**   v   **IRELAND   20 pts**

	Caps				Caps		
15	20th	G.H.Davies	(Wasps)	.	24th	H.P.McNeill	(London Irish)
14	4th	M.E.Harrison	(Wakefield)	.	20th	T.M.Ringland	(Ballymena)
13	6th	K.G.Simms	(Cambridge Univ)	.	7th	B.J.Mullin	(UC Dublin)
12	1st	F.J.Clough	(Cambridge Univ)	.	18th	M.J.Kiernan	(Dolphin)
11	11th	R.Underwood	(RAF/Leicester)	.	10th	K.D.Crossan	(Instonians)
10	8th	C.R.Andrew	(Nottingham)	.	1st	R.P.Keyes	(Cork Constitution)
9	8th	N.D.Melville (Capt)	(Wasps)	.	8th	M.T.Bradley	(Cork Constitution)
1	2nd	G.J.Chilcott	(Bath)	.	2nd & last	A.P.Kennedy	(London Irish)
2	12th	S.E.Brain	(Coventry)	.	24th	C.F.Fitzgerald (Capt)	(St Mary's College)
3	26th	G.S.Pearce	(Northampton)	.	4th	D.C.Fitzgerald	(Lansdowne)
4	9th	W.A.Dooley	(Preston G'hoppers)	.	2nd	B.W.McCall	(London Irish)
5	24th	M.J.Colclough	(Swansea)	.	21st	D.G.Lenihan	(Cork Constitution)
6	18th	P.J.Winterbottom	(Headingley)	.	2nd	R.D.Morrow	(Bangor)
7	3rd	G.W.Rees	(Nottingham)	.	6th	N.J.Carr	(Ards)
8	1st	D.Richards	(Leicester)	.	7th	B.J.Spillane	(Bohemians)

3rd & last   J.Palmer (Bath) for Simms -

Referee: C.Norling   (Wales)

SCORERS:

			0 - 4	T.M.Ringland	Try
	Penalty Try		4 - 4		
C.R.Andrew	Conversion		6 - 4		
			6 - 8	B.J.Mullin	Try
			6 - 10	M.J.Kiernan	Conversion
C.R.Andrew	Penalty Goal		9 - 10		
			Half-time		
			9 - 13	M.J.Kiernan	Penalty Goal
D.Richards	Try	(1st)	13 - 13		
C.R.Andrew	Conversion		15 - 13		
G.H.Davies	Try	(4th & last)	19 - 13		
C.R.Andrew	Conversion		21 - 13		
			21 - 16	M.J.Kiernan	Penalty Goal
D.Richards	Try	(2nd)	25 - 16		
			25 - 20	B.W.McCall	Try

POINTS:

C.R.Andrew	9 points	(86)	M.J.Kiernan	8 points
D.Richards	8 points	(8)	B.J.Mullin, B.W.McCall,	
G.H.Davies	4 points	(16)	and T.M.Ringland	4 points each

MATCH COMMENTARY:

Not surprisingly, the Selector's made six team and one positional change after the humiliation at Murrayfield.   This must have been one of the coldest days for an International rugby match for many years, but with snow on the pitch, the match was played and the revised English pack put up a sterling performance. No-one worked harder than Dean Richards, the newly capped Leicester No 8, and he was well rewarded with two tries.   The game was remarkably open considering the conditions and the handling, and six tries, were a credit to both teams.

61st match   **ENGLAND   10 pts**   v   **FRANCE   29 pts**

	Caps					Caps		
15	21st & last	G.H.Davies	(Wasps)	.		38th	S.Blanco	(Biarritz)
14	5th	M.E.Harrison	(Wakefield)	.		7th	J-B.Lafond	(Racing Club)
13	7th	K.G.Simms	(Cambridge Univ)	.		27th	P.Sella	(Agen)
12	2nd	F.J.Clough	(Cambridge Univ)	.		2nd	D.Charvet	(Toulouse)
11	12th	R.Underwood	(RAF/Leicester)	.		5th	E.Bonneval	(Toulouse)
10	9th	C.R.Andrew	(Nottingham)	.		10th	G.Laporte	(Graulhet)
9	9th	N.D.Melville (Capt)	(Wasps)	.		19th	P.Berbizier	(Lourdes)
1	3rd	G.J.Chilcott	(Bath)	.		4th	P.Marocco	(Montferrand)
2	13th & last	S.E.Brain	(Coventry)	.		12th	D.Dubroca (Capt)	(Agen)
3	27th	G.S.Pearce	(Northampton)	.		16th	J-P.Garuet-Lempirou	(Lourdes)
4	10th	W.A.Dooley	(Preston G'hoppers)	.		32nd	F.Haget	(Agen)
5	25th & last	M.J.Colclough	(Swansea)	.		25th	J.Condom	(Boucau)
6	19th	P.J.Winterbottom	(Headingley)	.		5th	E.Champ	(Toulon)
7	4th	G.W.Rees	(Nottingham)	.		22nd	D.Erbani	(Agen)
8	2nd	D.Richards	(Leicester)	.		46th	J-L.Joinel	(Brive)

5th	R.J.Hill (Bath) for Melville - 24	.
6th	S.Barnes (Bath) for Davies - 30	.

Referee: W.D.Bevan   (Wales)

SCORERS:

			0 - 4	G.Laporte	Try	
			0 - 7	G.Laporte	Penalty Goal	
			0 - 10	G.Laporte	Penalty Goal	
			Half-time			
			0 - 14	S.Blanco	Try	
			0 - 17	G.Laporte	Penalty Goal	
			0 - 21		Penalty Try	
			0 - 23	G.Laporte	Conversion	
S.Barnes	Penalty Goal		3 - 23			
S.Barnes	Penalty Goal		6 - 23			
W.A.Dooley	Try	(1st)	10 - 23			
			10 - 27	P.Sella	Try	
			10 - 29	G.Laporte	Conversion	

POINTS:

S.Barnes	6 points	(21)	G.Laporte	17 points	
W.A.Dooley	4 points	(4)	P.Sella	4 points	
			S.Blanco	4 points	

MATCH COMMENTARY:

Although England retained the same side which had performed so creditably against Ireland - albeit in very different conditions, they were thoroughly out-played and out-classed by a lively and enterprising French XV. England's weaknesses had been cruelly exposed, and these could be summed up as a lack of flexibility and mobility, and an apparent rigid adherence to an ill-conceived and unimaginative game plan. When the game plan became inappropriate, England seemed to have no other, nor the wit either to invent one or to improvise.

Although finishing in fourth, not last, place in the table, England had conceded 100 points in the Five Nations Championship, the highest points against total ever, exceeding the previous highest of 88 suffered by England in 1971-72.

SUMMARY OF THE SEASON - 1985 - 86:

England's results in the Five Nations Championship this year were in marked contrast one to another, not only in terms of the scores, but also interms of the means employed to those ends. No tries in the first two games, but the first a creditable victory and the second a sound thrashing. Next, conddifence apparently undiminished, a meritorious win over Ireland and finally a second drubbing, this time at the hands of the Welsh. Both wins were at home, and both thrashings away. But it was an unusual Five Nations series overall, in that there was an unprecedented total of points scored (360), and 34 tries - England's contribution being five and one of those was a penalty try.

The overriding lesson learned from the previous summer's tour to New Zealand was that forward power is all important, and the conclusion drawn was that England must have a large and heavy front five. Five such pillars of oak were selected and remained, with two exceptions, throughout the season. It could be argued too that these five were largely responsible for the wins over Wales and Ireland, but it had to be conceded also that their immobility and lack of pace around the field was largely responsible for England's downfall at Murrayfield and in Paris where lightwieght, mobile and fast forwards won the day by moving the ball in the hand and linking with the backs. The England backs too, proved barely mediocre in International terms and displayed the least flair and enterprise of all the Five Nations teams.

The side to play Wales in the opening match showed eight changes from that which was humiliated against New Zealand on tour, and there were two new caps. Nigel Melville was restored to the captaincy, and Rob Andrew to partner him at fly-half. The result was based on Dooley and Colclough's dominance in the lines-out which spread to other forward areas as the match progressed, and on Rob Andrew's boot. The Welsh came back to catch England and go into the lead in the second half, but England courageously kept at it and Andrew's final penalty goal and last ditch drop goal swung the game to England. It was a good but unimaginative performance, and did not prepare the same side for the culture shock which awaited them at Murrayfield. England tried the same tactics, but the front five did not achieve the expected dominance and Andrew's kicking was somewhat wayward. Consequently, Scotland led at half-time by 12 - 6 - all the scores being penalty goals. At that stage Scotland realised that England had run out of ideas and set about running them ragged such that, towards the end, many of the England side had run out of heart as well as ideas. It was Scotland's biggest ever victory over England and equalled England's biggest ever margin of defeat. But England bounced back after four changes to record their highest points total against the Irish since 1947. The juggernaut front five again held sway but this time aided and abetted by the newly capped Dean Richards whose influence was such that he scored two tries on his debut, both pushovers, and later a penalty try was added to the story of restored English forward dominance. But the same story from Murrayfield was repeated at Parc des Princes, the English pack was too slow by half and the backs too lacking in imagination and flair, both of which the French possessed in abundance and it really was no contest.

Thus England finished the season having won both their home games scoring 46 points and conceding 38 with tries shared four each. The away matches told a very different story, 16 points scored and 62 conceded, one try scored and seven conceded. In all England conceded 100 points during the Five Nations season, their worst record of all time. There were some notable individual achievements - Rob Andrew's 21 points against Wales was an individual match record for England, beating "Dusty" Hare's 19 scored in 1981 and 1982. and Gavin Hastings' 21 points at Murrayfield equalled Ollie Campbell's highest individual points score against England.

Twenty one players represented England during the season and four new caps were awarded, some of whom were to make a significant impact on the English game at all levels in future years, not least of whom was Dean Richards. Maurice Colclough was one of five players who, by the end of the season, had played for England for the last time. Colclough was the last of the 1980 Grand Slam side to retire and his International career had spanned eight years. He went on two Lions' tours, in 1980 and 1983, and played in all four Test Matches on both tours. Huw Davies, born of Welsh parents, nevertheless elected to play for England and was, undoubtedly, one of the most versatile players of his day. He earned 21 caps for England, six at full-back, six in the centre and eight at fly-half, plus one as a replacement, and scored a try on his debut against Scotland in 1981. Steve Brain, the Coventry hooker, won a total of thirteen caps and played a very significant part in the progress and development of the Rugby Club. Simon Smith, a rugby and athletics blue at Cambridge, won nine caps and scored a try on his debut against Romania in 1985. Graham Robbins, the Coventry No 8, gained two caps before yielding to Dean Richards for the Ireland game this season, and had made his mark at the back of the powerful Midlands pack in the Divisional Championships earlier in the season.

FIVE NATIONS CHAMPIONSHIP TABLE:

Won: **Nothing**

		Played	Won	Lost	Drawn	Points: For	Against	Tries: For	Against	Title Points
1 =	France	4	3	1	0	98	52	13	1	6
1 =	Scotland	4	3	1	0	76	54	7	4	6
3 =	Wales	4	2	2	0	74	71	4	8	4
3 =	**ENGLAND**	4	2	2	0	62	100	5	11	4
5	Ireland	4	0	4	0	50	83	5	10	0

Home Games: beat Wales 21 - 18, (no tries to one); beat Ireland 25 - 20, (four tries to three)

Away Games: lost to Scotland 6 - 33, (no tries to three); lost to France 10 - 29, (one try to four)

99th match   **ENGLAND   0 pts**   v   **IRELAND   17 pts**

	Caps					Caps		
15	6th	**W.M.H.Rose**	(Harlequins)	.	27th	**H.P.McNeill**	(Blackrock College)
14	6th	**M.E.Harrison**	(Wakefield)	.	23rd	**T.M.Ringland**	(Ballymena)
13	5th	**J.L.B.Salmon**	(Harlequins)	.	10th	**B.J.Mullin**	(Oxford University)
12	8th	**K.G.Simms**	(Liverpool)	.	21st	**M.J.Kiernan**	(Dolphin)
11	13th	**R.Underwood**	(RAF/Leicester)	.	13th	**K.D.Crossan**	(Instonians)
10	10th	**C.R.Andrew**	(Nottingham)	.	16th	**P.M.Dean**	(St Mary's College)
9	6th	**R.J.Hill (Capt)**	(Bath)	.	11th	**M.T.Bradley**	(Cork Constitution)
1	5th	**P.A.G.Rendall**	(Wasps)	.	52nd	**P.A.Orr**	(Old Wesley)
2	1st	**R.G.R.Dawe**	(Bath)	.	5th	**H.T.Harbison**	(Bective Rangers)
3	28th	**G.S.Pearce**	(Northampton)	.	7th	**D.C.Fitzgerald**	(Lansdowne)
4	3rd	**N.C.Redman**	(Bath)	.	24th	**D.G.Lenihan (Capt)**	(Cork Constitution)
5	1st & only	**D.A.Cusani**	(Orrell)	.	3rd	**J.J.Glennon**	(Skerries)
6	16th	**J.P.Hall**	(Bath)	.	7th	**P.M.Matthews**	(Wanderers)
7	20th	**P.J.Winterbottom**	(Headingley)	.	9th	**N.J.Carr**	(Ards)
8	3rd & last	**P.D.Simpson**	(Bath)	.	9th	**W.A.Anderson**	(Dungannon)

7th   S.Barnes (Bath) for Rose -

Referee: R.Hourquet   (France)

SCORERS:

0 - 3	**M.J.Kiernan**	Penalty Goal
0 - 7	**M.J.Kiernan**	Try
0 - 9	**M.J.Kiernan**	Conversion
Half-time		
0 - 13	**P.M.Matthews**	Try
0 - 17	**K.D.Crossan**	Try

POINTS:

M.J.Kiernan	9 points
K.D.Crossan	4 points
P.M.Matthews	4 points

MATCH COMMENTARY:

England had prepared assiduously and at some length of time for the new Five Nations season as well as for this match, as part of their build-up for the 1987 Inaugural World Cup to be held in the Antipodes early in the summer. In spite of that, surely not because of it, the England performance was an immense disappointment, and the reasons for it were not easily understood. There seemed to be no drive, co-ordination or even sense of purpose in the side, the half-backs were frail and indecisive, and Paul Simpson, out of position at No 8 looked lost. Neither Steve Bainbridge nor Wade Dooley were available because of injury, but the sterling efforts of Nigel Redman and Dave Cusani were negated by Renee Hourquet's *laissez-faire* refereeing. Ireland themselves did not play well but they did score three tries and as England tried to respond it seemed that Richard Hill continually took the wrong options and the spirit in the side faded away. Thus it was that England slipped to their worst defeat by Ireland for forty years.

Not for 74 games had England failed to score a point in an International match, the last occasion was in January 1973 when New Zealand won by nine points to nil at Twickenham.

62nd match   **ENGLAND   15 pts**   v   **FRANCE   19 pts**

	Caps					Caps		
15	7th	W.M.H.Rose	(Harlequins)	.		47th	S.Blanco	(Biarritz)
14	7th	M.E.Harrison	(Wakefield)	.		5th	P.Berot	(Agen)
13	6th	J.L.B.Salmon	(Harlequins)	.		37th	P.Sella	(Agen)
12	9th	K.G.Simms	(Liverpool)	.		9th	D.Charvet	(Toulouse)
11	14th	R.Underwood	(RAF/Leicester)	.		14th	E.Bonneval	(Toulouse)
10	11th	C.R.Andrew	(Nottingham)	.		4th	F.Mesnel	(Racing Club)
9	7th	R.J.Hill (Capt)	(Bath)	.		28th	P.Berbizier	(Lourdes)
1	6th	P.A.G.Rendall	(Wasps)	.		3rd	P.Ondarts	(Biarritz)
2	2nd	R.G.R.Dawe	(Bath)	.		21st	D.Dubroca (Capt)	(Agen)
3	29th	G.S.Pearce	(Northampton)	.		24th	J-P.Garuet-Lempirou	(Lourdes)
4	11th	W.A.Dooley	(Preston G'hoppers)	.		17th	A.Lorieux	(Grenoble)
5	14th	S.Bainbridge	(Gosforth)	.		34th	J.Condom	(Boucau)
6	21st	P.J.Winterbottom	(Headingley)	.		15th	E.Champ	(Toulon)
7	5th	G.W.Rees	(Nottingham)	.		28th	D.Erbani	(Agen)
8	17th	J.P.Hall	(Bath)	.		27th	L.Rodriguez	(Montferrand)

	4th	G.J.Chilcott (Bath) for Rendall -		.

Referee: J.M.Flemimg   (Scotland)

SCORERS:	W.M.H.Rose	Penalty Goal		3 - 0			
	W.M.H.Rose	Penalty Goal		6 - 0			
	W.M.H.Rose	Penalty Goal		9 - 0			
				9 - 3	F.Mesnel	Drop Goal
	C.R.Andrew	D'p Goal	(6th)	12 - 3		
				Half-time		
				12 - 6	S.Blanco	Drop Goal
				12 - 10	E.Bonneval	Try
				12 - 12	P.Berot	Conversion
				12 - 16	P.Sella	Try
	W.M.H.Rose	Penalty Goal		15 - 16		
				15 - 19	P.Berot	Penalty Goal

POINTS:	W.M.H.Rose	12 points	(53)	P.Berot	5 points
	C.R.Andrew	3 points	(89)	P.Sella and E.Bonneval	4 points each
				S.Blanco and F.Mesnel	3 points each

MATCH COMMENTARY:

The two first choice locks, Dooley and Bainbridge, were available again and the selectors replaced Paul Simpson with Gary Rees but put John Hall at No 8.   The result was a very much improved England performance up front and a bit more confidence at half-back, so much so that England led by 12 points to 3 at half-time.   But there was no penetration in the three-quarter line with Marcus Rose showing no inclination to enter the line.   In the second half the French pack squared up to their opponents, and started gaining better quality possession and further reduced England's chances of scoring a try.   Phillipe Sella's try summed up England's trials and tribulations when he intercepted a pass from Richard Hill to Rob Andrew and ran 65 yards to score.   Until then England led, but after that they were doomed.

92nd match   **ENGLAND**   **12 pts**   v   **WALES**   **19 pts**

	Caps					Caps		
15	8th	W.M.H.Rose	(Harlequins)	.		8th	M.A.Wyatt	(Swansea)
14	8th	M.E.Harrison	(Wakefield)	.		4th	G.M.C.Webbe	(Bridgend)
13	10th	K.G.Simms	(Liverpool)	.		9th	J.A.Devereux	(Bridgend)
12	7th	J.L.B.Salmon	(Harlequins)	.		3rd	K.Hopkins	(Swansea)
11	15th	R.Underwood	(RAF/Leicester)	.		2nd	I.C.Evans	(Llanelli)
10	12th	C.R.Andrew	(Nottingham)	.		11th	J.Davies	(Llanelli)
9	8th	R.J.Hill (Capt)	(Bath)	.		9th	R.N.Jones	(Swansea)
1	5th	G.J.Chilcott	(Bath)	.		15th	J.Whitefoot	(Cardiff)
2	3rd	R.G.R.Dawe	(Bath)	.		19th	W.J.James	(Aberavon)
3	30th	G.S.Pearce	(Northampton)	.		7th	S.Evans	(Neath)
4	12th	W.A.Dooley	(Preston G'hoppers)	.		4th	S.Sutton	(South Wales Police)
5	15th	S.Bainbridge	(Gosforth)	.		20th	R.L.Norster	(Cardiff)
6	22nd	P.J.Winterbottom	(Headingley)	.		7th	W.P.Moriarty	(Swansea)
7	6th	G.W.Rees	(Nottingham)	.		22nd	D.F.Pickering (Capt)	(Llanelli)
8	18th	J.P.Hall	(Bath)	.		11th	P.T.Davies	(Llanelli)
				.		1st	R.G.Collins (S Wales P'lce) for Davies -	

Referee: R.Megson   (Scotland)

SCORERS:

W.M.H.Rose	Penalty Goal	3 - 0			
		3 - 3	M.A.Wyatt	Penalty Goal	
		3 - 6	M.A.Wyatt	Penalty Goal	
		3 - 9	M.A.Wyatt	Penalty Goal	
W.M.H.Rose	Penalty Goal	6 - 9			
		6 - 12	M.A.Wyatt	Penalty Goal	
W.M.H.Rose	Penalty Goal	9 - 12			
		Half-time			
		9 - 15	M.A.Wyatt	Penalty Goal	
		9 - 19	S.Evans	Try	
W.M.H.Rose	Penalty Goal	12 - 19			

POINTS:

W.M.H.Rose	12 points	M.A.Wyatt	15 points
		S.Evans	4 points

MATCH COMMENTARY:

An unedifying and very indisciplined game in which several players, on either side, were lucky not to be sent off. The fists were flying from the first minute, and Richard Hill did little to exert a calming influence on his pack. The lines-out were the area of greatest contention where a mighty battle was fought for possession between Wade Dooley and Steve Bainbridge, for England, and Robert Norster and Steve Sutton for Wales, and this was where tempers became short and the physical contest went beyond the laws. When Wade Dooley flattened Phil Davies with a punch to the jaw, the match was almost out of control. Four England players were dropped as a disciplinary measure after the match, Dooley, Dawe, Chilcott and the captain Richard Hill. The fact that nine penalty goals were scored in the match, and only one try, says much for the quality of rugby on display. Wales probably had the edge because their half-back pairing of Robert Jones and Jonathan Davies kept their cool when all around were losing theirs.

103rd match
94th Calcutta Cup

ENGLAND   21 pts   v   SCOTLAND   12 pts

	Caps					Caps		
15	9th	W.M.H.Rose	(Harlequins)	.	9th	A.G.Hastings	(Watsonians)
14	9th	M.E.Harrison (Capt)	(Wakefield)	.	8th	M.D.F.Duncan	(West of Scotland)
13	3rd	S.J.Halliday	(Bath)	.	36th	K.W.Robertson	(Melrose)
12	8th	J.L.B.Salmon	(Harlequins)	.	26th	G.R.T.Baird	(Kelso)
11	16th	R.Underwood	(RAF/Leicester)	.	5th	I.Tukalo	(Selkirk)
10	1st	P.N.Williams	(Orrell)	.	41st	J.Y.Rutherford	(Selkirk)
9	4th	R.M.Harding	(Bristol)	.	40th	R.J.Laidlaw	(Jedforest)
1	7th	P.A.G.Rendall	(Wasps)	.	6th	D.M.B.Sole	(Bath)
2	1st	B.C.Moore	(Nottingham)	.	48th	C.T.Deans (Capt)	(Hawick)
3	31st	G.S.Pearce	(Northampton)	.	37th	I.G.Milne	(Heriot's)
4	4th	N.C.Redman	(Bath)	.	6th	D.B.White	(Gala)
5	16th	S.Bainbridge	(Gosforth)	.	29th	I.A.M.Paxton	(Selkirk)
6	19th	J.P.Hall	(Bath)	.	12th	J.Jeffrey	(Kelso)
7	7th	G.W.Rees	(Nottingham)	.	9th	F.Calder	(Stewart's-Melville)
8	3rd	D.Richards	(Leicester)	.	25th & last	J.R.Beattie	(Glasgow Acad'ls)
				.	44th	A.J.Tomes (Hawick) for Beattie - 45	

Referee: O.E.Doyle   (Ireland)

SCORERS:

			0 - 3	A.G.Hastings	Penalty Goal
W.M.H.Rose	Penalty Goal		3 - 3		
	Penalty Try		7 - 3		
W.M.H.Rose	Conversion		9 - 3		
			Half-time		
W.M.H.Rose	Penalty Goal		12 - 3		
W.M.H.Rose	Try	(2nd & last)	16 - 3		
W.M.H.Rose	Conversion		18 - 3		
			18 - 6	A.G.Hastings	Penalty Goal
W.M.H.Rose	Penalty Goal		21 - 6		
			21 - 10	K.W.Robertson	Try
			21 - 12	A.G.Hastings	Conversion

POINTS:

W.M.H.Rose	17 points	(82)		A.G.Hastings	8 points
Penalty Try	4 points			K.W.Robertson	4 points

MATCH COMMENTARY:

Scotland came to Twickenham yet again looking for a victory which would give them the Triple Crown - and with England's record so far this season, they had cause to be optimistic. Apart from the four disciplinary changes after Cardiff, England made three other changes, and whatever the reason, England rose to the occasion and the pack played magnificently. Conditions were very heavy and did not suit Scotland's light and mobile pack, and England were able to slow the tempo down and frustrate the Scots. England scored two tries, albeit one of them a penalty try, but the best try of the match was undoubtedly Keith Robertson's when Scotland were all but down and out. Last year's humiliation at Murrayfield had at least been avenged, and it seemed that all the good intentions and plans laid in the weeks before the Championship started had come to fruition in this match - but it had still been a very poor season for England.

SUMMARY OF THE SEASON - 1986 - 87:

The preparations for this season, and indirectly for the forthcoming World Cup, if they were intended to bring England to a peak of fitness and readiness for the World Cup, after the Five Nations Championship, then they could be said to have been successful. If, conversely, and as is most likely, they had been planned to generate a successful Five Nations performance as a stepping stone to a serious challenge for the World Cup, then they were an abject failure. In an unprecedented move, England had named a 40-man squad in the summer of 1986, and had given each member an individual training schedule prepared by Tom McNab, the British Olympic Coach. Then, in October, the whole squad were taken to Portugal for five days of training and preparation. The result, in the first three matches of the Championship at least, was a disaster. Indeed at that stage, England looked to be heading for their worst ever season, and a dreaded "whitewash" was imminent. They had lost three matches; they had lost their way completely at Cardiff, following which the RFU had declared that four players, including the Captain, would not be considered for selection for the last match of the season; and in three games they had failed to score a try.

The match against Ireland, notwithstanding the non-availability of Wade Dooley, Steve Bainbridge and Dean Richards, was calamitous and England looked like a third rate scratch regional side who had had no opportunity before the match to get to know each other.

Against France, with the return of Dooley and Bainbridge (but not Richards, John Hall moving to No 8) and against much stronger opponents, the whole side, especially the pack played with committment and courage, but they lacked inspiration and were still not good enough even to score a try, let alone win the match. There were signs, too, in the French match, of frustration leading to gratuitous violence, and, in fact, the French proved better disciplined than some of the English forwards. Gareth Chilcott for Paul Rendall was the only change made for Cardiff where an appalling exhibition of all that can be unacceptable about the game took place. It was a continuation of the reaction to frustration seen in the French match, fuelled by a desire not to be intimidated by the Welsh at Cardiff where England had not won since 1963, together with some injudicious motivational imprecations by the Captain in the team-talk immediately before the match. The outcome was nothing short of an inexcusable disgrace and the RFU were absolutely right to take the action they did. The appointment of Mike Harrison, "Burglar Bill" of the New Zealand tour, as Captain probably had more effect on the teams performance and on the match result than the seven team changes which were made, four pre-announced, for the final match of the season against Scotland. The spirit was different, the application and committment was greater and legitimate, and the result spoke for itself. Mike Harrison had had a most successful season in leading Yorkshire to memorable win in the County Championship Final over Middlesex - beating Lancashire by a record 42 points to 7 on the way, and in leading the North to the Divisional Championship. He appeared to give England direction, responsibility and a self-belief, and it was no surprise when he was appointed to lead England into the 1987 World Cup.

Scotland had come to Twickenham for the fifth time since 1947, in the hope of beating England and securing the coveted Triple Crown, and each time they had been thwarted. They had won only twice at Twickenham since 1947, in 1971 and 1983, and in each of those seasons they had lost every other Five Nations match.

England thus finished a very disappointing season with only two points and, although sharing fourth place in the Table with Wales, they had an inferior points difference and so were, to all intents an purposes, at the bottom of the pile. England have not now won a match away from Twickenham since February 1982, when they beat France in Paris. This represents a losing sequence of ten Five Nations matches and fourteen matches against all opposition, including the tours to South Africa and New Zealand.

Marcus Rose became the sixth England player to score fifty individual points in International matches when he kicked his third penalty goal against France in his seventh International match.

Twenty four players were engaged in the four Five Nations matches, and in addition Stuart Barnes was used as a replacement against Ireland. Four new caps were awarded; to Peter Williams, Brian Moore, Graham Dawe and Dave Cusani. In view of the imminence of the World Cup, it was not surprising that only two players were not to appear for England again, both, presumably, would not have wished it that way. Paul Simpson, whose greatest hour was his first cap against the All Blacks in 1983 when England won, and he took all the knocks which the All Blacks could throw at him and never stopped smiling, won three caps. Dave Cusani, the Orrell lock, was limited to only one.

FIVE NATIONS CHAMPIONSHIP TABLE:

Won: **Calcutta Cup**

		Played	Won	Lost	Drawn	Points: For	Against	Tries: For	Against	Title Points
1	France	4	4	0	0	82	59	10	4	8
2 =	Ireland	4	2	2	0	57	46	8	6	4
2 =	Scotland	4	2	2	0	71	76	7	8	4
4 =	Wales	4	1	3	0	54	64	4	6	2
4 =	**ENGLAND**	4	1	3	0	48	67	2	7	2

Home Games: lost to France 15 - 19, (no tries to two); beat Scotland 21 - 12, (two tries to one)

Away Games: lost to Ireland 0 - 17, (no tries to three); lost to Wales 12 - 19, (no tries to one)

THE WORLD CUP - 1987:

THE WORLD CUP SQUAD:

Manager:	M.P.Weston		Coach:		M.J.Green		Captain:		M.E.Harrison	

Full-backs:	W.M.H.Rose	(Harlequins)	9 caps	Forwards:	S.J.Bainbridge	(Fylde)	16 caps
	J.M.Webb	(Bristol)	no caps		G.J.Chilcott	(Bath)	5 caps
					R.G.R.Dawe	(Bath)	3 caps
Three-quarters:	M.D.Bailey	(Wasps)	2 caps		W.A.Dooley	(Fylde)	12 caps
	F.J.Clough	(Orrell)	2 caps		D.W.Egerton	(Bath)	no caps
	M.E.Harrison	(Wakefield)	9 caps		J.P.Hall	(Bath)	19 caps
	J.L.B.Salmon	(Harlequins)	8 caps		B.C.Moore	(Nottingham)	1 cap
	K.G.Simms	(Wasps)	10 caps		G.S.Pearce	(Northampton)	31 caps
	R.Underwood	(RAF/Leicester)	16 caps		J.A.Probyn	(Wasps)	no caps
					N.C.Redman	(Bath)	4 caps
Half-backs:	C.R.Andrew	(Wasps)	12 caps		G.W.Rees	(Nottingham)	7 caps
	R.M.Harding	(Bristol)	4 caps		P.A.G.Rendall	(Wasps)	7 caps
	R.J.Hill	(Bath)	8 caps		D.Richards	(Leicester)	3 caps
	P.N.Williams	(Orrell)	1 cap		P.J.Winterbottom	(Headingley)	22 caps
Replacements:	G.H.Davies	(Wasps)	21 caps		M.G.Skinner	(Harlequins)	no caps

ENGLAND - WORLD CUP RESULTS:

Pool 1 matches:

May 23rd	AUSTRALIA	at Concord Oval	LOST	6 - 19	(one try to two)
May 30th	JAPAN	at Concord Oval	WON	60 - 7	(ten tries to one)
June 3rd	U.S.A.	at Concord Oval	WON	34 - 6	(four tries to one)

Quarter Final:

June 8th	WALES	at Ballymore	LOST	3 - 16	(no tries to three)

WORLD CUP WINNERS:	NEW ZEALAND	beat FRANCE in the Final	29 - 9	(three tries to one)
		beat WALES in the Semi-Final	49 - 6	(eight tries to one)
RUNNER UP:	FRANCE	beat AUSTRALIA in the Semi-Final	30 - 24	(four tries to two)
3rd PLACE	WALES	beat AUSTRALIA in the Play-off	22 - 21	(three tries to two)
4th PLACE	AUSTRALIA			
BEATEN QUARTER FINALISTS:	ENGLAND	lost to WALES	3 - 16	(no tries to three)
	IRELAND	lost to AUSTRALIA	15 - 33	(two tries to four)
	FIJI	lost to FRANCE	16 - 31	(two tries to four)
	SCOTLAND	lost to NEW ZEALAND	3 - 30	(no tries to two)

WORLD CUP 1987 SUMMARY:

The Inaugural World Cup no doubt took the game of Rugby Union Football to new heights in terms of public exposure and awareness, and probably sowed the early seeds of professionalism which took a further eight years to flourish on the occasion of the third tournament in South Africa in 1995. But the first step on that road, rocky though it may prove to be, was the need to sell the game to a wider National and International audience, and the tournament succeeded in doing that with a series of matches, all of which were admirable advertisements for the game. All the matches were played in the best of spirits and some of them rose to sublime heights of achievement and spectacle. Most notable of these was probably the magnificent semi-final between France and Australia. There were organisational inadequacies, inevitably. The arrangements to hold the tournament in two centres, Australia and New Zealand, tended to reduce the impact in both; the refereeing arrangements and standards, particularly consistency of interpretation, created difficulties and some frustration and the omission of two of the best referees in the world, Clive Norling and Roger Quittenton from the list of those being considered for the last two matches of the tournament, the Final and the Third-place play-off, was, to say the least, difficult to understand. For the general public, the ticketing facilities and marketing services left much to be desired. Nevertheless, the legacy of the first World Cup will be a far-reaching and enthusiastic audience for the game generating wider participation upon which, in future, it will undoubtedly expand and prosper. The most profound of all the lessons from the first World Cup was, again, the gulf which undeniably exists between Southern Hemisphere at this time, New Zealand, rugby and that of the Northern Hemisphere. It seems that as standards of play and fitness increase in the north, they increase that little bit more in the south. New Zealand were unarguably the supreme Champions and they underlined that position emphatically by scoring 298 points and 43 tries in six matches, while conceding only 52 points. This represents an average match score of almost 50 points to 9 and seven tries in each match - and that against the best in the world !!

England's part in this bright shop-window for the game was destined to be unspectacular and to a degree unmemorable. One can be excused of harbouring the thought that the RFU, and possibly the Five Nations Committee, did not take the event as seriously as they might have done, and it is certainly true that they underestimated the impact that the event would have on both the game and its potential world-wide audience.

That apart, England's organisation in the tournament itself was somewhat hap-hazard and cavalier. Immediately after their opening match against Australia, the whole party went off to Hamilton Island for a few days relaxation when, surely, intense preparations should have been underway, not just for the two remaining pool games, but also for the sterner tests which would follow. The first of these was likely to be, and so it proved, a Quarter-final against Wales, which, considering what took place during the previous meeting of the two sides, was a trifle unfortunate. The defeat by Australia was England's fourteenth successive defeat away from home - they had not won away since 1982 in Paris. The two remaining pool matches were won without difficulty, the one against Japan yielding a record total score and record winning margin as well as a record post-war try count, but the Quarter-final against Wales saw England plumbing the depths of despair and mediocrity with a very, very poor performance. Wales, themselves, were far below their best, having suffered many injuries which had upset their rhythm and their continuity, but although they did not play well, they were plenty good enough to beat a poor England side. The pity was, apart from having to return home as nowhere near the first four in World Rugby rankings, many failed to realise the extent of the inadequacies in England's performance and organisation which had been so cruelly exposed in the tournament. In the close season, at home, Mike Weston was appointed as "Honorary" Team Manager, but within weeks he had resigned when he could not persuade the RFU to retain the services of Martin Green as a selector. In his place came Geoff Cooke with several new brooms and another chapter in the chequered history of English International Rugby was about to open.

Mike Harrison, as Captain for the World Cup, made the best of a bad job, in circumstances which were not easy. He was not a tactician, nor a deep thinker about the game, and his approach could be described as cavalier - as was his approach to his own personal play. In that sense, he was good for the side, but he had some mighty millstones round his neck, and not surprisingly failed to lift the team above its self-imposed level of mediocrity. Of the squad of 26 players, three, Dave Egerton, John Hall and Jeff Probyn did not play in a match, nor, for that matter did Huw Davies nor Micky Skinner who were summoned to join the squad following injuries. Five players played in all four matches, the captain, Mike Harrison, Jamie Salmon and the back row of Peter Winterbottom, Gary Rees and Dean Richards. In fact, Jonathan Webb also played in all the matches but he was a replacement for Marcus Rose in the first.

Four players called it a day after the World Cup. Steve Bainbridge had won 18 caps and his International career was doubtless abbreviated by his disciplinary record in having been sent off in first-class rugby three times in all. He went on the Lion's tour in 1983, as a late replacement for Donal Lenihan and played in two Tests. He was a schoolteacher in Newcastle. Jamie Salmon, 12 English caps, had also won three All Black caps during the time he spent in New Zealand in the late seventies and early eighties; he, too was a teacher. Fran Clough of Orrell, had won four caps and continued playing club rugby for many years to come, and Peter Williams, also of Orrell, and also having won four caps, signed for Salford Rugby League Club.

So ended a rather sad and depressing World Cup campaign for England, but, with hindsight, the match against Wales was probably the turning point in the chronicle of English International Rugby which was to lead to the successes of the Nineties.

THE ENGLAND 1987 WORLD CUP SQUAD.

Back Row: Official, K.G.Simms, R.M.Harding, C.R.Andrew, P.A.G.Rendall, W.M.H.Rose, G.W.Rees. R.G.R.Dawe, G.J.Chilcott, B.C.Moore, R.J.Hill,

Middle Row: Official, J.A.Probyn, M.D.Bailey, F.J.Clough, J.P.Hall, D.Richards, W.A.Dooley, S.Bainbridge, D.W.Egerton, N.C.Redman, J.M.Webb, P.N.Williams, and P.J.Winterbottom,

Seated:Official, Official, M.J.Green (Coach), G.S.Pearce, M.P.Weston (Manager), M.E.Harrison (Captain), A.Grimsdell (President RFU), R.Underwood, Official, J.L.B.Salmon and D.Wood (Secretary RFU)

13th match   # ENGLAND   6 pts   v   # AUSTRALIA   19 pts

	Caps				Caps		
15	10th & last	**W.M.H.Rose**	(Harlequins)	.	25th & last	**R.G.Gould**	(Queensland)
14	10th	**M.E.Harrison (Capt)**	(Wakefield)		21st	**P.C.Grigg**	(Queensland)
13	11th	**K.G.Simms**	(Wasps)		34th	**A.G.Slack (Capt)**	(Queensland)
12	9th	**J.L.B.Salmon**	(Harlequins)		9th	**B.Papworth**	(New South Wales)
11	17th	**R.Underwood**	(RAF/Leicester)		28th	**D.I.Campese**	(ACT)
10	2nd	**P.N.Williams**	(Orrell)	.	16th	**M.P.Lynagh**	(Queensland)
9	5th	**R.M.Harding**	(Bristol)		18th	**N.C.Farr-Jones**	(New South Wales)
1	8th	**P.A.G.Rendall**	(Wasps)	.	21st	**E.E.Rodriguez**	(New South Wales)
2	2nd	**B.C.Moore**	(Nottingham)		23rd	**T.A.Lawton**	(Queensland)
3	32nd	**G.S.Pearce**	(Northampton)		23rd	**A.J.McIntyre**	(Queensland)
4	13th	**W.A.Dooley**	(Preston G'hoppers)	.	20th	**S.A.G.Cutler**	(New South Wales)
5	5th	**N.C.Redman**	(Bath)		10th	**W.A.Campbell**	(Queensland)
6	23rd	**P.J.Winterbottom**	(Headingley)		42nd	**S.P.Poidevin**	(New South Wales)
7	8th	**G.W.Rees**	(Nottingham)		20th	**S.N.Tuynman**	(New South Wales)
8	4th	**D.Richards**	(Leicester)	.	1st	**T.Coker**	(Queensland)
	1st	J.M.Webb (Bristol) for Rose - 5		.	2nd	S.L.James (New South Wales) for Gould -	

Referee: K.H.Lawrence   (New Zealand)

SCORERS:

				0 - 3	M.P.Lynagh	Penalty Goal
				0 - 6	M.P.Lynagh	Penalty Goal
M.E.Harrison	Try	(3rd)		4 - 6		
J.M.Webb	Conversion			6 - 6		
				Half-time		
				6 - 10	**D.I.Campese**	Try
				6 - 13	**M.P.Lynagh**	Penalty Goal
				6 - 17	**S.P.Poidevin**	Try
				6 - 19	**M.P.Lynagh**	Conversion

POINTS:

M.E.Harrison	4 points	(12)		**M.P.Lynagh**	11 points
J.M.Webb	2 points	(2)		**S.P.Poidevin**	4 points
				D.I.Campese	4 points

MATCH COMMENTARY:

England put up a stout performance in their first World Cup tie and the match was a splendid advertisement for the game in general and this tournament in particular. England were certainly unfortunate to lose the match by thirteen points because this was not a correct indication of the difference between the two sides. Midway through the second half, the score was tied at six points each with England looking the better of the two sides, David Campese crossed the English line and was tackled by Peter Williams whereupon Campese lost control of the ball and certainly did not touch it down. Nevertheless the try was given by the New Zealand referee Keith Lawrence. He was particularly severe on the England line-out such that the penalty count for the match was 19 - 6 to Australia, exactly the same as the match score. This is not to say that England deserved to win, they did not, but they contributed to a magnificent match in which the England back row showed the world how to gain possession on the ground. Marcus Rose was concussed very early in the game, and Jonathan Webb proved an admirable alternative in winning his first cap for England.

1st match   **ENGLAND   60 pts**   v   **JAPAN   7 pts**

	Caps					Caps		
15	2nd	J.M.Webb	(Bristol)	.		D.Murai	(Marubeni)
14	11th	M.E.Harrison (Capt)	(Wakefield)	.		N.Taumoefolau	(Sanyo)
13	12th	K.G.Simms	(Wasps)	.		E.Kutsuki	(Toyota)
12	10th	J.L.B.Salmon	(Harlequins)	.		K.Matsuo	(Doshiba U)
11	18th	R.Underwood	(RAF/Leicester)	.		S.Onuki	(Suntory)
10	3rd	P.N.Williams	(Orrell)	.		S.Hirao	(Kobe Steel)
9	6th	R.M.Harding	(Bristol)	.		M.Hagimoto	
1	9th	P.A.G.Rendall	(Wasps)	.		T.Kimura	(World)
2	3rd	B.C.Moore	(Nottingham)	.		T.Fujita	(Nissan Steel)
3	6th	G.J.Chilcott	(Bath)	.		K.Horaguchi	(Nippon Steel)
4	6th	N.C.Redman	(Bath)	.		S.Kurihara	(Waseda University)
5	17th	S.Bainbridge	(Gossforth)	.		A.Oyagi	(World)
6	24th	P.J.Winterbottom	(Headingley)	.		K.Miyamoto	(Doshiba U)
7	9th	G.W.Rees	(Nottingham)	.		T.Hayashi (Capt)	(Kobe Steel)
8	5th	D.Richards	(Leicester)	.		M.Chida	(Nippon Steel)

	3rd	F.J.Clough (Cambridge Univ) for Simms -		.
	13th	C.R.Andrew (Wasps) for Williams -		.

Referee: R.Hourquet   (France)

SCORERS:

J.M.Webb	Penalty Goal		3 - 0			
J.M.Webb	Penalty Goal		6 - 0			
R.Underwood	Try	(3rd)	10 - 0			
G.W.Rees	Try	(1st)	14 - 0			
J.M.Webb	Conversion		16 - 0			
			16 - 3	K.Matsuo	Penalty Goal	
			Half-time			

England expanded their game in the second half to score eight further tries, six of them converted by Jonathan Webb. The try scorers were:

D.Richards (3rd), K.G.Simms (1st & only), N.C.Redman (1st & only), R.Underwood (4th), M.E.Harrison (4th, 5th and 6th), and J.L.B.Salmon (1st & only)
Japan's only try was scored by K.Miyamoto.

POINTS:

J.M.Webb	20 points	(22)		K.Miyamoto	4 points
M.E.Harrison	12 points	(24)		K.Matsuo	3 points
R.Underwood	8 points	(16)			
J.L.B.Salmon, D.Richards,		(4),(12)			
K.G.Simms, N.C.Redman	4 points	(4),(4)			
and G.W.Rees	each	(4)			

MATCH COMMENTARY:

It took the England pack fully thirty minutes to settle to the pace at which the Japanese started the game, but once that was done, then the tries came and the pack could ease off in the set piece and concentrate on getting to the breakdown as quickly as possible..Even so, England conceded fifteen penalties for which really there was no need nor any excuse. Mike Harrison's remarkable hat-trick of tries came within the space of thirteen minutes and Gary Rees and Peter Winterbottom had a field day and were both all over the field at considerable pace. Mike Weston and Martin Green, in anticipating the rule on tactical substitutions, took both Peter Williams and Kevin Simms off the fiel as a precautionary measure after minor injuries, but this did not stem the flow of tries and expansive running at all. To their credit, the Japanese tackled like dervishes and with considerable courage, but were unable to prevent a record score for England containing a record ten tries in the match.

1st match   **ENGLAND   34 pts**   v   **U.S.A.   6 pts**

	Caps					Caps	
15	3rd	**J.M.Webb**	(Bristol)	.		R.Nelson	(Pacific Coast)
14	12th	**M.E.Harrison (Capt)**	(Wakefield)	.		**M.Purcell**	(Pacific Coast)
13	4th & last	**F.J.Clough**	(Cambridge Univ)	.		**K.Higgins**	(Pacific Coast)
12	11th	**J.L.B.Salmon**	(Harlequins)	.		**T.Vinick**	(Eastern Union)
11	3rd	**M.D.Bailey**	(Wasps)	.		**G.Hein**	(Pacific Coast)
10	14th	**C.R.Andrew**	(Wasps)	.		**J.Clarkson**	(Pacific Coast)
9	9th	**R.J.Hill**	(Bath)	.		**M.Saunders**	(Pacific Coast)
1	7th	**G.J.Chilcott**	(Bath)	.		**R.Bailey**	(Pacific Coast)
2	4th	**R.G.R.Dawe**	(Bath)	.		**J.Everett**	(Pacific Coast)
3	33rd	**G.S.Pearce**	(Northampton)	.		**N.Brendel**	(Mid-Western Union)
4	14th	**W.A.Dooley**	(Preston G'hoppers)	.		**R.Causey**	(Eastern Union)
5	18th & last	**S.Bainbridge**	(Gosforth)	.		**E.Burlingham (Capt)**	(Pacific Coast)
6	25th	**P.J.Winterbottom**	(Headingley)	.		**G.Lambert**	(Eastern Union)
7	10th	**G.W.Rees**	(Nottingham)	.		**S.Finkel**	(Mid-Western Union)
8	6th	**D.Richards**	(Leicester)	.		**B.Vizard**	(Pacific Coast)

Referee: K.V.J.Fitzgerald   (Australia)

SCORERS:						
	J.M.Webb	Penalty Goal		3 - 0		
	P.J.Winterbottom	Try	(1st)	7 - 0		
	J.M.Webb	Conversion		9 - 0		
	J.M.Webb	Penalty Goal		12 - 0		
			Half-time			
	P.J.Winterbottom	Try	(2nd)	16 - 0		
	J.M.Webb	Penalty Goal		19 - 0		
	J.M.Webb	Penalty Goal		22 - 0		
	M.E.Harrison	Try	(7th)	26 - 0		
	J.M.Webb	Conversion		28 - 0		
				28 - 4	M.Purcell	Try
				28 - 6	R.Nelson	Conversion
	W.A.Dooley	Try	(2nd)	32 - 6		
	J.M.Webb	Conversion		34 - 6		

POINTS:						
	J.M.Webb	18 points	(40)		M.Purcell	4 points
	P.J.Winterbottom	8 points	(8)		R.Nelson	2 points
	M.E.Harrison and W.A.Dooley	4 points	(20),(8)			
		each				

MATCH COMMENTARY:

Messrs Weston and Green made eight changes from the side which had dealt so comprehensively with Japan four days previously, but, significantly the same back row of Peter Winterbottom, Gary Rees and Dean Richards stayed together, presumably to make assurance doubly sure. The Americans had beaten Japan and put up a solid performance against Australia so any slip up in this match was unthinkable. In the event, England ran out fairly easy winners by four tries to one, and the dreadful prospect of failing to qualify for the Quarter-finals was eliminated.

93rd match   **ENGLAND   3 pts**   v   **WALES   16 pts**

	Caps					Caps		
15	4th	J.M.Webb	(Bristol)	.	12th	P.H.Thorburn	(Neath)
14	13th	M.E.Harrison (Capt)	(Wakefield)	.	7th	I.C.Evans	(Llanelli)
13	13th	K.G.Simms	(Wasps)	.	14th	J.A.Devereux	(Bridgend)
12	12th & last	J.L.B.Salmon	(Harlequins)	.	15th	B.Bowen	(South Wales Police)
11	19th	R.Underwood	(RAF/Leicester)	.	20th	A.M.Hadley	(Cardiff)
10	4th & last	P.N.Williams	(Orrell)	.	17th	J.Davies	(Llanelli)
9	7th	R.M.Harding	(Bristol)	.	14th	R.N.Jones	(Swansea)
1	10th	P.A.G.Rendall	(Wasps)	.	2nd	A.Buchanan	(Llanelli)
2	4th	B.C.Moore	(Nottingham)	.	17th	A.J.Phillips	(Cardiff)
3	34th	G.S.Pearce	(Northampton	.	1st	D.Young	(Swansea)
4	15th	W.A.Dooley	(Preston G'hoppers)	.	20th	R.D.Moriarty (Capt)	(Swansea)
5	7th	N.C.Redman	(Bath)	.	25th	R.L.Norster	(Cardiff)
6	26th	P.J.Winterbottom	(Headingley)	.	6th	G.J.Roberts	(Cardiff)
7	11th	G.W.Rees	(Nottingham)	.	4th	R.G.Collins	(South Wales Police)
8	7th	D.Richards	(Leicester)	.	13th	W.P.Moriarty	(Swansea)
	8th	G.J.Chilcott (Bath) for Rendall -		.	3rd	H.D.Richards (Neath) for Norster -	

Referee: R.Hourquet   (France)

SCORERS:

			0 - 4	G.J.Roberts	Try
			0 - 6	P.H.Thorburn	Conversion
			Half-time		
			0 - 10	R.N.Jones	Try
J.M.Webb		Penalty Goal	3 - 10		
			3 - 14	J.A.Devereux	Try
			3 - 16	P.H.Thorburn	Conversion

POINTS:

J.M.Webb	3 points	(43)	G.J.Roberts	4 points
			R.N.Jones	4 points
			J.A.Devereux	4 points
			P.H.Thorburn	4 points

MATCH COMMENTARY:

Of all the games played between England and Wales, this, the 93rd, was arguably the most important, but England totally failed to rise to the occasion. The Welsh had suffered major problems with injuries and had to call up David Young into the side from grade Rugby in Sydney. England, on the other hand, had enjoyed a fairly smooth ride through their Group with all their games being played at the Concord Oval. In spite of their tribulations Welsh "hwyl" prevailed, they raised their game and saw off the English challenge with Robert Jones making as great a contribution as any behind an efficient pack.   But the victory was somewhat laboured, and Wales do not appear to offer any threat to New Zealand in the forthcoming semi-final. How much worse, then, were England in conceding three tries to a moderate Welsh side ? England were very poor because they seemed to have slipped back into the old habits of yore, making countless unforced errors and continually taking the wrong options on those infrequent occasions when they took any decision at all. Each of the Welsh tries came as a direct result of a mistake on England's part, and although they were never short of possession, they failed to impose any control whatsoever over the game. England will have to take the next World Cup a bit more seriously and without complacency, if such an embarrassing performance A29is not to be repeated on home soil in 1991.

FIVE NATIONS CHAMPIONSHIP, 1987-88   January 16th 1988, at Parc des Princes

63rd match   **ENGLAND   9 pts**   v   **FRANCE   10 pts**

	Caps				Caps		
15	5th	J.M.Webb	(Bristol)	.	56th	S.Blanco	(Biarritz)
14	14th	M.E.Harrison (Capt)	(Wakefield)	.	9th	P.Berot	(Agen)
13	1st	W.D.C.Carling	(Durham University)	.	46th	P.Sella	(Agen)
12	14th	K.G.Simms	(Wasps)	.	8th	M.Andrieu	(Nimes)
11	20th	R.Underwood	(RAF/Leicester)	.	18th & last	E.Bonneval	(Toulouse)
10	11th	L.Cusworth	(Leicester)	.	13th	F.Mesnel	(Racing Club)
9	10th	N.D.Melville	(Wasps)	.	37th	P.Berbizier	(Agen)
1	11th	P.A.G.Rendall	(Wasps)	.	12th	P.Ondarts	(Biarritz)
2	5th	B.C.Moore	(Nottingham)	.	30th	D.Dubroca (Capt)	(Agen)
3	1st	J.A.Probyn	(Wasps)	.	32nd	J-P.Garuet-Lempirou	(Lourdes)
4	8th	J.Orwin	(Bedford)	.	43rd	J.Condom	(Biarritz)
5	16th	W.A.Dooley	(Fylde)	.	3rd & last	P.Serriere	(Racing Club)
6	1st	M.G.Skinner	(Harlequins)	.	24th	E.Champ	(Toulouse)
7	27th	P.J.Winterbottom	(Headingley)	.	37th	D.Erbani	(Agen)
8	8th	D.Richards	(Leicester)	.	36th	L.Rodriguez	(Dax)

Referee: O.E.Doyle   (Ireland)

SCORERS:

			0 - 3	P.Berot	Penalty Goal
J.M.Webb	Penalty Goal		3 - 3		
			Half-time		
L.Cusworth	D'p Goal (4th & last)	6 - 3			
J.M.Webb	Penalty Goal		9 - 3		
			9 - 6	P.Berot	Penalty Goal
			9 - 10	L.Rodriguez	Try

POINTS:

J.M.Webb	6 points	(49)	P.Berot	6 points
L.Cusworth	3 points	(12)	L.Rodriguez	4 points

MATCH COMMENTARY:

After England's failure and France's success in the World Cup recently, England came to Paris as very much the underdogs, but they refused to accept that status, and gave the French a torrid time. Micky Skinner, gaining his first cap, and Peter Winterbottom played very powerful games and Dooley and Orwin controlled the lineout. England missed two try-scoring chances before half-time when, first, Will Carling mistimed his pass with a two man overlap and then Kevin Simms elected to try to pass when his momentum would probably have carried him over the line. Jonathan Webb, uncharacteristically, missed several penalty goal attempts. The scores were level at half-time, then France began to turn the screws in the second half and, although England did establish a six point lead, France gradually gained the upper hand. But England still had a three point lead when Serge Blanco chose to run the ball well within his own half. It went through several pairs of French hands before Andrieu kicked ahead and Mike Harrison had to chase back towards his own line. It was one of those bounces which deceive everybody and Laurent Rodriguez was on hand to dribble forward over the line and touch down. The conversion was missed but it didn't matter. All in all a worthy England performance with the three new caps acquitting themselves very well, but the fact remains, the match was lost.

ENGLAND   3 pts   v   WALES   11 pts

	Caps					Caps		
15	6th	J.M.Webb	(Bristol)	.		2nd	A.Clement	(Swansea)
14	15th & last	M.E.Harrison (Capt)	(Wakefield)	.		10th	I.C.Evans	(Llanelli)
13	2nd	W.D.C.Carling	(Durham University)	.		11th	M.G.Ring	(Pontypool)
12	15th & last	K.G.Simms	(Wasps)	.		18th	B.Bowen (Capt)	(South Wales Police)
11	21st	R.Underwood	(RAF/Leicester)	.		24th	A.M.Hadley	(Cardiff)
10	12th & last	L.Cusworth	(Leicester)	.		20th	J.Davies	(Llanelli)
9	11th	N.D.Melville	(Wasps)	.		18th	R.N.Jones	(Swansea)
1	12th	P.A.G.Rendall	(Wasps)	.		6th	S.T.Jones	(Pontypool)
2	6th	B.C.Moore	(Nottingham)	.		6th	K.H.Phillips	(Neath)
3	2nd	J.A.Probyn	(Wasps)	.		4th	D.Young	(Swansea)
4	9th	J.Orwin	(Bedford)	.		1st	P.S.May	(Llanelli)
5	17th	W.A.Dooley	(Fylde)	.		27th	R.L.Norster	(Cardiff)
6	2nd	M.G.Skinner	(Harlequins)	.		2nd	R.Phillips	(Neath)
7	28th	P.J.Winterbottom	(Headingley)	.		17th	W.P.Moriarty	(Swansea)
8	9th	D.Richards	(Leicester)	.		7th	R.G.Collins	(South Wales Police)
				.		1st	I.J.Watkins (Ebbw Vale) for K.Phillips -	

Referee: S.R.Hilditch   (Ireland)

SCORERS:

			0 - 0			
			Half-time			
			0 - 4	A.M.Hadley	Try	
			0 - 8	A.M.Hadley	Try	
			0 - 11	J.Davies	Drop Goal	
J.M.Webb		Penalty Goal	3 - 11			

POINTS: J.M.Webb   3 points   (52)   A.M.Hadley   8 points

J.Davies   3 points

MATCH COMMENTARY:

A lot was expected of the unchanged England XV after their impressive performance in Paris, but the Welsh, full of confidence after beating England in the World Cup, were up to the challenge. The first half was evenly contested but the Welsh backs looked the more threatening in attack and England never really got their backs moving because, on many occasions, the ball was dropped or possession was lost at a crucial stage. In the second half, the Welsh forwards began to exercise some control and the silken running and handling skills of the four fly-halves in the side, Mark Ring, Brendan Bowen, Anthony Clement and Jonathan Davies set up two tries for Adrian Hadley. England's only try scoring chance came when Nigel Melville broke from a maul and beat the first line of defence to sprint 50 yards upfield, but there was no support and the chance was lost. Jonathan Davies' drop goal confirmed the Welsh superiority in the closing stages and Jonathan Webb just managed to spare England the indignity of a blank score sheet by kicking a late penalty goal, and in so doing passed the total of fifty in his personal points tally for England in his sixth match. He was the seventh player so to do.

Not a good result for England, and the stark fact remains that yet again the first two matches in the Five Nations Championship have been lost and, to boot, England have not scored a try - only three penalty goals and a drop goal so far.

104th match
95th Calcutta Cup

ENGLAND 9 pts   v   SCOTLAND 6 pts

	Caps					Caps		
15	7th	J.M.Webb	(Bristol)	.	17th	A.G.Hastings	(Watsonians)
14	22nd	R.Underwood	(RAF/Leicester)	.	16th	M.D.F.Duncan	(West of Scotland)
13	3rd	W.D.C.Carling	(Durham University)	.	8th & last	A.V.Tait	(Kelso)
12	4th	S.J.Halliday	(Bath)	.	40th	K.Robertson	(Melrose)
11	1st	C.Oti	(Cambridge Univ)	.	12th	I.Tukalo	(Selkirk)
10	15th	C.R.Andrew	(Wasps)	.	2nd & last	A.M.B.Ker	(Kelso)
9	12th	N.D.Melville (Capt)	(Wasps)	.	47th & last	R.J.Laidlaw	(Jedforest)
1	13th	P.A.G.Rendall	(Wasps)	.	14th	D.M.B.Sole	(Edinburgh Acad'ls)
2	7th	B.C.Moore	(Nottingham)	.	5th	G.J.Callander	(Kelso)
3	3rd	J.A.Probyn	(Wasps)	.	13th & last	N.A.Rowan	(Boroughmuir)
4	10th	J.Orwin	(Bedford)	.	13th	D.B.White	(Gala)
5	18th	W.A.Dooley	(Fylde)	.	4th	D.F.Cronin	(Bath)
6	3rd	M.G.Skinner	(Harlequins)	.	3rd	D.J.Turnbull	(Hawick)
7	29th	P.J.Winterbottom	(Headingley)	.	17th	F.Calder	(Stewart's-Melville)
8	10th	D.Richards	(Leicester)	.	35th	I.A.M.Paxton	(Selkirk)

    12th   G.W.Rees (Nottingham) for Winterbottom - 15

Referee: W.Jones   (Wales)

SCORERS:

			0 - 0			
			Half-time			
			0 - 3	A.G.Hastings	Penalty Goal	
C.R.Andrew	D'p Goal	(7th)	3 - 3			
			3 - 6	A.G.Hastings	Penalty Goal	
J.M.Webb	Penalty Goal		6 - 6			
J.M.Webb	Penalty Goal		9 - 6			

POINTS:

J.M.Webb	6 points	(58)	A.G.Hastings	6 points	
C.R.Andrew	3 points	(92)			

MATCH COMMENTARY:

A very dreary game in which England again failed to score their first try of the season. Following the disappointing result against Wales, the selectors decided to retain the same pack but to change two of the three-quarters, including the captain, and the fly-half. Thus, Rob Andrew was restored to partner Nigel Melville, Simon Halliday came into the centre and Chris Oti went to the left wing with Rory Underwood moving across to the right. Nigel Melville assumed the captaincy again yet again. For the second successive match there was no score at half-time for two reasons. Firstly, Gavin Hasting was having an off-day with his boot and missed several possible penalty goal kicks, and secondly, England were incapable of turning their territorial advantage and the lion's share of possession into points. As against Wales, Nigel Melville made a break when he intercepted a pass from Matt Duncan, ran all of fifty yards and ran out of support. The second half produced 15 points but no better entertainment, and there were only occasional flashes of the skills that the Scots had shown to such good effect in the mighty match at Cardiff. Not for the last time, the Scots' Coach Derrick Grant criticised England's limited approach, and Geoff Cooke maintained that England had wanted to play open rugby but the Scots had prevented them from doing so !! In Edinburgh that evening the Calcutta Cup was used as a ball in an impromptu game of street rugby, and Dean Richards and John Jeffrey were called to account.

100th match   **ENGLAND   35 pts**   v   **IRELAND   3 pts**

	Caps					Caps		
15	8th	J.M.Webb	(Bristol)	.		36th	H.P.McNeill	(London Irish)
14	23rd	R.Underwood	(RAF/Leicester)	.	34th & last	T.M.Ringland	(Ballymena)
13	4th	W.D.C.Carling	(Durham University)	.	21st	B.J.Mullin	(Blackrock College)
12	5th	S.J.Halliday	(Bath)	.	31st	M.J.Kiernan	(Dolphin)
11	2nd	C.Oti	(Cambridge Univ)	.	24th	K.D.Crossan	(Instonians)
10	16th	C.R.Andrew	(Wasps)	.	25th	P.M.Dean	(St Mary's College)
9	13th & last	N.D.Melville (Capt)	(Wasps)	.	22nd	M.T.Bradley	(Constitution)
1	14th	P.A.G.Rendall	(Wasps)	.	2nd	T.P.J.Clancy	(Lansdowne)
2	8th	B.C.Moore	(Nottingham)	.	7th	T.J.Kingston	(Dolphin)
3	4th	J.A.Probyn	(Wasps)	.	17th	D.C.Fitzgerald	(Lansdowne)
4	11th	J.Orwin	(Bedford)	.	35th	D.G.Lenihan (Capt)	(Constitution)
5	19th	W.A.Dooley	(Fylde)	.	1st & only	M.M.F.Moylett	(Shannon)
6	4th	M.G.Skinner	(Harlequins)	.	2nd	W.D.McBride	(Malone)
7	13th	G.W.Rees	(Nottingham)	.	17th	P.M.Matthews	(Wanderers)
8	11th	D.Richards	(Leicester)	.	20th	W.A.Anderson	(Dungannon)

	8th	R.M.Harding (Bristol) for Melville - 40		

Referee: C.Norling   (Wales)

SCORERS:

			0 - 3	M.J.Kiernan	Drop Goal
			Half-time		
G.W.Rees	Try	(2nd & last)	4 - 3		
J.M.Webb	Penalty Goal		7 - 3		
C.Oti	Try	(1st)	11 - 3		
J.M.Webb	Conversion		13 - 3		
C.Oti	Try	(2nd)	17 - 3		
C.Oti	Try	(3rd)	21 - 3		
C.R.Andrew	Conversion		23 - 3		
R.Underwood	Try	(5th)	27 - 3		
C.R.Andrew	Conversion		29 - 3		
R.Underwood	Try	(6th)	33 - 3		
C.R.Andrew	Conversion		35 - 3		

POINTS:

C.Oti	12 points	(12)		M.J.Kiernan	3 points
R.Underwood	8 points	(24)			
C.R.Andrew	6 points	(98)			
J.M.Webb	5 points	(63)			
G.W.Rees	4 points	(8)			

MATCH COMMENTARY:

Six tries in this game very effectively scotched the rumours that England were incapable of scoring a try. The first half had given no indication of what was to come, when, following Nigel Melville's departure through injury at half-time, England suddenly found their flair and confidence and the hapless Irish, no slouches themselves in the back division, could only watch. A truly remarkable match, and a remarkable change of fortune for the English side which prompted the first tentative strains of "Swing low, Sweet Chariot...." to be heard in the stands !!

THE ENGLAND TEAM WHO BEAT IRELAND AT TWICKENHAM ON MARCH 19th 1988

Standing: C.Norling (Referee) J.A.Probyn, P.A.G.Rendall, M.G.Skinner, W.A.Dooley, J.Orwin, D.Richards, J.M.Webb,

Seated: C.Oti, S.J.Halliday, W.D.C.Carling, B.C.Moore,N.D.Melville (Captain), R.Underwood, G.W.Rees, C.R.Andrew.

101st match   **ENGLAND 21 pts**   v   **IRELAND 10 pts**

	Caps				Caps		
15	9th	J.M.Webb	(Bristol)	.	37th & last	H.P.McNeill	(London Irish)
14	1st	J.Bentley	(Sale)	.	1st	J.F.Sexton	(UC Dublin)
13	6th	S.J.Halliday	(Bath)	.	1st	V.J.G.Cunningham	(St Mary's College)
12	5th	W.D.C.Carling	(Harlequins)	.	22nd	B.J.Mullin	(Oxford University)
11	24th	R.Underwood	(RAF/Leicester)	.	32nd	M.J.Kiernan	(Dolphin)
10	17th	C.R.Andrew	(Wasps)	.	26th	P.M.Dean	(St Mary's College)
9	9th	R.M.Harding	(Bristol)	.	1st	L.F.P.Aherne	(Dolphin)
1	15th	P.A.G.Rendall	(Wasps)	.	3rd	T.P.J.Clancy	(Lansdowne)
2	9th	B.C.Moore	(Nottingham)	.	1st	S.J.Smith	(Ballymena)
3	5th	J.A.Probyn	(Wasps)	.	9th	J.J.McCoy	(Bangor)
4	12th	J.Orwin (Capt)	(Bedford)	.	36th	D.G.Lenihan (Capt)	(Constitution)
5	20th	W.A.Dooley	(Fylde)	.	21st	W.A.Anderson	(Dungannon)
6	14th	G.W.Rees	(Nottingham)	.	3rd & last	W.J.Sexton	(Garryowen)
7	5th	M.G.Skinner	(Harlequins)	.	18th	P.M.Matthews	(Wanderers)
8	1st	D.W.Egerton	(Bath)	.	10th & last	M.E.Gibson	(London Irish)

	9th	G.J.Chilcott (Bath) for Rendall -			.		

Referee: R.Hourquet   (France)

SCORERS:

J.M.Webb	Penalty Goal		3 - 0				
J.M.Webb	Penalty Goal		6 - 0				
R.Underwood	Try	(7th)	10 - 0				
J.M.Webb	Conversion		12 - 0				
			Half-time				
J.M.Webb	Penalty Goal		15 - 0				
			15 - 4		S.J.Smith	Try	
			15 - 6		M.J.Kiernan	Conversion	
			15 - 10		H.P.McNeill	Try	
R.M.Harding	Try	(1st & only)	19 - 10				
J.M.Webb	Conversion		21 - 10				

POINTS:

J.M.Webb	13 points	(76)	S.J.Smith	4 points	
R.Underwood	4 points	(28)	H.P.McNeill	4 points	
R.M.Harding	4 points	(4)	M.J.Kiernan	2 points	

MATCH COMMENTARY:

The Irish Millennium Celebration was certainly quite a party but, unfortunately, the weather conditions in the form of a strong cold wind inhibited the party spirit on the field. Ball handling and finishing were adversely affected by the chill temperature and the strong wind which tended to blow passes off course and limited the effectiveness of tactical kicking. Nevertheless 40,000 people entered into the spirit of the occasion at Lansdowne Road in this Digital sponsored match. The two new caps, John Bentley and David Egerton acquitted themselves well and the unfortunate Mickey Skinner suffered a broken nose from a punch in the first minute - some party spirit !! Not as entertaining a game, by any means, as the Five Nations fixture, but at least England recorded their third successive win for the first time in eight years !

SUMMARY OF THE SEASON - 1987 - 88:

When Geoff Cooke eventually took up the reins of control of English International Rugby, one of his first actions was to reduced the selection panel fron seven to three consisting of himself, Roger Uttley, the coach, and John Elliott. These three were to have first a stabilising and later an inspiring influence on the course of events. This, the first season, as could be expected was a roller coaster of emotions, but it became very apparent by the last match of the season that the side had some confidence, a sense of purpose and direction and a sense of security, and all this mainly because Cooke's philosophy of breaking down the barriers between players and officials, and allowing the players some say in their playing style and destiny, was beginning to pay dividends. Even then, the rough rides were not all over, for the tour to Australia and Fiji the following summer had its problems. But substantial progress was made during the course of this season.

The side selected to play France, away, in the opening match of the season, showed three new caps and five of the pack and four of the backs who had had that sobering experience against Wales in Brisbane the previous summer with Mike Harrison retaining the captaincy. Popular opinion gave England no chance, no chance at all, and perversely England all but won the match with little more than a disallowed try, several penalty goal misses and a cruel bounce to take away from the formidable Parc des Princes. But the reality was that this was the tenth successive Five Nations defeat away from home. The same side was given the opportunity to tackle Wales at Twickenham in what was hoped would be a better contest than last season's at Cardiff and a better result than Brisbane. But it was not to be, the roller-coaster had been switched on and all high expectations were deflated on the sharp needles of Welsh flair, clever running and fine handling skills. For Scotland, the pack remained the same but out went Mike Harrison, Kevin Simms and Les Cusworth in favour of Chris Oti, Simon Halliday and Rob Andrew. Nigel Melville took over the Captaincy, that poisoned chalice, once again. And a very dreary match it was too - but England won, away, for the first time since 1982, but still no try had been scored. Against Ireland with Gary Rees the only change, replacing the injured Peter Winterbottom, the only score aproaching half-time was Michael Kiernan's penalty goal when Nigel Melville sustained the last and probably the most painful of his many injuries on the field, a badly dislocated ankle. It all came good in the second half when England scored six tries, five of them from the wings. Rob Andrew said "there was a kind of emotional bonding among the team at half-time" and "we had.....a duty to Melville to go out and win this game, and win it in a manner which would have gained his approval." And so they did, and Twickenham saw, or rather heard, the first strains of "Swing low, Sweet Chariot...." for the first time. For forty minutes all the painful humiliations and frustrations of many disappointments were forgotten at a stroke, and surely, this was evidence aplenty that Geoff Cooke was leading England in the right direction - at last. The final fixture of the season was the Millennium match in Dublin for which three changes were made, one necessitated by Nigel Melville's injury, and the others with half an eye on the forthcoming tour to Australia and Fiji. John Bentley came in on the wing in place of Chris Oti, and Dave Egerton at No 8 in place of Dean Richards. The captaincy was given to John Orwin. The match was won comfortably in conditions not really conducive to attractive running rugby because the wind was too strong. Thus, a season of change finished moderately satisfactorily with some pattern and purpose to England's play and to team selection. Third place in the Championship Table, having won two and lost two, has been achieved only once in the past five seasons and was therefore a measure of improvement in performance and, hopefully, in fortunes. The score against Ireland is England's highest post-war points total in all Five Nations matches, and is also the highest winning margin. It is only the second time since the war that England have scored six tries in a Five Nations match. England used only nineteen players during the Five Nations season, eleven players appearing in all four matches, and four new caps were awarded during the season. The most notable achievement, of course , was Chris Oti's three tries in the match against Ireland - a feat not achieved in a Five Nations match since John Carleton scored three at Murrayfield in 1980.

Four players bade their farewells to international Rugby at the end of the season. Nigel Melville, whose career was tragically injury prone, won 13 caps and captained England seven times over four seasons. He was called as a replacement for Terry Holmes to the 1983 Lions in New Zealand but was injured in the second game he played having scored two tries in his first. Mike Harrison, "Burglar Bill" to his friends in the Antipodes, and a Bank employee, won 15 caps and led England on seven occasions. Kevin Simms, the sleekest of runners, also won 15 caps, and had three Cambridge Blues. Les Cusworth, 12 caps, the much under-rated Leicester fly-half, is currently an Assistant Coach to England with Jack Rowell.

FIVE NATIONS CHAMPIONSHIP TABLE:

Won: **Calcutta Cup**

		Played	Won	Lost	Drawn	Points: For	Against	Tries: For	Against	Title Points
1 =	Wales	4	3	1	0	57	42	7	4	6
1 =	France	4	3	1	0	57	47	8	3	6
3	**ENGLAND**	4	2	2	0	56	30	6	3	4
4 =	Scotland	4	1	3	0	67	68	6	7	2
4 =	Ireland	4	1	3	0	43	90	4	14	2

Home Games: lost to Wales 3 - 11, (no tries to two); beat Ireland 35 - 3, (six tries to nil)

Away Games: lost to France 9 - 10, (no tries to one); beat Scotland 9 - 6, (no tries)

ENGLAND TOUR TO AUSTRALIA and FIJI - 1988

THE TOUR PARTY:

Manager:	G.D.Cooke	Assistant Coaches:	A.B.C.Davies D.Robinson		Captain:	J.Orwin		

Full-backs:	R.Adamson	(Wakefield)	no caps	Forwards:	G.J.Chilcott	(Bath)	9 caps
	J.M.Webb	(Bristol)	9 caps		R.G.R.Dawe	(Bath)	4 caps
					W.A.Dooley	(Preston G'hoppers	20 caps
Three-quarters:	B.Barley	(Wakefield)	4 caps		D.W.Egerton	(Bath)	1 cap
	J.Bentley	(Sale)	1 cap		B.C.Moore	(Nottingham)	9 caps
	J.R.D.Buckton	(Saracens)	no caps		J.Orwin	(Bedford)	12 caps
	B.Evans	(Leicester)	no caps		G.S.Pearce	(Northampton)	34 caps
	S.J.Halliday	(Bath)	6 caps		J.A.Probyn	(Wasps)	5 caps
	R.Underwood	(RAF/Leicester)	24 caps		N.C.Redman	(Bath)	7 caps
					G.W.Rees	(Nottingham)	14 caps
Half-backs:	C.R.Andrew	(Wasps)	17 caps		P.A.G.Rendall	(Wasps)	15 caps
	S.Barnes	(Bath)	7 caps		D.Richards	(Leicester)	11 caps
	R.M.Harding	(Bristol)	9 caps		R.A.Robinson	(Bath)	no caps
	S.Robson	(Moseley)	no caps		M.G.Skinner	(Harlequins)	5 caps
Replacements:	W.D.C.Carling	(Harlequins)	5 caps				
	T.Buttimore	(Leicester)	no caps				

When Geoff Cooke selected his tour party he made several mistakes not least of which was the appointment of John Orwin as captain, and under his stewardship the team was never cohesive and motivated as they had been under Nigel Melville the previous season. In addition there were others selected who proved not to be of International standard, or anywhere near that, which helped to explain, for example, losing to a very moderate New South Wales side. But those shortcomings could not be held responsible for the fact that at no stage, yet often with no shortage of possession, the backs, and the half-backs, in particular, never held sway and imposed themselves on the field of play. Even the forwards, often providing that possession were shown up in the Tests against Australia, and particularly the first when they were unceremoniously shunted all over the field. It was a poor tour with poor results which did nothing to further the cause of the hoped for England revival. Geoff Cooke made another error of judgement before the tour party left the UK for Ausrralia, in announcing that the principal objective of the tour was to prove that England could be counted among the best teams in the world, and that the performance against Ireland was no flash-in-the-pan. If he later ate his words, there was no written acknowledgement of the fact.

Two players earned their first caps on the tour, Barry Evans and Andy Robinson, and five said their farewells to International Rugby on their return home. John Orwin, with 14 caps, had captained England on three occasions. He was a publican. Brian Barley, who won 7 caps, was a pillar of rugby in his native Yorkshire both at Club and County level - he played for Yorkshire 29 times. Richard Harding, 12 caps, had captained England only once in the match against Fiji on this tour. John Bentley, a policeman in Leeds, had 2 caps, and, later in the year, signed for Leeds Rugby League Club, and later represented Great Britain. Barry Evans, the fast Leicester winger, won 2 caps, both on this tour.

If there was one lesson to be learned from this escapade, it was that there appeared to be a dearth of young and developing players who could expect to form the nucleus of the England sides in,say, three years time - at least among those selected this time.

TOUR RESULTS:

May 17th	Queensland Country	at Mackay	WON	39 - 7	(five tries to one)
May 22nd	Queensland	at Ballymore	WON	22 - 19	(two tries to one)
May 25th	Queensland B	at Toowoomba	WON	19 - 7	(two tries to one)
May 29th	**AUSTRALIA**	**at Ballymore**	**LOST**	**16 - 22**	**(two tries to one)**
June 1st	S. Australia Invitation XV	at Adelaide	WON	37 - 10	(six tries to one)
June 5th	New South Wales	at Sydney	LOST	12 - 23	(no tries to three)
June 8th	New South Wales B	at Wollongong	WON	25 - 9	(three tries to one)
June 12th	**AUSTRALIA**	**at Sydney**	**LOST**	**8 - 28**	**(two tries to four)**
June 17th	**FIJI**	**at Suva**	**WON**	**25 - 12**	**(three tries to nil)**

THE ENGLAND SQUAD FOR THE NINE MATCH TOUR TO AUSTRALIA AND FIJI IN 1988

Back Row: R.A.Robinson, Official, R.Adamson, J.A.Probyn, B.Barley, G.J.Chilcott,

Middle Row: S.Barnes, S.Robson, J.Bentley, J.R.D.Buckton, D.Richards, D.W.Egerton, W.A.Dooley, M.G.Skinner, N.C.Redman, J.M.Webb, G.W.Rees, R.G.R.Dawe,

Seated: A.B.C.Davies (Coach) B.C.Moore, D.Robinson (Coach), P.A.G.Rendall, President RFU, J.Orwin (Captain), G.D.Cooke (Manager), G.S.Pearce, Official,

Not present: C.R.Andrew, R.Underwood, S.J.Halliday, B.Evans.

R.M.Harding, K.Murphy (Phsyio)

14th match   **ENGLAND   16 pts**   v   **AUSTRALIA   22 pts**

	Caps				Caps		
15	10th	J.M.Webb	(Bristol)	.	7th	A.J.S.Leeds	(New South Wales)
14	2nd & last	J.Bentley	(Sale)	.	3rd	I.N.Williams	(New South Wales)
13	7th	S.J.Halliday	(Bath)	.	1st	J.C.Grant	(New South Wales)
12	5th	B.Barley	(Wakefield)	.	4th	M.T.Cook	(Queensland)
11	25th	R.Underwood	(RAF/Leicester)	.	35th	D.I.Campese	(New South Wales)
10	18th	C.R.Andrew	(Wasps)	.	24th	M.P.Lynagh	(Queensland)
9	10th	R.M.Harding	(Bristol)	.	24th	N.C.Farr-Jones (Capt)	(New South Wales)
1	16th	P.A.G.Rendall	(Wasps)	.	1st	R.Lawton	(Queensland)
2	10th	B.C.Moore	(Nottingham)	.	31st	T.A.Lawton	(Queensland)
3	6th	J.A.Probyn	(Wasps)	.	30th	A.J.McIntyre	(Queensland)
4	13th	J.Orwin (Capt)	(Bedford)	.	28th	S.A.G.Cutler	(New South Wales)
5	21st	W.A.Dooley	(Preston G'hoppers)	.	4th	D.Frawley	(New South Wales)
6	2nd	D.W.Egerton	(Bath)	.	10th	J.S.Miller	(Queensland)
7	15th	G.W.Rees	(Nottingham)	.	2nd	J.M.Gardner	(Queensland)
8	12th	D.Richards	(Leicester)	.	1st	D.G.Carter	(New South Wales)

Referee: D.J.Bishop   (New Zealand)

SCORERS:

J.M.Webb	Penalty Goal		3 - 0			
			3 - 3	M.P.Lynagh	Penalty Goal	
R.Underwood	Try	(8th)	7 - 3			
J.Bentley	Try	(1st & only)	11 - 3			
J.M.Webb	Conversion		13 - 3			
			13 - 6	M.P.Lynagh	Penalty Goal	
			13 - 9	M.P.Lynagh	Penalty Goal	
			13 - 13	I.N.Williams	Try	
			Half-time			
			13 - 16	M.P.Lynagh	Penalty Goal	
			13 - 19	M.P.Lynagh	Penalty Goal	
			13 - 22	M.P.Lynagh	Penalty Goal	
J.M.Webb	Penalty Goal		16 - 22			

POINTS:

J.M.Webb	8 points	(84)	M.P.Lynagh	18 points	
R.Underwood	4 points	(32)	I.N.Williams	4 points	
J.Bentley	4 points	(4)			

MATCH COMMENTARY:

England had started their tour inauspiciously, winning all three games but not convincingly, so it was surprising to see them compile a healthy lead early in the game with two breakaway tries, both resulting from interceptions and a seventy yard chase upfield.   There was nearly a third too, but Rory Underwood was brought down by a superb tackle from his equally pacy opposite number, Ian Williams.   With a 13 - 3 lead England should have been able to hold on, but the Australian pack began to push England around and Michael Lynagh and Nick Farr-Jones exerted a degree of control and influence over the match which the English half-backs could not match.   Lynagh's boot secured the points and England lost a game which they had not deserved to win, despite the favourable 2 to 1 try count.

15th match   **ENGLAND** **8 pts**   v   **AUSTRALIA** **28 pts**

	Caps				Caps		
15	11th	**J.M.Webb**	(Bristol)		8th	**A.J.S.Leeds**	(New South Wales)
14	1st	**B.J.Evans**	(Leicester)		36th	**D.I.Campese**	(New South Wales)
13	6th	**W.D.C.Carling**	(Harlequins)		5th	**G.A.Ella**	(New South Wales)
12	6th	**B.Barley**	(Wakefield)		5th	**M.T.Cook**	(Queensland)
11	26th	**R.Underwood**	(RAF/Leicester)		4th	**I.N.Williams**	(New South Wales)
10	19th	**C.R.Andrew**	(Wasps)		25th	**M.P.Lynagh**	(Queensland)
9	11th	**R.M.Harding**	(Bristol)		25th	**N.C.Farr-Jones (Capt)**	(New South Wales)
1	17th	**P.A.G.Rendall**	(Wasps)		1st & only	**P.Kay**	(New South Wales)
2	11th	**B.C.Moore**	(Nottingham)		32nd	**T.A.Lawton**	(Queensland)
3	7th	**J.A.Probyn**	(Wasps)		31st	**A.J.McIntyre**	(Queensland)
4	14th & last	**J.Orwin (Capt)**	(Bedford)		29th	**S.A.G.Cutler**	(New South Wales)
5	22nd	**W.A.Dooley**	(Preston G'hoppers)		5th	**D.Frawley**	(New South Wales)
6	1st	**R.A.Robinson**	(Bath)		11th	**J.S.Miller**	(Queensland)
7	16th	**G.W.Rees**	(Nottingham)		2nd & last	**S.Lidbury**	(New South Wales)
8	13th	**D.Richards**	(Leicester)		2nd	**D.G.Carter**	(New South Wales)

Referee: D.J.Bishop   (New Zealand)

SCORERS:

R.Underwood	Try	(9th)	4 - 0			
			4 - 3	**M.P.Lynagh**	Penalty Goal	
			4 - 7	**D.G.Carter**	Try	
			4 - 9	**M.P.Lynagh**	Conversion	
			4 - 12	**M.P.Lynagh**	Penalty Goal	
			4 - 16	**Gary Ella**	Try	
			4 - 18	**M.P.Lynagh**	Conversion	
			Half-time			
			4 - 22	**D.I.Campese**	Try	
			4 - 24	**M.P.Lynagh**	Conversion	
D.Richards	Try	(4th)	8 - 24			
			8 - 28	**M.P.Lynagh**	Try	

POINTS:

R.Underwood	4 points	(36)		**M.P.Lynagh**	16 points
D.Richards	4 points	(16)		**D.I.Campese, Gary Ella,**	
				and D.G.Carter	4 points each

MATCH COMMENTARY:

This was a very poor English performance, because although the forwards won the greater share of possession, the backs were unable to do anything with it, and indeed looked very pedestrian compared with their Australian counterparts. Rory Underwood scored a fine try early in the match near the left-corner, but it was the only English movement of note in the whole match. With the score at 18 points to 4 against England at half-time, a fairly hefty defeat looked on the cards. The forwards, inspired by Dean Richards - not by John Orwin - improved their performance, particularly in defence, in the second half and confined the enterprising Australians to only two more tries. Dean Richards himself pulled one of those back as well, so Australia were pretty well contained in the second half. In both matches, England's back play had been poor, and none of the half-backs, in any of the matches, had managed to impose their authority on procedings.

1st match   **ENGLAND   25 pts**   v   **FIJI   12 pts**

		Caps				Caps	
15	20th	C.R.Andrew	(Wasps)	.	J.Kubu	(Easts, Sydney)	
14	2nd & last	B.J.Evans	(Leicester)	.	N.Baleiverata	(Suva)	
13	7th & last	B.Barley	(Wakefield)	.	S.Aria	(Nawdi)	
12	7th	W.D.C.Carling	(Harlequins)	.	N.Nadruku	(Nadroga)	
11	27th	R.Underwood	(RAF/Leicester)	.	T.Mitchell	(Army)	
10	8th	S.Barnes	(Bath)	.	S.Koroduadua	(Suva)	
9	12th & last	R.M.Harding (Capt)	(Bristol)	.	P.Tabulutu	(Nawdi)	
1	10th	G.J.Chilcott	(Bath)	.	M.Taga	(Suva)	
2	12th	B.C.Moore	(Nottingham)	.	S.Naivilawasa (Capt)	(Suva)	
3	35th	G.S.Pearce	(Northampton	.	I.Naituku	(Suva)	
4	8th	N.C.Redman	(Bath)	.	M.Rasari	(Nadroga)	
5	23rd	W.A.Dooley	(Preston G'hoppers)	.	A.Nadalo	(Suva)	
6	17th	G.W.Rees	(Nottingham)	.	S.Vonoilagi	(Rewa)	
7	2nd	R.A.Robinson	(Bath)	.	P.Gale	(Nadi)	
8	14th	D.Richards	(Leicester)	.	P.Naruma	(Suva)	

	3rd	D.W.Egerton (Bath) for Rees -

	Referee:	K.V.J.Fitzgerald	(Australia)

SCORERS:

B.Barley	Try	(1st & only)	4 - 0			
S.Barnes	Conversion		6 - 0			
			6 - 3	S.Koroduadua	Penalty Goal	
S.Barnes	Penalty Goal		9 - 3			
			9 - 6	S.Koroduadua	Penalty Goal	
			Half-time			
			9 - 9	S.Koroduadua	Drop Goal	
			9 - 12	S.Koroduadua	Penalty Goal	
R.Underwood	Try	(10th)	13 - 12			
S.Barnes	Conversion		15 - 12			
S.Barnes	Penalty Goal		18 - 12			
S.Barnes	Penalty Goal		21 - 12			
R.Underwood	Try	(11th)	25 - 12			

POINTS:

S.Barnes	13 points	(34)	S.Koroduadua	12 points	
R.Underwood	8 points	(44)			
B.Barley	4 points	(4)			

MATCH COMMENTARY:

England managed, with a much changed side, to salvage some shreds of respectability by winning the last match of what had turned out to be a demoralising tour. Again the English forwards won much more than their share of possession, yet the backs did little with it apart from providing Rory Underwood with two tries. But with the ball they had it should have been five times that. The England back row in particular, had an excellent game, themselves denying Fiji any opportunities to play an open game. Both the crowd and the Fijian side, understandably, became frustrated at the lack of enterprise and spectacle and frustration was the root cause of the Fijian prop, Taga being sent off for punching Gary Rees in the 8th minute of injury time !! So ended a tour of which much had been expected, but which achieved little.

16th match   **ENGLAND   28 pts**   v   **AUSTRALIA   19 pts**

	Caps				Caps		
15	12th	J.M.Webb	(Bristol)	.	12th	A.J.S.Leeds	(Paramatta/NSW)
14	1st & only	A.T.Harriman	(Harlequins)	.	4th & last	J.C.Grant	(Orange City/NSW)
13	8th	W.D.C.Carling (Capt)	(Harlequins)	.	1st & only	B.Girvan	(Norths/ACT)
12	8th	S.J.Halliday	(Bath)	.	9th	M.T.Cook	(University/Qu'land)
11	28th	R.Underwood	(RAF/Leicester)	.	40th	D.I.Campese	(Randwick/NSW)
10	21st	C.R.Andrew	(Wasps)	.	28th	M.P.Lynagh	(Brisbane/Qu'land)
9	1st	C.D.Morris	(Liverpool St Helens)	.	29th	N.C.Farr-Jones (Capt)	(Sydney Univ/NSW)
1	18th	P.A.G.Rendall	(Wasps)	.	9th	M.N.Hartill	(Gordon/NSW)
2	13th	B.C.Moore	(Nottingham)	.	36th	T.A.Lawton	(Souths/Queensland)
3	8th	J.A.Probyn	(Wasps)	.	35th	A.J.McIntyre	(University/Qu'land)
4	24th	W.A.Dooley	(Preston G'hoppers)	.	33rd	S.A.G.Cutler	(Gordon/NSW)
5	1st	P.J.Ackford	(Harlequins)	.	16th	W.A.Campbell	(Wests/Queensland)
6	4th	D.W.Egerton	(Bath)	.	14th	J.S.Miller	(University/Qu'land)
7	3rd	R.A.Robinson	(Bath)	.	4th & last	J.M.Gardner	(Wests/Queensland)
8	15th	D.Richards	(Leicester)	.	28th	S.N.Tuynman	(Eastwood/NSW)

1st   J.R.D.Buckton (Saracens) for Carling -

Referee: D.J.Bishop   (New Zealand)

SCORERS:

			0 - 4	A.J.S.Leeds	Try	
			0 - 6	M.P.Lynagh	Conversion	
			0 - 9	M.P.Lynagh	Penalty Goal	
J.M.Webb	Penalty Goal		3 - 9			
C.D.Morris	Try	(1st)	7 - 9			
J.M.Webb	Conversion		9 - 9			
			Half-time			
			9 - 13	D.I.Campese	Try	
R.Underwood	Try	(12th)	13 - 13			
R.Underwood	Try	(13th)	17 - 13			
J.M.Webb	Conversion		19 - 13			
J.M.Webb	Penalty Goal		22 - 13			
			22 - 17	J.C.Grant	Try	
			22 - 19	M.P.Lynagh	Conversion	
S.J.Halliday	Try	(1st)	26 - 19			
J.M.Webb	Conversion		28 - 19			

POINTS:

J.M.Webb	12 points	(96)	M.P.Lynagh	7 points	
R.Underwood	8 points	(52)	A.J.S.Leeds, D.I.Campese,		
C.D.Morris and S.J.Halliday	4 points each	(4),(4)	and J.C.Grant	4 points each	

MATCH COMMENTARY:

A first-rate performance and a convincing victory for England, all the sweeter after the disappointment of the tour to Australia and Fiji last summer. Will Carling's appointment as Captain made for a higher level of confidence about England's approach to the game and provided a magnificent match with some of the most exciting running with ball in hand that English supporters had seen for many a long day.
In fact this was the sixth successive match in which Rory Underwood had scored a try - but only two of those had been at Twickenham.

THE ENGLAND TEAM WHO BEAT AUSTRALIA AT TWICKENHAM ON NOVEMBER 5th 1988, IN WILL CARLING'S FIRST MATCH AS CAPTAIN.
Standing: Touch Judge, D.J.Bishop (Referee), S.M.Bates (Bench), G.W.Rees (Bench), K.Dunn (Bench), J.A.Probyn, P.A.G.Rendall, P.J.Ackford, D.W.Egerton, W.A.Dooley,
D.Richards, A.T.Harriman, J.R.D.Buckton (Bench), A.L.Thompson (Bench), G.J.Chilcott (Bench), Touch Judge,
Seated: C.D.Morris, J.M.Webb, S.J.Halliday, R.Underwood, W.D.C.Carling (Captain), B.C.Moore, C.R.Andrew, R.A.Robinson.

105th match   **ENGLAND   12 pts**   v   **SCOTLAND   12 pts**

96th Calcutta Cup

	Caps					Caps		
15	13th	J.M.Webb	(Bristol)	.		17th	P.W.Dods	(Gala)
14	29th	R.Underwood	(RAF/Leicester)	.		42nd	K.W.Robertson	(Melrose)
13	9th	W.D.C.Carling (Capt)	(Harlequins)	.		15th	S.Hastings	(Watsonians)
12	9th	S.J.Halliday	(Bath)	.		2nd	S.R.P.Lineen	(Boroughmuir)
11	3rd	C.Oti	(Wasps)	.		15th	I.Tukalo	(Selkirk)
10	22nd	C.R.Andrew	(Wasps)	.		2nd	C.M.Chalmers	(Melrose)
9	2nd	C.D.Morris	(Liverpool/St Helens)	.		3rd	G.Armstrong	(Jedforest)
1	19th	P.A.G.Rendall	(Wasps)	.		17th	D.M.B.Sole	(Edinburgh Acad'ls)
2	14th	B.C.Moore	(Nottingham)	.		2nd	K.S.Milne	(Heriot's FP)
3	9th	J.A.Probyn	(Wasps)	.		1st	A.P.Burnell	(London Scottish)
4	25th	W.A.Dooley	(Preston G'hoppers)	.		2nd	C.A.Gray	(Nottingham)
5	2nd	P.J.Ackford	(Harlequins)	.		7th	D.F.Cronin	(Bath)
6	4th	M.C.Teague	(Gloucester)	.		20th	J.Jeffrey	(Kelso)
7	4th	R.A.Robinson	(Bath)	.		19th	F.Calder (Capt)	(Stewart's-Melville)
8	16th	D.Richards	(Leicester)	.		16th	D.B.White	(Gala)

Referee: G.Maurette   (France)

SCORERS:	C.R.Andrew	Penalty Goal	3 - 0		
	C.R.Andrew	Penalty Goal	6 - 0		
			6 - 3	P.W.Dods	Penalty Goal
			6 - 7	J.Jeffrey	Try
			6 - 9	P.W.Dods	Conversion
			Half-time		
			6 - 12	P.W.Dods	Penalty Goal
	J.M.Webb	Penalty Goal	9 - 12		
	J.M.Webb	Penalty Goal	12 - 12		

POINTS:	C.R.Andrew	6 points	(104)	P.W.Dods	8 points
	J.M.Webb	6 points	(102)	J.Jeffrey	4 points

MATCH COMMENTARY:

The euphoria and optimism which followed the victory over Australia in November was exactly what was needed to inspire the Scots to take the "Auld Enemy" down a peg or two, and they succeeded in doing exactly that. Scotland spoiled everything and England allowed them to do it. The England back row, so effective against Australia, were sucked into a war of attrition by John Jeffrey and Finlay Calder and this effectively took them out of the game, Throughout the match M. Maurette awarded countless penalties for goings on at the bottom of rucks but Rob Andrew and Jonathan Webb between them missed seven penalty goal attempts. Tactically England were without direction, and when they found that they could not repeat the free-flowing movements of the match against Australia, because the Scots did not allow them to do so, no other options were forthcoming. Scotland scored the only try of the game when Jonathan Webb dropped a high ball and John Jeffrey won the race for the touchdown. In the second half, after Scotland had gone six points ahead, England rallied and caught up with two penalty goals but Rob Andrew missed the the final and decisive penalty goal attempt with the last kick of the game.

Jonathan Webb and Rob Andrew both passed the 100 total points mark for England in this match. But it was Webb's 13th match, and in that respect he emulated Dusty Hare, but Rob Andrew had taken 22 matches to get into three figures, but he was not always first choice kicker.

102nd match   **ENGLAND   16 pts**   v   **IRELAND   3 pts**

	Caps					Caps		
15	14th	J.M.Webb	(Bristol)			2nd	F.J.Dunlea	(Lansdowne)
14	30th	R.Underwood	(RAF/Leicester)			36th	M.J.Kiernan	(Dolphin)
13	10th	W.D.C.Carling (Capt)	(Harlequins)			27th	B.J.Mullin	(London Irish)
12	10th	S.J.Halliday	(Bath)			21st	D.G.Irwin	(Instonians)
11	4th	C.Oti	(Wasps)			30th	K.D.Crossan	(Instonins)
10	23rd	C.R.Andrew	(Wasps)			31st	P.M.Dean	(St Mary's College)
9	3rd	C.D.Morris	(Liverpool/St Helens)			6th	L.F.P.Aherne	(Lansdowne)
1	20th	P.A.G.Rendall	(Wasps)			8th	T.P.J.Clancy	(Lansdowne)
2	15th	B.C.Moore	(Nottingham)			6th	S.J.Smith	(Ballymena)
3	10th	J.A.Probyn	(Wasps)			14th	J.J.McCoy	(Bangor)
4	26th	W.A.Dooley	(Preston G'hoppers)			41st	D.G.Lenihan	(Cork Constitution)
5	3rd	P.J.Ackford	(Harlequins)			24th	W.A.Anderson	(Dungannon)
6	5th	M.C.Teague	(Gloucester)			23rd	P.M.Matthews (Capt)	(Wanderers)
7	5th	R.A.Robinson	(Bath)			4th	P.T.J.O'Hara	(Sunday's Well)
8	17th	D.Richards	(Leicester)			5th	N.P.Mannion	(Corinthians)

| | 11th | G.J.Chilcott (Bath) for Probyn - | | | | 13th & last | B.J.Spillane (Bohemians) for O'Hara - |

Referee: L.J.Peard   (Wales)

SCORERS:	C.R.Andrew	Penalty Goal		3 - 0			
	C.R.Andrew	Penalty Goal		6 - 0			
				Half-time			
	B.C.Moore	Try	(1st)	10 - 0			
				10 - 3	M.J.Kiernan	Penalty Goal	
	D.Richards	Try	(5th)	14 - 3			
	C.R.Andrew	Conversion		16 - 3			

POINTS:	C.R.Andrew	8 points	(112)		M.J.Kiernan	3 points
	B.C.Moore	4 points	(4)			
	D.Richards	4 points	(20)			

MATCH COMMENTARY:
After the frustration of being denied by Scotland, England fielded a unchanged side who were determined not to lose control of events, and the pack, in particular, never gave Ireland any room to manoeuvre and precious few opportunities. Wade Dooley and Paul Ackford made the lines-out their own and Dean Richards and Mike Teague swept up everything round the fringes and deprived the Irish of possession.

The English back play was less unsure than against the Scots, but was by no means dominant or influential and all the running was made by the pack from whose numbers came both tries. It was a bruising encounter altogether, but the team knew that they had to win to repair the damage done to several individual and their collective reputations and in doing so showed considerable character and self-belief.

Dean Richards' try epitomised that attitude when he charged through a scattered Irish defence after Chris Oti's fine run upfield, as if his life and that of the rest of the side depended on it.

Not a memorable match from anybody's point of view, containing as it did twenty penalty awards against England, but, nevertheless, England achieved the result they came for, even if not in the most spectacular fashion, and in so doing achieved their highest post-war margin of victory over Ireland in Dublin.

64th match   **ENGLAND   11 pts**   v   **FRANCE   0 pts**

	Caps					Caps		
15	15th	J.M.Webb	(Bristol)	.		67th	S.Blanco	(Biarritz)
14	31st	R.Underwood	(RAF/Leicester)	.		13th	J-B.Lafond	(Racing Club)
13	11th	W.D.C.Carling (Capt)	(Harlequins)	.		57th	P.Sella	(Agen)
12	11th	S.J.Halliday	(Bath)	.		19th	M.Andrieu	(Nimes)
11	5th	C.Oti	(Wasps)	.		29th	P.Lagisquet	(Bayonne)
10	24th	C.R.Andrew	(Wasps)	.		21st	F.Mesnel	(Racing Club)
9	4th	C.D.Morris	(Liverpool/St Helens)	.		45th	P.Berbizier (Capt)	(Agen)
1	21st	P.A.G.Rendall	(Wasps)	.		22nd	P.Ondarts	(Biarritz)
2	16th	B.C.Moore	(Nottingham)	.		48th	P.Dintrans	(Tarbes)
3	12th	G.J.Chilcott	(Bath)	.		3rd & last	C.Portolan	(Toulouse)
4	27th	W.A.Dooley	(Preston G'hoppers)	.		3rd	G.Bourguignon	(Narbonne)
5	4th	P.J.Ackford	(Harlequins)	.		53rd	J.Condom	(Biarritz)
6	6th	M.C.Teague	(Gloucester)	.		8th	M.Cecillon	(Bourgoin)
7	6th	R.A.Robinson	(Bath)	.		41st	D.Erbani	(Agen)
8	18th	D.Richards	(Leicester)	.		46th	L.Rodriguez	(Dax)
					.			
					.	37th	J-P.Garuet (Lourdes) for Portolan -	
					.	19th	D.Charvet (Toulouse) for Lagisquet -	

Referee: S.R.Hilditch   (Ireland)

SCORERS: W.D.C.Carling   Try   (1st)   4 - 0
                                                                         Half-time
                 C.R.Andrew   Penalty Goal   7 - 0
                 R.A.Robinson   Try   (1st & last)   11 - 0

POINTS: W.D.C.Carling   4 points   (4)
                 R.A.Robinson   4 points   (4)
                 C.R.Andrew   3 points   (115)

MATCH COMMENTARY:
England, again unchanged, except for the injured Probyn, who was concussed against Ireland, improved on their previous performance
with better discipline and even greater forward power. The French played badly and lacked a lineout jumper and a pacy open-side
flanker, but this should not detract from the much improved England performance. As the match wore on, France became tetchy and
aggressive but England did not rise to the bait and maintained their discipline as Roger Uttley had urged them to do, earlier in the season.
But again, there was little expansive rugby from the backs even though the pack were providing abundant possession, and it seems that
Dewi Morris has problems with his service to Rob Andrew and this places a restriction on the extent to which the English backs can start
free-flowing handling movements. The first try came from such a movement, however, which went wrong. It should have been a scissors
movement between Will Carling and Chris Oti, and Oti mistimed his run to such a degree that Carling never gave the pass and was able
to score himself as Oti drew the defence away. But the second was a fine effort between the back row and the scrum-half with Andy
Robinson making the touchdown.. An excellent result for England, and very well deserved.
It is ten long years since England scored a try against France away from home.

95th match   **ENGLAND   9 pts**   v   **WALES   12 pts**

	Caps					Caps		
15	16th	J.M.Webb	(Bristol)			24th	P.H.Thorburn (Capt)	(Neath)
14	32nd	R.Underwood	(RAF/Leicester)			18th	I.C.Evans	(Llanelli)
13	12th	W.D.C.Carling (Capt)	(Harlequins)			2nd	D.W.Evans	(Oxford University)
12	12th	S.J.Halliday	(Bath)			8th	M.R.Hall	(Cambridge Univ)
11	6th	C.Oti	(Wasps)			1st	A.Emyr	(Swansea)
10	25th	C.R.Andrew	(Wasps)			3rd & last	P.Turner	(Newbridge)
9	5th	C.D.Morris	(Liverpool/St Helens)			27th	R.N.Jones	(Swansea)
1	22nd	P.A.G.Rendall	(Wasps)			6th	M.Griffiths	(Bridgend)
2	17th	B.C.Moore	(Nottingham)			10th & last	I.J.Watkins	(Ebbw Vale)
3	13th	G.J.Chilcott	(Bath)			3rd	L.Delaney	(Llanelli)
4	28th	W.A.Dooley	(Preston G'hoppers)			21st	P.T.Davies	(Llanelli)
5	5th	P.J.Ackford	(Harlequins)			34th & last	R.L.Norster	(Cardiff)
6	7th	M.C.Teague	(Gloucester)			3rd	G.Jones	(Llanelli)
7	7th	R.A.Robinson	(Bath)			8th & last	D.J.Bryant	(Bridgend)
8	19th	D.Richards	(Leicester)			6th	M.A.Jones	(Neath)

18th   G.W.Rees (Nottingham) for Teague - 1

Referee: K.V.J.Fitzgerald   (Australia)

SCORERS:

C.R.Andrew	Penalty Goal		3 - 0		
			3 - 3	P.H.Thorburn	Penalty Goal
			3 - 6	P.H.Thorburn	Penalty Goal
C.R.Andrew	D'p Goal	(8th)	6 - 6		
C.R.Andrew	Penalty Goal		9 - 6		
			Half-time		
			9 - 10	M.R.Hall	Try
			9 - 12	P.H.Thorburn	Conversion

POINTS:

C.R.Andrew	9 points	(124)		P.H.Thorburn	8 points
				M.R.Hall	4 points

MATCH COMMENTARY:

History does indeed repeat itself, for again England came to Cardiff with high hopes, and again departed well beaten. It was a dull day and a dull game fraught with tension and not infrequent punch-ups. Geoff Cooke had decided that an unchanged team would take the field even though Jeff Probyn was fit again, and this proved to be a mistake for Gareth Chilcott, normally a loose head, was no match at tight head for the powerful scrummaging of Mike Griffiths, and this put England at a serious disadvantage. Then immediately after the kick-off, after a accidental collision, Mike Teague had to leave the field, and England had a real problem. With these advantages the Welsh pack played superbly and put England under all sorts of pressure. Morris and Andrew could make nothing of the messy possession which the forwards gave them, and with Robert Norster reigning supreme at the back of the line-out, and Robert Jones at his sniping, incisive best, England were going nowhere. But it was 9 - 6 to England at half-time, and all was not over until Paul Turner put up a high ball near touch on the England 22. Rory Underwood caught it with time to spare but between he and Jonathan Webb the ball went to ground, was hacked on and Wales scored the only try of the match. Thereafter, England were penned in their own half and every attempt they made to escape was foiled either by powerful Welsh tackling or nervous English handling and any hopes of a retaliatory score slipped away.

2nd match   **ENGLAND 58 pts**   v   **ROMANIA 3 pts**

	Caps					Caps	
15	1st	S.D.Hodgkinson	(Nottingham)	.	M.Toader		(Dynamo Bucharest)
14	7th	C.Oti	(Wasps)	.	N.Racean		(Timisoara)
13	13th	S.J.Halliday	(Bath)	.	A.Lungu		(Dynamo Bucharest)
12	1st	J.C.Guscott	(Bath)	.	N.Fulina		(Baia Mare)
11	33rd	R.Underwood	(RAF/Leicester)	.	D.Boldor		(Steaua)
10	26th	C.R.Andrew (Capt)	(Wasps)	.	G.Ignat		(Steaua)
9	1st & only	S.M.Bates	(Wasps)	.	D.Negea		(Dynamo Bucharest)
1	23rd	P.A.G.Rendall	(Wasps)	.	G.Leonte		(Steaua)
2	18th	B.C.Moore	(Nottingham)	.	V.Ion		(Dynamo Bucharest)
3	14th & last	G.J.Chilcott	(Wasps)	.	G.Dumitrescu		(Steaua)
4	6th	P.J.Ackford	(Harlequins)	.	S.Coriascu		(Steaua)
5	29th	W.A.Dooley	(Preston G'hoppers)	.	G.Caragea		(Dynamo Bucharest)
6	30th	P.J.Winterbottom	(Headingley)	.	F.Murariu (Capt)		(Steaua)
7	8th	M.C.Teague	(Gloucester)	.	A.Radulescu		(Steaua)
8	20th	D.Richards	(Leicester)	.	H.Dumitras		(Buzau)

	11th	J.A.Probyn (Wasps) for Chilcott - 3	.	C.Radacanu (Dynamo Bucharest) for Caragea
	19th	G.W.Rees (Nottingham) for Richards - 28	.	

Referee: J.B.Anderson   (Scotland)

SCORERS:

D.Richards	Try	(5th)	4 - 0		
S.D.Hodgkinson	Conversion		6 - 0		
J.C.Guscott	Try	(1st)	10 - 0		
S.D.Hodgkinson	Conversion		12 - 0		
			12 - 3	G.Ignat	Penalty Goal
S.D.Hodgkinson	Penalty Goal		15 - 3		
C.R.Andrew	D'p Goal	(9th)	18 - 3		
C.Oti	Try	(4th)	22 - 3		
S.D.Hodgkinson	Conversion		24 - 3		
			Half-time		
J.C.Guscott	Try	(2nd)	28 - 3		
S.D.Hodgkinson	Conversion		30 - 3		
C.Oti	Try	(5th)	34 - 3		
S.D.Hodgkinson	Conversion		36 - 3		
J.A.Probyn	Try	(1st)	40 - 3		
S.D.Hodgkinson	Conversion		42 - 3		
J.C.Guscott	Try	(3rd)	46 - 3		
S.D.Hodgkinson	Conversion		48 - 3		
C.Oti	Try	(6th)	52 - 3		
C.Oti	Try	(7th)	56 - 3		
S.D.Hodgkinson	Conversion		58 - 3		

POINTS:					
S.D.Hodgkinson	19 points	(19)	G.Ignat	3 points	
C.Oti	16 points	(28)			
J.C.Guscott	12 points	(12)			
D.Richards	4 points	(24)			
J.A.Probyn	4 points	(4)			
C.R.Andrew	3 points	(127)			

MATCH COMMENTARY:

England approached this match with some trepidation because, with one exception, this was the Romanian team which had beaten Wales at the Arms Park the previous December, and because the match was to be played in a temperature of well over 80 degrees and high humidity. In the event, England were totally dominant and the pack was much more mobile and faster about the pitch, so much so that there were often five English forwards at the line-out position before the first Romanian arrived.

This was England's second highest points total in all matches, and the highest ever margin of victory. Simon Hodgkinson's eight conversions beat the seven achieved by Jonathan Webb in the 1987 World Cup match against Japan. Jeremy Guscott's three tries on his debut was also an outstanding achievement, as was Chris Oti's feat in scoring four tries in the match much of which was due to Guscott's silken running and the exquisite timing of his pass.

SUMMARY OF THE SEASON - 1988 - 89:

After the immensely disappointing tour of Australia and Fiji the previous summer, Geoff Cooke decided that if England were going to build seriously for the 1991 World Cup then a framework for English International rugby had to be established within which a degree of continuity and around which individual and squad confidence could be built. He decided that the construction of the framework and the development of the confidence had to start with the appointment of a captain who would lead the side through the intervening period. Amidst speculation Will Carling, who had made a solid impression last season, was appointed and had every chance of holding his place in the side.

The beginning of Carling's tenure of office was almost a dream come true. Australia were touring England and Scotland and they came to Twickenham on Guy Fawkes Day only to succumb to an explosion of courageous and expansive rugby. It was a splendid effort, and appeared to be confirmation for all that Geoff Cooke had got it right and that England were really on their way. Ironically, the season was to take much the same shape as the previous one but in reverse. This time it started with a bang at Twickenham and ended with a whimper at Cardiff. Last time the whimpers came against France and Wales and the bang took place against Ireland.

There were unrealistically high expectations for the opening Five Nations match against Scotland at Twickenham, and the Scots saw to it that they were dashed. Spoiling has always been an effective Scottish tactic and this time it worked to perfection largely through the efforts of Finlay Calder and John Jeffrey (who, some say, was born off-side !) A victory over Ireland was therefore essential if the team was to retain any credibility and self-esteem, and it was achieved in a very tense and unspectacular match at Lansdowne Road and the forward power, to become so successful in future years, was beginning to develop. A strangely lack-lustre French side was seen off at Twickenham without themselves getting on to the scoreboard, and all that remained was the trip to Cardiff where victory would give England, not the Triple Crown, but the title outright irrespective of whether or not France beat Scotland on the same day. Thus another tense pressure match was in prospect at Cardiff where England had not won for 26 years. The game was all that England would not have wished it to be, and the Welsh pack facing England without Jeff Probyn, with Gareth Chilcott playing out of position against Mike Griffiths and with Mike Teague off the field within the first minute, got a grip of the match and never let go. There was nothing that England could do to retrieve the situation once Wales had scored the only try of the match following an unforced error on the part of Rory Underwood.

England finished in joint second place in the Championship Table, with Scotland, in a season which in its glorious opening stage promised very much more than that. But now, unlike previous years, there was a plan, there was the nucleus of a good side developing, and, probably of most importance, a vital and visible thread of continuity stretching into the foreseeable future.

The final match of the season, against Romania in Bucharest, without the injured Will Carling, was a potential pitfall. The Romanians had beaten Wales, at Cardiff, the previous December, 15 - 9, and it would have been all too easy for England to falter in high temperatures and high humidity at the 23 August Stadium. Thankfully they put on a very convincing display and scored nine tries without reply. On their debuts, Jeremy Guscott scored three tries and Simon Hodgkinson kicked 19 points including eight conversions.

In the four Five Nations matches, only sixteen players were called upon, and the side would have been unchanged throughout had it not been for the concussion sustained by Jeff Probyn in the Irish match which kept him out of the game for three weeks. In all six matches, twenty two players appeared plus John Buckton for his first cap as a replacement against Australia. Other new caps were Dewi Morris, try scorer on his debut, Paul Ackford and Andrew Harriman for the Australia match and Simon Hodgkinson, Jeremy Guscott and Steve Bates in Romania. Only three players were not to appear in International Rugby again. Steve Bates and Andrew Harriman earned their only caps this year, but Andrew Harriman was to captain the England VII who won the World Cup Sevens at Murrayfield in 1993. Gareth Chilcott won 14 caps and was to go on the forthcoming Lions tour. He was always a somewhat larger than life character, somewhat injury prone and became best known for his TV Commentary roles and his Pantomime performances in later years.

Ten England players were invited to join Gavin Hastings' Lions party in Australia in the summer of 1989, and seven of them were forwards. They were: Dean Richards, Mike Teague, Wade Dooley, Paul Ackford, Brian Moore, Andy Robinson ansd Gareth Chilcott. In the backs were Rory Underwood, Chris Oti and, at the time he was selected, the uncapped Jeremy Guscott. Rob Andrew was called as a replacement for Paul Dean. Eight played in the Tests, four in all three matches, Underwood, Moore, Ackford and Richards, and four in only the second and third, Guscott, Andrew, Dooley and Teague. Thus for two Tests, there were eight England players in the Lions' side.

FIVE NATIONS CHAMPIONSHIP TABLE:

Won: **Retained Calcutta Cup**

		Played	Won	Lost	Drawn	Points: For	Points: Against	Tries: For	Tries: Against	Title Points
1	France	4	3	1	0	76	47	11	3	6
2 =	**ENGLAND**	4	2	1	1	48	27	4	2	5
2 =	Scotland	4	2	1	1	75	59	9	7	5
4 =	Ireland	4	1	3	0	64	92	6	12	2
4 =	Wales	4	1	3	0	44	82	3	9	2

Home Games: beat France 11 - 0, (two tries to nil); drew with Scotland 12 - 12, (no tries to one)

Away Games: beat Ireland 16 - 3, (two tries to nil); lost to Wales 9 - 12, (no tries to one)

2nd match   **ENGLAND   58 pts**   v   **FIJI   23 pts**

	Caps					Caps	
15	2nd	**S.D.Hodgkinson**	(Nottingham)	.		**M.Natuilagilagi**	(Army & Suva)
14	4th	**M.D.Bailey**	(Wasps)	.		**T.Lovo**	(QVS OB Suva)
13	13th	**W.D.C.Carling (Capt)**	(Harlequins)	.		**L.Erenavula**	(Hyatt Nadroga)
12	2nd	**J.C.Guscott**	(Bath)	.		**N.Nadruku**	(Hyatt Nadroga)
11	34th	**R.Underwood**	(RAF/Leicester)	.		**T.Vonolagi**	(Army & Suva)
10	27th	**C.R.Andrew**	(Wasps)	.		**S.Koroduadua**	(Police/Suva)
9	10th	**R.J.Hill**	(Bath)	.		**L.Vasuvulagi**	(Baravi Nadroga)
1	1st & only	**A.R.Mullins**	(Harlequins)	.		**M.Taga**	(QVS OB Suva)
2	19th	**B.C.Moore**	(Nottingham)	.		**S.Naivilawasa**	(Police/Suva)
3	1st & only	**M.S.Linnett**	(Moseley)	.		**S.Naituko**	(Lomaiviti Suva)
4	7th	**P.J.Ackford**	(Harlequins)	.		**I Savai**	(QVS OB Suva)
5	30th	**W.A.Dooley**	(Preston G'hoppers)	.		**M.Rasari**	(Army & Suva)
6	31st	**P.J.Winterbottom**	(Harlequins)	.		**N.Matriawa**	(Army & Suva)
7	6th	**M.G.Skinner**	(Harlequins)	.		**A.Dere**	(Army & Suva)
8	5th	**D.W.Egerton**	(Bath)	.		**E.Teleni (Capt)**	(Army & Suva)

14th	S.J.Halliday (Bath) for Bailey -	
20th	G.W.Rees (Nottingham) for Winterbottom -	

Referee: B.W.Stirling   (Ireland)

SCORERS:

R.Underwood	Try	(14th)	4 - 0			
R.Underwood	Try	(15th)	8 - 0			
S.D.Hodgkinson	Conversion		10 - 0			
			10 - 4	L.Erenavula	Try	
			10 - 6	S.Koroduadua	Conversion	
			10 - 10	E.Teleni	Try	
R.Underwood	Try	(16th)	14 - 10			
S.D.Hodgkinson	Penalty Goal		17 - 10			
			17 - 13	S.Koroduadua	Penalty Goal	
S.D.Hodgkinson	Penalty Goal		20 - 13			
			Half-time			
M.G.Skinner	Try	(1st)	24 - 13			
S.D.Hodgkinson	Conversion		26 - 13			
M.D.Bailey	Try	(1st & only)	30 - 13			
S.D.Hodgkinson	Conversion		32 - 13			
M.S.Linnett	Try	(1st & only)	36 - 13			
S.D.Hodgkinson	Conversion		38 - 13			
R.Underwood	Try	(17th)	42 - 13			
			42 - 17	M.Rasari	Try	
R.Underwood	Try	(18th)	46 - 17			
S.D.Hodgkinson	Conversion		48 - 17			
			48 - 21	I.Savai	Try	
			48 - 23	S.Koroduadua	Conversion	
P.J.Ackford	Try	(1st & only)	52 - 23			
J.C.Guscott	Try	(4th)	56 - 23			
C.R.Andrew	Conversion		58 - 23			

POINTS:	R.Underwood	20 points	(72)		S.Koroduadua	7 points
	S.D.Hodgkinson	16 points	(35)		L.Erenevula, E.Teleni,	
	M.G.Skinner, M.D.Bailey,		(4),(4)		M.Rasari and I Savai	4 points each
	M.S.Linnett, P.J.Ackford	4 points	(4),(4)			
	and J.C.Guscott	each	(16)			
	C.R.Andrew	2 points	(129)			

MATCH COMMENTARY:

England's forward power totally denied Fiji any possession at all and gradually these normally high-spirited and cheerful souls became frustrated and disillusioned to the extent that they stopped tackling altogether and resorted to unlawful physical intimidation. After repeated warnings, Brian Stirling was compelled to send off two of the Fijian three-quarters, Tevita Vonolagi and Noa Nadruku, for reckless tackling. England found themselves playing touch rugby at times. Rory Underwood equalled D.Lambert's record of five tries in an International set in 1907 against France, and he also reached a personal total of 18 tries in Internationals which equalled Cyril Lowe's record.

All the running on and off the ball was a joy to watch, but as a match, it was hardly a contest.

Ten tries in the match equals the record set in the 1987 World Cup against Japan. This is the highest score ever at Twickenham against all opposition and also the highest aggregate score.

103rd match   **ENGLAND   23 pts**   v   **IRELAND   0 pts**

	Caps					Caps		
15	3rd	S.D.Hodgkinson	(Nottingham)		1st	K.J.Murphy	(Constitution)
14	5th	M.D.Bailey	(Wasps)		38th	M.J.Kiernan	(Dolphin)
13	14th	W.D.C.Carling (Capt)	(Harlequins)		30th	B.J.Mullin	(Blackrock College)
12	3rd	J.C.Guscott	(Bath)		24th	D.G.Irwin	(Instonians)
11	35th	R.Underwood	(RAF/Leicester)		30th	K.D.Crossan	(Instonians)
10	28th	C.R.Andrew	(Wasps)		1st	P.C.Russell	(Instonians)
9	11th	R.J.Hill	(Bath)		9th	L.F.P.Aherne	(Lansdowne)
1	24th	P.A.G.Rendall	(Wasps)		19th	D.C.Fitzgerald	(Lansdowne)
2	20th	B.C.Moore	(Nottingham)		9th	S.J.Smith	(Ballymena)
3	12th	J.A.Probyn	(Wasps)		1st	G.F.Halpin	(Wanderers)
4	8th	P.J.Ackford	(Harlequins)		6th	N.P.J.Francis	(Blackrock College)
5	31st	W.A.Dooley	(Preston G'hoppers)		26th	W.A.Anderson (Capt)	(Dungannon)
6	32nd	P.J.Winterbottom	(Harlequins)		26th	P.M.Matthews	(Wanderers)
7	7th	M.G.Skinner	(Harlequins)		6th	P.T.J.O'Hara	(Sunday's Well)
8	6th	D.W.Egerton	(Bath)		8th	N.P.Mannion	(Corinthians)
					2nd	J.P.McDonald (Malone) for Smith - 34	

Referee: P.Robin   (France)

SCORERS:

S.D.Hodgkinson	Penalty Goal		3 - 0
J.A.Probyn	Try	(2nd)	7 - 0
			Half-time
D.W.Egerton	Try	(1st & only)	11 - 0
S.D.Hodgkinson	Conversion		13 - 0
R.Underwood	Try	(19th)	17 - 0
J.C.Guscott	Try	(5th)	21 - 0
S.D.Hodgkinson	Conversion		23 - 0

POINTS:

S.D.Hodgkinson	7 points	(42)
J.A.Probyn, D.W.Egerton,	4 points	(8),(4)
R.Underwood and J.C.Guscott	each	(76),(20)

MATCH COMMENTARY:

The first half of this match gave the impression that it was going to be another dour inhibited struggle reminiscent of many games earlier in the Eighties. In the last ten minutes, however, there was a magical transformation and England scored sixteen points. This, though, was the consequence of unremitting pressure by the English pack. Gary Halpin, in his first International, was turned all over by Paul Rendall and Wade Dooley and Paul Ackford although not winning everything in the lines-out against Neil Francis, kept up the pressure. England played most of the last hour of the match in the Irish 22 and until the last ten minutes could get no further. But the pressure told and Ireland all but collapsed. England had gone into the match without Dean Richards who was still injured and Dave Egerton took up the No 8 position. It might have been different with Richards there, but for an hour England could make no impression on a very ordinary Irish side. At that stage they had only Jeff Probyn's try to show for sustained pressure and that came from following up a kick rather than from forward dominance. Then with eight minutes to go, Dave Egerton crashed over the Irish line after a series of tapped penalties, then Underwood, then Guscott scored and, at last, Ireland were finished. Rory Underwood's nineteenth try established a new record of tries scored by an England player beating Cyril Lowe's record set (also against Ireland) in 1923. This was England's second highest winning margin over Ireland.

65th match   **ENGLAND   26 pts**   v   **FRANCE   7 pts**

	Caps				Caps		
15	4th	S.D.Hodgkinson	(Nottingham)	.	73rd	S.Blanco	(Biarritz)
14	6th	M.D.Bailey	(Wasps)		25th	M.Andrieu	(Nimes)
13	15th	W.D.C.Carling (Capt)	(Harlequins)		65th	P.Sella	(Agen)
12	4th	J.C.Guscott	(Bath)		21st	D.Charvet	(Toulouse)
11	36th	R.Underwood	(RAF/Leicester)		37th	P.Lagisquet	(Bayonne)
10	29th	C.R.Andrew	(Wasps)		26th	F.Mesnel	(Racing Club)
9	12th	R.J.Hill	(Bath)		52nd	P.Berbizier (Capt)	(Agen)
1	25th	P.A.G.Rendall	(Wasps)		27th	P.Ondarts	(Biarritz)
2	21st	B.C.Moore	(Nottingham)		14th	L.Armary	(Lourdes)
3	13th	J.A.Probyn	(Wasps)		42nd & last	J-P Garuet-Lempirou	(Lourdes)
4	9th	P.J.Ackford	(Harlequins)		7th	T.Devergie	(Nimes)
5	32nd	W.A.Dooley	(Preston G'hoppers)		46th & last	D.Erbani	(Agen)
6	33rd	P.J.Winterbottom	(Harlequins)		35th	E.Champ	(Toulon)
7	8th	M.G.Skinner	(Harlequins)		53rd	L.Rodriguez	(Dax)
8	9th	M.C.Teague	(Gloucester)		4th	O.Roumat	(Dax)
					11th	P.Marocco (Montferrand) for Armary -

Referee: O.E.Doyle   (Ireland)

SCORERS:	S.D.Hodgkinson	Penalty Goal		3 - 0		
	S.D.Hodgkinson	Penalty Goal		6 - 0		
	S.D.Hodgkinson	Penalty Goal		9 - 0		
	R.Underwood	Try	(20th)	13 - 0		
				Half-time		
	J.C.Guscott	Try	(6th)	17 - 0		
	S.D.Hodgkinson	Conversion		19 - 0		
	S.D.Hodgkinson	Penalty Goal		22 - 0		
				22 - 4	D.Charvet	Try
				22 - 7	P.Lagisquet	Penalty Goal
	W.D.C.Carling	Try	(2nd)	26 - 7		

POINTS:	S.D.Hodgkinson	14 points	(56)		D.Charvet	4 points
	R.Underwood, J.C.Guscott	4 points	(80),(24)		P.Lagisquet	3 points
	and W.D.C.Carling	each	(8)			

MATCH COMMENTARY:

This was magnificently controlled rugby by the England team (256 caps amongst them) who totally outplayed a vastly more experienced French side (527 caps amongst them). They made France look poor. It was a total team effort, but Paul Ackford's line-out work, Peter Winterbottom's tackling and Skinner and Teague's back-row play in general were of the very highest order. In difficult, gusty conditions, Simon Hodgkinson scored with three immaculate goal kicks to give England a nine point lead midway through the first half, and this boosted England's confidence and demoralised the French. Late in the second half, France managed a response, but even that flicker of reaction was negated by the third England try by the captain. This was France's biggest ever defeat at Parc des Princes and was England's biggest winning margin over France for 74 years. Jeremy Guscott continued his commendable habit of scoring a try in each International match in which he plays. He has now scored six tries in four matches.

96th match   **ENGLAND 34 pts**   v   **WALES 6 pts**

	Caps					Caps		
15	5th	S.D.Hodgkinson	(Nottingham)	.		27th	P.H.Thorburn	(Neath)
14	15th	S.J.Halliday	(Bath)	.		15th	M.H.Titley	(Swansea)
13	16th	W.D.C.Carling (Capt)	(Harlequins)	.		19th	M.G.Ring	(Cardiff)
12	5th	J.C.Guscott	(Bath)	.		11th	M.R.Hall	(Cardiff)
11	37th	R.Underwood	(RAF/Leicester)	.		4th	A.Emyr	(Swansea)
10	30th	C.R.Andrew	(Wasps)	.		5th	D.W.Evans	(Cardiff)
9	13th	R.J.Hill	(Bath)	.		30th	R.N.Jones (Capt)	(Swansea)
1	26th	P.A.G.Rendall	(Wasps)	.		9th	M.Griffiths	(Cardiff)
2	22nd	B.C.Moore	(Nottingham)	.		10th	K.H.Phillips	(Neath)
3	14th	J.A.Probyn	(Wasps)	.		4th	L.Delaney	(Llanelli)
4	10th	P.J.Ackford	(Harlequins)	.		2nd	A.G.Allen	(Newbridge)
5	33rd	W.A.Dooley	(Preston G'hoppers)	.		2nd	G.O.Llewellyn	(Neath)
6	34th	P.J.Winterbottom	(Harlequins)	.		24th	P.T.Davies	(Llanelli)
7	9th	M.G.Skinner	(Harlequins)	.		12th	R.G.Collins	(Cardiff)
8	10th	M.C.Teague	(Gloucester)	.		9th	M.A.Jones	(Neath)

Referee: D.Leslie   (Scotland)

SCORERS:

S.D.Hodgkinson	Penalty Goal		3 - 0			
S.D.Hodgkinson	Penalty Goal		6 - 0			
W.D.C.Carling	Try	(3rd)	10 - 0			
S.D.Hodgkinson	Conversion		12 - 0			
R.Underwood	Try	(21st)	16 - 0			
			Half-time			
S.D.Hodgkinson	Penalty Goal		19 - 0			
R.Underwood	Try	(22nd)	23 - 0			
S.D.Hodgkinson	Conversion		25 - 0			
			25 - 4	P.T.Davies	Try	
			25 - 6	P.H.Thorburn	Conversion	
R.J.Hill	Try	(1st)	29 - 6			
S.D.Hodgkinson	Conversion		31 - 6			
S.D.Hodgkinson	Penalty Goal		34 - 6			

POINTS:

S.D.Hodgkinson	18 points	(74)	P.T.Davies	4 points
R.Underwood	8 points	(88)	P.H.Thorburn	2 points
W.D.C.Carling and R.J.Hill	4 points	(12),(4)		
	each			

MATCH COMMENTARY:

Another splendid display by a very well controlled and organised English team. The result - the highest ever score and the biggest ever point margin against Wales. England played with elan and panache and with increasing confidence as the game went on - yet this was not as competent a performance as had been seen against France, because many opportunities were created but by no means all were taken. Never before had England piled up a 25 - 0 lead over Wales at any time, and such was Wales' disgrace that their Coach, John Ryan, saw fit to resign only a few days after the match.

In gaining his 37th cap, Rory Underwood beat David Duckham's record of 36 caps as England's most capped back.

106th match   **ENGLAND   7 pts**   v   **SCOTLAND   13 pts**

97th Calcutta Cup

	Caps					Caps		
15	6th	S.D.Hodgkinson	(Nottingham)	.		24th	A.G.Hastings	(Watsonians)
14	16th	S.J.Halliday	(Bath)	.		6th	A.G.Stanger	(Hawick)
13	17th	W.D.C.Carling (Capt)	(Harlequins)	.		23rd	S.Hastings	(Watsonians)
12	6th	J.C.Guscott	(Bath)	.		10th	S.R.P.Lineen	(Boroughmuir)
11	38th	R.Underwood	(RAF/Leicester)	.		22nd	I.Tukalo	(Selkirk)
10	31st	C.R.Andrew	(Wasps)	.		9th	C.M.Chalmers	(Melrose)
9	14th	R.J.Hill	(Bath)	.		11th	G.Armstrong	(Jedforest)
1	27th	P.A.G.Rendall	(Wasps)	.		25th	D.M.B.Sole (Capt)	(Edinburgh Acad'ls)
2	23rd	B.C.Moore	(Nottingham)	.		10th	K.S.Milne	(Heriot's FP)
3	15th	J.A.Probyn	(Wasps)	.		9th	A.P.Burnell	(London Scottish)
4	11th	P.J.Ackford	(Harlequins)	.		10th	C.A.Gray	(Nottingham)
5	34th	W.A.Dooley	(Preston G'hoppers)	.		15th	D.F.Cronin	(Bath)
6	35th	P.J.Winterbottom	(Headingley)	.		28th	J.Jeffrey	(Kelso)
7	10th	M.G.Skinner	(Harlequins)	.		26th	F.Calder	(Stewart's-Melville)
8	11th	M.C.Teague	(Gloucester)	.		24th	D.B.White	(London Scottish)

7th & last   M.D.Bailey (Wasps) for Guscott -   .   4th   D.J.Turnbull (Hawick) for White -

Referee: D.Bishop   (New Zealand)

SCORERS:

				0 - 3	C.M.Chalmers	Penalty Goal
				0 - 6	C.M.Chalmers	Penalty Goal
J.C.Guscott	Try	(7th)		4 - 6		
				4 - 9	C.M.Chalmers	Penalty Goal
				Half-time		
				4 - 13	A.G.Stanger	Try
S.D.Hodgkinson	Penalty Goal			7 - 13		

POINTS:

J.C.Guscott	4 points	(28)	C.M.Chalmers	9 points	
S.D.Hodgkinson	3 points	(77)	A.G.Stanger	4 points	

MATCH COMMENTARY:

For the first time ever, between two British teams, the last match of the season would decide the Grand Slam. The atmosphere at Murrayfield was electric and the tension reached unparalleled heights as David Sole led his team at a deliberate walking pace to demonstrate their control and self-discipline. Two verses of "Flower of Scotland" were played, and sung with almost tangible emotion, to further intimidate England. England, it must be said, were a touch complacent and that proved fatal. Scotland, to a man, played magnificently and fully deserved their third Grand Slam. England will learn much from this bitter experience, not least that nemesis inevitably stalks and replaces hubris !!

From the kick-off it was evident that England were going to have demands made upon them which they would do well to recognise, let alone respond to. Scotland took the might of the England pack on face to face and concentrated their efforts in denying possession with John Jeffrey and Finlay Calder playing the key roles. England simply had no "Plan B" to fall back on and almost got to the point where they were trying too hard and beginning to lose control of themselves - but they never had control of the match. Jeremy Guscott's silken running produced a fine try, but it was never enough, and when Gary Armstrong made a break, and passed to Gavin Hastings who then chipped ahead for Tony Stanger to score, England were dead and buried and the only course open to them was to return home "tae think again" !! There is no question about who won and who lost this magnificent match; it was not lost, it was won - by Scotland, and there was never any doubt in any Scotsman's mind once David Sole walked his team onto the pitch - the doubts were sown in the minds of the English.

SUMMARY OF THE SEASON - 1989 - 90:

This was an excellent season for Five Nations Rugby, indeed for Northern Hemisphere Rugby, with high standards of play, thirty six tries in the ten Five Nations matches and high drama right to the final whistle. Intense joy for the Scots with their third Grand Slam, and their second in a period of only six years; intense disappointment for England having come so far and having played so well to get there and ending up with nothing; and abject despair for Wales who suffered their first ever "whitewash" in the Championship, losing every game and conceding 90 points and thirteen tries.

There is no doubt that the 1989 Lions' Tour to Australia did a great deal of good for those members of the England team who enjoyed that experience and whose confidence at International level had not, at that time, reached its peak. Among those who benefitted were Rob Andrew, Paul Ackford, Mike Teague, Jeremy Guscott and these four, in particular, showed that benefit in the 1990 International season. Rory Underwood and Wade Dooley already had the experience and the confidence, as did Dean Richards, who missed the whole of this International season through injury. Brian Moore had his own internal confidence generator. The combined effect on the England side was considerable, and it showed firstly in the calm and composed demolition of the Fijian side in November, when six of those Lions were in the side. Also recalled to the side was Richard Hill at scrum-half whose speed and length of pass behind a dominant pack gave Rob Andrew time and space to exercise his control over the game and the pairing stood England in very good stead from that point up to the World Cup final in 1991. Richard Hill had been capped first in 1984 in South Africa and had captained England in 1987 until the match at Cardiff, since which time he had been in the International wilderness.

Team confidence, therefore, going into the 1990 Five Nations Championship was high. The forwards in set piece, line-out and loose could provide athletic backs with fast quality ball, and, as had already been proved, they could run in the tries. In defence, there was not a weak link in the side, except possibly at full-back where Simon Hodgkinson was in the side to kick the goals when the opportunity presented itself. It took an hour in the first match against Ireland at Twickenham , for the confidence to become points on the board, but the last eight minutes of that match when sixteen points were scored, two goals and a further try, set the season alight and the level of expectation high. With Mike Teague replacing Dave Egerton, the side went to Paris and played magnificent rugby with Rory Underwood, Jeremy Guscott and Will Carling all scoring tries in a style which is normally exhibited by the French at Parc des Princes rather than by their opponents. Simon Hodgkinson's accurate goal kicking laid the foundation, and in so doing he amassed 50 individual points in only his fourth International match. Simon Halliday replaced Mark Bailey on the right wing for the match at Twickenham against Wales and the England supporters who had suffered so many disappointments and humiliations at the hands of the Welsh witnessed the destruction of a very poor Welsh side. This was the first time that England had scored four tries against the Welsh, and it was the side's fifth successive victory against all comers. Thus the Grand Slam and all that went with it beckoned at Murrayfield on March 17th 1990. It was 1980 all over again, but this time Scotland were in with a shout as well. England were on the crest of a wave and in their final training session at Peebles the day before, nothing went wrong, every pass went to hand and every ploy worked perfectly. Bill MacLaren, who was privileged to watch, was very impressed ! England were a trifle over-confident, the Scots, motivated by Ian McGeechan and David Sole were adamant that this was to be their day, and they thoroughly deserved it. They tackled like demons, they disrupted the English line-out very effectively by constantly changing line-out positions and they were absolutely determined that England would leave Murrayfield with nothing to show for their efforts; and they succeeded in a match that will forever be branded on the memories of those who saw it - and, indeed, of those who took part. Ironically, Jeremy Guscott's try was the first scored by England at Murrayfield since the Grand Slam match in 1980 ten years ago.

It was suggested at the time that because of the result of that one match, England's season had been a failure. This was certainly not the case. The whole side had played some splendid rugby, had matured and developed well beyond even the most optimistic expectations, had scored 12 tries, conceded only three and scored 90 points, more than in any other season since 1947.

But the experience of Murrayfield was certainly to influence the style and the approach to English International rugby for some time to come. Apart from the two props who played in the match against Fiji, whose first and last International it was to be in both cases, only Mark Bailey was to leave the International stage at the end of the season. He had won seven caps and is a Fellow at Queen's College, Cambridge. With the World Cup imminent, many players will doubtless regard that as their objective and their swansong.

FIVE NATIONS CHAMPIONSHIP TABLE:

Won: **Nothing**

		Played	Won	Lost	Drawn	Points: For	Points: Against	Tries: For	Tries: Against	Title Points
1	Scotland	4	4	0	0	60	26	6	3	8
2	**ENGLAND**	4	3	1	0	90	26	12	3	6
3	France	4	2	2	0	67	78	9	6	4
4	Ireland	4	1	3	0	36	75	4	11	2
5	Wales	4	0	4	0	42	90	5	13	0

Home Games: beat Ireland 26 - 7, (four tries to nil); beat Wales 34 - 6, (four tries to one)

Away Games: beat France 26 - 7, (three tries to one); lost to Scotland 7 - 13, (one try each)

ENGLAND TOUR TO ARGENTINA - 1990

THE TOUR PARTY:

Manager:	G.D.Cooke	Assistant Coach:	J.J.Elliott R.M.Uttley	Captain:	W.D.C.Carling

				Forwards:			
Full-backs:	J.Liley	(Leicester)	no caps	Forwards:	W.A.Dooley	(Preston G'hoppers)	34 caps
	S.D.Hodgkinson	(Nottingham)	6 caps		D.W.Egerton	(Bath)	6 caps
					R.Kimmins	(Orrell)	no caps
Three-quarters:	J.R.D.Buckton	(Saracens)	1 cap		J.Leonard	(Saracens)	no caps
	W.D.C.Carling	(Harlequins)	17 caps		M.S.Linnett	(Moseley)	1 cap
	G.C.Childs	(Northern)	no caps		B.C.Moore	(Nottingham)	23 caps
	N.J.Heslop	(Orrell)	no caps		C.J.Olver	(Harlequins)	no caps
	C.Oti	(Wasps)	7 caps		M.Poole	(Leicester)	no caps
	G.J.Thompson	(Harlequins)	no caps		J.A.Probyn	(Wasps)	15 caps
	T.Underwood	(Leicester)	no caps		N.C.Redman	(Bath)	8 caps
					R.A.Robinson	(Bath)	7 caps
Half-backs:	R.J.Hill	(Bath)	14 caps		T.A.K.Rodber	(Northampton)	no caps
	P.A.Hull	(Bristol)	no caps		D.Ryan	(Wasps)	no caps
	C.D.Morris	(Orrell)	5 caps		M.G.Skinner	(Harlequins)	10 caps
	D.Pears	(Harlequins)	no caps		V.E.Ubogu	(Bath)	no caps
					P.J.Winterbottom	(Harlequins)	35 caps
Replacements:	S.M.Bates	(Wasps)	1 cap				

This second tour to Argentina by England was apparently arranged without Geoff Cooke's knowledge, and at an inconvenient time of year for the England players in July and August. For this latter reason, eight senior England players declined the invitation to make the trip, and the only seasoned Internationals on the tour were Will Carling, Richard Hill, Wade Dooley, Brian Moore, Jeff Probyn and Peter Winterbottom. Who is to say which of them, with the advantage of hindsight, inwardly wished that they too had declined the invitation. The tour started on a down-beat note when the side was beaten by Banco Nacion who had Hugo Porter at fly-half, Porta kicked 21 points in the match and even though the try count was four to two, the match was lost. On the strength of this performance, Hugo Porta decided to make himself available for the reciprocal tour to England later in the year. The refereeing, generally, on the tour was, to say the least, unsatisfactory and at best wholly inconsistent, and in the penultimate match of the tour, John Olver, the acting captain, was within a whisker of bringing the players off the field because of the incomprehensible refereeing. Significantly in all seven matches, 50 penalty goals were scored, 23 by England, 27 by their opponents, and only 23 tries, 14 by England against 9.

The most disappointing aspect of the tour, however, was that several of the uncapped players showed either a disinclination or a lack of the necessary ability and application to step successfully from first-class rugby to International level. This phenomena was undoubtedly the greater because eight established Internationals had missed the tour anyway, but it was a sad commentary on England's strength in depth. That said, there were successes and not least that of Jason Leonard, who won his first cap in the first Test and has been present in the England side virtually ever since. Nigel Heslop, too, showed some determination and character as a wing three-quarter.

With the imminence of the World Cup, not one player decided to retire voluntarily from International rugby following this tour, but it did mark the end of two players' International careers. John Buckton, the Saracens centre, gained three caps, and was also a member of the 1988 side which toured Australia and Fiji. David Egerton, who won seven caps, might have won many more had he not been a contemporary of other notable No 8s, Dean Richards, Mike Teague and, on this tour, Dean Ryan.

After thr tour, during which he was trying desperately to recover his authority after the defeat at Murrayfield and the criticisms that followed, Will Carling received more than one serious offer from Rugby League clubs, but at least felt confident enough to turn them down.

TOUR RESULTS:

July 14th	Banco Nacion	at Buenos Aires	LOST	21 - 29	(four tries to two)
July 18th	Tucuman Selection	at Tucuman	WON	19 - 14	(one try to two)
July 21st	Buenos Aires Selection	at Buenos Aires	LOST	23 - 26	(four tries to three)
July 24th	Cuyo Selection	at Mendoza	LOST	21 - 22	(no tries to two)
July 28th	**ARGENTINA**	**at Buenos Aires**	**WON**	**25 - 11**	**(two tries to nil)**
July 31st	Cordoba	at Cordoba	WON	15 - 12	(one try to nil)
August 4th	**ARGENTINA**	**at Buenos Aires**	**LOST**	**13 - 15**	**(two tries to nil)**

THE ENGLAND SQUAD FOR THE SEVEN MATCH TOUR TO ARGENTINA IN 1990

Back Row: R.J.Hill, V.E.Ubogu, G.C.Childs, P.J.Winterbottom, M.G.Skinner, N.C.Redman, M.S.Linnett, J.Leonard, T.Underwood, P.A.Hull,

Middle Row: R.A.Robinson, J.Liley, J.R.D.Buckton, T.A.K.Rodber, D.W.Egerton, W.A.Dooley, R.Kimmins, M.Poole, C.D.Morris, C.Oti, C.J.Olver, G.J.Thompson,

Seated: N.J.Heslop, J.A.Probyn, B.C.Moore, J.J.Elliott (Coach) G.D.Cooke (Manager), President RFU, W.D.C.Carling, R.M.Uttley (Coach), D.Pears, S.D.Hodgkinson,
K.Murphy (Physio)

Not present: D.Ryan

3rd match   **ENGLAND   25 pts**   v   **ARGENTINA   12 pts**

	Caps					Caps	
15	7th	S.D.Hodgkinson	(Nottingham)		A.Scolni		(Alumni)
14	1st	N.J.Heslop	(Orrell)		H.Vidou		(Buenos Aires)
13	18th	W.D.C.Carling (Capt)	(Harlequins)		M.Loffreda (Capt)		(San Isidro Club)
12	2nd	J.R.D.Buckton	(Saracens)		D.Cuesta Silva		(San Isidro Club)
11	8th	C.Oti	(Wasps)		S.Salvat		(Alumni)
10	1st	D.Pears	(Harlequins)		R.Madero		(San Isidro Club)
9	15th	R.J.Hill	(Bath)		F.Gomez		(Banco Nacion)
1	1st	J.Leonard	(Saracens)		A.Rocca		(Buenos Aires)
2	24th	B.C.Moore	(Nottingham)		J-J.Angelillo		(San Isidro Club)
3	16th	J.A.Probyn	(Wasps)		L.Molina		(Tucuman LTC)
4	9th	N.C.Redman	(Bath)		E.Branca		(CAST)
5	35th	W.A.Dooley	(Preston G'hoppers)		A.Iachetti		(Hindu)
6	11th	M.G.Skinner	(Harlequins)		P.A.Garreton		(Tucuman UC)
7	36th	P.J.Winterbottom	(Harlequins)		M.Baeck		(Los Tordos, Cuyo)
8	1st	D.Ryan	(Wasps)		M.J.S.Bertranou		(Los Tordos, Cuyo)

Referee: B.Kinsey   (Australia)

SCORERS:	S.D.Hodgkinson	Penalty Goal		3 - 0		
	D.Ryan	Try	(1st)	7 - 0		
				7 - 3	H.Vidou	Penalty Goal
				7 - 6	H.Vidou	Penalty Goal
	S.D.Hodgkinson	Penalty Goal		10 - 6		
				10 - 9	H.Vidou	Penalty Goal
	S.D.Hodgkinson	Penalty Goal		13 - 9		
				Half-time		
	C.Oti	Try	(8th & last)	17 - 9		
	S.D.Hodgkinson	Conversion		19 - 9		
				19 - 12	H.Vidou	Penalty Goal
	S.D.Hodgkinson	Penalty Goal		22 - 12		
	S.D.Hodgkinson	Penalty Goal		25 - 12		

POINTS:	S.D.Hodgkinson	17 points	(94)	H.Vidou	12 points
	C.Oti	4 points	(32)		
	D.Ryan	4 points	(4)		

MATCH COMMENTARY:

After three embarrassing defeats in the first four matches of the tour, England won the first test without difficulty. There were four new caps in the side, and the whole knitted together commendably well. Forward domination, especially in the lines-out, was the basis of England's superiority together with the accuracy of Simon Hodgkinson's goal kicking. The first try by Ryan, following a blind-side break by Hill in the early minutes was undoubtedly the settling influence that England needed to allay their nervousness after a poor start to the tour.   But the match was undoubtedly won in the last twenty minutes when Argentina were moving the ball every way in an attempt to score and only truly demoniac tackling kept them out. No-one showed more committment in this respect than Mickey Skinner.

4th match   **ENGLAND   13 pts**   v   **ARGENTINA   15 pts**

	Caps					Caps		
15	8th	S.D.Hodgkinson	(Nottingham)	.		A.Scolni	(Alumni)
14	2nd	N.J.Heslop	(Orrell)	.		H.Vidou	(Buenos Aires)
13	19th	W.D.C.Carling (Capt)	(Harlequins)	.		M.Loffreda (Capt)	(San Isidro Club)
12	3rd & last	J.R.D.Buckton	(Saracens)	.		D.Cuesta Silva	(San Isidro Club)
11	9th	C.Oti	(Wasps)	.		S.Salvat	(Alumni)
10	2nd	D.Pears	(Harlequins)	.		R.Madero	(San Isidro Club)
9	16th	R.J.Hill	(Bath)	.		F.Gomez	(Banco Nacion)
1	2nd	J.Leonard	(Saracens)	.		M.Aguirre	(Alumni)
2	25th	B.C.Moore	(Nottingham)	.		J-J.Angelillo	(San Isidro Club)
3	17th	J.A.Probyn	(Wasps)	.		D.M.Cash	(San Isidro Club)
4	10th	N.C.Redman	(Bath)	.		E.Branca	(CAST)
5	36th	W.A.Dooley	(Preston G'hoppers)	.		A.Iachetti	(Hindu)
6	12th	M.G.Skinner	(Harlequins)	.		P.A.Garreton	(Tucuman UC)
7	37th	P.J.Winterbottom	(Harlequins)	.		M.Baeck	(Los Tordos, Cuyo)
8	2nd	D.Ryan	(Wasps)	.		M.J.S.Bertranou	(Los Tordos, Cuyo)

7th & last   D.W.Egerton (Bath) for Dooley - 50

Referee: B.Kinsey   (Australia)

SCORERS:

				0 - 3	H.Vidou	Penalty Goal
S.D.Hodgkinson	Try	(1st & only)	4 - 3		
S.D.Hodgkinson	Conversion		6 - 3		
			6 - 6	H.Vidou	Penalty Goal
N.J.Heslop	Try	(1st)	10 - 6		
			10 - 9	H.Vidou	Penalty Goal
		Half-time			
			10 - 12	H.Vidou	Penalty Goal
S.D.Hodgkinson	Penalty Goal		13 - 12		
			13 - 15	H.Vidou	Penalty Goal

POINTS:

S.D.Hodgkinson	9 points	(103)	H.Vidou	15 points
N.J.Heslop	4 points	(4)		

MATCH COMMENTARY:

Although England beat their opponents in the try count, 2 - 0, they could not get away from the deadly accuracy of Vidou's goal kicking. The turning point was probably Wade Dooley's departure with a rib injury ten minutes into the second half, and when Simon Hodgkinson missed two straight-forward penalty attempts late in the game, England found that the match had slipped away from them. Argentina proved yet again how difficult they can be to beat at home in the forbidding Velez Sarsfeld Stadium where France (three times) and Australia have lost since 1985. On this occasion, it was England's scalp which was captured, and it was not that the tackling was less effective than the previous week, but rather that the pressure was even greater and England had to kill the ball as a preventative measure and were penalised accordingly. Both the England tries were well worked and with his perfect conversion from the touchline of his own try, Simon Hodgkinson reached a personal tally of 100 International points, in only eight International matches. Each time England scored, either a try or a penalty goal, Vidou replied with his boot, and when Wade Dooley went off, Vidou kept scoring and England did not. Ironically, England had scored four tries to one in the Test series and yet had the dismal record of having played seven matches on the tour and lost four of them.

5th match   **ENGLAND   51 pts**   v   **ARGENTINA   0 pts**

	Caps					Caps		
15	9th	S.D.Hodgkinson	(Nottingham)	.		A.Scolni	(Alumni)
14	3rd	N.J.Heslop	(Orrell)	.		S.Ezcurra	(CUBA)
13	20th	W.D.C.Carling (Capt)	(Harlequins)	.		D.Cuesta Silva	(San Isidro Club)
12	7th	J.C.Guscott	(Bath)	.		M.Allen	(CASI)
11	39th	R.Underwood	(RAF/Leicester)	.		G.M.Jorge	(Pucara)
10	32nd	C.R.Andrew	(Wasps)	.		H.Porta (Capt)	(Banco Nacion)
9	17th	R.J.Hill	(Bath)	.		G.Camardon	(Alumni)
1	3rd	J.Leonard	(Harlequins)	.		F.Mendez	(Tucuman RC)
2	1st	C.J.Olver	(Northampton)	.		R.A.Le Fort	(Tucuman RC)
3	18th	J.A.Probyn	(Wasps)	.		D.M.Cash	(San Isidro Club)
4	12th	P.J.Ackford	(Harlequins)	.		G.Llanes	(La Plata)
5	37th	W.A.Dooley	(Preston G'hoppers)	.		P.Sporleder	(Curupayti)
6	20th	J.P.Hall	(Bath)	.		P.A.Garreton	(Tucuman UC)
7	38th	P.J.Winterbottom	(Harlequins)	.		A.M.Macome	(Tucuman RC)
8	21st	D.Richards	(Leicester)	.		M.J.S.Bertranou	(Los Tordos)

21st   G.W.Rees (Nottingham) for Ackford - 70

Referee: C.J.Hawke   (New Zealand)

SCORERS:

S.D.Hodgkinson	Penalty Goal		3 - 0
R.J.Hill	Try	(2nd & last)	7 - 0
S.D.Hodgkinson	Conversion		9 - 0
R.Underwood	Try	(23rd)	13 - 0
S.D.Hodgkinson	Conversion		15 - 0
			Half-time
S.D.Hodgkinson	Penalty Goal		18 - 0
S.D.Hodgkinson	Penalty Goal		21 - 0
R.Underwood	Try	(24th)	25 - 0
S.D.Hodgkinson	Conversion		27 - 0
J.C.Guscott	Try	(8th)	31 - 0
S.D.Hodgkinson	Conversion		33 - 0
J.C.Guscott	Try	(9th)	37 - 0
S.D.Hodgkinson	Conversion		39 - 0
J.P.Hall	Try	(2nd & last)	43 - 0
S.D.Hodgkinson	Conversion		45 - 0
R.Underwood	Try	(25th)	49 - 0
S.D.Hodgkinson	Conversion		51 - 0

POINTS:

S.D.Hodgkinson	23 points	(126)
R.Underwood	12 points	(100)
J.C.Guscott	8 points	(36)
R.J.Hill and J.P.Hall	4 points	(8),(8)
	each	

MATCH COMMENTARY:

England thoroughly outclassed Argentina by seven tries to none and totally avenged the defeat in the second Test at Buenos Aires the previous August. Simon Hodgkinson set a new English scoring record of 23 points beating Douglas Lambert's 22 points set in 1911 against France. The drama of the day was the dismissal of the 18 year old Argentinian prop, Frederico Mendez, for accurately placing a right hook on Paul Ackford's jaw during a break in play. It would not be unreasonable to assume that retaliation was the underlying motive. England's points came in three distinct phases; fifteen points in the first quarter of an hour; eighteen points in the first ten minutes of the second half; and finally a further eighteen points in the last eight minutes of the match after Mendez had been sent off.

The fact that Argentina were denied any points at all (only the second time in nearly 20 years that Hugo Porta has failed to score in an International match) must give an early indication of England's purpose in the forthcoming Five Nations Championship - this time there will be no mistakes !!

97th match   **ENGLAND   25 pts**   v   **WALES   6 pts**

	Caps					Caps		
15	10th	S.D.Hodgkinson	(Nottingham)	.		33rd	P.H.Thorburn (Capt)	(Neath)
14	4th	N.J.Heslop	(Orrell)	.		19th	I.C.Evans	(Llanelli)
13	21st	W.D.C.Carling (Capt)	(Harlequins)	.		25th	M.G.Ring	(Cardiff)
12	8th	J.C.Guscott	(Bath)	.		1st	I.S.Gibbs	(Neath)
11	40th	R.Underwood	(RAF/Leicester)	.		5th	S.P.Ford	(Cardiff)
10	33rd	C.R.Andrew	(Wasps)	.		1st	N.R.Jenkins	(Pontypridd)
9	18th	R.J.Hill	(Bath)	.		33rd	R.N.Jones	(Swansea)
1	4th	J.Leonard	(Harlequins)	.		4th	B.R.Williams	(Neath)
2	26th	B.C.Moore	(Harlequins)	.		16th	K.H.Phillips	(Neath)
3	19th	J.A.Probyn	(Wasps)	.		4th	P.Knight	(Pontypridd)
4	13th	P.J.Ackford	(Harlequins)	.		4th	G.D.Llewellyn	(Neath)
5	38th	W.A.Dooley	(Preston G'hoppers)	.		5th	G.O.Llewellyn	(Neath)
6	12th	M.C.Teague	(Gloucester)	.		1st	A.J.Carter	(Newport)
7	39th	P.J.Winterbottom	(Harlequins)	.		4th	P.Arnold	(Swansea)
8	22nd	D.Richards	(Leicester)	.		1st	G.M.George	(Newport)
						4th	C.J.Bridges (Neath) for Jones - 46	

Referee: R.J.Megson   (Scotland)

SCORERS:

			0 - 3	P.H.Thorburn	Penalty Goal
S.D.Hodgkinson	Penalty Goal		3 - 3		
S.D.Hodgkinson	Penalty Goal		6 - 3		
S.D.Hodgkinson	Penalty Goal		9 - 3		
S.D.Hodgkinson	Penalty Goal		12 - 3		
			Half-time		
S.D.Hodgkinson	Penalty Goal		15 - 3		
			15 - 6	N.R.Jenkins	Penalty Goal
S.D.Hodgkinson	Penalty Goal		18 - 6		
M.C.Teague	Try	(2nd)	22 - 6		
S.D.Hodgkinson	Penalty Goal		25 - 6		

POINTS:

S.D.Hodgkinson	21 points	(147)	P.H.Thorburn	3 points	
M.C.Teague	4 points	(8)	N.R.Jenkins	3 points	

MATCH COMMENTARY:

England's first win at Cardiff since 1963 was a story of dominant forward power and ruthlessly efficient goal kicking. As a spectacle, it was somewhat lacking and Wales' persistent indiscipline allowed Hodgkinson the opportunity to kick a record seven penalty goals.   Paul Thorburn, on the other hand, had a disastrous day with his boot. That England's performance was workmanlike was undeniable, but it was also undeniably boring.   As an exhibition of the game of Rugby Football, Cardiff 1991 will do the reputation and cause of English rugby no good at all. Yet, the result saw the laying of a ghost which had haunted successive English sides for 28 years and as such it should have been a joyous occasion.   But it was far from that.   The English pack played with commendable efficiency but they did not achieve the dominance they expected because the Welsh pack refused to be pushed around and Robert Jones, in a damage limitation exercise, showed what an expert player he is. But England had no plan "B" and dour persistence and obdurateness prevailed. In keeping with that, attitudes after the game were less than convivial, when the England squad petulantly refused to attend the usual post-match Press Conference.

107th match
98th Calcutta Cup

ENGLAND 21 pts   v   SCOTLAND 12 pts

	Caps					Caps		
15	11th	S.D.Hodgkinson	(Nottingham)	.	30th	A.G.Hastings	(Watsonians)
14	5th	N.J.Heslop	(Orrell)	.	12th	A.G.Stanger	(Hawick)
13	22nd	W.D.C.Carling (Capt)	(Harlequins)	.	16th	S.R.P.Lineen	(Boroughmuir)
12	9th	J.C.Guscott	(Bath)	.	29th	S.Hastings	(Watsonians)
11	41st	R.Underwood	(RAF/Leicester)	.	5th & last	A.Moore	(Edinburgh Acad'ls)
10	34th	C.R.Andrew	(Wasps)	.	15th	C.M.Chalmers	(Melrose)
9	19th	R.J.Hill	(Bath)	.	17th	G.Armstrong	(Jedforest)
1	5th	J.Leonard	(Harlequins)	.	31st	D.M.B.Sole (Capt)	(Edinburgh Acad'ls)
2	27th	B.C.Moore	(Harlequins)	.	15th	K.S.Milne	(Heriot's FP)
3	20th	J.A.Probyn	(Wasps)	.	13th	A.P.Burnell	(London Scottish)
4	14th	P.J.Ackford	(Harlequins)	.	16th	C.A.Gray	(Nottingham)
5	39th	W.A.Dooley	(Preston G'hoppers)	.	20th	D.F.Cronin	(Bath)
6	13th	M.C.Teague	(Gloucester)	.	7th	D.J.Turnbull	(Hawick)
7	40th	P.J.Winterbottom	(Harlequins)	.	34th	J.Jeffrey	(Kelso)
8	23rd	D.Richards	(Leicester)	.	29th	D.B.White	(London Scottish)

Referee: S.R.Hilditch   (Ireland)

SCORERS:

S.D.Hodgkinson	Penalty Goal		3 - 0			
S.D.Hodgkinson	Penalty Goal		6 - 0			
			6 - 3	C.M.Chalmers	Penalty Goal	
			6 - 6	C.M.Chalmers	Penalty Goal	
S.D.Hodgkinson	Penalty Goal		9 - 6			
			Half-time			
N.J.Heslop	Try	(2nd)	13 - 6			
S.D.Hodgkinson	Conversion		15 - 6			
			15 - 9	C.M.Chalmers	Penalty Goal	
			15 - 12	C.M.Chalmers	Penalty Goal	
S.D.Hodgkinson	Penalty Goal		18 - 12			
S.D.Hodgkinson	Penalty Goal		21 - 12			

POINTS:

S.D.Hodgkinson	17 points	(164)	C.M.Chalmers	12 points	
N.J.Heslop	4 points	(8)			

MATCH COMMENTARY:

An England side, unchanged from their dubious triumph in Cardiff four weeks earlier were grimly determined to erase the memory of the humiliation at Murrayfield last time around - at least the twelve who were involved on that never-to-be-forgotten day were so determined. Beyond determination, there was almost a paranoia that the experience be expunged from the memory, and that providing the end result was was achieved, any means would be justified. Thus the capacity crowd were treated to another grindingly efficient display about as exciting and emotive as a snail Grand Prix. The pack dominated, Simon Hodgkinson kicked and the match was won. The only redeeming feature and certainly the only memory for the 63,000 crowd was Nigel Heslop's try in the south-west corner the build up to which covered acres of ground and involved all of nine players after two successful English rucks and some very slick passing. It was a very good try. But one swallow does not make a summer. The Irish are next, and the Triple Crown may well be achieved, but there are sterner tests to come.

104th match   **ENGLAND   16 pts**   v   **IRELAND   7 pts**

	Caps					Caps		
15	12th	S.D.Hodgkinson	(Nottingham)	.		2nd	J.E.Staples	(London Irish)
14	6th	N.J.Heslop	(Orrell)	.		3rd	S.P.Geoghegan	(London Irish)
13	23rd	W.D.C.Carling (Capt)	(Harlequins)	.		36th	B.J.Mullin	(Blackrock College)
12	10th	J.C.Guscott	(Bath)	.		2nd	D.M.Curtis	(London Irish)
11	42nd	R.Underwood	(RAF/Leicester)	.		35th	K.D.Crossan	(Instonians)
10	35th	C.R.Andrew	(Wasps)	.		8th	B.A.Smith	(Leicester)
9	20th	R.J.Hill	(Bath)	.		3rd	R.Saunders (Capt)	(London Irish)
1	6th	J.Leonard	(Harlequins)	.		8th	J.J.Fitzgerald	(Young Munster)
2	28th	B.C.Moore	(Harlequins)	.		12th	S.J.Smith	(Ballymena)
3	21st	J.A.Probyn	(Wasps)	.		26th	D.C.Fitzgerald	(Lansdowne)
4	15th	P.J.Ackford	(Harlequins)	.		9th	N.P.J.Francis	(Blackrock College)
5	40th	W.A.Dooley	(Preston G'hoppers)	.		3rd	B.J.Rigney	(Greystones)
6	14th	M.C.Teague	(Gloucester)	.		30th	P.M.Matthews	(Wanderers)
7	41st	P.J.Winterbottom	(Harlequins)	.		3rd	G.F.Hamilton	(NIFC)
8	24th	D.Richards	(Leicester)	.		3rd	B.F.Robinson	(Ballymena)

Referee: A.Ceccon   (France)

SCORERS:

S.D.Hodgkinson	Penalty Goal		3 - 0		
			3 - 3	B.A.Smith	Penalty Goal
		Half-time			
			3 - 7	S.P.Geoghegan	Try
S.D.Hodgkinson	Penalty Goal		6 - 7		
R.Underwood	Try	(26th)	10 - 7		
S.D.Hodgkinson	Conversion		12 - 7		
M.C.Teague	Try	(3rd & last)	16 - 7		

POINTS:

S.D.Hodgkinson	8 points	(172)		S.P.Geoghegan	4 points
R.Underwood and M.C.Teague	4 points	(104),(12)		B.A.Smith	3 points
	each				

MATCH COMMENTARY:

Unchanged for the third successive match, the English steamroller went to Dublin convinvced that the dour tactics which had seen off both the Welsh and the Scots would serve them well again, and that the Triple Crown was there for the taking as long as they did not stumble on that fatal sliver of complacency which had cut so deep at Murrayfield in 1990.   Ireland, not sharing these dreams or illusions, played their usual terrier-like disruptive game and never allowed England to settle.   Such were the distractions of the hornets buzzing around their heads, and their feet, that the Irish took a four point lead from Simon Geoghegan's try early in the second half.   But England kept their cool and gradually, towards the end of the match, the English pack began to dominate and establish the platform from which Rory Underwood's invaluable try was scored with only ten minutes of the match remaining.   Hodgkinson was seriously off form with his kicking and England could not depend on him to score early points.   The Irish resistance was inspired and they missed some clear scoring opportunities, which, if taken, would have changed the course of the match.   When Rory Underwood crossed for his 26th International try there were audible sighs of relief from the stands and the terraces, and probably from the field as well, and from that moment, England knew that they had won.   Credit is certainly due to the England pack for refusing to give up or to deviate from their purpose and eventually the policy paid off with domination over Neil Francis in the line-out and with Mike Teague's try in the final minutes.   The Triple Crown is in the bag.

66th match   **ENGLAND   21 pts**   v   **FRANCE   19 pts**

	Caps					Caps		
15	13th	**S.D.Hodgkinson**	(Nottingham)	.		85th	**S.Blanco (Capt)**	(Biarritz)
14	7th	**N.J.Heslop**	(Orrell)	.		20th	**J-B.Lafond**	(Racing Club)
13	24th	**W.D.C.Carling (Capt)**	(Harlequins)	.		36th	**F.Mesnel**	(Racing Club)
12	11th	**J.C.Guscott**	(Bath)	.		72nd	**P.Sella**	(Agen)
11	43rd	**R.Underwood**	(RAF/Leicester)	.		7th	**P.Saint-Andre**	(Montferrand)
10	36th	**C.R.Andrew**	(Wasps)	.		26th	**D.Camberabero**	(Beziers)
9	21st	**R.J.Hill**	(Bath)	.		56th & last	**P.Berbizier**	(Agen)
1	7th	**J.Leonard**	(Harlequins)	.		4th	**G.Lascube**	(Agen)
2	29th	**B.C.Moore**	(Harlequins)	.		16th	**P.Marocco**	(Montferrand)
3	22nd	**J.A.Probyn**	(Wasps)	.		36th	**P.Ondarts**	(Biarritz)
4	16th	**P.J.Ackford**	(Harlequins)	.		3rd & last	**M.Tachdjian**	(Racing Club)
5	41st	**W.A.Dooley**	(Preston G'hoppers)	.		16th	**O.Roumat**	(Dax)
6	15th	**M.C.Teague**	(Gloucester)	.		5th & last	**X.Blond**	(Racing Club)
7	42nd	**P.J.Winterbottom**	(Harlequins)	.		5th	**A.Benazzi**	(Racing Club)
8	25th	**D.Richards**	(Leicester)	.		6th	**L.Cabannes**	(Agen)

14th   M.Cecillon (Bourgoin) for Tachdjian - 40

Referee: L.J.Peard   (Wales)

SCORERS:	S.D.Hodgkinson	Penalty Goal		3 - 0			
				3 - 4	P.Saint-Andre	Try	
				3 - 6	D.Camberabero	Conversion	
	C.R.Andrew	D'p Goal	(10th)	6 - 6			
	S.D.Hodgkinson	Penalty Goal		9 - 6			
				9 - 9	D.Camberabero	Penalty Goal	
	R.Underwood	Try	(27th)	13 - 9			
	S.D.Hodgkinson	Conversion		15 - 9			
	S.D.Hodgkinson	Penalty Goal		18 - 9			
				Half-time			
				18 - 13	D.Camberabero	Try	
	S.D.Hodgkinson	Penalty Goal		21 - 13			
				21 - 17	F.Mesnel	Try	
				21 - 19	D.Camberabero	Conversion	

POINTS:	S.D.Hodgkinson	14 points	(186)	D.Camberabero	11 points
	R.Underwood	4 points	(108)	P.Saint-Andre	4 points
	C.R.Andrew	3 points	(132)	F.Mesnel	4 points

MATCH COMMENTARY:

Both teams, unbeaten so far, stood to win the Grand Slam if they could win this match. And what a magnificent contest it turned out to be. Of the three French tries, two, the first by Saint-Andre, and the last by Mesnel, were supremely courageous, astonishingly inventive and perfectly executed and both made Rory Underwood's 27th international try, a good one by any other standards, look pedestrian. The quality England's play in this match was a vast improvement, and they deservedly took the Grand Slam, with an unchanged side throughout, but France took just as much credit for playing spectacular rugby. If this standard can be maintained for the World Cup, we are in for a treat.

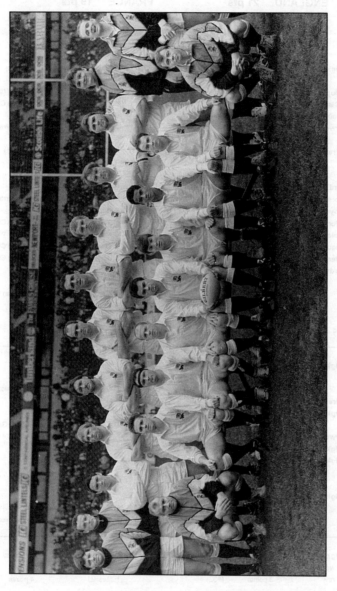

THE ENGLAND TEAM WHO WON THE "GRAND SLAM" IN 1991 BY BEATING FRANCE AT TWICKENHAM ON MARCH 16th.

Standing: S.J.Halliday (Bench), J.M.Webb (Bench), R.Underwood, P.J.Winterbottom, M.C.Teague, P.J.Ackford, W.A.Dooley, D.Richards, J.A.Probyn, J.Leonard, M.G.Skinner (Bench), C.D.Morris (Bench),

Seated: P.A.G.Rendall (Bench), N.J.Heslop, B.C.Moore, R.J.Hill, W.D.C.Carling (Captain), C.R.Andrew, J.C.Guscott, S.D.Hodgkinson, C.J.Olver (Bench).

SUMMARY OF THE SEASON - 1990 - 91:

There were probably three items on Geoff Cooke's agenda at the beginning of this season, each , no doubt, equally shared by the whole England squad. The first was to win the Grand Slam and to compensate for the failure at Murrayfield, and to do so in a manner within which the possibility of error was to be minimised. There was no doubt at all that the end would justify the means. The second item was to prepare adequately for the 1991 World Cup which was taking place in Britain and France in the following autumn. Thirdly, within all of that, there were scores to be settled with Argentina, for that defeat at Buenos Aires on the 1990 tour, with Wales, and a win at Cardiff after 28 years would not only scotch the snake, but kill it too, and, finally, there was the matter of Scotland who had to be made to pay for last year's impertinence and precociousness.

The season was a triumph for England, their objective was achieved, but they made no friends from the means they adopted to achieve it, although, at the time, nothing seemed more important. The later tour to Australia, the World Cup itself, and, indeed, the following season happily put the whole scenario into perspective.

In November 1990, the prospects were exciting and the intentions were focussed and extremely determined. Single-mindedness and application were the order of the day. Argentina were summarily despatched by 51 points to nil. England scored seven tries, and Simon Hodgkinson kicked 23 points to beat Rob Andrew's record of 21 scored against Wales at Twickenham in 1986. Rory Underwood scored a hat-trick of tries to reach 100 points in his career - only the fifth England player to do so - and all those points came from tries. Thus, the defeat at Buenos Aires the previous summer was properly avenged.

As the Five Nations season progressed, the prospects improved match by match. England won at Cardiff and exorcized that ghost and in so doing scored their highest points total ever at the Arms Park with Simon Hodgkinson kicking seven penalty goals. Four weeks later, Scotland were subjected to the same grindingly efficient treatment at Twickenham the singular objective of which was to avenge the traumatic experience at Murrayfield when David Sole, with panache, had outwitted fifteen Englishmen and picked up the Grand Slam and everything that went with it. Nigel Heslop's try was memorable, but it only served to emphasise the gulf between what England were capable of and what they chose to do, but, anyway, the third (and biggest) wrong had been righted. But it was not all a bed of roses in Dublin. The Irish were at their irritatingly disruptive and entertaining best, galloping about, as John Mason has more recently observed, scattering doubt and apprehension amongst their opponents. England were sorely pushed to emerge with their record intact. Rory Underwood's try, from virtually nothing was the decisive factor.

So, for the second successive season, England were poised for the Grand Slam, this time with the Triple Crown already in the bag, this time at Twickenham but, this time against France who had a similar interest in the outcome of the match and who had won on this ground three times in the last five visits. The day was fine and dry and conditions were perfect for a fast running game. And fast running there was in abundance - and mainly by France. Three magnificent French tries by Saint-Andre, Camberabero and Mesnel, to one by Rory Underwood reflected the difference in running rugby skills and pure flair between the two sides, with two of the French tries, the first by Saint-Andre, initiated by Serge Blanco from behind his own posts, and the third by Franck Mesnel were two of the best ever seen at Twickenham. But England took the spoils and rightly so - but it was close !!

England had fielded an unchanged side for the whole tournament and Geoff Cooke's faith and loyalty to his team was amply rewarded and wholly justified. As preparation for the World Cup, the season had been an outstanding success and against that background, the decision to tour Australia and Fiji in July, too far from the end of this domestic season and too far from the beginning of the next, was difficult to understand. Simon Hodgkinson scored 60 points during the course of the Five Nations season (83 in the five matches), easily surpassing "Dusty" Hare's record of 44 set in 1984.

There were, not surprisingly, no departures from the International scene at the end of the season, and indeed, during the course of it only one new cap was awarded - to John Olver in the opening match against Argentina.

There was visible evidence at Twickenham of the massive rebuilding programme, masterminded by Dudley Wood as RFU Secretary. The new three-tier north stand was now in place and totally dwarfed the previously impressive East and West stands. Spectators at the top of the new structure had almost a bird's eye view of the proceedings on the pitch some considerable distance below.

FIVE NATIONS CHAMPIONSHIP TABLE:

Won: **Grand Slam, Triple Crown, Championship Title and Calcutta Cup**

		Played	Won	Lost	Drawn	Points: For	Against	Tries: For	Against	Title Points
1	**ENGLAND**	4	4	0	0	83	44	5	4	8
2	France	4	3	1	0	91	46	11	2	6
3	Scotland	4	2	2	0	81	73	7	6	4
4 =	Ireland	4	0	3	1	66	86	8	11	1
4 =	Wales	4	0	3	1	42	114	5	13	1

Home Games: beat Scotland 21 - 12, (one try to nil); beat France 21 - 19, (one try to three)

Away Games: beat Wales 25 - 6, (one try to nil); beat Ireland 16 - 7, (two tries to one)

ENGLAND TOUR TO AUSTRALIA and FIJI - 1991

THE TOUR PARTY:

Manager:	G.D.Cooke		Coach:	R.M.Uttley		Captain:	W.D.C.Carling	
			Assistant:	R.Best				

Full-backs:	S.D.Hodgkinson	(Nottingham)	13 caps	Forwards:	P.J.Ackford	(Harlequins)	16 caps
	J.M.Webb	(Bath)	16 caps		M.C.Bayfield	(Northampton)	no caps
					W.A.Dooley	(Preston G'hoppers	41 caps
Three-quarters:	W.D.C.Carling	(Harlequins)	24 caps		J.P.Hall	(Bath)	20 caps
	J.C.Guscott	(Bath)	11 caps		J.Leonard	Saracens)	7 caps
	S.J.Halliday	(Harlequins)	16 caps		B.C.Moore	(Harlequins)	29 caps
	N.J.Heslop	(Orrell)	6 caps		C.J.Olver	(Northampton)	1 cap
	D.P.Hopley	(Wasps)	no caps		G.S.Pearce	(Northampton)	35 caps
	I.G.Hunter	(Northampton)	no caps		J.A.Probyn	(Wasps)	22 caps
	C.Oti	(Wasps)	9 caps		N.C.Redman	(Bath)	10 caps
	R.Underwood	(RAF/Leicester)	43 caps		G.W.Rees	(Nottingham)	21 caps
					P.A.G.Rendall	(Wasps)	27 caps
Half-backs:	C.R.Andrew	(Wasps)	36 caps		D.Richards	(Leicester)	25 caps
	R.J.Hill	(Bath)	21 caps		M.G.Skinner	(Harlequins)	12 caps
	C.D.Morris	(Orrell)	5 caps		M.C.Teague	(Gloucester)	15 caps
	D.Pears	(Harlequins)	2 caps		P.J.Winterbottom	(Harlequins)	42 caps

There was a strong body of opinion when this tour was announced that it would be likely to do more harm than good and that the England squad would have been well advised to lay off rugby altogether during the close season in the UK im preparation for the coming World Cup. However, the England management thought differently and the team embarked upon the tour early in July, and proceeded to lose the first match to New South Wales and two of the next three, first to Queensland and, even more alarmingly, to Fiji B a few days before the Test match in Suva. The performance in the latter match was far from satisfactory and at times England looked in complete disarray, rather embarrassing for the Grand Slam Champions. But worse was yet to come. In the final match of this mis-guided tour, England suffered their second heaviest defeat ever in an International match in conceding 40 points and five tries to Australia. The essential difference between the teams lay in the athleticism and mobility of the Australian pack who left the much vaunted England pack floundering and desperately short of breath. The match also illustrated to interested observers that Australian rugby had progressed in leaps and bounds since England's previous tour in 1988 and the Australian visit to Twickenham later the same year. Various encounters with France since then, had, nonetheless, given strong indications of that progress.

There were, nevertheless, at least two positive results to emerge from the tour. Martin Bayfield, in the absence of Wade Dooley, had established himself as a very strong contender for the middle line-out position in years to come, and Jonathan Webb had recovered all his poise and confidence and managed to oust Simon Hodgkinson from the full-back berth for the tour and the for the future - Simon Hodgkinson, despite his success in the previous season, was to gain only one more cap.

As preparation for the World Cup, this tour was a calamitous mistake, for the experience eroded England's confidence, and never was this more apparent than against Australia - in the final. Neither Geoff Cooke nor Roger Uttley subscribed to that view, both maintaining that the tour had pointed out unequivocally the lessons that had to be learned, and they would make sure that the squad learned them. The fact that Wales had also suffered a severe (and heavier) thrashing was not considered relevant to England's position.

Not surprisingly, not one player decided to hang up his boots at the end of the tour - there were bigger fish to fry, and the experience of a lifetime to look forward to in the Second World Cup.

TOUR RESULTS:

July 7th	New South Wales	at Sydney	LOST	19 - 21	(three tries to two)
July 10th	Victoria President's XV	at Melbourne	WON	26 - 9	(five tries to one)
July 14th	Queensland	at Ballymore	LOST	14 - 20	(three tries each)
Julky 16th	Fiji B	at Lautoka	LOST	13 - 27	(one try to three)
July 20th	**FIJI**	**at Suva**	**WON**	**28 - 9**	**(three tries to one)**
July 23rd	Emerging Australians	at Gosford	WON	36 - 3	(six tries to nil)
July 27th	**AUSTRALIA**	**at Sydney**	**LOST**	**15 - 40**	(one try to five)

3rd match   **ENGLAND   28 pts**   v   **FIJI   12 pts**

	Caps					Caps		
15	17th	**J.M.Webb**	(Bath)	.		**O.Turuva**	(Saunaka & Nadi)
14	44th	**R.Underwood**	(RAF/Leicester)	.		**T.Vonolagi**	(Army & Suva)
13	12th	**J.C.Guscott**	(Bath)	.		**J.Taqaiwai**	(Duavata & Rewa)
12	25th	**W.D.C.Carling (Capt)**	(Harlequins)	.		**V.Rauluni**	(Nabua & Suva)
11	10th	**C.Oti**	(Wasps)	. .		**F.Seru**	(Nabua & Suva)
10	37th	**C.R.Andrew**	(Wasps)	.		**W.Serevi**	(Nabua & Suva)
9	22nd	**R.J.Hill**	(Bath)	.		**P.Tabulutu**	(Nabua & Suva)
1	8th	**J.Leonard**	(Harlequins)	.		**E.Naituvau**	(Army & Suva)
2	30th	**B.C.Moore**	(Harlequins)	.		**S.Naiviliwasa**	(Police & Suva)
3	23rd	**J.A.Probyn**	(Wasps)	.		**M.Taga (Capt)**	(QVS OB & Suva)
4	11th	**N.C.Redman**	(Bath)	.		**S.Domoni**	(Waimanu & Suva)
5	1st	**M.C.Bayfield**	(Northampton)	.		**I.Savai**	(Regent & Nadi)
6	16th	**M.C.Teague**	(Gloucester)	.		**A.Dere**	(Army & Suva)
7	22nd	**G.W.Rees**	(Nottingham)	.		**M.G.Olsson**	(St J Marist & Suva)
8	26th	**D.Richards**	(Leicester)	.		**I.Tawake**	(Yalovata & Nadroga)

13th   M.G.Skinner (Harlequins) for Teague - 40   .

Referee: B.Kinsey   (Australia)

SCORERS:							
	J.M.Webb	Penalty Goal		3 - 0			
	J.A.Probyn	Try	(3rd & last)	7 - 0			
	J.M.Webb	Conversion		9 - 0			
				9 - 3	**W.Serevi**	Penalty Goal	
	C.R.Andrew	D'p Goal	(11th)	12 - 3			
				12 - 7	**F.Seru**	Try	
				12 - 9	**W.Serevi**	Conversion	
				Half-time			
				12 - 12	**W.Serevi**	Drop Goal	
	R.Underwood	Try	(28th)	16 - 12			
	J.M.Webb	Conversion		18 - 12			
	C.R.Andrew	D'p Goal	(12th)	21 - 12			
	J.M.Webb	Penalty Goal		24 - 12			
	C.R.Andrew	Try	(1st)	28 - 12			

POINTS:						
	C.R.Andrew	10 points	(142)		**W.Serevi**	8 points
	J.M.Webb	10 points	(112)		**F.Seru**	4 points
	J.A.Probyn	4 points	(12)			
	R.Underwood	4 points	(112)			

MATCH COMMENTARY:

England won comfortably and deservedly in the end, but at one stage when Fiji had drawn level at 12 - 12 in the second half, the result was very much in doubt. Had Fiji run the ball thereafter, they would surely have won, but they elected to try frequent, and unsuccessful, drops at goal and so lost the match. Sixteen points, including two tries, in the last fourteen minutes, assured England victory, but it was by no means a convincing one. With Dooley out and John Hall on his way home, Australia, next week, is going to be a daunting prospect on this form.

17th match   **ENGLAND   15 pts**   v   **AUSTRALIA   40 pts**

	Caps					Caps		
15	18th	**J.M.Webb**	(Bath)	.		2nd	**M.C.Roebuck**	(New South Wales)
14	45th	**R.Underwood**	(RAF/Leicester)	.		56th	**D.I.Campese**	(New South Wales)
13	13th	**J.C.Guscott**	(Bath)	.		9th	**T.J.Horan**	(Queensland)
12	26th	**W.D.C.Carling (Capt)**	(Harlequins)	.		8th	**J.S.Little**	(Queensland)
11	11th	**C.Oti**	(Wasps)	.		2nd	**R.H.Egerton**	(New South Wales)
10	38th	**C.R.Andrew**	(Wasps)	.		45th	**M.P.Lynagh**	(Queensland)
9	23rd	**R.J.Hill**	(Bath)	.		46th	**N.C.Farr-Jones**	(New South Wales)
1	9th	**J.Leonard**	(Harlequins)	.		12th	**A.J.Daly**	(New South Wales)
2	31st	**B.C.Moore**	(Harlequins)	.		12th	**P.N.Kearns**	(New South Wales)
3	24th	**J.A.Probyn**	(Wasps)	.		9th	**E.J.McKenzie**	(New South Wales)
4	17th	**P.J.Ackford**	(Harlequins)	.		11th	**R.J.McCall**	(Queensland)
5	2nd	**M.C.Bayfield**	(Northampton)	.		2nd	**J.A.Eales**	(Queensland)
6	17th	**M.C.Teague**	(Gloucester)	.		52nd	**S.P.Poidevin**	(New South Wales)
7	43rd	**P.J.Winterbottom**	(Harlequins)	.		5th	**V.Ofahengaue**	(New South Wales)
8	27th	**D.Richards**	(Leicester)	.		16th	**B.T.Gavin**	(New South Wales)
						3rd	P.J.Slattery (Q'sland) for Farr-Jones - 57	

Referee: K.H.Lawrence   (New Zealand)

SCORERS:

				0 - 3	M.P.Lynagh	Penalty Goal
				0 - 7	M.C.Roebuck	Try
				0 - 9	M.P.Lynagh	Conversion
J.C.Guscott	Try	(10th)		4 - 9		
J.M.Webb	Conversion			6 - 9		
				6 - 12	M.P.Lynagh	Penalty Goal
				Half-time		
				6 - 16	D.I.Campese	Try
				6 - 18	M.P.Lynagh	Conversion
J.M.Webb	Penalty Goal			9 - 18		
				9 - 22	D.I.Campese	Try
				9 - 25	M.P.Lynagh	Penalty Goal
J.M.Webb	Penalty Goal			12 - 25		
J.M.Webb	Penalty Goal			15 - 25		
				15 - 29	V.Ofahengaue	Try
				15 - 31	M.P.Lynagh	Conversion
				15 - 34	M.P.Lynagh	Penalty Goal
				15 - 38	V.Ofahengaue	Try
				15 - 40	M.P.Lynagh	Conversion

POINTS:

J.M.Webb	11 points	(123)		M.P.Lynagh	20 points
J.C.Guscott	4 points	(40)		D.I.Campese	8 points
				V.Ofahengaue	8 points
				M.C.Roebuck	4 points

MATCH COMMENTARY:

Australia's win by five tries to one was their biggest ever winning total and margin over England, and England have yet to win on Australian soil.   The Grand Slam winning pack had no answer to the power and mobility of the Australian eight, amongst whom Gavin, Ofahengaue and Eales were outstanding and the Australian backs could do almost what they liked, a situation much to the liking of David Campese who scored two splendid tries.   Willie Ofahengaue, too, took advantage.   England's decision to tour, out of season and just before the World Cup, was not vindicated by this result (Wales probably came to the same conclusion) and Carling and Cooke will have some hard work to do to restore morale and confidence before England meet New Zealand in the World Cup opener in October.

THE WORLD CUP - 1991:

THE WORLD CUP SQUAD:

Manager:	G.D.Cooke	Coach:	R.M.Uttley	Captain:	W.D.C.Carling

Full-backs:	S.D.Hodgkinson	(Nottingham)	13 caps	Forwards:	P.J.Ackford	(Harlequins)	17 caps
	J.M.Webb	(Bristol)	18 caps		W.A.Dooley	(Preston G'hoppers)	41 caps
					J.Leonard	(Harlequins)	9 caps
Three-quarters:	W.D.C.Carling	(Harlequins)	26 caps		B.C.Moore	(Harlequins)	31 caps
	J.C.Guscott	(Bath)	13 caps		C.J.Olver	(Northampton)	1 cap
	N.J.Heslop	(Orrell)	7 caps		G.S.Pearce	(Northampton)	35 caps
	S.J.Halliday	(Harlequins)	16 caps		J.A.Probyn	(Wasps)	24 caps
	C.Oti	(Wasps)	11 caps		N.C.Redman	(Bath)	11 caps
	R.Underwood	(RAF/Leicester)	45 caps		G.W.Rees	(Nottingham)	22 caps
					P.A.G.Rendall	(Wasps)	27 caps
Half-backs:	C.R.Andrew	(Wasps)	38 caps		D.Richards	(Leicester)	27 caps
	R.J.Hill	(Bath)	23 caps		M.G.Skinner	(Harlequins)	13 caps
	C.D.Morris	(Orrell)	5 caps		M.C.Teague	(Gloucester)	17 caps
	D.Pears	(Harlequins)	2 caps		P.J.Winterbottom	(Harlequins)	43 caps

---

ENGLAND - WORLD CUP RESULTS:

Pool 1 matches:

October 3rd	NEW ZEALAND	at Twickenham	LOST	12 - 18	(no tries to one)
October 8th	ITALY	at Twickenham	WON	36 - 6	(four tries to one)
October 11th	U.S.A.	at Twickenham	WON	37 - 9	(five tries to one)

Quarter Final:

October 19th	FRANCE	at Parc des Princes	WON	19 - 10	(two tries to one)

Semi Final:

October 26th	SCOTLAND	at Murrayfield	WON	9 - 6	(no tries)

Final:

November 2nd	AUSTRALIA	at Twickenham	LOST	6 - 12	(no tries to one)

WORLD CUP WINNERS:	AUSTRALIA	beat ENGLAND in the Final	12 - 6	(one try to nil)
		beat NEW ZEALAND in the Semi-Final	16 - 6	(two tries to nil)
RUNNER UP:	ENGLAND	beat SCOTLAND in the Semi-Final	9 - 6	(no tries)
3rd PLACE	NEW ZEALAND	beat SCOTLAND in the play-off	13 - 6	(one try to nil)
4th PLACE	SCOTLAND			
BEATEN QUARTER FINALISTS:	FRANCE	lost to ENGLAND	10 - 19	(one try to two)
	WESTERN SAMOA	lost to SCOTLAND	6 - 28	(no tries to three)
	IRELAND	lost to AUSTRALIA	18 - 19	(one try to three)
	CANADA	lost to NEW ZEALAND	13 - 29	(two tries to five)

WORLD CUP 1991 SUMMARY:

By any standards the 1991 World Cup was an outstanding success. Before the tournament started there were many doubts expressed and many more privately held, that perhaps the tournament was not going to have universal appeal; perhaps in the notoriously unreliable English autumn weather, matches would be ground out in a monotonous series of scrummages, partly because the ball would be wet and the pitches treacherous and partly because losing a match would have a finality not usually associated with the game; and, above all, could the appeal of the game be sustained in the broader public domain for a month ?

All such fears were allayed, however, the whole tournamnet had enormous appeal, and under the sharp focus of close media scrutiny, all aspects of the game as a whole emerged with credit and increased popularity. Above all thousands of rugby afficionados as well as the players displayed good humour, magnanimity in victory and not a trace of the ill-will, boorishness and vulgar irresponsibility which, regrettably, has been frequently evident around the fringes of other sports from time to time.

There were heroes and drama aplenty right from the early stages. Italy, who held the mighty All-Blacks to a mere 10 point margin at Leicester; the sheer impertinence, combined with hard-nosed pragmatism, of the Western Samoans who beat Wales at Cardiff, in the National Stadium, and effectively put them out of the tournament; the heroic efforts of Canada against both France and New Zealand in their Quarter-Final at Lille; the intense drama of the Dublin Quarter-Final when Gordon Hamilton scored a fine try to put Ireland in the lead with just five minutes to go, and Michael Lynagh's masterly achievement in scoring the winning try for Australia in the last minute.

England's progress through all the stages was not without moments of high drama either. But not so in the opening match which failed to live up to expectations. At that time there were no floodlights at Twickenham, so the match had to be played in the afternoon. This did not detract from the attendance - but why did it have to be held on a Thursday ? The afternoon started with a complete anti-climax when the opening ceremony - not an appropriate word - totally lacked any atmosphere or sense of occasion prior to the match. A little forethought and reflection on the spectacle of other opening ceremonies, the Olympics, the Soccer World Cup and European Championships, the Superbowl, and a little imagination and enterprise could have created an unforgettable occasion. As it was, those present had to rely upon the match to provide the spectacle and excitement. The reigning World Champions against the current Grand Slam winners should have been a clash of the Titans, but, if it was, it was neither dramatic nor exciting. England won the first half and New Zealand the second and in the end the mighty England pack were well beaten at their own game. Four tries in the Italian match, and especially Jeremy Guscott's second try, gave the slightly bewildered English supporters something to cheer, in spite of Italy's best endeavours to kill the ball and the game. Five tries against the USA and Will Carling beating Bill Beaumont's record of having led England on 21 occasions,was an even greater cause for celebration, but this was really kids' stuff compared with the battles yet to come

Parc des Princes was not a place for faint hearts when the Quarter-Final match was played, and there were certainly no faint hearts on the field that day. The match was as physical an encounter as had been seen for many a long day and the French set the scene and succumbed to the pressure when first Nigel Heslop, and then Mike Teague were roughed up in the early stages. Jonathan Webb rubbed salt in by converting both penalty goals and France never got off the back foot. Eventually, despite sterling efforts to gain the ascendancy, and despite Jean-Baptiste Lafond's try to pull the French level just after half-time, the French "sang-froid" deserted them and they lost their cool and lost the match. At Murrayfield, it was like the 1990 Grand Slam match all over again and the atmosphere wa was electric. Tension throughout and high drama when first Gavin Hastings, from in front of the posts, put a penalty attempt wide whic would have taken Scotland into a 9 - 6 lead with some twelve minutes left to play. Then, and not for the last time, Rob Andrew seized the day and dropped a goal to win the match. No tries were scored in this one, but for tension and emotive climax, the match lacked nothing. The Final was a spectacular conclusion to a memorable tournament, but the result did not go England's way because they got their game plan wrong in an attempt to play an expansive game when their success over the last two seasons has been based on powerful forward play, pulling the opposition in, retaining possession and driving forward again. Not spectacular but effective. Unfortunately, when the expansive plan failed to break a very resolute Australian defence, England could not revert to their previous. practice. It was a game of heroic endeavour in which every England player gave his all, but it was not enough and Nick Farr-Jones collected "Bill" and took it back to Sydney - and deservedly so.

When it was all over, it was still early in the British season, but even so, several England players decided that it was time to call it a day. Gary Pearce won 36 caps in a career which had spanned 13 seasons; Paul Rendall, 28 caps, and Gary Rees, 23 caps, had both been playing International rugby for eight seasons and, as well as Gary Pearce had all played in the 1987 World Cup four years ago. So had Richard Hill, 29 caps and former Captain and he, Simon Hodgkinson, 14 caps, and Chris Oti, 13, against their wishes, did not pull on an England jersey again. Paul Ackford, 22 caps, first capped three years ago, was the only British Lion amongst those retiring.

The Second World Cup had reflected the changing emphases in World Rugby. The dominance of New Zealand had been removed, again by Australia, who had one or two Bledisloe Cups to their name, and the once nigh invincible Welsh had been condemned to having to qualify for the 1995 event. How are the mighty fallen..... In parallel, Canada, Western Samoa and Italy emerged with much credit and bright futures in the game. But most important of all, on a World stage and under a powerful spotlight, the game and all those involved in it gained much popular appeal and interest which will stand the game in good stead in the future - whatever that may bring.

THE ENGLAND 1991 WORLD CUP SQUAD.

Back Row: S.D.Hodgkinson, C.D.Morris, J.C.Guscott, M.C.Teague, P.J.Winterbottom, N.J.Heslop, J.Leonard, B.C.Moore,
Middle Row: S.J.Halliday, J.M.Webb, D.Richards, P.J.Ackford, M.G.Skinner, W.A.Dooley, N.C.Redman, G.S.Pearce, J.A.Probyn, C.Oti,
Seated: D.Pears, R.Underwood, R.J.Hill, W.D.C.Carling (Captain), C.R.Andrew, P.A.G.Rendall, G.W.Rees, C.J.Olver.

16th match   **ENGLAND   12 pts**   v   **NEW ZEALAND   18 pts**

	Caps					Caps		
15	19th	J.M.Webb	(Bath)	.		27th	T.J.Wright	(Auckland)
14	46th	R.Underwood	(RAF/Leicester)	.		41st	J.J.Kirwan	(Auckland)
13	27th	W.D.C.Carling (Capt)	(Harlequins)	.		12th	C.R.Innes	(Auckland)
12	14th	J.C.Guscott	(Bath)	.		7th	B.J.McCahill	(Auckland)
11	12th	C.Oti	(Wasps)	.		4th	J.K.R.Timu	(Otago)
10	39th	C.R.Andrew	(Wasps)	.		32nd	G.J.Fox	(Auckland)
9	24th	R.J.Hill	(Bath)	.		14th	G.T.M.Bachop	(Canterbury)
1	10th	J.Leonard	(Harlequins)	.		36th	S.C.McDowell	(Auckland)
2	32nd	B.C.Moore	(Harlequins)	.		35th	S.B.T.Fitzpatrick	(Auckland)
3	25th	J.A.Probyn	(Wasps)	.		26th	R.W.Loe	(Waikato)
4	18th	P.J.Ackford	(Harlequins)	.		12th	I.D.Jones	(North Auckland)
5	42nd	W.A.Dooley	(Preston G'hoppers)	.		53rd	G.W.Whetton (Capt)	(Auckland)
6	18th	M.C.Teague	(Gloucester)	.		31st	A.J.Whetton	(Auckland)
7	44th	P.J.Winterbottom	(Harlequins)	.		20th	M.N.Jones	(Auckland)
8	28th	D.Richards	(Leicester)	.		10th	Z.V.Brooke	(Auckland)

10th   A.T.Earl (Canterbury) for Brooke - 70

Referee: J.M.Fleming   (Scotland)

SCORERS:	J.M.Webb	Penalty Goal		3 - 0			
				3 - 3	G.J.Fox	Penalty Goal	
				3 - 6	G.J.Fox	Penalty Goal	
	J.M.Webb	Penalty Goal		6 - 6			
				6 - 9	G.J.Fox	Penalty Goal	
	J.M.Webb	Penalty Goal		9 - 9			
	C.R.Andrew	D'p Goal	(13th)	12 - 9			
				Half-time			
				12 - 13	M.N.Jones	Try	
				12 - 15	G.J.Fox	Conversion	
				12 - 18	G.J.Fox	Penalty Goal	

POINTS:	J.M.Webb	9 points	(132)	G.J.Fox	14 points
	C.R.Andrew	3 points	(145)	M.N.Jones	4 points

MATCH COMMENTARY:

The opening match of the 1991 World Cup with the reigning World Champions facing the current Grand Slam winners was eagerly awaited and the build-up was intense. England fielded their entire Grand Slam pack upon whom so much reliance had been placed earlier in 1991, and for the first half of the game honours were even. England found themselves 3 points ahead after only 15 seconds from a penalty goal after a late tackle on Jonathan Webb by Micheal Jones. Penalty goals were then exchanged after a series of minor indiscretions and the score remained even until Rob Andrew cooly slotted his 13th International drop goal just before half-time to put England into a 12 - 9 lead at the break. But in the second half it was all New Zealand dominating up front, always going forward, always getting possession at the subsequent put in and then doing it all over again. New Zealand were always harder, more aggressive, more determined and none more so than the raw-boned flanker Michael Jones who took the inside pass from John Kirwan when all the England backs had been committed in the tackle, to score the only try of the match. Richard Hill, behind a beaten pack, lost confidence, and all the back line suffered. It was not a spectacular or exciting match but it was very competently won by New Zealand who just did not allow England to play to their strengths.

1st match   **ENGLAND   36 pts**   v   **ITALY   6 pts**

	Caps					Caps		
15	20th	**J.M.Webb**	(Bath)	.		**L.Troiani**	(Scavolini L'Aquila)
14	13th & last	**C.Oti**	(Wasps)	.		**P.Vaccari**	(Nutrilinea Calvisano)
13	28th	**W.D.C.Carling (Capt)**	(Harlequins)	.		**F.Gaetaniello**	(Ecomar Livorno)
12	15th	**J.C.Guscott**	(Bath)	.		**S.Barba**	(Amatori Mediolanum)
11	47th	**R.Underwood**	(RAF/Leicester)	.		**Marcello Cuttitta**	(Amatori Mediolanum)
10	40th	**C.R.Andrew**	(Wasps)	.		**D.Dominguez**	(Amatori Mediolanum)
9	25th	**R.J.Hill**	(Bath)	.		**I.Francescato**	(Pastajolly Tavisium)
1	11th	**J.Leonard**	(Harlequins)	.		**Massimo Cuttitta**	(Amatori Mediolanum)
2	33rd	**B.C.Moore**	(Harlequins)	.		**G.Pivetta**	(Iranian Loom San Dona)
3	26th	**J.A.Probyn**	(Wasps)	.		**F.Properzi-Curti**	(Amatori Mediolanum)
4	19th	**P.J.Ackford**	(Harlequins)	.		**R.Favaro**	(Benetton Treviso)
5	12th	**N.C.Redman**	(Bath)	.		**G.Croci**	(Amatori Mediolanum)
6	19th	**M.C.Teague**	(Gloucester)	.		**R.Saetti**	(Petrarca Padova)
7	45th	**P.J.Winterbottom**	(Harlequins)	.		**G.Zanon (Capt)**	(Benetton Treviso)
8	29th	**D.Richards**	(Leicester)	.		**M.Giovanelli**	(Amatori Mediolanum)

	28th & last	P.A.G.Rendall (Wasps) for Probyn - 53		.		M.Bonomi (Amatori Med'um) for Troiani - 48

Referee: J.B.Anderson   (Scotland)

SCORERS:

J.M.Webb	Penalty Goal		3 - 0			
J.M.Webb	Penalty Goal		6 - 0			
R.Underwood	Try	(29th)	10 - 0			
J.M.Webb	Conversion		12 - 0			
J.M.Webb	Penalty Goal		15 - 0			
J.M.Webb	Penalty Goal		18 - 0			
J.C.Guscott	Try	(11th)	22 - 0			
J.M.Webb	Conversion		24 - 0			
			Half-time			
J.C.Guscott	Try	(12th)	28 - 0			
J.M.Webb	Conversion		30 - 0			
			30 - 4		Marcello Cuttitta	Try
			30 - 6		D.Dominguez	Conversion
J.M.Webb	Try	(1st)	34 - 6			
J.M.Webb	Conversion		36 - 6			

POINTS:

J.M.Webb	24 points	(156)		Marcello Cuttitta	4 points
J.C.Guscott	8 points	(48)		D.Dominguez	2 points
R.Underwood	4 points	(116)			

MATCH COMMENTARY:

Something of a one sided match with Italy showing little of the enterprise with which they had beaten the United States only three days before and a marked cynicism and disrespect for the rules of the game. As a spectacle the match was ruined because Italy persisted in killing the ball "going over the top" and in doing so conceded 37 penalties most of which England ran only to be faced with solid and determined tackling which was by far the best feature of the Italian's game in this match. The second of Jeremy Guscott's two tries was a magnificent solo effort and Jonathan Webb's 24 points beat Simon Hodgkinson's record of 23 individual points in an International.

2nd match   **ENGLAND 37 pts**   v   **U.S.A. 9 pts**

	Caps					Caps	
15	14th & last	S.D.Hodgkinson	(Nottingham)			R.B.Nelson	(Belmont Shore)
14	8th	N.J.Heslop	(Orrell)			G.M.Hein	(Old Blues)
13	29th	W.D.C.Carling (Capt)	(Harlequins)			M.A.Williams	(Aspen)
12	17th	S.J.Halliday	(Harlequins)			K.G.Higgins	(Old Blues)
11	48th	R.Underwood	(RAF/Leicester)			P.Sheehy	(Washington)
10	41st	C.R.Andrew	(Wasps)			C.P.O'Brien	(Old Blues)
9	26th	R.J.Hill	(Bath)			M.D.Pidcock	(Pensacola)
1	12th	J.Leonard	(Harlequins)			L.Manga	(South Jersey)
2	2nd	C.J.Olver	(Northampton)			A.W.Flay	(Jersey Shore)
3	36th & last	G.S.Pearce	(Northampton)			N.Mottram	(Boulder)
4	43rd	W.A.Dooley	(Preston G'hoppers)			C.E.Tunnacliffe	(Belmont Shore)
5	13th	N.C.Redman	(Bath)			K.R.Swords (Capt)	(Beacon Hill)
6	14th	M.G.Skinner	(Harlequins)			S.Lipman	(Santa Monica)
7	23rd & last	G.W.Rees	(Nottingham)			A.M.Ridnell	(Old Puget Sound)
8	30th	D.Richards	(Leicester)			R.Farley (Phil	(Philadelphia W)

M.G.de Jong (Denver Baba's) for Higgins - 40
J.P.Wilkerson (Belmont Shore) for Farley - 75

Referee: L.J.Peard   (Wales)

SCORERS:

S.Hodgkinson	Penalty Goal		3 - 0			
R.Underwood	Try	(30th)	7 - 0			
S.Hodgkinson	Conversion		9 - 0			
S.Hodgkinson	Penalty Goal		12 - 0			
			12 - 3	M.A.Williams	Penalty Goal	
S.D.Hodgkinson	Penalty Goal		15 - 3			
W.D.C.Carling	Try	(4th)	19 - 3			
S.Hodgkinson	Conversion		21 - 3			
			Half-time			
			21 - 7	R.B.Nelson	Try	
			21 - 9	M.A.Williams	Conversion	
M.G.Skinner	Try	(2nd)	25 - 9			
S.Hodgkinson	Conversion		27 - 9			
N.J.Heslop	Try	(3rd & last)	31 - 9			
S.Hodgkinson	Conversion		33 - 9			
R.Underwood	Try	(31st)	37 - 9			

POINTS:

S.D.Hodgkinson	17 points	(203)	M.A.Williams	5 points
R.Underwood	8 points	(124)	R.B.Nelson	4 points
M.G.Skinner, N.J.Heslop	4 points	(8),(12)		
and W.D.C.Carling	each	(16)		

MATCH COMMENTARY:

An adequate performance by England guaranteeing them a place in the quarter-finals. This was Will Carling's 22nd match as England Captain thus breaking Bill Beaumont's previous record of 21 matches. Rory Underwood became the third highest try scorer in the history of the game, with 31 tries. Simon Hodgkinson became only the second England player to score more than 200 individual points.

67th match   **ENGLAND   19 pts**   v   **FRANCE   10 pts**

	Caps				Caps		
15	21st	**J.M.Webb**	(Bath)	.	93rd & last	**S.Blanco (Capt)**	(Biarritz)
14	9th	**N.J.Heslop**	(Orrell)	.	27th	**J-B.Lafond**	(Racing Club)
13	30th	**W.D.C.Carling (Capt)**	(Harlequins)	.	79th	**P.Sella**	(Agen)
12	16th	**J.C.Guscott**	(Bath)	.	44th	**F.Mesnel**	(Racing Club)
11	49th	**R.Underwood**	(RAF/Leicester)	.	14th	**P.Saint-Andre**	(Montferrand)
10	42nd	**C.R.Andrew**	(Wasps)	.	7th	**T.Lacroix**	(Dax)
9	27th	**R.J.Hill**	(Bath)	.	6th	**F.Galthie**	(Colomiers)
1	13th	**J.Leonard**	(Harlequins)	.	10th	**G.Lascube**	(Agen)
2	34th	**B.C.Moore**	(Harlequins)	.	21st & last	**P.Marocco**	(Montferrand)
3	27th	**J.A.Probyn**	(Wasps)	.	42nd	**P.Ondarts**	(Biarritz)
4	20th	**P.J.Ackford**	(Harlequins)	.	6th	**J-M.Cadieu**	(Toulouse)
5	44th	**W.A.Dooley**	(Preston G'hoppers)	.	23rd	**O.Roumat**	(Dax)
6	15th	**M.G.Skinner**	(Harlequins)	.	42nd & last	**E.Champ**	(Toulon)
7	46th	**P.J.Winterbottom**	(Harlequins)	.	11th	**L.Cabannes**	(Racing Club)
8	20th	**M.C.Teague**	(Gloucester)	.	18th	**M.Cecillon**	(Bourgoin)

Referee: D.J.Bishop   (New Zealand)

SCORERS:

J.M.Webb	Penalty Goal		3 - 0			
J.M.Webb	Penalty Goal		6 - 0			
			6 - 3	**T.Lacroix**	Penalty Goal	
R.Underwood	Try	(32nd)	10 - 3			
			10 - 6	**T.Lacroix**	Penalty Goal	
			Half-time			
			10 - 10	**J-B.Lafond**	Try	
J.M.Webb	Penalty Goal		13 - 10			
W.D.C.Carling	Try	(5th)	17 - 10			
J.M.Webb	Conversion		19 - 10			

POINTS:

J.M.Webb	11 points	(167)	**T.Lacroix**	6 points	
R.Underwood	4 points	(128)	**J-B.Lafond**	4 points	
W.D.C.Carling	4 points	(20)			

MATCH COMMENTARY:

A highly emotive encounter, in which the French lost their cool and lost the game, and England won well because they refused to be distracted. Within ten minutes, France were six points down as a result of two violent and unseemly indiscretions on first, Nigel Heslop and then Mike Teague. Webb slotted the goals and France were struggling. Two penalty goals to France and then Rory Underwood's fine try from a Will Carling break gave England a 10 - 6 lead at half-time. England had dropped Dean Richards, moved Mike Teague to No. 8 and introduced Mickey Skinner on the blind side, and it was he who , in one second, inspired England to greater heights just when France appeared to be gaining the ascendancy. Marc Cecillon was on a charge round the back of a five yard scrum determined to get to the English line when Skinner, standing directly in front of him, tackled him head on with such power that Cecillon went flying backwards and that, essentially, was the turning point. A further penalty goal and finally a try poached by Will Carling took England to the semi-finals. But it was a sorry, violent game totally unworthy of the occasion and an inappropriate end to Serge Blanco's distinguished career. The abuse in the tunnel of referee David Bishop by French Coach Daniel Dubroca did the game a further disservice as did the attempted cover-up by RWC.

108th match   **ENGLAND   9 pts**   v   **SCOTLAND   6 pts**

	Caps					Caps		
15	22nd	J.M.Webb	(Bath)	.	35th	A.G.Hastings	(Watsonians)
14	18th	S.J.Halliday	(Harlequins)	.	19th	A.G.Stanger	(Hawick)
13	31st	W.D.C.Carling (Capt)	(Harlequins)	.	35th	S.Hastings	(Watsonians)
12	17th	J.C.Guscott	(Bath)	.	22nd	S.R.P.Lineen	(Boroughmuir)
11	50th	R.Underwood	(RAF/Leicester)	.	30th	I.Tukalo	(Selkirk)
10	43rd	C.R.Andrew	(Wasps)	.	22nd	C.M.Chalmers	(Melrose)
9	28th	R.J.Hill	(Bath)	.	23rd	G.Armstrong	(Jedforest)
1	14th	J.Leonard	(Harlequins)	.	37th	D.M.B.Sole (Capt)	(Edinburgh Acad'ls)
2	35th	B.C.Moore	(Harlequins)	.	8th	J.Allan	(Edinburgh Acad'ls)
3	28th	J.A.Probyn	(Wasps)	.	20th	A.P.Burnell	(London Scottish)
4	21st	P.J.Ackford	(Harlequins)	.	21st	C.A.Gray	(Nottingham)
5	45th	W.A.Dooley	(Preston G'hoppers)	.	7th	G.W.Weir	(Melrose)
6	16th	M.G.Skinner	(Harlequins)	.	39th	J.Jeffrey	(Kelso)
7	47th	P.J.Winterbottom	(Harlequins)	.	33rd	F.Calder	(Stewart's Melville)
8	21st	M.C.Teague	(Gloucester)	.	25th	D.B.White	(London Scottish)

Referee: K.V.J.Fitzgerald   (Australia)

SCORERS:

			0 - 3	A.G.Hastings	Penalty Goal
			0 - 6	A.G.Hastings	Penalty Goal
J.M.Webb	Penalty Goal		3 - 6		
			Half-time		
J.M.Webb	Penalty Goal		6 - 6		
C.R.Andrew	D'p Goal	(14th)	9 - 6		

POINTS:

J.M.Webb	6 points	(173)	A.G.Hastings	6 points
C.R.Andrew	3 points	(148)		

MATCH COMMENTARY:

Almost as if the script had been written beforehand, the two semi-finals provided not only the opportunity to determine the leader in each hemisphere, but also the promise of a true world final when the leader from the northern hemisphere would be faced with their counterpart from the south.   As anticipated it was a dour and titanic struggle, with no quarter asked, or given.   It was only the second game in the Final stages of the World Cup (1987 or 1991) in which no tries were scored.   England retained the same pack who had exercised such control in Paris but had to replace the concussed Nigel Heslop with Simon Halliday.   Rory Underwood on the occasion of his 50th cap, led England out, and John Jeffrey, the almost apochryphal "White Shark", who had previously announced his retirement after the World Cup, led Scotland into a cacaphony of sound in the Murrayfield stadium.

The England pack established their ascendancy in both the set pieces and in the lines-out but not by any means in an overwhelming manner. Richard Hill, therefore, had some time and Gary Armstrong was hurried and hassled but also typically resilient.   Rather than kick to touch an risk losing possession, Scotland often put the ball into open spaces, but the English defence, although sometimes hurried, was adequate. Even so, Scotland were 6 points up after 30 minutes and 6 - 3 up at half time.   Early in the second half Jonathan Webb made the scores level with his second penalty goal and it was all to play for in the last quarter.   Then came Gavin Hastings' nightmare; he put a relatively straight-forward penalty attempt wide and missed the opportunity to take the lead, and before long Rob Andrew had done just that for England , and the match, always full of tension and intrigue, which neither side deserved to lose, was over.

18th match   **ENGLAND   6 pts**   v   **AUSTRALIA   12 pts**

	Caps					Caps		
15	23rd	**J.M.Webb**	(Bath)	.	10th	**M.C.Roebuck**	(NSW)
14	19th	**S.J.Halliday**	(Harlequins)	.	64th	**D.I.Campese**	(NSW)
13	32nd	**W.D.C.Carling (Capt)**	(Harlequins)	.	17th	**T.J.Horan**	(Queensland)
12	18th	**J.C.Guscott**	(Bath)	.	15th	**J.S.Little**	(Queensland)
11	51st	**R.Underwood**	(RAF/Leicester)	.	9th & last	**R.H.Egerton**	(NSW)
10	44th	**C.R.Andrew**	(Wasps)	.	53rd	**M.P.Lynagh**	(Queensland)
9	29th & last	**R.J.Hill**	(Bath)	.	53rd	**N.C.Farr-Jones (Capt)**	(NSW)
1	15th	**J.Leonard**	(Harlequins)	.	19th	**A.J.Daly**	(NSW)
2	36th	**B.C.Moore**	(Harlequins)	.	20th	**P.N.Kearns**	(NSW)
3	29th	**J.A.Probyn**	(Wasps)	.	16th	**E.J.A.McKenzie**	(NSW)
4	22nd & last	**P.J.Ackford**	(Harlequins)	.	18th	**R.J.McCall**	(Queensland)
5	46th	**W.A.Dooley**	(Preston G'hoppers)	.	10th	**J.A.Eales**	(Queensland)
6	18th	**M.G.Skinner**	(Harlequins)	.	59th	**S.P.Poidevin**	(NSW)
7	48th	**P.J.Winterbottom**	(Harlequins)	.	12th	**V.Ofahengaue**	(NSW)
8	22nd	**M.C.Teague**	(Gloucester)	.	9th	**T.Coker**	(Queensland)

Referee: W.D.Bevan   (Wales)

SCORERS:

			0 - 3	**M.P.Lynagh**	Penalty Goal
			0 - 7	**A.J.Daly**	Try
			0 - 9	**M.P.Lynagh**	Conversion
			Half-time		
J.M.Webb	Penalty Goal		3 - 9		
			3 - 12	**M.P.Lynagh**	Penalty Goal
J.M.Webb	Penalty Goal		6 - 12		

POINTS:

J.M.Webb	6 points	(179)	**M.P.Lynagh**	8 points
			A.J.Daly	4 points

MATCH COMMENTARY:

The final was a fitting and spectacular conclusion to an immensely successful tournament. England broke their shackles and played expansively moving the ball in the hand with skill and speed. They could not, however, penetrate a magnificent Australian defence, particularly in mid-field where Horan and Little tackled heroically. It could be argued, and it has been many times since, that Geoff Cooke and Will Carling made an immense tactical blunder in not playing to their undoubted strength in the pack and by apparently trying to play an open, fluent game instead. Had they played to their strengths, as they had in the Five Nations, they could well have won the World Cup. The match was electrifying, there were chances galore for both sides in the first twenty minutes and none more heart-stopping than David Campese's burst on to a short pass at speed, in his own half. A dozen strides more then a clever punt ahead could have given him a try had the bounce not been unfavourable. Then, following Lynagh's penalty goal, Tim Horan chose to run from his own 22, the crowd gasped and roared in excitement and wonder but Horan was bundled into touch only inches short. From the ensuing line-out, Willie "O" took a great two-handed catch and drove on, the pack supported and Tony Daly scored the only try of the afternoon. It remained a pulsating match of heroic endeavour and supreme effort in an atmosphere in which the crowd and the players were almost as one. England could not escape from the stranglehold of a tenacious defence and Australia thoroughly deserved their success, for they must be one of the finest teams ever to grace the game. Not least of their qualities is their sportsmanship, their dignity and the spirit in which they play the game.

THE ENGLAND TEAM WHO CONTESTED THE WORLD CUP FINAL AGAINST AUSTRALIA AT TWICKENHAM ON NOVEMBER 2nd 1991.
L to R : W.D.C.Carling (Captain), R.Underwood, C.R.Andrew, J.M.Webb, J.C.Guscott, S.J.Halliday,
P.J.Ackford, W.A.Dooley, P.J.Winterbottom. M.C.Teague, M.G.Skinner, C.D.Morris, J.A.Probyn, B.C.Moore, J.Leonard.

109th match   **ENGLAND   25 pts**   v   **SCOTLAND   7 pts**

99th Calcutta Cup

	Caps				Caps		
15	24th	J.M.Webb	(Bath)	.	37th	A.G.Hastings	(Watsonians)
14	20th	S.J.Halliday	(Harlequins)		21st	A.G.Stanger	(Hawick)
13	33rd	W.D.C.Carling (Capt)	(Harlequins)		37th	S.Hastings	(Watsonians)
12	19th	J.C.Guscott	(Bath)	.	24th	S.R.P.Lineen	(Boroughmuir)
11	52nd	R.Underwood	(RAF/Leicester)		32nd	I.Tukalo	(Selkirk)
10	45th	C.R.Andrew	(Wasps)		24th	C.M.Chalmers	(Melrose
9	6th	C.D.Morris	(Orrell)	.	1st	A.D.Nichol	(Dundee HSFP)
1	16th	J.Leonard	(Harlequins)		39th	D.M.B.Sole (Capt)	(Edinburgh Acad'ls)
2	37th	B.C.Moore	(Harlequins)	.	17th	K.S.Milne	(Heriot's FP)
3	30th	J.A.Probyn	(Wasps)	.	22nd	A.P.Burnell	(London Scottish)
4	3rd	M.C.Bayfield	(Northampton)	.	1st	N.G.B.Edwards	(Harlequins)
5	47th	W.A.Dooley	(Preston G'hoppers)	.	9th	G.W.Weir	(Melrose)
6	18th	M.G.Skinner	(Harlequins)	.	1st	D.J.McIvor	(Edinburgh Acad'ls)
7	49th	P.J.Winterbottom	(Harlequins)	.	1st	I.R.Smith	(Gloucester)
8	1st	T.A.K.Rodber	(Army/Northampton)	.	27th	D.B.White	(London Scottish)

31st   D.Richards (Leicester) for Rodber - 61

Referee: W.D.Bevan   (Wales)

SCORERS:

			0 - 3	A.G.Hastings	Penalty Goal
J.M.Webb	Penalty Goal		3 - 3		
J.M.Webb	Penalty Goal		6 - 3		
R.Underwood	Try	(33rd)	10 - 3		
			10 - 7	D.B.White	Try
			Half-time		
J.M.Webb	Penalty Goal		13 - 7		
J.M.Webb	Penalty Goal		16 - 7		
J.C.Guscott	D'p Goal	(1st)	19 - 7		
C.D.Morris	Try	(2nd)	23 - 7		
J.M.Webb	Conversion		25 - 7		

POINTS:

J.M.Webb	14 points	(193)		D.B.White	4 points
R.Underwood and C.D.Morris	4 points	(132),(8)		A.G.Hastings	3 points
J.C.Guscott	3 points	(51)			

MATCH COMMENTARY:

Scotland put some considerable pressure on England, who, after legal wrangles appeared in the traditional all-white strip, as if trying to avenge the World Cup semi-final defeat of the previous October. In the first half, the Scottish pack did not allow England any breathing space at all, pushed them all over the field and dominated the lines-out. The four Anglos in the Scottish pack thoroughly enjoyed themselves. Rory Underwood's try, set up by Simon Halliday, gave England the lead against the run of play, but the final indignity was to come when the English pack conceded a push-over try. In the second half things did not improve until Dean Richards came on to replace the unfortunate Tim Rodber and exerted a steadying influence, particularly in the loose. The second England try was again created by Simon Halliday, and scored by Dewi Morris shortly after Jeremy Guscott's towering drop goal had secured a comfortable lead. In the end, and contrary to early expectations, England won by a record margin at Murrayfield. But the day really belonged to the Scots defence.

105th match   **ENGLAND   38 pts**   v   **IRELAND   9 pts**

	Caps					Caps		
15	25th	J.M.Webb	(Bath)	.	11th	J.E.Staples	(London Irish)
14	21st	S.J.Halliday	(Harlequins)	.	3rd	R.M.Wallace	(Garryowen)
13	34th	W.D.C.Carling (Capt)	(Harlequins)	.	44th	B.J.Mullin	(Blackrock)
12	20th	J.C.Guscott	(Bath)	.	11th	D.M.Curtis	(London Irish)
11	53rd	R.Underwood	(RAF/Leicester)	.	9th	S.P.Geoghegan	(London Irish)
10	46th	C.R.Andrew	(Wasps)	.	7th	R.P.Keyes	(Cork Constitution)
9	7th	C.D.Morris	(Orrell)	.	13th	L.F.P.Aherne	(Lansdowne)
1	17th	J.Leonard	(Harlequins)	.	9th	N.J.Popplewell	(Greystones)
2	38th	B.C.Moore	(Harlequins)	.	20th	S.J.Smith	(Ballymena)
3	31st	J.A.Probyn	(Wasps)	.	3rd	G.F.Halpin	(London Irish)
4	4th	M.C.Bayfield	(Northampton)	.	5th	M.J.Galwey	(Shannon)
5	48th	W.A.Dooley	(Preston G'hoppers)	.	18th	N.P.J.Francis	(Blackrock)
6	19th	M.G.Skinner	(Harlequins)	.	37th	P.M.Matthews (Capt)	(Wanderers)
7	50th	P.J.Winterbottom	(Harlequins)	.	2nd	M.J.J.Fitzgibbon	(Shannon)
8	2nd	T.A.K.Rodber	(Northampton)	.	11th	B.F.Robinson	(Ballymena)

Referee: W.D.Bevan   (Wales)

SCORERS:

J.M.Webb	Try	(2nd)	4 - 0			
J.M.Webb	Conversion		6 - 0			
			6 - 4	R.P.Keyes	Try
			6 - 6	R.P.Keyes	Conversion
J.M.Webb	Penalty Goal		9 - 6			
			9 - 9	R.P.Keyes	Penalty Goal
C.D.Morris	Try	(3rd)	13 - 9			
J.M.Webb	Conversion		15 - 9			
J.C.Guscott	Try	(13th)	19 - 9			
J.M.Webb	Conversion		21 - 9			
			Half-time			
J.M.Webb	Penalty Goal		24 - 9			
R.Underwood	Try	(34th)	28 - 9			
S.J.Halliday	Try	(2nd & last)	32 - 9			
J.M.Webb	Try	(3rd)	36 - 9			
J.M.Webb	Conversion		38 - 9			

POINTS:

J.M.Webb	22 points	(215)	R.P.Keyes	9 points
R.Underwood, J.C.Guscott	4 points	(136),(55)		
C.D.Morris and S.J.Halliday	each	(12),(8)		

MATCH COMMENTARY:

To commemorate his 50th cap, Peter Winterbottom led England out to a tumultuous welcome from a capacity crowd who were to be treated to a fine spectacle of running rugby, with seven fine tries scored, six of them by England. Jonathan Webb scored England's, and his, first try after only three minutes, and within five minutes of that, Ralph Keyes had sold a classic dummy to the England middle five, and scored untouched. Six points each, two converted tries within ten minutes of the start of the match, and the crowd sat forward in their seats anticipating a feast. And they were not to be disappointed; the spectacle continued, with as fine a display by the England backs as had been seen in a Five Nations game since the same match four years ago.

This was England's highest post-war points total in a Five Nations match, and it is only the third time since that England have scored six tries in a match. Jonathan Webb's 22 points beat Rob Andrew's individual Five Nations record set in 1986. He is also the only England full-back to have scored two tries in an International match since 1947.

68th m   ENGLAND   31 pts   v   FRANCE   13 pts

	Caps					Caps		
15	26th	**J.M.Webb**	(Bath)	.		29th	**J-B.Lafond**	(Racing Club)
14	22nd	**S.J.Halliday**	(Harlequins)	.		15th	**P.Saint-Andre**	(Montferrand)
13	35th	**W.D.C.Carling (Capt)**	(Harlequins)	.		81st	**P.Sella (Capt)**	(Agen)
12	21st	**J.C.Guscott**	(Bath)	.		46th	**F.Mesnel**	(Racing Club)
11	54th	**R.Underwood**	(RAF/Leicester)	.		2nd	**S.Viars**	(Brive)
10	47th	**C.R.Andrew**	(Toulouse)	.		2nd	**A.Penaud**	(Brive)
9	8th	**C.D.Morris**	(Orrell)	.		8th	**F.Galthie**	(Colomiers)
1	18th	**J.Leonard**	(Harlequins)	.		12th	**G.Lascube**	(Agen)
2	39th	**B.C.Moore**	(Harlequins)	.		4th	**V.Moscato**	(Begles)
3	32nd	**J.A.Probyn**	(Wasps)	.		4th	**P.Gimbert**	(Begles)
4	5th	**M.C.Bayfield**	(Northampton)	.		20th	**M.Cecillon**	(Bourgoin)
5	49th	**W.A.Dooley**	(Preston G'hoppers)	.		2nd	**C.Mougeot**	(Begles)
6	20th	**M.G.Skinner**	(Harlequins)	.		3rd	**J-F.Tordo**	(Nice)
7	51st	**P.J.Winterbottom**	(Harlequins)	.		13th	**L.Cabannes**	(Racing Club)
8	32nd	**D.Richards**	(Leicester)	.		1st	**A.van Heerden**	(Tarbes)

	3rd	D.Pears (Harlequins) for Andrew - 34	.	3rd	J-L.Sadourny (Colomiers) for Sella - 55
			.	25th	O.Roumat (Dax) for Mougeot - 62
			.	1st	P.Montlaur (Agen) for Sadourny - 64

Referee: S.R.Hilditch   (Ireland)

SCORERS:

J.M.Webb	Penalty Goal		3 - 0			
			3 - 4	**S.Viars**	Try
	Penalty Try		7 - 4			
J.M.Webb	Conversion		9 - 4			
J.M.Webb	Try	(4th & last)	13 - 4			
J.M.Webb	Conversion		15 - 4			
			Half-time			
			15 - 7	**S.Viars**	Penalty Goal
J.M.Webb	Penalty Goal		18 - 7			
R.Underwood	Try	(35th)	22 - 7			
J.M.Webb	Conversion		24 - 7			
			24 - 11	**A.Penaud**	Try
			24 - 13	**S.Viars**	Conversion
J.M.Webb	Penalty Goal		27 - 13			
C.D.Morris	Try	(4th)	31 - 13			

POINTS:

J.M.Webb	19 points	(234)	**S.Viars**	9 points
C.D.Morris and R.Underwood	4 points	(16),(140)	**A.Penaud**	4 points
Penalty Try	each			

MATCH COMMENTARY:

The only change to the England side was the return of Dean Richards for Tim Rodber at No: 8, and with 63 points and eight tries under their collective belt, the team was cautiously optimistic in their approach to this match. They had won the last four encounters with France, but they were generally aware that France would be seeking revenge for the sound defeat they suffered in the World Cup Quarter-Final just four months ago. After an early penalty goal to England, the French pack exerted tremendous pressure mainly from loose play and England's defence was sorely stretched. After Viars' try, Gimbert was adjudged to have collapsed the scrum in retreat and England got the penalty try. Johnathan Webb broke through indecisive tackling to score before half-time and the French were in disarray. Thereafter, England gradually pulled away from France and controlled the match. Phillipe Sella had to retire with a badly cut head almost on the hour, and after that French discipline evaporated and the last ten minutes were very unsavoury. Steve Hilditch had no alternative in sending Lascube and Moscato off the pitch and Tordo and Gimbert were fortunate to avoid a similar fate. Brian Moore seemed to be the focus of the French front row's attention and doubtless he had been provoking them to their indiscretions as he is frequently wont against France ! Throughout this mayhem England calmly maintained their discipline and the sight of Steve Hilditch being escorted off the pitch by armed police painted a sorry picture to end what had otherwise been a magnificent match.

During the course of it, Jonathan Webb became England's most capped full-back with 26 caps, and Dean Richards their most capped No: 8 with 32 caps. A total of 94 points had now been accumulated in three matches so far this season, already four more than the previous record set by England last year.

France used all three permissible substitutes during the match, an unprecedented event, and, ironically, Jean-Luc Sadourny who replaced Phillipe Sella, himself had to be replaced after an accidental collision with Franck Mesnel when he had only been on the field for eight minutes or so ! In all respects another very sad day for France, following which Bernard Lapasset, the FFR President, saw fit to order, publically, the French team to put its house in order.

98th match   **ENGLAND   24 pts**   v   **WALES   0 pts**   98th match

	Caps				Caps		
15	27th	J.M.Webb	(Bath)		18th	A.Clement	(Swansea)
14	23rd & last	S.J.Halliday	(Harlequins)		30th	I.C.Evans (Capt)	(Llanelli)
13	36th	W.D.C.Carling (Capt)	(Harlequins)		7th	N.R.Jenkins	(Pontypridd)
12	22nd	J.C.Guscott	(Bath)		12th	I.S.Gibbs	(Swansea)
11	55th	R.Underwood	(RAF/Leicester)		20th	M.R.Hall	(Cardiff)
10	48th	C.R.Andrew	(Toulouse)		3rd	C.J.Stephens	(Llanelli)
9	9th	C.D.Morris	(Orrell)		41st	R.N.Jones	(Swansea)
1	19th	J.Leonard	(Harlequins)		21st	M.Griffiths	(Cardiff)
2	40th	B.C.Moore	(Harlequins)		7th	G.R.Jenkins	(Swansea)
3	33rd	J.A.Probyn	(Wasps)		11th	L.Delaney	(Llanelli)
4	6th	M.C.Bayfield	(Northampton)		10th	G.O.Llewellyn	(Neath)
5	50th	W.A.Dooley	(Preston G'hoppers)		3rd	A.H.Copsey	(Llanelli)
6	21st & last	M.G.Skinner	(Harlequins)		11th	M.S.Morris	(Neath)
7	52nd	P.J.Winterbottom	(Harlequins)		7th	R.E.Webster	(Swansea)
8	33rd	D.Richards	(Leicester)		3rd	S.Davies	(Swansea)

10th & last	N.J.Heslop (Orrell) for Carling - 72			4th	M.A.Rayer (Cardiff) for Clement - 40

Referee: R.J.Megson   (Scotland)

SCORERS:	W.D.C.Carling	Try	(6th)	4 - 0
	J.M.Webb	Conversion		6 - 0
	M.G.Skinner	Try	(3rd & last)	10 - 0
	J.M.Webb	Conversion		12 - 0
	J.M.Webb	Penalty Goal		15 - 0
			Half-time	
	W.A.Dooley	Try	(3rd & last)	19 - 0
	J.M.Webb	Conversion		21 - 0
	J.M.Webb	Penalty Goal		24 - 0

POINTS:	J.M.Webb	12 points	(246)
	W.D.C.Carling	4 points	(24)
	M.G.Skinner	4 points	(12)
	W.A.Dooley	4 points	(12)

MATCH COMMENTARY:

Wade Dooley, gaining his 50th cap, led England onto the field where, without too much trouble, they were to complete their second successive Grand Slam. Fittingly Captain Will Carling opened the scoring in the first minute of the match and Wade Dooley wrapped it up with a try in the last quarter, but in between, England did not live up to the promise of the matches against Ireland and France and stout, resolute Welsh defence and determination held the mighty English at bay.   England were 15 points up after half an hour, and then Wales decided to close it down and, again England could do very little about it until, with 12 minutes to go Wade Dooley took a short pass from Rob Andrew and crashed through the thin red line, to complete what he will doubtless regard as his finest hour.   The match was not an anti-climax, but it did not complete the season, and the second successive Grand Slam in quite the style that England would have wished. Too many handling errors occurred in the second half, from which England were always able to recover, but without them Wales may well have been at the wrong end of a severe beating. Nevertheless, the end to a highly satisfactory and record-breaking season for England.

SUMMARY OF THE SEASON - 1991 - 92:

By any standards this had been an outstandingly successful seasom for England, and, indeed, a memorable twelve months. During that time England had had the immensely disappointing, but nevertheless, invaluable tour to Fiji and Australia in June 1991, the elation of a successful World Cup, only to suffer the frustration of falling at the last hurdle, and finally a second successive Grand Slam in the Five Nations Championship. Of such stuff are dreams made.

The Five Nations, with which this summary is concerned, started and ended somewhat lamely, but caught fire with memorable performances in the middle in the matches against Ireland and France. But the outcome was a second successive Grand Slam, a feat only ever achieved twice before by England and once by Wales in the history of the Five Nations Championship, and the previous occasion was 58 years ago in 1923 and 1924 when W.J.A.Davies and W.W.Wakefield respectively led their teams to the same pinnacle of achievement. But it has never been achieved before under the same captain.

There were three changes from the World Cup final side for the first match of the new season at Murrayfield. Martin Bayfield came in for Paul Ackford who had retired, Tim Rodber replaced Mike Teague, and Dewi Morris left Richard Hill on the bench. It is a measure of Geoff Cooke's loyalty to his team, and the consistency of his selection policy that the same fifteen players played throughout the season except for Rodber and Richards who each played two matches at No: 8. Against Scotland, and despite the fact that England were pushed around for most of the first half, and yet won by an unprecedented margin, the match showed what a pillar of strength and what an influential player Dean Richards is. Until he came on to replace the unfortunate Rodber, England were rudderless, but, following his arrival, it was very different. The second Grand Slam saw a host of other records broken during the course of those four matches. The victory at Murrayfield was the highest post-war margin of victory on that ground. Against Ireland, England scored their highest points total in a Five Nations match since 1907, and scored six tries in a match for only the third time in that period - but for the second time in five years against Ireland. It was also the sixth successive win against Ireland, home or away. In Paris, England scored four tries against France for the first time post-war and amassed their highest post-war score both away from home and against France. It was also England's fourth successive win away from home - a feat never accomplished before. In that match, Jonathan Webb scored 22 points beating Rob Andrew's record of 21 in a Five Nations match set against Wales in 1986. Against France, Webb scored his 50th penalty goal for England: only "Dusty" Hare has scored more with 67.

By the end of the season, England had scored 118 points, easily beating the record set by Wales in 1976. They also scored 15 tries, the highest in any post war season by any team. Jonathan Werbb's 67 points in the season became the highest individual points total in a Five Nations season, beating the 60 scored by Simon Hodgkinson the previous season. Webb also became the highest individual total points scorer, with 246, beating "Dusty" Hare's previous record of 240 with his penultimate penalty goal against Wales.

England have now lost only one Five Nations match in the previous three seasons. However, in that time, they have lost twice to Australia, once at home and once away, lost once to New Zealand at home and once to Argentina away. The message must be that England still have some way to go to compete on equal terms with the southern hemisphere nations. Indeed, Geoff Cooke, who was re-appointed in April to continue as Team Manager until the World Cup in South Africa in 1995, said as much in his report at the end of the season, and cautioned that England could well slip to 4th place in the World Rankings behind Australia, New Zealand and South Africa.

It had been a lighter season than last when grim determination and Simon Hodgkinson's metronomic boot seemed to have taken some of the very soul of the game away for ever. The World Cup had its lighter moments, but basically it served to remind the Home Nations that there was still a long way to go to the top. England's performance in the 1992 Five Nations only re-emphasised that position. They were certainly capable of excellence, but they could not sustain it over a prolonged period as is vitally necessary in pursuit of world pre-eminence. The Five Nations opposition in 1992 was as weak as it had been for some time, and as such, flattered England to deceive, but the game as a whole had grown immensely, due in no small part to to England's successive Grand Slams, which, in fairness, in any circumstances, is no mean feat. At the end of the season, both Mickey Skinner and Simon Halliday, 21 and 23 caps respectively, had played their last match for England and returned, also respectively, to computer programming and stock-broking.

FIVE NATIONS CHAMPIONSHIP TABLE:

Won: **Grand Slam, Triple Crown, Championship Title and Calcutta Cup**

		Played	Won	Lost	Drawn	Points: For	Against	Tries: For	Against	Title Points
1	**ENGLAND**	4	4	0	0	118	29	15	4	8
2 =	France	4	2	2	0	75	62	10	5	4
2 =	Scotland	4	2	2	0	47	56	4	4	4
2 =	Wales	4	2	2	0	40	63	2	5	4
5	Ireland	4	0	4	0	46	116	3	16	0

Home Games: beat Ireland 38 -= 9, (six tries to one); beat Wales 24 - 0, (three tries to nil)

Away Games: beat Scotland 25 - 7, (two tries to one); beat France 31 - 13, (four tries to two).

1st match   **ENGLAND** **26 pts**   v   **CANADA** **13 pts**

	Caps					Caps		
15	28th	J.M.Webb	(Bath)	.		8th	S.Stewart	(UBC OBs)
14	1st	I.G.Hunter	(Northampton)	.		15th	S.Gray	(Kats)
13	37th	W.D.C.Carling (Capt)	(Harlequins)	.		1st	M.Williams	(Meralomas)
12	23rd	J.C.Guscott	(Bath)	.		15th	I.Stuart	(Vancouver RC)
11	1st	T.Underwood	(Leicester)	.		5th	D.Lougheed	(Toronto Welsh)
10	49th	C.R.Andrew	(Wasps)	.		19th	G.Rees	(Oak Bay Castaways)
9	10th	C.D.Morris	(Orrell)	.		7th	J.Graf	(UBC OBs)
1	20th	J.Leonard	(Harlequins)	.		8th	D.Jackart	(UBC OBs)
2	3rd & last	C.J.Olver	(Northampton)	.		15th	K.Svoboda	(Ajax Wanderers)
3	1st	V.E.Ubogu	(Bath)	.		18th	E.Evans	(UBC OBs)
4	7th	M.C.Bayfield	(Northampton)	.		1st	J.Knauer	(Meralomas)
5	51st	W.A.Dooley	(Preston G'hoppers)	.		12th	N.Hadley (Capt)	(UBC OBs)
6	3rd & last	D.Ryan	(Wasps)	.		3rd	I.Gordon	(James Bay)
7	53rd	P.J.Winterbottom	(Harlequins)	.		15th	G.MacKinnon	(Ex-Britannia Lions)
8	34th	D.Richards	(Leicester)	.		2nd	C.McKenzie	(UBC OBs)

Referee: G.Simmonds   (Wales)

SCORERS:

				0 - 3		G.Rees	Penalty Goal
I.G.Hunter	Try	(1st)	5 - 3			
J.C.Guscott	Try	(14th)	10 - 3			
			10 - 6		G.Rees	Penalty Goal
J.M.Webb	Penalty Goal		13 - 6			
J.M.Webb	Penalty Goal		16 - 6			
			Half-time			
P.J.Winterbottom	Try	(3rd & last)	21 - 6			
			21 - 11		J.Graf	Try
			21 - 13		G.Rees	Conversion
I.G.Hunter	Try	(2nd)	26 - 13			

POINTS:

I.G.Hunter	10 points	(10)		G.Rees	8 points
J.M.Webb	6 points	(252)		J.Graf	5 points
J.Guscott	5 points	(60)			
P.J.Winterbottom	5 points	(13)			

MATCH COMMENTARY:

The first Rugby Union International at Wembley Stadium, necessary because of re-building works at Twickenham was not a memorable occasion. The gap between the sides in experience and potential was immense, but, in the event, Canada played well and England played badly, and the match, as a spectacle, suffered. Despite their newly designed shirts, England were never able to take control of the game because Canada, to their credit, refused to let them and England submitted. Four tries to one flatters England; the difference between the two sides on the day is better measured by the points margin. Although it was only the opening match of the season, it was not a convinvcing display and the point was again clearly made - if England are denied the opportunity to do what they set out to do by their opponents, then England have no other option available and cannot, so to speak, think on their feet.

Ian Hunter did well to score two tries (now worth five points each) on his debut, emulating Dean Richards' feat in 1986.

10th match   **ENGLAND   33 pts**   v   **SOUTH AFRICA   16 pts**

	Caps					Caps		
15	29th	**J.M.Webb**	(Bath)	.	3rd	**J.T.J.van Rensberg**	(Transvaal)
14	2nd	**T.Underwood**	(Leicester)	.	5th	**J.T.Small**	(Transvaal)
13	38th	**W.D.C.Carling (Capt)**	(Harlequins)	.	24th & last	**D.M.Gerber**	(Western Province)
12	24th	**J.C.Guscott**	(Bath)	.	5th	**P.G.Muller**	(Natal)
11	56th	**R.Underwood**	(RAF/Leicester)	.	3rd	**J.Olivier**	(Northern Transvaal)
10	50th	**C.R.Andrew**	(Wasps)	.	28th & last	**H.E.Botha (Capt)**	(Transvaal)
9	11th	**C.D.Morris**	(Orrell)	.	7th & last	**G.D.Wright**	(Transvaal)
1	21st	**J.Leonard**	(Harlequins)	.	5th	**J.J.Styger**	(Orange Free State)
2	41st	**B.C.Moore**	(Harlequins)	.	3rd	**W.G.Hills**	(Northern Transvaal)
3	2nd	**V.E.Ubogu**	(Bath)	.	1st	**K.S.Andrews**	(Western Province)
4	8th	**M.C.Bayfield**	(Northampton)	.	3rd	**H.Hattingh**	(Northern Transvaal)
5	52nd	**W.A.Dooley**	(Preston G'hoppers)	.	7th & last	**A.W.Malan**	(Northern Transvaal)
6	23rd	**M.C.Teague**	(Moseley)	.	3rd	**C.P.Strauss**	(Western Province)
7	54th	**P.J.Winterbottom**	(Harlequins)	.	1st	**F.C.Smit**	(Western Province)
8	1st	**B.B.Clarke**	(Bath)	.	3rd	**A.Richter**	(Northern Transvaal)

1st   P.R.de Glanville (Bath) for T.Underwood - 55

Referee: S.R.Hilditch   (Ireland)

SCORERS:

J.M.Webb	Penalty Goal		3 - 0			
			3 - 3	**H.E.Botha**	Penalty Goal
			3 - 6	**H.E.Botha**	Penalty Goal
T.Underwood	Try	(1st)	8 - 6		
			8 - 9	**H.E.Botha**	Drop Goal
			8 - 14	**C.P.Strauss**	Try
			8 - 16	**H.E.Botha**	Conversion
J.M.Webb	Penalty Goal		11 - 16		
			Half-time		
J.C.Guscott	Try	(15th)	16 - 16		
J.M.Webb	Conversion		18 - 16		
J.M.Webb	Penalty Goal		21 - 16		
C.D.Morris	Try	5th & last	26 - 16		
J.M.Webb	Conversion		28 - 16		
W.D.C.Carling	Try	(7th)	33 - 16		

POINTS:

J.M.Webb	13 points	(265)	**H.E.Botha**	11 points
T.Underwood, J.C.Guscott	5 points	(5),(65)	**C.P.Strauss**	5 points
C.D.Morris and W.D.C.Carling	each	(21),(29)		

MATCH COMMENTARY:

In the first match between the two countries in Britain since 1969, South Africa held their own in the first half but were wholly out-played in the second, and conceded the greatest number of points in their history. England won comfortably, but not impressively, because in the first half they struggled in the set pieces and allowed South Africa in general, and Naas Botha in particular, to dictate events. In the second half however, it became a different story with Martin Bayfield assuming command in the lines-out and Peter Winterbottom immensely effective in the loose. Two of England's tries came from Rob Andrew's clever exploitation of the opposition backs lying up on, or in front of, the gain line.

69th match   **ENGLAND   16 pts**   v   **FRANCE   15 pts**

	Caps					Caps		
15	30th	J.M.Webb	(Bath)	.	33rd	J-B.Lafond	(Begles)
14	2nd	I.G.Hunter	(Northampton)	.	24th	P.Saint-Andre	(Montferrand)
13	39th	W.D.C.Carling (Capt)	(Harlequins)	.	85th	P.Sella	(Agen)
12	25th	J.C.Guscott	(Bath)	.	9th	T.Lacroix	(Dax)
11	57th	R.Underwood	(RAF/Leicester)	.	6th	P.Hontas	(Biarritz)
10	51st	C.R.Andrew	(Wasps)	.	34th	D.Camberabero	(Beziers)
9	12th	C.D.Morris	(Orrell)	.	9th	A.Heuber	(Toulon)
1	22nd	J.Leonard	(Harlequins)	.	30th	L.Armary	(Lourdes)
2	42nd	B.C.Moore	(Harlequins)	.	11th	J-F.Tordo	(Nice)
3	34th	J.A.Probyn	(Wasps)	.	4th	L.Seigne	(Merignac)
4	9th	M.C.Bayfield	(Northampton)	.	31st	O.Roumat	(Dax)
5	1st	M.O.Johnson	(Leicester)	.	15th	A.Benazzi	(Agen)
6	24th	M.C.Teague	(Moseley)	.	9th	P.Benetton	(Agen)
7	55th	P.J.Winterbottom	(Harlequins)	.	20th	L.Cabannes	(Racing Club)
8	2nd	B.B.Clarke	(Bath)	.	28th	M.Cecillon (Capt)	(Bourgoin)

		.	51st	F.Mesnel (Racing Club) for Sella - 32
		.	3rd	S.Ougier (Toulouse) for Lacroix - 50

Referee: J.Fleming   (Scotland)

SCORERS:

J.M.Webb	Penalty Goal		3 - 0			
			3 - 5	P.Saint-Andre	Try	
			3 - 7	D.Camberabero	Conversion	
J.M.Webb	Penalty Goal		6 - 7			
			6 - 12	P.Saint-Andre	Try	
I.G.Hunter	Try	rd & last)	11 - 12			
J.M.Webb	Conversion		13 - 12			
			Half-time			
J.M.Webb	Penalty Goal		16 - 12			
			16 - 15	D.Camberabero	Penalty Goal	

POINTS:

J.M.Webb	11 points	(276)	P.Saint-Andre	10 points	
I.G.Hunter	5 points	(15)	D.Camberabero	5 points	

MATCH COMMENTARY:

In pursuit of their third successive Grand Slam, England could not have had a more shaky start. Within fifteen minutes they were two tries down. First, Jonathan Webb dropped a high ball under his posts, Saint-Andre retrieved and touched down. Then Webb was out-jumped by the same Saint-Andre in going for another high ball with the same result. Later in the first half with France in a 12 point to 6 lead, and England struggling, Jonathan Webb hit the post with a penalty goal attempt and the rebound fell straight into the arms of Ian Hunter whose try, followed by Webb's conversion, put England into a one point lead at the break. Then England settled down and gained much more possession especially from Martin Johnson, Wade Dooley's last minute replacement, in the lines-out. A penalty goal for each side was the only scoring in the second half and England were just holding on to their slender lead when Lady Luck again had a significant say. In the closing minutes, Jean-Baptiste Lafond, from full-back, attempted a drop goal and the ball hit the cross-bar and bounced back, not into waiting French arms leading to a dramatic last-minute winning try, but harmlessly into space for England to clear and win the match. The French could rightly feel somewhat aggrieved.

99th match   **ENGLAND 9 pts**   v   **WALES 10 pts**

	Caps					Caps		
15	31st	J.M.Webb	(Bath)	.		6th	M.A.Rayer	(Cardiff)
14	3rd	I.G.Hunter	(Northampton)	.		33rd	I.C.Evans (Capt)	(Llanelli)
13	40th	W.D.C.Carling (Capt)	(Harlequins)	.		23rd	M.R.Hall	(Cardiff)
12	26th	J.C.Guscott	(Bath)	.		15th	I.S.Gibbs	(Swansea)
11	58th	R.Underwood	(RAF/Leicester)	.		2nd	W.T.Procter	(Llanelli)
10	52nd	C.R.Andrew	(Wasps)	.		9th	N.R.Jenkins	(Pontypridd)
9	13th	C.D.Morris	(Orrell)	.		44th	R.N.Jones	(Swansea)
1	23rd	J.Leonard	(Harlequins)	.		1st	R.L.Evans	(Llanelli)
2	43rd	B.C.Moore	(Harlequins)	.		1st	N.Meek	(Pontypool)
3	35th	J.A.Probyn	(Wasps)	.		7th	H.Williams-Jones	(South Wales Police)
4	10th	M.C.Bayfield	(Northampton)	.		13th	G.O.Llewellyn	(Neath)
5	53rd	W.A.Dooley	(Preston G'hoppers)	.		6th	A.H.Copsey	(Llanelli)
6	25th	M.C.Teague	(Moseley)	.		12th	E.W.Lewis	(Llanelli)
7	56th	P.J.Winterbottom	(Harlequins)	.		10th	R.E.Webster	(Swansea)
8	3rd	B.B.Clarke	(Bath)	.		6th	S.Davies	(Swansea)

2nd   P.R.de Glanville (Bath) for Hunter -

Referee: J.Dume   (France)

SCORERS:	J.M.Webb	Penalty Goal		3 - 0			
				3 - 3	N.R.Jenkins	Penalty Goal	
	J.M.Webb	Penalty Goal		6 - 3			
	J.C.Guscott	D'p Goal	(2nd)	9 - 3			
				9 - 8	I.C.Evans	Try	
				9 - 10	N.R.Jenkins	Conversion	
			Half-time				
				9 - 10			

POINTS:	J.M.Webb	6 points	(282)	N.R.Jenkins	5 points
	J.C.Guscott	3 points	(68)	I.C.Evans	5 points

MATCH COMMENTARY:

England had not been convincing winners against either Canada or South Africa, and they had been desperately lucky to beat France, and, this time, Wales exposed the inadequacies, but it was, as Alan Davies the Welsh coach said, " a majestic performance". England had no answer to Ieuan Evans' try nor to the ferocious and heroic Welsh tackling. Gareth Llewellyn more than matched Dooley and Bayfield in the lines-out, and the Welsh front row gave every bit as good as they got. All Wales, especially Scott Gibbs and Mike Hall, put on a defensive performance that surpassed anything in living memory, and England could not rise above it. England's response in the second half was very aggressive, and after the shock and the indignity of Ieuan Evans' splendid try, when Rory Underwood was caught almost literally napping, they demonstrated some considerable strength of character in doubling and redoubling their efforts to regain the lead. Outstanding in this respect was Dewi Morris who twice got desperately close to the line only to be thwarted by a heroic Welsh defence. Nor was he the only one to get close; time and again England assaulted the Welsh line and time and again every Welsh player dug that little bit deeper and kept them out. Cardiff had seen nothing like this almost in living memory. At long last in some respects, and in no time in others, Monsieur Dume blew the final whistle and the much-heralded Welsh revival had begun. English dreams had died yet again at Cardiff.

110th match
100th Calcutta Cup

ENGLAND   26 pts   v   SCOTLAND   12 pts

	Caps					Caps		
15	32nd	J.M.Webb	(Bath)	.	45th	A.G.Hastings (Capt)	(Watsonians)
14	3rd	T.Underwood	(Leicester)	.	30th	A.G.Stanger	(Hawick)
13	41st	W.D.C.Carling (Capt)	(Harlequins)	.	46th	S.Hastings	(Watsonians)
12	27th	J.C.Guscott	(Bath)	.	6th	A.G.Shiel	(Melrose)
11	59th	R.Underwood	(RAF/Leicester)	.	4th	D.A.Stark	(Boroughmuir)
10	9th	S.Barnes	(Bath)	.	33rd	C.M.Chalmers	(Melrose)
9	14th	C.D.Morris	(Orrell)	.	28th	G.Armstrong	(Jedforest)
1	24th	J.Leonard	(Harlequins)	.	5th	P.H.Wright	(Boroughmuir)
2	44th	B.C.Moore	(Harlequins)	.	25th	K.S.Milne	(Heriot's FP)
3	36th	J.A.Probyn	(Wasps)	.	29th	A.P.Burnell	(London Scottish)
4	11th	M.C.Bayfield	(Northampton)	.	4th	A.I.Reed	(Bath)
5	54th	W.A.Dooley	(Preston G'hoppers)	.	28th	D.F.Cronin	(London Scottish)
6	26th	M.C.Teague	(Moseley)	.	14th	D.J.Turnbull	(Hawick)
7	57th	P.J.Winterbottom	(Harlequins)	.	4th	I.R.Morrison	(London Scottish)
8	4th	B.B.Clarke	(Bath)	.	18th	G.W.Weir	(Melrose)

1st	G.P.J.Townsend (Gala) for Chalmers - 24
2nd	K.M.Logan (Stirling C) for S.Hastings - 65

Referee: B.Stirling   (Ireland)

SCORERS:

			0 - 3	A.G.Hastings	Penalty Goal
J.M.Webb	Penalty Goal		3 - 3		
			3 - 6	C.M.Chalmers	Drop Goal
J.C.Guscott	Try	(16th)	8 - 6		
J.M.Webb	Penalty Goal		11 - 6		
			Half-time		
R.Underwood	Try	(36th)	16 - 6		
T.Underwood	Try	(2nd)	21 - 6		
J.M.Webb	Conversion		23 - 6		
			23 - 9	A.G.Hastings	Penalty Goal
J.M.Webb	Penalty Goal		26 - 9		
			26 - 12	A.G.Hastings	Penalty Goal

POINTS:

J.M.Webb	11 points	(293)	A.G.Hastings	9 points
J.C.Guscott, R.Underwood	5 points	(73),(145)	C.M.Chalmers	3 points
and T.Underwood	each	(10)		

MATCH COMMENTARY:

England had made two changes following the surprise defeat at Cardiff in replacing Rob Andrew with Stuart Barnes, and Ian Hunter with Tony Underwood. The 100th Calcutta Cup match saw Scotland playing at Twickenham for the Triple Crown, a crusade which they had last fulfilled in 1938. In the event, Stuart Barnes masterminded three excellent English tries, and Scotland were well beaten. Craig Chalmers' departure with a broken arm after 20 minutes removed Scotland's play-maker, and thereafter they appeared unco-ordinated and lacking direction. Stuart Barnes, winning only his ninth cap in ten seasons, then did what he had said he would do all week - get the England backs moving. Guscott's and the two Underwood tries all came from sharp breaks by Stuart Barnes, but, it has to be said, also owed much to fine angled running and well-timed passes. They were sights for sore English eyes.

106th match   **ENGLAND   3 pts**   v   **IRELAND   17 pts**

	Caps					Caps		
15	33rd & last	J.M.Webb	(Bath)	.	3rd	C.P.Clarke	(Terenure College)
14	4th	T.Underwood	(Leicester)	.	10th	R.M.Wallace	(Garryowen)
13	42nd	W.D.C.Carling (Capt)	(Harlequins)	.	14th	V.J.G.Cunningham	(St Mary's College)
12	28th	J.C.Guscott	(Bath)	.	16th	P.P.A.Danaher	(Garryowen)
11	60th	R.Underwood	(RAF/Leicester)	.	16th	S.P.Geoghegan	(London Irish)
10	10th & last	S.Barnes	(Bath)	.	2nd	E.P.Elwood	(Lansdowne)
9	15th	C.D.Morris	(Orrell)	.	29th	M.T.Bradley (Capt)	(Cork Constitution)
1	25th	J.Leonard	(Harlequins)	.	18th	N.J.Popplewell	(Greystones)
2	45th	B.C.Moore	(Harlequins)	.	13th	T.J.Kingston	(Dolphin)
3	37th & last	J.A.Probyn	(Wasps)	.	3rd	P.M.Clohessy	(Young Munster)
4	12th	M.C.Bayfield	(Northampton)	.	8th	P.S.Johns	(Dungannon)
5	55th & last	W.A.Dooley	(Preston G'hoppers)	.	15th	M.J.Galwey	(Shannon)
6	27th & last	M.C.Teague	(Moseley)	.	14th	P.T.J.O'Hara	(Cork Constitution)
7	58th & last	P.J.Winterbottom	(Harlequins)	.	12th	W.D.McBride	(Malone)
8	5th	B.B.Clarke	(Bath)	.	18th	B.F.Robinson	(London Irish)

Referee: A.MacNeill   (Australia)

SCORERS:

			0 - 3	E.Elwood	Penalty Goal
	J.M.Webb	Penalty Goal	3 - 3		
			3 - 6	E.Elwood	Drop Goal
			Half-time		
			3 - 9	E.Elwood	Penalty Goal
			3 - 12	E.Elwood	Drop Goal
			3 - 17	M.J.Galwey	Try

POINTS:

	J.M.Webb	3 points	(296)	E.Elwood	12 points
				M.J.Galwey	5 points

MATCH COMMENTARY:

England were unchanged following their impressive win over Scotland, and knew that they had to beat Ireland by a substantial margin to have any chance of finishing with a better points difference than France. As it happened, fifteen Irishmen had other ideas for which England were woefully unprepared. The Irish played as only they can, like demented terriers, delighting in denting reputations, humbling the mighty and bringing everything down to earth. They all played magnificently, denying England everything, and Eric Elwood, winning only his second cap, conducted the orchestra and did the business with his boot until Mick Galwey's try finally put the boot in. The transformation in the side which had beaten Scotland was difficult to comprehend and those who had earned a sweet victory with consummate authority then, had now to swallow the bitter pill of defeat. It seemed that Stuart Barnes, playing Cinderella at the Twickenham Ball, could do nothing back in the kitchen at Lansdowne Road because the ugly sisters (with respect) just did not permit it. It is not as if England did not try, and cruised through the match with an air of detatched complacency. They did try, very hard indeed, but nothing went right and the fighting Irish were always half a second quicker in thought and deed - and probably in word too in the close exchanges. An astonishing Irish performance against the team who were quoted at 6-1 on in a local bookmakers in the morning. It would have been a memorable night in Dublin !!

SUMMARY OF THE SEASON - 1992 - 93:

In the close season, the ruck/maul laws had been changed and the points value of a try had been increased from four to five, in an attempt to open up the game, encourage try scoring and reduce the incidence of penalty goals. Whether or not the changes will be successful in doing that remains to be seen, but the first signs were not encouraging. It was also announced mid-season, that a new Five Nations Championship Trophy would be available and that if an outright winner did not emerge, the Title would be determined on points difference. The expectations for this season after the two successive Grand Slams in 1991 and 1992, were, without needing the advantage of hindsight, far too high and, as such, were, inevitably, destined to be unrealised. The cracks appeared against a very mediocre Canadian side in the first International Rugby Union match to be played at Wembley Stadium. These cracks spread a little further in the fortuitous victory over France at Twickenham, and the dream collapsed totally, much to the unconstrained delight of 60,000 or so Welshmen, in the debacle at Cardiff Arms Park. Those expectations were already faded memories when the Irish had their triumphant say at Lansdowne Road in March In the two pre-Five Nations games in the autumn, four new caps were awarded, and three of those players, Tony Underwood, Victor Ubogu and Ben Clarke were to make a significant mark on the International scene in seasons to come. But it was the fourth, Ian Hunter, who was to make the first impression by scoring two tries on his debut, the first player to do so since Dean Richards achieved that distinction against Ireland in 1986. Martin Johnson, the Leicester lock, won his first cap due to Wade Dooley's last minute withdrawal from the French match, and, inconspicuously, a future England captain, Phil de Glanville appeared on two occasions in an England jersey this season as a replacement. When England beat South Africa at Twickenham in November, for only the third time, England scored their highest ever points total in the series of matches between the two countries. In this match too, Rob Andrew gained his 50th cap, only the fourth English player ever to do so - and the other three, Rory Underwood, Peter Winterbottom and Wade Dooley were also in the side. The Five Nation's Championship was where Geoff Cooke's unintended prediction was fulfilled when England shot themselves in the foot, in conceding a critical score to Wales from which they were not allowed to recover. A brief glimpse of what might have been was there in the match against Scotland, but then came the "down-to -earth-with-a-bump" trip to Dublin and the end of an eminently forgettable season. Many observers attributed England's failure to the new ruck/maul laws, but the truth is that while the changes might have altered the basis on which the two previous seasons' successes had been founded, and that while the law change did not enhance the game, England failed to adapt successfully to the change, whereas others did so better.

The end of the season also saw the end of the International careers of several illustrious players, and one or two others. Peter Winterbottom who won 58 caps over eleven seasons, Wade Dooley, 55 caps spanning nine seasons, Jeff Probyn, 37 caps over six seasons and Mike Teague, 27 caps over nine seasons, all gave sterling service to the cause oif International rugby. Indeed, Winterbottom, Dooley and Probyn each held the record for the most caps gained in their respective positions. So too did Jonathan Webb, 33 caps at full-back, already a qualified surgeon and the holder of the English individual points scoring record in Internationals of 296 points. Stuart Barnes gained the last of his 10 caps against Ireland after gaining his first against Australia in 1984. He was a player of immense talent and flair, a major inspiration behind the success of the Bath Club in the late '80s and '90s, and he had always been an understudy to Rob Andrew's leading role, and had spent much of his time on the England bench. Never one to keep his thoughts to himself, Barnes had rebelled occasionally against this constraint and talked himself out of possible International selection. Strangely both he and Andrew had played on opposing sides in the 'Varsity matches in 1982 and 1983 and each gained three blues. John Olver, another understudy, always the reserve hooker, retired from the International scene with three caps to continue his career as a schoolmaster at Stamford School, and Dean Ryan, a back row forward of considerable aggression and talent, who gained only three caps because he was playing at a time when England had a collection of back row forwards of world class all at the same time.

It had been an immensely disappointing season for England, although it cannot be denied that the sights had been set unrealistically high by the media, and to a certain extent, the general public, which in itself placed the team under an unnecessary degree of pressure. Nevertheless, a little less complacency at the outset, and ever more application must be the rule for the future, and with the wealth of talent already knocking at the 1st XV door, so to speak, continued success must be a distinct possibility.

Disappointing season or not, sixteen English players were invited to tour with the British Lions to New Zealand in the summer.

FIVE NATIONS CHAMPIONSHIP TABLE:

Won: **Calcutta Cup**

		Played	Won	Lost	Drawn	Points: For	Against	Tries: For	Against	Title Points
1	France	4	3	1	0	73	35	8	2	6
2	Scotland	4	2	2	0	50	40	3	4	4
2	**ENGLAND**	4	2	2	0	54	54	4	4	4
2	Ireland	4	2	2	0	45	53	2	5	4
5	Wales	4	1	3	0	34	74	3	5	2

Home Games: beat France 16 - 15, (one try to two): beat Scotland 26 - 12, (three tries to nil)

Away Games: lost to Wales 9 - 10, (no tries to one); lost to Ireland 3 - 17, (no tries to one).

THE WORLD CUP SEVENS - 1993

THE WORLD CUP SEVENS SQUAD:

ANDY HARRIMAN (Captain)	(Harlequins)
ADEDAYO ADEBAYO	(Bath)
NICK BEAL	(Northampton)
JUSTYN CASSELL	(Saracens)
LAWRENCE DALLAGLIO	(Wasps)
MATT DAWSON	(Northampton)
DAMIEN HOPLEY	(Wasps)
TIM RODBER	(Northampton)
DAVE SCULLY	(Wakefield)
CHRIS SHEASBY	(Harlequins)

Manager: **Peter Rossborough**   Coach: **Les Cusworth**

WORLD CUP SEVENS RESULTS:

Group D matches:	beat HONG KONG	40 - 5
	beat SPAIN	31 - 0
	lost to WESTERN SAMOA	28 - 10
	beat CANADA	33 - 0
	beat NAMIBIA	24 - 5

Quarter Finals - Group 2:	beat NEW ZEALAND	21 - 12
	beat SOUTH AFRICA	14 - 7
	lost to AUSTRALIA	21 - 12

Semi-Finals:	beat FIJI	21 - 7

WORLD CUP SEVENS FINAL:	beat AUSTRALIA	21 - 17

It was not the best venue, Murrayfield was half finished and the whole of the west side of the ground was a builders yard; it was not the best of Scottish weather, it was mainly wet and always very cold; and the organisation and administration left much to be desired in that it was a punishing three day schedule for the players - England played ten games, five on the final day - and the facilities available for the considerable crowd were at best spartan and hopelessly inadequate. Nevertheless, the tournament was very successful, was thoroughly enjoyed by observer and player alike, and offered some spectacular fare and some heroic endeavour.

England's squad of ten young, fit, enthusiastic players - they had only three full International caps amongst them, two by Tim Rodber and one by Andy Harriman - excelled themselves and from a quiet start in the early stages blossomed into peak form in the final stages of the tournament. In losing to Western Samoa in the first Group stage, England found themselves in the quarter-final group, having to play New Zealand, South Africa and Australia in that order, and before they met Australia they had already qualified for the semi-finals by beating New Zealand having led 21 - 0 at half-time, and South Africa having been 0 - 7 down in the first half. In the semi-final, under intense pressure from Fiji, England absorbed it all and struck back with two tries from Andy Harriman, the first after a break by Lawrence Dallaglio and clever footwork from he and Harriman, and the second following a tremendous try saving tackle by Dave Scully on the Fiji giant Rasari, and an astute pick-up and precision pass from Adebayo. The final was a dream come true with Andy Harriman beating David Campese on the outside for a try in the first minute from which England did not look back.

Credit was due to every member of the squad and to the Coach Les Cusworth, who had so little time to prepare, but the achievement was based on Harriman's pace - and his twelve tries; Beal's kicking - he missed only one conversion out of thirteen on the final day; Rodber's tackling; Sheasby and Dallaglio's work-rate; Scully's tenacity and courage; and Adebayo's perception and vision. And a worthy effort it was. As Simon Jones observed, the tournament has great potential for the future, but it should be moved to Hong Kong.

17th match   **ENGLAND   15 pts**   v   **NEW ZEALAND   9 pts**

	Caps					Caps		
15	1st	J.E.B.Callard	(Bath)			20th	J.K.R.Timu	(Otago)
14	5th	T.Underwood	(Leicester)			2nd	J.W.Wilson	(Otago)
13	43rd	W.D.C.Carling (Capt)	(Harlequins)			16th	F.E.Bunce	(North Harbour)
12	3rd	P.R.de Glanville	(Bath)			8th	E.Clarke	(Auckland)
11	61st	R.Underwood	(Leicester)			19th	V.L.Tuigamala	(Auckland)
10	53rd	C.R.Andrew	(Wasps)			2nd	M.C.G.Ellis	(Otago)
9	1st	K.P.P.Bracken	(Bristol)			2nd	S.T.Forster	(Otago)
1	26th	J.Leonard	(Harlequins)			7th	C.W.Dowd	(Auckland)
2	46th	B.C.Moore	(Harlequins)			56th	S.B.T.Fitzpatrick(Capt)	(Auckland)
3	3rd	V.E.Ubogu	(Bath)			11th	O.M.Brown	(Auckland)
4	2nd	M.O.Johnson	(Leicester)			32nd	I.D.Jones	(North Auckland)
5	14th	N.C.Redman	(Bath)			2nd	S.B.Gordon	(Waikato)
6	3rd	T.A.K.Rodber	(Northampton)			13th	J.W.Joseph	(Otago)
7	6th	B.B.Clarke	(Bath)			23rd	Z.V.Brooke	(Auckland)
8	35th	D.Richards	(Leicester)			12th	A.R.B.Pene	(Otago)

Referee: F.Burger   (South Africa)

SCORERS:	J.E.B.Callard	Penalty Goal		3 - 0		
	J.E.B.Callard	Penalty Goal		6 - 0		
				Half-time		
				6 - 3	J.W.Wilson	Penalty Goal
	J.E.B.Callard	Penalty Goal		9 - 3		
				9 - 6	J.W.Wilson	Penalty Goal
	C.R.Andrew	D'p Goal	(15th)	12 - 6		
				12 - 9	J.W.Wilson	Penalty Goal
	J.E.B.Callard	Penalty Goal		15 - 9		

POINTS:	J.E.B.Callard	12 points	(12)		J.W.Wilson	9 points
	C.R.Andrew	3 points	(151)			

MATCH COMMENTARY:

England played highly disciplined controlled rugby to record only their fourth ever victory over the All Blacks. With nine changes from the last disastrous match against Ireland, two of them, Guscott and Morris, absent through injury and 'flu respectively, the England side had an unfamiliar look with eight of the side having only 24 caps between them. But, to a man, they were heroes, all. They attacked the All Blacks, so far unbeaten on this tour, and fresh from having put 51 points past Scotland only a week earlier, in all phases of the game. They drove into New Zealand with bruising first-time tackles and denied them any momentum. The big back row were superior to their opposite numbers in all respects; the lines-out were even in possession obtained but all the quality ball was England's, and Nigel Redman had the game of his life. Rob Andrew was immaculate at fly-half and he effectively controlled the game. The two new caps, Kyran Bracken and Jonathan Callard came through their baptisms of fire with full credit and Callard's goal-kicking, having missed only two, spoke volumes for his confidence and temperament. Will Carling emulated Nick Farr-Jones' record of having led his country 36 times, and now he shares the distinction with John Pullin of having led England to victory over each of the three senior Southern Hemisphere IRB members. He is also only the second International captain to have won against all senior members of the IRB. Not a spectacular match, but a tremendous achievement.

THE ENGLAND TEAM WHO BEAT NEW ZEALAND AT TWICKENHAM ON NOVEMBER 27th 1993

Standing: J.P.Hall (Bench), P.R.de Glanville, B.B.Clarke, M.O.Johnson, T.A.K.Rodber, N.C.Redman, D.Richards, V.E.Ubogu, J.Leonard, G.C.Rowntree (Bench)

Seated: R.G.R.Dawe (Bench) M.J.S.Dawson (Bench) K.P.P.Bracken, C.R.Andrew, B.C.Moore, W.D.C.Carling (Captain) T.Underwood, J.E.B.Callard, R.Underwood,

S.Barnes (Bench), I.G.Hunter (Bench)

111th match

ENGLAND   15 pts   v   SCOTLAND   14 pts

101st Calcutta Cup

	Caps					Caps		
15	2nd	J.E.B.Callard	(Bath)	.	48th	A.G.Hastings (Capt)	(Watsonians)
14	6th	T.Underwood	(Leicester)	.	33rd	A.G.Stanger	(Hawick)
13	44th	W.D.C.Carling (Capt)	(Harlequins)	.	48th	S.Hastings	(Watsonians)
12	4th	P.R.de Glanville	(Bath)	.	16th	D.S.Wylie	(Stewart's Melville)
11	62nd	R.Underwood	(Leicester)	.	5th	K.M.Logan	(Stirling County)
10	54th	C.R.Andrew	(Wasps)	.	3rd	G.P.J.Townsend	(Gala)
9	2nd	K.P.P.Bracken	(Bristol)	.	29th	G.Armstrong	(Jedforest)
1	27th	J.Leonard	(Harlequins)	.	1st	A.V.Sharp	(Bristol)
2	47th	B.C.Moore	(Harlequins)	.	28th	K.S.Milne	(Heriot's FP)
3	4th	V.E.Ubogu	(Bath)	.	32nd	A.P.Burnell	(London Scottish)
4	3rd	M.O.Johnson	(Leicester)	.	2nd	D.S.Munro	
5	13th	M.C.Bayfield	(Northampton)	.	5th	A.I.Reed	(Bath)
6	21st & last	J.P.Hall	(Bath)	.	1st	P.Walton	(Northampton)
7	1st	N.A.Back	(Leicester)	.	7th	R.I.Wainwright	(Edinburgh Acad'ls)
8	7th	B.B.Clarke	(Bath)	.	21st	G.W.Weir	(Melrose)

.	6th	I.R.Smith (Gloucester) for Wainwright - 67
.	3rd	I.C.Jardine (Stirling Co) for S.Hastings - 71
.	2nd	B.W.Redpath (Melrose) - temporary

Referee: L.L.McLauchlan   (New Zealand)

SCORERS:

J.E.B.Callard	Penalty Goal	3 - 0		
		3 - 5	R.I.Wainwright	Try
		Half-time		
		3 - 8	A.G.Hastings	Penalty Goal
J.E.B.Callard	Penalty Goal	6 - 8		
J.E.B.Callard	Penalty Goal	9 - 8		
		9 - 11	A.G.Hastings	Penalty Goal
J.E.B.Callard	Penalty Goal	12 - 11		
		12 - 14	G.P.J.Townsend	Drop Goal
J.E.B.Callard	Penalty Goal	15 - 14		

POINTS:

J.E.B.Callard	15 points	(27)	A.G.Hastings	6 points
			R.I.Wainwright	5 points
			G.P.J.Townsend	3 points

MATCH COMMENTARY:

England made three changes from the pack which had dominated the All Blacks in November, and gave the much vaunted Neil Back his first taste of International rugby. Scotland had some morale to restore after the trouncing by New Zealand and a very much less than adequate performance in Cardiff three weeks ago. In the first 20 minutes England moved the ball with purpose and, but for heroic and last-ditch Scottish defence, could have scored two tries. As it was, Scotland survived, and their defensive success seemed to inspire them and demoralise England. After 28 minutes, Rob Wainwright broke away from a maul on the right and ran 22 metres to score the only try of the match. Thereafter, England lost direction and could do nothing constructive but land penalty goals. When in the last minute of normal time, a soaring Townsend drop goal put Scotland back in the lead, Murrayfield joy was unconfined until with the last kick of the match, Jonathan Callard stole the spoils for England. All credit to him, but the Scots were well and truly robbed. If only Gavin Hastings had not missed five penalty kicks at goal, he would have shed no post-match tears and justice would have been done.

107th match   **ENGLAND 12 pts**   v   **IRELAND 13 pts**

	Caps					Caps		
15	3rd	**J.E.B.Callard**	(Bath)	.		4th	**C.M.P.O'Shea**	(Lansdowne)
14	7th	**T.Underwood**	(Leicester)	.		14th	**R.M.Wallace**	(Garryowen)
13	45th	**W.D.C.Carling (Capt)**	(Harlequins)	.		1st	**M.J.Field**	(Malone)
12	5th	**P.R.de Glanville**	(Bath)	.		20th	**P.P.A.Danaher**	(Garryowen)
11	63rd	**R.Underwood**	(RAF/Leicester)	.		20th	**S.P.Geoghegan**	(London Irish)
10	55th	**C.R.Andrew**	(Wasps)	.		6th	**E.P.Elwood**	(Lansdowne)
9	3rd	**K.P.P.Bracken**	(Bristol)	.		33rd	**M.T.Bradley (Capt)**	(Cork Constitution)
1	28th	**J.Leonard**	(Harlequins)	.		22nd	**N.J.Popplewell**	(Greystones)
2	48th	**B.C.Moore**	(Harlequins)	.		17th	**T.J.Kingston**	(Dolphin)
3	5th	**V.E.Ubogu**	(Bath)	.		6th	**P.M.Clohessy**	(Young Munster)
4	4th	**M.O.Johnson**	(Leicester)	.		17th	**M.J.Galwey**	(Shannon)
5	14th	**M.C.Bayfield**	(Northampton)	.		24th	**N.P.J.Francis**	(Old Belvedere)
6	4th	**T.A.K.Rodber**	(Northampton)	.		22nd	**B.F.Robinson**	(Ballymena)
7	2nd	**N.A.Back**	(Leicester)	.		15th	**W.D.McBride**	(Malone)
8	1st	**S.O.Ojomoh**	(Bath)	.		12th	**P.S.Johns**	(Dungannon)

Referee: P.Thomas   (France)

SCORERS:

J.E.B.Callard	Penalty Goal	3 - 0			
		3 - 3	E.P.Elwood	Penalty Goal
J.E.B.Callard	Penalty Goal	6 - 3		
		6 - 8	S.P.Geoghegan	Try
		6 - 10	E.P.Elwood	Conversion
		Half-time		
J.E.B.Callard	Penalty Goal	9 - 10		
		9 - 13	E.P.Elwood	Penalty Goal
J.E.B.Callard	Penalty Goal	12 - 13		

POINTS:

J.E.B.Callard	12 points	(39)	E.P.Elwood	8 points
			S.P.Geoghegan	5 points

MATCH COMMENTARY:

All fifteen Irishmen seemed determined to continue where they left off after rattling England's cage in Dublin at the end of last season. They were all knees, elbows and aggression and the ferocity of their onslaught right from the kick-off knocked the English pack out of step, and they never regained their composure. As a result, possession was slow from the set piece, from the loose it was almost non-existent and from the lines-out it was, at best, erratic so that Kyran Bracken got the ball and the Irish pack - not always in that order - and his confidence suffered. Even with poor ball, Rob Andrew was not starved of possession but he rarely did other than boot it upfield, and when it was seen that Ireland could cope with that, no alternative tactic was forthcoming. The Irish try was a perfectly executed set move undertaken at speed and Simon Geoghegan left Tony Underwood with consummate ease. From that point on it never seemed remotely likely that England would, or could, win the match. The Irish kept up the pressure but their frequent indiscretions on the ground gave Jonathan Callard ample opportunity to put points the board, but he failed with four kicks at goal, two of which hit the upright. Anyway, it would have been a travesty had England won their second successive game by this dubious means. This was England's first Five Nations defeat at Twickenham since Wales won in 1988, and it was the first defeat at Twickenham in the Five Nations under the captaincy of Will Carling.

70th match   **ENGLAND   18 pts**   v   **FRANCE   14 pts**

	Caps					Caps		
15	4th & last	D.Pears	(Harlequins)	.		18th	J-L.Sadourny	(Colomiers)
14	4th	I.G.Hunter	(Northampton)	.		1st	W.Techoueyres	(Begles)
13	46th	W.D.C.Carling (Capt)	(Harlequins)	.		97th	P.Sella	(Agen)
12	6th	P.R.de Glanville	(Bath)	.		20th	T.Lacroix	(Dax)
11	64th	R.Underwood	(RAF/Leicester)	.		34th	P.Saint-Andre	(Montferrand)
10	56th	C.R.Andrew	(Wasps)	.		19th	A.Penaud	(Brive)
9	16th	C.D.Morris	(Orrell)	.		14th	F.Galthie	(Colomiers)
1	29th	J.Leonard	(Harlequins)	.		1st	L.Benezech	(Racing Club)
2	49th	B.C.Moore	(Harlequins)	.		14th	J-M.Gonzales	(Bayonne)
3	6th	V.E.Ubogu	(Bath)	.		15th	P.Gallart	(Beziers)
4	5th	M.O.Johnson	(Leicester)	.		8th	O.Merle	(Grenoble)
5	15th	N.C.Redman	(Bath)	.		43rd	O.Roumat (Capt)	(Dax)
6	5th	T.A.K.Rodber	(Northampton)	.		23rd	A.Benazzi	(Agen)
7	8th	B.B.Clarke	(Bath)	.		27th	L.Cabannes	(Racing Club)
8	2nd	S.O.Ojomoh	(Bath)	.		20th	P.Benetton	(Agen)

Referee: S.R.Hilditch   (Ireland)

SCORERS:

	C.R.Andrew	Penalty Goal		3 - 0		
				Half-time		
	C.R.Andrew	Penalty Goal		6 - 0		
	C.R.Andrew	Penalty Goal		9 - 0		
	C.R.Andrew	D'p Goal	(16th)	12 - 0		
				12 - 3	T.Lacroix	Penalty Goal
				12 - 8	A.Benazzi	Try
				12 - 11	T.Lacroix	Penalty Goal
	C.R.Andrew	Penalty Goal		15 - 11		
				15 - 14	T.Lacroix	Penalty Goal
	C.R.Andrew	Penalty Goal		18 - 14		

POINTS:

	C.R.Andrew	18 points	(169)		T.Lacroix	9 points
					A.Benazzi	5 points

MATCH COMMENTARY:

Showing five changes from the side which dithered and was totally indecisive against Ireland only two weeks ago, this England side put up an astonishing performance of controlled tenacity, determined, solid defence and an almost visible sense of purpose to record their seventh successive win over France and their fourth successive triumph in Paris. No matter that, yet again, no tries were scored, this was the way that England had beaten France before and they believed that they could do so again, and they were right. The heroes of the hour were Rob Andrew, at his influential best; Will Carling whose leadership and tackling were exemplary; the entire pack, not least Nigel Redman and Victor Ubogu who was given a torrid time in the early set-pieces and courageously stood his ground. Dewi Morris excelled again and David Pears, at last at full-back, never put a foot wrong under a series of high balls. England's methodology achieved the result and effectively snuffed out the French flair by destroying their confidence. This tactic also stifles individual flair and talent in the England side, and the game, if not the result, suffers. Pierre Berbizier is right - Five Nations style rugby will never dominate the Southern Hemisphere sides. A week earlier, Geoff Cooke had announced his intention to resign in March, before the tour to South Africa - perhaps he agreed with Berbizier !!

100th match　　　**ENGLAND　15 pts**　　v　　**WALES　8 pts**

	Caps					Caps		
15	5th	I.G.Hunter	(Northampton)	.	15th	M.A.Rayer	(Cardiff)
14	8th	T.Underwood	(Leicester)	.	41st	I.C.Evans (Capt)	(Llanelli)
13	47th	W.D.C.Carling (Capt)	(Harlequins)	.	29th	M.R.Hall	(Cardiff)
12	7th	P.R.de Glanville	(Bath)	.	8th	N.G.Davies	(Llanelli)
11	65th	R.Underwood	(RAF/Leicester)	.	6th	N.Walker	(Cardiff)
10	57th	C.R.Andrew	(Wasps)	.	21st	N.R.Jenkins	(Pontypridd)
9	17th	C.D.Morris	(Orrell)	.	10th	R.H.St J.B.Moon	(Llanelli)
1	30th	J.Leonard	(Harlequins)	.	8th	R.L.Evans	(Llanelli)
2	50th	B.C.Moore	(Harlequins)	.	14th	G.R.Jenkins	(Swansea)
3	7th	V.E.Ubogu	(Bath)	.	10th	J.D.Davies	(Neath)
4	6th	M.O.Johnson	(Leicester)	.	39th	P.T.Davies	(Llanelli)
5	16th	N.C.Redman	(Bath)	.	25th	G.O.Llewellyn	(Neath)
6	6th	T.A.K.Rodber	(Northampton)	.	24th	E.W.Lewis	(Llanelli)
7	9th	B.B.Clarke	(Bath)	.	8th	M.A.Perego	(Llanelli)
8	36th	D.Richards	(Leicester)	.	5th	L.S.Quinnell	(Llanelli)
	1st	M.J.Catt (Bath) for Andrew - 77		.	11th	A.H.Copsey (Llanelli) for Lewis - 49

Referee:　J.M.Flemimg　　(Scotland)

SCORERS:	R.Underwood	Try	(37th)	5 - 0		
	C.R.Andrew	Conversion		7 - 0		
				7 - 3	N.R.Jenkins	Penalty Goal
				Half-time		
	T.A.K.Rodber	Try	(1st)	12 - 3		
	C.R.Andrew	Penalty Goal		15 - 3		
				15 - 8	N.Walker	Try

	R.Underwood	5 points	(150)		N.Walker	5 points	
	T.A.K.Rodber	5 points	(5)		N.R.Jenkins	3 points	
	C.R.Andrew	5 points	(174)				

MATCH COMMENTARY:

At the beginning of the season, it would have been impossible to imagine the scenario - Wales coming to Twickenham for the Grand Slam, and, on the same day, Scotland playing France for the Wooden Spoon !　England had reassembled the pack which had beaten New Zealand in November, and Ian Hunter had been chosen in his favourite, and club, position at full-back.　England needed to win by a margin of sixteen points if they were to deny Wales the title, and they started off with that objective clearly in mind. The opening score, and England's first try in six matches came in the thirteenth minute when Rory Underwood scored his 37th International from a dazzlig move at full pace. For the next half hour, Wales were torn apart with Richards and Redman time and again ripping possession from the Welsh grasp. Further vibrant attacking play saw Carling squeezed into touch just short of the line and minutes later Tim Rodber stole the ball from a Welsh throw and scored the second try. With a 15-3 lead, England should have sewn it up, but their lack of killer instinct allowed Wales to fight back and score a consolation try through Nigel Walker to ensure that, although they lost the match, they won the Championship Title and pushed England into second place.　Geoff Cooke retired on an apparently high note with four wins out of five in the season, but some of those were of dubious quality and, anyway, England scored only two tries in those five matches - but nineteen penalty goals !!

SUMMARY OF THE SEASON - 1993 - 94:

This season, the last of Geoff Cooke's successful stewardship if England's International fortunes, was one where England had every opportunity to take another Grand Slam, it would have been the third in four years, but they failed to do so, and possibly did not even consider the possibility because of a fundamental lack of self-belief. That was the only missing ingredient, they had talent in abundance in all positions on the field, yet lacked faith in themselves. The living proof of the old adage "If you think you can, you might, if you don't think you can, you wont". England didn't, and didn't.

After a host of seassoned players had retired from International rugby at the end of the previous season, fears were expressed that there were too few players of sufficient calibre waiting to succeed them, and that England, as a consequence, were in for a mediocre season. Not so, for the season started off very well. For the first match against New Zealand, Geoff Cooke schemed and plotted an England victory based on the, as it proved, correct theory that even the All Blacks would succumb to a totally dominant pack playing ten man rugby. And he was right. His foremost disciple of the day must have been Nigel Redman , who, in gaining his 14th cap, played the game of his life. So why should it be then that twelve of that same side should appear to be so hesitant and lacking confidence when they turn out at Murrayfield ? In the event, they scraped home by the narrowest of margins with the last kick of the match, where justice was certainly seen not to be done. With only two further changes, the same hesitancy and self-doubt emerged at Twickenham when the Irish came to play. England lost this one by a similarly narrow margin but never looked like winning the game at any stage. This time, as it should be, justice was definitely done and was seen to be done. On this performance, England would have no chance in Paris whatsoever and the Nation wondered what Geoff Cooke would do about it. What he did was the last thing that anybody expected - he resigned. His contract extended to the end of the World Cup in 1995, but Geoff decided it was time to go because, apparently, of his deteriorating relationships with the powers that be at Twickenham in the RFU. He announced five changes from the side who had lacked self-belief at home against Ireland. Out went Jon Callard, Tony Underwood, Kyran Bracken, Martin Bayfield and Neil Back and back came David Pears at full-back, Ian Hunter on the wing, Dewi Morris, Nigel Redman and Ben Clarke. Cooke convinced the side, as he had prior to the New Zealand match, that they could win in Paris playing ten man rugby hard, and they did just that without the irrelevance of scoring a try. Considering that six of the pack had not played at Parc des Princes before, it was a notable achievement. For the final match at Twickenham against Wales, (the 100th match between the two old adversaries, Wales having won 48, and England 39, so far,) Dean Richards' return meant that the same pack which had beaten New Zealand was now facing Wales who came with a somewhat improbable Grand Slam as their prize for winning at Twickenham this time around, and England, if they were to take the Title instead of Wales, had to win by a 16 point margin. England played well enough to win the match but not well enough to win the Title - a lack of self-belief again rearing its head. Rather incongruously, Ieuan Evans, on behalf of the beaten Welsh side , went up to collect the trophy, having lost the match. Had England won the match by the necessary sixteen point margin to take the title, it is conceivable that they could have done this, as they did in France, from the boot, and then would have won the title outright having scored, possibly, no tries at all. That would not have been a very satisfactory state of affairs.

The Welsh match marked Brian Moore's 50th cap for England; he is the fifth player to achieve this distinction.

There was only one departure from International rugby at the end of the season; John Hall, having won 21 caps over eleven seasons, turned all his attentions to furthering the cause of his beloved Bath where, on retiring, he became Director of Rugby.

After six and a half years at the helm, Geoff Cooke left the England structure and organisation infinitely stronger than he had found it in 1987. He had nurtured England to two Grand Slams and a World Cup Final, any one of which achievements would have been far from the wildest dreams of the most ardent England supporter at the time he took charge. The game itself had progressed with astonishing pace as well, and, in the circumstances, Cooke had done as much as he could to prepare his players for the advent of professionalism, and if he wished to stand down before that tide overwhelmed the game, his timing was commendable.

His successor, of course, was to be Jack Rowell, who had masterminded the Bath domination of English Club rugby for a decade and led them to five Courage League Championships and nine Pilkington Cup successes. His first task would be to manage the tour to South Africa in the summer, and his second and greater, would be to prepare England for the third World Cup, in South Africa in the summer of 1995.

FIVE NATIONS CHAMPIONSHIP TABLE:

Won: **Calcutta Cup**

		Played	Won	Lost	Drawn	Points: For	Against	Tries: For	Against	Title Points
1	Wales	4	3	1	0	78	51	7	4	6
2	**ENGLAND**	4	3	1	0	60	49	2	4	6
3	France	4	2	2	0	84	69	9	2	4
4	Ireland	4	1	2	1	49	70	1	5	3
5	Scotland	4	0	3	1	38	70	1	5	1

Home Games: lost to Ireland 12 - 13, (no tries to one): beat Wales 15 - 8, (two tries to one}

Away Games: beat Scotland 15 - 14, (no tries to two); beat France 18 - 14, (no tries to one)

ENGLAND TOUR TO SOUTH AFRICA - 1994

THE TOUR PARTY:

Manager:	J.Rowell	Assistant: Coaches:	J.Elliott R.Best & L.Cusworth	Captain:	W.D.C.Carling	

Full-backs:	P.A.Hull	(RAF/Bristol)	no caps	Forwards:	M.C.Bayfield	(Northampton)	14 caps
	D.Pears	(Harlequins)	4 caps		B.B.Clarke	(Bath)	9 caps
					R.G.R.Dawe	(Bath)	4 caps
Three-quarters:	A.A.Adebayo	(Bath)	no caps		L.B.N.Dallaglio	(Wasps)	no caps
	W.D.C.Carling	(Harlequins)	47 caps		M.O.Johnson	(Leicester)	6 caps
	M.J.Catt	(Bath)	2 caps		J.Leonard	(Harlequins)	30 caps
	P.R.de Glanville	(Bath)	7 caps		J.Mallett	(Bath)	1 cap
	D.P.Hopley	(Wasps)	no caps		B.C.Moore	(Harlequins)	50 caps
	S.Potter	(Leicester)	no caps		S.O.Ojomoh	(Bath)	2 caps
	R.Underwood	(RAF/Leicester)	65 caps		M.D.Poole	(Leicester)	no caps
	T.Underwood	(Leicester)	8 caps		N.C.Redman	(Bath)	16 caps
					D.Richards	(Leicester)	36 caps
Half-backs:	C.R.Andrew	(Wasps)	57 caps		T.A.K.Rodber	(Northamptom)	6 caps
	S.Barnes	(Bath)	10 caps		G.C.Rowntree	(Leicester)	no caps
	S.M.Bates	(Wasps)	1 cap		D.Ryan	(Wasps)	3 caps
	C.D.Morris	(Orrell)	17 caps		V.E.Ubogu	(Bath)	7 caps
Replacements:	J.E.B.Callard	(Bath)	3 caps		S.D.Shaw	(Bristol)	no caps

Jack Rowell, following his recent appointment, said little and saw everything on this disappointing tour of South Africa; no doubt he learned a great deal. England, too, learned a lot about the differences and the difficulties of playing on hard grounds and they became aware, painfully on some occasions, that percentage or ten man rugby is not the way to win matches in the southern hemisphere. There is rather more to it than that.

After four defeats in the first five matches of the tour, England went to Pretoria to face the might of the emerging South Africa. In the first quarter of an hour, England played, arguably, the finest rugby they have ever played in 124 years of International matches. Within those first sixteen minutes, England were twenty points up and the might of South Africa was humbled. The towering stands at Loftus Versfeld were silent and their mainly Afrikaans occupants were dumbfounded and speechless. The final margijn of the English victory was 17 points, exactly the same as it had been at Twickenham in 1992. Unfortunately, England could not keep it up, and South African revenge was sweet in Cape Town only one week later where the margin of victory was eighteen points - but the other way. Refereeing interpretations not infrequently disturbed England, and there can be little more frustrating than inconsistent application of the laws. But, by far the most disturbing incident came in the match against Eastern Province between the two Test matches. It was, at best, a very brutal match with the referee almost encouraging intimidation and violence. Jonathan Callard was at the bottom of a ruck and had his face raked by an Eastern Province boot. Tim Rodber saw it, and lost his temper. Consequence, Callard had 25 stiches above the eye, the perpetrator got a ticking off, and Tim Rodber was sent off - only the second player to experience this indignity in an English jersey. The respective disciplinary committees did nothing, and Rodber played in the Test four days later. As an example to others this is totally unacceptable, and the answer must lie in proper, effective, authoritative refereeing on the field and just and consistent administrative support for the referees off it, to eradicate such foul play.

The tour was a valuable lesson, especially for the World Cup in twelve months time, and it clearly showed that England have much ability, but that they need to be more flexible and adaptable, and above all, more consistent, to reap rewards at the very top level.

TOUR RESULTS:

May 18th	Orange Free State	at Bloenfontein	LOST	11 - 22	(one try to four)
May 21st	Natal	at Durban	LOST	6 - 21	(no tries)
May 25th	Western Transvaal	at Potchefstroom	WON	26 - 24	(two tries each)
May 28th	Transvaal	at Johannesburg	LOST	21 - 24	(two tries each)
May 31st	South Africa "A"	at Kimberley	LOST	16 - 19	(one try to two)
June 4th	SOUTH AFRICA	at Pretoria	WON	32 - 15	(two tries to nil)
June 7th	Eastern Province	at Port Elizabeth	WON	31 - 13	(three tries to one)
June 11th	SOUTH AFRICA	at Cape Town	LOST	9 - 27	(no tries to two)

THE ENGLAND SQUAD FOR THE EIGHT MATCH TOUR TO SOUTH AFRICA IN 1994

Back Row: D.Richards, T.Underwood, V.E.Ubogu, G.C.Rowntree, P.R.de Glanville, J.Mallett, R.G.R.Dawe, P.A.Hull, M.J.Catt, A.A.Adebayo, J.Leonard,

Middle Row: S.O.Ojomoh, J.C.Guscott, L.B.N.Dallaglio, B.B.Clarke, M.D.Poole, M.O.Johnson, M.C.Bayfield, T.A.K.Rodber, N.C.Redman, D.Ryan, D.P.Hopley, D.Pears, Official,

Seated: R.Underwood, T.Crystal (Team Doctor), C.D.Morris, L.Cusworth (Coach) B.C.Moore, J.Rowell (Manager), W.D.C.Carling (Captain), R.Best (Coach), C.R.Andrew, J.Elliott (Coach), S.Barnes, K.Murphy (Physio), S.M.Bates.

S.Potter replaced J.C.Guscott before departure.

11th match   **ENGLAND**   **32 pts**   v   **SOUTH AFRICA**   **15 pts**

	Caps				Caps		
15	1st	**P.Hull**	(RAF/Bristol)				
					4th	A.J.Joubert	(Natal)
14	9th	**T.Underwood**	(Leicester)				
13	48th	**W.D.C.Carling (Capt)**	(Harlequins)		13th	J.T.Small	(Natal)
12	8th	**P.R.de Glanville**	(Bath)		1st	B.Venter	(Orange Free State)
11	66th	**R.Underwood**	(RAF/Leicester)		13th	P.G.Muller	(Natal)
					2nd	C.M.Williams	(Western Province)
10	58th	**C.R.Andrew**	(Wasps)				
9	18th	**C.D.Morris**	(Orrell)		3rd	H.P.le Roux	(Transvaal)
					3rd	J.H.van der Westhuize	(North Transvaal)
1	31st	**J.Leonard**	(Harlequins)				
2	51st	**B.C.Moore**	(Harlequins)		1st	A.H.le Roux	(Orange Free State)
3	8th	**V.E.Ubogu**	(Bath)		4th	J.Allan	(Natal)
4	15th	**M.C.Bayfield**	(Northampton)		5th	I.S.Swart	(Transvaal)
5	17th	**N.C.Redman**	(Bath)		7th	J.J.Strydom	(Transvaal)
6	7th	**T.A.K.Rodber**	(Northampton)		3rd	S.Atherton	(Natal)
7	10th	**B.B.Clarke**	(Bath)		8th	J.F.Pienaar (Capt)	(Transvaal)
8	37th	**D.Richards**	(Leicester)		1st	F.J.van Heerden	(Western Province)
					11th	C.P.Strauss	(Western Province)
	3rd	S.O.Ojomoh (Bath) for Richards - 56					

Referee:	C.Hawke	(New Zealand)

SCORERS:

C.R.Andrew	Penalty Goal		3 - 0	
C.R.Andrew	Penalty Goal		6 - 0	
B.B.Clarke	Try	(1st)	11 - 0	
C.R.Andrew	Conversion		13 - 0	
C.R.Andrew	Try	(2nd & last)	18 - 0	
C.R.Andrew	Conversion		20 - 0	
C.R.Andrew	Penalty Goal		23 - 0	
			23 - 3	A.J.Joubert Penalty Goal
			23 - 6	A.J.Joubert Penalty Goal
			Half-time	
C.R.Andrew	Penalty Goal		26 - 6	
			26 - 9	A.J.Joubert Penalty Goal
			26 - 12	A.J.Joubert Penalty Goal
			26 - 15	A.J.Joubert Penalty Goal
C.R.Andrew	Penalty Goal		29 - 15	
C.R.Andrew	D'p Goal	(17th)	32 - 15	

POINTS:

C.R.Andrew	27 point	(201)		A.J.Joubert	15 points
B.B.Clarke	5 points	(5)			

MATCH COMMENTARY:

This was one of England's finest performances because the whole team played, as Jack Rowell said, "with one heartbeat", and especially in the first sixteen minutes when England scored 20 points, South Africa were demolished and totally demoralised. The pace was furious, the middle five totally dominant, the backs' defence was exemplary and nobody put a foot wrong. After four defeats on the tour so far, this win was sweet indeed. Rob Andrew's 27 points becomes a new English record and he is the first to score by all four means in the same match.

12th match   **ENGLAND   9 pts**   v   **SOUTH AFRICA   27 pts**

	Caps					Caps		
15	2nd	P.Hull	(RAF/Bristol)	.				
					5th	A.J.Joubert	(Natal)
14	10th	T.Underwood	(Leicester)	.				
13	49th	W.D.C.Carling (Capt)	(Harlequins)	.	14th	J.T.Small	(Natal)
12	9th	P.R.de Glanville	(Bath)	.	2nd	B.Venter	(Orange Free State)
11	67th	R.Underwood	(RAF/Leicester)	.	14th	P.G.Muller	(Natal)
					3rd	C.M.Williams	(Western Province)
10	59th	C.R.Andrew	(Wasps)	.				
9	19th	C.D.Morris	(Orrell)	.	4th	H.P.le Roux	(Transvaal)
					1st	J.P.Roux	(Transvaal)
1	32nd	J.Leonard	(Harlequins)	.				
2	52nd	B.C.Moore	(Harlequins)	.	6th	I.S.Swart	(Transvaal)
3	9th	V.E.Ubogu	(Bath)	.	5th	J.Allan	(Natal)
4	16th	M.C.Bayfield	(Northampton)	.	1st	J.H.S.le Roux	(Transvaal)
5	18th	N.C.Redman	(Bath)	.	1st	M.G.Andrews	(Natal)
6	8th	T.A.K.Rodber	(Northampton)	.	4th	S.Atherton	(Natal)
7	4th	S.O.Ojomoh	(Bath)	.	9th	J.F.Pienaar (Capt)	(Transvaal)
8	11th	B.B.Clarke	(Bath)	.	5th	I.Macdonald	(Transvaal)
					4th	A.Richter	(North Transvaal)
				.	4th	J.van der Westhuizen (North Transvaal)	
				.		for Williams - 69	
				.	2nd	F.J.van Heerden (Western Province)	
	Referee:	C.Hawke	(New Zealand)	.		for Macdonald - 69	

SCORERS:

C.R.Andrew	Penalty Goal	3 - 0			
		3 - 3	H.P.le Roux	Penalty Goal
		Half-time		
		3 - 6	H.P.le Roux	Penalty Goal
		3 - 9	A.J.Joubert	Penalty Goal
		3 - 12	H.P.le Roux	Penalty Goal
C.R.Andrew	Penalty Goal	6 - 12		
C.R.Andrew	Penalty Goal	9 - 12		
		9 - 17	H.P.le Roux	Try
		9 - 20	A.J.Joubert	Penalty Goal
		9 - 25	A.J.Joubert	Try
		9 - 27	A.J.Joubert	Conversion

POINTS:

C.R.Andrew	9 points	(210)	H.P.le Roux	14 points
			A.J.Joubert	13 points

MATCH COMMENTARY:

There was only one change from the team which won so emphatically and so dramatically in Pretoria, Steve Ojomoh replacing the injured Dean Richards, yet the England side put in a slovenly and inept performance, in total contrast to the purposefulness and committment of the previous week. South Africa opened the match ferociously and knocked England back on their heels, and they never recovered. Only England's defence was resolute and kept South Africa out until the last eleven minutes when England were only three points behind. Two fine tries then sealed England's fate and made the scoreline truly reflect the difference between the teams. Perhaps the drama of the mid-week match against Eastern Province, when Tim Rodber was sent off, had exacted its toll on English morale, but whatever the reason, the performance and the result marked the end of a disappointing tour - but for those golden first 20 minutes in Pretoria.

3rd match   **ENGLAND   54 pts**   v   **ROMANIA   3 pts**

	Caps				Caps		
15	3rd	P.Hull	(RAF/Bristol)	.	15th	V.Brici	(Farul Constanta)
14	11th	T.Underwood	(Leicester)	.	13th	G.Solomie	(Timisoara Univ)
13	50th	W.D.C.Carling (Capt)	(Harlequins)	.	1st	M.Vioreanu	(Timisoara Univ)
12	29th	J.C.Guscott	(Bath)	.	21st	S.Tofan	(Dinamo Bucharest)
11	68th	R.Underwood	(RAF/Leicester)	.	7th	R.Cioca	(Dinamo Bucharest)
10	60th	C.R.Andrew	(Wasps)	.	3rd	I.Ivancuic	(CSM Suceava)
9	20th	C.D.Morris	(Orrell)	.	34th	D.Neaga	(Dinamo Bucharest)
1	33rd	J.Leonard	(Harlequins)	.	1st	L.Costea	(Steaua Bucharest)
2	53rd	B.C.Moore	(Harlequins)	.	1st	I.Negreci	(CFR Constanta)
3	10th	V.E.Ubogu	(Bath)	.	18th	G.Vlad	(Gravita Bucharest)
4	17th	M.C.Bayfield	(Northampton)	.	29th	C.Cojocariu	(Bayonne)
5	7th	M.O.Johnson	(Leicester)	.	2nd	C.Branescu	(Farul Constanta)
6	9th	T.A.K.Rodber	(Northampton)	.	9th	T.Oroian	(Steaua Bucharest)
7	5th	S.O.Ojomoh	(Bath)	.	2nd	A.Gealapu	(Steaua Bucharest)
8	12th	B.B.Clarke	(Bath)	.	16th	T.Brinza (Capt)	(Cluj University)

5th	C.Draguceanu (Steaua B) for Oroian - 49	
1st	F.Marioara (Dinamo B) for Costea - 52	
2nd	C.Gheorghe (Grivita B) for Negreci - 69	
13th	A.Guranescu (Dinamo B) for Branescu - 78	

Referee: S.Neethling   (South Africa)

SCORERS:

				England	Romania	
				0 - 3	I.Ivancuic	Penalty Goal
C.R.Andrew	Penalty Goal		3 - 3		
C.R.Andrew	Penalty Goal		6 - 3		
C.R.Andrew	Penalty Goal		9 - 3		
C.R.Andrew	Penalty Goal		12 - 3		
T.Underwood	Try	(3rd)	17 - 3		
C.R.Andrew	Conversion		19 - 3		
W.D.C.Carling	Try	(8th)	24 - 3		
C.R.Andrew	Conversion		26 - 3		
			Half-time		
T.Underwood	Try	(4th)	31 - 3		
C.R.Andrew	Conversion		33 - 3		
	Penalty Try		38 - 3		
C.R.Andrew	Conversion		40 - 3		
T.A.K.Rodber	Try	(2nd)	45 - 3		
C.R.Andrew	Conversion		47 - 3		
R.Underwood	Try	(38th)	52 - 3		
C.R.Andrew	Conversion		54 - 3		

POINTS:

C.R.Andrew	24 points	(234)	I.Ivancuic	3 points
T.Underwood	10 points	(20)		
R.Underwood, T.A.K.Rodber	5 points	(155),(10)		
and W.D. and W.D.C.Carling	each	(34)		
Penalty Try	5 points			

MATCH COMMENTARY:

This was not an impressive performance by England in the first match played under Jack Rowell since he exercised his preference to take charge of coaching himself and got rid of Dick Best after the South Africa tour. The intention to play open fifteen-man attacking rugby was very evident but the execution against very mediocre opposition was poor. Too many passes went to ground, too many openings and overlaps were ignored and there was a distinct absence of flair. Jeremy Guscott, returning to the side after a year's absence, looked a bit out of sorts and was paired with Will Carling in the centre for the 29th time - an all-time record. Rob Andrew had a good start to the season, scoring with ten out of his eleven kicks at goal.

The open play concept is commendable and refreshing, but sterner tests will expose the weaknesses unless substantial improvement can be made in the awareness of what is going on round about them on the part of several players.

2nd match   **ENGLAND 60 pts**   v   **CANADA 19 pts**

	Caps					Caps		
15	4th & last	P.Hull	(Bristol)	.		17th	S.Stewart	(U.B.C. Old Boys)
14	12th	T.Underwood	(Leicester)	.		5th	R.Toews	(Meraloma)
13	51st	W.D.C.Carling (Capt)	(Harlequins)	.		7th	C.Stewart	(West'n Province SA
12	30th	J.C.Guscott	(Bath)	.		21st	I.Stuart (Capt)	(Vancouver RC)
11	69th	R.Underwood	(RAF/Leicester)	.		11th	D.Lougheed	(Toronto Welsh)
10	61st	C.R.Andrew	(Wasps)	.		27th	G.Rees	(Oxford University)
9	4th	K.P.P.Bracken	(Bristol)	.		15th	J.Graf	(U.B.C. Old Boys)
1	34th	J.Leonard	(Harlequins)	.		24th	E.Evans	(IBM Tokyo)
2	54th	B.C.Moore	(Harlequins)	.		10th	M.Cardinal	(James Bay)
3	11th	V.E.Ubogu	(Bath)	.		17th	D.Jackart	(U.B.C. Old Boys)
4	8th	M.O.Johnson	(Leicester)	.		4th	M.James	(Burnaby Lake)
5	18th	M.C.Bayfield	(Northampton)	.		14th	N.Hadley	(Wasps)
6	10th	T.A.K.Rodber	(Northampton)	.		9th	I.Gordon	(James Bay)
7	13th	B.B.Clarke	(Bath)	.		20th	G.McKinnon	(Ex Britannia Lions)
8	38th	D.Richards	(Leicester)	.		11th	C.McKenzie	(U.B.C. Old Boys)

	2nd	M.J.Catt (Bath) for Hull -		.		24th	S.Gray (Kats) - temporary
	10th	P.R.de Glanville (Bath) for T.Underwood -		.			and for Stuart - 56

Referee: W.J.Erickson   (Australia)

SCORERS:

C.R.Andrew	Penalty Goal		3 - 0			
C.R.Andrew	Penalty Goal		6 - 0			
C.R.Andrew	Penalty Goal		9 - 0			
C.R.Andrew	Penalty Goal		12 - 0			
C.R.Andrew	Penalty Goal		15 - 0			
			Half-time			
C.R.Andrew	Penalty Goal		18 - 0			
T.Underwood	Try	(5th)	23 - 0			
C.R.Andrew	Conversion		25 - 0			
R.Underwood	Try	(39th)	30 - 0			
C.R.Andrew	Conversion		32 - 0			
K.P.P.Bracken	Try	(1st)	37 - 0			
C.R.Andrew	Conversion		39 - 0			
			39 - 5	D.Loughheed	Try
M.J.Catt	Try	(1st)	44 - 5			
C.R.Andrew	Conversion		46 - 5			
			46 - 10	D.Loughheed	Try
			46 - 12	G.Rees	Conversion
R.Underwood	Try	(40th)	51 - 12			
C.R.Andrew	Conversion		53 - 12			
			53 - 17	E.Evans	Try
			53 - 19	G.Rees	Conversion
M.J.Catt	Try	(2nd)	58 - 19			
C.R.Andrew	Conversion		60 - 19			

POINTS:	C.R.Andrew	30 points	(264)	D.Loughheed	10 points
	R.Underwood and M.J.Catt	10 points	(165),(40)	E.Evans	5 points
	T.Underwood and K.P.P.Bracken	5 points	(25),(15)	G.Rees	4 points

MATCH COMMENTARY:

This was an exceptional England performance to record their highest score ever at Twickenham, but it did depend to a large extent on the confidence generated by Rob Andrew's impeccable boot in putting England 15 points up at half-time. In the second half, it was all England and courageous Canadian defence was called upon to keep out wave upon wave of England attacks, but the six tries that were scored, they could do nothing about.

Jack Rowell has not yet solved the back row problem, but it may well be that playing conditions, and the opposition, should determine who plays in which position. This performance augurs well for the next six months, but a severe test in Dublin is next.

Rob Andrew's 30 points sert a new English record, beating his own 27 points achieved against South Africa the previous summer.

108th match   **ENGLAND   20 pts**   v   **IRELAND   8 pts**

	Caps					Caps		
15	3rd	M.J.Catt	(Bath)	.		9th	C.M.P.O'Shea	(Lansdowne)
14	13th	T.Underwood	(Leicester)	.		25th	S.P.Geoghegan	(Bath)
13	52nd	W.D.C.Carling (Capt)	(Harlequins)	.		47th	B.J.Mullin (Capt)	(Blackrock College)
12	31st	J.C.Guscott	(Bath)	.		25th	P.P.A.Danaher	(Garryowen)
11	70th	R.Underwood	(RAF/Leicester)	.		3rd	N.K.P.J.Woods	(Blackrock College)
10	62nd	C.R.Andrew	(Wasps)	.		1st	P.A.Burke	(Cork Constitution)
9	5th	K.P.P.Bracken	(Bristol)	.		1st	N.A.Hogan	(Terenure)
1	35th	J.Leonard	(Harlequins)	.		25th	N.J.Popplewell	(Wasps)
2	55th	B.C.Moore	(Harlequins)	.		4th	K.G.M.Wood	(Garryowen)
3	12th	V.E.Ubogu	(Bath)	.		11th	P.M.Clohessy	(Young Munster)
4	9th	M.O.Johnson	(Leicester)	.		21st	M.J.Galwey	(Shannon)
5	19th	M.C.Bayfield	(Northampton)	.		29th	N.P.J.Francis	(Old Belvedere)
6	11th	T.A.K.Rodber	(Northampton)	.		1st	A.G.Foley	(Shannon)
7	14th	B.B.Clarke	(Bath)	.		4th	D.Corkery	(Cork Constitution)
8	39th	D.Richards	(Leicester)	.		17th	P.S.Johns	(Dungannon)

3rd   G.M.Fulcher (Cork Const) for Francis - 40

Referee: P.Thomas   (France)

SCORERS:

W.D.C.Carling	Try	(9th)	5 - 0				
C.R.Andrew	Conversion		7 - 0				
			7 - 3		P.A.Burke	Penalty Goal	
B.B.Clarke	Try	(2nd)	12 - 3				
			Half-time				
C.R.Andrew	Penalty Goal		15 - 3				
T.Underwood	Try	(6th)	20 - 3				
			20 - 8		A.G.Foley	Try	

POINTS:

W.D.C.Carling,	5	(39)		A.G.Foley	5 points
B.B.Clarke, C.R Andrew	points	(10),(269)		P.A.Burke	3 points
and T.Underwood	each	(30)			

MATCH COMMENTARY:

After losing their last two matches against Ireland, and for Jack Rowell's first Five nations game, England were in no mood to be trifled with. It was a dreadful day with a very strong wind blowing down the pitch and the ground was wet although drying quickly in the wind.   Will Carling, leading England for the 45th time, elected to play against the wind in the first half and fully justified his decision by scoring the first try within ten minutes.   In the first half, England's display was virtually faultless.   The back row, particularly Tim Rodber and Dean Richards were immense and there was little that the Irish could do.   In the second half, even having lost Neil Francis, Irish resistance stiffened as English resolve faded a little. Tony Underwood scored England's third try from some remarkable open play and both Kyran Bracken and Jeremy Guscott should have created tries but each hung on to the ball a fraction too long. But it was a very impressive performance. Ben Clarke had the distinction of becoming the first player in International Rugby to be shown the yellow card !

Rob Andrew's conversion of Will Carling's try was his 22nd successive successful kick at goal, a remarkable sequence which started with his third attempt at goal against Romania, through nine successful kicks in that match and a further twelve against Canada.

Rory Underwood's 70th cap took him past Mike Gibson's Home Nations record of 69 caps.

71st match   **ENGLAND   31 pts**   v   **FRANCE   10 pts**

	Caps					Caps		
15	4th	M.J.Catt	(Bath)	.	25th	J-L Sadourny	(Colomiers)	
14	14th	T.Underwood	(Leicester)	.	9th	P.Bernat-Salles	(Pau)	
13	53rd	W.D.C.Carling (Capt)	(Harlequins)	.	104th	P.Sella	(Agen)	
12	32nd	J.C.Guscott	(Bath)	.	27th	T.Lacroix	(Dax)	
11	71st	R.Underwood	(RAF/Leicester)	.	41st	P Saint-Andre (Capt)	(Montferrand)	
10	63rd	C.R.Andrew	(Wasps)	.	9th	C.Deylaud	(Toulouse)	
9	6th	K.P.P.Bracken	(Bristol)	.	5th	G.Accoceberry	(Begles)	
1	36th	J.Leonard	(Harlequins)	.	8th	L.Bezenech	(Racing Club)	
2	56th	B.C.Moore	(Harlequins)	.	21st	J-M Gonzalez	(Bayonne)	
3	13th	V.E.Ubogu	(Bath)	.	5th	C.Califano	(Toulouse)	
4	10th	M.O.Johnson	(Leicester)	.	3rd	O.Brouzet	(Grenoble)	
5	20th	M.C.Bayfield	(Northampton)	.	49th	O.Roumat	(Dax)	
6	12th	T.A.K.Rodber	(Northampton)	.	30th	A.Benazzi	(Agen)	
7	15th	B.B.Clarke	(Bath)	.	33rd	L.Cabannes	(Racing Club)	
8	40th	D.Richards	(Leicester)	.	27th	P.Benetton	(Agen)	
				.	1st	M.de Rougement (Toulon) temp		
				.	13th	L.Seigne (Brive) for Bezenech - 23		
				.	13th	S.Viars (Brive) for Sadourny - 37		
	Referee:	K.W.McCartney	(Scotland)					

SCORERS:

				0 - 3	J-L Sadourny	Penalty Goal	
C.R.Andrew	Penalty Goal			3 - 3			
C.R.Andrew	Penalty Goal			6 - 3			
J.C.Guscott	Try	(17th)		11 - 3			
C.R.Andrew	Conversion			13 - 3			
				Half-time			
				13 - 8	S.Viars	Try	
				13 - 10	T.Lacroix	Conversion	
C.R.Andrew	Penalty Goal			16 - 10			
C.R.Andrew	Penalty Goal			19 - 10			
T.Underwood	Try	(7th)		24 - 10			
T.Underwood	Try	(8th)		29 - 10			
C.R.Andrew	Conversion			31 - 10			

POINTS:

C.R.Andrew	16 points	(285)		S.Viars	5 points	
T.Underwood	10 points	(40)		J-L Sadourny	3 points	
J.C.Guscott	5 points	(78)		S.Viars	2 points	

MATCH COMMENTARY:

This was, without doubt, a magnificent England performance, because France were on the back foot throughout the match and their try, a spectacle of Gallic flamboyance and flair, only added to the England's triumph because it fitted the occasion.   Again the England back row were very impressive and if Jack Rowell insists that the jury is still out, his expectations are rather high.   Unlike two weeks ago in Dublin, England did not ease off and their reward was two tries in the last ten minutes.   This was England's eighth successive win against France and was their biggest winning margin since 1947.   It also equalled France's heaviest margin of defeat in that time. Three tries in successive Five Nations matches so England will be going to Cardiff next in the right frame of mind !

THE ENGLAND TEAM WHO BEAT FRANCE AT TWICKENHAM ON FEBRUARY 4th 1995

Standing: K.W.McCartney (Referee), Touch Judge, J.Rowell (Manager), C.D.Morris (Bench), G.C.Rowntree (Bench), V.E.Ubogu, D.Richards, J.E.B.Callard (Bench),
B.B.Clarke, M.C.Bayfield, M.O.Johnson, T.A.K.Rodber, S.O.Ojomoh (Bench), P.R.de Glanville (Bench), J.Leonard, R.G.R. Dawe (Bench), Touch Judge,
Seated: K.P.P.Bracken, J.C.Guscott, C.R.Andrew, W.D.C.Carling (Captain), B.C.Moore, R.Underwood, T.Underwood, M.J.Catt.

101st match   **ENGLAND   23 pts**   v   **WALES   9 pts**

	Caps					Caps		
15	5th	M.J.Catt	(Bath)	.		34th	A.Clement	(Swansea)
14	15th	T.Underwood	(Leicester)	.		49th	I.C.Evans (Capt)	(Llanelli)
13	54th	W.D.C.Carling (Capt)	(Harlequins)	.		17th	N.G.Davies	(Llanelli)
12	33rd	J.C.Guscott	(Bath)	.		3rd	M.Taylor	(Pontypool)
11	72nd	R.Underwood	(RAF/Leicester)	.		9th	N.Walker	(Cardiff)
10	64th	C.R.Andrew	(Wasps)	.		31st	N.R.Jenkins	(Pontypridd)
9	7th	K.P.P.Bracken	(Bristol)	.		50th	R.N.Jones	(Swansea)
1	37th	J.Leonard	(Harlequins)	.		30th	M.Griffiths	(Cardiff)
2	57th	B.C.Moore	(Harlequins)	.		24th	G.R.Jenkins	(Swansea)
3	14th	V.E.Ubogu	(Bath)	.		19th	J.D.Davies	(Neath)
4	11th	M.O.Johnson	(Leicester)	.		3rd	D.Jones	(Cardiff)
5	21st	M.C.Bayfield	(Northampton)	.		35th	G.O.Llewellyn	(Neath)
6	13th	T.A.K.Rodber	(Northampton)	.		9th	H.T.Taylor	(Cardiff)
7	16th	B.B.Clarke	(Bath)	.		26th	R.G.Collins	(Pontypridd)
8	41st	D.Richards	(Leicester)	.		31st	E.W.Lewis	(Cardiff)

.   2nd   M.Back (Bridgend) for Clement - 9

.   18th   R.H.St J.B.Moon (Llanelli) for Walker - 48

.   16th   H.Williams-Jones (Llanelli) for Taylor - 65

Referee: D.Mene   (France)

SCORERS:

			0 - 3	N.R.Jenkins	Penalty Goal
V.E.Ubogu	Try	(1st & only)	5 - 3		
C.R.Andrew	Conversion		7 - 3		
C.R.Andrew	Penalty Goal		10 - 3		
			Half-time		
			10 - 6	N.R.Jenkins	Penalty Goal
C.R.Andrew	Penalty Goal		13 - 6		
R.Underwood	Try	(41st)	18 - 6		
			18 - 9	N.R.Jenkins	Penalty Goal
R.Underwood	Try	(42nd)	23 - 9		

POINTS:

R.Underwood	10 point	(175)		N.R.Jenkins	9 points
C.R.Andrew	8 point	(293)			
V.E.Ubogu	5 point	(5)			

MATCH COMMENTARY:

An England side unchanged for the third successive match, paid scant respect to the "ghost" of Cardiff Arms Park and secured their second win at this famous ground in the last thirty two years. This was another mighty performance by the England pack, but the Welsh did not permit them to be as dominating as they had been against France. In the early minutes the Welsh were very lively and showed that they meant to attack and deservedly took the lead in 20 minutes with an immaculately struck penalty goal from Neil Jenkins. But then the England pack got going, Ubogu scored and the game was virtually over. Wales could only hang on. Even Robert Jones, earning his 50th cap, only the third Welshman to do so, and so often the scourge of England in the past, could do nothing. Rory Underwood's two tries, including his first at Cardiff in six visits, amply compensated for the mistakes of previous years, and the unnecessary sending off of John Davies, for stamping on Ben Clarke, was the only sour note of the afternoon. Wales were well beaten but, even so, the England backs were not at their best. Only Scotland, again, stand between England and the Grand Slam, at Twickenham, in four weeks time.

112th match   **ENGLAND   24 pts**   v   **SCOTLAND   12 pts**

102nd Calcutta Cup

	Caps				Caps		
15	6th	M.J.Catt	(Bath)		56th	A.G.Hastings (Capt)	(Watsonians)
14	16th	T.Underwood	(Leicester)		7th	C.A.Joiner	(Melrose)
13	55th	W.D.C.Carling (Capt)	(Harlequins)		12th	G.P.J.Townsend	(Gala)
12	34th	J.C.Guscott	(Bath)		53rd	S.Hastings	(Watsonians)
11	73rd	R.Underwood	(RAF/Leicester)		15th	K.M.Logan	(Stirling County)
10	65th	C.R.Andrew	(Wasps)		41st	C.M.Chalmers	(Melrose)
9	8th	K.P.P.Bracken	(Bristol)		10th	B.W.Redpath	(Melrose)
1	38th	J.Leonard	(Harlequins)		5th	D.I.W.Hilton	(Bath)
2	58th	B.C.Moore	(Harlequins)		36th	K.S.Milne	(Heriot's FP)
3	15th	V.E.Ubogu	(Bath)		11th	P.H.Wright	(Boroughmuir)
4	12th	M.O.Johnson	(Leicester)		27th	G.W.Weir	(Melrose)
5	22nd	M.C.Bayfield	(Northampton)		5th	S.J.Campbell	(Dundee HSFP)
6	14th	T.A.K.Rodber	(Northampton)		12th	R.I.Wainwright	(West Hartlepool)
7	17th	B.B.Clarke	(Bath)		11th	I.R.Morrison	(London Scottish
8	42nd	D.Richards	(Leicester)		5th	E.W.Peters	(Bath)

	21st	C.D.Morris (Orrell) temp			1st	J.J.Manson (Dundee HSFP) for Hilton - 45
	6th	S.O.Ojomoh (Bath) for Richards - 51				
	1st	G.C.Rowntree (Leicester) temp				

Referee: B.W.Stirling   (Ireland)

SCORERS:

			0 - 3	C.M.Chalmers	Drop Goal
C.R.Andrew	Penalty goal		3 - 3		
C.R.Andrew	Penalty goal		6 - 3		
			6 - 6	C.M.Chalmers	Drop Goal
C.R.Andrew	Penalty goal		9 - 6		
C.R.Andrew	Penalty goal		12 - 6		
			Half-time		
C.R.Andrew	Penalty goal		15 - 6		
			15 - 9	A.G.Hastings	Penalty Goal
C.R.Andrew	Penalty goal		18 - 9		
			18 - 12	A.G.Hastings	Penalty Goal
C.R.Andrew	Drop Goal	(18th)	21 - 12		
C.R.Andrew	Penalty goal		24 - 12		

POINTS: C.R.Andrew   24 points   (317)   A.G.Hastings   6 points

                                                                     C.M.Chalmers   6 points

MATCH COMMENTARY:

England fielded an unchanged side for the Championship, as they had in 1991, and repeated their Grand Slam triumph of that year and 1992, but not in the manner they would have wished. No tries in this match, and a demonstrated inability to rise above the opposition who lived on brink of off-side and inhibited the attainment of clean possession for their opponents. Such is the way the Scots play their game, when they consider it necessary, and England could not overcome it. There was an impressive kicking display from Rob Andrew who became England's highest ever points scorer, and the first to pass a total of 300 individual points in International matches.

Gavin Hastings' men deprived England, not of the glory, but of the deep satisfaction of a job well done and a game well won.

SUMMARY OF THE SEASON - 1994 - 95:

On the face of it, this appears to have been a very successful season for England in Jack Rowell's first season in full charge. Six matches were played and six matches were won. Six tries scored in each of the early season games, and nine in the Five Nations Championship which culminated in the Grand Slam triumph against Scotland at Twickenham; twenty one tries in total against only five, shades of 1992 and perhaps the dawn of another new era in English International rugby. But it was not all quite as rosy as that. The first two matches against Romania and Canada were ideal openers in good conditions and England had the opportunity to run the ball, to play an expansive game and to boost their confidence. But that confidence was a long time in coming because against Romania Rob Andrew had kicked four penalty goals before the first try was scored, and against Canada, whose resistance was much stiffer, six penalty goals, the last after half-time, were on the board before England really opened up. In the Five Nations, the first three matches were certainly won convincingly, two of them away from home, with England scoring three tries in each, but the last, against Scotland, perhaps illustrates the point. There appears to be little initiative and no competent play-maker in this England side. The 1991 malaise is not cured. If Plan "A" fails, there is no Plan "B" to fall back on, and, if there were, there appears to be no-one to decide when to do so. Scotland, at Twickenham, denied England their platform by depriving them of the second, third and fourth phase possession on which everything had depended in the previous three games. As a last resort, Scotland infringed to contain the situation and this enabled Rob Andrew to kick seven penalty goals to win the match. Negative tactics on the Scots' part certainly, but England had no answer. It is this apparent lack of resourcefulness in depth which may well be England's undoing in the forthcoming World Cup in South Africa.

The side selected had remained the same for the four Five Nations matches, as had been the case in 1991, and did not even require a replacement until the last match against Scotland. The incidence of injury which disrupts team harmony and interferes with selection can have a profound and disproportionate effect on a side, and England were lucky in that respect. Not so Paul Hull whose departure during the match against Canada gave Mike Catt his opportunity which he grasped with enthusiasm and no little success. Paul Hull had played extremely well on the tour to South Africa and could have expected to have established himself in the England side during the course of this season, but in the event, he could not and did not manage to get into the World Cup squad. Only nineteen players were used for the six matches and only one new cap was awarded during the course of the season to Graham Rowntree, the Leicester loose-head prop, who appeared as a temporary replacement in the match against Scotland. Needless to say, no player retired at the end of or during the season, with the World Cup looming and the unconfirmed promises of abundant riches thereafter.

Several milestones were passed during the season; Will Carling became the first Captain in the history of the Five Nations Championship to have led his side to three Grand Slams; he also gained his 50th cap in the first match of the season against Romania - only five others have passed this landmark, three of whom are still in the side; in the Scotland match the captain led his side for the 48th time, and for the 43rd successive time which in itself, is an English record for successive caps; Rob Andrew's kicking performance against Scotland took him past 300 individual points in International rugby and at the same time past Jonathan Webb's previous record of 296 points; with the win over Wales, Will Carling became the first English captain to win twice at Cardiff since the second World War; England have now won six matches in succession, only the third time that such a feat has been accomplished and each time it has been done under Carling's captaincy. It was, in northern hemisphere terms, a very successful season, but the game has become more global in recent years and, as a general rule now, that which is good enough in the northern context, will never be good enough in the broader sphere. Aspirations and dreams are often the basis of motivation, but the greatest enemy of all to overcome is complacency, and it is just possible that, after such a successful domestic season, England may have lured themselves into that trap yet again. Let us hope that Jack Rowell knows better than that.

Off the field, there were two regrettable incidents, one at the beginning of the season and one at the end, which showed the RFU in a very bad light indeed. The first was the ill-mannered and inconsiderate sacking of Dick Best as England's coach following Jack Rowell's declaration that he wanted total control as manager and coach; the second, more ludicrous than tragic, occurred on the day of the Pilkington Cup Final, and arose after a Radio interview in which Will Carling saw fit to refer to the RFU Committee as "57 old farts". The powers that be met in the East India Club on the Saturday morning and announced that Carling had been sacked as England Captain. On Sunday, Dennis Easby, the RFU President, confirmed that there was no way back for Carling, and on Monday, after a suitable uproar, he was re-instated !!

FIVE NATIONS CHAMPIONSHIP TABLE:

Won: **Grand Slam, Triple Crown, Championship Title and Calcutta Cup**

		Played	Won	Lost	Drawn	Points: For	Against	Tries: For	Against	Title Points
1	ENGLAND	4	4	0	0	98	39	9	2	8
2	Scotland	4	3	1	0	87	71	6	6	6
3	France	4	2	2	0	77	70	10	6	4
4	Ireland	4	1	3	0	44	83	5	9	2
5	Wales	4	0	4	0	43	86	1	8	0

Home Games: beat France 31 - 10, (three tries to one); beat Scotland 24 - 12, (no tries)

Away Games: beat Ireland 20 - 8, (three tries to one); beat Wales 23 - 9, (three tries to nil).

THE WORLD CUP - 1995

THE WORLD CUP SQUAD:

Manager:	J.Rowell	Coach:	L.Cusworth		Captain:	W.D.C.Carling	

Full-backs:	J.E.B.Callard	(Bath)	3 caps	Forwards:	N.A.Back	(Leicester)	2 caps
	M.J.Catt	(Bath)	6 caps		M.C.Bayfield	(Northampton)	23 caps
					B.B.Clarke	(Bath)	17 caps
Three-quarters:	W.D.C.Carling	(Harlequins)	55 caps		R.G.R.Dawe	(Bath)	4 caps
	P.R.de Glanville	(Bath)	10 caps		M.O.Johnson	(Leicester)	12 caps
	J.C.Guscott	(Bath)	34 caps		J.Leonard	(Harlequins)	38 caps
	I.G.Hunter	(Northampton)	5 caps		J.A.Mallett	(Bath)	no caps
	D.P.Hopley	(Wasps)	no caps		B.C.Moore	(Harlequins)	58 caps
	R.Underwood	(RAF/Leicester)	73 caps		S.O.Ojomoh	(Bath)	6 caps
	T.Underwood	(Leicester)	16 caps		D.Richards	(Leicester)	42 caps
					T.A.K.Rodber	(Northampton)	14 caps
Half-backs:	C.R.Andrew	(Wasps)	65 caps		G.C.Rowntree	(Leicester)	2nd
	K.P.P.Bracken	(Bristol)	8 caps		V.E.Ubogu	(Bath)	15 caps
	C.D.Morris	(Orrell)	21 caps		R.I.West	(Gloucester)	no caps
Repalcements:	A.C.T.Gomardall	(Wasps)					

ENGLAND - WORLD CUP RESULTS:

Pool B matches:

May 27th	ARGENTINA	at Durban	WON	24 - 18	(no tries to two)
May 31st	ITALY	at Durban	WON	27 - 20	(two tries each)
June 4th	WESTERN SAMOA	at Durban	WON	44 - 22	(four tries to three)

Quarter Final:

June 11th	AUSTRALIA	at Cape Tow	WON	25 - 22	(one try each)

Semi Final:

June 18th	NEW ZEALAND	at Cape Tow	LOST	29 - 45	(four tries to six)

Third place Play-off:

June 22nd	FRANCE	at Pretoria	LOST	9 - 19	(no tries to two)

WORLD CUP WINNERS:	SOUTH AFRICA	beat NEW ZEALAND in the Final	15 - 12	(no tries) aet
		beat FRANCE in the Semi-Final	19 - 15	(one try to nil)
RUNNER UP:	NEW ZEALAND	beat ENGLAND in the Semi-Final	45 - 29	(six tries to four)
3rd PLACE	FRANCE	beat ENGLAND in the Play-off	19 - 9	(two tries to nil)
4th PLACE	ENGLAND			
BEATEN QUARTER FINALISTS:	IRELAND	lost to FRANCE	12 - 36	(no tries to two)
	WESTERN SAMOA	lost to SOUTH AFRICA	14 - 42	(no tries to six)
	AUSTRALIA	lost to ENGLAND	22 - 25	(one try each)
	SCOTLAND	lost to NEW ZEALAND	30 - 18	(three tries to six)

WORLD CUP SUMMARY:

The 1995 World Cup was many things all rolled into one.   Not only was it an outstanding event, it was also a tribute to the emerging "Rainbow Nation" of South Africa, rid forever of the shackles of apartheid, and embarked on a new destiny.   It was also a threshold for the game of Rugby Union in that the forces of professionalism were already making, or had already made, depending on one's country of origin, a significant impact on the game which was, all too soon, to change it beyond recognition.   And yet still the die-hard traditionalists in their ivory towers in the northern hemisphere held out.   The tournament was awash with rumour and counter-rumour regarding the activities of Kerry Packer, Rupert Murdoch and Ross Turnbull who was apparently recruiting on the spot (or trying to) and astronomical sums were allegedly being offered to set up a World Rugby Circus amongst other fanciful ideas, and still the IRB, the RFU and the other Home Unions did nothing.

Thankfully the ideas remained fanciful and the rumours remained rumours, and those who were there for the express purpose of winning the World Cup got on with their business.   The pageant and the spectacle of the opening ceremony, and the result of the opening match, gave the tournamnet a dream start which could not have been anticipated.   South Africa, at their first attempt in the World Cup, swept past Australia in the opening game and the romantics present must have had a foretaste of what was yet to come.   And come it did.

Jack Rowell, after a successful Five Nations tournament which gave England their third Grand Slam in five years and flattered to deceive, promised a fluid opening game from England and whetted the appetites of the many supporters left at home with assurances that England would "hit the ground running" and make a real impact on the tournament.   The worldy wise would have recognised that the seeds for the destruction of Jack Rowell's dream were sown at Twickenham in March when England failed to impose their game on the Scots, and although they won the game, they failed to score a try.

That unhappy experience was repeated at Durban in England's opening match when the team again failed to impose themselves on a robust but unimaginative Argentinian team, and again failed to score a try, but conceded two.   The second Pool B match against Italy, four days later did little to boost England's flagging morale, and in spite of five changes to the side, it was still a disappointing performance. On the bright side, two tries were scored, but to counter that another two were conceded.   Against Western Samoa, matters improved, England won the try count 4 - 3 and won the match by a margin of 22 points.   But it was a very unreal match in which nine substitutes or replacements made their appearance and from which not a lot of confidence could be gained for the sterner tests which England were to face in the final knock-out stages of the tournament.

Because South Africa had beaten Australia in the opening game in Pool A, it became England's lot to face Australia in the second series of Quarter finals in Cape Town on Sunday, June 11th.   The game was, at least to all observers, a re-run of the 1991 Final, when England got their tactics all wrong and ended up losing a game they could well have won.   Half the players on the field had been at Twickenham that day, and there were certainly points to be made.   In the first half hour, England, belying their previous form and looking supremely confident, had opened up a ten point lead, including a Tony Underwood try, but Australia struck what seemed like a killer punch when Damien Smith gathered a superbly accurate kick from Michael Lynagh, and scored a try immediately after the interval which Lynagh converted to make the scores level again.   England were shaken and it was 13 points each.   Both sides raised their game, but neither gained the ascendancy, and extra time looked inevitable when with a supreme effort the England pack drove to the Australian 22, Morris fed Andrew in space with a quick accurate pass and one of the finest and most dramatic drop goals ever seen in International rugby sailed high between the posts and England were through to the Semi Finals.

But that was as far as they were going to get.   In an astonishing Semi Final New Zealand destroyed England with two tries in the first six minutes and shortly after England found themselves 25 points to nil down.   Nevertheless a spirited fight back in the last half hour was all to England's credit even though All Black motivation must have been a little jaded by then.   England scored four tries to give the scoreline substantially more respectability, but there was a gulf between the sides, and particularly between Jonah Lomu and whoever confronted him.   The Third Place play-off against France was a shattering anti-climax as all such events are, but France at least made an effort, and none but Dewi Morris on the England side were prepared to make any effort whatsoever.   This was a shameful performance on the part of the side, the Captain and the Manager and Coach.   In mitigation, Jack Rowell said at a Press Conference "to play Australia, New Zealand and France in such a short space of time is asking a lot".   Surprisingly, no one in the audience saw fit to remark that if you want to win the World Cup, that is exactly what you have to be prepared to do !!   Statistically, England's performance was little better than average. They scored 149 points and conceded 127; they scored 11 tries and conceded 14; but they outscored their opponents in penalty goals by 22 to 11 - shades of 1991 all over again.

But overall, it was a splendid tournament with every bit as much drama in the final match as there had been in the first.   It was South Africa's tournament, and South Africa's year and nothing should detract from that.   The point, however, was emphatically made that an even wider gulf has developed between northern and southern hemisphere rugby.   France would rightly argue with that; they had recently won a series in New Zealand in 1994 and in South Africa in 1993, although it appears that South Africa have learned a lot in two years. For England, and indeed for all four Home Nations, there are lessons to be learned, and soon, if we are ever to compete effectively - and paying players is not the answer.   But for the moment, to the Winner, the Glory, and richly deserved it was.

Four Stalwarts of English International Rugby played their last in the International arena in South Africa.   Rob Andrew, who later in the year was to announce his enforced retirement from International rugby on taking up a professional post with Newcastle as Director of Rugby. His career had spanned eleven seasons, he was England's most capped fly half, with 70 caps, and held the English record for points scored in Internationals, 396, and for drop goals, 21, in his career.   Brian Moore, 64 caps, is England's most capped hooker, is a Litigation partner with a London legal practice and was a thorn in the flesh of the RFU in the negotiations which regarding professionalism in the game.   Dewi Morris, 26 caps, was the only player to say after the World Cup "Now, I quit".   He was one of England's best scrum halves, and almost a ninth forward as well, the only chink in his armour being a, relatively, weak pass, but a team man through and through, as Orrell and later Sale, will testify.   Graham Dawe earned 5 caps in a period of nine years and gained caps in the 1st and the 3rd World Cups.

THE ENGLAND WORLD CUP SQUAD, 1995.

Back Row: V.E.Ubogu, N.A.Back, G.C.Rowntree, M.J.Catt, S.O.Ojomoh, I.G.Hunter, J.Mallett, P.R.de Glanville, J.E.B.Callard, J.Leonard,

Middle Row: K.P.P.Bracken, J.C.Guscott, D.Richards, B.B.Clarke, T.A.K.Rodber, M.C.Bayfield, R.I.West, M.O.Johnson, D.P.Hopley, R.G.R.Dawe, T.Underwood,

Seated: K.Murphy (Physio), T.Crystal (Team Doctor), R.Underwood, B.C.Moore, J.Rowell (Manager), W.D.C.Carling (Captain), J.Elliott (Coach), C.R.Andrew,

C.D.Morris, L.Cusworth (Coach), Official.

6th match   **ENGLAND**   **24 pts**   v   **ARGENTINA**   **18 pts**

	Caps					Caps		
15	7th	M.J.Catt	(Bath)			E.Jurado	(Jockey Rosario)
14	17th	T.Underwood	(Leicester)			M.J.Teran	(Tucuman RC)
13	56th	W.D.C.Carling (Capt)	(Harlequins)			F.Garcia	(Alumni BA)
12	35th	J.C.Guscott	(Bath)			S.Salvat (Capt)	(Alumni BA)
11	74th	R.Underwood	(RAF/Leicester)			D.Cuesta Silva	(San Isidro BA)
10	66th	C.R.Andrew	(Wasps)			L.Arbizu	(Belgrano BA)
9	22nd	C.D.Morris	(Orrell)			R.H.Crexell	(Jockey Rosario)
1	39th	J.Leonard	(Harlequins)			E.P.Noriega	(Hindu)
2	59th	B.C.Moore	(Harlequins)			F.E.Mendez	(Mendoza RC)
3	16th	V.E.Ubogu	(Bath)			M.E.Corral	(San Isidro BA)
4	13th	M.O.Johnson	(Leicester)			P.L.Sporleder	(Curupayti BA)
5	23rd	M.C.Bayfield	(Northampton)			G.A.Llanes	(La Plata RCBA)
6	15th	T.A.K.Rodber	(Northampton)			C.Viel	(Newman BA)
7	18th	B.B.Clarke	(Bath)			R.Martin	(San Isidro BA)
8	7th	S.O.Ojomoh	(Bath)			J.M.Santamarina	(Tucuman RC)

3rd	N.A.Back (Leicester) - temp		S.Irazoqui (Palermo BC) for Viel - 65
11th	P.R.de Glanville (Bath) for Carling - 78		

Referee: J.M.Fleming   (Scotland)

SCORERS:

C.R.Andrew	Penalty Goal		3 - 0			
C.R.Andrew	Penalty Goal		6 - 0			
C.R.Andrew	Penalty Goal		9 - 0			
C.R.Andrew	Penalty Goal		12 - 0			
		Half-time				
C.R.Andrew	D'p Goal	(19th)	15 - 0			
			15 - 3	L.Arbizu	Penalty Goal
C.R.Andrew	Penalty Goal		18 - 3			
			18 - 8	P.Noriega	Try
			18 - 10	L.Arbizu	Conversion
C.R.Andrew	D'p Goal	(20th)	21 - 10			
			21 - 13	L.Arbizu	Penalty Goal
C.R.Andrew	Penalty Goal		24 - 13			
			24 - 18	L.Arbizu	Try

POINTS:

C.R.Andrew	24 points	(341)		L.Arbizu	13 points
				P.Noriega	5 points

MATCH COMMENTARY:

Only two changes from the side which had seized the Grand Slam 10 weeks earlier - Steve Ojomoh replacing the injured Dean Richards at No 8 and Dewi Morris getting the nod over Kyran Bracken. Whether or not the changes were significant, one was left with the feeling that the build-up and the Grand Slam reputation had been too much for England to live up and the consequence was a humiliation. England were outplayed by two tries to none by a team who conceded penalties with no thought of the consequences but who had a very strong scrummage - on occasions they pushed the mighty England pack around. This was a deplorable result, demonstrating again that England cannot think on their feet and, had it not been for Rob Andrew, the humiliation would have been almost too much to bear.

2nd match   **ENGLAND   27 pts**   v   **ITALY   20 pts**

	Caps					Caps		
15	8th	**M.J.Catt**	(Bath)	.		**L.Troiani**	(L'Aquila)
14	18th	**T.Underwood**	(Leicester)	.		**P.Vaccari**	(Milan)
13	36th	**J.C.Guscott**	(Bath)	.		**I.Francescato**	(Treviso)
12	12th	**P.R.de Glanville**	(Bath)	.		**S.Bordon**	(Rovigo)
11	75th	**R.Underwood**	((RAF/Leicester)	.		**M.Gerosa**	(Piacenza)
10	67th	**C.R.Andrew (Capt)**	(Wasps)	.		**D.Dominguez**	(Milan)
9	9th	**K.P.P.Bracken**	(Bristol)	.		**A.Troncon**	(Treviso)
1	2nd	**G.C.Rowntree**	(Leicester)	.		**Massimo Cuttitta (Capt**	(Milan)
2	60th	**B.C.Moore**	(Harlequins)	.		**C.Orlandi**	(Piacenza)
3	40th	**J.Leonard**	(Harlequins)	.		**F.Properzi-Curti**	(Milan)
4	14th	**M.O.Johnson**	(Leicester)	.		**M.Giacheri**	(Treviso)
5	24th	**M.C.Bayfield**	(Northampton)	.		**P.Pedroni**	(Milan)
6	16th	**T.A.K.Rodber**	(Northampton)	.		**O.Arancio**	(Catania)
7	4th	**N.A.Back**	(Leicester)	.		**A.Sgorlon**	(San Dona)
8	19th	**B.B.Clarke**	(Bath)	.		**J.M.Gardner**	(Roma)

Referee: S.P.Hilditch   (Ireland)

SCORERS:							
	T.Underwood	Try	(9th)	5 - 0			
	C.R.Andrew	Conversion		7 - 0			
	C.R.Andrew	Penalty Goal		10 - 0			
				10 - 3	**D.Dominguez**	Penalty Goal	
	C.R.Andrew	Penalty Goal		13 - 3			
	C.R.Andrew	Penalty Goal		16 - 3			
				16 - 8	**P.Vaccari**	Try	
				16 - 10	**D.Dominguez**	Conversion	
				Half-time			
	R.Underwood	Try	(43rd)	21 - 10			
	C.R.Andrew	Penalty Goal		24 - 10			
	C.R.Andrew	Penalty Goal		27 - 10			
				27 - 13	**D.Dominguez**	Penalty Goal	
				27 - 18	**Massima Cuttitta**	Try	
				27 - 20	**D.Dominguez**	Conversion	

POINTS:						
	C.R.Andrew	17 points	(358)	**D.Dominguez**	10 points	
	T.Underwood	5 points	(45)	**P.Vaccari**	5 points	
	R.Underwood	5 points	(180)	**Massima Cuttitta**	5 points	

MATCH COMMENTARY:

With Will Carling and Dean Richards both missing through injury, and Bracken and Back recalled with Graham Rowntree being awarded his first full cap at loose head and Jason Leonard, in his 40th successive International, moving across to tight-head, England could not improve upon their lack-lustre performance against Argentina. Although the match was played in very wet and windy conditions, this was no excuse for another very poor England performance. Only Rob Andrew, again restoring respectability, and Martin Bayfield showed any composure and class, the rest were virtually headless chickens. Both Underwood tries were well executed but there should have been many more.

WORLD CUP, 1995   June 4th 1995, at Durban

1st match   **ENGLAND   44 pts**   v   **WESTERN SAMOA   22 pts**

	Caps					Caps		

	Caps					Caps		
15	4th	J.E.B.Callard	(Bath)	M.T.Umaga	(Wellington, NZ)
14	6th	I.G.Hunter	(Northampton)	B.Lima	(Auckland NZ)
13	57th	W.D.C.Carling (Capt)	(Harlequins)	T.Vaega	(Pukekohe, NZ)
1`2	13th	P.R.de Glanville	(Bath)	T.Fa'amasino	(Vaimoso)
11	76th	R.Underwood	(RAF/Leicester)	G.P.Leaupepe	(Auckland NZ)
10	9th	M.J.Catt	(Bath)	E.Puleitu	(Apia West)
9	23rd	C.D.Morris	(Orrell)	T.Nu'uali'itia	(Auckland, NZ)
1	3rd	G.C.Rowntree	(Leicester)	M.A.N.Mika	(Otage, NZ)
2	5th & last	R.G.R.Dawe	(Bath)	T.Leiasamaivao	(Moataa)
3	17th	V.E.Ubogu	(Bath)	G.Latu	(Vaimoso)
4	1st & only	R.I.West	(Gloucester)	D.R.Williams	(Colomiers, France)
5	15th	M.O.Johnson	(Leicester)	L.Falaniko	(Marist, NZ)
6	8th	S.O.Ojomoh	(Bath)	P.Leavasa	(Apia)
7	5th	N.A.Back	(Leicester)	M.Iupeli	(Marist, NZ)
8	43rd	D.Richards	(Leicester)	P.R.Lam (Capt)	(Auckland, NZ)

1st & only	J.A.Mallett (Bath) for Rowntree - 26	S.Tatupu (Ponsonby, NZ) for Leavasa - 31
17th	T.A.K.Rodber (Northampton) for Back - 33	F.Sini (Marist, NZ) for Puleitu - 40
1st	D.P.Hopley (Wasps) for Carling - 71	S.Lemamea (SCOPA) for Tatupu - 69
61st	B.C.Moore (Harlequins) for Rodber - 74	P.Fatialofa (Counties, NZ) for Latu - 76
10th	K.P.P.Bracken (Bristol) for Richards - 75	

Referee: P.Robin   (France)

SCORERS:

N.A.Back	Try	(1st)	5 - 0		
J.E.B.Callard	Penalty Goal		8 - 0		
M.J.Catt	D'p Goal	(1st)	11 - 0		
R.Underwood	Try	(44th)	16 - 0		
J.E.B.Callard	Conversion		18 - 0		
J.E.B.Callard	Penalty Goal		21 - 0		
			Half-time		
			21 - 3	T.Fa'amasino	Penalty Goal
			21 - 8	F.Sini	Try
			21 - 10	T.Fa'amasino	Conversion
J.E.B.Callard	Penalty Goal		24 - 10		
			24 - 15	F.Sini	Try
			24 - 17	T.Fa'amasino	Conversion
	Penalty Try		29 - 17		
J.E.B.Callard	Conversion		31 - 17		
J.E.B.Callard	Penalty Goal		34 - 17		
R.Underwood	Try	(45th)	39 - 17		
J.E.B.Callard	Conversion		41 - 17		
J.E.B.Callard	Penalty Goal		44 - 17		
			44 - 22	M.Umaga	Try

POINTS:	J.E.B.Callard	21 points	(60)	F.Sini	10 points
	R.Underwood	10 points	(190)	T.Fa'amasino	7 points
	N.A.Back	5 points	(5)	M.Umaga	5 points
	M.J.Catt	3 points	(13)		

MATCH COMMENTARY:

A very much improved performance by England although they allowed Western Samoa to approach within seven points just after half-time, hence the situation where Jonathan Callard was still kicking penalty goals with over thirty points on the board. The lead was 21 points to nil at half-time yet within less than fifteen minutes Western Samoa had scored two converted tries and a penalty goal. It was altogether a somewhat bizarre match with nine replacements appearing, three in the first half, one at half time and five in the last eleven minutes. England's record in these preliminary matches does not inspire confidence for the forthcoming knock out stages. In three matches they have scored 95 points and conceded 60, scored six tries and conceded seven and kicked 16 penalty goals. Argentina lost all their Pool matches yet in their match against England, they won the try count by two tries to none. Grand Slam Champions or not, this is not the kind of rugby which will ensure further progress in the competition.

19th match   **ENGLAND 25 pts**   v   **AUSTRALIA 22 pts**

	Caps				Caps		
15	10th	**M.J.Catt**	(Bath)		9th	**M.Burke**	(New South Wales)
14	19th	**T.Underwood**	(Leicester)		91st	**D.I.Campese**	(New South Wales)
13	58th	**W.D.C.Carling (Capt)**	(Harlequins)		35th	**J.S.Little**	(Queensland)
12	37th	**J.C.Guscott**	(Bath)		36th	**T.J.Horan**	(Queensland)
11	77th	**R.Underwood**	(RAF/Leicester)		16th	**D.P.Smith**	(Queensland)
10	68th	**C.R.Andrew**	(Wasps)		72nd & last	**M.P.Lynagh (Capt)**	(Queensland)
9	24th	**C.D.Morris**	(Orrell)		10th	**G.M.Gregan**	(ACT)
1	41st	**J.Leonard**	(Harlequins)		11th	**D.J.Crowley**	(Queensland)
2	62nd	**B.C.Moore**	(Harlequins)		47th	**P.N.Kearns**	(New South Wales)
3	18th	**V.E.Ubogu**	(Bath)		44th	**E.J.A.McKenzie**	(New South Wales)
4	16th	**M.O.Johnson**	(Leicester)		40th	**R.J.McCall**	(Queensland)
5	25th	**M.C.Bayfield**	(Northampton)		40th & last	**J.A.Eales**	(Queensland)
6	18th	**T.A.K.Rodber**	(Northampton)		25th	**V.Ofanhengaue**	(New South Wales)
7	20th	**B.B.Clarke**	(Bath)		27th & last	**D.J.Wilson**	(Queensland)
8	44th	**D.Richards**	(Leicester)		42nd	**B.T.Gavin**	(New South Wales)

9th   S.O.Ojomoh - temp

Referee: D.J.Bishop   (New Zealand)

SCORERS:

			0 - 3	M.P.Lynagh	Penalty Goal
C.R.Andrew	Penalty Goal		3 - 3		
C.R.Andrew	Penalty Goal		6 - 3		
T.Underwood	Try	(10th)	11 - 3		
C.R.Andrew	Conversion		13 - 3		
			13 - 6	M.P.Lynagh	Penalty Goal
			Half-time		
			13 - 11	D.P.Smith	Try
			13 - 13	M.P.Lynagh	Conversion
C.R.Andrew	Penalty Goal		16 - 13		
			16 - 16	M.P.Lynagh	Penalty Goal
			16 - 19	M.P.Lynagh	Penalty Goal
C.R.Andrew	Penalty Goal		19 - 19		
			19 - 22	M.P.Lynagh	Penalty Goal
C.R.Andrew	Penalty Goal		22 - 22		
C.R.Andrew	D'p Goal	(21st)	25 - 22		

POINTS:

C.R.Andrew	20 points	(378)	**M.P.Lynagh**	17 points
T.Underwood	5 points	(50)	**D.P.Smith**	5 points

MATCH COMMENTARY:

An astonishing match of extraordinary intensity and courage among those taking part. It had never been billed as a grudge match, but to the six Englishmen and the nine Australians who had played in the 1991 Final, and had not met since, there was a point to be made. England played magnificently to stretch to a 10 point lead after twenty minutes and had a 13 - 6 advantage at half-time. The difference at that stage was Tony Underwood's converted try which came when England pounced on a loose ball and Underwood raced 50 metres, just beating Damien Smith to the line. Based on the pack's dominance in the first half, England should have been futher ahead, not only because Rob Andrew had missed a straightforward drop goal attempt. Then within the first minute of the second half, Michael Lynagh's immaculately placed kick to the corner was snatched out of the air and out of Tony Underwood's grasp for Australia's first try, which Lynagh converted to level the scores. England then crept ahead with a penalty goal. Australia equalised a few minutes later and then themselves edged into the lead with another. 22 - 19 to Australia. With about five minutes to go, Rob Andrew levelled the scores again with another penalty. The eighty minute mark came and went, and the match was in injury time with everyone wondering exactly what the rules and regulations were about extra time, when England drove powerfully fully 25 metres from Martin Bayfield's possession at a line-out, the ball was whisked out to Andrew and from all of 45 metres a drop goal soared straight and true between the posts and Australia were beaten. The final whistle seconds later, was greeted momentarily with a stunned silence as the drama of what had happened dawned on those privileged to witness such a dramatic climax to a tense and enthralling encounter.

18th match   **ENGLAND 29 pts**   v   **NEW ZEALAND 45 pts**

	Caps					Caps		
15	11th	M.J.Catt	(Bath)	.		5th	G.M.Osborne	(North Harbour)
14	20th	T.Underwood	(Leicester)	.		8th	J.W.Wilson	(Otago)
13	59th	W.D.C.Carling (Capt)	(Harlequins)	.		27th	F.E.Bunce	(North Harbour)
12	38th	J.C.Guscott	(Bath)	.		30th	W.K.Little	(North Harbour)
11	78th	R.Underwood	(RAF/Leicester)	.		6th	J.Lomu	(Counties)
10	69th	C.R.Andrew	(Wasps)	.		5th	A.P.Mehrtens	(Canterbury)
9	25th	C.D.Morris	(Orrell)	.		28th	G.T.M.Bachop	(Canterbury)
1	42nd	J.Leonard	(Harlequins)	.		13th	C.W.Dowd	(Auckland)
2	63rd	B.C.Moore	(Harlequins)	.		67th	S.B.T.Fitzpatrick	(Auckland)
3	19th	V.E.Ubogu	(Bath)	.		22nd	O.M.Brown	(Auckland)
4	17th	M.O.Johnson	(Leicester)	.		42nd	I.D.Jones	(North Harbour)
5	26th	M.C.Bayfield	(Northampton)	.		16th	R.M.Brooke	(Auckland)
6	19th	T.A.K.Rodber	(Northampton)	.		29th	M.R.Brewer	(Canterbury)
7	21st	B.B.Clarke	(Bath)	.		5th	J.Kronfeld	(Otago)
8	45th	D.Richards	(Leicester)	.		31st	Z.V.Brooke	(Auckland)

13th   B.P.Larsen (N'th Harbour) for Z. Brooke - 64

Referee: S.R.Hilditch   (Ireland)

SCORERS:

			0 - 5	J.Lomu	Try	
			0 - 10	J.Kronfeld	Try	
			0 - 12	A.P.Mehrtens	Conversion	
			0 - 15	A.Mehrtens	Penalty Goal	
			0 - 18	Z.V.Brooke	Drop Goal	
			0 - 23	J.Lomu	Try	
			0 - 25	A.P.Mehrtens	Conversion	
C.R.Andrew	Penalty Goal		3 - 25			
			Half-time			
			3 - 30	J.Lomu	Try	
			3 - 35	G.T.M.Bachop	Try	
R.Underwood	Try	(46th)	8 - 35			
C.R.Andrew	Conversion		10 - 35			
W.D.C.Carling	Try	(10th)	15 - 35			
			15 - 40	J.Lomu	Try	
			15 - 42	A.P.Mehrtens	Conversion	
W.D.C.Carling	Try	(11th)	20 - 42			
C.R.Andrew	Conversion		22 - 42			
			22 - 45	A.Mehrtens	Drop goal	
R.Underwood	Try	(47th)	27 - 45			
C.R.Andrew	Conversion		29 - 45			

POINTS:

R.Underwood	10 points	(200)	J.Lomu	20 points	
W.D.C.Carling	10 points	(49)	A.Mehrtens	12 points	
C.R.Andrew	9 points	(387)	G.T.M.Bachop & J.Kronfeld	5 points each	
			Z.V.Brooke	3 points	

MATCH COMMENTARY:

Even though England had not acquitted themselves well in their Pool matches, whereas New Zealand had scored 29 tries in the early stages and a further six in the Quarter Final against Scotland, this match was expected to be a clash of the Titans with the victor very likely to go all the way. After all, England had disposed of the Australian challenge - why not New Zealand too ?

An astonishing first half onslaught by the All Blacks which yielded two tries in the first six minutes, knocked proud England sideways and that alone was ample testimony to the quality of this New Zealand side. Jonah Lomu's first try after two minutes when he ran through rather than round Will Carling, Tony Underwood and Mike Catt sounded the death knell and England were back pedalling for the next hour. A try from Josh Kronfeld, an amazing 40 metre drop goal from Zinzan Brooke and another try for Lomu set England back to the tune of 25 points to 3 at half-time. After 51 minutes, England were 35 points to three down, and disaster was staring them in the face. Then two things happened; Dewi Morris decided that this nonsense had to stop and tried ferociously to whip up even greater effort from the pack and to move the ball wide. The direct result of this initiative was England's first try by Rory Underwood. Then Zinzan Brooke, who had been a massive presence in the loose, particularly in turning over possession when England persisted in running ball close in with, mainly, the back row, had to leave the field in the 64th minute. Thereafter, England had a greater share of the ball and Dewi Morris decided to use it. When they moved the ball wide, and ran onto their passes, the England backs showed what they could do and scored three more tries with another for Rory Underwood and two fine tries for the captain. Nonetheless, and try as he might, Tony Underwood could not escape the the clutches and the influence of Jonah Lomu, who apart from unceremoniously dumping Underwood whenever he got the ball, also scored two more tries himself, to bring his match total to four tries - a formidable performance.

The England pack just about shared the honours, but nothing could compare with the spirit, enterprise and vision of the All Blacks, never better emphasised than when Zinzan Brooke dropped his goal. The final margin of 16 points flattered England, on the performance on the day, it should have been 40 points, but to their eternal credit, England did not give up and their efforts in the last fifteen minutes spoke volumes for their character.

72nd match   **ENGLAND   9 pts**   v   **FRANCE   19 pts**

	Caps					Caps		
15	12th	M.J.Catt	(Bath)		33rd	J-L.Sadourny	(Colomiers)
14	7th & last	I.G.Hunter	(Northampton)		13th	E.N'Tamack	(Toulouse)
13	60th	W.D.C.Carling (Capt)	(Harlequins)		111th & last	P.Sella	(Agen)
12	39th	J.C.Guscott	(Bath)		35th	T.Lacroix	(Dax)
11	79th	R.Underwood	(RAF/Leicester)		50th	P.Saint-Andre (Capt)	(Montferrand)
10	70th	C.R.Andrew	(Wasps)		56th & last	F.Mesnel	(Racing Club)
9	26th & last	C.D.Morris	(Orrell)		16th	F.Galthie	(Colomiers)
1	43rd	J.Leonard	(Harlequins)		12th	C.Califano	(Toulouse)
2	64th & last	B.C.Moore	(Harlequins)		29th	J-M.Gonzales	(Bayonne)
3	20th	V.E.Ubogu	(Bath)		11th	L.Benezech	(Racing Club)
4	18th	M.O.Johnson	(Leicester)		21st	O.Merle	(Montferrand)
5	27th	M.C.Bayfield	(Northampton)		55th	O.Roumat	(Dax)
6	20th	T.A.K.Rodber	(Northampton)		38th	A.Benazzi	(Agen)
7	22nd	B.B.Clarke	(Bath)		41st	L.Cabannes	(Racing Club)
8	10th	S.O.Ojomoh	(Bath)		1st & only	A.Cigagna	(Toulouse)
					9th	O.Brouzet (Grenoble) temp	

Referee: D.Bishop   (New Zealand)

SCORERS:

C.R.Andrew	Penalty Goal	3 - 0			
		3 - 3	T.Lacroix	Penalty Goal
		Half-time		
		3 - 6	T.Lacroix	Penalty Goal
C.R.Andrew	Penalty Goal	6 - 6		
		6 - 9	T.Lacroix	Penalty Goal
		6 - 14	O.Roumat	Try
C.R.Andrew	Penalty Goal	9 - 14		
		9 - 19	E.N'Tamack	Try

POINTS:

C.R.Andrew	9 points	(396)	T.Lacroix	9 points
			O.Roumat	5 points
			E.N'Tamack	5 points

MATCH COMMENTARY:

After the trauma of the defeat by New Zealand, it would have been difficult for any team to pick themselves up dust themselves down and start all over again. But then, France had lost a semi-final too. With astonishing naivete and insensitivity, Jack Rowell dropped Tony Underwood, whose humiliation was now complete, and selected all the other guilty parties for one final moment of glory. The consequence was a shattering anti-climax, as the third place play-off is always going to be, but this, from England's point of view was nothing short of dreadful. What Rowell should have done, of course, was to give those players who had been little called upon other than as tackle fodder for six weeks, the chance to avenge the National humiliation and continue the winning streak against France. All would have played their hearts out for the privilege. But as it was, the side appeared totally disinterested and demotivated. With the ball in hand, support was lacking everywhere, kicking still predominated, the lines-out were a shambles and no-one called the shots, no-one tried to control events, and leadership on the field and from the stand was conspicuous by its absence. England were not well beaten in this match as they had been in the previous encounter, they just never gave any indication that they wanted to win it, and for that the Manager and Captain must accept responsibility, but whether they will remains to be seen.

13th match   **ENGLAND   14 pts**   v   **SOUTH AFRICA   24 pts**

	Caps					Caps		
15	5th & last	J.E.B.Callard	(Bath)	.	19th	A.J.Joubert	(Natal)
14	2nd	D.P.Hopley	(Wasps)	.	12th	J.Olivier	(Northern Transvaal)
13	61st	W.D.C.Carling (Capt)	(Harlequins)	.	12th	J.C.Mulder	(Transvaal)
12	40th	J.C.Guscott	(Bath)	.	20th	H.P.le Roux	(Transvaal)
11	80th	R.Underwood	(RAF/Leicester)	.	16th	C.M.Williams	(Western Province)
10	13th	M.J.Catt	(Bath)	.	15th	J.T.Stransky	(Western Province)
9	11th	K.P.P.Bracken	(Bristol)	.	16th	J.H.van der Westhuizen	(Northern Transvaal)
1	44th	J.Leonard	(Harlequins)	.	2nd	A.van der Linde	(Western Province)
2	1st	M.P.Regan	(Bristol)	.	6th	J.Dalton	(Transvaal)
3	21st & last	V.E.Ubogu	(Bath)	.	6th	T.G.Laubscher	(Western Province)
4	19th	M.O.Johnson	(Leicester)	.	10th	J.J.Weise	(Transvaal)
5	28th	M.C.Bayfield	(Northampton)	.	16th	M.G.Andrews	(Natal)
6	21st	T.A.K.Rodber	(Northampton)	.	13th	R.J.Kruger	(Northern Transvaal)
7	8th & last	R.A.Robinson	(Bath)	.	5th	F.J.van Heerden	(Western Province)
8	23rd	B.B.Clarke	(Bath)	.	24th	J.F.Pienaar (Capt)	(Transvaal)

	1st	L.B.N.Dallaglio (Wasps) for Rodber - 66	.	26th	J.T.Small (Natal) for Olivier - 47
	14th	P.R.de Glanville (Bath) for Carling - 78	.	10th	R.A.W.Straeuli (Transvaal) for Kruger - 62

Referee: J.M.Fleming   (Scotland

SCORERS:

J.E.B.Callard	Penalty Goal	3 - 0			
		3 - 3	J.T.Stransky	Penalty Goal
		3 - 6	J.T.Stransky	Penalty Goal
J.E.B.Callard	Penalty Goal	6 - 6		
		6 - 11	C.M.Williams	Try
		Half-time		
		6 - 16	J.H.van der Westhuizen	Try
J.E.B.Callard	Penalty Goal	9 - 16		
		9 - 19	J.T.Stransky	Penalty Goal
		9 - 24	C.M.Williams	Try
P.R.de Glanville	Try	(1st) 14 - 24		

POINTS:

J.E.B.Callard	9 points	(69)	C.M.Williams	10 points
P.R.de Glanville	5 points	(5)	J.T.Stransky	9 points
			J.H.van der Westhuizen	5 points

MATCH COMMENTARY:

This was an exceedingly disappointing display by England who, for the second time in recent memory (the World Cup being the first) failed to live up to the pre-match promises of open expansive rugby. This does not detract from the South Africans whose defence was superb and whose attacking flair, led and encouraged by the admirable Pienaar, gave them three cracking tries. It could have been four had Jim Fleming been better sighted when Chester Williams touched down midway through the second half for a disallowed try. Had Joel Stransky been in kicking form the margin could have been 30 points. The England pack, especially the front five, won enough ball to feed an army, but the indecisive backs committed too many unforced errors and threw away the opportunities. There was a distinct lack of pace and vision at half-back. The new Twickenham saw the rightful World Champions in commanding form, and England (professional or not) way behind. The now completed 75,000 seat Twickenham stadium is a magnificent arena, it is a pity that the team's performance did not complement it.

2nd match   **ENGLAND   27 pts**   v   **WESTERN SAMOA   9 pts**

	Caps					Caps		
15	14th	M.J.Catt	(Bath)	.		V.Patu	(Vaiala)
14	3rd & last	D.P.Hopley	(Wasps)	.		B.Lima	(Marist)
13	62nd	W.D.C.Carling (Capt)	(Harlequins)	.		T.Vaega	(Te Atatu/Moataa)
12	41st	J.C.Guscott	(Bath)	.		G.Leaupepe	(Te Atuta)
11	81st	R.Underwood	(RAF/Leicester)	.		A.Telea	(Petone)
10	1st	P.J.Grayson	(Northampton)	.		D.Kellett	(Ponsonby/Marist)
9	1st	M.J.S.Dawson	(Northampton)	.		J.Filemu	(Wellington)
1	4th	G.C.Rowntree	(Leicester)	.		M.A.Mika	(Otago University)
2	2nd	M.P.Regan	(Bristol)	.		T.Leisasmaiva'o	(Wellington/Moataa)
3	45th	J.Leonard	(Harlequins)	.		P.Fatialofa	(Manukau/Marist)
4	20th	M.O.Johnson	(Leicester)	.		P.Leavasa	(Apia)
5	29th	M.C.Bayfield	(Northampton)	.		F.L.Falaniko	(Marist)
6	22nd	T.A.K.Rodber	(Northampton)	.		S.Kaleta	(Ponsonby)
7	2nd	L.B.N.Dallaglio	(Wasps)	.		S.Vaifale	(Marist)
8	24th	B.B.Clarke	(Bath)	.		P.Lam (Capt)	(Auckland/Marist)

S.Smith (Helensville) for Falaniko - 73

Referee: I.Roger   (South Africa)

SCORERS:

P.J.Grayson	Penalty Goal		3 - 0			
P.J.Grayson	Penalty Goal		6 - 0			
			6 - 3	D.Kellett	Penalty Goal	
P.J.Grayson	Penalty Goal		9 - 3			
			9 - 6	D.Kellett	Penalty Goal	
P.J.Grayson	Penalty Goal		12 - 6			
			Half-time			
P.J.Grayson	Penalty Goal		15 - 6			
			15 - 9	D.Kellett	Penalty Goal	
L.B.N.Dallaglio	Try	(1st)	20 - 9			
P.J.Grayson	Conversion		22 - 9			
R.Underwood	Try	(48th)	27 - 9			

POINTS:

P.J.Grayson	17 points	(17)		D.Kellett	9 points
L.B.N.Dallaglio	5 points	(5)			
R.Underwood	5 points	(205)			

MATCH COMMENTARY:

After the feeble performance against South Africa, Jack Rowell continued his pursuit of that elusive quality - expansive rugby, by making six changes, two of them positional for this important, yet insignifcant match. England had singularly failed to impress all through the World Cup (with the possible exception of the match against Australia) and since, and their followers were expecting a convincing display this afternoon. Regrettably they were to be disappointed yet again. So much so, that the unfortunate Paul Grayson, on his debut, when going for the fourth of his five penalty goals was roundly, and seriously, booed by the England faithful - at Twickenham. Unprecedented !!

There was a lot wrong with this England performance even though the front five showed commendable competence, and the newcomers, Dawson, Grayson and Dallaglio did well, the rest, to coin a phrase, were rubbish. Rowell has got to deliver soon, and perhaps he should force the issue by ensuring some dynamic leadership on the field, if only to compensate for the absence of same off it.

73rd match   **ENGLAND   12 pts**   v   **FRANCE   15 pts**

	Caps					Caps		
15	15th	M.J.Catt	(Bath)	.		39th	J-L.Sadourny	(Colomiers)
14	1st	J.M.Sleightholme	(Bath)	.		19th	E.N'Tamack	(Toulouse)
13	63rd	W.D.C.Carling (Capt)	(Harlequins)	.		5th	R.Dourthe	(Dax)
12	42nd	J.C.Guscott	(Bath)	.		5th	T.Castaignede	(Toulouse)
11	82nd	R.Underwood	(RAF/Leicester)	.		56th	P.Saint-Andre (Capt)	(Montferrand)
10	2nd	P.J.Grayson	(Northampton)	.		36th	T.Lacroix	(Dax)
9	2nd	M.J.S.Dawson	(Northampton)	.		5th	P.Carbonneau	(Toulouse)
1	5th	G.C.Rowntree	(Leicester)	.		1st	M.Perie	(Toulon)
2	3rd	M.P.Regan	(Bristol)	.		32nd	J-M.Gonzalez	(Bayonne)
3	46th	J.Leonard	(Harlequins)	.		17th	C.Califano	(Toulouse)
4	21st	M.O.Johnson	(Leicester)	.		56th	O.Roumat	((Dax)
5	30th	M.C.Bayfield	(Northampton)	.		27th	O.Merle	(Montferrand)
6	11th & last	S.O.Ojomoh	(Bath)	.		42nd	L.Cabannes	(Racing Club)
7	3rd	L.B.N.Dallaglio	(Wasps)	.		5th	F.Pelous	(Dax)
8	25th	B.B.Clarke	(Bath)	.		41st	A.Benazzi	(Agen)
	46th	D.Richards (temp)		.		11th	P.Bernat-Salles (Begles-Bordeaux) for	
				.			Sadourny - 55	
	Referee:	D.T.M.McHugh	(Ireland)					

SCORERS:

P.J.Grayson	Penalty Goal		3 - 0				
			3 - 3	T.Lacroix		Penalty Goal	
P.J.Grayson	Penalty Goal		6 - 3				
			Half-time				
			6 - 6	T.Lacroix		Drop goal	
			6 - 9	T.Lacroix		Penalty Goal	
P.J.Grayson	D'p Goal	(1st)	9 - 9				
			9 - 12	T.Lacroix		Penalty Goal	
P.J.Grayson	D'p Goal	(2nd)	12 - 12				
			12 - 15	T. Castaignede		Drop Goal	

POINTS:

P.J.Grayson	12 points	(29)		T.Lacroix	12 points	
				T. Castaignede	3 points	

MATCH COMMENTARY:

After two changes, Ojomoh for Rodber and Jon Sleightholme for Damien Hopley on the right wing, this was a much improved England performance, but although long on committment it was short on flair. The French decided to play England at their own game, 10 man rugby, and to maintain their discipline and they did both admirably. England's defence was impeccable and the best of a good bunch in that respect were Dallaglio, Carling, Guscott and Sleightholme. As a result, although they did not try to, France never looked like scoring a try. England had two chances and the unfortunate Rory Underwood was unsuccessfully involved in both. The first, when he narrowly failed to exert downward pressure due to the close attentions of N'Tamack and Saint-Andre, came in the first minute when Catt kicked ahead rather than keeping the ball in hand; and the second came some 15 minutes later when an inside pass from a good Carling break was taken by Rory and, instead of going for the line some eight yards away, he tried to pass inside to Catt and the poor pass went to ground. The French pack got the upper hand in the end, but Paul Grayson's second perfectly struck drop goal from 40 metres levelled the scores three minutes from time. Then the precocious 20-year old Thomas Castaignede won the game for France with flair, aplomb and a wobbly drop goal.

102nd match   **ENGLAND   21 pts**   v   **WALES   15 pts**

	Caps					Caps		
15	16th	M.J.Catt	(Bath)	.	4th	W.J.L.Thomas	(Llanelli)	
14	2nd	J.M.Sleightholme	(Bath)	.	58th	I.C.Evans	(Llanelli)	
13	64th	W.D.C.Carling (Capt)	(Harlequins)	.	2nd	L.B.Davies	(Neath)	
12	43rd	J.C.Guscott	(Bath)	.	21st	N.G.Davies	(Llanelli)	
11	83rd	R.Underwood	(RAF/Leicester)	.	20th	W.T.Proctor	(Llanelli)	
10	3rd	P.J.Grayson	(Northampton)	.	2nd	A.C.Thomas	(Bristol)	
9	3rd	M.J.S.Dawson	(Northampton)	.	1st	R.Howley	(Bridgend)	
1	6th	G.C.Rowntree	(Leicester)	.	2nd	A.L.P.Lewis	(Cardiff)	
2	4th	M.P.Regan	(Bristol)	.	6th	J.M.Humphreys (Capt)	(Cardiff)	
3	47th	J.Leonard	(Harlequins)	.	25th	J.D.Davies	(Neath)	
4	22nd	M.O.Johnson	(Leicester)	.	42nd	G.O.Llewellyn	(Neath)	
5	31st	M.C.Bayfield	(Northampton)	.	11th	D.Jones	(Cardiff)	
6	23rd	T.A.K.Rodber	(Northampton)	.	38th	E.W.Lewis	(Cardiff)	
7	4th	L.B.N.Dallaglio	(Wasps)	.	2nd	R.G.Jones	(Llanelli)	
8	26th	B.B.Clarke	(Bath)	.	17th	H.T.Taylor	(Cardiff)	

	15th	P.R de Glanville (Bath) for Carling - 53	.			
			.	2nd	S.Williams (Neath) temp	
			.	30th	G.R.Jenkins (Swansea) for Humphreys - 57	

Referee: K.W.McCartney   (Scotland)

SCORERS:

				0 - 5	H.T.Taylor	Try	
R.Underwood	Try	(49th & last)		5 - 5			
P.J.Grayson	Conversion			7 - 5			
			Half-time				
J.C.Guscott	Try	(18th)		12 - 5			
P.J.Grayson	Penalty Goal			15 - 5			
				15 - 8	A.C.Thomas	Penalty Goal	
P.J.Grayson	Penalty Goal			18 - 8			
P.J.Grayson	Penalty Goal			21 - 8			
				21 - 13	R.Howley	Try	
				21 - 15	A.C.Thomas	Conversion	

POINTS:

P.J.Grayson	11 points	(40)	H.T.Taylor, A.C.Thomas		
R.Underwood	5 points	(210)	and R.Howley	5 points each	
J.C.Guscott	5 points	(83)			

MATCH COMMENTARY:

Jack Rowell made only one change from the side beaten in Paris two weeks previously, bringing Tim Rodber back in place of the unfortunate Ojomoh. But, in the event, Steve Ojomoh might have considered himself fortunate not to have been associated with this match at all, for very few reputations were enhanced. It was a lumbering, clumsy performance by England who could make no impression against a keen youthful and exhuberent but inexperienced Welsh side who set out to enjoy themselves.   There were the briefest flashes of what might have been from England but there were too, long periods of directionless confusion, abysmally poor kicking and unco-ordinated forward play. England did nothing in the lines-out and little more with the ball in hand. Yet they won the penalty count by 19 to 10 - enough to win the match by 20 points in days gone by - but Grayson could not kick his goals either. England were 21 points to 8 up with fifteen minutes to go and then conceded a converted try and were struggling to hold on at the end.   Another unconvincing performance.

113th match   **ENGLAND   18 pts**   v   **SCOTLAND   9 pts**

103rd Calcutta Cup

	Caps					Caps		
15	17th	M.J.Catt	(Bath)	.		5th	R.J.S.Shepherd	(Melrose)
14	3rd	J.M.Sleightholme	(Bath)	.		16th	C.A.Joiner	(Melrose)
13	65th	W.D.C.Carling (Capt)	(Harlequins)	.		61st	S.Hastings	(Watsonians)
12	44th	J.C.Guscott	(Bath)	.		15th	I.C.Jardine	(Stirling County)
11	84th	R.Underwood	(RAF/Leicester)	.		8th	M.Dods	(Northampton)
10	4th	P.J.Grayson	(Northampton)	.		17th	G.P.J.Townsend	(Northampton)
9	4th	M.J.S.Dawson	(Northampton)	.		19th	B.W.Redpath	(Melrose)
1	7th	G.C.Rowntree	(Leicester)	.		14th	D.I.W.Hilton	(Bath)
2	5th	M.P.Regan	(Bristol)	.		8th	K.D.McKenzie	(Stirling County)
3	48th	J.Leonard	(Harlequins)	.		20th	P.H.Wright	(Boroughmuir)
4	23rd	M.O.Johnson	(Leicester)	.		13th	S.J.Campbell	(Dundee HSFP)
5	1st	G.S.Archer	(Bristol)	.		37th	G.W.Weir	(Newcastle Gosf
6	27th	B.B.Clarke	(Bath)	.		22nd	R.I.Wainwright (Capt)	(Watsonians)
7	5th	L.B.N.Dallaglio	(Wasps)	.		13th	E.W.Peters	(Bath)
8	47th	D.Richards	(Leicester)	.		16th	I.R.Smith	(Gloucester)

	24th	T.A.K.Rodber (Northampton)		.
		for Richards - 78		.

	Referee:	W.D.Bevan	(Wales)

SCORERS:

P.J.Grayson	Penalty Goal	3 - 0			
P.J.Grayson	Penalty Goal	6 - 0			
		6 - 3	M.Dods	Penalty Goal
P.J.Grayson	Penalty Goal	9 - 3			
P.J.Grayson	Penalty Goal	12 - 3			
		Half-time			
		12 - 6	M.Dods	Penalty Goal
		12 - 9	M.Dods	Penalty Goal
P.J.Grayson	Penalty Goal	15 - 9			
P.J.Grayson	Penalty Goal	18 - 9			

POINTS: | P.J.Grayson | 18 points | (58) | | M.Dods | 9 points |

MATCH COMMENTARY:

Jack Rowell made two changes from the side which had performed so unconvincingly against Wales in dropping Tim Rodber for the second time this season, and, more surprisingly, Martin Bayfield. Dean Richards' selection made the game plan patently obvious, but with Scotland going for a Grand Slam and at home, it wasn't going to be easy. The fact was, of course, that England had to win the match (at any price) to maintain Jack Rowell's position. Six years ago, when David Sole led the ominous walk out onto the pitch, Scotland sent the Auld Enemy homeward "tae think again". But not this time. Dean Richards saw to that. Again, he imposed his will and his character on the game and killed it. He did exactly what he was picked to do, slow the game down and exert dominant pressure through the pack and he is a past master at that. As such, it was a job very professionally done, as befits the new open game !! Professional but dull. Scotland played frenetically and tried to move the ball at all times, but their anxiety led to nervousness and indiscretion and Paul Grayson punished the offenders. As one pundit commented afterwards "One was left with the unacceptable impression that, having established total forward dominance, England had not got the imagination, the courage, or, God forbid, even the ability to score a try". England got a result, lost yet more friends, and Jack Rowell did not solve his problems, but he did buy some time. What a terrible price to pay !!

109th match   ENGLAND 28 pts   v   IRELAND 15 pts

	Caps					Caps		
15	18th	M.J.Catt	(Bath)	.	2nd	S.J.P.Mason	(Orrell)	
14	4th	J.M.Sleightholme	(Bath)	.	37th	S.P.Geoghegan	(Bath)	
13	66th	W.D.C.Carling (Capt)	(Harlequins)	.	14th	J.C.Bell	(Northampton)	
12	45th	J.C.Guscott	(Bath)	.	12th	M.J.Field	(Malone)	
11	85th & last	R.Underwood	(RAF/Leicester)	.	7th	N.K.P.J.Woods	(Blackrock College)	
10	5th	P.J.Grayson	(Northampton)	.	3rd	D.G.Humprhries	(London Irish)	
9	5th	M.J.S.Dawson	(Northampton)	.	8th	N.A.Hogan (Capt)	(Terenure College)	
1	8th	G.C.Rowntree	(Leicester)	.	38th	N.J.Popplewell	(Newcastle)	
2	6th	M.P.Regan	(Bristol)	.	3rd	A.T.H.Clarke	(Northampton)	
3	49th	J.Leonard	(Harlequins)	.	5th	P.S.Wallace	(Blackrock College)	
4	24th	M.O.Johnson	(Leicester)	.	16th	G.M.Fulcher	(Cork Constitution)	
5	2nd & last	G.S.Archer	(Bristol)	.	5th	J.W.Davidson	(Dungannon)	
6	28th	B.B.Clarke	(Bath)	.	13th	D.S.Corkery	(Cork Constitution)	
7	6th	L.B.N.Dallaglio	(Wasps)	.	25th	W.D.McBride	(Malone)	
8	48th & last	D.Richards	(Leicester)	.	4th	V.C.P.Costello	(St Mary's College)	

	25th	T.A.K.Rodber (Northampton) - temp	.	4th	C.M.McCall (Bangor) for Field - 16
	16th	P.R.de Glanville (Bath) for Carling - 35	.		

Referee: E.Murray   (Scotland)

SCORERS:

			0 - 3	D.G.Humphries	Drop Goal
			0 - 6	S.J.P.Mason	Penalty Goal
P.J.Grayson	Penalty Goal		3 - 6		
P.J.Grayson	Penalty Goal		6 - 6		
			6 - 9	S.J.P.Mason	Penalty Goal
			6 - 12	S.J.P.Mason	Penalty Goal
P.J.Grayson	Penalty Goal		9 - 12		
			9 - 15	S.J.P.Mason	Penalty Goal
P.J.Grayson	Penalty Goal		12 - 15		
			Half-time		
P.J.Grayson	Penalty Goal		15 - 15		
P.J.Grayson	D'p Goal	(3rd)	18 - 15		
P.J.Grayson	Penalty Goal		21 - 15		
J.M.Sleightholme	Try	(1st)	26 - 15		
P.J.Grayson	Conversion		28 - 15		

POINTS:

P.J.Grayson	23 points	(81)		S.J.P.Mason	12 points
J.M.Sleightholme	5 points	(5)		D.G.Humphries	3 points

MATCH COMMENTARY:

Will Carling had announced his intention to retire from the England Captaincy a week before this match, and, taking into account his wary relationship with Jack Rowell and the intense media scrutiny he had been under in connection with his divorce and sundry other personal matters, during the course of the season, it came as no surprise, and the news was greeted with both sympathy and understanding.

So it was that he led an unchanged England side for his 59th and last match as Captain, all of whom were acutely conscious of the need to redress the balance following the result of the last meeting at Twickenham, and there was a Triple Crown to be won as well. Ireland got off to a cracking start with a drop goal from David Humphries in the first minute and a further three points from a Simon Mason penalty goal only a few minutes later. But the opportunities came Paul Grayson's way and he levelled the score. Meanwhile, Will Carling was trying all he knew in continually running at the opposition and continually getting felled by resolute tackling because Grayson was not even drawing his man never mind creating half a gap. After Carling dramatically and anti-climactically had to leave the field with torn ankle ligaments, in the 33rd minute, Dean Richards took charge, slowed the game down and England ground into the lead. from being three points down at half-time Fortunately, to save everyone's face, with three minutes to go, Guscott and de Glanville set off on dummy runs, Sleightholme took the reverse pass and stormed through to score England's third try of the Championship. Even with only three tries, England took the Triple Crown and, thanks to Wales, who had beaten France, the title, but the manner of their doing so was less than satisfactory.

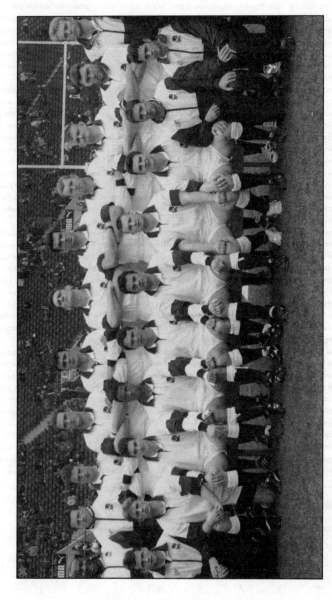

THE ENGLAND TEAM WHO BEAT IRELAND AT TWICKENHAM ON MARCH 16TH 1996, IN WILL CARLING'S LAST MATCH AS CAPTAIN.

Standing: V.E.Ubogu (Bench), R.G.R.Dawe (Bench), M.J.Catt, L.B.N.Dallaglio, B.B.Clarke, G.S.Archer, M.O.Johnson, D.Richards, G.C.Rowntree, J.Leonard, T.A.K.Rodber (Bench)

Seated: J.E.B.Callard (Bench) M.J.S.Dawson, P.J.Grayson. J.C.Guscott, R.Underwood, W.D.C.Carling (Captain), M.P.Regan, J.M.Sleightholme, P.R.de Glanville (Bench), K.P.P.Bracken (Bench)

SUMMARY OF THE SEASON - 1995 - 96:

Was this was another successful season for England, Jack Rowell and Will Carling ? They had won the Five Nations Championship on points difference over Scotland, won the Triple Crown for the nineteenth time, and for the fourth time under Will Carling's stewardship, and, of course, the Calcutta Cup. But a better perspective of the season as a whole can be gained when the two matches played before Christmas are taken into account as well. The defeat at the hands of South Africa, when abundant possession meant that the game was there for the taking, and the disappointing, totally negative performance against Western Samoa, demonstrated that neither the team, the Captain nor the Manager had learned the lessons offered by the unsatisfactory yet instructive experience of the World Cup. The more charitable might argue that the humiliation at the hands of New Zealand would take some time to get over, but professional teams must be able to rise above and learn from such sobering experiences.

There was depressing evidence throughout the season that England did not have a strategy, There was talk aplenty by both Carling and Rowell about a young team settling in to play expansive rugby to release the pace and experience of a formidable back division, and yet in the whole season, England scored only six tries in six games, but converted twenty five penalty goals. In two of the games, the last two, and in desperation, England elected to abandon the idea of expansive rugby, hence the recall of Dean Richards. There was inconsistency in selection. Mike Catt failed at fly-half, his club position, and Rowell should have known his capabilities in that respect; Martin Bayfield, a middle jumper, was dropped in favour of Gareth Archer, a front jumper, and the back row dilemma was never resolved. The unfortunate Tim Rodber was dropped twice during the season, and Andy Robinson and Steve Ojomoh each played only once. Only for the last two matches did the same back row combination play in successive matches and by that time it was being openly admitted that the ends were more important than the means and that expansive rugby, by implication beyond the capability of the side, would have to take a back seat. The strategy reverted to forward dominance and slowing the pace of the game down at which Dean Richards is a past master. As a result only one try was scored in those two games and they were won because that strategy in the Five Nations is successful, but it was clearly demonstrated in South Africa in 1994 and 1995 that it will not work on the world stage.

There was an undefined suspicion during the course of the season that perhaps all was not well between the Manager, Jack Rowell, and the Captain, Will Carling. Whether or not that was the case ceased to matter when, one week before the final match of the season, Will Carling announced his intention to stand down from the Captaincy after the Ireland match, but not yet to retire from International rugby. By any standards, Carling had been an outstanding Captain for England since his surprising appointment by Geoff Cooke in 1988 at the tender age of 22. He had led England on 59 occasions, won three Grand Slams and four Triple Crowns. Under his leadership, England have won 44 matches and lost 14, with one draw. During those eight seasons, Carling has missed only two matches. His tenure of office far exceeds that of any other International Captain, Nick Farr Jones being the next in line having led Australia 36 times, followed by Sean Fitzpatrick of New Zealand with 33 to date. It was a cruel twist of fate (and of ankle ligaments), that he should have to leave the field at Twickenham in his last match as Captain, on a stretcher. He ranks as England's third highest try scorer with 11 tries in 66 matches so far, and was always a strong running centre, fearless and resolute in defence, but without the vision of a true play-maker.

England used 23 players in total during the course of the six match season, and 18 in the Five Nations matches, plus the unfortunate Phil de Glanville who gained three caps as a substitute but never started a match. There were eight players who played in two matches or less, and eight, conversely who played in all six. Six new caps were awarded during the season, and all of those six played in the last two matches Five players came to the end of their International careers, for various reasons, at the end of the season. Rory Underwood won a record 85 caps for England, and scored a record 49 tries. He had been playing International rugby for 13 seasons since gaining his first cap against Ireland in 1984 and in that time he had missed only nine matches and had played in all but one of all England's World Cup matches in 1987, 1991 and 1995. A remarkable record. The mighty Dean Richards had won 48 caps, spanning 11 seasons and had been in and out of the England side on numerous occasions. Victor Ubogu, 21 caps, Andy Robinson, 8, Jonathan Callard, 5, and Damien Hopley, 3 caps, were the others. The season for England never lived up to its optimistic promise, nor, with hindsight, was it ever likely to do so. The game is still in the throes of agonising change, but it is professional, and it must be professionally run by the National Unions, by the Managers and Coaches, and, indeed by the referees, all of whom should be as professional, in all respects, as the players. There is still a long way to go.

FIVE NATIONS CHAMPIONSHIP TABLE:

Won: **Triple Crown, Championship Title and Calcutta Cup**

		Played	Won	Lost	Drawn	Points: For	Against	Tries: For	Against	Title Points
1	**ENGLAND**	4	3	1	0	79	54	3	2	6
2	Scotland	4	3	1	0	60	56	5	3	6
3	France	4	2	2	0	89	57	10	3	4
4	Wales	4	1	3	0	62	82	6	9	2
5	Ireland	4	1	4	0	65	106	5	12	2

Home Games: beat Wales 21 - 15, (two tries each); beat Ireland 28 - 15, (one try to nil)

Away Games: lost to France 12 - 15, (no tries); beat Scotland 18 - 9, (no tries)

3rd match   **ENGLAND   54 pts**   **v**   **ITALY   21 pts**

	Caps					Caps		
15	1st	**T.R.G.Stimpson**	(Newcastle)	.		5th	**J.Pertile**	(Roma Olimpic)
14	5th	**J.M.Sleightholme**	(Bath)	.		38th	**P.Vaccari**	(Calvisano)
13	67th	**W.D.C.Carling**	(Harlequins)	.		27th	**S.Bordon**	(Rovigo)
12	17th	**P.R.de Glanville (Capt)**	(Bath)	.		32nd	**I.Francescato**	(Benetton Treviso)
11	1st	**A.A.Adebayo**	(Bath)	.		3rd	**L.Manteri**	(Benetton Treviso)
10	19th	**M.J.Catt**	(Bath)	.		32nd	**D.Dominguez**	(Milan)
9	1st	**A.C.T.Gomarsall**	(Wasps)	.		23rd	**A.Troncon**	(Benetton Treviso)
1	9th	**G.C.Rowntree**	(Leicester)	.		50th	**M.Cuttitta**	(Milan)
2	7th	**M.P.Regan**	(Bristol)	.		30th	**C.Orlandi**	(Milan)
3	50th	**J.Leonard**	(Harlequins)	.		36th	**F.P.Curti**	(Milan)
4	25th	**M.O.Johnson**	Leicester)	.		7th	**W.Christofoletto**	(Benetton Treviso)
5	1st	**S.D.Shaw**	(Bristol)	.		34th	**C.Checchinato**	(Benetton Treviso)
6	26th	**T.A.K.Rodber**	(Northampton)	.		35th	**M.Giovanelli (Capt)**	(P.U.C.France)
7	7th	**L.B.N.Dallaglio**	(Wasps)	.		19th	**C.Covi**	(Padova)
8	1st	**C.M.A.Sheasby**	(Wasps)	.		22nd	**O.Arancio**	(Milan)

1st	R.J.K.Hardwick (Coventry) for Leonard - 71	.	2nd	G.Guidi (Livorno) for Troncon - 32
1st	P.B.T.Greening (Gloucester) for Regan - 76	.	23rd	A.Sgorlon (Benetton Treviso) for Covi - 56
12th	K.P.P.Bracken (Saracens) for Gomarsall - 80	.	2nd	A.Barattin (Tarvisium) for Checchinato - 81

Referee: P.Deluca   (Argentina)

SCORERS:

M.J.Catt	Penalty Goal		3 - 0			
M.J.Catt	Penalty Goal		6 - 0			
A.C.T.Gomarsall	Try	(1st)	11 - 0			
M.J.Catt	Conversion		13 - 0			
M.J.Catt	Penalty Goal		16 - 0			
J.M.Sleightholme	Try	(2nd)	21 - 0			
L.B.N.Dallaglio	Try	(2nd)	26 - 0			
M.J.Catt	Conversion		28 - 0			
			Half-time			
M.O.Johnson	Try	(1st)	33 - 0			
M.J.Catt	Conversion		35 - 0			
			35 - 5	**P.Vaccari**	Try	
			35 - 7	**D.Dominguez**	Conversion	
A.C.T.Gomarsall	Try	(2nd)	40 - 7			
M.J.Catt	Conversion		42 - 7			
			42 - 12	**A.Troncon**	Try	
			42 - 14	**D.Dominguez**	Conversion	
			42 - 19	**O.Arancio**	Try	
			42 - 21	**D.Dominguez**	Conversion	
T.A.K.Rodber	Try	(3rd)	47 - 21			
M.J.Catt	Conversion		49 - 21			
C.M.A.Sheasby	Try	(1st)	54 - 21			

POINTS:	M.J.Catt	19 points	(32)	D.Dominguez	6 points
	A.C.T.Gomarsall	10 points	(10)	P.Vaccari, A Troncon	
	C.M.A.Sheasby, L.B.N.Dallaglio,		(5),(10)	and O.Arancio	5 points each
	M.O.Johnson, T.A.K.Rodber	5 points	(5),(15)		
	and J.M.Sleightholme	each	(10)		

MATCH COMMENTARY:

Even five new caps in the England side failed to ignite this match into any form of spectacle at all. With 25,000 seats empty at Twickenham, the atmosphere was distinctly lacking and a very flat match bore witness to that. England won, but lost direction in the third quarter and allowed the opposition to score three tries within fifteen minutes, and then came good again. But it really was not good enough and many questions remain to be answered. The five new caps acquitted themselves well enough, with Chris Sheasby and Andy Gomarsall scoring tries in their debut match. In scoring two tries Andy Gomarsall became one of only five players to have scored two tries in their debut International match, the others being Ian Hunter, against Canada in 1992, Dean Richards, against Ireland in 1986, Bob Lloyd, against New Zealand in 1967, and Jim Roberts, against Wales in 1960.

In no respect did the match inspire or improve the prospects for England, in terms of a potentially winning Five Nations season to come, nor for Italy in their determined pursuit of a place in a re-structured Six Nations European competition.

1st match   **ENGLAND   19 pts**   v   **N.Z. BARBARIANS 34 pts**

(The RFU decreed that Caps would not be awarded for this match)

15	T.R.G.Stimpson	(Newcastle)		C.M.Cullen	(Manawatu)
14	J.M.Sleightholme	(Bath)		J.Vidiri	(Counties)
13	W.D.C.Carling	(Harlequins)		A.I.Ieremia	(Wellington)
12	P.R.de Glanville (Capt)	(Bath)		L.Stensness	(Auckland)
11	A.A.Adebayo	(Bath)		J.T.Lomu	(Counties)
10	M.J.Catt	(Bath)		A.P.Mehrtens	(Canterbury)
9	A.C.T.Gomarsall	(Wasps)		J.W.Marshall	(Canterbury)
1	G.C.Rowntree	(Leicester)		M.R.Allen	(Taranaki)
2	M.P.Regan	(Bristol)		S.B.T.Fitzpatrick (Capt)	(Auckland)
3	J.Leonard	(Harlequins)		O.M.Brown	(Auckland)
4	M.O.Johnson	(Leicester)		I.D.Jones	(North Harbour)
5	S.D.Shaw	(Bristol)		R.M.Brooke	(Auckland)
6	T.A.K.Rodber	(Northampton)		M.N.Jones	(Auckland)
7	L.B.N.Dallaglio	(Wasps)		A.Blowers	(Auckland)
8	C.M.A.Sheasby	(Wasps)		T.C.Randell	(Otago)

D.G.Mika (Auckland) for Randell - 56
C.J.Spencer (Auckland) for Mehrtens - 60
G.M.Osborne (North Harbour) for Vidiri - 80

Referee: C.Thomas   (Wales)

SCORERS:

M.J.Catt	Penalty Goal	3 - 0			
		3 - 5	R.M.Brooke	Try	
		3 - 8	A.P.Mehrtens	Penalty Goal	
M.J.Catt	Penalty Goal	6 - 8			
M.J.Catt	Penalty Goal	9 - 8			
		Half-time			
		9 - 13	A.Blowers	Try	
J.M.Sleightholme	Try	14 - 13			
T.R.G.Stimpson	Try	19 - 13			
		19 - 16	A.P.Mehrtens	Penalty Goal	
		19 - 19	C.J.Spencer	Penalty Goal	
		19 - 22	C.J.Spencer	Penalty Goal	
		19 - 27	C.J.Spencer	Try	
		19 - 29	C.J.Spencer	Conversion	
		19 - 34	J.Vidiri	Try	

POINTS:

M.J.Catt	9 points		C.J.Spencer	13 points
J.M.Sleightholme	5 points		A.P.Mehrtens	6 points
T.R.G.Stimpson	5 points		R.M.Brooke, A.Blowers and J.Vidiri	5 points each

MATCH COMMENTARY:

The RFU had decided in their infinite wisdom that caps would not be awarded for this match, although it would undoubtedly be the hardest match against the strongest opponents that England would face up to this season.

England performed remarkably well, but not well enough to win the match. As one astute commentator observed "England won the show-piece match 19 - 13, but lost the real game 21 - 0". The speed at which the whole Barbarians side played proved too much for England in the last twenty minutes, and the arrival of Spencer to replace Mehrtens drove the final nails in the coffin. The forwards competed well but possession from the tight and from the loose came back too slowly to be other than a disadvantage to the half-backs of whom Mike Catt, in particular, looked out of sorts and out of place at this level. After England took the lead in the third quarter with two well-taken tries, to establish that 19 - 13 score, it seemed that New Zealand recognised the need, raised their game and nearly trebled their score in the last twenty minutes. This performance was testimony to their ability and to their fitness and England should, indeed must, learn from having been on the receiving end. It was surely not without significance that New Zealand replaced both their No 8 and their fly-half just before the last quarter onslaught began. Whether these were injury provoked substitutes or tactical replacements is not clear, and no matter, but the fact is that replacements were made and they must have played a significant part in the extent to which New Zealand were able to raise their game. Herein lies another lesson for the England Management, Coaches and Captain - now that tactical substitutes are allowed, use that facility to best advantage, it can be an invaluable weapon in the professional contest.

7th match   **ENGLAND   20 pts**   v   **ARGENTINA   18pts**

	Caps					Caps		
15	1st	N.D.Beal	(Northampton)	.	11th	E.Jurado	(Jockey de Rosario)
14	6th	J.M.Sleightholme	(Bath)	.	23rd	G.F.Camardon	(Asociacion Alumni)
13	68th	W.D.C.Carling	(Harlequins)	.	4th	E.Simone	(Liceo Naval)
12	46th	J.C.Guscott	(Bath)	.	42nd	L.Arbizu (Capt)	(Belgrano A.C.)
11	21st	T.Underwood	(Newcastle)	.	8th	D.L.Albanese	(San Isidro)
10	20th	M.J.Catt	(Bath)	.	5th	G.Quesada	(Hindu Club)
9	2nd	A.C.T.Gomarsall	(Wasps)	.	9th	N.Fernandez-Miranda	(Hindu Club)
1	10th	G.C.Rowntree	(Leicester)	.	13th	R.Grau	(Liceo R.C.)
2	8th	M.P.Regan	(Bristol)	.	5th	C.Promanzio	(Duendes R.C.)
3	51st	J.Leonard (Capt)	(Harlequins)	.	4th	M.Reggiardo	(Castres)
4	26th	M.O.Johnson	(Leicester)	.	42nd	P.L.Sporleder	(Curupayti)
5	2nd	S.D.Shaw	(Bristol)	.	33rd	G.A.Llanes	(La Plata Rugby)
6	27th	T.A.K.Rodber	(Northampton)	.	26th	R.A.Martin	(San Isidro)
7	8th	L.B.N.Dallaglio	(Wasps)	.	15th	P.J.Camerlinckx	(Regatas Bella Vista)
8	2nd	C.M.A.Sheasby	(Wasps)	.	4th	P.Bouza	(Duendes R.C.)

29th   B.B.Clarke (Richmond) for Sheasby - 56

Referee: T.Henning   (South Africa)

SCORERS:

			0 - 3		G.Queseda	Penalty Goal
M.J.Catt	Penalty Goal		3 - 3			
M.J.Catt	Penalty Goal		6 - 3			
			6 - 6		G.Queseda	Penalty Goal
M.J.Catt	Penalty Goal		9 - 6			
			9 - 9		G.Queseda	Penalty Goal
			Half-time			
M.J.Catt	Penalty Goal		12 - 9			
			12 - 12		G.Queseda	Penalty Goal
			12 - 15		G.Queseda	Penalty Goal
			12 - 18		G.Queseda	Penalty Goal
M.J.Catt	Penalty Goal		15 - 18			
J.Leonard	Try	(1st)	20 - 18			

POINTS:

M.J.Catt	15 points	(47)		G.Queseda	18 points
J.Leonard	5 points	(5)			

MATCH COMMENTARY:

With Tim Stimpson, Adedeyo Adebeyo and, later, Captain Phil de Glanville, all *'hors de combat'* Jack Rowell had to pedal backwards from his preferred selection, and allow Jeremy Guscott to play at centre. It was still not a capacity crowd at Twickenham and those who stayed away must have been mightily relieved for, from England's point of view, it was a dreadful game. Mike Catt proved beyond reasonable doubt that he is not an International fly-half, and with him the England machine spluttered and almost died. The most humiliating of defeats was avoided only by the pack's sterling effort in driving Jason Leonard over for the winning try with six minutes to go to the end of the match. On this evidence, the pre-Christmas matches have complicated issues rather than clarified them, and the promise of world-class rugby at Twickenham is as much of a pipe dream as ever it was. A lot of changes in attitude and direction are necessary before the Five Nations.

114th match   **ENGLAND   41 pts   v   SCOTLAND   13 pts**
104th Calcutta Cup

	Caps					Caps		
15	2nd	T.R.G.Stimpson	(Newcastle)	.	11th	R.J.S.Shepherd	(Melrose)
14	7th	J.M.Sleightholme	(Bath)	.	8th	D.A.Stark	(Melrose)
13	69th	W.D.C.Carling	(Harlequins)	.	43rd	A.G.Stanger	(Hawick)
12	18th	P.R.de Glanville (Capt)	(Bath)	.	3rd	B.R.S.Ericksson	(London Scottish)
11	22nd	T.Underwood	(Newcastle)	.	28th	K.M.Logan	(Stirling County)
10	6th	P.J.Grayson	(Northampton)	.	23rd	G.P.J.Townsend	(Northampton)
9	3rd	A.C.T.Gomarsall	(Wasps)	.	22nd	B.W.Redpath	(Melrose)
1	11th	G.C.Rowntree	(Leicester)	.	1st	T.J.Smith	(Watsonians)
2	9th	M.P.Regan	(Bristol)	.	2nd	D.G.Ellis	(Currie)
3	52nd	J.Leonard	(Harlequins)	.	4th	M.J.Stewart	(Northampton
4	27th	M.O.Johnson	(Leicester)	.	43rd	G.W.Weir	(Newcastle)
5	3rd	S.D.Shaw	(Bristol)	.	12th	A.I.Reed	(Wasps)
6	9th	L.B.N.Dallaglio	(Wasps)	.	8th	P.Walton	(Newcastle)
7	1st	R.A.Hill	(Saracens)	.	21st	I.R.Smith	(Gloucester)
8	28th	T.A.K.Rodber	(Northampton)	.	26th	R.I.Wainwright (Capt)	(Watsonians)

Referee: P.O'Brien   (New Zealand)

SCORERS:

P.J.Grayson	Penalty Goal		3 - 0			
	Penalty Try		8 - 0			
P.J.Grayson	Conversion		10 - 0			
			10 - 5	B.R.S.Ericksson	Try	
			10 - 7	R.J.S.Shepherd	Conversion	
P.J.Grayson	Penalty Goal		13 - 7			
			13 - 10	R.J.S.Shepherd	Penalty Goal	
P.J.Grayson	Penalty Goal		16 - 10			
			Half-time			
			16 - 13	R.J.S.Shepherd	Penalty Goal	
P.J.Grayson	Penalty Goal		19 - 13			
P.J.Grayson	Penalty Goal		22 - 13			
A.C.T.Gomarsall	Try	(3rd)	27 - 13			
P.J.Grayson	Conversion		29 - 13			
W.D.C.Carling	Try	12th & last)	34 - 13			
P.R.de Glanville	Try	(2nd)	39 - 13			
P.J.Grayson	Conversion		41 - 13			

POINTS:

P.J.Grayson	21 point	(102)		R.J.S.Shepherd	8 points
A.C.T.Gomarsall, W.D.C.Carling	5 point	(15),(54)		B.R.S.Ericksson	5 points
and P.R.de Glanville	each	(10)			
Penalty Try					

MATCH COMMENTARY:

England's opening Five Nations match against Scotland had been eagerly awaited by friend and foe alike, primarily to see whether England's stuttering performance in the three pre-Christmas Internationals was to continue in that vein or no. In the event, both parties were to some extent satisfied. This was a commendable win for England by a record margin against Scotland and the highest score ever achieved by England in a Five Nations match. The first hour of the match was workman-like, tedious and uninspiring. The score at that time was 22 - 13 with five penalty goals from Paul Grayson, and a converted but very dubious penalty try. England appeared to be trying too hard, the ball was coming back too slowly, frustration was creeping in and confidence was almost visibly waning. Meanwhile, Scotland were tackling like demons but taking, generally, a fearful physical battering. Then the floodgates opened and England scored three tries through Andy Gomarsall, Will Carling and Phil de Glanville within six minutes, and the game was over. Then England lapsed into unconvincing mode once again. For the second match in succession, Scotland had conceded three tries in the middle of the second half. For England, those three tries demonstrated what was possible, and the remaining minutes before and after, clearly demonstrated why the possible had not been achieved before. But one cannot argue with the score, and, hopefully, the recycling of possession at a faster rate can be improved in training and if so, then the prospects for the remainder of this season are bright indeed, notwithstanding the trips to both Dublin and Cardiff yet to come.

THE ENGLAND TEAM WHO BEAT SCOTLAND AT TWICKENHAM ON FEBRUARY 1ST 1997

Standing: B.B.Clarke (Bench), W.D.C.Carling, R.A.Hill, T.R.G.Stimpson, S.D.Shaw, M.O.Johnson, T.A.K.Rodber, L.B.N.Dallaglio, G.C.Rowntree, J.Leonard, D.J.Garforth (Bench),

Seated: P.B.T.Greening (Bench), M.P.Regan, T.Underwood, P.J.Grayson, P.R.de Glanville (Captain), A.C.T.Gomarsall, J.M.Sleightholme, J.C.Guscott (Bench), A.Healey (Bench), M.J.Catt (Bench)

110th match   **ENGLAND   46 pts   v   IRELAND   6 pts**

	Caps				Caps		
15	3rd	T.R.G.Stimpson	(Newcastle)		25th	J.E.Staples (Capt)	(Harlequins)
14	8th	J.M.Sleightholme	(Bath)		2nd	D.Hickie	(St Mays's College)
13	70th	W.D.C.Carling	(Harlequins)		20th	J.C.Bell	(Northampton)
12	19th	P.R.de Glanville (Capt)	(Bath)		16th	M.J.Field	(Malone)
11	23rd	T.Underwood	(Newcastle)		5th	J.A.Topping	(Ballymena)
10	7th	P.J.Grayson	(Northampton)		19th	E.P.Elwood	(Lansdowne)
9	4th	A.C.T.Gomarsall	(Wasps)		12th	N.A.Hogan	(Terenure)
1	12th	G.C.Rowntree	(Leicester)		44th	N.J.Popplewell	(Newcastle)
2	10th	M.P.Regan	(Bristol)		2nd	R.P.Nesdale	(Newcastle)
3	53rd	J.Leonard	(Harlequins)		11th	P.S.Wallace	(Saracens)
4	28th	M.O.Johnson	(Leicester)		11th	J.W.Davidson	(London Irish)
5	4th	S.D.Shaw	(Bristol)		33rd	P.S.Johns	(Saracens)
6	10th	L.B.N.Dallaglio	(Wasps)		20th	D.S.Corkery	(Bristol)
7	2nd	R.A.Hill	(Saracens)		31st	W.D.McBride	(Malone)
8	29th	T.A.K.Rodber	(Northampton)		4th	E.R.P.Miller	(Leicester)

1st	A.Healey (Leicester) for Gomarsall - 73			9th	A.G.Foley (Shannon) for Miller - 12	
47th	J.C.Guscott (Bath) for Carling - 77			7th	D.G.Humphreys (L Irish) for Elwood - 25	
				3rd	B.F.O'Meara (Cork Const) for Hogan - 66	

Referee: C.J.Hawke   (New Zealand)

SCORERS:

			0 - 3	E.P.Elwood	Penalty Goal	
P.J.Grayson	Penalty Goal		3 - 3			
			3 - 6	E.P.Elwood	Penalty Goal	
J.M.Sleightholme	Try	(3rd)	8 - 6			
P.J.Grayson	Penalty Goal		11 - 6			
			Half-time			
P.J.Grayson	Penalty Goal		14 - 6			
P.J.Grayson	Penalty Goal		17 - 6			
A.C.T.Gomarsall	Try	(4th)	22 - 6			
P.J.Grayson	Conversion		24 - 6			
J.M.Sleightholme	Try	(4th)	29 - 6			
R.A.Hill	Try	(1st)	34 - 6			
T.Underwood	Try	(11th)	39 - 6			
P.J.Grayson	Conversion		41- 6			
T.Underwood	Try	(12th)	46 - 6			

POINTS:

P.J.Grayson	16 points	(118)	E.P.Elwood	6 points	
T.Underwood	10 points	(60)			
J.M.Sleightholme	10 points	(20)			
A.C.T.Gomarsall and R.A.Hill	5 points	(20),(5)			
	each				

MATCH COMMENTARY:

The eager anticapation with this fixture was awaited was worthy of a Championship decider, but it was not that. It was, though, a revived Ireland after the fortuitous victory at Cardiff, against a confident, unchanged England side after their impressive win over a poor Scotland. It was also Jack Rowell versus his erstwhile colleague at Bath, Brian Ashton who had been appointed Coaching Adviser to the Irish team only three weeks previously. The Irish, as always, started frenetically and there was no advantage to either side until fate in the form of injury struck at Ireland. First Eric Miller and then Eric Elwood had to leave the field which diminished Ireland's confidence and, one suspects, their potential. However it was only 11 - 6 at half-time but Ireland were beginning to look ragged. During parts of the third quarter, Ireland showed promising signs of taking the game to England with vigorous thrusts from Hickie, Topping and Field in quick succession, but Foley and Corkery were also giving away unnecessary penalties from which Grayson kept the score moving and the gap widening. But the climax came after Gomarsall's try when England scored four more tries in the last eight minutes of the match, when Ireland were totally bewildered. Significantly, two tactical replacements played a major part in three of those four tries. Austin Healey's speed from the base of the scrum only seconds after he came on to the field, led directly to Richard Hill's try, and Jeremy Guscott's slick passing out of the tackle was certainly responsible for both Tony Underwood's tries. A selection dilemma of even greater proportions is looming for the England Coach because surely, no justification now exists for Jeremy Guscott's continued omission from the side.

This was Englands's highest ever score and biggest winning margin in any Five Nations match, and it is the first time in fifty years that England have scored six tries away from home in the Five Nations Championship.

74th match   **ENGLAND   20 pts   v   FRANCE   23 pts**

	Caps					Caps		
15	4th	T.R.G.Stimpson	(Newcastle)			50th	J-L.Sadourny	(Colomiers)
14	9th	J.M.Sleightholme	(Bath)			3rd	L.Leflamand	(Bourgoin)
13	71st	W.D.C.Carling	(Harlequins)			4th	C.Lamaison	(Brive)
12	20th	P.R.de Glanville (Capt)	(Bath)			11th	S.Glas	(Bourgoin)
11	24th	T.Underwood	(Newcastle)			6th	D.Venditti	(Brive)
10	8th	P.J.Grayson	(Northampton)			28th	A.Penaud	(Brive)
9	5th	A.C.T.Gomarsall	(Wasps)			13th	P.Carbonneau	(Brive)
1	13th	G.C.Rowntree	(Leicester)			28th	C.Califano	(Toulouse)
2	11th	M.P.Regan	(Bristol)			7th	M.Dal Maso	(Agen)
3	54th	J.Leonard	(Harlequins)			11th	F.Tournaire	(Narbonne)
4	29th	M.O.Johnson	(Leicester)			36th	O.Merle	(Montferrand)
5	5th	S.D.Shaw	(Bristol)			5th	H.Moirin	(Toulouse)
6	11th	L.B.N.Dallaglio	(Wasps)			52nd	A.Benazzi (Capt)	(Agen)
7	3rd	R.A.Hill	(Saracens)			2nd	O.Magne	(Dax)
8	30th	T.A.K.Rodber	(Northampton)			16th	F.Pelous	(Dax)
						7th	R.Castel (Beziers) for Miorin - 49	
						11th	M.de Rougemont (Toulon) for Benazzi - 66	

Referee: J.M.Fleming   (Scotland)

SCORERS:

			0 - 3	C.Lamaison	Penalty Goal
P.J.Grayson	Penalty Goal		3 - 3		
P.J.Grayson	Penalty Goal		6 - 3		
P.J.Grayson	Penalty Goal		9 - 3		
			9 - 6	C.Lamaison	Drop Goal
L.B.N.Dallaglio.	Try	(3rd)	14 - 6		
			Half-time		
P.J.Grayson	D'p Goal	(4th)	17 - 6		
P.J.Grayson	Penalty Goal		20 - 6		
			20 - 11	L.Leflamand	Try
			20 - 13	C.Lamaison	Conversion
			20 - 18	C.Lamaison	Try
			20 - 20	C.Lamaison	Conversion
			20 - 23	C.Lamaison	Penalty Goal

POINTS:

P.J.Grayson	15 points	(133)	C.Lamaison	18 points
L.B.N.Dallaglio.	5 points	(15)	L.Leflamand	5 points

MATCH COMMENTARY:

England fielded an unchanged side for the third match in succession, and there was widespread expectation that the side would continue the running game which had graced the last twenty minutes of the Ireland match - indeed Jack Rowell implied that this would certainly be so. But it was a quite extraordinary game in which England in moving to a 20 - 6 lead within the hour had then to spend most of the second half defending desperately against a French side, who, far from losing the place and their tempers, became more resolute as the game went on. The first half was played at a very fast pace with England driving for second, third and fourth phase ball very successfully, but when they did attempt to move tha ball wide, Grayson did not get his three-quarters moving, the French mid-field tackling was effective and neither wing received a pass worthy of the name.   Merle and Pelous certainly shared the honours in the lines-out and England possession from that area was rarely crisp nor potentially dangerous.   Lawrence Dallaglio's try was well worked but it came from loose play with Phil de Glanville going left and, again, cutting back inside to find Dallaglio coming up at pace on the inside.   That put England 14 points to 6 up at half-time.

A Paul Grayson drop goal and a further penalty had all spectators present, and the multitude watching on TV, expecting England to pile a heap of points on top of their now commanding 20 - 6 lead.   But, not so.   England did not visibly slacken, but the French very visibly stepped up their game, and even when Captain Abdelatif Benazzi went off the field, following an earlier tactical substitute, the two replacements Castel and de Rougemont noticably further livened up the pace, and England began to struggle.   There were no tactical substitutions from the England bench, presumably because there was perceived to be no need, or because the need was not recognised. Two superb second-half tries, one by Christophe Lamaison who converted both and struck the winning penalty goal with three minutes remaining were France's just reward for some very courageous rugby.   Why England lost control and lost the match will be the subject of many a post-mortem but, whatever the reason, France won the match because they believed that they could - and they did.   England lacked that conviction.

Thus occured France's third successive win over England, and an ignominious end to an England run of seven succesive wins in all matches.   Never before have England suffered such a reversal in establishing a 14 point lead, and from that position, losing the match.

FIVE NATIONS CHAMPIONSHIP, 1996-97   March 15th 1997, at Cardiff Arms Park

103rd match   **ENGLAND   34 pts**   v   **WALES   13 pts**

	Caps					Caps		
15	5th	T.R.G.Stimpson	(Newcastle)	.	50th	N.R.Jenkins	(Pontypridd)
14	10th	J.M.Sleightholme	(Bath)	.	11th	S.D.Hill	(Cardiff)
13	72nd & last	W.D.C.Carling	(Harlequins)	.	9th	A.G.Bateman	(Richmond)
12	21st	P.R.de Glanville (Capt)	(Bath)	.	29th	N.G.Davies	(Llanelli)
11	25th	T.Underwood	(Newcastle)	.	17th	G.Thomas	(Bridgend)
10	21st	M.J.Catt	(Bath)	.	32nd & last	J.Davies	(Cardiff)
9	2nd	A.Healey	(Leicester)	.	16th	R.Howley	(Cardiff)
1	14th	G.C.Rowntree	(Leicester)	.	14th	C.D.Loader	(Swansea)
2	12th	M.P.Regan	(Bristol)	.	19th	J.M.Humphries (Capt)	(Cardiff)
3	55th	J.Leonard	(Harlequins)	.	21st	D.Young	(Cardiff)
4	30th	M.O.Johnson	(Leicester)	.	57th	G.O.Llewellyn	(Harlequins)
5	6th	S.D.Shaw	(Bristol)	.	3rd	M.J.Voyle	(Llanelli)
6	30th	B.B.Clarke	(Richmond)	.	14th	S.M.Williams	(Neath)
7	4th	R.A.Hill	(Saracens)	.	6th	K.P.Jones	(Ebbw Vale)
8	31st	T.A.K.Rodber	(Northampton)	.	14th	L.S.Quinell	(Richmond)

48th	J.C.Guscott (Bath) for Sleightholme - 40	.	29th	W.T.Proctor (Llanelli) for Jenkins - 15
2nd	P.B.T.Greening (Gloucester) for Regan - 40	.	3rd	S.C.John (Llanelli) for Loader - 23
3rd	C.M.A.Sheasby (Wasps) for Clarke - 70	.	2nd	D.L.M.McIntosh (Pontypridd) for Jones - 65
71st & last	C.R.Andrew (Newcastle) for Catt - 73	.	6th	J.C.Quinnell (Richmond) for Voyle - 69
1st	D.J.Garforth (Leicester) for Rowntree - 78	.		

Referee: J.Dume   (France)

SCORERS:

	M.J.Catt	Penalty Goal		3 - 0			
	M.J.Catt	Penalty Goal		6 - 0			
				6 - 3	J.Davies	Penalty Goal	
				Half-time			
	T.R.G.Stimpson	Try	(1st)	11 - 3			
	M.J.Catt	Conversion		13 - 3			
	T.Underwood	Try	(13th)	18 - 3			
	M.J.Catt	Conversion		20 - 3			
				20 - 6	J.Davies	Penalty Goal	
	R.A.Hill	Try	(2nd)	25 - 6			
	M.J.Catt	Conversion		27 - 6			
	P.R.de Glanville	Try	(3rd)	32 - 6			
	M.J.Catt	Conversion		34 - 6			
				34 - 11	R.Howley	Try	
				34 - 13	J.Davies	Conversion	

POINTS:

	M.J.Catt	14 points	(61)	J.Davies	8 points
	T.R.G.Stimpson, T.Underwood	5 points	(5),(65)	R.Howley	5 points
	P.R de Glanville and R.A.Hill	each	(15),(10)		

MATCH COMMENTARY:

This was to be the last International Rugby match at Cardiff Arms Park prior to the demolition of the existing stadium, only finally completed in the early Eighties, and the erection of a new, larger capacity arena in time for the 1999 World Cup. It was an emotive occasion for that reason, but probably one which the Welsh would rather forget for their side were beaten out of sight, by a record margin at Cardiff, and by four tries to one. Wales were sorely stricken by injuries both before and during the match, but England, who had changed both half-backs following the disaster in the second half against France two weeks previously, and were without Lawrence Dallaglio who had to withdraw at the last minute, were vastly superior once they got their line-out problems sorted out early in the second half. Mike Catt was recalled at fly-half in place of the injured Paul Grayson, and Austin Healey replaced Andy Gomarsall as his partner. Both played very well in the intimidating atmosphere of Cardiff Arms Park, especially Mike Catt whose confidence would have been at a low ebb anyway, the more so because Jack Rowell had seen fit to invite Rob Andrew to the England bench, the implication being that Catt's kicking might fail yet again.

In the first half Wales competed vigorously, and especially in the lines-out where Gareth Llewellyn and Mike Voyle allowed Martin Johnson and Simon Shaw very little latitude. The match, therefore, was somewhat pedestrian and uninspiring at that stage and three penalty goals, and several misses, were all there was to report at half-time.

At that point Jeremy Guscott replaced Jon Sleightholme who was suffering from double vision, and in the second half, England began to get clean possession from the lines-out, and the England backs found space in which to run. In this situation, Jeremy Guscott thrived, as he had against Ireland, and within ten minutes had created a try for Tim Stimpson and, twenty minutes later, another for Richard Hill with an immaculately timed pass out of the tackle. England scored four tries in the second half with a powerful and convincing performance of open fifteen-man rugby to which Wales had no answer at all and they visibly wilted in the closing stages. Some dignity was restored when Robert Howley scored Wales' only try from fully fifty yards with an exceptional break and elusive running and awareness of the highest class, and Jonathan Davies converted the try with the last kick of the match.

England used five substitutes and Wales four, in this remarkable match, from which the unfortunate Neil Jenkins had to retire with a broken arm. After a successful return to the front line, Mike Catt was withdrawn and Rob Andrew entered the game for the last seven minutes, to earn his 71st, and surely now his last, cap. Darren Garforth was also given a run very late in the game to earn his first cap.

England's win at Cardiff was their second successive win on Welsh soil, only ever achieved once before, and it was their fourth successive win over Wales which gave them their third successive Triple Crown and their fifth in the last seven years.

SUMMARY OF THE SEASON - 1996 - 97:

This was undoubtedly one of the most exciting, surprising and spectacular Five Nations Championships for many years. During the course of the season, Wales won in Edinburgh, Ireland won, again, in Cardiff, England led France by 20 points to 6 at Twickenham and lost the match, England won their third successive Triple Crown and France deservedly won their fifth Grand Slam. During the course of the season, over ten matches, 511 points were scored substantially more than the previous highest points total of 363 in 1991, and 53 tries were scored, more than any other season on record except 1911 when the total was 55.

It was a almost a very successful season for England who only had themselves to blame for failing to win another Grand Slam. They scored a record 141 points and fifteen tries in the Five Nations, won at Cardiff for the second successive time, and played some spectacular rugby. But their season had started disappointingly with less than satisfactory results against Italy and Argentina, and a sound thrashing against the New Zealand Barbarians for which match International caps were not awarded although the opposition was close to a full strength New Zealand side. The Five Nations tournament for England, was really a story of second halves, for in the four matches, England scored 47 points and three tries in the first half of the four matches and 94 points and 12 tries in the second periods. In all the games there were periods of excellence and in most cases these were preceded by dour efforts to establish a platform from which to launch the final assault. This was certainly so in the matches against Scotland, Ireland and Wales, but it did not work out that way against France.

Jack Rowell's selection policy still does not convince the majority of observers. He made a rod for his own back in October by appointing Phil de Glanville as Captain for the whole season, thus forcing himself to choose between Carling and Guscott for the other centre spot. In most games, particularly in Rugby Union, the Captain **must** be fully deserving of his place in the side against all comers. Will Carling was undoubtedly playing well enough to command a place in the side, but surely there is no other Team Manager in the world who would not include Jeremy Guscott in his starting line-up. On the two occasions when he came on as a replacement for an injured player, Guscott fashioned four tries in forty five minutes total playing time, two for Tony Underwood against Ireland and one each for Tim Stimpson and Richard Hill against Wales. No side can afford to deny itself such outstanding talent. Rowell also failed to solve the eternal dilemma of being able to play an attacking fly-half and still retain the services of a reliable goal kicker. This latter problem, however, is not of his making, and will not be resolved in the future if overseas players continue to be recruited into Courage League rugby as readily as has been the case this season. Tactical substitution opportunities were almost completely ignored except in the Ireland match, despite the lessons which were there for the learning in the New Zealand Barbarians match. Such substitutions could have been used to good effect in both the Barabrians game and, in particular, against France in that fatal second half.

In all six matches (i.e. excluding the "no caps" match against the New Zealand Barbarians), England used 22 players in all and a further five as replacements only, and for the Five Nations matches 18 players were used and a further five replacements. Were it not for the injuries to Lawrence Dallaglio and Paul Grayson which rendered them unavailable for the last match against Wales, only one change would have been made in the Five Nations season, that of Austin Healey replacing Andy Gomarsall at scrum-half for the Wales match. Four replacements, Rob Hardwick and Phil Greening against Italy and Rob Andrew and Darren Garforth against Wales, were on the field of play for all of 22 minutes in total as token replacements - a practice which does nothing to further the merit of gaining an England cap. Eleven new caps were awarded during the season, seven as original selections and four as replacements. Of the seven original selections, Nick Beal and Adedayo Adebayo played only one match. Only Will Carling announced his retirement at the end of the season; details of his career can be found in Section 4 under England Captains. However, it is unlikely that Rob Andrew will add further to his 71 caps !! Eighteen England players were invited to tour South Africa with the British Lions in the summer of 1997 (and four more were to be called upo as replacements) and Martin Johnson was given the Captaincy of the Touring Party. Never before has England's representation in a Lions' squad been as high as 18 although 16 were on the 1993 tour to New Zealand under Gavin Hastings. All eight of the England pack as represented in the Five Nations were included. In addition, in May/June 1997, Jack Rowell will take an England Squad to Argentina for a two-Test tour under the Captaincy of Phil de Glanville and that experience should prove invaluable for the second string England pack while their seniors are again under scruting in South Africa although this time in a different guise. A one-off match against Australia in Sydne on July 12th is also scheduled for the close season. One cannot avoid the feeling that this might just be a match too far !

FIVE NATIONS CHAMPIONSHIP TABLE:

Won: **Triple Crown, and Calcutta Cup**

		Played	Won	Lost	Drawn	Points: For	Against	Tries: For	Against	Title Points
1	France	4	4	0	0	129	77	14	6	8
2	**ENGLAND**	4	3	1	0	141	55	15	4	6
3	Wales	4	1	3	0	94	106	11	12	2
4	Scotland	4	1	3	0	90	132	9	13	2
5	Ireland	4	1	3	0	57	141	4	18	2

Home Games: beat Scotland 41 - 13, (four tries to one); lost to France 20 - 23, (one try to two)

Away Games: beat Ireland 46 - 6, (six tries to nil); beat Wales 34 - 13, (four tries to one)

THE WORLD CUP SEVENS - 1997

THE WORLD CUP SEVENS SQUAD:

TIM RODBER (Captain)	(Northampton)
ADEDAYO ADEBAYO	(Bath)
NEIL BACK	(Leicester)
NICK BEAL	(Northampton)
MIKE CATT	(Bath)
AUSTIN HEALEY	(Leicester)
RICHARD HILL	(Saracens)
DAVE SCULLY	(Wakefield)
CHRIS SHEASBY	(Harlequins)
JONATHAN SLEIGHTHOLME	(Bath)

Manager: **Andy Harriman**   Coach: **Les Cusworth**

WORLD CUP SEVENS RESULTS:

Preliminary Matches: Pool A	beat Canada	33 - 12	(five tries to two)
	beat Zimbabwe	26 - 7	(four tries to one)
2nd Round Pool Matches:	beat Canada	30 - 7	(six tries to one)
	beat Cook Islands	29 - 10	(five tries to two)
Quarter Finals:	**lost to Western Samoa**	5 - 21	(one try to three)

England never looked as if they were going to be successful in defending the World Sevens Title which they had so handsomely won in the inaugural World Cup Sevens Tournament at Murrayfield in 1993. In the Preliminary matches over the first two days, they did not look confident and the fact that very little time had been spent in preparation became very apparent. Lawrence Dallaglio had had to withdraw from the squad and from the Captaincy in the preceding week because of a heavy cold, and Tim Rodber was promoted to lead the side. There were five of the victorious 1993 squad seeking to defend the title in Hong Kong, but the lack of adequate preparation, and an intense club and International match schedule took its toll (seven of the squad, including Dallaglio, had played against Wales the day before the squad left for Hong Kong).

The tournament organisation left something to be desired in that several of the Quarter-finalists had to play the same opponents twice in the first two days as part of the seeding and screening process which determined the eight teams to progress to the final day knock-out stage. England survived this somewhat tedious process and in so doing had to face Canada twice, once on each of the two days. The desired result was achieved, but it was not exactly adequate preparation for the sterner tests to come.

As it was, England's first game on the final day against Western Samoa was a bitter disappointment. As the skipper, Tim Rodber, observed "We let ourselves down badly, the game was there for the taking. Western Samoa were a side we should have beaten". That may well be so, but the fact is that England failed to do so with a lack-lustre display and the score was only made partially respectable following a very late consolation try from Austin Healey.

The Tournament as a whole was much more successful for being played in Hong Kong despite persistent rain and sultry conditions, but this did not detract from the excitement nor the spectacle. Fiji won the Title deservedly and with panache, beating South Africa in the final by 24 points to 21, and, indeed, they had dominated the tournament throughout. In their seven matches they scored 323 points, including 49 tries, and conceded only 35 points.

The four Home Nations were certainly "not in the frame" in terms of the Fijiian and the South African squads' performances. The much vaunted gulf still exists, and it is becoming increasingly evident that the running skills and awareness required in sevens are being applied to a greater extent in the 15-a-side game. England will ignore this trend at their peril.

England's leading try scorer was Austin Healey with five tries, followed by Chris Sheasby with four.

ENGLAND TOUR TO ARGENTINA - 1997

THE TOUR PARTY:

| Manager: | J.Rowell | Coach: | J.Rowell | Captain: | P.R.de Glanville |

Asst Coaches:: **L.Cusworth and M.A.C.Slemen**

Full-backs:	J.Mallinder	(Sale)	no caps	Forwards:	D.Baldwin	(Sale)	no caps
	M.S.Mapletoft	(Gloucester)	no caps		B.B.Clarke	(Richmond)	30 caps
					R.Cockerill	(Leicester)	no caps
Three-quarters:	A.A.Adebayo	(Bath)	1 cap		M.Corry	(Bristol)	no caps
	M.C.Allen	(Northampton)	no caps		A.J.Diprose	(Saracens)	no caps
	J.Baxendell	(Sale)	no caps		D.J.Garforth	(Leicester)	1 cap
	P.R.de Glanville	(Bath)	21 caps		P.B.T.Greening	(Gloucester)	2 caps
	N.J.J.Greenstock	(Wasps)	no caps		D.Grewcock	(Coventry)	no caps
	D.O'Leary	(Harlequins)	no caps		M.Haag	(Bath)	no caps
	D.Rees	(Sale)	no caps		R.J.K.Hardwick	(Coventry)	1 cap
	J.M.Sleightholme	(Bath)	10 caps		R.Jenkins	(Harlequins)	no caps
					J.Mallett	(Bath)	1 cap
Half-backs:	K.P.P.Bracken	(Saracens)	12 caps		S.O.Ojomoh	(Bath)	11 caps
	M.J.Catt	(Bath)	21 caps		N.C.Redman	(Bath)	18 caps
	A.C.T.Gomarsall	(Wasps)	5 caps		C.M.A.Sheasby	(Wasps)	3 caps
	A.D.King	(Wasps)	no caps		K.Yates	(Bath)	no caps
Replacements:	J.E.B.Callard	(Bath)	5 caps		W.Green	(Wasps)	no caps
					S.Diamond	(Sale)	no caps

This was a much depleted England squad because there were 18 England players involved in the British Lions' tour to South Africa at the same time. As a result, of the 30 players on this tour, 16 were uncapped. Nevertheless, overall, it was a very successful tour, did a great deal for team-building in the lead up to the 1999 World Cup, showed that England have an encouraging strength in depth at International level, and gave cause to many of the 18 English Lions to look over their shoulders at the advancing competition for their places in the side next season. England could consider themselves a trifle unfortunate in that both Mike Catt and Nigel Redman had been called as replacements for the Lions in South Africa between the first and second Tests in Argentina. Both had played a considerable part in the first Test victory (not least Mike Catt with 21 points) and, although it cannot be said that with both in the team for the second Test, England would have won the match, their sudden absence must have had some effect on the side.

In the provincial matches, the performances were convincing with 22 tries being scored in the four matches. Even in the match which England lost, against Buenos Aires, England scored three tries to one and lost only because the place kicking of both Alex King and Mark Mapletoft was woefully unreliable. In all in that match, eight penalty kicks at goal were missed and one conversion was charged down. There were several outstanding successes on the tour with Tony Diprose and Kevin Yates in the pack both showing remarkable agility and ability, Kyran Bracken at scrum-half back to his best form and Adedayo Adebayo demonstrating his power on the wing in scoring two tries in the first Test before injury constrained his performance in the second.

Jack Rowell could be well satisfied with his second string squad's performance in trying circumstances, and, no doubt, many of this squad will be bound for Australia for the single Test in Sydney on July 12th, together with those English Lions who have sufficieint energy left to make the trip !!A19

TOUR RESULTS:

May 21st	Cordoba	Chateau Carreras Stadium	WON	38 - 21	(five tries to two)
May 24th	Buenos Aires	Cricket & Rugby Club, Buenos Aires	LOST	21 - 23	(three tries to one)
May 27th	Argentina "A"	Cricket & Rugby Club, Buenos Aires	WON	58 - 17	(eight tries to three)
May 31st	**ARGENTINA**	**FCO Ground, Buenos Aires**	**WON**	**40 - 16**	**(six tries to three)**
June 3rd	Cuyo	Mendoza	Won	37 - 8	(six tries to one)
June 7th	**ARGENTINA**	**FCO Ground, Buenos Aires**	**LOST**	**13 - 33**	**(two tries to four)**

8th match   **ENGLAND   46 pts**   v   **ARGENTINA   20 pts**

Caps   Caps

15	1st	J.Mallinder	(Sale)	.	E.Jurado	(Jockey de Rosario)

14	11th	J.M.Sleightholme	(Bath)	.	T.Solari	(Hindu Club)
13	1st	N.J.J.Greenstock	(Wasps)	.	E.Simone	(Licoe Naval)
12	22nd	P.R.de Glanville (Capt)	(Bath)	.	L.Arbizu (Capt)	(Belgrano A.C.)
11	2nd	A.A.Adebayo	(Bath)	.	F.Soler	(Tala)

10	22nd	M.J.Catt	(Bath)	.	G.Quesada	(Hindu Club)
9	13th	K.P.P.Bracken	(Saracens)	.	N.Fernandez-Miranda	(Hindu Club)

1	1st	K.Yates	(Bath)	.	R.Grau	(Gauteng Lions)
2	3rd	P.B.T.Greening	(Gloucester)	.	F.Mendez	(Bath)
3	2nd	D.J.Garforth	(Leicester)	.	M.Reggiardo	(Castres)
4	19th	N.C.Redman	(Bath)	.	G.A.Llanes	(Bath)
5	1st	M.Haag	(Bath)	.	P.L.Sporleder	(Curupayti)
6	1st	M.Corry	(Bristol)	.	R.A.Martin	(San Isidro)
7	1st	A.J.Diprose	(Saracens)	.	P.J.Camerlinckx	(Regatas Bella Vista)
8	31st	B.B.Clarke	(Richmond)	.	P.Bouza	(Duendes R.C.)

	1st	R.Cockerill (Leicester) for Greening - 25	.	C.Promanzio (Duendes R.C.) for Mendez - 38
	4th	C.M.A.Sheasby (Wasps) for Corry - 59	.	I.Fernandes-Lobbe (Liceo N) for Sporleder - 65
			.	O.Hasan-Jalil (Natacio y Gimansia)
				for Reggiardo - 70

Referee: I.Rogers   (South Africa)

SCORERS:

	N.J.J.Greenstock	Try	(1st)	5 - 0		
	M.J.Catt	Conversion		7 - 0		
				7 - 5	G.Queseda	Try
				7 - 8	G.Queseda	Drop Goal
	M.J.Catt	Penalty goal		10 - 8		
				10 - 13	L.Arbizu	Try
	A.J.Diprose	Try	(1st)	15 - 13		
	M.J.Catt	Conversion		17 - 13		
				Half-time		
	A.A.Adebayo	Try	(1st)	22 - 13		
	M.J.Catt	Conversion		24 - 13		
	B.B.Clarke	Try	(3rd)	29 - 13		
	M.J.Catt	Try	(3rd)	34 - 13		
	M.J.Catt	Conversion		36 - 13		
				36 - 18	T.Solari	Try
				36 - 20	G.Quesada	Conversion
	M.J.Catt	Penalty Goal		39 - 20		
	A.A.Adebayo	Try	(2nd)	44 - 20		
	M.J.Catt	Conversion		46 - 20		

POINTS:

M.J.Catt	21 points	(82)	G.Queseda	10 points
A.A.Adebayo	10 points	(10)	L.Arbizu	5 points
A.J.Diprose and B.B.Clarke	5 points	(5),(15)	T.Solari	5 points
and N.J.J.Greenstock	each	(5)		

MATCH COMMENTARY:

With so many England players responding to the call of the British Lions in South Africa, it was perhaps surprising that there were only six new caps in the side as originally selected for what was expected to be a very tough match against a formidable Argentinian pack. Twelve of the Argentinian side who had held England so close at Twickenham the previous December were appearing again, and added to their ranks was Frederico Mendez, a front-row forward of immense stature in any company.

The match started very badly for England when Mike Catt put his kick-off out on the full and then, moments, later dropped a perfect pass from his scrum half, and the few England supporters present feared a repetition of his performance against Argentina last time round. But it was not to be, England steadied themselves, applied themselves, and in spite of being behind on two occasions in the first half, took the lead with Tony Diprose's converted try just before half-time. That try dispirited Argentina, and during the break, the England side recognised this. The pressure applied early in the second half secured three tries for England in the space of 12 minutes and Argentina were dead in the water. The third of those tries by Mike Catt was one of the finest possible, when he made a break from a set piece, chipped over the Argentinian full-back, and caught the ball on the full to run in 50 metres to score under the posts. Even after that, England kept the pressure on, and scored a further 10 points before the end of the match.

A thoroughly competent display by England despite the very shaky start, and ample evidence that English rugby is now developing a formidable strength in depth.

9th match   **ENGLAND 13 pts**   **v**   **ARGENTINA 33 pts**

Caps   Caps

15	2nd	J.Mallinder	(Sale)		E.Jurado	(Jockey de Rosario)
14	12th	J.M.Sleightholme	(Bath)		T.Solari	(Hindu Club)
13	2nd	N.J.J.Greenstock	(Wasps)		E.Simone	(Liceo Naval)
12	23rd	P.R.de Glanville (Capt)	(Bath)		L.Arbizu (Capt)	(Belgrano A.C.)
11	3rd	A.A.Adebayo	(Bath)		F.Soler	(Tala)
10	1st	M.S.Mapletoft	(Gloucester)		G.Quesada	(Hindu Club)
9	14th	K.P.P.Bracken	(Saracens)		N.Fernandez-Miranda	(Hindu Club)
1	2nd	K.Yates	(Bath)		R.Grau	(Gauteng Lions)
2	2nd	R.Cockerill	(Leicester)		C.Promanzio	(Duendes R.C.)
3	3rd	D.J.Garforth	(Leicester)		M.Reggiardo	(Castres)
4	1st	D.J.Grewcock	(Coventry)		G.A.Llanes	(Bath)
5	2nd	M.Haag	(Bath)		P.L.Sporleder	(Curupayti)
6	2nd	M.Corry	(Bristol)		R.A.Martin	(San Isidro)
7	2nd	A.J.Diprose	(Saracens)		I.Fernandes-Lobbe	(Liceo Naval)
8	32nd	B.B.Clarke	(Richmond)		P.J.Camerlinckx	(Regatas Bella Vista)

5th	C.M.A.Sheasby (Wasps) for Corry - 54	O.Hasaan-Jalil (Natacio y Gimansia)
1st	A.D.King (Wasps) for Mallinder - 58	for Reggiardo - 59
6th	A.C.T.Gomarsall (Wasps) for Adebayo - 67	G.Aristide (Jockey de Rosario) for Solari - 68
		C.Veil (Newman) for Martin - 75

Referee: J.Kaplan   (South Africa)

SCORERS:

			0 - 3	G.Queseda	Penalty Goal
			0 - 6	G.Queseda	Penalty Goal
			0 - 11	F.Soler	Try
			0 - 13	G.Queseda	Conversion
M.S.Mapletoft	Penalty Goal		3 - 13		
			Half-time		
			3 - 16	G.Queseda	Penalty Goal
			3 - 21	R.Grau	Try
			3 - 23	G.Queseda	Conversion
			3 - 28	F.Soler	Try
A.D.King	Try	(1st)	8 - 28		
			8 - 33	E.Simone	Try
D.J.Grewcock	Try	(1st)	13 - 33		

POINTS:

A.D.King	5 points	(5)		G.Queseda	13 points
D.J.Grewcock	5 points	(5)		F.Soler	10 points
M.S.Mapletoft	3 points	(3)		R.Grau & E.Simone	5 points each

MATCH COMMENTARY:

There were three changes from the side which had won the opening match of the two match series the previous week, two of which were occasioned by Fran Cotton's call for Mike Catt and Nigel Redman to join the Lions in South Africa. The third was the retention of Richard Cockerill as hooker in place of the concussed Phil Greening. Although undoubtedly, these enforced changes had some effect on the performance of the side, they were not in themselves, instrumental in the sound beating which the rejuvenated and inspired Argentinan side handed out to England. England were never off the back foot and, in the first half, were rarely out of their own half, such was the pressure and intensity of the Argentinian onslaught. England did survive the first quarter and found themselves only six points down, with Queseda having kicked two and missed two penalty goals, and the Argentinian back row having been denied a try when Haag and de Glanville managed to prevent Fernandes-Lobbe scoring by holding him up when over the line.

But then came the fatal mistake which severely damaged English morale, and inspired Argentina, when Mallinder and Adebayo between them managed to leave the ball on the ground after an elabotate scissors attempt, and Soler simply had to pick it up and run 40 metres to score. Thereafter, it was all Argentina, and they were 28 points to 3 ahead midway through the second half. Two late tries from Alex King and Darren Grewcock, both on the occasion of their first caps, restored some respectability to the score, but, nonetheless, England were well beaten.

For the second successive visit, England shared the two match series with Argentina, but, considering the circumstances of selection, with 18 players on tour with the Lions, it was a commendable achievement.

20th match   **ENGLAND   6 pts**   v   **AUSTRALIA   25 pts**

	Caps					Caps	
15	6th	T.R.G.Stimpson	(Newcastle)			M.Burke	(New South Wales)
14	3rd	J.Bentley	(Newcastle)			B.Tune	(Queensland)
13	24th	P.R.de Glanville (Capt)	(Bath)			J.S.Little	(Queensland)
12	3rd	N.J.J.Greenstock	(Wasps)			J.Holbeck	(ACT)
11	2nd	N.D.Beal	(Northampton			J.Roff	(ACT)
10	23rd	M.J.Catt	(Bath)			T.J.Horan	(Queensland)
9	6th	M.J.S.Dawson	(Northampton)			G.M.Gregan	(ACT)
1	15th	G.C.Rowntree	(Leicester)			C.Blades	(New South Wales)
2	13th	M.P.Regan	(Bristol)			M.Foley	(Queensland)
3	4th	D.J.Garforth	(Leicester)			E.J.A.McKenzie	(ACT)
4	7th	S.D.Shaw	(Bristol)			G.Morgan	(Queensland)
5	20th	N.C.Redman	(Bath)			J.A.Eales (Capt)	(Queensland)
6	12th	L.B.N.Dallaglio	(Wasps)			D.Manu	(ASW)
7	5th	R.A.Hill	(Saracens)			B.Robinson	(ACT)
8	32nd	T.A.K.Rodber	(Northampton)			T.Coker	(Queensland)

	3rd	A.Healey (Leicester) for Dawson - 40		D.J.Wilson (Queensland) for Coker - temporar
	33rd	B.B.Clarke (Richmond) for Hill - 68		A.Blades (NSW) for McKenzie - 68

Referee: P.O'Brien   (New Zealand)

SCORERS:

			0 - 5	M.Burke	Try
			0 - 8	J.A.Eales	Penalty goal
T.R.G.Stimpson	Penalty goal		3 - 8		
M.J.Catt	Drop Goal	(2nd)	6 - 8		
			Half-time		
			6 - 13	B.Tune	Try
			6 - 15	M.Burke	Conversion
			6 - 20	G.M.Gregan	Try
			6 - 25	T.J.Horan	Try

POINTS:

T.R.G.Stimpson	3 points	(8)	M.Burke	8 points
M.J.Catt	3 points	(85)	B.Tune, G.M.Gregan	
			and T.J.Horan	5 points each.
			J.A.Eales	3 points

MATCH COMMENTARY:

The Cook Trophy is the reward in this newly established series between England and Australia to be contested twice yearly in future.
Notwithstanding the anticlimax and the long trip from South Africa undertaken by the 12 Lions in the side only three days prior to this match,
this was a poor performance by an England team conspicuously lacking in attacking ideas and imagination. The first half was all Australia
and they effectively denied England any worthwhile possession, and spent 35 of the 40 minutes in the England half of the field. England's
defence was courageous and very effective, and largely as a result of this England did well to be only 3 points to 8 down at half-time.
But apart from brief surges, mainly originated by Austin Healey, who replaced Matt Dawson at the break, England did little to impress in
the second half, and Australia ran in three further and excellent tries against a rapidly tiring and increasingly dispirited England defence.
Southern hemisphere competition is vitally necessary for England, but not in the close season, nor immediately after a Lions' Tour !